D1393939

Ralf Kuhlen | Rui Moreno
Marco Ranieri | Andrew Rhodes
(Eds.)

Controversies
in Intensive Care
Medicine

Medizinisch Wissenschaftliche Verlagsgesellschaft

Ralf Kuhlen | Rui Moreno
Marco Ranieri | Andrew Rhodes
(Eds.)

Controversies in Intensive Care Medicine

with contributions from:

MG Abate | L Abrahão Hajjar | S Afonso | F Álvarez-Lerma | P Amado | PJD Andrews | D Annane
D De Backer | J Bakker | O Barbosa da Silva | G Bellingan | K Bendjelid | A Biasi Cavalcanti
L Blanch | SI Blot | M Borelli | J Brokmann | C Bruel | C Brun-Buisson | J Carlet | J Chastre
BP Cholley | G Citerio | G Colin | A Combes | RC Costa Filho | C Cozowicz | BH Cuthbertson
D Crippen | J Cruz | R Dembinski | P Devos | J-M Domínguez-Roldán | G Ferreyra
S Finfer | H Flaatten | MJ Garcia Monge | E Gayat | T Geeraerts | FRB Gomes Galas | RD Griffiths
ABJ Groeneveld | O Grottke | O Hamzaoui | GT Henriques Filho | M Hiesmayr | M Imhoff
TC Jansen | AL Jardim | M Jonas | C Jones | JA Kellum | R Kitzberger | E Knobel | M Knobel | L Kramer
K Kranzer | S Kreyer | R Kuhlen | M Leone | A Liolios | T Lisboa | B Lortat Jacob | U Lucangelo
C-E Luyt | MR Macleod | R Maio | C Martin | FO Martins | V Maxime | A Mebazaa | DK Menon
TM Merz | B Misset | I Morales | RP Moreno | T Muders | AP Neves | P Olaechea | G Ospina-Tascon
HM Oudemans-van Straaten | M Palomar | AE Pesaro | F Philippart | J Poelaert | KH Polderman
LF Poli-de-Figueiredo | J-C Preiser | RJ Price | C Putensen | VM Ranieri | J Rello | A Rhodes
JL da Rocha Paranhos | A Rodriguez | J-A Romand | R Rossaint | HU Rothen | D Schmidlin
K Singbartl | JMA Sousa | CL Sprung | M Tavares | JF Teixeira | J-L Trouillet | RJ Trof | V Umbrain
A Valentin | DM Vandijck | J-L Vincent | C Waldmann | J Wernerman | J Woods | H Wrigge

Medizinisch Wissenschaftliche Verlagsgesellschaft

Editors

Ralf Kuhlen, MD, Prof.
Klinik für Intensivmedizin
Helios Klinikum Berlin Buch
Hobrechtsfelder Chaussee 100
13125 Berlin, Germany

Rui P. Moreno, MD, PhD
Unidade de Cuidados Intensivos Polivalente
Hospital de Santo António dos Capuchos
Centro Hospitalar de Lisboa Central E.P.E.
Alameda de Santo António dos Capuchos
1169-050 Lisboa, Portugal

V. Marco Ranieri, MD, Prof.
Università di Torino
Dipartimento di Anestesia e Rianimazione
Ospedale S. Giovanni Battista-Molinette
Corso Dogliotti 14
10126 Torino, Italy

Andrew Rhodes, FRCA, FRCP
Department of Intensive Care Medicine
St George's Hospital
Blackshaw Road
London SW17 0QT, UK

EUROPEAN SOCIETY
OF INTENSIVE CARE
MEDICINE

European Society of Intensive Care Medicine
40 Avenue Joseph Wybran
1070 Bruxelles, Belgium
Tel: 0032 2 559 03 50 – Fax: 0032 2 527 00 62
e-mail: public@esicm.org
www.esicm.org

MWV Medizinisch Wissenschaftliche Verlagsgesellschaft OHG
Zimmerstraße 11
D-10969 Berlin
www.mwv-berlin.de

ISBN 978-3-939069-61-4

These publications are listed in: Deutsche Nationalbibliothek
Detailed bibliographical information is available via internet http://dnb.d-nb.de.

Medicine is an ever-changing science. As new research and clinical experience broaden our knowledge, changes in treatment and drug therapy are required. The editors and the publisher of this work have checked with sources believed to be reliable in their efforts to provide information that is complete and generally in accordance with the standards accepted at the time of publication. However, in view of the possibility of human error or changes in medical sciences, neither the editors nor the publisher nor any other party who has been involved in the preparation or publication of this work warrants, that the information contained herein is in every respect accurate or complete, and they disclaim all responsibility for any errors or omissions or for the results obtained from use of the information contained in this work. Readers are encouraged to confirm the information contained herein with other sources. For example and in particular, readers are advised to check the product information sheet included in the package of each drug they plan to administer to be certain that the information contained in this work is accurate and that changes have not been made in the recommended dose or in the contraindications for administration. This recommendation is of particular importance in connection with new or infrequently used drugs.

Any necessary errata are published at the publisher's website www.mwv-berlin.de.

Project management: Claudia Leonhardt, Berlin
Editorial office: Monika Laut-Zimmermann, Berlin
Product management: Nina Heinlein, Berlin
Copy editing: M. May-Lee Sia, Berlin | Jan K. Schwing, readytoread.de | Laura Stöver, Berlin
Layout and typesetting: Elena Frecot | Silvio Patzner, eScriptum GmbH & CoKG – Publishing Services, Berlin
Printing: druckhaus köthen GmbH, Köthen

Reply and complaints to:
MWV Medizinisch Wissenschaftliche Verlagsgesellschaft OHG, Zimmerstraße 11, D-10969 Berlin, lektorat@mwv-berlin.de

Preface

Last year, the European Society of Intensive Care Medicine (ESICM) celebrated its 25th anniversary in combination with its 20th annual congress. On that occasion we published a book entitled "25 Years of Progress and Innovation in Intensive Care Medicine", which was given to all conference attendees and also every member of the society as an anniversary present. The feedback from our members and also from other readers of the book was extremely positive, with many requests asking us to repeat the exercise in 2008 and future years. This year's annual congress is entitled "Controversies in Intensive Care Medicine" and will be held in Lisbon, Portugal, in September. The editors, the executive committee of the society, the publisher and all the people involved with last year's project were easily convinced to accept the challenge of producing another book that will again accompany the annual conference and will be distributed to society members. As in the past year, the title of the book reflects the theme of the congress, focusing on areas of controversy within our specialty.

How should controversial issues in intensive care be presented? The first idea was to identify the topic of the controversy and then have pro and con chapters reflecting the two respective standpoints. Although this approach could have been very interesting and entertaining, we thought that highlighting the topic of the controversy within one chapter would be more helpful for the reader to understand the background and see how different conclusions may be drawn from the scientific evidence on the issue. Therefore, we were looking for authors who are not only experts in their field but who were also willing to produce an objective description of the different, conflicting views one might have on a controversial issue. We asked authors to describe the "school of thought" in favour and against an argument with equal emphasis and finally to draw a conclusion which at its best would be helpful for the reader to resolve the controversy when thinking about it at the bedside. Within

the ESICM, and also among our worldwide circle of friends and colleagues it was easy to find authors who could deliver such an article within a tight deadline. For that we are extremely grateful. It is a special pleasure for us to be able to thank all of these individuals for the excellent work they have done in preparing their manuscripts, reading and editing their chapters and especially for being as balanced with their views as possible. Without them this book would never have become a reality. We would also like to thank the ESICM office staff for their help with editing and Thomas Hopfe and his wonderful team at MWV in Berlin, Germany, especially Claudia Leonhardt and Nina Heinlein, for their excellent support from the publishing house. Without their friendly but crucial efforts to keep all of us within our timeframes we would not have been able to present the book in time for our Lisbon meeting.

The book tries to address the many controversial topics that we face within our specialty. Although we neither intended nor hoped to cover every controversy in intensive care medicine we are happy that many of the most relevant topics have been addressed. The respective chapters are organised in sections on acute respiratory failure, acute circulatory failure, acute kidney injury, sepsis and infection, neuro-intensive care, acute bleeding, organisational issues, surgical intensive care and trauma, and adjunctive issues. We hope that the readers will find their way through all of these controversial areas and learn something helpful that will be of use in daily clinical practice. We hope that you, the reader, will enjoy reading this book as much as we have enjoyed producing it!

Ralf Kuhlen (Chair of the Editorial and Publishing Committee)
Rui P. Moreno (President Elect of the ESICM)
V. Marco Ranieri (President of the ESICM)
Andrew Rhodes (Chair of the Division of Scientific Affairs)

Content

A. Acute respiratory failure

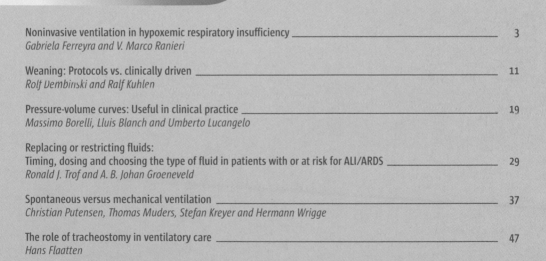

Gabriela Ferreyra and V. Marco Ranieri

Noninvasive ventilation in hypoxemic respiratory insufficiency

Introduction

Since its introduction into clinical practice, noninvasive ventilation (NIV) has been a major advantage in the management of acute respiratory failure caused by chronic obstructive pulmonary disease (1, 2, 3) and sleep hypoventilation disorders (4).

In recent years, there has been an increase in this technique as a first-line ventilation modality in the acute care setting (5). However, although NIV has showed to be effective in acute respiratory failure, there is still a controversy over its benefits in hypoxemic respiratory failure.

Hypoxemic respiratory failure is defined as a condition in which the respiratory system fails in its gas exchange function of oxygenation, PaO_2/FIO_2 less than 200, respiratory rate greater than 35 breaths per minute and active contraction of the accessory muscles of respiration (6). Patients who develop hypoxemic respiratory failure, requiring endotracheal intubation and sedation, show a high rate of ventilator-associated pneumonia (6), prolonging mechanical ventilation with increased morbidity and mortality (7). Therefore, NIV has recently been proposed in patients with hypoxemic respiratory failure to avoid endotracheal intubation, decrease ICU and hospital length of stay and mortality through respiratory muscle unloading and gas exchange improvement.

Is NIV effective and safe in all forms of hypoxemic respiratory failure?

In patients with various forms of hypoxemic respiratory failure, the beneficial effects of NIV remain controversial. An international consensus conference held in 2001 analysed data on the use of NIV in patients with acute respiratory failure (8) from several studies. This expert analysis concluded that based on current data, the use of NIV does not consistently improve clinical outcomes in patients with hypoxemic respiratory failure, and therefore cannot be recommended at this time. Although some select patient populations may have benefits, the conference committee's main concern was that larger controlled studies are still required to determine the potential benefit and safety of using this type of ventilation and thereby avoiding endotracheal intubation during hypoxemic acute respiratory failure. Currently, five years after the original consensus conference analysis, two surveys have re-examined the use of NIV outside clinical trials and have confirmed that NIV success varies in different types of hypoxemic respiratory failure. Specifically, Schettino et al. (9) recorded data over one year examining the use of NIV in a standard medical care routine in the

ICU, emergency ward, and general medical-surgical units. More than 449 patients with acute respiratory failure were enrolled in this study; NIV prevented intubation in 62 % of the patients and was correlated with improved survival. Examination of different pathologies found that NIV successfully prevented intubation in patients with cardiogenic pulmonary oedema (82 %) and COPD exacerbation (76 %). However, due to other causes, it was much less successful during hypoxemic respiratory failure, which had the lowest rate of prevented intubation (40 %). Moreover, intubated patients in this category had a high mortality rate (64 %). A more recent prospective survey evaluated the use of NIV over three weeks in 70 French intensive care units. Among patients receiving NIV, only 38 % subsequently required endotracheal intubation, showing that NIV prevented ETI in 62 % of patients, which is similar to previous result (9, 10, 11). However, NIV failure in hypoxemic patients was lower (54 %) than in the former study (5).

Early studies in patients with hypoxemic respiratory failure from heterogeneous categories were promising (12, 13), although improvements in outcome were only observed when hypercapnia was present (14). Subsequently, the comparison of NIV and conventional ventilation in acute hypoxemic, not hypercapnic, respiratory failure due to various causes was studied in a randomised controlled trial. Only 31 % of the NIV group needed intubation. More patients in the conventional group had serious complications. Nonetheless, mortality was not different in both groups (6). On the contrary, in a similar population treated with continuous positive airway pressure (CPAP), there were no improved outcomes in comparison with the patients in the oxygen group. Moreover, higher rates of adverse events were found in the CPAP group (15).

The application of NIV in patients with acute cardiogenic pulmonary oedema (ACPE) has showed beneficial effects in comparison with standard treatment (16–18). However, higher myocardial infarction rate was associated with non-invasive positive pressure ventilation (NPPV) in one of the studies (19). In contrast, most recently several studies have shown that neither continuous positive airway pressure (CPAP) nor NPPV had an effect on new myocardial infarction rates (9, 20, 21). Several meta-analyses and systematic reviews (20, 22–25) have been performed over the last few years to confirm the overall beneficial effect of NIV on clinical outcomes and to determine whether CPAP and NPPV is more advantageous in the treatment of respiratory failure due to ACPE. Overall, NIV was associated with a significant reduction in the need for invasive mechanical ventilation, and decreased mortality in comparison with standard therapy. However, although a trend towards less mortality was shown with NPPV alone, it did not result in a significant reduction, which was probably due to the low power related to the limited number of patients in the studies (20, 23).

The superior effect of NPPV in comparison with CPAP in patients with hypercapnic ACPE, through the investigation of its potential superiority due to respiratory muscle unloading, has been further analysed in the meta-analysis published by Winck et al. (20). The authors performed a subgroup analysis by dividing patients according to their $PaCO_2$ levels (below or above 50 mmHg), finding that NPPV again showed only a small trend towards a decreased mortality rate and a reduced need of ETI. However, because these results did not reach significance the authors conclude that there is no superiority of NPPV, even in the more severe hypercapnic ACPE patients ($PaCO_2$ above 50 mmHg).

To date, the extended literature suggests that both modes are safe and efficient ways to improve clinical outcomes in cardiogenic pulmonary oedema; although the simplicity of CPAP makes it the logical choice as a first-line technique. However, if the patient fails to improve or experiences accessory muscle overload, NPPV should be applied. Moreover, the literature suggests that in patients with cardiogenic pulmonary oedema it is both safe and effective to use NIV in the emergency ward (9, 26).

Other forms of hypoxemic respiratory failure

There is a significant debate concerning the precise indications for NIV in patients with hypoxemic respiratory failure not due to cardiogenic pulmonary oedema or chronic obstructive pulmonary disease (27).

In a recent meta-analysis, Keenan et al. evaluated the effect of NIV in patients with hypoxemic respiratory failure of various causes. NIV was associated with a reduction of endotracheal intubation, ICU length of stay and mortality rate. Similar results were found in an interim analysis when patients with cardiogenic pulmonary oedema and COPD were excluded. Notwithstanding, because of the few studies and the heterogeneity found in the population analysed, strong conclusions could not be reached. The authors suggest that some selected populations such as patients with immunosuppression (28) or specific postoperative conditions (29, 30) had the best outcomes (27).

Several studies reported SAPS II > 31 or 32, $PaO_2/FiO_2 < 175$ to 200 as indicators of noninvasive ventilation failure (9, 11, 31, 32). Accordingly, patients with hypoxemic respiratory failure and SAPS II < 31 or 32, $PaO_2/FiO_2 > 175$ to 200, would be better candidates for successful NIV.

Is it safe and effective to use NIV in patients with ALI/ARDS and pneumonia?

Whether to use NIV in these patients has been a matter of debate. A recent physiologic study with acute respiratory distress syndrome (ARDS) patients demonstrated a reduction of muscle effort and improved oxygenation when noninvasive pressure support combined with positive end expiratory pressure was applied (33). Moreover, clinical improvements in patients with ARDS and pneumonia were reported with the use of NIV in earlier randomised and non-randomised studies (12, 34). One of the first cohort studies analysing NIV in patients with ALI/ARDS showed that 66 % of the patients could avoid intubation when NIV was used as a first intervention prior to endotracheal intubation (12). Furthermore, in selected patients with community-acquired pneumonia, NIV was associated with a reduction in intubation rate (34). However, most recently, Pneumonia and ARDS have been identified as independent risk factors for NIV failure. Intubation rates in patients with ARDS and community-acquired pneumonia were 51 % and 50 % respectively (31). Honrubia et al. found similar results in another RCT. Patients received either NPPV or conventional invasive ventilation. The intubation rate was lower in the NIV group, but no further benefits were confirmed. Despite a tendency towards reduction in mortality (23 % in the noninvasive group and 39 %

in the conventional group), it did not reach significance. In addition, in a subgroup analysis all the patients with pneumonia failed NIV and 66 % died in the ICU (35). The poor outcome of patients with pneumonia is consistent with previous studies (11, 14, 36).

Despite these trials, different results have been observed in another study. Ferrer et al. conducted a randomised trial in patients with acute hypoxemic respiratory failure compared with oxygen therapy; NIV decreased the need for intubation, incidence of septic shock and ICU mortality. Interestingly, a separate analysis showed a significant reduction of the intubation rate in patients with pneumonia, which was not the case in patients with ARDS where NIV was associated with an increased risk of intubation (37).

In a recent multi-centre survey, the application of NIV as a first-line intervention was investigated in selected patients with early ARDS (32). The study was conducted over a period of 25 months and included 147 patients with sepsis as the primary cause of ARDS. The authors reported that 54 % of ARDS patients avoided intubation. Patients who required intubation had an ICU mortality of 53 %. However, the overall ICU mortality including patients with NIV success and failure was 28 %, lower than recently published literature about prediction of death in ARDS patients (38). This data is not consistent with other published studies (9). One important difference in this trial is that applied PEEP levels were higher (12 cmH_2O) than in the former study (5 cmH_2O). Predictive values of NIV failure were higher SAPS II, older age, and higher levels of ventilator pressure. The authors suggest that ARDS patients with SAPS II < 34 and a $PaO_2/FiO_2 > 175$ are likely to benefit from the use of NIV.

Immunocompromised patients

Hilbert et al. in a RCT comparing NIV with standard therapy in immunosuppressed patients with type 1 respiratory failure have shown a reduction not only in intubation rate but also in mortality. Fewer patients in the NIV group than in the standard treatment group required endotracheal intubation and had serious complications. Moreover, ICU and hospital mortality were lower in the treatment group (28).

Surgical patients

Several early studies on the use of NIV as CPAP or NPPV to prevent or treat hypoxemic respiratory failure in postoperative patients reported physiologic benefits in the first stage of hypoxemia (39–41). However, clinical outcomes were less clear. In recent years, randomised controlled trials have also reported improvement in clinical outcomes. CPAP, when used prophylactically after thoracoabdominal aneurysm repair was shown to reduce pulmonary complications and length of hospital stay (42). Similarly, Squadrone et al. evaluated the effectiveness of continuous positive airway pressure in patients with early hypoxemia after major abdominal surgery in comparison with oxygen and standard therapy. Pneumonia and intubation rate were lower in the CPAP group and a trend toward shorter ICU stay was reported. Three patients died in hospital among the group of patients who received oxygen alone, but none in the treatment group died (43).

NIV has also been applied to prevent hypoxemia after cardiac surgery, with improvement in lung function and oxygenation (40, 41). Pasquina et al. conducted a study comparing CPAP and NPPV. Less atelectasis were found in the NPPV group. However, the absence of a control group with standard therapy did not allow for a conclusion (44). To date, there is no data to support that NIV or CPAP improve clinical outcomes in cardiac surgery. On the contrary, in the postoperative setting of patients with hypoxemic respiratory failure after lung resection, comparing NIV with standard therapy, a reduction of intubation rate and mortality was reported in 50 % of the patients in the control group versus 20 % in the NIV group. The investigators recommended NIV to improve survival in such patients (30).

Comparable benefits were reported in a randomised controlled trial of NIV in comparison with standard therapy with oxygen administration in solid organ transplantation (29). There was a faster improvement in oxygenation and a reduction in intubation rate with NIV in comparison with standard therapy. However, mortality did not differ between groups.

Weaning and postextubation respiratory failure

NPPV as a weaning strategy

Weaning failure and reintubation are considered risk factors for higher pneumonia and mortality rates (7). Favourable impact has been described in several studies on the use of NIV as a mode of early extubation (45, 46).

Lately, in a heterogeneous population of patients, two RCTs have demonstrated beneficial effects of NIV compared to standard therapy in preventing respiratory failure after extubation in high-risk patients. There was a lower rate of intubation, and a trend to lower mortality when NIV was applied for at least 48 hours (47). In a similar study, comparing prophylactic NIV with conventional therapy for at least 24 hours, the authors reported a reduction of respiratory failure and lower ICU mortality in the treatment group (48). A recent meta-analysis evaluated the role of NIV in facilitating early extubation. NIV compared to invasive mechanical ventilation resulted in decreased ventilator-associated pneumonia, shorter hospital length of stay and less mortality; however, most of the studies included in the meta-analysis had a high percentage of COPD patients (49). Therefore, information about hypoxemic, not hypercapnic, patients remains less ambiguous.

The use of NIV when extubation failure is already established has been less clear over the years. Promising results of NIV on postextubation failure with the application of NIV were suggested at the international consensus conference (8). However, there was not enough evidence to recommend NIV in this population, suggesting the need for further studies. Recently, two randomised trials were conducted in this field. Keenan et al. published the first randomised controlled trial examining the use of NIV in comparison with standard therapy in a heterogeneous population of patients who developed acute respiratory failure after extubation. There was no difference in the rates of reintubation and hospital mortality for both groups. However, the criterion for reintubation was not hypoxemia but other clinical signs (50). Similar results were observed by Esteban et al. in a larger multi-centre randomised controlled trial evaluating NIV versus conventional therapy in postextubation respiratory failure. There was no difference in reintubation rate in the control and NIV groups. Moreover, there no further benefit was found in the subgroup analysis of hypoxemic patients. In addition, patients who failed NIV and were reintubated had a higher mortality rate than the control group. What is of interest is that the time from the development of respiratory distress to the reintubation was higher in the NIV group (51).

Comments

Broad literature on the use of NIV in an acute setting has emerged over the last years in the fervour to avoid endotracheal intubation, ventilator-associated pneumonia and hospital mortality. NIV was shown to play an important role as an adjunctive therapy to standard treatment in many forms of acute respiratory failure. However, the question whether NIV is safe and efficient in an overall population of patients with hypoxemic respiratory failure remains unanswered.

The setting and how NIV is applied, as well as the heterogeneity of the population studied, may have influenced the effectiveness of noninvasive ventilation in different studies.

NIV as a ventilatory mode to prevent or treat early stages of hypoxemia in the postoperative abdominal period is supported by published articles and a meta-analysis.

Selected patient populations, such as immuno-compromised patients (28), and postoperative respiratory failure (29, 30) have shown clinical benefits.

The question of whether to use NIV in patients with ARDS and pneumonia remains unanswered. Although a recent survey reported that half of the treated patients with ARDS avoided endotracheal intubation, further studies are needed to confirm the benefit of NIV as a ventilatory mode in this challenging population of patients.

Recent data from everyday practice outside the clinical trials in one survey has shown that although well-trained respiratory staff was involved, a high percentage of patients with hypoxemic respiratory failure failed to improve clinical outcome and had a mortality rate when noninvasive ventilation was applied (9). This data is consistent with the statement of the consensus conference held in 2001 (8). Noninvasive ventilation, although attractive in the intensive care unit setting, cannot be recommended as a first-line therapy for an overall population with hypoxemic respiratory failure.

The authors

Gabriela Ferreyra
V. Marco Ranieri, MD, Prof.
Dipartimento di Anestesia e Rianimazione |
Università di Torino | Ospedale
S. Giovanni Battista-Molinette | Torino, Italy

Address for correspondence
V. Marco Ranieri
Università di Torino
Dipartimento di Anestesia e Rianimazione
Ospedale S. Giovanni Battista-Molinette
Corso Dogliotti 14
10126 Torino, Italy
e-mail: marco.ranieri@unito.it

References

1. Brochard L, Isabey D, Piquet J, Amaro P, Mancebo J, Messadi AA et al. Reversal of acute exacerbations of chronic obstructive lung disease by inspiratory assistance with a face mask. N Engl J Med. 1990;323(22): 1523–30.
2. Plant PK, Owen JL, Elliott MW. Early use of non-invasive ventilation for acute exacerbations of chronic obstructive pulmonary disease on general respiratory wards: a multicentre randomised controlled trial. Lancet. 2000;355(9219):1931–5.
3. Keenan SP, Sinuff T, Cook DJ, Hill NS. Which patients with acute exacerbation of chronic obstructive pulmonary disease benefit from noninvasive positive-pressure ventilation? A systematic review of the literature. Ann Intern Med. 2003;138(11):861–70.
4. Kerby GR, Mayer LS, Pingleton SK. Nocturnal positive pressure ventilation via nasal mask. Am Rev Respir Dis. 1987;135(3):738–40.
5. Demoule A, Girou E, Richard JC, Taille S, Brochard L. Increased use of noninvasive ventilation in French intensive care units. Intensive Care Med. 2006;32(11): 1747–55.
6. Antonelli M, Conti G, Rocco M, Bufi M, De Blasi RA, Vivino G et al. A comparison of noninvasive positive-pressure ventilation and conventional mechanical ventilation in patients with acute respiratory failure. N Engl J Med. 1998;339(7):429–35.
7. Epstein SK, Ciubotaru RL, Wong JB. Effect of failed extubation on the outcome of mechanical ventilation. Chest. 1997;112(1):186–92.
8. Evans TW. International Consensus Conferences in Intensive Care Medicine: non-invasive positive pressure ventilation in acute respiratory failure.Organised jointly

by the American Thoracic Society, the European Respiratory Society, the European Society of Intensive Care Medicine, and the Societe de Reanimation de Langue Francaise, and approved by the ATS Board of Directors, December 2000. Intensive Care Med. 2001; 27(1):166-78.

9. Schettino G, Altobelli N, Kacmarek RM. Noninvasive positive-pressure ventilation in acute respiratory failure outside clinical trials: experience at the Massachusetts General Hospital. Crit Care Med. 2008; 36(2):441-7.

10. Antro C, Merico F, Urbino R, Gai V. Non-invasive ventilation as a first-line treatment for acute respiratory failure: "real life" experience in the emergency department. Emerg Med J. 2005;22(11):772-7.

11. Demoule A, Girou E, Richard JC, Taille S, Brochard L. Benefits and risks of success or failure of noninvasive ventilation. Intensive Care Med. 2006;32(11):1756-65.

12. Rocker GM, Mackenzie MG, Williams B, Logan PM. Noninvasive positive pressure ventilation: successful outcome in patients with acute lung injury/ARDS. Chest. 1999;115(1):173-7.

13. Pennock BE, Crawshaw L, Kaplan PD. Noninvasive nasal mask ventilation for acute respiratory failure. Institution of a new therapeutic technology for routine use. Chest. 1994;105(2):441-4.

14. Wysocki M, Tric L, Wolff MA, Millet H, Herman B. Noninvasive pressure support ventilation in patients with acute respiratory failure. A randomized comparison with conventional therapy. Chest. 1995;107(3):761-8.

15. Delclaux C, L'Her E, Alberti C, Mancebo J, Abroug F, Conti G et al. Treatment of acute hypoxemic nonhypercapnic respiratory insufficiency with continuous positive airway pressure delivered by a face mask: A randomized controlled trial. Jama. 2000;284(18):2352-60.

16. Masip J, Betbese AJ, Paez J, Vecilla F, Canizares R, Padro J et al. Non-invasive pressure support ventilation versus conventional oxygen therapy in acute cardiogenic pulmonary oedema: a randomised trial. Lancet. 2000; 356(9248):2126-32.

17. Nava S, Carbone G, DiBattista N, Bellone A, Baiardi P, Cosentini R et al. Noninvasive ventilation in cardiogenic pulmonary edema: a multicenter randomized trial. Am J Respir Crit Care Med. 2003;168(12):1432-7.

18. L'Her E, Duquesne F, Girou E, de Rosiere XD, Le Conte P, Renault S et al. Noninvasive continuous positive airway pressure in elderly cardiogenic pulmonary edema patients. Intensive Care Med. 2004;30(5):882-8.

19. Mehta S, Jay GD, Woolard RH, Hipona RA, Connolly EM, Cimini DM et al. Randomized, prospective trial of bilevel versus continuous positive airway pressure in acute pulmonary edema. Crit Care Med. 1997;25(4):620-8.

20. Winck JC, Azevedo LF, Costa-Pereira A, Antonelli M, Wyatt JC. Efficacy and safety of non-invasive ventilation in the treatment of acute cardiogenic pulmonary edema –

a systematic review and meta-analysis. Crit Care. 2006; 10(2):R69.

21. Ferrari G, Olliveri F, De Filippi G, Milan A, Apra F, Boccuzzi A et al. Noninvasive positive airway pressure and risk of myocardial infarction in acute cardiogenic pulmonary edema: continuous positive airway pressure vs noninvasive positive pressure ventilation. Chest. 2007; 132(6):1804-9.

22. Masip J, Roque M, Sanchez B, Fernandez R, Subirana M, Exposito JA. Noninvasive ventilation in acute cardiogenic pulmonary edema: systematic review and meta-analysis. Jama. 2005;294(24):3124-30.

23. Peter JV, Moran JL, Phillips-Hughes J, Graham P, Bersten AD. Effect of non-invasive positive pressure ventilation (NIPPV) on mortality in patients with acute cardiogenic pulmonary oedema: a meta-analysis. Lancet. 2006; 367(9517):1155-63.

24. Ho KM, Wong K. A comparison of continuous and bi-level positive airway pressure non-invasive ventilation in patients with acute cardiogenic pulmonary oedema: a meta-analysis. Crit Care. 2006;10(2):R49.

25. Moritz F, Brousse B, Gellee B, Chajara A, L'Her E, Hellot MF et al. Continuous positive airway pressure versus bilevel noninvasive ventilation in acute cardiogenic pulmonary edema: a randomized multicenter trial. Ann Emerg Med. 2007;50(6):666-75, 675 e1.

26. Collins SP, Mielniczuk LM, Whittingham HA, Boseley ME, Schramm DR, Storrow AB. The use of noninvasive ventilation in emergency department patients with acute cardiogenic pulmonary edema: a systematic review. Ann Emerg Med. 2006;48(3):260-9, 269 e1-4.

27. Keenan SP, Sinuff T, Cook DJ, Hill NS. Does noninvasive positive pressure ventilation improve outcome in acute hypoxemic respiratory failure? A systematic review. Crit Care Med. 2004;32(12):2516-23.

28. Hilbert G, Gruson D, Vargas F, Valentino R, Gbikpi-Benissan G, Dupon M et al. Noninvasive ventilation in immunosuppressed patients with pulmonary infiltrates, fever, and acute respiratory failure. N Engl J Med. 2001; 344(7):481-7.

29. Antonelli M, Conti G, Bufi M, Costa MG, Lappa A, Rocco M et al. Noninvasive ventilation for treatment of acute respiratory failure in patients undergoing solid organ transplantation: a randomized trial. Jama. 2000;283(2): 235-41.

30. Auriant I, Jallot A, Herve P, Cerrina J, Le Roy Ladurie F, Fournier JL et al. Noninvasive ventilation reduces mortality in acute respiratory failure following lung resection. Am J Respir Crit Care Med. 2001;164(7): 1231-5.

31. Antonelli M, Conti G, Moro ML, Esquinas A, Gonzalez-Diaz G, Confalonieri M et al. Predictors of failure of noninvasive positive pressure ventilation in patients with acute hypoxemic respiratory failure: a multi-center study. Intensive Care Med. 2001;27(11):1718-28.

32. Antonelli M, Conti G, Esquinas A, Montini L, Maggiore SM, Bello G et al. A multiple-center survey on the use in clinical practice of noninvasive ventilation as a first-line intervention for acute respiratory distress syndrome. Crit Care Med. 2007;35(1):18–25.

33. L'Her E, Deye N, Lellouche F, Taille S, Demoule A, Fraticelli A et al. Physiologic effects of noninvasive ventilation during acute lung injury. Am J Respir Crit Care Med. 2005;172(9):1112–8.

34. Confalonieri M, Potena A, Carbone G, Porta RD, Tolley EA, Umberto Meduri G. Acute respiratory failure in patients with severe community-acquired pneumonia. A prospective randomized evaluation of noninvasive ventilation. Am J Respir Crit Care Med. 1999;160 (5 Pt 1):1585–91.

35. Honrubia T, Garcia Lopez FJ, Franco N, Mas M, Guevara M, Daguerre M et al. Noninvasive vs conventional mechanical ventilation in acute respiratory failure: a multicenter, randomized controlled trial. Chest. 2005;128(6):3916–24.

36. Jolliet P, Abajo B, Pasquina P, Chevrolet JC. Non-invasive pressure support ventilation in severe community-acquired pneumonia. Intensive Care Med. 2001;27(5): 812–21.

37. Ferrer M, Esquinas A, Leon M, Gonzalez G, Alarcon A, Torres A. Noninvasive ventilation in severe hypoxemic respiratory failure: a randomized clinical trial. Am J Respir Crit Care Med. 2003;168(12):1438–44.

38. Rubenfeld GD, Caldwell E, Peabody E, Weaver J, Martin DP, Neff M et al. Incidence and outcomes of acute lung injury. N Engl J Med. 2005;353(16):1685–93.

39. Lindner KH, Lotz P, Ahnefeld FW. Continuous positive airway pressure effect on functional residual capacity, vital capacity and its subdivisions. Chest. 1987;92(1): 66–70.

40. Kindgen-Milles D, Buhl R, Loer SA, Muller E. Nasal CPAP therapy: effects of different CPAP levels on pressure transmission into the trachea and pulmonary oxygen transfer. Acta Anaesthesiol Scand. 2002;46(7):860–5.

41. Matte P, Jacquet L, Van Dyck M, Goenen M. Effects of conventional physiotherapy, continuous positive airway pressure and non-invasive ventilatory support with bilevel positive airway pressure after coronary artery bypass grafting. Acta Anaesthesiol Scand. 2000;44(1): 75–81.

42. Kindgen-Milles D, Muller E, Buhl R, Bohner H, Ritter D, Sandmann W et al. Nasal-continuous positive airway pressure reduces pulmonary morbidity and length of hospital stay following thoracoabdominal aortic surgery. Chest. 2005;128(2):821–8.

43. Squadrone V, Coha M, Cerutti E, Schellino MM, Biolino P, Occella P et al. Continuous positive airway pressure for treatment of postoperative hypoxemia: a randomized controlled trial. Jama. 2005;293(5):589–95.

44. Pasquina P, Merlani P, Granier JM, Ricou B. Continuous positive airway pressure versus noninvasive pressure support ventilation to treat atelectasis after cardiac surgery. Anesth Analg. 2004;99(4):1001–8, table of contents.

45. Nava S, Ambrosino N, Clini E, Prato M, Orlando G, Vitacca M et al. Noninvasive mechanical ventilation in the weaning of patients with respiratory failure due to chronic obstructive pulmonary disease. A randomized, controlled trial. Ann Intern Med. 1998;128(9):721–8.

46. Girault C, Daudenthun I, Chevron V, Tamion F, Leroy J, Bonmarchand G. Noninvasive ventilation as a systematic extubation and weaning technique in acute-on-chronic respiratory failure: a prospective, randomized controlled study. Am J Respir Crit Care Med. 1999;160(1):86–92.

47. Nava S, Gregoretti C, Fanfulla F, Squadrone E, Grassi M, Carlucci A et al. Noninvasive ventilation to prevent respiratory failure after extubation in high-risk patients. Crit Care Med. 2005;33(11):2465–70.

48. Ferrer M, Valencia M, Nicolas JM, Bernadich O, Badia JR, Torres A. Early noninvasive ventilation averts extubation failure in patients at risk: a randomized trial. Am J Respir Crit Care Med. 2006;173(2):164–70.

49. Burns KE, Adhikari NK, Meade MO. A meta-analysis of noninvasive weaning to facilitate liberation from mechanical ventilation. Can J Anaesth. 2006;53(3): 305–15.

50. Keenan SP, Powers C, McCormack DG, Block G. Noninvasive positive-pressure ventilation for postextubation respiratory distress: a randomized controlled trial. Jama. 2002;287(24):3238–44.

51. Esteban A, Frutos-Vivar F, Ferguson ND, Arabi Y, Apezteguia C, Gonzalez M et al. Noninvasive positive-pressure ventilation for respiratory failure after extubation. N Engl J Med. 2004;350(24):2452–60.
Gabriela Ferreyra and V. Marco Ranieri

Rolf Dembinski and Ralf Kuhlen

Weaning: Protocols vs. clinically driven

Introduction to the topic

Depending on its duration mechanical ventilation affects morbidity and mortality of patients in the intensive care unit due to life-threatening complications (1). Most important, mechanical ventilation may cause severe lung injury due to pulmonary baro- and volutrauma (2) and is associated with the occurrence of nosocomial pneumonia (3). The incidence of these complications increases with every day passing on mechanical ventilation (4) resulting in concomitant increased mortality (5). Vice versa, complications of mechanical ventilation usually prolong the ventilation period due to gas exchange disorders. Consequently, all efforts should be made from the start to shorten the duration of mechanical ventilation as much as possible.

However, even when the reason for the onset of mechanical ventilation has been treated successfully and severe complications have been avoided or adequately treated, discontinuation after prolonged mechanical ventilation often cannot be performed instantaneously due to weakness of the respiratory musculature. Therefore, a certain time period is necessary for ventilator withdrawal to accustom patients to breathing without mechanical assistance, a process referred to as weaning from mechanical ventilation.

In patients ventilated for longer than 24 hours about 40–92 % of the duration of mechanical ventilation is dedicated to weaning (1, 6, 7). However, reasons for prolonged weaning are not only related to medical problems such as gas exchange disorders and/or muscle weakness but are also associated with logistic problems such as the clinicians' delay in recognizing the ability of a patient to have mechanical ventilation discontinued. The latter issue has been strikingly disclosed in studies demonstrating a reintubation rate of only 60 % in patients self-extubated during mechanical ventilation (8). This is probably due to the fact that no single factor or measurement is able to predict successful discontinuation from mechanical ventilation (9). Moreover, it should not be forgotten that extubation failure as well is accompanied with increased mortality (10).

In contrast to single parameters, the completion of a combination of several discrete criteria has been shown to improve the likelihood of successful discontinuation from mechanical ventilation (11). Therefore, it is suggested to screen a bundle of parameters frequently in all ventilated patients to provide early identification of patients who are 'ready to wean'. In all patients complying with these requirements successful spontaneous breathing trials have been demonstrated to further increase the probability of successful discontinuation from ventilation (12–14). Thus, daily spontaneous breathing trials are recommended in patients who are ready to wean.

With the aim of simplifying this screening process, increasing efficiency, and decreasing physicians' workload, most experts in the field recommend the use of weaning protocols (see fig. 1). This position seems to be maintained by the results of several clinical trials in which weaning protocols revealed beneficial effects compared to usual care (15–17). However, other studies failed to reveal improvements of outcome parameters after implementation of weaning protocols (18). Thus, there is ongoing controversy about the impact of weaning protocols compared to clinical decision making based on more or less standardised parameters. The following contribution highlights the most important arguments alleged within this discussion.

Controversial position 1: Weaning by protocols

Weaning protocols are mainly compiled on the basis of statistically significant results. Up until today four major randomised controlled trials including a total number of more than 1,000 patients revealed a significant reduction of the duration of mechanical ventilation due to weaning protocols (15–17, 19).

In the first of these studies presented by Wesley Ely and colleagues in 1996 daily screening followed by spontaneous breathing trials in medical and coronary intensive care units reduced the du-

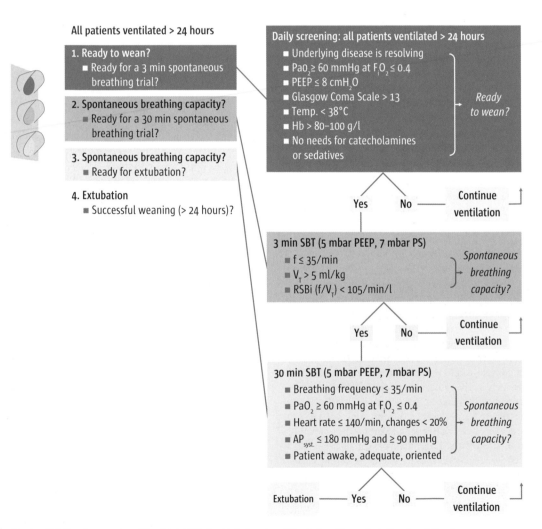

Fig. 1   SBT: Spontaneous breathing trial, RSBi: Rapid shallow breathing index, AP$_{syst.}$: Systolic arterial blood pressure

ration of ventilation from a median of 6.0 to 4.5 in 300 patients (15). Moreover, complications and total costs for the intensive care unit were lower in the protocol group when compared to controls.

In 1997 Marin Kollef and co-workers published data of 357 patients from medical and surgical intensive care units randomised to protocol-directed or physician-directed weaning (16). Like Ely et al., they found reduced length of stay on mechanical ventilation from 2.9 to. 4.3 days and hospital cost savings for patients in the protocol-directed group.

These results were confirmed again by Gregory Marelich et al. in 335 medical and surgical intensive care medicine patients by a reduction from 5.2 to 2.8 days of mechanical ventilation due to the use of a respiratory care practitioner- and registered nurse-driven protocol.

More recently, François Lellouche and his group could demonstrate a reduction of the duration of mechanical ventilation from 12.0 to 7.5 days in 144 medical and surgical intensive care medicine patients due to the use of a computer-driven weaning protocol in comparison to physician-directed weaning without a protocol (19).

According to these results there should be no doubt about the usefulness of weaning protocols as long as evidence-based medicine is considered in clinical practice. However, beside statistical significance it is crucial for the discussion to recognise the numerous content-related advantages potentially responsible for the beneficial effects of weaning protocols in controlled trials:

First, application of protocols allows obtaining and processing of more parameters at a time when compared to individual human capacity. Thereby, an inadvertent loss of relevant data can be avoided. Moreover, measurements and data collection are always performed in the same manner according to a preset sequence and predefined methods. Therefore, individual differences in recording data can be minimised. Furthermore, protocols provide exact definitions and threshold values thereby avoiding misunderstandings and misinterpretations. Thus, following a weaning protocol there should be exactly one predefined way to frequently measure, record, process and interpret all relevant data within a short time period. Consequently, screening patients by using a weaning protocol does not require a physician but can be nurse-directed instead. Besides cost savings due

to the reduced length of stay on ventilation this decrease of physicians' workload may further save total costs for the intensive care unit.

According to the data obtained in the screening process, protocols furthermore dictate straightforward practical results. In contrast, even with identical findings during individual examination, barriers to adherence probably avoid practical results. The lack of adherence to the low tidal volume strategy in patients with acute respiratory distress syndrome (ARDS) is a good example of this problem: Eight years ago a large-sized multicenter trial of the American ARDS-Network revealed a marked and significant decrease of mortality in ARDS patients due to the reduction of tidal volumes from 12 to 6 ml kg^{-1} bodyweight (20). Therefore, an analogous reduction of tidal volumes has been strongly recommended by all experts and critical care societies. However, several observational studies demonstrated only poor adherence to this guideline even years later (21, 22). On the other hand, protocol-guided limitation of tidal volumes has been proven to be more effective and successful (23). Thus, protocols provide practical conformity thereby avoiding different treatment due to individual barriers or local specialists. This is also important as high practice variability implies high error rates. "To err is human"; thus even specialists make mistakes. Weaning protocols may effectively avoid costly and life-threatening errors even in optimally staffed clinics and therefore improve the quality of treatment.

Criticism of protocols often raises the loss of importance of individual knowledge, experience, and expertise. However, weaning protocols actually reflect the knowledge, experience, and expertise of numerous clinical experts proven by corresponding results in controlled clinical trials. Thus, as individual decision making depends on individual expertise, protocols provide a maximum of expertise as they reflected condensed and evidence proved knowledge and experience of several experts. Essentially, a weaning protocol is the result of multiple individual observations investigated and proven to be beneficial in randomised controlled studies.

In contrast to guidelines that allow different decisions by different physicians for the same clinical situation according to their qualification and experience a protocol is more explicit and must lead to the same decisions by multiple physicians. Actually, protocols should be so explicit that they could be implemented in a computer program. Accordingly, the use of a computer-driven closed-loop weaning protocol has been shown to markedly reduce duration of ventilation in a randomised controlled trial (19). This should be viewed as a decrease of clinicians' workload rather than a restriction on the freedom of decision and treatment. Moreover, explicit protocols may serve as effective educational tools by determining relevant parameters to be considered, definitely fixing thresholds and their value for decisionmaking.

Apart from the quality of clinical treatment, scientific progress and thereby the quality of treatment in the future depends on the use of weaning protocols as well. Only by using standardised protocols are controlled clinical studies that compare and improve current thinking able to be realised, thereby optimising the therapy of patients in the intensive care medicine. Recently, this has been demonstrated in a randomised multicenter study combining a current weaning protocol with a daily wake-up trial to achieve additional beneficial effects (24). In this study presented by Timothy Girard et al., patients with combined treatment spent more days breathing without assistance during the 28-day study period, and were discharged from intensive care and the hospital earlier than were those with a weaning protocol alone.

In summary, weaning protocols offer the most efficient and effective method to implement evidence-based medicine into clinical practice. Their application provides optimal intensive care according to current knowledge with a maximum of safety. Additionally, the use of weaning protocols contributes to saving personal and financial recourses, facilitate education, and may help to improve medical progress. Thus, to use or not to use weaning protocols is a matter of good or bad clinical practice.

Controversial position 2:
Weaning clinically driven

Several randomised controlled studies revealed a shortened duration of mechanical ventilation due to the use of weaning protocols. However, several others did not. Moreover, even the major positive trials most often cited in the discussion did not reveal any other beneficial effects to outcome apart from the duration of mechanical ventilation. Finally, the validity of these studies is limited due to major deficiencies of their design and performance.

For instance, no beneficial effects on mortality or length of stay either on intensive care or in the hospital could be demonstrated in the study by Ely et al. (15). Obviously, shortening the duration of mechanical ventilation by 1.5 days had only limited effects on outcome in this trial. In both groups daily screening was performed but resulted in spontaneous breathing trials only in the intervention group. In this group the patients' physicians were notified if the trial was successful. However, in the control group no spontaneous breathing trials were performed at all. However, according to the results of two randomised studies presented 1994 by Laurent Brochard et al. (12) and 1995 by Andrés Esteban et al. (13) it was already known at the time of patients' recruitment between June 1995 and February 1996 that spontaneous breathing trials may decrease the duration of ventilation. Thus, the results of the study reflect beneficial effects of weaning protocols including spontaneous breathing trials rather than advantages of weaning protocols per se. Moreover, 33 % of patients in the control group were ventilated with intermittent mandatory ventilation although this mode was accompanied with the worst outcome in both previous studies by Brochard and Esteban. Strictly speaking, treatment of patients in the control group possibly reflected usual care at that time but did not met the requirements of evidence-based medicine in those days.

In the study by Kollef et al. the use of weaning protocols shortened total duration of ventilation by 1.4 days and reduced hospital costs but any other significant advantages due to intervention could not be determined (16). Worth noting is the fact that duration of ventilation before start of weaning already showed significant differences of 0.7 days in favour of the intervention group. Thus, groups were possibly not very well matched in this trial. More important, three different weaning protocols were applied in four intensive care units participating in this study to facilitate acceptance of the weaning protocols within the individual intensive care units. Differences included the ventilation mode thereby using intermittent mandatory ventilation, pressure support ventilation and assisted control ventilation and the weaning strategy applying spontaneous breathing trials in not even 30 % of patients of both groups. In summary, the results of this study have to be interpreted carefully, considering patient selection bias and different treatment algorithms within the groups.

Marelich et al. and Lellouche et al. also failed to reveal any other beneficial effects on outcome in their studies apart from the length of stay on mechanical ventilation (17, 19). In several other randomised controlled trials not even beneficial effects on the duration of ventilation could be revealed when comparing protocol-directed and physician-directed weaning (18, 25–27). For example, in a randomised study by Jerry Krishnan et al. the implementation of a weaning protocol in a single centre intensive care unit with generous physician staffing and structured rounds had no effects at all despite a prolonged duration of spontaneous breathing trials prior to successful extubation (18). Moreover, a trend toward higher mortality has been found in three other studies (17, 19, 27).

In summary, evidence of beneficial effects due to weaning protocols derived by randomised controlled clinical studies is limited and effectiveness appears to be strongly dependent on the individual institution.

Furthermore, implementation of weaning protocols may not be as successful as expected even after a one-year training period driven by experts in the field in a university hospital (28). In a study presented by Ely and co-workers in 1999 the percentage of patients who received a spontaneous breathing trial after having passed the daily screen successfully was only 29 % after a one-year implementation period. In fact, there was a trend towards prolonged length of stay on mechanical ventilation in this study. Obviously, adherence to good clinical care is not always ensured by the implementation of weaning protocols alone.

Protocols per se carry the risk of loss of variability and individuality. This may not be relevant when protocols are used to ensure that simple instructions are carried out. However, weaning from mechanical ventilation is a complex process with numerous aspects which can not be condensed into a simple protocol. There are always different routes to achieve a goal and only individual decision making based on individual experience may result in the best way to success for each individu-

al clinical scenario. The replacement of specialists by less educated and less skilled assistants fulfilling oversimplified protocols is accompanied with the risk of missing the occurrence of complications, not to mention their adequate therapy. This may especially be relevant in closed loop computer systems without any physician feedback.

In summary, the use of weaning protocols is less supplied by evidence than commonly suggested because none of the positive randomised controlled studies has ever found any beneficial effect apart from a reduction of the duration of ventilation. Moreover, several trials even failed to reveal this effect. On the other hand, weaning protocols are difficult to implement in clinical practice and may be unnecessary in intensive care units with adequate physician staffing and structured rounds. By nature protocols represent a possibly dangerous tool with the risk of lost control and the occurrence of complications which can not be recognised and adequately treated without the presence of a well-educated, trained, and experienced physician. Thus, to use or not to use weaning protocols is a question of accepting or not accepting an unnecessary risk in clinical practice.

Summary

Weaning protocols are valuable tools to standardise, control and thereby shorten the duration of withdrawal from mechanical ventilation and saving costs. Furthermore, physicians' workload is probably reduced due to the use of protocols. However, none of the several randomised controlled trials were able to demonstrate any other beneficial effects on patient's outcome apart from a reduced length of stay on mechanical ventilation. Thus, evidence for the use of protocols is limited especially in well-staffed units with regular structured rounds in daily practice. Moreover, implementation of weaning protocols is difficult and time-consuming and requires detailed planning and surveillance according to individual conditions. Nevertheless, in less well staffed wards with higher workload, weaning protocols appear to be a reasonable method to improve quality of treatment. Probably, this applies to the majority of intensive care units in Europe.

Essentially, all previous trials unveiled that the standard procedure of weaning from mechanical ventilation may be improved by using protocols. Possibly, this reflects more strongly that there is a certain level of disorganisation in standard care than the medical advantages of protocols. Thus, further studies evaluating weaning protocols should focus on the comparison to other methods of process optimisation to properly determine their significance for clinical practice.

Key points for clinical practice

- Weaning protocols may reduce the duration of mechanical ventilation.
- Other beneficial effects on outcome parameters have not been proven so far.
- Weaning protocols may also save costs and probably reduce physicians' workload.
- Effectiveness, however, depends on local conditions including staffing and structure.
- Implementation of weaning protocols is also difficult and requires surveillance.
- Probably, advantages outbalance drawbacks in the majority of intensive care units and should therefore be recommended.

The authors

Rolf Dembinski, MD, PhD[1]
Ralf Kuhlen, MD, Prof.[2]
[1]Klinik für Operative Intensivmedizin | Universitätsklinikum der RWTH Aachen, Germany
[2]Klinik für Intensivmedizin | Helios Klinikum Berlin Buch, Germany

Address for correspondence
Rolf Dembinski
Klinik für Operative Intensivmedizin
Universitätsklinikum der RWTH Aachen
Pauwelsstraße 30
52074 Aachen, Germany
e-mail: rolf.dembinski@post.rwth-aachen.de

References

1. Esteban A, Anzueto A, Frutos F, Alia I, Brochard L, Stewart TE et al. Characteristics and outcomes in adult patients receiving mechanical ventilation: a 28-day international study. JAMA. 2002;287:345–55.
2. Oeckler RA, Hubmayr RD. Ventilator-associated lung injury: a search for better therapeutic targets. Eur Respir J. 2007;30:1216–26.
3. Davis KA. Ventilator-associated pneumonia: a review. J Intensive Care Med. 2006;21:211–26.
4. Ibrahim EH, Ward S, Sherman G, Schaiff R, Fraser VJ, Kollef MH. Experience with a clinical guideline for the treatment of ventilator-associated pneumonia. Crit Care Med. 2001;29:1109–15.
5. Ibrahim EH, Ward S, Sherman G, Kollef MH. A comparative analysis of patients with early-onset vs late-onset nosocomial pneumonia in the ICU setting. Chest. 2000; 117:1434–42.
6. Esteban A, Alia I, Ibanez J, Benito S, Tobin MJ. Modes of mechanical ventilation and weaning. A national survey of Spanish hospitals. The Spanish Lung Failure Collaborative Group. Chest. 1994;106:1188–93.
7. Esteban A, Ferguson ND, Meade MO, Frutos-Vivar F, Apezteguia C, Brochard L et al. Evolution of mechanical ventilation in response to clinical research. Am J Respir Crit Care Med. 2008;177:170–7.
8. Boulain T. Unplanned extubations in the adult intensive care unit: a prospective multicenter study. Association des Reanimateurs du Centre-Ouest. Am J Respir Crit Care Med. 1998;157:1131–7.
9. Meade M, Guyatt G, Cook D, Griffith L, Sinuff T, Kergl C et al. Predicting success in weaning from mechanical ventilation. Chest. 2001;120:400S–24S.
10. Epstein SK. Extubation failure: an outcome to be avoided. Crit Care. 2004;8:310–2.
11. Ely EW, Baker AM, Evans GW, Haponik EF. The prognostic significance of passing a daily screen of weaning parameters. Intensive Care Med. 1999;25:581–7.
12. Brochard L, Rauss A, Benito S, Conti G, Mancebo J, Rekik N et al. Comparison of three methods of gradual withdrawal from ventilatory support during weaning from mechanical ventilation. Am J Respir Crit Care Med. 1994;150:896–903.
13. Esteban A, Frutos F, Tobin MJ, Alia I, Solsona JF, Valverdu I et al. A comparison of four methods of weaning patients from mechanical ventilation. Spanish Lung Failure Collaborative Group. N Engl J Med. 1995;332:345–50.14.
14. Esteban A, Alia I, Gordo F, Fernandez R, Solsona JF, Vallverdu I et al. Extubation outcome after spontaneous breathing trials with T-tube or pressure support ventilation. The Spanish Lung Failure Collaborative Group. Am J Respir Crit Care Med. 1997;156:459–65.
15. Ely EW, Baker AM, Dunagan DP, Burke HL, Smith AC, Kelly PT et al. Effect on the duration of mechanical ventilation of identifying patients capable of breathing spontaneously. N Engl J Med. 1996;335:1864–9.
16. Kollef MH, Shapiro SD, Silver P, St John RE, Prentice D, Sauer S et al. A randomized, controlled trial of protocol-directed versus physician-directed weaning from mechanical ventilation. Crit Care Med. 1997;25: 567–74.

17. Marelich GP, Murin S, Battistella F, Inciardi J, Vierra T, Roby M. Protocol weaning of mechanical ventilation in medical and surgical patients by respiratory care practitioners and nurses: effect on weaning time and incidence of ventilator-associated pneumonia. Chest. 2000;118:459–67.

18. Krishnan JA, Moore D, Robeson C, Rand CS, Fessler HE. A prospective, controlled trial of a protocol-based strategy to discontinue mechanical ventilation. Am J Respir Crit Care Med. 2004;169:673–8.

19. Lellouche F, Mancebo J, Jolliet P, Roeseler J, Schortgen F, Dojat M et al. A multicenter randomized trial of computer-driven protocolized weaning from mechanical ventilation. Am J Respir Crit Care Med. 2006;174: 894–900.

20. ARDS Network. Ventilation with lower tidal volumes as compared with traditional tidal volumes for acute lung injury and the acute respiratory distress syndrome. N Engl J Med. 2000;342:1301–8.

21. Young MP, Manning HL, Wilson DL, Mette SA, Riker RR, Leiter JC et al. Ventilation of patients with acute lung injury and acute respiratory distress syndrome: has new evidence changed clinical practice? Crit Care Med. 2004; 32:1260–5.

22. Gillis RC, Weireter LJ, Jr., Britt RC, Cole FJ, Jr., Collins JN, Britt LD. Lung protective ventilation strategies: have we applied them in trauma patients at risk for acute lung injury and acute respiratory distress syndrome? Am Surg. 2007;73:347–50.

23. Yilmaz M, Keegan MT, Iscimen R, Afessa B, Buck CF, Hubmayr RD et al. Toward the prevention of acute lung injury: protocol-guided limitation of large tidal volume ventilation and inappropriate transfusion. Crit Care Med. 2007;35:1660–6.

24. Girard TD, Kress JP, Fuchs BD, Thomason JW, Schweickert WD, Pun BT et al. Efficacy and safety of a paired sedation and ventilator weaning protocol for mechanically ventilated patients in intensive care (Awakening and Breathing Controlled trial): a randomised controlled trial. Lancet. 2008;371:126–34.

25. Hendrix H, Kaiser ME, Yusen RD, Merk J. A randomized trial of automated versus conventional protocol-driven weaning from mechanical ventilation following coronary artery bypass surgery. Eur J Cardiothorac Surg. 2006;29:957–63.

26. McKinley BA, Moore FA, Sailors RM, Cocanour CS, Marquez A, Wright RK et al. Computerized decision support for mechanical ventilation of trauma induced

ARDS: results of a randomized clinical trial. J Trauma. 2001;50:415–24.

27. Namen AM, Ely EW, Tatter SB, Case LD, Lucia MA, Smith A et al. Predictors of successful extubation in neurosurgical patients. Am J Respir Crit Care Med. 2001;163:658–64.

28. Ely EW, Bennett PA, Bowton DL, Murphy SM, Florance AM, Haponik EF. Large scale implementation of a respiratory therapist-driven protocol for ventilator weaning. Am J Respir Crit Care Med. 1999;159:439–46.

29. Schultz TR, Lin RJ, Watzman HM, Durning SM, Hales R, Woodson A et al. Weaning children from mechanical ventilation: a prospective randomized trial of protocol-directed versus physician-directed weaning. Respir Care. 2001;46:772–82.

30. Randolph AG, Wypij D, Venkataraman ST, Hanson JH, Gedeit RG, Meert KL et al. Effect of mechanical ventilator weaning protocols on respiratory outcomes in infants and children: a randomized controlled trial. JAMA. 2002;288:2561–8.

31. Foster GH, Conway WA, Pamulkov N, Lester JL, Magilligan DJ Jr. Early extubation after coronary artery bypass: brief report. Crit Care Med. 1984;12:994–6.

32. Wood G, MacLeod B, Moffatt S. Weaning from mechanical ventilation: physician-directed vs a respiratory-therapist-directed protocol. Respir Care. 1995;40:219–24.

33. Saura P, Blanch L, Mestre J, Valles J, Artigas A, Fernandez R. Clinical consequences of the implementation of a weaning protocol. Intensive Care Med. 1996;22:1052–6.

34. Burns SM, Marshall M, Burns JE, Ryan B, Wilmoth D, Carpenter R et al. Design, testing, and results of an outcomes-managed approach to patients requiring prolonged mechanical ventilation. Am J Crit Care. 1998;7:45–57.

35. Horst HM, Mouro D, Hall-Jenssens RA, Pamukov N. Decrease in ventilation time with a standardized weaning process. Arch Surg. 1998;133:483–8.

36. Dries DJ, McGonigal MD, Malian MS, Bor BJ, Sullivan C. Protocol-driven ventilator weaning reduces use of mechanical ventilation, rate of early reintubation, and ventilator-associated pneumonia. J Trauma. 2004;56: 943–51.

37. Tonnelier JM, Prat G, Le GG, Gut-Gobert C, Renault A, Boles JM et al. Impact of a nurses' protocol-directed weaning procedure on outcomes in patients undergoing mechanical ventilation for longer than 48 hours: a prospective cohort study with a matched historical control group. Crit Care. 2005;9:R83–R89.

Massimo Borelli, Lluis Blanch and Umberto Lucangelo

Pressure-volume curves: Useful in clinical practice

Introduction

Translational research has shown that overdistension and repetitive opening and closing of alveolar units contribute to progressive lung injury, and this damage is not distinguishable from the original disease in patients with acute respiratory distress syndrome (ARDS) receiving mechanical ventilation. Ventilator strategies focused on preventing alveolar end-expiratory collapse and limiting the tidal volume (VT) of each breath can attenuate overdistension and ventilator-induced lung injury (VILI). Pressure-volume (PV) curves of the respiratory system performed at the bedside can help clinicians to accomplish these endpoints (1, 5).

In the last decade, technological developments and new commercially available ventilators have enabled the use of PV curves at the bedside even in unspecialised intensive care units. The complicated, cumbersome and time-consuming supersyringe method of tracing PV curves has been superseded by a friendly approach to PV curve analysis in mechanically ventilated patients accomplished through automatic maneuvers associated with digital data collecting and computer elaboration. In the era of protective ventilatory strategy, the versatility of computer-controlled ventilators should allow personalised treatment tailored to the pathophysiology of individual patients (7).

Mathematical approximation to respiratory system pressure-volume curves

The respiratory PV curve is the result of the elastic behavior of the lung and the chest wall. The basic principle of elasticity is explained by Hooke's law, which adapted to the respiratory system can be written in the form:

$$\frac{F}{S} = Y \cdot \left(\frac{\Delta L}{L_\circ} \right)$$

where the tension developed by the stretching, defined as the force F over the cross-sectional area, S, of the element is proportional to the ratio between the displacement ΔL and the rest length $L_\circ$ by means of a proportional quantity, Y, called Young's module. As this equation is unidimensional, applying it to the elastic behaviour of three-dimensional anatomic structures is not straightforward. Therefore, physiologists prefer to study pulmonary elasticity, or better its reciprocal quantity called compliance, expressed by the ratio between the change in volume ΔV over the change in pressure ΔP:

$$C = \frac{\Delta V}{\Delta P}$$

Compliance values, C, do not remain constant during a respiratory act; instead, they generate a characteristic S-shaped curve. From a mathematical point of view, PV curves can be drawn on a scatter plot considering the discrete sequence of a pair: volume is considered the dependent variable and is plotted on the vertical axis, while pressure represents the independent variable. Several questions could be posed about this curve, but the most natural is: can one find an explicit function that "describes" the plot obtained? In other words, given the pressure value P, can one predict the volume V during a respiratory act? One possible approach is to analyze the plot statistically, i.e. to find the best fitting curve in the sense of ordinary least mean squares.

Venegas et al. (40) proposed to describe the set of points by means of a continuous sigmoidal function whose shape can be controlled by four numerical parameters, a, b, c, d and whose analytic expression is the following:

$$V = a + \frac{b}{1 + e^{-\frac{P-c}{d}}} \equiv a + b \cdot \left\{ 1 + e^{-(P-c)/d} \right\}^{-1}$$

In figure 1, the fitting of the inspiratory limb of the PV curve is represented. Actually, it is not sim-

ple to find the suitable values for a, b, c, d to ensure the best goodness-of-fit of the curve "by paper and pencil": the presence of sums, multiplications and exponentials makes it necessary to use a numerical iterative approach to determine the best parameters. Typically, the Levenberg-Marquardt algorithm is adopted (14) and the responses obtained are excellent, if measured by the determination coefficient R^2 (often greater than 99%). From a geometric point of view, the parameter a represents the lower asymptotic value of the sigmoidal curve, while $a + b$ represents the upper one. The parameter c represents the pressure value in which the curve changes its behavior from convex to concave: this is the inflexion point

$$\left(c, a + \frac{b}{2} \right),$$

which is also the symmetrical center of the curve and the point at which the second derivative is null. Lastly, the parameter d modifies the slope of the sigmoidal model, and it is possible to prove that at the inflexion point the derivative of the curve equals

$$\frac{b}{4d}.$$

The clinical interpretation of this last quantity represents the maximum compliance of the total respiratory system:

$$C_{max} = \frac{b}{4d}.$$

Several more recent attempts have been made to find the model that fits the PV curve best, and various solutions have been proposed (22, 23, 33). Although there is no unanimous agreement about the optimal solution from the clinical point of view, it should be noted that some models (23, 33) require the lower asymptote to be equal to zero, i.e. they require zero lung volume at atmospheric airway pressure and thus do not allow for positive values of functional residual capacity (23). Another model (22) introduces a fifth shape parameter; although this generally leads to slight improvements in fitting, it does not seem to be clearly grounded in clinical reality. A further advantage of the original Venegas model is that it can be ob-

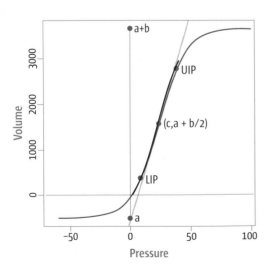

Fig. 1   The inspiratory limb of a PV curve (solid black): the sigmoidal model (—) and the inflection tangent line (—). The slope of the tangent line represents the maximum compliance of the system.

tained as the unique smooth solution of a first order differential equation (32).

Ideally, it is possible to recognise three distinct regions in a PV curve. In the lower left region, increasing pressure levels involve small variations in volume, and from a dynamic point of view the acceleration of the system is positive. The upper right region is characterised by negative acceleration and by increasing pressure levels that cannot be supported by further volume variations. In the intermediate region, in which the model is approximately linear, increasing pressure levels result in nearly proportional volume variations. Identifying those borderline points between the distinct regions of the curve "by cye" can lead to discrepancies and high inter- and intra-observer variability (21); therefore, Venegas et al. (40) proposed to choose the two points in which the sigmoidal model achieves its maximal geometrical curvature, i.e. the points at which the third derivative is null. These points are usually called the lower (LIP) and upper inflection points (UIP), although lower and upper maximum curvature points would be more appropriate terms. These points are located where pressure is equal to

$$c \pm 1.32 \cdot d.$$

Considering different regression models, the UIP and LIP also vary: this can mask different degrees of lung injury that require the tailored choice of ventilatory settings (2, 3). These considerations should be taken in account when different models or different techniques are used to analyse and record PV curves.

The loop described by the inflation and the deflation limbs of the PV curve quantifies hysteresis. This phenomenon represents the lung elastic energy loss occurring between inspiration and expiration, considering the lung as an imperfect elastic body. Several physiopathological conditions can contribute to hysteresis: for example, the opening and closing of lung units, stress relaxation and stress recovery of airways and lung parenchyma, or volume and time-dependent molecular reorganisation of the surface active material that coats air-liquid interfaces in alveoli and conducting airways (11, 12).

In a simplified isolated lung model, hysteresis involves two components of the elastic recoil forces: the surface forces at the air-liquid interfaces and the tissue forces. In the saline-filled lung model, the effects of surface forces are eliminated, so that the pressure required to inflate the lung is only that necessary to overcome the tissue forces: in this case the hysteresis is strongly reduced to close to zero.

Reading PV curves at the bedside

Several studies have demonstrated that the inspiratory limb of the PV curve is parallel to both aeration and recruitment curves (4, 10). For inspiratory pressures between 0 cmH_2O and the inspiratory LIP, the increase in lung volume is mainly due to aeration of normally and poorly aerated areas. When airway pressure increases above the LIP, recruitment starts. Therefore, the LIP reflects the onset of recruitment of nonaerated areas in the lung (15). It has been reported that the presence of an LIP in the curve indicates significant potential for recruitment (41). As detecting this potential could have important consequences for patient management (17), it is tempting to speculate that PV curves could be a useful tool at the bedside (2).

Clinical evolution and the appropriate ventilatory setting should be monitored daily by comparison with a reference PV curve (usually the first PV cure obtained) and its temporal geometrical modification. From the clinical point of view, the elements of particular interest provided by the PV curve are the LIP, UIP, deflation maximum curvature and total respiratory system compliance C_{max}. At the beginning, the PV curve is flat and reflects very low compliance (LIP), the following segment is characterised by a steeper slope that represents C_{max}. At the end of inflation (UIP), when the respiratory system is completely distended, the decrease in compliance suddenly approaches zero.

Recruitment pressures have a Gaussian distribution that is responsible for the steeper part of the curve (33), with the inspiratory UIP reflecting the end of this massive recruitment. However, some recruitment takes place at pressures higher than this point (4, 8). It is useful to detect the UIP to obtain an upper pressure ventilatory limit to avoid overdistension, although some studies suggest that the UIP might indicate the end of alveolar recruitment and not necessarily the beginning of overdistension (28, 29). In every case where the aim is to protect the lung, ventilatory settings should be chosen to achieve a plateau pressure (Pplat) below the UIP.

The LIP occurs at the beginning of lung inflation, where alveoli are less distensible and require high insufflation pressures to reopen. The application of positive end-expiratory pressure (PEEP) values chosen slightly above than LIP pressure value prevents end-expiratory alveolar collapse and avoids shear stress trauma caused by periodic alveolar opening and closing. Immediate gas exchange and intrapulmonary shunt improvement are usually the clinical result of appropriate PEEP applications.

Until a few years ago, LIP determination was considered only of scientific interest; however, nowadays LIP determination has become important to ensure the correct application of PEEP. This has brought about significant improvements in outcome (5) and has established the central role of PEEP in lung protective ventilation strategies (38). Moreover, LIP analysis is an easy way to detect homogeneous lung disease in which recruitment through PEEP application is still possible, even if the optimal level of PEEP cannot be deduced (24, 25, 29). Nevertheless, it is not possible to perform a PEEP titration when the LIP is not identifiable on the PV curve, as occurs in late-stage ARDS patients (2 weeks after onset), presumably because fibrosis replaces edema (34).

In the linear part of the PV curve, the ratio between pressure and volume variations is almost constant. In these conditions, tidal volume ventilation is desirable to minimise VILI.

It is important to point out that the PV curve represents a dynamic phenomenon that reflects alveolar distension of open units and recruitment of previous closed lung units. As suggested by Jonson (24, 25), the volume change in a lung (ΔV) is the sum of two components: $\Delta V = (\Delta V_D + \Delta V_R)$, where ΔV_D represents the continuous distension of open lung units under increasing pressure and ΔVR represents the volume increments when the critical opening pressure of one or more collapsed lung units is overcome and the units are recruited.

With compliance (C) defined as the ratio between volume change (ΔV) and pressure change (ΔP), in accordance with the above consideration, alveolar recruitment is a continuous process that contributes to compliance as described by the following equations:

$$C = \frac{\Delta V}{\Delta P} = \frac{\Delta V_D + \Delta V_R}{\Delta P}$$

Although the best mathematical equation to describe PV curve has yet to be defined, from a clinical point of view it is important to be aware of the limitations of the mathematical models used. For instance, the Venegas model imposes symmetry between the LIP and UIP with respect to the inflection point: this assumption does not fit all clinical conditions. An asymmetric PV curve can be analyzed using a mathematical model with higher degrees of freedom (37), but few physicians have the skills or time for the routine management of these complex mathematical models. For clinical purposes, irrespective of the model used, a rough estimate of the LIP and UIP could be obtained by monitoring a volume-versus-compliance plot (CV curve) together with the PV curve.

During lung filling, the CV curve presents two flat portions (corresponding to the LIP and UIP) separate from a linear segment with a steeper slope that represents C_{max} (see fig. 2).

The physiological meaning of hysteresis was explained in the previous section. From the clinical point of view, hysteresis depends upon both the volume and the maximum pressure reached during the PV maneuver. Hysteresis is increased in the presence of edema in the early stage of ARDS. To allow comparison between and within patients, it could be useful to use the normalised hysteresis ratio HR, which is defined as the quotient between the hysteresis area A and the product of the total pressure variation ΔP multiplied by the total inflated volume V (6):

$$HR = \frac{A}{\Delta P \cdot V}$$

Because ARDS patients are characterised by rapid change in respiratory system mechanics over the course of the illness, multiple PV curve measurement over time may be required to set the ventilator appropriately (23).

If a moderate/high PEEP level is used in an attempt to keep all alveoli open, the level of tidal volume should not exceed the UIP in the PV curve because recruitment beyond this point is non-

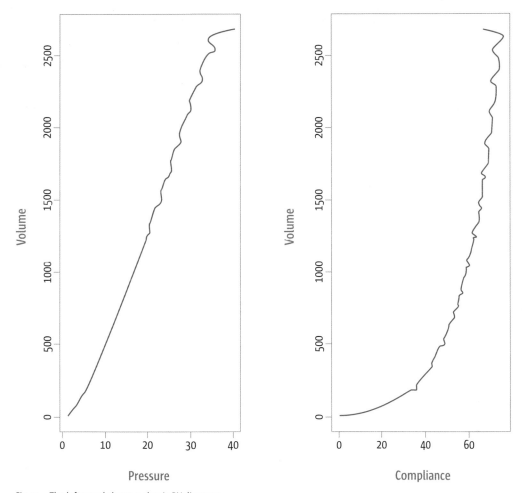

Fig. 2   The left panel shows a classic PV diagram:
The LIP, UIP and linear part of the curve are identifiable by comparing the behavior on a CV plot (right panel).

significant and further hyperinflation is clearly caused, as has been demonstrated by CT scan (26). Roupie et al. (36) observed a mean UIP value of 26 ± 6 cm H$_2$O in 25 ARDS patients and when a tidal volume of 10 ml/kg was used, 80 % showed a plateau pressure that exceeded the UIP value. Based on this criterion, many patients would need a reduction in tidal volume that would result in hypercapnia. Recently, Terragni et al. (39) found that limiting tidal volume to 6 ml/kg of predicted body weight and plateau pressure to 30 cm H$_2$O may not be sufficient to avoid superimposed lung injury in ARDS patients characterised by a larger nonaerated compartment. Therefore, the protocol for mechanical ventilation set-

tings proposed by the Acute Respiratory Distress Syndrome Network to ventilate ARDS patients (1, 9) could be further improved by periodic assessment of respiratory mechanics and the effects of PEEP on recruitment with PV curves at the bedside. Moreover, the advanced technology built into ventilators allows PV curves to be constructed with acceptable variability under anaesthesia alone and no serious adverse effects (43). Finally, in non-responding mechanically ventilated ARDS patients, an unconventional ventilatory technique such as high frequency ventilation (HFV) is required to improve gas exchange. In this case, the LIP is used to set the mean pressure applied to the respiratory system at the beginning of HFV

(27). The range of increment of mean airway pressure during HFV has to be set according to the linear part of the PV curve and to the patient's hemodynamic conditions.

Pressure-volume curves at the bedside: Clinical studies

Mechanical ventilation is lifesaving in patients with severe hypoxemia diagnosed with ARDS. Nevertheless, studies from experimental and clinical fields have shown that positive pressure breathing can worsen pre-existing lung injury by inducing tidal inspiratory opening of alveolar units that close again at end-expiration, and high airway pressures at end-inspiration can also cause overdistension of ventilated alveoli. This phenomenon has been named VILI or ventilation-associated lung injury. Furthermore, repetitive overdistension and/or closing and reopening alveoli can cause or trigger a pulmonary and systemic inflammatory reaction that may further predispose to injury of other organs. Thus, mechanical ventilation can contribute to multisystem organ failure.

There is evidence that lung protective mechanical ventilatory strategies reduce mortality in patients with ARDS. These strategies typically involve the use of small tidal volumes to avoid high alveolar pressures at end-inspiration and alveolar overdistension together with the use of moderate or high PEEP levels to keep alveoli open at end-expiration and thus maintain alveolar recruitment.

Recent studies compared the traditional lower end-expiratory pressure strategy with a higher end-expiratory pressure strategy (FiO_2 and PEEP were predefined in each arm) in patients with ARDS ventilated with low tidal volumes. Interestingly, no effect on mortality (9, 30) was found, although high PEEP ventilation was associated with fewer episodes of severe hypoxemia and decreased use of rescue therapies (30). In parallel, Mercat et al. (31) in a French multicenter randomised trial found that a strategy for setting PEEP aimed at increasing alveolar recruitment while limiting hyperinflation did not significantly reduce mortality but improved lung function and reduced the duration of mechanical ventilation and the duration of organ failure. Although it seems that the optimal PEEP strategy has yet to be determined, ventilatory strategies with higher

levels of PEEP appear safe and probably beneficial, especially in patients with acute lung injury and ARDS in the most critical condition, whereas strategies with lower levels of PEEP may worsen outcomes (16).

The question that clinicians have in mind is: can PV curves refine ventilator set up in the framework of low tidal volume and adequate PEEP selection? Selecting tidal volume and PEEP in accordance with the findings obtained from PV curves drawn in zero PEEP conditions yielded better ventilator tuning and seemed to have a positive effect on outcome in several studies. Amato et al (5) provided the first demonstration that setting the ventilator according to the measured mechanics of the respiratory system can have a significant impact on clinical outcome in patients with ARDS. As compared with conventional ventilation, the protective strategy of setting the PEEP above the LIP and tidal ventilation (6 ml/kg) in the linear portion of the respiratory system PV curve was associated with improved survival at 28 days. In a recent study, Villar et al. (42) found that a mechanical ventilation strategy consisting of setting PEEP level above the LIP on day 1 and maintaining a low tidal volume had a more beneficial impact on outcome in patients with severe and persistent ARDS than a strategy with a higher tidal volume and relatively low PEEP. Finally, Ranieri et al. (35) found that the group of ARDS patients randomised to receive tidal volume and PEEP based on the PV curve had a reduction in plasma and bronchoalveolar lavage concentrations of IL-6, soluble TNF-alpha receptor 75, and IL-1 receptor antagonist, whereas an increase in these concentrations was detected in the control group. Moreover, Grasso et al. (18, 19) have shown the importance of considering both the distribution of loss of aeration and the physiologic effects of PEEP when ventilating patients with ARDS. Both PV curves and stress index measurements are better physiologic approaches for setting PEEP than the PEEP-FIO_2 table described in recent studies (1, 9).

Summary

In patients with ARDS, it is important to assess respiratory system mechanics and to choose appropriate ventilator settings. In most patients with ARDS, the information obtained from static inflation PV curves of the respiratory system could be used to select an appropriate tidal volume and PEEP levels that might improve outcome. Nevertheless, important questions remain to be investigated, including the optimal periodicity of PV curve measurement and uncertainties regarding its interpretation. Mathematical approaches to PV interpretation stress the importance of eliminating subjectivity to determine the correct ventilatory parameters; however, clinical practice provides suitable criteria to individualise these parameters by observing PV and CV curves to avoid VILI. This apparent dichotomy could be effectively resolved when a satisfactory respiratory mechanical model is found.

Key points for clinical practice

1. *Static PV curves correlate with the changes in lung morphology during passive inflation and deflation in patients with ARDS. The different techniques available to trace static PV curves at the bedside yield quite reproducible results, although there is variability in the assessment of the different inflection points.*
2. *The physiological data obtained by measuring static PV curves has helped clinicians to better understand the behavior of the respiratory system when positive-pressure ventilation is applied in patients with ARDS receiving mechanical ventilation.*
3. *In modern ventilators, a complete PV curve can be traced in a short time without ventilator disconnection, under sedation alone, and the results are immediate. Usually, the inflation and deflation limbs can be obtained and minimal PEEP can be used to avoid lung derecruitment.*

The authors

Massimo Borelli, MSc[1]
Lluis Blanch, MD, PhD[2]
Umberto Lucangelo, MD[3]
    [1]Department of Mathematics and Computer Science | Trieste University | Trieste, Italy
    [2]Critical Care Center | CIBER Enfermedades Respiratorias | Hospital de Sabadell, Corporació Sanitaria Parc Tauli | Institut Universitari Fundació Parc Tauli | Universitat Autònoma de Barcelona, Spain
    [3]Department of Perioperative Medicine | Intensive Care and Emergency | Cattinara Hospital | Trieste University School of Medicine | Trieste, Italy

Address for correspondence
    Lluis Blanch
    Critical Care Center
    Hospital de Sabadell
    Corporació Sanitaria Parc Tauli
    08208 Sabadell, Spain
    e-mail: lblanch@tauli.cat

References

1. [No authors listed]. Ventilation with lower tidal volumes as compared with traditional tidal volumes for acute lung injury and the acute respiratory distress syndrome. The Acute Respiratory Distress Syndrome Network. N Engl J Med. 2000;342:1301–1308.
2. Albaiceta GM, Blanch L, Lucangelo U. Static pressure-volume curves of the respiratory system: were they just a passing fad? Curr Opin Crit Care. 2008;14:80–86.
3. Albaiceta GM, Garcia E, Taboada F. Comparative study of four sigmoid models of pressure-volume curve in acute lung injury. Biomed Eng Online. 2007 Feb 14;6:7.
4. Albaiceta GM, Taboada F, Parra D, Luyando LH, Calvo J, Menendez R et al. Tomographic study of the inflection points of the pressure-volume curve in acute lung injury. Am J Respir Crit Care Med. 2004;170:1066–72.
5. Amato MB, Barbas CS, Medeiros DM, Magaldi RB, Schettino GP, Lorenzi-Filho G et al. Effect of a protective-ventilation strategy on mortality in the acute respiratory distress syndrome. N Engl J Med. 1998;338:347–354.
6. Bachofen H, Hildebrant J. Area analysis of pressure volume hysteresis in mammalian lungs. J Appl. Physiol. 1971;30:493–497.
7. Blanch L, López-Aguilar J, Villagrá A. Bedside evaluation of pressure-volume curves in patients with acute respiratory distress syndrome. Curr Opin Crit Care. 2007; 13:332–337.
8. Borges JB, Okamoto VN, Matos GF, Caramez MP, Arantes PR, Barros F et al. Reversibility of lung collapse and hypoxemia in early acute respiratory distress syndrome. Am J Respir Crit Care Med. 2006;174:268–1278.
9. Brower RG, Lanken PN, MacIntyre N, Matthay MA, Morris A, Ancukiewicz M et al. Higher versus lower positive end-expiratory pressures in patients with the acute respiratory distress syndrome. N Engl J Med. 2004; 351:327–336.
10. Crotti S, Mascheroni D, Caironi P, Pelosi P, Ronzoni G, Mondino M et al. Recruitment and derecruitment during acute respiratory failure: a clinical study. Am J Respir Crit Care Med. 2001;164:131–40.
11. Chiumello D, Carlesso E, Aliverti A, Dellacà RL, Pedotti A, Pelosi PP, et al. Effects of volume shift on the pressure-volume curve of the respiratory system in ALI/ARDS patients. Minerva Anestesiol. 2007;73:109–118.

12. de Chazal I, Hubmayr RD. Novel aspects of pulmonary mechanics in intensive care. Br J Anaesth. 2003;91; 81–91.

13. Decailliot F, Demoule A, Maggiore SM, Jonson B, Duvaldestin P, Brochard L. Pressure-volume curves with and without muscle paralysis in acute respiratory distress syndrome. Intensive Care Med. 2006;32: 1322–1328.

14. Dennis JE, Schnabel RB. Numerical methods for unconstrained optimization and nonlinear equations. Prentice-Hall, Inc., New Jersey. 1983.

15. Downie JM, Nam AJ, Simon BA. Pressure-volume curve does not predict steady-state lung volume in canine lavage lung injury. Am J Respir Crit Care Med. 2004;169: 957–962.

16. Gattinoni L, Caironi P. Refining ventilatory treatment for acute lung injury and acute respiratory distress syndrome. JAMA. 2008;299:691–693.

17. Gattinoni L, Caironi P, Cressoni M, Chiumello D, Ranieri VM, Quintel M et al. Lung recruitment in patients with the acute respiratory distress syndrome. N Engl J Med. 2006;354:1775–1786.

18. Grasso S, Fanelli V, Cafarelli A, Anaclerio R, Amabile M, Ancona G et al. Effects of high versus low positive end-expiratory pressures in acute respiratory distress syndrome. Am J Respir Crit Care Med. 2005;171:1002–1008.

19. Grasso S, Stripoli T, De Michele M, Bruno F, Moschetta M, Angelelli G et al. ARDSnet ventilatory protocol and alveolar hyperinflation: role of positive end-expiratory pressure. Am J Respir Crit Care Med. 2007;176:761–767.

20. Harris RS. Pressure-Volume Curves of the Respiratory System. Respir Care. 2005;50:78–98.

21. Harris RS, Hess DR, Venegas JG. An objective analysis of the pressure-volume curve in the acute respiratory distress syndrome. Am J Respir Crit Care Med. 2000;161:432–439.

22. Heller H, Brandt S, Schuster KD. Development of an algorithm for improving the description of the pulmonary pressure-volume curve. J Appl Physiol. 2002;92:1770;author reply 1770–1.

23. Henzler D, Orfao S, Rossaint R, Kuhlen R. Modification of a sigmoidal equation for the pulmonary pressure-volume curve for asymmetric data. J Appl Physiol. 2003;95:2183–4;author reply 2184.

24. Jonson B. Elastic pressure-volume curves in acute lung injury and acute respiratory distress syndrome. Intensive Care Med. 2005;31:205–212.

25. Jonson B, Svantesson C. Elastic pressure-volume curves: what information do they convey? Thorax. 1999;54: 82–87.

26. Lu Q, Constantin JM, Nieszkowska A, Elman M, Vieira S, Rouby JJ. Measurement of alveolar derecruitment in patients with acute lung injury computerized tomography versus pressure-volume curve. Crit Care. 2006;10(3):R95. Epub 2006 Jun 22.

27. Luecke T, Meinhardt JP, Herrmann P, Weisser G, Pelosi P, Quintel M. Setting mean airway pressure during high-frequency oscillatory ventilation according to the static pressure-volume curve in surfactant-deficient lung injury: a computed tomography study Anesthesiology. 2003;99:1313–1322.

28. Maggiore SM, Jonson B, Richard JC, Jaber S, Lemaire F, Brochard L. Alveolar derecruitment at decremental positive end-expiratory pressure levels in acute lung injury: comparison with the lower inflection point, oxygenation, and compliance. Am J Respir Crit Care Med. 2001;164:795–801.

29. Maggiore SM, Richard JC, Brochard L. What has been learnt from P/V curves in patients with acute lung injury/acute respiratory distress syndrome. Eur Respir J. 2003;42:22s–26s.

30. Meade MO, Cook DJ, Guyatt GH, Slutsky AS, Arabi YM, Cooper DJ et al. Ventilation strategy using low tidal volumes, recruitment maneuvers, and high positive end-expiratory pressure for acute lung injury and acute respiratory distress syndrome: a randomized controlled trial. JAMA. 2008;299:637–645.

31. Mercat A, Richard JC, Vielle B, Jaber S, Osman D, Diehl JL et al. Positive end-expiratory pressure setting in adults with acute lung injury and acute respiratory distress syndrome: a randomized controlled trial. JAMA. 2008; 299:646–655.

32. Narusawa U. General characteristics of the sigmoidal model equation representing quasi-static pulmonary P-V curves. J Appl Physiol. 2001;91:201–210.

33. Pelosi P, Goldner M, McKibben A, Adams A, Eccher G, Caironi P et al. Recruitment and derecruitment during acute respiratory failure: an experimental study. Am J Respir Crit Care Med. 2001;164:122–130.

34. Puybasset L, Cluzel P, Gusman P, Grenier P, Preteux F, Rouby JJ. Regional distribution of gas and tissue in acute respiratory distress syndrome. I. Consequences for lung morphology. CT Scan ARDS Study Group. Intensive Care Med. 2000;26:857–869.

35. Ranieri VM, Suter PM, Tortorella C, De Tullio R, Dayer JM, Brienza A et al. Effect of mechanical ventilation on inflammatory mediators in patients with acute respiratory distress syndrome: a randomized controlled trial. JAMA. 1999;282:54–61.

36. Roupie E, Dambrosio M, Servillo G, Mentec H, el Atrous S, Beydon L et al. Titration of tidal volume and induced hypercapnia in acute respiratory distress syndrome. Am J Respir Crit Care Med. 1995;152:121–128.

37. Svantesson C, Drefeldt B, Sigurdsson S, Larsson A, Brochard L, Jonson B. A single computer-controlled mechanical insufflation allows determination of the pressure-volume relationship of the respiratory system. J Clin Monit Comput. 1999;15:9–16.

38. Takeuchi M, Goddon S, Dolhnikoff M, Shimaoka M, Hess D Amato MB et al. Set positive end-expiratory

pressure during protective ventilation affects lung injury. Anesthesiology. 2002;97:682–692.

39. Terragni PP, Rosboch G, Tealdi A, Corno E, Menaldo E, Davini O et al. Tidal hyperinflation during low tidal volume ventilation in acute respiratory distress syndrome. Am J Respir Crit Care Med. 2007;175:160–166.

40. Venegas JG, Harris RS, Simon BA. A comprehensive equation for the pulmonary pressure-volume curve. J Appl Physiol. 1998;84:389–395.

41. Vieira SR, Puybasset L, Lu Q, Richecoeur J, Cluzel P, Coriat P et al. A scanographic assessment of pulmonary morphology in acute lung injury. Significance of the lower inflection point detected on the lung pressure-volume curve. Am J Respir Crit Care Med. 1999;159: 1612–23.

42. Villar J, Kacmarek RM, Pérez-Méndez L, Aguirre-Jaime A. A high positive end-expiratory pressure, low tidal volume ventilatory strategy improves outcome in persistent acute respiratory distress syndrome: a randomized, controlled trial. Crit Care Med. 2006;34: 1311–1318.

43. Decailliot F, Demoule A, Maggiore SM, Jonson B, Duvaldestin Ph, Brochard L. Pressure-volume curves with and without muscle paralysis in acute respiratory distress syndrome. Intensive Care Med 2006;32: 1322–1328.

Ronald J. Trof and A. B. Johan Groeneveld

Replacing or restricting fluids: Timing, dosing and choosing the type of fluid in patients with or at risk for ALI/ARDS

Introduction

The ongoing debate on fluid resuscitation includes the timing, dosing, and choosing the type of fluid and effects on pulmonary hydration status, particularly during (impending) acute lung injury (ALI)/acute respiratory distress syndrome (ARDS), when pulmonary capillary permeability may be increased (1).

From physiological considerations, animal and limited clinical observations, it can be assumed that extravasation of fluids in vivo is governed by pericapillary hydrostatic and colloid osmotic pressures (COP), and permeability. This does not necessarily equate with oedema formation, however, when increased lymph flow (up to a factor of 9 in normal lungs) may offset increased fluid filtration. Additionally, the effect of plasma COP to attenuate filtration (or a low COP to increase filtration) is expected to increase when hydrostatic pressure increases and drives fluids out of the bloodstream (2). Furthermore, an increased permeability and a resultant decrease in the pericapillary COP gradient may attenuate potential differences between fluid types, decreasing (crystalloids) and maintaining or even increasing plasma COP (colloids), respectively. Figure 1 illustrates these concepts, based on filtration forces rather than adaptations in lymph flow and suggests that differences in fluid types are expected to be less in modulating pulmonary oedema

formation in the steep part of the cardiac function curve, which is associated with a relatively low hydrostatic filtration pressure in the lungs.

Both pulmonary capillary permeability and oedema can be measured at the bedside; many ALI and all ARDS patients meeting accepted criteria have a measurably increased pulmonary capillary permeability but only up to 70 % have a supranormal extravascular lung water (EVLW) (3–7). Indeed, the single transpulmonary thermal dilution technique is currently the reference standard for measuring and monitoring extravascular thermal volume in the lungs as a measure of accessible lung water – EVLW – at the bedside. This technique has shown excellent correlation with the gravimetric method (8) and may have prognostic significance (6, 9). With this technique, however, pleural fluid is not measured. CT scanning gives an indirect measure of oedema but is, by nature, intermittent at best, involving transportation and interruption of, for instance, renal replacement therapy instituted to attenuate fluid overloading. There is some evidence that EVLW (plus pulmonary blood volume) fairly correlates to tissue lung weights (i.e. pulmonary blood plus extravascular fluid volumes) estimated from CT scans (10). CT scanning carries the advantage of assessing pleural fluid also. Indeed, accumulation of pleural fluid in mechanically ventilated patients is common and physiology predicts that this may serve as an overflow system for increased intrapulmonary fluid filtration, when draining lymph flow is overwhelmed. Increased pleural pressure hampering parietal resorption in the course of mechanical ventilation may further contribute.

After elaborating on these basic physiologic principles, we will now address the major controversial issues of fluid resuscitation, when clinically needed, in ALI/ARDS or in patients at high risk for these syndromes. We will focus on clinical studies.

Controversy 1: Guiding fluid resuscitation and avoiding overhydration

The goals of fluid resuscitation, when needed, in (impending) ALI/ARDS are aimed at preventing or decreasing new organ failures and ultimately survival. However, intermediate haemodynamic and metabolic endpoints aimed at reaching those goals vary among studies. In any case, overhydration, particularly with crystalloids, is a serious threat and may, among other adverse effects, confound diagnosing and aggravate pulmonary oedema in ALI/ARDS (11–13). Fluid overloading is probably also a common cause of pleural fluid which in turn may compress the lungs, thereby, together with an increased permeability, aggravate oedema, contributing to ventilatory dependency in ALI/ARDS. Fluid overloading leading to an abdominal compartment syndrome may further compromise pulmonary function (12).

Fluid overloading can be prevented by defining goals of fluid resuscitation and refining monitoring techniques. Indeed, predicting fluid responsiveness (i.e. a rise in stroke volume, cardiac output and thus oxygen delivery upon fluid loading) by dynamic or static preload indicators or their combination may help to decide on fluid challenges, provided that there is a clinical problem likely ameliorated by increased oxygen delivery (1, 14–21). Obviously, instead of measuring and monitoring preload indicators as surrogate markers of fluid responsiveness, semi-continuous measurements of stroke volume or cardiac output could serve that purpose as well, provided that they are accurate (14–19, 21–23). Fluid loading should be continued until direct or indirect measures reach a particular point likely associated with improved and sufficient tissue oxygenation. To this end, regional as well as global parameters can be used, together with a careful clinical as-

sessment, including near infrared spectroscopy/tissue oxymetry, microcirculatory imaging and gastrointestinal PCO_2 tonometry for the former, or central or mixed venous oxymetry for the latter (19, 20, 24, 25). Adequate, optimal, goal-directed, goal-oriented or targeted fluid therapy/resuscitation, terms used in the literature, are not unequivocally defined, but may nevertheless imply similar or related endpoints for resuscitation, albeit varying among studies (14, 16–21, 23, 24). In any case, continuing fluid loading when cardiac output does not further increase on the plateau of the cardiac function curve, might result in harmful fluid overloading, particularly in the lungs, deteriorating gas exchange and compliance, while fluid loading in the steep part of the cardiac function curve may not (measurably) increase oedema formation, even in case of mildly increased permeability oedema and ALI after major surgery (1, 4, 11; conform fig. 1). However, when using refined monitoring tools, including EVLW measurements, in patients with or at risk for ALI/ARDS, after major surgery for instance, the amount of fluid given and the duration of mechanical ventilation were, paradoxically, greater than when fluid loading was based on traditional filling pressure measurements (22). Yet, there is no single, universally accepted tool to prevent fluid overloading, when fluid resuscitation is deemed to be necessary.

Controversy 2: Is 'dry' better than 'wet' in preventing/ameliorating pulmonary oedema in ALI/ARDS?

Whereas completely withholding fluids or deliberately overhydrating patients for some time will certainly overwhelm physiological (renal) compensation mechanisms and carry a fatal outcome, restrictive and liberal fluid therapy may be relatively meaningless if departing from different fluid regimens. Hence, the use of fixed, for instance perioperative, fluid dosages is probably also less useful than individual optimisation. Thus the key question is the adequacy of fluid resuscitation, as elaborated above, rather than the relative superiority of a restrictive or liberal regimen.

Nevertheless, authors have advocated perioperative restricted rather than liberal fluid therapy, in order, among others, to prevent occasionally fa-

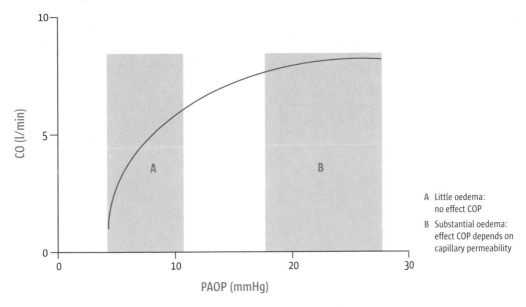

Fig. 1   Schematic representation of the classical cardiac function curve: Cardiac output (CO) versus pulmonary artery occlusion pressure (PAOP). A. denotes the area in which only little oedema occurs regardless of the colloid osmotic pressure (COP). B. denotes the area in which substantial pulmonary oedema may occur in which the effect of COP depends on capillary permeability.

tal postoperative pulmonary oedema, associated with too liberal fluid therapy and not preceded by any warning signs (26–29). Indeed, the widely held belief that surgery may be associated with contraction of the extracellular fluid volume necessitating liberal fluid therapy, may be incorrect (30). When departing from fixed-dose liberal fluid therapy, some fluid restriction can indeed reduce some morbidity (but not mortality) of surgical patients (27–29), whereas a more liberal (as in individualised goal-directed) fluid therapy better maintained tissue oxygenation and decreased morbidity after surgery, as compared to a more restricted or standard policy in other studies (14, 16–21, 24, 25, 29, 31). However, the effect on pulmonary (permeability) oedema and even gas exchange remained unclear in most of these latter studies on patients often at risk for ALI/ARDS after surgery (14, 16–19, 21, 24, 25, 28, 29, 31, 32). The discussion on restricted versus liberal fluid therapy otherwise also applies to trauma/haemorrhagic shock, in which, when bleeding cannot be immediately controlled, small rather than large volume resuscitation may be recommended (33).

The restricted and liberal policies may affect the lungs in keeping them 'dry' or rendering them 'wet', respectively, even though some studies on liberal policies, paradoxically reported unchanged or even diminished duration of ventilation after surgery, associated with improved ventilatory function (20, 27, 31, 32). More complete resuscitation may thus shorten ventilation and ICU durations of stay (14, 21, 23). Nevertheless, a positive fluid balance has been associated with an increasing EVLW, prolonged mechanical ventilation/ICU stay and a worse outcome in sepsis and ALI/ARDS, and vice versa, but this does not necessarily imply cause-effect relationships (13, 22, 34–37). Refining and guiding fluid resuscitation in the course of (impending) ALI/ARDS may benefit from predicting fluid responsiveness and monitoring EVLW in order to prevent oedema formation and thus prolonged need for mechanical ventilation (1, 4, 11, 13, 22, 23, 34, 38). In patients requiring pulmonary artery catheter monitoring who had an elevated EVLW, a fluid strategy based on EVLW measurements, for instance, resulted in less fluid balance positivity and a shorter ventilation duration / ICU stay than a strategy based on the pulmonary artery occlusion pressure (38). In patients with risk factors for ALI/ARDS, such as sepsis and major surgery, or those with established pulmonary oedema or ALI/ARDS, restricting fluids after the initial phase of resuscitation may be beneficial (13, 39). In fact, the ARDS Network trial suggests that, after initial resuscitation, a regimen aimed at less positivity of 7-daily and cumulative fluid balance may improve lung function (oedema?) and reduce ventilator/ICU days but may not reduce mortality in the first 28 days, in patients with ALI/ARDS (39). Obviously, keeping the lungs 'dry' rather than 'wet' should be weighted against potential hypoperfusion of extrapulmonary, injured or vital organs such as the kidneys (13). This may require additional attention and monitoring, but, apparently, additional organ failure was minimal in the restricted fluid group of the ARDS network trial (39). Taken together, timing and dosing fluid therapy in patients with or at risk for ALI/ARDS is still a controversial issue.

Controversy 3: Colloid versus crystalloid in preventing/ameliorating pulmonary oedema during ALI/ARDS

It follows from physiology that the 'dry' and 'wet' issue should also include a discussion on potential merits and detriments of fluid types (crystalloids versus colloids) in ALI/ARDS or patients with an elevated risk for these syndromes (40, 41). Although, roughly speaking, colloids may not confer a survival benefit nor prevent pulmonary oedema as compared to crystalloids in mixed patients populations, albumin administration may be associated with less pulmonary complications, according to meta-analyses, even though oedema was not directly measured (40–42). Hence, the controversy on colloid and crystalloids, when used for fluid resuscitation in ALI/ARDS is ongoing. Notwithstanding, adverse effects of gross overhydration are, obviously, independent of fluid types.

In a small series of mechanically ventilated ALI/ARDS patients with hypoproteinemia and presumably a low COP, albumin and furosemide versus furosemide alone ameliorated gas exchange and some other surrogate indices of pulmonary oedema, which again was not directly measured (43). In critically ill, hypoalbuminemic

patients with a presumably low COP, albumin administration was associated with less positive fluid balance and improved pulmonary function (37). Verheij et al. used a bedside technique for measuring pulmonary permeability for proteins that is specific for ALI/ARDS (4). They showed in postoperative, presumably hypovolemic patients with ALI, in half of them accompanied by mild permeability oedema, that the type of fluids (saline versus gelatin, albumin or starch) did not affect pulmonary oedema formation in the presence of an increased cardiac output, i.e. in the steep part of the cardiac function curve (as in fig. 1). Alternatively, increased permeability may have diminished the contribution of plasma COP on oedema formation, thereby diminishing differences between fluid types, or adaptation of Starling forces and increased lymph flow may have fully compensated for slightly increased fluid transport, or both.

Controversy 4: Colloid versus colloid in preventing or ameliorating pulmonary oedema and lung injury in ALI/ARDS

Among the colloids, albumin and high-molecular weight starch preparations have potential anti-inflammatory and anti-permeability properties, respectively, as suggested by animal experiments. Indeed, HES as compared to gelatin used after abdominal aortic surgery was suggested to ameliorate some gas exchange and other respiratory abnormalities, used as surrogate indices of oedema (44). Verheij et al. (4) confirmed a mild attenuation of directly measured permeability in the lungs, in patients after major surgery, but the clinical consequences remained unclear. Conversely, the favourable effects of albumin suggested by others (37, 43) could have been caused, in part, by a mild anti-inflammatory effect rather than by amelioration of hypoproteinemia, a low COP and pulmonary oedema. However, sufficient clinical data to decide in this matter are lacking.

Summary

Many questions regarding fluid resuscitation during ALI/ARDS remain unanswered, and this is partly related to the frequent use of surrogate indicators of pulmonary oedema, including gas exchange parameters and chest radiography, which may not reflect pulmonary oedema. This calls for using direct measures of permeability and oedema, with proven feasibility at the bedside (4), in evaluating fluid resuscitation in patients with or at risk for ALI/ARDS after sepsis, trauma or major surgery.

Key points for clinical practice

1. *The timing, dosing and choosing of the type of fluid therapy, when clinically needed, in patients with or at risk for ALI/ARDS, is best accomplished by carefully weighing potential benefits and hazards for the individual patient in the course of disease. There is no consensus on this issue.*

2. *Fluid resuscitation remains the treatment of choice, provided that the patient is likely to be fluid responsive, in case of hypotension and tissue hypooxygenation (accompanied by clinical signs). Adequate fluid resuscitation may ameliorate morbidity/mortality and prevent harmful fluid overloading.*

3. *While relative fluid restriction, after initial resuscitation, may ameliorate pulmonary oedema formation and shorten ventilator days particularly when permeability is increased (in ALI/ARDS), this is likely to benefit only when haemodynamically tolerated and when tissue oxygenation and renal perfusion are unlikely to be severely diminished.*

4. *In the steep part of the cardiac function curve, the type (and dose) of fluid used for resuscitation, i.e. colloid or crystalloid, probably does not have a major impact on fluid accumulation in the lungs, regardless of permeability. Predicting and monitoring fluid responsiveness as well as EVLW may prevent (further) pulmonary oedema formation and may guide fluid loading, when needed, during ALI/ARDS, regardless of dose and type of fluid.*

The authors

Ronald J. Trof, MD
A. B. Johan Groeneveld, MD, PhD, FCCP, FCCM
    Department of Intensive Care | Vrije Universiteit
    Medical Center | Amsterdam, Netherlands

Address for correspondence
    A. B. Johan Groeneveld
    Department of Intensive Care
    Vrije Universiteit Medical Center
    De Boelelaan 1117
    1081 HV Amsterdam, The Netherlands
    e-mail: johan.groeneveld@vumc.nl

References

1. Grocott MPW, Mythen MG, Gan TJ. Perioperative fluid management and clinical outcomes in adults. Anesth Analg. 2005;100:1093–1106.
2. Groeneveld ABJ. Vascular pharmacology of acute lung injury and acute respiratory distress syndrome. Vasc Pharmacol. 2003;39:247–256.
3. Groeneveld ABJ, Verheij J. Extravascular lung water to blood volume ratios as measures of permeability in sepsis-induced ALI/ARDS. Intensive Care Med. 2006;32: 1315–1321.
4. Verheij J, Van Lingen A, Raijmakers PGHM, Rijnsburger ER, Veerman DP, Wisselink W, Girbes ARJ, Groeneveld ABJ. Effect of fluid loading with saline or colloids on pulmonary permeability, oedema and lung injury score after cardiac and major vascular surgery. Br J Anaesth. 2006;96:21–30.
5. Khan S, Trof RJ, Groeneveld AJ. Transpulmonary dilution-derived extravascular lung water as a measure of lung edema. Curr Opin Crit Care. 2007;13:303–307.
6. Michard F. Bedside assessment of extravascular lung water by dilution methods: temptations and pitfalls. Crit Care Med. 2007;35:1186–1192.
7. Phillips CR, Chesnutt MS, Smith SM. Extravascular lung water in sepsis-associated acute respiratory distress syndrome: indexing with predicted body weight improves correlation with severity of illness and survival. Crit Care Med. 2008;36:69–73.
8. Katzenelson R, Perel A, Berkenstadt H et al. Accuracy of transpulmonary thermodilution versus gravimetric measurement of extravascular lung water. Crit Care Med. 2004;32:1150–1554.
9. Sakka SG, Klein M, Reinhart K, Meier-Hellmann A. Prognostic value of extravascular lung water in critically ill patients. Chest. 2002;122:2080–2086.
10. Patroniti N, Bellani G, Maggioni E, Manfio A, Marcora B, Pesenti A. Measurement of pulmonary edema in patients with acute respiratory distress syndrome. Chest. 2005; 33:2547–2554.
11. Groeneveld ABJ, Polderman KH. Acute lung injury, overhydration or both? Crit Care. 2005;9:136–137.
12. Cotton BA, Guy JS, Morris JA, Abumrad NN. The cellular, metabolic, and systemic consequences of aggressive fluid resuscitation strategies. Shock. 2006;26:115–121.
13. Durairaj L, Schmidt GA. Fluid therapy in resuscitated sepsis. Less is more. Chest. 2008;133:252–263.
14. Gan TJ, Soppitt A, Maroof M, El-Moalem H, Robertson KM, Moretti E, Dwane P, Glass PSA. Goal-directed

intraoperative fluid administration reduces length of hospital stay after major surgery. Anesthesiology. 2002; 97:820–826.

15. McKendry M, McGloin H, Saberi D, Caudwell L, Brady AR, Singer M. Randomised controlled trial assessing the impact of a nurse delivered, flow monitored protocol for optimisation of circulatory status after cardiac surgery. Br Med J. 2004;329:258–262.

16. Pearse R, Dawson D, Fawcett J, Rhodes A, Grounds RM, Bennett ED. Early goal-directed therapy after major surgery reduces complications and duration of hospital stay. A randomised, controlled trial. Crit Care. 2005;9: R687–R693.

17. Wakeling HG, McFall MR, Jenkins CS, Woods WGA, Miles WFA, Barclay GR, Fleming SC. Intraoperative oesophageal Doppler guided fluid management shortens postopera- tive hospital stay after major bowel surgery. Br J Anaesth. 2005;95:634–642.

18. Noblett SE, Snowden CP, Shenton BK, Horgan AF. Randomized clinical trial assessing the effect of Doppler-optimized fluid management on outcome after elective colorectal resection. Br J Surg. 2006;93: 1069–1076.

19. Bundgaard-Nielsen M, Holte K, Secher NH, Kehlet H. Monitoring of peri-operative fluid administration by individualized goal-directed therapy. Acta Anaesthesiol Scand. 2007;51:331–340.

20. Donati A, Loggi S, Preiser J-C, Orsetti G, Münch C, Gabbanelli V, Pelaia P, Pietropaoli P. Goal-directed intraoperative therapy reduces morbidity and length of hospital stay in high-risk surgical patients. Chest. 2007; 132:1817–1824.

21. Lopes MR, Oliveira MA, Pereira VOS, Lemos IPB, Auler JOC, Michard F. Goal-directed management based on pulse pressure variation monitoring during high-risk surgery: a pilot randomized controlled trial. Crit Care. 2007;11:R100.

22. Uchino S, Bellomo R, Morimatsu H, Sugihara M, French C, Stephens D, Wendon J, Honore P, Mulder J, Turner A and the PULSE study group. Pulmonary artery catheter versus pulse contour analysis: a prospective epidemio- logical study. Crit Care. 2006;10:R174.

23. Goepfert SMG, Reuter DA, Akyol D, Lamm P, Kilger E, Goetz AE. Goal-directed fluid management reduces vasopressor and catecholamine use in cardiac surgery patients. Intensive Care Med. 2007;33: 96–103.

24. Pölönen P, Ruokonen E, Hippeläinen M, Pöyhönen M, Takala J. A prospective, randomized study of goal-orient- ed hemodynamic therapy in cardiac surgical patients. Anesth Analg. 2000;90:1052–1059.

25. Arkiliç CF, Taguchi A, Sharma N, Ratnaraj J, Sessler DI, Read TE, Fleshman JW, Kurz A. Supplemental perioantiopera- tive fluid administration increases tissue oxygen pressure. Surgery. 2003;133:49–55.

26. Arieff A. Fatal postoperative pulmonary edema. Pathogenesis and literature review. Chest. 1999;115: 1371–1377.

27. Brandstrup B, Tønnesen H, Beier-Holgersen R, Hjortsø E, Ørding H, Lindroff-Larsen K, Rasmussen MS, Lanng C, Wallin L and the Danish Study Group on perioperative fluid therapy. Effects of intravenous fluid restriction on postoperative complications: comparison of two perioperative fluid regimens. A randomized assessor- blinded multicenter trial. Ann Surg. 2003;238:641–648.

28. Nisanevich V, Felsenstein I, Almogy G, Weissman C, Einav S, Matot I. Effect of intraoperative fluid manage- ment on outcome after intraabdominal surgery. Anesthesiology. 2005;103:25–32.

29. Holte K, Foss NB, Andersen J, Valentiner L, Lund C, Bie P, Kehlet H. Liberal or restrictive fluid administration in fast-track colonic surgery: a randomized, double-blind study. Br J Anaesth. 2007;99:500–508.

30. Brandstrup B, Svensen C, Engquist A. Hemorrhage and operation cause a contraction of the extracellular space needing replacement-evidence and implications/ A systematic review. Surgery. 2006;139:41–432.

31. Holte K, Klarskov B, Christensen DS, Lund C, Nielsen KG, Bie P, Kehlet H. Liberal versus restrictive fluid administra- tion to improve recovery after laparoscopic cholecystec- tomy. A randomized, double-blind study. Ann Surg. 2004;240:892–899.

32. Holte K, Kristensen BB, Valantiner L, Foss NB, Husted H, Kehlet H. Liberal versus restrictive fluid management in knee arthroplasty: a randomized, double-blind study. Anesth Analg. 2007;105:465–474.

33. Stern SA. Low-volume fluid resuscitation for presumed hemorraghic shock: helpful or harmful ? Curr Opin Crit Care. 2001;7:422–430.

34. Schuller D, Mitchell JP, Calandrino FS, Schuster DP. Fluid balance during pulmonary edema. Is fluid gain a marker or a cause of poor outcome ? Chest. 1991;100: 1068–1075.

35. Alsous F, Khamiees M, DeGirolamo A, Amoateng- Adjepong Y, Manthous CA. Negative fluid balance predicts survival in patients with septic shock. A retrospective study. Chest. 2000;117:1749–1754.

36. Sakr Y, Vincent J-L, Reinhart K, Groeneveld J, Michalo- poulos A, Sprung CL, Artigas A, Ranieri VM. High tidal volume and positive fluid balance are associated with worse outcome in acute lung injury. Chest. 2005;128: 3098–3108.

37. Dubois M-J, Orellana-Jimenez C, Mélot C, De Backer D, Berré J, Leeman M, Brimioulle S, Appoloni O, Créteur J, Vincent J-L. Albumin administration improves organ function in critically ill hypoalbuminemic patients: a prospective, randomized, controlled pilot study. Crit Care Med. 2006;34:2536–2540.

38. Mitchell JP, Schuller D, Calandrino FS, Schuster DP. Improved outcome based on fluid management in

critically ill patients requiring pulmonary artery catheterization. Am Rev Respir Dis. 1992;145:988–989.

39. NHLB institute ARDS clinical trials network. Comparison of two fluid-management strategies in acute lung injury. N Engl J Med. 2006;354:2564–2575.

40. Choi PT-L, Yip G, Quinonez LG, Cook D. Crystalloids vs. colloids in fluid resuscitation: a systematic review. Crit Care Med. 1999;27:200–210.

41. Perel P, Roberts I. Colloids versus crystalloids for fluid resuscitation in critically ill patients. Cochrane Database Syst Rev. 2007.

42. Vincent J-L, Navickis RJ, Wilkes MM. Morbidity in hospitalized patients receiving human albumin: a meta-analysis of randomized, controlled trials. Crit Care Med. 2004;32:2029–2038.

43. Martin GS, Moss M, Wheeler AP, Mealer M, Morris JA, Bernard GR. A randomized, controlled trial of furosemide with or without albumin in hypoproteinemic patients with acute lung injury. Crit Care Med. 2005;33:1161–1687.

44. Rittoo D, Gosling P, Burnley S, Bonnici C, Millns P, Simms MH, Smith SR, Vohra RK. Randomized study comparing the effects of hydroxyethyl starch solution with Gelofusine on pulmonary function in patients undergoing abdominal aortic aneurysm surgery. Br J Anaesth. 2004;92:61–66.

Christian Putensen, Thomas Muders, Stefan Kreyer
and Hermann Wrigge

Spontaneous versus mechanical ventilation

Introduction

Controlled mechanical ventilation (CMV) via an artificial airway is generally provided to completely unload the patient from the work of breathing and to assure adequate gas exchange during the acute phase of respiratory insufficiency until the underlying respiratory dysfunction has resolved (1, 2). Based on recent research, the criteria used to determine when to terminate mechanical ventilation should be based on standardised weaning protocols rather on the clinical and often subjective judgment of the attending intensive care physician (1, 3, 4). The actual process of weaning the patient from CMV is carried out by allowing spontaneous breathing attempts with T-piece or continuous positive airway pressure (CPAP), or by gradually reducing mechanical ventilator assistance (5, 6). Not surprisingly, gradual discontinuation with partial ventilator support has been demonstrated to be beneficial only in patients with difficulties in tolerating unassisted spontaneous breathing (5, 7). Although introduced as weaning techniques, partial ventilator support modes are increasingly applied as primary mechanical ventilator support in critically ill patients during the acute phase of respiratory insufficiency.

Spontaneous versus controlled mechanical ventilation

Viires colleagueset al. (8) demonstrated in shock models that complete unloading from the work of breathing with CMV resulted in a reduction of the blood flow to the respiratory muscles and improved organ perfusion when compared with unassisted spontaneous breathing. As a consequence, blood lactate and arterial pH values indicated improved tissue oxygenation with CMV (8). Furthermore, Ebihara et al. (9) observed in a septic shock model that unassisted spontaneous breathing contributes to myofibril damage, which can be prevented by resting of the respiratory muscles with CMV. Based on these findings and case reports it is generally believed that in critically ill patients CMV is beneficial in the acute phase of respiratory insufficiency.

Sassoon et al. (10) showed that diaphragm inactivity with CMV within 24 hours significantly decreases diaphragm force and produces myofibril damage contributing to the reduced force. Preserving diaphragmatic contractions during assist-controlled ventilation (ACV) attenuates the force loss induced by complete inactivity in CMV (11). Recently, Levine (12) reported diaphragm muscle atrophy in brain-dead organ donors undergoing CMV for 18 to 69 hours when compared to patients undergoing lung surgery who had received only 2 to 3 hours of mechanical ventilation. Consistent with previous animal studies, diaphragm inactivity with CMV induced marked atrophy of diaphragm fibres, an increase in oxidative stress, and activation of degradation pathways. Based on this, some degree of diaphragm contraction during partial ventilator support should be of advantage in critically ill patients even in the acute phase of respiratory insufficiency.

Support of spontaneous ventilation

During ACV and pressure support ventilation (PSV) every inspiratory effort is mechanically supported by the ventilator. By contrast, airway pressure release Ventilation (APRV) (13) ventilates by time-cycled switching between two pressure levels in a high flow or demand valve continuous positive airway pressure (CPAP) circuit and therefore allows unrestricted spontaneous breathing in any phase of the mechanical ventilator cycle. Whereas PSV has been demonstrated to facilitate weaning in patients with difficulties in tolerating unassisted spontaneous breathing (5, 7), comparisons between partial ventilator support modalities in the acute phase of respiratory insufficiency are lacking.

Physiologic effects of assisted spontaneous breathing

Ventilation distributions

Radiological studies demonstrate that ventilation is distributed differently during pure spontaneous breathing and CMV (14). During spontaneous breathing, the posterior muscular sections of the diaphragm move more than the anterior tendon plate (see fig. 1) (14). Consequently, in patients in the supine position, the dependent lung regions tend to be better ventilated during spontaneous breathing. If the diaphragm is relaxed, it will be moved by the weight of the abdominal cavity and the intra-abdominal pressure towards the cranium and the mechanical V_T will be distributed more to the anterior, non-dependent and less perfused lung regions (15). When compared with spontaneous breathing, both in patients with healthy lungs and patients undergoing mechanical ventilation this leads to lung areas in the dorsal lung regions close to the diaphragm being less ventilated or atelectatic. Recent results demonstrate that the posterior muscular sections of the diaphragm move more than the anterior tendon plate when large breaths or sighs are present during spontaneous breathing (16).

Computed tomography (CT) of patients with acute respiratory distress syndrome (ARDS) has demonstrated radiographic densities corresponding to alveolar collapse localised primarily in the dependent lung regions that correlates with intrapulmonary shunting and accounts entirely for the observed arterial hypoxemia (17, 18). Formation of radiographic densities has been attributed to alveolar collapse caused by superimposed

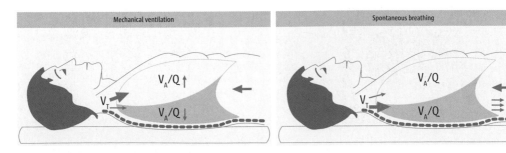

Fig. 1   Distribution of ventilation during purely mechanical and spontaneous ventilation.

pressure on the lung and a cephalad shift of the diaphragm most evident in dependent lung areas during CMV (19). The cephalad shift of the diaphragm may be even more pronounced in patients with ARDS and reduced chest wall elastance, in whom an increase in intra-abdominal pressure is invariably observed. Persisting spontaneous breathing has been considered to improve distribution of ventilation to dependent lung areas and thereby ventilation-perfusion (V_A/Q) matching, presumably by diaphragmatic contraction opposing alveolar compression (14, 20). This concept is supported by CT observations in anaesthetised patients demonstrating that contractions of the diaphragm induced by phrenic nerve stimulation favor distribution of ventilation to dependent, well-perfused lung areas and decrease atelectasis formation (21).

Spontaneous breathing with APRV in experimentally-induced lung injury was associated with less atelectasis formation in end-expiratory spiral CT of the whole lungs and in CT scans above the diaphragm (see fig. 2) (22). Although other inspiratory muscles may also contribute to improvement in aeration during spontaneous breathing, the cranio-caudal gradient in aeration, aeration differences, and the marked differences in aeration in regions close to the diaphragm between airway pressure release ventilation (APRV) with and without spontaneous breathing suggest a predominant role of diaphragmatic contractions in the observed aeration differences (22). Spontaneous breathing resulted in significant improvement of end-expiratory lung volume in experimental lung

injury (22). Experimental data suggest that recruitment of dependent lung areas may be caused essentially by an increase in transpulmonary pressure (P_{TP}) due to the decrease of pleural pressure with spontaneous breathing during APRV (23). Because the posterior muscular sections of the diaphragm move more than the anterior tendon plate, decrease in intrapleural pressure and hence, increase in P_{TP} should be maximal in the dependent lung regions during spontaneous breathing. This concept is supported by CT observations in experimentally-induced lung injury demonstrating that during spontaneous with APRV a large portion of the V_T is distributed to the initially collapsed dependent lung regions (24).

Pulmonary gas exchange

In patients with ARDS, APRV with spontaneous breathing of 10 to 30 % of the total minute ventilation (V_E) accounted for an improvement in V_A/Q matching, intrapulmonary shunting and arterial oxygenation (20). These results confirm earlier investigations in animals with induced lung injury (25, 26) demonstrating improvement in intrapulmonary shunt and arterial oxygenation during spontaneous breathing with APRV. Increase in arterial oxygenation in conjunction with greater pulmonary compliance indicates recruitment of previously non-ventilated lung areas. Clinical studies in patients with ARDS show that spontaneous breathing during APRV does not necessarily lead to instant improvement in gas exchange but to a con-

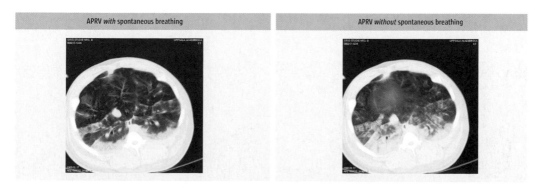

Fig. 2   Computed tomography of a lung region above the diaphragm at end-expiration in oleic acid-induced lung injury with and without spontaneous breathing during APRV. Atelectasis formation is reduced with spontaneous breathing.

tinuous improvement in oxygenation within 24 hours after start of spontaneous breathing (27).

In patients at risk of developing ARDS, maintained spontaneous breathing with APRV resulted in lower venous admixture and better arterial blood oxygenation over an observation period of more than 10 days as compared to CMV with subsequent weaning (28). These results show that even in patients requiring ventilator support, maintained spontaneous breathing can counteract progressive deterioration in pulmonary gas exchange.

The effect of breath-to-breath assisted spontaneous inspiration efforts on gas exchange based on animal studies is conflicting (25, 26, 29). In patients with ARDS, PSV did not produce significant improvement in intrapulmonary shunt, V_A/Q matching or gas exchange when compared to CMV (20). This is in agreement with the results of Cereda et al. demonstrating comparable gas exchange in patients with acute lung injury during CMV and PSV (30). Apparently, spontaneous contribution on a mechanically assisted breath was not sufficient to counteract V_A/Q maldistribution of positive pressure lung insufflations. Whether a decrease of the pressure support level would improve gas exchange has not been tested in patients with ARDS.

Work of breathing

Work of spontaneous breathing depends highly on the level of ventilator support. Patient data indicate that breath-to-breath synchronised ventilator support with PSV may reduce the work of spontaneous breathing more efficiently than intermittent ventilator support with APRV or IMV. In addition, asynchronous interferences between spontaneous and mechanical ventilation may increase the work of breathing and reduce the effectiveness of ventilator support, while leading to deteriorating gas exchange. Improved recruitment and thus, gas exchange, does not seem to correlate with the increase in work of breathing.

Cardiovascular effects

Application of a mechanical ventilator breath generates an increase in airway- and, therefore, in intrathoracic pressure, which in turn reduces venous return to the heart. In normo- and hypovolaemic patients, this produces a reduction in right- and left-ventricular filling and results in decreased stroke volume, cardiac output, and oxygen delivery (DO_2) (31). To normalise systemic blood flow during mechanical ventilation, intravascular volume often needs to be increased and/ or the cardiovascular system needs pharmacological support. Reducing mechanical ventilation to a level which provides adequate support for existing spontaneous breathing should help to reduce the cardiovascular side effects of ventilator support (32).

Periodic reduction of intrathoracic pressure resulting from maintained spontaneous breathing during mechanical ventilator support promotes venous return to the heart and right and left ventricular filling, thereby increasing cardiac output and DO_2 (33). Experimental (23, 25, 26, 34) and clinical (20, 27, 35) studies show that during APRV with spontaneous breathing of 10 to 40 % of total V_E at unchanged V_E or airway pressure limits results in an increase in cardiac index. A simultaneous rise in right ventricular end-diastolic volume during spontaneous breathing with APRV indicates improved venous return to the heart (20). In addition, the outflow from the right ventricle, which depends mainly on the lung volume, which is the major determinant of pulmonary vascular resistance, may benefit from decrease in intrathoracic pressure during APRV (20, 35).

Patients with left ventricular dysfunction may not benefit from augmentation of venous return to the heart and increased left ventricular afterload as a result of reduced intrathoracic pressure. Thus, switching abruptly from CMV to PSV with simultaneous reduction in airway pressure has been demonstrated to result in decompensation of existing cardiac insufficiency (36). Räsänen et al. (37, 38) showed the need of adequate ventilator support and CPAP-levels in patients with respiratory and cardiogenic failure. Providing that spontaneous breathing receives adequate support and sufficient CPAP-levels are applied, maintenance of spontaneous breathing during APRV should not prove disadvantageous and is not *per se* contraindicated in patients with ventricular dysfunction (37, 39).

Oxygen supply and demand balance

Increase in cardiac index and PaO_2 during APRV improved the relationship between tissue oxygen supply and demand because oxygen consumption remained unchanged despite the work of spontaneous breathing. In accordance with previous experimental (25, 26) and clinical findings (20) total oxygen consumption is not measurably altered by adequately supported spontaneous breathing in patients with low lung compliance. Increased DO_2 with unchanged oxygen consumption indicates an improved tissue oxygen supply and demand balance as reflected by a decrease in oxygen extraction rate and higher mixed venous SO_2. However, inadequately adjusted ventilator assistance may result in marked increase in inspiratory efforts, work of breathing, and oxygen consumption. Measurement of mixed or central venous SO_2 has to be recommended to detect increase in oxygen consumption with insufficient tissue oxygen supply with assisted spontaneous breathing.

Organ perfusion

By reducing cardiac index and venous return to the heart, CMV can have negative effects on the perfusion and functioning of extrathoracic organ systems. Increase in venous return and cardiac index, due to the periodic fall in intrathoracic pressure during spontaneous inspiration, should significantly improve organ perfusion and function during partial ventilator support. In patients with ARDS, spontaneous breathing with intermittent mandatory ventilation (IMV) leads to an increase in glomerular filtration rate and sodium excretion (40). Compatible with these results in patients with ARDS kidney perfusion and glomerular filtration rate improve during spontaneous breathing with APRV (41).

Direct measurement of intestinal perfusion is not possible in critically ill patients. Therefore, animal experiments are necessary to evaluate the effect of ventilator support on intestinal perfusion. The coloured microsphere technique is a standard experimental method to determine regional blood and is therefore an appropriate method to determine blood flow in different anatomic regions of the gut (42, 43). Hering et al. (44, 45) observed in an induced lung injury model that spontane-

ous breathing improves systemic blood flow and mucosal-submucosal blood flow in the duodenum, the ileum, and the colon when compared to CMV with and without permissive hypercapnia. Improvements were more pronounced in the mucosal-submucosal layer. Muscularis-serosal perfusion decreased during CMV support applying high tidal volume in comparison with APRV with spontaneous breathing (44, 45).

Side effects

A frequently raised question is whether spontaneous breathing might be harmful by contributing to ventilator-induced lung injury. In the diseased lung, the distribution of stress and the strain, which are the triggers of ventilator-induced lung injury, is not homogeneous (46, 47). Strain is defined as elongation of the lung structure compared with its resting position. Thus, an appropriate surrogate for lung strain might be the ratio between V_T and the end-expiratory lung volume (EELV) (46). Stress is defined as tension of the lung skeleton fibre system. An indicator for the stress applied to the lung parenchyma is P_{TP} which equals airway pressure minus intrapleural pressure (P_{PL}) (46, 47). Stress and strain should be higher in well-ventilated lung areas regions than the collapsed lung regions, which are believed to be somewhat protected because these lung areas bear stress but no strain (46, 47).

During spontaneous breathing tidal ventilation is preferentially distributed to dependent lung regions close to the diaphragm (see fig. 3) (14, 16, 24, 48). Because the posterior muscular sections of the diaphragm contract more than the anterior tendon plate, decrease in PPL and the concomitant increase in PTP is maximal in the dependent lung areas adjunct to the diaphragm. This localised increase in PTP explains entirely the successful recruitment of atelectasis formations in adjunct to the diaphragm with spontaneous breathing (21). In the apical lung regions, differences in tidal volume distribution between dependent and non-dependent lung is not significantly different with spontaneous breathing (24). Inhomogeneous distribution of tidal ventilation, as shown earlier in patients with ALI (49–51), may be explained by regional differences in PTP and can be affected by spontaneous breathing.

PTP decreases with a cephalocaudal gradient. Thus, lower PTP will be observed in the caudal than in the cephalad parts of the lungs. This cephalocaudal decrease in PTP may be explained by the transmission of abdominal pressure to the thoracic cavity (19) which decreases from base to apex. Furthermore, transmission of abdominal pressure to the thoracic cavity should be maximal in the dependent regions in a supine individual. In addition, compression of lung tissue by the weight of the heart may occur (52). Although increase in PTP caused by spontaneous breathing is maximal in the dependent lung areas in adjunct to the diaphragm it is unlikely that the resulting absolute P_{TP} in the dependent lung regions is higher than in cephalad lung areas in the absence of spontaneous breathing. This concept is supported by findings that gas volume and aeration is not higher in the dependent lung regions with spontaneous breathing than in cephalad lung areas in the absence of spontaneous breathing (24, 48).

Tidal recruitment is observed in the presence and absence of spontaneous breathing. In the absence of spontaneous breathing tidal recruitment is more than twice as high in dependent lung regions near the diaphragm (see fig. 4) (24). This cyclic alveolar collapse and reopening in the absence of spontaneous breathing causes a regional increase in P_{TP} and shear forces with transmural pressures of up to 100 cmH$_2$O applied to lung cells (53). In an open lung, according to the model of Mead et al. (53), the stress and strain should be more homogeneously distributed throughout the lung parenchyma, preventing the triggering of the inflammatory reaction.

Increase in P_{TP} and/or shear forces due to cyclic opening of lung units during inspiration and closure during expiration causes mechanical stress and may contribute to ventilator-associated lung injury including aggravation of pulmonary and systemic inflammation (54, 55). Another mechanism which may aggravate pulmonary and systemic inflammation is the cyclic strain applied to the lung tissue.

Regional strain is equivalent to the local increase in the ratio between tidal ventilation and EELV (46, 47). Regional analyses of attenuation distribution suggest that improved EELV is mostly due to alveolar recruitment in dependent juxtadiaphragmatic lung regions with spontaneous breathing (22, 24). Thus, the concomitant increase in tidal ventilation and EELV should not result in a higher strain in the dependent lung regions close to the diaphragm than in non-dependent or apical lung regions.

Preliminary data demonstrate no difference in histologically-based lung injury scores and pulmonary and systemic cytokine response between APRV with and without spontaneous breathing in a pulmonary and extrapulmonary induced lung injury model (56). These data suggest that spontaneous breathing when carefully applied should not contribute to ventilator-induced lung injury.

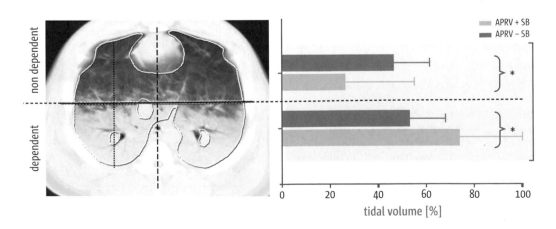

Fig. 3   Distribution of tidal volume with and without spontaneous breathing during APRV

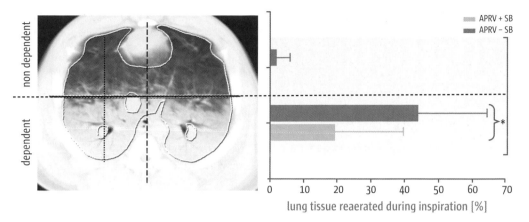

Fig. 4   Tidal recruitment with and without spontaneous breathing during APRV

Limitations

Based on the observed physiologic findings, spontaneous breathing with APRV may be advantageous to recruit atelectasis in adjunct to the diaphragm and thereby improves pulmonary gas exchange in patients with acute lung injury, ARDS, and atelectasis formation after major surgery. Because lower levels of sedation are required to allow spontaneous breathing, partial ventilator support should not be used in patients that do require deep sedation for management of their underlying disease (e.g. cerebral edema with increased intracranial pressure). In patients with obstructive lung disease, the advantage of spontaneous breathing in the acute phase of respiratory insufficiency until the underlying respiratory dysfunction has resolved is not supported by clinical research.

Adjustments of partial pressure support

ACV using V_T of not more than 6 ml/kg ideal body weight has been shown to improve outcome in patients with ARDS (57, 58). Based on these results V_T of not more than 6 ml/kg ideal body weight should be used regardless of the ventilator support modality used. Positive end-expiratory pressure (PEEP) levels should prevent end-expiratory alveolar collapse and tidal alveolar overdistension (57, 58). However, based on recent clinical trials, high PEEP levels can improve arterial oxygenation but are not associated with an improved survival rate.

Analgesia and sedation

Analgesia and sedation is used not only to ensure sufficient pain relief and anxiolysis but also to adapt the patient to mechanical ventilation (59, 60). The level of analgesia and sedation required during CMV is equivalent to a Ramsay score between 4 and 5, i.e. a deeply sedated patient unable to respond when spoken to and who has no sensation of pain. A Ramsay score between 2 and 3 has to be targeted, i.e. an awake, responsive and cooperative patient, allowing for spontaneous breathing. In patients with acute lung injury (28), maintaining spontaneous breathing leads to a significantly lower need of analgesics and sedatives compared to initial use of CMV followed by weaning. Higher doses of analgesics and sedatives used exclusively to adapt patients to CMV required not only higher doses of vasopressors and positive inotropes to keep cardiovascular function stable but was also associated with significantly fewer days on ventilator support, earlier extubation, and a shorter stay in the intensive care unit (28). Sedation has been reported to be associated with the development of delirium in critically ill patients (61). However, whether less deep sedation while maintaining spontaneous breathing is associated with a lower incidence of delirium has not been investigated.

Summary

Based on available data, it can be suggested that spontaneous breathing during ventilator support does not need to be suppressed even in patients with severe pulmonary dysfunction if no contraindications are present. Experimental data do not support the contention that spontaneous breathing aggravates ventilator-induced lung injury. Improvements in pulmonary gas exchange, systemic blood flow, and oxygen supply to the tissue which have been observed when spontaneous breathing was allowed during adequately adjusted ventilator support are reflected in a decrease in days on ventilator support and time of stay in the intensive care unit.

The authors

Christian Putensen, MD
Thomas Muders, MD
Stefan Kreyer, MD
Hermann Wrigge, MD
    Department of Anaesthesiology and
    Intensive Care Medicine | University of Bonn,
    Germany

Address for correspondence
    Christian Putensen
    Department of Anaesthesiology and
    Intensive Care Medicine
    University of Bonn
    Sigmund-Freud-Str. 35
    53105 Bonn, Germany
    e-mail: putensen@uni-bonn.de

References

1. MacIntyre NR. Evidence-based ventilator weaning and discontinuation. Respir Care. 2004;49:830–836.
2. Esteban A, Ferguson ND, Meade MO et al. Evolution of mechanical ventilation in response to clinical research. Am J Respir Crit Care Med. 2008;177:170–177.
3. Ely EW, Baker AM, Dunagan DP et al. Effect on the duration of mechanical ventilation of identifying patients capable of breathing spontaneously. N Engl J Med. 1996;335:1864–1869.
4. Kollef MH, Shapiro SD, Silver P et al. A randomized, controlled trial of protocol-directed versus physician-directed weaning from mechanical ventilation. Crit Care Med. 1997;25:567–574.
5. Brochard L, Rauss A, Benito S et al. Comparison of three methods of gradual withdrawal from ventilatory support during weaning from mechanical ventilation [see comments]. Am J Respir Crit Care Med. 1994;150:896–903.
6. Esteban A, Alia I, Gordo F et al. Extubation outcome after spontaneous breathing trials with T-tube or pressure support ventilation. The Spanish Lung Failure Collaborative Group. Am J Respir Crit Care Med. 1997;156:459–465.
7. Esteban A, Alia I, Tobin MJ et al. Effect of spontaneous breathing trial duration on outcome of attempts to discontinue mechanical ventilation. Spanish Lung Failure Collaborative Group. Am J Respir Crit Care Med. 1999;159:512–518.
8. Viires N, Sillye G, Aubier M, Rassidakis A, Roussos C. Regional blood flow distribution in dog during induced hypotension and low cardiac output. Spontaneous breathing versus artificial ventilation. J Clin Invest. 1983;72:935–947.
9. Ebihara S, Hussain SN, Danialou G, Cho WK, Gottfried SB, Petrof BJ. Mechanical ventilation protects against diaphragm injury in sepsis: interaction of oxidative and mechanical stresses. Am J Respir Crit Care Med. 2002;165:221–228.
10. Sassoon CS, Caiozzo VJ, Manka A, Sieck GC. Altered diaphragm contractile properties with controlled mechanical ventilation. J Appl Physiol. 2002;92:2585–2595.
11. Sassoon CS, Zhu E, Caiozzo VJ. Assist-control mechanical ventilation attenuates ventilator-induced diaphragmatic dysfunction. Am J Respir Crit Care Med. 2004;170:626–632.
12. Levine S, Nguyen T, Taylor N et al. Rapid disuse atrophy of diaphragm fibers in mechanically ventilated humans. N Engl J Med. 2008;358:1327–1335.
13. Baum M, Benzer H, Putensen C, Koller W. Biphasic positive airway pressure (BIPAP) – a new form of augmented ventilation. Anaesthesist. 1989;38:452–458.
14. Froese AB, Bryan AC. Effects of anesthesia and paralysis on diaphragmatic mechanics in man. Anesthesiology. 1974;41:242–255.
15. Reber A, Nylund U, Hedenstierna G. Position and shape of the diaphragm: implications for atelectasis formation. Anaesthesia. 1998;53:1054–1061.
16. Kleinman BS, Frey K, VanDrunen M et al. Motion of the Diaphragm in Patients with Chronic Obstructive Pulmonary Disease while Spontaneously Breathing versus during Positive Pressure Breathing after Anesthesia and Neuromuscular Blockade. Anesthesiology. 2002;97:298–305.
17. Bernard GR, Artigas A, Brigham KL et al. Report of the American-European consensus conference on ARDS: definitions, mechanisms, relevant outcomes and clinical trial coordination. Intensive Care Med. 1994;20:225–232.
18. Gattinoni L, Presenti A, Torresin A et al. Adult respiratory distress syndrome profiles by computed tomography. J Thorac Imaging. 1986;1:25–30.

19. Puybasset L, Cluzel P, Chao N, Slutsky AS, Coriat P, Rouby JJ. A computed tomography scan assessment of regional lung volume in acute lung injury. The CT Scan ARDS Study Group. Am J Respir Crit Care Med. 1998;158: 1644–1655.

20. Putensen C, Mutz NJ, Putensen-Himmer G, Zinserling J. Spontaneous breathing during ventilatory support improves ventilation- perfusion distributions in patients with acute respiratory distress syndrome. Am J Respir Crit Care Med. 1999;159:1241–1248.

21. Hedenstierna G, Tokics L, Lundquist H, Andersson T, Strandberg A. Phrenic nerve stimulation during halothane anesthesia. Effects of atelectasis. Anesthesiology. 1994;80:751–760.

22. Wrigge H, Zinserling J, Neumann P et al. Spontaneous Breathing Improves Lung Aeration in Oleic Acid-induced Lung Injury. Anesthesiology. 2003;99:376–384.

23. Henzler D, Dembinski R, Bensberg R, Hochhausen N, Rossaint R, Kuhlen R. Ventilation with biphasic positive airway pressure in experimental lung injuryInfluence of transpulmonary pressure on gas exchange and haemodynamics. Intensive Care Med. 2004.

24. Wrigge H, Zinserling J, Neumann P et al. Spontaneous breathing with airway pressure release ventilation favors ventilation in dependent lung regions and counters cyclic alveolar collapse in oleic-acid-induced lung injury: a randomized controlled computed tomography trial. Crit Care. 2005;9:R780-R789.

25. Putensen C, Rasanen J, Lopez FA. Effect of interfacing between spontaneous breathing and mechanical cycles on the ventilation-perfusion distribution in canine lung injury. Anesthesiology. 1994;81:921–930.

26. Putensen C, Rasanen J, Lopez FA. Ventilation-perfusion distributions during mechanical ventilation with superimposed spontaneous breathing in canine lung injury. Am J Respir Crit Care Med. 1994;150:101–108.

27. Sydow M, Burchardi H, Ephraim E, Zielmann S. Long-term effects of two different ventilatory modes on oxygenation in acute lung injury. Comparison of airway pressure release ventilation and volume-controlled inverse ratio ventilation. Am J Respir Crit Care Med. 1994;149:1550–1556.

28. Putensen C, Zech S, Wrigge H et al. Long-term effects of spontaneous breathing during ventilatory support in patients with acute lung injury. Am J Respir Crit Care Med. 2001;164:43–49.

29. Henzler D, Pelosi P, Bensberg R et al. Effects of partial ventilatory support modalities on respiratory function in severe hypoxemic lung injury. Crit Care Med. 2006;34: 1738–1745.

30. Cereda M, Foti G, Marcora B et al. Pressure support ventilation in patients with acute lung injury. Crit Care Med. 2000;28:1269–1275.

31. Pinsky MR. The effects of mechanical ventilation on the cardiovascular system. Crit Care Clin. 1990;6:663–678.

32. Kirby RR, Perry JC, Calderwood HW, Ruiz BC. Cardiorespiratory effects of high positive end-expiratory pressure. Anesthesiology. 1975;43:533–539.

33. Downs JB, Douglas ME, Sanfelippo PM, Stanford W. Ventilatory pattern, intrapleural pressure, and cardiac output. Anesth Analg. 1977;56:88–96.

34. Falkenhain SK, Reilley TE. Improvement in cardiac output during airway pressure release ventilation. Crit Care Med. 1992;20:1358–1360.

35. Kaplan LJ, Bailey H, Formosa V. Airway pressure release ventilation increases cardiac performance in patients with acute lung injury/adult respiratory distress syndrome. Crit Care. 2001;5:221–226.

36. Lemaire F, Teboul JL, Cinotti L et al. Acute left ventricular dysfunction during unsuccessful weaning from mechanical ventilation. Anesthesiology. 1988;69: 171–179.

37. Rasanen J, Heikkila J, Downs J, Nikki P, Vaisanen I, Viitanen A. Continuous positive airway pressure by face mask in acute cardiogenic pulmonary edema. Am J Cardiol. 1985;55:296–300.

38. Rasanen J, Nikki P. Respiratory failure arising from acute myocardial infarction. Ann Chir Gynaecol Suppl. 1982; 196:43-47.

39. Nikki P, Tahvanainen J, Rasanen J, Makelainen A. Ventilatory pattern in respiratory failure arising from acute myocardial infarction. II. PtcO$_2$ and PtcCO$_2$ compared to PaO$_2$ and PaCO$_2$ during IMV4 vs IPPV12 and PEEP0 vs PEEP10. Crit Care Med. 1982;10: 79-81.

40. Steinhoff HH, Kohlhoff RJ, Falke KJ. Facilitation of renal function by intermittent mandatory ventilation. Intensive Care Med. 1984;10:59–65.

41. Hering R, Peters D, Zinserling J, Wrigge H, von Spiegel T, Putensen C. Effects of spontaneous breathing during airway pressure release ventilation on renal perfusion and function in patients with acute lung injury. Intensive Care Med. 2002;28:1426–1433.

42. Revelly JP, Liaudet L, Frascarolo P, Joseph JM, Martinet O, Markert M. Effects of norepinephrine on the distribution of intestinal blood flow and tissue adenosine triphosphate content in endotoxic shock. Crit Care Med. 2000; 28:2500–2506.

43. Kowallik P, Schulz R, Guth BD et al. Measurement of regional myocardial blood flow with multiple colored microspheres. Circulation. 1991;83:974–982.

44. Hering R, Viehofer A, Zinserling J et al. Effects of spontaneous breathing during airway pressure release ventilation on intestinal blood flow in experimental lung injury. Anesthesiology. 2003; 99:1137–1144.

45. Hering R, Bolten JC, Kreyer S et al. Spontaneous breathing during airway pressure release ventilation in experimental lung injury: effects on hepatic blood flow. Intensive Care Med. 2008;34:523–527.

46. Marini JJ, Gattinoni L. Ventilatory management of acute respiratory distress syndrome: a consensus of two. Crit Care Med. 2004;32:250–255.

47. Gattinoni L, Caironi P, Carlesso E. How to ventilate patients with acute lung injury and acute respiratory distress syndrome. Curr Opin Crit Care. 2005;11: 69–76.

48. Neumann P, Wrigge H, Zinserling J et al. Spontaneous breathing affects the spatial ventilation and perfusion distribution during mechanical ventilatory support. Crit Care Med. 2005;33:1090–1095.

49. Gattinoni L, D'Andrea L, Pelosi P, Vitale G, Pesenti A, Fumagalli R. Regional effects and mechanism of positive end-expiratory pressure in early adult respiratory distress syndrome. JAMA. 1993;269:2122–2127.

50. Gattinoni L, Pelosi P, Vitale G, Pesenti A, D'Andrea L. Body position changes redistribute lung computed-tomographic density in patients with acute respiratory failure. Anesthesiology. 1991;74:15–23.

51. Puybasset L, Gusman P, Muller JC, Cluzel P, Coriat P, Rouby JJ. Regional distribution of gas and tissue in acute respiratory distress syndrome. III. Consequences for the effects of positive end-expiratory pressure. CT Scan ARDS Study Group. Adult Respiratory Distress Syndrome. Intensive Care Med. 2000;26:1215–1227.

52. Malbouisson LM, Busch CJ, Puybasset L, Lu Q, Cluzel P, Rouby JJ. Role of the heart in the loss of aeration characterizing lower lobes in acute respiratory distress syndrome. CT Scan ARDS Study Group. Am J Respir Crit Care Med. 2000;161:2005–2012.

53. Mead J, Takishima T. Stress distribution in lungs: a model of pulmonary elasticity. J Appl Physiol. 1970;28:596–608.

54. Ranieri VM, Suter PM, Tortorella C et al. Effect of mechanical ventilation on inflammatory mediators in patients with acute respiratory distress syndrome: a randomized controlled trial [see comments]. JAMA. 1999;282:54–61.

55. Stuber F, Wrigge H, Schroeder S et al. Kinetic and reversibility of mechanical ventilation-associated pulmonary and systemic inflammatory response in patients with acute lung injury. Intensive Care Med. 2002;28:834–841.

56. Varelmann D, Wrigge H, Zinserling J, Muders T, Uhlig S, Hedenstierna G, Putensen C. Inflammatory response to spontaneous breathing in two different models of acute lung injury. Intensive Care Med. 2005;31:S21.

57. Amato MB, Barbas CS, Medeiros DM et al. Effect of a protective-ventilation strategy on mortality in the acute respiratory distress syndrome. N Engl J Med. 1998;338: 347–354.

58. The Acute Respiratory Distress Syndrome Network. Ventilation with lower tidal volumes as compared with traditional tidal volumes for acute lung injury and the acute respiratory distress syndrome. N Engl J Med. 2000; 342:1301–1308.

59. Wheeler AP. Sedation, analgesia, and paralysis in the intensive care unit. Chest. 1993;104:566–577.

60. Burchardi H, Rathgeber J, Sydow M. The concept of analgo-sedation depends on the concept of mechanical ventilation. In: Vincent JL, editor. Yearbook of intensive care and emergency medicine. Berlin, Heidelberg, New York: Springer-Verlag. 1995: 155–164.

61. Pandharipande P, Shintani A, Peterson J et al. Lorazepam is an independent risk factor for transitioning to delirium in intensive care unit patients. Anesthesiology. 2006;104:21–26.

Hans Flaatten

The role of tracheostomy in ventilatory care

Introduction

The history of tracheostomy dates back to the Greek physicians Galen and Aretaeus in the 2nd Century. Until the year 1546 there was however no record of a successful case in a human (1). The procedure was infrequently used, and usually reported with a very high mortality rate until the early 19th century. At that time, Jackson standardised the technique and indication of operative tracheostomy (2). In the beginning, the procedure was only used in cases of mechanical laryngeal obstructions (3). First, in 1943 a "new" indication was "born" when there was a case report on its use to facilitate suction of secretions from the bronchial tree in patients with bulbar poliomyelitis. During the Scandinavian epidemic of poliomyelitis in 1952–3, use of tracheostomy in the treatment of respiratory insufficiency was used in a large scale. The next milestone in the history of tracheostomy was the description of a percutaneous approach using a guide-wire and Seldinger technique in 1969 (4). During the 1990's the methods were refined, and became increasingly used in the ICU worldwide.

Methods

The traditional method of tracheostomy is the *surgical (open) method*. Using this method a horizontal skin incision is performed below the cricoid cartilage, and a midline vertical incision is performed to divide the strap muscles. If necessary, thyroid isthmus must be divided between ligatures. The cricoid is elevated (cricoid hook) and one of several methods is used for the tracheal incision, usually at the level of the 2nd and 3rd tracheal ring. The tracheostomy tube is then inserted through the tracheal incision, with concomitant withdrawal of the endotracheal tube. The wound is partially closed with sutures, and often stay sutures are used to keep the tube in place.

There are various *percutaneous methods* in use. Probably the guide wire and Seldinger technique is the most frequently used method (often called Ciaglia method after its inventor) (5). Another frequently used technique is the guide wire and dilating forceps technique of Grigg (6). In both methods the trachea are punctured with a needle, to advance a metal guide-wire into the trachea. Often a flexible bronchoscopy is performed simultaneously through the endotracheal tube in order to assure a correct midline puncture before proceeding further with this method. The guide-wire is then used as a guide for dilatation, with dilatators or a forceps according to the chosen technique. A channel is then created through the tissue where the tracheal cannula then subsequently is introduced, again with concomitant withdrawal of the endotracheal tube.

In all procedures the patient is usually given general anaesthesia, often with a muscle relaxant to prevent movement of the trachea during the procedure. Usually two physicians and an assistant are required, one responsible for the ventilation and endotracheal tube (and bronchoscopy if performed), the other to perform the tracheostomy. Traditionally surgical tracheostomies are performed in the operating theatre by a surgeon or ENT physician, while the percutaneous methods are performed bedside in the ICU by an intensivist.

Epidemiology

The use of tracheostomy in the ICU has increased during the last two decades, but large epidemiological data is difficult to find (as an example from national ICU databases). Figure 1 shows the use of tracheostomy per year in our unit from 1997 to 2007.

Both the absolute and relative numbers are increased from (numbers given with reference to all admitted ICU patients), with a mean in the period of 16.2 %. This corresponds to 23 % of all intubated and ventilated patients in the period, and 36.2 % of all patients ventilated for more than 24 h.

In table 1, the reported incidence of tracheostomy in ICU patients in some recent studies is given. Note that the denominator is different from study to study. Some use all ICU patients, while others give the number based on ventilated patients only, or patients ventilated above a certain time (usually 12–24 hours). One study from North Carolina has in addition studied the population based incidence of tracheostomy for prolonged mechanical ventilation (7) and found a nearly three fold increase from 8.3/100.000 in 1993 to 24.2/100.000 in 2002.

Indications (general)

The classical indication is upper airway obstruction, and was the only reason to perform a tracheostomy before World War 2. In ICU patients this

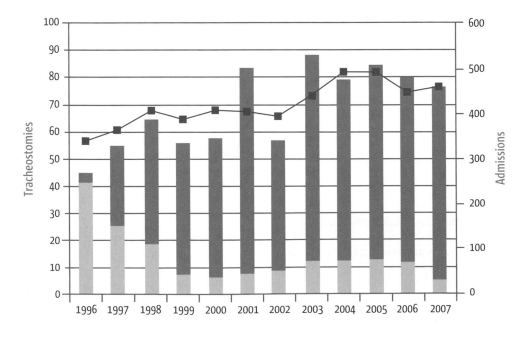

Fig. 1   Use of tracheostomy at the ICU Haukeland University Hospital, 1996–2007

Tab. 1 Recent published incidence of tracheostomy in ICU patients

Author and year	ICU population	Time period	Incidence %
Flaatten 2006 (8)	All ICU patients	1997–2003	17.7 (mean)
Blot 2005 (9)	All ventilated pts	2000	7.2 (median)
Frutos-Vivar 2005 (10)	Ventilated >12h	1998 (one month)	10.7
Arabi 2004 (11)	Trauma patients	1999–2004	21
Engoren 2004 (12)	All ventilated pts	1998–2000	8.3
Cox 2004 (7)	All ventilated pts	1993–2002	4.3 to 7.7
Fischler 2000 (13)	Ventilated >24h	1995–1996	10
Simpson 1999 (14)	All ICU patients	1991–1997	16.8 (median)
Kollef 1999 (15)	Ventilated >24 h	1996	9.8

is still an important indication, but has been surpassed by other indications:

Recent indication for tracheostomy in the ICU

- Replacement for long-term endotracheal intubation
- Weaning from ventilator
- To shorten ICU stay in intubated patients
- Failed extubation

Controversies regarding tracheostomy in the ICU

There are several controversies regarding the use of tracheostomy in ICU patients. Some have not yet been resolved. The three most important are:

- The use of prolonged endotracheal intubation or tracheostomy in ICU patients
- The timing of tracheostomy, early or late
- The method of tracheostomy, surgical or percutaneous

Controversy 1 and 2: Tracheostomy plays an important role in the ICU

Pros

Long-term tracheal intubation has been demonstrated to give sequelae. More than 20 years ago Whited reported laryngotracheal sequelae after long-term intubation (16).

Laryngotracheal problems (after Whited (16))

Intubation	Documented findings
2–5 days	Injury to the posterior commissure of the larynx
6–10 days	Increased incidence, and continuous damage from the posterior glottis through the cervical trachea
11–24 days	Increased incidence and severity of problems leading to stenosis

In a prospective study from 1995, all patients intubated for > 24 h were submitted to bronchoscopy on the day of extubation (17). They found long-term sequelae in 8.6 % of their patients. In a more recent study of 654 ICU patients, 11 % of patients intubated revealed laryngotracheal injuries at follow up 6–12 months after discharge from the ICU (18). The length of oro-tracheal intubation was the most important factor in that study. In addition, in a prospective randomised study comparing early with late tracheostomies in 120 ICU patients, more damage to mouth and larynx was found in the prolonged translaryngeal intubation group (19).

There is also evidence that prolonged intubation leads to more heavily sedated patients and loss of autonomy, and that a tracheostomy may rapidly change this situation (20).

Hence, long term oro-tracheal intubation may lead to more laryngotracheal lesions, in addition to more sedated patients. The latter can obviously lead to increased time on the ventilator and hence increased LOS in the ICU.

Several large retrospective studies have recently been published, where a group of ICU patients receiving a tracheostomy have been compared with patients ventilated without the use of tracheostomy (8, 15, 21). The time to perform tracheostomy varies from median 6 to median 12 days,

Tab. 2   Data from studies comparing ventilated patients with and without tracheostomy.
All data mean values, * = SAPS II score, # = APACHE II score

Study	Group	Size	Age Year	Severity	Vent.day Days	LOS Days	Mortality % ICU	Mortality % Hosp	Mortality % 1 year
Combes 2007 (21)	Trach[1]	166	59	53*	35	41	33	37	
	Tube >3d	340	59	53*	12	15	42	48	
Kollef 1999 (15)	Trach[2]	51	53.1	19.2 #	19.5	18.8	NA	13.7	
	Tube >12h	470	57.9	17.8#	4.1	5.7	NA	26.4	
Flaatten 2006 (8)	Trach[3]	461	53.5	46.6*	11.4	14.8	11.2	27.1	36.8
	Tube >1d	855	47.1	48.3*	3.9	5.5	29.0	36.8	43.2

1. Median time 12 days 2. Mean time 9.7 days 3. Median time 6 days

and inclusion criteria vary from ventilated more than 12 hours to more than 3 days. The pattern regarding survival is however the same, a strong tendency to reduced mortality in the group offered a tracheostomy. The main results from these studies are shown in table 2.

Many studies have been aimed at finding the optimal time for performing a tracheostomy in the ICU patient. American guidelines from 2001 advocate the use of tracheostomy if the expected time on mechanical ventilation is judged to exceed 21 days (22). Recently, these guidelines have been criticised (23), and several new studies, including a systematic review have been published after the publication of these guidelines. The systematic review found no significant reduction in mortality, but concluded that: "*In critically ill adult patients who require prolonged mechanical ventilation, performing a tracheostomy at an earlier stage than is currently practised, may shorten the duration of artificial ventilation and LOS in intensive care*" (24).

Cons

To date, no large prospective study has proven a beneficial effect of tracheostomy in general, not even when performed early. Most data originates from retrospective studies, or open prospective studies with a small sample size.

On the other hand, performing a tracheostomy has its own morbidity and mortality.

There are reports of major intra-operative complications or deaths during and immediately after tracheostomy (25–29), and probably the reports of procedure-related deaths is only the tip of the iceberg. In his review of nearly 10,000 patients with tracheostomy from 65 studies, Dulguerov et al (30) found the highest complication rate in older studies using the surgical technique, while in more recent studies perioperative complications were more common with the percutaneous method (10 % vs. 3 %) and postoperative complications more frequent with the surgical technique (10 % vs. 7 %). Although more recent studies demonstrate a very low complication rate, it will probably never reach zero.

In a systematic review comparing surgical and percutaneous tracheostomy in 1212 patients, the long-term complications in 288 patients completing follow up were as shown in table 3 (31). This indicates that long-term sequelae after tracheostomy in general are comparable with sequelae after long-term intubation, although the profile of problems are different.

Before one clearly can demonstrate a reduction in other causes of mortality using tracheostomy, the procedure related deaths and major morbidity may counteract the possible benefits.

Controversy 3: The percutaneous method should be used if possible

Pros

Since the introduction of alternatives to open or surgical tracheostomy, one of the main arguments

Tab. 3 Type and frequency of long-term complications after tracheostomy; ST = surgical tracheostomy, PDT = percutaneous dilatation tracheostomy. Modified from: Delaney A, Bagshaw SM, Nalos M. Percutaneous dilatational tracheostomy versus surgical tracheostomy in critically ill patients: a systematic review and meta-analysis. Critical care (London, England). 2006;10(2):R55.

Type of complication	ST (n = 145)	PDT (n = 133)
Delayed closure	13	8
Tracheal stenosis	18	11
Cosmetic deformity	17	5
Airway symptoms/stridor	20	19
Other	4	2
Sum long-term complications	72 (49.6 %)	45 (33.8 %)

in favour of the new technique was its potential for use bedside in the ICU. This has several advantages:
- No need to transport the patients from the ICU to the OR
- Less time used on the procedure, no transport and no lifting to and from an operating table
- Less time from decision making to completed procedure

Tab. 4 Summary of the findings (all comparisons percutaneous method against open (surgical) method). Modified from: Delaney A, Bagshaw SM, Nalos M. Percutaneous dilatational tracheostomy versus surgical tracheostomy in critically ill patients: a systematic review and meta-analysis. Critical care (London, England). 2006;10(2):R55.

	OR	95 % CI
Wound infection	0.37	0.22 to 0.62
Unfavorable scarring	0.44	0.23 to 0.83
Overall complications	0.57	0.37 to 0.88
Decannulation/ obstruction	2.79	1.29 to 6.03
	Mean difference	95 % CI
Cost-effectiveness ($)	−456	−482 to −430
Case length (min)	−4.59	−5.39 to −3.79

The early reports confirmed these advantages; in addition the procedure itself took less time compared with the surgical technique. When calculating the cost, including use of the OR, the new techniques proved to be less expensive.

Because the Seldinger technique is widely used by intensivists, the new technique was easy to learn.

Several systematic reviews have been published on this subject, also in non-intensive care journals. The most recent from Laryngoscope concludes with *"Percutaneous tracheotomies are more cost-effective and provide greater feasibility in terms of bedside capability and nonsurgical operation"* (32)

Cons

There are no significant or clinical differences between the two methods regarding major morbidity and mortality. If the open (surgical) technique could be performed bedside in the ICU, much of the difference regarding cost-effectiveness would also disappear. Because the safety of the percutaneous method has not been firmly documented for important ICU sub-groups like children, morbidly obese and patients who have had previous operations in the area, the surgical method still must have its place in all ICUs. It could hence be argued that one group of physicians, primarily the ENT surgeons, should perform all tracheostomies so as to concentrate as much experience as possible in few hands. In addition, there is also still a question about mortality, because procedure-related mortality has been reported by several authors regarding the percutaneous method.

In the small ICU where such procedures are performed only infrequently, one should also discuss if the surgical technique should be the method of choice, at least if the hospital has surgeons with experience in this technique.

Conclusion

Tracheostomy have become a frequent procedure in the ICU in the last decades, and most intensivists will claim its advantage regarding shortened time on the ventilator, better patient comfort and reduced LOS in the ICU. This last is an important attainment that reduces costs and make the ICU more efficient. However, we do not have definite proof regarding its benefit in long-term outcomes. Most evidence from epidemiological studies and small open prospective studies often yields the same results, showing associated improvement in overall mortality also, with the use of (early) tracheostomy. Two large scale prospective clinical trials are presently running to answer the controversy about the timing of tracheostomy (33, 34). Until these two studies are completed and their results published, we will probably not have the answer about what the optimal timing is to perform a tracheostomy in the ICU population.

The controversy regarding the technique has been less prominent lately. In experienced hands, both methods are safe and the perioperative complications are not very different. However, if the OR is used for the surgical procedure, this increases costs, and total time spent on the procedure (including transportation time and lifting from the bed to the operating table) considerably. Given this fact, there are advantages in using the percutaneous method. However, this method is not without serious complications, and it is necessary to give physicians performing this procedure in the ICU enough experience.

The author

Hans Flaatten, MD, PhD
Department of Anaesthesia
and Intensive Care
Department of Surgical Sciences
University Hospital of Bergen
N-5021 Bergen, Norway
e-mail: hans.flaatten@helse-bergen.no

References

1. Borman J, Davidson J. A history of tracheostomy. Brit J Anaesth. 1963;35:388–90.
2. Jackson C. Tracheotomy. Am Laryng Rhin Otol. 1909:337.
3. Jackson C. Tracheotomy. Am J Surg. 1939;46:519.
4. Toy FJ, Weinstein JD. A percutaneous tracheostomy device. Surgery. 1969 Feb;65(2):384–9.
5. Ciaglia P, Firsching R, Syniec C. Elective percutaneous dilatational tracheostomy. A new simple bedside procedure; preliminary report. Chest. 1985 Jun;87(6):715–9.
6. Griggs WM, Worthley LI, Gilligan JE, Thomas PD, Myburg JA. A simple percutaneous tracheostomy technique. Surgery, gynecology & obstetrics. 1990 Jun;170(6):543–5.
7. Cox CE, Carson SS, Holmes GM, Howard A, Carey TS. Increase in tracheostomy for prolonged mechanical ventilation in North Carolina, 1993–2002. Critical care medicine. 2004 Nov;32(11):2219–26.
8. Flaatten H, Gjerde S, Heimdal JH, Aardal S. The effect of tracheostomy on outcome in intensive care unit patients. Acta anaesthesiologica Scandinavica. 2006 Jan; 50(1):92–8.
9. Blot F, Melot C. Indications, timing, and techniques of tracheostomy in 152 French ICUs. Chest. 2005 Apr;127(4): 1347–52.
10. Frutos-Vivar F, Esteban A, Apezteguia C, Anzueto A, Nightingale P, Gonzalez M et al. Outcome of mechanically ventilated patients who require a tracheostomy. Critical care medicine. 2005 Feb;33(2):290–8.
11. Arabi Y, Haddad S, Shirawi N, Al Shimemeri A. Early tracheostomy in intensive care trauma patients improves resource utilization: a cohort study and literature review. Critical care (London, England). 2004 Oct;8(5):R347–52.
12. Engoren M, Arslanian-Engoren C, Fenn-Buderer N. Hospital and long-term outcome after tracheostomy for respiratory failure. Chest. 2004 Jan;125(1):220–7.
13. Fischler L, Erhart S, Kleger GR, Frutiger A. Prevalence of tracheostomy in ICU patients. A nation-wide survey in Switzerland. Intensive care medicine. 2000 Oct;26(10): 1428–33.
14. Simpson TP, Day CJ, Jewkes CF, Manara AR. The impact of percutaneous tracheostomy on intensive care unit practice and training. Anaesthesia. 1999 Feb;54(2):186–9.
15. Kollef MH, Ahrens TS, Shannon W. Clinical predictors and outcomes for patients requiring tracheostomy in the intensive care unit. Critical care medicine. 1999 Sep;27(9):1714–20.
16. Whited RE. A prospective study of laryngotracheal sequelae in long-term intubation. The Laryngoscope. 1984 Mar;94(3):367–77.
17. Thomas R, Kumar EV, Kameswaran M, Shamim A, al Ghamdi S, Mummigatty AP et al. Post intubation laryngeal sequelae in an intensive care unit. The Journal of laryngology and otology. 1995 Apr;109(4):313–6.
18. Esteller-More E, Ibanez J, Matino E, Adema JM, Nolla M, Quer IM. Prognostic factors in laryngotracheal injury following intubation and/or tracheotomy in ICU patients. Eur Arch Otorhinolaryngol. 2005 Nov;262(11): 880–3.
19. Rumbak MJ, Newton M, Truncale T, Schwartz SW, Adams JW, Hazard PB. A prospective, randomized, study comparing early percutaneous dilational tracheotomy to prolonged translaryngeal intubation (delayed tracheotomy) in critically ill medical patients. Critical care medicine. 2004 Aug;32(8):1689–94.
20. Nieszkowska A, Combes A, Luyt CE, Ksibi H, Trouillet JL, Gibert C et al. Impact of tracheotomy on sedative administration, sedation level, and comfort of

mechanically ventilated intensive care unit patients. Critical care medicine. 2005 Nov;33(11):2527–33.

21. Combes A, Luyt CE, Nieszkowska A, Trouillet JL, Gibert C, Chastre J. Is tracheostomy associated with better outcomes for patients requiring long-term mechanical ventilation? Critical care medicine. 2007 Mar;35(3): 802–7.

22. MacIntyre NR, Cook DJ, Ely EW Jr., Epstein SK, Fink JB, Heffner JE et al. Evidence-based guidelines for weaning and discontinuing ventilatory support: a collective task force facilitated by the American College of Chest Physicians; the American Association for Respiratory Care; and the American College of Critical Care Medicine. Chest. 2001 Dec;120(6 Suppl):375S–95S.

23. Tobin MJ, Jubran A. Meta-analysis under the spotlight: focused on a meta-analysis of ventilator weaning. Critical care medicine. 2008 Jan;36(1):1–7.

24. Griffiths J, Barber VS, Morgan L, Young JD. Systematic review and meta-analysis of studies of the timing of tracheostomy in adult patients undergoing artificial ventilation. BMJ. Clinical research ed. 2005 May 28; 330(7502):1243.

25. Klein M, Agassi R, Shapira AR, Kaplan DM, Koiffman L, Weksler N. Can intensive care physicians safely perform percutaneous dilational tracheostomy? An analysis of 207 cases. Isr Med Assoc J. 2007 Oct;9(10):717–9.

26. Bowen CP, Whitney LR, Truwit JD, Durbin CG, Moore MM. Comparison of safety and cost of percutaneous versus surgical tracheostomy. The American surgeon. 2001 Jan;67(1):54–60.

27. Pandit RA, Jacques TC. Audit of over 500 percutaneous dilational tracheostomies. Crit Care Resusc. 2006 Jun;8(2):146–50.

28. Patel A, Swan P, Dunning J. Does a percutaneous tracheostomy have a lower incidence of complications compared to an open surgical technique? Interactive cardiovascular and thoracic surgery. 2005 Dec;4(6): 563–8.

29. Tan CC, Lee HS, Balan S. Percutaneous dilational tracheostomy – a 3 year experience in a general hospital in Malaysia. The Medical journal of Malaysia. 2004 Dec;59(5):591–7.

30. Dulguerov P, Gysin C, Perneger TV, Chevrolet JC. Percutaneous or surgical tracheostomy: a meta-analysis. Critical care medicine. 1999 Aug;27(8):1617–25.

31. Delaney A, Bagshaw SM, Nalos M. Percutaneous dilatational tracheostomy versus surgical tracheostomy in critically ill patients: a systematic review and meta-analysis. Critical care (London, England). 2006; 10(2):R55.

32. Higgins KM, Punthakee X. Meta-analysis comparison of open versus percutaneous tracheostomy. The Laryngoscope. 2007 Mar;117(3):447–54.

33. ClinicalTrials.gov. Early versus late Tracheostomy. 2008.

34. ClinicalTrials.gov. Early Percutanous Tracheostomy for Cardiac Surgery. 2008.

B. Acute circulatory failure

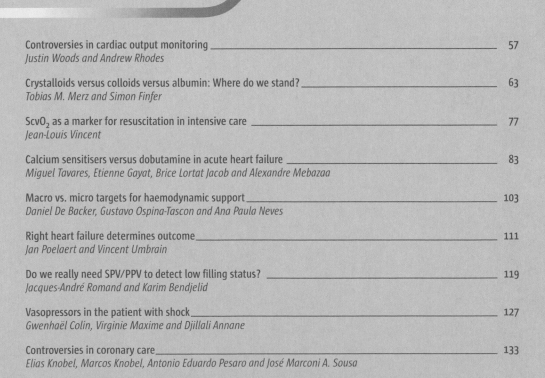

Justin Woods and Andrew Rhodes

Controversies in cardiac output monitoring

Introduction

Cardiovascular instability is a common cause of morbidity and subsequent mortality in critically ill patients. Appropriately chosen therapy requires an understanding of the pathophysiological disturbance, which can often only be fully understood with advanced haemodynamic monitoring. Although some studies where protocolised therapy has been started early in the patient's disease progression have shown benefit, others have not (1–6). Retrospective studies of pulmonary artery catheters have elicited harm leading to some authors calling for a moratorium on these devices until benefit can be unequivocally shown (7–10). There is no doubt that the ideal of a device being able to help us to modify our interventions is laudable, however, often we lack the evidence base to justify the primacy that these devices are given. The basis for our presumption of benefit is that knowledge of the cardiovascular derangement, and the ability to track subsequent change following an intervention, will lead to an improved outcome for our patient. Sadly, this evidence base remains lacking in many clinical scenarios and is considered by many to be unachievable due to the extensive use of these devices in everyday practice (11).

What the debate is focused on now is not so much the need for the information, but how that is subsequently interpreted and used to influence outcome. A haemodynamic monitoring device remains just that, irrespective of the underlying pathology, until it is paired with a clinical intervention designed to influence pathophysiology. The device itself has no bearing on the outcome but instead provides the vehicle for active intervention. The underlying issues are more in keeping with the accuracy of the device, utilisation of the information obtained and the morbidity and mortality caused by the devices.

Controversy 1: The pulmonary artery catheter is harmful

The flow-directed pulmonary artery catheter has been available for over thirty years (12). It essentially monitors three primary variables (pressure, cardiac output and mixed venous oxygen saturation) and then derives many others. It is used for both diagnosis and treatment but it has no intrinsic properties that allow it to independently improve outcome without an associated change in treatment strategy. Although ingrained in critical care practice, its use has been questioned due to the worrying detrimental effects demonstrated in several observation studies (7, 8, 13). Gore, Zion and Connors all conducted retrospective analyses which appear to show that use of the device is associated with harm, although this could be ascribed to the severity of the underlying illness (7, 8, 13, 14). What can be difficult to dissect is whether there is a chance that the patient may have survived irrespective of the use of the monitoring.

More recently there have been a number of prospectively performed randomised controlled studies which were designed to confirm or refute this suggestion of harm that had been raised in the observational studies (15–18). All of these have been criticised for being underpowered to adequately detect small differences in outcome directly related to the catheter. However, not one of them has been able to confirm the previous concerns of harm. It is worth noting, though, that none of these studies directed clinicians in how to use the data from the catheter. It is perhaps not surprising, therefore, that none of them were to prove beneficial to the patients. It seems likely that the direct harm related to this tool is not significant, and it is far more pertinent how the clinicians use the data acquired.

It should be remembered that the pulmonary artery catheter is simply a monitoring device that acquires information about a patient's haemodynamic status. It is not surprising, therefore, that it has proven to be difficult to demonstrate benefit to patient outcome with this tool. In order for this to happen a number of steps must have occurred together. These include the correct acquisition of data, the appropriate understanding of physiological variables (so that the acquired data can be put into a relevant clinical context) and following that, a logical and appropriate clinical decision based on the data and the relevant physiological and pharmacological treatments available.

With the pulmonary artery catheter, there are problems with each of these steps that limit its utility to prove benefit. These include a failure of clinicians to interpret the waveforms such as a pulmonary artery occlusion pressure trace appropriately (19, 20), a lack in understanding of how the occlusion pressure relates to preload (21) and a failure of clinicians to interpret the variables appropriately within a clinical context (22, 23).

The pulmonary artery occlusion pressure has been used as a measure of preload for decades (24, 25). It relates end diastolic pressures in the left atrium to volumes and, subsequently, to compliance of the ventricle. The underlying assumption is that a continuous column of blood exists between the catheter tip and the left atrium and that the measured pressure is that of the left atrium and, by inference, the left ventricle. The re-

lationship that is desired is that at a given time, for a given compliance, the myocardial fibre length is proportional to the load applied which reflects the end diastolic volume. Unfortunately, static measures are of limited value and catheter malplacement, mechanical ventilation, valvular stenosis, cardiomyopathies (all causes) and dynamic changes in compliance all influence the preload approximation (26). An additional problem is that the occlusion pressure incorrectly assumes no interdependence between the right and left heart, however, in right-heart pathological states the ventricular interdependence may actually reverse, altering the myocardial dynamics (27). Thus, when interpreting the value, even as a trend, the overall physiology and evolving changes have to be borne in mind (28). Kumar has shown that pulmonary artery occlusion pressures are poor predictors of volume response and, along with central venous pressures, are poorly correlated with end diastolic volumes (21). Thus, using pulmonary artery occlusion pressures to guide therapy is of restricted value.

In order for the pulmonary artery catheter to be of positive use to patients, the risks attached to the device must be outweighed by the likely positive benefits of knowing the data. This implies that the data is being acquired at a time when therapy may still influence the outcome. It can be seen in the work of Rivers and colleagues (4) that early targeted therapy in septic shock can lead to mortality reductions, whereas delaying treatment even when targeted can lead to either no effect at all (6) or even a worsening of the clinical condition (5). That the pulmonary artery catheter has complications associated with its insertion and in vivo presence is undoubted. The complications may be related to duration of use (infection and thromboembolus) and insertion (haematoma, dysrhythmia, valvular and pulmonary injury) (16, 18, 29–32). The cumulative effect of these complications for patients remains obscure, with a meta-analysis by Ivanov concluding that there were no new organ failures attributable to catheter use and that there was a trend towards fewer complications in the catheter-treated groups (29).

The failure of clinical trials to find a beneficial niche for the pulmonary artery catheter, together with the known risks and complications, have led many senior opinion leaders to suggest it should not be used in critical care practice (33). This view remains contested and controversial. However, many clinicians perceive the tool as nothing but a monitor and therefore any complications arising as due only to malpractice or a clinician's misunderstanding of the physiology and pharmaceutics. It should be remembered that no other monitoring device has ever been able to demonstrate outcome improvement on its own (34). The pulmonary artery catheter, although perhaps more invasive than some other monitors, should be viewed in a similar fashion and not put onto a pedestal of its own.

Controversy 2: Minimally invasive cardiac output monitoring is safe and therefore mandated over the pulmonary artery catheter

A recent international consensus conference has suggested that to date there is limited data either describing the accuracy (efficacy) or the usability (efficaciousness) of the newer generation of less invasive haemodynamic monitoring devices in critically ill or shocked patients (35). The need for such a conference has arisen due to the ongoing controversies surrounding the pulmonary artery catheter and the plethora of new less invasive devices that are in the market place. New techniques, especially if they are perceived to be less invasive to patients, are always seen as exciting and 'sexy'. However, it is incumbent on us to carefully evaluate these new devices to prevent similar debates surrounding their use, as is the case with the pulmonary artery catheter. These new devices mainly relate to the techniques described by pulse pressure analysis and are typified by the PICCO^{TM} system, the LiDCO*plus*^{TM} and Vigileo monitors, but also includes Doppler analysis and thoracic bio-impedance.

The criticism surrounding this new generation of devices essentially can be described in terms of two main issues. Firstly, there is no good data describing their accuracy and precision in the patients where they are likely to be used, and secondly, much like the pulmonary artery catheter, there is very little evidence to show how they can be used to improve patient outcomes.

If we focus on the pulse pressure devices, as they are the most widely used, it can be seen that most of the validation studies have been performed in cardiac surgery patients (36–38). This is perhaps not surprising as this patient population is easy to study and has a ready indication for a reference comparison technique such as the pulmonary artery catheter. It must be borne in mind, however, that no matter how good the data is in this group caution is advised before extrapolating these studies to other patient categories such as severe sepsis or septic shock. Some of the devices are now being assessed in the mixed bag of medical intensive care patients (39, 40) where the accuracy is still acceptable although not as good as previously thought, but more data is still eagerly awaited.

Many of these devices also need an independent measurement of cardiac output as a reference technique, for instance, the PICCO^{TM} utilises trans-pulmonary thermodilution and the LIDCO*plus*^{TM} lithium dilution. Although calibration is beneficial as it resets the baseline and provides clinicians with a level of reassurance, it can be fraught with problems. The accuracy and precision of the calibration needs to be understood in order to prevent increased errors entering the system (41), but also it is important to understand when each device needs to have a calibration performed in order to be happy with the continuous data. Recent studies have suggested that this is perhaps within a couple of hours of a baseline calibration when haemodynamic changes have occurred (40), but further clarification with other devices and techniques is needed.

The second issue surrounds these tools' ability to influence patient outcomes. It is likely that the issues here are exactly the same as for the pulmonary artery catheter. If cardiac output is to be used to influence outcome, it must be correctly measured, interpreted and acted upon. These new devices can measure this variable with a less invasive methodology. This should reduce the risks to patients; however, perhaps the more important facet is how we act upon the knowledge rather than how we acquire it. Studies demonstrating how we should use this data to improve outcomes in shocked patients in the intensive care unit are still awaited.

Whilst these new devices can provide information concerning the patient's haemodynamic status in an easier fashion than previously and with a less invasive method, it is important to remember that the data supporting their use is still limited. It is absolutely necessary for clinicians to fully acquaint themselves with these new technologies including all the limitations and pitfalls behind their use. This learning phase, although understood, was sadly lacking with the pulmonary artery catheter (19), but the same mistakes must not be made again.

Conclusions

In order for any monitor to be able to benefit a patient, several truths need to be understood. These include the fact that (1) every monitor has risks for the patient, from pulmonary artery rupture through to electrocution, (2) the monitor cannot provide benefit on its own, it requires a sensible clinician to use the device appropriately, identify when and when not to assess the data and how to interpret it, (3) monitoring without treatment will not change the patient's status, and (4) it is only when the benefits outweigh the risks that the monitoring device should be used. These truths are the same for whatever monitoring device is used.

It is too simplistic to conclude that one particular monitor is better or worse than another. They all have particular aspects that benefit some situations more than others. The pulmonary artery catheter has particular advantages for patients with right ventricular dysfunction (27), whereas the less invasive devices may be better for less sick patients. The most important point, however, is that clinicians need to learn how to use the specific tools that they have available to them in order to minimise the risks and maximise the potential benefits. If this occurs, we can expect positive impacts for our patients in the future.

The authors

Justin Woods, research Fellow
Andrew Rhodes, FRCA, FRCP, Consultant in Intensive Care Medicine
    Department of Intensive Care Medicine |
    St George's Hospital | London, SW17 0QT, UK

Address for correspondence
    Andrew Rhodes
    Department of Intensive Care Medicine
    St George's Hospital
    Blackshaw Road
    London, SW17 0QT, UK
    e-mail: andyr@sgul.ac.uk

References

1. Berlauk JF, Abrams JH, Gilmour IJ, O'Connor SR, Knighton DR, Cerra FB. Preoperative optimization of cardiovascular hemodynamics improves outcome in peripheral vascular surgery. A prospective, randomized clinical trial. Ann Surg. 1991;214(3):289–297; discussion 298–289.
2. Pearse R, Dawson D, Fawcett J, Rhodes A, Grounds RM, Bennett ED. Early goal-directed therapy after major surgery reduces complications and duration of hospital stay. A randomised, controlled trial [ISRCTN38797445]. Crit Care. 2005;9(6):R687–693.
3. Boyd O, Grounds RM, Bennett ED A randomized clinical trial of the effect of deliberate perioperative increase of oxygen delivery on mortality in high-risk surgical patients. JAMA. 1993;270(22):2699–2707.
4. Rivers E, Nguyen B, Havstad S, Ressler J, Muzzin A, Knoblich B, Peterson E, Tomlanovich M. Early goal-directed therapy in the treatment of severe sepsis and septic shock. N Engl J Med. 2001;345(19):1368–1377.
5. Hayes MA, Timmins AC, Yau EH, Palazzo M, Hinds CJ, Watson D. Elevation of systemic oxygen delivery in the treatment of critically ill patients. N Engl J Med. 1994; 330(24):1717–1722.
6. Gattinoni L, Brazzi L, Pelosi P, Latini R, Tognoni G, Pesenti A, Fumagalli R. A trial of goal-oriented hemodynamic therapy in critically ill patients. SvO2 Collaborative Group. N Engl J Med. 1995;333(16): 1025–1032.
7. Connors AF, Jr., McCaffree DR, Gray BA. Evaluation of right-heart catheterization in the critically ill patient without acute myocardial infarction. N Engl J Med. 1983; 308(5):263–267.
8. Gore JM, Goldberg RJ, Spodick DH, Alpert JS, Dalen JE. A community-wide assessment of the use of pulmonary artery catheters in patients with acute myocardial infarction. Chest. 1987;92(4):721–727.
9. Robin ED. Death by pulmonary artery flow-directed catheter. Time for a moratorium? Chest. 1987, 92(4): 727–731.
10. Dalen JE, Bone RC. Is it time to pull the pulmonary artery catheter? JAMA. 1996;276(11):916–918.
11. Pinsky MR. Hemodynamic evaluation and monitoring in the ICU. Chest. 2007;132(6):2020–2029.
12. Swan HJ, Ganz W, Forrester J, Marcus H, Diamond G, Chonette D. Catheterization of the heart in man with use of a flow-directed balloon-tipped catheter. N Engl J Med. 1970;283(9):447–451.
13. Zion MM, Balkin J, Rosenmann D, Goldbourt U, Reicher-Reiss H, Kaplinsky E, Behar S. Use of pulmonary artery catheters in patients with acute myocardial infarction. Analysis of experience in 5,841 patients in the SPRINT Registry. SPRINT Study Group. Chest. 1990;98(6): 1331–1335.

14. Friese RS, Shafi S, Gentilello LM. Pulmonary artery catheter use is associated with reduced mortality in severely injured patients: a National Trauma Data Bank analysis of 53,312 patients. Crit Care Med. 2006;34(6): 1597–1601.

15. Rhodes A, Cusack RJ, Newman PJ, Grounds RM, Bennett ED. A randomised, controlled trial of the pulmonary artery catheter in critically ill patients. Intensive Care Med. 2002;28(3):256–264.

16. Sandham JD, Hull RD, Brant RF, Knox L, Pineo GF, Doig CJ, Laporta DP, Viner S, Passerini L, Devitt H et al. A randomized, controlled trial of the use of pulmonary-artery catheters in high-risk surgical patients. N Engl J Med. 2003;348(1):5–14.

17. Harvey S, Harrison DA, Singer M, Ashcroft J, Jones CM, Elbourne D, Brampton W, Williams D, Young D, Rowan K. Assessment of the clinical effectiveness of pulmonary artery catheters in management of patients in intensive care (PAC-Man): a randomised controlled trial. Lancet. 2005;366(9484):472–477.

18. Richard C, Warszawski J, Anguel N, Deye N, Combes A, Barnoud D, Boulain T, Lefort Y, Fartoukh M, Baud F et al. Early use of the pulmonary artery catheter and outcomes in patients with shock and acute respiratory distress syndrome: a randomized controlled trial. JAMA. 2003;290(20):2713–2720.

19. Iberti TJ, Fischer EP, Leibowitz AB, Panacek EA, Silverstein JH, Albertson TE. A multicenter study of physicians' knowledge of the pulmonary artery catheter. Pulmonary Artery Catheter Study Group. JAMA. 1990;264(22):2928–2932.

20. Iberti TJ, Daily EK, Leibowitz AB, Schecter CB, Fischer EP, Silverstein JH. Assessment of critical care nurses' knowledge of the pulmonary artery catheter. The Pulmonary Artery Catheter Study Group. Crit Care Med. 1994;22(10):1674–1678.

21. Kumar A, Anel R, Bunnell E, Habet K, Zanotti S, Marshall S, Neumann A, Ali A, Cheang M, Kavinsky C et al. Pulmonary artery occlusion pressure and central venous pressure fail to predict ventricular filling volume, cardiac performance, or the response to volume infusion in normal subjects. Crit Care Med. 2004;32(3):691–699.

22. Pinsky MR, Teboul JL. Assessment of indices of preload and volume responsiveness. Curr Opin Crit Care. 2005; 11(3):235–239.

23. Gnaegi A, Feihl F, Perret C. Intensive care physicians' insufficient knowledge of right-heart catheterization at the bedside: time to act? Crit Care Med. 1997;25(2): 213–220.

24. Shoemaker WC, Appel PL, Kram HB, Waxman K, Lee TS. Prospective trial of supranormal values of survivors as therapeutic goals in high-risk surgical patients. Chest. 1988;94(6):1176–1186.

25. Durham R, Neunaber K, Vogler G, Shapiro M, Mazuski J. Right ventricular end-diastolic volume as a measure of

preload. J Trauma. 1995;39(2):218–223; discussion 223–214.

26. Gomez CM, Palazzo MG. Pulmonary artery catheterization in anaesthesia and intensive care. Br J Anaesth. 1998;81(6):945–956.

27. Woods J, Monteiro P, Rhodes A. Right ventricular dysfunction. Curr Opin Crit Care. 2007;13(5):532–540.

28. Pinsky MR. Clinical significance of pulmonary artery occlusion pressure. Intensive Care Med. 2003;29(2): 175–178.

29. Ivanov R, Allen J, Calvin JE. The incidence of major morbidity in critically ill patients managed with pulmonary artery catheters: a meta-analysis. Crit Care Med. 2000;28(3):615–619.

30. Boyd KD, Thomas SJ, Gold J, Boyd AD. A prospective study of complications of pulmonary artery catheterizations in 500 consecutive patients. Chest. 1983;84(3):245–249.

31. Sise MJ, Hollingsworth P, Brimm JE, Peters RM, Virgilio RW, Shackford SR. Complications of the flow-directed pulmonary artery catheter: A prospective analysis in 219 patients. Crit Care Med. 1981;9(4):315–318.

32. Connors AF Jr, Castele RJ, Farhat NZ, Tomashefski JF, Jr. Complications of right heart catheterization. A prospective autopsy study. Chest. 1985;88(4):567–572.

33. Finfer S, Delaney A. Pulmonary artery catheters. BMJ. 2006;333(7575):930–931.

34. Pedersen T, Pedersen P, Moller AM. Pulse oximetry for perioperative monitoring. Cochrane Database Syst Rev. 2001(2):CD002013.

35. Antonelli M, Azoulay E, Bonten M, Chastre J, Citerio G, Conti G, De Backer D, Lemaire F, Gerlach H, Groeneveld J et al. Year in review in Intensive Care Medicine. 2007. II. Haemodynamics, pneumonia, infections and sepsis, invasive and non-invasive mechanical ventilation, acute respiratory distress syndrome. Intensive Care Med. 2008; 34(3):405–422.

36. Godje O, Hoke K, Goetz AE, Felbinger TW, Reuter DA, Reichart B, Friedl R, Hannekum A, Pfeiffer UJ. Reliability of a new algorithm for continuous cardiac output determination by pulse-contour analysis during hemodynamic instability. Crit Care Med. 2002;30(1): 52–58.

37. Linton R, Band D, O'Brien T, Jonas M, Leach R. Lithium dilution cardiac output measurement: a comparison with thermodilution. Crit Care Med. 1997;25(11): 1796–1800.

38. Button D, Weibel L, Reuthebuch O, Genoni M, Zollinger A, Hofer CK. Clinical evaluation of the FloTrac/Vigileo system and two established continuous cardiac output monitoring devices in patients undergoing cardiac surgery. Br J Anaesth. 2007;99(3):329–336.

39. Cecconi M, Fawcett J, Grounds RM, Rhodes A. A prospective study to evaluate the accuracy of pulse power analysis to monitor cardiac output in critically ill patients. BMC Anesthesiol. 2008;8(1):3.

40. Hamzaoui O, Monnet X, Richard C, Osman D, Chemla D, Teboul JL. Effects of changes in vascular tone on the agreement between pulse contour and transpulmonary thermodilution cardiac output measurements within an up to 6-hour calibration-free period. Crit Care Med. 2008; 36(2):434–440.

41. Cecconi M, Grounds M, Rhodes A. Methodologies for assessing agreement between two methods of clinical measurement: are we as good as we think we are? Curr Opin Crit Care. 2007;13(3):294–296.

Tobias M. Merz and Simon Finfer

Crystalloids versus colloids versus albumin: Where do we stand?

Introduction

Administration of intravenous fluid to increase or maintain intravascular volume is a cornerstone in the therapy of critically ill patients. In a multinational "point-prevalence" study of over 5000 intensive care unit (ICU) patients in 390 hospitals in 24 countries, approximately 35 % of ICU patients received resuscitation fluids on a single day (SAFE TRIPS investigators – unpublished data). As so many thousands of ICU patients receive resuscitation fluids each day, very small differences in outcomes attributable to the choice of fluid could have a substantial impact on the global burden of disease and both the survival and health-related quality of life of critically ill patients. Resuscitation fluids fall into three broad categories, crystalloids, synthetic colloids and albumin-containing solutions, and available data suggest that there is wide variation in the type of fluids clinicians use. In a questionnaire survey of 451 ICUs in Germany 43 % of respondents reported using exclusively colloids for volume resuscitation, hydroxy-ethyl starch (HES) was the most commonly used colloid solution, albumin-containing solutions were rarely the first choice fluid (1). In contrast, in a survey of 364 clinicians from medical and surgical specialties in the Canadian province of Ontario, 70 % of respondents reported using crystalloids for volume expansion more than 90 % of the time, albumin was the most common colloid used followed by HES (2). In a survey of more than 2400 ICU doctors from the European and French Intensive Care Societies, 65 % of clinicians reported using a mixture of crystalloids and colloids for volume resuscitation; isotonic crystalloids, HES, and gelatins were the most common fluids used (3). In a Europe-based inception cohort study of 687 shocked patients treated in 115 ICUs, 17 % received crystalloid resuscitation alone, 67 % received a mixture of colloid and crystalloid fluids and 16 % received colloids alone; 48 % of patients received starch, 38 % received gelatin, 28 % received plasma, 15 % received albumin and 3 % received dextran (F. Schortgen – personal communication). A recent survey of European burns units confirms significant practice variation in this more specialised patient population and suggests that uncertainty over the choice of fluids remains widespread (4).

Ideally the choice of any medical treatment is based on an analysis of the balance of risk and benefit that is relevant to the patient to be treated; the analysis of risk and benefit is best informed by the results of large-scale randomised controlled trials (5). In the absence of such data clinicians may extrapolate the results of smaller clinical studies or be influenced by laboratory studies or studies examining surrogate endpoints. A number of studies have suggested that early or pre-emptive fluid resuscitation may improve outcome in groups of critically ill and surgical patients (6–8), and so data that one or other fluid may provide more rapid or persistent intravascular volume expansion may underpin a convincing argument to prefer one fluid over another. As exposure to a drug detailer has been found to influence clinicians' choice of fluids, advancing such arguments may be effective in altering clinicians' behaviour (2).

In the discussion below we review both the basic science arguments and, more importantly, the clinical trial data that support the use of crystalloids, synthetic colloids or albumin. We discuss two controversial positions:

1. There is currently insufficient evidence to advocate the use of synthetic colloids in modern clinical practice.
2. If you really must use a colloid, perhaps you should use albumin.

Controversial point 1: There is currently insufficient evidence to advocate the use of synthetic colloids in modern clinical practice

Basic science

Determinants of fluid flux: Physicians asked to specify the circumstances in which they prefer to use colloid instead of crystalloid resuscitation fluids often report manipulation of colloid osmotic pressure (COP) and more rapid expansion of intravascular volume with lower total infusion volume to be the most important reasons for their decision (2). These preferences are based on the classical Starling model of microvascular fluid exchange, which builds on the concept of passive transendothelial filtration driven by differences in capillary and interstitial hydrostatic and oncotic pressure and a fixed endothelial fluid permeability. In contrast to this model, newer findings suggest that fluid and solute filtration and absorption are closely balanced by active mechanisms such as transcellular protein transport, adjusted changes in intercellular fluid flow and reabsorption of fluids in specialised tissues (9). In light of these more complex processes COP loses its position as the most important determinant of microvascular fluid exchange.

Effects of synthetic colloids on vascular permeability and inflammatory processes: At microvascular level, critical illness and systemic inflammatory response syndrome (SIRS) is associated with increased vascular permeability and tissue oedema formation, increased neutrophil activation and endothelial adherence and with changes in coagulation properties. An ideal resuscitation fluid would, apart from restoring intravascular volume, positively modulate these inflammatory reactions. To influence these inflammatory processes, resuscitation fluids must exhibit specific properties to allow for interaction with blood components or the capillary wall. Indeed, such interactions have been described in tissue and animal models of microvascular fluid exchange. Exchange of fluid and solutes from the endoluminal space to the interstitium requires passage through the endothelial cell surface glycocalyx, which consists of a network of membrane-bound and soluble proteoglycans and glycoproteins covering the intraluminal surface of the microvascular endothelium (10, 11). The endothelial glycocalyx serves as a competent barrier for water and colloids, only after its destruction do changes in endothelial cellular morphology, such as after ischaemia or inflammation, determine capillary permeability (12–15). In addition to its capacity to influence endothelial permeability to fluids and solutes, the glycocalyx also plays an important role in blood cell–endothelial interactions (16, 17). Whereas in normal conditions the endothelial leukocyte adhesion molecules are shielded by glycosaminglycan chains and the soluble components of the glycocalyx, they appear to be uncovered after degradation of the glycocalyx through enzymes, cytokines, or ischaemia and reperfusion, thus allowing leukocyte adhesion and transmigration (16, 18, 19). Colloids in resuscitation fluids interact with the endothelial glycocalyx in a specific manner, depending on different properties such as molecular size and structure and charge (12, 13, 20) and thus have at least the potential to influence capillary permeability and blood cell–endothelial interactions.

Depending on molecular weight and charge, colloids may remain excluded from the glycocalyx (e.g. large anionic or neutral dextran molecules (13)), or may penetrate the glycocalyx and influence its properties (e.g. hydroxyethyl starch (20)). When compared to saline and Ringer's solution, hydroxyethyl starch (HES) (20) and dextran (21) bind to the endothelial glycocalyx surface layer and induce a sealing effect, thus influencing transcapillary fluid flux independently of their action on intraluminal COP.

Resuscitation fluids can affect different steps of blood cell–endothelium interactions and thus alter inflammatory processes. Hypertonic and isotonic saline, dextrans and Ringer's solution can induce pro-inflammatory changes in gene expression of human leucocytes and increase neutrophil intracellular oxidative burst activity (22–24). Resuscitation with HES may be associated with a decrease in neutrophil–endothelial interaction, an effect that was attributed to changes in glycocalyx properties (25) and restoration of macrophage integrity (26).

Effects on the coagulation system: All plasma substitutes interfere with the physiological mechanisms of haemostasis through a non-specific effect correlated to the degree of haemodilution. Progressive haemodilution using crystalloids or colloids has been shown to induce an initial hypercoagulable state after substitution of 20–30 % of total blood volume in several in vitro (27–29) and in vivo (30, 31) studies. The type of resuscitation fluid does not seem to influence the degree of initial hypercoagulable state (32, 33). This phenomenon has been attributed to a decrease in the concentration of coagulation inhibitors and can be attenuated by maintaining normal anti-thrombin III (ATIII) (34) and magnesium levels (35). At 30–40 % dilution with a crystalloid solution coagulation returns to normal; dilution has to exceed 50 % before coagulation is again impaired. The dilutional effect of crystalloid infusion is reversed over time and coagulation returns to normal (36). In the case of synthetic colloids, coagulopathy develops at a dilution ratio higher than 30 % (33). Other non-specific effects of haemodilution on coagulation include a decrease in platelet count and dilution of red blood cells, both of which play an important role in haemostasis.

Specific actions of plasma substitutes on haemostasis relate to the direct action on coagulation proteins, platelet function and the fibrinolytic system and are only described for colloids. Dextrans and HES have more significant effects, depending on their molecular weight and – in the case of HES – molar substitution ratio; gelatins show lesser impact on haemostasis (37, 38). Plasma substitution with dextran induces a more pronounced decrease in levels of von Willebrand factor (vWF)

and associated factor VIII (VIII:c) than is accounted for by dilutional effects. This effect has been attributed to the adsorption of vWF and VIII:c on dextran molecules resulting in a structural alteration (39). Like dextrans, starches interfere with normal haemostasis at different levels. They induce a decrease in vWF and VIII:c, which is related to the in vivo molecular weight (Mw) of the specific HES (40–42). Additionally, HES seems to reduce platelet aggregation by decreasing the expression of the platelet receptor GPIIb/IIIa (43), and to enhance fibrinolysis, possibly by diminishing α2-antiplasmin-plasmin interactions (44). The generally accepted belief that gelatins have no specific effects on haemostasis has been challenged by studies reporting a decrease in vWF and inhibition of GPIIb/IIIa-mediated platelet aggregation and thus impairment of clot formation (45, 46). In clinical settings, bleeding complications have been observed with the use of dextran and HES, especially in preparations featuring high in vivo Mw (47, 48) but not with gelatins (49, 50). In the recently published Efficacy of Volume Substitution and Insulin Therapy in Severe Sepsis (VISEP) study, which compared fluid resuscitation with HES and Ringer's lactated in patients with severe sepsis, patients assigned to HES had significantly lower platelets counts and higher transfusion requirements (51). More recently developed HES solutions with lower average Mw and lower molar substitution may have less marked effects on coagulation (52).

Outcome data from clinical trials

Effects on renal function: Acute renal failure (ARF) occurs in 5–10 % of critically ill patients, and known predisposing factors include sepsis, major surgery, circulatory failure and the administration of nephrotoxic drugs (53). The most common predisposing factor is septic shock, and overall mortality for ICU patients with renal failure exceeds 60 % (53). In recent years it has become apparent that the choice of resuscitation fluid and especially the use of HES might contribute to the occurrence of renal failure, particularly in patients with severe sepsis (54, 55). When compared to gelatins, fluid resuscitation of brain-dead kidney donors with HES is associated with more frequent impairment of immediate renal function in the transplant recipients (56), and results in an increased incidence of renal failure and oliguria in ICU patients with severe sepsis and septic shock (54). In the VISEP study, fluid resuscitation with HES resulted in more rapid normalisation of central venous pressure but also in a significantly higher rate of acute renal failure (34.9% vs. 22.8%; p = 0.002) and more days on which renal replacement therapy (18.3% vs. 9.2%) was necessary, when compared with fluid resuscitation with modified Ringer's lactate solution (51). Again, some studies that have examined effects on surrogate outcome measures have questioned whether these effects are seen with more recently developed starch solutions (57), and the results of larger trials are awaited (58). Occurrence of ARF has also been reported with the use of dextrans in heterogeneous patient populations, although only in few small studies and case reports (59–61).

Effects on pulmonary function: The optimal fluid management in patients with acute lung injury (ALI) and acute respiratory distress syndrome (ARDS) requires a balance between adequate fluid resuscitation to assure sufficient systemic tissue perfusion and too liberal administration promoting pulmonary oedema in the setting of increased pulmonary vascular permeability. Intravascular hydrostatic pressure and COP are altered by fluid administration, and formation of pulmonary oedema is enhanced by reduced COP and elevated hydrostatic pressures (62–64). Higher cumulative fluid balance has been associated with further impairment of pulmonary function and increased mortality in ARDS (65, 66), and a recent high quality trial reported improved oxygenation and increased "ventilator-free days" in patients assigned to a conservative fluid resuscitation strategy (67). Cautious fluid administration seems beneficial in patients with ARDS (67, 68), but to date clinical trials have not demonstrated a beneficial effect of colloids as compared to crystalloids in the context and outcome of ALI/ARDS.

Effect on Mortality: Despite the long-running controversy, many trials and subsequent meta-analyses, there is no convincing evidence that resuscitation with synthetic colloids offers a mortality benefit over resuscitation with crystalloids. Unfortunately, most studies have had inadequate statistical power to definitively confirm or exclude

mortality differences and many have suffered from methodological flaws (69). To date the VISEP Study, which was stopped early after inclusion of 537 patients because of increased rates of renal failure in the HES group, represents the largest trial in the field. The rate of death at 28 days did not differ significantly between the HES group and the Ringer's lactate group (26.7% vs. 24.1%), but there was a trend to increased mortality at 90 days in the HES group (41.0% vs. 33.9%, p = 0.09).

Figure 1 shows sample size, mortality and statistical power of the ten largest published trials comparing crystalloids and synthetic colloids in adult intensive care patients (51, 70–78). None of these trials reached the generally accepted minimum of 80% power in demonstrating a mortality difference between fluid resuscitation strategies. Additionally, the trials inconsistently favour crystalloids or colloids and the mortality differences between resuscitation groups are variable and may not be representative of a heterogeneous population of intensive care patients. The Paris-based CRISTAL study is a randomised controlled trial that plans to recruit 3010 participants (79); participants will be assigned to fluid resuscitation with either crystalloid or colloid with the precise choice of fluid being left to the treating clinicians. This trial should provide valuable data on the relative merits of colloids as a class but the design may not allow definitive conclusions regarding the efficacy or safety of individual colloid solutions. There will be particular interest in whether it can resolve the controversy surrounding the safety of HES solutions as ongoing trials of HES solutions are generally too small or examine only surrogate outcome measures (80).

Even after completion of the CRISTAL study, it is likely that meta-analyses will provide the most reliable information to clinicians. A number of meta-analyses have already examined how the choice of resuscitation fluid influences outcome (81–86). The most comprehensive is the recent update from the Cochrane Library (86); relative risk (RR) of death for HES compared to crystalloids was 1.05 (95% confidence interval [CI] 0.63–1.75), for dextrans compared to crystalloids a RR of 1.24 (95% CI 0.94–1.65) and for gelatins compared to crystalloids a RR of 0.9 (95% CI 0.49–1.72) was reported. The authors concluded that resuscitation with colloids is not associated with reduced

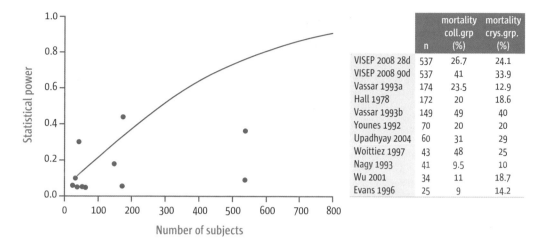

	n	mortality coll.grp (%)	mortality crys.grp. (%)
VISEP 2008 28d	537	26.7	24.1
VISEP 2008 90d	537	41	33.9
Vassar 1993a	174	23.5	12.9
Hall 1978	172	20	18.6
Vassar 1993b	149	49	40
Younes 1992	70	20	20
Upadhyay 2004	60	31	29
Woittiez 1997	43	48	25
Nagy 1993	41	9.5	10
Wu 2001	34	11	18.7
Evans 1996	25	9	14.2

Fig. 1   Crystalloids versus synthetic colloids – statistical power as a function of sample size.
Number of subjects and statistical power of the ten largest published trials comparing crystalloids and synthetic colloids (51, 70–78). Statistical power was calculated using actual group size and mortality from the individual studies. The line indicates statistical power as a function of sample size in detecting a 10% mortality difference assuming a baseline mortality of 20% (two-tailed alpha 0.05, beta 0.2). None of the trials reaches 80% power. Three trials exhibit higher statistical power for their sample size than calculated for the example function, indicating a higher baseline mortality than 20% and/or a mortality difference between fluid resuscitation groups of > 10%. The VISEP trial (51) reported 28-day and 90-day mortality, both analyses did not reach 80% power.

mortality in either critical care patients in general or in the evaluated subgroups of patients with trauma, burns or following surgery.

Thus, even in recent meta-analyses the 95% confidence intervals for the relative risk of death include the possibility that fluid resuscitation with synthetic colloids causes a substantial increase in mortality; until large-scale trials confirm their safety we must conclude that there is insufficient evidence to advocate the use of synthetic colloids in modern clinical practice.

Controversial point 2: If you must use a colloid, perhaps you should use albumin

Effect of albumin on vascular permeability and inflammatory processes: Albumin exerts a variety of potentially beneficial effects on vascular permeability and inflammatory processes. Due to its electrostatic properties, albumin penetrates and binds to the endothelial surface glycocalyx and influences its barrier function by decreasing hydraulic conductivity (13, 87, 88). The resulting sealing effect attenuates fluid extravasation independently of the oncotic properties of albumin (20, 21). Additionally, albumin can reduce vascular permeability by suppressing the oxidative burst of neutrophils (89), binding inflammatory mediators such as arachidonic acid (90), and by scavenging free radicals (91). Albumin is the principal extracellular antioxidant and maintains the redox state of the plasma, mostly by exposing a single thiol group (92, 93). Additionally, albumin exhibits modest intrinsic non-thiol-dependent anti-inflammatory properties in vitro (91). In patients with acute lung injury, albumin administration favourably influences plasma thiol-dependent antioxidant status as well as levels of protein oxidative damage (94). In an animal model of haemorrhagic shock, albumin improved mesenteric microcirculation and global haemodynamics and attenuated leukocyte rolling and endothelial adhesion (95). In an ischaemia-reperfusion model albumin reduced capillary permeability and tissue oedema when compared to Ringer's solution (96).

Effects on the coagulation system: Albumin has modest anti-thrombotic and anticoagulant effects which have been attributed to its capacity to bind nitric oxide (NO), thereby inhibiting the inactivation of NO and prolonging its anti-platelet effect (97). In vitro studies showed that albumin can inhibit platelet aggregation and alter fibrin polymerisation although these changes do not necessarily affect overall clot formation as assessed by thrombo-elastometry (38, 98, 99). In clinical settings, use of albumin does not seem to be associated with increased bleeding (49, 50).

Effects on renal function: In interleukin-2-associated capillary leak syndrome fluid resuscitation with albumin exerts a protective effect on renal function as compared to crystalloids (100). In large-volume paracentesis fluid replacement with albumin reduces the risk of renal dysfunction compared to detaining fluids and to fluid replacement using synthetic colloids (101–103). Similarly, in spontaneous bacterial peritonitis albumin administration has been shown to reduce renal impairment and mortality compared to no fluid resuscitation (104). The beneficial effects of albumin administration on systemic haemodynamic and renal function in spontaneous bacterial peritonitis may result from both an improvement in cardiac function and a decrease in the degree of arterial vasodilatation (105). When the occurrence of renal insufficiency was evaluated as secondary outcome measure in studies comparing use of albumin or crystalloids in general intensive care patients, none of the trials reported a significant effect of choice of fluid on renal function (106–108).

Effects on pulmonary function: According to Starling's law a higher COP should exert a protective effect on pulmonary fluid balance and thus on pulmonary oedema formation. In hypovolaemic and septic shock albumin is effective in raising COP and maintaining COP-pulmonary artery occlusion pressure (PAOP) gradient, whereas saline decreases the COP-PAOP gradient (62). A decrease in COP-PAOP gradient may be associated with occurrence of pulmonary oedema and increased mortality in critically ill patients (63). Additionally, albumin improves endothelial barrier function and this might further reduce pulmonary capillary permeability (87, 88). Hypoproteinaemic patients with established ALI show improvements of oxygenation and a trend towards reduced mortality with albumin substitution and concomitant treatment with frusemide to induce negative fluid balance (109). However, albumin administration does not produce clinically relevant differences in measures such as duration of mechanical ventilation or lung injury scores in a variety of patient populations, for example after cardiac surgery (110, 111), in patients with ALI/ARDS (106), burns (107) and in heterogeneous populations of critically ill patients (106, 107).

Effects on mortality: Until recently, only relatively small trials have addressed the issue of albumin administration and mortality in critically ill patients. A meta-analysis published by the Cochrane Injuries Group Albumin Reviewers in 1998 included 24 studies involving a total of 1419 patients and suggested that the administration of albumin-containing fluids, in comparison to crystalloid solutions, resulted in a 6% increase in the absolute risk of death (112).

In 2004 the results of the Saline versus Albumin Fluid Evaluation (SAFE) study were published; the SAFE study compared the effects of fluid resuscitation with 4% albumin or normal saline on mortality in 6997 ICU patients (106). The trial sought to minimise random error by including a sufficient number of patients to provide 90% power to detect a 3 percent absolute difference in mortality from an expected baseline rate of 15 percent. Effectively concealed random allocation and blinding of patients, clinicians and researchers combined with excellent compliance was thought to have guaranteed reliable results (113). Mortality did not differ significantly between the patients assigned to albumin and those assigned to saline (relative risk [RR] of death for albumin compared to saline, 0.99; 95% CI, 0.91–1.09). Secondary outcomes – survival time, rates of new organ dysfunction, the duration of mechanical ventilation, the duration of renal replacement therapy, and the length of stay in the intensive care unit and in the hospital – were also similar. A priori subgroup analyses consisted of patients with trauma, severe sepsis and ARDS at baseline.

The SAFE study indicated the presence of heterogeneity of treatment effects among patients who did and did not have a diagnosis of trauma; this evidence resulted from an increased number of deaths among patients with traumatic brain injury who received albumin. In a post-hoc study including only patients with traumatic brain injury (defined as a history of trauma, evidence of brain trauma on a computed tomographic [CT] scan, and a Glasgow Coma Scale score [GCS] of 13 or less), fluid resuscitation with albumin was associated with higher mortality rates than was resuscitation with saline (114). At 24 months post-randomisation, 33.2% of patients assigned albumin had died, as compared with 20.4% of those assigned saline (RR 1.63; 95% CI 1.17–2.26; p = 0.003). Among patients with severe brain injury (GCS 3–8), 41.8% of patients assigned albumin died, compared to 22.2% of those assigned saline (RR 1.88; 95% CI 1.31–2.70; p < 0.001). The authors note that, as yet, the mechanism by which albumin might increase mortality in patients with traumatic brain injury is not known. In their conclusions the authors recommend that albumin should not be used as resuscitation fluid in the intensive care unit treatment of traumatic brain injury.

In contrast with the findings in patients with traumatic brain injury, the 28-day mortality rate in patients in the SAFE study who had severe sepsis at baseline was lower in those assigned albumin (30.7% vs. 35.3%; p = 0.09); comparing the RR of death in those with and without sepsis (0.87 for those with severe sepsis versus 1.05 for those without severe sepsis), using the test for common relative risk, the probability that the difference occurred by chance is 0.06. The editorial accompanying the publication of the SAFE study results noted that this borderline result suggests that further study of albumin in patients with severe sepsis is warranted (113).

Use of albumin in patients with hypoalbuminaemia: In patients with acute illness, serum albumin concentration is inversely related to mortality risk (115–117). A systematic review of studies including patients with different acute or chronic illness reported an estimated increase of mortality by 24% to 56% for each 2.5 g/l decrease in serum albumin concentration (118). Thus the use of albumin as a resuscitation fluid for hypoalbuminaemic patients seems intuitively attractive. However, in an updated meta-analysis the Cochrane Injuries Group Albumin Reviewers concluded that there is no evidence for reduction of mortality by administration of albumin as resuscitation fluid, but reported a possible increase of the risk of death in the subgroup of patients with hypoalbuminaemia and burns; the meta-analysis included the data from the SAFE study in the subgroup of stud-

ies where albumin was deemed to be indicated for treatment of hypovolaemia (81).

Using the data from the SAFE study, the SAFE study investigators addressed the question whether the treatment effect of albumin versus saline for fluid resuscitation is influenced by baseline serum albumin concentration and whether the use of either resuscitation fluid could be recommended based on a patient's serum albumin concentration (119). In this post-hoc analysis, baseline serum albumin concentration of 25g/l or lower was independently associated with a higher mortality (OR 1.3, 95% CI 1.16–1.51, p = 0.0009). Among patients with a serum albumin concentration of 25 g/l or less, whilst the 28-day mortality was lower in patients assigned to albumin as compared to saline (23.7% vs. 26.2%, odds ratio 0.87, 95% CI 0.73–1.05), the difference was not statistically significant (p = 0.14). The odds ratios for death for albumin versus saline for patients with a baseline serum albumin concentration of 25 g/l or less and more than 25 g/l were 0.87 and 1.09, respectively; the ratio of odds ratios was 0.80, (95% confidence interval 0.63 to 1.02; p = 0.08 for heterogeneity). No significant interaction was found between baseline serum albumin concentration as a continuous variable and the effect of albumin and saline on mortality. Again, further research examining the effects of albumin administration in patients with hypoalbuminaemia appears warranted.

Why prefer albumin over synthetic colloids? In patients with traumatic brain injury it is prudent to avoid albumin administration during acute resuscitation; for all other patient groups the data suggesting that albumin should be preferred to crystalloids is either absent or inconclusive. However, albumin remains the only colloid solution to have its safety and efficacy tested in a large high quality randomised controlled trial (see fig. 2). Despite the lack of safety and efficacy data for other colloid solutions, surveys suggest that a substantial proportion of clinicians continue to administer colloids to large numbers of critically ill patients. Those clinicians who wish to use colloid solutions can be far more certain of the effects of albumin on their patients than they can be for synthetic colloids; for this reason, albumin should be preferred to synthetic colloids if a colloid solution is to be used for fluid resuscitation.

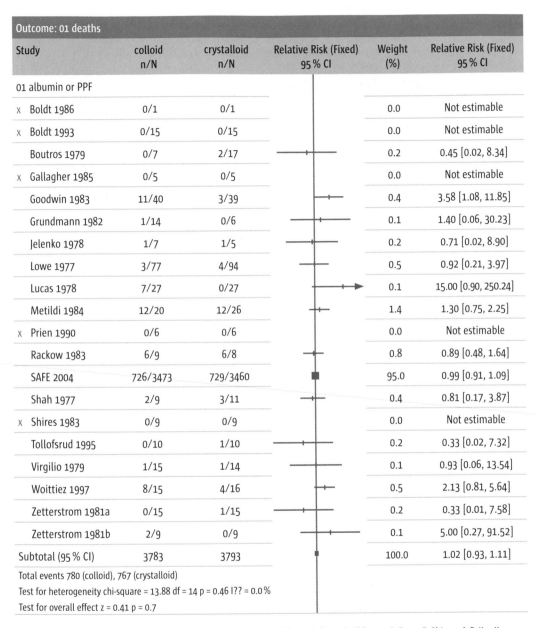

Outcome: 01 deaths					
Study	colloid n/N	crystalloid n/N	Relative Risk (Fixed) 95 % CI	Weight (%)	Relative Risk (Fixed) 95 % CI
01 albumin or PPF					
x Boldt 1986	0/1	0/1		0.0	Not estimable
x Boldt 1993	0/15	0/15		0.0	Not estimable
Boutros 1979	0/7	2/17		0.2	0.45 [0.02, 8.34]
x Gallagher 1985	0/5	0/5		0.0	Not estimable
Goodwin 1983	11/40	3/39		0.4	3.58 [1.08, 11.85]
Grundmann 1982	1/14	0/6		0.1	1.40 [0.06, 30.23]
Jelenko 1978	1/7	1/5		0.2	0.71 [0.02, 8.90]
Lowe 1977	3/77	4/94		0.5	0.92 [0.21, 3.97]
Lucas 1978	7/27	0/27		0.1	15.00 [0.90, 250.24]
Metildi 1984	12/20	12/26		1.4	1.30 [0.75, 2.25]
x Prien 1990	0/6	0/6		0.0	Not estimable
Rackow 1983	6/9	6/8		0.8	0.89 [0.48, 1.64]
SAFE 2004	726/3473	729/3460		95.0	0.99 [0.91, 1.09]
Shah 1977	2/9	3/11		0.4	0.81 [0.17, 3.87]
x Shires 1983	0/9	0/9		0.0	Not estimable
Tollofsrud 1995	0/10	1/10		0.2	0.33 [0.02, 7.32]
Virgilio 1979	1/15	1/14		0.1	0.93 [0.06, 13.54]
Woittiez 1997	8/15	4/16		0.5	2.13 [0.81, 5.64]
Zetterstrom 1981a	0/15	1/15		0.2	0.33 [0.01, 7.58]
Zetterstrom 1981b	2/9	0/9		0.1	5.00 [0.27, 91.52]
Subtotal (95 % CI)	3783	3793		100.0	1.02 [0.93, 1.11]

Total events 780 (colloid), 767 (crystalloid)
Test for heterogeneity chi-square = 13.88 df = 14 p = 0.46 I?? = 0.0 %
Test for overall effect z = 0.41 p = 0.7

Fig. 2   Effect of albumin versus crystalloid on mortality. Adapted from: Roberts I, Alderson P, Bunn F, Chinnock P, Ker K, Schierhout G. Colloids versus crystalloids for fluid resuscitation in critically ill patients. Cochrane Database Syst Rev 2004;(4):CD000567. Copyright Cochrane Collaboration, reproduced with permission.

Summary

Synthetic colloids have specific characteristics not exclusively related to their effect on oncotic pressure that may influence vascular permeability and inflammatory processes, but the clinical relevance of these properties has not been sufficiently evaluated (12, 20). Restoration of intravascular volume and tissue perfusion in shock states occurs more rapidly when using colloids, although without proven survival benefit (51, 62, 95). Synthetic colloids affect the coagulation system (48) and can induce anaphylactoid reactions (120). Additionally, there is growing evidence that certain synthetic colloids can be associated with increase of morbidity and potentially even mortality in subgroups of critically ill patients; the most striking example relates to the use of HES solutions in patients with severe sepsis (51). Whilst synthetic colloids, including the more recently developed HES solutions, may be safe and efficacious, as yet there is inadequate evidence to reach that conclusion. There is a pressing need for large scale randomised controlled trials and hopefully the CRISTAL study will provide data that will aid clinicians' decision-making. Given the higher costs of synthetic colloids and the dearth of evidence that their use has beneficial effects not obtained from cheaper crystalloid solutions, it is hard to defend their continued use outside of high quality randomised controlled trials.

Albumin binds to the endothelial surface glycocalyx and influences its barrier function by inducing a sealing effect (13). It has modest anti-inflammatory and anti-thrombotic effects, does not adversely affect renal function and may have beneficial effects on pulmonary transcapillary fluid loss. The SAFE study remains the only published trial with sufficient power to provide reasonable certainty over the comparative effects of resuscitation fluids on mortality. The SAFE study provides evidence that, with the exception of patients with traumatic brain injury, albumin can be considered as safe as saline; further study of albumin in patients with severe sepsis and those with hypoalbuminaemia is warranted.

Despite its demonstrated safety, in most countries albumin is expensive and similar clinical outcomes can be achieved by the administration of much cheaper crystalloid solutions. However, in contrast to artificial colloids and with the notable exception of patients with severe traumatic brain injury, fluid resuscitation with albumin is not associated with an increased risk of harm. Whether selected populations of critically ill patients, such as patients with severe sepsis or hypoalbuminaemia, can derive benefit from albumin administration requires further study.

Key points for clinical practice

- *As around 35% of patients in intensive care units receive resuscitation fluids each day, small differences in outcome attributable to the type of fluid used may result in substantial effects on morbidity and mortality. Such effects may only be detectable by large trials.*

- *Survey data demonstrate widespread practice variation in the choice of resuscitation fluids.*
- *With the exception of the SAFE study, published trials suffer from being too small to provide adequate statistical power. Many trials have significant methodological flaws; too many small trials report the effects of fluids on laboratory or physiological variables or on surrogate outcomes.*
- *There are insufficient data to conclude that synthetic colloids are safe in the critically ill or to recommend their use when cheaper crystalloid solutions are available.*
- *Other than in patients with traumatic brain injury, administration of albumin to critically ill patients produces similar outcomes to administration of saline; saline is considerably cheaper.*
- *Hydroxyethyl starch solutions should be avoided in patients with severe sepsis and septic shock; the safety of more recently developed HES solutions in this population should be tested in large trials examining mortality and effects on renal function.*
- *Albumin should be avoided in patients with traumatic brain injury; whether synthetic colloids are safe in this population is not known.*
- *In haemodynamically stable patients with ALI/ARDS, a restrictive fluid resuscitation strategy is appropriate, as is the combination of colloids and diuretics in hypooncotic patients.*
- *Future clinical trials should examine the efficacy of albumin in patients with severe sepsis and in patients with hypoalbuminaemia; it remains possible, but unproven, that albumin is beneficial in these settings.*
- *Large high quality trials of synthetic colloids in both heterogeneous and selected patient populations are required.*

The authors

Tobias M. Merz, MD[1]
Simon Finfer, MBBS, FRCP, FRCA, FJFICM[1,2]
  [1]Staff Specialist in Intensive Care |
  Department of Intensive Care Medicine |
  Royal North Shore Hospital of Sydney |
  St Leonards, Australia
  [2]Professor | The George Institute for International Health | Faculty of Sydney | Sydney, Australia

Address for correspondence
  Simon Finfer
  Senior Staff Specialist in Intensive Care

Department of Intensive Care Medicine
Royal North Shore Hospital of Sydney
St Leonards
2065 NSW, Australia
e-mail: sfinfer@george.org.au

References

1. Boldt J, Lenz M, Kumle B, Papsdorf M. Volume replacement strategies on intensive care units: results from a postal survey. Intensive Care Med. 1998 Feb;24(2): 147–51.

2. Miletin MS, Stewart TE, Norton PG. Influences on physicians' choices of intravenous colloids. Intensive Care Med. 2002 Jul;28(7):917–24.

3. Schortgen F, Deye N, Brochard L. Preferred plasma volume expanders for critically ill patients: results of an international survey. Intensive Care Med. 2004 Dec; 30(12):2222–9.

4. Boldt J, Papsdorf M. Fluid management in burn patients: Results from a European survey-More questions than answers. Burns. 2008 Jan 15.

5. Collins R, MacMahon S. Reliable assessment of the effects of treatment on mortality and major morbidity, I: clinical trials. Lancet. 2001 Feb 3;357(9253):373–80.

6. Rivers E, Nguyen B, Havstad S, Ressler J, Muzzin A, Knoblich B, et al. Early goal-directed therapy in the treatment of severe sepsis and septic shock. N Engl J Med. 2001 Nov 8;345(19):1368–77.

7. Sinclair S, James S, Singer M. Intraoperative intravascular volume optimisation and length of hospital stay after repair of proximal femoral fracture: randomised controlled trial. Bmj. 1997 Oct 11;315(7113):909–12.

8. Wakeling HG, McFall MR, Jenkins CS, Woods WG, Miles WF, Barclay GR, et al. Intraoperative oesophageal Doppler guided fluid management shortens postoperative hospital stay after major bowel surgery. Br J Anaesth. 2005 Nov;95(5):634–42.

9. Michel CC. Starling: the formulation of his hypothesis of microvascular fluid exchange and its significance after 100 years. Exp Physiol. 1997 Jan;82(1):1–30.

10. Reitsma S, Slaaf DW, Vink H, van Zandvoort MA, oude Egbrink MG. The endothelial glycocalyx: composition, functions, and visualization. Pflugers Arch. 2007 Jun; 454(3):345–59.

11. Raman R, Sasisekharan V, Sasisekharan R. Structural insights into biological roles of protein-glycosaminogly-can interactions. Chem Biol. 2005 Mar;12(3):267–77.

12. Rehm M, Zahler S, Lotsch M, Welsch U, Conzen P, Jacob M et al. Endothelial glycocalyx as an additional barrier determining extravasation of 6 % hydroxyethyl starch or 5 % albumin solutions in the coronary vascular bed. Anesthesiology. 2004 May;100(5):1211–23.

13. Vink H, Duling BR. Capillary endothelial surface layer selectively reduces plasma solute distribution volume. Am J Physiol Heart Circ Physiol. 2000 Jan;278(1):H285–9.

14. Bruegger D, Jacob M, Rehm M, Loetsch M, Welsch U, Conzen P et al. Atrial natriuretic peptide induces shedding of endothelial glycocalyx in coronary vascular bed of guinea pig hearts. Am J Physiol Heart Circ Physiol. 2005 Nov;289(5):H1993–9.

15. Adamson RH, Lenz JF, Zhang X, Adamson GN, Weinbaum S, Curry FE. Oncotic pressures opposing filtration across non-fenestrated rat microvessels. J Physiol. 2004 Jun 15;557(Pt 3):889–907.

16. Vink H, Duling BR. Identification of distinct luminal domains for macromolecules, erythrocytes, and leukocytes within mammalian capillaries. Circ Res. 1996 Sep;79(3):581–9.

17. Vink H, Constantinescu AA, Spaan JA. Oxidized lipoproteins degrade the endothelial surface layer: implications for platelet-endothelial cell adhesion. Circulation. 2000 Apr 4;101(13):1500–2.

18. Constantinescu AA, Vink H, Spaan JA. Endothelial cell glycocalyx modulates immobilization of leukocytes at the endothelial surface. Arterioscler Thromb Vasc Biol. 2003 Sep 1;23(9):1541–7.

19. Henry CB, Duling BR. TNF-alpha increases entry of macromolecules into luminal endothelial cell glycocalyx. Am J Physiol Heart Circ Physiol. 2000 Dec;279(6):H2815–23.

20. Jacob M, Bruegger D, Rehm M, Welsch U, Conzen P, Becker BF. Contrasting effects of colloid and crystalloid resuscitation fluids on cardiac vascular permeability. Anesthesiology. 2006 Jun;104(6):1223–31.

21. Berg S, Golster M, Lisander B. Albumin extravasation and tissue washout of hyaluronan after plasma volume expansion with crystalloid or hypooncotic colloid solutions. Acta Anaesthesiol Scand. 2002 Feb;46(2): 166–72.

22. Gushchin V, Stegalkina S, Alam HB, Kirkpatrick JR, Rhee PM, Koustova E. Cytokine expression profiling in human leukocytes after exposure to hypertonic and isotonic fluids. J Trauma. 2002 May;52(5):867–71.

23. Rhee P, Burris D, Kaufmann C, Pikoulis M, Austin B, Ling G et al. Lactated Ringer's solution resuscitation causes neutrophil activation after hemorrhagic shock. J Trauma. 1998 Feb;44(2):313–9.

24. Koustova E, Stanton K, Gushchin V, Alam HB, Stegalkina S, Rhee PM. Effects of lactated Ringer's solutions on human leukocytes. J Trauma. 2002 May;52(5):872–8.

25. Handrigan MT, Burns AR, Donnachie EM, Bowden RA. Hydroxyethyl starch inhibits neutrophil adhesion and transendothelial migration. Shock. 2005 Nov;24(5): 434–9.

26. Schmand JF, Ayala A, Morrison MH, Chaudry IH. Effects of hydroxyethyl starch after trauma-hemorrhagic shock: restoration of macrophage integrity and prevention of

increased circulating interleukin-6 levels. Crit Care Med. 1995 May;23(5):806–14.

27. Mardel SN, Saunders FM, Ollerenshaw LD, Buddeley DT. Haemodilution induces a hypercoagulable state. Br J Anaesth. 1996 Nov;77(5):700–1.

28. Konrad C, Markl T, Schuepfer G, Gerber H, Tschopp M. The effects of in vitro hemodilution with gelatin, hydroxyethyl starch, and lactated Ringer's solution on markers of coagulation: an analysis using SONOCLOT. Anesth Analg. 1999 Mar;88(3):483–8.

29. Petroianu GA, Liu J, Maleck WH, Mattinger C, Bergler WF. The effect of In vitro hemodilution with gelatin, dextran, hydroxyethyl starch, or Ringer's solution on Thrombelastograph. Anesth Analg. 2000 Apr;90(4): 795–800.

30. Ng KF, Lam CC, Chan LC. In vivo effect of haemodilution with saline on coagulation: a randomized controlled trial. Br J Anaesth. 2002 Apr;88(4):475–80.

31. Jones SB, Whitten CW, Despotis GJ, Monk TG. The influence of crystalloid and colloid replacement solutions in acute normovolemic hemodilution: a preliminary survey of hemostatic markers. Anesth Analg. 2003 Feb;96(2):363–8, table of contents.

32. Boldt J, Haisch G, Suttner S, Kumle B, Schellhase F. Are lactated Ringer's solution and normal saline solution equal with regard to coagulation? Anesth Analg. 2002 Feb;94(2):378–84, table of contents.

33. Ekseth K, Abildgaard L, Vegfors M, Berg-Johnsen J, Engdahl O. The in vitro effects of crystalloids and colloids on coagulation. Anaesthesia. 2002 Nov;57(11):1102–8.

34. Ruttmann TG, Jamest MF, Lombard EH. Haemodilution-induced enhancement of coagulation is attenuated in vitro by restoring antithrombin III to pre-dilution concentrations. Anaesth Intensive Care. 2001 Oct;29(5):489–93.

35. Ruttmann TG, Montoya-Pelaez LF, James MF. The coagulation changes induced by rapid in vivo crystalloid infusion are attenuated when magnesium is kept at the upper limit of normal. Anesth Analg. 2007 Jun;104(6):1475–80, table of contents.

36. Ruttmann TG, Lemmens HJ, Malott KA, Brock-Utne JG. The haemodilution enhanced onset of coagulation as measured by the thrombelastogram is transient. Eur J Anaesthesiol. 2006 Jul;23(7):574–9.

37. Egli GA, Zollinger A, Seifert B, Popovic D, Pasch T, Spahn DR. Effect of progressive haemodilution with hydroxyethyl starch, gelatin and albumin on blood coagulation. Br J Anaesth. 1997 Jun;78(6):684–9.

38. Niemi TT, Suojaranta-Ylinen RT, Kukkonen SI, Kuitunen AH. Gelatin and hydroxyethyl starch, but not albumin, impair hemostasis after cardiac surgery. Anesth Analg. 2006 Apr;102(4):998–1006.

39. Batlle J, del Rio F, Lopez Fernandez MF, Martin R, Lopez Borrasca A. Effect of dextran on factor VIII/von Willebrand factor structure and function. Thromb Haemost. 1985 Oct 30;54(3):697–9.

40. Jamnicki M, Bombeli T, Seifert B, Zollinger A, Camenzind V, Pasch T et al. Low- and medium-molecular-weight hydroxyethyl starches: comparison of their effect on blood coagulation. Anesthesiology. 2000 Nov;93(5): 1231–7.

41. Felfernig M, Franz A, Braunlich P, Fohringer C, Kozek-Langenecker SA. The effects of hydroxyethyl starch solutions on thromboelastography in preoperative male patients. Acta Anaesthesiol Scand. 2003 Jan;47(1):70–3.

42. Nielsen VG. Colloids decrease clot propagation and strength: role of factor XIII-fibrin polymer and thrombin-fibrinogen interactions. Acta Anaesthesiol Scand. 2005 Sep;49(8):1163–71.

43. Franz A, Braunlich P, Gamsjager T, Felfernig M, Gustorff B, Kozek-Langenecker SA. The effects of hydroxyethyl starches of varying molecular weights on platelet function. Anesth Analg. 2001 Jun;92(6):1402–7.

44. Nielsen VG. Hydroxyethyl starch enhances fibrinolysis in human plasma by diminishing alpha2-antiplasmin-plasmin interactions. Blood Coagul Fibrinolysis. 2007 Oct; 18(7):647–56.

45. de Jonge E, Levi M, Berends F, van der Ende AE, ten Cate JW, Stoutenbeek CP. Impaired haemostasis by intravenous administration of a gelatin-based plasma expander in human subjects. Thromb Haemost. 1998 Feb;79(2):286–90.

46. Evans PA, Glenn JR, Heptinstall S, Madira W. Effects of gelatin-based resuscitation fluids on platelet aggregation. Br J Anaesth. 1998 Aug;81(2):198–202.

47. Van der Linden P, Ickx BE. The effects of colloid solutions on hemostasis. Can J Anaesth. 2006 Jun;53(6 Suppl): S30–9.

48. de Jonge E, Levi M. Effects of different plasma substitutes on blood coagulation: a comparative review. Crit Care Med. 2001 Jun;29(6):1261–7.

49. Tigchelaar I, Gallandat Huet RC, Korsten J, Boonstra PW, van Oeveren W. Hemostatic effects of three colloid plasma substitutes for priming solution in cardiopulmonary bypass. Eur J Cardiothorac Surg. 1997 Apr;11(4): 626–32.

50. Mortelmans YJ, Vermaut G, Verbruggen AM, Arnout JM, Vermylen J, Van Aken H et al. Effects of 6 % hydroxyethyl starch and 3 % modified fluid gelatin on intravascular volume and coagulation during intraoperative hemodilution. Anesth Analg. 1995 Dec; 81(6):1235–42.

51. Brunkhorst FM, Engel C, Bloos F, Meier-Hellmann A, Ragaller M, Weiler N et al. Intensive insulin therapy and pentastarch resuscitation in severe sepsis. N Engl J Med. 2008 Jan 10;358(2):125–39.

52. Gandhi SD, Weiskopf RB, Jungheinrich C, Koorn R, Miller D, Shangraw RE et al. Volume replacement therapy during major orthopedic surgery using Voluven (hydroxyethyl starch 130/0.4) or hetastarch. Anesthesiology. 2007 Jun;106(6):1120–7.

53. Uchino S, Kellum JA, Bellomo R, Doig GS, Morimatsu H, Morgera S et al. Acute renal failure in critically ill patients: a multinational, multicenter study. Jama. 2005 Aug 17;294(7):813–8.

54. Schortgen F, Lacherade JC, Bruneel F, Cattaneo I, Hemery F, Lemaire F et al. Effects of hydroxyethylstarch and gelatin on renal function in severe sepsis: a multicentre randomised study. Lancet. 2001 Mar 24;357(9260):911–6.

55. Van Biesen W, Yegenaga I, Vanholder R, Verbeke F, Hoste E, Colardyn F et al. Relationship between fluid status and its management on acute renal failure (ARF) in intensive care unit (ICU) patients with sepsis: a prospective analysis. J Nephrol. 2005 Jan–Feb;18(1): 54–60.

56. Cittanova ML, Leblanc I, Legendre C, Mouquet C, Riou B, Coriat P. Effect of hydroxyethylstarch in brain-dead kidney donors on renal function in kidney-transplant recipients. Lancet. 1996 Dec 14;348(9042):1620–2.

57. Boldt J, Brosch C, Ducke M, Papsdorf M, Lehmann A. Influence of volume therapy with a modern hydroxyethylstarch preparation on kidney function in cardiac surgery patients with compromised renal function: a comparison with human albumin. Crit Care Med. 2007 Dec;35(12):2740–6.

58. BaSES Trial: Basel Starch Evaluation in Sepsis. [cited 2008 February 16]; Available from: http://clinicaltrials.gov/ct2/show/NCT00273728.

59. Biesenbach G, Kaiser W, Zazgornik J. Incidence of acute oligoanuric renal failure in dextran 40 treated patients with acute ischemic stroke stage III or IV. Ren Fail. 1997 Jan;19(1):69–75.

60. Kato A, Yonemura K, Matsushima H, Ikegaya N, Hishida A. Complication of oliguric acute renal failure in patients treated with low-molecular weight dextran. Ren Fail. 2001 Sep;23(5):679–84.

61. Tsang RK, Mok JS, Poon YS, van Hasselt A. Acute renal failure in a healthy young adult after dextran 40 infusion for external-ear reattachment surgery. Br J Plast Surg. 2000 Dec;53(8):701–3.

62. Rackow EC, Falk JL, Fein IA, Siegel JS, Packman MI, Haupt MT, et al. Fluid resuscitation in circulatory shock: a comparison of the cardiorespiratory effects of albumin, hetastarch, and saline solutions in patients with hypovolemic and septic shock. Crit Care Med. 1983 Nov;11(11):839–50.

63. Rackow EC, Fein IA, Siegel J. The relationship of the colloid osmotic-pulmonary artery wedge pressure gradient to pulmonary edema and mortality in critically ill patients. Chest. 1982 Oct;82(4):433–7.

64. Rackow EC, Weil MH, Macneil AR, Makabali CG, Michaels S. Effects of crystalloid and colloid fluids on extravascular lung water in hypoproteinemic dogs. J Appl Physiol. 1987 Jun;62(6):2421–5.

65. Sakr Y, Vincent JL, Reinhart K, Groeneveld J, Michalopoulos A, Sprung CL, et al. High tidal volume and positive fluid balance are associated with worse outcome in acute lung injury. Chest. 2005 Nov;128(5):3098–108.

66. Simmons RS, Berdine GG, Seidenfeld JJ, Prihoda TJ, Harris GD, Smith JD, et al. Fluid balance and the adult respiratory distress syndrome. Am Rev Respir Dis. 1987 Apr;135(4):924–9.

67. Wiedemann HP, Wheeler AP, Bernard GR, Thompson BT, Hayden D, deBoisblanc B, et al. Comparison of two fluid-management strategies in acute lung injury. N Engl J Med. 2006 Jun 15;354(24):2564–75.

68. Mitchell JP, Schuller D, Calandrino FS, Schuster DP. Improved outcome based on fluid management in critically ill patients requiring pulmonary artery catheterization. Am Rev Respir Dis. 1992 May;145(5): 990–8.

69. Roberts I, Alderson P, Bunn F, Chinnock P, Ker K, Schierhout G. Colloids versus crystalloids for fluid resuscitation in critically ill patients. Cochrane Database Syst Rev. 2004(4):CD000567.

70. Vassar MJ, Perry CA, Holcroft JW. Prehospital resuscitation of hypotensive trauma patients with 7.5 % NaCl versus 7.5 % NaCl with added dextran: a controlled trial. J Trauma. 1993 May;34(5):622–32; discussion 32–3.

71. Vassar MJ, Fischer RP, O'Brien PE, Bachulis BL, Chambers JA, Hoyt DB et al. A multicenter trial for resuscitation of injured patients with 7.5 % sodium chloride. The effect of added dextran 70. The Multicenter Group for the Study of Hypertonic Saline in Trauma Patients. Arch Surg. 1993 Sep;128(9):1003–11; discussion 11–3.

72. Hall KV, Sorensen B. The treatment of burn shock: results of a 5-year randomized, controlled clinical trial of Dextran 70 v Ringer lactate solution. Burns. 1978;5(1): 107–12.

73. Younes RN, Aun F, Accioly CQ, Casale LP, Szajnbok I, Birolini D. Hypertonic solutions in the treatment of hypovolemic shock: a prospective, randomized study in patients admitted to the emergency room. Surgery. 1992 Apr;111(4):380–5.

74. Upadhyay M, Singhi S, Murlidharan J, Kaur N, Majumdar S. Randomized Evaluation of Fluid Resuscitation with Crystalloid (saline) and Colloid (polymer from degraded Gelatin in saline) in Pediatric Septic Shock[†]. Indian Pediatrics. 2004;42:223–31

75. Hondenbrink Y JL, Oude Nijhuis J, Woittiez AJJ. Restoration of colloid osmotic pressure in hypoalbuminaemic patients. Intensive Care Med. 1997;23 (Supp 1): S184.

76. Nagy KK, Davis J, Duda J, Fildes J, Roberts R, Barrett J. A comparison of pentastarch and lactated Ringer's solution in the resuscitation of patients with hemorrhagic shock. Circ Shock. 1993 Aug;40(4):289–94.

77. Wu JJ, Huang MS, Tang GJ, Kao WF, Shih HC, Su CH, et al. Hemodynamic response of modified fluid gelatin compared with lactated ringer's solution for volume expansion in emergency resuscitation of hypovolemic

shock patients: preliminary report of a prospective, randomized trial. World J Surg. 2001 May;25(5): 598–602.

78. Evans PA, Garnett M, Boffard K, Kirkman E, Jacobson BF. Evaluation of the effect of colloid (Haemaccel) on the bleeding time in the trauma patient. J R Soc Med. 1996 Feb;89(2):101P-4P.

79. Clinical trials of hydroxyethyl starch on ClinicalTrials.gov. [cited 2008 February 16]; Available from: http://clinicaltrials.gov/ct2/show/NCT00337805?term=hydroxyethyl+starch.

80. Clinical trials of hydroxyethyl starch on Current controlled trials. [cited 2008 February 16]; Available from: http://www.controlled-trials.com/isrctn/search.html?srch=hydroxyethyl+starch.

81. Alderson P, Bunn F, Lefebvre C, Li WP, Li L, Roberts I et al. Human albumin solution for resuscitation and volume expansion in critically ill patients. Cochrane Database Syst Rev. 2004(4):CD001208.

82. Choi PT, Yip G, Quinonez LG, Cook DJ. Crystalloids vs. colloids in fluid resuscitation: a systematic review. Crit Care Med. 1999 Jan;27(1):200–10.

83. Schierhout G, Roberts I. Fluid resuscitation with colloid or crystalloid solutions in critically ill patients: a systematic review of randomised trials. Bmj. 1998 Mar 28;316(7136):961–4.

84. Wilkes MM, Navickis RJ. Patient survival after human albumin administration. A meta-analysis of randomized, controlled trials. Ann Intern Med. 2001 Aug 7;135(3): 149–64.

85. Velanovich V. Crystalloid versus colloid fluid resuscitation: a meta-analysis of mortality. Surgery. 1989 Jan; 105(1):65–71.

86. Perel P, Roberts I. Colloids versus crystalloids for fluid resuscitation in critically ill patients. Cochrane Database Syst Rev. 2007(4):CD000567.

87. Schneeberger EE, Lynch RD, Neary BA. Interaction of native and chemically modified albumin with pulmonary microvascular endothelium. Am J Physiol. 1990 Feb;258(2 Pt 1):L89–98.

88. Schneeberger EE, Hamelin M. Interaction of serum proteins with lung endothelial glycocalyx: its effect on endothelial permeability. Am J Physiol. 1984 Aug;247(2 Pt 2):H206–17.

89. Nathan C, Xie QW, Halbwachs-Mecarelli L, Jin WW. Albumin inhibits neutrophil spreading and hydrogen peroxide release by blocking the shedding of CD43 (sialophorin, leukosialin). J Cell Biol. 1993 Jul;122(1): 243–56.

90. Beck R, Bertolino S, Abbot SE, Aaronson PI, Smirnov SV. Modulation of arachidonic acid release and membrane fluidity by albumin in vascular smooth muscle and endothelial cells. Circ Res. 1998 Nov 2;83(9):923–31.

91. Lang JD, Jr., Figueroa M, Chumley P, Aslan M, Hurt J, Tarpey MM, et al. Albumin and hydroxyethyl starch

92. Moran LK, Gutteridge JM, Quinlan GJ. Thiols in cellular redox signalling and control. Curr Med Chem. 2001 Jun;8(7):763–72.

93. Quinlan GJ, Margarson MP, Mumby S, Evans TW, Gutteridge JM. Administration of albumin to patients with sepsis syndrome: a possible beneficial role in plasma thiol repletion. Clin Sci (Lond). 1998 Oct;95(4): 459–65.

94. Quinlan GJ, Mumby S, Martin GS, Bernard GR, Gutteridge JM, Evans TW. Albumin influences total plasma antioxidant capacity favorably in patients with acute lung injury. Crit Care Med. 2004 Mar;32(3):755–9.

95. Horstick G, Lauterbach M, Kempf T, Bhakdi S, Heimann A, Horstick M et al. Early albumin infusion improves global and local hemodynamics and reduces inflammatory response in hemorrhagic shock. Crit Care Med. 2002 Apr;30(4):851–5.

96. Nielsen VG, Tan S, Brix AE, Baird MS, Parks DA. Hextend (hetastarch solution) decreases multiple organ injury and xanthine oxidase release after hepatoenteric ischemia-reperfusion in rabbits. Crit Care Med. 1997 Sep;25(9):1565–74.

97. Simon DI, Stamler JS, Jaraki O, Keaney JF, Osborne JA, Francis SA et al. Antiplatelet properties of protein S-nitrosothiols derived from nitric oxide and endothelium-derived relaxing factor. Arterioscler Thromb. 1993 Jun;13(6):791–9.

98. Kim SB, Chi HS, Park JS, Hong CD, Yang WS. Effect of increasing serum albumin on plasma D-dimer, von Willebrand factor, and platelet aggregation in CAPD patients. Am J Kidney Dis. 1999 Feb;33(2):312–7.

99. Galanakis DK. Anticoagulant albumin fragments that bind to fibrinogen/fibrin: possible implications. Semin Thromb Hemost. 1992 Jan;18(1):44–52.

100. Pockaj BA, Yang JC, Lotze MT, Lange JR, Spencer WF, Steinberg SM et al. A prospective randomized trial evaluating colloid versus crystalloid resuscitation in the treatment of the vascular leak syndrome associated with interleukin-2 therapy. J Immunother Emphasis Tumor Immunol. 1994 Jan;15(1):22–8.

101. Gines P, Tito L, Arroyo V, Planas R, Panes J, Viver J, et al. Randomized comparative study of therapeutic paracentesis with and without intravenous albumin in cirrhosis. Gastroenterology. 1988 Jun;94(6):1493–502.

102. Gines A, Fernandez-Esparrach G, Monescillo A, Vila C, Domenech E, Abecasis R et al. Randomized trial comparing albumin, dextran 70, and polygeline in cirrhotic patients with ascites treated by paracentesis. Gastroenterology. 1996 Oct;111(4):1002–10.

103. Altman C, Bernard B, Roulot D, Vitte RL, Ink O. Randomized comparative multicenter study of hydroxyethyl starch versus albumin as a plasma expander in cirrhotic patients with tense ascites treated

with paracentesis. Eur J Gastroenterol Hepatol. 1998 Jan;10(1):5–10.

104. Sort P, Navasa M, Arroyo V, Aldeguer X, Planas R, Ruiz-del-Arbol L, et al. Effect of intravenous albumin on renal impairment and mortality in patients with cirrhosis and spontaneous bacterial peritonitis. N Engl J Med. 1999 Aug 5;341(6):403–9.

105. Fernandez J, Navasa M, Garcia-Pagan JC, J GA, Jimenez W, Bosch J, et al. Effect of intravenous albumin on systemic and hepatic hemodynamics and vasoactive neurohormonal systems in patients with cirrhosis and spontaneous bacterial peritonitis. J Hepatol. 2004 Sep;41(3):384–90.

106. Finfer S, Bellomo R, Boyce N, French J, Myburgh J, Norton R. A comparison of albumin and saline for fluid resuscitation in the intensive care unit. N Engl J Med. 2004 May 27;350(22):2247–56.

107. Cooper AB, Cohn SM, Zhang HS, Hanna K, Stewart TE, Slutsky AS. Five percent albumin for adult burn shock resuscitation: lack of effect on daily multiple organ dysfunction score. Transfusion. 2006 Jan;46(1):80–9.

108. Dubois MJ, Orellana-Jimenez C, Melot C, De Backer D, Berre J, Leeman M, et al. Albumin administration improves organ function in critically ill hypoalbuminemic patients: A prospective, randomized, controlled, pilot study. Crit Care Med. 2006 Oct;34(10):2536–40.

109. Martin GS, Mangialardi RJ, Wheeler AP, Dupont WD, Morris JA, Bernard GR. Albumin and furosemide therapy in hypoproteinemic patients with acute lung injury. Crit Care Med. 2002 Oct;30(10):2175–82.

110. Verheij J, van Lingen A, Raijmakers PG, Rijnsburger ER, Veerman DP, Wisselink W et al. Effect of fluid loading with saline or colloids on pulmonary permeability, oedema and lung injury score after cardiac and major vascular surgery. Br J Anaesth. 2006 Jan;96(1):21–30.

111. Tollofsrud S, Svennevig JL, Breivik H, Kongsgaard U, Ozer M, Hysing E, et al. Fluid balance and pulmonary functions during and after coronary artery bypass surgery: Ringer's acetate compared with dextran, polygeline, or albumin. Acta Anaesthesiol Scand. 1995 Jul;39(5):671–7.

112. Human albumin administration in critically ill patients: systematic review of randomised controlled trials. Cochrane Injuries Group Albumin Reviewers. Bmj. 1998 Jul 25;317(7153):235–40.

113. Cook D. Is albumin safe? N Engl J Med. 2004 May 27;350(22):2294–6.

114. Myburgh J, Cooper DJ, Finfer S, Bellomo R, Norton R, Bishop N, et al. Saline or albumin for fluid resuscitation in patients with traumatic brain injury. N Engl J Med. 2007 Aug 30;357(9):874–84.

115. Mangialardi RJ, Martin GS, Bernard GR, Wheeler AP, Christman BW, Dupont WD, et al. Hypoproteinemia predicts acute respiratory distress syndrome development, weight gain, and death in patients with sepsis. Ibuprofen in Sepsis Study Group. Crit Care Med. 2000 Sep;28(9):3137–45.

116. Blunt MC, Nicholson JP, Park GR. Serum albumin and colloid osmotic pressure in survivors and nonsurvivors of prolonged critical illness. Anaesthesia. 1998 Aug; 53(8):755–61.

117. Yap FH, Joynt GM, Buckley TA, Wong EL. Association of serum albumin concentration and mortality risk in critically ill patients. Anaesth Intensive Care. 2002 Apr;30(2):202–7.

118. Goldwasser P, Feldman J. Association of serum albumin and mortality risk. J Clin Epidemiol. 1997 Jun;50(6): 693–703.

119. Finfer S, Bellomo R, McEvoy S, Lo SK, Myburgh J, Neal B et al. Effect of baseline serum albumin concentration on outcome of resuscitation with albumin or saline in patients in intensive care units: analysis of data from the saline versus albumin fluid evaluation (SAFE) study. Bmj. 2006 Nov 18;333(7577):1044.

120. Ring J. Anaphylactoid reactions to plasma substitutes. Int Anesthesiol Clin. 1985 Fall;23(3):67–95.

Jean-Louis Vincent

ScvO$_2$ as a marker for resuscitation in intensive care

Introduction

Adequate tissue oxygenation is known to be a key factor in determining tissue survival. Resuscitation efforts in critically ill patients therefore target restoration, normalisation and maintenance of regional blood flow and oxygenation. However, the difficulty lies in how best to monitor this parameter, as tissue hypoxia can persist despite apparent normalisation of global haemodynamic and oxygenation parameters (1, 2). The mixed venous oxygen saturation (SvO$_2$) could represent a useful guide for the adequacy of tissue oxygenation, especially when combined with cardiac output measurements. The SvO$_2$ is the oxygen saturation of the mixed venous blood, i.e., blood collected from all parts of the body, mixed in the right heart chambers and arriving in the pulmonary artery ready to be oxygenated. An SvO$_2$ value therefore reflects the oxygen that has been extracted from the body, i.e., the balance between the oxygen that was supplied (DO$_2$) and the oxygen that has been consumed (VO$_2$) (3). The Fick equation defines VO$_2$ as the product of cardiac output (CO) and the arteriovenous oxygen difference (CaO$_2$–CvO$_2$). Hence, as the oxygen content of the blood is basically dependent on the amount of haemoglobin and its oxygen saturation, by rearranging the equation, we can see that SvO$_2$ is influenced by the arterial oxygen saturation and the balance between the VO$_2$ and the cardiac output and haemoglobin concentration ([Hb]).

$$SvO_2 = SaO_2 - [VO_2/(CO \times [Hb \times 13.9])]$$

where SaO$_2$ is the arterial oxygen saturation (13.9 is a constant value related to the amount of oxygen bound to 1g of haemoglobin, multiplied by 10 to correspond to a VO$_2$ in ml/min). Therefore, SvO$_2$ decreases if there is a decrease in SaO$_2$, cardiac output or haemoglobin concentration, or an increase in VO$_2$. Hence, a decrease in SvO$_2$ is not necessarily pathological, as it occurs during exercise. Likewise, a low SvO$_2$ should not always be corrected, as it would necessitate excessive use of blood transfusions or inotropic agents. There are people with heart failure or chronic anaemia who are walking around with a low SvO$_2$.

Obviously, to have access to the mixed venous blood in the pulmonary artery for measurement of SvO$_2$, a pulmonary artery catheter is needed, which is an invasive technique. With recent concerns about the pulmonary artery catheter and its risk/benefit ratio in critically ill patients (4–8), and with the continuing trend towards using less invasive monitoring strategies wherever possible, attention has turned towards other parameters that could be used to assess regional oxygenation. The blood in the pulmonary artery is a mixture of blood from the superior vena cava, the inferior vena cava, and the coronary sinus. Blood in the superior vena cava can be accessed via a central venous catheter, insertion of which is often used in acutely ill patients to facilitate administration of fluids and medications and to measure the central venous pressure (CVP). Measurement of the oxygenation in the superior vena caval blood, the so-called central venous oxygen saturation (ScvO$_2$), could provide some information about oxygen extraction by the tissues as it will reflect the degree of oxygen extracted from the brain and the upper body. In this paper, we will consider the pros and cons of using $ScvO_2$ compared to SvO_2 as a resuscitation marker in critically ill patients.

The pro: $ScvO_2$ CAN replace SvO_2 as a marker for resuscitation

A central venous catheter is routinely placed in most critically ill patients to facilitate venous access and measure CVP, and is easily performed in ICU and non-ICU settings. In addition, placement of a central venous catheter is associated with fewer complications than insertion of a pulmonary artery catheter (9). Perhaps not surprisingly, various clinical studies in different groups of patients have shown a reasonably good correlation between SvO_2 and $ScvO_2$ with correlation coefficients of 0.88–0.945 (10–14). It is, of course, logical that there would be some relationship between $ScvO_2$ and SvO_2. After all, the mixed venous blood includes the blood sampled in the superior vena cava. If DO_2 is reduced, oxygen extraction should increase in all parts of the body to maintain VO_2. Even if single values of SvO_2 cannot be determined from single $ScvO_2$ values, trends in $ScvO_2$ over time do follow trends in SvO_2, and continuous $ScvO_2$ monitoring could, therefore, reliably replace continuous SvO_2 monitoring (14, 15).

Several recent studies have documented the value of $ScvO_2$ monitoring in critically ill patients. Perhaps the most well-known of these is the landmark study by Rivers et al. in which continuous $ScvO_2$ monitoring was used to guide the early resuscitation of patients with severe sepsis and septic shock (16). In this study (16), patients attending the emergency room with severe sepsis or septic shock were randomised to receive either six hours of early "goal-directed" therapy or standard therapy before admission to the intensive care unit (ICU). In addition to standard resuscitation measures, patients in the goal-directed group were given fluids, vasoactive agents, and red cell transfusions to keep $ScvO_2$ at 70% or above. The goal-directed protocol patients received more fluids, more dobutamine, and more blood transfusions in the first 6 hours than the standard treatment group and had lower mortality rates (31% versus

47%, p=0.009). Trzeciak et al. demonstrated that the early goal-directed protocol end-points can be easily achieved in an emergency department, and several studies have now confirmed the benefit of an early-goal directed protocol, including the $ScvO_2$ target, in patients with severe sepsis and septic shock (17–20). In an observational cohort study, Nguyen et al. (19) assessed the impact on outcomes of a bundle of interventions, including completion of early-goal directed therapy within 6 hours, in patients presenting to the emergency department with severe sepsis and septic shock. Patients in whom the whole bundle of interventions was completed had lower in-hospital mortality than patients in whom the bundle was not completed (20.8 vs. 39.5%, p<0.01). In multivariate analysis, completing early goal-directed therapy within 6 hrs was the only bundle component with a significant odds ratio (OR) for decreased mortality (OR, 0.36; 95% CI, 0.17–0.79; $p=0.01$).

As a result of these studies, the Surviving Sepsis Campaign Guidelines recommend that the goals of initial resuscitation of sepsis-induced hypoperfusion should include a CVP of 8–12 mmHg, an MAP > 65 mmHg, a urine output > 0.5 ml/kg/hr, and a $ScvO_2 > 70\%$ or $SvO_2 > 65\%$, noting that "The consensus panel judged central venous and mixed venous oxygen saturation to be equivalent" (21).

Recently, a multicenter study demonstrated that a low $ScvO_2$ during the peri- and postoperative period was associated with an increased risk of postoperative complications in high-risk patients undergoing major surgery (22). The authors suggested that in these patients also, protocols targeting $ScvO_2$ may, therefore, be useful to improve outcomes, and a randomised controlled study comparing $ScvO_2$ guided intraoperative fluid therapy with standard perioperative fluid therapy in patients undergoing elective bowel surgery is currently underway (ClinicalTrials.gov identifier: NCT00468793).

The con: $ScvO_2$ CANNOT replace SvO_2 as a marker for resuscitation

Although, as seen above, there is clearly some relationship between $ScvO_2$ and SvO_2, the specific nature of that relationship is actually quite complex. Venous oxygen saturation differs among different organ systems, as they each extract different amounts of oxygen (see fig. 1). In physiological conditions, oxygen extraction by the kidneys is very low, so that the oxygen saturation in the inferior vena cava is relatively high and the ScvO$_2$ is lower

than the SvO$_2$ (23). In pathological conditions, however, regional blood flow is redistributed away from the hepatosplanchnic region and towards the coronary and cerebral circulations such that cerebral perfusion is usually better preserved and renal and splanchnic blood flows generally reduced. The oxygen demand of the hepato-splanchnic region may also be increased. All these factors result in an ScvO$_2$ that is usually higher than the SvO$_2$ in the acutely ill patient (10–14) (see fig. 2). This may explain why the correlation between ScvO$_2$ and SvO$_2$ is actually suboptimal. Several authors have evaluated the relationship between ScvO$_2$ and SvO$_2$ as unreliable, even when the correlation between the two is apparently good. Martin et al. (24) reported that in 50 % of measurements, there was a greater than 5 % difference between ScvO$_2$ and SvO$_2$, and that abrupt changes in SvO$_2$ were not detected by ScvO$_2$ monitoring in 18 % of the measurements. Reinhart et al. (14) noted that despite

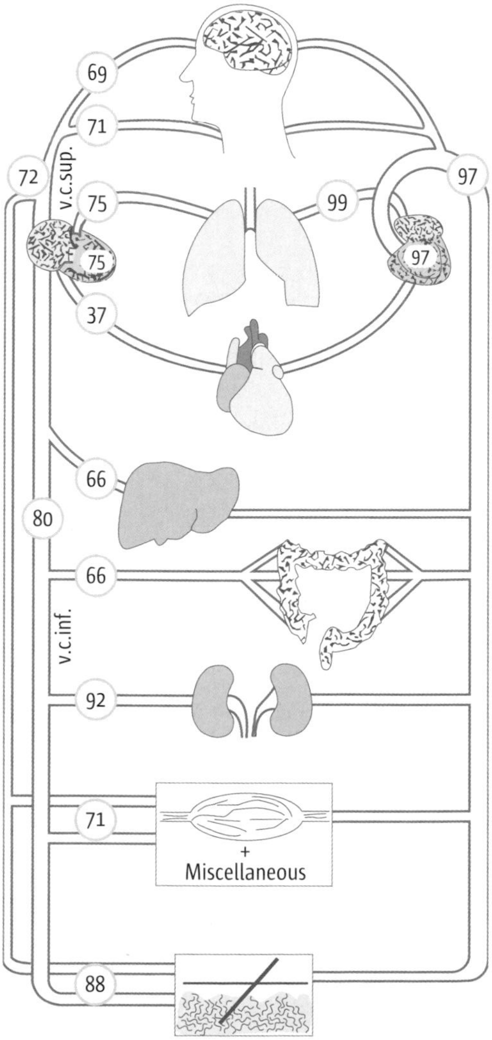

Fig. 1   Arterial (shown on the right) and venous (left) oxygen saturations (in %) in various vascular regions. V.c.inf: inferior vena cava; v.c.sup: superior vena cava. Adapted from: Reinhart K, Eyrich K, Eds, Clinical aspects of O$_2$ transport and tissue oxygenation. 1989, 195–211, Monitoring oxygen transport and tissue oxygenation in critically ill patients, Reinhart K. With kind permission of Springer Science and Business Media.

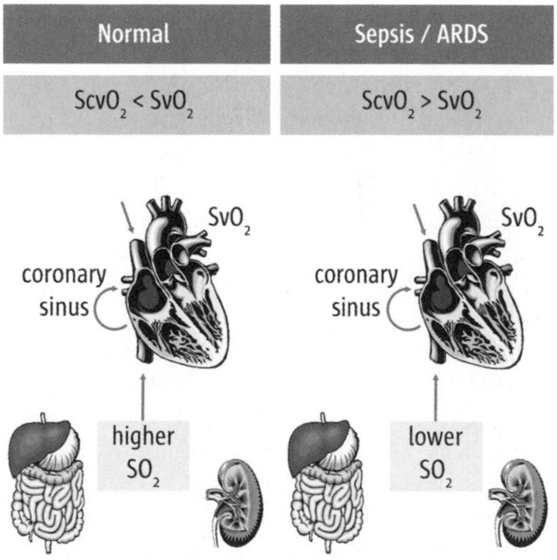

Fig. 2   ScvO$_2$ and SvO$_2$ in physiological conditions and in acutely ill patients. In physiological conditions (left panel) oxygen extraction by the kidneys is very low, so that the oxygen saturation (SO$_2$) in the inferior vena cava is relatively high and the ScvO$_2$ is lower than the SvO$_2$. In pathological conditions (right panel), however, cerebral perfusion is usually preserved and renal and splanchnic blood flows generally reduced. The oxygen demand of the hepatosplanchnic region may also be increased. All these factors result in an ScvO$_2$ that is usually higher than the SvO$_2$ in the acutely ill patient.

reasonable correlations of 0.88 for single measurements and 0.81 for continuous measurements, precise determination of SvO_2 from $ScvO_2$ was not possible and reported a bias of 7 and a precision of 8. Similarly, Chawla et al. (13), despite reporting an overall correlation of 0.88, noted a bias of 5.2% and concluded that $ScvO_2$ is not a reliable surrogate for SvO_2. Dueck and colleagues (15) found that some individual measurements of $ScvO_2$ differed by more than 10% from corresponding SvO_2 values, and, in patients undergoing cardiac surgery, Sander et al. (25) noted that there was a clinically unacceptable correlation between $ScvO_2$ and SvO_2 (r^2 0.38–0.46) with a low mean bias (0.3%), but clinically unacceptably high limits of agreement (–11.9 to +12.4%). Even trend analysis may not be so reliable (12).

The use of $ScvO_2$ as a resuscitation target was shown to be helpful in the study by Rivers et al. (16), but this was a single-centre study with a limited number of patients, and a rather high mortality rate in the control group. Importantly, too, even if $ScvO_2$ is a valid target in very early resuscitation, whether or not this applies later in the resuscitation process is uncertain. Indeed, studies using SvO_2 to guide haemodynamic therapy in critically ill patients have not shown a benefit (26).

Summary

The use of $ScvO_2$ or SvO_2 as a marker of resuscitation in critically ill patients must still be considered a grey area. Although there is a well-expected relation between $ScvO_2$ and SvO_2, this relation is rather loose. This has been recognised for years (27). One must also recognise that comparison of the results of different studies is difficult, as they included varied groups and numbers of patients; some measured $ScvO_2$ and SvO_2 simultaneously while others measured them sequentially as the pulmonary artery catheter is advanced; and they used different statistical approaches. The exact position of the tip of the central venous catheter is also an important issue. $ScvO_2$ monitoring is certainly attractive as it requires only a central venous catheter instead of the more invasive pulmonary artery catheter that is needed to measure SvO_2. However, the correlation between $ScvO_2$ and SvO_2 is not perfect, especially in patients with circulatory shock; even trends are approximations. Nevertheless, even approximations may sometimes be helpful when the situation is unclear. $ScvO_2$ monitoring may be particularly helpful in the early resuscitation of septic patients, but is not precise enough to be used for any fine haemodynamic tuning and, in complex cases, insertion of a pulmonary artery catheter should still be considered. However, even the use of the SvO_2 as a guide for resuscitation is complex (28), and indeed, it would be naïve to consider simple algorithms, as these may result in excessive transfusions or overzealous administration of dobutamine. Importantly, whichever measure is used, SvO_2 or $ScvO_2$, values should not be interpreted in isolation but used to complement multiple other measures and markers of perfusion and oxygenation including cardiac output and blood lactate levels.

The author

Jean-Louis Vincent, MD, PhD
Department of Intensive Care
Erasme University Hospital
Route de Lennik 808
1070 Brussels, Belgium
e-mail: jlvincent@ulb.ac.be

References

1. Rady MY, Rivers EP, Nowak RM. Resuscitation of the critically ill in the ED: Responses of blood pressure, heart rate, shock index, central venous oxygen saturation, and lactate. Am J Emerg Med. 1996;14(2):218–225.
2. Vincent JL, De Backer D. Oxygen transport-the oxygen delivery controversy. Intensive Care Med. 2004;30(11): 1990–1996.
3. Vincent JL. The relationship between oxygen demand, oxygen uptake, and oxygen supply. Intensive Care Med. 1990; 16 Suppl. 2:S145–S148.
4. Sandham JD, Hull RD, Brant RF, Knox L, Pineo GF, Doig CJ et al. A randomized, controlled trial of the use of pulmonary-artery catheters in high-risk surgical patients. N Engl J Med. 2003;348(1):5–14.
5. Richard C, Warszawski J, Anguel N, Deye N, Combes A, Barnoud D et al. Early use of the pulmonary artery catheter and outcomes in patients with shock and acute respiratory distress syndrome: A randomized controlled trial. JAMA. 2003;290(20):2713–2720.
6. Yu DT, Platt R, Lanken PN, Black E, Sands KE, Schwartz JS et al. Relationship of pulmonary artery catheter use to mortality and resource utilization in patients with severe sepsis. Crit Care Med. 2003;31(12):2734–2741.
7. Connors AF, Jr., Speroff T, Dawson NV, Thomas C, Harrell FE, Wagner D et al. The effectiveness of right

heart catheterization in the initial care of critically ill patients. JAMA. 1996;276:889–897.

8. Harvey S, Harrison DA, Singer M, Ashcroft J, Jones CM, Elbourne D et al. Assessment of the clinical effectiveness of pulmonary artery catheters in management of patients in intensive care (PAC-Man): a randomised controlled trial. Lancet. 2005;366(9484):472–477.

9. The National Heart, Lung, and Blood Institute Acute Respiratory Distress Syndrome (ARDS) Clinical Trials Network. Pulmonary-artery versus central venous catheter to guide treatment of acute lung injury. N Engl J Med. 2006;354(21):2213–2224.

10. Berridge JC. Influence of cardiac output on the correlation between mixed venous and central venous oxygen saturation. Br J Anaesth. 1992;69(4):409–410.

11. Ladakis C, Myrianthefs P, Karabinis A, Karatzas G, Dosios T, Fildissis G et al. Central venous and mixed venous oxygen saturation in critically ill patients. Respiration. 2001;68(3):279–285.

12. Varpula M, Karlsson S, Ruokonen E, Pettila V. Mixed venous oxygen saturation cannot be estimated by central venous oxygen saturation in septic shock. Intensive Care Med. 2006;32(9):1336–1343.

13. Chawla LS, Zia H, Gutierrez G, Katz NM, Seneff MG, Shah M. Lack of equivalence between central and mixed venous oxygen saturation. Chest. 2004;126(6): 1891–1896.

14. Reinhart K, Kuhn HJ, Hartog C, Bredle DL. Continuous central venous and pulmonary artery oxygen saturation monitoring in the critically ill. Intensive Care Med. 2004; 30:1572–1578.

15. Dueck MH, Klimek M, Appenrodt S, Weigand C, Boerner U. Trends but not individual values of central venous oxygen saturation agree with mixed venous oxygen saturation during varying hemodynamic conditions. Anesthesiology. 2005;103(2):249–257.

16. Rivers E, Nguyen B, Havstad S, Ressler J, Muzzin A, Knoblich B et al. Early goal-directed therapy in the treatment of severe sepsis and septic shock. N Engl J Med. 2001;345(19):1368–1377.

17. Kortgen A, Niederprum P, Bauer M. Implementation of an evidence-based "standard operating procedure" and outcome in septic shock. Crit Care Med. 2006;34(4):943–949.

18. Micek ST, Roubinian N, Heuring T, Bode M, Williams J, Harrison C et al. Before-after study of a standardized hospital order set for the management of septic shock. Crit Care Med. 2006;34(11):2707–2713.

19. Nguyen HB, Corbett SW, Steele R, Banta J, Clark RT, Hayes SR et al. Implementation of a bundle of quality indicators for the early management of severe sepsis and septic shock is associated with decreased mortality. Crit Care Med. 2007;35(4):1105–1112.

20. Jones AE, Focht A, Horton JM, Kline JA. Prospective external validation of the clinical effectiveness of an emergency department-based early goal-directed therapy protocol for severe sepsis and septic shock. Chest. 2007;132(2):425–432.

21. Dellinger RP, Levy MM, Carlet JM, Bion J, Parker MM, Jaeschke R et al. Surviving Sepsis Campaign: International guidelines for management of severe sepsis and septic shock: 2008. Crit Care Med. 2008; 36:296–327.

22. Collaborative Study Group on Perioperative ScvO$_2$ Monitoring. Multicentre study on peri- and postoperative central venous oxygen saturation in high-risk surgical patients. Crit Care. 2006;10(6):R158.

23. Barratt-Boyes BG, WOOD EH. The oxygen saturation of blood in the venae cavae, right-heart chambers, and pulmonary vessels of healthy subjects. J Lab Clin Med. 1957;50(1):93–106.

24. Martin C, Auffray JP, Badetti C, Perrin G, Papazian L, Gouin F. Monitoring of central venous oxygen saturation versus mixed venous oxygen saturation in critically ill patients. Intensive Care Med. 1992; 18(2): 101–104.

25. Sander M, Spies CD, Foer A, Weymann L, Braun J, Volk T et al. Agreement of central venous saturation and mixed venous saturation in cardiac surgery patients. Intensive Care Med. 2007;33(10):1719–1725.

26. Gattinoni L, Brazzi L, Pelosi P, Latini R, Tognoni G, Pesenti A et al. A trial of goal-oriented hemodynamic therapy in critically ill patients. SvO$_2$ Collaborative Group. N Engl J Med. 1995;333:1025–1032.

27. Vincent JL. Does central venous oxygen saturation accurately reflect mixed venous oxygen saturation? Nothing is simple, unfortunately. Intensive Care Med. 1992;18(7):386–387.

28. Pinsky MR, Vincent JL. Let us use the PAC correctly and only when we need it. Crit Care Med. 2005;33: 1119–1122.

29. Reinhart K. Monitoring oxygen transport and tissue oxygenation in critically ill patients. In: Reinhart K, Eyrich K, editors. Clinical Aspects of O$_2$ Transport and Tissue Oxygenation. Berlin: Springer, 1989:195–211.

Miguel Tavares, Etienne Gayat, Brice Lortat Jacob
and Alexandre Mebazaa

Calcium sensitisers versus dobutamine in acute heart failure

Introduction

Acute heart failure definition

During the past decade there has been a marked increase of interest in what has become known as "acute heart failure" (AHF), a term describing a heterogeneous syndrome that includes new onset heart failure and worsening chronic heart failure (CHF) (1).

Until recently, the clinical characteristics, management patterns, and outcomes of patients admitted with AHF have been poorly defined, due to lack of specific data, and AHF was not considered as a separate entity with distinct epidemiology and pathophysiology. During the past years, several large registries and trials have generated a considerable amount of data and new concepts have been suggested by the epidemiology, diagnosis and treatment of AHF in the short time since their inception. Although included patients may be quite different in terms of severity, data from these registries and trials shows the poor short- and long-term prognosis, especially for the most severe patients admitted to intensive care, with in-hospital mortality that may be as high as 28 %

and post-discharge mortality that may reach 62.5 % at 1 year (2) (see tab. 1).

In 2005, the European Society of Cardiology (ESC) and the European Society of Intensive Care Medicine (ESICM) published new guidelines for diagnosis and treatment of AHF, and defined AHF as a rapid onset or change in heart failure (HF) signs and symptoms, resulting in the need for urgent therapy (16). The underlying mechanism may be cardiac or extra-cardiac, the cardiac dysfunction can be related to systolic or diastolic dysfunction, to abnormalities in cardiac rhythm, or to pre-load and after-load mismatch. This is a complex syndrome that has many different etiologies, and as such, it is the result of diverse pathophysiological processes encompassing a large spectrum of patients that present with evidence of increased intra-cardiac pressures and disrupted myocardial oxygen balance, with or without low cardiac output (CO). This leads to pulmonary and tissue congestion and hypoperfusion, and who have significant morbidity and mortality.

Heart failure has classically been considered to be a clinical syndrome associated with impaired cardiac contractility and cardiac dilatation (17). However, according

Tab. 1 Clinical characteristic of patients hospitalised with acute heart failure syndromes in US and European registries

	US Registries		European Registries				
	ADHERE (3)	OPTIMIZE-HF (4)	EHFS-I (5)	EHFS-II (6)	FINN-AKVA (7)	EFICA (2)	Italian AHFS (8)
Patients (n)	187,565	48,612	11,327*	3,580	620	599	2,807
Age (mean)	75	73	71	70	75	73	73
Male Gender (%)	49	48	53	61	50	59	60
Prior HF (%)/Previous AHF hospitalisation (%)	76/33	88	65/44	63/45	51/20	66/53	56
Hypertension (%)	74	71	53	63	55	60	66
CAD** (%)/AMI** (%)	57/31	50	68/39	54	55/28	46/22	46/37
Diabetes Mellitus (%)	44	42	27	32	32.3	27	38
Atrial Fibrilation (%)	31	31				25	21
Renal Insufficiency (creatinine levels > 2 mg/dl) (%)	30	20	17	17	9	53	25
Preserved LVEF (%)	53	49		34		27	34
Admitted to ICU/CCU (%)	19		7	50	51	100	69
Cardiogenic shock (%)	2		<1	4	2	32	8
In-hospital mortality (%)	4	4	7	7	7	28	7
Post-Discharge mortality (%)		10 (n=5791) (60–90 days)	14 (n = 10,434)	20 (1-year)		43 (4-week) 62 (1-year)	
Post-Discharge Rehospitalisation (%)		30 (n=5791) (60–90 days)					

* Only 40% had AHF as a primary cause of admission
** CAD – Coronary Artery Disease, AMI – Acute Myocardial Infarction

to data from AHF registries and clinical trials, one-third to half of these patients have a relatively normal systolic function with preserved ejection fraction (EF) (2–8). This entity is attributed to abnormalities of diastolic function, although the exact mechanism is debated (18, 19). The prevalence of HF with preserved EF (HFPEF) seems to be changing as a result of changes in population demographics and in the prevalence and treatment of risk factors for HF. The average prevalence of preserved EF among 4596 AHF patients at the Mayo Clinic Hospitals in Olmsted County, Minnesota, from 1987 through 2001, increased over time from 38 percent to 47 percent to 54 percent in three consecutive five-year periods included in the study, and the increase in the prevalence of HFPEF was due to an increase in the number of patients admitted with HFPEF (20). The prevalence rates of hypertension, atrial fibrillation (AF), and diabetes among patients with AHF increased significantly over the same time (20). These patients are usually older than patients with systolic dysfunction, more likely to be female, to have a higher mean body mass index, more likely to be obese and to have lower haemoglobin than those with systolic dysfunction. The prevalence rates of hypertension and AF are higher among patients with HFPEF than among those with reduced EF. These patients have significant cardiac and non-cardiac comorbidities like hypertension, valvular disease, coronary artery disease (CAD), arrhythmia, especially AF, diabetes, renal insufficiency and they have a similar post-discharge event rate when compared to patients with systolic dysfunction. Several observational studies have shown contradictory data regarding the prognosis of HFPEF compared with HF with systolic dysfunction. Available data on HFPEF are mostly based on ambulatory populations, with less information on hospitalised patients and these patients have often been excluded from HF clinical trials. (21–23). Some studies show a better survival in patients with HFPEF (21, 24–26), while others find similar survival rates in both kinds of patients (23, 27–32). Most of these studies were observational retrospective studies (21, 27, 32–34). In a French cohort of 662 consecutive patients hospitalised for a first episode of HF followed prospectively, 5-year survival rates were not different in patients with HFPEF and patients with reduced EF (35).

AHF pathophysiology

In AHF, acute congestion, myocardial injury, renal and other end organ damage, all progressively exacerbate each other in a vicious circle where time plays a determinant role (see fig. 1).

When cardiac output is reduced, several compensatory neurohumoral mechanisms are stimulated. This includes the sympathetic nervous system, the RAAS, endothelin and vasopressin pathways. Stimulation of those four pathways may induce peripheral vasoconstriction, increase LV afterload and worsen LV systolic function. In addition, decreased renal perfusion and glomerular filtration together with renal congestion increase renal sodium and osmotic and non-osmotic water retention, which increase pulmonary and venous congestion, decreasing oxygenation, increasing myocardial wall stress and decreasing cardiac performance.

The heart pumping function maintains low end diastolic pressure (EDP) allowing systemic and pulmonary venous return. Increased left ventricular (LV) EDP leads to pulmonary congestion and poorer oxygenation. Increased right ventricular (RV) EDP leads to peripheral edema, increased liver, kidney and mesenteric vein pressures, with worsened function in these organs. Because they share a common septum, increased pressures in one side of the heart push the septum, increasing pressure and decreasing telediastolic volume in the other side, further compromising stroke volume (SV) and CO. This is particularly important with hypoxia, consequent to lung congestion, which may markedly increase pulmonary vascular resistance (PVR), causing an increase in RV EDP that will further contribute to increased LV EDP and decreased LV diastolic volume (36). If there are other causes that may compromise ventricular filling, as in HF with preserved ejection fraction (HFPEF), hypoxia or ischemia will further increase EDP.

Increased EDP increases wall tension, decreasing at the same time coronary blood flow when oxygen consumption is greater. In the AHF patient with lung congestion, this becomes more noticeable due to poorer blood oxygenation, and in each episode the heart oxygen balance is further compromised by decreased myocardial perfusion due to increased EDP, increased heart rate and/or arrhythmia, leading to further impairment of cardiac contractility and enhancing the process of pulmonary congestion.

Minor myocardial damage detected by Troponin T (TnT) is a powerful predictor of long-term prognosis in patients with AHF (37). In a study with patients with pulmonary edema (PE) without acute myocardial infarction (AMI), more than half had elevated cardiac TnT levels, suggesting ongoing myocardial injury. In this study, elevated TnT was an independent predictor of long-term mortality (38). Congestion and myocardial injury progressively exacerbate each other, thus contributing to irrevocable cardiac damage. In the end stage heart failure

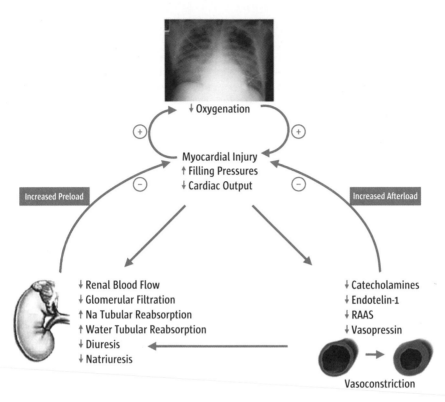

Fig. 1   Vicious circle of worsening heart failure
Congestion and myocardial injury progressively exacerbate each other during each AHF episode. Increased EDP increases wall tension, impairing coronary blood flow while myocardial oxygen consumption is increasing. Poorer blood oxygenation, due to pulmonary congestion, further compromises the already disrupted heart oxygen balance. Decreased myocardial perfusion due to increased heart rate and/or arrhythmia worsens impaired cardiac contractility and enhances pulmonary congestion. Pulmonary congestion and hypoxia increase RV afterload and RV EDP, pushing the septum and increasing left-sided pressures. Right-sided congestion leads to venous, renal, hepatic and mesenteric congestion worsening organ function. Modified from: Tavares M, Rezlan E, Vostroknoutova I, Khouadja H, Mebazaa A. New pharmacologic therapies for acute heart failure. Crit Care Med. 2008;36:S112–120.

(ESHF) patient, where low CO is prevalent, low systolic blood pressure (SBP) adds a critical component, especially in patients with coronary artery disease (CAD), aggravating myocardial perfusion. In each episode the bigger the oxygenation compromise and the bigger the hypotension, the greater the myocardial injury.

Venous congestion and increased intra-abdominal pressure impair renal tubular function, and may play a more important role than the systolic dysfunction, as renal dysfunction occurs with equal frequency in low Ejection Fraction (EF) and preserved EF patients. Sodium and water retention increase pulmonary and venous congestion, decreasing oxygenation, increasing myocardial wall stress and decreasing cardiac performance. In patients with decreased CO, renal renin-angiotensin-aldosterone

system (RAAS) activation increases vasoconstriction, decreases glomerular filtration with further sodium and fluid retention, increases secretion of vasopressin release by the pituitary gland with consequent water retention, and endothelin-1 release by endothelial cells increasing vasoconstriction which imposes extra work on a failing myocardium.

Comorbidities associated with AHF may each play a role in worsening oxygenation and cardiac function like hypertension, CAD, arrhythmia, diabetes, renal insufficiency, chronic obstructive pulmonary disease, obstructive apnea or anemia. New arrhythmia during an exacerbation of HF identifies a high-risk group with higher intra-hospital and 60-day morbidity and mortality (39). Renal dysfunction in patients with HF is common and is increasingly recognised as an independent risk factor for morbidity and mortality, and the level of renal dysfunction is a potent independent predictor of death or AHF admission (40–44). AHF is commonly associated with renal dysfunction with requirement of higher diuretic doses at discharge (11). According to data from HF registries and clinical trials, arterial hypertension is the more common comorbidity present in 50 to 74 % of AHF patients, followed by CAD in about 50 %. In a landmark paper, left ventricular ejection fraction (LVEF) during an episode of acute hypertensive PE was shown to be similar to LVEF measured after treatment, after blood pressure control, and in these AHF patients acute hypertensive PE was not associated with systolic dysfunction or severe acute mitral regurgitation (45).

The progression of CHF is characterised by frequent AHF episodes requiring hospitalisation, and high mortality. Clinical deterioration is triggered by many factors that promote and add more myocardial damage. In each episode of AHF, left and right congestion, myocardial injury, increased afterload and several common comorbidities like hypertension, CAD and renal insufficiency progressively exacerbate each other, contributing to irrevocable cardiac damage and worsening long-term prognosis.

Acute heart failure treatment

Most patients with AHF present to the emergency room with a relatively high blood pressure and pulmonary and systemic congestion without signs of systemic hypoperfusion. In addition, data from the Acute Decompensated Heart Failure National Registry (ADHERE) showed that about half of the patients admitted with AHF had a relatively preserved systolic function (43). These patients have a higher incidence of hypertension, LV hypertrophy, and diabetes than patients admitted with systolic dysfunction (46).

The way we manage AHF is important because long-term mortality and morbidity may be influenced by our therapeutic choices that are used only for hours or days. Immediate treatment priorities are meant to improve short-term survival by restoring oxygenation and improving organ perfusion, improving haemodynamics and symptoms while avoiding or limiting cardiac, renal and other organ damage that may adversely affect morbidity and mortality. Early intervention and patient stabilisation should provide a window of opportunity to provide specific treatment, if there is one, or to initiate and/or gradually optimise long-term HF therapies that have extensive proven evidence for improving long-term outcomes like

β-blockers, angiotensin converter inhibitors or spironolactone.

Acute congestion, myocardial injury, renal and other end organ damage all progressively exacerbate each other in a vicious circle where time plays a determinant role and early intervention is key. As in other medical emergencies, AHF needs a rapid, initial integrative approach where assessment and management are provided in the shortest time, in a parallel way, in order to stop an episode that continues damaging the heart after presentation, and, like thrombolysis or aspirin in patients with AMI, short-term intervention can lead to long-term benefit.

Data from ADHERE shows that early administration of intravenous vasoactive therapy in the ED was associated with significantly lower mortality, fewer transfers to critical care, decreased necessity of invasive procedures, shorter in-hospital and critical care unit median length of stay, and fewer of these patients required prolonged hospitalisation (47, 48).

Several therapies in AHF management have an unacceptably high incidence of hypotension that may *per se* increase cardiac, renal and other organ damage. Their use should require frequent, or preferably, continuous blood pressure monitoring and pre-emptive measures to avoid it.

Non-invasive ventilation (NIV) should be given early to every patient admitted with AHF, as it is the only tool with proven improvement in morbidity and mortality (49–69). If the respiratory acidosis is associated with mental status impairment, endotracheal intubation and mechanical ventilation should be considered early. Failure to improve acute respiratory failure in 1 to 2 hours is an indication to consider intubation, and delay in intubating a patient who does not improve with NIV is associated with increased mortality (70).

Although consensus guidelines provide evidence-based strategies for the treatment of CHF, the current drug therapy of AHF is largely empirical and has traditionally been transposed from CHF, where HF patients were usually considered as having systolic dysfunction and where sodium and water retention play a central role for the presenting symptoms. ESC guidelines highlight the lack of evidence upon which to base much of current therapy. Morphine, loop diuretics, and inotropic agents have been used for many years without sound evidence from randomised studies on their benefit on morbidity or survival, and, although these drugs may exert acute favorable haemodynamic and clinical effects, there is either lack of evidence or conflicting evidence about its outcome benefit. This is especially true for inotropes or inodilators which lately have been consistently associated with decreased survival. Indeed, all patients are not created equal, and in euvolemic or hypovolemic patients, loop diuretics may induce marked decreases in SV and CO, hypotension or worsening renal function, while inotropes used in patients with HFPEF may markedly increase mortality and hospital stay. Data from ADHERE shows that patients with HFPEF may respond differently to treatment with inotropes compared to those with impaired LVEF. In this registry approximately 14 % of the patients were treated with at least 1 infusion of inotrope or inodilator (dobutamine 6 %, dopamine 6 %, and milrinone 3 %) (71). Among these, 15 % of patients receiving inodilators had HFPEF (72). In this subgroup analysis, HFPEF patients who received inotropic agents had a significantly longer length of hospital stay (12.9 vs. 9.6 days; p < 0.0001) and higher mortality rate (19 vs. 14 %; p < 0.002) than all other inotrope-treated patients. HFPEF patients who received inotropic agents had more than double the length of stay (12.9 vs. 5.8 days; p < 0.0001) and a near tenfold increase in mortality rate (19 vs. 2 %; p < 0.0001) compared with HFPEF patients who were not treated with inotropes (72).

If a rhythm disorder is the likely cause of PE or acute coronary syndrome (ACS), one should consider emergency cardioversion. Bradycardia should be addressed if it is the cause of symptomatic low CO.

Patients with ACS or any serious mechanical cardiac disorder should proceed rapidly to angiography and catheterisation for therapeutic measures including percutaneous coronary intervention (PCI) or surgery (16).

Controversial position 1: Inotrope/inodilator use in AHF

The "recommended" indication for short-term inotrope use in AHF is organ hypoperfusion often associated with hypotension and systolic dysfunction, not improved by IV vasodilators or diuretics. Inotropic therapy is often required in the emergency context of these patients who show evidence of critical hypoperfusion, such as lactic acidosis, obtundation or oliguria. They may require rapid institution of inotropic and/or vasopressor therapy until the cause of shock is determined and definitive therapy implemented. The benefits and risks are quite immediate in this situation and these agents can be lifesaving for patients with rapidly progressive haemodynamic collapse.

Of note, preserved EF patients usually do not benefit from inotropic therapy and may markedly worsen SV and CO if inotropes are used.

In general, the use of inotropes has long been a subject of controversy, mainly because of the lack of alternative therapies and lack of prospective, placebo-controlled trials. Their use remains common, but is highly variable and site-dependent (73). Data available from randomised controlled trials on short-term, intermittent, and long-term use of IV inotropic and inodilator agents (dobutamine, dopamine, and milrinone) failed to show benefit with current medications and suggested that their acute, intermittent, or continuous infusion use may increase morbidity and mortality in patients with AHF, particularly in patients with preserved left ventricular function (10, 72, 74–80).

Traditional inotropes and inodilator agents

Traditional inotropes and inodilator agents such as endogenous catecholamines, β-agonists like dobutamine or dopamine, and phosphodiesterase (PDE) inhibitors like milrinone or amrinone exert their action through a common pathway of increased intracellular cyclic adenosine monophosphate (cAMP) and calcium concentrations in cardiac myocytes, lowering filling pressures and enhancing CO, improving haemodynamics and symptoms. Cardiac glycosides block the sodium pump, and the rise in intracellular sodium leads to increased intracellular calcium by the sodium-calcium exchanger. β receptor occupancy by β agonists increases cAMP through the action of a coupled G protein and adenyl-cyclase. PDE inhibitors reduce the activity of PDE, thus reducing the rate of cAMP breakdown. Both elevate cAMP and cause phosphorylation of intracellular proteins. Several proteins are phosphorylated by increased cAMP: the surface membrane calcium channel, which increases calcium entry and hence sarcoplasmic reticulum loading, Troponin I and phospholambam, which accelerate the relaxation rate. Increased intracellular calcium leads to increased sarcoplasmic reticulum calcium load and calcium release by the action potential. Both increase myocardial oxygen consumption, making hearts less efficient. β-adrenergic agonists and PDE inhibitors cause a 2-fold, even 3-fold, increase in activation heat and work through an uneconomical process to generate more force (81). This intracellular calcium overload leads to increased risk of arrhythmia, and to the activation of maladaptive calcium-dependent signaling cascades that accelerate myocardial cell injury.

Dobutamine has been used for the last 30 years as an inotrope in AHF patients. It is a synthetic catecholamine that acts on α-1, β-1 and β-2 adrenergic receptors, and its mechanisms of action are complex. It is given as the racemic mixture. The l-isomer is a potent agonist at α-1 receptors, while the d-isomer is a potent α-1 antagonist. Both isomers are β receptor agonists with greater selectivity for β-1 than β-2 receptors. The net result of administration of the racemic mixture is more or less selective β agonist effects. In the heart, stimulation of these receptors produces a relatively strong, additive inotropic effect and a relatively weak chronotropic effect. In the vasculature, α-1 agonist activity balances the β-2 agonist effect. Systemic vascular resistance (SVR) is not much affected, presumably by the counterbalancing effects of β-2 agonist-mediated vasodilatation, and α-1 agonist mediated vasoconstriction.

In clinical use, dobutamine has a rapid onset of action and a short half-life (82). Its haemodynamic effects are an increase in CO and a decrease in SVR without significant change in arterial pressure. Dobutamine has largely replaced agents with rather profound toxicity, such as isoproterenol and epinephrine. As a β-1 receptor agonist, although it may have less tachycardia or arrhythmia incidence compared to older β agonists, it increases heart rate and it significantly increases SV, CO, aortic dp/dt, urine flow and urine sodium concentration with a significant reduction in SVR and PVR, translated to lower pulmonary capillary wedge pressure (PCWP) and lower right atrial pressure. Like other usual inotropic agents, dobutamine increases myocardial oxygen demand.

Milrinone, amrinone, vesnarinone and enoximone, among others, selectively inhibit PDE, the enzyme that breaks down intracellular cAMP to its inactive metabolite 5-AMP, leading to increased intracellular cAMP. This results in increased intracellular calcium concentration and myocardial contractility as well as acceleration of myocardial relaxation. Increased cAMP peripherally produces vasodilatation in both the arterial

and venous circulation. The end result is an inotropic and vasodilator effect increasing CO and decreasing systemic and pulmonary vascular resistances, thus decreasing LV and RV filling pressures, which made these drugs an attractive option in AHF treatment.

Given the limitations of high-dose diuretic and vasodilator use in these patients, several new pharmacologic and non pharmacologic interventions have been introduced, while others are under development or in preclinical investigation for the treatment of pulmonary and systemic congestion and restoration of CO in the setting of AHF (83).

Calcium sensitisers: Levosimendan

Levosimendan belongs to the Class II calcium sensitiser agents. It acts on interaction of Troponin-tropomyosin with actin reactions and thereby facilitates actin regulation. They induce myofilament calcium sensitising action, but do not increase the affinity of Troponin C – calcium binding. They stabilise the calcium-induced conformational change of Troponin C (TnC) only during systole by stereoselective binding to the calcium binding conformation of calcium-saturated TnC (84).

Its binding site on TnC was hypothesised at a hydrophobic region of the N-domain of this thin filament regulatory protein (85–87). This leads to calcium-dependent binding of the drug to TnC without increasing the affinity of calcium to TnC, avoiding undesired effects of calcium sensitisation on cardiac relaxation during diastole (88).

Among calcium sensitisers, levosimendan is the most studied and has been introduced in several countries for the treatment of acutely decompensated HF.

It differs from classic inodilators because of its ability to improve myocardial efficiency without significantly increasing myocardial oxygen demand, its antistunning properties, its effects on coronary blood flow, and its lack of negative lusitropic effects (89). Levosimendan increases myocardial contractility, in a dose-dependent fashion, in healthy subjects, patients with LV dysfunction, and patients who have undergone coronary artery bypass graft (CABG) surgery (90–92).

Beneficial effects of levosimendan are also related to its vasodilatatory effect on systemic, coronary, pulmonary, renal, splanchnic and cerebral arteries, and on systemic and portal veins (93–101). This effect is mediated by an adenosine tri-phosphate (ATP) -dependent potassium channel-opening effect in an ATP-dependent manner in arterial smooth muscle cells of the small resistance arteries and by a calcium-activated potassium and voltage-dependent potassium channel opening effect in large conductance vessels (102–104). Membrane hyperpolarisation induced by the open potassium channels inhibits calcium entry and activates sodium-calcium exchange, decreasing intracellular calcium and inducing vasodilatation. This induced decrease in right and left ventricular afterload seems to be beneficial in failing hearts (105, 106).

Interestingly, the circulating metabolites OR-1855 and OR-1896 are formed slowly, and their maximum concentrations are seen on average 24 to 48 hours after terminating the infusion. OR-1896 has an elimination half-life of 75–78 hours in patients with HF New York Heart Association (NYHA) Class III–IV, is excreted by the kidney, and prolongs the duration of the haemodynamic effects of the parent compound (107, 108).

Controversial position 2: Levosimendan versus dobutamine use in AHF

Clinical studies

Acute heart failure

Several clinical trials have shown the beneficial effect of levosimendan on short-term haemodynamic and clinical signs in patients with AHF (see tab. 2).

The Levosimendan Infusion versus Dobutamine (LIDO) study enrolled 203 patients with severe low-output HF and compared the effects of levosimendan with those of dobutamine in a double-blind fashion over 24 hours. The primary end point of haemodynamic improvement (an increase of 30% or more in CO and a decrease of 25% or more in PCWP) was achieved by 28% of the levosimendan patients and 15% of the dobutamine patients (p=0.022). At 31 days, all-cause mortality was significantly lower with levosimendan compared to dobutamine (17 vs.

6.8%) (HR 0.43 [95% CI 0.18–1.00] p=0.049). The patients were also followed retrospectively for 180 days and this analysis revealed that 26% of the levosimendan patients had died compared with 38% in the dobutamine group (HR 0.57 [95% CI 0.34–0.95] p=0.029) (110).

The inodilatory effects of levosimendan were accentuated by concomitant use of β-blocking agents in the LIDO study, where a subgroup analysis demonstrated that the use of β-blockers enhanced the haemodynamic effects of levosimendan but reduced the haemodynamic effects of dobutamine (110).

The two recent large-scale randomised trials, Multicenter Evaluation of Intravenous Levosimendan Efficacy (REVIVE)-2 and Survival of Patients with Acute Heart Failure In Need of Intravenous Inotropic Support (SURVIVE), showed no effect of levosimendan on 90- and 180-day mortality respectively (12, 13). However, REVIVE-2 data showed benefit in the primary endpoint of change in clinical dyspnea through 5 days in the levosimendan group vs. placebo, greater B-type natriuretic peptide (BNP) decrease at 24 hours, and a shorter hospital stay in the levosimendan group. In SURVIVE, at 31 days, in the 88% of patients with a prior history of heart failure, there was a trend to lower risk of death in the levosimendan group compared with the dobutamine group, while in the subgroup of patients without a prior history of HF (12%) there was a mortality increase in the levosimendan group (13). There was also a survival difference in favor of levosimendan (HR 0.72 [95% CI 0.44–1.16]) at 5 days in a post-hoc analysis associated with a great decrease in plasma BNP after levosimendan treatment. The early beneficial effect of levosimendan over dobutamine was striking during the first 5 days in patients chronically treated with a β-blocker, but it was not evident in 180-day survival.

After PCI or after CABG

In patients undergoing elective CABG, levosimendan increases CO and SV and decreases SVR without increasing myocardial oxygen consumption or causing myocardial substrate utilisation to deteriorate (92, 95). Levosimendan improves coronary blood flow, and myocardium performance while the heart is ischemic (92, 95, 113–119). This

Tab. 2 Randomised clinical trials comparing the effects of levosimendan with dobutamine in acute heart failure

Study	Patients	Dosage (LD + I)	Comparator	Aim	Outcomes
Nieminem et al. (109)	151 with NYHA II–IV	3–36 µg/kg + 0.05–0.6 µg/kg/min	Dobutamine (6 µg/kg/min) and placebo	Proportion of patients achieving in each treatment at 24 h at least : >15 % increase in SV >25 % decrease in PCWP and >4 mmHg >40 % increase in CO with change in HR<20 % >50 % decrease in PCWP	Levosimendan treatment was associated with dose-dependent favourable haemodynamic responses
LIDO Trial (110)	103 with AHF	24 µg/kg + 0.1 µg/kg/min(l)	Dobutamine (5 µg/kg/min)	Effects on haemodynamics and outcomes	Levosimendan improved haemodynamics and survival at 180 days
REVIVE Trial (111)	100 with HF and symptoms at rest	0.1–0.2 µg/kg/min(l)	Dobutamine	Effects on composite clinical endpoints	Levosimendan produced an early greater symptom response and decreased creatinine and BNP levels
REVIVE-2 Trial (112)	600 with HF and symptoms at rest	0.1–0.2 µg/kg/min(l)	Dobutamine	Effects on composite clinical endpoints	Levosimendan produced an early greater symptom response, reduction in ICU & Hospital LOS and decreased creatinine and BNP levels
SURVIVE Trial (13)	1327 with AHF requiring inotropes	12 µg/kg + 0.1–0.2 µg/kg/min(l)	Dobutamine (5–40 µg/kg/min)	Effects on mortality at 180 days	No differences in terms of global mortality between levosimendan and dobutamine but Decreased BNP levels Decreased 5 and 31 days mortality Decreased mortality in CHF (prespecified subgroup analysis)

was first shown in animals (113–115, 119) and healthy humans (95), but was later shown in patients with congestive HF and after AMI in patients with LV dysfunction, improving the left ventricular diastolic function of stunned myocardium in these patients (116, 117, 120, 121).

In the Randomized Study on Safety and Effectiveness of Levosimendan in Patients with Left Ventricular Failure after an Acute Myocardial Infarct (RUSSLAN) trial in 504 patients with AHF after AMI, a significant dose-related decrease in worsening HF or death over the first 24 hours was observed in patients treated with levosimendan compared with placebo (4.0 vs. 8.8 %). At 14 days, mortality was significantly lower with levosimendan compared with placebo (11.4 vs. 8.8 %) (122).

In a retrospective matched-pair analysis of 52 patients undergoing emergency CABG for AMI, with cardiogenic shock diagnosed in 52 % of the patients in both groups, levosimendan added to catecholamines reduced morbidity compared to the control group treated with catecholamines only. Levosimendan-treated patients had fewer intra-aortic balloon pumps inserted (33 % vs. 76 %, P 0.05) and lower need for dialysis (11 % levosimendan; 32 % control, p > 0.05) but no reductions in mortality or length of stay (123).

Levosimendan has also been used to restore right or left ventricular function in patients after cardiac surgery (124) and in unresponsive cardiogenic shock patients after heart transplantation primary graft failure (125, 126).

Diastolic heart failure

In animal and human preclinical studies, levosimendan has been shown to improve diastolic function and its inotropic effect is associated with an increased rate of relaxation and reduced relaxation time, thus improving diastolic filling (131–134).

In severe HF patients with restrictive left ventricular filling assessed both by pulsed-wave Doppler echocardiography of the mitral flow and simultaneous pulmonary artery catheterisation, levosimendan improved both systolic and diastolic function, increasing left ventricular filling, SV (−24 % ± 9) and CO (29 % ± 14) while decreasing PCWP (−29 % ± 6). The percentage changes of the early/late transmitral diastolic peak flow velocity (E/A) ratio and the percentage changes

of the isovolumetric relaxation time were independent predictors of the increase in CO in this series (135).

Peripartum cardiomyopathy

Using new drugs in patients with rare diseases is always difficult, and there are only a few anecdotal reports describing the successful use of levosimendan in peripartum cardiomyopathy patients (136–138). AHF is a life-threatening event that occurs in rare instances during or after childbirth. In these published reports, in patients with a severe episode of AHF, levosimendan improved cardiac performance which was associated both with symptomatic relief and haemodynamic or echocardiographic improvement in ventricular function. Levosimendan induced a steady decline of increased PCWP, followed by a definitive increase in cardiac SV and patient recovery (136–138).

Right ventricular dysfunction in ARDS

In patients with acute respiratory distress syndrome (ARDS), pulmonary hypertension and RV dysfunction have been associated with poor outcome (139–141). In a prospective, randomised, placebo-controlled pilot study of septic shock patients requiring mechanical respiratory support due to ARDS, levosimendan was shown to decrease mean pulmonary artery pressure, PVR and RV end-systolic volume, increasing CO, right ventricular ejection fraction and mixed venous oxygen saturation (105).

Natriuretic peptides change after levosimendan administration

In patients with CHF decompensation, BNP levels at admission and discharge, as well as the magnitude of BNP change during treatment, are predictors of an adverse outcome in terms of re-hospitalisation, death, and worsening of heart failure, and the extent of the acute neurohormonal response after a single levosimendan administration may predict the clinical outcome in patients with decompensated CHF (142, 143).

Several studies have shown that the serum levels of BNP or NT-proBNP are significantly decreased when levosimendan is administered to these patients. The magnitude of levosimendan-induced reduction in plasma BNP levels at 48 hrs. was recently recognised as a predictor of 6-month survival, and lower BNP levels at the time of discharge are associated with improved post-discharge outcomes (142, 144–151).

In the SURVIVE trial, compared to dobutamine, levosimendan showed a greater BNP decrease at 24 hours and a lower 5 and 31 days mortality in AHF patients with a prior history of HF. However, it may be unrealistic to expect such benefits to last for 180 days post-discharge.

Arrhythmia risk with levosimendan

Data from SURVIVE showed an unexpected higher incidence of atrial fibrillation (AF) and ventricular extrasystoles in the levosimendan arm, when beforehand one could expect a higher incidence of arrhythmia in the dobutamine group due to its increase of intracellular calcium concentration and greater increase of myocardial oxygen demand.

This is interesting, because levosimendan-increased AF risk was not described in earlier trials where levosimendan was compared to dobutamine. As SURVIVE was a large, randomised, double-blind trial with similar baseline patient characteristics between the two arms, this suggests a drug-related reason.

Although there was no significant difference in the number of hypotension episodes between the two groups, systolic and diastolic blood pressure initially declined more until cessation of the study drug infusion, and heart rate increased more and remained more elevated through 5 days in the levosimendan group. This might explain a higher incidence of AF. In addition, the high incidence of AF was associated with a high incidence of hypokalemia. This could be another mechanism of AF.

Key points for clinical practice

- *Patients hospitalised for AHF carry a high risk of death and re-hospitalisation in the months following admission.*

- *In AHF, acute congestion, myocardial injury, renal and other end organ damage all progressively exacerbate each other in a vicious circle where time plays a determinant role and early intervention is key to treatment success.*

- *HFPEF is a underrecognised condition, is increasing, and recent data shows that it may be present in one-third to half of the patients. These patients should not receive inotropes as LVEF is preserved.*

- *Inotropic therapy may be lifesaving for patients with rapidly progressive haemodynamic collapse who have evidence of critical hypoperfusion until the cause of shock is determined and definitive therapy implemented.*

- *Compared to dobutamine, levosimendan showed a marked BNP level decrease at 24 hours through 5 days and improved short- and medium-term survival, especially for patients with a previous history of HF allowing concomitant use of ß-blocker therapy*

- *In countries where it is available, early levosimendan infusion can be considered for AHF patients who remain symptomatic with dyspnea at rest despite initial therapy, particularly those with history of chronic HF or chronically treated with ß-blockers (152)*

- *However, as a powerful vasodilator, levosimendan may be a harmful drug. Although this drug influences little myocardial oxygen demand per se, in patients with active ischemia or obstructive CAD, levosimendan-induced hypotension, especially in the hypovolemic patient, may precipitate tachycardia, aggravate ischemia and increase myocardial damage.*

- *Acutely decompensated CHF, NYHA class III/IV, ischemic cardiomyopathy, SBP >100 mm Hg, absence of concomitant hypotensive or arrhythmogenic therapies, BNP reduction >50% or BNP <700 pg/ml at discharge after levosimendan administration, have all been associated with improved outcome in patients who had levosimendan.*

Abbreviations

ACS	Acute coronary syndrome
ADHERE	Acute Decompensated Heart Failure National Registry
AF	Atrial fibrillation
AHF	Acute heart failure
AMI	Acute myocardial infarction
ARDS	Acute respiratory distress syndrome
BNP	B-type natriuretic peptide
cAMP	Cyclic adenosine monophosphate
CAD	Coronary artery disease

CABG	Coronary artery bypass graft
CHF	Chronic heart failure
CO	Cardiac output
EDP	End diastolic pressure
EF	Ejection fraction
ESC	European Society of Cardiology
ESHF	End stage heart failure
ESICM	European Society of Intensive Care Medicine
HF	Heart failure
HFPEF	Heart failure with preserved ejection fraction
LIDO	Levosimendan Infusion versus Dobutamine
LV	Left ventricle
LVEF	Left ventricular ejection fraction
NIV	Non-invasive ventilation
NYHA	New York Heart Association
PCI	Percutaneous coronary intervention
PE	Pulmonary edema
PDE	Phosphodiesterase
PCWP	Pulmonary capillary wedge pressure
PVR	Pulmonary vascular resistance
RASS	Renin-angiotensin-aldosterone system
RV	Right ventricle
REVIVE	Randomized Multicenter Evaluation of Intravenous Levosimendan Efficacy
SBP	Systolic blood pressure
SURVIVE	Survival of Patients with Acute Heart Failure In Need of Intravenous Inotropic Support
SV	Stroke volume
SVR	Systemic vascular resistance
TnC	Troponin C
TnT	Troponin T

Key words

Acute Heart Failure, Inotropes, Inodilators, Dobutamine, Levosimendan, Calcium Sensitizers, Acute heart failure therapy

Financial support

Ministère de l'Enseignement Supérieur et de la Recherche (EA 322)

The authors

Miguel Tavares, MD[1]
Etienne Gayat[2]
Brice Lortat Jacob[2]

Alexandre Mebazaa, MD, PhD[2]
[1]Department of Anaesthesiology and Critical Care | Hospital Geral de Santo António | Porto, Portugal.
[2]University Paris 7 Denis Diderot | Department of Anaesthesiology and Critical Care Medicine | Lariboisière Hospital, AP-HP | Paris, France

Address for correspondence
Alexandre Mebazaa
University Paris 7 Denis Diderot
AP-HP
Department of Anaesthesiology and
Critical Care Medicine
Lariboisière Hospital 2
Rue Ambroise Paré
75010 Paris, France
e-mail: alexandre.mebazaa@lrb.aphp.fr

References

1. Schiff GD, Fung S, Speroff T, McNutt RA. Decompensated heart failure: symptoms, patterns of onset, and contributing factors. Am J Med. 2003;114:625–630.
2. Zannad F, Mebazaa A, Juillierc Y, Cohen-Solal A, Guize L, Alla F, Rouge P, Blin P, Barlet MH, Paolozzi L, Vincent C, Desnos M, Samii K. Clinical profile, contemporary management and one-year mortality in patients with severe acute heart failure syndromes: The EFICA study. Eur J Heart Fail. 2006;8:697–705.
3. Yancy CW, Lopatin M, Stevenson LW, De Marco T, Fonarow GC. Clinical presentation, management, and in-hospital outcomes of patients admitted with acute decompensated heart failure with preserved systolic function: a report from the Acute Decompensated Heart Failure National Registry (ADHERE) Database. J Am Coll Cardiol. 2006;47:76–84.
4. No authors listed. The OPTIMIZE-HF Registry. Final Data Report. Duke Clinical Research Institute.
5. Cleland JG, Swedberg K, Follath F, Komajda M, Cohen-Solal A, Aguilar JC, Dietz R, Gavazzi A, Hobbs R, Korewicki J, Madeira HC, Moiseyev VS, Preda I, van Gilst WH, Widimsky J, Freemantle N, Eastaugh J, Mason J. The EuroHeart Failure survey programme – a survey on the quality of care among patients with heart failure in Europe. Part 1: patient characteristics and diagnosis. Eur Heart J. 2003;24:442–463.
6. Nieminen MS, Brutsaert D, Dickstein K, Drexler H, Follath F, Harjola VP, Hochadel M, Komajda M, Lassus J, Lopez-Sendon JL, Ponikowski P, Tavazzi L. EuroHeart

Failure Survey II (EHFS II): a survey on hospitalized acute heart failure patients: description of population. Eur Heart J. 2006;27:2725–2736.

7. Siirila-Waris K, Lassus J, Melin J, Peuhkurinen K, Nieminen MS, Harjola VP. Characteristics, outcomes, and predictors of 1-year mortality in patients hospitalized for acute heart failure. Eur Heart J. 2006;27:3011–3017.

8. Tavazzi L, Maggioni AP, Lucci D, Cacciatore G, Ansalone G, Oliva F, Porcu M. Nationwide survey on acute heart failure in cardiology ward services in Italy. Eur Heart J. 2006;27:1207–1215.

9. VMACInvestigators. Intravenous nesiritide vs nitroglycerin for treatment of decompensated congestive heart failure: a randomized controlled trial. Jama. 2002; 287:1531–1540.

10. Cuffe MS, Califf RM, Adams KF, Jr., Benza R, Bourge R, Colucci WS, Massie BM, O'Connor CM, Pina I, Quigg R, Silver MA, Gheorghiade M. Short-term intravenous milrinone for acute exacerbation of chronic heart failure: a randomized controlled trial. Jama. 2002;287: 1541–1547.

11. Binanay C, Califf RM, Hasselblad V, O'Connor CM, Shah MR, Sopko G, Stevenson LW, Francis GS, Leier CV, Miller LW. Evaluation study of congestive heart failure and pulmonary artery catheterization effectiveness: the ESCAPE trial. Jama. 2005;294:1625–1633.

12. Cleland JG, Freemantle N, Coletta AP, Clark AL. Clinical trials update from the American Heart Association: REPAIR-AMI, ASTAMI, JELIS, MEGA, REVIVE-II, SURVIVE, and PROACTIVE. Eur J Heart Fail. 2006;8:105–110.

13. Mebazaa A, Nieminen MS, Packer M, Cohen-Solal A, Kleber FX, Pocock SJ, Thakkar R, Padley RJ, Poder P, Kivikko M. Levosimendan vs dobutamine for patients with acute decompensated heart failure: the SURVIVE Randomized Trial. Jama. 2007;297:1883–1891.

14. McMurray JJ, Teerlink JR, Cotter G, Bourge RC, Cleland JG, Jondeau G, Krum H, Metra M, O'Connor CM, Parker JD, Torre-Amione G, van Veldhuisen DJ, Lewsey J, Frey A, Rainisio M, Kobrin I. Effects of tezosentan on symptoms and clinical outcomes in patients with acute heart failure: the VERITAS randomized controlled trials. Jama. 2007;298:2009–2019.

15. Konstam MA, Gheorghiade M, Burnett JC, Jr., Grinfeld L, Maggioni AP, Swedberg K, Udelson JE, Zannad F, Cook T, Ouyang J, Zimmer C, Orlandi C. Effects of oral tolvaptan in patients hospitalized for worsening heart failure: the EVEREST Outcome Trial. Jama. 2007;297:1319–1331.

16. Nieminen MS, Bohm M, Cowie MR, Drexler H, Filippatos GS, Jondeau G, Hasin Y, Lopez-Sendon J, Mebazaa A, Metra M, Rhodes A, Swedberg K, Priori SG, Garcia MA, Blanc JJ, Budaj A, Cowie MR, Dean V, Deckers J, Burgos EF, Lekakis J, Lindahl B, Mazzotta G, Morais J, Oto A, Smiseth OA, Garcia MA, Dickstein K, Albuquerque A, Conthe P, Crespo-Leiro M, Ferrari R, Follath F, Gavazzi A, Janssens U, Komajda M, Morais J,

Moreno R, Singer M, Singh S, Tendera M, Thygesen K. Executive summary of the guidelines on the diagnosis and treatment of acute heart failure: the Task Force on Acute Heart Failure of the European Society of Cardiology. Eur Heart J. 2005;26:384–416.

17. Hunt SA, Abraham WT, Chin MH, Feldman AM, Francis GS, Ganiats TG, Jessup M, Konstam MA, Mancini DM, Michl K, Oates JA, Rahko PS, Silver MA, Stevenson LW, Yancy CW, Antman EM, Smith SC, Jr., Adams CD, Anderson JL, Faxon DP, Fuster V, Halperin JL, Hiratzka LF, Jacobs AK, Nishimura R, Ornato JP, Page RL, Riegel B. ACC/AHA 2005 Guideline Update for the Diagnosis and Management of Chronic Heart Failure in the Adult: a report of the American College of Cardiology/American Heart Association Task Force on Practice Guidelines (Writing Committee to Update the 2001 Guidelines for the Evaluation and Management of Heart Failure): developed in collaboration with the American College of Chest Physicians and the International Society for Heart and Lung Transplantation: endorsed by the Heart Rhythm Society. Circulation. 2005;112:e154–235.

18. Vasan RS, Levy D. Defining diastolic heart failure: a call for standardized diagnostic criteria. Circulation. 2000; 101:2118–2121.

19. Zile MR, Gaasch WH, Carroll JD, Feldman MD, Aurigemma GP, Schaer GL, Ghali JK, Liebson PR. Heart failure with a normal ejection fraction: is measurement of diastolic function necessary to make the diagnosis of diastolic heart failure? Circulation. 2001;104:779–782.

20. Owan TE, Hodge DO, Herges RM, Jacobsen SJ, Roger VL, Redfield MM. Trends in prevalence and outcome of heart failure with preserved ejection fraction. N Engl J Med. 2006;355:251–259.

21. Cohn JN, Johnson G. Heart failure with normal ejection fraction. The V-HeFT Study. Veterans Administration Cooperative Study Group. Circulation. 1990;81:III48–53.

22. Masoudi FA, Havranek EP, Smith G, Fish RH, Steiner JF, Ordin DL, Krumholz HM. Gender, age, and heart failure with preserved left ventricular systolic function. J Am Coll Cardiol. 2003;41:217–223.

23. Vasan RS, Larson MG, Benjamin EJ, Evans JC, Reiss CK, Levy D. Congestive heart failure in subjects with normal versus reduced left ventricular ejection fraction: prevalence and mortality in a population-based cohort. J Am Coll Cardiol. 33:1948–1955.

24. Ghali JK, Kadakia S, Bhatt A, Cooper R, Liao Y. Survival of heart failure patients with preserved versus impaired systolic function: the prognostic implication of blood pressure. Am Heart J. 1992;123:993–997.

25. Aronow WS, Ahn C, Kronzon I. Prognosis of congestive heart failure in elderly patients with normal versus abnormal left ventricular systolic function associated with coronary artery disease. Am J Cardiol. 1990;66:1257–1259.

26. Aronow WS. Epidemiology, pathophysiology, prognosis, and treatment of systolic and diastolic heart failure in elderly patients. Heart Dis. 2003;5:279–294.

27. Senni M, Tribouilloy CM, Rodeheffer RJ, Jacobsen SJ, Evans JM, Bailey KR, Redfield MM. Congestive heart failure in the community: a study of all incident cases in Olmsted County, Minnesota, in 1991. Circulation. 1998; 98:2282–2289.

28. Taffet GE, Teasdale TA, Bleyer AJ, Kutka NJ, Luchi RJ. Survival of elderly men with congestive heart failure. Age and ageing. 1992;21:49–55.

29. McDermott MM, Feinglass J, Lee PI, Mehta S, Schmitt B, Lefevre F, Gheorghiade M. Systolic function, readmission rates, and survival among consecutively hospitalized patients with congestive heart failure. Am Heart J. 1997; 134:728–736.

30. McAlister FA, Teo KK, Taher M, Montague TJ, Humen D, Cheung L, Kiaii M, Yim R, Armstrong PW. Insights into the contemporary epidemiology and outpatient management of congestive heart failure. Am Heart J. 1999;138:87–94.

31. Pernenkil R, Vinson JM, Shah AS, Beckham V, Wittenberg C, Rich MW. Course and prognosis in patients ≥ 70 years of age with congestive heart failure and normal versus abnormal left ventricular ejection fraction. Am J Cardiol. 1997;79:216–219.

32. Warnowicz MA, Parker H, Cheitlin MD. Prognosis of patients with acute pulmonary edema and normal ejection fraction after acute myocardial infarction. Circulation. 1983;67:330–334.

33. Bhatia RS, Tu JV, Lee DS, Austin PC, Fang J, Haouzi A, Gong Y, Liu PP. Outcome of heart failure with preserved ejection fraction in a population-based study. N Engl J Med. 2006;355:260–269.

34. Blackledge HM, Tomlinson J, Squire IB. Prognosis for patients newly admitted to hospital with heart failure: survival trends in 12 220 index admissions in Leicestershire 1993–2001. Heart. 2006;89:615–620.

35. Tribouilloy C, Rusinaru D, Mahjoub H, Souliere V, Levy F, Peltier M, Slama M, Massy Z. Prognosis of heart failure with preserved ejection fraction: a 5 year prospective population-based study. Eur Heart J. 2008;29:339–347.

36. Atherton JJ, Moore TD, Lele SS, Thomson HL, Galbraith AJ, Belenkie I, Tyberg JV, Frenneaux MP. Diastolic ventricular interaction in chronic heart failure. Lancet. 1997;349:1720–1724.

37. Perna ER, Macin SM, Cimbaro Canella JP, Alvarenga PM, Rios NG, Pantich R, Augier N, Farias EF, Jantus E, Brizuela M, Medina F. Minor myocardial damage detected by troponin T is a powerful predictor of long-term prognosis in patients with acute decompensated heart failure. Int J Cardiol. 2005;99:253–261.

38. Perna ER, Macin SM, Parras JI, Pantich R, Farias EF, Badaracco JR, Jantus E, Medina F, Brizuela M. Cardiac troponin T levels are associated with poor short- and long-term prognosis in patients with acute cardiogenic pulmonary edema. Am Heart J. 2002;143:814–820.

39. Benza RL, Tallaj JA, Felker GM, Zabel KM, Kao W, Bourge RC, Pearce D, Leimberger JD, Borzak S, O'Connor C M, Gheorghiade M. The impact of arrhythmias in acute heart failure. J Card Fail. 2004;10:279–284.

40. Hillege HL, Girbes AR, de Kam PJ, Boomsma F, de Zeeuw D, Charlesworth A, Hampton JR, van Veldhuisen DJ. Renal function, neurohormonal activation, and survival in patients with chronic heart failure. Circulation. 2000;102:203–210.

41. Bibbins-Domingo K, Lin F, Vittinghoff E, Barrett-Connor E, Grady D, Shlipak MG. Renal insufficiency as an independent predictor of mortality among women with heart failure. J Am Coll Cardiol. 2004;44:1593–1600.

42. Ezekowitz J, McAlister FA, Humphries KH, Norris CM, Tonelli M, Ghali WA, Knudtson ML. The association among renal insufficiency, pharmacotherapy, and outcomes in 6,427 patients with heart failure and coronary artery disease. J Am Coll Cardiol. 2004;44: 1587–1592.

43. Adams KF, Jr., Fonarow GC, Emerman CL, LeJemtel TH, Costanzo MR, Abraham WT, Berkowitz RL, Galvao M, Horton DP. Characteristics and outcomes of patients hospitalized for heart failure in the United States: rationale, design, and preliminary observations from the first 100,000 cases in the Acute Decompensated Heart Failure National Registry (ADHERE). Am Heart J. 2005; 149:209–216.

44. Hillege HL, Nitsch D, Pfeffer MA, Swedberg K, McMurray JJ, Yusuf S, Granger CB, Michelson EL, Ostergren J, Cornel JH, de Zeeuw D, Pocock S, van Veldhuisen DJ. Renal function as a predictor of outcome in a broad spectrum of patients with heart failure. Circulation. 2006;113:671–678.

45. Gandhi SK, Powers JC, Nomeir AM, Fowle K, Kitzman DW, Rankin KM, Little WC. The pathogenesis of acute pulmonary edema associated with hypertension. N Engl J Med. 2001;344:17–22.

46. Fonarow GC. The Acute Decompensated Heart Failure National Registry (ADHERE): opportunities to improve care of patients hospitalized with acute decompensated heart failure. Rev Cardiovasc Med. 2003;4 Suppl 7: S21–30.

47. Emerman CL. Treatment of the acute decompensation of heart failure: efficacy and pharmacoeconomics of early initiation of therapy in the emergency department. Rev Cardiovasc Med. 2003;4 Suppl 7:S13–20.

48. Peacock WFt, Fonarow GC, Emerman CL, Mills RM, Wynne J. Impact of early initiation of intravenous therapy for acute decompensated heart failure on outcomes in ADHERE. Cardiology. 20067;107:44–51.

49. Bersten AD, Holt AW, Vedig AE, Skowronski GA, Baggoley CJ. Treatment of severe cardiogenic pulmonary edema with continuous positive airway pressure

delivered by face mask. N Engl J Med. 1991;325: 1825–1830.

50. Crane SD, Elliott MW, Gilligan P, Richards K, Gray AJ. Randomised controlled comparison of continuous positive airways pressure, bilevel non-invasive ventilation, and standard treatment in emergency department patients with acute cardiogenic pulmonary oedema. Emerg Med J. 2004;21:155–161.

51. Kelly CA, Newby DE, McDonagh TA, Mackay TW, Barr J, Boon NA, Dargie HJ, Douglas NJ. Randomised controlled trial of continuous positive airway pressure and standard oxygen therapy in acute pulmonary oedema; effects on plasma brain natriuretic peptide concentrations. Eur Heart J. 2002;23:1379–1386.

52. Kelly AM, Georgakas C, Bau S, Rosengarten P. Experience with the use of continuous positive airway pressure (CPAP) therapy in the emergency management of acute severe cardiogenic pulmonary oedema. Aust N Z J Med. 1997;27:319–322.

53. L'Her E, Duquesne F, Girou E, de Rosiere XD, Le Conte P, Renault S, Allamy JP, Boles JM. Noninvasive continuous positive airway pressure in elderly cardiogenic pulmonary edema patients. Intensive Care Med. 2004; 30:882–888.

54. Lin M, Yang YF, Chiang HT, Chang MS, Chiang BN, Cheitlin MD. Reappraisal of continuous positive airway pressure therapy in acute cardiogenic pulmonary edema. Short-term results and long-term follow-up. Chest. 1995; 107:1379–1386.

55. Park M, Sangean MC, Volpe Mde S, Feltrim MI, Nozawa E, Leite PF, Passos Amato MB, Lorenzi-Filho G. Randomized, prospective trial of oxygen, continuous positive airway pressure, and bilevel positive airway pressure by face mask in acute cardiogenic pulmonary edema. Crit Care Med. 2004;32:2407–2415.

56. Park M, Lorenzi-Filho G. Noninvasive mechanical ventilation in the treatment of acute cardiogenic pulmonary edema. Clinics. 2006;61:247–252.

57. Park M, Lorenzi-Filho G, Feltrim MI, Viecili PR, Sangean MC, Volpe M, Leite PF, Mansur AJ. Oxygen therapy, continuous positive airway pressure, or noninvasive bilevel positive pressure ventilation in the treatment of acute cardiogenic pulmonary edema. Arq Bras Cardiol. 2001;76:221–230.

58. Rasanen J, Heikkila J, Downs J, Nikki P, Vaisanen I, Viitanen A. Continuous positive airway pressure by face mask in acute cardiogenic pulmonary edema. Am J Cardiol. 1985;55:296–300.

59. Takeda S, Takano T, Ogawa R. The effect of nasal continuous positive airway pressure on plasma endothelin-1 concentrations in patients with severe cardiogenic pulmonary edema. Anesth Analg. 1997;84: 1091–1096.

60. Takeda S, Nejima J, Takano T, Nakanishi K, Takayama M, Sakamoto A, Ogawa R. Effect of nasal continuous

positive airway pressure on pulmonary edema complicating acute myocardial infarction. Jpn Circ J. 1998;62:553–558.

61. Levitt MA. A prospective, randomized trial of BiPAP in severe acute congestive heart failure. J Emerg Med. 2001;21:363–369.

62. Masip J, Betbese AJ, Paez J, Vecilla F, Canizares R, Padro J, Paz MA, de Otero J, Ballus J. Non-invasive pressure support ventilation versus conventional oxygen therapy in acute cardiogenic pulmonary oedema: a randomised trial. Lancet. 2000;356:2126–2132.

63. Nava S, Carbone G, DiBattista N, Bellone A, Baiardi P, Cosentini R, Marenco M, Giostra F, Borasi G, Groff P. Noninvasive ventilation in cardiogenic pulmonary edema: a multicenter randomized trial. Am J Respir Crit Care Med. 2003;168:1432–1437.

64. Bellone A, Monari A, Cortellaro F, Vettorello M, Arlati S, Coen D. Myocardial infarction rate in acute pulmonary edema: noninvasive pressure support ventilation versus continuous positive airway pressure. Crit Care Med. 2004;32:1860–1865.

65. Bellone A, Vettorello M, Monari A, Cortellaro F, Coen D. Noninvasive pressure support ventilation vs. continuous positive airway pressure in acute hypercapnic pulmonary edema. Intensive Care Med. 2005;31:807–811.

66. Cross AM, Cameron P, Kierce M, Ragg M, Kelly AM. Non-invasive ventilation in acute respiratory failure: a randomised comparison of continuous positive airway pressure and bi-level positive airway pressure. Emerg Med J. 2003;20:531–534.

67. Mehta S, Jay GD, Woolard RH, Hipona RA, Connolly EM, Cimini DM, Drinkwine JH, Hill NS. Randomized, prospective trial of bilevel versus continuous positive airway pressure in acute pulmonary edema. Crit Care Med. 1997;25:620–628.

68. Peter JV, Moran JL, Phillips-Hughes J, Graham P, Bersten AD. Effect of non-invasive positive pressure ventilation (NIPPV) on mortality in patients with acute cardiogenic pulmonary oedema: a meta-analysis. Lancet. 2006;367:1155–1163.

69. Winck JC, Azevedo LF, Costa-Pereira A, Antonelli M, Wyatt JC. Efficacy and safety of non-invasive ventilation in the treatment of acute cardiogenic pulmonary edema – a systematic review and meta-analysis. Crit Care. 2006;10:R69.

70. Truwit JD, Bernard GR. Noninvasive ventilation – don't push too hard. N Engl J Med. 2004;350:2512–2515.

71. Fonarow GC, Yancy CW, Heywood JT. Adherence to heart failure quality-of-care indicators in US hospitals: analysis of the ADHERE Registry. Arch Intern Med. 2005;165: 1469–1477.

72. Adams K, Marco TD, Berkowitz R. Inotrope use and negative outcomes in treatment of acute heart failure in patients with preserved systolic function: data from the ADHERE database. Circulation. 2003;108(Suppl. IV):695.

73. Elkayam U, Tasissa G, Binanay C, Stevenson LW, Gheorghiade M, Warnica JW, Young JB, Rayburn BK, Rogers JG, DeMarco T, Leier CV. Use and impact of inotropes and vasodilator therapy in hospitalized patients with severe heart failure. Am Heart J. 2007; 153:98-104.

74. Felker GM, Benza RL, Chandler AB, Leimberger JD, Cuffe MS, Califf RM, Gheorghiade M, O'Connor CM. Heart failure etiology and response to milrinone in decompensated heart failure: results from the OPTIME-CHF study. J Am Coll Cardiol. 2003;41:997-1003.

75. Thackray S, Easthaugh J, Freemantle N, Cleland JG. The effectiveness and relative effectiveness of intravenous inotropic drugs acting through the adrenergic pathway in patients with heart failure-a meta-regression analysis. Eur J Heart Fail. 2002;4:515-529.

76. O'Connor CM, Gattis WA, Uretsky BF, Adams KF, Jr., McNulty SE, Grossman SH, McKenna WJ, Zannad F, Swedberg K, Gheorghiade M, Califf RM. Continuous intravenous dobutamine is associated with an increased risk of death in patients with advanced heart failure: insights from the Flolan International Randomized Survival Trial (FIRST). Am Heart J. 1999;138:78-86.

77. Bayram M, De Luca L, Massie MB, Gheorghiade M. Reassessment of dobutamine, dopamine, and milrinone in the management of acute heart failure syndromes. Am J Cardiol. 2005;96:47G-58G.

78. Cuffe MS, Califf RM, Adams KF, Bourge RC, Colucci W, Massie B, O'Connor CM, Pina I, Quigg R, Silver M, Robinson LA, Leimberger JD, Gheorghiade M. Rationale and design of the OPTIME CHF trial: outcomes of a prospective trial of intravenous milrinone for exacerbations of chronic heart failure. Am Heart J. 2000;139: 15-22.

79. Shin DD, Brandimarte F, De Luca L, Sabbah HN, Fonarow GC, Filippatos G, Komajda M, Gheorghiade M. Review of current and investigational pharmacologic agents for acute heart failure syndromes. Am J Cardiol. 2007;99: S4-S23.

80. Ewy GA. Inotropic infusions for chronic congestive heart failure: medical miracles or misguided medicinals? J Am Coll Cardiol. 1999;33:572-575.

81. Endoh M. Mechanisms of action of novel cardiotonic agents. J Cardiovasc Pharmacol. 2002;40:323-338.

82. Vallet B, Dupuis B, Chopin C. [Dobutamine: mechanisms of action and use in acute cardiovascular pathology]. Ann Cardiol Angeiol (Paris). 1991;40:397-402.

83. Tavares M, Rezlan E, Vostroknoutova I, Khouadja H, Mebazaa A. New pharmacologic therapies for acute heart failure. Crit Care Med. 2008;36:S112-120.

84. Holubarsch C. New inotropic concepts: rationale for and differences between calcium sensitizers and phosphodiesterase inhibitors. Cardiology. 1997;88 Suppl 2:12-20.

85. Sorsa T, Pollesello P, Rosevear PR, Drakenberg T, Kilpelainen I. Stereoselective binding of levosimendan to cardiac troponin C causes Ca2+-sensitization. Eur J Pharmacol. 2004;486:1-8.

86. Pollesello P, Ovaska M, Kaivola J, Tilgmann C, Lundstrom K, Kalkkinen N, Ulmanen I, Nissinen E, Taskinen J. Binding of a new Ca2+ sensitizer, levosimendan, to recombinant human cardiac troponin C. A molecular modelling, fluorescence probe, and proton nuclear magnetic resonance study. J Biol Chem. 1994;269: 28584-28590.

87. Sorsa T, Pollesello P, Solaro RJ. The contractile apparatus as a target for drugs against heart failure: interaction of levosimendan, a calcium sensitiser, with cardiac troponin c. Mol Cell Biochem. 2004;266:87-107.

88. Duncker DJ, Verdouw PD. Inotropic therapy of heart failure. Editorial comments on: Vasodilation and mechanoenergetic inefficiency dominates the effect of the "Ca2+ sensitizer" MCI-154 in intact pigs. Scand Cardiovasc J. 2002;36:131-135.

89. Toller WG, Stranz C. Levosimendan, a new inotropic and vasodilator agent. Anesthesiology. 2006;104:556-569.

90. Lilleberg J, Sundberg S, Hayha M, Akkila J, Nieminen MS. Haemodynamic dose-efficacy of levosimendan in healthy volunteers. Eur J Clin Pharmacol. 1994;47:267-274.

91. Lilleberg J, Sundberg S, Nieminen MS. Dose-range study of a new calcium sensitizer, levosimendan, in patients with left ventricular dysfunction. J Cardiovasc Pharmacol. 1995;26 Suppl 1:S63-69.

92. Lilleberg J, Nieminen MS, Akkila J, Heikkila L, Kuitunen A, Lehtonen L, Verkkala K, Mattila S, Salmenpera M. Effects of a new calcium sensitizer, levosimendan, on haemodynamics, coronary blood flow and myocardial substrate utilization early after coronary artery bypass grafting. Eur Heart J. 1998;19:660-668.

93. Slawsky MT, Colucci WS, Gottlieb SS, Greenberg BH, Haeusslein E, Hare J, Hutchins S, Leier CV, LeJemtel TH, Loh E, Nicklas J, Ogilby D, Singh BN, Smith W. Acute hemodynamic and clinical effects of levosimendan in patients with severe heart failure. Study Investigators. Circulation. 2000;102:2222-2227.

94. Pagel PS, Hettrick DA, Warltier DC. Influence of levosimendan, pimobendan, and milrinone on the regional distribution of cardiac output in anaesthetized dogs. Br J Pharmacol. 1996;119:609-615.

95. Michaels AD, McKeown B, Kostal M, Vakharia KT, Jordan MV, Gerber IL, Foster E, Chatterjee K. Effects of intravenous levosimendan on human coronary vasomotor regulation, left ventricular wall stress, and myocardial oxygen uptake. Circulation. 2005;111:1504-1509.

96. Kaheinen P, Pollesello P, Levijoki J, Haikala H. Levosimendan increases diastolic coronary flow in isolated guinea-pig heart by opening ATP-sensitive potassium channels. J Cardiovasc Pharmacol. 2001;37:367-374.

97. Gruhn N, Nielsen-Kudsk JE, Theilgaard S, Bang L, Olesen SP, Aldershvile J. Coronary vasorelaxant effect of

levosimendan, a new inodilator with calcium-sensitizing properties. J Cardiovasc Pharmacol. 1998;31:741–749.

98. De Witt BJ, Ibrahim IN, Bayer E, Fields AM, Richards TA, Banister RE, Kaye AD. An analysis of responses to levosimendan in the pulmonary vascular bed of the cat. Anesth Analg. 2002;94:1427–1433, table of contents.

99. Hohn J, Pataricza J, Petri A, Toth GK, Balogh A, Varro A, Papp JG. Levosimendan interacts with potassium channel blockers in human saphenous veins. Basic Clin Pharmacol Toxicol. 2004;94:271–273.

100. Pagel PS, Hettrick DA, Warltier DC. Comparison of the effects of levosimendan, pimobendan, and milrinone on canine left ventricular-arterial coupling and mechanical efficiency. Basic Res Cardiol. 1996;91:296–307.

101. Pataricza J, Hohn J, Petri A, Balogh A, Papp JG. Comparison of the vasorelaxing effect of cromakalim and the new inodilator, levosimendan, in human isolated portal vein. J Pharm Pharmacol. 2000;52: 213–217.

102. Yokoshiki H, Katsube Y, Sunagawa M, Sperelakis N. Levosimendan, a novel Ca2+ sensitizer, activates the glibenclamide-sensitive K+ channel in rat arterial myocytes. Eur J Pharmacol. 1997;333:249–259.

103. Pataricza J, Krassoi I, Hohn J, Kun A, Papp JG. Functional role of potassium channels in the vasodilating mechanism of levosimendan in porcine isolated coronary artery. Cardiovasc Drugs Ther. 2003;17: 115–121.

104. Yokoshiki H, Sperelakis N. Vasodilating mechanisms of levosimendan. Cardiovasc Drugs Ther. 2003;17:111–113.

105. Morelli A, Teboul JL, Maggiore SM, Vieillard-Baron A, Rocco M, Conti G, De Gaetano A, Picchini U, Orecchio-ni A, Carbone I, Tritapepe L, Pietropaoli P, Westphal M. Effects of levosimendan on right ventricular afterload in patients with acute respiratory distress syndrome: a pilot study. Crit Care Med. 2006;34:2287–2293.

106. Kerbaul F, Rondelet B, Demester JP, Fesler P, Huez S, Naeije R, Brimioulle S. Effects of levosimendan versus dobutamine on pressure load-induced right ventricular failure. Crit Care Med. 2006;34:2814–2819.

107. Kivikko M, Antila S, Eha J, Lehtonen L, Pentikainen PJ. Pharmacokinetics of levosimendan and its metabolites during and after a 24-hour continuous infusion in patients with severe heart failure. Int J Clin Pharmacol Ther. 2002;40:465–471.

108. Lehtonen L, Poder P. The utility of levosimendan in the treatment of heart failure. Ann Med. 2007;39:2–17.

109. Nieminen MS, Akkila J, Hasenfuss G, Kleber FX, Lehtonen LA, Mitrovic V, Nyquist O, Remme WJ. Hemodynamic and neurohumoral effects of continuous infusion of levosimendan in patients with congestive heart failure. J Am Coll Cardiol. 2000;36:1903–1912.

110. Follath F, Cleland JG, Just H, Papp JG, Scholz H, Peuhkurinen K, Harjola VP, Mitrovic V, Abdalla M, Sandell EP, Lehtonen L. Efficacy and safety of intravenous levosimendan compared with dobutamine in severe low-output heart failure (the LIDO study): a randomised double-blind trial. Lancet. 2002;360:196–202.

111. Packer M, Colucci W, Fisher L. Development of a comprehensive new endpoint for the evaluation of new treatments for acute decompensated heart failure: results with levosimendan in the REVIVE-1 study. (Abstract). J Card Fail. 2003;9:S61.

112. Packer M, The Randomized multicenter EValuation of Intravenous leVosimendan Efficacy-2 (REVIVE-2) trial. Late-breaking Clinical Trials. American Heart Association, Annual Scientific Session, Dallas, TX, 13–16 November 2005.

113. Tassani P, Schad H, Heimisch W, Bernhard-Abt A, Ettner U, Mendler N, Lange R. Effect of the calcium sensitizer levosimendan on the performance of ischaemic myocardium in anaesthetised pigs. Cardiovasc Drugs Ther. 2002;16:435–441.

114. Jamali IN, Kersten JR, Pagel PS, Hettrick DA, Warltier DC. Intracoronary levosimendan enhances contractile function of stunned myocardium. Anesth Analg. 1997; 85:23–29.

115. Grossini E, Caimmi PP, Molinari C, Teodori G, Vacca G. Hemodynamic effect of intracoronary administration of levosimendan in the anesthetized pig. J Cardiovasc Pharmacol. 2005;46:333–342.

116. De Luca L, Proietti P, Celotto A, Bucciarelli-Ducci C, Benedetti G, Di Roma A, Sardella G, Genuini I, Fedele F. Levosimendan improves hemodynamics and coronary flow reserve after percutaneous coronary intervention in patients with acute myocardial infarction and left ventricular dysfunction. Am Heart J. 2005;150: 563–568.

117. Kersten JR, Montgomery MW, Pagel PS, Warltier DC. Levosimendan, a new positive inotropic drug, decreases myocardial infarct size via activation of K(ATP) channels. Anesth Analg. 2000;90:5–11.

118. Harkin CP, Pagel PS, Tessmer JP, Warltier DC. Systemic and coronary hemodynamic actions and left ventricular functional effects of levosimendan in conscious dogs. J Cardiovasc Pharmacol. 1995;26:179–188.

119. du Toit E, Hofmann D, McCarthy J, Pineda C. Effect of levosimendan on myocardial contractility, coronary and peripheral blood flow, and arrhythmias during coronary artery ligation and reperfusion in the in vivo pig model. Heart. 2001;86:81–87.

120. Ukkonen H, Saraste M, Akkila J, Knuuti J, Karanko M, Iida H, Lehikoinen P, Nagren K, Lehtonen L, Voipio-Pulkki LM. Myocardial efficiency during levosimendan infusion in congestive heart failure. Clin Pharmacol Ther. 2000;68:522–531.

121. De Luca L, Sardella G, Proietti P, Battagliese A, Benedetti G, Di Roma A, Fedele F. Effects of levosi-mendan on left ventricular diastolic function after

primary angioplasty for acute anterior myocardial infarction: a Doppler echocardiographic study. J Am Soc Echocardiogr. 2006;19:172–177.

122. Nieminen M, Moiseyev V, Andrejevs N. Randomized study on safety and effectiveness of levosimendan in patients with left ventricular failure after an acute myocardial infarction (RUSSLAN Trial) [abstract no. 3404]. Circulation. 1996;100: I-646.

123. Lehmann A, Kiessling AH, Isgro F, Zeitler C, Thaler E, Boldt J. Levosimendan in patients with acute myocardial ischaemia undergoing emergency surgical revascularization. European journal of anaesthesiology. 2008;25: 224–229.

124. De Luca L, Colucci WS, Nieminen MS, Massie BM, Gheorghiade M. Evidence-based use of levosimendan in different clinical settings. Eur Heart J. 2006;27: 1908–1920.

125. Mebazaa A, Karpati P, Renaud E, Algotsson L. Acute right ventricular failure – from pathophysiology to new treatments. Intensive Care Med. 2004;30:185–196.

126. Petaja LM, Sipponen JT, Hammainen PJ, Eriksson HI, Salmenpera MT, Suojaranta-Ylinen RT. Levosimendan reversing low output syndrome after heart transplantation. Ann Thorac Surg. 2006;82:1529–1531.

127. Plochl W, Rajek A. The use of the novel calcium sensitizer levosimendan in critically ill patients. Anaesth Intensive Care. 2004;32:471–475.

128. Labriola C, Siro-Brigiani M, Carrata F, Santangelo E, Amantea B. Hemodynamic effects of levosimendan in patients with low-output heart failure after cardiac surgery. Int J Clin Pharmacol Ther. 2004;42:204–211.

129. Nijhawan N, Nicolosi AC, Montgomery MW, Aggarwal A, Pagel PS, Warltier DC. Levosimendan enhances cardiac performance after cardiopulmonary bypass: a prospective, randomized placebo-controlled trial. J Cardiovasc Pharmacol. 1999;34:219–228.

130. Barisin S, Husedzinovic I, Sonicki Z, Bradic N, Barisin A, Tonkovic D. Levosimendan in off-pump coronary artery bypass: a four-times masked controlled study. J Cardiovasc Pharmacol. 2004;44:703–708.

131. Barraud D, Faivre V, Damy T, Welschbillig S, Gayat E, Heymes C, Payen D, Shah AM, Mebazaa A. Levosimendan restores both systolic and diastolic cardiac performance in lipopolysaccharide-treated rabbits: comparison with dobutamine and milrinone. Crit Care Med. 2007;35:1376–1382.

132. Tachibana H, Cheng HJ, Ukai T, Igawa A, Zhang ZS, Little WC, Cheng CP. Levosimendan improves LV systolic and diastolic performance at rest and during exercise after heart failure. Am J Physiol Heart Circ Physiol. 2005;288:H914–922.

133. Hasenfuss G, Pieske B, Kretschmann B, Holubarsch C, Alpert NR, Just H. Effects of calcium sensitizers on intracellular calcium handling and myocardial energetics. J Cardiovasc Pharmacol. 1995;26 Suppl 1: S45–51.

134. Givertz MM, Andreou C, Conrad CH, Colucci WS. Direct myocardial effects of levosimendan in humans with left ventricular dysfunction: alteration of force-frequency and relaxation-frequency relationships. Circulation. 2007;115:1218–1224.

135. Dernellis J, Panaretou M. Effects of levosimendan on restrictive left ventricular filling in severe heart failure: a combined hemodynamic and Doppler echocardiographic study. Chest. 2005;128:2633–2639.

136. Benlolo S, Lefoll C, Katchatouryan V, Payen D, Mebazaa A. Successful use of levosimendan in a patient with peripartum cardiomyopathy. Anesth Analg. 2004; 98:822–824.

137. Benezet-Mazuecos J, de la Hera J. Peripartum cardiomyopathy: A new successful setting for levosimendan. Int J Cardiol. 2007.

138. Nguyen HD, McKeown B. Levosimendan for post-partum cardiomyopathy. Crit Care Resusc. 2005;7:107–110.

139. Villar J, Blazquez MA, Lubillo S, Quintana J, Manzano JL. Pulmonary hypertension in acute respiratory failure. Crit Care Med. 1989;17:523–526.

140. Monchi M, Bellenfant F, Cariou A, Joly LM, Thebert D, Laurent I, Dhainaut JF, Brunet F. Early predictive factors of survival in the acute respiratory distress syndrome. A multivariate analysis. Am J Respir Crit Care Med. 1998; 158:1076–1081.

141. Squara P, Dhainaut JF, Artigas A, Carlet J. Hemodynamic profile in severe ARDS: results of the European Collaborative ARDS Study. Intensive Care Med. 1998; 24:1018–1028.

142. Avgeropoulou C, Andreadou I, Markantonis-Kyroudis S, Demopoulou M, Missovoulos P, Androulakis A, Kallikazaros I. The Ca2+-sensitizer levosimendan improves oxidative damage, BNP and pro-inflammatory cytokine levels in patients with advanced decompensated heart failure in comparison to dobutamine. Eur J Heart Fail. 2005;7:882–887.

143. Maeda K, Tsutamoto T, Wada A, Mabuchi N, Hayashi M, Tsutsui T, Ohnishi M, Sawaki M, Fujii M, Matsumoto T, Kinoshita M. High levels of plasma brain natriuretic peptide and interleukin-6 after optimized treatment for heart failure are independent risk factors for morbidity and mortality in patients with congestive heart failure. J Am Coll Cardiol. 2000;36:1587–1593.

144. Giannakoulas G, Giannoglou G, Vassilikos V, Martiadou K, Kalpidis P, Parharidis G, Louridas G. Clinical significance of acute neurohormonal response after levosimendan treatment. Am J Cardiol. 2006;98: 1123–1124.

145. Logeart D, Thabut G, Jourdain P, Chavelas C, Beyne P, Beauvais F, Bouvier E, Solal AC. Predischarge B-type natriuretic peptide assay for identifying patients at high

risk of re-admission after decompensated heart failure. J Am Coll Cardiol. 2004;43:635–641.

146. Mueller T, Gegenhuber A, Haltmayer M. Levosimendan reduces plasma amino terminal proBNP in patients with decompensated heart failure. Int J Cardiol. 2005;104:355–356; author reply. 357–358.

147. Parissis JT, Panou F, Farmakis D, Adamopoulos S, Filippatos G, Paraskevaidis I, Venetsanou K, Lekakis J, Kremastinos DT. Effects of levosimendan on markers of left ventricular diastolic function and neurohormonal activation in patients with advanced heart failure. Am J Cardiol. 2005;96:423–426.

148. Kyrzopoulos S, Adamopoulos S, Parissis JT, Rassias J, Kostakis G, Iliodromitis E, Degiannis D, Kremastinos DT. Levosimendan reduces plasma B-type natriuretic peptide and interleukin 6, and improves central hemodynamics in severe heart failure patients. Int J Cardiol. 2005;99:409–413.

149. Moertl D, Berger R, Huelsmann M, Bojic A, Pacher R. Short-term effects of levosimendan and prostaglandin E1 on hemodynamic parameters and B-type natriuretic peptide levels in patients with decompensated chronic heart failure. Eur J Heart Fail. 2005;7:1156–1163.

150. McLean AS, Huang SJ, Nalos M, Ting I. Duration of the beneficial effects of levosimendan in decompensated heart failure as measured by echocardiographic indices and B-type natriuretic peptide. J Cardiovasc Pharmacol. 2005;46:830–835.

151. Gegenhuber A, Mueller T, Firlinger F, Lenz K, Poelz W, Haltmayer M. Time course of B-type natriuretic peptide (BNP) and N-terminal proBNP changes in patients with decompensated heart failure. Clin Chem. 2004;50:454–456.

152. Follath F, Franco F, Cardoso JS. European experience on the practical use of levosimendan in patients with acute heart failure syndromes. Am J Cardiol. 2005;96:80G-85G.

Daniel De Backer, Gustavo Ospina-Tascon and Ana Paula Neves

Macro vs. micro targets for haemodynamic support

Introduction

Acute circulatory failure, or shock, is one of the top pre-occupations of intensivists: it is one of the leading causes for ICU admission, and haemodynamic monitoring will be provided in most ICU patients. Shock is associated with a state of inadequate supply or inappropriate use of oxygen and nutrients by the cells that may result in tissue hypoxia and lactic acidosis. Unless transient, this will lead to irreversible tissue damage and death. In order to minimise tissue necrosis and definitive organ injury, adaptations in organ metabolism are likely to occur, shutting down some less essential metabolic pathways in order to preserve vital functions. This will lead to the development of multiple organ failure, which can be reversed if circulatory failure and its cause can be cured. The rationale for haemodynamic support, or resuscitation, is to provide tissues with sufficient amounts of oxygen and nutriments in order to ameliorate organ dysfunction, or at least to prevent further deterioration in organ function.

Global haemodynamic alterations, blood flow redistribution, microvascular blood flow alterations, and direct cellular injury may play a crucial role in the development of multiple organ failure in these patients. It is difficult to prioritise these factors. It is obvious that when the heart is not beating anymore, flow and oxygen cannot reach the cells, whatever the integrity of the other components of the circulation. However, when some

minimal values of cardiac output and pressure are achieved, the role of the other factors may become predominant, and trying to further increase cardiac index or blood pressure may then become useless. Even though the role of mitochondrial dysfunction should not be neglected, hypoxia can further impair mitochondrial function (1). In addition, haemodynamic resuscitation blunts the activation of the inflammation, coagulation and apoptosis (2). The crucial issue will be to determine the targets for haemodynamic resuscitation and the time window during which these should be implemented.

In this chapter we will review the impact of global and regional targeted haemodynamic resuscitation. It will not focus only on outcome, as a recent international consensus conference is available on this topic (3); we will mostly focus on the implications of macrocirculatory and microcirculatory alterations on organ function, and how targets may be proposed. We will focus this review on sepsis even though alterations in macro- and microcirculations have been observed in other conditions than sepsis, as most of the data available were obtained in the field of sepsis.

Controversial position 1: Global haemodynamic alterations and endpoints are important

Septic shock is a complex syndrome characterised by profound cardiovascular derangements, associating alterations in cardiac function, decreased vascular tone, hypovolaemia (related to volume losses related to vascular permeability and to blood pooling in large capacitance veins, and especially in the splanchnic area), altered venous compliance, and myocardial dysfunction (systolic and diastolic). In addition, regional blood flow alterations may occur, especially in the splanchnic area.

What are the consequences of these alterations for haemodynamic monitoring? The combination of hypovolaemia, vasoplegia and myocardial dysfunction leads to inadequate tissue perfusion. Many experimental studies have shown that cardiac output is initially low and that the hyperdynamic state can only be observed after fluid resuscitation (4, 5). In addition, several studies have reported that the severity and duration of hypotension and inadequacy of cardiac output are associated with an impaired outcome (6–8, 9), it is thus likely that the impaired oxygen delivery plays a role in the development of organ dysfunction. The main haemodynamic targets used at the macrocirculatory level are mean arterial pressure and cardiac index and its determinants.

Mean arterial pressure

Mean arterial pressure (MAP) is used as an indices of tissue perfusion. It neglects the outflow pressure (venous pressure, in most cases equal to central venous pressure) and the interstitial pressure of the organ, which can usually be neglected when the patient does not have compartmental syndrome.

Although MAP is usually decreased in septic shock, it can usually be restored by administration of fluids and vasopressors. But what is the target level for MAP? Varpula et al. (9) evaluated the impact of hypotension on outcome in 111 patients with septic shock. Four levels of MAP were used to define hypotension: 60, 65, 70 and 75 mmHg. The duration and severity of hypotension was defined as the area under the predefined level during the first 6 and 48 hours of admission to the ICU. A MAP of 65 mmHg better separated survivors and non-survivors at both time points. However, very few studies have evaluated this target.

In a small study including 10 patients with septic shock, increasing MAP from 65 to 75 and 85 mmHg failed to alter tissue perfusion, evidenced as lactate levels, gastric tonometry and urine output (10). Similar results were subsequently observed in a small randomised trial including 28 patients (11). However, in 14 patients with severe hypotension (MAP around 55 mmHg), correction of hypotension was associated with an increase in urine output and creatinine clearance (12). Altogether these studies included less than 50 patients, we should thus refrain from generalising these data with respect to all patients. Individual factors are likely to affect this goal; a MAP of 65 mmHg seems reasonable for the majority of patients, but some patients may tolerate lower values while others will require higher target values. This was nicely illustrated in a recent study by Deruddre et al. (13). These authors evaluated renal perfusion with echography and observed a huge variability in the response of the patients, even though there was no significant effect for the entire population. Thus, if target values other than 65 mmHg are used, the benefit of using these different targets should always be documented.

Do strategies aiming at restoring a MAP of 65 mmHg improve outcome? In a randomised trial including 224 patients in septic shock, Lin et al. (14) evaluated a protocol based on achievement of a MAP of 65 mmHg to standard therapy. These authors observed a decrease in hospital mortality from 72 % in the control arm to 54 % in the protocol arm.

Cardiac output

Control of perfusion pressure is often insufficient to restore tissue perfusion. Experimental studies have shown that cardiac output is low in the absence of resuscitation and becomes hyperdynamic only when large amounts of fluids are administered. In addition, cardiac output may subsequently decrease, due to myocardial depression. Cardiac output is usually lower in non-survivors than in survivors so that monitoring of cardiac output may be proposed, especially when signs of hypoperfusion persist (3).

However, one of the problems with cardiac output measurement is its interpretation: A given cardiac output value may be adequate for a patient sufficiently and mechanically ventilated, but insufficient for a febrile patient breathing spontaneously. It is therefore not unexpected that no definite value can be considered safe or no specific goal can be defined. Another aspect is timing of interventions: Early interventions seem to be welcome, but for how long should attempts to increase cardiac output be made? Several trials attempting to increase cardiac output have failed (15, 16), and several reasons may be considered to explain this failure: timing issues (optimisation initiated relatively late but maintained for a long period of time), very high doses (up to 200 mcg/kg.min) of dobutamine, target value of cardiac output, and ineffective intervention.

Is it therefore useless to measure cardiac output? Probably not, but no specific goal can be proposed for it. Thus, cardiac output should never be considered in isolation, but our interpretation of cardiac output should always take into account signs of hypoperfusion. When one is willing to try to improve tissue perfusion, then measurements of cardiac output can be useful to detect alterations in whole body blood flow and to ensure that therapies aiming at increasing global perfusion effectively do so.

Venous oxygen saturation

Mixed-venous (SvO_2), and more recently, superior vena cava ($ScvO_2$) O_2 saturations have been proposed in the monitoring of septic shock. SvO_2 reflects the balance between oxygen demand and oxygen supply. Are SvO_2 and $ScvO_2$ equivalent? Probably not, and especially in sepsis, as desaturated blood coming from the inferior vena cava is not taken into account in the measurements of $ScvO_2$.

In a series of 111 patients with septic shock invasively monitored, multivariate analysis identified the time spent with a blood pressure below 65 mmHg but also the time spent during the first 6 and 48 hours of admission to the ICU with a SvO_2 below 65 % as an independent predictor of outcome (9). As a SvO_2 of 65 % is thought to be equivalent to a $ScvO_2$ of 70 %, does this mean that SvO_2 should be maintained above 65 % or $ScvO_2$ above 70 % in patients with septic shock? Probably not. These values can only be used as indicators of global tissue perfusion, patients with lower values of $S(c)vO_2$ may not present signs of hypoperfusion. In addition, timing is a crucial is-

sue. Maintenance of $ScvO_2$ above 70 % already at emergency department admission and for a brief period of time (6 hours) has been shown to improve outcome (17) while later maintenance of SvO_2 above 65 %, and for a long period of time, has proven to be useless (15).

Central venous pressure and other indices of preload

The Surviving Sepsis Guidelines suggest to monitor Central venous pressure (CVP) as an estimate of preload, and that a value of 10 to 12 mmHg should be achieved (18). This issue is highly controversial. CVP and other static measurements of preload (pulmonary artery occluded pressure or cardiac volumes) poorly predict the response to fluids (19). Other and better-performing indices of fluid responsiveness may be used to better predict the response to fluids; however, the key issue is that no specific goal can be recommended. Indeed, increasing preload is mandatory to optimise cardiac output, but preload should not be further increased when cardiac output is considered to be adequate. CVP, and the other indices of preload and indices of fluid responsiveness, are a means to achieve the goal, namely tissue perfusion optimisation via optimisation of cardiac index, but should by no means be a goal in itself.

Macrocirculatory targets for resuscitation – a summary

Early haemodynamic optimisation is associated with a decreased risk of new onset organ failure and death (17). What component of the increased oxygen delivery is the most relevant? Early administration of fluids prolongs survival time in animals (20), but the role of fluid administration in patients with septic shock, and especially in prolonged shock, remains unclear. The role of inotropic agents is also controversial. Combining the findings of the studies by Rivers et al. (17) and Gattinoni et al. (15) it has been proposed that haemodynamic optimisation using fluids, inotropic agents and probably with red blood cell transfusions may be beneficial in the early phases of sepsis (3, 18). In the late stages of sepsis, maintaining oxygen delivery at high levels may not to be beneficial especially when signs of tissue hy-poperfusion are lacking, and fluid restriction may even be considered in some selected cases (21). Nevertheless, it sounds reasonable to avoid tissue hypoperfusion. The lowest tolerable level of oxy-gen delivery has to be defined on an individual basis. The issue will be to detect tissue hypoper-fusion. When signs of tissue hypoperfusion per-sist despite achievement of satisfactory global haemodynamic endpoints, it may be useful to as-sess microcirculatory perfusion (see fig. 1).

Controversial point 2: Microvascular alterations and endpoints are important

Information gained from global haemodynamics may fail to detect alterations in organ perfusion that occur at the organ level. Indeed, microcircu-latory alterations may compromise tissue per-fusion, even when microcirculatory targets are achieved. The microcirculation plays a key role in organ perfusion as it is the primary site for gas and nutrient exchange. In addition, microcircula-tory oxygen delivery cannot be predicted from glo-bal haemodynamic measurements, as haemat-ocrit in capillaries is lower than systemic haema-tocrit and is not linearly distributed, and the con-trol of microcirculation is influenced by different mechanisms.

Multiple experimental studies have demon-strated microvascular alterations characterised by a decrease in total and functional capillary densi-ty, and heterogeneity of blood flow with perfused capillaries in close vicinity of non-perfused capil-laries. These microvascular dysfunctions can lead to cellular alterations (22).

Patients with septic shock also show a marked decrease in the density of total and perfused small vessels (mostly capillaries) and an increase in het-erogeneity of flow (23, 24). These alterations were independent of systemic alterations (25) and can-not be predicted from global haemodynamic mon-itoring. Importantly, the impairment of microcir-culation was more severe in non-survivors (23, 24), and persistent microvascular alterations were associated with development of organ failure and death (26). In the latter study the improvement in microvascular perfusion from day 1 to day 2 was more predictive of outcome than changes in glo-bal haemodynamics or lactate levels.

These alterations can be manipulated, but as stated above, the control of the microcircula-tion is governed by mechanisms differing from macrocirculation. Hence, specific interventions should be expected to be more potent than usual vasoactive agents. Several interventions have al-ready been proven to affect microcirculation, but the effects were sometimes highly variable. The characterisation of the interventions able to im-prove the microcirculation of septic patients is still in progress.

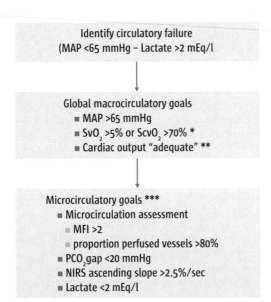

Fig. 1   Tentative goals for resuscitation of macro- and microcirculation in septic shock
* within 6 hours of admission according to Rivers protocol (17) and Surviving Sepsis Guidelines (18).
** after 6 hours (unproven benefit)
*** Goals inferred from observational studies only, no proof of benefit for active manipulation of these variables

Visualisation of microcirculation with small handheld cameras

Orthogonal Polarisation Spectral (OPS) and Side-stream Dark Field (SDF) imaging techniques have recently been introduced and allow the direct vis-ualisation of the microcirculation. These are small handheld microscopes that can be directly applied on superficial tissues covered by a thin epithelial layer such as sublingual mucosa, but ileostomies and colostomies, rectal and vaginal mucosa can also be investigated. Even though observational data clearly identified different microcirculatory patterns in survivors and in non-survivors (23, 24), no specific goal has been validated at this stage. The goals proposed in figure I are inferred from these studies, but these should be validated in interventional studies. In addition, one may consider that achieving a 7% improvement in microvascular perfusion in response to resuscitation manoeuvres would be a reasonable goal (26). This is probably premature as these data have to be confirmed in other observational studies and, if possible, also by prospective interventional studies. However, we are far from this point, as we are still in a process of characterising the interventions that may effectively improve the microcirculation. In addition, these techniques may not yet be ready for widespread use as a monitoring techniques. Firstly, it requires some training particularly to prevent pressure artifacts. Secondly, the semi-quantitative actual scores used have very good reproducibility but are time-consuming (27). Computer-assisted analysis is currently in development, but it still requires major human intervention. Finally, it can mostly be used only on the sublingual area, and this area can be visualised only in sedated or calm patients not supported by non-invasive mechanical ventilation. Having said that, this technique can be used like echocardiography, using some gross evaluation of microvascular perfusion for clinical practice while more refined measurements are needed for research purposes.

Near-infrared spectroscopy (NIRS)

NIRS measures oxygen saturation in tissues, the measurement representing the aggregate of oxygen saturations in the sampling volume (mostly venous blood). This measurement is of limited use in conditions of heterogeneous blood flow, as in sepsis, but an occlusion test can be conducted to evaluate the microvascular response to hypoxia. Several studies have shown that speed of flow recovery after transient occlusion is altered in patients with sepsis (28, 29). This slope mostly but not exclusively reflects the capacity of the micro-

vasculature to recruit arterioles and capillaries, but is also affected by oxygen consumption of the tissues and, at least theoretically, by haemoglobin and O_2 content of the vessels. These alterations were more severe and had a different evolution in non-survivors compared to survivors (30). These techniques are easy to use and easily available. However, goals and interventions still need to be defined.

Reflectance spectroscopy

Reflectance spectroscopy is another technique that can be used to measure tissue SO_2. This technique uses a microlight guide of monochromatic light generated at different wavelengths in the range of 502 to 628 nm, allowing SO_2 measurement due to absorbtion of light by oxy- and deoxyhaemoglobin. The advantage of this technique is that the resolution of the probe allows SO_2 measurements in a very small area while the beam scans a broad piece of tissue. A histogram of tissue SO_2 can be generated, which provides information on heterogeneity in tissue oxygenation and allows disclosure of tiny zones of tissue hypoxia. Reporting only the mean value of tissue SO_2 is misleading, as the advantage of the technique to take into account tissue heterogeneity would be lost. Unfortunately, this error is frequently made by some investigators (31), and no conclusions can the be drawn on the presence or absence of hypoxic areas. Initially, this technique was mostly used under experimental conditions. Embedding this technique on an endoscope, measurements of human gastric SO_2 have shown a huge heterogeneity of gastric mucosal SO_2 in shock (32). Recent developments of the technique have permitted a miniaturisation of the technique, making it suitable for measurement of skin and sublingual SO_2. Although this technique is promising, it can actually only be proposed for research purposes, as normal behavior and key pathophysiological alterations have to be better defined.

Tissue CO₂ measurements

Tissue CO_2 represents the balance between CO_2 production and flow to the tissue. As it is influenced by arterial CO_2, the tissue to arterial gradient, or PCO_2 gap, is usually calculated. The PCO_2 gap can be considered as an indice of the adequacy of flow more than an indice of tissue hypoxia, unless very large PCO_2 gap values are reached (33). Gastric tonometry was the first to be used, but this technique has almost been abandoned, mostly due to technical problems (interference of duodeno-gastric reflux and feeding with PCO_2 measurements), even though some consider it to actually be the only monitoring technique that has proven to improve outcome (27). A gastric PCO_2 gap above 20 mmHg has been found to discriminate survivors from non-survivors (34). Recently, sublingual and buccal PCO_2 monitoring has been developed (35). Sublingual PCO_2 is altered in sepsis, and non-survivors present more severe alterations (36). Using this technique, we demonstrated that sublingual PCO_2 tracks microvascular blood flow, as the sublingual PCO_2 gap is inversely related with the proportion of perfused capillaries (37). Although attractive, this technique is not widely available.

Lactate measurements

Lactate measurements can be used to assess the impact of tissue perfusion on cellular metabolism, even though other causes than tissue hypoxia are sometimes responsible for the increased lactate levels (38). Lactate levels can be used to identify patients at risk of developing organ failure and death (39, 40). Several groups have reported that the magnitude of the decrease in lactate levels under the influence of resuscitative procedures.

As macro- and microcirculatory alterations often coexist, it is difficult to discriminate which is more likely to contribute to lactic acidosis. We recently demonstrated that the decrease in lactate levels induced by dobutamine administration was proportional to the improvement in microcirculation while it was not related to the changes in cardiac index and blood pressure, suggesting that microcirculation was a key determinant of tissue perfusion and hence lactic acidosis (25).

Summary and discussion

Macro- versus microcirculatory goals for resuscitation?

It is of course difficult to prioritise macro- and microcirculatory alterations. The microcirculation, as a whole, is crucial as it is the place where oxygen exchanges take place. On the other hand, the macrocirculation is also important as it provides flow to the microcirculation. Few studies compared the prognostic value of global and microcirculatory alterations (23, 26, 41). In a small series of 28 critically ill patients, Poeze et al. (41) observed that global haemodynamic variables were rather the strongest predictors of outcome on admission, while after haemodynamic stabilisation gastric tonometric variables and liver indocyanine green clearance became important predictors of outcome. In a series of 49 patients with septic shock, we observed that changes in microvascular perfusion between day of admission and subsequent days were more closely associated with outcome than changes in any other global haemodynamic variable (26). However, it should be noted that that in both cases minimal haemodynamic resuscitation based on global haemodynamic variables was already undertaken in the Emergency Department.

It may thus be logical to propose some initial and thus, early, haemodynamic resuscitation. Once these goals are achieved, we would propose to assess the microcirculation, especially if signs of tissue hypoperfusion or organ dysfunction are present (see fig. 1).

One goal for all or patient-centered resuscitation?

Multiple studies have shown that perioperative haemodynamic optimisation improves outcome in high-risk surgery patients, and this was achieved using various haemodynamic targets including optimisation of cardiac output, SvO_2, and preload. In the less severely ill patients optimisation of preload with fluids (reaching a point at which stroke volume can not be further increased by additional fluids) seems sufficient, while in the most severe patients reaching a fixed value of DO_2 has to be targeted, using inotropic agents if needed.

In patients with septic shock, such an approach has failed (15, 16), with the exception of the Rivers study (17). Although timing is important, one should also take into account the huge heterogeneity of the patients. Patients with sepsis present a greater heterogeneity compared to patients in the perioperative setting who are submitted to standard procedures, including anaesthetic regimen.

Accordingly, it is likely that individualised approaches would be more adapted than standardised approaches. This is likely to be true for macro- and microcirculatory variables. Accordingly, one should always be very cautious when using predefined goals.

Key points for clinical practice

- *Macro- and microvascular alterations are a hallmark of circulatory failure and especially of septic shock.*
- *Both have been shown to be more severe in non-survivors.*
- *No specific macro- or microvascular target can be recommended in septic shock, with the exception of macrocirculatory goals for initial resuscitation.*
- *After the initial phase of resuscitation, it may be reasonable to prevent further tissue hypoperfusion.*
- *Macrovascular targets should include a mean arterial pressure above 65 mmHg and a reasonably adapted cardiac index.*
- *Microvascular alterations may be present even when these reasonable macrovascular goals have been achieved. Actually, no specific microvascular target can be provided even though it may appear logical to try to minimise these alterations.*

Key words

Shock, microcirculation, lactate, outcome, tissue oxygenation, organ failure.

The authors

Daniel De Backer, MD, PhD
Gustavo Ospina-Tascon, MD
Ana Paula Neves, MD
    Department of Intensive Care | Erasme
    University Hospital | Université Libre
    de Bruxelles (ULB), Belgium

Address for correspondence
    Daniel De Backer
    Department of Intensive Care
    Erasme University Hospital
    Route de Lennik 808
    1070 Brussels, Belgium
    e-mail: ddebacke@ulb.ac.be

References

1. Frost MT, Wang Q, Moncada S, Singer M. Hypoxia accelerates nitric oxide-dependent inhibition of mitochondrial complex I in activated macrophages. Am J Physiol Regul Integr Comp Physiol.2005;288:R394–R400.
2. Rivers EP, Kruse JA, Jacobsen G, Shah K, Loomba M, Otero R et al. The influence of early hemodynamic optimization strategies on biomarker patterns of severe sepsis and septic shock. Crit Care Med. 2007;35: 2016–2024.
3. Antonelli M, Levy M, Andrews PJ, Chastre J, Hudson LD, Manthous C et al. Hemodynamic monitoring in shock and implications for management: International Consensus Conference, Paris, France, 27–28 April 2006. Intensive Care Med. 2007.
4. Cholley BP, Lang RM, Berger DS, Korcarz C, Payen D, Shroff SG. Alterations in systemic arterial mechanical properties during septic shock: role of fluid resuscitation. Am J Physiol. 1995;269:H375–H384.
5. De Backer D, Zhang H, Cherkhaoui S, Borgers M, Vincent JL. Effects of dobutamine on hepato-splanchnic hemodynamics in an experimental model of hyperdynamic endotoxic shock. Shock 2001;15:208–214.
6. Shoemaker WC, Appel PL, Kram HB, Bishop MH, Abraham E. Sequence of physiologic patterns in surgical septic shock. Crit Care Med. 1993;21:1876–1889.
7. Shoemaker WC, Appel PL, Kram HB, Bishop MH, Abraham E. Temporal hemodynamic and oxygen transport patterns in medical patients: septic shock. Chest. 1993;104:1529–1536.
8. Tuchschmidt J, Fried J, Astiz M, Rackow E. Elevation of cardiac output and oxygen delivery improves outcome in septic shock. Chest. 1992;102:216–220.
9. Varpula M, Tallgren M, Saukkonen K, Voipio-Pulkki LM, Pettila V. Hemodynamic variables related to outcome in septic shock. Intensive Care Med. 2005;31:1066–1071.
10. LeDoux D, Astiz ME, Carpati CM, Rackow EC. Effects of perfusion pressure on tissue perfusion in septic shock. Crit Care Med. 2000;28:2729–2732.
11. Bourgoin A, Leone M, Delmas A, Garnier F, Albanese J, Martin C. Increasing mean arterial pressure in patients with septic shock: effects on oxygen variables and renal function. Crit Care Med. 2005;33:780–786.
12. Albanese J, Leone M, Garnier F, Bourgoin A, Antonini F, Martin C. Renal effects of norepinephrine in septic and nonseptic patients. Chest. 2004;126:534–539.
13. Deruddre S, Cheisson G, Mazoit JX, Vicaut E, Benhamou D, Duranteau J. Renal arterial resistance in septic shock: effects of increasing mean arterial pressure with norepinephrine on the renal resistive index assessed with Doppler ultrasonography. Intensive Care Med. 2007;33:1557–1562.
14. Lin SM, Huang CD, Lin HC, Liu CY, Wang CH, Kuo HP. A modified goal-directed protocol improves clinical

outcomes in intensive care unit patients with septic shock: a randomized controlled trial. Shock. 2006;26: 551–557.

15. Gattinoni L, Brazzi L, Pelosi P, Latini R, Tognoni G, Pesenti A et al. A trial of goal-oriented hemodynamic therapy in critically ill patients. N Engl J Med. 1995;333: 1025–1032.

16. Hayes MA, Timmins AC, Yau EHS, Palazzo M, Hinds CJ, Watson D. Elevation of systemic oxygen delivery in the treatment of critically ill patients. N Engl J Med. 1994; 330:1717–1722.

17. Rivers E, Nguyen B, Havstadt S, Ressler J, Muzzin A, Knoblich B et al. Early goal-directed therapy in the treatment of severe sepsis and septic shock. N Engl J Med. 2001;345:1368–1377.

18. Dellinger RP, Levy MM, Carlet JM, Bion J, Parker MM, Jaeschke R et al. Surviving Sepsis Campaign: International guidelines for management of severe sepsis and septic shock: 2008. Intensive Care Med. 2008;34:17–60.

19. Osman D, Ridel C, Ray P, Monnet X, Anguel N, Richard C et al. Cardiac filling pressures are not appropriate to predict hemodynamic response to volume challenge. Crit Care Med. 2007;35:64–68.

20. Hollenberg SM, Dumasius A, Easington C, Colilla SA, Neumann A, Parrillo JE. Characterization of a hyper-dynamic murine model of resuscitated sepsis using echocardiography. Am J Respir Crit Care Med. 2001; 164:891–895.

21. Wiedemann HP, Wheeler AP, Bernard GR, Thompson BT, Hayden D, deBoisblanc B et al. Comparison of two fluid-management strategies in acute lung injury. N Engl J Med. 2006;354:2564–2575.

22. Eipel C, Bordel R, Nickels RM, Menger MD, Vollmar B. Impact of leukocytes and platelets in mediating hepatocyte apoptosis in a rat model of systemic endotoxemia. Am J Physiol Gastrointest Liver Physiol. 2004;286:G769–G776.

23. De Backer D, Creteur J, Preiser JC, Dubois MJ, Vincent JL. Microvascular blood flow is altered in patients with sepsis. Am J Respir Crit Care Med. 2002;166:98–104.

24. Trzeciak S, Dellinger RP, Parrillo JE, Guglielmi M, Bajaj J, Abate NL et al. Early Microcirculatory Perfusion Derangements in Patients With Severe Sepsis and Septic Shock: Relationship to Hemodynamics, Oxygen Transport, and Survival. Ann Emerg Med. 2007;49:88–98.

25. De Backer D, Creteur J, Dubois MJ, Sakr Y, Koch M, Verdant C et al. The effects of dobutamine on microcircula-tory alterations in patients with septic shock are independent of its systemic effects. Crit Care Med. 2006;34: 403–408.

26. Sakr Y, Dubois MJ, De Backer D, Creteur J, Vincent J-L. Persistant microvasculatory alterations are associated with organ failure and death in patients with septic shock. Crit Care Med. 2004;32:1825–1831.

27. De Backer D, Hollenberg S, Boerma C, Goedhart P, Buchele G, Ospina-Tascon G et al. How to evaluate the microcirculation: report of a round table conference. Crit Care. 2007;11:R101.

28. Pareznik R, Knezevic R, Voga G, Podbregar M. Changes in muscle tissue oxygenation during stagnant ischemia in septic patients. Intensive Care Med. 2006;32:87–92.

29. De Blasi RA, Palmisani S, Alampi D, Mercieri M, Romano R, Collini S et al. Microvascular dysfunction and skeletal muscle oxygenation assessed by phase-modula-tion near-infrared spectroscopy in patients with septic shock. Intensive Care Med. 2005;31:1661–1668.

30. Creteur J, Carollo T, Soldati G, Buchele G, De Backer D, Vincent JL. The prognostic value of muscle StO(2) in septic patients. Intensive Care Med. 2007;33:1549–1556.

31. Albuszies G, Radermacher P, Vogt J, Wachter U, Weber S, Schoaff M et al. Effect of increased cardiac output on hepatic and intestinal microcirculatory blood flow, oxygenation, and metabolism in hyperdynamic murine septic shock. Crit Care Med. 2005;33:2332–2338.

32. Temmesfeld-Wollbrück B, Szalay A, Mayer K, Olschewski H, Seeger W, Grimminger F. Abnormalities of gastric mucosal oxygenation in septic shock. Am J Respir Crit Care Med. 1998;157:1586–1592.

33. Schlichtig R, Bowles SA. Distinguishing between aerobic and anaerobic appearance of dissolved CO_2 in intestine during low flow. J Appl Physiol. 1994;76:2443–2451.

34. Levy B, Gawalkiewicz P, Vallet B, Briancon S, Nace L, Bollaert PE. Gastric capnometry with air-automated tonometry predicts outcome in critically ill patients. Crit Care Med. 2003;31:474–480.

35. Weil MH, Nakagawa Y, Tang W, Sato Y, Ercoli F, Finegan R et al. Sublingual capnometry: a new noninvasive measurement for diagnosis and quantitation of severity of circulatory shock. Crit Care Med. 1999;27:1225–1229.

36. Marik PE. Sublingual capnography: a clinical validation study. Chest. 2001;120:923–927.

37. Creteur J, De Backer D, Sakr Y, koch M, Vincent JL. Sublingual capnometry tracks microcirculatory changes in septic patients. Intensive Care Med. 2006;32:516–523.

38. De Backer D. Lactic acidosis. Intensive Care Med. 2003;29:699–702.

39. Trzeciak S, Dellinger RP, Chansky ME, Arnold RC, Schorr C, Milcarek B et al. Serum lactate as a predictor of mortality in patients with infection. Intensive Care Med. 2007;33:970–977.

40. Howell MD, Donnino M, Clardy P, Talmor D, Shapiro NI. Occult hypoperfusion and mortality in patients with suspected infection. Intensive Care Med. 2007;33: 1892–1899.

41. Poeze M, Solberg BC, Greve JW, Ramsay G. Monitoring global volume-related hemodynamic or regional variables after initial resuscitation: What is a better predictor of outcome in critically ill septic patients? Crit Care Med. 2005;33:2494–2500.

Jan Poelaert and Vincent Umbrain

Right heart failure determines outcome

The right ventricle has an intriguing function within the cardiovascular system. Although the importance of its role has long been denied, during the last decades research has shown its importance in critical disease states. With respect to outcomes of the critically ill, the role of the right ventricle can be investigated as part of the whole cardiac function, or whether the right ventricle itself plays an interfering factor. Acute disease may interfere strongly with right ventricular function. A combination of diminished function based on myocardial ischaemia and increased afterload could hamper outcome considerably, not in the least by burdening left ventricular filling.

The right ventricle (RV) has been considered the minor cardiac chamber since long ago. This opinion has been revised as recent investigations over the past three decades have demonstrated the importance of the RV in particular in critically ill patients with cardiac failure.

The aim of the current review is to provide an update on the importance of the RV with respect to outcome. Some physiologic and pathophysiologic reflections will be reviewed. Moreover, we present a framework for assessing the RV and discuss some RV supportive measures.

Introduction

Both anatomical and physiological features have to be described to allow proper understanding of RV function in disease.

Anatomy

The RV is a thin-walled structure with a muscular mass of $\pm 15\%$ in comparison with the LV mass and a RV stroke work $\pm 25\%$ of LV capacity. The RV can be imagined as a flattened inversed tetrahedron mounted upon a tubular structure. The first part represents the inlet and is actually crescent shaped; the second tubular part is the outlet of the RV. The combination of both structures already demonstrates the geometrical difficulty in imaging this part of the heart. The tetrahedron is built up of four walls (inferior and septal walls, the tricuspid valve and the interventricular septum). At the level of the transition of the tetrahedronic and tubular structure, a crista supraventricularis, a U-shaped band, is present separating the rough surface of the RV inlet component and the smooth RV outlet element, besides a smaller moderator band connecting the distal interventricular septum and the free wall of the RV. The outlet part ends at the pulmonary valve.

Pathophysiology

Several issues with respect to the optimal perception of cardiac function have to be considered:

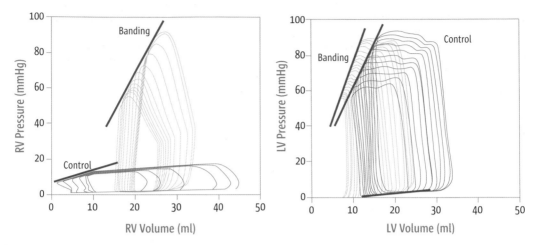

Fig. 1   Right ventricular (left panel) and left ventricular (right panel) pressure-volume loops before (control) and after induction of acute pulmonary arterial hypertension (banding). From: Leeuwenburgh BPJ et al. Biventricular systolic function in young lambs subject to chronic systemic right ventricular pressure overload. Am J Physiol – Heart Circ Physiol. 2001;281:H2697-H2704. Used with permission from The American Physiological Society.

1. pumping function,
2. preloading conditions,
3. afterload.

The venous return fills the RV mainly in early diastole, after which RA contraction finalises RV filling. The contraction pattern of the RV is complex, comprising subsequently descent of the tricuspid valve, contraction of the free RV wall and contraction of the interventricular septum. A peristalsis movement propels the blood into the right ventricular outflow tract; the pulmonary valve opens when RV systolic pressure exceeds pulmonary diastolic pressure.

RV systolic performance is not in the least determined by the same factors. The RV is characterised by a low pressure-high volume making it very sensitive to dysfunction and dilatation with increased afterloading conditions. These characteristics make RV physiology much different from left heart physiology. In normal physiological conditions, pulmonary vascular resistance is only 10 % of the systemic vascular resistance, albeit the initial parts of the pulmonary vascular bed has a larger compliance than main systemic arteries. Whereas the LV easily handles pressure alterations over a wide range, it hardly can resist large volume changes. In contrast, the RV suffers rapidly from pressure overload and will cope with

larger volume shifts. Hence, preload determines primarily RV systolic function according to the Frank-Starling curve (see fig. 1).

The RV ejection continues even when RV pressure declines resulting in typical triangular pressure-volume loops. The isovolumic contraction time is the time between the opening of both valves and is very short. The perfusion of the RV muscle occurs throughout the whole cardiac cycle with two phases, in contrast to the LV in which coronary perfusion occurs only in diastole. The longer myocardial perfusion is advantageous as the oxygen extraction ratio of the RV myocardium is higher than of the LV muscle.

RV function may be hampered by three major issues: myocardial ischaemia, volume overload and/or pressure overload. Often, several of these issues are involved with RV failure. Volume overload is either due to congenital or acquired disease as there is atrial septum defect, persistent left superior caval vein or important tricuspid regurgitation. Always, volume overload will lead to dilation of the RV with subsequent decompensation. Acute pressure overload is the consequence of pulmonary embolism, severely decreased pulmonary compliance as with atelectasis, extensive pneumonia, ARDS etc. With RV ischaemia, the dilatation of the RV will diminish and disappear over a period of several weeks/months (1, 2). In contrast, acute pulmonary hypertension will initiate RV contractile dysfunction following pressure overload, however, without arguments of RV ischaemia (3). Not the extent of PHT but the integrity of the RV and the way the RV copes with this pressure overload will determine outcome.

Secondary tricuspid regurgitation could result in additional volume overload. Prolonged dilatation of the RV will certainly lead to decreased coronary perfusion, hampering further pumping function and aggravating RV failure. The dilatation of the RV is then a concomitant factor augmenting the tricuspid regurge flow, which often originates initially from increased pulmonary artery pressures.

The sole reaction to acute disease of the RV is dysfunction and dilation. Dysfunction relates to a significantly reduced kinesis of the RV free wall and RVOT, without dilation of the RV. Dilation includes bulging of the free RV wall and flattening of the interventricular septum, increasing the RV end-diastolic volume considerably. The differential diagnosis between dysfunction and dilatation of the RV can be most easily made at the bedside with echocardiography (vide infra). With dilation of the RV, the triangular shape of the pressure-volume loop shifts towards a quadrangular structure, similar to the LV function loops (see fig. 1). The biphasic pattern of the coronary perfusion is reduced to a diastolic perfusion, similar to LV muscle perfusion. With progression of acute disease, the RV will hypertrophy when chronicity of the disease persists. Figure 1 exemplifies the dilation of the RV in normal and diseased circumstances. With stiffening of the interventricular septum, LV compliance will also become severely hampered.

Myocardial ischaemia

RV ischaemia occurs in ± 50 % of patients with acute infero-posterior myocardial infarction, sometimes resulting in severe burden of circulation, with systemic hypotension, low cardiac output and cardiogenic shock (4). Perfusion of the right coronary artery (RCA) will be hampered whenever occlusion of this vessel occurs; furthermore, acute albeit prolonged dilatation of the right chamber will squeeze the RCA, hindering adequate perfusion to the myocardium.

Acute right coronary artery (RCA) occlusion proximal to the RV branches results in right ventricular free wall dysfunction, in conjunction with the posterior two-thirds of the interventricular septum and the postero-inferior wall segments. The pumping function of the RV will be disabled, strongly hampering also the function of the LV and decreasing LV preload. The ischaemic RV has a low compliance, is dilated, and volume dependent, resulting in pandiastolic RV dysfunction and septally-mediated alterations in LV compliance, which are exacerbated by elevated intrapericardial pressure. Under these conditions, RV pressure generation and output are dependent on LV-septal contractile contributions, governed by both primary septal contraction and paradoxical septal motion.

When the culprit coronary lesion is distal to the right atrial (RA) branches, augmented RA contractility enhances RV performance and optimises cardiac output (2). Conversely, more proximal occlusions result in ischaemic depression of RA contractility, which impairs RV filling, thereby resulting in further depression of RV performance and more severe haemodynamic compromise. Bradyarrhythmias limit the output generated by the rate-dependent noncompliant ventricles. Patients with right ventricular infarction and haemodynamic compromise often respond to volume resuscitation and restoration of a physiological rhythm. Vasodilators and diuretics should generally be avoided. In some, inotropic or even vasopressor stimulation may be required. The latter will improve coronary perfusion, which will enable recovery of RV systolic function.

RV function assessment

The complexity of the RV chamber makes it difficult to properly assess RV function. Right ventricular ejection fraction has been used as a measure of right ventricular function but has been found to be dependent on loading conditions and ventricular interaction as well as on myocardial structure. Right ventricular function and regional wall motion can be determined with right ventricular angiography, radionuclide ventriculography, two-dimensional echocardiography or magnetic resonance imaging. However, the intricate structure of the RV and its pronounced translational movements render quantification difficult. True regional wall motion analysis is, however, possible with myocardial tagging based on magnetic resonance techniques. With this technique a baso-apical shear motion of the RV was observed which was enhanced in patients with aortic stenosis (5). However, all these techniques are not very useful in ICU patients, with high PEEP ventilation and severe hypoxaemia. Therefore bedside techniques such as echocardiography should be primarily preferred in assessing RV systolic and diastolic function. Tricuspid annular plane systolic excursion (6) is a relatively easy echocardiographic technique, providing a good prognostic indicator in ischaemic cardiomyopathy (7). Haemodynamic monitoring including a pulmonary artery catheter should be combined with intermittent echo-Doppler, whenever haemodynamically important PHT is present. This suggests that acute PHT necessitates to the association of techniques in a second plan, whereas chronic states of permanently increased afterload will be tolerated much better. Table 1 provides a framework on how to assess the RV in clinical practice.

Tab. 1   Simple framework to assess the right ventricle with echocardiography in a critically ill patient

1. Assessment of RV dilation:
    start short axis; comparison of LV and RV. Once the RV is > 60 % of the diameter of the LV, RV dilation is present;

2. Evaluation of tricuspid forward flow and presence of tricuspid regurge flow;

3. Four chamber view to assess the interventricular and interatrial septum; bulging towards the left, suggests higher pressure in the right heart;

4. Visualization of the inferior caval vein:
    large variation (> 50 %) in a mechanically ventilated patient suggests fluid responsiveness and adequate RV function; in dilated RV, the ventilation induced diameter variation will be (nearly) absent.

Right heart failure has minor influence on outcome

From the above stated physiological and pathophysiological explanations, it is clear that right heart failure may interfere with normal homeostasis, including the normal functioning of the LV.

In a risk-stratified study of patients admitted with RV myocardial infarction, it was obvious that more than 60 % did not suffer from RV failure, in contrast to 12 % with cardiogenic shock and 23 % with RV failure (8). Neither interventional nor thrombolytic therapy did have an effect on outcome in the subsets with absence of RV failure or RV failure without cardiogenic shock. In particular those patients suffering from cardiogenic shock in conjunction with a RV myocardial infarction, known to have a comparable mortality as those suffering from LV infarction (4), should be considered for immediate interventional management (9).

The RV has, however, intrinsic protection mechanisms. RV ischaemia occurs in about half of the patients presenting with an inferoposterior myocardial infarction (1). Cardiogenic shock following right ventricular ischaemia, in ± 25 % of these patients present, is characterised by initially normal LV systolic function albeit low output, diminished left-sided preload and disproportionately increased right-sided filling pressures (4). Still, right heart failure may have a good outcome due to some compensatory mechanisms. With a dysfunctional RV free wall, the RV systolic pressure will be generated mainly by LV septal wall contractions. In addition, as long as the RA perfusion is not hindered, this chamber will still participate in the RV filling with increased contractility, reinforcing the atrial 'kick'. Loss of this atrial contribution compromises RV filling considerably (10, 11). Furthermore, whenever right ventricular perfusion could be restored by thrombolysis or any other PCI technique, many patients recover and survive. Even in patients with cardiogenic shock secondary to predominant LV failure, the presence of RV dilatation and dysfunction identifies a subgroup of patients with predominant inferior myocardial infarction and an improved long-term prognosis (12).

A point of discussion remains the reaction of the RV against increased afterload: some investigators claim the RV increases contractility as reaction on afterload increase (13) or shows a tendency of augmented function (14), although this thesis is contradicted in autonomically blocked conscious dogs by others (15). A protagonist study showed thoracic epidural anaesthesia (sympatholysis) inhibits the native positive inotropic response of the right ventricle to increased afterload and deteriorates the haemodynamic effects of acute pulmonary hypertension (16).

One of the important issues with respect to survival is the adequacy of LV filling in patients with manifest RV failure and pulmonary hypertension. Once LV filling is hampered rapid deterioration may occur with significant RV myocardial wall hypoperfusion and subsequent failure. Superposing pulmonary hypertension is often the major problem. The structure, geometry and abruptness of the increase of pulmonary artery pressures, the RV will dictate whether the RV can cope with PHT. Mild PHT is characterised by a mean pulmonary artery pressure (PAP) less than 30 mmHg; moderate PHT corresponds to a PAP of 30–45 mmHg; severe PHT relates to PAP > 45 mmHg. Acute PHT, lasting less than 2 h, does not direct the RV into irreversible dysfunction, as was shown in an animal study (3), without any change in epi/endo blood flow ratio, coronary sinus pH or lactate content. However, hypoxic pulmonary vasoconstriction, pulmonary fibrosis, ARDS, in conjunction with high PEEP ventilation or/and presence of pulmonary oedema are common causes of PHT, inducing long-lasting effects on the RV and the circulation in general.

Selective vasodilators were extensively tested in various settings. Administration of NO to patients with RV myocardial infarction and signs of cardiogenic shock, permits rapid recovery and restoration of perfusion pressure (17). NO induces selective pulmonary vasodilation, with subsequent improved RV performance and restoration of perfusion and cardiac output, preventing any haemodynamic effect on the systemic circulation. This again implies improvement of coronary perfusion at the RV side. After initial proper support, prognosis of RV myocardial infarction patients is good (18, 19). In contrast, epoprostenol (20), another pulmonary vascular dilator, appears to have marked negative influence on RV contractility in an experimental setting of acute PHT (21). Nevertheless, although knowledge identifying important factors influencing improved outcome in cardiac failure is built up progressively (22), larger trials on the effects of specific medication to improve RV failure are still lacking.

The sole field the predictive value of the response of the RV has been really tested is preoperative evaluation of cardiac transplant candidates (23, 24). In patients with advanced chronic heart failure and PHT, testing the reversibility of the PHT portends useful information on the short-term outcome (25). This evaluation must include RV function testing: an improvement of RV performance with acute RV afterload reduction suggests a better outcome than reduction of the pulmonary vascular resistance as such. Furthermore, as the pulmonary venous pressure determines the degree of PHT in potential cardiac transplant patients, a reduction of this pulmonary venous pressure appears the key point in this setting (26).

Right heart failure plays a major role in the outcome of the critically ill

The importance of the RV as a determinant of clinical symptoms, exercise capacity, perioperative survival and postoperative outcome has been underestimated for a long time. Altered LV function in patients with valvular disease influences RV performance mainly by changes in afterload but also by ventricular interaction.

From a pathophysiological point of view, it is obvious that PHT will interfere with the proper activity of the RV by serial and parallel interaction. Moderate PHT may induce an increase of RV contractility, increasing the flow. However, the present PHT reduces the venous return to the LV, hampering optimal cardiac output (serial interaction). This output is further decreased due to a leftward shift of the interventricular septum due to RV dilation (parallel interaction). The pressure overload within the RV will also induce volume overload following important tricuspid regurgitation. Finally, perfusion of the myocardium is hampered by a reduction of the perfusion pressure, following reduced cardiac output and will further hinder optimal activity of the RV, in particular against an increased afterload.

Although the RV may have an in-built mechanism to overcome these problems, it appears that the balance between preload, systolic function and afterload could become unsteady. Dysregulation of the whole balance will induce further deterioration of the circulation leading rapidly or progressively to an irreversible collapse. Hence, RV function is one of the key issues determining the course of the haemodynamics. Besides RV function, LV contractile function and relaxation properties in response to PHT may deteriorate (27), explaining in part why volume therapy may not help to support the circulation. The latter study suggests that optimalisation of LV preload is an important key issue in restoring the imbalance between RV and LV, besides the afterload reduction at the level of the right heart.

The critical balance between all these variables may be best observed in patients after cardiopulmonary bypass, in whom the right ventricular myocardium was not perfectly preserved and/or cooled with cardioplegic solution (28). Moderate PHT after bypass could already induce important RV failure and unbalance RV/LV interaction (29). The present preoperative optimization before and postoperative follow up after cardiac transplantation is another pertinent example of this critical balance between RV afterload, RV function and LV preloading conditions (25, 30, 31). At multivariate analysis, independent predictors of transplant-free survival were found to be RV systolic function (RVEF (p = 0.001), RV stroke work index (p = 0.015), RV end-diastolic volume (p = 0.034) and LV preload (left ventricular end-diastolic volume (p = 0.048)), but not LVEF (30).

In patients with functional moderate to severe mitral regurgitation, RV function has a decisive role with respect to outcome (32). Both RV systolic function, assessed by the tricuspid annular plane systolic excursion, and LV ejection fraction were predictive of death from all causes. Although data show a significant difference between the groups of patients with different tricuspid annular plane systolic excursion with respect to aminoterminal pro-B natriuretic peptide (BNP), clinical decision making for outcome determination remains difficult because of a large overlap between patient data. After 24 months, survival was only 45% in patients with the worst RV function whereas in patients with good RV function outcome was up to 82% (32).

Also, in congenital cardiac surgical patients after correction of transposition of great arteries including a ventricular septum defect, RV failure exemplified by severe tricuspid regurgitation and persistent augmented central venous pressure above 15 mmHg, caused by persistent PHT, indicate a bad prognosis (33, 34).

Correction of tricuspid valve regurgitation in patients with severely decreased RV function will hamper successful recovery. Presence of tricuspid valve regurgitation seems not to affect outcome, on the condition this regurge is only related to a gauge to overfilling/high pressure (35). On the contrary, pulmonary valve insufficiency could indicate a bad prognosis in patients after repair of tetralogy of Fallot with RV outflow tract patching. In this pathology, the role of the RV outflow tract function is highlighted: pulmonary valve insufficiency may induce RV dilation only late in the disease process when the function of the RV outflow tract is preserved (36).

The importance of the influence of PHT in patients with RV failure has also been underlined in patients with advanced heart failure (25). This study was designed to assess whether testing of potential reversibility of pulmonary hypertension (PHT) may be a useful means of defining the short-term prognosis of patients with advanced heart failure and elevated pulmonary artery pressure. In such patients, the reversibility of PHT after acute vasodilator administration is associated with a low early mortality rate after heart transplantation. In a series of haemodynamically stable patients suffering from thromboembolic events, BNP showed a cut-off level of 1.25 pmol L(-1) with a sensitivity and specificity of 60% and 62%, respectively (37). These data suggest that for every patient correctly receiving thrombolytic therapy at this cut-off, 16 patients will receive this therapy unnecessarily. For clinical purposes BNP does not attain sufficient clinical sensitivity and specificity (37). Further studies are warranted with respect to determining the value of BNP on outcome in chronic thromboembolic patients with RV failure (38). However, on a short term, BNP correlates with RV remodelling (38), and provides insight in the presence of RV overload (37). The prognostic evaluation of patients with advanced heart failure and PHT should also include the assessment of the changes of right ventricular ejection fraction over time after acute afterload reduction (25, 37).

Key points

It is generally acknowledged that the RV systolic function plays a key role in a variety of diseases in the critically ill. The RV dysfunction can be summarised on the basis of three important issues:

1. *myocardial ischaemia with involvement of RV;*
2. *volume overload;*
3. *pressure overload. The first and the third element appear to be the most important in the critically ill, mechanically ventilated patient.*

Although the RV may have an implicit safety margin against pressure overload with initial increase of contractility, it is clear that the RV plays a critical role in the determination of outcome in patients with acute and chronic heart failure, rather than the degree of developed PHT. Rapid diagnosis of RV failure and presence of pulmonary hypertension is therefore warranted. Echocardiography plays a key function in this respect. Consequent therapeutic interventions should therefore be implemented at the earliest convenience to salvage myocardial tissue and unload the dilated RV.

The authors

Jan Poelaert, MD, PhD
Vincent Umbrain, MD
    Department Anaesthesiology and
    Perioperative and Pain Medicine |
    UZ-Brussels, Belgium

Address for correspondence
Jan Poelaert
Department Anaesthesiology
Perioperative and Pain Medicine
UZ-Brussels
Laarbeeklaan 101
1090 Brussels, Belgium
e-mail: jan.poelaert@uzbrussel.be

References

1. Goldstein JA. Right heart ischemia: pathophysiology, natural history, and clinical management. Prog Cardiovasc Dis. 1998;40(4):325–41.
2. Goldstein JA. Pathophysiology and management of right heart ischemia. J Am Coll Cardiol. 2002;40(5):841–53.
3. Greyson C et al. Right ventricular dysfunction persists following brief right ventricular pressure overload. Cardiovasc Res. 1997;34(2):281–8.
4. Jacobs AK et al. Cardiogenic shock caused by right ventricular infarction: A report from the SHOCK registry. Journal of the American College of Cardiology. 2003; 41(8):1273–1279.
5. Nagel E, Stuber M, Hess OM. Importance of the right ventricle in valvular heart disease. Eur Heart J. 1996; 17(6):829–36.
6. Kaul S et al. Assessment of right ventricular function using two-dimensional echocardiography. Am Heart J. 1984;107(3):526–31.
7. Ghio S et al. Prognostic usefulness of the tricuspid annular plane systolic excursion in patients with congestive heart failure secondary to idiopathic or ischemic dilated cardiomyopathy. Am J Cardiol. 2000; 85(7):837–42.
8. Lupi-Herrera E et al. Acute right ventricular infarction: clinical spectrum, results of reperfusion therapy and short-term prognosis. Coron Artery Dis. 2002;13(1): 57–64.
9. Pfisterer M. Right ventricular involvement in myocardial infarction and cardiogenic shock. Lancet. 2003; 362(9381):392–4.
10. Goldstein JA et al. Determinants of hemodynamic compromise with severe right ventricular infarction. Circulation. 1990;82(2):359–68.
11. Goldstein JA et al. Right atrial ischemia exacerbates hemodynamic compromise associated with experimental right ventricular dysfunction. J Am Coll Cardiol. 1991; 18(6):1564–72.
12. Mendes LA et al. Cardiogenic shock: predictors of outcome based on right and left ventricular size and function at presentation. Coron Artery Dis. 2005;16(4): 209–15.
13. de Vroomen M et al. Improved contractile performance of right ventricle in response to increased RV afterload in newborn lamb. Am J Physiol Heart Circ Physiol. 2000; 278(1):H100–5.
14. Langeland S et al. Experimental validation of a new ultrasound method for the simultaneous assessment of radial and longitudinal myocardial deformation independent of insonation angle. Circulation. 2005; 112(14):2157–62.
15. Karunanithi MK et al. Right ventricular preload recruitable stroke work, end-systolic pressure-volume, and dP/dtmax-end-diastolic volume relations compared as indexes of right ventricular contractile performance in conscious dogs. Circ Res. 1992;70(6):1169–79.
16. Rex S et al. Thoracic epidural anesthesia impairs the hemodynamic response to acute pulmonary hypertension by deteriorating right ventricular-pulmonary arterial coupling. Crit Care Med. 2007;35(1): 222–9.
17. Inglessis I et al. Hemodynamic effects of inhaled nitric oxide in right ventricular myocardial infarction and cardiogenic shock. Journal of the American College of Cardiology. 2004;44(4):793–798.
18. Bowers TR et al. Effect of reperfusion on biventricular function and survival after right ventricular infarction. N Engl J Med. 1998;338(14):933–40.
19. Zehender M, Kasper W, Kauder E. Right ventricular infarction as an independent predictor of prognosis after acute inferior myocardial infarction. N Engl J Med. 1993; 328:981–8.
20. Langer F et al. Treatment of a case of acute right heart failure by inhalation of iloprost, a long-acting prostacyclin analogue. Eur J Anaesthesiol. 2001;18(11): 770–3.

21. Rex S et al. Epoprostenol treatment of acute pulmonary hypertension is associated with a paradoxical decrease in right ventricular contractility. Intensive Care Med. 2008;34(1):179–89.

22. Komajda M et al. The EuroHeart Failure Survey programme – a survey on the quality of care among patients with heart failure in Europe. Part 2: treatment. Eur Heart J. 2003;24(5):464–74.

23. Levine TB et al. Impact of medical therapy on pulmonary hypertension in patients with congestive heart failure awaiting cardiac transplantation. Am J Cardiol. 1996; 78(4):440–3.

24. Van Trigt P et al. Mechanisms of transplant right ventricular dysfunction. Ann Surg. 1995;221(6):666–75; discussion 675–6.

25. Gavazzi A et al. Response of the right ventricle to acute pulmonary vasodilation predicts the outcome in patients with advanced heart failure and pulmonary hypertension. Am Heart J. 2003;145(2):310–6.

26. Naeije R et al. Nature of pulmonary hypertension in congestive heart failure. Effects of cardiac transplantation. Am J Respir Crit Care Med. 1994;149(4 Pt 1): 881–7.

27. Ama R et al. Acute pulmonary hypertension causes depression of left ventricular contractility and relaxation. Eur J Anaesthesiol. 2006;23(10):824–31.

28. Bhayana JN et al. Combined antegrade/retrograde cardioplegia for myocardial protection: a clinical trial. J Thorac Cardiovasc Surg. 1989;98(5 Pt 2):956–60.

29. Dembinski R, Rossaint R, Kuhlen R. Modulating the pulmonary circulation: an update. Curr Opin Anaesthesiol. 2003;16(1):59–64.

30. La Vecchia L et al. Right ventricular function predicts transplant-free survival in idiopathic dilated cardiomyopathy. J Cardiovasc Med (Hagerstown). 2006; 7(9):706–10.

31. Bittner HB et al. Right ventricular function in orthotopic total atrioventricular heart transplantation. J Heart Lung Transplant. 1998;17(8):826–34.

32. Dini FL et al. Right ventricular dysfunction is a major predictor of outcome in patients with moderate to severe mitral regurgitation and left ventricular dysfunction. Am Heart J. 2007;154(1):172–9.

33. Freeman J et al. Acute pulmonary hypertension complicating the arterial switch procedure. Pediatr Cardiol. 1995;16(6):297–300.

34. Kiraly L, Hartyanszky I, Prodan Z. Right ventricle failure and outcome of simple and complex arterial switch operations in neonates. Croat Med J. 2002;43(6):660–4.

35. Bove T et al. Outcome analysis of major cardiac operations in low weight neonates. Ann Thorac Surg. 2004;78(1):181–7.

36. d'Udekem Y, Rubay J, Ovaert C. Failure of right ventricular recovery of fallot patients after pulmonary valve replacement: delay of reoperation or surgical technique? J Am Coll Cardiol. 2001;37(7):2008–9.

37. Pieralli F et al. Usefulness of bedside testing for brain natriuretic peptide to identify right ventricular dysfunction and outcome in normotensive patients with acute pulmonary embolism. Am J Cardiol. 2006;97(9):1386–90.

38. Reesink HJ et al. Brain natriuretic peptide as noninvasive marker of the severity of right ventricular dysfunction in chronic thromboembolic pulmonary hypertension. Ann Thorac Surg. 2007;84(2):537–43.

Jacques-André Romand and Karim Bendjelid

Do we really need SPV/PPV to detect low filling status?

Do we really need SPV/PPV to detect low filling status? In deeply sedated, mechanically ventilated patients, the answer can be yes, or sometimes. In spontaneously breathing patients the response is no, because they are inaccurate.

Hypotension is often observed in critically ill patients and is always a challenge to the medical team. Indeed, to normalise blood pressure the first question to be asked must be "is the intravascular volume adequate?" But to diagnose hypovolaemia it is not always necessary to have sophisticated indices. During acute haemorrhage, hypovolaemia is obvious and an increased blood pressure after volume expansion (VE) confirms the adequacy of the treatment and directs the volume resuscitation. Similarly, during an early stage of severe sepsis or septic shock, hypovolaemia is always present and fluid resuscitation may be directed by observing in parallel arterial lactate decrease and systemic arterial pressure increase following VE, considering arterial oxygen saturation as the limiting factor to continue fluid resuscitation (1). On the other hand, a patient presenting with multiple morbidities and in whom hypotension occurs could benefit from not receiving useless VE. Indeed, when volume expansion is unnecessary, a protective approach which could avoid aggravating heart failure and pulmonary oedema must be applied (2, 3). Moreover, in patients in whom generalised hypervolaemia is already present avoiding unnecessary fluid challenge is useful (3).

Why is the assessment of a decrease in intravascular volume such a challenge?

Well, this simple question is more complicated to answer than it seems (4). Indeed, to restore normal blood pressure by fluid therapy, the cardiovascular filling (preload defined as end-diastolic volume of both ventricular chambers), cardiac function (inotropism), and vascular resistance (afterload), must be estimated or better, measured (5). The difficulty of establishing the status of the intravascular volume brings many physicians to systematically administer a fluid challenge to treat potential or latent hypovolaemia (6). This method consists of infusing a defined amount of fluid over a brief period of time. The response to the intravascular volume loading can be monitored by invasive monitoring with the measurements of cardiac output. If cardiac output (CO) increases, the patient is a "responder", whereas if CO does not change, the patient is a "non-responder" (7). The state of responder or non-responder is the basis of the concept of fluid responsiveness. The rationale for fluid challenge is related to the physiological "law" which states that following VE ventricular stroke volume increases when preload is low (responder). Thus, increasing ventricular stroke volume ultimately will normalise blood pressure in the presence of invariable systemic vascular resistances. But the Frank-Starling curve has two components and after reaching a maximal SV, further fluid administration will not bring more benefit and even has the potential to be harmful (non-responder, see fig. 1). Moreover, the slope of the relationship between ventricular preload and stroke volume also depends on ventricular contractility and thus the pre-infusion cardiac preload is not the only factor influencing the response to a volume load (8). In these conditions, cardiac preload and fluid responsiveness are not synonymous but express different physiological concepts (8). Consequently, measuring or estimating preload cannot predict fluid responsiveness. To the contrary, measuring preload is certainly a valuable tool to confirm that the volume infused has reached the cardiac chambers and thus informs about cardiac preload responsiveness in the presence of capillary leak (9).

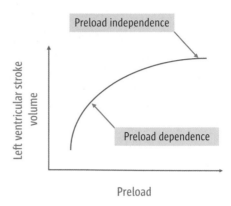

Fig. 1   Relationship between left ventricular preload and cardiac output. The initial part of this relationship demonstrates fluid responsiveness whereas no change in cardiac output is observed in the second part of the slope.

Fluid responsiveness assessment

Different methodologies have been used to assess fluid responsiveness. These can be grouped into two categories: static and dynamic measurements.

Static indices to assess fluid responsiveness

They include information derived through measurement of cardiac intra-cavitary pressures such as right atrial pressure (RAP), pulmonary artery occlusion pressure (Paop) or the estimation of the cardiac chambers volumes such as right or left-ventricular-end diastolic volumes obtained either by a modified pulmonary artery catheter, trans-pulmonary themodilution (Picco^{TM}, Pulsion, Munich, Germany) and echocardiography (surfaces and volumes). The term "static indices" refers to measuring a variable at a determined time. Even if static measurements have been used by clinician for decades, it is well established that neither the pressure nor the volume measurements as a surrogate of preload are able to predict fluid responsiveness (1, 10). This means that preload measurements which have often been proposed to estimate intravascular volume and to predict cardiac output increase after fluid challenge are not accurate in predicting fluid re-

sponsiveness. Many factors explain it, particularily for RAP. Indeed, the right ventricle works in unstressed volume conditions and is able to adapt its stroke volume to quite a broad spectrum of venous return without affecting RAP value if the tricuspid valve is competent. It is also due to the fact that the Frank-Starling relation between preload and stroke volume following VE (preload change) depends not only on the preload value but also on the ventricular function curve (slope of the curve) (8). And this is true in either deeply sedated, mechanically ventilated patients (1, 10) and/or spontaneously breathing patients (9). Osman et al. recently reviewed the fluid responsiveness prediction in critically ill patients and found that neither RAP nor Paop are able to predict fluid responsiveness, confirming the results of previous studies (11). They also demonstrated that combining what is considered as low RAP and Paop did not increase the predictability of CO increase following VE (11). They also observed that when septic patients presented with a RAP < 8 mmHg and a Paop < 11 mmHg, sensitivity to be a responder to VE was 35%, with a specificity of 71% (11). Moreover, the positive and negative predicting values were 54% and 63% respectively (11) (see fig. 2). It is interesting, however, to observe that the updated sepsis guidelines still consider RAP as tools not only to assess preload but also to target fluid resuscitation

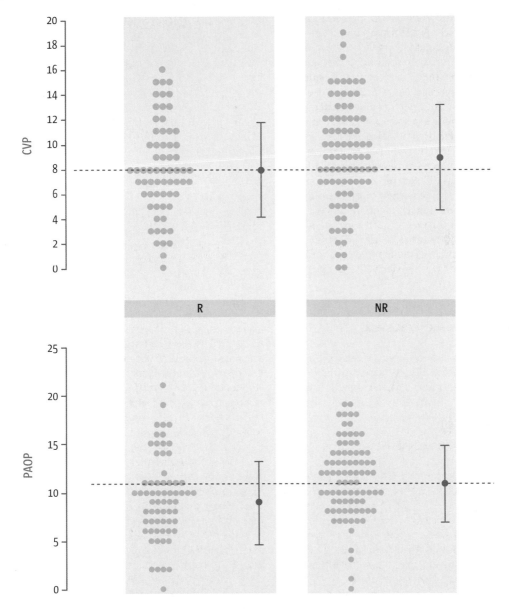

Fig. 2   Non-differentiation of either central venous pressure (CVP) or pulmonary artery occlusion pressure (Paop) to predict fluid responsiveness in septic patients. Modified from: Osman D, Ridel C, Ray P et al. Cardiac filling pressures are not appropriate to predict hemodynamic response to volume challenge. Crit Care Med. 2007;35(1):64–8. With kind permission from Lippincott Williams & Wilkins.

(Grade 1C) (12). In summary, considering the work of Osman et al., the international recommendations propose to use a "gold standard" to direct fluid therapy in septic patients that "works" one out of two times! We can conclude that using only intravascular static pressures to guide fluid therapy can lead to inappropriate therapeutic decisions. Various other methods which are also considered as static indexes, such as modified flow-directed pulmonary artery catheter, transpulmonary thermodilution (13), radionuclide angiography, trans-thoracic and trans-oesophageal echocardiography, have been used to measure cardiac volumes in the chambers as indicators of preload (1). However, even if ventricular volumes should reflect preload dependency more accurately than pressure indices, conflicting results have been reported so far and ventricular volume assessments are not a recommended guide to fluid responsiveness (1). In summary, current evidence does not support the use of static measurement to predict FR neither during mechanical ventilation with positive pressure nor during spontaneous breathing (1, 9).

Dynamic indices to assess fluid responsiveness

They consist of observing the cyclic changes in intra-thoracic and transpulmonary pressures, either during spontaneous breath or mechanical positive pressure breath. The resulting cycling pressure gradient generated transiently affects ventricular preload, leading to cyclic changes in stroke volume in preload-dependent, but not in preload-independent, patients (1, 10). The rationale for guiding fluid therapy by heart-lung interaction indices is that the haemodynamic changes induced by positive pressure ventilation are greater when central blood volume is low than when it is normal or high (14). Bendjelid et al. and Coudray et al. have reviewed these indices both in conditions of controlled mechanical ventilation and during spontaneous breathing (1, 9).

Dynamic indices in deeply sedated, mechanically ventilated, critically ill patients

In deeply sedated, mechanically ventilated, critically ill patients, the results in respiratory changes in stroke volume (15), systolic pressure (16, 17), pulse pressure (18), preejection period (19, 20) and vena cava diameter (21–23) (see fig. 3) have been studied. In different patient populations, all of them have identified decreased-preload hypotension and allow distinguishing between responders and non-responders to fluid challenge. However, Dalibon et al. (24) demonstrated that even normotensive anesthetised patients could present respiratory change in systolic pressure

values higher than what is accepted as cut-off value differentiating between R and NR to VE, but without demonstrating evidence of intravascular fluid depletion (24). Others have also found that dynamic indices as indexes of fluid responsiveness show false-positives in deeply sedated mechanically ventilated patients, for example in the presence of cor pulmonale (25, 26). A possible explanation for these cor pulmonale-induced false-positives is that the right ventricle was over-distended and an increase in pleural pressure and the rise in right ventricular impedance during inspiration decreased venous return and decompressed the right ventricle, allowing improved left ventricular ejection and producing the cyclic changes of the dynamic indexes (inter-ventricular interdependence). Furthermore, major limitations preclude the utilisation of dynamic indexes, such as arrhythmias (1), presence of spontaneous breath (1), and the magnitude of positive pressure tidal volume (27, 28). It is also important to mention that to date no studies have demonstrated the utility of these methods against relevant clinical outcomes (1).

Dynamic indices during spontaneous breath

During spontaneous breathing (SB) a very different heart-lung interaction is observed than when patients are deeply sedated and mechanically ventilated because intra-thoracic pressure is negative during inspiration (25, 29) and the respiratory rate is variable. Moreover, the amplitude of the intra-thoracic pressure swings in patients with no heart diseases is much lower in SB than in MV patients (30). Respiratory-induced variation in RAP was investigated by Magder et al. as a predictor of fluid responsiveness (31, 32). The hypothesis was that when the heart is not volume-responsive, i.e. in the flat portion of the Starling curve, RAP will not fall during inspiration nor will the CO rise after VE. This hypothesis was tested in a population of spontaneously breathing patients where respiratory change in RAP was defined by a fall > 1 mmHg during inspiration to be considered positive for respiratory variations, and where patients were excluded if the respiratory effort was not sufficient to generate at least a 2 mmHg fall in Paop during inspiration. Using these criteria, Magder

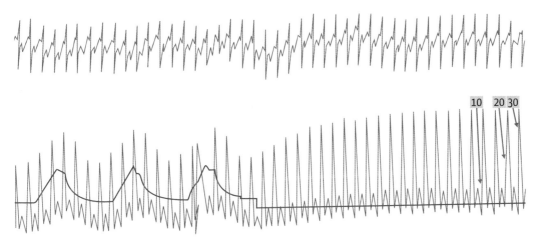

Fig. 3   Arterial pressure variation induced by intermittent positive pressure ventilation and during an apnoeic period. Top:
         ECG trace. Bottom: Arterial and airway pressure tracings resulting from positive pressure breath and during apnoea.
         Modified from: Vieillard-Baron A, Chergui K, Augarde R, 2003, Cyclic Changes in Arterial Pulse during Respiratory
         Support Revisited by Doppler Echocardiography, American Journal of Respiratory and Critical Care Medicine, 168,
         671–676. With kind permission from the authors and the American Thoracic Society.

et al. (31) found that respiratory change in central venous pressure was a good predictor of fluid responsiveness in spontaneously breathing patients. However, more recently Heenet et al. found that respiratory change in RAP does not predict fluid responsiveness in spontaneously breathing patients (33). Teboul and colleagues explored the possibility to predict fluid responsiveness in spontaneous breathing patients or triggering the ventilator. Monnet et al. found that passive leg raising more accurately predicts fluid responsiveness than pulse pressure variation in spontaneously breathing hypovolaemic critically ill patients with a sensitivity of 97 % and a specificity of 94 % (34). They also confirm that in spontaneous breathing patients a poor correlation is observed between pulse pressure variation and fluid responsiveness, precluding the use of dynamic indices of preload assessment in such patients (34). This fact has also been confirmed by Heenet et al. who found that respiratory change in pulse pressure does not predict fluid responsiveness in spontaneously breathing patients (33). More recently, Lamia form the Teboul team demonstrated that in critically ill patients with spontaneous breathing activity the response of echocardiographic stroke volume to passive leg raising was a good predictor of volume responsiveness (35).

Conclusion

In conclusion we can say that currently no universal methods allow predicting fluid responsiveness in critically ill patients and this is true both for static and dynamic methods. A promising method is the leg raising test which seems to overcome many limitations observed with the other methods. We need prospective value to demonstrate that this simple method is useful and modifies outcome in critically ill patients. In the meantime "le bon sens paysan" must prevail and, paraphrasing Milic-Emily, we can say that fluid responsiveness is not a science but an art (36).

The authors

Jacques-André Romand, MD, FCCM
Karim Bendjelid, PD, MD, MS,
Médecins Adjoints Agrégés
    Intensive Care Service | Geneva University
    Hospital | Geneva, Switzerland

Address for correspondence
    Jacques-André Romand
    Intensive Care Division
    Geneva University Hospital
    1211 Geneva 14, Switzerland
    e-mail: Jacques-andre.romand@hcuge.ch

References

1. Bendjelid K, Romand JA. Fluid responsiveness in mechanically ventilated patients: a review of indices used in intensive care. Intensive Care Med. 2003;29: 352-60.
2. Arieff AI. Fatal postoperative pulmonary edema: pathogenesis and literature review. Chest. 1999;115: 1371-7.
3. Boussat S, Jacques T, Levy B et al. Intravascular volume monitoring and extravascular lung water in septic patients with pulmonary edema. Intensive Care Med. 2002;28:712-8.
4. Hahn RG. Fluid therapy might be more difficult than you think. Anesth Analg. 2007;105:304-5.
5. Boldt J, Lenz M, Kumle B et al. Volume replacement strategies on intensive care units: results from a postal survey. Intensive Care Med. 1998;24:147-51.
6. Horst HM, Obeid FN. Hemodynamic response to fluid challenge: a means of assessing volume status in the critically ill. Henry Ford Hosp Med J. 1986;34:90-4.
7. Stetz CW, Miller RG, Kelly GE et al. Reliability of the thermodilution method in the determination of cardiac output in clinical practice. Am Rev Respir Dis. 1982;126: 1001-4.
8. Michard F, Reuter DA. Assessing cardiac preload or fluid responsiveness? It depends on the question we want to answer. Intensive Care Med. 2003;29:1396; author reply 7.
9. Coudray A, Romand JA, Treggiari M et al. Fluid responsiveness in spontaneously breathing patients: a review of indexes used in intensive care. Crit Care Med. 2005;33:2757-62.
10. Michard F, Teboul JL. Predicting fluid responsiveness in ICU patients(*): a critical analysis of the evidence. Chest. 2002;121:2000-8.
11. Osman D, Ridel C, Ray P et al. Cardiac filling pressures are not appropriate to predict hemodynamic response to volume challenge. Crit Care Med. 2007;35(1):64-8.
12. Dellinger RP, Levy MM, Carlet JM et al. Surviving Sepsis Campaign: international guidelines for management of severe sepsis and septic shock: 2008. Crit Care Med. 2008;36:296-327.
13. Michard F, Alaya S, Zarka V et al. Global end-diastolic volume as an indicator of cardiac preload in patients with septic shock. Chest. 2003;124:1900-8.
14. Gunn SR, Pinsky MR. Implications of arterial pressure variation in patients in the intensive care unit. Curr Opin Crit Care. 2001;7:212-7.
15. Reuter DA, Felbinger TW, Schmidt C et al. Stroke volume variations for assessment of cardiac responsiveness to volume loading in mechanically ventilated patients after cardiac surgery. Intensive Care Med. 2002;28:392-8.
16. Perel A, Pizov R, Cotev S. Systolic blood pressure variation is a sensitive indicator of hypovolemia in ventilated dogs subjected to graded hemorrhage. Anesthesiology. 1987;67:498-502.
17. Tavernier B, Makhotine O, Lebuffe G et al. Systolic pressure variation as a guide to fluid therapy in patients with sepsis-induced hypotension [see comments]. Anesthesiology. 1998;89:1313-21.
18. Michard F, Boussat S, Chemla D et al. Relation between respiratory changes in arterial pulse pressure and fluid responsiveness in septic patients with acute circulatory failure. Am J Respir Crit Care Med. 2000;162:134-8.
19. Bendjelid K, Suter PM, Romand JA. The respiratory change in preejection period: a new method to predict fluid responsiveness. J Appl Physiol. 2004;96:337-42.
20. Feissel M, Badie J, Merlani PG et al. Pre-ejection period variations predict the fluid responsiveness of septic ventilated patients. Crit Care Med. 2005;33:2534-9.
21. Barbier C, Loubieres Y, Schmit C et al. Respiratory changes in inferior vena cava diameter are helpful in pre-dicting fluid responsiveness in ventilated septic patients. Intensive Care Med. 2004;30:1740-6.
22. Vieillard-Baron A, Chergui K, Rabiller A et al. Superior vena caval collapsibility as a gauge of volume status in ventilated septic patients. Intensive Care Med. 2004; 30:1734-39.
23. Feissel M, Michard F, Faller JP et al. The respiratory variation in inferior vena cava diameter as a guide to fluid therapy. Intensive Care Med. 2004;30:1834-7.
24. Dalibon N, Guenoun T, Journois D et al. The clinical relevance of systolic pressure variations in anesthetized nonhypotensive patients. J Cardiothorac Vasc Anesth. 2003;17:188-92.
25. Magder S. Clinical usefulness of respiratory variations in arterial pressure. Am J Respir Crit Care Med. 2004; 169:151-5.
26. Vieillard-Baron A, Prin S, Chergui K et al. Hemodynamic instability in sepsis: bedside assessment by Doppler echocardiography. Am J Respir Crit Care Med. 2003;168: 1270-6.
27. De Backer D, Heenen S, Piagnerelli M et al. Pulse pressure variations to predict fluid responsiveness: influence of tidal volume. Intensive Care Med. 2005;31:517-23.
28. Reuter DA, Bayerlein J, Goepfert MS et al. Influence of tidal volume on left ventricular stroke volume variation measured by pulse contour analysis in mechanically ventilated patients. Intensive Care Med. 2003;29:476-80.
29. Magder S. More respect for the CVP. Intensive Care Med. 1998;24:651-3.
30. Guyton AC. Regulation of cardiac output. N Engl J Med. 1967;277:805-12.
31. Magder S, Georgiadis G, Cheong T. Respiratory variations in right atrial pressure predict the response to fluid challenge. J Crit Care. 1992;7:76-85.
32. Magder S, Lagonidis D. Effectiveness of albumin versus normal saline as a test of volume responsiveness in post-cardiac surgery patients. J Crit Care. 1999;14:164-71.

33. Heenen S, De Backer D, Vincent JL. How can the response to volume expansion in patients with spontaneous respiratory movements be predicted? Crit Care. 2006;10:R102.

34. Monnet X, Rienzo M, Osman D et al. Passive leg raising predicts fluid responsiveness in the critically ill. Crit Care Med. 2006;34:1402–7.

35. Lamia B, Ochagavia A, Monnet X et al. Echocardiographic prediction of volume responsiveness in critically ill patients with spontaneously breathing activity. Intensive Care Med. 2007;33:1125–32.

36. Milic-Emili J. Is weaning an art or a science? Am Rev Respir Dis. 1986;134:1107–8.

Gwenhaël Colin, Virginie Maxime and Djillali Annane

Vasopressors in the patient with shock

Introduction to the topic

Septic shock is the most severe form of sepsis, and is commonly define by a combination of severe sepsis and hypotension which is refractory to fluid replacement and the need for vasopressor therapy to maintain a mean arterial pressure at 65 mmHg. A number of drugs can be considered as vasopressors including mainly catecholamines, vasopressin and analogs, and nitric oxide inhibitors. Although endogenous vasopressin levels may be inappropriate in sepsis, and administration of replacement dose of vasopressin may result in significant haemodynamic improvement (1) this drug cannot be used as a first line vasopressor in septic shock patients. While nonselective nitric oxide inhibitors had detrimental effects in patients with septic shock (2), benefit from selective inhibitors seen in experimental models (3, 4) remains to be investigated in clinical trials. Among the various catecholergic agents, phenylephrine has not been evaluated in any randomised controlled study. The current review will focus on the use of dopamine, norepinephrine and epinephrine.

Recent international guidelines recommend that dopamine and norepinephrine should be used as a first line vasopressor and that epinephrine should be given only to patients poorly responsive to norepinephrine (5).

In a prospective, double-blind, randomised trial, Martin et al. (6) compared haemodynamic and metabolic effects of dopamine and norepinephrine in hyperdynamic septic shock. Adults with persistent hyperdynamic septic shock despite adequate fluid resuscitation were included if they had:
1. a systolic blood pressure of less than 90 mmHg,
2. a cardiac index above 4 l/min/m^2,
3. evidence of organ hypoperfusion (encephalopathy prior to sedation or an urine output below 30 ml/h), arterial lactate above 2.5 mmol/l, and
4. evidence of infection.

The study drugs were titrated to achieve and maintain for at least 6 consecutive hours all of the following:
1. systemic vascular resistance index > 1,100 dynes.s/cm^5.m^2 and/or mean arterial pressure $\geq$ 80 mmHg,
2. a cardiac index $\geq$ 4.0 l/min/m^2,
3. an oxygen delivery > 550 ml/min/m^2, and
4. an oxygen uptake > 150 ml/min/m^2.

Patients were assigned to receive either dopamine (2.5 to 25 µg/kg/min) or norepinephrine (0.5 to 5.0 µg/kg/min). The haemodynamic and metabolic goals were achieved in only 5/16 dopamine treated patients (31 %) compared to 15/16 norepinephrine-treated patients (93 %) (dose of 1.5 ± 1.2 µg/kg/min) (p < .001). Ten of the 11 patients who did not respond to dopamine were switched to norepinephrine and subsequently successfully resuscitated.

In a prospective, multicenter, observational study, Levy et al. (7) investigated the prognostic value of the haemodynamic response to dopamine in septic shock patients. Patients were graded as having dopamine-resistant septic shock when mean arterial pressure was less than 70 mmHg despite the use of 20 µg/kg/min of dopamine. Adequately fluid resuscitated patients received rapidly increasing doses of dopamine from 10 to 20 µg/kg/min in 10 to 15 minutes. Patients with dopamine-resistant septic shock were promptly switched to receive norepinephrine or epinephrine. One-hundred and ten patients were included and 66 (60%) had dopamine-resistant shock. The crude 28-day mortality was 54% in the whole population. Only 7/44 (16%) dopamine-sensitive patients died compared to 52/66 (78%) dopamine-resistant patients (p = .0006). In multivariate analysis, independent predictors of death included resistance to dopamine (odds ratio, 9.5; 95% confidence interval, 3–25), arterial lactate > 3.5 mmol/l (odds ratio, 1.75; 95% confidence interval, 1.06–2.55), and Sepsis-related Organ Failure Assessment score > 10 (odds ratio, 1.40; 95% confidence interval, 1.07–2.12). The authors concluded that an early dopamine response test may allow recognition of more severe septic shock patients, who may benefit from adjunctive therapy.

A study of regional haemodynamic in septic shock, suggested better splanchnic haemodynamic in norepinephrine-treated patients compared to dopamine (8). The multinational, observational SOAP cohort study suggested that the use of dopamine was an independent predictor of death in patients with acute circulatory failure. This study led to a dramatic decrease in the use of dopamine in septic shock (9). However, the recently completed, multinational, randomised controlled study by the SOAP investigators did not show any evidence for a difference in mortality in shock patients treated with dopamine or norepinephrine. Therefore, the current literature support the use of either dopamine or norepinephrine in the initial management of septic shock. One may consider using the dopamine response test as proposed by Levy et al. to decide which patients should receive norepinephrine (7).

Approximately 50% of patients with severe sepsis and septic shock may present with impaired left ventricular systolic function (10). Current guidelines suggested that such patients should be given dobutamine in addition to norepinephrine (5). Alternately, physicians may consider using epinephrine which has both vasoconstrictive and inotropic properties. People have worried about impaired splanchnic blood in septic shock despite adequate fluid replacement and the use of vasopressors (11). Two randomised controlled studies, performed on parallel groups, have compared the effects of epinephrine to the combination of norepinephrine plus dobutamine on the splanchnic bed (12, 13).

Levy et al. (12) performed a prospective, randomised clinical trial comparing the effects of norepinephrine and dobutamine to those of epinephrine in hyperdynamic dopamine-resistant septic shock. This study included 30 patients who had a cardiac index > 3.5 l/min/m² and a mean arterial pressure ≤ 60 mmHg after fluid replacement and infusion of dopamine at a dose of 20 µg/kg/min and, who had either oliguria or increased arterial lactate levels. Patients were randomised to norepinephrine-dobutamine or epinephrine which were titrated to maintain mean arterial blood pressure greater than 80 mmHg with a stable or increased cardiac index. Therapeutic goals were reached in all patients. No statistical difference was found between epinephrine and norepinephrine-dobutamine for systemic hemodynamic measurements. Epinephrine infusion was associated with an increase in lactate levels (from 3.1 ± 1.5 to 5.9 ± 1.0 mmol/l; p < 0.01), while they decreased in the norepinephrine-dobutamine group (from 3.1 ± 1.5 to 2.7 ± 1.0 mmol/l). The lactate/pyruvate ratio significantly increased in the epinephrine group (from 15.5 ± 5.4 to 21 ± 5.8; p < 0.01) and did not change in the norepinephrine-dobutamine group (13.8 ± 5 to 14 ± 5.0). Epinephrine was associated with a significant decrease in gastric mucosal pH and a rise in the partial pressure of carbon dioxide gap (tonometer PCO_2-arterial PCO_2). In the norepinephrine-dobutamine group, gastric mucosal pH and tonometer PCO_2-arterial PCO_2 were normalised within 6 hours (p < 0.01). However, the metabolic changes observed in the epinephrine group were transient, and 24 hours after randomisation there was no more difference between norepinephrine and dobutamine, and epinephrine on splanchnic hemodynamic. The authors concluded that epinephrine was as effective as the combination of norepinephrine-dobutamine. Nevertheless, because of the transient perturbation in splanchnic perfusion and oxygenation, they suggested that the combination of norepinephrine and dobutamine should be preferred to epinephrine. Several cross-over studies found comparable results (13–15). Finally, dopexamine may have comparable effects than dobutamine (16).

Seguin et al. (17) compared epinephrine with a combination of dobutamine (5 µg/kg/min) and norepinephrine on gastric perfusion in patients with septic shock in another prospective randomised study that included 22 patients who met all of the following criteria:
1. evidence of infection;
2. at least 3 criteria of systemic inflammatory response;

3. at least 2 of: plasma lactate > 2 mmol/l or unexplained metabolic acidosis (pH < 7.3), hypoxemia, urine output < 30 ml/h for at least 2 hours despite > 500ml of fluid replacement, platelet count < 100,000/mm^3 or a 50 % decrease from previous value or unexplained coagulopathy;

4. systolic blood pressure < 90 mmHg and pulmonary capillary wedge pressure > 12 mmHg. Epinephrine and norepinephrine were titrated to achieve a mean arterial pressure of 70 to 80 mmHg. There were no significant difference in-between groups, except for greater values of gastric mucosal blood flow in epinephrine-treated patients. Treatment with epinephrine was also associated with slightly higher cardiac index (5.0 ± 1.6 versus 4.2 ± 1.5 l/m^2) and oxygen transport (617 ± 166 versus 481 ± 229ml/min/m^2). The authors concluded that epinephrine-related increase in cardiac index may have favoured the gastric mucosal blood flow.

Most (if not all) of the published studies suggested that norepinephrine plus dobutamine and epinephrine were equally effective in achieving general haemodynamic goals and that deleterious effects on splanchnic perfusion were more likely observed with the use of epinephrine.

Annane et al. (18), in a prospective, multicenter (involving 19 French intensive care units), randomised, double-blind study compared in 330 septic shock patients the efficacy and safety of norepinephrine plus dobutamine (whenever needed) versus epinephrine alone. Drugs were titrated to maintain mean blood pressure at 70 mmHg or more. The primary outcome was 28-day all-cause mortality. Adults were included if they met the following criteria for less than 7 days: evidence of infection, at least two of four criteria of systemic inflammatory response syndrome, and at least two signs of hypoperfusion or organ dysfunction (ratio of arterial oxygen tension over inspired fraction of oxygen less than 280 mmHg, urinary output below 0.5 ml/kg/h or 30 ml/h for at least one hour, arterial lactate concentration above 2 mmol/l or platelet count below 100,000/mm^3). Additionally, patients had to meet the three following criteria for less than 24 hours: a systolic blood pressure below 90 mmHg or a mean arterial pressure below 70 mmHg, administration of > 1000 ml of fluid bolus or a capillary wedge pressure between 12 and 18 mmHg, and need for more than 15 µg/kg/min of dopamine or any dose of epinephrine or norepinephrine. At day 28, mortality was 40 % in the epinephrine group and 34 % deaths in the norepinephrine-dobutamine group (p = 0.31; relative risk 0.86, 95 % CI 0.65–1.14). There was no significant difference between the two groups in mortality rates at discharge from intensive care, and hospital, and at day 90. Time to haemodynamic success (defined by the time to restore a mean arterial pressure of at least 70 mmHg for at least 12 consecutive hours), time to vasopressor withdrawal, and time course of SOFA score were not different between the two treatment arms. Finally, there was no evidence for a difference in the rate of serious adverse events between the two groups. The authors concluded that there was no evidence for superiority of norepinephrine (plus dobutamine whenever needed) over epinephrine. Thus, physicians may consider either strategy for the routine management of septic shock.

The Australian and New Zealand CAT study was presented at international meeting by Myburgh, JA (and is currently submitted to a peer-reviewed journal). This study has included 280 patients with acute circulatory failure (76 % being septic shock) and compared norepinephrine to epinephrine. The authors did not find any evidence for a superiority of norepinephrine over epinephrine regarding survival, time to shock reversal, haemodynamic parameters, ventilation time, or length of hospital stay. Epinephrine-treated patients had higher arterial lactate levels at day 1. These results were in keeping with those of the CATS study (18).

The transient elevation of arterial lactate during epinephrine infusion resulted from increased Na/K ATPase activity with high ADP levels activating the pyruvate kinase, rather than from tissue dysoxia (19).

Controversial position 1

The physiological approach

Given the potential deleterious effects of epinephrine on splanchnic perfusion and oxygenation, many physicians prefer using norepinephrine as a first line agent, and whenever needed they will add dobutamine. The combination of the two drugs may allow independent adjustment of cardiac index and systemic vascular resistance.

Controversial position 2

The pragmatic approach

Based on the CATS study (18) and the CAT study, which showed that epinephrine and norepinephrine are equipotent and had comparable efficacy and safety profiles, many physicians will use epinephrine as a first line agent. In addition, epinephrine is less expensive than norepinephrine and/or dobutamine, is easier to titrate and does not request immediate monitoring of cardiac index.

Summary

Along with fluid perfusion, vasopressor therapy is critical for haemodynamic management of septic shock. Norepinephrine may be more effective than dopamine to restore an adequate haemodynamic status (6). Neverthe-

Tab. 1   Summary of the main clinical trials on catecholamines for shock patients

Studies	Arms	Primary endpoints	Number of patients	Population	Main results
Martin et al.	Norepinephrine Dopamine	To achieve and maintain for 6 h all: SVRI > 1,100 dynes.s/cm^5.m^2 MBP > 80 mmHg Cardiac index ≥ 4,0 l/min/m^2 Oxygen delivery > 550 ml/min/m^2	16 16	Hyperdynamic septic shock	Norepinephrine is more effective than dopamine
Levy et al.	Dopa-S Dopa-R	28-days mortality	44 66	Septic shock	Dopa-S septic shock patients have a better prognosis than Dopa-R
Levy et al.	Norepinephrine + Dopamine Epinephrine	Haemodynamics lactate metabolism gastric tonometric variables in hyperdynamic dopamine resistant septic shock	30	Septic shock	Haemodynamic effects are similar Inadequate splanchnic oxygen utilisation and metabolic change in the epinephrine group
Seguin et al.	Norepinephrine + Dopamine Epinephrine	Cardiac index Gastric mucosal blood flow	11 11	Septic shock	Trend toward greater values for cardiac index in the epinephrine group Significant higher gastric mucosal blood flow in the epinephrine group
CATS Annane et al.	Norepinephrine +/– Dobutamine Epinephrine	28-days all causes mortality	169 161	Septic shock	No evidence from a difference in efficacy and safety
Zhou et al.	Random succession of epinephrine, norepinephrine and norepinephrine-dobutamine (cross-over)	Gastric mucosal value Oxygen extraction Ratio Cardiac Index Arterial lactate	16	Septic shock	Gastric mucosal perfusion improvement by norepinephrine plus dobutamine Deleterious effect of epinephrine and dopamine

less a short dopamine response test may help in selecting the sickest patients who could benefit from adjunctive therapy (7). Most of the clinical trials comparing epinephrine and norepinephrine plus dobutamine effects on splanchnic perfusion suggested that epinephrine is more deleterious on this vascular bed (12–15).

However, two multicenter, randomised, double-blind studies (CATS and CAT) did not show any evidence for different clinical outcomes between patients who received epinephrine and those who received norepinephrine plus dobutamine.

Key points for clinical practice

According to recent international guidelines (5):
- *"We recommend either norepinephrine or dopamine as the first choice vasopressor agent to correct hypotension in septic shock (administered through a central catheter as soon as one is available) (Grade 1C).*
- *We suggest that epinephrine, phenylephrine, or vasopressin should not be administered as the initial vasopressor in septic shock (Grade 2C). Vasopressin .03 units/min may be subsequently added to norepinephrine with anticipation of an effect equivalent to norepinephrine alone.*
- *We suggest that epinephrine be the first chosen alternative agent in septic shock that is poorly responsive to norepinephrine or dopamine (Grade 2B)."*

According to CATS, CAT, and SOAP, randomised controlled studies, physicians may use either dopamine, norepinephrine or epinephrine depending on adequate fluid replacement and adequate haemodynamic goals. The choice between these three drugs may also rely on physicians' own experience and local resources.

The authors

Gwenhaël Colin, MD
Virginie Maxime, MD
Djillali Annane, MD, PhD
General Intensive Care Unit | Department of Acute Medicine and Surgery Raymond Poincaré Hospital (AP-HP) |
University of Versailles SQY (UniverSud Paris) |
Garches, France

Address for correspondence
Djillali Annane
General Intensive Care Unit
Raymond Poincaré Hospital (AP-HP)
University of Versailles SQY
(UniverSud Paris)
104 boulevard Raymond Poincaré
92380 Garches, France
e-mail: Djillali.annane@rpc.aphp.fr

References

1. Lauzier F et al. Vasopressin or norepinephrine in early hyperdynamic septic shock: a randomized clinical trial. Intensive Care Med. 2006;32(11):1782–9.
2. Lopez A et al. Multiple-center, randomized, placebo-controlled, double-blind study of the nitric oxide synthase inhibitor 546C88: effect on survival in patients with septic shock. Crit Care Med. 2004;32(1):21–30.
3. Levy B. et al. Comparative effects of vasopressin, norepinephrine, and L-canavanine, a selective inhibitor of inducible nitric oxide synthase, in endotoxic shock. Am J Physiol Heart Circ Physiol. 2004;287(1):H209–15.
4. Kadoi, Y. and F. Goto, Selective inducible nitric oxide inhibition can restore hemodynamics, but does not improve neurological dysfunction in experimentally-induced septic shock in rats. Anesth Analg. 2004. 99(1): p. 212–20.
5. Dellinger RP et al. Surviving Sepsis Campaign: International guidelines for management of severe sepsis and septic shock: 2008. Intensive Care Med. 2008; 34(1):17–60.
6. Martin C et al. Norepinephrine or dopamine for the treatment of hyperdynamic septic shock? Chest. 1993; 103(6): 1826–31.
7. Levy B et al. Cardiovascular response to dopamine and early prediction of outcome in septic shock: a prospective multiple-center study. Crit Care Med. 2005; 33(10): 2172–7.
8. Marik PE, Mohedin M. The contrasting effects of dopamine and norepinephrine on systemic and splanchnic oxygen utilization in hyperdynamic sepsis. Jama, 1994;272(17):1354–7.
9. Sak Y et al. Does dopamine administration in shock influence outcome? Results of the Sepsis Occurrence in Acutely Ill Patients (SOAP) Study. Crit Care Med. 2006; 34(3):589–97.
10. Charpentier J et al. Brain natriuretic peptide: A marker of myocardial dysfunction and prognosis during severe sepsis. Crit Care Med. 2004;32(3):660–5.
11. Oud L, Haupt MT. Persistent gastric intramucosal ischemia in patients with sepsis following resuscitation from shock. Chest. 1999;115(5):1390–6.

12. Levy B et al. Comparison of norepinephrine and dobutamine to epinephrine for hemodynamics, lactate metabolism, and gastric tonometric variables in septic shock: a prospective, randomized study. Intensive Care Med. 1997;23(3):282–7.

13. Zhou SX et al. Effects of norepinephrine, epinephrine, and norepinephrine-dobutamine on systemic and gastric mucosal oxygenation in septic shock. Acta Pharmacol Sin. 2002;23(7):654–8.

14. Duranteau J et al. Effects of epinephrine, norepinephrine, or the combination of norepinephrine and dobutamine on gastric mucosa in septic shock. Crit Care Med. 1999; 27(5):893–900.

15. Meier-Hellmann A et al. Epinephrine impairs splanchnic perfusion in septic shock. Crit Care Med. 1997;25(3):399–404.

16. Seguin P et al. Dopexamine and norepinephrine versus epinephrine on gastric perfusion in patients with septic shock: a randomized study [NCT00134212]. Crit Care. 2006;10(1):R32.

17. Seguin P et al. Effects of epinephrine compared with the combination of dobutamine and norepinephrine on gastric perfusion in septic shock. Clin Pharmacol Ther. 2002;71(5):381–8.

18. Annane D et al. Norepinephrine plus dobutamine versus epinephrine alone for management of septic shock: a randomised trial. Lancet. 2007;370(9588):676–84.

19. Levy B et al. Relation between muscle Na+K+ATPase activity and raised lactate concentrations in septic shock: a prospective study. Lancet. 2005;365(9462): 871–5.

Elias Knobel, Marcos Knobel, Antonio Eduardo Pesaro
and José Marconi A. Sousa

Controversies in coronary care

Introduction

The advent of coronary care units in the early 1960s led to a marked reduction in mortality due to arrhythmia in the acute phase of a myocardial infarction. More recently, there has been a focus directed at limiting the loss of cardiac muscle through early reperfusion strategies. Among these strategies, thrombolytic therapy and percutaneous coronary intervention (PCI) are routinely used today in patients with acute myocardial infarction (AMI), resulting in reduced morbidity and mortality. Several studies have demonstrated the efficacy of PCIs versus fibrinolysis, especially when this procedure is conducted in a timely fashion. The treatment with antithrombotics, antiplatelets and other medication has been fundamental to maintain coronary blood flow in patients referred to PCI, usually with stent implantation. However, there are controversies and unanswered questions regarding this subject, and some of them will be briefly discussed in this chapter.

Primary percutaneous coronary intervention for all patients with ST-elevation acute myocardial infarction (STEMI)?

A planned reperfusion strategy using primary PCI or full-dose fibrinolytic therapy improves survival in patients with ST-elevation myocardial infarction (STEMI) (1). The main goal of the treatment is to minimise total ischaemic time, which is defined as the time from the onset of symptoms to initiation of reperfusion therapy. When PCI capability is available, the best outcomes are achieved by employing this strategy, however many hospital systems do not have the capability of meeting the time goal for primary PCI. A decision must be made between the local administration of fibrinolytic therapy or transfer to another institution for primary PCI. Both strategies are discussed here.

PCI is better

PCI is superior to fibrinolytic therapy when performed in a timely fashion by an experienced team (1, 2). Fibrinolytic therapy carries a greater risk of minor and major bleeding. Intracranial haemorrhage is the most serious of these risks; occurring in approximately 0.7 percent of patients treated with fibrinolytics (3).

The door-to-balloon time is a key indicator of quality of care for patients with STEMI who are treated with primary PCI. Longer intervals between the onset of symptoms and balloon time have been correlated with poorer outcomes in several studies of primary PCI (4, 5). However some studies have suggested that delays in the delivery of primary PCI are important only within the first 2 to 3 hours after the onset of symptoms. Among 29,222 patients with STEMI, McNamara et al. found a strong relationship between door-to-balloon time and in-hospital mortality (5). When treatment was started within 90 minutes after arrival, in-hospital mortality was 3.0 %; it increased to 4.2 %, 5.7 %, and 7.4 % when delays were 91 to 120 minutes, 121 to 150 minutes, and more than 150 minutes, respectively. Adjusted for differences in patient characteristics, each 15-minute reduction in door-to-balloon time from 150 to less than 90 minutes was associated with 6.3 fewer deaths per 1,000 patients treated. Guidelines from the European Society of Cardiology and ACC-AHA recommend a treatment goal of 90 minutes or less for door-to-balloon time (or the time from initial medical contact to treatment) (6), This measure has been incorporated in hospital performance and quality indicator reports.

Two situations that deserve more special attention are patients in whom STEMI develops after admission to the hospital and patients who are transferred from another hospital for primary PCI. Several clinical trials have shown promising results of emergency transfer for primary PCI as compared with on-site fibrinolytic therapy (7). The choice to use primary PCI could substantially delay access to reperfusion for some patients with STEMI who otherwise could immediately be given fibrinolytic therapy.

The potential benefit of transfer for primary PCI compared to fibrinolysis was demonstrated in a meta-analysis (8). Primary PCI was associated with a significant reduction in the incidence of the combined end point of death, reinfarction, or stroke compared to fibrinolysis (relative risk 0.58, 95 % CI 0.47–0.71). In all of the trials analyzed, transfer time for primary PCI was always less than three hours. It has been suggested that, if delay beyond two hours is expected, transfer for primary PCI may be the best choice for high risk patients: patients with large infarctions, cardiogenic shock, Killip class 3 or 4, and failed fibrinolysis (9). However, a pooled analysis from 22 trials, including 6,763 STEMI patients, suggested that primary PCI was superior to fibrino-

lytic, regardless of the time to presentation and PCI-related delay (10).

Another point is the PCI-related delay that is the difference between the door-to-balloon time and the door-to-needle time. However, this measure overestimates the reperfusion delay for PCI, since PCI reperfusion is immediate while fibrinolytic therapy generally does not reestablish perfusion for about 30 minutes.

In conclusion, in order to perform primary PCI in all patients, first it is necessary establish hospital-based strategies to reduce door-to-balloon time; second, when both reperfusion strategies can be rapidly performed, current evidence from clinical trials and registries strongly supports the use of primary PCI, based on its superiority in re-establishing coronary blood flow and the lower risks of re-infarction and intracerebral haemorrhage (2). PCI is also the best option for patients with cardiogenic shock and the only option for those with contraindications to fibrinolytic therapy.

Fibrinolys may be better

Given the substantial resources required, many hospitals in Europe lack PCI capabilities, and even fewer provide round-the-clock staffing for these procedures. The benefit of fibrinolytic therapy is greatest when given within the first four hours, particularly within the first 2 to 3 hours after the onset of symptoms (11).

Fibrinolytic therapy remains a practical option for a large number of patients when there is no immediate access to a catheterization laboratory, particularly since the reduced mortality associated with primary PCI may be restricted to high-risk patients (12).

The relevant question is, how long a delay in access to primary PCI would make fibrinolytic therapy the preferred reperfusion therapy. Several studies have examined this issue (13). Although results vary substantially, all suggest that differences between reperfusion therapies with respect to mortality favor primary PCI but diminish as PCI-related delays increase, potentially reaching equivalence between 60 and 120 minutes.

Because of the lack of definitive data, there is no consensus on the selection of reperfusion therapy in situations in which primary PCI is not readily available.

Rapid administration of fibrinolytic therapy within 30 minutes after arrival at the hospital is recommended when door-to-balloon times of more than 90 minutes are anticipated with primary PCI. However, depending on the clinical scenario, the equivalence between the strategies may occur with delays of as much as 120 minutes or more in access to primary PCI.

Evaluating time to treatment

In the community, door-to-balloon times and PCI-related delays are significantly longer than those in randomised clinical trials.

A review of 23 randomised trials of primary PCI versus fibrinolysis, which enrolled a total of 7,739 patients, have shown the following results: primary PCI was associated with a 2 percent absolute reduction in short-term mortality with significant reductions in nonfatal re-infarction and stroke (14). The magnitude of the survival benefit at four to six weeks declined as the mean PCI-related delay increased. When this time was more than 62 minutes there was no survival advantage to primary PCI over fibrinolysis.

Non-patient-related factors which appear to increase the PCI delay are door-to-door transfer times and off-hour presentation. In a review of 68,439 patients treated for an STEMI with either fibrinolytic therapy or primary PCI, among patients who presented off-hours (weekdays 5 PM to 7 AM and weekends), there was a significant increase in time to treatment with PCI (door-to-balloon time 116 versus 95 minutes with presentation during regular hours) (15).

PCI-related delay greater than 60 to 90 minutes appears to eliminate the survival benefit of primary PCI over fibrinolysis. Interpretation of these results should consider confounding factors associated with both increased PCI-related delay and worse outcomes, such as the experience of hospitals and operators. Furthermore when reinfarction and stroke is added to survival as a combined end point, the advantage of primary PCI over fibrinolysis may be retained with slightly greater PCI-related delay.

In conclusion fibrinolytic therapy is recommended within 30 minutes after arrival at the hospital when door-to-balloon times of more than 90 minutes are anticipated with primary PCI.

Data from the CAPTIM randomised clinical trial show that in patients within 2 hours from onset of symptoms, fibrinolytic therapy may be the therapeutic choice (16).

Summary

The main goal of reperfusion therapy in STEMI is to minimise total ischaemic time, which is defined as the time from onset of symptoms to initiation of reperfusion. To perform primary PCI in all patients it is necessary to establish hospital-based strategies to reduce door-to-balloon time. When both reperfusion strategies can be rapidly performed, current evidence from clinical trials and registries strongly supports the use of primary PCI. PCI is also the best option for patients with cardiogenic shock and the only option for those with contraindications to fibrinolytic therapy. Otherwise, fibrinolytic therapy is recommended within 30 minutes after arrival at the hospital when door-to-balloon times of more than 90 minutes are anticipated with primary PCI. Further data from one study show that in patients within 2 hours from symptoms onset, fibrinolytic therapy may be the therapeutic choice (16).

Key points for clinical practice

- Reperfusion strategy using primary PCI or full-dose fibrinolytic therapy improves survival in patients with STEMI.
- Fibrinolytic therapy carries a greater risk of minor and major bleeding.
- PCI is superior to fibrinolytic therapy when performed in a timely fashion by expert teams.
- PCI is the best option for patients with cardiogenic shock and the only option for those with contraindications to fibrinolytic therapy.
- Fibrinolytic therapy is recommended within 30 minutes after arrival at the hospital when door-to-balloon times of more than 90 minutes are anticipated with primary PCI.

Invasive stratification strategy is the best option after UA/NSTEMI?

What is the best stratification strategy after Unstable Angina/Non ST Elevation Myocardial Infarction (UA/NSTEMI)? Over the past ten years, the medical establishment has conducted several trials to elucidate this issue, but controversy persists. Guidelines published in 2002 favored the invasive strategy for high-risk patients. However, recent studies have again highlighted this controversy and new guidelines were modified in 2007 (17).

Invasive strategy: Con

Routine invasive stratification was not better than conservative stratification after UA/NSTEMI in several relevant trials (18, 19). In 1994, the TIMI IIIB trial randomly assigned 1,473 patients to an early invasive strategy versus an early conservative strategy. The end point for the comparison of the two strategies (death, myocardial infarction, or an unsatisfactory symptom-limited exercise stress test at 6 weeks) occurred in 18.1% of patients assigned to the early conservative strategy and 16.2% of patients assigned to the early invasive strategy (P = NS). Subsequently, in the VANQWISH trial, the primary end point (death or nonfatal myocardial infarction) was more frequent in the invasive-strategy group. On the other hand, the MATE study didn't show differences between invasive or non-invasive strategies (20).

In the last ten years great improvement was achieved in medical therapy. Statins, beta-blockade and thienopiridines were included in UA/NSTEMI treatment. However, an important modern study confirmed the results of previous trials. In 2005 the ICTUS study (21) randomised 1,200 high-risk NSTEMI patients for invasive versus selective invasive management. Myocardial infarction was significantly more frequent in the group assigned to early invasive management. After one year of follow-up, researchers were unable to find a difference in end points between the two groups.

Non-invasive coronary management evaluates functional ischaemic status, which is more useful than isolated anatomic information. An angioplasty based on functional ischaemic evaluation avoids unnecessary interventions in intermediate non-ischaemic lesions. Additionally, conservative management might prevent coronary angiography complications as femoral artery damage and renal toxicity.

In conclusion, UA/NSTEMI patients (troponin positive or not) may be safely treated under a conservative strategy, as long as initial medical therapy is successful, and patient remains stable.

Invasive strategy: Pro

Routine invasive stratification is the best choice in high risk UA/NSTEMI patients. Several trials have successfully demonstrated that some studies in the 1990s (TIMI IIIB VANQWISH, MATE) were not conclusive about this controversy. However, patients in the invasive group were not treated with current "full" therapy in these old trials. Clopidogrel, GP IIb/IIIa inhibitors and stents were not available at that time. Nowadays, we know that these therapies are fundamental to reduce thrombosis and restenosis after angioplasty.

More recently, an array of trials (FRISC II, TRUCS, RITA-3, TIMI-18) have shown that an early invasive strategy (angiography in the first 24–48 h) is better than a conservative approach when one is dealing with high-risk UA/NSTEMI patients. These studies have shown that patients treated with an early invasive strategy were submitted to angioplasty and stents more often than those in the conservative group. One of the most important of these trials was the TACTICS-TIMI 18 (22). In this study, death, MI, or re-hospitalisation at six months occurred in 15.9% of patients assigned to the invasive strategy versus 19.4% assigned to the conservative one (beneficial in patients with troponin elevation, ST-segment deviation, or TIMI risk score greater than 3).

On the other hand, in 2005 the ICTUS study did not show differences in mortality between invasive or conservative management in UA/NSTEMI patients. A plausible explanation for this result, the opposite of TACTICS TIMI 18, is the high rate of cross over, with revascularisation performed in 47% of the patients in the selective invasive group. ICTUS had also used a controversial definition for post-procedural MI (minimal, asymptomatic CK-MB elevation).

Recently, a meta-analysis of contemporary randomised trials in NSTEMI, including ICTUS, demonstrated benefits of an early invasive strategy in comparison to a conservative strategy (23). According to this study, the early invasive strategy reduces mortality (RR = 0.75), nonfatal MI (RR 0.83) and hospitalisation (RR = 0.69) at 2 years.

In conclusion, high-risk UA/NSTEMI patients should be managed with early intervention strategy, as this option may reduce the risk of death or myocardial infarction.

Summary

Given all this uncertainty, how do we decide to be invasive or not? This article approaches three points.

First, invasive stratification seems to be the best strategy for clinically unstable patients (e.g. pulmonary edema, hypotension, ventricular arrhythmias).

Second, it also appears to be the best strategy for really high-risk patients and therefore, accurate early risk stratification is fundamental. The higher the risk score, the larger the intervention benefit. However, isolated troponin elevation may not be enough to determine high risk, so it is possible to use other scores (such as GRACE, TIMI, and Braunwald) to help in the decision-making.

Third, the conservative strategy seems to be safe for most patients who are stable after initial medical treatment. Therefore a delay for invasive procedures (even in troponin positive patients) is possible even when co-morbidities are present (e.g. renal impairment).

In conclusion, and considering the unresolved nature of the debate, key variables for rational decision-making are accurate early risk scores, clinical stability, hospital available resources, associated diseases, and patient preferences.

Key points for clinical practice

- *Invasive stratification after UA/NSTEMI seems to be the best strategy for clinically unstable patients (e.g. pulmonary edema, hypotension, ventricular arrhythmias).*
- *UA/NSTEMI patients may be safely conducted in a conservative strategy, when initial medical therapy is successful, and the patient remains stable.*
- *The higher the risk score after UA/NSTEMI is, the larger the intervention benefit. However, isolated troponin elevation may not be enough to determine high risk, and therefore other scores may be used (such as GRACE, TIMI, and Braunwald) to help in decision-making.*
- *Key variables for decision-making of invasive or non-invasive strategy after UA/NSTEMI are accurate early risk scores, clinical stability, hospital available resources, associated diseases, and patient preferences.*

Clopidogrel: Should be used early in all Non ST-Elevation acute coronary syndromes (UA/NSTEMI) patients?

Today, clopidogrel is one of the major therapeutic tools in UA/NSTEMI, responsible for a significant reduction of cardiovascular events (24, 25). Due to its strong antiplatelet action, one of the limitations to its wider use is a higher incidence of bleeding (surgical and non-surgical), an issue that has caused controversy in its early use.

Pro

Clopidogrel has gained notoriety and generated controversy in the treatment of UA/NSTEMI at the time the CURE trial (Clopidogrel in Unstable angina to prevent Recurrent Events) (26) was conducted. This trial analysed its effect combined with aspirin versus placebo in NSTEACS in 12,562 patients, during the first 24 hours of symptom onset, for 3 to 12 months. Aspirin with clopidogrel reduced the risk of combined cardiovascular events (AMI, cardiovascular death and cerebral vascular accident) by around 20 %. The value of an early use of clopidogrel is the dissociation from the mortality curve, already by the first two hours of randomisation. The relative risk reduction reached 30 % on patients submitted to angioplasty and stent implantation. The benefit occurred with low, medium and high-risk patients likewise. Clopidogrel began to be indicated for UA/NSTEMI starting with a 300 mg loading dose followed by a 75 mg/day (based on the CURE and CREDO trials (26, 27) for 1 to 9 months. Usage of the medication for patients that received bare metal stents is recommended for at least 1 month, whereas medication for those who received pharmacological stents should be maintained for at least 3 to 6 months, and up to 12 months in patients with low risk of bleeding. Studies do not demonstrate excessive risk of bleeding from the combination of clopidogrel and GP IIb/IIIa inhibitors or antithrombotics. Today, clopidogrel has the precise indication for UA/NSTEMI (Class I, level of evidence A), and should be used as early as possible (28).

Con

Due to its mechanism of action, while it has the benefit of reducing ischaemic events, clopidogrel is more prone to cause bleeding which can limit its use in UA/NSTEMI.

In the CURE trial (26) the incidence of major bleeding, was more frequent in the clopidogrel group when compared to placebo (3.6 % x 2.7 %, p = 0,003). There were no significant differences in life-threatening bleeding; however, the incidence of minor bleedings was significantly greater in the clopidogrel group (15.3 % x 8.6 %, p < 0,0001). In the cases where the patient underwent myocardial revascularization surgery within five days of clopidogrel use, there was a strong trend towards more bleeding in the clopidogrel group (9.6 % x 6.3 %, p < 0,06). However, in patients undergoing an early invasive stratification and who may be indicated for surgical revascularization, it is acceptable to postpone the initiation of therapy with clopidogrel until cinecoronariography is performed (25, 28). This strategy avoids postponing surgical procedures, once the medication should be withheld 5 to 7 days before major surgeries. In these cases, the early use of glycoprotein IIb/IIIa inhibitors such as tirofiban and epitifibatide is an acceptable alternative according to the last guidelines, since 6 hours after discontinuing the anti-platelet effect is inexistent.

Summary

The issue of early clopidogrel use must be individualised, based on the characteristics of the service. Those presenting a high number of coronary artery bypass graft surgery (CABG) in ACS patients, may opt for the definition of the coronary anatomy and thus start with clopidogrel or not. Nevertheless, we always advise the early use of clopidogrel, due to the huge benefit this medication offers to patients during the very first hours of ischaemic profile onset, outweighing the possible haemorrhagic risks of a small portion of patients referred to CABG.

Key points for clinical practice

- The early administration of clopidogrel in UA/NSTEMI reduces the incidence of major cardiac events.
- Clopidogrel should be withheld 5 to 7 days before CABG.
- The incidence of minor bleeding is significantly higher in patients that used clopidogrel.

Prasugrel or clopidogrel: Which is the ideal anti-platelet in patients with ACS undergoing PCI?

Since the PCI – CURE study (29), clopidogrel has been a mandatory drug for patients with ACS undergoing PCI (29–31). A new recently-developed ADP receptor antagonist, Prasugrel, is under clinical development in the USA and has just had its first clinical results published in the TRITON – TIMI 38 study (32), which compared the efficacy and safety of this novel drug against clopidogrel in this clinical scenario.

Prasugrel

Prasugrel is not available for sale yet, but in the final stages of development, prasugrel has demonstrated proven efficacy in reducing cardiovascular events according to data generated by the TRITON – TIMI 38 study (32). This study analyzed more than 13,000 patients with moderate- to high-risk UA/NSTEMI and STEACS scheduled to PCI and randomised to receive either a pre-PCI 60-mg loading dose of prasugrel, followed by a 10-mg daily maintenance dose for 6 to 15 months, or a 300-mg loading dose of clopidogrel followed by a 75-mg daily maintenance dose over the same period. Efficacy end points were encouraging for the prasugrel group. There were no differences regarding cardiovascular death, nonfatal cerebral vascular accident and all-cause mortality; however, there was a significant benefit regarding mortality /MI / cerebral vascular accident end points (Prasugrel 9.9 % vs Clopidogrel 12.1 % p < 0,001), nonfatal MI (Prasugrel 7.3 % vs Clopidogrel 9.5 % p < 0,001), urgent target-vessel revascularization (Prasugrel 2.5 % vs Clopidogrel 3.7 % p < 0,001), and stent thrombosis (Prasugrel 1.1 % vs Clopidogrel 2.4 % p < 0,001). Based on these efficacy data we were able to verify that for each 1,000 patients treated with prasugrel, 23 myocardial infarctions were prevented compared to Clopidogrel.

Recently, preliminary data of the PRINCIPLE TIMI 44 trial (34) were made public. The purpose of this study was to investigate the action of prasugrel (60-mg loading dose and 10-mg maintenance dose) and that of clopidogrel (600-mg loading dose and 75-mg maintenance dose) in platelet inhibition and P2Y12 receptor antagonism in patients with stable coronary disease. Prasugrel achieves greater and faster P2Y12 receptor-mediated platelet inhibition than clopidogrel due to more efficient generation of its active metabolite. Such findings, despite not being clinical end points, suggest enormous potential for the use of prasugrel in clinical practice.

Clopidogrel

Clopidogrel is an antiplatelet agent that has been in our sphere for almost a decade, and we are fully aware of its mechanism of action and its adverse side effects according to the clinical picture and the administered dosage (29–31, 33). When compared to prasugrel its efficacy may not have been superior, nevertheless regarding safety prasugrel showed significant increase in bleeding, which makes us reflect about the need of a safe and known drug for this group of patients – in this case, clopidogrel. Clopidogrel was significantly safer than prasugrel regarding all types of bleeding: fatal bleeding (Prasugrel 0.4 % vs Clopidogrel 0.1 % p = 0.002), TIMI major or minor bleeding (Prasugrel 5.0 % vs Clopidogrel 3.8 % p = 0.002), Bleeding requiring blood transfusion(Prasugrel 4.0 % vs Clopidogrel 3.0 % p < 0.001) and TIMI major bleeding related to CABG (Prasugrel 13.4 % vs Clopidogrel 3.2 % p < 0.001). In subgroup analysis of patients with prior stroke history, elderly older than 75 and less than 60 kg in weight were classified as those bearing the highest risk of bleeding when treated with prasugrel. The drug is contraindicated in these cases.

Summary

Recent results with prasugrel are of the utmost importance, since this drug is only beginning to be researched. A relevant aspect is that in high-risk patients, such as diabetic patients with low bleeding risk, prasugrel would be the drug of choice, whereas those with low risk of ischaemic events and high risk of bleeding would benefit from clopidogrel. We still do not have a guideline recommending the use of prasugrel in clinical practice and many doubts regarding its future use will be elucidated by new specific clinical trials in which the drug will be tested under different scenarios of acute coronary syndromes.

Key points for clinical practice

- In the TRITON – TIMI 38 trial, Prasugrel presented greater efficacy in cardiovascular end points when compared to clopidogrel.
- Prasugrel was associated with a higher incidence of all types of bleeding in comparison with clopidogrel.
- Patients with prior stroke history, elderly older than 75 and those less than 60 kg in weight presented a higher risk of bleeding when treated with prasugrel.

The authors

Elias Knobel, MD, PhD, FAHA, FACP, FCCM[1]
Marcos Knobel, MD[2]
Antonio Eduardo Pesaro, MD[2]
José Marconi A. Sousa, MD[2]
   [1]Director emeritus and founder of the ICU |
   Vice-president of the board of directors |
   Hospital Israelita Albert Einstein |
   São Paulo, Brazil
   [2] From the staff of the ICU | Hospital
   Israelita Albert Einstein | São Paulo, Brazil

Address for correspondence
   Elias Knobel
   Hospital Israelita Albert Einstein
   Av. Albert Einstein, 627/701 – CEP 05651-901
   Morumbi, São Paulo, Brazil
   e-mail: knobel@einstein.br

References

1. Keeley EC, Hillis LD. Primary PCI for myocardial infarction with ST-segment elevation. N Engl J Med. 2007;356:47–54.
2. Cucherat M, Bonnefoy E, Tremeau G. WITHDRAWN: Primary angioplasty versus intravenous thrombolysis for acute myocardial infarction. Cochrane Database Syst Rev. 2007;18(3):CD001560.

3. Huynh T, Cox JL, Massel D et al. FASTRAK II Network. Predictors of intracranial hemorrhage with fibrinolytic therapy in unselected community patients: a report from the FASTRAK II project. Am Heart J 2004;148:86–91.

4. De Luca G, Suryapranata H, Ottervanger JP, Antman EM. Time delay to treatment and mortality in primary angioplasty for acute myocardial infarction: every minute of delay counts. Circulation. 2004;109:1223–5.

5. McNamara RL, Wang Y, Herrin J et al. NRMI Investigators. Effect of door-to-balloon time on mortality in patients with ST-segment elevation myocardial infarction. J Am Coll Cardiol. 2006;47:2180–6.

6. Antman EM, Hand M, Armstrong PW et al. 2007 Focused Update of the ACC/AHA 2004 Guidelines for the Management of Patients with ST-Elevation Myocardial Infarction: a report of the American College of Cardiology/American Heart Association Task Force on Practice Guidelines: developed in collaboration With the Canadian Cardiovascular Society endorsed by the American Academy of Family Physicians: 2007 Writing Group to Review New Evidence and Update the ACC/AHA 2004 Guidelines for the Management of Patients With ST-Elevation Myocardial Infarction, Writing on Behalf of the 2004 Writing Committee. Circulation. 2008;117:296–329.

7. Dalby M, Bouzamondo A, Lechat P, Montalescot G. Transfer for primary angioplasty versus immediate thrombolysis in acute myocardial infarction: a meta-analysis. Circulation. 2003;108:1809–14.

8. Andersen HR, Nielsen TT, Rasmussen K et al. A comparison of coronary angioplasty with fibrinolytic therapy in acute myocardial infarction. N Engl J Med. 2003;349:733–42.

9. Herrmann HC. Transfer for primary angioplasty: the importance of time. Circulation 2005;111:718–20.

10. Boersma E. The Primary Coronary Angioplasty vs. Thrombolysis Group. Does time matter? A pooled analysis of randomized clinical trials comparing primary percutaneous coronary intervention and in-hospital fibrinolysis in acute myocardial infarction patients. Eur Heart J. 2006;27:779–88.

11. Edmond JJ, French JK, Aylward PE et al., for the HERO-2 Investigators. Variations in the use of emergency PCI for the treatment of re-infarction following intravenous fibrinolytic therapy: impact on outcomes in HERO-2Eur Heart J. 2007;28:1418–24.

12. Thune JJ, Hoefsten DE, Lindholm MG et al. and Danish Multicenter Randomized Study on Fibrinolytic Therapy Versus Acute Coronary Angioplasty in Acute Myocardial Infarction (DANAMI)-2 Investigators. Simple risk stratification at admission to identify patients with reduced mortality from primary angioplasty. Circulation. 2005;112:2017–21.

13. Gibson CM, Pinto DS, Cutlip D. Selecting a reperfusion strategy for acute ST elevation (Q wave) myocardial infarction. Available at www.uptodate.com.

14. Nallamothu BK, Bates ER. Percutaneous coronary intervention versus fibrinolytic therapy in acute myocardial infarction: is timing (almost) everything? Am J Cardiol. 2003;92:824–6.

15. Magid DJ, Wang Y, Herrin J et al. Relationship between time of day, day of week, timeliness of reperfusion, and in-hospital mortality for patients with acute ST-segment elevation myocardial infarction. JAMA. 2005;294:803–12.

16. Steg PG, Bonnefoy E, Chabaud S et al. Impact of time to treatment on mortality after prehospital fibrinolysis or primary angioplasty: data from the CAPTIM randomized clinical trial Circulation. 2003;108:2851–6.

17. Bassand JP, Hamm CW, Ardissino D et al. ESC 2007 Guidelines for the diagnosis and treatment of non-ST-segment elevation acute coronary syndromes. Rev Esp Cardiol. 2007;60:1070.e1–80.

18. The TIMI IIIB Investigators. Effects of tissue plasminogen activator and a comparison of early invasive and conservative strategies in unstable angina and non-Q-wave myocardial infarction: results of the TIMI IIIB Trial. Thrombolysis in Myocardial Ischemia. Circulation. 1994;89:1545–56.

19. Boden WE, O'Rourke RA, Crawford MH et al. Outcomes in patients with acute non-Q-wave myocardial infarction randomly assigned to an invasive as compared with a conservative management strategy. Veterans Affairs Non-Q-Wave Infarction Strategies in Hospital (VAN-QWISH) Trial Investigators. N Engl J Med. 1998;338:1785–92.

20. McCullough PA, O'Neill WW, Graham M et al. A prospective randomized trial of triage angiography in acute coronary syndromes ineligible for thrombolytic therapy. Results of the medicine versus angiography in thrombolytic exclusion (MATE) trial. J Am Coll Cardiol. 1998;32:596–605.

21. de Winter RJ, Windhausen F, Cornel JH et al. Early invasive versus selectively invasive management for acute coronary syndromes. N Engl J Med. 2005;353:1095–104.

22. Cannon CP, Weintraub WS, Demopoulos LA et al. Comparison of early invasive and conservative strategies in patients with unstable coronary syndromes treated with the glycoprotein IIb/IIIa inhibitor tirofiban. N Engl J Med. 2001;344:1879–87.

23. Mehta SR, Cannon CP, Fox KA et al. Routine vs selective invasive strategies in patients with acute coronary syndromes: a collaborative meta-analysis of randomized trials. JAMA. 2005;293:2908–17.

24. Plosker GL, Lyseng-Williamson KA. Clopidogrel: a review of its use in the prevention of thrombosis. Drugs. 2007;67(4):613–46. Review.

25. Elsässer A, Nef H, Möllmann H, Hamm CW. Clopidogrel in acute coronary syndrome: when, how much, how long? Z Kardiol. 2005 Jun;94(6):377–82. Review.

26. Yusuf S, Mehta SR, Zhao F et al. Clopidogrel in unstable angina to prevent recurrent events Trial Investigators. Circulation. 2003 Feb 25;107(7):966–72.

27. Brener SJ, Steinhubl SR, Berger PB et al. for the CREDO Investigators. Prolonged dual antiplatelet therapy after percutaneous coronary intervention reduces ischemic events without affecting the need for repeat revascularization: insights from the CREDO trial. J Invasive Cardiol. 2007 Jul;19(7):287–90.

28. Anderson JL, Adams CD, Antman EM et al. ACC/AHA 2007 guidelines for the management of patients with unstable angina/non-ST-Elevation myocardial infarction: a report of the American College of Cardiology/American Heart Association Task Force on Practice Guidelines. J Am Coll Cardiol. 2007 Aug 14; 50(7):e1–e157.

29. Mehta SR, Yusuf S, Peters RJG et al. Effects of pretreatment with clopidogrel and aspirin followed by long-term therapy in patients undergoing percutaneous coronary intervention: the PCI-CURE study. Lancet. 2001;358:527–33.

30. Yusuf S, Mehta SR, Zhao F et al. Clopidogrel in unstable angina to prevent recurrent events Trial Investigators. Circulation. 2003 Feb 25;107(7):966–72.

31. Peters RJ, Mehta SR, Fox KA et al. Clopidogrel in unstable angina to prevent recurrent events (CURE) Trial Investigators. Effects of aspirin dose when used alone or in combination with clopidogrel in patients with acute coronary syndromes: observations from the Clopidogrel in Unstable angina to prevent Recurrent Events (CURE) study. Circulation. 2003 Oct 7;108(14): 1682–7.

32. Wiviott SD, Braunwald E, McCabe CH et al. TRITON-TIMI 38 Investigators. Prasugrel versus clopidogrel in patients with acute coronary syndromes. N Engl J Med. 2007 Nov 15;357(20):2001–15. Epub 2007 Nov 4.

33. Anderson JL, Adams CD, Antman EM et al. ACC/AHA 2007 guidelines for the management of patients with unstable angina/non-ST-Elevation myocardial infarction: a report of the American College of Cardiology/American Heart Association Task Force on Practice Guidelines. J Am Coll Cardiol. 2007 Aug 14;50(7):e1–e157.

34. Stephen D, Wiviott DT, Andrew LF et al. for the PRINCIPLE-TIMI 44 Investigators. Prasugrel Compared With High Loading- and Maintenance-Dose Clopidogrel in Patients With Planned Percutaneous Coronary Intervention: The Prasugrel in Comparison to Clopidogrel for Inhibition of Platelet Activation and Aggregation – Thrombolysis in Myocardial Infarction 44 Trial. Circulation December 18/25, 2007;116:2923–32.

C. Acute kidney injury

Kai Singbartl and John A. Kellum

Renal replacement therapies:
When, how, and how much?

Introduction to the topic

Acute kidney injury (AKI) represents a frequent, steadily increasing challenge in critically-ill patients (1, 2). AKI greatly contributes to hospital morbidity and mortality, independent of the underlying disease process. It is now widely accepted that patients die because of AKI; not just simply 'with' AKI (3, 4). This change in perspective means that achieving a comprehensive understanding of AKI and appropriate management of patients with AKI is an even higher priority than before. Complications of AKI, such as uremia, electrolyte abnormalities, and fluid overload, have been managed by means of renal replacement therapy (RRT) for more than 50 years. Nonetheless, there are still substantial controversies surrounding the use of RRT, especially in critically-ill patients. Right timing, correct mode, optimal dose of RRT are still not completely known or agreed upon amongst experts.

Better early than late? – When to initiate RRT

Potentially life-threatening complications of AKI, such as severe metabolic acidosis, hyperkalemia or gross hypervolemia (pulmonary edema), are well-accepted indications to initiate RRT. Beyond these so-called emergent indications, there is

great debate but only scarce data as to when to begin with RRT. Given the overall need for control of electrolyte, acid-base and fluid homeostasis in these patients, and the growing appreciation of the clinical consequences of AKI, one might be inclined to view RRT as renal support, similar to respiratory support, and favor an "early" initiation of therapy. On the other side, one can argue that many patients with AKI recover renal function without the need for RRT; that overly aggressive initiation of 'early' RRT will therefore pose unnecessary risks to a substantial number of patients. Similar to other aspects of AKI, the indications for initiation of RRT have been derived from findings in patients with end-stage renal disease (ESRD). Critically-ill patients with AKI greatly differ from patients with ESRD in several key aspects, including higher urea generation rate due to increased catabolism as well as non-steady volumes of distribution. It has been conventional clinical practice to start RRT at BUN levels of 100 mg/dl or greater. However, these recommendations stem from older clinical studies (5–9) that do not meet today's criteria of evidence-based medicine, as they were, for example, either statistically under-powered or retrospective or both (see tab. 1).

Over the past decade, several observational studies have also addressed the effect of timing of initiation of continuous RRT (CRRT) on outcome from AKI (see tab. 1) (10–15). Gettings et al. found a survival benefit in patients receiving early CRRT (39 % survival) as compared to those receiving late CRRT (20 % survival) (10). Demirkilic et al. (12) as well as Elahi et al. (13) reported similar findings. In multi-variable analysis of factors contributing to survival in a randomised trial of RRT dosing by Ronco et al. (discussed below) (16) the BUN at the start of RRT was again found to be an independent predictor – where the higher the BUN, the worse the survival. Contrary to these findings, Liu et al. could not find a significant survival benefit in patients receiving early RRT (15). Recently, Bagshaw and colleagues have shown that when RRT is initiated more than five days after ICU admission mortality is roughly twice that of when RRT is initiated within 24 hours of ICU admission (17). Unfortunately, none of these studies (12, 13) are capable of answering the question, "does early initiation of RRT improve outcome?". This is because there is significant indication bias as to why clinicians begin RRT in a given patient. Furthermore, and perhaps most damning for these sorts of analyses, studies that compare early RRT to late RRT do not account for those in the "late" group who are excluded because they never receive RRT. These patients usually have somewhat lower mortality than those who receive RRT; thus excluding them from the "late" group would falsely increase the mortality in this group. In order to answer this important question, a randomised trial will be needed.

So far, the only randomised prospective trial to address the effect of timing of RRT on outcome was a very small study by Bouman et al. (11). This study included 106 critically-ill patients with AKI from two centers. Patients were randomised to either early high-volume continuous veno-venous hemofiltration (CVVH, n = 35, 72–96 l per 24 h) or early low-volume CVVH (n = 35, 24–36 l per 24) or late low-volume CVVH (n = 36, 24–36 l per 24 h). In the early treatment groups, CVVH was started within 12 h of either diuretic-resistant oliguria for more than 6 h or measured creatinine clearance less than 20 ml/min. In the late treatment group, CVVH was not started until BUN greater than 112 mg/dl, serum K^+ concentration greater than 6.5 mmol/l or frank pulmonary edema. There were no significant differences in survival between the groups. Interestingly, 28-day mortality for patients in this study was only 27 %; thus significantly lower than that usually reported for critically-ill patients with AKI, indicating a less critically-ill population. This study was also greatly underpowered to detect any differences in outcome.

Tab. 1   Clinical studies addressing the effect of timing of RRT on patient outcome

| Study | RRT Mode | Study Design | Number of Patients | Patient Survival (%) | |
				Early	Late
Parsons et al. (5)	IHD	Retrospective	33	75	12
Fischer et al. (6)	IHD	Retrospective	162	43	26
Kleinknecht et al. (7)	IHD	Retrospective	500	73	58
Conger at al. (8)	IHD	RCT	18	64	20
Gillum et al. (9)	IHD	RCT	34	41	53
Gettings et al. (10)	CRRT	Retrospective	100	39	20
Bouman et al. (11)	CRRT	RCT	106	69	75
Demirkilic et al. (12)	CRRT	Retrospective	61	77	45
Elahi et al. (13)	CRRT	Retrospective	64	78	57
Piccinni et al. (14)	CRRT	Retrospective	80	55	28
Liu et al. (15)	CRRT & IHD	Observation	243	65	59

Therefore, currently available data remain insufficient to provide sound information regarding correct timing of RRT in critically-ill patients with AKI. Only a well-designed, large randomised clinical trial (RCT) will ultimately be able to answer the question of when to initiate RRT. However, all future trials will face the same challenge as long as one crucial problem remains unsolved. There is, to date, no appropriate marker to identify patients with serious, persistent AKI early in the disease process. Without early identification of this patient population, many patients that would otherwise recover renal function without RRT would be subjected to the "early RRT" study arm, and thus to the risks of RRT, unnecessarily. However, this may not pose such an unusual burden, given the substantial risk of death seen with AKI and the relatively small risk associated with RRT it would seem an acceptable strategy to randomise patients with, for example, RIFLE-Failure criteria (18) to have RRT initiated as soon as criteria are met versus only when more traditional criteria develop. In any case there is wide consensus that the question of when to start RRT is of paramount importance (19).

Is there a "one mode fits all" technique? How to perform RRT

Although roughly 4% of all critically-ill patients admitted to ICU receive RRT for severe AKI (1), there is still great debate about the initial modality, i.e. CRRT versus intermittent haemodialysis (IHD). Considerable variation in RRT practice patterns around the world attests to this ongoing controversy (20). The theoretical advantages of CRRT over IHD include increased time-averaged dialysis dose, more haemodynamic stability, and, possibly, removal of inflammatory cytokines. Numerous non-randomised trials have shown better metabolic control as well as higher renal recovery and survival rates with CRRT than with IHD (21–32). Some non-randomised trials, however, failed to show any benefit of CRRT over IHD; some have demonstrated higher costs of CRRT (33–37).

A recently published meta-analysis analyzed nine qualifying RCT (38–44), including two abstracts, with respect to the effect of CRRT and IHD on mortality, renal recovery, and treatment-related side effects (see tab. 2) (45). The authors could not find a difference in mortality by RRT modality (pooled odds ratio 0.99; 95% confidence interval 0.78–1.26; $p = 0.91$). There was also no statistical difference in recovery of renal function by RRT modality. However, CRRT was associated with significantly less episodes of haemodynamic instability and a trend towards fewer arrhythmic complications. IHD was associated with a greater cumulative fluid balance. This meta-analysis also found several flaws in the design and execution of the original trials that limit the overall strength of this study. There were selection biases by excluding haemodynamically unstable patients, differences in baseline characteristics, or high crossover rates between RRT modes. Finally, no trial had a standardised protocol for the dose of RRT delivered or the timing of initiation of RRT.

As result of inconclusive studies or meta-analyses, clinicians and scientists frequently ask for larger, better RCT to answer the remaining questions. In their meta-analysis, Bagshaw and colleagues also concluded that a larger, more sophisticated RCT to compare CRRT and IHD is warranted (45). To plan and conduct another but larger, better RCT comparing CRRT versus IHD appears reasonable on first sight. However, a critical interpretation of all available data also allows for alternative conclusions. As either modality appears to be safe and effective in critically-ill patients when used by skilled clinicians, each physician or each intensive care unit can choose the

Tab. 2   Peer-reviewed RCTs addressing the effect of RRT mode on patient outcome – odds ratios from seven trials as analyzed in Bagshaw et al. (45) (Odds ratio < 1 favors CRRT, odds ratio > 1 favors IHD).

Study	Number of patients	Odds ratio	Confidence interval
Kierdorf (38)	100	0.81	0.36–1.82
John et al. (41)	30	1.00	0.19–5.24
Mehta et al. (59)	166	1.89	1.01–3.52
Gasparovic et al. (40)	104	1.67	0.74–3.78
Augustine et al. (39)	80	0.89	0.35–2.29
Uehlinger et al. (43)	125	0.91	0.45–1.85
Vinsonneau et al. (44)	359	0.95	0.61–1.48

modality that works best for them (46). Moreover, only a few centers employ only one modality; most centers are capable of and employ both CRRT and IHD. The decision whether to use CRRT or IHD is largely driven by the individual patient's clinical status, i.e. the priority of the respective goals that need to be achieved. CRRT appears to be superior regarding haemodynamic stability as well as total water and solute removal over 24 hours. IHD, on the other hand, can remove substantially more water and solute per hour, may require less anticoagulation, and does not immobilise patients for most of the day. The latter issue is particularly crucial, as the efficiency of CRRT is greatly reduced by prolonged or repeated interruption (47, 48). Thus, we prefer to look at IHD and CRRT as tools, each better at performing a specific job (49), rather than viewing them as interchangeable therapies. Indeed, CRRT was developed precisely because some patients are unable to be adequately treated with IHD.

Research and development efforts over the past years have also made CRRT and IHD more alike giving rise to the concept of 'slow low-efficiency daily dialysis' (SLEDD) (50–52), a so-called hybrid technique. SLEDD uses a modified dialysis monitor; allows for daily adaptations of treatment conditions, such as duration, blood and dialysate flow, modes of clearance, and choice of filter. In theory SLEDD offers greater flexibility compared to either CRRT or IHD and could reduce costs (53). However, there is currently not enough clinical data to determine the role of SLEDD in critically-ill patients that require RRT. While the option to perform both slow, extended treatments and short, more intensive treatments with only one machine has the potential to significantly improve hospital logistics, more data are needed before this approach can be advocated.

The more, the better? – Dose of RRT

As mentioned before, many recommendations for the management of RRT in critically-ill patients stem from patients with ESRD. This is also true for the dose of RRT. No optimal dose has been established yet, but it is widely accepted that the delivered dose should at least be equal to that recommended for ESRD. This assumption is intuitive, as critically-ill patients with AKI are inherently more ill, malnourished, and catabolic. With IHD, the dose is given by the unitless index Kt/V, where K represents urea clearance, t the duration of diaylsis, and V the volume of distribution of urea. In CRRT, total effluent flow closely approximates the clearance of low molecular weight solutes. The dose of CRRT is therefore given by the sum of ultrafiltrate and dialysate flow rates equaling the total effluent flow rate. A general problem with RRT in critically-ill patients is that both IHD and CRRT do not reach the levels prescribed. A retrospective analysis found that merely 68 % of the prescribed CRRT dose was actually delivered, largely due to reductions in treatment times (48).

Several prospective studies, most of them using CRRT, have been conducted to identify the optimal dose of RRT in patients with AKI. Schiffl and colleagues assigned 160 critically-ill, but haemodynamically stable, patients with AKI to either daily or every other day IHD (54). Patients in the daily IHD group displayed an overall mortality of 28 %, whereas those in the 'every other day' group revealed an overall mortality of 46 % (p = 0.01). Daily IHD had also significantly better metabolic control, greater haemodynamic stability during treatment sessions, and faster recovery from AKI. This study, however, suffers from several limitations: exclusion of haemodynamically unstable patients, lack of randomisation, below normal dose of treatment in the every-other-day group.

To date, there are three RCTs addressing the effect of dose of CRRT on clinically relevant outcome parameters (see tab. 3) (11, 16, 55). Ronco and colleagues randomised a total of 452 critically-ill patients at one center to continuous venovenous hemofiltration (CVVH) with three different ultrafiltration rates: 20, 35 or 45 ml/kg/h (16). The survival rates were 41 %, 57 %, and 58 %, respectively. The recovery rate of renal function was similar in all three groups. A smaller RCT by Bouman and colleagues, discussed above, failed to show a survival benefit with high volume CVVH (11). As mentioned above, this study clearly suffers from a small sample size that does not have sufficient statistical power to detect differences in outcome. Finally, Saudan and colleagues, in the most recent study, found a higher survival rate in patients receiving high-volume CVVH (55). This single center RCT included 206 patients randomised to either CVVH with a mean ultrafiltration rate of 25 ± 5 ml/kg/h (n = 104) or continuous veno-ve-

Tab. 3   RCT evaluating the effect of CRRT dose on survival

Study	Number of patients	Total effluent flow rate (ml/kg/h)		Patient survival (%)	
		Low dose	High dose	Low dose	High dose
Ronco et al. (16)	435	20	35	41	57
Bouman et al. (11)	106	19	48	72	74
Saudan et al. (55)	206	25	42	39	59

nous hemodiafiltration (CVVHDF, n = 102) with a total effluent flow rate of 42 ml/kg/h (mean ultrafiltration rate 24 ± 6 ml/kg/h, mean dialysate flow rate 15 ± 5ml/kg/h). 28-day survival rate was 39 % in the CVVH group but 59 % in the CVVH-DF group. Renal recovery was identical between the two groups. One might argue that randomizing patients to either CVVH or CVVHDF resembles a comparison of RRT modes rather a comparison of RRT doses. To be a true mode-comparing study without any dose effect, the total effluent doses would have needed to be identical. Saudan and colleagues, instead, show that augmentation of small solute clearance with continuous dialysis, when added to filtration substantially improves survival. Indeed the net effect on survival was very similar between the Saudan and Ronco studies. Pooled estimates from all four of the above studies suggest the odds ratio for surviving is nearly 2 favoring a higher dose (56).

However, all of the above studies are single-centered trials; the other limitations described make the optimal dose of RRT for critically-ill patients with AKI still uncertain. However, best available evidence to date supports the use of at least 35 ml/kg/h total effluent flow rates for CVVH/CVVHDF (56). Two large, multi-center RCTs are currently underway and should be able to provide strong clinical evidence regarding the optimal dose of RRT. The VA/NIH Acute Renal Failure Trial Network (ATN) study in the USA compares two different levels of RRT intensity in more than 1,100 patients; finished enrolling patients last year (57). Here, haemodynamically-unstable patients received CVVHDF or SLEDD and haemodynamically-stable patients received IHD. Intensive RRT consisted of either CVVHDF with a total effluent rate of 35 ml/kg/h or IHD/SLEDD six times per week. Conventional dose RRT included CVHDF with a total effluent rate of

20 ml/kg/h or IHD/SLEDD three times per week. Results from this study will be available later in 2008. The Randomized Evaluation of Normal Versus Augmented Level of RRT (RENAL) study in Australia and New Zealand is currently in the process of randomizing 1,500 patients to CVVH-DF (58). Augmented CVVHDF is performed with total effluent flow rates of 40 ml/kg/h, normal CVVHDF with total effluent flow rates of 25 ml/kg/h. Conclusion of enrollment is scheduled for spring/summer 2008.

Summary and key points for clinical practice

Timing of RRT: No definite answer can currently be given with regards to whether "early" initiation of RRT results in better outcome than conventional initiation of RRT. Larger RCTs will be helpful in answering this question, but only if they also reach and adhere to consensus regarding the definitions of "early" and "late" initiation. We recommend a study design that uses RIFLE criteria as the point of initiation in at least one experimental arm.

Mode of RRT: Both CRRT and IHD appear to be effective in critically-ill patients with AKI and should be used according to individual patients' needs and local preferences. Despite the remaining uncertainty as to which mode of RRT is superior, our view is that both modalities have a role in the management of critically ill patients with AKI. Finally, more data are needed with respect to the newer, so-called hybrid techniques, e.g. SLEDD.

Dose of RRT: Although current data do not allow for a definite answer as to what the optimal dose of RRT in critically-ill patients with AKI is, best available data support the use of either total effluent flow rates of at least 35 ml/kg/h in CVVH/CVVHDF or daily IHD. However, lower or so-called 'conventional' doses might still be safe and effective, but their use should now be restricted to research protocols that specifically address the issue of RRT doses – fortunately such trials are nearing completion.

The authors

Kai Singbartl, MD[1]
John A. Kellum, MD, FACP, FCCM, FCCP[2]
[1]Assistant Professor of Critical Care
Medicine and Anaesthesiology | The
CRISMA Laboratory | Department of Critical
Care Medicine | University of Pittsburgh |
Pittsburgh, USA
[2]Professor of Critical Care Medicine and
Medicine | The CRISMA Laboratory |
Department of Critical Care Medicine |
University of Pittsburgh | Pittsburgh, USA

Address for correspondence
John A. Kellum
Department of Critical Care Medicine
608 Scaife Hall
University of Pittsburgh School of Medicine
3550 Terrace Street
Pittsburgh, PA 15261, USA
e-mail: kellumja@ccm.upmc.edu

References

1. Uchino S, Kellum JA, Bellomo R, Doig GS, Morimatsu, H, Morgera, S, Schetz M, Tan I, Bouman C, Macedo E, Gibney N, Tolwani A, Ronco C. Acute renal failure in critically ill patients: a multinational, multicenter study. JAMA. 2005;294:813–8.
2. Brivet FG, Kleinknecht DJ, Loirat P, Landais PJ. Acute renal failure in intensive care units–causes, outcome, and prognostic factors of hospital mortality; a prospective, multicenter study. French Study Group on Acute Renal Failure. Crit Care Med. 1996;24:192–8.
3. Metnitz P, Krenn C, Steltzer H, Lang T, Ploder J, Lenz K, Le Gall J, Druml W. Effect of acute renal failure requiring renal replacement therapy on outcome in critically ill patients. Crit Care Med. 2002;30:2051–8.
4. Kellum, JA, Angus, DC. Patients are dying of acute renal failure. Crit Care Med. 2002;30:2156–7.
5. Parsons FM, Hobson SM, Blagg CR, McCracken BH. Optimum time for dialysis in acute reversible renal failure. Description of an improved dialyser with large surface area. Lancet. 1961;1:129–34.
6. Fischer RP, Griffen WO, Reiser M, Clark DS. Early dialysis in the treatment of acute renal failure. Surg Gynecol Obstet. 1966;123:1019–23.
7. Kleinknecht D, Jungers P, Chanard J, Barbanel C, Ganeval D. Uremic; non-uremic complications in acute renal failure: Evaluation of early; frequent dialysis on prognosis Kidney Int. 1972;1:190–6.
8. Conger JD. A controlled evaluation of prophylactic dialysis in post-traumatic acute renal failure J Trauma. 1975;15:1056–63.
9. Gillum DM, Dixon BS, Yanover MJ, Kelleher SP, Shapiro MD, Benedetti RG, Dillingham MA, Paller MS, Goldberg JP, Tomford RC. The role of intensive dialysis in acute renal failure (1986) Clin Nephrol. 1986;25:249–55.
10. Gettings LG, Reynolds HN, Scalea T. Outcome in post-traumatic acute renal failure when continuous renal replacement therapy is applied early vs. late Intensive Care Med. 1999;25:805–13.
11. Bouman CS, Oudemans-Van Straaten HM, Tijssen JG, Zandstra DF, Kesecioglu J. Effects of early high-volume continuous venovenous hemofiltration on survival; recovery of renal function in intensive care patients with acute renal failure: a prospective, randomized trial (2002) Crit Care Med. 2002;30:2205–11.
12. Demirkilic U, Kuralay E, Yenicesu M, Cacalar K, Oz BS, Cingaz F, Gafracanay C, Yildirim V, Ceylan S, Arslan M, Vural A, Tatar H. Timing of replacement therapy for acute renal failure after cardiac surgery J Card Surg. 2004;19:17–20.
13. Elahi MM, Lim MY, Joseph RN, Dhannapuneni RR, Spyt TJ. Early hemofiltration improves survival in post-cardioto-my patients with acute renal failure. Eur J Cardiothorac Surg. 2004;26:1027–31.
14. Piccinni P, Dan M, Barbacini S, Carraro R, Lieta E, Marafon S, Zamperetti N, Brendolan A, D'Intini V, Tetta C, Bellomo R, Ronco C. Early isovolaemic haemofiltration in oliguric patients with septic shock. Intensive Care Med. 2006;32:80–6.
15. Liu KD, Himmelfarb J, Paganini E, Ikizler TA, Soroko SH, Mehta RL, Chertow GM. Timing of initiation of dialysis in critically ill patients with acute kidney injury. Clin J Am Soc Nephrol. 2006;1:915–9.
16. Ronco C, Bellomo R, Homel P, Brendolan A, Dan M, Piccinni P, La Greca G. Effects of different doses in continuous veno-venous haemofiltration on outcomes of acute renal failure: a prospective randomised trial. Lancet. 2000;356:26–30.
17. Bagshaw SM, Uchino SM, Bellomo R, Morimatsu H, Morgera S, Schetz M, Tan I, Bouman C, Macedo E, Gibney N, Tolwani A, Oudemans-van Straaten HM, Ronco C, Kellum JA. Beginning and Ending Supportive Therapy for the Kidney (BEST Kidney) Investigators. Septic acute kidney injury in critically ill patients: clinical characteristics and outcomes. Clin J Am Soc Nephrol. 2007;2:431–439.
18. Bellomo R, Ronco C, Kellum JA, Mehta RL, Palevsky P. Acute renal failure – definition, outcome measures, animal models, fluid therapy and information technology needs: the Second International Consensus Conference of the Acute Dialysis Quality Initiative (ADQI) Group. Crit Care. 2004;8:R204–12.
19. Kellum JA, Mehta RL, Levin A, Molitoris BA, Warnock DG, Shah SV, Joannidis M, Ronco C, for the Acute Kidney Injury Network (AKIN). Development of a Clinical

Research Agenda for Acute Kidney Injury Using an International, Interdisciplinary, Three-Step Modified Delphi Process. Clin J Am Soc Nephrol. 2008: CJN.04891107.

20. Ricci Z, Ronco C, D'Amico G, De Felice R, Rossi S, Bolgan I, Bonello M, Zamperetti N, Petras D, Salvatori, G, Dan M, Piccinni P. Practice patterns in the management of acute renal failure in the critically ill patient: an international survey. Nephrol Dial Transplant. 2006;21:690–6.

21. Jacka MJ, Ivancinova X, Gibney RT. Continuous renal replacement therapy improves renal recovery from acute renal failure. Can J Anaesth. 2005;52:327–32.

22. Waldrop J, Ciraulo DL, Milner TP, Gregori D, Kendrick AS, Richart CM, Maxwell RA, Barker DE. A comparison of continuous renal replacement therapy to intermittent dialysis in the management of renal insufficiency in the acutely Ill surgical patient. Am Surg. 2005;71:36–9.

23. Bellomo R, Boyce N. Continuous venovenous hemodia-filtration compared with conventional dialysis in critically ill patients with acute renal failure. ASAIO J. 1993;39:M794–7.

24. Bellomo R, Farmer M, Bhonagiri S, Porceddu S, Ariens M, M'Pisi D, Ronco C. Changing acute renal failure treatment from intermittent hemodialysis to continuous hemofiltration: impact on azotemic control. Int J Artif Organs. 1999;22:145–50.

25. Bellomo R, Farmer M, Wright C, Parkin G, Boyce N. Treatment of sepsis-associated severe acute renal failure with continuous hemodiafiltration: clinical experience; comparison with conventional dialysis. Blood Purif. 1995; 13:246–54.

26. Bellomo R, Mansfield D, Rumble S, Shapiro J, Parkin G, Boyce N. Acute renal failure in critical illness. Conven-tional dialysis versus acute continuous hemodia-filtration. ASAIO J. 1992;38:M654–7.

27. Swartz RD, Bustami RT, Daley JM, Gillespie BW, Port FK. Estimating the impact of renal replacement therapy choice on outcome in severe acute renal failure. Clin Nephrol. 2005;63:335–45.

28. Gangji AS, Rabbat CG, Margetts PJ. Benefit of continuous renal replacement therapy in subgroups of acutely ill patients: a retrospective analysis. Clin Nephrol. 2005; 63:267–75.

29. Chang JW, Yang WS, Seo JW, Lee JS, Lee SK, Park SK. Continuous venovenous hemodiafiltration versus hemodialysis as renal replacement therapy in patients with acute renal failure in the intensive care unit. Scand J Urol Nephrol. 2004;38:417–21.

30. Hirayama Y, Hirasawa H, Oda S, Shiga H, Nakanishi K, Matsuda K, Nakamura M, Hirano T, Moriguchi T, Watanabe E, Nitta M, Abe R, Nakada T. The change in renal replacement therapy on acute renal failure in a general intensive care unit in a university hospital; its clinical efficacy: a Japanese experience. Ther Apher Dial. 2003;7:475–82.

31. Uchino S, Bellomo R, Kellum JA, Morimatsu H, Morgera S, Schetz MR, Tan I, Bouman C, Macedo E, Gibney N, Tolwani A, Oudemans-Van Straaten HM, Ronco C. Patient; kidney survival by dialysis modality in critically ill patients with acute kidney injury. Int J Artif Organs. 2007;30:281–92.

32. Uchino S, Bellomo R, Ronco C. Intermittent versus continuous renal replacement therapy in the ICU: impact on electrolyte and acid-base balance. Intensive Care Med. 2001;27:1037–43.

33. Cho KC, Himmelfarb J, Paganini E, Ikizler TA, Soroko SH, Mehta RL, Chertow GM. Survival by dialysis modality in critically ill patients with acute kidney injury. J Am Soc Nephrol. 2006;17:3132–8.

34. Guerin C, Girard R, Selli JM, Ayzac L. Intermittent versus continuous renal replacement therapy for acute renal failure in intensive care units: results from a multicenter prospective epidemiological survey. Intensive Care Med. 2002;28:1411–8.

35. Rialp G, Roglan A, Betbese A, Perez-Marquez M, Balus J, Lopez-Velarde G, Santos JA, Bak E, Net A. Prognostic indexes; mortality in critically ill patients with acute renal failure treated with different dialytic techniques. Ren Fail. 1996;18:667–75.

36. Vitale C, Bagnis C, Marangella M, Belloni G, Lupo M, Spina G, Bondonio P, Ramello A. Cost analysis of blood purification in intensive care units: continuous versus intermittent hemodiafiltration. J Nephrol. 2003;16:572–9.

37. Manns B, Doig CJ, Lee H, Dean S, Tonelli M, Johnson D, Donaldson C. Cost of acute renal failure requiring dialysis in the intensive care unit: clinical; resource implications of renal recovery. Crit Care Med. 2003;31:449–55.

38. Kierdorf HP. Einfluß der kontinuierlichen Hämofiltration auf Proteinkatabolismus und Prognose des akuten Nierenversagens im Multiorganversagen. (1994) Thesis, RWTH Aachen, Germany.

39. Augustine JJ, Sandy D, Seifert TH, Paganini EP. A randomized controlled trial comparing intermittent with continuous dialysis in patients with ARF. Am J Kidney Dis. 2004;44:1000–7.

40. Gasparovic V, Filipovic-Grcic I, Merkler M, Pisl Z. Continuous renal replacement therapy (CRRT) or intermittent hemodialysis (IHD) – what is the procedure of choice in critically ill patients?. Ren Fail. 2003;25:855–62.

41. John S, Griesbach D, Baumgärtel M, Weihprecht H, Schmieder RE, Geiger H. Effects of continuous haemofiltration vs intermittent haemodialysis on systemic haemodynamics; splanchnic regional perfusion in septic shock patients: a prospective, randomized clinical trial. Nephrol Dial Transplant. 2001;16:320–7.

42. Mehta RL, Kellum JA, Shah SV, Molitoris BA, Ronco C, Warnock DG, Levin A. Acute Kidney Injury Network: report of an initiative to improve outcomes in acute kidney injury. Crit Care. 2007;11:R31.

43. Uehlinger DE, Jakob SM, Ferrari P, Eichelberger M, Huynh-Do U, Marti HP, Mohaupt MG, Vogt B, Rothen, HU Regli B, Takala J, Frey FJ. Comparison of continuous; intermittent renal replacement therapy for acute renal failure. Nephrol Dial Transplant. 2005;20:1630–7.

44. Vinsonneau C, Camus C, Combes A, Costa de Beauregard MA, Klouche K, Boulain T, Pallot JL, Chiche JD, Taupin P, Landais P, Dhainaut JF. Continuous venovenous haemodiafiltration versus intermittent haemodialysis for acute renal failure in patients with multiple-organ dysfunction syndrome: a multicentre randomised trial. Lancet. 2006;368:379–85.

45. Bagshaw SM, Berthiaume LR, Delaney A, Bellomo R. Continuous versus intermittent renal replacement therapy for critically ill patients with acute kidney injury: a meta-analysis. Crit Care Med. 2008;36:610–7.

46. Van Biesen W, Veys N, Vanholder R. Intermittent hemodialysis for renal replacement therapy in intensive care: new evidence for old truths. Contrib Nephrol. 2007; 156:304–8.

47. Uchino S, Fealy N, Baldwin I, Morimatsu H, Bellomo R. Continuous is not continuous: the incidence and impact of circuit "down-time" on uraemic control during continuous veno-venous haemofiltration. Intensive Care Med. 2003;29:575–8.

48. Venkataraman R, Kellum JA, Palevsky P. Dosing patterns for continuous renal replacement therapy at a large academic medical center in the United States. J Crit Care. 2002;17:246–50.

49. Kellum JA, Palevsky PM. Renal support in acute kidney injury. Lancet. 2006;368:344–345.

50. Van Biesen W, Vanholder R, Lameire N. Dialysis strategies in critically ill acute renal failure patients. Curr Opin Crit Care. 2003;9:491–5.

51. Vanholder R, Van Biesen W, Lameire N. What is the renal replacement method of first choice for intensive care patients? J Am Soc Nephrol. 2001;12 Suppl 17:S40–3.

52. Fliser D, Kielstein JT. Technology Insight: treatment of renal failure in the intensive care unit with extended dialysis. Nat Clin Pract Nephrol. 2006;2:32–9.

53. Berbece AN, Richardson RM. Sustained low-efficiency dialysis in the ICU: cost, anticoagulation, and solute removal. Kidney Int. 2006;70:963–8.

54. Schiffl H, Lang SM, Fischer R. Daily hemodialysis and the outcome of acute renal failure. N Engl J Med. 2002;346: 305–10.

55. Saudan P, Niederberger M, De Seigneux S, Romand J, Pugin J, Perneger T, Martin PY. Adding a dialysis dose to continuous hemofiltration increases survival in patients with acute renal failure. Kidney Int. 2006;70: 1312–7.

56. Kellum JA. Renal replacement therapy in critically ill patients with acute renal failure: does a greater dose improve survival?. Nat Clin Pract Nephrol. 2007;3: 128–129.

57. Palevsky PM, O'Connor T, Zhang JH, Star RA, Smith MW. Design of the VA/NIH Acute Renal Failure Trial Network (ATN) Study: intensive versus conventional renal support in acute renal failure. Clin Trials. 2005;2: 423–35.

58. Bellomo R. Do we know the optimal dose for renal replacement therapy in the intensive care unit?. Kidney Int. 2006;70:1202–4.

59. Mehta RL, McDonald B, Gabbai FB, Pahl M, Pascual MT, Farkas A, Kaplan RM. A randomized clinical trial of continuous versus intermittent dialysis for acute renal failure. Kidney Int. 2001;60:1154–63.

Heleen M. Oudemans-van Straaten

Anticoagulation for renal replacement therapy: Heparin or citrate

Introduction

Acute renal failure (ARF) is a severe complication of critical illness, generally developing as a component of multiple organ failure. Prognosis depends on the severity of the acute disease and underlying comorbidities. ARF confers an independent risk for mortality if renal replacement is required (1). Among the components of RRT, the use of biocompatible membranes (2) and an adequate RRT dose (3, 4) have shown to improve clinical outcome. Given the high mortality of these patients, further improvement of the intervention is wanted.

To prevent clotting in extracorporeal RRT circuits anticoagulation is generally required. Heparins are the classic choice. Their main drawback is bleeding as a result of systemic anticoagulation (5). Critically ill patients are at risk for bleeding due to recent surgery, trauma, mucosal lesions and coagulopathy. Regional anticoagulation with citrate seems an attractive alternative. Citrate is administered in the extracorporeal circuit and inhibits the generation of thrombin by chelating calcium. Citrate is partially removed by filtration or dialysis (6, 7), and the remains are rapidly metabolised. As a result, systemic coagulation is unaffected. However, metabolism of citrate requires adequate liver function and muscle perfusion (8). As a result, some patients do not tolerate citrate. Furthermore citrate is substrate for buffer as

well, making its use complex and prone to metabolic derangement (9, 10).

Altogether, the decision whether to use heparin or citrate for anticoagulation of RRT circuits remains controversial. The present contribution aims to highlight the pitfalls of the two regimes in order to support clinical decision-making.

Controversial position of heparins

Unfractionated heparin (UFH) is a mixture of molecules with sizes ranging from 5 to 30 kDa, while low molecular heparins (LMWH) are derived from UFH conferring a molecular weight ranging from 2 to 6 kD (11). The major side effect of heparins is bleeding associated with systemic anticoagulation. Other side effects include interference with inflammation, heparin-induced thrombocytopenia, hypoaldosteronism, and effects on serum lipids and bone resorption (11–13).

Heparins and anticoagulation (11, 14)

Heparins are glucosaminoglycans exerting a complex of anticoagulant effects, mainly by the binding of the pentasaccharide domain to anti-thrombin (AT). Binding to AT potentiates the natural anticoagulant properties of AT, which include inhibition of the coagulation factors II (thrombin), IXa, Xa, IXa and XIIa. For the simultaneous binding of heparin to AT and thrombin a minimal chain length of 18 saccharides is required. As a result only the larger heparin fragments of UFH have anti-IIa activity, while the smaller fragments of UFH and the LMWHs preferentially inhibit Xa activity. The anti-IIa to anti-Xa activity varies between 1:2 to 1:5 among the different compounds. Heparins additionally inhibit the generation of factor VIIa and factor VIIa-tissue factor (TF) complex, stimulate the release of tissue factor pathway inhibitor (TFPI) from vascular sites, and potentiate TFPI inhibition of the VIIa/TF complex. Since the anti-Xa effect of LMWH is stronger than the anti-IIa effect, the anticoagulant effect of LMWH can only partially be neutralised by protamine.

Heparins and bleeding

Critically ill patients have an increased risk of bleeding. The use of heparins will augment this risk. Studies report a bleeding incidence of 0% to 50% (summarised in 9, 15). A retrospective analysis found increased bleeding if systemic aPTT is higher than 45 seconds (5). However a reliable test to predict bleeding is not available (11).

Heparins and inflammation

The binding of heparin to AT does not only potentiate its anticoagulant effects but additionally prohibits the anti-inflammatory actions of AT. AT exerts anti-inflammatory effects by binding to glucosaminoglycans on endothelial membranes, which enhances prostacyclin formation, diminishes the adherence and migration of leukocytes, reduces platelet aggregation and decreases proinflammatory cytokine production. (16, 17). Furthermore, heparins can mobilise myeloperoxidase, not only from neutrophils adhered to and activated by the dialysis membrane but also from circulating and inflammation primed leukocytes adhering to the vascular endothelium (18). These pro-inflammatory effects of heparins may espe-cially be pronounced in inflammatory states. On the other hand, heparins have anti-inflammatory properties as well. Post hoc analysis of the major sepsis trials suggests that low-dose heparin might have favorable effects on survival (summarised in reference (12). However, for the prevention of extracorporeal clotting higher doses of heparins are required, increasing the risk of side effects (13).

Heparin binding to other compounds

A further problem with the use of heparins is its binding to other molecules than AT. The non-specific binding of heparin to plasma proteins and cells decreases its anticoagulant activity. Since several of these proteins are acute phase reactants, the anticoagulant response to heparin among critically ill patients is highly variable (11, 19, 20). LMWHs exert less binding to plasma proteins than UFH.

Heparin-induced thrombocytopenia

A feared side effect of heparins is the development of heparin-induced thrombocytopenia (HIT), related to the binding of heparin to platelet factor-4 (PF4), released from activated platelets. Some patients develop antibodies against this heparin–PF4 complex. The antibody-PF4-heparin complex subsequently binds to platelets inducing platelet activation, aggregation and activation of the blood-coagulation pathways. This sequence results in a loss of circulating platelets and a pro-thrombotic state (21). Depending on the dose and type of heparin, the population and the criteria used, < 1% to 5% of treated patients develop HIT (22–24). LMWHs confer less antibody development than UFH (25).

Pitfals with dosing and monitoring of heparins

Anticoagulant effects of heparins are unpredictable in the critically ill as a consequence of low levels of antithrombin and the nonspecific binding of heparins to proteins and cells. Due to less non-specific binding LMWHs have more predictable pharmacokinetics (11). Clinical studies show that acquired AT deficiency in critically ill patients receiving UFH during CRRT is associated with premature filter clotting while supplementation of AT improves filter lifespan (26, 26, 27).

Half life of UFH is about 90 min, while normal half-life of LMWHs is 2–4 hours. However, clearance of heparins is complex. The larger heparin fragments (anti-IIa) are cleared from the circulation more rapidly than the smaller (anti-Xa), resulting in prolongation of the anti-Xa effect in vivo which is not detetected by APTT. Furthermore renal insufficiency increases half life of the smaller fragments, which is a well-recognised phenomenon for LMWHs (28), but also accounts for the smaller fragments of UFH (29). Because anti-Xa measurement is not generally available, this accumulation goes undetected. It should be noted that a recent small study indicates that LMWHs are eliminated by CRRT (30). LMWHs may therefore not accumulate if CRRT is applied.

Although many factors in critically ill patients confound the relation between heparin dose and anticoagulant effects or bleeding (11), monitoring of UFH with aPTT is still the best option. To minimise the risk of bleeding, it seems prudent to keep target aPTT below 45 seconds (5) or less than 1.5 times normal (9). At this low level of anticoagulation ACT is relatively insensitive (31). Normal aPTT does however not exclude the presence of an anti-Xa effect. For UFH, a loading dose of 30 U/kg followed by a continuous infusion of 5–10 U/kg/h may be considered. The 5 U/kg dose is often associated with normal APTT (32).

The anticoagulant effect of LMWHs can be monitored by measuring anti-Xa activity. A correlation between anti-Xa level and circuit survival time was found in one study (33), but not in other studies (34, 35). Therefore, routine monitoring of anticoagulation might not be necessary to achieve optimal circuit survival. In addition, anti-Xa seems an unreliable predictor of bleeding as well (33) and anti-Xa determinations are not generally available. Therefore, a fixed dosing regimen of LMWH is often applied (36). Alternatively, a loading dose of 25–50 U/kg followed by a continuous infusion of about 5 IU/kg/h may be considered, aiming at systemic anti-Xa levels of 0.25–0.35 U/ml.

UFH versus LMWH

The major advantages of UFH are its low costs, ease of administration, simple monitoring and reversibility with protamine. LMWHs exhibit several advantages including lower incidence of HIT (21), less platelet and polymorphnuclear cell activation (13), less protein binding leading to higher and more constant bioavailability (11) and lack of metabolic side effect (37). However half life of LMWHs is longer and protamine only reversed their anti-IIa effect. There are two small randomised studies comparing UFH to LMWH. Circuit survival is reported to be similar (36) or longer with LMWHs (33). Studies are too small to compare bleeding complications. The main drawback of both heparins is systemic anticoagulation and the lack of a reliable predictor of bleeding and anti-thrombotic efficacy (11).

Pitfalls with the use of heparins for anticoagulation in CRRT

- Bleeding
- No reliable test to predict bleeding
- Unreliable anticoagulant effects in the critically ill due to
  - antithrombin deficiency
  - non-specific binding to plasma proteins and cells
- Heparin-induced thrombocytopenia
- Pro-inflammatory effects related to
  - AT binding
  - myeloperoxidase release
- Anti-inflammatory effects

Citrate

Citrate and anticoagulation

Citrate chelates calcium and thereby decreases ionised calcium in the extracorporeal circuit. Because calcium is a cofactor in the coagulation cascade, the generation of thrombin is inhibited. Citrate is partially removed by convection or diffusion and partially enters the systemic circulation, where ionised calcium rises again due to the dilution of extracorporeal blood, the liberation of chelated calcium when citrate is metabolised, and the replacement of calcium. As a result, systemic effects on coagulation do not occur.

Citrate and acid base

Apart from being an anticoagulant, citrate is buffer substrate. The generation of buffer is related to the conversion of sodium citrate to citric acid:

$$Na_3citrate + 3H_2CO_3$$
$$\rightarrow Citric\ acid\ (C_6H_8O_7) + 3NaHCO_3$$

Citric acid enters the mitochondria and is metabolised in the Krebs cycle, mainly in the liver, but also in skeletal muscle and renal cortex, leaving sodium bicarbonate. The *buffer* strength of the citrate solution is thus related to the conversion of tri-sodium citrate to citric acid. One mole of trisodium citrate provides three moles of bicarbonate. In some solutions, e.g. the ACD-A solution, part of the sodium is replaced by hydrogen, which reduces buffer strength (9, 10).

Citrate and biocompatibility

The use of citrate appears to attenuate dialysis membrane-induced inflammation as well. Exposure of blood to foreign material initiates a series of humoral and cellular reactions. Protein adsorption, triggering of the coagulation and complement cascade, and activation of leukocytes and platelets play a role. Activated leukocytes release inflammatory mediators that induce oxidative stress, thereby transforming lipids and proteins and contributing to endothelial injury. Activated platelets aggregate and enhance thrombin generation. The cascades of inflammation and thrombosis are highly linked at molecular level (38–40).

In intermittent haemodialysis, citrate anticoagulation (compared to heparin or dalteparin) almost completely abolishes both polymorphnuclear and platelet degranulation and lowers plasma oxidised-LDL indicating less cellular activation and lipid peroxidation (41–43). This anti-inflammatory effect of citrate seems to be mediated by extracellular hypocalcemia, which not only inhibits the generation of thrombin, but also influences intracellular calcium signaling and may thus down-regulate the foreign material induced inflammation (44–46).

Feasibility of citrate

After the first reports of Mehta and Ward (47), a wide variety of citrate systems for CRRT have been described. More than 50 hits are encountered in a Medline search. Among them are systems for continuous venovenous haemodialysis (CVVHD), pre- and postdilution continuous haemofiltration (CVVH), continous haemodiafiltration (CVVHDF) and for different doses of CRRT (1.5 to 4 l/h) (summarised in the electronic supplemental material of reference 9). Each has its specified composition of dialysis and replacement fluids. Studies compete in the degree of safety, feasibility and flexibility. However, none of the systems has proven superiority and none of the proposed systems can attain perfect acid-base control using a single standard citrate-, replacement- or dialysis solution. Each protocol has its own rules to titrate anticoagulation, correct metabolic acidosis or alkalosis, hypo- or hypercalcemia, depending on the modality and the solutions in use (10).

Tolerance, metabolic complications and limitations

Tolerance of citrate is related to the metabolic conversion of citrate, which is diminished in conditions of liver failure or poor tissue perfusion (8, 48). If metabolism is insufficient, citrate accumulates decreasing ionised calcium and increasing total to ionised calcium ratio in the blood (49–51). In addition, metabolic acidosis will ensue because citrate is not used as a buffer. Accumulation of citrate is easily detectable with standard monitoring. A rise of total to ionised calcium ratio above 2.25 should warn the clinician to reduce citrate dose.

Different options [summarised in (9)]

Before implementation of citrate, several decisions have to be made. First, it should be decided whether to use haemofiltration, haemodialysis or haemodilfiltration. Second, whether citrate is infused separately before the filter and an adjusted replacement fluid is given, or alternatively, whether citrate is added to the replacement fluid, which is administered in predilution. Third, whether citrate is either administered in a fixed relation to blood flow, or citrate dose is adjusted according to postfilter ionised calcium measurements. The latter option may optimise anticoagulation, but complicates the intervention and causes variations in the amount of buffer entering the patient. Fourth, whether metabolic acidosis or alkalosis are adjusted by varying the dose of citrate, or whether the buffer content of the replacement fluids is altered. In the first option, the level of anticoagulation varies and may cause early filter clotting. Fifth, the clinician should verify whether the method is appropriate for the presently recommended dose of CRRT (52–54).

Dosing and monitoring

For optimal anticoagulation, citrate flow is adjusted to blood flow, targeting at a concentration of 3–5 mmol/l in the filter. Post-filter iCa can be used for fine tuning of the level of anticoagulation aiming at a concentration of iCa < 0.35 mmol/l. However, other protocols prefer a fixed citrate dose, and do not monitor iCa in the circuit [summarised in (9)]. Minimal biochemical monitoring of citrate includes assessment of systemic acid base balance and ionised calcium at 6-h interval. Total calcium should be measured at least at 24-h intervals to calculate the total calcium to ionised calcium ratio and detect citrate accumulation. In patients at risk for citrate accumulation more frequent monitoring is recommended. In patients with liver failure, a first check two hours after initation of the treatment is recommended. If the ratio increases, the attending physician can decide to reduce citrate dose. If citrate accumulation persists, CRRT can often be continued without anticoagulation because the patient generally has liver failure and coagulapathy.

Pitfalls with the use of citrate for anticoagulation in CRRT

- *Citrate is both anticoagulant and buffer*
- *Changing anticoagulant dose infuences buffer supply to the patient*
- *The use of citrate requires*
  - *implementation of a strict protocol*
  - *training and understanding*
- *Metabolic conversion is reduced in case of liver failure and poor tissue perfusion*

Citrate versus heparin: Safety and effectivity

A huge amount of studies describe the feasibility of citrate for CRRT. Some of the published studies compare circuit life and bleeding complications with citrate to historical or contemporary non-randomised controls receiving heparin (9, 55–57). Groups are generally not comparable, because the citrate patients often had a higher risk of bleeding. Three small randomised controlled studies comparing citrate to heparin in critically ill patients have been published in full paper (54, 58, 59). Our recent randomised controlled trial including 200 critically ill patients with ARF without an increased risk of bleeding and or underlying liver failure comparing citrate to the LMWH nadroparin has not been published yet. I will summarise the safety and efficacy of the two anticoagulant strategies below.

- *Safety.* The primary rationale for the use of citrate is to reduce bleeding complications. The four randomised studies excluded patients with an increased risk of bleeding. Bleeding was significantly reduced in one (59) and non-significantly reduced in the other randomised trials, while transfusion rate was significantly less in one of three randomised studies (54). In one of the studies, the relative risk of bleeding was significantly lower in de citrate patients after adjustment for severeity of illness and AT concentration (58). In a non-randomised cohort study citrate patients had less bleeding despite their higher risk of bleeding (56).
- *Efficacy.* Circuit life is influenced by a myriad of factors, among these are the patient's acute illness, which often causes activation of coagulation and or a reduced coagulation capacity; platelet count, modality of CRRT (dialysis or filtration), dose and filtration fraction of haemofiltration, quality of the vascular access, the local protocol of disconnection and logistic events needing discontinuation of the circuit. In two of the three randomised studies comparing citrate to heparin, circuit life was significantly longer with citrate (54, 58), while circuit life was similar in the other two.
- *Tolerance.* Tolerance of citrate is a matter of concern. However, in our randomised controlled trial, tolerance for citrate was better than for the low LMWH nadroparin even though

we excluded four times more patients for anticipated adverse events to nadroparin than to citrate. After randomisation, we had to discontinue nadroparin for predefined adverse events more frequently than citrate.

- *Metabolic control.* Metabolic complications depend on the rules and flexibility of the local protocol. The majority of the studies report excellent or adequate metabolic control with citrate. Some report metabolic alkalosis or hypernatremia. These complications are sometimes related to protocol violation, sometimes to shortcomings of the protocol and generally easy to correct by adjustment of bicarbonate replacement or citrate dose. In our randomised controlled trial we observed equal efficacy in correcting metabolic acidosis and less metabolic alkalosis with citrate.
- *Patient survival.* The primary incentive to perform a large randomised controlled trial was our concern whether citrate would be safe. Unexpectedly, the study showed a fifteen percent absolute 3-month survival benefit for citrate on intention to treat analysis.

Summary

Anticoagulation is required to prevent clotting in the extracorporeal circuit of CRRT. Heparins are most popular. The major advantages of UFH are its low costs, ease of administration, simple monitoring and reversibility with protamine. LMWHs have the advantage of better bioavailability and more reliable pharmacokinetics, less platelet and polymorphnuclear cell activation, lower incidence of HIT and lack of metabolic side effects. However. LMWHs have a longer half life and are only partially neutralised by protamine. The main drawback of both is that heparins cause systemic anticoagulation and thereby increase the risk of bleeding, while a reliable predictor of bleeding is not available.

Regional anticoagulation with citrate is at least as effective as heparins and does not increase the patient's risk of bleeding. Comparative studies report a similar or longer circuit survival time and less bleeding with citrate. Complexity of the intervention is its main drawback. Safe performance of citrate anticoagulation requires the implementation of a local protocol, adequate training and understanding of the method. Safety will further improve as a citrate module is incorporated in the CRRT device. With these precautions, citrate is well-tolerated, provides good metabolic control and may even improve patient survival.

Key points for clinical practice

- Take precautions to reduce the side effects of anticoagulation for CRRT.
- Both UFH and LMWHs increase the risk of bleeding.
- To limit the risk of bleeding
  - use UFH in a low dose and limit prolongation of APTT to a maximum of 45 seconds or 1.5 times normal
  - use LMWHs in a low dose and limit prolongation of ant-Xa to a maximum of 0.40 U/ml
  - preferably use citrate
- Regional anticoagulation with citrate
  - is at least as effective as heparins
  - reduces the patient's risk of bleeding.
  - seems to mitigate membrane-induced cellular activation
  - may even improve patient survival.
- To limit the metabolic risks of citrate
  - use a strict protocol adjusted to the desired dose and mode of CRRT
  - provide regular training to nurses and doctors to improve practical skills and understanding of the method

The author

Heleen M. Oudemans-van Straaten, MD, PhD
  Department of Intensive Care Medicine
  Onze Lieve Vrouwe Gasthuis
  Oosterpark 10
  1091 AC Amsterdam, The Netherlands
  e-mail: h.m.oudemans-vanstraaten@olvg.nl

References

1. Metnitz PG, Krenn CG, Steltzer H, Lang T, Ploder J, Lenz K et al. Effect of acute renal failure requiring renal replacement therapy on outcome in critically ill patients. Crit Care Med. 2002;30:2051–8.
2. Himmelfarb J, Tolkoff RN, Chandran P, Parker RA, Wingard RL, Hakim R. A multicenter comparison of dialysis membranes in the treatment of acute renal failure requiring dialysis. J Am Soc Nephrol. 1998;9:257–66.
3. Ronco C, Bellomo R, Homel P, Brendolan A, Dan M, Piccinni P et al. Effects of different doses in continuous veno-venous haemofiltration on outcomes of acute renal

failure: a prospective randomised trial. Lancet. 2000; 356:26–30.

4. Saudan P, Niederberger M, De Seigneux S, Romand J, Pugin J, Perneger T et al. Adding a dialysis dose to continuous hemofiltration increases survival in patients with acute renal failure. Kidney Int. 2006;70:1312–7.

5. van de Wetering J, Westendorp RG, van der Hoeven JG, Stolk B, Feuth JD, Chang PC. Heparin use in continuous renal replacement procedures: the struggle between filter coagulation and patient hemorrhage. J Am Soc Nephrol. 1996;7:145–50.

6. Swartz R, Pasko D, O'Toole J, Starmann B. Improving the delivery of continuous renal replacement therapy using regional citrate anticoagulation. Clin Nephrol. 2004;61: 134–43.

7. Chadha V, Garg U, Warady BA, Alon US. Citrate clearance in children receiving continuous venovenous renal replacement therapy. Pediatr Nephrol. 2002;17:819–24.

8. Apsner R, Schwarzenhofer M, Derfler K, Zauner C, Ratheiser K, Kranz A. Impairment of citrate metabolism in acute hepatic failure. Wien Klin Wochenschr. 1997; 109:123–7.

9. Oudemans-van Straaten HM, Wester JP, de Pont AC, Schetz MR. Anticoagulation strategies in continuous renal replacement therapy: can the choice be evidence based? Intensive Care Med. 2006;32:188–202.

10. Joannidis M, Oudemans-van Straaten HM. Clinical review: Patency of the circuit in continuous renal replacement therapy. Crit Care. 2007;11:218.

11. Hirsh J, Warkentin TE, Shaughnessy SG, Anand SS, Halperin JL, Raschke R et al. Heparin and low-molecular-weight heparin: mechanisms of action, pharmacokinetics, dosing, monitoring, efficacy, and safety. Chest. 2001; 119(1 Suppl):64S–94S.

12. Cornet AD, Smit EG, Beishuizen A, Groeneveld AB. The role of heparin and allied compounds in the treatment of sepsis. Thromb Haemost. 2007;98:579–86.

13. Leitienne P, Fouque D, Rigal D, Adeleine P, Trzeciak MC, Laville M. Heparins and blood polymorphonuclear stimulation in haemodialysis: an expansion of the biocompatibility concept. Nephrol Dial Transplant. 2000; 15:1631–7.

14. Samama MM, Gerotziafas GT. Comparative pharmacokinetics of LMWHs. Semin Thromb Hemost. 2000;26 Suppl 1:31–8.

15. Schetz M. Anticoagulation for continuous renal replacement therapy. Curr Opin Anaesthesiol. 2001;14: 143–9.

16. Okajima K, Uchiba M. The anti-inflammatory properties of antithrombin III: new therapeutic implications. Semin Thromb Hemost. 1998;24:27–32.

17. Warren BL, Eid A, Singer P, Pillay SS, Carl P, Novak I et al. Caring for the critically ill patient. High-dose antithrombin III in severe sepsis: a randomized controlled trial. JAMA. 2001;286:1869–78.

18. Borawski J. Myeloperoxidase as a marker of hemodialysis biocompatibility and oxidative stress: the underestimated modifying effects of heparin. Am J Kidney Dis. 2006; 47:37–41.

19. Young E, Podor TJ, Venner T, Hirsh J. Induction of the acute-phase reaction increases heparin-binding proteins in plasma. Arterioscler Thromb Vasc Biol. 1997;17: 1568–74.

20. Cosmi B, Fredenburgh JC, Rischke J, Hirsh J, Young E, Weitz JI. Effect of nonspecific binding to plasma proteins on the antithrombin activities of unfractionated heparin, low-molecular-weight heparin, and dermatan sulfate. Circulation. 1997;95:118–24.

21. Warkentin TE. Heparin-induced thrombocytopenia: diagnosis and management. Circulation. 2004;110: e454–e458.

22. Verma AK, Levine M, Shalansky SJ, Carter CJ, Kelton JG. Frequency of heparin-induced thrombocytopenia in critical care patients. Pharmacotherapy. 2003;23:745–53.

23. Selleng K, Warkentin TE, Greinacher A. Heparin-induced thrombocytopenia in intensive care patients. Crit Care Med. 2007;35:1165–76.

24. Selleng S, Selleng K, Wollert HG, Muellejans B, Lietz T, Warkentin TE et al. Heparin-induced thrombocytopenia in patients requiring prolonged intensive care unit treatment after cardiopulmonary bypass. J Thromb Haemost. 2007, Dec [Epub ahead of print].

25. Lindhoff-Last E, Nakov R, Misselwitz F, Breddin HK, Bauersachs R. Incidence and clinical relevance of heparin-induced antibodies in patients with deep vein thrombosis treated with unfractionated or low-molecular-weight heparin. Br J Haematol. 2002;118:1137–42.

26. du Cheyron D, Bouchet B, Bruel C, Daubin C, Ramakers M, Charbonneau P. Antithrombin supplementation for anticoagulation during continuous hemofiltration in critically ill patients with septic shock: a case-control study. Crit Care. 2006;10:R45.

27. Lafargue M, Joannes-Boyau O, Honore PM, Gauche B, Grand H, Fleureau C et al. Acquired deficit of antithrombin and role of supplementation in septic patients during continuous veno-venous hemofiltration. ASAIO J. 2008;54:124–8.

28. Lim W, Dentali F, Eikelboom JW, Crowther MA. Meta-analysis: low-molecular-weight heparin and bleeding in patients with severe renal insufficiency. Ann Intern Med. 2006;144:673–84.

29. Thorevska N, Amoateng-Adjepong Y, Sabahi R, Schiopescu I, Salloum A, Muralidharan V et al. Anticoagulation in hospitalized patients with renal insufficiency: a comparison of bleeding rates with unfractionated heparin vs enoxaparin. Chest. 2004;125: 856–63.

30. Isla A, Gascon AR, Maynar J, Arzuaga A, Corral E, Martin A et al. In vitro and in vivo evaluation of enoxaparin removal by continuous renal replacement therapies with

acrylonitrile and polysulfone membranes. Clin Ther. 2005;27:1444–51.

31. De Waele JJ, van Cauwenberghe S, Hoste E, Benoit D, Colardyn F. The use of the activated clotting time for monitoring heparin therapy in critically ill patients. Intensive Care Med. 2003;29:325–8.

32. Tan HK, Baldwin I, Bellomo R. Continuous veno-venous hemofiltration without anticoagulation in high-risk patients. Intensive Care Med 2000;26:1652–7.

33. Joannidis M, Kountchev J, Rauchenzauner M, Schusterschitz N, Ulmer H, Mayr A et al. Enoxaparin vs. unfractionated heparin for anticoagulation during continuous veno-venous hemofiltration: a randomized controlled crossover study. Intensive Care Med. 2007; 33:1571–9.

34. Journois D, Safran D, Castelain MH, Chanu D, Drevillon C, Barrier G. Comparison of the antithrombotic effects of heparin, enoxaparin and prostacycline in continuous hemofiltration. Ann Fr Anesth Reanim. 1990;9:331–7.

35. de Pont AC, Oudemans-van Straaten HM, Roozendaal KJ, Zandstra DF. Nadroparin versus dalteparin anticoagulation in high-volume, continuous venovenous hemofiltration: a double-blind, randomized, crossover study. Crit Care Med. 2000;28:421–5.

36. Reeves JH, Cumming AR, Gallagher L, O'Brien JL, Santamaria JD. A controlled trial of low-molecular-weight heparin (dalteparin) versus unfractionated heparin as anticoagulant during continuous venovenous hemodialysis with filtration. Crit Care Med. 1999;27: 2224–8.

37. Elisaf MS, Germanos NP, Bairaktari HT, Pappas MB, Koulouridis EI, Siamopoulos KC. Effects of conventional vs. low-molecular-weight heparin on lipid profile in hemodialysis patients. Am J Nephrol. 1997;17:153–7.

38. Hakim RM. Clinical implications of biocompatibility in blood purification membranes. Nephrol Dial Transplant. 2000;15 Suppl 2:16–20.

39. Chanard J, Lavaud S, Randoux C, Rieu P. New insights in dialysis membrane biocompatibility: relevance of adsorption properties and heparin binding. Nephrol Dial Transplant. 2003;18:252–7.

40. Gorbet MB, Sefton MV. Biomaterial-associated thrombosis: roles of coagulation factors, complement, platelets and leukocytes. Biomaterials. 2004;25: 5681–703.

41. Bos JC, Grooteman MP, van Houte AJ, Schoorl M, van Limbeek J, Nube MJ. Low polymorphonuclear cell degranulation during citrate anticoagulation: a comparison between citrate and heparin dialysis. Nephrol Dial Transplant. 1997;12:1387–93.

42. Gritters M, Grooteman MP, Schoorl M, Schoorl M, Bartels PC, Scheffer PG et al. Citrate anticoagulation abolishes degranulation of polymorphonuclear cells and platelets and reduces oxidative stress during haemodialysis. Nephrol Dial Transplant. 2006;21:153–9.

43. Böhler J, Schollmeyer P, Dressel B, Dobos G, Horl WH. Reduction of granulocyte activation during hemodialysis with regional citrate anticoagulation: dissociation of complement activation and neutropenia from neutrophil degranulation. J Am Soc Nephrol. 1996;7: 234–41.

44. Berridge MJ, Bootman MD, Roderick HL. Calcium signalling: dynamics, homeostasis and remodelling. Nat Rev Mol Cell Biol. 2003;4:517–29.

45. Hofer AM, Brown EM. Extracellular calcium sensing and signalling. Nat Rev Mol Cell Biol. 2003;4:530–8.

46. Böhler J, Donauer J, Birmelin M, Schollmeyer PJ, Horl WH. Mediators of complement-independent granulocyte activation during haemodialysis: role of calcium, prostaglandins and leukotrienes. Nephrol Dial Transplant. 1993;8:1359–65.

47. Mehta RL, McDonald BR, Aguilar MM, Ward DM. Regional citrate anticoagulation for continuous arteriovenous hemodialysis in critically ill patients. Kidney Int. 1990;38:976–81.

48. Kramer L, Bauer E, Joukhadar C, Strobl W, Gendo A, Madl C et al. Citrate pharmacokinetics and metabolism in cirrhotic and noncirrhotic critically ill patients. Crit Care Med. 2003;31:2450–5.

49. Bakker AJ, Boerma EC, Keidel H, Kingma P, van der Voort PH. Detection of citrate overdose in critically ill patients on citrate-anticoagulated venovenous haemofiltration: use of ionised and total/ionised calcium. Clin Chem Lab Med. 2006;44:962–6.

50. Meier-Kriesche HU, Gitomer J, Finkel K, DuBose T. Increased total to ionized calcium ratio during continuous venovenous hemodialysis with regional citrate anticoagulation. Crit Care Med. 2001;29:748–52.

51. Hetzel GR, Taskaya G, Sucker C, Hennersdorf M, Grabensee B, Schmitz M. Citrate plasma levels in patients under regional anticoagulation in continuous venovenous hemofiltration. Am J Kidney Dis. 2006;48: 806–11.

52. Oudemans-van Straaten HM. Review and guidelines for regional anticoagulation with citrate in continuous hemofiltration. Neth J Crit Care. 2004;8:146–56.

53. Tolwani AJ, Prendergast MB, Speer RR, Stofan BS, Wille KM. A practical citrate anticoagulation continuous venovenous hemodiafiltration protocol for metabolic control and high solute clearance. Clin J Am Soc Nephrol. 2006;1:79–87.

54. Monchi M, Berghmans D, Ledoux D, Canivet JL, Dubois B, Damas P. Citrate vs. heparin for anticoagulation in continuous venovenous hemofiltration: a prospective randomized study. Intensive Care Med. 2004;30:260–5.

55. Bagshaw SM, Laupland KB, Boiteau PJ, Godinez-Luna T. Is regional citrate superior to systemic heparin anticoagulation for continuous renal replacement therapy? A prospective observational study in an adult regional critical care system. J Crit Care. 2005;20:155–61.

56. Van der Voort PH, Postma SR, Kingma WP, Boerma EC, Van Roon EN. Safety of citrate based hemofiltration in critically ill patients at high risk for bleeding: a comparison with nadroparin. Int J Artif Organs. 2006;29: 559-63.

57. Spronk PE, Steenbergen H, ten KM, Rommes JH. Re: Regional citrate anticoagulation does not prolong filter survival during CVVH. J Crit Care. 2006;21:291-2.

58. Kutsogiannis DJ, Gibney RT, Stollery D, Gao J. Regional citrate versus systemic heparin anticoagulation for continuous renal replacement in critically ill patients. Kidney Int. 2005;67:2361-7.

59. Betjes MG, van Oosterom D, van Agteren M, van de WJ. Regional citrate versus heparin anticoagulation during venovenous hemofiltration in patients at low risk for bleeding: similar hemofilter survival but significantly less bleeding. J Nephrol. 2007;20:602-8.

D. Sepsis and infection

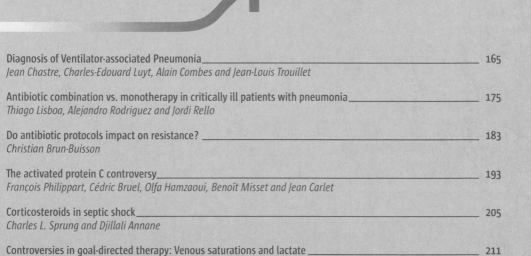

Jean Chastre, Charles-Edouard Luyt, Alain Combes
and Jean-Louis Trouillet

Diagnosis of Ventilator-associated Pneumonia

Introduction

Ventilator-associated pneumonia (VAP) is the most frequent ICU-acquired infection among patients receiving
mechanical ventilation (1). Although the attributable
mortality rate for VAP is still debated, it has been shown
that these infections prolong both the duration of ventilation and the duration of intensive care unit (ICU) stay
(1, 2). Approximately 50% of all antibiotics prescribed in
an ICU are administered for respiratory tract infections
(3). Because several studies have shown that appropriate
antimicrobial treatment of patients with VAP significantly improves outcome, more rapid identification of infected patients and accurate selection of antimicrobial
agents represent important clinical goals (1). Consensus,
however, on appropriate diagnostic strategies for VAP
has yet to be reached. Ideally, any diagnostic strategy
intended to be used in patients clinically suspected of
having developed VAP should be able to reach the three
following objectives:
1. to accurately identify patients with true pulmonary
   infection and, in case of infection, to isolate the causative microorganisms (in order to initiate immediate
   appropriate antimicrobial treatment and then to optimise therapy based on pathogen susceptibility patterns);
2. to identify patients with extrapulmonary sites of infection; and

3. to withhold and/or withdraw antibiotics in patients
   without infection.

This report reviews the potential advantages and drawbacks of using bronchoscopic techniques compared with
using non-invasive modalities and/or clinical evaluation
alone for the diagnosis of VAP, based on our personal experience and major additions to the literature that have
appeared in recent years.

The invasive strategy

Concern about the inaccuracy of clinical approaches to VAP recognition and the impossibil-
ity of using such a strategy to avoid over-prescrip-
tion of antibiotics in the ICU has led numerous
investigators to postulate that "specialised" diagnostic methods, including quantitative cultures
of specimens obtained with bronchoscopic or
non-bronchoscopic techniques, such as bronchoalveolar lavage (BAL) and/or protected specimen
brush (PSB), could improve identification of patients with true VAP and facilitate decisions
whether or not to treat, and thus affect clinical
outcome (2, 4, 5). Using such a strategy, therapeutic decisions are made within tight protocols,
based on results of direct examination of distal

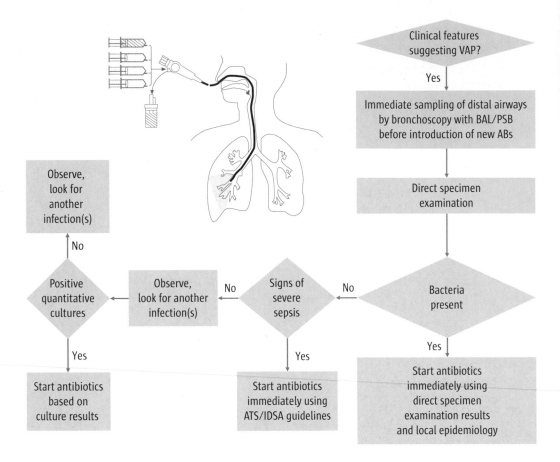

Fig. 1   The invasive strategy

pulmonary samples and results of quantitative cultures (see fig. 1).

The use of invasive techniques, coupled with quantitative cultures of PSB or BAL specimens allows for the precise identification of the offending organisms and their susceptibility patterns. Such data are invaluable for optimal antibiotic selection. Recent studies have found that initial, empiric antibiotic treatment often requires modification when quantitative culture results are available (4, 6–8). They also increase the confidence and comfort level of health care workers in managing patients with suspected nosocomial pneumonia (9). Therefore, antibiotic therapy that is directed by quantitative cultures results may be more effective than empiric treatment.

The second most compelling argument for invasive bronchoscopic techniques is that they can reduce excessive antibiotic use. There is little disagreement that the clinical diagnosis of nosocomial pneumonia is overly sensitive and leads to the unnecessary use of broad-spectrum antibiotics. Because bronchoscopic techniques may be more specific, their use would reduce antibiotic pressure in the intensive care unit, thereby limiting the emergence of drug-resistant strains and the attendant increased risks of superinfection (5). Most epidemiologic investigations have clearly demonstrated that the indiscriminate use of antimicrobial agents in ICU patients may have immediate as well as long-term consequences, which contribute to the emergence of multi-resistant pathogens and increase the risk of serious superinfections (10, 11). This increased risk is not limited to one patient but may increase the risk of colonisation or infection by multi-drug-resistant bacterial strains in patients throughout the ICU and even the entire hospital. Virtually all reports emphasise that better antibiotic control programs to limit bacterial resistance are urgently needed in ICUs and that patients without true infection should not receive antimicrobial treatment (12–14).

The more targeted use of antibiotics also could reduce overall costs, despite the expense of bronchoscopy and quantitative cultures, and minimise antibiotic-related toxicity. This is particularly true in the case of patients who have late-onset ventilator-associated pneumonia, in whom expensive combination therapy is recommended by most authorities in the field. A conservative cost analysis performed in a trauma ICU suggested that the discontinuation of antibiotics upon the return of negative bronchoscopic quantitative culture results could lead to a savings of more than $ 1,700 per patient suspected of VAP (15).

Finally, probably the most important risk of not performing bronchoscopy for the patient is that another site of infection may be missed. The major benefit of a negative bronchoscopy may in fact be to direct attention away from the lungs as the source of fever. Many hospitalised patients with negative bronchoscopic cultures have other potential sites of infection that can be identified via a simple diagnostic protocol. In a study of 50 patients with suspected ventilator-associated pneumonia who underwent a systematic diagnostic protocol designed to identify all potential causes of fever and pulmonary densities, Meduri et al. confirmed that lung infection was present in only 42 % of cases and that the frequent occurrence of multiple infectious and noninfectious processes justifies a systematic search for the source of fever in this setting (16). Delay in the diagnosis or definitive treatment of the true site of infection may lead to prolonged antibiotic therapy, more antibiotic-associated complications, and induction of further organ dysfunction.

Reasons not to use invasive diagnostic techniques include the following: First, the accuracy of bronchoscopic techniques is questionable in patients on prior antibiotics, especially when new antibiotics have been introduced after the onset of the symptoms suggestive of nosocomial pneumonia, before pulmonary secretions were collected. In fact, as demonstrated by Johanson et al. and other investigators, culture results of respiratory secretions are mostly not modified when pneu-

monia develops as a superinfection in patients who have been receiving systemic antibiotics for several days before the appearance of the new pulmonary infiltrates, the reason being that the bacteria responsible for the new infection are then resistant to the antibiotics given previously (17, 18). On the other hand, performing microbiologic cultures of pulmonary secretions for diagnostic purposes after initiation of new antibiotic therapy in patients suspected of having developed nosocomial pneumonia can clearly lead to a high number of false-negative results, regardless of the way in which these secretions are obtained (18–20). In fact, all microbiological techniques are probably of little value in patients with a recent pulmonary infiltrate who have received new antibiotics for that reason, even for less than 24 h. In this case, a negative finding could indicate either that the patient has been successfully treated for pneumonia and the bacteria are eradicated, or that he had no lung infection to begin with.

Second, bronchoscopy may transiently worsen patient's status, although several studies suggest that the incidence of such complications is quite low (21, 22). Third, an invasive approach to diagnosing nosocomial pneumonia may increase costs of caring for critically ill patients, at least in some institutions in which fees for bronchoscopy are very high. Fourth, while patient management may change based on results from invasive tests, undisputable data suggesting that these changes lead to an improvement in patient outcome are lacking. Some experts also question the willingness of physicians to stop antibiotic therapy in the face of a negative bronchoscopic culture. Indeed, as cited below, there is evidence that physicians are reluctant to discontinue antibiotics for suspected nosocomial pneumonia solely because of a negative culture. The development of algorithms incorporating clinical suspicion into the interpretation of culture results may improve the acceptability of negative results.

Several investigators also argue that the use of bronchoscopy in the evaluation of nosocomial pneumonia is limited by the lack of standardised, reproducible methods and diagnostic criteria (23). Although a general consensus has emerged on the use of 10^3 cfu/ml as the cutoff for a PSB culture, and 10^4 cfu/ml for BAL specimens, concern has been raised about their reproducibility, particularly near the diagnosis thresholds (23, 24). Whether the clinical suspicion of VAP should influence the interpretation of quantitative culture results also has not been entirely clarified. Many microbiology laboratories may not be able to promptly and accurately process quantitative cultures, although the techniques used can be very similar to those applied routinely to urine cultures.

One major technical problem with all bronchoscopic techniques is proper selection of the sampling area in the tracheobronchial tree. Usually, the sampling area is selected based on the location of infiltrate on chest radiograph or the segment visualised during bronchoscopy as having purulent secretions (25). In patients with diffuse pulmonary infiltrates or minimal changes in a previously abnormal chest radiograph, determining the correct airway to sample may be difficult. In these cases, sampling should be directed to the area where endobronchial abnormalities are maximal. In case of doubt, and because autopsy studies indicate that ventilator-associated pneumonia frequently involve the posterior portion of the right lower lobe, this area should probably be sampled in priority (26).

Others have suggested that any potential value of bronchoscopy in the management of nosocomial pneumonia would be limited to late-onset infections, as infections that occur within 4 days of admission often are caused by community-acquired pathogens, and are easier to diagnose and manage than is pneumonia occurring later in the hospital course. Although it is true that community-acquired pathogens often are identified in early-onset pneumonia, hospital-acquired pathogens cannot be excluded in the early time frame (27).

The clinical strategy

The second option is to treat every patient clinically suspected of having a pulmonary infection with new antibiotics, even when the likelihood of infection is low, arguing that several studies showed that immediate initiation of appropriate antibiotics was associated with reduced mortality (6, 28, 29). Using this strategy, the selection of appropriate empirical therapy is based on risk factors, local resistance patterns, and involves qualitative testing to identify possible pathogens, antimicrobial therapy being adjusted according to culture results or clinical response (see fig. 2). Anti-

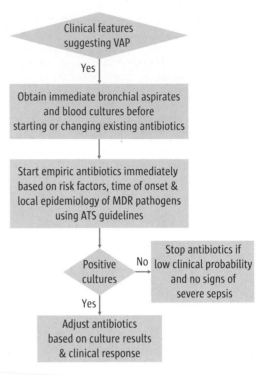

Fig. 2   The clinical strategy

microbial treatment is discontinued if and only if the following three criteria are fulfilled on day 3:
1. clinical diagnosis of HAP is unlikely (there are no definite infiltrates found on chest radiography at follow-up and no more than one of the three following findings: temperature > 38.3°C, leukocytosis or leukopenia, and purulent tracheobronchial secretions) or an alternative noninfectious diagnosis is confirmed,
2. tracheobronchial aspirate culture results are non-significant, and
3. there is no severe sepsis or shock (30).

This "clinical" approach has two undisputable advantages: first, no specialised microbiologic techniques are requested, and, second, the risk of missing a patient who needs antimicrobial treatment is minimal, at least when all suspected patients are treated with new antibiotics. Many investigators continue to state that bronchoscopy is an invasive, time-consuming, and expensive procedure, which is not readily available on a 24-hour basis in all institutions. They insist that these techniques may result in exposure to some false negative results and that they should first be validated in prospective, randomised trials demonstrating that they improve survival or other meaningful endpoints, such as antimicrobial resistance, antibiotic complications, or costs compared with clinical diagnosis (31). The appropriateness of diagnostic tools may also differ depending on whether the goal is to prevent the spread of resistant organisms, compare incidence rates of pneumonia, or prescribe treatment for a patient. For example, for calculating incidence rates, one should use a definition that is applicable to all patients over prolonged time periods. Infection-control personnel should be able to make the diagnosis based on common clinical and laboratory findings. Definitions that require the performance of specialised diagnostic tests are not universal enough to produce comparable rates in most health care settings.

Such a clinical strategy, however, leads to overestimation of the incidence of VAP because tracheobronchial colonisation and non-infectious processes mimicking it are included (7). Qualitative endotracheal aspirate cultures contribute indisputably to the diagnosis of VAP only when they are completely negative for a patient with no modification of prior antimicrobial treatment. In such a case, the negative-predictive value is very high and the probability of the patient having pneumonia is close to zero (32).

While the simple qualitative culture of endotracheal aspirates (EA) is a technique with a high percentage of false-positive results due to bacterial colonisation of the proximal airways observed in most ICU patients, some recent studies using quantitative culture techniques suggest that EA cultures may have a reasonable overall diagnostic accuracy, similar to that of several other more invasive techniques (33). Inherent advantages of these techniques are less invasiveness, availability to nonbronchoscopists, lower initial cost than bronchoscopy, less compromise of patient gas exchange during the procedure and availability to patients with small endotracheal tubes. Disadvantages include the potential sampling errors inherent in a blind technique and the lack of airway visualisation.

Another option is to follow the strategy described by Singh et al. (34), in which decisions regarding antibiotic therapy are based on a clinical score constructed from seven variables, the clinical pulmonary infection score (CPIS). Patients with CPIS > 6 are treated as having VAP with antibiotics for 10 to 21 days (see fig. 3), antibiotics are discontinued if CPIS is ≤ 6 at 3 days. Such an approach avoids prolonged treatment of patients with a low likelihood of infection, while allowing immediate treatment of patients with VAP. Two conditions, however, must be respected rigorously when implementing this strategy. First, selection of initial antimicrobial therapy should be based on flora responsible for most VAP at each institution. Ciprofloxacin is unlikely to be the right choice in numerous institutions because of a high prevalence of MRSA infections (35). Second, physicians should reevaluate antimicrobial treatment on day 3, when susceptibility patterns of the microorganism(s) considered to be VAP-causative are available, in order to select treatment with a narrower spectrum.

Summary of the evidence

Other than decision-analysis studies (36–38) and one retrospective study (9), only five trials assessed the impact of a diagnostic strategy on antibiotic use and outcome of patients suspected of having hospital-acquired pneumonia using a randomised scheme (5, 39–42). One of the first studies to clearly demonstrate a benefit in favor of the bacteriological strategy was a prospective cohort study conducted in 10 Canadian ICUs (9). The authors compared 92 patients with suspected pneumonia who underwent fiberoptic bronchoscopy and 49 patients who did not. Mortality among bronchoscopy patients was 19% versus 35% for controls (p = 0.03). Patients managed with a bacteriological strategy received fewer antibiotics and more patients had all antibiotics discontinued compared to the control group.

No differences in mortality and morbidity were found when either invasive (PSB and/or BAL) or non-invasive (quantitative endotracheal aspirate cultures) techniques were used to diagnose VAP in three Spanish randomised studies (39–41). Those studies, however, were based on relatively few patients (51, 76 and 88, respectively). Antibiotics were continued in all patients despite negative cultures, thereby neutralizing one potential advantage of any diagnostic test in patients with suspected VAP. Concerning the latter, several prospective studies have concluded that antibiotics can be stopped in patients with negative quantitative cultures, without adversely affecting the recurrence of pneumonia and mortality (4, 43).

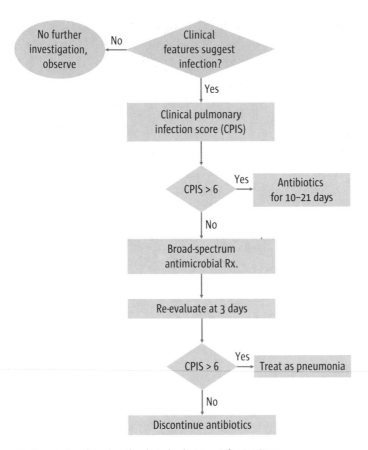

Fig. 3   Strategy based on the clinical pulmonary infection Score

A large, prospective, randomised trial compared clinical versus bacteriological strategy for the management of 413 patients suspected of having VAP (5). The clinical strategy included empirical antimicrobial therapy, based on clinical evaluation and the presence of bacteria on direct examination of tracheal aspirates, and possible subsequent adjustment or discontinuation according to the results of qualitative (not semi-quantitative) cultures of endotracheal aspirates. The bacteriological strategy consisted of fiberoptic bronchoscopy with direct examination of BAL and/or PSB samples, and empirical therapy initiated only when results were positive. Definitive diagnosis, based on quantitative culture results of samples obtained with PSB or BAL, was awaited before adjusting, discontinuing, or, for some patients with negative direct examination (no bacteria identified on cytocentrifuge preparation of BAL fluid or PSB samples) and positive quantitative cultures (> 10^3 cfu/ml for the PSB and > 10^4 cfu/ml for BAL), starting therapy (see fig. 1). Em-

pirical antimicrobial therapy was initiated in 91 % of patients in the clinical strategy group and in only 52 % of those in the bacteriological strategy group. Compared with patients managed clinically, those receiving bacteriological management had a lower mortality rate on day 14 (25 % and 16 %; p = 0.02), lower sepsis-related organ failure assessment scores on day 3 and 7 (p = 0.04), and less antibiotic use (mean number of antibiotic-free days, 2 ± 3 and 5 ± 5; p < 0.001). Pertinently, 22 non-pulmonary infections were diagnosed in the bacteriological strategy group and only 5 in the clinical strategy group, suggesting that overdiagnosis of VAP may lead to missed non-pulmonary infections.

A recent trial conducted by the Canadian Critical Care Trials Group also investigated the impact of different diagnostic approaches on outcomes of 740 patients suspected of having VAP (42). Patients previously colonised or infected with MRSA or *Pseudomonas* species and of those having previously received the "study drugs", i.e., meropenem and/or ciprofloxacin were excluded, resulting in less than 12 % of difficult-to-treat pathogens, such as *P. aeruginosa*, *Acinetobacter* spp., *S. maltophilia*, and/or MRSA, as compared to more than 30 % in the French study. There was no significant difference in the primary outcome (28-day mortality rate) between the BAL group and the endotracheal-aspiration group (18.9 % and 18.4 %, respectively; p = 0.94). The BAL group and the endotracheal-aspiration group also had similar rates of targeted therapy on day 6 (74.2 % and 74.6 %, respectively; p = 0.90), days alive without antibiotics (10.4 ± 7.5 and 10.6 ± 7.9, p = 0.86), and maximum organ-dysfunction scores (mean [± SD], 8.3 ± 3.6 and 8.6 ± 4.0; p = 0.26). The two groups did not differ significantly in the length of stay in the ICU or hospital. Unfortunately, information on how decision algorithms were followed in the two arms once cultures were available (as soon as day 2 or day 3) was not given. Because the rate of targeted therapy was only 74.2 % in the BAL arm on day 6, it is highly probable that in many patients managed using this diagnostic technique early de-escalation was not performed although clearly indicated. Thus, in contrast to previous recommendations concerning the use of quantitative BAL, many patients with quantitative culture results below the cut-off of 10^4 cfu/ml continued to receive antibiotics, even after day 3. This could entirely explain why there was a similar use of antibiotics in the two study arms. Obviously, the potential benefit of using a diagnostic tool such as BAL for safely restricting unnecessary antimicrobial therapy in such a setting can only be obtained when decisions regarding antibiotics are closely linked to both bacteriological direct examination and culture-results.

Though the results of the Canadian study are consistent with those of the three Spanish trials, in which antimicrobial treatment was also initiated in all suspected patients and rarely withheld in patients with negative cultures, additional studies will be needed before concluding that a strategy based on the systematic collection of distal pulmonary secretions before introduction of new antibiotics and quantitative culture techniques is useless.

Key points for clinical practice

All experts interested in this field agree that the major goals of any management strategy are early, appropriate antibiotics in adequate doses of patients with true VAP, while avoiding excessive antibiotics and the emergence of multi-drug-resistant strains.

The only way to do that is to follow 3 steps:

- *To obtain a lower respiratory tract sample for culture (quantitative or semi-quantitative) and microscopy before introduction of new antibiotics;*
- *To immediately start empiric antimicrobial treatment, unless there are both a negative microscopy and no signs of severe sepsis; and*
- *To re-evaluate treatment on day 2 or 3, based on microbiologic culture results and clinical outcome.*

Because even a few doses of a new antimicrobial agent can negate results of microbiologic cultures, pulmonary secretions in patients suspected of having developed VAP should always be obtained before new antibiotics are administered.

Empirical treatment of patients with VAP should be selected based on available epidemiologic characteristics, information provided by direct examination of pulmonary secretions, intrinsic antibacterial activities of antimicrobial agents and their pharmacokinetic characteristics.

Once the microbiological data become available, antimicrobial therapy should be re-evaluated in order to avoid prolonged use of a broader spectrum of antibiotic therapy than is justified by the available information. For many patients, including those with late-onset infection, the culture data will not show the presence of highly resistant pathogens, and in these individuals therapy can be narrowed, or even reduced, to a single agent in light of the susceptibility pattern of the causative pathogens without risking inappropriate treatment.

The authors

Jean Chastre, MD
Charles-Edouard Luyt, MD
Alain Combes, MD
Jean-Louis Trouillet, MD
    Service de Réanimation Médicale | Institut de Cardiologie | Hôpital Pitié-Salpêtrière | Paris Cedex 13, France

Address for correspondence
    Jean Chastre
    Service de Réanimation Médicale
    Institut de Cardiologie
    Hôpital Pitié-Salpêtrière
    43–87 bd de l'Hôpital
    75651 Paris Cedex 13, France
    e-mail: jean.chastre@psl.aphp.fr

References

1. Guidelines for the Management of Adults with Hospital-acquired, Ventilator-associated, and Healthcare-associated Pneumonia. Am J Respir Crit Care Med. 2005; 171:388–416.
2. Chastre J, Fagon JY. Ventilator-associated pneumonia. Am J Respir Crit Care Med. 2002;165:867–903.
3. Bergmans DC, Bonten MJ, Gaillard CA, van Tiel FH, van der Geest S, de Leeuw PW, Stobberingh EE. Indications for antibiotic use in ICU patients: a one-year prospective surveillance. J Antimicrob Chemother. 1997;39:527–35.
4. Bonten MJ, Bergmans DC, Stobberingh EE, van der Geest S, De Leeuw PW, van Tiel FH, Gaillard CA. Implementation of bronchoscopic techniques in the diagnosis of ventilator-associated pneumonia to reduce antibiotic use. Am J Respir Crit Care Med. 1997;156:1820–4.
5. Fagon JY, Chastre J, Wolff M, Gervais C, Parer-Aubas S, Stephan F, Similowski T, Mercat A, Diehl JL, Sollet JP, Tenaillon A. Invasive and noninvasive strategies for management of suspected ventilator-associated pneumonia. A randomized trial. Ann Intern Med. 2000; 132:621–30.
6. Rello J, Gallego M, Mariscal D, Sonora R, Valles J. The value of routine microbial investigation in ventilator-associated pneumonia. Am J Respir Crit Care Med. 1997; 156:196–200.
7. Fagon JY, Chastre J, Hance AJ, Domart Y, Trouillet JL, Gibert C. Evaluation of clinical judgment in the identification and treatment of nosocomial pneumonia in ventilated patients. Chest. 1993;103:547–53.
8. Shorr AF, Sherner JH, Jackson WL, Kollef MH. Invasive approaches to the diagnosis of ventilator-associated pneumonia: A meta-analysis. Crit Care Med. 2005; 33:46–53.
9. Heyland DK, Cook DJ, Marshall J, Heule M, Guslits B, Lang J, Jaeschke R. The clinical utility of invasive diagnostic techniques in the setting of ventilator-associated pneumonia. Canadian Critical Care Trials Group. Chest. 1999;115:1076–84.
10. McGowan JE. Antimicrobial resistance in hospital organisms and its relation to antibiotic use. Rev Infect Dis. 1983;5:1033–48.
11. Kollef MH, Fraser VJ. Antibiotic resistance in the intensive care unit. Ann Intern Med. 2001;134:298–314.
12. Murthy R. Implementation of strategies to control antimicrobial resistance. Chest. 2001;119:405S–411S.
13. Paterson DL. The role of antimicrobial management programs in optimizing antibiotic prescribing within hospitals. Clin Infect Dis. 2006;42 Suppl 2:S90–5.
14. Goldmann DA, Weinstein RA, Wenzel RP, Tablan OC, Duma RJ, Gaynes RP, Schlosser J, Martone WJ. Strategies to Prevent and Control the Emergence and Spread of Antimicrobial-Resistant Microorganisms in Hospitals. A challenge to hospital leadership. Jama. 1996;275:234–40.
15. Croce MA, Fabian TC, Shaw B, Stewart RM, Pritchard FE, Minard G, Kudsk KA, Baselski VS. Analysis of charges associated with diagnosis of nosocomial pneumonia: can routine bronchoscopy be justified? J Trauma. 1994; 37:721–7.
16. Meduri GU, Mauldin GL, Wunderink RG, Leeper KV, Jr., Jones CB, Tolley E, Mayhall G. Causes of fever and pulmonary densities in patients with clinical manifestations of ventilator-associated pneumonia. Chest. 1994; 106:221–35.
17. Johanson WG, Jr., Seidenfeld JJ, Gomez P, de los Santos R, Coalson JJ. Bacteriologic diagnosis of nosocomial pneumonia following prolonged mechanical ventilation. Am Rev Respir Dis. 1988;137:259–64.
18. Souweine B, Mom T, Traore O, Aublet-Cuvelier B, Bret L, Sirot J, Deteix P, Gilain L, Boyer L. Ventilator-associated sinusitis: microbiological results of sinus aspirates in patients on antibiotics. Anesthesiology. 2000;93: 1255–60.
19. Montravers P, Fagon JY, Chastre J, Lecso M, Dombret MC, Trouillet JL, Gibert C. Follow-up protected specimen brushes to assess treatment in nosocomial pneumonia. Am Rev Respir Dis. 1993;147:38–44.
20. Prats E, Dorca J, Pujol M, Garcia L, Barreiro B, Verdaguer R, Gudiol F, Manresa F. Effects of antibiotics on protected specimen brush sampling in ventilator-associated pneumonia. Eur Respir J. 2002;19:944–51.
21. Trouillet JL, Guiguet M, Gibert C, Fagon JY, Dreyfuss D, Blanchet F, Chastre J. Fiberoptic bronchoscopy in ventilated patients. Evaluation of cardiopulmonary risk under midazolam sedation. Chest. 1990;97:927–33.
22. Steinberg KP, Mitchell DR, Maunder RJ, Milberg JA, Whitcomb ME, Hudson LD. Safety of bronchoalveolar lavage in patients with adult respiratory distress syndrome. Am Rev Respir Dis. 1993;148:556–61.
23. Marquette CH, Herengt F, Mathieu D, Saulnier F, Courcol R, Ramon P. Diagnosis of pneumonia in mechanically ventilated patients. Repeatability of the protected specimen brush. Am Rev Respir Dis. 1993;147:211–4.
24. Gerbeaux P, Ledoray V, Boussuges A, Molenat F, Jean P, Sainty JM. Diagnosis of nosocomial pneumonia in mechanically ventilated patients: repeatability of the bronchoalveolar lavage. Am J Respir Crit Care Med. 1998;157:76–80.
25. Meduri GU, Chastre J. The standardization of bronchoscopic techniques for ventilator-associated pneumonia. Chest. 1992;102:557S–564S.
26. Rouby JJ. Histology and microbiology of ventilator-associated pneumonias. Semin Respir Infect. 1996;11:54–61.
27. Giantsou E, Liratzopoulos N, Efraimidou E, Panopoulou M, Alepopoulou E, Kartali-Ktenidou S, Minopoulos GI, Zakynthinos S, Manolas KI. Both early-onset and late-onset ventilator-associated pneumonia are caused mainly by potentially multiresistant bacteria. Intensive Care Med. 2005.

28. Alvarez-Lerma F. Modification of empiric antibiotic treatment in patients with pneumonia acquired in the intensive care unit. ICU-Acquired Pneumonia Study Group. Intensive Care Med. 1996;22:387–94.

29. Iregui M, Ward S, Sherman G, Fraser VJ, Kollef MH. Clinical importance of delays in the initiation of appropriate antibiotic treatment for ventilator-associated pneumonia. Chest. 2002;122:262–8.

30. Torres A, Ewig S. Diagnosing ventilator-associated pneumonia. N Engl J Med. 2004;350:433–5.

31. Niederman MS. Bronchoscopy for ventilator-associated pneumonia: show me the money (outcome benefit)! [editorial; comment]. Crit Care Med. 1998;26:198–9.

32. Kirtland SH, Corley DE, Winterbauer RH, Springmeyer SC, Casey KR, Hampson NB, Dreis DF. The diagnosis of ventilator-associated pneumonia: a comparison of histologic, microbiologic, and clinical criteria. Chest. 1997;112:445–57.

33. Cook D, Mandell L. Endotracheal aspiration in the diagnosis of ventilator-associated pneumonia. Chest. 2000;117:195S–197S.

34. Singh N, Rogers P, Atwood CW, Wagener MM, Yu VL. Short-course empiric antibiotic therapy for patients with pulmonary infiltrates in the intensive care unit. A proposed solution for indiscriminate antibiotic prescription. Am J Respir Crit Care Med. 2000;162:505–11.

35. Ibrahim EH, Ward S, Sherman G, Schaiff R, Fraser VJ, Kollef MH. Experience with a clinical guideline for the treatment of ventilator-associated pneumonia. Crit Care Med. 2001;29:1109–15.

36. Baker AM, Bowton DL, Haponik EF. Decision making in nosocomial pneumonia. An analytic approach to the interpretation of quantitative bronchoscopic cultures. Chest. 1995;107:85–95.

37. Sterling TR, Ho EJ, Brehm WT, Kirkpatrick MB. Diagnosis and treatment of ventilator-associated pneumonia – impact on survival. A decision analysis. Chest. 1996;110:1025–34.

38. Babcock HM, Zack JE, Garrison T, Trovillion E, Kollef MH, Fraser VJ. Ventilator-associated pneumonia in a multi-hospital system: differences in microbiology by location. Infect Control Hosp Epidemiol. 2003;24:853–8.

39. Sanchez-Nieto JM, Torres A, Garcia-Cordoba F, El-Ebiary M, Carrillo A, Ruiz J, Nunez ML, Niederman M. Impact of invasive and noninvasive quantitative culture sampling on outcome of ventilator-associated pneumonia: a pilot study [see comments] [published erratum appears in Am J Respir Crit Care Med 1998 Mar;157(3 Pt 1):1005]. Am J Respir Crit Care Med. 1998;157:371–6.

40. Ruiz M, Torres A, Ewig S, Marcos MA, Alcon A, Lledo R, Asenjo MA, Maldonaldo A. Noninvasive versus invasive microbial investigation in ventilator-associated pneumonia: evaluation of outcome. Am J Respir Crit Care Med. 2000;162:119–25.

41. Sole Violan J, Fernandez JA, Benitez AB, Cardenosa Cendrero JA, Rodriguez de Castro F. Impact of quantitative invasive diagnostic techniques in the management and outcome of mechanically ventilated patients with suspected pneumonia. Crit Care Med. 2000;28:2737–41.

42. Heyland D, Dodek P, Muscedere J, Day A. A randomized trial of diagnostic techniques for ventilator-associated pneumonia. N Engl J Med. 2006;355:2619–30.

43. Croce MA, Fabian TC, Waddle-Smith L, Melton SM, Minard G, Kudsk KA, Pritchard FE. Utility of Gram's stain and efficacy of quantitative cultures for posttraumatic pneumonia: a prospective study. Ann Surg. 1998;227:743–51; discussion 751–5.

Thiago Lisboa, Alejandro Rodriguez and Jordi Rello

Antibiotic combination vs. monotherapy in critically ill patients with pneumonia

Introduction

Combination therapy in critically ill patients is believed to increase the likelihood of therapeutic success through a synergistic effect of associated antimicrobial agents and assuring an adequate coverage of more likely causative pathogens by an extended spectrum of activity (1, 2).

However, the added benefits of the combination therapy approach, besides its intuitive appeal, are unclear. Available evidence is not conclusive and clinical benefit appears to be more associated with enhancement of appropriateness of empirical therapy than with synergy effects. Moreover, potential disadvantages to using combination therapy include a greater risk of drug toxicity, increased costs and potential emergence of resistant pathogens (2, 3).

We review the available evidence for combination therapy in severe community-acquired pneumonia admitted to ICU and ventilator-associated pneumonia and discuss possible mechanisms and potential benefits of this approach.

Combination therapy in severe community-acquired pneumonia

Severe community-acquired pneumonia is defined as a pneumonia contracted outside a hospital setting that requires admission to the ICU. It corresponds to 10 % of all hospitalised patients with CAP, but in terms of mortality (> 30 %), it is the most important strata. Community-acquired pneumonia can be caused by a wide variety of pathogens. However, *Streptococcus pneumoniae*, *Legionella sp.* and *Haemophilus influenzae* are the main pathogens to cover (4). Until more accurate and rapid diagnostic methods are available, the initial treatments for most patients remain empirical, and physicians should consider specific risk factors for Gram negative pathogen in each patient (5, 6).

The optimal therapy for CAP remains controversial. Since pneumococci are consistently identified as the most common pathogen in CAP, all current guidelines (7–9) for empirical therapy include an antipneumococcal antibiotic. Several surveillance studies report increasing in vitro resistance of *S. pneumoniae* to a plethora of antimicrobial agents including beta-lactams and fluoroquinolones (10, 11). However, in clinical practice, patients who do not respond to therapy with these agents are very infrequently reported, and these remain an exception rather than the rule.

The impact of combination therapy on mortality in critically ill patients with SCAP is still debated. Whether dual therapy contributes to improved survival, or if they are secondary to benefit from aggressive initial therapy (12) is an open question. The benefit of combination therapy may be due to:

1. the presence of undetected co-pathogens, as atypical bacteria,
2. antibiotic synergy, or
3. immunomodulatory effects of macrolides or fluoroquinolones.

Monotherapy or combination therapy in community-acquired pneumonia patients

The most recent IDSA/ATS Guidelines (7) recommended for patients admitted to ICU to begin with a wide spectrum antibiotic treatment. The combination therapy with two different antibiotics that include a potent antipneumococcal β-lactam (cefotaxime, ceftriaxone or ampicillin-sulbactam) plus a macrolide (level II evidence) or a respiratory fluoroquinolone (level I evidence) is the treatment suggested for critically ill patients. Because septic shock and mechanical ventilation are the clearest indications for ICU admission, the majority of ICU patients would still require dual therapy. However, these recommendations were not obtained from clinical trials and have been extrapolated from non-severe cases, in conjunction with case series and retrospective analyses of cohorts with SCAP (7). In fact, many of these trials involved a discretionary use of antibiotic and most were pharmaceutical trials that deliberately excluded ICU patients. Thus, the implications of empirical antibiotic therapy for ICU patients with severe CAP remain unknown.

Combination therapy: What is the evidence?

In the last 10 years, many different studies have evaluated the impact of the dual antibiotic treatment for SCAP on mortality. Mufson and Stanek (13) in 1999 reported their experience of 20 years with bacteremic pneumococcal pneumonia. When mortality was compared between regimes containing a macrolided and a β-lactam with those containing β-lactam alone, there was a significant difference in mortality. Other retrospective and observational studies (14, 15) have showed higher rates of survival in patients who are treated with a combination antibiotic therapy. However, the studied population included patients with pneumococcal bacteremic CAP and their conclusions might not be extrapolated to the treatment of all patients with SCAP. Three of these retrospective studies (14–16) reported that the benefit was higher in patients with SCAP who received a combination therapy. Indeed, Waterer et al. (14) observed an 11.3 % absolute mortality difference (18.2 % vs 6.9 %, p = 0.02) favouring the dual therapy. After controlling for comorbidities and the APACHE II score predicted mortality, there was a 6.4 times increase in risk of death associated with monotherapy (95 % CI 1.9–21.7). However, all deaths occurred in patients with a PSI score over 90, and therefore there was no mortality difference between antibiotic strategies in milder disease. In addition, Baddour et al. (15) reported that there was a substantial 14-day survival advantage in favour of combination therapy when the analysis was restricted to patients with severe disease (23.4 % vs. 55.3 %, p = 0.001). Finally, Martinez et al. (16) examined 409 patients with bacteremic pneumococcal pneumonia. The authors evaluated the outcome of patients according to the use of monotherapy with a β-lactam or combination therapy with a β-lactam plus a macrolide. After a stepwise logistic regression analysis, shock, age > 65 years, infection with resistant pathogens, and dual therapy were associated with mortality. The association between initial combination therapy and a lower in-hospital mortality rate remained significant after the exclusion of patients who died < 48 h after admission (OR: 0.4, CI 0.17–0.92).

Although the consistent findings of these studies are very suggestive, they all suffer from one or more significant limitations, predominantly arising from the retrospective nature and the special population considered. The lack of controlled trial data in SCAP admitted to ICU is also a problem with respect to the assessment of the impact of antibiotic therapy on survival according to different levels of illness. Recently, our group

(17) demonstrated, in a secondary analysis of a prospective multicenter and observational cohort study including 529 ICU patients with SCAP, that the adjusted 28-day in-ICU mortality was similar (p = 0.99) for the combination antibiotic therapy and the monotherapy in the absence of shock. On the other hand, in patients with shock, combination antibiotic therapy was associated with significantly higher 28-day adjusted in-ICU survival (hazard ratio, 1.69; 95% CI, 1.09–2.6; p = 0.01). These data suggest that ICU patients at higher risk of death (in shock) will derive greater benefit from therapeutic interventions focusing on survival (18). In contrast, these findings strongly suggest that combination therapy does not increase ICU survival in CAP patients with a lower risk of death (without shock). Thus, the potential benefits of combination therapy may be limited to the most severely ill patients.

Do specific pathogens matter in the choice of combination regimen?

Suggested antibiotic regimens for inpatients include a β-lactam combined with a macrolide or monotherapy with a respiratory fluoroquinolone (7). Although *S. pneumoniae* remains to be the leading pathogen in CAP, the rationale for a macrolide supplement or fluoroquinolone monotherapy lies in its ability to cover intracellular (atypical) pathogens as *Legionella pneumophila*; *Chlamydia pneumoniae* and *Mycoplasma pneumoniae*. However, only coverage for L pneumophila is recommended for patients in intensive care units.

Atypical pathogens

Controversy still exists in the literature regarding the need to use antimicrobials covering atypical pathogens when initially treating hospitalised CAP patients. There is some transatlantic controversy between North American physicians, who support the importance of covering atypical organisms and European physicians, who are yet to be convinced of benefit of the systematic use of macrolide (19). A recent international multicenter study (20) observed a significant global presence (about 20%) of atypical pathogens in CAP.

The authors reported that patients treated with atypical coverage had lower time to clinical stability (3.2 vs 3.7 days, p < 0.001), lower length of stay (6.1 vs 7.1 days, p < 0.01) and lower CAP-related mortality (3.8% vs 6.4%, p = 0.05). In contrast, two recent meta-analysis (21, 22) found no difference in mortality between regimens with coverage of atypical pathogens and regimens without such coverage, persisting in all subgroup analysis. In addition, there was a non-significant trend toward clinical success when covering the atypical pathogens, but this advantage disappeared when they evaluated high quality methodological studies alone. Waterer et al. (14) observed that the coverage of these microorganisms did not contribute to the apparent benefit of dual therapy after the multivariate analysis. Our findings (4) agree with the study of Mundy et al. (23) who observed infrequent identification of atypical pathogens in a prospective series of patients hospitalised at the Johns Hopkins. Thus, the impact of the atypical pathogens in critically ill patients in SCAP seems to be scarce.

Pseudomonas aeruginosa

In patients with certain risk factors like severe structural lung disease (bronchiectasias), recent antibiotic exposure, or recent hospitalisation, *P. aeruginosa* can be present in the setting of SCAP (6, 8). Probably in this subset of patients treatment with anti-pseudomonal agents should be considered.

Immunomodulation: A target for combination therapy

The immunomodulatory effect of the macrolide or fluoroquinolone is independent of their antibacterial activity. Although some fluoroquinolones exhibit some immunomodulatory effects, macrolides have been the most extensively investigated. Experimental and clinical data on the anti-inflammatory effects of macrolides was recently reported (14, 24, 25). Macrolides have been shown to reduce the tumor necrosis factor (TNF) and IL-6 production by whole blood after stimuli with heat-killed pneumococci (25). In addition, macrolides appear to enhance polimorphonuclear activity against pneumococci even when the isolates are macrolide resistant, (26) and to reduce the IgG mediated lung damage in rats, again probably by the reduction in both TNF and IL-1β release from the alveolar macrophages (27). It is worth noting that macrolides have become widely used in pan-bronchiolitis and cystic fibrosis with their efficacy attributed to immunomodulation rather than anti-bacterial effects (28). All fluoroquinolones mod-estly impair rat macrophage chemotaxis (29) and transendothelial neutrophil and monocyte migra-tion (30). However, only moxifloxacin and gati-floxacin inhibited IL-8 production. These actions on endothelial cells may contribute to the inhibi-tory effects of fluoroquinolones seen in experi-mental sepsis models, but their clinical relevance is uncertain (31).

Combined therapy:
What is the best combination?

The controversy about which is the best dual ther-apy for SCAP treatment remains unresolved. Sev-eral studies (14–16) have found that the use of a β-lactam plus a macrolide is associated with sig-nificantly lower mortality. Conversely, few studies have examined the combination of β-lactam with fluoroquinolones versus other combination ther-apies. A recent study (32) observed that the em-piric use of a β-lactam plus a fluoroquinolone was associated with higher 30-day mortality when compared to other guideline-concordant regimes for patients hospitalised with SCAP. This study has common limitations to observational and ret-rospective analysis. However, it is in accordance with a recent study of Metersky et al. (33) who studied the relationship between the initial anti-biotic regimen and mortality in a large cohort of Medicare beneficiaries who were hospitalised with bacteremic pneumonia. These authors ob-served that, compared to patients who received no atypical coverage, patients treated with a mac-rolide had a lower risk of adjusted in-hospital mor-tality (OR = 0.59, 95 % IC, 0.40–0.88; p = 0.01) and 30-day mortality (OR = 0.61, 95 % IC: 0.43–0.87; p = 0.007). Interestingly, there were no significant associations between fluoroqui-nolones and patient outcome (OR = 0.94, 95 % IC: 0.69–1.28). Conversely, other studies (34, 35) found no significant differences between the use

of this combination and others. Nevertheless, the mortality rate observed in these trials is much lower than the mortality rate reported for CAP critically ill patients, and it is possible that the pa-tients included in these trials are different from those included in observational studies. Since most studies showing the importance of adding a macrolide to a β-lactam regimen for SCAP are retrospective, only a prospective randomised dou-ble-blind trial would be welcome to clarify wheth-er combination therapy is truly more effective than monotherapy for SCAP. The strength of the association demonstrated in observational studies provides significant justification to suggest that combination therapy with a macrolide should be the first line option of antibiotic treatment for ICU patients with SCAP.

Combination or monotherapy in
ventilator-associated pneumonia

Several studies demonstrate that empirical anti-biotic treatment appropriateness is the key deter-minant for VAP patient outcome (36–39). The treatment strategy in these patients has moved from the old paradigm of starting with narrow spectrum antibiotics and modifying choices after microbiology data are available to a new paradigm based in the "right first time" (40, 41). It justifies starting with broad-spectrum antibiotic therapy in order to assure a maximum coverage and minimizing the risk of an appropriate empirical therapy (41, 42). Empirical antimicrobial treat-ment choice should be patient-specific, based on risk factors and comorbidities, and individualised, considering local microbiologic data (42). Anti-biotic selection in early-onset VAP without risk factors for multi-drug resistant pathogens in-cludes mostly single agent with a narrow-spec-trum while late-onset episodes should consider the possibility of multiresistant organisms and a broad-spectrum treatment strategy.

Some authors argue that a combination regi-men would increase likelihood of therapeutic suc-cess through a wider coverage and potential anti-microbial synergy. Moreover, it would assure a broader coverage not only in monomicrobial epi-sodes of VAP but, mainly polymicrobial episodes (43), which constitute roughly a half of VAP epi-sodes in some series (44). On the other hand, some studies suggest that combination therapy is more expensive and is associated with greater toxicity and with emergence of multi-resistant microorganisms. Whether a broad-spectrum treatment obtained through combined therapy improves outcomes in patients with VAP diagnosis remains controversial.

What is the evidence?

Few studies have compared monotherapy versus combination antibiotic therapy in critically ill patients with VAP (45–48). The major drawback of these older studies is that the beta-lactam used in combination arm is generally an agent with a narrow spectrum of activity compared with the agent of monotherapy group (43). Moreover, these studies used to be designed to prove the effectiveness of the agent used in monotherapy and results are nearly the same, i.e. monotherapy is at least as effective as a combination antibiotic regimen (43).

Recently, Heyland et al. (49) describes a randomised clinical trial comparing a strategy of combination therapy (meropenem plus ciprofloxacin) versus a strategy of monotherapy (only meropenem) with broad-spectrum antibiotics for suspected late ventilator-associated pneumonia. The study included 740 patients and found no difference in 28-day mortality between combination and monotherapy groups. Moreover, no difference was found in LOS in ICU or hospital, clinical and microbiological treatment response nor emergence of antibiotic-resistant bacteria. This

study excluded patients known to be colonised with *Pseudomonas* or MRSA. However, when evaluated a subgroup of patients with multidrug resistant Gram-negative bacteria, microbiological eradication of infecting organisms was significantly higher in the combination therapy group, but there were no differences in clinical outcomes. This can probably be explained by the significant difference in the antibiotic adequacy between both groups (Combination = 84.2% vs Monotherapy = 18.8%). An important question to be answered is if such a difference in microbiological eradication would persist after antibiotic adequacy adjustment.

Interestingly, Garnacho-Montero et al. (50) described similar findings in an observational study comparing use of monotherapy versus combination as empiric therapy for monomicrobial VAP episodes due to *Pseudomonas aeruginosa* in 5 sites (Canarias Island, Lleida, Mallorca, Sevilla and Tarragona). In this study, initial use of combination therapy reduced the likelihood of inappropriate therapy compared with monotherapy (9.5% vs 43.3%). Nevertheless, considering only appropriate therapy, there was no difference in outcomes comparing monotherapy and combination therapy groups. Moreover, monotherapy or combination therapy did not influence length of stay or resistance emergence. An important conclusion derived from this study is the safety of de-escalation in patients with *Pseudomonas* infection, as the effect of combination therapy is related only to antibiotic appropriateness. Table 1 shows a comparison of North-American (49) and Spanish (50) studies.

Tab. 1   Comparison of studies of combination therapy for VAP

Study	Heyland (49)		Garnacho-Montero (50)	
Variables	Monotherapy	Combination	Monotherapy	Combination
Country	Canada and US		Spain	
Number of sites	28		5	
Number of patients	370	369	67	116
Prevalence of *P. aeruginosa* (%)	–	–·	100	100
Prevalence of polymicrobial VAP (%)	24.3	21.4	–	–
Appropriateness of antibiotic (%)	85.1	93.1	56.7	90.5
Mortality (%)	18.1	19.2	50.7	37.1

A meta-analysis (51) recently demonstrated that monotherapy is not inferior to combination therapy in the empirical treatment of VAP. However, data quality was limited and further studies are necessary to clarify such a question.

Available evidence is not conclusive if combination therapy affects VAP patient outcomes. In clinical practice, combination therapy should be considered according to local microbiologic data, in patients with a high-risk to multidrug-resistant pathogens such as *Pseudomonas aeruginosa* in order to assure an appropriate empirical therapy which is the key determinant of mortality risk in these patients.

Synergy: Does it justify combination?

Although appealing, the possibility that antibiotic combination has a synergistic effect on killing activity is difficult to support (43). Technical difficulties interfere with a real measurement of such an effect. Although there is some evidence of in vitro synergistic effect between agents (e.g. penicillin plus aminoglycoside or fluoroquinolone) against some pathogens, extrapolation of these results to clinical practice is not always possible. Moreover, it is unlikely that its effect could be demonstrated in terms of mortality (2). Effectiveness of combination therapy was evaluated using clinical and inflammatory parameters (C-reactive protein) by Damas et al. (52) and no difference was observed regarding the time course of temperature, leukocytosis or C-reactive protein level between patients treated with monotherapy or combined therapy. Again, no difference was observed in length of stay in ICU, free-ventilator-days or mortality between monotherapy or combination therapy groups.

Although synergy possibility is a very attractive hypothesis to consider when selecting an antibiotic regimen in VAP patients, its usefulness should be assessed in further clinical studies.

Summary

Current recommendations for critically ill patients with SCAP treatment include a combination of two antibiotics: a β-lactam plus a macrolide or fluoroquinolones. These recommendations, however, have been extrapolated from non-severe cases. Data from observational studies support that the addition of a macrolide to a β-lactam improves outcomes in critically ill patients with SCAP. *L. pneumophila* coverage is recommended for patients with SCAP. In intubated CAP patients with special risk factors (severe structural lung disease) two antipseudomonal agents should be considered in order to cover higher risk of multi-drug resistant Gram-negative microorganisms. The empirical initial antibiotic treatment for critically ill patients with CAP should provide appropriate coverage for penicillin-resistant *S. pneumoniae* and *Legionella sp.*, the most frequent pathogens observed in severe CAP, and in patients with shock, combination therapy is recommended.

In patients with ventilator-associated pneumonia the most important factor affecting outcome is appropriateness of empirical antibiotic treatment. Recent studies did not demonstrate any difference in clinical outcomes in patients receiving monotherapy or combined therapy. In patients with high risk for multidrug-resistant pathogens, use of combined therapy may allow a broader coverage, increasing the likelihood of appropriate empirical antibiotic therapy.

Key points

- In patients with shock and severe community-acquired pneumonia combination therapy should always be considered.
- The impact of atypical pathogens in critically ill patients with SCAP seems to be scarce.
- Observational studies support that the addition of a macrolide to a β-lactam appears to result in improved survival in critically ill patients with CAP.
- In ventilator-associated pneumonia, the key determinant of mortality is an appropriate empirical therapy.
- In VAP patients with high-risk for multidrug resistant pathogens, empirical combination therapy is recommended to assure appropriateness of empirical treatment.

Supported by AGAUR (05/SGR/920), Fondo de Investigaciones Sanitarias (PI 04/1500), and MARATO TV3.

The authors

Thiago Lisboa, MD
Alejandro Rodriguez, MD, PhD
Jordi Rello, MD, PhD
  Critical Care | Joan XXIII University Hospital |
  University Rovira & Virgili | Institut Pere
  Virgili | CIBER Enfermedades Respiratorias |
  Tarragona, Spain

Address for correspondence
  Jordi Rello
  Critical Care, Joan XXIII University Hospital
  Carrer Dr. Mallafre Guasch 4
  43007 Tarragona, Spain
  e-mail: jrello.hj23.ics@gencat.cat

References

1. Safdar N, Handelsman J, Maki DG. Does combination antimicrobial therapy reduce mortality in Gram-negative bacteremia? Lancet Infect Dis. 2004;4:519–527.

2. Paul M, Benuri-Silbiger I, Soares-Weiser K et al. Beta-lactam monotherapy versus beta-lactam aminoglycoside combination therapy for sepsis in immunocompetent patients: Systematic review and meta-analysis of randomized trials. BMJ. 2004;328: 668–682.

3. Leibovici L, Paul M. Aminoglycoside/beta-lactam combinations in clinical practice. J Antimicrob Chemother. 2007;60:911–912.

4. Bodí M, Rodríguez A, Solé-Violan et al. Antibiotic prescription for community-acquired pneumonia in the intensive care unit: Impact of adherence to Infectious Diseases Society of America Guidelines on survival. Clin Infect Dis. 2005;41:1709–16.

5. Rello J, Rodríguez R, Jubert P et al. Severe community-acquired pneumonia in the elderly: epidemiology and prognosis. Clin Infect Dis. 1996;23:723–728.

6. Rello J, Bodí M, Mariscal D et al. Microbiogical testing and outcome of patients with severe community-acquired pneumonia. Chest. 2003;123:174–180.

7. Mandell LA, Wunderink RG, Anzueto A et al. Infectious Disease Society of America/American Thoracic Society Consensus Guidelines on the management of community-acquired pneumonia in adults. Clin Infect Dis. 2007;44:S27–72.

8. Bartlett JG, Dowell SF, Mandell LA et al. Practice guidelines for the management of community-acquired pneumonia in adults. Clin Infect Dis. 2000;31:347–82.

9. British Thoracic Society (2001) BTS guidelines for the management of community-acquired pneumonia in adults. Thorax. 56:iv1–iv64.

10. Jacobs MR, Felmingham D, Appelbaum PC et al. The Alexander project 1998–2000: Susceptibility of pathogens isolated from community-acquired respiratory infection to commonly used antimicrobial agents. J Antimicrob Chemother. 2003;52:229–46.

11. Aspa J, Rajas O, Rodriguez de castro F et al. Drug-resistant pneumococcal pneumonia: Clinical relevance and related factors. Clin Infec Dis. 2004;38:787–98.

12. Hook EW, Horton CA, Schaberg DR. Failure of intensive care unit support to influence mortality from pneumococcal bacteremia. JAMA. 1983;249:1055–57.

13. Mufson MA, Stanek RJ. Bacteremic pneumococcal pneumonia in one American city: a 20-year longitudinal study, 1978–1997. Am J Med. 1999;107:34S–43S.

14. Waterer GW, Somes GW, Wunderink RG. Monotherapy may be suboptimal for severe bacteriemic pneumococcal pneumonia. Arch Intern Med. 2001,161(15):1837–1842.

15. Baddour LM, Yu VL, Klugman KP et al. Combinations antibiotic therapy lowers mortality among severely ill patients with pneumoccocal bacteriemia. Am J Respir Crit Care Med. 2004;170:440–444.

16. Martínez JA, Horcajada JP, Almela M et al. Addition of macrolide to a β-lactam-based empirical antibiotic regimen is associated with lower in-hospital mortality for patients with bacteremic pneumococcal pneumonia. Clin Infect Dis. 2003;36:389–95.

17. Rodríguez A, Mendia A, Sirvent JM et al. Combination antibiotic therapy improves survival in patients with community-acquired pneumonia and shock. Crit Care Med. 2007,35:1493–1499.

18. Rello J, Rodriguez A. Improving survival for sepsis: On the cutting edge. Crit Care Med. 2003;31:2807–08.

19. Weiss K, Tillotson GS. The controversy of combination vs monotherapy in the treatment of hospitalized community-acquired pneumonia. Chest. 2005;128: 940–46.

20. Arnold FW, Summersgill JT, Lajoie AS et al. A worldwide perspective of atypical pathogens in community-acquired pneumonia. Am J Respir Crit Care Med. 2007; 175:1086–93.

21. Shefet D, Robenshtok E, Mical P , Leibovici L. Empirical atypical coverage for inpatients with community-acquired pneumonia. Systematic review of randomized controlled trials. Arch Intern Med. 2005;165:1992–2000.

22. Robenshtok E, Shefet D, Gafter-Gvili A, Paul M, Vidal L, Leibovici L. Empiric antibiotic coverage of atypical pathogens for community acquired pneumonia in hospitalized adults. Cochrane Database Syst Rev. 2008; 23:CD004418.

23. Mundy LM, Oldach D, Auwaerter PG et al. Implications for macrolide treatment in community-acquired pneumonia. Chest. 1998;113:1201–06.

24. Lode H, Grossman C, Choudhri S et al. Sequential IV/PO moxifloxacin treatment of patients with severe community-acquired pneumonia. Respir Med. 2003;97: 1134.

25. Schultz MJ, Speerlman P, Zaat S et al. Erythromycin inhibits tumor necrosis factor alpha and interleukin 6 production induced by heat-killed Streptocuccus pneumoniae in whole blood. Antimicrob Agents Chemother. 1998;42:1605–09.

26. Cuffini AM, Tullio V, Mandras N et al. Clarithromycin mediated the expression of polimorphonuclear granulocyte response against Streptocuccus pneumoniae strains with different patterns of susceptibility and resistance to penicillin and Clarithromycin. Int J Tissue React. 2002;24:37–44.

27. Tamaoki J, Kondo M, Kohri K et al. Macrolide antibiotic protect against immune complex-induced lung injury in rats: role of nitric oxide form alveolar macrophages. J. Immunol. 1999;163:2909–15.

28. Schultz MU. Macrolide activities beyond their antimicrobial effects: macrolides in diffuse panbronchiolitis and cystic fibrosis. J Antimicrob Chemother. 2004; 54:21–28.

29. Labro MT. Interference of antibacterial agents with phagocytic functions: immunomodulation or "immuno-fairy tales" ?. Clin Microbiol Rev. 2000;13:615–50.

30. Uriarte SM, Molestina RE, Miller RD et al. Effects of fluoroquinolones on the migration of human phagocytes through Chlamydia pneumoniae-infected and tumor necrosis factor alpha-stimulated endothelial cells. Antimicrob Agents Chemother. 2004;48:2538–43.

31. Parnham MJ. Immunomodulatory effects of antimicrobials in the therapy of respiratory tract infections. Curr Opin Infect Dis. 2005;18:125–131.

32. Mortensen EM, Restrepo I, Anzueto A, Pugh J. The impact of empiric antimicrobial therapy with a β-lactam and fluoroquinolone on mortality for patients hospitalized with severe pneumonia. Crit Care. 2006;10:R8.

33. Metersky ML, Ma A, Houck PM, Bratzler DW. Antibiotic for bacteremic pneumonia: Improved outcome with macrolide but not fluoroquinolones. Chest. 2007;131:466–73.

34. Gleason PP, Meehan TP, Fine JM et al. Association between initial antimicrobial therapy and medical outcomes for hospitalized elderly patients with pneumonia. Arch Intern Med. 1999;159:2562–72.

35. Burgess DS, Lewis JS. Effect of macrolides as part of initial empiric therapy on medical outcomes for hospitalized patients with community-acquired pneumonia. Clin Ther. 2000;22:872–78.

36. Kollef MH, Sherman G, Ward S et al. Inadequate antimicrobial treatment of infections: A risk factor for hospital mortality among critically ill patients. Chest. 1999;115:462–474.

37. Dupont H, Mentec H, Sollet JP et al. Impact of appropriateness of initial antibiotic therapy on the outcome of ventilator-associated pneumonia. Intensive Care Med. 2001;27:355–362.

38. Leone M, Garcin F, Bouvenot J et al. Ventilator-associated pneumonia: breaking the vicious circle of antibiotic overuse. Crit Care Med. 2007;35:379–385.

39. Park DR. Antimicrobial treatment of ventilator-associated pneumonia. Respir Care. 2005;50:932–952.

40. Sandiumenge A, Diaz E, Bodi M, Rello J. Therapy of ventilator-associated pneumonia. A patient-based approach based on the ten rules rules of "The Tarragona Strategy". Intensive Care Med. 2003;29:876–883.

41. Hoffken G, Niederman MS. Nosocomial pneumonia: The importance of a De-escalating strategy for antibiotic treatment of pneumonia in the ICU. Chest. 2002;122: 2183–2196.

42. Diaz E, Muñoz E, Agbaht K, Rello J. Management of ventilator-associated pneumonia caused by multi-resistant bacteria. Curr Opin Crit Care. 2007;13:45–50.

43. Wolff M. Role of Aminoglycosides in the treatment of Ventilator-associated pneumonia. Clin Pulm Med. 2000; 7:120–127.

44. Trouillet JL, Chastre J, Vuagnat A et al. Ventilator-associated pneumonia caused by potentially drug-resistant bacteria. Am J Respir Crit Care Med. 1998;157:531–539.

45. Sieger B, Berman SJ, Geckler RW et al. Empiric treatment of hospitalized-acquired lower respiratory tract infections with meropenem or ceftazidime with tobramycin. Crit Care Med. 1997;25:1663–1667.

46. Fink MP, Snydman DR, Niederman MS et al. Treatment of severe pneumonia in hospitalized patients: results of a multicenter, randomized, double blind trial comparing intravenous ciprofloxacin with imipenem-cilastatin. Antimicrob Agents Chemother. 1994;38:547–557.

47. Cometta A, Baumgartner JD, Lew D et al. Prospective randomized comparison of imipenem monotherapy with imipenem plus netilmicin for treatment of severe infections in non-neutropenic patients. Antimicrob Agents Chemother. 1994;38:1309–1313.

48. Rubinstein E, Lode H, Grassi C et al. Ceftazidime monotherapy versus ceftriaxone/tobramycin for serious acquired gram-negative infections. Clin Infect Dis. 1995;20:1217–1228.

49. Heyland DK, Dodek P, Muscedere J et al. Randomized trial of combination versus monotherapy for the empiric treatment of suspected ventilator-associated pneumonia. Crit Care Med. 2008; [Epub ahead of print].

50. Garnacho-Montero J, Sa-Borges M, Sole-Violan J et al. Optimal management therapy for Pseudomonas aeruginosa ventilator-associated pneumonia: an observational, multicenter study comparing monotherapy with combination antibiotic therapy. Crit Care Med. 2007;35:1888–1895.

51. Aarts MW, Hancock JN, Heyland D et al. Empiric antibiotic therapy for suspected ventilator-associated pneumonia: A systematic review and meta-analysis of randomized trials. Crit Care Med. 2008; [Epub ahead of print].

52. Damas P, Garweg C, Monchi M et al. Combination therapy versus monotherapy: A randomized pilot study on the evolution of inflammatory parameters after ventilator-associated pneumonia. Crit Care. 2006;28:R52.

Christian Brun-Buisson

Do antibiotic protocols impact on resistance?

Introduction

Although there are large disparities across countries and regions, antimicrobial resistance is of growing concern worldwide (1–3). Addressing this problem is both urgent and mandatory, unless we risk facing a situation were we are confronted with infection for which there is no therapy available. Indeed, two factors concur with this potential risk: the unremitting emergence of new resistance problems, both in gram-positive (4) and gram-negative microorganisms (5, 6) on one hand, and the decreased output of new therapeutic classes by the pharmaceutical industry (7). Therefore, the only option at this time is to make sure that antibiotics are used prudently and as appropriately as possible through antibiotic stewardship (1, 8). Intensivists have a special responsibility in antibiotic stewardship in the hospital, as ICUs are areas where antibiotic consumption is highest and of course, where resistance rates are also highest, therefore leading to more broad-spectrum antibiotics being prescribed and to "spiralling resistance" (1, 9–11).

However, the intensivist is confronted with the dilemma of treating the patient in the best way and taking no risks in the face of serious and potentially life-threatening infection, through often prescribing antibiotics with broader-than-needed spectrum, yet still aiming at preserving the future efficacy of the drugs used and limiting the risk of resistance to these agents (8). As discussed by Paterson and Rice, three major options are available, aimed at reducing resistance rates in the hospital (8):

1. drug restriction, which entails eliminating some antibiotics from the hospital formulary (or raising strong barriers to their routine prescription),
2. de-escalation, which means allowing to use broad-spectrum drugs empirically, but downgrading to narrower-spectrum drugs whenever and as soon as possible, and
3. antibiotic rotation (or cycling), which means changing the class of antibiotics prescribed for empiric therapy of specific infections at fixed intervals.

Cycling antibiotic use actually derives from the first option, by using multiple successive restrictions of antimicrobials: its rationale is to expect a reduction of resistance rate to the cycled antimicrobial agents following their withdrawal for a substantial duration, so that they can be reintroduced later on with improved effectiveness for therapy of infection, after reduced resistance rates to that agent (12). The underlying assumptions are that there is a direct link between "antibiotic pressure" from a specific drug or class of drugs and resistance to this agent(s), and that withdrawing this pressure in a given environment after a while will both limit the magnitude of resistance and restore susceptibility to that agent for future use. Questions are whether these premises hold true for all classes of drugs, and what are the optimal durations of exposure/withdrawal periods for this strategy to be effective. While there is a clear relationship between prolonged exposure to several agents and resistance rates, for example to cephalosporins and fluoroquinolones in gram-negative bacilli, or imipenem in *Pseudomonas*, this relationship is less obvious for other drug/microorganisms combination; in addition, multiple combined resistance traits may be present in different bacterial species, so that exposure to one drug or class may foster resistance to other agents or classes. Accordingly, there is ongoing debate of the actual clinical efficacy of cycling, which will be the essential discussion in this chapter, as well as its place among other options of creating protocols for antibiotic use in the ICU.

Antibiotic rotation decrease resistance: Pro

The clinical experience with antibiotic rotation is usually reported as dating back to the availability of the then new aminoglycoside amikacin, i.e., back to the seventies (13). At that time, resistance to formerly available aminoglycosides (gentamycin, tobramycin) was an increasingly worrisome problem among Gram negative bacilli. Gerding et al. (13) reported on the evolution of resistance to gentamycin, tobramycin and amikacin when switching to amikacin as the first-line agent instead of gentamycin, and back to gentamycin during two successive cycles over a 4-year period. They showed decreasing gentamycin resistance with increasing amikacin usage, without increase in amikacin resistance during its preferential use. A similar experience of antibiotic rotation within the same class (i.e., aminoglycosides) was reported in 1985 by Young et al, during a 3-year experience of switching from gentamycin to amikacine (14).

The topic was then laid to rest for several years, possibly because of the availability of new and more active agents capable of opposing the resistance mechanisms prevalent at that time. The re-emergence of multi-drug resistant GNB and VRE in the mid-1990's, fostered renewed interest in antibiotic rotation protocols in ICUs.

The first study to suggest the efficacy of antibiotic rotation in ICUs was published from M. Kollef's group (15), which has produced several of the recent papers on the topic. In this study, the authors reported on two successive 6-month periods when ceftazidime was the preferred prescribed first-line agent for VAP, then substituted for ciprofloxacine. The overall VAP rate was almost halved and VAP caused by MRGNB decreased from 4.0% to 0.9% in the second period. This was clearly a very impressive result, although

the study period was short, and no controls were provided before or after the one-year period of study. In a follow-up paper (16), the same group reported on three 6-month periods during which ceftazidime, ciprofloxacine, and cefepime were consecutively used as the recommended first-line agent for therapy of severe infections in the ICU. In this more detailed study, it was apparent that although the recommended agent was preferentially used within its class, it accounted for no more than 30% of antibiotic use in each period. The positive result was a reduction of the rate of inadequate empiric therapy throughout the study (from 4.4% to 2.1% and 1.6%). However, the was a small but significant increase in resistance rate of GNB to each of the preferential agents during each corresponding period of use, and no impact on VAP or BSI rates, or on outcome of patients.

The second most impressive paper supporting cycling came from a French group in Bordeaux (17). Gruson et al. examined the effects of cycling of major first-line broad-spectrum antibiotics for empiric therapy of VAP. After a 2-year baseline period during which Ceftazidime + ciprofloxacin were used empirically, the authors used monthly rotation of first-line agents (with consecutive use of cefepime, piperacilline-tazobactam, imipenem, ticarcillin-clavulanic acid, together with rotating the first-line aminoglycoside agent) during the subsequent 2-year period (17). In addition to rotation, fluoroquinolone use was drastically reduced, de-escalation was performed routinely, and duration of therapy was limited to 15 days overall including 5 days of combined therapy. The main results were a reduction in the incidence rate of VAP (suspected and confirmed) and reduced rates of infection caused by high-risk micro organisms (*B. cepacia*, *S. maltophilia*, and *A. baumannii*), but not of *P. aeruginosa* (although their resistance rates to beta-lactams and aminoglycosides were lower) or MRSA. It should be noted that the most striking change in antibiotic use occurring during the cycling period was a near 90% overall reduction in fluoroquinolone use during the cycling period, together with a shift from imipenem to piperacillin-tazobactam.

In a subsequent report, the same group described their experience with routinely rotating antibiotics over the 3 years following this first study (18). Different first-line beta-lactam antibiotics were rotated monthly for either early-onset or late-onset VAP, while fluoroquinolones remained avoided. While the effects of the program recorded during the first study were maintained overall, with relatively low levels of infection or resistance rates, no substantial further improvement was recorded; however, the rate of isolation of potentially drug-resistant GNB tended to return to the initial level.

Other subsequent studies of antibiotic cycling have been published by M. Kollef's group and colleagues. Warren et al. and Merz et al. (19, 20) performed a detailed study where rectal colonisation with antimicrobial-resistant GNB (enterobacteriaceae and *Pseudomonas*) were analysed through weekly samples during a baseline 5-month period and a subsequent 24-month period of rotating antibiotics. Four classes of agents including 3 beta-lactams (cefepime, carbapenem, and extended-spectrum penicillins) and fluoroquinolones were cycled at 3–4 month intervals. Overall, 48% of total cycle antibiotic days were compliant with the cycling protocol (Merz 04).

In aggregate, there was no significant difference in the ICU-acquired infection rates or colonisation rates with potentially resistant GNB during the period with and without cycling. However, the interpretation of these results is limited by the fact that patients admitted during the cycling period appeared more severely ill than those admitted during the baseline period.

Bennett et al. examined the impact of cycling in a SICU (21), using a monthly rotation protocol of 4 drugs (piperacillin-tazobactam, imipenem, and ceftazidime; ciprofloxacine was initially included as a fourth option, but later withdrawn from the cycles because of relatively high resistance rates) during a 2-year period. They found that the resistance rates of GNB to major first-line agents was generally lower during the cycling period than before (especially for *P. aeruginosa*), but with no impact on infection rates. Such changes were not observed in the "control" nearby MICU, where cycling was not used.

One expected benefit from cycling is reduced resistance rates to first line agents administered for empiric therapy and cycled, resulting in a lesser rate of inappropriate antibiotic therapy during cycling. Conversely, it is necessary to check that the recommendation to use a given agent during each cycle does not result in adverse outcomes for patients thus treated. This important outcome

has been evaluated by Merz et al. (22), using data recorded during the study previously reported by Warren et al. where 3–4 month cycling periods of 3 beta-lactams and fluoroquinolones were used sequentially (23, 24). Among 1,123 patients admitted over a 28-month period, 59 bloodstream infections (BSIs), 17 ventilator-associated pneumonias (VAPs), and 101 urinary tract infections (UTIs) involving Gram-negative bacteria were recorded among 139 patients. Only 15 (11%) patients received initially inappropriate empiric therapy, and this rate did not differ between the baseline and cycling period (15% vs. 10%, p = 0.4), and actually tended to be lower in the latter, especially for therapy of suspected VAP. However, low overall infection rates and some imbalances between the 2 groups make the interpretation of the results difficult (see tab. 1). In addition, mortality tended to be higher, not lower in the cycling group, despite similar initial severity of illness.

Tab. 1 Characteristics, outcomes and infection rates before and during cycling. Modified from Merz LR, Warren DK, Kollef MH, Fraser VJ. Effects of an antibiotic cycling program on antibiotic prescribing practices in an intensive care unit. Antimicrob Agents Chemother. 2004;48:2861–65 and Warren DK, Hill HA, Merz LR, Kollef MH, Hayden MK, Fraser VJ et al. Cycling empirical antimicrobial agents to prevent emergence of antimicrobial-resistant Gram-negative bacteria among intensive care unit patients. Crit Care Med. 2004;32:2450–2456.
Abbreviations: ICU: Intensive care unit; LOS: Length of stay; VAP: Ventilator-associated pneumonia; BSI: Bloodstream infection; CVC: Central-venous catheter.

Period (no. of patients)	Baseline (n = 242)	Cycling (n = 930)	p value
APACHE II, mean (range)	22.5 (5–47)	23.3 (5–45)	0.06
In-ICU mortality, n (%)	38 (16)	198 (21)	0.06
ICU LOS, mean days (range)	7.7 (1–40)	8.7 (3–64)	0.01
VAP rate, p. 1,000 pt-d	6.1	3.0	.15
BSI rate, p. 1,000 pt-d	14.9	16.8	.66
CVC-related BSI episodes, p. 1,000 pt-d	12.9	13.9	.98
C.difficile-associated diarrhea, n (%)	16 (7)	69 (7)	.78

The third study showing a benefit from antibiotic rotation in the ICU was published by Raymond et al.(25) These authors compared a 1-year baseline period to a subsequent 1-year study of quarterly antibiotic rotation, where beta-lactam drugs (piperacillin-tazobactam, carbapenem, cefepime) or ciprofloxacin, with or without clindamycin were cycled in a surgical ICU. A specific feature of that study is that different drugs were used in a given cycle for empiric therapy of pneumonia or intra-abdominal infection, thus introducing a mixing of different drugs at the same time (e.g., carbapenem for pneumonia together with ciprofloxacine + clindamycin for peritonitis or sepsis of unknown origin). During the cycling period, there were less infections caused by resistant GPC (32.5 vs. 20.5 p.1000 pt-d) or resistant GNB (17.2 vs. 6.6 p.1000 pt-d, $p < 0.001$), although the overall incidence density rate of ICU-acquired infection did not vary significantly; while a decrease in overall mortality was not reported by the authors, they did report a reduced mortality "attributable" to infection, with fewer deaths occurring in infected patients during therapy of infection (38.1% vs. 15.5%, $p = 0.035$), likely associated with less resistance of responsible pathogens. A multivariate analysis of factors associated with mortality showed that antibiotic rotation was associated with a reduced risk. Furthermore, antibiotic use and costs tended to decrease during the cycling period.

In a follow-up study, the same group examined the impact of antibiotic rotation in the ICU on the incidence and characteristics of infections occurring in wards where ICU patients were transferred (26). Indeed, they found a decreased incidence of infection compared to the pre-cycling period, and a decreased incidence of infections caused by antibiotic-resistant GPC or GNB. However, a separate analysis of patients transferred from the ICU or admitted from other wards or the community showed that the reduction of infection occurred mostly in the latter group. The authors' interpretation of this somewhat surprising finding was that cross-transmission of antibiotic-resistant microorganism may have been reduced during the rotation period, perhaps because of a lesser carriage rate in patients coming from the ICU, or of some other confounding factor.

Antibiotic rotation reduces resistance: Con

The potential impact of cycling antibiotics has been examined from a theoretical perspective, using population epidemiology and mathematical modeling by Lipstich and others (27, 28). Studies performed both in community and hospital settings suggest that cycling may not be effective and even actually favour the selection of resistant organisms. When switching from one drug to another, the resistance rate to the newly introduced drug is relatively low, and this new drug is temporarily more effective, while resistance to the former drug declines. However, resistance rises soon after the introduction of the new drug. The shorter the interval between cycling period, the lesser the proportion of resistant strains in the total hospital population, and modeling shows that cycling results in about 30% more resistance than a strategy "mixing" the use of different drugs (i.e., equivalent to cycling at very short intervals) (27).

Moss et al. examined the effects of 3-month cycles of antibiotic rotation over a 18-month period in a pediatric ICU at the Johns Hopkins hospital in the US (29). Three beta-lactams were rotated as first-line therapy and continued if the isolate was susceptible. The major endpoint was colonisation with "antibiotic-resistant bacteria". In this limited pilot study of 441 children, there was no substantial change in resistance of colonizing microorganisms over time; the authors however noted a downward trend to less resistance in infants studied during the cycling period.

Van Loon et al. examined the effect on resistance rate among gram-negative bacilli of rotating 2 beta-lactams (Piperacillin-tazobactam and cefepime) and a fluoroquinolone (levofloxacin) during four 4-month periods in a surgical ICU (30). Importantly, the study design controlled for the relative importance of cross-transmission and overall antibiotic use. The protocol was well adhered to, as 96% (range 88 to 100%) of all antibiotic courses were prescribed in accordance with antibiotics specified in the protocol during each period; however, the authors also noted that overall, only 27% to 49% of all antibiotic use was due to the cycled antibiotics. In addition, total antibiotic use increased by 24% during the cycling period (30). The primary end-point was colonisation with antibiotic-resistant bacteria to each antibiotic cycled. The use of fluoroquinolones and piperacillin-tazobactam were clearly associated with increased antibiotic resistance to the cycled drug in use, especially for the fluroquinolone (see tab. 2); in addition, acquisition rates for any of the three cycled antibiotics tended to be higher during fluoroquinolone use (29.6 and 37.9/1,000 days at risk) than during beta-lactam use (16.8 and 19.5/1,000 days at risk) (RR 1.4; 95% CI: 0.9–2.3, p = 0.20), thus tending to confirm a higher risk of selection of resistance associated with fluoroquinolone use. Withdrawal of drug was not followed by a rapid decrease in resistance to any one drug, which was likely explained by the presence of combined resistance traits to different classes of drugs within bacteria.

Differences observed were statistically significant, except during cefpirome exposure.

A cycling strategy was compared to a mixing strategy in a relatively short-term study performed in two ICUs in Spain (31). In a cross-over design, one ICU started with mixing and the other with cycling, both during two successive 4-month periods; cefepime/ceftazidime, ciprofloxacin, carbapenem, and piperacillin were used sequentially every month during the cycling periods, and "mixing" used the same antibiotics in sequence for consecutive patients. The primary end-point was acquisition rate of enteric and nonfermentative Gramnegative bacilli resistant to the antibiotics under intervention or to amikacin. *Pseudomonas aeruginosa*, *A. baumannii*, other nonfermentative Gram-negative bacilli, extended-spectrum beta-lactamase producing *Escherichia coli* or *Klebsiella*, and species of *Enterobacteriaceae* different from *E. coli*, *Klebsiella*, and *Proteus mirabilis* were considered as potentially resistant (PRGNB). There was no difference in nosocomial infection rates, nor in the acquisition rate of ARGNB or PRGNB, or of ARGPC. However, the authors report that a significantly higher proportion of patients acquired a strain of *P. aeruginosa* resistant to cefepime during mixing, and there was a trend toward a more frequent acquisition of resistance to ceftazidime, imipenem, meropenem, and any beta-lactam (20 of 179, 11% vs. 9 of 167, 5% during cycling, p = .052).

Similar to the observation made in the study by van Loon, the antibiotics cycled never represented > 45% of the anti-pseudomonal agents prescribed. There were differences in use of various antibiotics during the 2 periods, with higher overall use

Tab. 2 Acquisition rate of resistance to each cycled antibiotic during periods of exposure or non-exposure to a given cycled antibiotic. Modified from: van Loon HJ, Vriens MR, Fluit AC, Troelstra A, van der WC, Verhoef J et al. Antibiotic rotation and development of gram-negative antibiotic resistance. Am J Respir Crit Care Med. 2005;171:480–487. Differences observed were statistically significant, except during cefpirome exposure.

	Levofloxacin	Piperacillin-tazobactam	Cefpirome
Exposure	19.6	16.3	14.8
Non-exposure	5.2	9.0	13.3
Relative risk	3.2 [1.4–7.1]	2.4 [1.2–4.8]	0.9 [0.4–1.7]

during cycling (31). The interpretation of this study is unfortunately confounded by two factors:
1. an outbreak of multi-resistant *Acinetobacter baumannii* (except to carbapenem) which occurred at the initiation of the study, and affected both units together with antibiotic use;
2. the unexplained finding of a substantially higher mortality in one of the two ICUs during cycling as compared to during mixing (42% vs. 17%, p = 0.001), resulting in an overall difference in mortality when comparing the cycling (31%) with the mixing (20%, p = 0.01) periods grouped between the 2 ICUs.

In a prospective observational study, Damas et al. analysed the effects of rotating first-line antibiotics in 3 subunits of one ICU during 2 years (32). A cephalosporin, a fluoroquinolone and an extended-spectrum beta-lactam + inhibitor were used over cycles of 8 months, starting with a different drug in a cross-over design in each of the 3 subunits. There was no significant change in overall antibiotic susceptibility observed over the 2-year time of the study. However, when grouping periods when each individual class was used, reduced susceptibility to the antibiotics used preferentially was observed, specifically for *P. aeruginosa* and fluoroquinolones during use of the latter, and for inducible Enterobacteriaceae and cefotaxime during cephalosporin use, or during piperacillin-tazobactam use. Of note, resistance to imipenem also increased during fluoroquinolone use.

Discussion

It is difficult to draw firm conclusions from these conflicting studies. There are indeed major problems with their interpretation and comparison, which relate to methodological issues, and differences in protocols used.

A common problem is that all studies have used a before-after design, with variable degrees of sophistication; because of the nature of the question addressed it is not feasible to perform a randomised control study. The only alternative design which would strengthen the generalizability of the observations would be a cluster-randomised trial involving a sufficiently large number of ICUs where ICUs would be allocated to rotation or usual mixing, possibly within a cross-over design. Such a study has not been performed. In addition, as emphasised by Nijssen et al. (33), there are a number of confounding factors that need to be controlled for when performing such studies, in order to interpret the observed changes in resistance rates associated with cycling antibiotics or other related interventions. In addition to potential changes in case-mix and overall antibiotic use, a major confounder is the adherence to infection control practices and control of cross-transmission. Increased awareness and changes in infection control practices at initiation of the study is common in association with the antibiotic policy tested. Conversely, in several of the studies reviewed above, the authors mention that an outbreak occurred during the study, which may have variably affected the results.

It is also not uncommon that changes in overall antibiotic prescribing policies occur in association with implementation of the antibiotic rotation protocol. For example, in the study by Gruson et al. (17), a drastic reduction (by almost 90%) of overall fluoroquinolone use occurred during the study, and antibiotic policies regarding the use of combination therapy and duration were also altered. In the study by Raymond et al. (25), an antibiotic therapy team was introduced during the study, and prevention of cross-transmission also likely improved with the introduction of dispensable alcoholic hand rubs.

While the results of some early studies of rotation appear impressive, it must be recognised that these also had several of these problems. The first study by Kollef's group was of short duration, and rather described the switch from one drug to another – a strategy often shown to be effective in the short term for control of outbreaks, but not in the long term – than a true cycling study (15). The subsequent study by the same group is indeed much less impressive. As mentioned above, Gruson et al. combined rotation with restriction (of fluoroquinolones) and other measures of antibiotic stewardship (17). Although these authors showed in a subsequent study that their favourable results were maintained in the long term, it is unknown whether this was due to continued rotation or the other measures taken (16, 18).

All studies show an increase in resistance to the drug in use, to a variable extent, depending on the specific drug and duration of cycling. It is apparent from the studies using different duration of cycling that the longer the cycling period, the more apparent the resistance (32). If cycling is to be used, it seems that short periods (i.e., one month) might lessen this risk (18). These observations are concordant with the model predicting increased resistance with increased duration of cycling.

Another issue relates to the drugs cycled and their relative risk of fostering resistance, and whether cycling should use drugs of different classes or can use several drugs of the same class. All studies show markedly increased resistance to fluoroquinolones among GNB with their use, consistent with the known relationship between fluoroquinolone use and resistance (34). Similar observations, although to a somewhat lesser extent, are true for imipenem (35). There appears to be however, a differential risk with cephalosporins, with a trend to a higher risk for ceftazidime than for cefepime (16), an expected finding given the increased activity of the latter and its lesser susceptibility to known bacterial resistance mechanisms of GNB. In addition, cross-resistance to different classes of drugs can emerge when using one of them. This again seems particularly true with fluoroquinolones (16, 36).

Given the limitations of cycling and uncertain effectiveness, are there other antibiotic strategies available to help contain resistance? The overall objective of such strategies is to reduce exposure to antibiotics, particularly to broad-spectrum agents, which are most prone to favour the emergence of further problem microorganisms and infection in the ICU population.

The most widely applied strategy is de-escalation, which allows for both limiting the risk of inappropriate empiric antibiotic therapy, and limiting time of exposure to broad-spectrum agents. Can this strategy be applied in clinical practice? Yes, to some extent; observational studies show that such de-escalation is appropriate and safe in about 30 % to 50 % of patients started with broad-spectrum therapy (37, 38). Therefore, it is of extreme importance that the antibiotic regimen be re-assessed at 48 h–72 h, when microbiological results are available, to ask whether de-escalation can be used, or even withdrawal in patients without documented or severe presentation. This requirement goes along with the need for having obtained adequate samples for culture before starting antibiotics for a given infection, and this clearly is an essential part of the de-escalation strategy (39). However, in some patients started on empiric therapy because of suspicion of infection, it is also possible to withdraw therapy altogether based on clinical evaluation only. In patients suspected of pneumonia, Singh et al. showed that when the suspicion of infection is weak (based on a clinical pulmonary infection score of < 6), that infection does not seem to be confirmed and the patient's condition does not worsen after 3 days, antibiotics can be safely stopped after 3 days (40). Interestingly in this randomised study, patients receiving a shorter course of therapy had less super-infection with resistant microorganisms and even a trend toward reduced 28-day mortality, as compared to patients receiving the usual full course of therapy. Again, re-evaluation of both the need for therapy and of antibiotics prescribed at 2–3 days is an important, effective, and simple component of an antibiotic policy.

In addition to de-escalation, paying special attention to duration of therapy is useful and effective. Whereas most prior recommendations advocate a course of 10–15 days, we have now learned that most infections can be effectively treated with shorter courses, even in the critically ill. This is apparent from the multicentre randomised controlled trial comparing a 15-day to a 8-day course in patients with VAP (41), where the latter was shown equivalent to the former, providing similar outcome for patients, together with indicators of reduced selection pressure for resistance. In support of this concept, Micek et al. performed a randomised controlled trial (42) where a routine policy of encouraging early discontinuation of antibiotics was implemented. As a result, patients received a mean of 2 days antibiotic less, without adverse effects (no increased relapse rate, and similar length of stay in ICU and mortality). The concept of shortening the duration of therapy is also indirectly supported by the recent studies testing the added value of procalcitonin measurements in the management of infections, resulting in shorter duration of therapy with PCT-guided therapy (43, 44).

Conclusion

Antibiotic stewardship is an essential part of containing antibiotic resistance in the ICU, together with adherence to infection control measures aiming at curtailing cross-transmission. Prominent among useful steps to this end are early antibiotic regimen re-evaluation and limiting exposure through de-escalation and withdrawal of antibiotics in patients in whom the need for therapy does not prove to be confirmed, as well as reducing the duration of therapy, with the possible help of biomarkers. The potential role of antibiotic formulary manipulation through cycling within a global antibiotic policy is unclear in the absence of an outbreak.

The author

Christian Brun-Buisson, Prof.
    Service de Réanimation Médicale
    Groupe Hospitalier Albert Chenevier –
    Henri Mondor, AP-HP
    University Paris 12, Créteil
    94010 Créteil, France
    e-mail: christian.brun-buisson@hmn.aphp.fr

References

1. Kollef MH, Fraser VJ. Antibiotic resistance in the intensive care unit. Ann Intern Med. 2001;134:298–314.
2. Diekema DJ, Pfaller MA, Jones RN, Doern GV, Kugler KC, Beach ML et al. Trends in antimicrobial susceptibility of bacterial pathogens isolated from patients with bloodstream infections in the USA, Canada and Latin America. SENTRY Participants Group. Int J Antimicrob Agents. 2000;13:257–71.

3. Fluit AC, Jones ME, Schmitz FJ, Acar J, Gupta R, Verhoef J. Antimicrobial susceptibility and frequency of occurrence of clinical blood isolates in Europe from the SENTRY antimicrobial surveillance program, 1997 and 1998. Clin Infect Dis. 2000;30:454–60.

4. Tenover FC, Lancaster MV, Hill BC, Steward CD, Stocker SA, Hancock GA et al. Characterization of staphylococci with reduced susceptibilities to vancomycin and other glycopeptides. J Clin Microbiol. 1998;36:1020–7.

5. Jacoby GA, Munoz-Price LS. The new beta-lactamases. N Engl J Med. 2005;352:380–391.

6. Robicsek A, Jacoby GA, Hooper DC. The worldwide emergence of plasmid-mediated quinolone resistance. Lancet Infect Dis. 2006;6:629–40.

7. Spellberg B, Powers JH, Brass EP, Miller LG, Edwards JE, Jr. Trends in antimicrobial drug development: implications for the future. Clin Infect Dis. 2004;38:1279–86.

8. Paterson DL, Rice LB. Empirical antibiotic choice for the seriously ill patient: are minimization of selection of resistant organisms and maximization of individual outcome mutually exclusive? Clin Infect Dis. 2003;36: 1006–12.

9. Dellit TH, Owens RC, McGowan JE, Jr., Gerding DN, Weinstein RA, Burke JP et al. Infectious Diseases Society of America and the Society for Healthcare Epidemiology of America guidelines for developing an institutional program to enhance antimicrobial stewardship. Clin Infect Dis. 2007;44:159–77.

10. Goldmann DA, Weinstein RA, Wenzel RP, Tablan OC, Duma RJ, Gaynes RP et al. Strategies to Prevent and Control the Emergence and Spread of Antimicrobial-Resistant Microorganisms in Hospitals. A challenge to hospital leadership. JAMA. 1996;275:234–40.

11. Owens RC, Jr., Rice L. Hospital-based strategies for combating resistance. Clin Infect Dis. 2006;42 Suppl 4: S173–S181.

12. Kollef MH. Is there a role for antibiotic cycling in the intensive care unit? Crit Care Med. 2001;29:N135–N142.

13. Gerding DN. Antimicrobial cycling: lessons learned from the aminoglycoside experience. Infect Control Hosp Epidemiol. 2000;21:S12–S17.

14. Young EJ, Sewell CM, Koza MA, Clarridge ME. Antibiotic resistance patterns during aminoglycoside restriction. Am J Med Sci. 1985;290:223–27.

15. Kollef MH, Vlasnik J, Sharpless L, Pasque C, Murphy D, Fraser VJ. Scheduled change of antibiotic classes. A strategy to decrease the incidence of ventilator-associated pneumonia. Am J Respir Crit Care Med. 1997;156:1040–1048.

16. Kollef MH, Ward S, Sherman G, Prentice D, Schaiff R, Huey W et al. Inadequate treatment of nosocomial infections is associated with certain empiric antibiotic choices. Crit Care Med. 2000;28:3456–64.

17. Gruson D, Hilbert G, Vargas F, Valentino R, Bebear C, Allery A et al. Rotation and restricted use of antibiotics in a medical intensive care unit. Impact on the incidence of ventilator-associated pneumonia caused by antibiotic-resistant gram-negative bacteria. Am J Respir Crit Care Med. 2000;162: 837–43.

18. Gruson D, Hilbert G, Vargas F, Valentino R, Bui N, Pereyre S et al. Strategy of antibiotic rotation: long-term effect on incidence and susceptibilities of Gram-negative bacilli responsible for ventilator-associated pneumonia. Crit Care Med. 2003;31:1908–14.

19. Warren DK, Hill HA, Merz LR, Kollef MH, Hayden MK, Fraser VJ et al. Cycling empirical antimicrobial agents to prevent emergence of antimicrobial-resistant Gram-negative bacteria among intensive care unit patients. Crit Care Med. 2004;32:2450–2456.

20. Merz LR, Warren DK, Kollef MH, Fraser VJ. Effects of an antibiotic cycling program on antibiotic prescribing practices in an intensive care unit. Antimicrob Agents Chemother. 2004;48:2861–65.

21. Bennett KM, Scarborough JE, Sharpe M, Dodds-Ashley E, Kaye KS, Hayward TZ, III et al. Implementation of antibiotic rotation protocol improves antibiotic susceptibility profile in a surgical intensive care unit. J Trauma. 2007;63:307–11.

22. Merz LR, Warren DK, Kollef MH, Fridkin SK, Fraser VJ. The impact of an antibiotic cycling program on empirical therapy for gram-negative infections. Chest. 2006;130: 1672–78.

23. Merz LR, Warren DK, Kollef MH, Fraser VJ. Effects of an antibiotic cycling program on antibiotic prescribing practices in an intensive care unit. Antimicrob Agents Chemother. 2004;48:2861–65.

24. Warren DK, Hill HA, Merz LR, Kollef MH, Hayden MK, Fraser VJ et al. Cycling empirical antimicrobial agents to prevent emergence of antimicrobial-resistant Gram-negative bacteria among intensive care unit patients. Crit Care Med. 2004;32:2450–2456.

25. Raymond DP, Pelletier SJ, Crabtree TD, Gleason TG, Hamm LL, Pruett TL et al. Impact of a rotating empiric antibiotic schedule on infectious mortality in an intensive care unit. Crit Care Med. 2001;29:1101–8.

26. Hughes MG, Evans HL, Chong TW, Smith RL, Raymond DP, Pelletier SJ et al. Effect of an intensive care unit rotating empiric antibiotic schedule on the development of hospital-acquired infections on the non-intensive care unit ward. Crit Care Med. 2004;32:53–60.

27. Bergstrom CT, Lo M, Lipsitch M. Ecological theory suggests that antimicrobial cycling will not reduce antimicrobial resistance in hospitals. Proc Natl Acad Sci USA. 2004;101: 13285–90.

28. Levin BR, Bonten MJ. Cycling antibiotics may not be good for your health. Proc Natl Acad Sci USA. 2004;101:13101–2.

29. Moss WJ, Beers MC, Johnson E, Nichols DG, Perl TM, Dick JD et al. Pilot study of antibiotic cycling in a pediatric intensive care unit. Crit Care Med. 2002;30: 1877–82.

30. van Loon HJ, Vriens MR, Fluit AC, Troelstra A, van der WC, Verhoef J et al. Antibiotic rotation and development of gram-negative antibiotic resistance. Am J Respir Crit Care Med. 2005;171:480–487.

31. Martinez JA, Nicolas JM, Marco F, Horcajada JP, Garcia-Segarra G, Trilla A et al. Comparison of antimicrobial cycling and mixing strategies in two medical intensive care units. Crit Care Med. 2006;34:329–36.

32. Damas P, Canivet JL, Ledoux D, Monchi M, Melin P, Nys M et al. Selection of resistance during sequential use of preferential antibiotic classes. Intensive Care Med. 2006; 32: 67–74.

33. Nijssen S, Bootsma M, Bonten M. Potential confounding in evaluating infection-control interventions in hospital settings: changing antibiotic prescription. Clin Infect Dis. 2006;43:616–23.

34. Neuhauser MM, Weinstein RA, Rydman R, Danziger LH, Karam G, Quinn JP. Antibiotic resistance among gram-negative bacilli in US intensive care units: implications for fluoroquinolone use. JAMA. 2003;289: 885–88.

35. Harbarth S, Harris AD, Carmeli Y, Samore MH. Parallel analysis of individual and aggregated data on antibiotic exposure and resistance in gram-negative bacilli. Clin Infect Dis. 2001;33:1462–68.

36. Trouillet JL, Vuagnat A, Combes A, Kassis N, Chastre J, Gibert C. Pseudomonas aeruginosa Ventilator-Associated Pneumonia: Comparison of Episodes Due to Piperacillin-Resistant versus Piperacillin-Susceptible Organisms. Clin Infect Dis. 2002;34:1047–54.

37. Giantsou E, Liratzopoulos N, Efraimidou E, Panopoulou M, Alepopoulou E, Kartali-Ktenidou S et al. De-escalation therapy rates are significantly higher by bronchoalveolar lavage than by tracheal aspirate. Intensive Care Med. 2007;33:1533–40.

38. Rello J, Vidaur L, Sandiumenge A, Rodriguez A, Gualis B, Boque C et al. De-escalation therapy in ventilator-associated pneumonia. Crit Care Med. 2004;32:2183–90.

39. Chastre J, Fagon JY. State of the Art: Ventilator-associated pneumonia. Am J Respir Crit Care Med. 2002;165: 867–903.

40. Singh N, Rogers P, Atwood CW, Wagener MM, Yu VL. Short-course Empiric Antibiotic Therapy for Patients with Pulmonary Infiltrates in the Intensive Care Unit. A proposed solution for indiscriminate antibiotic prescription. Am J Respir Crit Care Med. 2000;162: 505–11.

41. Chastre J, Wolff M, Fagon JY, Chevret S, Thomas F, Wermert D et al. Comparison of 8 vs 15 days of antibiotic therapy for ventilator-associated pneumonia in adults: a randomized trial. JAMA. 2003;290:2588–98.

42. Micek ST, Ward S, Fraser VJ, Kollef MH. A randomized controlled trial of an antibiotic discontinuation policy for clinically suspected ventilator-associated pneumonia. Chest. 2004;125:1791–99.

43. Christ-Crain M, Stolz D, Bingisser R, Muller C, Miedinger D, Huber PR et al. Procalcitonin guidance of antibiotic therapy in community-acquired pneumonia: a randomized trial. Am J Respir Crit Care Med. 2006;174: 84–93.

44. Nobre V, Harbarth S, Graf JD, Rohner P, Pugin J. Use of Procalcitonin to Shorten Antibiotic Treatment Duration in Septic Patients. A Randomized Trial. Am J Respir Crit Care Med. 2008 (in press).

François Philippart, Cédric Bruel, Olfa Hamzaoui,
Benoît Misset and Jean Carlet

The activated protein C controversy

*"There are more tears shed over answered prayers than
over unanswered prayers."*

Saint Teresa of Ávila

At the end of the first decade of the 21st century, sepsis
and particularly septic shock remain a public health concern because mortality still remains significant. Despite
a large and daily increasing amount of data becoming
available concerning sepsis pathophysiology (1), very few
therapeutic innovations are solid discoveries for clinical
practice.

Protein C pathway

Protein C is a serine protease which is produced
by the liver in an inactive zymogen form. Activated protein C (APC) is obtained by conversion of
protein C zymogen to the active form on the endothelial cell surface. thrombomodulin (TM) is a
surface endothelial cell receptor for thrombin, and
the direct activation of protein C to its active form
by TM-thrombin complex was demonstrated
more than twenty years ago (2). This reaction is
greatly enhanced by another endothelium membrane-bound protein, endothelial protein C receptor (EPCR), which binds with a high affinity inactive and activated forms of protein C (3). After its
activation, APC dissociates from EPCR and binds
to its cofactor protein S. In association with
protein S, APC induces a proteolytic inactivation
of activated factor V (Va) (4) and VIII (VIIIa) (5),
inhibits the synthesis of the plasminogen-activa-
tor inhibitor (PAI-1) (6) and blocks further generation of thrombin (7, 8).

Sepsis: Activated Protein C pathophysiology

Coagulation plays a central role during inflammatory processes, particularly infectious ones (9).
Sepsis is associated with a large range of coagulation abnormalities (10). In the most severe forms
of sepsis, such as septic shock, many of these
mechanisms are altered, and decreases of protein
C, protein S, antithrombin and tissue factor-path-
way inhibitor (TFPI) are observed. Once activated,
the inflammatory and coagulation pathways interact with one another to further amplify the host
response (11–13). This convergence of coagulation
and innate immunity contributes to the pathogenesis of septic shock (14). Moreover, the association
between coagulation alterations and sepsis evolution (15) is currently widely admitted.

APC plays a major role in coagulation regulation, either on homeostasis or during sepsis. During sepsis, decreased protein C production by the liver, endothelial cell alterations and low availability of protein S are responsible for a significant alteration in APC formation.

The decrease in protein C activation by endothelial cells is a multifactorial phenomenon. An alteration of the endothelial expression of thrombomodulin and to a lesser extent, EPCR, lead to an impairment of the activation of protein C (16). Moreover, endothelial cell-bound activated neutrophils release oxidant radicals that reduce the ability of thrombomodulin to bind thrombin and to activate protein C (17). Finally, such activated leukocytes are able to release proteases that can proteolytically shed thrombomodulin from the endothelial surface (18). At the same time there is an increase in plasminogen activator inhibitor 1 (PAI-1) (19), and a decrease in its inhibition by APC (20), leading to a procoagulant state (21).

Apart from its coagulation modulator properties, APC has numerous inflammatory modulation properties. APC contributes to the inflammatory response modulation by decreasing proinflammatory cytokine (such as TNF-α) production, either by animal (22) or human monocytes (23). Recombinant human APC (rhAPC), named drotrecogin alpha (activated) (DrotAA) has been show to modulate NF-κB-dependent gene expression by suppression of p50 and p52 NF-κB subunits in endothelial cells(24). This is of particular importance because, these modifications are responsible for a dose-dependent decrease in adhesion molecules such as intercellular adhesion molecule 1 (ICAM-1), vascular cell adhesion molecule 1 (VCAM-1) or E-selectin (24). DrotAA is associated with an inhibition of leukocytes adhesion to E-selectins (25) and a decrease in leukocyte tissular infiltration (26). Moreover, DrotAA decreases endothelial cell apoptosis (24).

The decrease in endogenous activated protein C during sepsis was confirmed (15, 27) and associated with outcome (27–29). *In vivo* mechanisms of actions of a therapeutic intervention in humans are beginning to be elucidated (30), even if they largely remain unclear (31), probably due to the wide difference between the endotoxemia model (DrotAA started before lipopolysaccharide in healthly volunteers) and the real sepsis process. These observations were of particular interest in the understanding of pathophysiology of coagulopathy associated with sepsis and severe sepsis (32), and part of the initial enthusiasm concerning the potential of DrotAA in the most severe infections.

Initial hopes ...

In vivo, DrotAA has been shown to attenuate coagulopathy, hepathopathy, and mainly to increase survival of baboons challenged with an *Escherichia coli* bacteremia (33). These observations were corroborated by the first human phase II trials (34, 35).

Due to these promising results, the recombinant human activated PROtein C Worldwide Evaluation in Severe Sepsis (PROWESS) trial, a large multicentre study, was initiated (36). After 1,520 randomised inclusions, the study was interrupted at the second interim analysis, because of the reduction in risk of death. DrotAA was shown to reduce the absolute risk of death of 6.1%, and the relative risk of death of 19.4% (36). Of particular interest, the clinical observations were correlated to pathophysiology and expected efficiency on coagulation and sepsis markers. Thus, plasma D-Dimers concentration decreased faster and remained lower in the intervention group from day 1 to day 7, and in the same way, the decrease in serum interleukin-6 was greater at each time point.

These encouraging results were secondary confirmed by a phase 3B study, Extended Evaluation of Recombinant Human Activated Protein C United States Trial (ENHANCE US) (37), using a single-arm observation of DrotAA efficacy and safety. Two hundred seventy-three adult patients were enrolled in this study, and the 28-day all-cause mortality rate, which was the main endpoint, was 26.4% (95% CI, 21.1 to 31.6%). These results were consistent with those of the PROWESS study (i.e. 24.7% in the treatment group). Moreover, the objective severity of these patients seemed comparable considering APACHE II scores (23.4 ± 7.4 in the intervention group, 24.8 ± 7.5 in the DrotAA group of the PROWESS study and 25.6 ± 7.8, in the placebo group). These results were also similar to those observed in other interventional studies on sepsis. Due to the extensive discussion about severity of patients, septic shock and number of organ failures were noted. There was no statistical difference between the groups in the number of patients requiring vasopressors, even if slightly more catecholamines were infused in the DrotAA group. Surprisingly, the percentage of patients receiving these vasopressors was lower than the percentage of patients included in the septic shock group (Septic shock, 74.0% (DrotAA/ENHANCE); 65.1% (DrotAA/PROWESS); 70.5% (placebo/PROWESS) and use of any vasopressor 63.7% (DrotAA/ENHANCE); 50.6% (DrotAA/PROWESS); 55.2% (placebo/PROWESS). On the other hand, patients with two or more organ failures were quite similar and patients with three or more visceral failures are slightly more numerous in the study group than in the two PROWESS groups (39.9% vs. 29.5% and 34.6%). This raised the possibility of better efficacy of DrotAA in the more severe patients.

The good initial results were confirmed by the evolution of survival patients, with persisting benefits in survival of the DrotAA group from hospital to 2.5 years in the most severe subgroup patients (APACHE II ≥ 25)(38). The comparison of multi-versus mono-organ failure patients, however, did not confirm such a survival advantage in the less severe patients, and the difference of the two global groups (DrotAA and placebo) disappears from the first time point follow-up (3 months): DrotAA: 66.1% vs. placebo 62.4% (p = 0.11)(38).

Because of these optimistic results in so deadly a pathology as severe sepsis, many professionals expected DrotAA to be quickly available for clinical use (39) – and their wish was granted.

... Secondary disappointments

Immediately after the initial enthusiasm, concerns began to appear from everywhere, directed along three major axes: the cost of this therapy, the reality of the results, and the real hemorrhagic risk for patients.

The cost problem, even if this question needs to be answered locally, was rapidly studied, with comparable information on both sides of the Atlantic. Angus et al. concluded that DrotAA has a cost-effectiveness profile similar to that of many well-accepted health care strategies and below commonly quoted thresholds, at $ 48,800

per quality-adjusted life-year, and a decrease in cost if only the more severe patients are treated (APACHE II ≥ 25) (40). Manns found consistent results, insisting on the necessity of further studies to determine the cost-effectiveness of DrotAA in the less severe patients (41). This favorable cost-effectiveness ratio was also retrieved in Europe (42, 43), upon condition that "treatment [was] targeted to those patients most likely to achieve the greatest benefit" (42). The disappointing secondary results brought back the relevance of the cost-benefit ratio of this treatment (44), particularly regarding the cheaper option given by hydrocortisone (45). A new shadow of doubt, unfortunately, looms over these other results (46).

The quality problem remained the source of a huge discussion. First of all, it centered on the "Lilly label" of the initial study, and the footprint of Eli Lilly & Company in the subsequent Surviving Sepsis Campain guidelines (47). In the particular case of sepsis, and singularly in the most severe pattern of infectious diseases, introducing a new and "saving lives" treatment seems to be a safe attitude. Thus, rather than asking for a confirmatory study, which would undoubtedly have been requested 10 years ago, both the Food and Drug Administration (FDA) and the European Agency for the Evaluation of Medicinal Products (EMEA) decided to approve the drug for specific patient subgroups. Nonetheless, like in other new therapeutic interventions reducing mortality in sepsis and more generally in intensive care (45, 48), the agreement was associated with the decision to conduct new trials to confirm the first results, it was decided (49) to shed light on the hemorrhagic risk, with a focus on pediatric patients and less severe adult patients. For both insulin and hydrocortisone, the results of these subsequent trials failed to confirm prior results (46, 50). This again underlines the need for a confirmatory trial for such a controversial molecule as DrotAA.

Secondly, there were two interfering phenomena during the PROWESS trial (51):

1. In order to better exclude patients that were expected not to benefit from DrotAA, an amendment was presented to and approved by the FDA (49). This amendment raised the question of the therapeutic effect of DrotAA in patients with comorbidities (52). Interestingly, patients with comorbidities ("significant underlying disorders") seemed to benefit from

DrotAA in the PROWESS trial, and these observations were confirmed by latter observations (53). The lack of precision concerning these associated pathologies (54), and the presence of conflicts of interest of the main authors (53, 54) probably decreased the thrust of this message, which certainly needs to be studied. Notably this amendment was approved seven months before the first interim analysis (51).

2. A technical modification in DrotAA production occurred two months after the amendment. Whereas the first intermediate analysis did not show any difference between groups (360 patients in each group, mortality 28.33% in DrotAA group vs. 30.28% in placebo group; p = 0.57), the difference appeared after these two interventions (490 patients in the DrotAA group and 480 in the placebo group, mortality 22.04% in DrotAA group vs. 31.25% in placebo group; p = 0.0001; RR = 0.71 and 95% CI 0.57 to 0.87) for 28 days mortality (51).

In addition to the previous issues, the question of the precocity of the interruption of was raised. Such an interruption is known to be associated with an increased risk of overestimation of good results (55), even in the case of a predefined interim analysis. This point was probably amplified by the unfortunate experience of the Tifacogin study (56). However, if the number of events seriously limit the risk of such an error, this interruption could be responsible for the significant discrepancy between the two groups of patients (57).

Antibiotherapy was also a subject of controversy. Patients were included if they received antibiotics within the first 48 hours after the diagnosis. The delay in itself is surprising, considering the potential severity of a delayed antibiotic introduction (58). Moreover, the appropriateness of antibiotherapy was established by a blinded clinical evaluation committee (36), but as underlined by Marti-Carvajal et al., all members of that committee were selected by the sponsors of the PROWESS trial (51).

Comorbidities were the root of another discussion. In the whole population, small non-significant differences were observed between placebo and treated patients regarding underlying diseases (36). Larger baseline differences occurred in the subgroups selected by FDA and EMEA criteria. Concerning patients with two or more organ dysfunctions (EMEA criterion), placebo patients were more likely to have comorbidities than DrotAA patients (59), particularly liver and cardiovascular diseases, which are known to strongly influence mortality after the first 3 days of sepsis (60, 61). In patients with an APACHE II score greater than 25 (FDA criterion) the patients were older and more likely to have cancer, diabetes and cardiovascular diseases in the placebo group. In summary, the therapeutic effect of DrotAA was probably overestimated in the more severe patients, because baseline differences between treated and placebo patients made the health of the placebo group chronically worse.

As noted previously, the subsequent studies were done, rather reinforcing the initial data and aggravating the first concerns and questions. ADDRESS (ADministration of DRotrecogin alfa [activated] in Early stage Severe Sepsis) (62), initially designed to explore the relevance of treatment in less severe patients was unable to find any difference between the groups. On the one hand, it was an expected observation, comfirming the subgroup analysis of PROWESS. The difference in DrotAA indication determined by EMEA and FDA justified the possibility to include patients estimated as "low risk of death" even if they had APACHE II ≥ 25 or two or more organ dysfunctions in European and North American countries respectively. Because of the presence of that discrepancy between inclusions, post-hoc subgroup analysis was conducted to confirm PROWESS results, in smaller groups with elevated APACHE II and/or multiple organ dysfunctions. None of these groups showed any statistical difference between DrotAA and placebo-treated patients, neither in 28-day mortality nor in hospital mortality (62). Nonetheless, the relevance of subgroups depends on their design a priori (63). Besides the limitations of a post-hoc analysis, this observation underlines the necessity of a clear and reproducible definition of severity. Moreover, these a posteriori subgroups must not stamp the lower mortality of the whole population 28-day mortality either at day 28 (17.0% in the placebo group vs. 18.5% in the DrotAA group; p = 0.34) or at hospital discharge (20.5% vs. 20.6%; p = 0.98) confirming the lowest severity of the ADDRESS patients in comparison with the PROWESS ones (30.8% in the placebo group vs. 24.7% in the DrotAA group;

p = 0.005 at day 28 and (34.9% in the placebo group vs. 29.7% in the DrotAA group; p = 0.03 at hospital discharge) (36, 40). Specifically, we must take into account the lower global severity of the patients, in other words, a patient with two or more organ dysfunctions but APACHE II less than 25 is probably younger or has less chronic health impairment. On the other hand, a patient with APACHE II scores higher but has less than two organ dysfunctions, is probably more chronically ill, but with a less severe acute sepsis.

These overall data, the lack of a clear and reproducible definition of acute severity and of the chronic health status, led to unexpected and non-reproducible results. Another major concern is the notion of sepsis itself. Usually in critical care research, infections are wholly grouped under a large designation of "sepsis" regardless of the primary organ infected. Prognosis is not the same, according to the different infectious sites (64). In this way, patients with bacteriemia or pneumonia seem to benefit from DrotAA. Conversely, patients suffering from urinary tract and intra-abdominal infections do not (51).

Of note in the Cochrane meta-analysis, a potential efficacy could be observed in older patients (more than 55 years old: RR 0.79, 95% CI 0.67 to 0.93), in more severe cases (at least 3 organ dysfunctions: RR 0.77, 95% CI 0.63 to 0.94) and during bacteriemic infections (RR 0.8, 95% CI 0.65 to 0.97). This notion is in accordance with previous observations with other therapeutic interventions in sepsis (65).

A long-term analysis of the ADDRESS population would be interesting, regarding the troubling results observed by Angus et al. concerning less severe patients of the PROWESS study. In patients with an APACHE II score of less than 25 an increasing 1-year mortality was observed in the treated group (28% vs. 34.5%, p = 0.04) (38). Once again, this probably illustrates the great limitations of *post-hoc* analysis. However, it remains unclear whether using DrotAA in less severe patients is not only inefficient and costly, but also detrimental to the long-term survival of the patients. Nevertheless, this discrepancy disappears at the end of the follow-up (2.5 years: 36.2% in the placebo group vs. 40.8% in the DrotAA group) (38). Interestingly, in clinical practice, the lower-risk patients (among patients presenting a therapeutic indication) are associated with a delayed

initiation of DrotAA. A single organ dysfunction, the absence of mechanical ventilation and the absence of catecholamine are associated with the start of DrotAA on day 2 (after diagnosis) or beyond (53). Moreover, in the same study Wheeler et al. pointed out a very important notion: While the patients' mortality was quite the same as in the PROWESS treated group, APACHE II was lower, but the number of comorbidities was more important. There was a clear association between the presence of more than one comorbidity and the observed mortality, and this association existed whatever the delay between sepsis and DrotAA initiation (53).

Drotrecogin alpha (activated) and bleeding

Activated protein C is an anticoagulant therapy. As usual with this kind of molecule, particular attention was focused on hemorrhagic risk. The incidence of severe bleeding, defined as any intracranial hemorrhage, life-threatening bleeding or need of three or more units of packed red blood cells on any two consecutive days, was notably low in the PROWESS study (placebo 17 (2%) vs. DrotAA 30 (3.5%)), with a trend toward higher risk associated with treatment (p = 0.06) (36). In the initial tolerance study there were not more serious bleeding events in the whole group of DrotAA treated patients with high or low dose than in the placebo group at day 28 (4% rhAPC, 5% placebo, p > 0.999) (35), but they were associated with higher incidence in both studied and placebo groups. In the ENHANCE study, the same range of values was observed for the study drug infusion period (4.0%; 95% CI, 1.7 to 6.4%) and during the 28-day study period (5.5%; 95% CI, 2.8 to 8.2%) (37).

Similar values were found in other observational studies (53). Recent survey studies give prominently more important bleeding events, around 10% (66, 67). These high levels could at least partially be explained by the off-label use of the drug (66), particularly in contraindications (44). In the same way, another American survey showed a higher mortality and a higher number of drug-related adverse events with DrotAA use than observed in the treated group of the PROWESS trial in patients of similar severity, but 37% of included patients would have contraindications or warnings that would have precluded their enrolment in the PROWESS trial (44). Once more, these observation underline the major necessity of a clear-cut indication and non-indication pattern of use if future results confirm the real survival benefit of this drug.

Great attention was given to the central nervous system, because severe hemorrhagic events were shown to be potentially more frequent with DrotAA. However, except in ENHANCE, CNS bleeding is lower than 1% in adult studies, even in association with heparin (62).

In the ADDRESS study, with less severe patients than in PROWESS, ENHANCE or phase IV observational studies, incidence of serious bleeding is lower during the infusion period (1.2% in DrotAA vs 2.4% in placebo) and during 28-day follow-up (2.2% in DrotAA vs 3.9% in placebo), but remains statistically significant (p = 0.02 and p = 0.01) (67). Of note, in this study no difference was observed in CNS-involved bleeding neither during the infusion period nor during the 28-day follow-up.

The observation of a significant deleterious effect in the *post-hoc* subgroup of surgical patients (surgery within the 30 days before the inclusion) with a single organ deficiency in the ADDRESS trial (314 patients in the placebo group and 321 in the DrotAA group; 28 days mortality: 14.1% vs. 20.7%, p = 0.03; hospital mortality: 19.8% vs. 23.4%, p = 0.26) confirmed the non-significant observations of the PROWESS study and raises the need for precise indications concerning surgical patients. DrotAA was also associated with higher risk of mortality in scheduled surgery patients (53). Increased death in this group could be associated with a lack of efficiency due to the delay in use and the low severity. Unfortunately no data are available concerning the association between bleeding and death in this particular subgroup. Recently, another retrospective study confirmed the connection between surgery and mortality (53). Interestingly, in this retrospective study there was no modification in mortality considering the introduction delay of DrotAA.

A notable global missing is the information about haemostasis. A great number of questions exist about the real anticoagulation activity of the molecule, its action on in vivo coagulation, perturbation of coagulation test variables, interaction with platelet levels (68). Whereas ample information is now available on the place of APC (notably DrotAA) in haemostasis, very few data were include in the PROWESS study (D-dimer evolution, which is an indirect marker, reflected more plasmin activation than thrombin inhibition) (36), and nothing was noted in the ENHANCE trial (37) or ADDRESS (56). What is more dramatic is the absence of any coagulation parameter concerning thrombosis and hemostasis in the XPRESS study (69). The authors underline the potential interest of data surrounding the hemostasis variation, notably the thrombin activation, and fibrinolysis evolution, but acknowledged these data as absent from the study design. In the RESOLVE trial, prothrombin time, activated partial thromboplastin time and INR (international normalized ratio) were recorded at patient inclusion, but nothing was specified about the modification during treatment (70).

Thus, the bleeding problem seems to be due more to the benefit/risk ratio than to the hemorrhagic risk itself (71). The anticoagulant properties of the DrotAA are the primary activity of this molecule and this interference with haemostasis is associated with hemorrhagic risk (72). In this way, two notions have to be clarified: Does the (survival) benefit really exceed the (bleeding) risk? And what is the real place of DrotAA in surgical patients, especially in the less severe ones?

Drotrecogin alpha (activated) and delay

Notably, as previously discussed, precocity of therapeutical intervention, usually known as "golden hour(s)" plays a central role in patient outcome (73). This is of paramount importance in sepsis, as has been widely shown (70, 74). Such a notion is of particular interest regarding numerous positive results concerning DrotAA. In the preclinical study, whereas antibiotics were started two hours after the E. coli challenge, protein C was administered in the same time as bacteria (33). This procedure could partly explain the good results. Interestingly, in the PROWESS study, APACHE II of the patient was obtained after inclusion and beginning of the treatment. In other words, patients were included in the first 24 hours of the severe sepsis (17.5 ± 12.8), and patients treated in the first 24 hours of organ dysfunction had a higher survival rate than patients treated later (58).

During the ADDRESS trial, the mean delay before starting treatment was longer (22.5 ± 13.6 in the DrotAA group) (56). Even if this could probably not justify the absence of positive results of the ADDRESS study, the association of a later treatment and a lower severity of patients could partially explain the inefficiency of DrotAA in this indication. In the particular case of pediatric severe sepsis, a 12-hour inclusion period did not permit a demonstration of any benefit of DrotAA (66), while a recent survey suggests the precocity of this therapeutic intervention is beneficial (53). Another recent retrospective observational study clearly shows that measured mortality is associated with a delay in starting DrotAA (mortality if initiation of treatment was on D0, D1 or D2 and beyond, was 33%, 40% and 52% respectively) (53). The interpretation of such results is quite difficult because of the retrospective and observational nature of the data, but they remain interesting due to their "real life" reflection.

A particular case: The children

The REsearching severe Sepsis and Organ dysfunction in children: a gLobal perspectiVE (RESOLVE) study, failed to find any difference between groups (70). This study, however, did not use a mortality end point, hopefully quite low in this group of patients, but a composite score, the Composite Time to Complete Organ Failure Resolution (CTCOFR) score, addressing respiratory, hemodynamic and renal failure resolution. Once more, lower severity is probably associated with lower efficiency of DrotAA. Nonetheless, the case mix could be considered as favorable to the studied product, considering that 50% of patients presented with a disseminated intravascular coagulation and 32.9% with a clinical purpura.

Conversely, even if bleeding risk was similar, or slightly lower (51) than the one observed in adults, the serious bleeding events were significantly more frequent at 6 (0.4% vs. 3.3%; p = 0.04) and 28 days (0.8% vs. 4.2%; p = 0.04) (75). The CNS was importantly implicated in these bleeding events, notably in children less than 60 days, and even though not significantly different, tended to be more frequent in DrotAA treatment (11 vs. 5 cases; p = 0.13). The Cochrane review, however, underlines the unclear relationship between

CNS bleeding and DrotAA (RR 2.17, 95% CI 0.77 to 6.16)(51). The major remaining concern thus is knowing whether there is a benefit for pediatric patients, and as in adult patients, if severity of disease and precocity of treatment have an impact on therapeutic effect.

Back to the future

Recent additional data mandated a reappraisal of regulatory agency decisions regarding patient selection, and in fact probably also patient safety and benefit from DrotAA therapy (75). These questions were stressed again by the recent publication of an extensive meta-analysis by the Cochrane collaboration concerning the clinical use of DrotAA. Its authors conclude that given the actual state of knowledge concerning DrotAA, this molecule should not be used for treating patients with severe sepsis or septic shock (51).

Many things remain to be done before writing the chronicle of this supposed announced death. First of all, protein C is known to have a real implication in sepsis pathophysiology, and its decrease during sepsis is associated with the severity of sepsis and risk of death. In the first studies (36, 37), an abnormal level of protein C at inclusion was found in 75.5% (DrotAA); 82.1% (DrotAA/PROWESS); 77.0% (placebo/PROWESS). Conversely, this data was not available in the ADDRESS study. On the other hand, biological interventions are known to be linked to the basal level of the molecule, enzymatic activity or response to stress ability (45). Studying the clinical response as a function of the protein C levels, or APC levels, should be an interesting issue.

The main weakness of sepsis studies probably stems from the disorder itself, and the way we diagnose it and measure its severity (76). Of paramount importance is the notion of definitions. The first problem of definition is the "sepsis" one. Anybody knows that the severity of infection is not the same regarding the location of the aggression (64), and, for example, the evolution of a severe pneumonia will not be identical to other infection processes (77). Sepsis is not a disease, but an extremely heterogeneous syndrome, differing in pathophysiological mechanisms and in outcome, function of pathogens and location. Moreover, outcome depends on many underlying conditions and events constituting the patient history. Considering the difficulties to grade the severity and the balance between chronic and acute parameters in a given patient, the recently developed PIRO (Predisposing factors, (nature of the) Insult, (intensity of) Response, (number of) Organ dysfunctions) grading system (78) could represent an interesting help regarding the homogenisation of patients in the studies to come. Noteworthy regarding the identification of potential beneficiary patients of a DrotAA treatment, a simple and reproducible biological test is Interleukin-6 (IL-6) measurement. Although IL-6 has not been validated as an official severity indicator, the greatest therapeutic effect was seen in the 402 patients with low IL-6 levels (14.6% mortality reduction) (59, 79).

The endpoint should be chosen with great caution. If 28-day mortality is a classical and widely accepted endpoint, it is, however, open to criticism, since 30% of surviving sepsis patients remain hospitalised on day 28 (73) and because this length of survival is not the endpoint for any intensivist.

Another major part of any trial design is the constitution of study groups, and subgroups. Subgroups will exist and physicians will ask for particular results. Because we know the necessity of population sample size and that a *post-hoc* interpretation has a very low value, a determination of effective studies has to take this notion into account. In another words, if the PROWESS study was undoubtedly an RCT with a very high methodological quality, patients were not stratified according to the subgroups proposed by FDA and EMEA, and this subgroup analysis considerably decreased the strength of the results. A solution was proposed by Ely et al. by selecting a target patient population using a multivariate prognostic model (79).

Finally, two variables need to be identified, even if we can suppose an equal repartition among groups: the bacteria (64), notably their virulence potentials and human polymorphisms concerning pathogen recognition and fighting, as well as coagulation pathways polymorphisms (Factor V Leyden, protein C, PAI-1 etc.).

These studies are in progress, with a new "Lilly study" centered on septic shock patients and a French one, the Activated PROtein C, low doses of Corticosteroids and their combination for treatment of Human Septic shock (APROCCHS) trial, which compares corticosteroids, DrotAA, both or none in septic shock patients with at least two organ dysfunctions.

At any rate, we cannot deprive ourselves of a new efficient therapy in sepsis even if it involves a tight part of the whole moving target of sepsis. In order to avoid the misuse of a therapy with an uncertain efficiency, it will be essential to contribute to such studies, to reinforce one or the other conviction about efficiency and change conviction into evidence-based medicine.

Summary

Pharmacologic efficiency of DrotAA is certitude and its molecular pathways are in fast progress, the question remains, however, to know whether such a modification could have a beneficial effect within the immense complexity of pathophysiological events that occur during sepsis and, thus, if adding it to the therapeutic arsenal against severe infections makes sense.

The authors

François Philippart, MD
Cédric Bruel, MD
Olfa Hamzaoui, MD
Benoît Misset, MD
Jean Carlet, MD
    Service de Réanimation Polyvalente | Groupe Hospitalier Paris Saint Joseph | Paris, France

Address for correspondence
    François Philippart
    Service de Réanimation Polyvalente
    Groupe Hospitalier Paris Saint Joseph
    185 rue R. Losserand
    75014 Paris, France
    e-mail: fphilipp@pasteur.fr

References

1. Annane D, Bellissant E, Cavaillon JM. Septic shock. Lancet. 2005;365(9453):63–78.
2. Owen WG, Esmon CT. Functional properties of an endothelial cell cofactor for thrombin-catalyzed activation of protein C. J Biol Chem. 1981;256(11):5532–5.

3. Fukudome K, Ye X, Tsuneyoshi N, Tokunaga O, Sugawara K, Mizokami H et al. Activation mechanism of anticoagulant protein C in large blood vessels involving the endothelial cell protein C receptor. J Exp Med. 1998;187(7):1029–35.

4. Walker FJ, Sexton PW, Esmon CT. The inhibition of blood coagulation by activated Protein C through the selective inactivation of activated Factor V. Biochim Biophys Acta. 1979;571(2):333–42.

5. Fulcher CA, Gardiner JE, Griffin JH, Zimmerman TS. Proteolytic inactivation of human factor VIII procoagulant protein by activated human protein C and its analogy with factor V. Blood. 1984;63(2):486–9.

6. van Hinsbergh VW, Bertina RM, van Wijngaarden A, van Tilburg NH, Emeis JJ, Haverkate F. Activated protein C decreases plasminogen activator-inhibitor activity in endothelial cell-conditioned medium. Blood. 1985;65(2):444–51.

7. Esmon C. The protein C pathway. Crit Care Med. 2000;28(9 Suppl):S44–8.

8. van't Veer C, Golden NJ, Kalafatis M, Mann KG. Inhibitory mechanism of the protein C pathway on tissue factor-induced thrombin generation. Synergistic effect in combination with tissue factor pathway inhibitor. J Biol Chem. 1997;272(12):7983–94.

9. Philippart F, Cavaillon JM. Sepsis mediators. Curr Infect Dis Rep. 2007;9(5):358–65.

10. Levi M, ten Cate H, van der Poll T, van Deventer SJ. Pathogenesis of disseminated intravascular coagulation in sepsis. Jama. 1993;270(8):975–9.

11. Aird WC. The role of the endothelium in severe sepsis and multiple organ dysfunction syndrome. Blood. 2003;101(10):3765–77.

12. Johnson K, Choi Y, DeGroot E, Samuels I, Creasey A, Aarden L. Potential mechanisms for a proinflammatory vascular cytokine response to coagulation activation. J Immunol. 1998;160(10):5130–5.

13. Stouthard JM, Levi M, Hack CE, Veenhof CH, Romijn HA, Sauerwein HP et al. Interleukin-6 stimulates coagulation, not fibrinolysis, in humans. Thromb Haemost. 1996;76(5):738–42.

14. Opal SM. Phylogenetic and functional relationships between coagulation and the innate immune response. Crit Care Med. 2000;28(9 Suppl):S77–80.

15. Lorente JA, Garcia-Frade LJ, Landin L, de Pablo R, Torrado C, Renes E et al. Time course of hemostatic abnormalities in sepsis and its relation to outcome. Chest. 1993;103(5):1536–42.

16. Liaw PC, Esmon CT, Kahnamoui K, Schmidt S, Kahnamoui S, Ferrell G et al. Patients with severe sepsis vary markedly in their ability to generate activated protein C. Blood. 2004;104(13):3958–64.

17. Glaser CB, Morser J, Clarke JH, Blasko E, McLean K, Kuhn I et al. Oxidation of a specific methionine in thrombomodulin by activated neutrophil products blocks cofactor activity. A potential rapid mechanism for modulation of coagulation. J Clin Invest. 1992;90(6):2565–73.

18. Boehme MW, Deng Y, Raeth U, Bierhaus A, Ziegler R, Stremmel W et al. Release of thrombomodulin from endothelial cells by concerted action of TNF-alpha and neutrophils: in vivo and in vitro studies. Immunology. 1996;87(1):134–40.

19. Paramo JA, Fernandez Diaz FJ, Rocha E. Plasminogen activator inhibitor activity in bacterial infection. Thromb Haemost. 1988;59(3):451–4.

20. Idell S. Endothelium and disordered fibrin turnover in the injured lung: newly recognized pathways. Crit Care Med. 2002;30(5 Suppl):S274–80.

21. Levi M, van der Poll T. Recombinant human activated protein C: current insights into its mechanism of action. Crit Care. 2007;11 Suppl 5:S3.

22. Murakami K, Okajima K, Uchiba M, Johno M, Nakagaki T, Okabe H et al. Activated protein C prevents LPS-induced pulmonary vascular injury by inhibiting cytokine production. Am J Physiol. 1997;272(2 Pt 1):L197–202.

23. Grey ST, Tsuchida A, Hau H, Orthner CL, Salem HH, Hancock WW. Selective inhibitory effects of the anticoagulant activated protein C on the responses of human mononuclear phagocytes to LPS, IFN-gamma, or phorbol ester. J Immunol. 1994;153(8):3664–72.

24. Joyce DE, Gelbert L, Ciaccia A, DeHoff B, Grinnell BW. Gene expression profile of antithrombotic protein c defines new mechanisms modulating inflammation and apoptosis. J Biol Chem. 2001;276(14):11199–203.

25. Grinnell BW, Hermann RB, Yan SB. Human protein C inhibits selectin-mediated cell adhesion: role of unique fucosylated oligosaccharide. Glycobiology. 1994;4(2):221–5.

26. Taylor FB, Jr., Stearns-Kurosawa DJ, Kurosawa S, Ferrell G, Chang AC, Laszik Z et al. The endothelial cell protein C receptor aids in host defense against Escherichia coli sepsis. Blood. 2000;95(5):1680–6.

27. Fourrier F, Chopin C, Goudemand J, Hendrycx S, Caron C, Rime A et al. Septic shock, multiple organ failure, and disseminated intravascular coagulation. Compared patterns of antithrombin III, protein C, and protein S deficiencies. Chest. 1992;101(3):816–23.

28. Yan SB, Helterbrand JD, Hartman DL, Wright TJ, Bernard GR. Low levels of protein C are associated with poor outcome in severe sepsis. Chest. 2001;120(3):915–22.

29. Mesters RM, Helterbrand J, Utterback BG, Yan B, Chao YB, Fernandez JA et al. Prognostic value of protein C concentrations in neutropenic patients at high risk of severe septic complications. Crit Care Med. 2000;28(7):2209–16.

30. Gupta A, Berg DT, Gerlitz B, Richardson MA, Galbreath E, Syed S et al. Activated protein C suppresses adrenomedullin and ameliorates lipopolysaccharide-induced hypotension. Shock. 2007;28(4):468–76.

31. Derhaschnig U, Reiter R, Knobl P, Baumgartner M, Keen P, Jilma B. Recombinant human activated protein C (rhAPC; drotrecogin alfa [activated]) has minimal effect on markers of coagulation, fibrinolysis, and inflammation in acute human endotoxemia. Blood. 2003;102(6):2093–8.

32. Faust SN, Levin M, Harrison OB, Goldin RD, Lockhart MS, Kondaveeti S et al. Dysfunction of endothelial protein C activation in severe meningococcal sepsis. N Engl J Med. 2001;345(6):408–16.

33. Taylor FB, Jr., Chang A, Esmon CT, D'Angelo A, Vigano-D'Angelo S, Blick KE. Protein C prevents the coagulopathic and lethal effects of Escherichia coli infusion in the baboon. J Clin Invest. 1987;79(3):918–25.

34. Rivard GE, David M, Farrell C, Schwarz HP. Treatment of purpura fulminans in meningococcemia with protein C concentrate. J Pediatr. 1995;126(4):646–52.

35. Bernard GR, Ely EW, Wright TJ, Fraiz J, Stasek JE Jr., Russell JA et al. Safety and dose relationship of recombinant human activated protein C for coagulopathy in severe sepsis. Crit Care Med. 2001;29(11):2051–9.

36. Bernard GR, Vincent JL, Laterre PF, LaRosa SP, Dhainaut JF, Lopez-Rodriguez A et al. Efficacy and safety of recombinant human activated protein C for severe sepsis. N Engl J Med. 2001;344(10):699–709.

37. Bernard GR, Margolis BD, Shanies HM, Ely EW, Wheeler AP, Levy H et al. Extended evaluation of recombinant human activated protein C United States Trial (ENHANCE US): a single-arm, phase 3B, multicenter study of drotrecogin alfa (activated) in severe sepsis. Chest. 2004;125(6):2206–16.

38. Angus DC, Laterre PF, Helterbrand J, Ely EW, Ball DE, Garg R et al. The effect of drotrecogin alfa (activated) on long-term survival after severe sepsis. Crit Care Med. 2004;32(11):2199–206.

39. Matthay MA. Severe sepsis – a new treatment with both anticoagulant and antiinflammatory properties. N Engl J Med. 2001;344(10):759–62.

40. Angus DC, Linde-Zwirble WT, Clermont G, Ball DE, Basson BR, Ely EW et al. Cost-effectiveness of drotrecogin alfa (activated) in the treatment of severe sepsis. Crit Care Med. 2003;31(1):1–11.

41. Manns BJ, Lee H, Doig CJ, Johnson D, Donaldson C. An economic evaluation of activated protein C treatment for severe sepsis. N Engl J Med. 2002;347(13):993–1000.

42. Burchardi H, Schneider H. Economic aspects of severe sepsis: a review of intensive care unit costs, cost of illness and cost effectiveness of therapy. Pharmacoeconomics. 2004;22(12):793–813.

43. Sacristan JA, Prieto L, Huete T, Artigas A, Badia X, Chinn C et al. [Cost-effectiveness of drotrecogin alpha [activated] in the treatment of severe sepsis in Spain]. Gac Sanit. 2004;18(1):50–7.

44. Deans KJ, Minneci PC, Banks SM, Natanson C, Eichacker PQ. Substantiating the concerns about recombinant human activated protein C use in sepsis.

45. Annane D, Sebille V, Charpentier C, Bollaert PE, Francois B, Korach JM et al. Effect of treatment with low doses of hydrocortisone and fludrocortisone on mortality in patients with septic shock. Jama. 2002;288(7):862–71.

46. Sprung CL, Annane D, Keh D, Moreno R, Singer M, Freivogel K et al. Hydrocortisone therapy for patients with septic shock. N Engl J Med. 2008;358(2):111–24.

47. Eichacker PQ, Natanson C, Danner RL. Surviving sepsis-practice guidelines, marketing campaigns, and Eli Lilly. N Engl J Med. 2006;355(16):1640–2.

48. van den Berghe G, Wouters P, Weekers F, Verwaest C, Bruyninckx F, Schetz M et al. Intensive insulin therapy in the critically ill patients. N Engl J Med. 2001;345(19):1359–67.

49. FDA. Drotrecogin alpha (activated): Product Approval Information – Licensing Action. http://www.fda.gov/cder/biologics/products/droteli112101.htm 2001.

50. Brunkhorst FM, Engel C, Bloos F, Meier-Hellmann A, Ragaller M, Weiler N et al. Intensive insulin therapy and pentastarch resuscitation in severe sepsis. N Engl J Med. 2008;358(2):125–39.

51. Marti-Carvajal A, Salanti G, Cardona AF. Human recombinant activated protein C for severe sepsis. Cochrane Database Syst Rev. 2007(3):CD004388.

52. Gardlund B. Activated protein C (Xigris) treatment in sepsis: a drug in trouble. Acta Anaesthesiol Scand. 2006;50(8):907–10.

53. Wheeler A, Steingrub J, Schmidt GA, Sanchez P, Jacobi J, Linde-Zwirble W et al. A retrospective observational study of drotrecogin alfa (activated) in adults with severe sepsis: comparison with a controlled clinical trial. Crit Care Med. 2008;36(1):14–23.

54. Dhainaut JF, Laterre PF, LaRosa SP, Levy H, Garber GE, Heiselman D et al. The clinical evaluation committee in a large multicenter phase 3 trial of drotrecogin alfa (activated) in patients with severe sepsis (PROWESS): role, methodology, and results. Crit Care Med. 2003;31(9):2291–301.

55. Montori VM, Devereaux PJ, Adhikari NK, Burns KE, Eggert CH, Briel M et al. Randomized trials stopped early for benefit: a systematic review. Jama. 2005;294(17):2203–9.

56. Abraham E, Reinhart K, Opal S, Demeyer I, Doig C, Rodriguez AL et al. Efficacy and safety of tifacogin (recombinant tissue factor pathway inhibitor) in severe sepsis: a randomized controlled trial. Jama. 2003;290(2):238–47.

57. Friedrich JO, Adhikari NK, Meade MO. Drotrecogin alfa (activated): does current evidence support treatment for any patients with severe sepsis? Crit Care. 2006;10(3):145.

58. Kumar A, Roberts D, Wood KE, Light B, Parrillo JE, Sharma S et al. Duration of hypotension before initiation of effective antimicrobial therapy is the critical

Crit Care Med. 2004;32(12):2542–3.

determinant of survival in human septic shock. Crit Care Med. 2006;34(6):1589–96.

59. Carlet J. Drotrecogin alfa (activated) administration: too many subgroups. Crit Care Med. 2003;31(10):2564; author reply. 2564–5.

60. Brun-Buisson C, Doyon F, Carlet J, Dellamonica P, Gouin F, Lepoutre A et al. Incidence, risk factors, and outcome of severe sepsis and septic shock in adults. A multicenter prospective study in intensive care units. French ICU Group for Severe Sepsis. Jama. 1995;274(12):968–74.

61. Brun-Buisson C, Meshaka P, Pinton P, Vallet B. EPISEPSIS: a reappraisal of the epidemiology and outcome of severe sepsis in French intensive care units. Intensive Care Med. 2004;30(4):580–8.

62. Abraham E, Laterre PF, Garg R, Levy H, Talwar D, Trzaskoma BL et al. Drotrecogin alfa (activated) for adults with severe sepsis and a low risk of death. N Engl J Med. 2005;353(13):1332–41.

63. Assmann SF, Pocock SJ, Enos LE, Kasten LE. Subgroup analysis and other (mis)uses of baseline data in clinical trials. Lancet. 2000;355(9209):1064–9.

64. Cohen J, Cristofaro P, Carlet J, Opal S. New method of classifying infections in critically ill patients. Crit Care Med. 2004;32(7):1510–26.

65. Eichacker PQ, Parent C, Kalil A, Esposito C, Cui X, Banks SM et al. Risk and the efficacy of antiinflammatory agents: retrospective and confirmatory studies of sepsis. Am J Respir Crit Care Med. 2002;166(9):1197–205.

66. Kanji S, Perreault MM, Chant C, Williamson D, Burry L. Evaluating the use of Drotrecogin alfa (activated) in adult severe sepsis: a Canadian multicenter observational study. Intensive Care Med. 2007;33(3):517–23.

67. Bertolini G, Rossi C, Anghileri A, Livigni S, Addis A, Poole D. Use of Drotrecogin alfa (activated) in Italian intensive care units: the results of a nationwide survey. Intensive Care Med. 2007;33(3):426–34.

68. Farmer JC. Drotrecogin alfa (activated) treatment in severe sepsis: a "journal club" review of the global ENHANCE trial. Crit Care Med. 2005;33(10):2428–31.

69. Levi M, Levy M, Williams MD, Douglas I, Artigas A, Antonelli M et al. Prophylactic heparin in patients with severe sepsis treated with drotrecogin alfa (activated). Am J Respir Crit Care Med. 2007;176(5):483–90.

70. Nadel S, Goldstein B, Williams MD, Dalton H, Peters M, Macias WL et al. Drotrecogin alfa (activated) in children with severe sepsis: a multicentre phase III randomised controlled trial. Lancet. 2007;369(9564):836–43.

71. Eichacker PQ, Natanson C. Increasing evidence that the risks of rhAPC may outweigh its benefits. Intensive Care Med. 2007;33(3):396–9.

72. Levine MN, Raskob G, Beyth RJ, Kearon C, Schulman S. Hemorrhagic complications of anticoagulant treatment: the Seventh ACCP Conference on Antithrombotic and Thrombolytic Therapy. Chest. 2004;126(3 Suppl):287S–310S.

73. Dellinger RP, Levy MM, Carlet JM, Bion J, Parker MM, Jaeschke R et al. Surviving Sepsis Campaign: international guidelines for management of severe sepsis and septic shock: 2008. Crit Care Med. 2008;36(1):296–327.

74. Rivers E, Nguyen B, Havstad S, Ressler J, Muzzin A, Knoblich B et al. Early goal-directed therapy in the treatment of severe sepsis and septic shock. N Engl J Med. 2001;345(19):1368–77.

75. Marti-Carvajal A, Salanti G, Cardona AF. Human recombinant activated protein C for severe sepsis. Cochrane Database Syst Rev. 2008(1):CD004388.

76. Carlet J. Prescribing indications based on successful clinical trials in sepsis: a difficult exercise. Crit Care Med. 2006;34(2):525–9.

77. Vincent JL, Sakr Y, Sprung CL, Ranieri VM, Reinhart K, Gerlach H et al. Sepsis in European intensive care units: results of the SOAP study. Crit Care Med. 2006;34(2):344–53.

78. Levy MM, Fink MP, Marshall JC, Abraham E, Angus D, Cook D et al. 2001 SCCM/ESICM/ACCP/ATS/SIS International Sepsis Definitions Conference. Crit Care Med. 2003;31(4):1250–6.

79. Ely EW, Laterre PF, Angus DC, Helterbrand JD, Levy H, Dhainaut JF et al. Drotrecogin alfa (activated) administration across clinically important subgroups of patients with severe sepsis. Crit Care Med. 2003;31(1):12–9.

Charles L. Sprung and Djillali Annane

Corticosteroids in septic shock

Introduction to the topic

The use of corticosteroids in patients with septic shock has been controversial for several decades (1). High dose steroids became standard therapy in the late 1970s and early 1980s (1). During the late 1980s and 1990s, a new consensus developed recommending that pharmacologic doses of corticosteroids in sepsis and septic shock should not be used because they did not improve survival and may have increased morbidity and mortality (3–6).

The importance of recognizing inadequate adrenal corticosteroid production or tissue resistance to corticosteroids has become important over the last decade, especially since the use of exogenous glucocorticoids for sepsis has decreased and the use of drugs altering adrenal cortex function has increased (7). In fact, recent studies demonstrated benefits with lower doses of steroids for longer periods of time (8–13).

Unfortunately, the use of steroids in the critically ill is not without adverse affects. Studies have shown an association between steroid therapy and superinfections (1) and the incidence of critical illness polyneuromyopathy (14, 15).

Studies with small patient numbers showed improved haemodynamics in patients receiving steroid therapy (8, 9, 11, 12, 13). Bollaert et al. (8),

examined whether hydrocortisone (100 mg intravenously every 8 hours for at least 5 days) could improve haemodynamics in patients with late septic shock. The corticosteroid-treated group had more shock reversal at 7 and 28 days, and there was a trend toward decreased mortality. Briegel et al. (9) treated patients with hyperdynamic septic shock with low doses of hydrocortisone (100 mg intravenously followed by 0.18 mg/kg/hr for 6 days) and subsequent tapering. There was a decrease in the time to vasopressor therapy cessation and a trend to earlier resolution of organ dysfunction (9). Overall shock reversal and mortality, however, were not affected (9). Keh et al. conducted a crossover trial in which 40 norepinephrine-treated patients received hydrocortisone (100 mg intravenously followed by 10 mg/hr for 3 days) or a placebo in a random order (11). There was a rapid decrease in the dose and duration of norepinephrine with significant improvement in mean arterial pressure and systemic vascular resistance whereas cardiac index was not affected. Oppert et al. (12) gave patients with early hyperdynamic septic shock hydrocortisone (50 mg intravenously followed by 0.18 mg/kg/hr until shock reversal) with subsequent tapering. Time to cessation of vasopressor support was shorter in the steroid-treated patients. Finally, Cicarelli et al. randomised 29 patients with septic shock to receive an intravenous infusion of 0.2 mg/kg of dexamethasone every 36 hours for five days (13). The duration of vasopressor therapy was significantly reduced in the dexamethasone treated patients. Similarly, there was a significant reduction in 7-day mortality with a trend for fewer deaths at 28 day in the steroids group.

Annane et al. (10) performed a multicenter, randomised, placebo-controlled, double-blind study to evaluate low dose corticosteroids in patients with severe early septic shock. Inclusion criteria included all the following criteria:

1. documented site (or at least strong suspicion) of infection, as evidenced by one or more of the following: presence of polymorphs in a normally sterile body fluid (except blood), positive culture or Gram stain of a normally sterile body fluid, clinical focus of infection (e.g., fecal peritonitis), wound with purulent discharge, pneumonia or other clinical evidence of systemic infection (e.g., purpura fulminans);
2. temperature higher than 38.3°C or lower than 35.6°C;
3. heart rate greater than 90 beats per minute;
4. systolic arterial pressure lower than 90 mmHg for at least 1 hour despite adequate fluid replacement and more than 5 μg/kg of body weight of dopamine or current treatment with epinephrine or norepinephrine;
5. urinary output of less than 0.5 ml/kg of body weight for at least 1 hour or ratio of arterial oxygen tension to the fraction of inspired oxygen (PaO_2/FIO_2) of less than 280 mmHg;
6. arterial lactate levels higher than 2 mmol/l; and
7. need for mechanical ventilation. Patients were randomised within 8 hours from shock onset to receive 50 mcg hydrocortisone intravenously every 6 hours and 50 mg fludrocortisone enterally for 7 days.

Patients were categorised into "non-responders" or "responders" based on their response to a 250 μg corticotropin stimulation test; non-responders defined by a cortisol increase ≤ 9 μg/dl (248 nmol/l). A total of 300 patients were randomised and 299 analyzed. The primary source of infection was the lung. Few patients had multi-resistant bacteria or fungi as causative pathogens,

and more than 90 % of patients received appropriate antibiotic within 11 hours on average. Reversal of shock occurred more commonly (57 %) in steroid-treated patients than placebo patients (40 %), and more rapidly (on average 2 days earlier). 28-day mortality was decreased by steroid therapy in the overall group (61 % vs. 55 %) and non-responder group (63 % vs. 53 %) (10). The rates of adverse events were comparable in the placebo and steroid groups (22 % vs. 21 %). The proportion of patients with superinfection at any time between randomisation and hospital discharge was similar in the two treatment arms (18 % vs. 15 %). Regardless of the site for a new infection, there was no evidence for a difference between the two groups. There was no evidence for steroid-induced neuromuscular weakness. However, there was no prospectively defined systematic screening for this complication. Based on the Annane study (10), the use of steroids in septic shock increased tremendously. Primarily based on the Annane study, the Surviving Sepsis Campaign recommended the use of low dose hydrocortisone for septic shock (16) as did recent meta-analyses (17, 18).

The use of steroids and corticotropin testing was evaluated in the Corticus study, a multicenter, randomised, placebo-controlled, double-blind study of hydrocortisone in septic shock patients (19). The Corticus study also evaluated non-responders and responders to a corticotropin stimulation test using the same definitions as the Annane study (10) previously cited. Inclusion criteria included:

1. Clinical evidence of infection within the previous 72 hours with either presence of polymorphonuclear cells in a normally sterile body fluid (excluding blood); culture or Gram stain of blood, sputum, urine or normally sterile body fluid positive for a pathogenic micro-organism; focus of infection identified by visual inspection (e.g. ruptured bowel with the presence of free air or bowel contents in the abdomen found at the time of surgery, wound with purulent drainage); or other clinical evidence of infection – treated community acquired pneumonia, purpura fulminans, necrotising fasciitis, etc.;
2. Evidence of a systemic response to infection defined by the presence of two or more of the following signs within the previous 24 hours: fever

(temperature >38.3°C) or hypothermia (rectal temperature < 35.6°C); tachycardia (heart rate of > 90 beats/min); tachypnea (respiratory rate > 20 breaths/min, $PaCO_2$< 32 mmHg) or need for invasive mechanical ventilation; alteration of the white cell count >12,000 cells/mm³, <4,000 cells/mm³ or > 10 % immature neutrophils (bands);

3. Evidence of shock within the previous 72 hours defined by (both A + B required): A. a systolic blood pressure (SBP) < 90 mmHg or a decrease in SBP of more than 50 mmHg from baseline in previous hypertensive patients (for at least one hour) despite adequate fluid replacement OR need for vasopressors for at least one hour (infusion of dopamine ≥ 5 mcg/kg/min or any dose of epinephrine, norepinephrine, phenylephrine or vasopressin) to maintain a SBP ≥ 90 mmHg [SBP did not have to be < 90 mmHg for more than one hour as the Annane study (10)]; and B. Hypoperfusion or organ dysfunction attributable to sepsis, including one of:

- Sustained oliguria (urine output < 0.5 ml/kg/hr for a minimum of 1 hour);
- Metabolic acidosis [pH of < 7.3, or arterial base deficit of ≥ 5.0 mmol/l, or an increased lactic acid concentration (> 2 mmol/l)];
- Arterial hypoxemia (PaO_2/FIO_2 < 280 in the absence of pneumonia) (PaO_2/FIO_2 < 200 in the presence of pneumonia);
- Thrombocytopenia – platelet count ≤ 100,000 cells/mm³;
- Acute altered mental status (Glasgow Coma Scale < 14 or acute change from baseline); and Informed consent according to local regulations.

A total of 500 patients were randomised and 499 analyzed. The primary source of infection was the gastrointestinal tract. At the time of enrollment 99 % of patients were receiving vasopressors and study treatment was started within 12 hours of this time in 77 % of patients. Corticus found that there were no differences in 28-day mortality in nonresponders (39 % hydrocortisone, 36 % placebo), responders (29 % hydrocortisone, 29 % placebo) or all patients (34 % hydrocortisone, 32 % placebo) (19). In patients who reversed shock, hydrocortisone hastened the time to shock reversal in nonresponders, responders and all patients

(19). Hydrocortisone failed to increase the proportion of patients with shock reversal in the total population or either corticotropin subset (17). There were more episodes of superinfection including new sepsis or septic shock in the hydrocortisone group but no evidence of increased neuromuscular weakness (19). Although investigators were reminded repeatedly to check for neuromuscular weakness, there was no prospectively defined systematic screening for this complication.

Controversial position 1

Based on the Annane study (10), many physicians worldwide continue to use steroids for patients in septic shock requiring vasopressors.

Controversial position 2

Based on the Corticus study (19) whose study criteria represent the majority of septic patients, many physicians have stopped using steroids for patients in septic shock.

Summary

The use of corticosteroids in patients with septic shock has been controversial for several decades and continues to be controversial despite two recent, large, well-performed studies. The two studies evaluated different patient populations and came to opposite conclusions. Similarities between the two studies included steroids' beneficial effects on time to shock reversal, no evidence for increased risk of neuromuscular weakness, and hyperglycaemia. Differences between the two studies include for Annane (10) and Corticus (19) respectively: entry window (8 vs. 72 hours; SBP < 90 mmHg (> 1 hour vs. < 1 hour); additional treatment (fludrocortisone vs., no fludrocortisone); treatment duration (7 vs. 11 days); weaning (none vs. present); SAPS II scores (59 vs. 49); non-responders to corticotropin (77 % vs. 47 %); differences in steroids effects according to the response to corticotropin (yes vs. no);increased risk of superinfection (no vs. yes) and study occurred after practice guidelines published recommending steroids (no vs. yes) (see fig. 1).

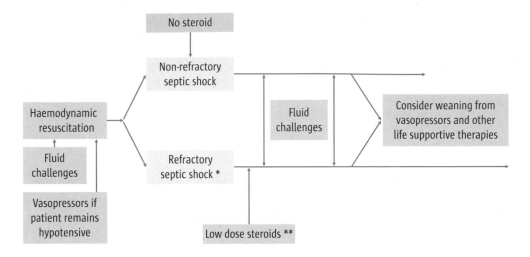

* Dr Annane defines refractory septic shock as the need for more than 0.5 µg/kg/min of norepinephrine or epinephrine which corresponds to the first quartile of non-responders for the baseline dose of epinephrine or norepinephrine in reference 10 and Dr Sprung defines refractory septic shock as a systolic blood pressure less than 90 mmHg for greater than one hour despite adequate fluid replcement and vasopressor the was the entry criteria for reference 10.

** Dr Annane recommends giving 50 mg intravenous bolus every six hours for 7 days as per reference 10 and Dr Sprung recommends giving 50 mg intravenous bolus every six hours for 5 days, then tapered to 50 mg intravenously every 12 hours for days 6–8, 50 mg every 24 hours for days 9–11 and then stopped as per reference 19.

Fig. 1   Decision tree for the use of corticosteroids in septic shock

Key points for clinical practice

The updated Surviving Sepsis campaign has given the following recommendation "We suggest intravenous hydrocortisone be given only to adult septic shock patients after blood pressure is identified to be poorly responsive to fluid resuscitation and vasopressor therapy (20)." Additional recommendations are

1) *fludrocortisone is optional when hydrocortisone is used and*
2) *steroid therapy should not be guided by the corticotropin test results (20).*

In fact another international task force came up with similar recommendations – "Hydrocortisone should be considered in the management strategy of patients with septic shock, particularly those patients who have responded poorly to fluid resuscitation and vasopressor agents (21)."

The authors

Charles L. Sprung, MD[1]
Djillali Annane, MD, PhD[2]
[1]General Intensive Care Unit | Department of Anaesthesiology and Critical Care Medicine | Hadassah Hebrew University Medical Center
[2]General Intensive Care Unit | Department of Acute Medicine and Surgery | Raymond Poincaré Hospital (AP-HP) | University of Versailles SQY, France

Address for correspondence
Charles L. Sprung
General Intensive Care Unit
Department of Anaesthesiology and
Critical Care Medicine
Hadassah Hebrew University Medical Center
P.O. Box 12000
Jerusalem, Israel 91120
e-mail: sprung@cc.huji.ac.il

References

1. Schein RMH, Sprung CL. The use of corticosteroids in the sepsis syndrome. Critical Care – State of the Art 1986; The Society of Critical Care Medicine. Fullerton. 1986;7: 131–149.
2. Schumer W. Steroids in the treatment of clinical septic shock. Ann Surg. 1976;184:333–341.
3. Bone RC, Fisher CJ Jr, Clemmer TP et al. A controlled clinical trial of high-dose methylprednisolone in the treatment of severe sepsis and septic shock. N Engl J Med. 1987;317:653–658.
4. The Veterans Administration Systemic Sepsis Cooperative Study Group. Effect of high-dose glucocorticoid therapy on mortality in patients with clinical signs of systemic sepsis. N Engl J Med. 1987;317.659–65.
5. Lefering R, Neugebauer EAM. Steroid controversy in sepsis and septic shock: a meta-analysis. Crit Care Med. 1995;23:1294–1303.
6. Cronin L, Cook DJ, Carlet J et al. Corticosteroid treatment for sepsis: A critical appraisal and meta-analysis of the literature. Crit Care Med. 1995;24:1430–1439.
7. Lamberts SWJ, Bruining HA, de Jong FH. Corticosteroid therapy in severe illness. New Engl J Med. 1997;337: 1285–1292.
8. Bollaert PE, Charpentier C, Levy S et al. Reversal of late septic shock with supraphysiologic doses of hydrocortisone. Crit Care Med. 1998;26:645–50.
9. Briegel J, Frost H, Haller M et al. Stress doses of hydrocortisone reverse hyperdynamic septic shock: A prospective, randomized, double-blind, single center study. Crit Care Med. 1999;27:723–32.
10. Annane D, Sebille V, Charpentier C, et al. Effect of treatment with low doses of hydrocortisone and fludrocortisone on mortality in patients with septic shock. JAMA. 2002;288:862–870.
11. Keh D, Boehnke T, Weber–Cartens S, Schulz C, Ahlers O, Bercker S, Volk HD, Doecke WD, Falke KJ, Gerlach H. Immunologic and hemodynamic effects of "low-dose" hydrocortisone in septic shock: a double-blind, randomized, placebo-controlled, crossover study. Am J Respir Crit Care Med. 2003;167(4):512–20.
12. Oppert M, Schindler R, Husung C et al. Low dose hydrocortisone improves shock reversal and reduces cytokine levels in early hyperdynamic septic shock. Crit Care Med. 2005;33:2457–2464.
13. Cicarelli DD, Viera JE, Martin Besenor FE. Early dexamethasone treatment for septic shock patients: a prospective randomized clinical trial. Sao Paulo Med J. 2007;125:237–41.
14. De Jonghe B, Sharshar T, Lefaucheur JP et al. Paresis acquired in the intensive care unit: a prospective multicenter study. JAMA. 2002;288:2859–2867.
15. Herridge MS, Cheung AM, Tansey CM et al. One-year outcomes in survivors of the acute respiratory distress syndrome. N Engl J Med. 2003;348:683–693.
16. Dellinger P, Carlet JM, Masur H et al. Surviving Sepsis Campaign guidelines for the management of severe sepsis and septic shock. Crit Care Med. 2004;32:858–873.
17. Annane D, Bellissant E, Bollaert PE et al. Corticosteroids for severe sepsis and septic shock: a systematic review and meta-analysis. BMJ. 2004;329:480–488.
18. Minneci PC, Deans KJ, Banks SM et al. Meta-analysis: The effects of steroids on survival and shock during sepsis depends on the dose. Ann Intern Med. 2004;141:47–56.
19. Sprung CL, Annane D, Keh D, Moreno R, Singer M, Sorenson F, Weiss Y, Benbenishty J, Kalenka A, Forst H, Laterre PF, Reinhart K, Cuthbertson B, Payen D, Briegel J. For the Corticus Study Group. The CORTICUS randomized, double-blind, placebo-controlled study of hydrocortisone therapy in patients with septic shock. N Engl J Med. 2008;358:111–124.
20. Dellinger RP, Levy MM, Carlet JM et al. for the International Surviving Sepsis Campaign Guidelines Committee. Surviving Sepsis Campaign: International guidelines for management of severe sepsis and septic shock: 2008. Crit Care Med. 2008;36:296–327.
21. Marik PE, Pastores SM, Annane D, Meduri GU, Artl W, Sprung CL, Keh D, Briegel J, Beishuizen A, Dimopoulou I, Tsagarakis S, Singer M, Chrousos GP, Zaloga G, Bokhari F, Vogeser M. Clinical practice guidelines for the diagnosis and management of corticosteroid insufficiency in critical illness: Recommendations of an international task force. Submitted for publication.

Tim C. Jansen and Jan Bakker

Controversies in goal-directed therapy: Venous saturations and lactate

Introduction

An important goal in the early treatment of critically ill patients with circulatory failure is to maintain or restore the balance between oxygen demand and oxygen supply. Both venous oxygen saturation and blood lactate level could reflect a disturbance in this balance and could thus represent useful clinical monitors in the early treatment of critically ill patients.

The use of central ($ScvO_2$) rather than mixed (SvO_2) venous oxygen saturation has attracted the attention of many ICU clinicians. This particularly gained popularity after the publication of the early goal-directed therapy trial of Rivers et al. (1). Central venous catheters are routinely inserted for central venous pressure recording and the infusion of vasoactive drugs or parenteral nutrition and consequently, $ScvO_2$ measurement does not involve extra risks and is less time-consuming compared with SvO_2 measurement that requires the placement of a pulmonary artery catheter. However, due to concerns on the numerical equivalence between $ScvO_2$ and SvO_2, it remains controversial whether therapy to balance oxygen delivery (DO_2) to oxygen demand can be guided by the surrogate $ScvO_2$ or only by the "golden standard" SvO_2? Controversy 1 focuses on this subject.

However, also the use of blood lactate levels represents a controversy that is relevant to everyday clinical practice in the ICU. Blood lactate levels are frequently monitored in critically ill patients, usually aiming to detect tissue hypoxia. However, other processes not related to tissue hypoxia and subsequent anaerobic metabolism can also result in increased blood lactate levels, complicating clinical interpretation and therapy. Due to this debate, some clinicians use normalisation of blood lactate levels as a resuscitation endpoint to balance oxygen delivery with oxygen demand whereas others hardly measure lactate. Therefore the question whether we should monitor blood lactate levels in the critically ill and if so, when it should be measured, what the therapeutic action should be and what the clinical impact of this process could be, remains unresolved. Controversy 2 addresses these questions.

Controversy 1: Can $ScvO_2$ replace SvO_2 in goal-directed therapy?

Numerical value of SvO_2 versus $ScvO_2$

The central venous catheter sampling site usually resides in the superior vena cava. Blood from the inferior vena cava (e.g. effluent from intra-abdominal organs) is therefore mainly neglected and $ScvO_2$ thus represents upper body oxygen balance. Venous oxygen saturations differ among several organ systems since different organs extract different amounts of oxygen (2). In healthy conditions, SvO_2 exceeds $ScvO_2$ by about 2–3 % (3). However, this difference is reversed in conditions of circulatory shock. In shock, $ScvO_2$ exceeds SvO_2 by about 5 % (4, 5). During redistribution in low-flow shock, splanchnic, mesenteric and renal blood flow decrease, resulting in an increase in oxygen extraction in these regions and a subsequent decrease in inferior vena cava oxygen saturation. In hyperdynamic septic shock, increased regional splanchnic metabolism rather than reduced perfusion, leads to lower oxygen saturation in lower body venous return (6). Contrary to blood flow to the abdominal organs, cerebral flow is preserved over some period in shock, resulting in a delayed or absent drop of $ScvO_2$ compared with SvO_2.

Another possible explanation of a lower level of SvO_2 in shock patients in comparison with $ScvO_2$ is the mixing of atrial blood with blood from the coronary sinus. Although coronary sinus flow may only be a fraction of total blood flow, the effluent from the coronary sinus has a very low oxygen saturation (7). In shock, coronary blood flow is increased as a consequence of coronary vasodilatation while oxygen extraction of the myocardium remains high (8), thereby reducing SvO_2 in comparison with $ScvO_2$.

The difference between $ScvO_2$ and SvO_2 is not equal in different ranges of cardiac output. A reversed correlation of the magnitude of the $ScvO_2$–SvO_2 difference to CI and DO_2 has been found (4, 9). Again, distribution of blood flow in low-flow conditions away from renal, splanchnic and mesenteric areas towards the brain and myocardium could likely explain this phenomenon.

Prognostic value of SvO_2 and $ScvO_2$

A low SvO_2 is regarded as a warning signal for the development of tissue hypoxia and has been associated with adverse outcome. For instance, the area of SvO_2 values under 70 % during the first 48 hours of septic shock treatment in the ICU has been found to be a significant independent predictor of mortality (10). Even in hyperdynamic septic shock patients, SvO_2 was found to have prognostic significance, as temporary re-

ductions have been associated with increased mortality (11, 12).

Many studies have focussed on a similar clinical utility of $ScvO_2$. For instance, after normalisation of vital signs following resuscitation of shock patients, the majority of the patients continued to have a low $ScvO_2$ and required additional therapy (13, 14). In trauma patients with stable vital signs, $ScvO_2$ was a reliable indicator of severity of injury and the amount of blood loss (15). A significant subset of patients with decompensated end-stage congestive heart failure (CHF) had an $ScvO_2$ as low as 30 % at presentation in the emergency department. These patients were clinically indistinguishable from those with mildly decompensated or stable CHF and, once identified, required aggressive alternative management (16). In addition, $ScvO_2$ has been found to assess the adequacy of cardiopulmonary resuscitation (17, 18) and prediction of short-term outcome (19). Finally, reductions in $ScvO_2$ have been independently associated with post-operative complications in surgical patients (20).

Efficacy of SvO_2 or $ScvO_2$ directed therapy

Although mortality has been related to low venous saturations, increasing SvO_2 or $ScvO_2$ will not necessarily improve outcome. The treatment algorithm associated with the monitoring is to provide the benefit to the patient. Some randomised controlled studies have used SvO_2 as a resuscitation endpoint. The study of Gattinoni et al. (21), aiming at achieving a normal SvO_2 (> 70 %) did not reduce morbidity or mortality in critically ill patients. In the preoperative setting, optimisation to achieve an SvO_2 of more than 65 % in vascular surgery patients neither resulted in reduction of complications (22). However, the study of Pölönen et al. in cardiac surgery patients showed that a treatment algorithm aiming at both a normal SvO_2 (> 70 %) and a normal lactate level (< 2.0 mmol/l) resulted in a significant reduction in complication rate and length of stay (23). This algorithm was started immediately on arrival in the ICU and lasted for 8 hours. In patients with severe sepsis and septic shock, Rivers et al. showed that a treatment algorithm that maintained $ScvO_2$ above 70 % (in addition to a CVP 8–12 mmHg, MAP > 65 mmHg, and urine output > 0.5 ml/kg/hour) resulted in a 16 % absolute reduction in mortality compared to standard treatment that did not use monitoring of $ScvO_2$ (1). In this study, $ScvO_2$ guided therapy was provided during the first 6 hours of treatment in the emergency department.

Comparison of studies using either SvO_2 or $ScvO_2$ guided treatment algorithms is difficult as the timing and the baseline conditions of the different studies were not comparable. The negative trial of Gattinoni et al. was started much later during ICU admission and lasted for five days (21). In addition, there was a striking difference in baseline value of venous saturation; $ScvO_2$ was 49 % in the Rivers study (1) whereas baseline SvO_2 was 70 % in the Gattinoni study (21).

Could ScvO₂ replace SvO₂ in goal-directed therapy?

Although a single measurement of $ScvO_2$ and SvO_2 may differ, changes over time in $ScvO_2$ parallel changes in SvO_2 in a wide range of hemodynamic conditions (24–26). In addition, the 5 % numerical difference usually found between SvO_2 and $ScvO_2$ values seems to be consistent, yet less important when addressing severe cases of oxygen imbalance (27). A low $ScvO_2$ – the range in which Rivers' goal-directed therapy was beneficial (1) – would result in even lower SvO_2 values. Thus, irrespective of whether $ScvO_2$ equals SvO_2, the presence of a low $ScvO_2$ level is associated with adverse outcome, and correcting this value could improve this. Insertion of a pulmonary artery catheter can be time-consuming (28), whereas a central venous catheter can be introduced faster or has already been inserted prior to ICU admission (in the operating room or emergency department). Therefore, the lack of accuracy of $ScvO_2$ measurement may be compensated by a positive outcome effect due to a possible earlier start of $ScvO_2$-based therapy (29).

Many clinicians have argued, however, that $ScvO_2$ cannot replace SvO_2 monitoring due to the lack of numerical equivalence (4, 5, 30, 31). Biases (mean of the differences) between the two sample sites ranged from 1 % (30) to 7 % (24) but more importantly, 95 % confidence intervals of these biases were often clinically unacceptable (4, 5, 25, 31). In a study with a mean bias of –5 % and a 95 % confidence interval of +5 % to –16 % (5),

a $ScvO_2$ measurement of 74 % would on average correspond to an SvO_2 of 69 % with an uncertainty of the estimate ranging from 58 to 79 %. It thus demonstrates a great variability between individual absolute values, and such variability would possibly urge the clinician to take inappropriate actions, especially when the $ScvO_2$ value is around the normal limit of 70 %.

The lack of numerical equivalence between SvO_2 and $ScvO_2$ is evident, particularly in circulatory shock. However, it is not the absolute value that matters, but rather its clinical utility. In this regard, $ScvO_2$ can probably be used as a warning signal in various clinical scenarios. Furthermore, the use of central instead of mixed venous saturation as a resuscitation endpoint seems to be acceptable in the early phase of hemodynamic optimisation of critically ill patients. The Surviving Sepsis Campaign has acknowledged this by recommending using either SvO_2 (target 65 %) or $ScvO_2$ (target 70 %) in the early resuscitation of patients with severe sepsis and septic shock (32). Following initial resuscitation, however, it is uncertain whether definite treatment can be based on $ScvO_2$ instead of SvO_2 measurement.

Controversy 2: Should lactate be used as a resuscitation endpoint?

An increase in lactate levels can be the result of increased production or decreased clearance or a combination of both processes. In addition, increased production of lactate can be the result of both anaerobic and aerobic metabolism.

Hyperlactataemia: Anaerobic aetiology

Experimental studies have clearly confirmed the causal relationship between tissue hypoxia and hyperlactataemia (33–35). These studies demonstrated that by reducing the components of systemic DO_2 (haemoglobin level, oxygen saturation and cardiac output) until oxygen demand could no longer be met, oxygen consumption was limited by DO_2 and this coincided with a sharp increase in lactate levels. Similarly, a study on withdrawal of life support in critically ill patients in a terminal state of disease described a sharp increase in lactate level at the moment that oxygen demand could no longer be met by increased oxygen extraction and oxygen consumption started to fall (36). Several other clinical observations pointed to an anaerobic origin of hyperlactataemia in critically ill patients. For example, patients in the early stages of catecholamine-treated septic shock or patients with cardiogenic shock had increased lactate-to-pyruvate ratios (37). Another study showed that hyperlactataemia was accompanied by the presence of oxygen supply dependency in the early phase of septic shock, (38). Finally, Rivers et al. illustrated that the hyperlactataemia in severe sepsis or septic shock prior to resuscitation was associated with signs of poor DO_2 and that increases in DO_2 were associated with reductions in lactate (1).

In the absence of low *systemic* DO_2 relative to *systemic* metabolic demand, microcirculatory processes hampering oxygen utilisation at the tissue level may also raise lactate levels. This is illustrated by a correlation between an increase in capillary perfusion and a reduction in lactate levels in patients with septic shock, independent of changes in systemic haemodynamic variables (39).

Hyperlactataemia: Aerobic aetiology

Besides anaerobic glycolysis, other aerobic mechanisms may account for the accumulation of lactate in critically ill patients:

1. increased aerobic glycolysis by catecholamine-stimulated Na-K pump hyperactivity (40),
2. mitochondrial dysfunction (41),
3. impaired pyruvate dehydrogenase activity (in sepsis) (42),
4. thiamin deficiency (beriberi disease) (43),
5. liver dysfunction (44, 45), also in sepsis (46),
6. (aerobic) pulmonary lactate production (47, 48),
7. alkalosis (49) and finally,
8. various medications and intoxications such as nucleosidic reverse transcriptase inhibitors (50), methformin (particularly in the presence of renal insufficiency) (51) and cyanide, methanol or ethylene-glycol intoxications (52).

Different mechanisms related to aerobic metabolism may thus cause hyperlactataemia in critically ill patients.

Prognostic value of blood lactate levels

Irrespective of the origin of increased blood lactate levels, the presence of hyperlactataemia in critically ill patients is always associated with an unfavourable outcome when compared to similar patients with normal blood lactate levels. Many studies have related increased blood lactate levels, and/or a lack of normalisation during treatment, to significant morbidity and a manyfold increased mortality. This has been shown in septic (53, 54), trauma (55), surgical (56) and post-cardiac surgery (57) patients, but also in heterogeneous ICU patients (58) and emergency department populations (59). Even in haemodynamically stable patients with hyperlactataemia, a condition referred to as compensated shock or occult hypo-perfusion, increased blood lactate levels are associated with increased morbidity and mortality (60, 61).

Efficacy of lactate-directed therapy

Given the above-mentioned aetiologies of increased blood lactate levels it is not immediately clear whether specific therapy should be instituted in hyperlactataemic patients and what this therapy should consist of to improve patient outcome. Improving pyruvate metabolism by the administration of dichloroacetate decreases lactate levels. However, in a randomised controlled study, the significant decrease in lactate in the patients receiving dichloroacetate was not associated with a clinical benefit to these patients (62). This probably indicates that the detrimental outcome associated with hyperlactataemia is more likely to be determined by the underlying cause than by the hyperlactataemia itself. In general, the treatment aimed to reduce lactate levels has focused on increasing systemic DO_2. Blow et al. designed a treatment protocol for hemodynamically stable trauma patients with increased lactate levels that consisted of augmenting oxygen content (red blood cell transfusion) and blood flow (fluids, dobutamine) (63). They showed that in patients in whom hyperlactataemia was not corrected by this therapy mortality was significantly higher than in those in whom lactate levels were normalised. Others showed that similar therapeutic strategies in children undergoing cardiac surgery reduced morbidity and mortality in comparison with a historical control group (64). Rivers et al. showed that early goal-directed therapy, mainly aiming at improving systemic DO_2 in patients with severe sepsis and increased lactate levels, significantly reduced lactate levels and improved outcome (1). Chytra et al. showed that optimisation of fluid management using esophageal Doppler in multiple-trauma patients was associated with a decrease in blood lactate levels, a lower incidence of infectious complications and a reduction in ICU and hospital length of stay (65). Only one randomised controlled trial has studied the effect of optimising systemic DO_2 aiming to normalise blood lactate levels. In cardiac surgery patients, Polonen et al. reported a decrease in morbidity associated with this therapeutic strategy (23).

Should we use lactate-guided therapy in critically ill patients?

The causal link between the phenomenon of oxygen supply dependency and hyperlactataemia in experimental studies is evident (33–35). In addition, also clinical studies have provided support for the use of lactate as a resuscitation endpoint, either indirectly (1, 63–65) or directly (23). As different aerobic mechanisms may result in hyperlactataemia in critically ill patients, lactate is a sensitive but rather aspecific marker of tissue hypoxia. It is therefore questionable whether increasing DO_2 is beneficial in all hyperlactatemic patients (66). Furthermore, the only randomised controlled trial that evaluated lactate-directed optimisation of oxygen delivery was conducted in post-cardiac surgery patients (23), which cannot be extrapolated to the general ICU setting. Furthermore, the timing of lactate-directed DO_2 therapy could be an important factor, the rationale being that early in the course of critical illness the likelihood of an anaerobic origin of hyperlactataemia is probably higher. For instance, Friedman et al. showed that oxygen supply dependency was present in the early phase of septic shock but absent in the later phase following stabilisation (38). The effective therapy of Polonen et al. started early and lasted for only eight hours (23). The study by Rivers et al. also took place in the early phase of severe sepsis (in the emergency department) and lasted for only six hours (1). Following initial resuscitation, especially when other clinical parameters of hy-

poperfusion (i.e. low SvO_2, poor peripheral perfusion, decreased urine output, etc.) are not present, non-anaerobic mechanisms may be a more likely cause of hyperlactataemia and increasing systemic DO_2 may be less likely to have positive effects on outcome parameters. However, conclusive data on this controversy are lacking. Currently, a randomised controlled multi-centre trial (n = 350) on the efficacy of early lactate-directed therapy in the ICU has been finalised (http://clinicaltrials.gov/ct2/show/NCT00270673). The primary objective of this study was to assess the effect of lactate-directed therapy (compared with non-lactate directed therapy) on in-hospital mortality when given in the first eight hours of ICU stay to patients with a lactate level of ≥ 3,0 mmol/l upon ICU admission. As data analysis is ongoing, for now it still remains controversial whether the use of lactate as a resuscitation endpoint in goal-directed therapy to balance oxygen delivery with oxygen demand improves patient outcomes.

Key points

Controversy 1:
Can $ScvO_2$ replace SvO_2 in goal-directed therapy?
- *In circulatory shock, $ScvO_2$ exceeds SvO_2 by about 5 %, with a large confidence interval*
- *$ScvO_2$ can be used as a warning signal in critically ill patients*
- *The use of $ScvO_2$ instead of SvO_2 in goal-directed therapy seems to be acceptable in the early phase of hemodynamic optimisation*
- *Following initial resuscitation, it is uncertain whether goal-directed therapy can be based on $ScvO_2$ instead of SvO_2*

Controversy 2:
Should lactate be used as a resuscitation endpoint?
- *Tissue hypoxia causes hyperlactataemia*
- *Lactate is a rather aspecific marker of tissue hypoxia due to other aerobic mechanisms of hyperlactataemia in critically ill patients*
- *Increased blood lactate levels, and a lack of decrease during treatment, are associated with increased morbidity and mortality*
- *Studies provide indirect support for the use of lactate in goal-directed therapy*
- *Currently, there is insufficient direct evidence for the use of lactate as a resuscitation endpoint*

The authors

Tim C. Jansen, MD
Jan Bakker, MD, PhD
    Department of Intensive Care | Erasmus MC
    University Medical Center Rotterdam |
    The Netherlands

Address for correspondence
    Jan Bakker
    Erasmus MC University Medical Center
    Department of Intensive Care
    (room Hs – 3.20)
    P.O. Box 2040
    3000 CA, Rotterdam, The Netherlands
    e-mail: jan.bakker@erasmusmc.nl

References

1. Rivers E, Nguyen B, Havstad S, Ressler J, Muzzin A, Knoblich B et al. Early goal-directed therapy in the treatment of severe sepsis and septic shock. N Engl J Med. 2001;345(19):1368–1377.
2. Reinhart K (1989) Monitoring O_2 transport and tissue oxygenation in critically ill patients. In: Reinhart K, Eyrich K (eds). Clinical aspects of O_2 transport and tissue oxygenation. Springer, Berlin/Heidelberg/New York, pp 195–211.
3. Bloos F, Reinhart K. Venous oximetry. Intensive Care Med. 2005;31(7):911–913.
4. Varpula M, Karlsson S, Ruokonen E, Pettila V. Mixed venous oxygen saturation cannot be estimated by central venous oxygen saturation in septic shock. Intensive Care Med. 2006;32(9):1336–1343.
5. Chawla LS, Zia H, Gutierrez G, Katz NM, Seneff MG, Shah M. Lack of equivalence between central and mixed venous oxygen saturation. Chest. 2004;126(6):1891–1896.
6. Dahn MS, Lange MP, Jacobs LA. Central mixed and splanchnic venous oxygen saturation monitoring. Intensive Care Med. 1988;14:373–378.
7. Beltrame JF, Limaye SB, Wuttke RD, Horowitz JD. Coronary hemodynamic and metabolic studies of the coronary slow flow phenomenon. Am Heart J. 2003;146(1):84–90.
8. Dhainaut JF, Huyghebaert MF, Monsallier JF, Lefevre G, Dall'Ava-Santucci J, Brunet F et al. Coronary hemodynamics and myocardial metabolism of lactate, free fatty acids, glucose, and ketones in patients with septic shock. Circulation. 1987;75(3):533–541.
9. Turnaoglu S, Tugrul M, Camci E, Cakar N, Akinci O, Ergin P. Clinical applicability of the substitution of mixed venous oxygen saturation with central venous oxygen

saturation. J Cardiothorac Vasc Anesth. 2001;15(5): 574–579.
10. Varpula M, Tallgren M, Saukkonen K, Voipio-Pulkki LM, Pettila V. Hemodynamic variables related to outcome in septic shock. Intensive Care Med. 2005;31(8):1066–1071.
11. Heiselman D, Jones J, Cannon L. Continuous monitoring of mixed venous oxygen saturation in septic shock. J Clin Monit. 1986;2(4):237–245.
12. Krafft P, Steltzer H, Hiesmayr M, Klimscha W, Hammerle AF. Mixed venous oxygen saturation in critically ill septic shock patients. The role of defined events. Chest. 1993; 103(3):900–906.
13. Rady MY, Rivers EP, Nowak RM. Resuscitation of the critically ill in the ED: responses of blood pressure, heart rate, shock index, central venous oxygen saturation, and lactate. Am J Emerg Med. 1996;14(2):218–225.
14. Rady MY, Rivers EP, Martin GB, Smithline H, Appelton T, Nowak RM. Continuous central venous oximetry and shock index in the emergency department: use in the evaluation of clinical shock. Am J Emerg Med. 1992;10(6): 538–541.
15. Scalea TM, Hartnett RW, Duncan AO, Atweh NA, Phillips TF, Sclafani SJ et al. Central venous oxygen saturation: a useful clinical tool in trauma patients. J Trauma. 1990; 30(12):1539–1543.
16. Ander DS, Jaggi M, Rivers E, Rady MY, Levine TB, Levine AB et al. Undetected cardiogenic shock in patients with congestive heart failure presenting to the emergency department. Am J Cardiol. 1998;82(7):888–891.
17. Rivers EP, Martin GB, Smithline H, Rady MY, Schultz CH, Goetting MG et al. The clinical implications of continuous central venous oxygen saturation during human CPR. Ann Emerg Med. 1992;21(9):1094–1101.
18. Nakazawa K, Hikawa Y, Saitoh Y, Tanaka N, Yasuda K, Amaha K. Usefulness of central venous oxygen saturation monitoring during cardiopulmonary resuscitation. A comparative case study with end-tidal carbon dioxide monitoring. Intensive Care Med. 1994; 20(6):450–451.
19. Snyder AB, Salloum LJ, Barone JE, Conley M, Todd M, DiGiacomo JC. Predicting short-term outcome of cardiopulmonary resuscitation using central venous oxygen tension measurements. Crit Care Med. 1991; 19(1):111–113.
20. Pearse R, Dawson D, Fawcett J, Rhodes A, Grounds RM, Bennett ED. Changes in central venous saturation after major surgery, and association with outcome. Crit Care. 2005;9(6):R694–R699.
21. Gattinoni L, Brazzi L, Pelosi P, Latini R, Tognoni G, Pesenti A et al. A trial of goal-oriented hemodynamic therapy in critically ill patients. SvO_2 Collaborative Group. N Engl J Med. 1995;333(16):1025–1032.
22. Ziegler DW, Wright JG, Choban PS, Flancbaum L. A prospective randomized trial of preoperative "optimization" of cardiac function in patients undergoing elective

peripheral vascular surgery. Surgery. 1997;122(3): 584–592.

23. Pölönen P, Ruokonen E, Hippelainen M, Poyhonen M, Takala J. A prospective, randomized study of goal-oriented hemodynamic therapy in cardiac surgical patients. Anesth Analg. 2000;90(5):1052–1059.

24. Reinhart K, Kuhn HJ, Hartog C, Bredle DL. Continuous central venous and pulmonary artery oxygen saturation monitoring in the critically ill. Intensive Care Med. 2004; 30(8):1572–1578.

25. Dueck MH, Klimek M, Appenrodt S, Weigand C, Boerner U. Trends but not individual values of central venous oxygen saturation agree with mixed venous oxygen saturation during varying hemodynamic conditions. Anesthesiology. 2005;103(2):249–257.

26. Reinhart K, Rudolph T, Bredle DL, Hannemann L, Cain SM. Comparison of central-venous to mixed-venous oxygen saturation during changes in oxygen supply/ demand. Chest. 1989;95(6):1216–1221.

27. Rivers E. Mixed vs central venous oxygen saturation may be not numerically equal, but both are still clinically useful. Chest. 2006;129(3):507–508.

28. Lefrant JY, Muller L, Bruelle P, Pandolfi JL, L'Hermite J, Peray P et al. Insertion time of the pulmonary artery catheter in critically ill patients. Crit Care Med. 2000; 28(2):355–359.

29. Lundberg JS, Perl TM, Wiblin T, Costigan MD, Dawson J, Nettleman MD et al. Septic shock: an analysis of outcomes for patients with onset on hospital wards versus intensive care units. Crit Care Med. 1998;26(6): 1020–1024.

30. Martin C, Auffray JP, Badetti C, Perrin G, Papazian L, Gouin F. Monitoring of central venous oxygen saturation versus mixed venous oxygen saturation in critically ill patients. Intensive Care Med. 1992;18(2):101–104.

31. Edwards JD, Mayall RM. Importance of the sampling site for measurement of mixed venous oxygen saturation in shock. Crit Care Med. 1998;26(8):1356–1360.

32. Dellinger RP, Levy MM, Carlet JM, Bion J, Parker MM, Jaeschke R et al. Surviving Sepsis Campaign: international guidelines for management of severe sepsis and septic shock: 2008. Crit Care Med. 2008 Jan;36(1):296–327.

33. Cain SM. Appearance of excess lactate in anesthetized dogs during anemic and hypoxic hypoxia. Am J Physiol. 1965;209:604–608.

34. Cain SM. Oxygen delivery and uptake in dogs during anemic and hypoxic hypoxia. J Appl Physiol. 1977;42: 228–234.

35. Zhang H, Vincent JL. Oxygen extraction is altered by endotoxin during tamponade-induced stagnant hypoxia in the dog. Circ Shock. 1993;40:168–176.

36. Ronco JJ, Fenwick JC, Tweeddale MG et al. Identification of the critical oxygen delivery for anaerobic metabolism in critically ill septic and nonseptic humans. JAMA. 1993;270:1724–1730.

37. Levy B, Sadoune LO, Gelot AM et al. Evolution of lactate/ pyruvate and arterial ketone body ratios in the early course of catecholamine-treated septic shock. Crit Care Med. 2000;28:114–119.

38. Friedman G, De Backer D, Shahla M et al. Oxygen supply dependency can characterize septic shock. Intensive Care Med. 1998;24:118–123.

39. De Backer D, Creteur J, Dubois MJ et al. The effects of dobutamine on microcirculatory alterations in patients with septic shock are independent of its systemic effects. Crit Care Med. 2006;34:403–408.

40. Levy B, Gibot S, Franck P et al. Relation between muscle Na+K+ ATPase activity and raised lactate concentrations in septic shock: a prospective study. The Lancet. 2005; 365:871–875.

41. Brealey D, Brand M, Hargreaves I et al. Association between mitochondrial dysfunction and severity and outcome of septic shock. Lancet. 2002;360:219–23.

42. Vary TC. Sepsis-induced alterations in pyruvate dehydrogenase complex activity in rat skeletal muscle: effects on plasma lactate. Shock. 1996;6:89–94.

43. Naidoo DP, Gathiram V, Sadhabiriss A et al. Clinical diagnosis of cardiac beriberi. S.Afr.Med.J. 1990;77: 125–127.

44. Woll PJ, Record CO. Lactate elimination in man: effects of lactate concentration and hepatic dysfunction. Eur.J.Clin. Invest. 1979;9:397–404.

45. Almenoff PL, Leavy J, Weil MH et al. Prolongation of the half-life of lactate after maximal exercise in patients with hepatic dysfunction. Critical Care Medicine. 1989; 17:870–873.

46. Levraut J, Ciebiera JP, Chave S et al. Mild hyperlactataemia in stable septic patients is due to impaired lactate clearance rather than overproduction. Am J Respir Crit Care Med. 1998;157:1021–1026.

47. De Backer D, Creteur J, Zhang H et al. Lactate production by the lungs in acute lung injury. Am J Respir Crit Care Med. 1997;156:1099–1104.

48. Routsi C, Bardouniotou H, Delivoria-Ioannidou V et al. Pulmonary lactate release in patients with acute lung injury is not attributable to lung tissue hypoxia. Crit Care Med. 1999;27:2469–2473.

49. Druml W, Grimm G, Laggner AN et al. Lactic acid kinetics in respiratory alkalosis. Crit Care Med. 1991;19: 1120–1124.

50. Claessens YE, Cariou A, Monchi M et al. Detecting life-threatening lactic acidosis related to nucleoside-analog treatment of human immunodeficiency virus-infected patients, and treatment with L-carnitine. Crit Care Med. 2003;31:1042–1047.

51. Salpeter SR, Greyber E, Pasternak GA et al. Risk of fatal and nonfatal lactic acidosis with metformin use in type 2 diabetes mellitus: systematic review and meta-analysis. Arch. Intern. Med. 2003;163:2594–2602.

52. Morgan TJ, Clark C, Clague A. Artifactual elevation of measured plasma L-lactate concentration in the presence of glycolate. Crit Care Med. 1999;27:2177–9.

53. Bakker J, Gris P, Coffernils M et al. Serial blood lactate levels can predict the development of multiple organ failure following septic shock. Am. J. Surg. 1996;171: 221–226.

54. Nguyen HB, Rivers EP, Knoblich BP et al. Early lactate clearance is associated with improved outcome in severe sepsis and septic shock. Crit Care Med. 2004;32:1637–1642.

55. Cerović O, Golubović V, Spec-Marn A, Kremzar B, Vidmar G. Relationship between injury severity and lactate levels in severely injured patients.Intensive Care Med. 2003 Aug;29(8):1300–5.

56. Husain FA, Martin MJ, Mullenix PS, Steele SR, Elliott DC. Serum lactate and base deficit as predictors of mortality and morbidity. Am.J.Surg. 2003;185:485–491.

57. Maillet JM, Le Besnerais P, Cantoni M, Nataf P, Ruffenach A, Lessana A, Brodaty D. Frequency, risk factors, and outcome of hyperlactataemia after cardiac surgery. Chest. 2003;123:1361–1366.

58. Smith I, P Kumar, S Molloy et al. Base excess and lactate as prognostic indicators for patients admitted to intensive care. Intensive Care Med. 2001;27:74–83.

59. Shapiro NI, Howell MD, Talmor D, Nathanson LA, Lisbon A, Wolfe RE, Weiss JW. Serum lactate as a predictor of mortality in emergency department patients with infection. Ann Emerg Med. 2005;45:524–528

60. Howell MD, Donnino M, Clardy P, Talmor D, Shapiro NI. Occult hypoperfusion and mortality in patients with suspected infection. Intensive Care Med. 2007; Nov;33(11):1892–9.

61. Meregalli A, Oliveira RP, Friedman G. Occult hypoperfusion is associated with increased mortality in hemodynamically stable, high-risk, surgical patients. Crit Care. 2004;8 R60–R65.

62. Stacpoole PW, Wright EC, Baumgartner TG et al. A controlled clinical trial of dichloroacetate for treatment of lactic acidosis in adults. The Dichloroacetate-Lactic Acidosis Study Group. N Engl J Med. 1992;327:1564–1569.

63. Blow O, Magliore L, Claridge JA et al. The golden hour and the silver day: detection and correction of occult hypoperfusion within 24 hours improves outcome from major trauma. J.Trauma. 1999;47:964–969.

64. Rossi AF, Khan DM, Hannan R et al. Goal-directed medical therapy and point-of-care testing improve outcomes after congenital heart surgery. Intensive Care Med. 2005;31:98–104.

65. Chytra I, Pradl R, Bosman R, Pelnar P, Kasal E, Zidkova A. Esophageal Doppler-guided fluid management decreases blood lactate levels in multiple-trauma patients: a randomized controlled trial. Crit Care. 2007;11:R24

66. James JH, Luchette FA, McCarter FD, Fischer JE. Lactate is an unreliable indicator of tissue hypoxia in injury or sepsis. Lancet. 1999 Aug 7;354(9177):505–8.

Marc Leone and Claude Martin

Starting and stopping antibiotic therapy

More than 75 % of patients admitted to intensive care unit (ICU) receive at least one antibiotic during their stay (1). Prompt initiation of appropriate antimicrobial therapy, which is defined by the effectiveness of treatment against the microorganisms responsible for the infection, saves lives and money in severely ill patients (2). However, the emergence of multiresistant bacteria is related to excessive antimicrobial use (3). Thus, the balance between benefit and harm should be evaluated before starting antibiotic therapy. After starting antibiotic therapy, the next challenge is to elicit the best time for discontinuing this treatment. We will review thereafter the indications for starting and stopping antibiotics in the ICU.

Before starting antibiotic therapy

Diagnostic procedure

The diagnostic procedure depends on the degree of urgency for starting antibiotics, the patient's condition, the site of infection, the prior administration of antibiotic therapy, the potential impact of the procedure on timing of antibiotic therapy. In community-acquired meningitis, a lumbar puncture before starting antibiotics is performed. In case of intracranial hypertension, however, lumbar puncture will be delayed and antibiotics are given immediately after blood has been obtained for culture. In community-acquired pneumonia, two blood culture specimens (30 min interval between sets), and potentially infected body fluids including pleural fluid should be taken before starting antibiotics. Sputum examination is a simple and inexpensive procedure. Fiber-optic bronchoscopy is debatable and this procedure may be dangerous in hypoxemic non-intubated patients. In ventilator-associated pneumonia (VAP), the microbiological diagnosis is made by using quantitative cultures before starting or changing antibiotics.

Gram stain may offer useful guidance in the choice of initial empirical antibiotic treatment. This technique should be used in all samples obtained from normally sterile fluids and from drained collections. This procedure has several limitations. The interpretation may be difficult. For example, *Acinetobacter baumanii* may appear as coccoid cell, or as staphylococci. In polymicrobial infections, the clinical pertinence of this procedure remains limited.

Choice of antibiotics

A judicious choice of antimicrobial therapy should be based on the host characteristics, the site of infection, the local ecology, and the pharmacokinetics/pharmacodynamics of antibiotics. The best option between monotherapy and combination of antibiotics remains under debate. An inappropriate antibiotic therapy is associated with increased mortality in patients with severe sepsis and septic shock, VAP or meningitis. Hence, considerations on timing of antibiotics may be elaborated only in the setting of an appropriate choice of these drugs.

Starting antibiotics

Antibiotics serve to reduce the mortality and morbidity associated with infections. According to each patient, the timing for starting an antibiotic therapy can be considered as emergent, urgent, and delayed. Emergent is defined by the need for starting antibiotics within 1 hour after diagnosis has been performed. Urgent is defined by the need for starting antibiotics within 6 to 8 hours. Delayed antibiotic therapy is defined by the start of antibiotics from 8 to 24 hours after admission or diagnosis. The patients who receive emergent or urgent antibiotic therapy warrant broad-spectrum therapy until the causative organism and its antibiotic susceptibilities are defined. However, one should keep in mind that restricting the use of broad-spectrum antibiotics is important for limiting superinfection and decreasing the development of multidrug resistant pathogens.

Emergent indications for starting antibiotic therapy

The patients with severe sepsis or septic shock must receive appropriate antibiotics within the first hour after diagnosis. Each hour of delay in antibiotic administration over the ensuing 6 hours after diagnosis has been associated with an average decrease in survival of 7.6% (2). In the patients with septic shock, delayed adequate antibiotic therapy was found as the only independent predictor of in-hospital mortality (4). Infections known to have a fulminant course, such as meningococcemia should be treated even before hospital admission. Parallel, antibiotics should be immediately given if bacterial meningitis is suspected (5, 6). In patients with pneumococcal meningitis,

survivors and nonsurvivors did not differ with respect to cerebrospinal fluid characteristics. By contrast, non survivors had a longer median interval between hospital admission and antibiotic therapy. An interval between admission and antibiotic therapy > 3 hours was the strongest indicator of mortality, with an odds ratio of 14 (5). Sepsis in splenectomised or neutropenic patients should be treated without delay. In splenectomised patients, pneumococcal infections accounted for 50% to 90% of cases reported in the literature and may be associated with a mortality of up to 60%. *Haemophilus influenzae* type B, meningococcus, and group A Streptococci have accounted for an additional 25% of infections (7). In these patients, diagnostic work-up should never delay the use of empiric therapy. Expert opinion recommends use of broad-spectrum antibiotic therapy active against penicillin-resistant pneumococci, beta-lactamase-producing *H. influenzae* and other possible organisms, such as *Escherichia coli* and *Salmonella*. Any local resistance patterns should be taken into account in selecting an initial empirical regimen (7).

In the Emergency Department, several approaches have been described to reduce the delay of antibiotic administration: guidelines on handling patients with serious infections and on ordering immediate treatment, guidelines on obtaining culture samples, lectures to medical and nursing staff, improvement of availability of antibiotics in the emergency department, and removal of financial restraints on stocking and ordering of antibiotics. Implementing this educational program resulted in a decrease from 54% to 32% of the percentage of patients whose first dose of antibiotic was delayed (8). However, it is of importance to underline that the indications for emergent antibiotic therapy should be restrictive. They concern only the patients with an infection involving a risk of death. In our opinion, prescription of an emergent antibiotic therapy should be based on a written procedure elaborated by a local expert team.

Urgent indications for starting antibiotic therapy

Urgent antibiotic therapy is probably the most frequent condition encountered in ICU. In this pattern, samples are collected before starting antibiotics. For instance, it has been shown that the administration of antibiotics within 4 hours does not reduce the time to clinical stability in adult patients with moderate-to-severe community-acquired pneumonia (9). The effects of undetermined factors can explain some conflicting findings. Among 451 patients with community-acquired pneumonia, univariate analysis showed that a time to the first antibiotic dose of > 4 hours was associated with increased mortality (10). After eliminating confounding factors, only an altered mental state was an independent factor for mortality. However, antibiotic administration within 8 hours has been shown to reduce 30-day mortality in patients older than 65 years (11). With respect to severe VAP, progressive change in the clinical picture over hours can favour the starting of antibiotic therapy. In practice, the onset of antibiotic therapy is frequently decided on the assessment of a clinical score such as clinical pulmonary infection score (12, 13). Gram stain results may be included in the "urgent choice" strategy. This picture is frequent in mechanically ventilated patients with fever, in whom the images on chest X-ray worsen over the day. Sometimes, other investigations, such as computed tomography scan or ultrasound may serve to confirm the diagnosis. Hence, antibiotics should be administered within 4 to 8 hours after diagnosis has been made and microbiological samples have been collected. Of course, antibiotics should be used in these patients immediately if infection is obvious or the patient is unstable.

Delayed indications for starting antibiotic therapy

Although delay is reported as a cause of increased mortality in septic patients, there is no need for starting antibiotics within the first hour in all patients with fever. In most patients, the aim is to perform the appropriate diagnostic procedures before starting antibiotic therapy. If the patient is stable and the diagnosis of VAP is only suspected, it seems wise to wait for the results of Gram examination before starting antibiotics, without exceeding 24 hours after diagnosis. Inadequate therapy is defined by the administration of inappropriate antibiotic therapy, i.e. inactive against the bacteria responsible for VAP, or a 24-hour delay in the administration of antibiotics. A study made

the point on this issue. Among 76 patients with VAP, 52 received an inadequate therapy, including 36 delayed treatments. The mortality rate was approximately 30 % in the group treated with adequate antibiotics, whereas it was around 60 % for those receiving inadequate therapy (75 % for inappropriate therapy and 58 % for delayed therapy). There were no differences for other factors like age, severity score at admission, pathogens, days prior mechanical ventilation (14). Hence, treatment of VAP can be delayed but the delay should not exceed 24 hours.

In the patients with bacteraemia, starting antibiotics may be considered as urgent. However, the literature softens this statement in the patients with haemodynamic stability. Indeed, the delays which are reported in the literature for starting antibiotics frequently exceed 8 hours. A delay in the administration of effective therapy increased the mortality rate among patients with methicillin resistant *Staphylococcus aureus* bacteraemia. However, one should note that the breakpoint was 44 hours (15). In patients with *Pseudomonas aeruginosa* bacteraemia, a trend toward higher mortality with increasing length of delay is demonstrated (16), but the delay was considered only after 24 hours. In another study, the breakpoint between early and delayed treatment was 52 hours (17).

In the field of other infections, there is a paucity of data on the best timing of antibiotic onset. It has been shown that in asymptomatic patients with positive urine culture, the administration of antibiotics does not affect the outcomes. Hence, this result probably suggests that there is no role for emergent antibiotic therapy in the stable patients with urinary tract infection (18).

Strategies according to patient's disease

The literature does not provide abundant data on the need to urgently start an antibiotic therapy, except in specific populations of patients (see fig. 1). Antibiotic therapy should be started without delay in patients with haemodynamic instability, those developing infections associated with high risk of mortality or morbidity, such as meningococcemia, and those with a prior medical history of splenectomy or neutropenia. Emergent antibiotic therapy is probably the most frequent pattern in the ICU. This strategy makes it possible

Starting antibiotics

Suspicion of infection in patient with:
✓ haemodynamic instability
✓ neuromeningeal symptoms
✓ neutropenia
✓ splenectomy

Severe VAP in stable patient
Stable patient with confirmed infection

Stable patient with suspected infection

Fig. 1   Indications and best timing for starting antibiotic therapy

to collect adequate microbiological samples before starting antibiotics. In practice, a delay of approximately 6 hours in the administration of antibiotics has a low impact on the outcomes of most stable patients. In the patients without any risk of complications, antibiotics can be started from 8 to 24 hours after diagnosis confirmation. This delay can be used to balance the benefits and harms associated with the use of antibiotics.

Stopping antibiotics

General considerations

In ICU, new findings suggest an early use of antibiotics in patients with haemodynamic instability. At the individual level, the early use of antibiotics is associated with improved outcomes. This strategy leads to the use of antibiotics in a large number of patients. At the collective level, overuse of antibiotics can increase the development of multidrug resistant pathogens. Thus, patients may develop superinfections due to difficult-to-treat pathogens. Experts in the field have developed strategies to limit the exposure of patients to antibiotics. Briefly, it is presently suggested to shorten dramatically the duration of antibiotic therapy. An interesting retrospective study showed that shorter courses of antibiotics were associated with sim-

ilar or fewer complications than prolonged therapy. Hence, in general, adopting a strategy of a fixed duration of therapy, rather than basing duration on resolution of fever or leukocytosis, appeared to yield similar outcomes with less antibiotic use (19). Short courses of antibiotic therapy have been successful in typhoid fever, meningococcal meningitis (3 days), VAP (8 days), and uncomplicated intra-abdominal infections (3 to 5 days). In contrast, intravenous catheter-associated infections require a 14-day treatment course (20).

Pre-determined fixed strategies

In the patients with documented infection, a reduced duration of antimicrobial therapy minimises the emergence of resistance. A randomised clinical trial was aimed at determining whether 8 days is as effective as 15 days of antibiotic treatment of patients with microbiologically proven VAP. Among patients who had received appropriate initial empirical therapy, with the possible exception of those developing nonfermenting gramnegative bacillus infections, comparable clinical effectiveness against VAP was obtained with the 8- and 15-day treatment regimens. Among patients who developed recurrent infections, multiresistant pathogens emerged less frequently in those who had received 8 days of antibiotics (21). Since this study, the duration of antibiotic therapy for the patients with VAP is 8 days. However, an observational study brought additional suggestions. In this observational study, the cohort of patients with VAP received around 10 days of antibiotic therapy. The patients with VAP due to *P. aeruginosa* were treated more frequently with an inappropriate empirical treatment than those with VAP due to other bacteria. However, when antibiotics therapy was appropriate, no difference was observed in terms of clinical response to treatment. In contrast, the clinical response of the patients who were appropriately treated for VAP due to *S. aureus* remained significantly poorer than that of patients with VAP due to other bacteria. These results suggest the need for further studies to determine the best duration of treatment with specific bacteria, such as *S. aureus* (22).

For patients with spontaneous bacterial peritonitis, there are no advantages to provide cefotaxime more than five days (23). For the patients with intra-abdominal infections, although no randomised clinical trials were available, observational data suggest to reduce the duration of antibiotics (19). In patients with community-acquired intra-abdominal infection, a 3-day course of ertapenem had the same clinical and bacteriological efficacy as a 5-day course (24). In conclusion, reducing the duration of antimicrobial therapy in proven infection is an efficient way to curtail the development of antimicrobial-resistance. Standard durations of antibiotic therapy are summarised in table 1.

Dynamic strategies

Several strategies aimed at shortening the duration of antibiotic therapy are based on the assessment of both the clinical, biological and microbiological courses. These strategies have been developed in the patients with VAP. In a randomised clinical trial, clinical pulmonary infection score (12) was used as operational criteria for decision-making regarding antibiotic therapy. Patients with clinical pulmonary infection score ≤ 6 were randomised to receive either standard therapy or ciprofloxacin monotherapy with reevaluation at day 3, with discontinuation of ciprofloxacin if clinical pulmonary infection score remained ≤ 6 at day 3. Antibiotics were continued beyond day 3 in 90 % of the patients in the standard therapy as compared with 28 % in the experimental therapy group. Antimicrobial resistance, or superinfections, or both, developed in 15 % of the patients in the experimental versus 35 % of the patients in the

Tab. 1   Pre-determined duration of antibiotic therapy

Site of infection	Duration of antibiotic therapy
Lung infections	
Community-acquired pneumonia due to *S. pneumoniae*	8 days
Ventilator-associated pneumonia	8 days
Ventilator-associated pneumonia and immunodepression	14 days
Pneumonia due to *L. pneumophila*	21 days
Pneumonia with lung necrosis	≥ 28 days
Intra-abdominal infections	
Community peritonitis	< 8 days
Post-operative peritonitis	14 days
Central nervous system infections	
Meningococcemia	< 8 days
Meningitis due to *S. pneumoniae*	10–14 days
Post-operative meningitis due to *S. epidermidis* or enterobacteriacae	14 days
Meningitis due to *L. monocytogenes*	21 days
Post-operative meningitis due to *S. aureus* or *P. aeruginosa*	21 days
Brain abscess	≥ 28 days
Catheter-related bacteremia	
S. epidermidis or enterobacteriacae (uncomplicated)	< 8 days
S. aureus / Candida sp (uncomplicated)	14 days
S. aureus (complicated)	> 28 days

standard therapy group (13). Hence, consideration of a simple score at the bedside may favourably impact on the duration of treatment. In another study, a policy of antibiotic discontinuation for patients with VAP was compared with a conventional policy based on the treating physician's decision. In the "discontinuation" group, the antibiotics were discontinued in the patients with a noninfectious etiology for infiltrates or resolution of signs or symptoms suggesting active infection. This policy resulted in a shorter duration of antibiotic therapy (25).

Some authors elaborated strategies based on the microbiological results to guide the therapy duration. In a case-control study, antibiotics were discontinued if pathogen growth was < 10,000 colony forming units per ml on repeat bronchoalveolar lavage performed on day 4 of antibiotic therapy. Although the duration of treatment seems excessive in the control group (16 ± 7 days), the duration of antibiotic therapy was reduced by around 6 days in this group, as compared with a control group (26). However, one should note that the bacterial eradication on microbiological samples is not a relevant goal for guiding the treatment. In a prospective follow-up of patients with suspected VAP and culture-negative bronchoalveolar lavage,

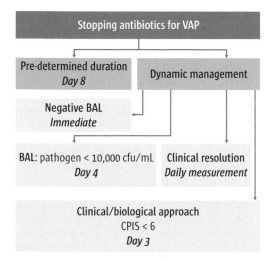

Fig. 2   Suggested parameters for stopping antibiotic for patients with ventilator-associated pneumonia BAL: bronchoalveolar lavage; CFU: colony-forming units; CPIS: clinical pulmonary infection score; VAP: ventilator-associated pneumonia

discontinuation of antibiotics before day 3 appears to be safe (27).

Procalcitonin is a biomarker which may be useful in the diagnosis of infection. It has been shown that serum procalcitonin levels are strong predictors for unfavorable outcome in patients with VAP (28). In patients with community-acquired pneumonia, procalcitonin guidance reduced total antibiotic exposure, antibiotic treatment duration, compared to patients treated according to guidelines (29). In a randomised clinical trial, antibiotics were discontinued when procalcitonin levels had decreased by 90 % or more. As compared to conventional regimen, patients assigned to the procalcitonin group had 3.5 days shorter median duration of antibiotic therapy. In patients in whom a decision could be taken based on serial procalcitonin measurements, procalcitonin guidance resulted in a 4-day reduction in the duration of antibiotic therapy (30). Although not demonstrated in the ICU patients, procalcitonin may be an option to discontinue antibiotic therapy in selected patients. Future investigations are required in order to guide the antibiotic therapy with biological markers.

Hence, the daily assessment of patients, using clinical, biological and microbiological examinations, can serve to determine the optimal duration of antibiotic therapy. However, in real life conditions, using a fixed pre-determined duration of antibiotic therapy according to the site of infection appears to be more realistic and easy-to-manage. Whatever the strategy, antibiotics can be safely ended in the stable patients with negative quantitative culture results (see fig. 2).

Conclusion

Starting early antibiotic therapy has been associated with improved outcomes in a few numbers of circumstances: septic shock, meningococcemia, patients with splenectomy or neutropenia. In the vast majority of cases, physicians have a window of 6–8 hours to collect microbiological samples before starting treatment. This situation is typically represented in the case of patients with VAP. In stable patients with fever, antibiotic therapy should be started after diagnosis has been made, rather within the 24 hours. Overall, one should underline the importance to treat only the patients clinically infected, and not those who are colonised without any clinical impact. The challenge is to have an anticipated approach in order to discontinue antibiotics as soon as possible. Antibiotic therapy should be ended each time the cultures remain negative. Excessive duration of treatment is associated with emergence of multidrug resistant pathogens, without evidence for any clinical improvement. Hence, the need for antibiotic continuation should be evaluated on a daily basis.

The authors

Marc Leone, MD, PhD
Claude Martin, MD
  Service d'Anesthésie et de Réanimation |
  Pôle Rauc, Hôpital Nord | Assistance Publique –
  Hôpitaux de Marseille and Faculté de Méde-
  cine de Marseille | Marseille, France

Address for correspondence
  Marc Leone
  Service d'Anesthésie et de Réanimation
  CHU Nord, Chemin des Bourrely
  13915 Marseille cedex 20, France
  e-mail: marc.leone@ap-hm.fr

References

1. Warren MM, Gibb AP, Walsh TS. Antibiotic prescription practice in an intensive care unit using twice-weekly collection of screening specimens: a prospective audit in a large UK teaching hospital. J Hosp Infect. 2005;59: 90–5.
2. Kumar A, Roberts D, Wood KE, Light B, Parrillo JE, Sharma S, Suppes R, Feinstein D, Zanotti S, Taiberg L, Gurka D, Kumar A, Cheang M. Duration of hypotension before initiation of effective antimicrobial therapy is the critical determinant of survival in human septic shock. Crit Care Med. 2006;34:1589–96.
3. Yu VL, Singh N. Excessive antimicrobial usage causes measurable harm to patients with suspected ventilator-associated pneumonia. Intensive Care Med. 2004;30:735–8.
4. Garnacho-Montero J, Aldabo-Pallas T, Garnacho-Montero C, Cayuela A, Jiménez R, Barroso S, Ortiz-Leyba C. Timing of adequate antibiotic therapy is a greater determinant of outcome than are TNF and IL-10 polymorphisms in patients with sepsis. Crit Care. 2006;10:R111.
5. Auburtin M, Wolff M, Charpentier J, Varon E, Le Tulzo Y, Girault C, Mohammedi I, Renard B, Mourvillier B, Bruneel F, Ricard JD, Timsit JF. Detrimental role of delayed antibiotic administration and penicillin-nonsusceptible strains in adult intensive care unit patients with pneumococcal meningitis: the PNEUMOREA prospective multicenter study. Crit Care Med. 2006;34:2758–65.
6. Aronin SI, Peduzzi P, Quagliarello VJ. Community-acquired bacterial meningitis: risk stratification for adverse clinical outcome and effect of antibiotic timing. Ann Intern Med. 1998;129:862–9.
7. Brigden ML, Pattullo AL. Prevention and management of overwhelming postsplenectomy infection – an update. Crit Care Med. 1999;27:836–42.
8. Natsch S, Kullberg BJ, van der Meer JW, Meis JF. Delay in administering the first dose of antibiotics in patients admitted to hospital with serious infections. Eur J Clin Microbiol Infect Dis. 1998;17:681–4.
9. Silber SH, Garrett C, Singh R, Sweeney A, Rosenberg C, Parachiv D, Okafo T. Early administration of antibiotics does not shorten time to clinical stability in patients with moderate-to-severe community-acquired pneumonia. Chest. 2003;124:1798–804.
10. Waterer GW, Kessler LA, Wunderink RG. Delayed administration of antibiotics and atypical presentation in community-acquired pneumonia. Chest. 2006;130:11–5.
11. Meehan TP, Fine MJ, Krumholz HM, Scinto JD, Galusha DH, Mockalis JT, Weber GF, Petrillo MK, Houck PM, Fine JM. Quality of care, process, and outcomes in elderly patients with pneumonia. JAMA. 1997;278:2080–4.
12. Pugin J, Auckenthaler R, Mili N, Janssens JP, Lew PD, Suter PM. Diagnosis of ventilator-associated pneumonia by bacteriologic analysis of bronchoscopic and nonbroncho-scopic "blind" bronchoalveolar lavage fluid. Am Rev Respir Dis. 1991;143(5 Pt 1):1121–9.
13. Singh N, Rogers P, Atwood CW, Wagener MM, Yu VL. Short-course empiric antibiotic therapy for patients with pulmonary infiltrates in the intensive care unit. A proposed solution for indiscriminate antibiotic prescription. Am J Respir Crit Care Med. 2000;162(2 Pt 1): 505–11.
14. Luna CM, Aruj P, Niederman MS, Garzón J, Violi D, Prignoni A, Ríos F, Baquero S, Gando S. Grupo Argentino de Estudio de la Neumonía Asociada al Respirador group. Appropriateness and delay to initiate therapy in ventilator-associated pneumonia. Eur Respir J. 2006;27: 158–64.
15. Lodise TP, McKinnon PS, Swiderski L, Rybak MJ. Outcomes analysis of delayed antibiotic treatment for hospital-acquired Staphylococcus aureus bacteremia. Clin Infect Dis. 2003;36:1418–23.
16. Kang CI, Kin SH, Kim HB, Park SW, Choe YJ, Oh MD, Kim EC, Choe KW. Pseudomonas aeruginosa bacteremia: risk factors for mortality and influence of delayed receipt of effective antimicrobial therapy on clinical outcome. Clin Infect Dis. 2003;37:745–51.
17. Lodise TP Jr, Patel N, Kwa A, Graves J, Furuno JP, Graffunder E, Lomaestro B, McGregor JC. Predictors of 30-day mortality among patients with Pseudomonas aeruginosa bloodstream infections: impact of delayed appropriate antibiotic selection. Antimicrob Agents Chemother. 2007;51:3510–5.

18. Leone M, Perrin AS, Granier I, Visintini P, Blasco V, Antonini F, Albanèse J, Martin C. A randomized trial of catheter change and short course of antibiotics for asymptomatic bacteriuria in catheterized ICU patients. Intensive Care Med. 2007;33:726–9.

19. Hedrick TL, Evans HL, Smith RL, McElearney ST, Schulman AS, Chong TW, Pruett TL, Sawyer RG. Can we define the ideal duration of antibiotic therapy? Surg Infect. (Larchmt) 2006;7:419–32.

20. Rubinstein E. Short antibiotic treatment courses or how short is short? Int J Antimicrob Agents. 2007;30 Suppl 1: S76–9.

21. Chastre J, Wolff M, Fagon JY, Chevret S, Thomas F, Wermert D, Clementi E, Gonzalez J, Jusserand D, Asfar P, Perrin D, Fieux F, Aubas S, PneumA Trial Group. Comparison of 8 vs 15 days of antibiotic therapy for ventilator-associated pneumonia in adults: a randomized trial. JAMA. 2003;290:2588–98.

22. Leone M, Garcin F, Bouvenot J, Boyadjev I, Visintini P, Albanèse J, Martin C. Ventilator-associated pneumonia: breaking the vicious circle of antibiotic overuse. Crit Care Med. 2007;35:379–85.

23. Runyon BA, McHutchison JG, Antillon MR, Akriviadis EA, Montano AA. Short-course versus long-course antibiotic treatment of spontaneous bacterial peritonitis. A randomized controlled study of 100 patients. Gastroenterology. 1991;100:1737–42.

24. Basoli A, Chirletti P, Cirino E, D'Ovidio NG, Doglietto GB, Giglio D, Giulini SM, Malizia A, Taffurelli M, Petrovic J, Ecari M, Italian Study Group. A prospective, double-blind, multicenter, randomized trial comparing ertapenem 3 vs ≥5 days in community-acquired intraabdominal infection. J Gastrointest Surg. 2008;12: 592–600.

25. Micek ST, Ward S, Fraser VJ, Kollef MH. A randomized controlled trial of an antibiotic discontinuation policy for clinically suspected ventilator-associated pneumonia. Chest. 2004;125:1791–9.

26. Mueller EW, Croce MA, Boucher BA, Hanes SD, Wood GC, Swanson JM, Chennault SK, Fabian TC. Repeat bronchoalveolar lavage to guide antibiotic duration for ventilator-associated pneumonia. J Trauma. 2007;63:1329–37.

27. Kollef MH, Kollef KE. Antibiotic utilization and outcomes for patients with clinically suspected ventilator-associated pneumonia and negative quantitative BAL culture results. Chest. 2005;128:2706–13.

28. Luyt CE, Guérin V, Combes A, Trouillet JL, Ayed SB, Bernard M, Gibert C, Chastre J. Procalcitonin kinetics as a prognostic marker of ventilator-associated pneumonia. Am J Respir Crit Care Med. 2005;171:48–53.

29. Christ-Crain M, Stolz D, Bingisser R, Müller C, Miedinger D, Huber PR, Zimmerli W, Harbarth S, Tamm M, Müller B. Procalcitonin guidance of antibiotic therapy in community-acquired pneumonia: a randomized trial. Am J Respir Crit Care Med. 2006;174:84–93.

30. Nobre V, Harbarth S, Graf JD, Rohner P, Pugin J. Use of procalcitonin to shorten antibiotic treatment duration in septic patients. A randomized trial. Am J Respir Crit Care Med. 2007;E-Pubmed.

Katharina Kranzer and Geoff Bellingan

MRSA control

There is huge variation in MRSA rates across Europe and the reasons for this are not clear. All agree that control policies should include effective barrier precautions and hand hygiene. Although increasingly used, the place for rapid screening remains to be clarified and the evidence for topical decontamination is also unclear with a real risk for mupirocin resistance. Screening is typically coupled with source isolation although this has been challenged in units where there is endemic MRSA. Most agree that effective restriction of antibiotic use is important although again it has been difficult to convincingly show a reduction in MRSA related to such changes.

Part of the problem in defining an ideal control policy is lack of knowledge of the processes through which transmission occurs. We do not properly understand the importance of different sites of the body as reservoirs, the degree to which the environment contributes to transmission, the relative risks of different management procedures or the importance of immunosuppression in acquisition. The other problem is that accurate subtyping of MRSA to allow detailed epidemiological studies to be made is complex and not routinely available.

Epidemiology

The prevalence of MRSA in hospitals varies greatly within geographical regions and hospitals. According to the most recent EARSS report half the European countries reported MRSA rates of up to 25 %. These countries included most of the southern countries, the United Kingdom and Ireland. Many northern European countries however had MRSA rates below 4 %. In most countries, despite the political profile of MRSA and other hospital acquired infections suggesting to the contrary, rates over the last few years have been largely stable. However, 27 out of 30 countries reported significantly higher MRSA proportions in ICU isolates compared to non-ICU isolates. In some southern European countries the proportion of MRSA found among ICU isolates was higher than 60 % (1). A recent study from the United Kingdom reported an MRSA prevalence among ICU patients of 16.2 % with great variability according to region (2).

There are multiple endemic MRSA (EMRSA) strains with variable abilities to compete with other strains. More recently dominance of EMRSA-15 and -16 both in ICU and non-ICU settings has been described in the UK and Ireland (3). Strains closely related to EMRSA-15 and -16 have been found in other European countries (4). The significance of the increased frequency of certain epidemic strains remains currently unclear, as do the reasons why other strains have declined.

Patients admitted to medical ICUs have a high frequency of risk factors associated with MRSA carriage e.g. multiple hospital admissions, older age, nursing home residency and renal replacement therapy. MRSA prevalence in this patient population is higher than in patients admitted to surgical ICUs or non-ICU wards (5). However ICU stay in itself is a risk factor for acquiring MRSA due to high antibiotic consumption, presence of intravenous devices and mechanical ventilation (6, 7). Decreased resistance to infection or "immunoparesis" must also play a part though the relative importance of this is not clear. Overall, most studies suggest MRSA colonisation and/or infection is associated with increased mortality and length of hospital stay (8–10).

MRSA transmission

The route of transmission of MRSA is poorly understood. There is surprisingly little data on the spread of a particular MRSA strain from patient to patient. How readily MRSA is disseminated from an index case to other patients in the ICU is not known, despite this being essential data for devising effective infection control strategies. It is thought that patients act as the main reservoirs. In patients colonised with MRSA the pathogen is found in wounds, gastrointestinal and respiratory tract and healthy skin, typically the anterior nares, hand and inguinal areas (11, 12). Healthcare workers colonised with MRSA in the nares might also act as a reservoir (13). More recent studies have shown that the ICU environment is commonly colonised with MRSA, including near bedside equipment (14–16). What is fascinating is that the strains found in this environment are often not the same as that found on the patient. MRSA remains viable on dry surface areas for weeks to months (17, 18) and some epidemic strains of MRSA have been shown to survive longer and at higher concentration than non-epidemic strains (19). The frequency of environmental contamination seems to depend on the body sites at which patients are colonised or infected (14). The situation is complicated by importation of community acquired MRSA (CA-MRSA) into healthcare facilities by patients and healthcare workers. More recently pigs and pig farmers have been found to be colonised with MRSA, raising concerns about a zoonotic reservoir for CA-MRSA (20).

The main vehicle through which patients acquire MRSA is thought to be from the hands of health care workers either contaminated through patient contact, from the environment or from their own noses (21). This implies poor hand hygiene is one of the most important factors in MRSA transmission. Evidence of transmission from the environment to patients has been inconclusive (12, 16). Some studies reported that cleaning a contaminated environment terminated MRSA outbreaks suggesting the environment plays a role in transmission (22). Health care workers colonised with MRSA have been found to be index cases in outbreaks (23) but direct transmission from one patient to another through contaminated hands of healthcare workers has not been commonly proven although this does not mean it is not potentially the most important place on which to focus infection control measures. As noted later, there are real difficulties in tracking MRSA transmission due to difficulty in identifying subtypes with sufficient accuracy for good epidemiology. Other routes for transmission can occur and here airborne spread of MRSA is of particular interest having been shown to occur during bed making and endotracheal suctioning (24).

Factors influencing individuals' susceptibility to become colonised remain unclear. Some patients never acquire MRSA even after prolonged ICU stays whereas others acquire the pathogen within days.

Despite uncertainty and lack of evidence concerning MRSA transmission infection control measures remain important. History has shown that infection control is achievable even under circumstances where neither the pathogen nor the route of transmission is clearly established (25).

Control measures

There are numerous local, national and international guidelines for prevention and control of MRSA, recommending various sets of control measures.

All of these guidelines recommend vigorous hand hygiene and contact precautions: using gloves, gowns and masks for direct contact with the patient. Non-compliance with hand hygiene and/or contact precautions remains a major problem. A review of 34 published studies showed that the average rate of adherence with recommended hand hygiene policies was only 40% (26). Similarly compliance with contact precautions was found to be less than 30% (27). However interventions to improve hand hygiene including education, motivation and introduction of alcohol/chlorhexidine hand hygiene solution were effective in increasing hand hygiene compliance and more importantly reduced nosocomial infections (28–30). There is some evidence that use of contact precautions reduces MRSA spread (31). Most studies investigating contact precautions implemented them as part of a wider infection control program variably including active surveillance, improved hand hygiene and eradication of MRSA carriage. Some of these studies were conducted in outbreak settings making generalisation of these results difficult (32).

The effectiveness of isolating MRSA positive patients either in single rooms or cohort nursing is debated. A review of studies investigating the effectiveness of isolation policies to reduced MRSA transmission concluded that the role of isolation measures alone cannot be assessed due to major methodological weaknesses and inadequate reporting in published research (32). More recently a study investigating single room isolation of MRSA positive patients in two ICUs in England showed no reduction in cross-infection (33), whereas studies from Italy and Germany showed an effect from isolation (34, 35). Isolation of patients in the English study was only initiated when surveillance cultures became positive for MRSA. Thus there was at least a 2-day window where patients were non-isolated despite being colonised with MRSA. This, together with the fact that measures implemented in ICUs are unlikely to change the broader epidemiology of MRSA in a hospital, might explain the ineffectiveness of single room isolation.

Most MRSA control programs such as "search & destroy" contain active surveillance as one of their components. In fact some of the other measures including barrier precautions and isolation only work if these patients are identified. Identification of patients colonised with MRSA has been shown to be incomplete using clinical microbiology cultures, as they fail to identify 85% of MRSA colonised patients (36). Active surveillance strategies differ with regards to screened population, screening sites, screening frequency and micro-

biology test applied to samples. Most ICUs obtain surveillance samples from patients on admission (37), but other hospital departments need to be more selective about whom to screen mainly due to cost implications. In Dutch hospitals MRSA screening is applied to health workers as well as patients (23). Nares and skin lesions are common screening sites (38); others include oral, inguinal and perianal areas (31, 36, 37). Results for MRSA detection by standard culture methods take 48–72 hours. Rapid culture-based tests and molecular-based PCR assays take 1–24 hours for results to become available (39–41). A recent study provided evidence that PCR screening on ICU admission is associated with significant reduction in MRSA transmission (42). However high costs and operator skill requirements remain obstacles to widespread use of molecular tests and cost-effectiveness has yet to be proven (43). In summary, active surveillance is part of most control programs without consistency regarding when, whom, where and how to screen due to lack of evidence.

Decontamination of carriers and environment is thought to reduce transmission by diminishing the MRSA reservoir. Decontamination has mainly been targeted at patients (37) and to a lesser extent health workers (23, 44). Nasal mupirocin and chlorhexidine for body wash are the most commonly used decontamination measures. Randomised controlled trials evaluating the efficacy of nasal mupirocin and washing with chlorhexidine for eradicating MRSA carriage in patients (45–47) and health care workers (44) showed mixed results. A Cochrane review concluded that there is insufficient evidence to support use of topical or systemic antimicrobial therapy (48). More recently intranasal mupirocin and chlorhexidine bathing in ICU was associated with decreased MRSA (49). Concerns have been raised about rates of mupirocin resistance both at institutional (50) and national level (51) in the context of widespread mupirocin use; resistance ranging from 4%–65% (52). There are no reports of chlorhexidine resistance so far (49). It is increasingly being questioned whether 0.5% chlorhexidine is sufficiently efficacious or whether 2% chlorhexidine should be used. Using a different approach, targeting the gastrointestinal tract as a potential reservoir and treating with oral vancomycin (53) has been shown to prevent MRSA pneumonia and to control an MRSA outbreak among ventilated patients; both studies are limited by sample size (54, 55).

Increased cleaning of environment and equipment has been shown to control MRSA outbreaks (56, 57). Cleaning the environment using detergents and disinfectants failed to eradicate MRSA (58). Decontamination of ICU with hydrogen peroxide vapor is highly effective in MRSA eradication, but rapid recontamination and the necessity to remove patients before decontamination makes this impracticable (58, 59). Studies investigating the association between cleaning, time and MRSA transmission are currently underway.

Once more evidence showing decontamination by use of topical or oral antibiotics as a measure to reduce MRSA transmission is sparse, but nevertheless it remains an integral part of most infection control programs.

It is generally accepted that antibiotic resistance is a consequence of antibiotic use. The high volumes of antibiotics used in agricultural settings have resulted in the development of resistance and the spread of resistant strains (60). High prevalence of MRSA in pigs and pig farmers (20) might be attributed to extensive use of antibiotics in pigs.

It is well-documented that use of antimicrobials is associated with increased incidence of MRSA acquisition both at an individual and group level (61, 62); quinolones being the most important culprit. Reduction of excessive and inappropriate antibiotic use has long been advocated. One study has found a short-term benefit of reduced antibiotic use on MRSA transmission (63), others have found little change in MRSA after implementation of antibiotic management programs (64). Rotation of antibiotics has been shown to be effective for controlling resistant Gram-negative infections (65), but influence on MRSA transmission is unknown.

Although the significance of antibiotics in the context of MRSA control is recognised, evidence-based strategies to reduce antibiotic usage at local and national level are currently lacking.

Control strategies are ineffective

Control measures are clearly ineffective as the spread of MRSA continues despite the existence of infection control programs and national and international guidelines. The failure of control programs might be due to intrinsic or extrinsic factors. Intrinsic factors are control measures that do not work. Examples are failure of MRSA decontamination with nasal mupurocin in patients colonised with mupurocin resistant strains (66, 67) or delay in screening results due to use of conventional culture techniques. Extrinsic factors are non-adherence or poor compliance by staff implementing, running and participating in control programs or factors not influenced by infection control programs. Extrinsic factors include non-compliance with hand hygiene and contact precautions by healthcare workers, lack of side rooms and functional pressure and importation of CA MRSA into health care facilities.

Control measures are hampered by lack of definitive tools for accurate epidemiological studies. Several molecular typing methods have been developed including phage typing, Pulse Field Gel Electrophoresis (PFGE) and Multi Locus Sequence Typing (MLST). Phage typing provides excellent discrimination between strains, but may change too rapidly to allow reliable identification of relationships between MRSA strains. There are also often a few dominant strains, so discriminating as to route of transmission can be difficult. Pulse field gel electrophoresis (PFGE) is good for investigating local epidemiology, but is labour-intensive, difficult to standardise between laboratories and remains a research tool. MLST is a molecular technique based on DNA sequencing of housekeeping genes that allows ready comparison between different laboratories but, due to the dominance of EMRSA-15 and -16 MLST lacks the discriminatory power for investigating local epidemiology of MRSA. These problems mean that is can be very difficult to determine the impact of specific changes unless there is a significant change in overall levels of MRSA.

This raises yet another issue, that of the "currency" used for reporting MRSA and the accuracy of such reporting. Many patients can be colonised with MRSA but remain without clinical infection hence when reporting MRSA it needs to be carefully defined whether this is colonisation or infection and how this is defined. This is important because even infection can be confusing, does this refer to bacteraemia alone or any infection and if any infection how is this defined? Many colonised patients are treated with anti-staphylococcal agents if they develop a new sepsis, despite lack of definitive evidence that it is MRSA causing this clinical change. This practice is not unreasonable as most patients with MRSA infection have preceding topical colonisation but does make it difficult to be accurate about the true incidence of MRSA and poses more uncertainly about results when studying impact of control measures. This problem is probably greatest when national death certification is used as the inclusion of MRSA on the death certificate, in the UK at least, is more as a matter of the political profile than clinical relevance of this pathogen.

Control strategies are effective

Infection control programs have been effective in reducing MRSA transmission in ICUs, but restriction of these programs to ICUs is unlikely to solve the problem. Some Scandinavian countries and The Netherlands have maintained low prevalence of nosocomial MRSA which is attributed to early implementation of nationwide "search & destroy" policies to identify carriage and specific infection control measures managing colonised patients (68, 69). Even though evaluation of the effectiveness of specific parts of infection control programs is difficult there is convincing evidence that packages of measures including surveillance, improved hand hygiene, contact precaution and isolation, decontamination of carriers and environment are effective in reducing MRSA transmission (31, 38, 70). The probability that the reduction in MRSA transmission is attributable to chance alone is unlikely considering the number of studies showing effectiveness of control programs. Encouraging reports from Belgium and Denmark show that control programs are capable of reducing prevalence (71, 72). A study using stochastic modeling concluded that endemicity could be reduced to less than 1 % in countries with high nosocomial endemicity within 6 years after concerted implementation of "search & control" strategies (73).

Cost of prevention and spread are higher in countries with high endemicity; the question of affordability remains crucial for implementation of control measures. Some studies suggest that costs of MRSA infection and spread exceeds the cost of prevention, however cost-effectiveness varies between countries, hospitals and departments depending on epidemiology, control program and resources available. Latent periods before the recognition of positive effects of control programs are considerable and present a challenge for staff motivation and continuing dedication and support from politicians.

Summary

MRSA is gaining an increasingly large profile although changes in MRSA by country may not reflect the column inches written. The backbone of MRSA control remains hand hygiene, coupled with rigorous contact precautions. The recent introduction of rapid screening tools are of interest but their place remains to be clarified, mainly because the relative importance of source isolation and the best method for topical decontamination (the two measured allied with any positive screen) have yet to be defined. A powerful, rapid and highly discriminatory test for MRSA subtypes to allow good epidemiological studies would be a major breakthrough. While we wait ... wash your hands.

Key points for clinical practice

- When reporting MRSA it needs to be clear whether this is colonisation or infection.
- All MRSA control measures include excellent hand hygiene and contact precautions.
- All units should monitor compliance with hand hygiene and contact precautions.
- The relative importance of routes for MRSA spread are not well documented though it is believed the main vehicle through which patients acquire MRSA is from the hands of healthcare workers.
- Other routes of spread, in particular airborne spread have been documented and should not be discounted.

The authors

Katharina Kranzer, MD
Geoff Bellingan MD, PhD, FRCP
    Critical Care Unit |
    University College London Hospitals HHS

Address for correspondence
Geoff Bellingan
Divisional Clinical Director
Critical Care and Theatres
Maples Bridge Link, Podium 3
University College London Hospitals NHS
Foundation Trust
235 Euston Rd
NW1 2BU London, UK
e-mail: geoff.bellingan@uclh.nhs.uk

References

1. EARSS. EARSS Annual Report 2006;2006.
2. Hails J, Kwaku F, Wilson AP, Bellingan G, Singer M. Large variation in MRSA policies, procedures and prevalence in English intensive care units: a questionnaire analysis. Intensive Care Med. 2003;29(3):481–3.
3. Johnson AP, Pearson A, Duckworth G. Surveillance and epidemiology of MRSA bacteraemia in the UK. J Antimicrob Chemother. 2005;56(3):455–62.
4. Potel C, Alvarez M, Alvarez P, Otero I, Fluiters E. Evolution, antimicrobial susceptibility and assignment to international clones of methicillin-resistant Staphylo-coccus aureus isolated over a 9-year period in two Spanish hospitals. Clin Microbiol Infect. 2007;13(7): 728–30.
5. Lucet JC, Chevret S, Durand-Zaleski I, Chastang C, Regnier B. Prevalence and risk factors for carriage of methicillin-resistant Staphylococcus aureus at admission to the intensive care unit: results of a multicenter study. Arch Intern Med. 2003;163(2):181–8.
6. Fridkin SK. Increasing prevalence of antimicrobial resistance in intensive care units. Crit Care Med. 2001; 29(4 Suppl):N64–8.
7. Ibelings MM, Bruining HA. Methicillin-resistant Staphylococcus aureus: acquisition and risk of death in patients in the intensive care unit. Eur J Surg. 1998;164(6):411–8.
8. Cosgrove SE, Qi Y, Kaye KS, Harbarth S, Karchmer AW, Carmeli Y. The impact of methicillin resistance in Staphylococcus aureus bacteremia on patient outcomes: mortality, length of stay, and hospital charges. Infect Control Hosp Epidemiol. 2005;26(2):166–74.
9. Cosgrove SE, Sakoulas G, Perencevich EN, Schwaber MJ, Karchmer AW, Carmeli Y. Comparison of mortality associated with methicillin-resistant and methicillin-sus-ceptible Staphylococcus aureus bacteremia: a meta-analysis. Clin Infect Dis. 2003;36(1):53–9.
10. Shorr AF, Combes A, Kollef MH, Chastre J. Methicillin-resistant Staphylococcus aureus prolongs intensive care unit stay in ventilator-associated pneumonia, despite initially appropriate antibiotic therapy. Crit Care Med. 2006;34(3):700–6.
11. Hill RL, Duckworth GJ, Casewell MW. Elimination of nasal carriage of methicillin-resistant Staphylococcus aureus with mupirocin during a hospital outbreak. J Antimicrob Chemother. 1988;22(3):377–84.
12. Coello R, Jimenez J, Garcia M, Arroyo P, Minguez D, Fernandez C et al. Prospective study of infection, colonization and carriage of methicillin-resistant Staphylococcus aureus in an outbreak affecting 990 patients. Eur J Clin Microbiol Infect Dis. 1994;13(1):74–81.
13. Reagan DR, Doebbeling BN, Pfaller MA, Sheetz CT, Houston AK, Hollis RJ et al. Elimination of coincident Staphylococcus aureus nasal and hand carriage with intranasal application of mupirocin calcium ointment. Ann Intern Med. 1991;114(2):101–6.
14. Boyce JM, Potter-Bynoe G, Chenevert C, King T. Environmen-tal contamination due to methicillin-resistant Staphylococ-cus aureus: possible infection control implications. Infect Control Hosp Epidemiol. 1997;18(9):622–7.
15. Hardy KJ, Oppenheim BA, Gossain S, Gao F, Hawkey PM. A study of the relationship between environmental contamination with methicillin-resistant Staphylococcus aureus (MRSA) and patients' acquisition of MRSA. Infect Control Hosp Epidemiol. 2006;27(2):127–32.
16. Wilson AP, Hayman S, Whitehouse T, Cepeda J, Kibbler C, Shaw S et al. Importance of the environment for patient acquisition of methicillin-resistant Staphylococcus aureus in the intensive care unit: a baseline study. Crit Care Med. 2007;35(10):2275–9.
17. Duckworth GJ, Jordens JZ. Adherence and survival properties of an epidemic methicillin-resistant strain of Staphylococc-us aureus compared with those of methicillin-sensitive strains. J Med Microbiol. 1990;32(3):195–200.
18. Beard-Pegler MA, Stubbs E, Vickery AM. Observations on the resistance to drying of staphylococcal strains. J Med Microbiol. 1988;26(4):251–5.
19. Farrington M, Brenwald N, Haines D, Walpole E. Resistance to desiccation and skin fatty acids in outbreak strains of methicillin-resistant Staphylococcus aureus. J Med Microbiol. 1992;36(1):56–60.
20. Khanna T, Friendship R, Dewey C, Weese JS. Methicillin resistant Staphylococcus aureus colonization in pigs and pig farmers. Vet Microbiol. 2007.
21. Cookson BD. Methicillin-resistant Staphylococcus aureus in the community: new battlefronts, or are the battles lost? Infect Control Hosp Epidemiol. 2000;21(6):398–403.
22. Cotterill S, Evans R, Fraise AP. An unusual source for an outbreak of methicillin-resistant Staphylococcus aureus on an intensive therapy unit. J Hosp Infect. 1996;32(3): 207–16.
23. Blok HE, Troelstra A, Kamp-Hopmans TE, Gigengack-Baars AC, Vandenbroucke-Grauls CM, Weersink AJ et al. Role of healthcare workers in outbreaks of methicillin-resistant Staphylococcus aureus: a 10-year evaluation from a Dutch university hospital. Infect Control Hosp Epidemiol. 2003;24(9):679–85.

24. Shiomori T, Miyamoto H, Makishima K, Yoshida M, Fujiyoshi T, Udaka T et al. Evaluation of bedmaking-related airborne and surface methicillin-resistant Staphylococcus aureus contamination. J Hosp Infect. 2002;50(1):30–5.

25. Mackie P, Sim F. Hypothesis, analysis and action in public health. Public Health. 2004;118(6):385–6.

26. Boyce JM, Pittet D. Guideline for Hand Hygiene in Health-Care Settings. Recommendations of the Healthcare Infection Control Practices Advisory Committee and the HICPAC/SHEA/APIC/IDSA Hand Hygiene Task Force. Society for Healthcare Epidemiology of America/Association for Professionals in Infection Control/Infectious Diseases Society of America. MMWR Recomm Rep. 2002;51(RR-16):1–45, quiz CE1–4.

27. Afif W, Huor P, Brassard P, Loo VG. Compliance with methicillin-resistant Staphylococcus aureus precautions in a teaching hospital. Am J Infect Control. 2002;30(7): 430–3.

28. Hugonnet S, Perneger TV, Pittet D. Alcohol-based handrub improves compliance with hand hygiene in intensive care units. Arch Intern Med. 2002;162(9): 1037–43.

29. Pittet D, Hugonnet S, Harbarth S, Mourouga P, Sauvan V, Touveneau S et al. Effectiveness of a hospital-wide programme to improve compliance with hand hygiene. Infection Control Programme. Lancet. 2000;356(9238): 1307–12.

30. Pittet D, Allegranzi B, Sax H, Dharan S, Pessoa-Silva CL, Donaldson L et al. Evidence-based model for hand transmission during patient care and the role of improved practices. Lancet Infect Dis. 2006;6(10):641–52.

31. Jernigan JA, Titus MG, Groschel DH, Getchell-White S, Farr BM. Effectiveness of contact isolation during a hospital outbreak of methicillin-resistant Staphylococcus aureus. Am J Epidemiol. 1996;143(5):496–504.

32. Cooper BS, Stone SP, Kibbler CC, Cookson BD, Roberts JA, Medley GF et al. Isolation measures in the hospital management of methicillin resistant Staphylococcus aureus (MRSA): systematic review of the literature. Bmj. 2004;329(7465):533.

33. Cepeda JA, Whitehouse T, Cooper B, Hails J, Jones K, Kwaku F et al. Isolation of patients in single rooms or cohorts to reduce spread of MRSA in intensive-care units: prospective two-centre study. Lancet. 2005; 365(9456):295–304.

34. Gastmeier P, Schwab F, Geffers C, Ruden H. To isolate or not to isolate? Analysis of data from the German Nosocomial Infection Surveillance System regarding the placement of patients with methicillin-resistant Staphylococcus aureus in private rooms in intensive care units. Infect Control Hosp Epidemiol. 2004;25(2):109–13.

35. Raineri E, Crema L, De Silvestri A, Acquarolo A, Albertario F, Carnevale G et al. Meticillin-resistant Staphylococcus aureus control in an intensive care unit: a 10 year analysis. J Hosp Infect. 2007;67(4):308–15.

36. Salgado CD, Farr BM. What proportion of hospital patients colonized with methicillin-resistant Staphylococcus aureus are identified by clinical microbiological cultures? Infect Control Hosp Epidemiol. 2006;27(2): 116–21.

37. Gould IM, MacKenzie FM, MacLennan G, Pacitti D, Watson EJ, Noble DW. Topical antimicrobials in combination with admission screening and barrier precautions to control endemic methicillin-resistant Staphylococcus aureus in an Intensive Care Unit. Int J Antimicrob Agents. 2007;29(5):536–43.

38. Lucet JC, Paoletti X, Lolom I, Paugam-Burtz C, Trouillet JL, Timsit JF et al. Successful long-term program for controlling methicillin-resistant Staphylococcus aureus in intensive care units. Intensive Care Med. 2005;31(8): 1051–7.

39. Johnson G, Millar MR, Matthews S, Skyrme M, Marsh P, Barringer E et al. Evaluation of BacLite Rapid MRSA, a rapid culture based screening test for the detection of ciprofloxacin and methicillin resistant S. aureus (MRSA) from screening swabs. BMC Microbiol. 2006;6: 83.

40. Harbarth S, Masuet-Aumatell C, Schrenzel J, Francois P, Akakpo C, Renzi G et al. Evaluation of rapid screening and pre-emptive contact isolation for detecting and controlling methicillin-resistant Staphylococcus aureus in critical care: an interventional cohort study. Crit Care. 2006;10(1):R25.

41. Huletsky A, Giroux R, Rossbach V, Gagnon M, Vaillancourt M, Bernier M et al. New real-time PCR assay for rapid detection of methicillin-resistant Staphylococcus aureus directly from specimens containing a mixture of staphylococci. J Clin Microbiol. 2004;42(5):1875–84.

42. Cunningham R, Jenks P, Northwood J, Wallis M, Ferguson S, Hunt S. Effect on MRSA transmission of rapid PCR testing of patients admitted to critical care. J Hosp Infect. 2007;65(1):24–8.

43. Hardy KJ, Szczepura A, Davies R, Bradbury A, Stallard N, Gossain S et al. A study of the efficacy and cost-effectiveness of MRSA screening and monitoring on surgical wards using a new, rapid molecular test (EMMS). BMC Health Serv Res. 2007;7:160.

44. Fernandez C, Gaspar C, Torrellas A, Vindel A, Saez-Nieto JA, Cruzet F et al. A double-blind, randomized, placebo-controlled clinical trial to evaluate the safety and efficacy of mupirocin calcium ointment for eliminating nasal carriage of Staphylococcus aureus among hospital personnel. J Antimicrob Chemother. 1995;35(3):399–408.

45. Wendt C, Schinke S, Wurttemberger M, Oberdorfer K, Bock-Hensley O, von Baum H. Value of whole-body washing with chlorhexidine for the eradication of methicillin-resistant Staphylococcus aureus: a randomized, placebo-controlled, double-blind clinical trial. Infect Control Hosp Epidemiol. 2007;28(9):1036–43.

46. Mody L, Kauffman CA, McNeil SA, Galecki AT, Bradley SF. Mupirocin-based decolonization of Staphylococcus aureus carriers in residents of 2 long-term care facilities: a randomized, double-blind, placebo-controlled trial. Clin Infect Dis. 2003;37(11):1467–74.

47. Harbarth S, Dharan S, Liassine N, Herrault P, Auckenthaler R, Pittet D. Randomized, placebo-controlled, double-blind trial to evaluate the efficacy of mupirocin for eradicating carriage of methicillin-resistant Staphylococcus aureus. Antimicrob Agents Chemother. 1999;43(6):1412–6.

48. Loeb M, Main C, Walker-Dilks C, Eady A. Antimicrobial drugs for treating methicillin-resistant Staphylococcus aureus colonization. Cochrane Database Syst Rev. 2003;(4):CD003340.

49. Ridenour G, Lampen R, Federspiel J, Kritchevsky S, Wong E, Climo M. Selective use of intranasal mupirocin and chlorhexidine bathing and the incidence of methicillin-resistant Staphylococcus aureus colonization and infection among intensive care unit patients. Infect Control Hosp Epidemiol. 2007;28(10):1155–61.

50. Miller MA, Dascal A, Portnoy J, Mendelson J. Development of mupirocin resistance among methicillin-resistant Staphylococcus aureus after widespread use of nasal mupirocin ointment. Infect Control Hosp Epidemiol. 1996;17(12):811–3.

51. Upton A, Lang S, Heffernan H. Mupirocin and Staphylococcus aureus: a recent paradigm of emerging antibiotic resistance. J Antimicrob Chemother. 2003;51(3):613–7.

52. Vivoni AM, Santos KR, de-Oliveira MP, Giambiagi-deMarval M, Ferreira AL, Riley LW et al. Mupirocin for controlling methicillin-resistant Staphylococcus aureus: lessons from a decade of use at a university hospital. Infect Control Hosp Epidemiol. 2005;26(7):662–7.

53. Boyce JM, Havill NL, Otter JA, Adams NM. Widespread environmental contamination associated with patients with diarrhea and methicillin-resistant Staphylococcus aureus colonization of the gastrointestinal tract. Infect Control Hosp Epidemiol. 2007;28(10):1142–7.

54. Silvestri L, van Saene HK, Milanese M, Fontana F, Gregori D, Oblach L et al. Prevention of MRSA pneumonia by oral vancomycin decontamination: a randomised trial. Eur Respir J. 2004;23(6):921–6.

55. Silvestri L, Milanese M, Oblach L, Fontana F, Gregori D, Guerra R et al. Enteral vancomycin to control methicillin-resistant Staphylococcus aureus outbreak in mechanically ventilated patients. Am J Infect Control. 2002;30(7):391–9.

56. Rampling A, Wiseman S, Davis L, Hyett AP, Walbridge AN, Payne GC et al. Evidence that hospital hygiene is important in the control of methicillin-resistant Staphylococcus aureus. J Hosp Infect. 2001;49(2):109–16.

57. Boyce JM. Environmental contamination makes an important contribution to hospital infection. J Hosp Infect. 2007;65 Suppl 2:50–4.

58. French GL, Otter JA, Shannon KP, Adams NM, Watling D, Parks MJ. Tackling contamination of the hospital environment by methicillin-resistant Staphylococcus aureus (MRSA): a comparison between conventional terminal cleaning and hydrogen peroxide vapour decontamination. J Hosp Infect. 2004;57(1):31–7.

59. Hardy KJ, Gossain S, Henderson N, Drugan C, Oppenheim BA, Gao F et al. Rapid recontamination with MRSA of the environment of an intensive care unit after decontamination with hydrogen peroxide vapour. J Hosp Infect. 2007;66(4):360–8.

60. Borgen K, Simonsen GS, Sundsfjord A, Wasteson Y, Olsvik O, Kruse H. Continuing high prevalence of VanA-type vancomycin-resistant enterococci on Norwegian poultry farms three years after avoparcin was banned. J Appl Microbiol. 2000;89(3):478–85.

61. Muller A, Mauny F, Talon D, Donnan PT, Harbarth S, Bertrand X. Effect of individual- and group-level antibiotic exposure on MRSA isolation: a multilevel analysis. J Antimicrob Chemother. 2006;58(4):878–81.

62. Muller AA, Mauny F, Bertin M, Cornette C, Lopez-Lozano JM, Viel JF et al. Relationship between spread of methicillin-resistant Staphylococcus aureus and antimicrobial use in a French university hospital. Clin Infect Dis. 2003;36(8):971–8.

63. Frank MO, Batteiger BE, Sorensen SJ, Hartstein AI, Carr JA, McComb JS et al. Decrease in expenditures and selected nosocomial infections following implementation of an antimicrobial-prescribing improvement program. Clin Perform Qual Health Care. 1997;5(4):180–8.

64. Cook PP, Catrou PG, Christie JD, Young PD, Polk RE. Reduction in broad-spectrum antimicrobial use associated with no improvement in hospital antibiogram. J Antimicrob Chemother. 2004;53(5):853–9.

65. Warren DK, Hill HA, Merz LR, Kollef MH, Hayden MK, Fraser VJ et al. Cycling empirical antimicrobial agents to prevent emergence of antimicrobial-resistant Gram-negative bacteria among intensive care unit patients. Crit Care Med. 2004;32(12):2450–6.

66. Cookson BD. The emergence of mupirocin resistance: a challenge to infection control and antibiotic prescribing practice. J Antimicrob Chemother. 1998;41(1):11–8.

67. Simor AE, Phillips E, McGeer A, Konvalinka A, Loeb M, Devlin HR et al. Randomized controlled trial of chlorhexidine gluconate for washing, intranasal mupirocin, and rifampin and doxycycline versus no treatment for the eradication of methicillin-resistant Staphylococcus aureus colonization. Clin Infect Dis. 2007;44(2):178–85.

68. Faria NA, Oliveira DC, Westh H, Monnet DL, Larsen AR, Skov R et al. Epidemiology of emerging methicillin-resistant Staphylococcus aureus (MRSA) in Denmark: a nationwide study in a country with low prevalence of MRSA infection. J Clin Microbiol. 2005;43(4):1836–42.

69. Vriens M, Blok H, Fluit A, Troelstra A, Van Der Werken C, Verhoef J. Costs associated with a strict policy to eradicate methicillin-resistant Staphylococcus aureus in a Dutch University Medical Center: a 10-year survey. Eur J Clin Microbiol Infect Dis. 2002;21(11):782–6.

70. Huang SS, Rifas-Shiman SL, Warren DK, Fraser VJ, Climo MW, Wong ES et al. Improving methicillin-resistant Staphylococcus aureus surveillance and reporting in intensive care units. J Infect Dis. 2007;195(3):330–8.

71. Struelens MJ, Ronveaux O, Jans B, Mertens R. Methicillin-resistant Staphylococcus aureus epidemiology and control in Belgian hospitals, 1991 to 1995. Groupement pour le Depistage, l'Etude et la Prevention des Infections Hospitalieres. Infect Control Hosp Epidemiol. 1996;17(8): 503–8.

72. Farr BM, Salgado CD, Karchmer TB, Sherertz RJ. Can antibiotic-resistant nosocomial infections be controlled? Lancet Infect Dis. 2001;1(1):38–45.

73. Bootsma MC, Diekmann O, Bonten MJ. Controlling methicillin-resistant Staphylococcus aureus: quantifying the effects of interventions and rapid diagnostic testing. Proc Natl Acad Sci USA. 2006;103(14):5620–5.

E. Neuro-intensive care

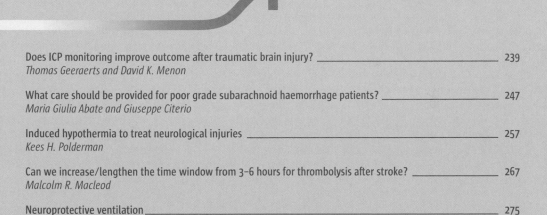

Thomas Geeraerts and David K. Menon

Does ICP monitoring improve outcome after traumatic brain injury?

Introduction

The first description of clinical continuous monitoring of intracranial pressure (ICP) was performed more than 50 years ago (1). ICP monitoring is now widely used for the care of severe traumatic brain injury (TBI) patients. In parallel the mortality in TBI patients has decreased over the past decade. Nevertheless, attributing the improved outcomes to ICP remains problematic as this question has never been subjected to a prospective, controlled randomised trial.

In Europe and the USA, a significant proportion (30 %) of severe TBI patients are admitted to non-neuro-surgical centres, and managed in general ICUs without neurosurgical facilities or ICP monitoring (2, 3). Moreover, a survey study showed that one fifth of neurosurgeons in Canada have a low level of confidence that, in severe TBI patients, routine ICP monitoring improves outcome (4). As ICP monitoring is an invasive and not risk-free method, the question of its efficacy in improving outcomes then remains of interest.

Arguments for the use of ICP monitoring after severe TBI to improve outcome

Raised ICP is frequent and difficult to predict after TBI

Lundberg showed in 1960 that ICP can rise to very high levels after TBI, and that this increase cannot be predicted by clinical examination (5, 6). Moreover, Lundberg also showed that ICP could vary considerably over time, highlighting the importance of having continuous recordings.

Prediction of high ICP remains difficult. In sedated (and paralyzed) patients, neurological examination has some limitations, due to lack of sensitivity at detecting changes in ICP (5, 7). The incidence of raised ICP is high (more than 50 %) for comatose patients (GCS ≤ 8) with an abnormal computed tomography (CT) scan (8). If the CT scan is normal, this incidence falls to 13 %. The head CT classification described by Marshall et al. was designed to predict the risk of elevated ICP and mortality rate (9). However, prediction of initial ICP or mean ICP remains difficult by examining ventricle size, sulcal size, transfalcine herniation, and gray/white differentiation (10, 11).

Compressed or absent basal cisterns indicate a threefold risk of raised intracranial pressure and is related to outcome. Subarachnoid hemorrhage on CT is also significantly correlated with the risk of elevated ICP (12). Nevertheless, raised ICP can occur in comatose TBI patients with normal initial CT scan (13). Therefore elevated ICP can not be ruled out with a normal CT scan (14, 15). Routinely repeated CT scan appears to be time-consuming and costly, and in the absence of clinical indicators this strategy does not alter patient management (16).

Raised ICP is associated with poor neurological outcomes

The association between elevated ICP and poor neurological outcome after TBI has been clearly demonstrated since the 1980s (17–20). As brain injury can lead to impairment or loss of autoregulation, raised ICP can impair cerebral blood flow and contribute to secondary ischemic damage to the brain. The ICP threshold related to neurological outcomes is probably 20–25 mmHg (21). The time of ICP over 20 mmHg is a strong predictor of outcomes after TBI (22, 23).

Early detection of secondary insults

Raised ICP after TBI reflects the altered cerebral compliance in relation with post-traumatic brain edema, contusions, hematoma or hydrocephalus. Increase in ICP can be the first indicator of worsening intracranial lesions after TBI needing surgical evacuation. In a study of 110 patients, identified as high risk based on the presence of traumatic subarachnoid haemorrhage, ICP elevation was the first indication of clinical deterioration in 20% of patients, about a quarter of whom required surgical intervention (24). The importance of early treatment of secondary insults after TBI is well-known (25). Early detection and evacuation of intracranial lesions with significant mass effect is an essential part of the treatment of TBI patients. ICP monitoring has been shown to help decision to surgery (26). However the potential benefit of very early ICP monitoring (< 6 hrs post-TBI) has never been investigated.

ICP monitoring allows goal-directed therapy

Information obtained by ICP monitoring allows therapeutic management. Eddy et al. showed in a retrospective study of 98 TBI patients that 81% of patients had therapeutic interventions based on ICP monitoring (27). There is a large body of clinical evidence showing that protocol-driven neurocritical care improves outcomes. Saul et al., in a retrospective study comparing two periods (before and after aggressive treatment based on ICP monitoring), showed a significant reduced mortality during the aggressive treatment period (28). Aggressive therapeutic protocols, with ICP monitoring as an integral part of the patient management, showed an improved survival after TBI (28, 29). Justification of ICP monitoring received important support when the pivotal role of cerebral perfusion pressure (CPP) was shown by Rosner (30). CPP is the difference between mean arterial pressure (MAP) and ICP. CPP actively maintained above 70 mmHg was associated with a low mortality rate in severe TBI patients (21%) (30). When CPP is below the lower limit of pressure autoregulation, cerebral blood flow becomes dependant on CPP, and cerebral ischemia can occur (31). Patel et al. in a retrospective study comparing two periods (pre- and post- neuroscience critical care unit creation with ICP/CPP driven protocols) demonstrated improvement in favorable neurological outcomes in severe TBI patients (59.6% vs. 40.4%, p = 0.036) (32). This difference between both periods could not be attributed to differences in trauma severity, age, or incidence of arterial hypotension at admission. During the second period ICP was monitored in 95% of patients, whereas in the initial period it was in 59% of patients. The overall mortality was not different between both periods. In another large retrospective study also performed in the UK, Patel showed that the mortality of TBI patients with comparable injury severity was lower when they were admitted to neurosurgical center, rather than retained in a referring non-specialist hospital (2). Even for patients not requiring surgical treatment, outcome may be improved by specialist neuro-ICU. In the USA, severe TBI patients admitted to "aggressive" trauma centers (in which ICP monitoring is used for more than 50% of patients) have a reduced mortality compared to non-aggressive trauma centers (27% vs. 45%) (see fig. 1) (33). These data are particularly interesting, since centres in this study were characterised based on a threshold of using ICP monitoring in > 50 % of TBI patients, suggesting a central role for such monitoring as a part of specialist neuro-critical care in TBI.

Outcome after TBI seems to be improved by organised secondary insults program based on ICP/CPP monitoring (34). Fakhry et al. in a retrospective comparison of outcome and mortality after severe TBI found that implementation of protocols based on the Brain Trauma Foundation guidelines with high compliance significantly decrease mortality and increase functional outcome (35). For ICP monitoring, these guidelines are (36):

- ICP should be monitored in all salvageable patients with a severe traumatic brain injury (GCS score of 3–8 after resuscitation) and an abnormal computed tomography (CT) scan (Level II recommendations).
- ICP monitoring is indicated in patients with severe TBI with a normal CT scan if two or

more of the following features are noted at admission: age over 40 years, unilateral or bilateral motor posturing, or systolic blood pressure <90 mmHg (Level III recommendations).

ICP can be therapeutic and avoid excessive therapy

By allowing the release of cerebrospinal fluid (CSF), ventriculostomy can reduce ICP and be a first therapeutic step in case of raised ICP. Intraparenchymal catheters do not permit CSF drainage. In centers using routinely CSF drainage for ICP control, the mortality after TBI is lower than in those using it never or occasionally (see fig. 2) (37). ICP monitoring could avoid excessive therapy. The administration of therapy based on "guidelines principles" and monitoring of ICP, could minimise the application of barbiturates and prolonged hyperventilation (38). However, this fact was not confirmed by other studies.

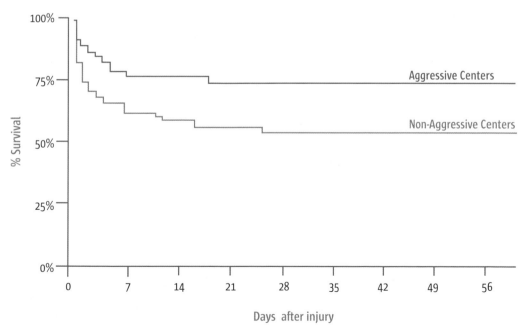

Fig. 1   Kaplan-Meyer curve (% of survival) for severe TBI patients managed in aggressive (in which ICP monitoring is used for more than 50 % of patients) and in non-aggressive trauma centers. Adapted from: Bulger EM, Nathens AB, Rivara FP, Moore M, MacKenzie EJ, Jurkovich GJ. Management of severe head injury: institutional variations in care and effect on outcome. Crit Care Med. 2002;30(8):1870–6. With kind permission from Lippincott Williams & Wilkins.

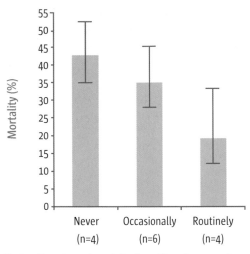

Fig. 2   Mean (range) mortality from US centers regarding the use of CSF drainage for ICP control. Modified from: The Brain Trauma Foundation. Guidelines for the Management of Severe Traumatic Brain Injury. J Neurotrauma. 2007;24:S1–S106

been described as a complication in the case of major coagulation disorders (42).

ICP monitoring malfunction may occur when ventricles collapse around ventriculostomy or in the case of subarachnoidal haemorrhage. Intraventricular drains remain the gold standard of ICP monitoring (43), mainly because they measure the global ICP and can be recalibrated. Intraparenchymal probes (fiber optic or strain gauge catheters) present a small drift of the zero reference as less than 1 mmHg after 5 days (43).

Infections of ICP probes are not exceptional, with an increased risk when ventriculostomies are used. Ventriculostomy-related infections can also occur with a 6–11% incidence (44). In TBI patients, 85% of ventriculitis related to ICP occurred in patients who have been monitored over 5 days (44). For intraparenchymal probes, the incidence of ventriculitis is lower (< 3%) (45). The incidence of bacterial colonisation of intraparenchymal probes (positive cultures without clinical signs of ventriculitis) is approx. 10% (45, 46).

Arguments against the ICP use after severe TBI to improve outcome

Lack of randomised control study

A publication from the *Cochrane Collaboration* in 2001 found no studies meeting the criteria of randomised controlled studies of real-time ICP monitoring by invasive or semi-invasive means in acute coma (traumatic or nontraumatic aetiology) versus no ICP monitoring (that is, clinical assessment of ICP) (39). This lack of level I evidence for the use of ICP monitoring is probably one of the principal explanations for the important variation in the use of ICP monitoring among trauma centers.

ICP monitoring is not risk-free

The first complication is failure of correct placement of ventriculostomy in the case of collapsed ventricles. The incidence of failure can rise to 10%, even in an experienced team (8, 40). In the case of multiple attempts, the risk of intracerebral haematoma increases to 2–4% (8, 41). Intracerebral hemorrhages after ICP placement have also

Outcome without ICP monitoring

Stuart et al. in 1983 reported a prospective series of 100 consecutive severe head injuries without ICP monitoring. The mortality rate was 34% and the outcome compared favorably with series in which ICP monitoring was performed (47).

More recently, Cremer et al., in a retrospective observational study of 333 patients with severe TBI from 1996 to 2001, comparing two trauma centers in the Netherlands, found that in survivors beyond 24 hrs following TBI, ICP/CPP-guided intensive care was not associated with improved functional status or survival compared to clinical and CT findings-guided intensive care (48). ICP monitoring was used in 67% of patients in ICP/CPP-guided intensive care, and in 0% of patients in the other center, in which MAP was maintained to 90 mmHg. Interestingly, sedative, vasopressors, mannitol and barbiturates were used more frequently in the ICP/CPP-guided intensive care unit. In this study, the increased intensity of care induced by ICP/CPP guided therapy was not associated with better outcomes.

ICP/CPP guided therapies are not risk-free

A monitoring method can not be separated from therapeutic implications, which may have beneficial or deleterious consequences. One randomised clinical trial has examined the consequences of different levels of CPP (49). In one group CPP was kept > 70 mmHg, and in the other it was kept > 50 mmHg. The incidence of secondary ischemic events was reduced by approximately 50 % in the high CPP group. However, the incidence of acute respiratory distress syndrome also increased fivefold in this group. Cardiopulmonary complications related to CPP guided therapy could have counterbalanced the beneficial effect, as the long-term neurological outcome was not improved. Similarly, hyperventilation, when inappropriately applied, may increase the risk of critical ischaemia in the injured brain (50).

Methological considerations

In critical care patients, the question of the effect of monitoring on outcome is difficult to answer. In general, randomised controlled trials study the effect of therapeutic measures, not of monitoring tools. Studies demonstrating a positive effect due to monitoring strategy are lacking. For example, there is no evidence that pulse oximetry affects the outcome of anaesthesia, but it has been adopted all over the world in clinical practice (51).

The Brain Trauma Foundation, in a recent analysis of this issue, made the following point:

> "A randomized trial of ICP monitoring with and without treatment is unlikely to be carried out. Similarly, a trial for treating or not treating systemic hypotension is not likely. Both hypotension and raised ICP are the leading causes of death in severe TBI, and are treated if either is suspected, regardless of whether ICP or blood pressure is monitored." (36).

The important methodological limitations of the published studies (not randomised, not controlled, comparison to historical series) are shared by pro and con ICP positions. In TBI patients a randomised controlled trial to show a 10 % reduction in mortality from 35 to 25 % (α = 5 %, power = 80 %) would require a sample size of 768 patients (52). Such a study should be multicentric and last more than 4 years. The fact that severe TBI patients are heterogeneous, and that optimal CPP (and ischemic threshold) could significantly differ among patients and over time complicates this study design.

Moreover, it is almost impossible to discriminate between the effect of a monitoring strategy and the therapy induced by this monitoring. How does one evaluate the effect of a monitoring tool without taking into consideration the related therapeutic procedures? As ICP monitoring becomes an integral part of the therapeutic management of severe TBI patients, the question *"Does ICP monitoring improve outcome?"* is probably not adequately focused enough to provide the basis for a useful study. What we need is better evidence on ICP thresholds and treatment modalities that result in improved outcomes. The first of these issues has been addressed in some previous studies, and a threshold of 20–25 mmHg seems sensible in an overall analysis. However, not all of the interventions used to decrease ICP are equally efficacious. Perhaps more importantly, the range and severity of side effects varies between ICP lowering interventions. A rational use of ICP as a guide to therapy must not only take account of the absolute threshold for treatment, but also the risk/benefit balance of the intervention used to treat it. Thus, hypothermia has no benefit when used prophylactically in all patients with TBI (53), but can clearly improve outcome when intracranial hypertension is refractory to therapy (54). This suggests that, for the side effects of hypothermia to be mitigated, its beneficial impact needs to be of a substantial magnitude, as is the case in the patients with very high ICP. This proposition is further supported by the finding that outcome is *worsened* by using hypothermia in patients with low ICP following TBI (55).

A consideration of these issues suggests more appropriate research question(s). For example, in the context of hypothermia, a critical question might be "Can ICP thresholds be used to identify patients in whom the risks of hypothermia are offset by physiological benefit, with an overall improvement in clinical outcome?".

Conclusion

ICP, as a monitoring tool, could not by itself improve outcomes. Information obtained by ICP monitoring is critical, and allows informed therapeutic decisions. ICP monitors should be placed in patients at risk for raised ICP, if the conditions leading to raised ICP are amenable, and if a care plane is associated with ICP measurements. ICP/CPP driven protocols are the cornerstone of modern neuro-ICU practice, and may improve outcome after TBI. However, intracranial pressure monitoring is a tool, and we need to think of it as such – its impact on outcomes will be determined by the way in which it is used.

Summary

Raised ICP after severe TBI is frequent in relation to altered cerebral compliance. Information obtained by ICP monitoring allows early detection of high ICP, and goal-directed therapy. There is a large body of clinical evidence showing that protocol-driven neurocritical care improves outcomes. However, ICP monitoring and ICP/CPP-guided therapy are not risk-free. A monitoring method can not be separated from therapeutic implications, which may have beneficial or deleterious consequences. A rational use of ICP as a guide to therapy must not only take account of the absolute threshold for treatment, but also the risk/benefit balance of the intervention used to treat it.

Key points for clinical practice

- *Raised ICP is associated with poor neurological outcomes after TBI.*
- *Prediction of high ICP using clinical or radiological signs remains difficult.*
- *Early detection and treatment of high ICP is an essential part of the treatment of TBI patients.*
- *Outcome after TBI can be improved by an organised secondary insults program based on ICP/CPP monitoring.*
- *Not all of the interventions used to decrease ICP are equally efficacious or deleterious.*
- *ICP should be monitored after severe TBI (GCS score of 3–8 after resuscitation)*
  - *in all salvageable patients with an abnormal computed tomography (CT) scan (Level II recommendations of the Brain Trauma Foundation)*
  - *in patients with a normal CT scan if two or more of the following features are noted at admission: age*

over 40 years, unilateral or bilateral motor posturing, or systolic blood pressure < 90 mmHg (Level III recommendations).

Acknowledgments

Professor David K. Menon was supported by grants from the Medical Research Council (UK), Royal College of Anaesthetists, Wellcome Trust, NIHR, and Queens' College Cambridge. Dr Thomas Geeraerts was supported by grants from the Société Française d'Anesthésie et de Réanimation (SFAR) and from Journées d'Enseignement Post-Universitaire d'Anesthésie-Réanimation (JEPU)-Novo Nordisk.

The authors

Thomas Geeraerts, MD, PhD
David K. Menon, MD, PhD, FRCP, FRCA, FMedSci
University Department of Anaesthesia | Addenbrooke's Hospital and University of Cambridge | Cambridge CB2 2QQ, UK

Address for correspondence
David K. Menon
University Department of Anaesthesia
Addenbrooke's Hospital and
University of Cambridge
Cambridge CB2 2QQ, UK
e-mail: dkm13@wbic.cam.ac.uk

References

1. Guillaume J, Janny P. Continuous intracranial manometry; physiopathologic and clinical significance of the method. Presse Med. 1951;59:953–5.
2. Patel HC, Bouamra O, Woodford M, King AT, Yates DW, Lecky FE. Trends in head injury outcome from 1989 to 2003 and the effect of neurosurgical care: an observational study. Lancet. 2005;366:1538–44.
3. MacKenzie EJ, Rivara FP, Jurkovich GJ, Nathens AB, Frey KP, Egleston BL et al. A national evaluation of the effect of trauma-center care on mortality. N Engl J Med. 2006; 354:366–78.
4. Sahjpaul R, Girotti M. Intracranial pressure monitoring in severe traumatic brain injury – results of a Canadian survey. Can J Neurol Sci. 2000;27:143–7.
5. Lundberg N. Continuous recording and control of ventricular fluid pressure in neurosurgical practice. Acta Psychiatr Scand Suppl. 1960;36:1–193.

6. Lundberg N, Troupp H, Lorin H. Continuous recording of the ventricular-fluid pressure in patients with severe acute traumatic brain injury. A preliminary report. J Neurosurg. 1965;22:581–90.

7. Suarez JI. Outcome in neurocritical care: advances in monitoring and treatment and effect of a specialized neurocritical care team. Crit Care Med. 2006;34:S232–8.

8. Narayan RK, Kishore PR, Becker DP, Ward JD, Enas GG, Greenberg RP et al. Intracranial pressure: to monitor or not to monitor? A review of our experience with severe head injury. J Neurosurg. 1982;56:650–9.

9. Marshall LF, Marshall SB, Klauber MR, Van Berkum Clark M, Eisenberg H, Jane JA et al. The diagnosis of head injury requires a classification based on computed axial tomography. J Neurotrauma. 1992;9 Suppl 1:S287–92.

10. Miller MT, Pasquale M, Kurek S, White J, Martin P, Bannon K et al. Initial head computed tomographic scan characteristics have a linear relationship with initial intracranial pressure after trauma. J Trauma. 2004;56: 967–72.

11. Hiler M, Czosnyka M, Hutchinson P, Balestreri M, Smielewski P, Matta B et al. Predictive value of initial computerized tomography scan, intracranial pressure, and state of autoregulation in patients with traumatic brain injury. J Neurosurg. 2006;104:731–7.

12. Eisenberg HM, Gary HE, Jr., Aldrich EF, Saydjari C, Turner B, Foulkes MA et al. Initial CT findings in 753 patients with severe head injury. A report from the NIH Traumatic Coma Data Bank. J Neurosurg. 1990;73:688–98.

13. O'Sullivan MG, Statham PF, Jones PA, Miller JD, Dearden NM, Piper IR et al. Role of intracranial pressure monitoring in severely head-injured patients without signs of intracranial hypertension on initial computerized tomography. J Neurosurg. 1994;80:46–50.

14. Lobato RD, Sarabia R, Rivas JJ, Cordobes F, Castro S, Munoz MJ et al. Normal computerized tomography scans in severe head injury. Prognostic and clinical management implications. J Neurosurg. 1986;65:784–9.

15. Stein SC, Spettell C, Young G, Ross SE. Delayed and progressive brain injury in closed-head trauma: radiological demonstration. Neurosurgery. 1993;32: 25–30.

16. Kaups KL, Davis JW, Parks SN. Routinely repeated computed tomography after blunt head trauma: does it benefit patients? J Trauma. 2004;56:475–80.

17. Miller JD, Becker DP, Ward JD, Sullivan HG, Adams WE, Rosner MJ. Significance of intracranial hypertension in severe head injury. J Neurosurg. 1977;47:503–16.

18. Choi SC, Muizelaar JP, Barnes TY, Marmarou A, Brooks DM, Young HF. Prediction tree for severely head-injured patients. J Neurosurg. 1991;75:251–5.

19. Narayan RK, Greenberg RP, Miller JD, Enas GG, Choi SC, Kishore PR et al. Improved confidence of outcome prediction in severe head injury. A comparative analysis of the clinical examination, multimodality evoked potentials, CT scanning, and intracranial pressure. J Neurosurg. 1981;54:751–62.

20. Balestreri M, Czosnyka M, Hutchinson P, Steiner LA, Hiler M, Smielewski P et al. Impact of intracranial pressure and cerebral perfusion pressure on severe disability and mortality after head injury. Neurocrit Care. 2006;4:8–13.

21. Struchen MA, Hannay HJ, Contant CF, Robertson CS. The relation between acute physiological variables and outcome on the Glasgow Outcome Scale and Disability Rating Scale following severe traumatic brain injury. J Neurotrauma. 2001;18:115–25.

22. Juul N, Morris GF, Marshall SB, Marshall LF. Intracranial hypertension and cerebral perfusion pressure: influence on neurological deterioration and outcome in severe head injury. The Executive Committee of the International Selfotel Trial. J Neurosurg. 2000;92:1–6.

23. Marmarou A, Saad A, Aygok G, Rigsbee M. Contribution of raised ICP and hypotension to CPP reduction in severe brain injury: correlation to outcome. Acta Neurochir Suppl. 2005;95:277–80.

24. Servadei F, Antonelli V, Giuliani G, Fainardi E, Chieregato A, Targa L. Evolving lesions in traumatic subarachnoid hemorrhage: prospective study of 110 patients with emphasis on the role of ICP monitoring. Acta Neurochir Suppl. 2002;81:81–2.

25. Chesnut RM, Marshall LF, Klauber MR, Blunt BA, Baldwin N, Eisenberg HM et al. The role of secondary brain injury in determining outcome from severe head injury. J Trauma. 1993;34:216–22.

26. Strege RJ, Lang EW, Stark AM, Scheffner H, Fritsch MJ, Barth H et al. Cerebral edema leading to decompressive craniectomy: an assessment of the preceding clinical and neuromonitoring trends. Neurol Res. 2003;25:510–5.

27. Eddy VA, Vitsky JL, Rutherford EJ, Morris JA, Jr. Aggressive use of ICP monitoring is safe and alters patient care. Am Surg. 1995;61:24–9.

28. Saul TG, Ducker TB. Effect of intracranial pressure monitoring and aggressive treatment on mortality in severe head injury. J Neurosurg. 1982;56:498–503.

29. Colohan AR, Alves WM, Gross CR, Torner JC, Mehta VS, Tandon PN et al. Head injury mortality in two centers with different emergency medical services and intensive care. J Neurosurg. 1989;71:202–7.

30. Rosner MJ, Daughton S. Cerebral perfusion pressure management in head injury. J Trauma. 1990;30:933–40.

31. Robertson CS. Management of cerebral perfusion pressure after traumatic brain injury. Anesthesiology. 2001;95:1513–7.

32. Patel HC, Menon DK, Tebbs S, Hawker R, Hutchinson PJ, Kirkpatrick PJ. Specialist neurocritical care and outcome from head injury. Intensive Care Med. 2002;28:547–53.

33. Bulger EM, Nathens AB, Rivara FP, Moore M, MacKenzie EJ, Jurkovich GJ. Management of severe head injury: institutional variations in care and effect on outcome. Crit Care Med. 2002;30(8):1870–6.

34. Elf K, Nilsson P, Enblad P. Outcome after traumatic brain injury improved by an organized secondary insult program and standardized neurointensive care. Crit Care Med. 2002;30:2129–34.

35. Fakhry SM, Trask AL, Waller MA, Watts DD. Management of brain-injured patients by an evidence-based medicine protocol improves outcomes and decreases hospital charges. J Trauma. 2004;56:492–9.

36. The Brain Trauma Foundation. Guidelines for the Management of Severe Traumatic Brain Injury. J Neurotrauma. 2007;24:S1–S106.

37. The Brain Trauma Foundation. Indications for intracranial pressure monitoring. J Neurotrauma. 1996;13:667–79.

38. Vukic M, Negovetic L, Kovac D, Ghajar J, Glavic Z, Gopcevic A. The effect of implementation of guidelines for the management of severe head injury on patient treatment and outcome. Acta Neurochir (Wien) 1999; 141:1203–8.

39. Forsyth RJ, Rodriguez B. Routine intracranial pressure monitoring in acute coma. Cochrane Database of Systematic Reviews. 2001;Issue 3.

40. Clark WC, Muhlbauer MS, Lowrey R, Hartman M, Ray MW, Watridge CB. Complications of intracranial pressure monitoring in trauma patients. Neurosurgery. 1989; 25:20–4.

41. Ghajar J. Intracranial pressure monitoring techniques. New Horiz. 1995;3:395–9.

42. Blei AT, Olafsson S, Webster S, Levy R. Complications of intracranial pressure monitoring in fulminant hepatic failure. Lancet. 1993;341:690–1.

43. Steiner LA, Andrews PJ. Monitoring the injured brain: ICP and CBF. Br J Anaesth. 2006;97:26–38.

44. Mayhall CG, Archer NH, Lamb VA, Spadora AC, Baggett JW, Ward JD et al. Ventriculostomy-related infections. A prospective epidemiologic study. N Engl J Med. 1984;310: 553–9.

45. Martinez-Mañas RM, Santamarta D, de Campos JM, Ferrer E. Camino intracranial pressure monitor: prospective study of accuracy and complications. J Neurol Neurosurg Psychiatry. 2000;69:82–6.

46. Rosner MJ, Becker DP. ICP monitoring: complications and associated factors. Clin Neurosurg. 1976;23:494–516.

47. Stuart GG, Merry GS, Smith JA, Yelland JD. Severe head injury managed without intracranial pressure monitoring. J Neurosurg. 1983;59:601–5.

48. Cremer OL, van Dijk GW, van Wensen E, Brekelmans GJ, Moons KG, Leenen LP et al. Effect of intracranial pressure monitoring and targeted intensive care on functional outcome after severe head injury. Crit Care Med. 2005; 33:2207–13.

49. Robertson CS, Valadka AB, Hannay HJ, Contant CF, Gopinath SP, Cormio M et al. Prevention of secondary ischemic insults after severe head injury. Crit Care Med. 1999;27:2086–95.

50. Muizelaar JP, Marmarou A, Ward JD, Kontos HA, Choi SC, Becker DP et al. Adverse effects of prolonged hyperventilation in patients with severe head injury: a randomized clinical trial. J Neurosurg. 1991;75:731–9.

51. Pedersen T, Pedersen P, Moller AM. Pulse oximetry for perioperative monitoring. Cochrane Database Syst Rev. 2001:CD002013.

52. The Brain Trauma Foundation. The American Association of Neurological Surgeons. The Joint Section on Neurotrauma and Critical Care. Indications for intracranial pressure monitoring. J Neurotrauma. 2000;17:479–91.

53. Clifton GL, Miller ER, Choi SC, Levin HS, McCauley S, Smith KRJ et al. Lack of effect of induction of hypothermia after acute brain injury. N Engl J Med. 2001;344: ≤556–63.

54. Polderman KH, Tjong Tjin Joe R, Peederman SM, Vandertop WP, Girbes AR. Effects of therapeutic hypothermia on intracranial pressure and outcome in patients with severe head injury. Intensive Care Med. 2002;28:1563–73.

55. Shiozaki T, Hayakata T, Taneda M, Nakajima Y, Hashiguchi N, Fujimi S et al. A muticenter prospective randomized controlled trial of the efficacy of mild hypothermia for severe head injury patients with low intracranial pressure. Mild Hypothermia Study Group in Japan. J Neurosurg. 2001;94:50–4.

Maria Giulia Abate and Giuseppe Citerio

What care should be provided for poor grade subarachnoid haemorrhage patients?

Introduction to the topic

Spontaneous subarachnoid haemorrhage (SAH) is a neurosurgical emergency caused by the extravasated blood in the subarachnoid space (1), in 85% of cases arising from the rupture of an intracranial aneurysm. The worldwide incidence of SAH is about 9/100,000/year (2), accounting for one in every 20 strokes.

In recent decades, SAH management has become increasingly multidisciplinary, involving neurosurgeons, neuroradiologists, anaesthesiologists and intensivists. After the initial stabilisation, aimed at restoring respiratory and cardiovascular function, the main treatment goals are the prevention and treatment of rebleeding (by either coiling or clipping) and the management of neurological and extracranial complications.

It is widely recognised that clinical outcome of patients with SAH is influenced by factors related to the patient physiology, the severity of the bleeding itself and treatments provided. Neurological status at the time of the bleed has significant prognostic implications with more severe cases, i.e. poor-grade or high-grade (defined as WFNS grades (3) IV and V), more likely to develop complications along with a longer stay in ICU and to have a poor outcome. Nowadays the prognosis remains poor: the overall case fatality rate is about 50%, with a trend towards gradual improvement (4, 5). It is widely recognised

that clinical outcome of patients with SAH is influenced by factors related to the patient physiology, the severity of bleeding itself and treatments provided (see fig. 1).

Historically, the outcome for poor-grade SAH is fateful and the majority of these patients have been treated conservatively. Nevertheless, in the last decade a trend toward active management of disease in patients with poor-grade SAH has been developed, with treatments including immediate ventriculostomy, early surgery and aggressive medical treatments (1, 6). The optimal surgical approach (clipping vs. coiling) is still controversial (7) but its discussion is beyond the scope of this chapter.

The main controversial point is the question of whether an already expected worse outcome should bear a different treatment. In this chapter, we will highlight some of the controversial aspects of the poor-grade SAH treatment, introducing the concept that a more aggressive treatment could produce a less unfavourable outcome than expected (8, 9).

Controversial position 1:
Vasospasm, delayed ischaemic neurological deficit and early cerebral ischaemia

Following SAH, incapacitating neurological complications, defined as delayed ischaemic neuro-

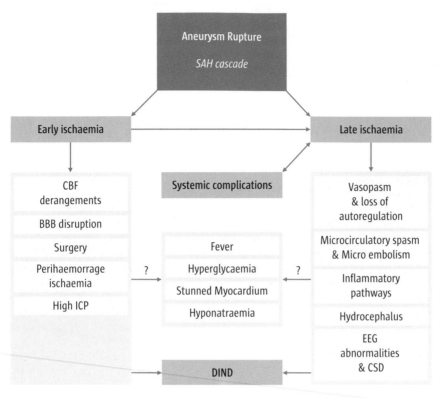

Fig. 1   Systemic and intracranial complication following SAH

logical deficit (DIND), occurs in 25–30 % of patients. Cerebral vasospasm (VS) is one of the primary causes of DIND and refers to intracranial vasoconstriction and spasm of affected arteries with marked increase in vasomotor tone. VS afflicts 30 % of patients with peak incidence between days 6–8 post haemorrhage, it worsens clinical outcome and it is correlated with a 1.5- to 3-fold increase in mortality (10). Moreover, the distinction between symptomatic VS and angiographic VS is crucial, being that the negative outcome related at the symptomatic VS and the latter not being treated traditionally. The amount of blood on computed tomography (CT), graded with the Fisher scale (11), is the most reliable prognostic factor for developing VS (12). Oxyhaemoglobin, resulting from degradation of blood products, is a prerequisite for the induction of VS but, even if many pathways have been described, it is still a matter of controversy how it produces VS (13). Coiling and clipping apparently carry the same risk of incidence and duration of VS occurrence (14).

The gold standard in detecting VS is cerebral angiography. Transcranial Doppler is commonly used as a practical bedside tool even if it has low specificity and sensitivity in detecting VS (15). Recent CBF studies have shown the feasibility and accuracy of VS detection with perfusion CT (16, 17).

Therapy of VS is still controversial and challenging. In the past years, the mainstay of VS therapy has been the hypervolaemic approach including haemodilution, hypertension and hypervolaemia (so called "triple H" therapy). Although this paradigm has gained widespread diffusion in the neurosurgical community, the efficacy of triple-H therapy and its precise role in the management of VS has been critically re-evaluated and, nowadays, remains uncertain (18, 19). A systematic meta-nalysis of the current literature concludes that at present "*There is no evidence that administration of large volume of fluids is beneficial in patients with subarachnoid haemorrhage*" (13). Vasopressor-induced elevation of mean arterial pressure remains

What care should be provided for poor grade subarachnoid haemorrhage patients?

E

a therapeutical option because it produces an increase of regional cerebral blood flow and brain tissue oxygenation in patients with subarachnoid haemorrhage (20).

Oral nimodipine (21) is the only medication for which consensus has been reached (22). It is administered to prevent and to treat VS even if the mechanisms of beneficial effect are controversial, including neuroprotection via reduction of calcium-dependent excitotoxicity, reduced platelet aggregation, dilatation of small arteries, inhibition of ischaemia triggered OHb, or some combination of these actions. A recent Cochrane review asserted that "*The evidence for nimodipine is not beyond all doubt, but given the potential benefits and modest risks of this treatment, oral nimodipine is currently indicated in patients with aneurismal SAH*" (23).

Moreover, a number of agents are under investigation for the prevention of VS, including the endothelin (ET) receptor antagonists (clazosentan), magnesium sulfate, nicardipine prolonged-release implants and statins, with the potential of inducing the up-regulation of the nitric oxide synthase that improves cerebral vasomotor reactivity (24, 25).

When VS is refractory to medical approaches, transluminal balloon angioplasty and intra-arterial vasodilators are possible options (22).

Processes other than VS contribute to CBF disturbances and negative outcome in patients with poor grade SAH. Among these global ischaemia, blood brain barrier (BBB) disruption, inflammatory pathways, autoregulatory failure and cortical spreading depression (26) have been found present in patients suffering from DIND. All these findings clearly point to alternative mechanisms of DIND and require different therapeutical approaches. As an example, persistent autoregulatory failure after SAH is independently associated with the occurrence of delayed cerebral infarction and may be an important cofactor in addition to VS itself. In fact, an early brain injury occurs at the onset of the bleed due to cessation or marked reduction in CBF (acute global ischaemia), that leads to neuronal apoptosis and BBB disruption, release of glutamate (with the potential of citotoxic oedema development), microcirculatory compromise and thrombus formation as a result of endothelium damage. It is reasonable to think of the DIND as the endpoint of a cascade

initiated at the onset of SAH when a dramatic reduction in CBF is likely to occur (27), then followed by VS and other derangements in brain metabolism. Patients with poor grade SAH are more likely to experience the complexity of this occurrence. Therapeutic intervention, currently under investigation, could therefore be directed at either intercepting the cascade before the patient deteriorates, or at compensating for the deficiencies incurred by VS.

Controversial position 2:
ICP and CPP monitoring and treatment

Pathophysiology of intracranial hypertension in patients with SAH is complex and it is usually due to acute hydrocephalus, reactive hyperemia and global ischaemic insult (i.e. brain oedema) that occur at the onset of the bleeding. Poor grade patients are more likely to experience this latter complication. Sudden discharge of blood into the basal cisterns with an acute rise in intracranial pressure (ICP) and reduction in cerebral blood flow (CBF) can be immediately fatal. If the patient survives, hydrocephalus (HC) is likely to happen because of either obstruction of CSF flow by blood clot, or a reduction of CSF reabsorption. Drain of CSF avoids fatal rise in ICP and is a cornerstone of SAH therapy. External ventricular drain (EVD) is the most widely used but the lumbar drain has been increasingly used as thought to be more physiological in favouring the CSF washout. Preliminary clinical research indicate that the incidence of VS is less in patients treated with lumbar drains than in patients treated with EVD alone (28). These findings have to be confirmed in larger series and the potential hazards of a lumbar CSF removal have to be kept in mind.

Placing an EVD in poor grade patients is part of the management and allows intermittent ICP monitoring but in severely ill patients a continuous ICP measurement, with a solid state sensor, is required. Continuous ICP values are needed as increasing MAP might be the only means to sustain the cerebral perfusion pressure (CPP) and maintain adequate perfusion. On the other hand, elevated blood pressure can be harmful as the acute vasoparalysis leading to direct transmission of arterial pressure to the parenchyma may occur. Therefore optimal CPP management is still controversial and requires integration of the monitoring data and individualisation of treatment.

Controversial position 3: Fever

Fever is a stereotyped adaptive response, coordinated by the hypothalamus, to a multiplicity of stimuli and leads to a variety of physiological perturbations, the most evident of which is a rise in body temperature. Among the different pathologies admitted in the NeuroIntensive Care Unit (NICU), SAH is the most strongly associated with fever, being present in up to 70% of cases (29), and body temperature rhythm has been shown to be altered (30). Significant associations have been described between fever and poor grade SAH, Fisher grade and development of VS. Wartenberg (31) studied medical complications after SAH and their impact on outcome and found that fever, anaemia, and hyperglycaemia were independent significant predictors of poor outcome. Epidemiological studies indicate that fever after acute neurological injury is associated with significantly increased mortality and impairment of functional outcome. The cause of this relationship is probably multifactorial. A large body of evidence indicates that, experimentally, even small increases in temperature can exacerbate ischaemic brain damage, and temperature elevations have also been associated with cerebral hyperaemia, oedema worsening and elevated intracranial pressure after SAH.

Fever among patients with subarachnoid haemorrhage is frequently non-infectious (48% vs. 18% compared to other NICU patients) and it has been associated with VS (32). Compared with infective fever, non-infectious fever begins earlier, within the first 48–72 h of admission, and this early occurrence significantly predicted negative evaluation for infection.

These considerations have prompted interest in the therapeutic effects of temperature reduction measures. While the feasibility and safety of temperature reduction drugs and devices in the ICU has been evaluated, there are no published data regarding the impact of this intervention on outcome. Nevertheless, one therapeutical aim in poor-grade patients is to reduce the burden of this secondary insult and, therefore, to maintain normothermia, mainly during the first week after SAH.

Controversial position 4: Hyponatraemia

Hyponatraemia (HNa) is a common complication after SAH, observed in 30 to 43% of patients in the acute phase. HNa is a severity marker of SAH, being more frequent in poor grade patients, and it contributes significantly to patient morbidity and mortality. In fact, acute HNa has been identified as a cause of increased intracranial hypertension and three-fold risk of cerebral infarction compared to patients with normal serum sodium levels. The differential diagnosis of HNa in SAH patients includes the syndrome of inappropriate antidiuretic hormone secretion (SIADH) and the cerebral salt-wasting syndrome (CSWS). The two conditions have different pathophysiologies and intravascular volume status, and require therefore different therapies. SIADH, caused by elevated serum vasopressin activity, is a euvolaemic hyponatraemic state. On the contrary, CSWS, defined as the renal loss of sodium during intracranial disease, is a hypovolaemic hyponatraemic condition linked with natriuresis and decrease in extracellular fluid volume. Because the volume depletion caused by CSWS is associated with decreased circulating ADH, CSWS is thought to be due to circulating atrial natriuretic peptides (ANP and BNP) that promote both volume contraction and sodium loss. Studies have focused on the association between hyponatraemia due to CSWS and both ANP and BNP. BNP secretion in SAH patients is closely related to the bleeding intensity and VS severity as well as to development of DIND and a progressive and marked increase during the clinical course in patients who eventually develop cerebral ischemia has been demonstrated. Increasing evidence suggests that the natriuretic peptides family plays an important role in the pathogenesis of CSWS, especially in the setting of SAH.

Clinically, the main difference between CSW and SIADH is the intravascular volume status, which is not easily measured at the bedside. A practical approach is to estimate intravascular volume integrating multiple factors including physical examination, trends of serum BUN/creatinine ratio, serum haemoglobin and cardiac filling pressures.

The key to the appropriate treatment of hyponatremia in the neurosurgical patient lies in the diagnosis of its cause as the management re-

What care should be provided for poor grade subarachnoid haemorrhage patients?

E

quired, is the opposite of the above mentioned conditions. From a probabilistic point of view in poor grade SAH, CSW is the more frequent cause of this electrolytes disturbance. Fluid restriction in SIADH is indicated but it has to be used with extreme caution because it has been associated with an incidence of cerebral infarction greater than 80%. Fluid resuscitation, even with hypertonic saline, is indicated in patients with CSWS and frequent serum sodium determination (i.e. every 6–12 hours) is mandatory. The sodium balance has to be calculated daily and hydrocortisone could be used in more severe cases and to overcome the excessive natriuresis (33).

Controversial position 5: Hyperglycaemia

Hyperglycaemia (HG) is common after SAH and prolonged HG is associated with increased ICU length of stay, increased risk of death or severe disability. Once adjusting for Hunt-Hess grade, aneurysm size, and age, HG remains an independent predictor of death or severe disability (34, 35). An independent association of HG with symptomatic VS and with poor outcome at discharge has also been described.

Since the detrimental effects of HG on outcome in critically ill patients are not controversial and so far the associations of HG with regional complications (i.e. VS) have been widely investigated, little is known about the consequences of HG, and its tight control, on brain metabolism (36).

Despite convincing evidence of the benefit of intensive glycaemic control in critically ill patients, questions may be arising regarding the effect of a potential substrate glucose deprivation in patients with a primarily injured brain.

The delivery and utilisation of glucose in patients with SAH has been investigated with microdyalisis (MD). A definition of metabolic and ischaemic derangements that happen in SAH is beyond the scope of this chapter. However, a better insight into brain metabolic effects of tight glycaemic control can identify patients with higher potential for recovery and who can benefit from more aggressive treatments

One MD study considered whether the decrease in cerebral glucose was eventually related to insulin administration in patients with poor grade SAH (37). The intensive glycaemic control with insulin resulted in a decrease of cerebral glucose and in a slight increase in glycerol (markers of cells distress). Despite the interesting results, whether low cerebral glucose is due to DIND or insulin itself is still a matter of controversy, together with the role of insulin receptors' sensitivity in the brain. Vespa et al. (36) demonstrated that intensive glycaemic control did not lead to reduction in cerebral metabolic rate but leads to increased MD markers of cellular metabolic distress (Lactate-Piruvate ratio and Glutamate) and, interestingly, no functional outcome advantage was disclosed in this group of patients, compared with the group that was treated with a less strict insulin regimen.

In addition Cesarini et al. (38) showed that, in a population of poor grade SAH with Fisher grade 3–4, the patients who had better recovery showed a biphasic MD pattern, with initial increase of lactate and piruvate and decrease of glucose. The detection of favourable prognostic metabolic patterns that reflect the potential of recovery in individual patients is fascinating. These preliminary findings point out that new monitoring tool such as MD can be useful in identifying which patients may benefit from a different insulin regimen and answer the question of who should be treated. These studies hint at the potential of new monitoring but at this stage there is no evidence that tolerance of HG is beneficial therefore glycaemic levels below 180 mg/dl are desirable (31).

Controversial position 6: Stunned myocardium

Cardiac dysfunction after SAH is referred to as "neurogenic stunned myocardium" (NSM) and may have a major impact on the haemodynamic management in NICU. Recognition of NSM unique features permits optimal management of patients with SAH and the identification of overlapping syndromes, ranging from acute myocardial infarction to the rare left ventricle (LV) balloon syndrome (39). Cardiopulmonary complications usually develop immediately after the bleeding and clinical findings range from asymptomatic mild troponin enzymes increase to cardiogenic shock, impaired LV function, congestive heart failure and pulmonary oedema (PO, in approximately 10% of patients) (40). The typical onset of NSM includes electrocardiogram (EKG) abnormalities, short-lasting modest serum cardiac necrosis marker increase, CXR suggestive of pulmonary oedema, echocardiogram documenting regional wall motion abnormalities (RWMA) beyond a singular vascular territory. Once performed, coronary angiogram documents normal coronary arteries.

EKG changes are the most common, non-specific, variable finding (25–75%) in NSM. Female sex and hypokalaemia are proven to be independent risk factors for severe QT prolongation. A correlation between QT (QTc) interval and HH grade has been shown only in one study depending on the QTc formula used to adjust the QT interval for the heart rate. Cardiac arrhythmias occur after SAH, with sinus bradycardia and sinus tachycardia being the most common (41).

The incidence of Troponin (cTnI) release in patients with SAH ranges from 20–42% (42) (peaking on the day of the bleeding) with 100% sensitivity in detecting LV dysfunction. Troponin increase is more pronounced in patients with high HH grade (43), worse baseline Fisher grade and in older females. Patients with abnormal cTnI are more likely to die (55% vs. 27%) and to have a worse GCS on discharge. Peak cTnI and admission GCS score of < 12 are independent predictors of death at discharge. These data support the idea that cTnI should be measured in all patients with SAH. B-Type natriuretic peptide also increases and is associated with RWMA (8%) (44), reduced Ejection fraction (EF), diastolic dysfunction, PO, cTnI elevation and early in-hospital mortality.

In the SAH population, there is also a likely significant overlap of neurogenic stress cardiomyopathy and neurogenic pulmonary oedema (NPO), the causes of which are still controversial. NPO is considered to be due to a combination of increased vascular permeability and concomitant LV dysfunction, with pulmonary wedge pressure increasing within hours after the onset of pulmonary oedema (45).

The pathogenesis of SAH-induced myocardial dysfunction is still controversial. There are three main theories:

1. A multi-vessel coronary artery spasm leading to ischaemia.
2. Micro-vascular dysfunction that postulates a decreased perfusion in myocardium.
3. Catecholamine hypothesis.

The last one is the most widely accepted theory. A sudden rise in ICP at the moment of bleeding may cause sympathetic activation via hypothalamic ischaemia. Increase in plasma norepinephrine within 48 hours that persists during the first week and normalises by 6 months along with elevated cardiac enzymes has been demonstrated. Animal models showed that the peak values of CK-MB and cTnI correlate positively with the catecholamine peak suggesting an elevated sympathetic activity in the acute phase of SAH as contributor to the cardiac dysfunction. Further support to the catecholamine's theory comes from histological studies. The SAH-induced NSM shows myocardial changes, known as myocardial contraction band necrosis (CBN), which refers to a specific form of myocyte injury with hypercontracted sarcomeres and interstitial mononuclear inflammatory response. CBN is also present in other conditions of dramatic sympathetic discharge (i.e. pheochromocytoma). Interestingly, a recent work of VH Lee e coll., propose an alternative terminology for NCM: "neurogenic stress cardiomyopathy" (NSC). NSC definition more accurately reflects the suspected pathophysiology of this complication, assuming that the catecholamine surge is crucial to producing cardiac injury rather than coronary occlusion (46). Given that the aetiology of NSM is still controversial, a clear definition of NSC is more than academic and carries great implications in terms of therapy.

The treatment of neurogenic stressed myocardium is supportive, as the condition has the potential for improvement with time (even to full function recovery) (46). Moreover, the optimal CPP is one of the main therapeutic targets in SAH patients to avoid secondary DIND. Therefore mean arterial pressure (MAP) must be sustained with fluid and vasopressors (usually with phenylephrine). However, if catecholamine themselves cause NSM, then phenylephrine (possibly dopamine, epinephrine, and norepinephrine) may be harmful. The clinicians have to balance between catecholamine infusion and MAP target. If inotropes are required then other strategies should be integrated to sustain CPP or cardiac output after SAH (i.e. dobutamine).

In SAH-related cardiac dysfunction some controversies do remain. Further studies need to clarify if the serum or CSF catecholamine levels can predict NSM, if the exogenous catecholamine administration increases cTnI, if sympatholic agents (labetalol) can reduce severity of NSM. The answers will facilitate our understanding of acute neurocardiology derangements in patients with SAH.

Summary

The optimal management of poor grade SAH has not been fully established yet. Several controversies remain in terms of aetiology of the main general and neurological complications and in terms of the best therapeutic options. What is not controversial at all is that the ruptured aneurysm should be treated in a timely fashion and that the complications are more likely to occur in patients presenting with a poor grade SAH. The challenging decision on who should be treated is difficult to answers at this stage. All throughout the European countries the burden of the neurological outcome is felt in a different fashion and this may explain the differences in making the decision of who should be treated.

Efforts to improve SAH outcome should be focused on the medical complications that also contribute to poor outcomes together with DIND.

Given the composite nature underling the occurrence of DIND and the cascade of events beginning at the onset of bleeding (CBF reduction) new monitoring tools as continuous EEG, microdyalisis and PtiO$_2$ should be routinely promoted to optimise cerebral physiology.

Once all the controversies and questions that need to be answered are sorted, then we might be able to tailor a cut-off for patients who can benefit from more aggressive therapies, despite the severity of the bleed. At this stage, poor grade SAH seems to be the population of patients that can most benefit from a better insight and understanding into SAH compliance and treatment.

Key points for clinical practice

1. *Poor grade SAH could be treated. Efforts to improve SAH outcome should be focused on the medical complications that also contribute to poor outcomes together with DIND.*

2. *Hypoxaemia, hyperglycaemia, cardiovascular instability and fever have been independently associated with increased poor outcome (death or disability) in patients with poor grade SAH. A mainstay of treatment should focus on their detection and prompt treatment.*

3. *Oral nimodipine is the only medication recommended*

and, despite the fact that the mechanism is still controversial; it has been associated with improved outcome.

4. *Mechanisms other than vasospasm contribute to the occurrence of DIND. Monitoring brain physiology (i.e. continuous EEG, microdialysis, PtiO$_2$ and pressure reactivity index) is therefore recommended to detect metabolic and functional derangements that likely contribute to poor outcome.*

5. *Clinical and radiological findings should drive the clinician to the opportunity of a continuous ICP monitoring as brain oedema with dramatic intracranial hypertension is frequent in poor grade SAH.*

The authors

Maria Giulia Abate, MD[1]
Giuseppe Citerio, MD[2]
[1]Resident in Anaesthesia and Intensive Care | University of Milano Bicocca-Italy & Research Fellow | Department of Anaesthesia University of Cambridge-UK
[2]Director Neuroanaesthesia and Neurointensive Care | Department of Perioperative Medicine and Intensive Care | San Gerardo Hospital | Monza, Italy

Address for correspondence

Giuseppe Citerio
UO Neuroanestesia e Neurorianimazione
Dipartimento di Medicina Perioperatoria
e Terapie Intensive
H San Gerardo
Via Pergolesi 33
20052 Monza (Mi), Italy
e-mail: g.citerio@hsgerardo.org

References

1. van Gijn J, Kerr RS, Rinkel GJ. Subarachnoid haemorrhage. Lancet. 2007;369(9558):306–18.
2. de Rooij NK et al., Incidence of subarachnoid haemorrhage: a systematic review with emphasis on region, age, gender and time trends. J Neurol Neurosurg Psychiatry. 2007;78(12):1365–72.
3. Report of World Federation of Neurological Surgeons Committee on a Universal Subarachnoid Hemorrhage Grading Scale. J Neurosurg. 1988;68(6):98–6.
4. Hop JW et al. Case-fatality rates and functional outcome after subarachnoid hemorrhage: a systematic review. Stroke. 1997;28(3):660–4.

5. Stegmayr B, Eriksson M, Asplund K. Declining mortality from subarachnoid hemorrhage: changes in incidence and case fatality from 1985 through 2000. Stroke. 2004; 35(9):2059–63.
6. Laidlaw JD, Siu KH. Poor-grade aneurysmal subarachnoid hemorrhage: outcome after treatment with urgent surgery. Neurosurgery. 2003;53(6):1275–80; discussion 1280–2.
7. van der Schaaf I et al. Endovascular coiling versus neurosurgical clipping for patients with aneurysmal subarachnoid haemorrhage. Cochrane Database Syst Rev. 2005(4):CD003085.
8. Naval NS et al. Controversies in the management of aneurysmal subarachnoid hemorrhage. Crit Care Med. 2006;34(2):511–24.
9. Al-Shahi R et al. Subarachnoid haemorrhage. Bmj. 2006;333(7561):235–40.
10. Macdonald RL, Pluta RM, Zhang JH. Cerebral vasospasm after subarachnoid hemorrhage: the emerging revolution. Nat Clin Pract Neurol. 2007;3(5):256–63.
11. Fisher CM, Kistler JP, Davis JM. Relation of cerebral vasospasm to subarachnoid hemorrhage visualized by computerized tomographic scanning. Neurosurgery. 1980;6(1):1–9.
12. Komotar RJ et al. Advances in vasospasm treatment and prevention. J Neurol Sci. 2007;261(1–2):134–42.
13. Hansen-Schwartz J. Cerebral vasospasm: a consideration of the various cellular mechanisms involved in the pathophysiology. Neurocrit Car. 2004;1(2):235–46.
14. Goddard AJ, Raju PP, Gholkar A. Does the method of treatment of acutely ruptured intracranial aneurysms influence the incidence and duration of cerebral vasospasm and clinical outcome? J Neurol Neurosurg Psychiatry. 2004;75(6):868–72.
15. Sloan MA et al. Assessment: transcranial Doppler ultrasonography: report of the Therapeutics and Technology Assessment Subcommittee of the American Academy of Neurology. Neurology. 2004;62(9):1468–81.
16. Schubert GA, Thome C. Cerebral blood flow changes in acute subarachnoid hemorrhage. Front Biosc. 2008;13: 1594–603.
17. Binaghi S et al. CT angiography and perfusion CT in cerebral vasospasm after subarachnoid hemorrhage. AJNR Am J Neuroradiol. 2007;28(4):750–8.
18. Lee KH, Lukovits T, Friedman JA. "Triple-H" therapy for cerebral vasospasm following subarachnoid hemorrhage. Neurocrit Care. 2006;4(1):68–76.
19. Hunt MA, Bhardwaj A. Caveats for triple-H therapy in the management of vasospasm after aneurysmal subarachnoid hemorrhage. Crit Care Med. 2007;35(8): 1985–6.
20. Muench E et al. Effects of hypervolemia and hypertension on regional cerebral blood flow, intracranial pressure, and brain tissue oxygenation after subarachnoid hemorrhage. Crit Care Med. 2007;35(8):1844–51; quiz 1852.
21. Kassell NF et al. Randomized, double-blind, vehicle-controlled trial of tirilazad mesylate in patients with aneurysmal subarachnoid hemorrhage: a cooperative study in Europe, Australia, and New Zealand. J Neurosurg. 1996;84(2):221–8.
22. Weyer GW, Nolan CP, Macdonald RL. Evidence-based cerebral vasospasm management. Neurosurg Focus. 2006;21(3):E8.
23. Dorhout Mees SM et al. Calcium antagonists for aneurysmal subarachnoid haemorrhage. Cochrane Database Syst Rev. 2007(3):CD000277.
24. Tseng MY et al. Effects of acute pravastatin treatment on intensity of rescue therapy, length of inpatient stay, and 6-month outcome in patients after aneurysmal subarachnoid hemorrhage. Stroke. 2007;38(5):1545–50.
25. Trimble JL, Kockler DR. Statin treatment of cerebral vasospasm after aneurysmal subarachnoid hemorrhage. Ann Pharmacother. 2007;41(12):2019–23.
26. Dreier, JP et al. Delayed ischaemic neurological deficits after subarachnoid haemorrhage are associated with clusters of spreading depolarizations. Brain. 2006; 129(Pt 12):3224–37.
27. Roos YB et al. Complications and outcome in patients with aneurysmal subarachnoid haemorrhage: a prospective hospital based cohort study in the Netherlands. J Neurol Neurosurg Psychiatry. 2000;68(3): 337–41.
28. Hoekema D, Schmidt RH, Ross I. Lumbar drainage for subarachnoid hemorrhage: technical considerations and safety analysis. Neurocrit Care. 2007;7(1):3–9.
29. Fernandez A et al. Fever after subarachnoid hemorrhage: risk factors and impact on outcome. Neurology. 2007; 68(13):1013–9.
30. Kirkness CJ et al. Temperature Rhythm in Aneurysmal Subarachnoid Hemorrhage. Neurocrit Care. 2007.
31. Wartenberg KE, Mayer SA. Medical complications after subarachnoid hemorrhage: new strategies for prevention and management. Curr Opin Crit Care. 2006; 12(2):78–84.
32. Rabinstein AA, Sandhu K. Non-infectious fever in the neurological intensive care unit: incidence, causes and predictors. J Neurol Neurosurg Psychiatry. 2007;78(11): 1278–80.
33. Katayama Y et al. A randomized controlled trial of hydrocortisone against hyponatremia in patients with aneurysmal subarachnoid hemorrhage. Stroke. 2007; 38(8):2373–5.
34. Frontera JA et al. Hyperglycemia after SAH: predictors, associated complications, and impact on outcome. Stroke. 2006;37(1):199–203.
35. McGirt MJ et al. Persistent perioperative hyperglycemia as an independent predictor of poor outcome after aneurysmal subarachnoid hemorrhage. J Neurosurg. 2007;107(6):1080–5.

What care should be provided for poor grade subarachnoid haemorrhage patients?

E

36. Vespa P et al. Intensive insulin therapy reduces microdialysis glucose values without altering glucose utilization or improving the lactate/pyruvate ratio after traumatic brain injury. Crit Care Med. 2006;34(3):850–6.

37. Schlenk F et al. Insulin-related decrease in cerebral glucose despite normoglycemia in aneurysmal subarachnoid hemorrhage. Crit Care. 2008;12(1):R9.

38. Cesarini KG et al. Early cerebral hyperglycolysis after subarachnoid haemorrhage correlates with favourable outcome. Acta Neurochir (Wien).≤ 2002;144(11): 1121–31.

39. Lee VH et al. Mechanisms in neurogenic stress cardiomyopathy after aneurysmal subarachnoid hemorrhage. Neurocrit Care. 2006;5(3):243–9.

40. Friedman JA et al. Pulmonary complications of aneurysmal subarachnoid hemorrhage. Neurosurgery. 2003;52(5):1025–31; discussion 1031–2.

41. Kawahara E et al. Role of autonomic nervous dysfunction in electrocardio-graphic abnormalities and cardiac injury in patients with acute subarachnoid hemorrhage. Circ J. 2003;67(9):753–6.

42. Naidech AM et al. Cardiac troponin elevation, cardiovascular morbidity, and outcome after subarachnoid hemorrhage. Circulation. 2005;112(18): 2851–6.

43. Tung P et al. Predictors of neurocardiogenic injury after subarachnoid hemorrhage. Stroke. 2004;35(2):548–51.

44. Tung PP et al. Plasma B-type natriuretic peptide levels are associated with early cardiac dysfunction after subarachnoid hemorrhage. Stroke. 2005;36(7):1567–9.

45. Fontes RB et al. Acute neurogenic pulmonary edema: case reports and literature review. J Neurosurg Anesthesiol. 2003;15(2):144–50.

46. Macmillan CS, Grant IS, Andrews PJ. Pulmonary and cardiac sequelae of subarachnoid haemorrhage: time for active management? Intensive Care Med. 2002;28(8): 1012–23.

Kees H. Polderman

Induced hypothermia to treat neurological injuries

Introduction

From the 1940s onwards various case reports, case series and uncontrolled studies have reported possible benefits of induced hypothermia on neurological outcome following various types of neurological injury. In the 1940s and 1950s moderate hypothermia (26–32°C) was used in the treatment of post-anoxic injuries following drowning or cardiac arrest, as well as in patients with traumatic brain injury (TBI) and other categories of patients. Several small clinical trials and numerous case reports were published during this period, which by and large reported positive results (6, 19, 61). However, these early studies were severely hampered by the side effects of hypothermia, which were extremely difficult to handle in a context without intensive care facilities. The first intensive care units in Europe were established only in the early 1950s (in Copenhagen, Denmark (8)) and in the late 1950s in the United States (in Baltimore, 1957). Thus, ICUs were not yet available in most hospitals between 1938 and 1960, when the first hypothermia studies were being done. This meant that hypothermia was being used in general wards, with neither ventilatory or circulatory support. In addition, it was (erroneously) believed that body temperature needed to be lowered as far as possible (usually below 30°C) to achieve benefits, because protective effects were presumed to be due solely to de-

creases in brain metabolism and oxygen demand. Hypothermia therefore remained a controversial treatment because of the combination of severe side effects and mixed study results.

The last two decades have seen a resurgence of interest in therapeutic hypothermia, but also a resurgence of the controversies. Animal experiments performed in the mid-1980s and early 1990s demonstrated that deep hypothermia was not needed to achieve benefits; protective effects were observed in neurological injury models when mild-to-moderate hypothermia (31–35°C) was used, with far fewer side effects. In addition, the advent of ICU and high care facilities has made it possible to deal with the most important potential side effects (discussed below) far more effectively. Presently, clinical use of hypothermia is far more widespread, but it is still not generally accepted even where the evidence seems quite strong (45, 49). This article will discuss three of these potential indications, and the controversies surrounding them.

Induced hypothermia for cardiac arrest

Fifteen non-randomised studies (reviewed in 49) and two randomised, controlled, multi-centred trials (7, 27) have reported that neurological outcome can be improved by using mild hypothermia in patients who have had a witnessed cardiac arrest with an initial rhythm of ventricular fibrillation (VF) or ventricular tachycardia (VT) with no measurable output. Bernard and co-workers (7) enrolled 77 patients following cardiac arrest who were cooled within 2½ hours of return of spontaneous circulation (ROSC) to a core temperature of 33°C for a period of 12 hours. Good neurological outcome was observed in 49% (n=21/43) of patients in the hypothermia group vs. 26% (n = 29/34) in the control group (p=0.046). The odds ratio (OR) for good outcome was 5.25 (95% CI 1.47–18.76, p=0.011) for hypothermia patients vs. controls after adjustment for case mix. Survival was higher in the hypothermia group, but this difference was not statistically significant (21/43 vs. 11/34, p=0.145).

The second RCCT was performed in Europe and enrolled 273 patients (27). Favourable neurological outcome was observed in 55% (n=75/136) of patients treated with hypothermia (target temperature 32–34°C), versus 39% (n=54/137) of controls (relative risk 1.40, 95% CI 1.08–1.81); mortality rates were 41% vs. 55% (rr 0.74; 95% CI 0.58–0.95) for hypothermia vs. controls, respectively. Target temperatures were reached only after an average period of eight hours in this study. Hypothermia was maintained for 24 hours.

The results of these studies were published in 2002. Several non-randomised studies published between 1997 and 2002 (mostly using historical controls) and one additional RCT that was underpowered to detect statistical significance (22) also reported trends or significant benefits of cooling in patients with cardiac arrest (reviewed in 49). Several implementation studies (before-after introduction of hypothermia) were published between 2003 and 2007; all seem to confirm potential benefits, with reported absolute increases in rates of favourable outcome ranging from 16% to 54% (49). Two databases registering the outcomes of patients treated with hypothermia have found that absolute rates of good outcome were similar or better than those reported in the two RCT's, suggesting that the results of the RCTs can be translated and applied in daily clinical practice (64, 37).

All this has led to a formal recommendation by the European Resuscitation Council (ERC) and the American Heart Association (AHA) to use hy-

pothermia following cardiac arrest if the initial rhythm was VT or VF, and consideration of its use for other rhythms (38, 39). A recently published meta-analysis concluded that the number-needed-to-treat (NNT) to allow one additional patient meeting the study criteria to leave the hospital with good neurological recovery was 6, with a 95% CI of 4–13 (26).

In spite of all this, recent surveys indicate that hypothermia remains underused in Europe (10, 65) and even more so in the United States (1, 34). These surveys indicate various reasons for non-usage of hypothermia, ranging from technical and logistical hurdles to not being convinced by the available evidence (34). Indeed, the two RCCTs underpinning the use of hypothermia in cardiac arrest have been criticised for a number of reasons. One study (7) used block randomisation to allocate hypothermia treatment; this means that patients were randomly assigned to hypothermia or normothermia according to the day of the month, with patients receiving hypothermia on odd-numbered days. The use of this method of randomisation was subsequently criticised; most statisticians agree that some allocation bias is possible when block randomisation rather than patient-by-patient randomisation is used. For this reason, the American Heart Association has based its recommendation to use hypothermia following cardiac arrest solely on the results of the European study (27), and has given it "only" a level IIa recommendation. In contrast, the European Resuscitation Council accepted the results of both studies and gave a level I recommendation to use hypothermia after cardiac arrest (39).

In addition, although final neurological outcome was assessed by observers that were blinded to which treatment the patients had received, for technical reasons the physicians treating the patients were aware which patients were being treated with hypothermia in both RCTs. Therefore, strictly speaking neither of the two studies was double-blinded.

Finally, the inclusion criteria for the two studies were relatively strict; only patients who had witnessed cardiac arrests, relatively rapid arrival of the ambulance, initial rhythms of VT/VF and no persistent hypotension or hypoxia could be enrolled. Only ± 10% of screened patients met these eligibility criteria. Thus controversy exists on the applicability of these findings to other patient populations (those with an initial rhythm of asystole, or unwitnessed arrests). Preliminary data suggest that such patients might also benefit from therapeutic hypothermia (22, 44, 49), but this remains uncertain.

Induced hypothermia for traumatic brain injury

Induced hypothermia has also been used to treat patients with *traumatic brain injury* (TBI). The neurological outcome and degree of permanent injury following severe TBI is determined in large part by so-called *secondary injury*, a collective term used to describe the destructive processes unfolding in the injured brain in the hours and days following the initial trauma. The most important mechanisms that drive secondary injury are local and global *ischaemia/reperfusion*, local or generalised *swelling* of the brain (cytotoxic oedema), inadequate or excessive perfusion of injured brain areas (*hypo/hyperperfusion*), local or systemic *obstruction of spinal fluid drainage* and local hematoma formation.

Numerous animal experiments in different models have shown that hypothermia mitigates secondary injury and improves outcome after experimental TBI. It has been tested in various animal models with different protocols, and has shown highly significant and robust neuroprotective effects (4, 45, 48–49). This has led to much clinical interest, and several clinical studies have used hypothermia to improve neurological outcome following severe TBI. However, these studies enrolled widely diverging patient populations and used widely diverging treatment protocols (45, 49). The duration of cooling varied from 24 hours to more than five days, with some studies using ICP to guide depth and duration of treatment; rates of re-warming and the responses to rebound intracranial hypertension differed markedly; time to target temperature also varied considerably. Many studies were performed in patients with high intra-cranial pressure (ICP), but some enrolled patients with normal ICP. These differences in study design complicate the interpretation, comparison, and aggregation of the results of the studies assessing the efficacy of mild-to-moderate hypothermia in TBI.

An important and often underappreciated aspect of this issue is the general ICU management

in these patients, and how it interacts with potentially neuroprotective strategies. This includes co-interventions such as osmotic therapy, sedation, analgesia and paralysis, as well as the targets for MAP and CPP. Studies assessing hypothermia as a potentially neuroprotective treatment have to deal with the potential side effects of cooling, particularly during prolonged usage as is necessary when patients with severe TBI are treated. The success in managing side effects has varied, and this may be an important factor in determining efficacy and successful use of cooling. This should be kept in mind when evaluating the results of various studies.

To date, twenty-eight clinical studies have been performed to assess the efficacy of hypothermia in adult patients with severe TBI (review: 49). Nineteen of these were controlled. Three studies (enrolling 131 patients) were performed in patients with normal ICP. Only one of these reported outcome data; in a study in 91 patients (45 cooled and 46 controls) Shiozaki et al. (58) reported no significant differences in rates of favourable outcome at 3 months following injury (47 % vs. 59 %, p = 0.251).

To date, 18 studies with a total number of 1,860 patients have used hypothermia in patients with high ICP that was refractory to "conventional" treatments (sedation/analgesia, paralysis, osmotic therapy, and sometimes barbiturates). Treatment duration in these studies ranged from 24 hours to five days. All reported a decrease in intracranial pressure when hypothermia was induced. Thirteen reported statistically significant favourable effects on neurological outcome associated with hypothermia; four reported non-significant favourable trends. All of the studies reporting favourable results were performed in specialised neurotrauma centres, with extensive experience in using hypothermia and managing its side effects.

In contrast, the authors of a well-designed multi-centred RCT (the NABISH-1 study) published in 2001 did not observe any favourable effects on outcome (12). Although decreases in ICP were seen in the hypothermia group and although there was an apparent benefit in a subgroup of patients (those in whom hypothermia was already present upon admission), the overall result of this study was clearly negative. Moreover, there were more days with complications in the intervention group.

The publication of this study in a prestigious medical journal led to the current controversy regarding the use of hypothermia in patients with severe TBI. The study was subsequently criticised for the way in which the side effects of hypothermia had been managed during cooling (42, 43), and for the way in which hypothermia had been used (relatively late start, slow speed of cooling, with an average time to target temperature of > 8 hours, rewarming after 48 hours regardless of rebound increases in intracranial hypertension). These issues are important because, for example, hypothermia can lead to hypovolaemia (through cold-induced diuresis) and thereby to hypotension; hypotension is associated with adverse outcome in TBI patients (11, 17, 20, 60). Indeed, prolonged hypotensive episodes (≥ 2 hours) occurred 3–4 times more frequently in the hypothermia group in the NABISH-1 study, while briefer episodes were not registered but probably also occurred more frequently in the hypothermia group. Other potential side effects of hypothermia include electrolyte disorders, hyperglycaemia, and increased infection rates (46, 50). All of these can adversely affect outcome in patients with TBI. In principle, it is possible to prevent all or most of these side effects; however, this requires a detailed protocol and a reasonable standard of ICU care. Lack of attention to side effects can easily lead to the benefits of cooling being diminished or even completely negated.

That such practical issues did indeed play a role in the negative outcome of the NABISH-1 study is confirmed by a subsequent report by the authors of NABISH-1. The authors stated that outcomes in their study had been far better in centres with high enrolment rates that had extensive experience in the use of hypothermia. When a sub-analysis was performed assessing outcome in patients admitted to the high-enrolment centres in this study (> 90 % of the total number of patients), there was a statistically significant difference in the rates of good neurological outcome in favour of the hypothermia group (12). Far more side effects had occurred in the hypothermia group in small centres, and it appeared that both data collection and patient management had been poorer. The authors concluded that "participation of small centres increased inter-centre variance and diminished the quality of data" (13). Proponents of the use of hypothermia in TBI have put forward that the side effects of hypothermia can be well and relatively easily managed in the context of good intensive care, and thus should not be regarded as "inevitable consequences" of hypothermia. They have argued that a novel treatment should be evaluated in the context of proper basic intensive care, and point to the subsequent sub-analysis of the NABISH 1 study suggesting that benefits were observed in more experienced centres (12, 42, 43). Opponents have argued that studies such as NABISH 1 reflect real life, and as such a treatment that is overly difficult to use should have no place in the treatment of TBI at this time. They have argued that sub-analyses can be no more than hypothesis-generating, and should not be used to undermine the overall conclusion of a study (14, 59).

Five meta-analyses looking at the issue of hypothermia in TBI patients were published between 2000 and 2007 (see tab. 1) (3, 10, 23, 24, 33). These analyses included differing numbers of clinical trials, based on the authors' assessment of methodology and quality of randomisation. Two also looked at the effect of differences in treatment protocol and patient selection. All of these analyses noted a trend to favourable effects of cool-

Tab. 1 Summary of the five meta-analyses assessing the efficacy of hypothermia in patients with TBI

	No. of patients	Odds ratio for poor neurological outcome (hypothermia vs. controls)	High ICP (normal ICP)	Assessment of protocol details
Harris 2002 (23)	n = 692	OR 0.61, 95 % CI 0.26–1.46	674 (16)	No
Henderson 2003 (24)	n = 748	OR 0.75, 95 % CI 0.56–1.01	641 (107)	No
McIntyre 2003 (33)	n = 1,069	OR 0.78, 95 % CI 0.63–0.98	962 (107)	Yes
Alderson 2004 (3)	n = 746	OR 0.75, 95 % CI 0.56–1.00	639 (107)	No
BTF 2007 (10)	n = 694	OR 0.68, 95 % CI 0.52–0.89	694 (0)	Yes

ing on neurological outcome; however, statistical significance was reached in only two reviews (10, 33). The authors of these two reviews concluded that there was sufficient evidence for the use of hypothermia in some categories of patients with TBI. One of the reviews also concluded that the duration of cooling and speed of re-warming were key factors in determining the efficacy of therapeutic hypothermia (33). The other three reviews concluded that there was insufficient evidence to recommend the use of therapeutic hypothermia at this time (3, 23, 24).

This issue remains hotly debated within the neurointensive care community. A new study, applying hypothermia for prolonged periods in patients with high ICP under well-controlled circumstances with high-quality ICU care, will probably be required to conclusively settle the issue. The European Society of Intensive Care Medicine is currently considering the initiation of such a study. What is somewhat less controversial is whether or not fever should be (symptomatically) treated in TBI patients. The topic of fever management will not be discussed in detail here, but various studies have shown a strong correlation between development of fever in various types of neurological injury and adverse outcome; this link persists after correcting for factors such as the severity of injury and presence or absence of infection (49).

In conclusion, what is not in dispute is that hypothermia is effective in controlling intracranial hypertension (class I evidence). However, lowering ICP does not necessarily equal improved outcome; positive effects on survival and neurological outcome have been achieved only in large referral centres with experience in the use of hypothermia, when treatment was applied within a few hours after injury and used for prolonged periods (3–5 days) in patients with elevated ICP. Management of side effects such as hypovolaemia is of key importance; re-warming should be accomplished very slowly, over a period of at least 24 hours. TBI patients with mild hypothermia (33–35°C) at admission who are haemodynamically stable should be allowed to remain hypothermic. Although hypothermia can also be used to control ICP in later stages following TBI, there is currently no evidence that neurological outcome can be improved by such delayed application of hypothermia.

Induced hypothermia for ischaemic stroke

The mechanisms of ischaemic injury in severe stroke are different from those in global anoxia. In severe stroke a central area of brain tissue experiences profound and prolonged ischaemia which, if left untreated, inevitably leads to necrosis. This core zone is surrounded by a so-called penumbra-zone which is hypoperfused but not (yet) irreversibly damaged. In theory the penumbra-zone can be salvaged as long it has not become necrotic. The salvageable zone can increase if (partial) reperfusion occurs, for instance following administration of clot-dissolving drugs; conversely the core (necrotic) zone and penumbra zone can extend outward if ischaemia persists.

Application of mild-to-moderate hypothermia significantly improves outcome in ischaemic stroke models (4, 45, 49, 51). In animal models the therapeutic time window for intervention has varied from 1–2 hours to up to 5 hours, depending on the type of animal model and on whether full or partial reperfusion was restored (as would be the case in stroke patients treated with thrombolytic agents or angiographic intervention). It should be realised that the human brain could be either more or less susceptible to ischaemic injury than the brains of the most frequently used animal models, depending on which post-ischaemic mechanisms of injury play the greatest role in the developing injury. Some experiments suggest that late-developing mechanisms such as neuroinflammation and development of apoptosis may play a greater role in human brain injury than in animals; because these mechanisms begin relatively late after injury (and continue for prolonged periods of time) this would imply a longer therapeutic window for neuroprotective interventions such as hypothermia.

In spite of the positive results from clinical trials in global anoxic injury and the observations in stroke models described above, no RCTs assessing the efficacy of hypothermia in patients with ischaemic stroke have yet been performed. Seven non-randomised studies enrolling a total number of 145 patients have been performed (29, 30, 52, 53, 54, 55, 57). Most of these were done in patients with middle cerebral artery infarction and brain oedema, a severe subtype of acute stroke. In these studies hypothermia was used to control delayed-onset intracranial hypertension, which meant that cooling was initiated only many hours after admission. All of these studies reported reductions in brain oedema and ICP during cooling, and found that the treatment had limited and well-manageable side effects. They also observed a decrease in mortality rates compared to historical controls (38 % vs. 80 % in the largest study enrolling 50 patients (54)). However, none of these studies was properly controlled. Variable protocols were used, with treatment durations ranging from 24 to 96 hours; co-interventions differed, and in all studies cooling was started long after the onset of stroke (22 ± 9 hours in the largest study, with a range of 4–75 hours). Thus hypothermia was used more as a method to control intracranial hypertension than as a primary method of neuroprotection. Some of the observed effects could well have been due to effective fever management. Only one small study has looked at the effects of combining the use of hypothermia with thrombolysis (30). This would seem to be a logical approach; thrombolysis restores blood flow, hypothermia is used to mitigate post-ischaemic and reperfusion injury. A larger clinical trial combining these two treatments is currently underway (62). Prospective studies assessing *early* use of hypothermia in severe as well as milder forms of ischaemic stroke are urgently needed.

An important logistical challenge is the fact that proper use of hypothermia and effective control of side effects may require ICU admission. A number of side effects are difficult to manage outside the ICU setting (see below), and most stroke patients are currently managed outside the ICU in neurology wards and stroke units. If effective use of hypothermia indeed requires treatment in the ICU, this would significantly complicate the organisation of hypothermia studies especially in less severe ischaemic stroke, as these patients are not routinely admitted to the ICU. Although two small case series have suggested that induction of mild hypothermia (33–35.5°C) in awake, non-ventilated patients could be feasible (21, 28), careful monitoring and aggressive patient management remain vital in obtaining good outcomes. There is some evidence that use of invasive (endovascular) cooling methods may slightly lower the shivering threshold in awake patients, which would be a potential advantage; however, this issue too needs to be more rigorously assessed in larger and properly controlled studies.

In summary, animal experiments and preliminary clinical data suggest that hypothermia could limit neurological injury in stroke. However, no RCCTs have yet been performed, and it is unclear whether this treatment could be safely administered outside the intensive care setting. Such studies (combining hypothermia with reperfusion through thrombolytics or angioplasty) are urgently needed. The available evidence *does* suggest that therapeutic hypothermia can be used to decrease brain oedema and control ICP in the subcategory of patients with medial cerebral artery infarction and cerebral oedema.

Practical aspects

As discussed above, in spite of the almost universally positive results from animal studies and the excellent results achieved in some clinical trials, the area of therapeutic temperature management remains one of the most controversial areas in intensive care medicine. Many of the problems related to past studies can be linked to difficulties in patient management, especially in the context outside (proper) intensive care. A detailed discussion of side effects and practical issues is beyond the scope of this article, but some of the more important ones will be briefly mentioned here.

It should be remembered that any gains in therapeutic results can be easily lost through improper application and poor patient management. For traumatic brain injury there is strong evidence suggesting that early induction and prolonged duration of treatment (3–5 days) are key aspects in determining the efficacy of cooling as a neuroprotective agent. Rapid induction can be achieved by combining the use of a (surface or intravascular) cooling device with rapid infusion of *cold (4°C) fluids* (1,500–3,000 ml of saline or Ringer's lactate) to "jump-start" the cooling process (47). Standard ICU care should include prevention of hypovolaemia/hypotension, tight control of glucose and electrolyte levels, prevention of infectious complications, adjustment of doses of various drugs (including sedatives and opiates), prevention of shivering, and other interventions (50). During the *maintenance phase the patients' core temperature should be* tightly controlled, with no or minor fluctuations (maximum 0.2–0.5°C).

Cardiac arrhythmias and/or cardiac shock should not be regarded as counterindications for cooling. Hypothermia does not cause hypotension; indeed, it has been used in five small clinical studies to treat refractory cardiac shock (15, 16, 35, 36, 34), and (although cardiac output *does* usually decrease, in conjunction with metabolism) the balance between oxygen supply and demand usually improves significantly during cooling (45, 50). Cooling *increases* membrane stability provided that core temperature remains >30°C (4, 45), and hypothermia has been used in animal experiments and small clinical studies to treat refractory arrhythmias (5, 41, 40).

An issue of special importance is the *speed of warming* in the re-warming phase. In this phase great care should be taken to avoid rapid re-warming; the target rate should be 0.2–0.30 C/hr, with a maximum of 0.5°C/hr in cardiac arrest patients. Warming should be even slower in TBI patients. The reason for this is that numerous animal experiments have shown that rapid re-warming can adversely affect outcome, whereas slow re-warming preserves the benefits of cooling (2, 25, 32).

Injury mechanisms such as apoptosis, neuroinflammation, reperfusion and membrane leakage can be re-triggered by rapid warming, causing the protective effects of cooling to be lost (49). Animal studies (18) and clinical observations (31) suggest that rapid re-warming may cause transient imbalances between cerebral blood flow and oxygen consumption (i.e. increased oxygen consumption relative to perfusion). Rapid warming also increases the risk of hyperkalaemia) (46, 50). Studies using rapid re-warming in TBI patients have had worse results than those using slow re-warming (33).

Summary and conclusions

There are numerous potential indications for therapeutic temperature management. Apart from the ones discussed above, hypothermia has been tested in *acute myocardial infarction* (to reduce infarct size following AMI and coronary reperfusion), *spinal cord injury* (perioperatively during high aortic cross surgery and following traumatic injury such as spinal cord contusion), *hepatic encephalopathy, ARDS, grand mal seizures, acute disseminated encephalomyelitis*, prevention of *radiocontrast nephropathy*, refractory cardiac shock following

cardiac surgery, and various others (review 49). Hypothermia remains widely underused even for those indications (such as cardiac arrest) where the evidence is strong, and where guidelines recommend its use. Clearly, there is a need for dissemination of the evidence and for more education. Equally clearly, many of the other potential applications have not been studied well enough, and the controversies surrounding hypothermia treatment for these treatments is likely to continue for some time.

All in all, it seems fair to say that mild hypothermia presents an important breakthrough in the treatment of at least some types of neurological injury. Its efficacy in the treatment of global post-ischaemic injuries has been clearly demonstrated, and it has been shown to be effective in lowering intracranial pressure in various types of brain injury. Controversies continue to surround its usage in TBI and stroke, and further studies will be needed to determine its place in the treatment for these and other indications. Other areas where the initial data seem highly promising are spinal cord protection in thoraco-abdominal aneurysm repair and decrease of myocardial injury following myocardial infarction. These topics require further and rigorous investigation as soon as possible. Other areas of research should include finding the optimum depth and duration of cooling, and determining what the optimum cooling methods are for different potential indications and patient categories. This will be the challenge for the next decade; much work remains to be done.

The author

Kees H. Polderman, MD, PhD
   Senior Consultant and Associate Professor of
   Intensive Care Medicine | Vice Chairman of
   the Department of Intensive Care | University Medical Center Utrecht, The Netherlands

Address for correspondence
   Kees H. Polderman
   Q 04.4.60
   P.O. Box 85500
   3508 GA Utrecht, The Netherlands
   e-mail: K.Polderman@tip.nl

References

1. Abella BS, Rhee JW, Huang KN, Vanden Hoek TL, Becker LB. Induced hypothermia is underused after resuscitation from cardiac arrest: a current practice survey. Resuscitation. 2005;64:181–6.
2. Alam HB, Rhee P, Honma K et al. Does the rate of rewarming from profound hypothermic arrest influence the outcome in a swine model of lethal hemorrhage? J Trauma. 2006;60:134–46.
3. Alderson P, Gadkary C, Signorini DF. Therapeutic hypothermia for head injury. Cochrane Database Syst Rev. 2004;4:CD001048.
4. Auer RN. Non-pharmacologic (physiologic) neuroprotection in the treatment of brain ischemia. Ann N Y Acad Sci. 2001;939:271–82 (review).
5. Bash SE, Shah JJ, Albers WH, Geiss DM. Hypothermia for the treatment of postsurgical greatly accelerated junctional ectopic tachycardia. J Am Coll Cardiol. 1987; 10:1095–9.
6. Benson DW, Williams GR, Spencer FC. The use of hypothermia after cardiac arrest. Anesth Analg. 1958;38: 423–428.
7. Bernard SA, Gray TW, Buist MD, Jones BM, Silvester W, Gutteridge G, Smith K. Treatment of comatose survivors of out-of-hospital cardiac arrest with induced hypothermia. N Engl J Med. 2002;346:557–63.
8. Berthelsen PG, Cronqvist M. The first intensive care unit in the world: Copenhagen. 1953. Acta Anaesthesiol Scand. 2003;47:1190–1195.
9. Boerrigter MG, Girbes ARJ, Polderman KH. European survey on the use of induced hypothermia in ICU's in Europe. Intensive Care Med. 2006;32:S7 [Abstract 9].
10. Brain Trauma Foundation; American Association of Neurological Surgeons; Congress of Neurological Surgeons; Joint Section on Neurotrauma and Critical Care, AANS/CNS. Guidelines for the management of severe traumatic brain injury. III. Prophylactic hypothermia. J Neurotrauma. 2007;24 Suppl 1:S21–5.
11. Chesnut RM, Marshall SB, Piek J, Blunt BA, Klauber MR, Marshall LF. Early and late systemic hypotension as a frequent and fundamental source of cerebral ischemia following severe brain injury in the Traumatic Coma Data Bank. Acta Neurochir Suppl (Wien). 1993;59:121–5.
12. Clifton GL, Miller ER, Choi SC, Levin HS, McCauley S, Smith KR, Muizelaar JP, Wagner FC, Marion DW, Luerssen TG, Chesnut RM, Schwartz M. Lack of Effect of Induction of Hypothermia after Acute Brain Injury. N Engl J Med. 2001;344:556–563.
13. Clifton GL, Choi SC, Miller ER, Levin HS, Smith jr KR, Muizelaar JP, Wagner FC, Marion DW, Luerssen TG. Intercenter variance in clinical trials of head trauma – experience of the national acute brain injury study: hypothermia. J Neurosurg. 2001;95:751–55.
14. Clifton GL. Is keeping cool still hot? An update on hypothermia in brain injury. Curr Opin Crit Care. 2004; 10:116–9.
15. Dalrymple-Hay MJ, Deakin CD, Knight H, Edwards JC, Keeton B, Salmon AP, Monro JL. Induced hypothermia as salvage treatment for refractory cardiac failure following paediatric cardiac surgery. Eur J Cardiothorac Surg. 1999; 15:515–8.
16. Deakin CD, Knight H, Edwards JC, Monro JL, Lamb RK, Keeton B, Salmon AP. Induced hypothermia in the postoperative management of refractory cardiac failure following paediatric cardiac surgery. Anaesthesia. 1998; 53:848–53.
17. Ducrocq SC, Meyer PG, Orliaguet GA, Blanot S, Laurent-Vannier A, Renier D, Carli PA. Epidemiology and early predictive factors of mortality and outcome in children with traumatic severe brain injury: experience of a French pediatric trauma center. Pediatr Crit Care Med. 2006;7:461–7.
18. Enomoto S, Hindman BJ, Dexter F, Smith T, Cutkomp J. Rapid Rewarming Causes an Increase in the Cerebral Metabolic Rate for Oxygen that Is Temporarily Unmatched by Cerebral Blood Flow: A Study during Cardiopulmonary Bypass in Rabbits. Anesthesiology. 1996;84:1392–1400.
19. Fay T. Observations on generalized refrigeration in cases of severe cerebral trauma. Assoc Res Nerv Ment Dis Proc. 1943;24:611–19.
20. Fearnside MR, Cook RJ, McDougall P, McNeil RJ. The Westmead Head Injury Project outcome in severe head injury. A comparative analysis of pre-hospital, clinical and CT variables. Br J Neurosurg. 1993;7:267–279.
21. Guluma KZ, Hemmen TM, Olsen SE, Rapp KS, Lyden PD. A trial of therapeutic hypothermia via endovascular approach in awake patients with acute ischemic stroke: methodology. Acad Emerg Med. 2006;13:820–7.
22. Hachimi-Idrissi S, Corne L, Ebinger G, Michotte Y, Huyghens L. Mild hypothermia induced by a helmet device: a clinical feasibility study. Resuscitation. 2001; 51:275–81.
23. Harris OA, Colford JM Jr, Good MC, Matz PG. The role of hypothermia in the management of severe brain injury: a meta-analysis. Arch Neurol. 2002;59:1077–83.
24. Henderson WR, Dhingra VK, Chittock DR, Fenwick JC, Ronco JJ. Hypothermia in the management of traumatic brain injury. A systematic review and meta-analysis. Intensive Care Med. 2003;29:1637–44.
25. Hildebrand F, van Griensven M, Giannoudis P et al. Effects of hypothermia and re-warming on the inflammatory response in a murine multiple hit model of trauma. Cytokine. 2005;31:382–93.
26. Holzer M, Bernard SA, Hachimi-Idrissi S, Roine RO, Sterz F, Mullner M; on behalf of the Collaborative Group on Induced Hypothermia for Neuroprotection After Cardiac Arrest. Hypothermia for neuroprotection after

cardiac arrest: systematic review and individual patient data meta-analysis. Crit Care Med. 2005;33:414–8.

27. Hypothermia after Cardiac Arrest Study Group. Mild therapeutic hypothermia to improve the neurologic outcome after cardiac arrest. N Engl J Med. 2002;346: 549–56.

28. Kammersgaard LP, Rasmussen BH, Jørgensen HS, Reith J, Weber U, Olsen TS. Feasibility and safety of inducing modest hypothermia in awake patients with acute stroke through surface cooling: a case-control study: the Copenhagen Stroke Study. Stroke. 2000;31: 2251–2256

29. Kollmar R, Schabitz WR, Heiland S, Georgiadis D, Schellinger PD, Bardutzky J, Schwab S. Neuroprotective effect of delayed moderate hypothermia after focal cerebral ischemia: an MRI study. Stroke. 2002;33: 1899–904.

30. Krieger DW, De Georgia MA, Abou-Chebl A, Andrefsky JC, Sila CA, Katzan IL, Mayberg MR, Furlan AJ. Cooling for acute ischemic brain damage (cool aid): an open pilot study of induced hypothermia in acute ischemic stroke. Stroke. 2001;32:1847–54.

31. Lavinio A, Timofeev I, Nortje J, Outtrim J, Smielewski P, Gupta A, Hutchinson PJ, Matta BF, Pickard JD, Menon D, Czosnyka M. Cerebrovascular reactivity during hypothermia and rewarming. Br J Anaesth. 2007;99: 237–44.

32. Maxwell WL, Watson A, Queen R, Conway B, Russell D, Neilson M, Graham DI. Slow, medium, or fast re-warming following post-traumatic hypothermia therapy? An ultrastructural perspective. J Neurotrauma. 2005;22: 873–84.

33. McIntyre LA, Fergusson DA, Hebert PC, Moher D, Hutchison JS. Prolonged therapeutic hypothermia after traumatic brain injury in adults: a systematic review. JAMA. 2003;289:2992–9.

34. Merchant RM, Soar J, Skrifvars MB, Silfvast T, Edelson DP, Ahmad F, Huang KN, Khan M, Vanden Hoek TL, Becker LB, Abella BS. Therapeutic hypothermia utilization among physicians after resuscitation from cardiac arrest. Crit Care Med. 2006;34:1935–40.

35. Moat NE, Lamb RK, Edwards JC, Manners J, Keeton BR, Monro JL. Induced hypothermia in the management of refractory low cardiac output states following cardiac surgery in infants and children. Eur J Cardiothorac Surg. 1992;6:579–84.

36. Moriyama Y, Iguro Y, Shimokawa S, Saigenji H, Toyohira H, Taira A. Successful application of hypother-mia combined with intra-aortic balloon pump support to low-cardiac-output state after open heart surgery. Angiology. 1996;47:595–9.

37. Nielsen N, for the Hypothermia Network Steering Group. Induced hypothermia after cardiac arrest – analysis of the Northern Hypothermia Network Registry. Intensive Care Med. 2006;32:S7 [Suppl. 1], Abstract 10.

38. Nolan JP, Morley PT, Hoek TL, Hickey RW; Advancement Life support Task Force of the International Liaison committee on Resuscitation. Therapeutic hypothermia after cardiac arrest. An advisory statement by the Advancement Life support Task Force of the International Liaison committee on Resuscitation. Resuscitation. 2003; 57:231–5.

39. Nolan JP, Deakin CD, Soar J, Bottiger BW, Smith G; European Resuscitation Council. European Resuscitation Council guidelines for resuscitation 2005. Section 4. Adult advanced life support. Resuscitation. 2005;67 Suppl 1:S39–86.

40. Otake H, Shite J, Paredes OL et al. Catheter-based transcoronary myocardial hypothermia attenuates arrhythmia and myocardial necrosis in pigs with acute myocardial infarction. J Am Coll Cardiol. 2007;49:250–60.

41. Pfammatter JP, Paul T, Ziemer G, Kallfelz HC. Successful management of junctional tachycardia by hypothermia after cardiac operations in infants. Ann Thorac Surg. 1995;60:556–60.

42. Polderman KH, Ely EW, Badr AE, Girbes AR. Induced hypothermia in traumatic brain injury: considering the conflicting results of meta-analyses and moving forward. Intensive Care Med. 2003;29:1637–44.

43. Polderman KH, Girbes AR, Peerdeman SM, Vandertop WP. Hypothermia. J Neurosurg. 2001;94:853–8.

44. Polderman KH, Sterz F, van Zanten ARH et al. Induced hypothermia improves neurological outcome in asystolic patients with out-of-hospital cardiac arrest. Circulation. 2003;108:IV-581 [abstract 2646].

45. Polderman KH. Therapeutic hypothermia in the Intensive Care unit: problems, pitfalls and opportunities. Part 1: indications and evidence. Intensive Care Medicine. 2004;30:556–75 (review).

46. Polderman KH. Application of therapeutic hypothermia in the intensive care unit. Opportunities and pitfalls of a promising treatment modality – Part 2: Practical aspects and side effects. Intensive Care Med. 2004;30:757–69 (review).

47. Polderman KH, Rijnsburger ER, Peerdeman SM, Girbes AR. Induction of hypothermia in patients with various types of neurologic injury with use of large volumes of ice-cold intravenous fluid. Crit Care Med. 2005;33:2744–51.

48. Polderman KH. Mechanisms and potential side effects of therapeutic mild hypothermia. In: Cardiac Arrest: the Science and Practice of Resuscitation Medicine, 2ND edition; Paradis N, Halperin H, Kern K, Wenzel V, Chamberlain D, editors; Cambridge university press. 2007;859–70.

49. Polderman KH. Induced hypothermia and fever control for prevention and treatment of neurological injuries. Lancet. 2008;371:1955–1969.

50. Polderman KH, Herold I. Therapeutic hypothermia and controlled normothermia in the ICU: practical

considerations, side effects and cooling methods. Crit Care Med. 2008 (in press).

51. Schaller B, Graf R. Hypothermia and stroke: the pathophysiological background. Pathophysiology. 2003; 10:7–35.

52. Schwab S, Schwarz S, Aschoff A, Keller E, Hacke W. Moderate hypothermia and brain temperature in patients with severe middle cerebral artery infarction. Acta Neurochir Suppl (Wien). 1998;71:131–4

53. Schwab S, Schwarz S, Spranger M, Keller E, Bertram M, Hacke W. Moderate hypothermia in the treatment of patients with severe middle cerebral artery infarction. Stroke. 1998;29:2461–6.

54. Schwab S, Georgiadis D, Berrouschot J, Schellinger PD, Graffagnino C, Mayer SA. Feasibility and safety of moderate hypothermia after massive hemispheric infarction. Stroke. 2001;32:2033–5.

55. Park CK, Jun SS, Kim MC, Kang JK. Effects of systemic hypothermia and selective brain cooling on ischemic brain damage and swelling. Acta Neurochir Suppl (Wien). 1998;71:225–8.

56. Safar P, DeKornfeld TJ, Person JM. The intensive care unit. Anaesthesia. 1961;16:275–84.

57. Steiner T, Friede T, Aschoff A, Schellinger PD, Schwab S, Hacke W. Effect and feasibility of controlled rewarming after moderate hypothermia in stroke patients with malignant infarction of the middle cerebral artery. Stroke. 2001;32:2833–5.

58. Shiozaki T, Hayakata T, Taneda M, Nakajima Y, Hashiguchi N, Fujimi S, Nakamori Y, Tanaka H, Shimazu T, Sugimoto H. A multicenter prospective randomized controlled trial of the efficacy of mild hypothermia for severely head injured patients with low intracranial pressure. Mild Hypothermia Study Group in Japan. J Neurosurg. 2001;94:50–4.

59. Stocchetti N, Zanaboni C, Colombo A, Citerio G, Beretta L, Ghisoni L, Zanier ER, Canavesi K. Refractory intracranial hypertension and "second-tier" therapies in traumatic brain injury. Intensive Care Med. 2008;34:461–7.

60. Vavilala MS, Bowen A, Lam AM, Uffman JC, Powell J, Winn HR, Rivara FP. Blood pressure and outcome after severe pediatric traumatic brain injury. J Trauma. 2003; 55:1039–44.

61. Williams GR Jr, Spencer FC. The clinical use of hypothermia following cardiac arrest. Ann Surg. 1958;148:462–8.

62. www.clinicaltrials.gov. Intravenous Thrombolysis Plus Hypothermia for Acute Treatment of Ischemic Stroke. ClinicalTrials.gov Identifier: NCT00283088, http://clinicaltrials.gov/ct/show/NCT00283088?order=1.

63. Yahagi N, Kumon K, Watanabe Y, Tanigami H, Haruna M, Hayashi H, Imanaka H, Takeuchi M, Ohashi Y, Takamoto S. Value of mild hypothermia in patients who have severe circulatory insufficiency even after intra-aortic balloon pump. J Clin Anesth. 1998;10:120–5.

64. Arrich J; European Resuscitation Council Hypothermia After Cardiac Arrest Registry Study Group. Clinical application of mild therapeutic hypothermia after cardiac arrest. Crit Care Med. 2007;35:1041–7.

65. Laver SR, Padkin A, Atalla A, Nolan JP. Therapeutic hypothermia after cardiac arrest: a survey of practice in intensive care units in the United Kingdom. Anaesthesia. 2006; 61:873–7.

Malcolm R. Macleod

Can we increase/lengthen the time window from 3–6 hours for thrombolysis after stroke?

Thrombolysis with intravenous tissue plaminogen activator (tPA) is one of only 4 effective treatments for acute ischaemic stroke. While thrombolysis is highly effective, its use is limited by the small proportion of patients presenting within 3 hours of symptom onset who are eligible for treatment. Strategies to increase the number of patients who might benefit from this treatment might have a substantial effect on death and disability. Such strategies include the demonstration of efficacy in unselected patients beyond 3 hours; the demonstration that it is possible to select patients according to certain (for instance imaging) criteria beyond three hours in whom efficacy is maintained; the use of intra-arterial thrombolysis; and the use of co-treatments which might extend the therapeutic window of thrombolysis. While each of these represents a promising approach, at present there is only randomised controlled trial evidence to support the efficacy of intra-arterial thrombolysis up to 6 hours after symptom onset.

Despite decades of research activity, acute ischaemic stroke remains a leading cause of death and disability. At present, 4 effective and well-evidenced treatments are available. The International Stroke Trial and the Chinese Acute Stroke Trial tested the efficacy of aspirin and/or heparin in the first 48 hours, and showed a significant benefit with aspirin but not heparin. A number of studies, summarised in meta-analyses conducted by the Stroke Unit Trialists Collaboration, demonstrated that management in a dedicated Stroke Unit resulted in a substantial improvement in death and disability. More recently, the DESTINY, DECIMAL and HAMLET studies have been combined in meta-analysis to show that, in patients with malignant MCA infarction, decompressive hemicraniectomy resulted in substantial reductions in mortality and reduced disability.

However, the intervention which has attracted the most attention for the treatment of acute ischaemic stroke is intravenous thrombolysis with tissue plasminogen activator. When given within 3 hours of stroke, tPA reduces the composite outcome of death or disability from around 45 % to 36 %, a relative reduction of 20 % and such that only 11 patients need to be treated to prevent one becoming dead or disabled. When treatment is initiated within 90 minutes of symptom onset the benefits are even more pronounced, with a Number Needed to Treat of only 7. By way of comparison, the pivotal trials of intravenous thrombolysis in the treatment of myocardial infarction which did so much to change the management of myocardial infarction were associated with an

NNT of 50, and treatment of meningococcal meningitis with penicillin has an NNT of 6.

Current use of tPA within 3 hours

There is substantial efficacy to support the use of tPA in selected patients with acute ischaemic stroke within 3 hours of symptom onset (1). However, a number of important factors need to be taken into account when determining whether an individual patient may benefit. The pivotal NINDS study (2) excluded patients considered to be at high risk of bleeding, and on this basis tPA is not licenced for use in patients with hypertension (a systolic BP above 185 mmHg or a diastolic BP above 110 mmHg); those with marked hypoglycaemia (blood sugar more than 22.2 mmol/l) and the elderly (over 80). In addition, patients held to be at high risk of bleeding either because of recent trauma or surgery; a known site at high risk of bleeding (e.g. oesophageal varicies); or a hypocoagulable state (low plateletes, known bleeding diathesis, warfarin treatment or recent treatment with heparin with an abnormal thromboplastin time) are considered to have contra-indications to the use of tPA within three hours.

Identification of the time at which the stroke occurred is a crucial, but sometimes elusive, piece of information. Where symptoms are present on waking from sleep the best that can be inferred is that the stroke occurred some time after the patient went to sleep, but with no greater precision than that. Strokes involving the non-dominant hemisphere may result in a lack of awareness of (usually) the left side of the body, and so the patient's recollection of when symptoms began may not reflect when the stroke occurred. Where a non-dominant hemisphere stroke appears radiologically older than the patient's history would suggest, one should identify the time of stroke onset with caution. Finally, patients with dominant hemisphere strokes may develop speech and language difficulties which render them unable to relate the history of their stroke. Under these circumstances, identifying someone who can give a firsthand eyewitness account of events can be crucial, and that person should be asked to accompany the patient to hospital and to remain with them until immediate management decisions have been concluded.

It is likely that the potential for benefit of treatment will be reduced and the risk of harm increased in patients who approach these cut-offs, and so the decision to proceed with thrombolysis requires careful consideration of the risks and potential benefits as they apply to the individual patient, and for this reason the decision should be taken by a physician skilled and experienced in the diagnosis, treatment and management of patients with stroke.

These complexities mean that only a small proportion of stroke patients receive thrombolysis. In Centres admitting unselected patients with stroke the best that can be achieved is around 10%, and even in Centres admitting an enriched population of patients (selected because they are potential candidates for thrombolysis) the best that can be achieved is 30–40%. However, such is the impact of the treatment that the introduction of a thrombolysis service might be expected to prevent 11 patients dying or becoming disabled per 1,000 strokes occuring in the community, compared with 46 per 1,000 for stroke unit care and 6 per 1,000 for immediate treatment with aspirin (see fig. 1) (3).

The development of strategies which broaden the pool of eligible patients whilst preserving efficacy would therefore represent a substantial advance in the treatment of stroke.

Extending the time window with evidence

The randomised controlled trials of tPA in acute ischaemic stroke have allowed delays from stroke onset to the initiation of treatment of up to 6 hours. A combined analysis of data from these trials confirms the efficacy of treatment within 3 hours, but suggests that there may be some benefit, albeit reduced, in similar patients treated within 6 hours of symptom onset (see fig. 2). Because the effect of thrombolysis is probably smaller, larger studies would be required to demonstrate significant superiority over standard care, and two studies are testing this hypothesis.

The third European Co-operative Acute Stroke Study (ECASS-3) is a randomised comparison of treatment with intravenous thrombolysis initiated between 3 and 4.5 hours of symptom onset. Eligibility is restricted to the terms of the licence for treatment within 3 hours, and

Can we increase/lengthen the time window from 3–6 hours for thrombolysis after stroke?

E

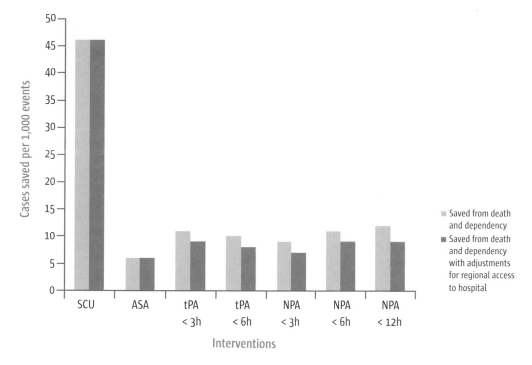

Fig. 1 The potential benefits of stroke care units SCUs, aspirin (ASA), tissue plasminogen activator (tPA) and neuroprotective agent (NPA) per 1,000 strokes in the community. NPAs are unproven therapies still being further investigated and for this analysis the potential impact was based on hypothetical absolute risk reductions from sample size calculations from previous clinical trials. From: Gilligan AK, Thrift AG, Sturm JW, Dewey HM, Macdonell RAL and Donnan G. Cerebroavascular Diseases 2005:20: 239–244, with permission from S. Karger, Basel.

patients over 80 are specifically excluded. Recruitment continues, and the first results are expected in 2009.

The third International Stroke Trial (IST-3) is a randomised trial comparing intravenous thrombolysis with tPA initiated within 6 hours of symptom onset with standard care (4). As well as providing information on treatment initiated between 3 and 6 hours of symptom onset it is also possible to randomise patients at earlier times where the treating physician is uncertain of the balance between risk and potential benefit, for instance in the elderly. Over 1,028 patients had been recruited by early 2008, making IST-3 the largest ever clinical trial of thrombolysis for tPA; with over 330 patients over the age of 80 randomised in the trial it will provide the first reliable evidence regarding efficacy in this group. The study aims to recruit 3,100 patients by 2011, with results expected in 2012.

Extending the time window with patient selection

The therapeutic principle underlying thrombolysis is that, at the time of vessel reperfusion, there are important brain volumes where neuronal survival is reversibly compromised, that is to say where reversal of ischaemia might lead to recovery of normal neuronal function. Evidence from experimental stroke (with all the caveats which must be placed on such data (5)) suggests that there are indeed regions of the brain with reduced perfusion where the potential for neuronal survival is maintained, at least for a time (6, 7); this is the region referred to as the ischaemic penumbra. Observational studies in stroke patients suggest that a penumbra may well exist in some patients with ischaemic stroke, and that in some patients it may persist for many hours (8). If the regions thus identified do truly represent poten-

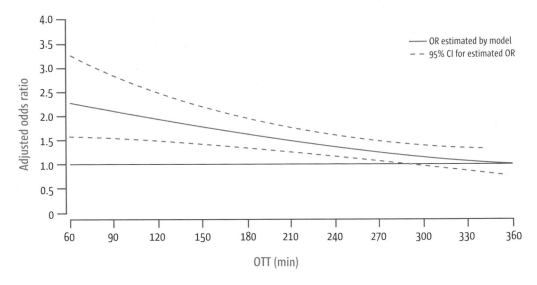

Fig. 2   Model estimating odds ratio for a favourable outcome at 3 months in patients receiving thrombolysis compared with controls, stratified by Onset to treatment Time (OTT). Reprinted from The Lancet, 363, Hacke W, Donnan G, Fieschi C, Kaste M, von KR, Broderick JP et al. Association of outcome with early stroke treatment: pooled analysis of ATLANTIS, ECASS, and NINDS rt-PA stroke trials, 768–74, 2004, with permission from Elsevier.

tially salvageable brain tissue, then patients with evidence of persisting penumbra might benefit from reperfusion even at later timepoints.

These considerations have formed the basis of strategies whereby patients have been selected for treatment based on MRI findings, usually some measure of a mismatch between tissue perfusion and tissue damage (for instance diffusion weighted imaging). These strategies have been tested in trials of an alternative thrombolytic agent, desmoteplase; despite some promise in earlier trials, selection of patients up to 9 hours after stroke on the basis of MRI criteria did not appear to identify a subgroup of patients in whom the benefits of early treatment were also seen at later times (9, 10).

The Echo Planar Imaging THrombolyis Evaluation Trial (EPITHET) was a randomised study of 100 patients allocated tPA or placebo between 3 and 6 hours designed to test the hypothesis that certain patterns of perfusion-diffusion mismatch on MRI scanning might predict those patients most likely to respond to thrombolysis. There was a non-significant improvement in outcome (44% vs. 42%) in all patients receiving thrombolysis, and this was more marked (45% vs. 40%) in the subgroup of patients with perfusion-diffusion mismatch. Importantly, reperfusion was observed in 56% of treated patients compared with only 26% of controls; reperfusion is known to be associated with improved functional outcome, so the results of EPITHET do suggest that thrombolysis beyond 3 hours may well be effective, and that selection of patients using MRI criteria may be useful. Further, larger trials testing this hypothesis are required.

It seems, therefore, that the currently available imaging selection criteria are not yet able reliably to identify patients at later timepoints who might benefit from thrombolysis. It may be that these selection criteria are not yet sufficiently robust, quick or sensitive to be effective. Alternative approaches might include CT based imaging modalities. However, it may be that that the limiting factor is not whether or not viable brain tissue exists at the time of reperfusion but rather the state of the downstream vasculature and in particular the vascular endothelium when it has been subjected to ischaemia for more than 3 to 6 hours. The time-related limiting factor may be an increased risk of harm in the form of haemorrhage rather a reduced chance of benefit, and indeed there is some evidence both from experimental data (11) and from clinical trial data (12)

Can we increase/lengthen the time window from 3–6 hours for thrombolysis after stroke?

E

to support this hypothesis. The selection criteria for "late" thrombolyis might therefore have to include not only a marker of salvageable brain but also some measure of endothelial health.

Extending the time window with different approaches

As discussed above, the efficacy of thrombolysis depends on both the ability to reinstate perfusion to still-viable brain and on the risk of harm. The greatest potential for harm comes from the risk of intracranial haemorrhage, and this is known to increase both with the dose of thrombolytic used and, as discussed above, with the delay to treatment. An alternative approach to intravenous thrombolysis is the intra-arterial approach. While this is technically more complex, it has a number of potential benefits. Firstly, the intra-arterial approach allows the delivery of a higher concentration of tPA in the vicinity of the clot along with a lower total dose of thrombolytic, and this may be important, particularly where there is an established risk of haemorrhage in other vascular beds. Secondly, the introduction of a catheter to the cranial circulation allows the deployment of other devices including mechanical devices to aid clot dissolution or to allow clot retrieval. This may be particularly important where a clot has formed and matured extracranially (for instance in the left atrial appendage of patients with atrial fibrillation) and may be substantially more resistant to the thrombolytic effects of tPA than is a freshly formed clot. Finally, the ability to determine angiographically when reperfusion has been achieved allows the dose of tPA to be limited to the minimum required.

The second PRO-urokinase for Acute Cerebral Thromboembolism study (PROACT II) tested the efficacy of intra-arterial thrombolysis in anterior circulation stroke when treatment was initiated up to 6 hours after symptom onset (13). Patients randomised were in general more severely affected by their stroke than patients in the intravenous thrombolysis trials. There the proportion of patients with a good outcome (a score on the Modified Rankin Scale of 0, 1 or 2) increased from 25% to 40%, and this was associated with an increase in the rate of middle cerebral artery reperfusion from 18% to 66%. However, there was no difference in mortality (25% versus 27%).

It has been argued that brain regions supplied by the posterior circulation (i.e. the brain stem, cerebellum, pons and mid-brain) might be more tolerant of ischaemia, and therefore that the time-window over which the benefits of treatments might exceed the risks would be prolonged. To date this hypothesis has been tested only in one small clinical trial where treatment was initiated within 24 hours of symptom onset (14); although the results were consistent with a substantial benefit the numbers of patients recruited was far too small to allow reliable conclusions to be drawn. Lindsberg and Mattle have reviewed reports of intravenous and intra-arterial approaches to posterior circulation thrombolysis where treatment was initiated up to 48 hours after symptom onset (15). Summarising a number of case reports and case series they reported good outcomes in 37% of patients with demonstrated recanalisation compared with only 2% of patients without.

One potential drawback of the intra-arterial approach is that the inevitable delay in preparing the patient for angiography means that treatment will be initiated later than would be the case if an intravenous approach were to be used. It has been suggested that this problem might be overcome if patients were to receive intravenous treatment as a "bridging" strategy while being prepared for angiography, and this approach is currently being tested in the third Interventional Management of Stroke study (IMS-3).

Extending the time window with alternative thrombolytic drugs

The benefits for thrombolysis depend on the balance between the potential to improve neurological outcome and the risk of harm. Tissue Plasminogen Activator is an endogenous protein found not only in the circulation but also within the brain. Here it has a number of roles not restricted to the vasculature, including the activation of matrix metalloproteinase 9 (16). The observed benefits of thrombolysis might therefore be moderated by these non-vascular effects, and the use of an alternative thrombolytic agent without such properties might be expected to perform better, particularly at longer delays to treatment where risk/benefit considerations become more balanced.

These considerations have lead to the development of desmoteplase, a plasminogen activator found in the saliva of the European vampire bat. The first and second Desmoteplase in Acute Stroke (DIAS) studies and the Dose Escalation study of Desmoteplase in Acute ischaemic Stroke study (DEDAS) have tested the efficacy of desmoteplase treatment initiated 3 to 9 hours after the onset of symptoms in patients with MRI findings suggesting the presence of an ischaemic penumbra (see above). Both DEDAS (9) and DIAS I (10) suggested that this strategy might be effective, but the larger DIAS II study designed to confirm these findings did not in fact do so (17). The DIAS II results were unusual in that patients in the Control group did much better than expected; in a post hoc analysis the investigators found that rates of MCA occlusion were substantially lower than anticipated, and suggest that in those patients with MCA occlusion desmoteplase may indeed have had some efficacy; further studies will be required to confirm or refute this hypothesis.

Extending the time window with co-treatments

It might be possible to augment the efficacy of neuroprotective drugs with thrombolysis, or to use drugs that reduce the risks of adverse events caused by thrombolysis. Most neuroprotective treatment strategies rely on intravenous drug delivery, and one reason advanced for the failure of such agents in clinical trial is that the concentration of drug achieved in brain was lower than achieved in animal studies. Clearly, where drug is delivered via the circulation and where cerebral perfusion is impaired, drug delivery will not be optimal; and conversely, strategies to increase perfusion of injured brain (such as thrombolysis) might result in increased delivery of drug to its site of intended action. There is substantial evidence across a range of drugs tested in animal models of stroke that combination treatment with thrombolytic and neuroprotectant retains efficacy at longer delays to treatment, at times when neither treatment alone retains efficacy. While there have been some attempts to test this hypothesis in clinical trials, this has usually been in subgroup analysis rather than the primary purpose of the trial, and results to date have been disappointing. Given that we do not yet have a neuroprotective interven-

tion which is effective at any time point, and given the effect that requiring an eligibility for thrombolysis would have on trial recruitment in the crucial 3 to 6 hour time scale and the ethical need to offer open label thrombolysis to eligible patients within three hours, I do not believe that studies testing the efficacy of combination treatments are currently practicable; first, get a neuroprotectant!

It has been suggested that the reinstatement of cerebral blood flow might create conditions which actually promote neuronal damage, in the form of so-called "reperfusion injury", held to be due in large part to an oxidative storm of free radicals at a time when endogenous free radical scavenging mechanisms are impaired (18). The existence of reperfusion injury remains a matter of debate, and it may simply represent injury which is observed to occur at the time of reperfusion, and which would have happened even if reperfusion had not occurred. Reperfusion injury has not been convincingly demonstrated in human stroke, but if it did exist then treatments directed at providing exogenous scavenging of free radicals – such as NXY-059 – might be expected to confer benefit in patients undergoing thrombolysis, and this is emphatically not the case (19).

A further consideration is the effect of drugs on the ischaemic vasculature. The major risk associated with the use of tPA is that of intracranial haemorrhage, and this risk increases with the delay to treatment meaning that it is a major determinant of the balance between risk and benefit at these later time points. At least part of the increased risk of haemorrhage at later time points is due to the effect of ischaemia on the vasculature, and drug treatments which promoted vascular health might reduce the risk of haemorrhage and therefore increase the safety, and therefore efficacy, of thrombolysis. Indeed, such effects have been reported for "neuroprotective" drugs including NXY-059 (11). In the SAINT II study the average delay between initiation of thrombolysis and initiation of treatment with NXY-059 or placebo was over 80 minutes (19), and so the hypothesis that simultaneous treatment might reduce the risk of haemorrhage has not been tested.

Conclusion

Currently, there is good evidence to support the efficacy of thrombolysis up to 3 hours post stroke onset. Research

Can we increase/lengthen the time window from 3-6 hours for thrombolysis after stroke?

E

effort now should focus on determining the efficacy at later times, on better methods to select these patients who might benefit, and on developing interventions to reduce the risks associated with thrombolysis at later time points.

The author

Malcolm R. Macleod, MD
Clinical Neurosciences
University of Edinburgh
Western General Hospital
Crewe Road, Edinburgh
EH10 5EY, UK
e-mail: malcolm.macleod@ed.ac.uk

References

1. Hacke W, Donnan G, Fieschi C, Kaste M, von KR, Broderick JP et al. Association of outcome with early stroke treatment: pooled analysis of ATLANTIS, ECASS, and NINDS rt-PA stroke trials. Lancet. 2004 Mar 6;363(9411): 768–74.
2. Tissue plasminogen activator for acute ischemic stroke. The National Institute of Neurological Disorders and Stroke rt-PA Stroke Study Group. N Engl J Med. 1995 Dec 14;333(24):1581–7.
3. Gilligan AK, Thrift AG, Sturm JW, Dewey HM, Macdonell RA, Donnan GA. Stroke units, tissue plasminogen activator, aspirin and neuroprotection: which stroke intervention could provide the greatest community benefit? Cerebrovasc Dis. 2005;20(4):239–44.
4. Whiteley W, Lindley R, Wardlaw J, Sandercock P. Third International Stroke Trial. International Journal of Stroke 2006 Aug;1:172–6.
5. Sena E, van der Worp HB, Howells D, Macleod M. How can we improve the pre-clinical development of drugs for stroke? Trends Neurosci. 2007 Sep;30(9):433–9.
6. Giffard C, Young AR, Kerrouche N, Derlon JM, Baron JC. Outcome of acutely ischemic brain tissue in prolonged middle cerebral artery occlusion: a serial positron emission tomography investigation in the baboon. J Cereb Blood Flow Metab. 2004 May;24(5):495–508.
7. Dirnagl U, Iadecola C, Moskowitz MA. Pathobiology of ischaemic stroke: an integrated view. Trends Neurosciences. 1999 Sep;22(9):391–7.
8. Takasawa M, Jones PS, Guadagno JV, Christensen S, Fryer TD, Harding S et al. How Reliable Is Perfusion MR in

Acute Stroke?. Validation and Determination of the Penumbra Threshold Against Quantitative PET. Stroke. 2008 Feb 7;STROKEAHA.
9. Furlan AJ, Eyding D, Albers GW, Al-Rawi Y, Lees KR, Rowley HA et al. Dose Escalation of Desmoteplase for Acute Ischemic Stroke (DEDAS): evidence of safety and efficacy 3 to 9 hours after stroke onset. Stroke. 2006 May;37(5): 1227–31.
10. Hacke W, Albers G, Al-Rawi Y, Bogousslavsky J, Davalos A, Eliasziw M et al. The Desmoteplase in Acute Ischemic Stroke Trial (DIAS): a phase II MRI-based 9-hour window acute stroke thrombolysis trial with intravenous desmoteplase. Stroke. 2005 Jan;36(1):66–73.
11. Culot M, Rentfel M, Dehouck MP, Lundquist S, Cecchelli R. NXY-059, a free radical-trapping neuroprotectant protects the blood brain barrier (BBB) in ischaemic conditions in vitro. Society for Neuroscience abstracts 2006;1:679–13.
12. Hacke W, Donnan G, Fieschi C, Kaste M, von KR, Broderick JP et al. Association of outcome with early stroke treatment: pooled analysis of ATLANTIS, ECASS, and NINDS rt-PA stroke trials. Lancet. 2004 Mar 6;363(9411): 768–74.
13. Furlan A, Higashida R, Wechsler L, Gent M, Rowley H, Kase C et al. Intra-arterial prourokinase for acute ischemic stroke. The PROACT II study: a randomized controlled trial. Prolyse in Acute Cerebral Thromboembolism. JAMA. 1999 Dec 1;282(21):2003–11.
14. Macleod MR, Davis SM, Mitchell PJ, Gerraty RP, Fitt G, Hankey GJ et al. Results of a multicentre, randomised controlled trial of intra-arterial urokinase in the treatment of acute posterior circulation ischaemic stroke. Cerebrovasc Dis. 2005;20(1):12–7.
15. Lindsberg PJ, Mattle HP. Therapy of Basilar Artery Occlusion: A Systematic Analysis Comparing Intra-Arterial and Intravenous Thrombolysis. Stroke. 2006 Mar 1;37(3):922–8.
16. Kelly MA, Shuaib A, Todd KG. Matrix metalloproteinase activation and blood-brain barrier breakdown following thrombolysis. Exp Neurol. 2006 Jul;200(1):38–49.
17. Hacke W, Furlan A. Results from the phase III study of Desmoteplase In Acute Ischemic Stroke Trial 2 (DIAS 2). European Stroke Conference, Glasgow. 2007. Ref Type: Abstract.
18. Dietrich WD. Morphological manifestations of reperfusion injury in brain. Ann N Y Acad Sci 1994 Jun 17; 723: 15–24.:15–24.
19. Shuaib A, Lees KR, Grotta J, Lyden P, Davalos A, Davis SM et al. SAINT II: Results of the second randomized, multicenter, placebo-controlled, double-blind study of NXY-059 treatment in patients with acute ischemic stroke. Stroke. 2007;38(2):471.

Odin Barbosa da Silva, Gustavo Trindade Henriques Filho
and Jorge Luiz da Rocha Paranhos

Neuroprotective ventilation

Introduction

Cerebral metabolism depends on the presence of adequate cerebral blood flow (CBF). Through this, satisfactory provision of oxygen (O_2) and glucose is ensured, along with the removal of cerebral metabolism products. The cerebral blood volume (CBV) varies proportionally in relation to the CBF (1).

Physiologically, this flow is 50 to 60 millilitres per 100 grams of cerebral tissue per minute, which corresponds to approximately 15–20% of the cardiac output. This allows the brain to consume oxygen at a rate of 3.3 ml/100g/min, which is close to 18–20% of the entire body's consumption, even though the brain only corresponds to 2% of total body weight (2). The CBF is kept relatively constant by means of the inherent properties of the cerebral vasculature, such as pressure autoregulation, which optimises the equilibrium between the CBF and the cerebral perfusion pressure (CPP) according to variations in intracranial pressure (ICP) and mean arterial pressure (MAP); metabolic autoregulation or metabolic coupling, which optimises the equilibrium between the flow and the cortical consumption (or activity); and vasoreactivity to perivascular carbon dioxide (CO_2) and to arterial oxygen pressure (1).

Autoregulation of the cerebral vessels is characterised by the capacity to keep the CBF stable within a range of MAP variation between 60 and 150 mmHg, by means of cerebral vasoconstriction when the pressure is high or vasodilatation when it is low (3). Through this, there will not be any increases in CBF or CBV (hyperaemia) with consequent brain swelling and intracranial hypertension (ICH). Nor will there be any reduction in CBF and CBV (oligaemia) with secondary ischemic lesions.

Metabolic coupling allows the CBF to be adapted according to the variation in metabolic demand, i.e. in relation to greater or lesser need for O_2 and glucose provision. During activation of the cortex, for example, the increased consumption of these metabolic substrates is compensated by a concomitant increase in the regional CBF, and the opposite occurs during sedation, anaesthesia and hypothermia. These adjustments are regulated through the sympathetic and parasympathetic innervation, the partial pressures of O_2 and CO_2 and the concentration of hydrogen ions (H^+), lactic acid, extracellular potassium, prostacyclin, adenosine, nitric oxide and thromboxane A_2, among others (4).

Thus, the O_2 levels are very important for maintaining the CBF and CBV, with small variations in PaO_2 between 50 and 300 mmHg. Hypoxaemia of lower than 50 mmHg not only leads to cerebral hypoxia but also leads to cerebral vasodilatation and increased CBF and CBV. This may give rise to ICH through engorgement of the microcirculation and cerebral oedema through extravasation of cerebral spinal fluid (CSF) across the blood-brain barrier consequent to lesions caused by the ischaemic event. From a physiopathological point of view, this level of hypoxaemia leads to an anaerobic glucose cycle, with lactic acidosis and accumulation of free H^+ in the perivascular CSF. This causes precapillary vasoplegia, which may vary in intensity depending on changes in the perivascular K^+ and Ca^{++} levels. On the other hand, experimental studies have been unable to demonstrate that hyperoxia of more than 300 mmHg would give rise to vasoconstriction with low cerebral flow, considering that the graphical relationship between CBF and PaO_2 is a curve that characteristically tends towards infinity (4).

CO_2 has a vasodilatory effect on the cerebral arterioles, through the perivascular H^+ levels (5). Thus, reductions in $PaCO_2$ lead to increases in perivascular pH, followed by cerebral vasoconstriction with consequent reduction in CBF and CBV and, depending on the intensity and the coupling between flow and consumption, cerebral hypoxia. The risk of hypoxia is also worsened by the effect of systemic alkalosis on the oxygen dissociation curve, thereby reducing the release of O_2 to the organs (6). The effect of the pH occurs through mediators, and the ones most frequently implicated are nitric oxide, prostanoids, cyclic nucleotides, intracellular calcium and potassium channels (7). With $PaCO_2$ values between 20 and 80 mmHg, in patients with brain trauma, each millimetre change in $PaCO_2$ causes the CBF to change by 1–2 ml/100g/min. However, this change only persists for a few hours while the metabolic compensation mechanisms correct the pH and normalise the CBF (8). Studies on anaesthetised animals have shown that, within six hours, the CBF returns to normal values because the pH has been corrected by the fall in extravascular bicarbonate in the brain (9, 10). Likewise, hyperaemia may occur when the $PaCO_2$ values rise (11).

Physiologically, the ICP is maintained by means of an equilibrium between the intracranial components (blood, CSF and cerebral tissue), as established by the Monro-Kellie doctrine (12, 13). In situations of increased intracranial volume (tumours, haematomas or oedema, for example), CSF and venous blood are displaced so that there is no acutely raised ICP. The ICH occurs when this compensatory mechanism (cerebral compliance) is exhausted. Furthermore, in patients with severe acute neurological disease presenting altered cerebral compliance and loss of autoregulatory and metabolic coupling properties, the physiological maintenance of cerebral perfusion is impaired such that the CPP depends directly on the MAP (14, 15). In such cases, after the primary neu-

rological injury has occurred, low CBF and lowering of the level of consciousness frequently occur. These need to be promptly corrected, given that it is important for the patient's prognosis to maintain an adequate CBF level (1, 16).

Therefore, it is clear that mechanical ventilation is an important part of the treatment of severely neurocritical patients. It is essential to know how to manage the ventilation correctly, regarding both its protective and its therapeutic characteristics, and how to avoid its potential deleterious effects, particularly the risk of ischaemic brain injury.

Ventilation and cerebral protection in neurocritical patients

There are several indications for tracheal intubation and mechanical ventilation in acute neurological patients, from the mere need for airway protection in patients with a score of less than nine on the Glasgow Coma Scale (4, 14), to loss of ventilatory drive, weakness of the respiratory musculature and inefficiency of gas exchange. Some authors have demonstrated, in an evaluation of several intensive care units around the world, that around 20 % of patients on mechanical ventilation had a neurological indication (14).

Neurological patients on mechanical ventilation can be divided into three groups: those who will receive ventilation for a short time, for example following a surgery; those who have a neuromuscular disease and are dependent on prolonged ventilation to maintain adequate gas exchange; and those who require mechanical ventilation as a therapeutic strategy for cerebral protection, in order to ensure that gas exchange takes place and assist in controlling the ICP, as in cases of brain trauma and stroke.

Mechanical ventilation needs to follow certain basic guidelines. These guidelines must be used to ventilate the first two groups of patients, but for the third group, other ventilatory strategies may be needed, as described in the following.

1. Ventilation mode: controlled ventilation must be instituted in patients without a good ventilatory drive, either due to lesions of the respiratory centre (trauma, ischaemia, bleeding or tumours) or because of the need for sedation to reduce the cerebral metabolism, to ensure adequate minute-ventilation. Assisted or con-

trolled-assisted ventilation should be used preferentially in patients presenting with a good drive, in order to avoid asynchronism and to allow the muscles to work, thereby avoiding atrophy of the respiratory musculature. Ventilatory asynchronism and respiratory exertion may lead to increased ICP (4, 16).

2. PEEP: positive end-expiratory pressure is important in mechanical ventilation in order to improve the airflow to non-recruited areas of the lungs, achieve better pulmonary compliance, reduce pulmonary shunt and raise arterial oxygenation. However, the increase in intrathoracic pressure is reflected in the jugular veins, with a consequent reduction in the cerebral venous return and ICH. Thus, physiological PEEP should always be used (around 5 cmH$_2$O), and increasing this when necessary for neurocritical patients must be guided by adequate monitoring of ICP (17, 18).

3. Plateau pressure: it is known that mechanical ventilation may by itself lead to lung injury. Therefore, keeping the plateau pressure under 30 cmH$_2$O is a strategy indicated both for reducing the risk of such injury and for improving the evolution of patients with associated pulmonary oedema (4).

4. FiO$_2$: when neurocritical patients are intubated and mechanical ventilation is initiated for them, 100% O$_2$ must be used. However, FiO$_2$ must be gradually reduced to levels that ensure both adequate oxygenation and absence of pulmonary lesions caused by O$_2$. FiO$_2$ less than 50% should be preferentially sought for this purpose (4).

5. Oxygenation: the peripheral oxygen saturation (SpO$_2$) should be kept greater than 94%, to ensure adequate O$_2$ delivery and avoid both direct hypoxic lesions and oligaemic intracranial hypertension due to failure of metabolic coupling, with increased need for O$_2$ and relatively low CBF, which would cause high cerebral extraction of oxygen (CEO$_2$) (1, 11, 12). Severe hyperoxia (PaO$_2$ > 300 mmHg) may also lead to deleterious vasoconstriction in neurocritical patients (4), but less severe rises may sometimes be beneficial, as we will discuss further on (19).

6. Ventilation: PaCO$_2$ should routinely be kept between 35 and 40 mmHg, to avoid cerebral vasodilatation in cases of hypercarbia, or vaso-

constriction due to hypocapnia followed by oligaemia and ischaemic hypoxia (14, 20).

Reduction of PaCO$_2$ may, however, be an appropriate therapeutic strategy in some situations. In 1942, White et al. (21) reported increased CBF and CBV secondary to hypercapnia. The first report on the therapeutic use of hyperventilation was by Furness, in the British Journal of Anaesthesia, in 1957 (22). The first study in which the relationship between PaCO$_2$ and ICP was measured and confirmed, during neurosurgical procedure, was by Lundberg et al. in 1959 (23). Until then, all comparisons had been made with patients ventilating spontaneously during surgical treatment.

Today, it is known that in situations of severe ICH, with pending cerebral herniation, the decrease in ICP needs to be rapid in order to avoid irreversible lesions or even brain death (14, 24, 25). It is also clear that the longer duration of cerebral ischaemia is directly related to worse prognosis (4, 14). One of the therapeutic methods used in this neurological emergency situation, in addition to osmotherapy, is hyperventilation. This should be done while keeping the PaCO$_2$ levels at around 30 mmHg, until the herniation has been reversed, thereby avoiding permanent neurological damage and making it possible for the cause of the ICH to be discovered and treated (1, 4, 14, 19, 24).

More intensive hyperventilation, in which PaCO$_2$ is kept between 25 and 30 mmHg or even lower than this, can be carried out safely according to some authors (26). To lessen the risk of low CBF and cerebral ischaemia this procedure must be associated with monitoring of the jugular bulb oxygen saturation (SjO$_2$) and mensuration of the cerebral extraction of oxygen (CEO$_2$), despite the limitation that this method evaluates overall O$_2$ consumption and not regional consumption (14, 24, 25, 26). This treatment is known as optimised hyperventilation (1).

This strategy is indicated in situations of refractory ICH, to assist in choosing the best method for controlling the ICP, as has been well-described among patients who were victims of severe brain trauma. For such patients, concomitant monitoring of SjO$_2$ and ICP is better than monitoring of ICP alone (14, 24, 25, 26, 27).

Thus, when ICH occurs with high SjO$_2$ (> 75%) and low CEO$_2$ (< 24%), and sample contamination due to catheter displacement or rapid aspiration has been ruled out, i.e., cases of hyper-aemic intracranial hypertension, reduction of the $PaCO_2$ is indicated (1, 27).

In situations of intracranial hypertension with normal SjO_2 and CEO_2 (55–75% and 24–42% respectively), hyperventilation associated with osmotherapy should be carried out with the aim of not deviating these values either towards oligaemia or towards cerebral hyperaemia; the latter with worse prognosis (4, 27).

Furthermore, some authors have suggested the hypothesis that one of the causes of the disorders in CBF regulation that exist when there is cerebral injury may be the consequent cerebral vasodilatation. Moller et al. evaluated nine patients with bacterial meningitis and were able to improve four patients' autoregulation after 30 minutes of hyperventilation (28).

Finally, three further important points require attention. The first of these is that the measurement of SjO_2 needs to be sequential, given that single measurements do not allow trustworthy conclusions and that corrections to the therapeutic management of ICH should be made regularly (1, 4, 27). Secondly, during neurosurgery, the use of hyperventilation helps to control ICH, improve the surgical field through reducing the cerebral volume and counterbalance the vasodilatory effects of the anaesthetics inhaled (29, 30). Lastly, studies on SjO_2 monitoring, both transoperatively during neurosurgical procedures and following brain trauma, have suggested that hyperoxia (PaO_2 between 200 and 250 mmHg) in association with hyperventilation reduces the risk of cerebral hypoxia by increasing the O_2 delivery to the brain tissue, as reflected by increased SjO_2. This strategy may be beneficial in clinical practice (20).

Risks of hyperventilation in neurocritical patients

Alveolar hypoventilation has the consequences of hypercapnia and hypoxemia, which are both harmful to the brain. As described earlier, hypoxemia leads to neuronal lesions due to hypoxia (secondary neurological lesions), which will worsen the lesions already established by the acute neurological event (primary lesion). It has been shown that, in cases of brain trauma, hypoxemia (PaO_2 < 60 mmHg) is an independent factor for mortality (4, 24).

In turn, hypercapnia leads to acidosis and cerebral vasodilatation. In neurocritical patients, this may cause hyperaemia, cerebral oedema and ICH.

Thus, the cerebral vasoconstricting effect of hyperventilation would reduce the CBF, and would therefore reduce the CBV and consequently the ICP. This reasoning was used for more than 20 years in treating acute neurological diseases, although it has been discouraged by more recent studies (1, 14, 25, 19).

In cases of traumatic brain injury, the CBF is decreased over the first 24 hours. Some authors have questioned whether this necessarily represents cerebral ischaemia and have made the interpretation that this response could be linked with decreased metabolism (7). With this reduced flow, the hypocapnia would probably be harmful at that moment. Studies have shown signs of cerebral ischaemia secondary to hyperventilation, such as increased CEO_2 and decreased phosphocreatinine in the brain (31). Thus, prophylactic hyperventilation in neurocritical patients should be avoided, given that this may worsen the overall or regional low CBF, even if performed for short periods, as demonstrated in studies with microdialysis (32).

In the only prospective randomised study on the effects of hyperventilation among neurological patients so far published, Muizelaar et al. showed that patients who, independent of the level of the ICP, underwent routine hyperventilation to attain a $PaCO_2$ of 25 mmHg over the first five days after suffering traumatic brain injury had a worse prognosis three and six months later than did the control group. However, there was no difference in the evaluation after one year; this was attributed to the small number of survivors (33). Coles et al. used positron emission tomography (PET) and showed that mild hyperventilation reducing the $PaCO_2$ to less than 34 mmHg gave rise to decreased flow and increased hypoperfused area of the brain (34).

Furthermore, in cases of ICH associated with oligaemia, in which the CEO_2 is high because of a relative or absolute decrease in CBF, as occurs in situations of hypoxaemia, hypovolaemia, arterial hypotension, anaemia, hyperthermia, convulsion, vasospasm and even hypocarbia, the hyperventilation may lead to neurological worsening due to intensification of the fall in CBF and CBV, thus leading to hypoxic and ischaemic lesions. In these situations of low SjO$_2$ (< 55%) and high CEO$_2$ (> 42%), hyperventilation is contraindicated, given that, as described earlier, it will worsen the ischaemic cerebral hypoxia. In these cases, the best therapy would be osmotherapy and haemodynamic optimisation (4, 27).

This hyperventilation can also be correlated with the oxygen pressure in the brain (PbrO$_2$) (24). This is a regional measurement of O$_2$ pressure by means of electrodes placed directly on the injured cerebral tissue or in the penumbra area. It is known that the normal values of PbrO$_2$ should be greater than 20 mmHg, and experimental and clinical studies (35, 36) have shown that these values are reduced during prolonged hyperventilation.

Most studies on the effects of hyperventilation have been carried out on patients with traumatic brain injury. Nevertheless, other neurological events have also been studied. Among patients with subarachnoid haemorrhage, those with severe vasospasm present reduced responsiveness to CO$_2$, while those without vasospasm or with mild spasms maintain this response intact (37). Thus, the clinical condition of the latter could be worsened through hyperventilation.

Among stroke patients, and particularly ischemic stroke patients, hyperventilation should be used even more cautiously, since there are few published studies and a possible ischaemic event could be very harmful to areas of the brain that are already hypoperfused (38, 39). The latest guidelines from the American Heart Association, released in 2007, suggest that if hyperventilation is used on intracranial haemorrhage patients, it should only be used for a few hours and the PaCO$_2$ should not be less than 30 to 35 mmHg (40). Moreover, whereas the interpretation of the results from CEO$_2$ through monitoring SjO$_2$ is well-validated among patients with traumatic brain injury, it still awaits further evidence among patients with other types of severe cerebral lesion (28, 41, 42).

It must be borne in mind that patients with cerebral lesions, especially those with traumatic brain injury, often present systemic lesions that may be worsened through hyperventilation (with the likelihood of high thoracic pressures) and hy-

pocapnia, such as those in a state of circulatory shock and those in risk of acute lung injury (43).

Finally, it needs to be emphasised that, during abrupt withdrawal of hyperventilation, significant perivascular acidosis tends to occur, which is produced by elevation of the PaCO$_2$ associated with a low level of cerebral extracellular bicarbonate (44). This acidosis triggers vasodilatation and consequently increased CBF, which must be avoided by performing gradual suspension over a minimum period of four to six hours (7).

Summary

Oxygen and glucose are the principal substrates for cerebral metabolism. Their provision needs to be maintained through adequate cerebral blood flow (CBF), which depends on the physiological properties of the cerebral vasculature. In situations of brain injury, some of these properties are lost, and control over CBF is deficient. Maintenance of cerebral perfusion pressure thus becomes directly dependent on the mean arterial pressure.

Low CBF and lowering of the level of consciousness, which are associated with hypoxemia and hypercapnia, frequently occur after primary neurological injury and need to be rapidly corrected to avoid secondary lesions, which have high mortality. Thus, mechanical ventilation is an important therapeutic method for managing neurocritical patients.

Several ventilatory parameters need to be adjusted, among which the minute ventilation, which determines the PaCO$_2$. This should be kept between 35 and 40 mmHg so that it does not lead to excessive vasodilatation with consequent hyperaemia if too high, or to vasoconstriction with cerebral ischaemia if too low.

Mild hyperventilation (PaCO$_2$ between 30 and 35 mmHg) should be carried out in situations of high intracranial pressure with herniation until the condition has been improved. Thus, it should be done for short periods, given that the benefit from controlling the intracranial hypertension outweighs the risk from temporary reduction in CBF.

Optimised hyperventilation, with monitoring of SjO$_2$ and CEO$_2$, should be considered in cases of refractory intracranial hypertension, when there is a condition of cerebral hyperaemia, or in association with osmotherapy when the SjO$_2$ is normal.

Hyperoxia improves O$_2$ delivery to the cerebral tissue during periods of hyperventilation.

Key points for clinical practice

- Tracheal intubation and mechanical ventilation must be performed in acute neurological patients who require airway protection (Glasgow Coma Scale less than nine), who present loss of ventilatory drive, patients with weakness of the respiratory musculature, and with inefficient gas exchange.
- The ventilation must be of controlled type in patients with an inadequate ventilatory drive and assisted or controlled-assisted type in patients with good ventilatory drive.
- Avoid asynchronism and respiratory exertion, which may raise the intracranial pressure.
- Use physiological PEEP. Use higher values only in situations of real need, and under monitoring of the intracranial pressure.
- Ventilate with plateau pressure less than 30 cmH$_2$O.
- Start with FiO$_2$ of 100 % and progressively reduce it to the lowest level that ensures that the SpO$_2$ is greater than 94 %, with an FiO$_2$ level preferably less than 50 %.
- Keep the PaCO$_2$ between 35 and 40 mmHg. Prophylactic or routine hyperventilation should not be used.
- Hyperventilation should be avoided during the first 24 hours after traumatic brain injury because of the reduction in CBF consequent to the primary damage.
- Special care is required in relation to patients with ischaemic stroke, since hyperventilation may worsen the cerebral injury in the most affected areas.
- Perform mild to moderate hyperventilation (PaCO$_2$ around 30 mmHg), in association with osmotherapy, in emergency situations of intracranial hypertension with signs of herniation, until the condition has been reversed.
- Perform optimised hyperventilation, with monitoring of SjO$_2$ and CEO$_2$ or PbrO$_2$ when there is refractory intracranial hypertension with cerebral hyperaemia, or in association with osmotherapy when there is refractory intracranial hypertension with normal SjO$_2$ and CEO$_2$. In these cases, the possibility of cerebral ischaemia must be borne in mind, and the monitoring of SjO$_2$ and CEO$_2$ should be sequential in order to assure better therapeutic results.
- Withdrawal of hyperventilation needs to be done gradually, over a four to six-hour period, to avoid a rebound effect with vasodilatation and increased CBF.
- Hyperoxia (PaO$_2$ between 200 and 250 mmHg) can be used together with hyperventilation to improve the O$_2$ delivery to the cerebral tissue.

The authors

Odin Barbosa da Silva, MD[1]
Gustavo Trindade Henriques Filho, MD[2]
Jorge Luiz da Rocha Paranhos, MD[3]
[1]Intensive Care Medicine | Hospital Santa Joana | HEMOPE | Hospital da Restauração | Recife-PE, Brasil
[2]Intensive Care Medicine | Hospital Santa Joana | HEMOPE | Hospital Universitário Oswaldo Cruz | Recife-PE, Brasil
[3]Intensive Care Medicine | Santa Casa da Misericórdia | São João del Rey-MG, Brasil

Address for correspondence
Odin Barbosa da Silva
Intensive Care Medicine
Hospital Santa Joana, HEMOPE
Hospital da Restauraçã
Rua Paulino Gomes de Souza 136/1201
52050-250 Recife-PE, Brasil
e-mail: odinbs@terra.com.br

References

1. Paranhos JLR. Traumatismo crânio-encefálico: Assistência Intensiva. In: David CM (Ed.). Medicina Intensiva – AMIB. Ed. Revinter. Rio de Janeiro. 2004:784–91.
2. Young WL, Ornstein E. Cerebral and spinal cord blood flow. In: Cottrell JE, Smith DS (Eds.). Anesthesia and Neurosurgery, 3rd ed. St. Louis: Mosby-Year Book Inc. 1994:17–57.
3. Reivich M. Arterial PaCO$_2$ and cerebral hemodynamics. Am.J.Physiol. 1964;206:25–35.
4. Réa-Neto A, Maciel FMB, Paranhos JLR, Silveira RR, Plotnik R. CITIN – Curso de Imersão em Terapia Intensiva Neurológica. AMIB. 2006.
5. Dietrich HH, Dacey RG Jr. Effects of extravascular acidification and extravascular alkalinization on constriction and depolarization in rat cerebral arterioles in vitro. J Neurosurg. 1994;81:437–42.
6. Nunn JF. Applied respiratory physiology. 3rd ed. Cambridge, UK: Butterworth & Co. 1987.
7. Brian JE Jr. Carbon dioxide and the cerebral circulation. Anesthesiology. 1998;88:1365–1386.
8. Obrist WD, Marion DW. Xenon techniques for CBF measurement in clinical head injury. In: Narayan RK, Wilberger J, Povlishock JT, (Eds.) New York, NY: McGraw-Hill. 1996;471–485.
9. Sato M, Pawlik G, Heiss W-D. Comparative studies of regional CNS blood flow autoregulation and responses to CO$_2$ in the cat. Stroke. 1984;15:91–7.

10. Warner DS, Turner DM, Kassell NF. Time-dependent effects of prolonged hypercapnia on cerebrovascular parameters in dogs: Acid-base chemistry. Stroke. 1987;18:142–9.

11. Obrist WD, Langfitt TW, Jaggi JL, Cruz J, Gennarelli TA. Cerebral blood flow and metabolism in comatose patients with acute head injury. J Neurosurg. 1984;61: 241–53.

12. Monro A. Observations on the structure and function of the nervous system. Edinburgh, Creech & Johnson. 1823;page 5.

13. Kellie G. An account of the appearances observed in the dissection of two of the three individuals presumed to have perished in the storm of the 3rd, and whose bodies were discovered in the vicinity of Leith on the morning of the 4th November 1821 with some reflections on the pathology of the brain. The Transactions of the Medico-Chirurgical Society of Edinburgh. 1824;1:84–169.

14. Vincent JL, Berré J. Primer on medical management of severe brain injury. Crit Care Med. 2005;33(6):1392–9.

15. Mayer SA, Chong JY. Critical Care Management of Increased Intracranial Pressure. Journal of Intensive Care Medicine Vol 17 No 2 March/April 2002.

16. McDonagh DL, Borel CO. Ventilatory management in the neurosciences critical care unit. In: Suarez JI. Critical care neurology and neurosurgery. Humana Press Inc. New Jersey. 2004;151–66.

17. McGuire G, Crossley D, Richards J et al. Effects of varying levels of positive end-expiratory pressure on intracranial pressure and cerebral perfusion pressure. Crit Care Med. 1997;25:1059–62.

18. Huynh T, Messer M, Sing RF, et al. Positive end-expiratory pressure alters intracranial and cerebral perfusion pressure in severe traumatic brain injury. J Trauma. 2002;53:488–92.

19. Valadka AB, Robertson CS. Surgery of cerebral trauma and associated critical care. Neurosurgery. 2007;61(S1):203–21.

20. Thiagarajan A, Goverdhan PD, Chari P, Somasunderam K. The effect of hyperventilation and hyperoxia on cerebral venous oxygen saturation in patients with traumatic brain injury. Anesth Analg. 1998;87:850–3.

21. White JC, Verlot M, Selverstone B, Beecher HK. Changes in brain volume during anesthesia: The effect of anoxia and hypercapnia. Arch Surg. 1942;44:1–21.

22. Furness DN. Controlled respiration in neurosurgery. Br J Anaesth. 1957;29:415–8.

23. Lundberg N, Kjallquist A, Bien C. Reduction of increased intracranial pressure by hyperventilation. Acta Psychiatr Neurol Scand. 1959;34(suppl 139):1–64.

24. Stocchetti N, Maas A, Chieregato A, van der Plas A. Hyperventilation in Head Injury – A Review. Chest. 2005; 127:1812–1827.

25. Brain Trauma Foundation. Guidelines for the management of severe traumatic brain injury, 3rd ed. Journal of Neurotrauma. 2007.

26. Cruz J. The first decade of continuous monitoring of jugular bulb oxyhemoglobin saturation: management strategies and clinical outcome. Crit Care Med. 1998;26:344–351.

27. Carneiro CC, Paranhos JLR. Monitorização do bulbo da jugular. In: David CM. Medicina Intensiva – AMIB. Ed. Revinter. Rio de Janeiro. 2004;808–11.

28. Moller K, Skinhoj P, Knudsen G, Larsen, FS. Effect of Short-Term Hyperventilation on Cerebral Blood Flow Autoregulation in Patients with Acute Bacterial Meningitis. Stroke. May 2000;31(5):1116–1122.

29. Kaieda R, Todd MM, Warner DS. The effects of anesthetics and PaCO$_2$ on the cerebrovascular, metabolic and electroencephalographic responses to nitrous oxide in the rabbit. Anesth Analg. 1989;68: 135–43.

30. Matta BF, Lam AM, Mayberg TS, Eng CC, Strebel S. Cerebrovascular response to carbon dioxide during sodium nitroprusside-and isoflurane-induced hypotension. Br J Anaesth. 1995;74:296–300.

31. Sutton LN, McLaughlin AC, Dante S et al. Cerebral venous oxygen content as a measure of brain energy metabolism with increased intracranial pressure and hyperventilation. J Neurosurg. 1990;73:927–32.

32. Marion DW, Puccio A, Wisniewski SR et al. Effect of hyperventilation on extracellular concentrations of glutamate, lactate, pyruvate, and local cerebral blood flow in patients with severe traumatic brain injury. Crit Care Med. 2002;30:2619–25.

33. Muizelaar JP, Marmarou A, Ward JD et al. Adverse effects of prolonged hyperventilation in patients with severe head injury: a randomized clinical trial. J Neurosurg. 1991;75: 731–739.

34. Coles JP, Minhas PS, Fryer TD et al. Effect of hyperventilation on cerebral blood flow in traumatic head injury: clinical relevance and monitoring correlates. Crit. Care Med. 2002;30:1950–59.

35. Manley GT, Pitts LH, Morabito D, et al. Brain tissue oxygenation during hemorrhagic shock, resuscitation, and alterations in ventilation. J Trauma. 1999;46:261–267.

36. van Santbrink H, Maas AI, Avezaat CJ. Continuous monitoring of partial pressure of brain tissue oxygen in patients with severe head injury. Neurosurgery. 1996;38: 21–31.

37. Voldby B, Enevoldsen EM, Jensen FT. Cerebrovascular reactivity in patients with ruptured intracranial aneurysms. J Neurosurg. 1985;62:59–67.

38. Fisher M. Antiedema Therapy in Ischemic Stroke. Stroke. 2007;38:3084–3094.

39. Silva OB. Acidente Vascular Cerebral Isquêmico. In: David CM. Medicina Intensiva – AMIB. Ed. Revinter. Rio de Janeiro. 2004;827–34.

40. Broderick J, Connolly S, Feldmann E et al. Guidelines for the Management of Spontaneous Intracerebral Hemorrhage in Adults – 2007 Update: A Guideline from

the American Heart Association/American Stroke Association Stroke Council, High Blood Pressure Research Council, and the Quality of Care and Outcomes in Research Interdisciplinary Working Group. Circulation. 2007;116:e391–e413.

41. Paulson OB, Brodersen P, Hansen EL et al. Regional cerebral blood flow, cerebral metabolic rate of oxygen, and cerebrospinal acid base variables in patients with acute meningitis and with acute encephalitis. Acta Med Scand. 1974;196:191–198.

42. Keller E, Steiner T, Fandino J et al. Jugular Venous Oxygen Saturation Thresholds in Trauma Patients May Not Extrapolate to Ischemic Stroke Patients: Lessons From a Preliminary Study. Journal of Neurosurgical Anesthesiology. 2002;14(2):130–136.

43. Bratton SL, Davis RL. Acute lung injury in isolated traumatic brain injury. Neurosurgery. 1997;40:707–12.

44. Albrecht RF, Miletich DJ, Ruttle M. Cerebral effects of extended hyperventilation in unanesthetized goats. Stroke. 1987;18:649–55.

F. Acute bleeding

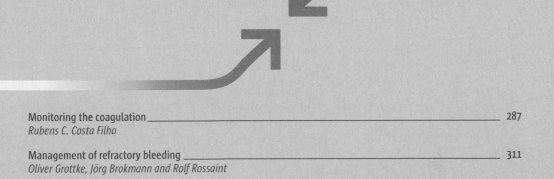

Rubens C. Costa Filho

Monitoring the coagulation

Introduction

In the early 60s two authors proposed a waterfall and cascade model of coagulation composed of sequential series of proteolytic steps in which plasma zymogens of serine proteases are transformed into active enzymes, which consequently lead to the activation of another zymogen in a blood chain reaction. The final result of this event is the formation of thrombin which converts a soluble protein, fibrinogen, into an insoluble polymer, fibrin, that forms and structures the clot (1, 2). These enzymes act to convert their pro-cofactor substrates to cofactors (V and VIII), which assemble these proteases on cell surfaces.

In the modern versions of the coagulation cascade, the interactions of the proteins are outlined in a Y-shaped scheme, with distinct "intrinsic" and "extrinsic" pathways initiated by factor XII (FXII) and FVIIa/tissue factor (TF), respectively. The pathways converge on a "common" pathway at the FVa/FXa (prothrombinase) complex. The coagulation complexes are generally noted to require phospholipids and calcium for their activity. This scheme was not actually proposed as a literal model of the haemostatic process in vivo. However, many physicians and students still consider the cascade as a model of physiology. Only after 35 years, some authors have proposed that coagulation occurs not as a "cascade", but in three overlapping stages (see fig. 1):

1. Initiation, which occurs on a tissue factor bearing cell;

2. Amplification, in which platelets and cofactors are activated to set the stage for large scale thrombin generation; and

3. Propagation, in which large amounts of thrombin are generated on the platelet surface. This cell-based model explains some aspects of haemostasis that a protein-centric model does not (3).

In order to give an example of how membranes are so important in clinical practice, we have chosen a Scott syndrome, which is a defect in the platelet membrane that causes bleeding complications once it is associated with a shortage of procoagulant sites on the activated platelets membrane. Platelets from these individuals have normal phospholipids content but do not express sites for prothrombinase [FVa/FXa] and intrinsic tenase [FVIIIa/FIXa] complexes assembly or shed micro-vesicles on stimulation. In Scott syndrome, the platelets demonstrate normal secretion and aggregation, indicating that associated bleeding disorder may result from abnormalities in the putative Ca^{2+}-mediated transbilayer movement of anionic phospholipids on platelet stimulation (4). This is one more piece of evidence which demonstrates that platelet membranes provide the most quantitatively abundant cellular surface for expression of the haemostatic response.

It is important to emphasise that the partial thromboplastin time (PTT), formerly utilised to discern moderate or even mild cases of haemophilia A and B, is now

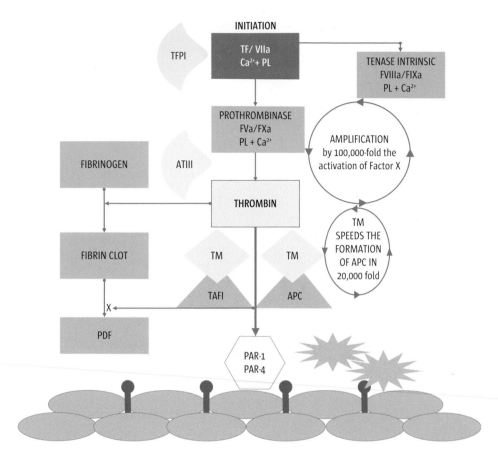

Fig. 1 Overview of cell-based model of coagulation and its kinetics. The normal endothelium maintains blood fluidity by inhibiting blood coagulation and platelet aggregation and promoting normal endogenous fibrinolysis.
It also provides a protective barrier which separates blood cells and plasma factors from highly reactive elements in the deeper layers of the vessel wall.
In disease and injury, these adhesive proteins are exposed, promoting platelet adhesion and expression of TF (Tissue Factor) over the surface of smooth muscle, fibroblasts, macrophages, leucocytes and endothelium, which are together called TF-bearing cells, trigger blood coagulation as depicted in this figure. Human platelets express PAR-1 and 4 which are activated by thrombin, even in low concentrations. They are fundamental for platelet activation and signaling which trigger local generation of proteases, and via PARs, activate the endothelium. (23, 24). It is important to emphasise the participation of platelets in haemostasis as a fundamental component of this physiological process. The reactions include adhesion to the cut end of a blood vessel, spreading of adherent platelets over the exposed subendothelial surface, secretion of stored platelet constituents such as molecules involved in haemostasis and wound healing, and the formation of larger platelet aggregates, which require von Willebrand and fibrinogen among other molecules which interact over their membranes.
TM (Thrombomodulin); TFPI (Tissue-Type Plasminogen activator); TAFI (Thrombin-Activatable Fibrinolysis Inhibitor or procarboxypeptidase U); PDF (Products of Degradations of Fibrin); ATIII (Antithrombin III); PAR-1 (Protease-Activated Receptors 1 and 4); APC (Activated Protein C); PL (phospholipids over cellular Membranes).

also used to diagnose several newly discovered abnormalities in the intrinsic system from normal patterns (5), where the presence of calcium and phospholipids were adjuvant.

Our task in this chapter is staggering because it depicts all the ways of monitoring coagulation, with of all these steps hidden from our sight, and pointing out controversies related to them is a real challenge. Due to this fact, we intend to describe main aspects regarding the most important issues in critical care, more bleeding than thrombotic patients. Furthermore, laboratory testing in the management of any clinical condition is only relevant if it can be demonstrated to indicate and to guide appropriately the institution of therapeutic measures to forestall or control the primary pathological source.

Clinical bleeding dilemma in ICU

The evaluation of individuals with a possible systemic bleeding diathesis is usually undertaken in one of the following categories:

1. Patients with active or history of unforeseen bleeding who require diagnostic investigation.
2. Patients may be found by chance to have abnormalities during screening lab tests of haemostasis and the need of explanation emerges.
3. Patients without previous coagulation problems often undergo routine screening for bleeding risk before the performance of invasive procedures or surgery.
4. Patients with necessary anticoagulation who will undergo invasive procedures.

On various occasions, in the scenario of bleeding the first question that must be considered is whether this situation is most likely caused by a systemic coagulopathy or by an anatomic or mechanical abnormality of the blood vessels. This kind of dilemma is mostly encountered in individuals who start haemorrhaging unexpectedly after any invasive procedure or surgery. In the majority of cases, a cautious and detailed consultation, usually forgotten, must focus on patient's history together with a physical examination, which would yields important diagnostic clues. Additionally, a careful investigation of drug use must be made. Patients who have been taking, aspirin and a variety of non-steroidal anti-inflammatory drugs, often neglect to advise the in-

terviewer about self-medication, and therefore, could develop platelet dysfunction by inhibiting platelet thromboxane A2 production (see tab. 1) (6). Accordingly, acquired haemostatic defects may be caused by some underlying systemic disorders such as renal failure, metabolic acidosis, hypocalcaemia and hypothermia, which are associated with impaired platelet-vascular interactions and prolongation of bleeding time (7). On some occasions, diseases could be manifested with haematological dysfunction such as liver disease in which thrombocytopenia, dysfibrinogenemia and intravascular coagulation may occur simultaneously, causing our analysis to stem from wrong assumptions.

In general, patients who bleed from multiple locations and on multiple occasions are more prone to have an underlying systemic defect of haemostasis; and those whose bleeding is located at a single injured site are certainly more likely to have an anatomic cause of bleeding. However, physicians have to be aware that even considering these statements they could overlap each other (see fig. 2).

The importance of monitoring bleeding

Bleeding is a feared and harmful complication of critical illness. Normal blood coagulation exists to halt excessive blood loss in a balanced manner. However, it is paradoxical that surgery or trauma simultaneously represent major risk factors for both haemorrhagic and thrombotic complications. For instance, it was estimated that surgery and trauma increase the baseline risk of thrombosis up to a hundred-fold (8). Whilst there is no doubt that some bleeding symptoms are more commonly associated with disease, especially

Underlying systemic effects
■ Bleeding from multiple locations and various occasions
A single injuried site
■ More likely to have an anatomic site as cause of bleeding

Fig. 2   Types of bleeding in general

Tab. 1   Examples of the interference on platelet function promoted by various therapeutic agents, commonly used in clinical practice. Modified from Michelson AD. Platelets. In chapter 58. Acquired disorders of platelets function. Academic Press in Canada: Elsevier. 2007.

Drugs that affect platelet function (class)	Example of type of drugs
Cyclooxigenase inhibitors	Aspirin, non-steroidal anti-inflammatory drugs
ADP receptor antagonists	Ticlopidine, Clopidogrel
GPIIb/IIIa antagonists	Abciximab, Tirofiban, Eptifibatide
Drugs that increase platelet cyclic AMP or cyclic GMP	Prostaglandin I_2 and analogues, Phosphodiesterase inhibitors (Dipyridamol, Aminophylline, Cilostazol) Nitric Oxide and NO donors
Antimicrobials	Penicillins, Cephalosporins, Miconazole, Hydroxychloroquine, Nitrofurantoin
Anticoagulants	Heparins
Cardiovascular	ß- Adrenergic blockers, Nitroglycerin, Nitroprusside, Furosemide, Quinidine, ACE-inhibitors (captopril, perindopril) Calcium channel blockers (Verapamil, Diltiazen)
Thrombolytic	Streptokinase, Tissue Plasminogen activator, Urokinase
Anaesthetics	Halothane
Psychotropics	Tricyclic antidepressants (Imipramine, Amytriptiline, Nortriptyline) Phenothiazines (Chlorpromazine, Prometazine, etc.) Selective serotonin reuptake inhibitors (Fluoxetine, Paroxetine, etc.)
Chemotherapeutic Agents	Mithramycin, BCNU*, Daunorubicin
Miscellaneous agents	Volume expanders (Dextrans and Hydroxyethil Starch) Lipid Lowering agents (clofibrate, halofenato), Epsilon-aminocaproic acid, Antihistamines, Ethanol, Vitamin E, Radiographic contrast agents, Herbal Medicines

*1.3–Bis(2-chloroethyl)-1-nitrosurea (BCNU)

menorrhagia and bleeding after surgical interventions, it is equally certain that such symptoms do not always reflect the presence of a systemic disorder of coagulation or haemostasis.

The characteristics of the bleeding events particularly as they are related to the sites and timing after any injury have to be followed and monitored on observational analysis beyond laboratory screening (see fig. 3).

Individuals with primary haemostasis disturbances usually exhibit problems related to platelet-vessel wall interactions (thrombocytopenia, abnormal platelet function) that manifest in a way usually called "easy bruising". Roughly 10% of men and 20% of women may report this problem if the interviewer asks leading questions regarding facility to bruise more easily than others when hurting themselves (9). Other disorders related to secondary haemostasis are manifested, which could combine fibrinolysis and coagulopathy (hepatic failure or DIC) (see tab. 2).

The epidemiology of bleeding problems

In the first prospective, one-centre study about clinical bleeding in intensive care unit (10), carried out in 1988, which evaluated 1,328 consecu-

The major issues to be determined from questions are:				
Is a pathological bleeding tendency present?	Is it congenital, familial or acquired?	Is it principally a defect of primary hemostasis (platelet or vessel wall dependent) or of fibrin formation and stability (dependent on the fluid phase of coagulation)?	Is there systemic disease causing or exacerbating any bleeding tendency?	Is increased bleeding induced or exacerbated by pharmaceutical drugs use?

Fig. 3   The bleeding history. Modified from: Greaves M, Watson HG. Approach to the diagnosis and management of mild bleeding disorders. J Thromb Haemost. 2007;5 (Suppl. 1):167–74.

tive patients admissions to a general medical/surgical ICU, over one year. It was found that one hundred and thirty-eight (10.4 %) critically ill patients developed at least one episode of bleeding after their admission, and three hundred and eighty-eight (29.2 %) patients bled coincidentally with their ICU admission. Furthermore, the group whose initial bleeding occurred after ICU admissions was older (p < 0.001), stayed longer both in the ICU and hospital (p < 0.001) and had a higher disease severity score with greater risk of death (p < 0.001) than those who never bled after admission. The upper GI tract was the single most common site for bleeding in almost 35 % of the

patients. Additionally, over 25 % of them bled from either urinary tract or had suspected bleeding, and at least 10 % bled from pulmonary, diffuse, or skin-wound sites.

Another way to perceive this problem is by looking at anaemia that has been documented and rarely investigated and consequently found to be very common and prevalent among critically ill patients, inclusively appearing early during the admission to ICU and hospital (11, 12). Recent evidence, leads critical care physicians to develop a widespread and more liberal attitude regarding transfusion, as is well described in two important observational studies which reported that roughly

Tab. 2   Characteristics of the bleeding disorders according to coagulopathy involved

Characteristics	Disorders of primary haemostasis (Platelet-Vascular Factor)	Disorders of secondary haemostasis (Coagulation Factor)
Onset of bleeding	Spontaneous and immediately after trauma	Delayed after trauma
Sites of bleeding	Superficial surfaces	Deep tissues
Skin	Petechiae, ecchymoses	Haematomas
Mucous membranes	Common (nasal, oral, gastrointestinal and genitourinary)	Rare
Other sites	Rare	Common (joint, muscle and retroperitoneal)
Clinical examples	Thrombocytopenia, functional platelet defect, vascular fragility	Congenital coagulation factor deficiency, acquired inhibitor, anticoagulation
	Disseminated intravascular coagulation (DIC), liver failure	DIC, Liver failure

35 to 45 % of patients admitted to critical care setting received around five units of red blood cells (RBC) while in ICU (13, 14) for various reasons. Approximately 14 million units of blood are annually collected in the United States, and about 12 million are used for transfusion; 25 % to 30 % in the ICU (15). However, this liberal approach led others to raise serious concerns regarding any form of transfusions because of its relationship with harm, such as nosocomial infections, immunoparalysis, cancer, adverse reactions from haemotransfusions with an increased mortality (16, 17, 18). A new bleeding assessment tool called HEME (HEmorhage MEasurement) was designed for the critically ill population (19) in such a way as to shed some light based on clinical bleeding characteristics and its comprehension about frequency and severity of bleeding during the patients ICU stay. Critical care medicine involves heterogeneous population and different medical approaches within resources. Moreover, there is a lack of standardised definitions of what major and minor bleeding means. Bleeding events have been classified variously as fatal, major, life-threatening, excessive, overt or a nuisance among others, and also, its monitoring has been confusing. On behalf of ISTH SCC, many authors contributed to give a more uniform definition of major bleeding based on objective criteria, but these criteria have not been designed for the critical care setting reality (20).

Clinical bleeding monitoring using a measuring tool, such as HEME, should be applied to critical care field not only as a guide for the clinician to better understand the risk of bleeding, its behaviour, severity, incidence from all anatomical sites, duration, causes and consequences, but also helps to diminish our subjective and arbitrary analysis of this hidden prevalence and still important common complication, even in non-surgical complex critically ill patients.

The HEME tool (19) (see fig. 4) is superior to existing bleeding scales including WHO (World Health Organisation) (21), among roughly more than dozens of bleeding scales already published (22); due to the fact that it provides descriptive details about the site, risks and severity of bleeding in a time frame. However, it was designed to be applied in ICU patients and could be utilised as a daily check-list although its validation needs to be proved in larger randomised trials.

To rigorously evaluate the efficacy of interventions designed to prevent bleeding, or the safety of each intervention that may promote bleeding, a baseline reference and monitoring is needed for comparison and evaluation such as described in HEME.

Another prospective study which involved 100 patients (19), approximately 10 % of the population of the former one in 1988 (10), it has maintained the same proportion of observed bleedings, whose majority was gastrointestinal in origin (52 %). However, for minor bleedings, HEME study was more precise relating to vascular catheter insertion sites (40.4 %), endotracheal tubes (16.3 %) and surgical wounds (14.3 %), giving us a much truer prospect about the necessity of a good monitoring tool in order to thoroughly understand the epidemiology of bleeding in the complex critical care patients setting. Thus, it would be possible to identify other risks factors and its combinations to discover a more predictive major bleeding in different ICU population.

Bleeding in critical care has been perceived to be an important issue, although few studies have addressed its impact on clinical grounds as a primary outcome. The literature agrees that major bleedings is more prone to produce harm in various scenarios (10, 19, 25, 26, 27, 28, 29), but it is not clear whether major bleeding is a cause or consequence of mortality, mainly in critical care in which comorbidities invariably are associated with bleeding. The prolongation of PTTa (HR of 1.2, 95 % CI: 1.1 to 1.3 for every 10 second increase) and a reduction in platelet count (HR of 1.7, 95 % CI: 1.2 to 2.3, for every 50 X 10^9/l decrease) were identified as risk factors for major bleeding (19), however it has to be validated in a larger population or combined with others screening exams, which could be generalised and applied more appropriately into our practise (31).

Thrombosis dilemma in critical care

Haemostasis is a defense mechanism which protects the organism from loss of blood by plugging injured vessels (1, 2). If this protective mechanism goes amiss, abnormal haemostasis may lead to bleeding disorders. Moreover, if the reactions that are supposed to protect the organism occur excessively inside the blood vessel, or in an inappropriate location, it may result in life threatening disease called thrombosis, partially or completely blocking the vessel (30).

Hemker's Law formulated 10 years ago would say:

"The more thrombin the more thrombosis but the less bleeding, the less thrombin the less thrombosis but the more bleeding" (32).

BLEEDING SITE

☐ **1. Vascular catheter or insertion site,** Specify side: ☐ Right ☐ Left

        Specify site: ☐ a. peripheral vein-arm ☐ d. PICC line ☐ f. jugular
                        ☐ b. peripheral vein-leg ☐ e. femoral ☐ g. subclavian
                        ☐ c. other: _____

☐ **2. Other skin bleeding** (not CVC-related): ☐ a. bruising ☐ b. petechiae ☐ c. non-surgical wound

☐ **3. Gastrointestinal:** ☐ a. NG blood ☐ b. Hematemesis ☐ c. melena ☐ d. hematochezia

☐ **4. Respiratory:** ☐ a. tracheostomy ☐ b. ETT aspirate ☐ c. hemoptysis ☐ d. chest tube

☐ **5. Surgical Site:** ☐ a. incision ☐ b. drain

☐ **6. Genitourinary:** ☐ a. gross hematuria ☐ b. vaginal ☐ c. bleeding around a urinary catheter

☐ **7. Retroperitoneal:**   ☐ **11. Pericardial**

☐ **8. Intracranial:**   ☐ **12. Intraarticular (non-traumatic)**

☐ **9. Intraspinal or eqidural**   ☐ **13. Other (describe)**

☐ **10. Intraocular (not subconjunctival):**

BLEEDING SEVERITY

☐ **Fatal Bleeding** description: _____

☐ **Major Bleeding**
    1. Overt bleeding with ANY ONE of the following in the absence of other causes:
        ☐ Decrease in hemoglobin of 20g/L or more
        ☐ Transfusion of 2 or more units of RBCs with no increase in Hg
        ☐ Decrease in systolic BP by 10mmHg or more while patient sitting up
        ☐ Spontaneous decrease in systolic BP of 20 mmHg or more
        ☐ Increase in heart rate by 20 bpm or more
    2. Bleeding at ANY ONE of the following critical sites:
        ☐ Intracranial   ☐ Intraspinal
        ☐ Intraocular (not subconjunctival)   ☐ Pericardial
        ☐ Retroperitoneal   ☐ Intraarticular (non-traumatic)
    3. Wound related bleeding requiring an intervention:
        ☐ Specify interventions:_____

☐ **Minor Bleeding**   ☐ Bleeding that did not meet criteria for major or fatal bleeding

TIMING ☐ New ☐ Ongoing ☐ Recurrent bleed at same site

        Start date: _____   Stop date: _____
        Start time: _____   Stop time: _____

Started proir to study day?   ☐ Yes   ☐ No

Fig. 4   HEME bleeding assessment tool. From: Arnold DM, Donahoe L, Clarke FJ, Traczyk AJ, Heels-Ansdell D, Cook DJ et cols. Bleeding during critical illness: A prospective cohort study using a new measurement tool. Clin Invest Med. 2007;30(2): E93–E102. With kind permission from Clinical and Investigative Medicine.

To address this statement, it is necessary to consider how the activity of thrombin is controlled by its structure. Once bound together as the thrombin-thrombomodulin complex (see fig. 1), its substrate specificity is redirected from procoagulant to anticoagulant reactions or even to antifibrinolitic action by blocking the plasmin action by TAFI reaction. Moreover, this "anticoagulant profile" could be accelerated by substrates such as PF4 (platelet Factor 4) secreted by platelet granules during activation or the glycosaminoglycans heparin and heparin sulfate available over the normal endothelium. Furthermore, the endothelial cell phenotypes vary in space and time (24, 33). According to this information, monitoring only thrombin generation would not mirror what really is going on above the endothelium which reacts in different ways and magnitude (34, 35).

Regarding the effect of thrombosis in western countries, it is frequent and prevalent (36), including within critical care where it happens mostly in silence.

Approximately, 200,000 patients have been studied in randomised controlled trials regarding the utilisation of anti-platelet agents for cardiovascular diseases, including primary and secondary prevention of thromboembolic diseases. Venous thromboembolism (VTE), which includes both deep vein thrombosis (DVT) and pulmonary embolism (PE), is a common complication in ICU, because it frequently requires surgery, catheter insertion, heavy sedation and paralysis with neuromuscular blocking drugs, which produce long periods of immobilisation, or even vasoactive drugs (36, 37).

Our habits in dealing with these syndromes could be reflected in a recent survey (38) conducted in Canada involving 79 Canadian intensivists which tried to determine which characteristics of DVT are considered to be clinically important. Within this study, interesting points were raised. Firstly, this survey confirmed that intensivists use different criteria to assign clinical significance than nonintensivists, particularly thrombosis experts. For example, asymptomatic DVT detected on screening ultrasonography in critically ill patients with severely impaired cardiorespiratory reserve were considered of substantial clinical importance inside ICU, whereas the significance of these thrombi would be debated by clinicians working outside the ICU setting.

Secondly, ultrasonographic (US) features may influence clinicians' interpretation of the importance of a DVT in the ICU setting. However, it has not been used routinely as a diagnostic and monitoring tool as other parameters such as pretest probability, and D-Dimer test. (39, 40). In addition, US has been applied more at the discharge than during the course of ICU evolution. Thirdly, it was shown that even the use of appropriate VTE prophylaxis, 15–30 % of patients undergoing major orthopedic surgery, for example will be discharged from the hospital with venographically detectable calf or more proximal DVT. Finally, this survey provides us with more information about treatment thresholds used by intensivists (although we cannot generalise these results), which may be lower than the thresholds employed by other specialists, even outside ICU. This survey helps us to understand about boundaries of our practice and trade-offs. In reality weighing the risks of bleeding and thrombosis are always considered, especially when deciding with what, when and how to treat DVT. These choices will influence the associated morbidity and mortality of venous thromboembolism in the ICU, along with different situations, patients and complications they are coping with.

The first Prospective randomised stratified concealed blinded multicenter trial (PROTECT: The PROphylaxis for ThromboEmbolism in Critical Care Trial) is ongoing. No previous trials have compared these two drugs in medical-surgical critically ill patients. Many controversies were raised by many authors in this particular situation (in Brazil there are at least 6 centers involved, including ours). Until now more than 1,000 patients have been included worldwide.

The main objective is to evaluate the effect of LMWH (low-molecular weight heparin) vs UFH (unfractionated heparin) on the primary disease: proximal leg DVT – diagnosed by compression ultrasound performed at least two times a week – and on the secondary objective of identifying the incidence of PE (pulmonary embolism), bleeding in general, and HIT (heparin-induced thrombocytopenia).

This study will objectively confirm venous thrombosis at any site through compressive ultrasonography (see at – http://clarityresearch.ca/protect/).

Many expert opinions have been requesting a larger trial similar to this one (40, 41, 42, 43, 44, 45). Moreover, only a large randomised trial like PROTECT will shed some light on scientific uncertainty and controversy in our practice.

Laboratory screening tests: A consideration in debate

The screening tests designed to be applied in haemostasiology have increased in number and quality along the last decade. There has not been a steady stream of new assays. Laboratory medicine has made remarkable advances along with improvements to the accuracy of existing ones. In spite of, the availability of numerous commercial assays and tests that exist on the market, we have been inundated with literature which provides us with more doubts and controversies. For example, there are various measurements assays of aPL (antiphospholipid antibodies) and β2-GPI (β2-Glycoprotein I) with lack of standardisation which cannot identify the same group of samples as positive. Consequently, the choice of the commercial supplier determines whether a patient has APS (antiphospholipid syndrome) or not. Furthermore, the inter-laboratory reproducibility of aCL (anticardiolipin) and β2-GPI screening is unacceptably poor (46, 47, 48, 49, 50). Moreover, APS cannot be defined, as well as other diseases, based solely on clinical patterns, which makes it impossible to produce studies on the relation between the clinical manifestations and the quality of the commercial assays.

In an ideal world, test improvements would lead to improved patient care. Additionally, development of a technically accurate assay is only the first step. The benefit of a laboratory test and monitoring it closely is defined by its accuracy or even by its correlation to a disease state. However, the real benefit is defined by the improvement in a patient's downstream health status. All of these actions require that physicians request exams for patients where it is indicated, not unnecessarily when it is not indicated, and interpret the tests or any results of monitoring through them, appropriately in light of clinical factors, limitations, timeliness, and availability. Also, nowadays, clinicians have to be updated with the advantages and limitations of the huge amount of assays flooded

on the market. Modern health care needs coordination of efforts among an enormous range of demands inside complex services, thus joining well prepared teams. Physicians have an obligation to patients, ensuring at least that the appropriate services are delivered safely, timely, effectively, efficiently and equally to all.

Recently, a number of studies have attempted directly to evaluate overuse, underuse, or misuse of laboratory screening. In one survey (51) 5 % of inpatients on unfractionated heparin therapy did not have any coagulation monitoring in the first 12 hours, and 13 % did not have a platelet count within the first 72 hours. Overall, a review of 44 published clinical audits of laboratory use found compelling evidence of significant misuse across a wide variety of tests (52).

Point-of-care coagulation monitoring is becoming important for a wide range of applications in the management of bleeding situations in order to improve outcome, treatments and cost reductions. In addition, its acceptance among anaesthesiologists, critical care physicians, cardiologists and clinicians has been increasing in the last few years.

In spite of great technological advances and greater understanding of the physiological nature of complex diseases states it has been traditional to divide the coagulation system into intrinsic and extrinsic pathways, although such a division does not occur in vivo, because TF/FVIIa complex, for example, is a potent activator of both FIX and FX as has been previously described.

Due to the existence of huge quantities and varieties of exams, we will select a few more common ones, related to our practice in critical care field. Furthermore, we will highlight their strengths and weaknesses.

These tools which mainly analyse whole blood rapidly, have been applied at "bedside" in order to provide a decision analysis and allocation of therapeutic resources to ensure more rational guidance. Therefore, these techniques may also supply medical information not only regarding clot formation and structure, but also for platelet function, displayed in real time. In a didactic way these instruments could be divided into those which provide data on *plasmatic coagulation* (e.g. activated clotting times [ACT, ACT plus, PTTa, PT] or heparin management devices [Hemochron Response, HMS plus]); *platelet function analysers*

[PFA-100, Veryfynow, Multiplate] or combinations of these techniques in which it is possible to assess as a whole the plasmatic coagulation, platelet function and fibrinolytic system [ROTEM® systems, Thromboelastography or Sonoclot], called viscoelastic analysers techniques which are increasing their utilisation for perioperative, intraoperative complex surgeries, trauma, obstetric bleeding complications and critical care patients. (see tab. 3)

Tab. 3   Monitoring stat devices

Plasmatic Coagulation Tools	References
ACTALYKE® XL (ACT)	http://www.helena.com/catalog/actalykexl.htm
CASCADE® POC	http://www.helena.com/catalog/cascadepoc.html
ACT PLUS	http://www.medtronic.com/cardsurgery/bloodmgmt/actplus_timer.html
HEOMOCHRON 401	http://www.itcmed.com/products_1b.html#anch1
HEMOCHRON RESPONSE	http://www.itcmed.com/products_1.html
HMS PLUS	http://www.medtronic.com/cardsurgery/bloodmgmt/hmsplus.html
TECHNOTHROMBIN® TGA Kit	http://www.technoclone.com
Platelet Function Tools	
MULTIPLATE®	http://www.multiplate.net/
CHRONO-LOG 700	http://www.chronolog.com/
PLATELETWORKS	http://www.helena.com/Platelet/plateletworks.htm
DiaMed Impact-R®	http://www.diamed.com/product_detail.aspx?id=894&navvis=
FLOW CYTOMETRY ASSAYS *Coulter EPICS® XL-MCL (CD62P) *VAST (PLT VASP/P2Y12 assay)	http://www.beckmancoulter.com/products/instrument/flowcytometry/epicsxl.asp http://www.biocytex.fr/product/kitpage.asp?CAT=7014
PFA-100	http://www.dadebehring.com
*Aspirin Resistance Serum TXB2 Urinary 11-dehydro TXB2	http://www.aspirinworks.com/LaboratoryInformation/PrincipleofAspirinWorksTest/tabid/67/Default.aspx
VERYFYNOW® (RPFA) VerifyNow Aspirin Assay VerifyNow P2Y212 Assay VerifyNow IIb/IIIa Assay	http://www.accumetrics.com/
Viscoelastic Analysis Tools (Mix)	
ROTEM® SYSTEMS	http://www.rotem.de/
TEG® 5000 with PlateletMapping®	http://www.haemoscope.com/
HAEMOSTASIS ANALYSIS SYSTEM®	http://www.hemodyne.com/
SONOCLOT®	http://www.sienco.com/

* Not Point-of-Care tools

The bleeding time

The bleeding time is prolonged by defects of either platelets or the plasma protein cofactors which are necessary for their function, including von Willebrand factor (vWF) and fibrinogen.

The procedure is usually performed with a disposable template device that produces one or two standardised incisions on the forearm. A sphygmomanometer is placed around the upper arm and inflated to 40 mmHg to standardise the intracapillary pressure. The time required for bleeding to cease is determined by carefully blotting the blood emerging from the wounds with filter paper at 30-second intervals, without touching the wounds. The bleeding time is a problematic test because it is influenced by technique, has an imprecise end point, and is generally prolonged in patients with platelet counts of less than 100,000/uL. Furthermore, the test is invasive, poorly sensitive to mild platelet function abnormalities, poor predictor of surgical bleeding (53). Although the bleeding test could be physiologically relevant, it is non-specific (e.g., affected by von Willebrand factor), has a high inter-operator variability, is insensitive and frequently produces scar formation. In spite of current knowledge, it has been estimated that more than 90% of all bleeding times performed in the United States are used preoperatively in an attempt to predict bleeding risk even though they are unreliable. An alternative is to screen for platelet functional defects using semi-automated platelet function analysers such as PFA-100. It remains to be seen whether such screening tests may also correlate with clinical bleeding or thrombotic risk (54, 55).

Platelet monitoring

Platelets play a central role in haemostasis and thrombosis. Thrombocytopenia is pivotal in various inherent disorders, acquired bleeding and thrombotic events. Furthermore, mortality rates as high as 38–54% have been observed, and have been reported to be proportional to the nadir of the platelet count in critical patients (56, 57, 58). There is a body of evidence suggesting that a platelet count less than $50 \times 10^9/l$ is associated with a poor outcome. Moreover, guidelines for platelet transfusion (59) have proposed that the threshold value of 50×10^9 platelets/l is indicative of platelet transfusion requirement in surgical patients.

In severe sepsis, the current recommendation is to administer platelets when counts are $5,000/mm^3$ (or $5 \times 10^9/l$) regardless of apparent bleeding.

Platelets transfusions may be considered when counts are $5,000–30,000/mm^3$ (or $5–30 \times 10^9/l$) and there is significant risk of bleeding.

Higher platelet counts ($50,000/mm^3$ [or $50 \times 10^9/l$]) are required for surgery or invasive procedures (55). In many fields of medicine, monitoring platelet numbers is crucial to avoid bleeding complications or even the opposite, as in the case of HIT (heparin-induced thrombocytopenia) (61).

Furthermore, clinicians should place more emphasis on platelet counting. The four main analytical procedures for platelet counting are:
1. Manual counting using phase contrast microscopy
2. Impedance analysis
3. Optical Light scatter/fluorescence analysis using various commercial analysers
4. Immunoplatelet counting by flow cytometry.

Although manual methods are the gold standard, it has been largely replaced by automated blood instrumentation; but some centres are still using it as a method of calibration of platelet count on automated blood cell counters and quality control material. However, this method is not only time-consuming, subjective, and time demanding, the results produce high levels of imprecision with inter-observer coefficient of variations (CV) in the range of 10 to 25% (62). In this context, there are two main issues that deserve to be considered. Firstly, the confidence and reliability of impedance platelet count progressively diminish below a count around $20 \times 10^9/l$ (63, 64). Secondly, there is a possibility that the interference might compromise the accuracy of a platelet count which is considerably higher in individuals who have thrombocytopenia. These interferences result from the presence of sample particles with sizes or optical characteristics similar to platelets that can not be discriminated from the real platelets. There are limitations of all impedance measurements (see tab. 4). Optical methods using two dimensions of light scatter are less prone to these problems, thus it is possible that a severe thrombocytopenia could be missed because clinicians believe that the platelet count is above the trigger point for any intervention, which could lead them to a wrong decision. In order to avoid this, it would be advisable, at least, to check low platelet numbers using manual methods in the case of patients at risk, even been aware of its inherent limitations, beyond the scope of the problem of pseudothrombocytopenia. One must be aware of potentially false readings from automated methods. Platelet numbers can be artificially low if platelets aggregate with each other or bind to neutrophils, which is called Platelet Satellitism. Such pseudothrombocytopenia may be spontaneously induced by the utilisation of EDTA (ethylenediaminetetraacetic acid) inside the blood collection tube or by agglutinins in the patient's blood. In case of suspicion of pseudothrombocytopenia we have to draw blood in tubes using alternative anticoagulants such as acid citrate dextrose or heparin (65). The full blood count is essential in the analysis of patients because modern blood counters can detect abnormalities in platelet number, platelet size distribution or even platelet volume, which could be flagged by these instruments. Therefore, a more precise inspection of patient's blood must be carried out (62).

Tab. 4 Selection of few reported interferences on platelet counting. Modified from Kunz D. Possibilities and Limitations of Automated Platelet Counting Procedures in the Thrombocytopenic Range. Semin Thromb Hemost. 2001;27:229–236.

Interferences
Cell Fragmentation of Acute Myeloid Leukaemia
Cytoplasmatic fragments of lymphoma cells
Microcytosis of red blood cells
Gross Lipidaemia or Protein Aggregates
Crioglobulinaemia Type I
Schistocytes, Fragmentocytes and white Cell fragments

Platelet function monitoring

Platelets can easily be activated or damaged by physical manipulation, thus samples drawn for platelet function studies are critical. Vacutainer™ (Becton Dickinson) collection of blood is not con-

sidered suitable for platelet aggregation measurements as increased responsiveness to low-dose ADP is typically observed from vacutainer versus syringe (66). Several new platelet function analysers such as the point-of-care (POC) have been developed recently for screening for platelet function abnormalities and monitoring anti-platelets therapy. Sodium citrate, a weak calcium chelator (0.102 M, 0.129 M citrate, buffered and non-buffered) at ratio 9:1 is typically chosen for platelet aggregation tests, which act by chelating Ca^{2++}. Higher concentrations of citrate over-chelate Ca^{2++} interfere with platelet studies (66, 67). Others studies have shown that individuals with a high haematocrit, an aggregating agent is necessary to produce an effect due to the decreased amount of free calcium available in the plasma, thus suggesting this formula $[5/(1- 0. htc)]$ = amount of whole blood to add to 1.0 ml anticoagulant (67). Other anticoagulants have been used such as corn trypsin inhibitor (an inhibitor of factor XII). However, EDTA should be avoided for platelet function studies because it disassembles the integrin $\alpha_{IIb}\beta_3$. Nonchelating anticoagulants (e.g. D-Phe-Pro-Arg-chloromethylketone – PPACK- a direct thrombin inhibitor) may be preferable for the monitoring of GP IIb/IIIa antagonist therapy (71). Furthermore, tubes should be carried upright without agitation, be maintained at room temperature (20–26°C) during transport and storage, and interestingly, manual transport is preferred instead of pneumatic tube systems transportation (69, 70). There are at least 33 available tests which could be carried out to evaluate platelet function, and global haemostatic tests with a significant dependence on platelet number and function. Analyses of all these tests could be seen elsewhere (69). Thrombocytopenia rarely causes a bleeding diathesis if platelet function is normal; thus the measurement of platelet count may not be as crucial as the platelet function according to this author (72). However, more recently, an interesting study showed that the thrombocytopenia, induced experimentally and only in whole blood from healthy people, produced the opposite effect. Since the amount of plasma, red cells and white cells were not altered in the model, the coagulopathy induced by platelet loss was mainly dependent on the reduction in platelet density itself in whole blood (73). These are examples only to illustrate the magnitude of controversies only in the preanalytic procedures.

Platelet aggregometry was developed in 1962 (74) and since then, has become the gold standard method for platelet function. This test could be measured by turbidimetry or whole blood by electrical impedance. The advantage of platelet aggregometry is that it measures the most important function in ex vivo systems, which is its aggregation, which work by using a glycoprotein (GP) IIb/IIIa [integrin $\alpha_{IIb} \beta_3$] in a dependent manner (75).

As shown in table 3 there are many point-of-care tests available in the market today. Those, represent few in staggering list of POC tests. Due to this, clinicians have to understand their advantages, limitations and possibilities in order to use them in their clinical practice. There is no "perfect test", neither an ideal scenario to apply each of them systematically.

For example, monitoring antiplatelet therapy such as thienopyridines (clopidogrel and aspirin) is an exam in demand mainly in invasive cardiovascular field.

Hereby, a recently study (76) was carried out to analyse and compare clopidogrel resistance through four methods using the whole blood impedance aggregometry, the novel (Multiple platelet function Analyser) Multiplate® analyser (Dynabyte, medical, Munich, Germany):

- Multiplate® with ADP agonist
- Multiplate® with ADP plus PG (prostaglandin) which gives a better performance to displayed clopidogrel action

Including two more flow cytometric methods:

- The determination of surface expression of P-selectin (CD62P) (Coulter EPICS® XL-MCL, Coulter Corporation, Miami, FL, USA)
- Flow cytometric assay for the measurement of vasodilator stimulated phosphoprotein, called VASP phosphorylation (PLT VASP/P2Y12 assay) (BioCytex Inc., Marseille, France)

The phosphorylation of this vasodilator stimulated phospho-protein (VASP), an intraplatelet actin regulatory protein, is dependent on the level of activation of the platelet $P2Y_{12}$ receptor, the drug target. Clopidogrel is a prodrug which is metabolised by cytochrome P450 (CYP3A4) in the liver to an active metabolite that specifically and irreversibly blocks the platelet ADP $P2Y_{12}$ receptor, thereby blocking the activation of GP IIb/IIIa.

Therefore, the amount of phosphorylation of VASP is highly correlated to the degree of P2Y12 receptor inhibition, whereas its non-phosphorylation state correlates with the active form of the P2Y12 receptor.

Nevertheless this study has raised discrepancies among these four methods regarding the clopidogrel effect and resistance in a heterogeneous cardiac population. The Multiplate® ADP+PG test displayed a better performance for detecting clopidogrel action than the Multiplate® ADP test alone and also the P-selectin assay in the present work. Moreover, the PLT VASP/P2Y12 assay was more specific to detect the blockade of the P2Y12 receptor than the others. Thus the 77 patients included in this observational study have shown a non-responder rate of 73 % in the Multiplate® ADP test, a 43 % in the Multiplate® ADP+PG test (more sensitive), a 63 % in the P-selectin assay, but only 38 % in the PLT VASP/P2Y12 assay, almost 2 times less incidence of resistance. Therefore, questions need to be elucidated by performing further clinical trials in a less heterogeneous population, with more reliable and comparable tests and methods in order to identify the occurrence of adverse cardiovascular events. Appropriate cut off values have to be selected for the diagnosis of response or non-response to clopidogrel or even other therapies.

Laboratory responses to clopidogrel and other P2Y12 inhibitors, as shown, are largely based upon monitoring ADP-stimulated responses. The POC tests have the advantage of being rapid (Multiplate takes 6 minutes to complete). However, its specificity and applicability in different scenarios and populations have to be discovered through better understanding of designed methodology and better correlation with cut-off values.

Recently, it has been proposed for example, that the term aspirin resistance should only be utilised as a description of the failure of aspirin to inhibit TXA_2 (thromboxane A2) production, irrespective of a nonspecific test of platelet function (77). Hereby, both drugs frequently used in the cardiology and neurology field could be labelled in terms of "resistance" according to their responsiveness or non-responsiveness detected by one of these tests.

Furthermore, even those few tests described in table 3, should ideally be performed pre and post intervention (e.g., drug administration), in a quality controlled scenario, with trained and well prepared personal, and mainly, along with expert's consultation in order to receive good interpretation of results. Moreover, if POC tests were applied at bedside in these contexts, it would generate less controversy regarding their results, interpretation, applicability and reliability.

Additional problems could be found with some non-POC tests such as LTA (Light Transmittance Aggregometry) because they are time-consuming, difficult and cannot be performed realistically on large numbers of patients in routine practise. However, the simpler tests of platelet function could offer the possibility of rapid and reliable identification of aspirin non-responsive patients, for example, without the requirement of a specialised laboratory (68).

While antiplatelet agents are used routinely by more individuals than any other drug, they remain one of very few classes in which the treatment is not monitored based on individual response since these antiplatelet agents have been very difficult to measure. However, some of the new POC platelet function instruments have been used increasingly in surgical setting, including those frequently mentioned in table 3, in spite of conflicting reports on their utility mainly regarding their prediction of bleeding and therapy (78, 79, 80, 81). The best correlation of the antiplatelet therapy with clinical efficacy and safety remains unclear. However, some advances in the laboratorial medicine together with our knowledge about haemostasiology, patient models, technological advances (82, 83) in addition to further work is warranted to establish their enormous potential. Perhaps all of these could eliminate our present inability to measure their effects. Ongoing trials certainly will shed some light on defining how to deal with monitoring aspirin, $P2Y_{12}$ inhibitors, GPIIb/IIIa antagonists or their combinations in different individuals.

The problem of PTT and PT (global tests of coagulation)

A variety of POC monitors have already been described in table 3, which analyses PTTa, PT among other parameters. Additionally, some are depicted as useful to determine the patient at risk of bleeding after cardiac surgery (72, 77); others have cited these tests as a useful instrument for transfusion algorithms (72, 84, 85).

Arguably, it is recommended that the laboratory tests be requested in order to answer a particular question based on the pre-test probability (on clinical grounds) combined to test result (post test probability) which may favour one approach or action, whereas another result relying on it would suggest a different clinical management. Due to this, the clinician should not request a test unless he knows what action he will take with either a positive or negative result.

Moreover, the PTT (activated partial thromboplastin time) is one of the most frequently requested tests in hospitals, without any reason to support that practice. There is no evidence to demonstrate whether a given patient will bleed or not, in a multitude of clinical scenarios. The original reason for asking for the PTT has evolved from "why does this patient bleed?" (because it was developed to assist the diagnostic process for patients with haemophilia) to "will this patient bleed?" (question for which it has never been designed since 1913 through the work of Lee and White) (86, 87, 88).

The literature has demonstrated that routine preoperative coagulation tests are not only irrational and useless, but also the prolongation of them (PTT and PT) used for screening are more often than not ignored but also not acted upon (86, 89, 90).

In table 5, the poor correlation of PTT results and haemorrhagic potential are described.

Thus, PTT suffers a wide range of interferences regarding the techniques and inherited and acquired diseases, not so uncommon in clinical practise. It serves fairly well as a surrogate marker for monitoring therapeutic heparin administration (86).

Viscoelastic coagulation monitoring

Viscoelastic techniques were designed to measure and monitor coagulation through the rapid assessment of whole blood (some could be done in plasma) collected and usually performed at bedside in critical care or in the operating room during

Tab. 5 Correlation of the PTT results and Bleeding in clinical practice. Modified from: Kitchens CS. To bleed or not to bleed? Is that the question for the PTT? J Thromb Haemost. 2005;3:2607–2611.

Bleeding	PTT normal	PTT prolonged
No	Healthy individuals	Deficiency of FXII, FXI, HMWK, PK
		Lupus Anticoagulant (LA)
		Alloantibodies from bovine thrombin against FV and thrombin
		Rattlesnake envenom
		Technical Errors (Erythrocytosis, heparin contamination, interfering substances)
Yes	Deficiency of FVII, FXIII	Deficiency of FVIII, FIX, FXI
	VonWillebrand disease	Alloantibodies from bovine thrombin against: FV and thrombin
	LMWH administration	Deficiency of fibrinogen, FII, FV, X
	Hyperfibrinolysis caused by: Acute Promyelocytic Leukaemia, Prostate Cancer, Alfa2-Plasmin inhibitor	Disseminated Intravascular Coagulation
		Hepatic dysfunction
		Vitamin K deficiency (malnutrition)
		Therapeutic heparin and warfarin

PK: Prekallikrein; HMWK: High molecular weight kininogen; LMWH: Low molecular weight heparin

anaesthesia in complex surgeries. This analysis gathers information *ex vivo* from plasma coagulation (soluble component part of the coagulation), regarding the dynamic of clot formation and structure and the status of clot dissolution (endogenous fibrinolysis). The milieu where this technique is performed (around 300–360 µl of whole blood) is closer than the actual patient status, during any procedure performed, regarding PH, temperature, metabolic profile, in addition with minimal manipulation of the sample.

These techniques are not new. Sonoclot® coagulation and platelet function analyser (see tab. 5) were introduced in 1975 (91) and thromboelastography in 1948 (92).

The principle of TEG® or ROTEM® gives a graphic representation of clot dynamic formation and subsequent lysis (see fig 5). Blood is incubated at 370 C in a heated cup (but the operator can adjust to the patient temperature with great flexibility). Inside the cup a suspended pin is connected to a detector system. This is a torsion wire in the case of TEG and an optical detector in RO-TEM®. The cup and pin are oscillated relative to each other through an angle of 4,045'. The movement is initiated from either the cup (TEG®) or the pin (ROTEM®). As fibrin forms between the cup and pin, it transmits rotation from the cup to the pin (TEG®) or impedes the rotation of the pin (ROTEM®) which is detected by the pin and a tracing is generated according to the increase in resistance (see fig. 5).

In typical thromboelastographic or thromboeleastometric tests, however, not all types of platelet defects can be detected. The reason for this is that thrombin is the most important platelet activator and is generated during the test which involves all blood cells. Therefore, mild defects such as the inhibition of platelet cyclo-oxygenase-1 (COX-1) by aspirin or of ADP-receptor antagonists cannot be reliably detected. Additional techniques should be used in those cases. Von Willebrand factor is also not detected in typical thrombelastographic or thromboeleastometric tracings. More recent advances include an expansion in the range of activators used to initiate aggregation rather than coagulation, such as the platelet mapping system® using ADP and arachidonic acid, making the Haemoscope TEG® – theoretically more sensitive to antiplatelet drugs than the conventional ones. The Sonoclot® analyser (Sienco, Arvada, CO, USA) also measures changes in the dynamic structure of a clot in a whole blood activated by celite. There is evidence to suggest that this instrument could also be indicated to analyse platelet numbers and functions (93, 94). The principle

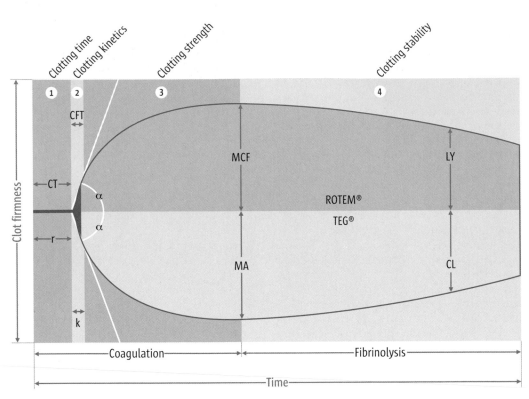

Parameter	Influence primarily by
1	Activity of coagulation factors: Anticoagulant drugs (e.g. heparin) Fibrinogen and platelets
2	Platelet function (interaction with fibrin) Fibrinogen
3	Platelets, Fibrinogen and FXIII
4	Endogenous fibrinolytic activity Hyperfibrinolysis

Fig. 5   Thromboelastometry/Thromboelastography tracing

of Sonoclot is similar to the thromboelastography (pin and torsion wired) and rotational thromboelastometry (optical and electromechanical transducer). Its difference consists of the introduction of a heated probe into 360 µl of whole blood sample added to the cuvette containing different coagulation activators/inhibitors and calcium, after an automated mixing procedure. Thus, the probe immersed into the sample, oscillates vertically, generating a qualitative graph, known as the sonoclot signature clot profile. However, this system has been criticised because of its unreliable results influenced by patient variables such as age, sex, and number of platelets. In addition, older studies have shown poor reproducibility of the measured parameters (95, 96, 97). Other authors have recently mentioned that Sonoclot® is a valuable and reliable resource in patients undergoing cardiac surgical procedures with an accuracy close to that of thromboelastography, with a parameter's coefficient of variation (CV %) roughly less than 10 % (98, 99, 100, 101).

It is only recently that the TEG/ROTEM have been used within haemostasis laboratories and spread more inside operation room and critical care facilities. The poor acceptance of the technology stems largely from the lack of agreement with standard laboratory variables described in older studies (102). Nowadays, more controlled variables were introduced such as quality control measurements; improved and simpler maintenance; technological improvements such as implementation of electronic pipettes and robustness against movement and shock; user friendly and well designed softwares (103) to deal with information and manage them together with appropriate therapy based on well structured and validated algorithms (104, 105, 106); but mainly, the development of a new array of reagents in which tests could be performed more safely and reliably (107, 111) (see fig. 6). A recent multi-centric study (107) demonstrated that the technique of reagent-supported thromboelastometry (ROTEM®) was reproducible, and the results were quite consistent with the 6 centres enrolled in Europe. They found more accuracy reference ranges which could serve as guideline for clinical application and support clinical decisions.

Speed evaluation at bedside or operation theatre to assist in therapeutic decision.

Meets the demand at bedside and operating theatre regarding bleed and more safety use of transfusions.

Include all the cells involved in coagulation system (not only plasma).

Real time assessment at bedside
(for example, for volume resuscitation with different solutions and the risk of bleeding) (see fig. 7).

Guide therapeutic actions through algorithms to monitor drug actions (see fig. 8 and 9).

Assist haemotransfusion choices in real-time.

Have been used for prediction of thrombosis and bleeding.

Fig. 6   Some advantages provide by Thromboelastography for routine practice (109, 110, 111, 112)

Moreover, viscoelastic point-of-care coagulation monitoring is being used in various clinical situations such as intensive care, trauma centres, operation theatre especially in the management of complex surgeries, in a large different settings where massive hemorrhage or hyper- or hypocoagulable states may be present, in addition to monitoring pharmacological treatment with anti- or procoagulant agents, in a way to better titrate treatments (112). (see also examples in fig. 7 and 8).

Conclusions and final considerations

Dissenting point of views in Medicine is a cornerstone to evolution and research. The basis of coagulation understanding is inseparable from any monitoring discussed here, or perhaps designed for a heterogeneous clinical practice. In spite of enormous advances in the field of haemostasiology, in which we have made great progress in its comprehension, we are still in the dark concerning the ideal way of monitoring since the earlier discoveries.

The occurrence of thrombosis or coagulopathy is the results of interacting genetic and acquired causes where we have covered a lot of ground. More knowledge of risk factors, however, particularly of the interactions of risk factors, will enable us to customise therapeutic actions (mainly in high-risk individuals), and in that way reach individualised guidelines for thrombosis or bleeding prevention, as well as adequate treatments (see example in fig. 9 for cardiac surgery). Utilisation of many of these instruments in monitoring haemostasiology has resulted in, at least until now, the development of algorithms for the appropriate haemotransfusions and pharmacologic interventions, mainly in bleeding patients.

Although the majority of medical decisions might be based on lab results, a large number of individuals affected by them could be identified by the application of a well structured and validated questionnaire. The use of standardised questions and a physical exam and, if indicated, other specific tests not only to ensure the detection of increased risk of bleeding in almost every case could also result in lower costs and more efficiency. (113).

New trials and research have been able to and will continue to obtain ideas and experiences to improve our understanding and development of the best practices based on good scientific evidence.

We ought to see the patient as a whole, and develop our ability to judge and consider all aspects of any prob-

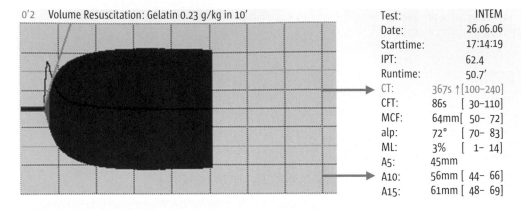

0'2 Volume Resuscitation: Gelatin 0.23 g/kg in 10'		
Test:		INTEM
Date:		26.06.06
Starttime:		17:14:19
IPT:		62.4
Runtime:		50.7'
CT:	367s ↑	[100–240]
CFT:	86s	[30–110]
MCF:	64mm	[50– 72]
alp:	72°	[70– 83]
ML:	3%	[1– 14]
A5:	45mm	
A10:	56mm	[44– 66]
A15:	61mm	[48– 69]

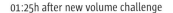

01:25h after new volume challenge

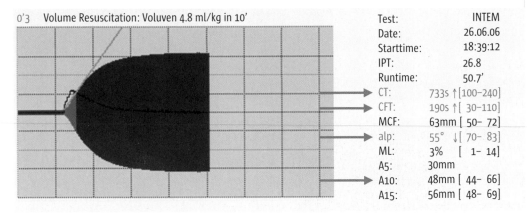

0'3 Volume Resuscitation: Voluven 4.8 ml/kg in 10'		
Test:		INTEM
Date:		26.06.06
Starttime:		18:39:12
IPT:		26.8
Runtime:		50.7'
CT:	733s ↑	[100–240]
CFT:	190s ↑	[30–110]
MCF:	63mm	[50– 72]
alp:	55° ↓	[70– 83]
ML:	3%	[1– 14]
A5:	30mm	
A10:	48mm	[44– 66]
A15:	56mm	[48– 69]

Fig. 7 Severe sepsis ROTEM tracings. Intervention described in the figure.
Two different colloids administered in 10 minutes based on kg and patient need. Two different behaviors on coagulation shown: Upper tracing: modified fluid gelatin do not cause profile modification immediately after the infusion
Lower tracing: 6 % hydroxyethyl starch 130/0.4 in 0.9 % sodium chloride injection – showing modification to a hypocoagulability (see the arrows indicating the value of parameters).

lem in the right perspective. Lastly, and most importantly, we have to weigh up medical evidence more than the detailed knowledge of some rare syndrome or any aspect of laboratorial monitoring.

Acknowledgements

I would like to thank the complete Critical Care Team from Pro Cardiaco Hospital for stimulating my work on haemostasiology in the critical care field, especially Dr. João Luiz Ferreira Costa coordinator of the routine staff along with Dr. José Roberto Martins, Dr. Felipe Saddy and Dr. Plinio Gomes.

To Dr. Fernando Gutierrez, ICU research coordinator, who gave me valuable suggestions for this chapter. To Margaret Corson for helping me with my written English and corrections. To Thiago Carmo Costa, my son, for designing the figures and tables, and lastly to the team of Trombocore Centre at Pro Cardiaco Hospital (Dra. Erica Távora Leite and Dr. Edimilson Assunção e Silva and Sonia Simões, RN).

(Patient 1) Severe sepsis with drotrecogin alpha activated infusion
without LMWH thromboprophylasis

0'1

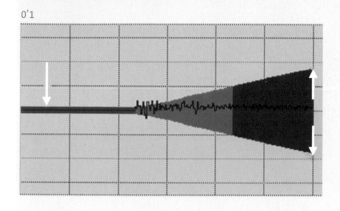

Test:	NATEM
Date:	27.01.06
Starttime:	18:32:49
IPT:	1.3↓ [6– 16]
Runtime:	60.2'
CT:	1411s↑ [300–999]
CFT:	1202s↑ [150–700]
MCF:	35mm [35– 65]

A5:	6mm
A10:	10mm
A15:	15mm

(Patient 2) Severe sepsis with drotrecogin alpha activated infusion
without LMWH thromboprophylasis

0'2

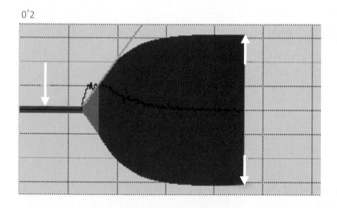

Test:	NATEM
Date:	30.01.06
Starttime:	19:14:44
IPT:	24.4↑[6– 16]
Runtime:	46.0'
CT:	764s [300–999]
CFT:	206s [150–700]
MCF:	63mm [35– 65]
alp:	54° [30– 70]

A5:	29mm
A10:	49mm
A15:	57mm

Fig. 8   Two Patients with severe sepsis during drotrecogin (DAA) infusion (Day 2).
(Note: Platelets count were similar) Upper tracing. Patient 1 – developed an important hypocoagulability status under infusion (DAA) High CFT Value C (lot Formation Time) Lower tracing. Patient 2 – showing a normal tracing during the infusion DAA even with concomitant use of enoxiparin for thromboprophylasis (Normal CFT value)

Conflicts of interests

I declare there are no conflicts of interests.

The author

Rubens C. Costa Filho, MD, FCCP, MBA
Director of Critical Care of Hospital Pró
Cardíaco | Director of Trombocore® –
Haemostasis/Thrombosis analysis in
critically ill patients by Rotational
Thromboelastometry (ROTEM®)

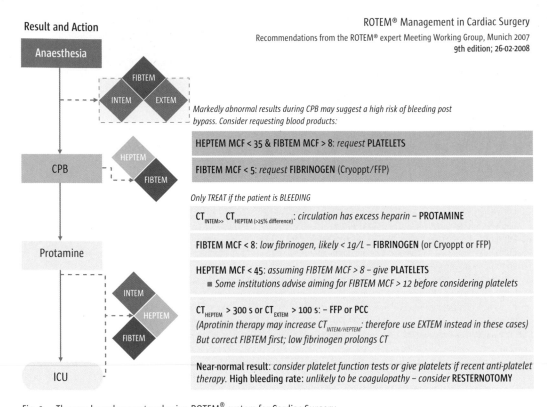

Result and Action

Anaesthesia

FIBTEM

INTEM   EXTEM

Markedly abnormal results during CPB may suggest a high risk of bleeding post bypass. Consider requesting blood products:

HEPTEM MCF < 35 & FIBTEM MCF > 8: *request* **PLATELETS**

HEPTEM

CPB

FIBTEM

FIBTEM MCF < 5: *request* **FIBRINOGEN** (Cryoppt/FFP)

Only TREAT if the patient is BLEEDING

$CT_{INTEM>>}$ $CT_{HEPTEM\ (>25\%\ difference)}$: *circulation has excess heparin –* **PROTAMINE**

Protamine

FIBTEM MCF < 8: *low fibrinogen, likely < 1g/L –* **FIBRINOGEN** (or Cryoppt or FFP)

HEPTEM MCF < 45: *assuming FIBTEM MCF > 8 – give* **PLATELETS**
- *Some institutions advise aiming for FIBTEM MCF > 12 before considering platelets*

INTEM

HEPTEM

CT_{HEPTEM} > 300 s *or* CT_{EXTEM} > 100 s: *–* **FFP or PCC**
(Aprotinin therapy may increase $CT_{INTEM/HEPTEM}$: therefore use EXTEM instead in these cases)
But correct FIBTEM first; low fibrinogen prolongs CT

FIBTEM

ICU

Near-normal result: *consider platelet function tests or give platelets if recent anti-platelet therapy.* **High bleeding rate**: *unlikely to be coagulopathy – consider* **RESTERNOTOMY**

Fig. 9   Therapy based on protocol using ROTEM® system for Cardiac Surgery.
The INTEM, EXTEM, HEPTEM and FIBTEM reagents tests were used for the diagnosis of perioperative coagulopathy disturbances during complex cardiac surgery. This algorithm was modified due to recommendations from the ROTEM® Expert Working Group, Munich 2007. Algorithms such as this one were designed to serve as the starting point for users. From K. Görlinger, R. Kong, A. Nimmo, B. Sørensen for the ROTEM® Expert Meeting Working Group (2007); Recommendations for using the ROTEM® in the management of non-cardiac surgery and trauma. The ROTEM® Expert Working Group is currently coordinated by Dr Robert Kong, Dr. Klaus Gorlinger, Dr. Alastair Nimmo and Dr. Benny Sørensen who kindly gave us permission for this publication (http://www.essener-runde.de/publikationen.html). The quest for ideal test monitoring would involve safety, cost-utility, reliability, rapidity and facility to interpret. Moreover, many types of POC monitoring are providing better global assessment of both primary, secondary haemostasis and fibrinolysis.

Address for correspondence
Rubens C. Costa Filho
Praça Atahualpa n. 86 apart 102 – Leblon
Rio de Janeiro, RJ – Brazil
e-mail: rubens1956@gmail.com

References

1. MacFarlane RG. An enzyme cascade in the blood clotting mechanism, and its function as a biochemical amplifier. Nature. 1964;202:498–499.

2. Davie EW, Ratnoff OD. Waterfall sequence for intrinsic blood clotting. Science 1964; 145:1310–1312.
3. Hoffman M, Monroe DM. A Cell-based Model of Hemostasis. Thromb Haemost. 2001;85:958–65.
4. Solum NO. Procoagulant expression in platelets and defects leading to clinical disorders. Arerioscler Thromb Vasc Biol. 1999; 19:2841–2846.
5. Langdell RD, Wagner RH, Brinkhous KM. Effect of anti-hemophilic factor on one-stage clotting tests: a presumptive test for hemophilia and a simple one-stage anti-hemophilic factor assay procedure. J Lab Clin Med. 1953;41: 637–47.

6. Michelson AD. Platelets. In chapter 58. Acquired disorders of platelets function. Academic Press in Canada: Elsevier. 2007.

7. Noris M, Remuzzi G. Uremic bleeding: closing the circle after 30 years of controversies? Blood. 1999;158: 2200–2211.

8. Kearon C, Hirsh J. Management of anticoagulation before and after elective surgery. N Engl J Med. 1997;336: 1506–1511.

9. Sham RL, Francis CW. Evaluation of mid bleeding disorders and easy bruising. Blood Rev. 1994;8:98–104.

10. Brown RB, Klar J, Teres D, Lemeshow S, sands M. Prospective study of clinical bleeding in intensive care unit patients. Crit Care Med. 1988;16:1171–1182.

11. Corwin HL, Parsonnet KC, Gettinger A. RBC transfusion in the ICU: is there a reason? Chest. 1995;108:767–71.

12. Rodriguez RM, Corwin HL, Gettinger A, Corwin MJ, Gubler D, Pearl RG. Nutritional deficiencies and blunted erythropoietin response as causes of the anemia of critical illness. J Crit Care. 2001;16:36–41.

13. Vincent JL, Baron JF, Reinhart K, Gattinoni L, Thijs L, Webb A, Meier-Hellmann A, Nollet G, Peres-Bota D. ABC (Anemia and Blood Transfusion in Critical Care) Investigators. Anemia and blood transfusion in critically ill patients. JAMA. 2002;288:1499–1507.

14. Corwin HL, Gettinger A, Pearl RG et al. The CRIT Study: anemia and blood transfusion in the critically ill – current clinical practice in the United States. Crit Care Med. 2004;32:39–52.

15. Goodnough LT, Brecher ME, Kanter MH, AuBuchon JP. Transfusion medicine. First of two parts – blood transfusion. N Engl J Med. 1999;340:438–447.

16. Hébert PC, Wells G, Blajchman MA, Marshall J, Martin C, Pagliarello G, Tweeddale M, Schweitzer I, Yetisir E. A multicenter, randomized, controlled clinical trial of transfusion requirements in critical care. N Engl J Med. 1999;340:409–417.

17. Napolitano LM, Corwin HL. Efficacy of red blood cell transfusion in the critically ill. Crit Care Clin. 2004;20: 255–68.

18. National Anemia Action Council. Anemia in the critically ill. 2004. Available at http://www.anemia.org/ professionals/resources/slides/critically_ill.pdf. Accessed January 22, 2007.

19. Arnold DM, Donahoe L, Clarke FJ, Traczyk AJ, Heels-Ansdell D, Cook DJ et cols. Bleeding during critical illness: A prospective cohort study using a new measurement tool. Clin Invest Med. 2007;30(2): E93–E102.

20. Schulman S, Kearon C. Definition of major bleeding in clinical investigations of antihemostatic medicinal products in non-surgical patients. J Thromb Haemost. 2004;3:692–694.

21. Miller AB, Hoogstraten B, Staquet M, Winkler A. Reporting results of cancer treatment. Cancer. 1981;47: 207–214.

22. Koreth R, Weinert C, Weisdorf DJ, Key NS. Measurement of bleeding severity: a critical review. Transfusion. 2004; 44: 605–617.

23. Coughlin SR. Thrombin signalling and protease-activated receptors. Nature. 2000;407,258–264.

24. Lane DA, Philippou H, Huntington JA. Directing thrombin. Blood. 2005;106:2605–2612.

25. Nevo S, Swan V, Enger C, Wojno KJ, Bitton R, Shabooti M, Fuller AK et al. Acute Bleeding After Bone Marrow Transplantation (BMT)- Incidence and Effect on Survival. A Quantitative Analysis in 1,402 Patients. Blood. 1998; 91:1469–1477.

26. Levine MN, Raskob G, Beyth RJ, Kearon C, Schulman S. Hemorrhage complications of anticoagulant treatment. Chest. 2004;126:S287–S310.

27. Penning-van Beest FJA, Erkens J, Petersen KU, Koelz HR, Herings RMC. Main comedications associated with major bleeding during anticoagulant therapy with coumarins. Eur J Clin Pharmacol. 2005;61(5–6):439–44.

28. Nieto JN, Tuesta AD, Marchena PJ, Tiberio G, Todoli JA, Samperiz AL, Monreal M. Clinical outcome of patients with venous thromboembolism and recent major bleeding: findings from a prospective registry (RIETE). J Thromb Haemost. 2005;3:703–09.

29. Penning-van Beest FJA, Koerselman J, Herings RMC. Risk of major bleeding during concomitant use of antibiotic drugs and coumarin anticoagulants. J Thromb Haemost. 2008;6:284–90.

30. Jagadeeswaran P, Kulkarni V, Carrillo M, Kim S. Zebrafish: from hematology to hydrology. J Thromb Haemost. 2007; 5(Suppl. 1):300–4.

31. Greaves M, Watson HG. Approach to the diagnosis and management of mild bleeding disorders. J Thromb Haemost. 2007;5 (Suppl. 1):167–74.

32. Hemker HC. Recollections on thrombin generation. J Thromb Haemost. 2008;6:219–26.

33. Di Cera E. Thrombin as procoagulant and anticoagulant. J Thromb Haemost. 2007;5 (Suppl. 1):196–202.

34. Levi M, Ten Cate H, van der Poll T. Endothelium: Interface between coagulation and inflammation. Crit Care Med. 2002;30:S220–S224.

35. Aird WC. Endothelial cell heterogeneity. Crit Care Med. 2003;31(4 Suppl):S221–S230.

36. Ibrahim EH, Iregui M, Prentice D, Sherman G, Kollef M, Shannon W. Deep vein thrombosis during prolonged mechanical ventilation despite prophylaxis. Crit Care Med. 2002,30:771–774.

37. Cook DJ, Crowther M, Meade M, Rabbat C, Schiff D, Geerts W, Griffith L, Guyatt GH. Deep venous thrombosis in medical-surgical ICU patients: prevalence, incidence and risk factors. Crit Care. 2003, Suppl 2:S54.

38. Cook D, Meade M, Guyatt G, Griffith L, Granton J, Geerts W et al. Clinically important deep vein thrombosis in the intensive care unit: a survey of intensivists. Critical Care. 2004;8:R145–R152.

39. Geerts WH, Heit JA, Clagett P, Pineo GF, Colwell CW, Anderson FA, Wheeler HB. Prevention of venous thromboembolism. Sixth ACCP Antithrombotic Consensus Conference on Antithrombotic Therapy. Chest. 2001;119(1 Suppl):132S–175S.

40. Robinson SK, Anderson DR, Gross M, Petrie D, Leighton R, Stanish W et al. Ultrasonographic screening before hospital discharge for deep venous thrombosis after arthroplasty. Ann Intern Med. 1997;127:439–445.

41. Kearon C, Julian JA, Newman TE et al. Noninvasive diagnosis of deep venous thrombosis. McMaDiagnostic Imaging Practice Guidelines Initiative. Ann Intern Med. 1998;128:663–677.

42. Lacherade JC, Cook D. Canadian ICU Directors Groups. Prevention of venous thromboembolism in critically ill medical patients: A Franco-Canadian cross-sectional study. J Crit Care. 2003;18(4):228–37.

43. Langham J, Thompson. identification and assessment of quality. Clinical Intensive Care. 2002;13(2–3):73–83.

44. Goldhaber SZ. Venous thromboembolism in the intensive care unit [editorial]. Chest. 1998;113:5–7.

45. Samama MM, Cohen AT, Darmon JY et al, for the Prophylaxis in Medical Patients with Enoxaparin Group. A comparison of enoxaparin versus placebo for the prevention of venous thromboembolism acutely ill medical patients. N Engl J Med. 1999;341:793–800.

46. Galli M, Reber G, Moerloose de P, Groot PG. Invitation to a debate on the serological criteria that define antiphospholipid syndrome. J Thromb Haemost. 2008; 6:399–401.

47. Tincani A, Allegri F, Sanmarco M, Cinquini M, Taglietti M, Balestrieri G, Koike T, Ichikawa K, Meroni P, Boffa MC. Anticardiolipin antibody assay: a methodological analysis for a better consensus in routine determinations – a cooperative project of the European Antiphospholipid Forum. Thromb Haemost. 2001;86:575–83.

48. Tincani A, Allegri F, Balestrieri G, Reber G, Sanmarco M, Meroni P, Boffa MC. Minimal requirements for antiphospholipid antibodies ELISAs proposed by the European Forum on antiphospholipid antibodies. Thromb Res. 2004;114:553–8.

49. Reber G, Shousboe I, Tincani A, Sanmarco M, Kveder T, de Moerloose P, Boffa MC, Arvieux J. Inter-laboratory variability of anti-beta2-glycoprotein I measurement. A collaborative study in the frame of the European Forum on Antiphospholipid Antibodies Standardization Group. Thromb Haemost. 2002;88:66–73.

50. Reber G, Tincani A, Sanmarco M, de Moerloose P, Boffa MC; European Forum on Antiphospholipid Antibodies Standardization Group. Variability of anti-beta2-glycoprotein I measurement by commercial assays. Thromb Haemost. 2005;94:665–72.

51. Valenstein PN, Walsh MK, Meier F et al. Heparin monitoring and patient safety: a college of american pathologists Q-probes study of 3431 patients at 140 institutions. arch Pathol Lab Med. 2004;128;397–402.

52. van Walraven C, Naylor CD. Do we know what inappropriate laboratory utilization is? A systematic review of laboratory clinical audits. JAMA. 1998;280(6): 550–558.

53. Gewirtz AS, Miller ML, Keys TF. The clinical usefulness of the preoperative bleeding time. Arch Pathol Lab Med. 1996;120(4):353–356.

54. Posan E, McBane RD, Grill DE et al. Comparison of PFA-100 testing and bleeding time for detecting platelet hypofunction and von Willebrand disease in clinical practice. Thromb Haemost. 2003;90(3):483–490.

55. Peerschke EIB. The laboratory evaluation of platelet dysfunction. Clin Lab Med. 2002;22:405–420.

56. Baughman RP, Lower EE, Flessa HC, Tollerud DJ. Thrombocytopenia in the intensive care unit. Chest. 1993;104(4):1243–1247.

57. Lee KH, Hui KP, Tan WC. Thrombocytopenia in sepsis: a predictor of mortality in the intensive care unit. Singapore Med J. 1993, 34:245–246.

58. Hanes SD, Quarles DA, Boucher BA. Incidence and risk factors of thrombocytopenia in critically ill trauma patients. Ann Pharmacother. 1997;31:285–289.

59. Practice guidelines for blood component therapy. A report by the American Society of Anesthesiologists task force on blood component therapy. Anesthesiology. 1996;84:732–747.

60. Dellinger RP, Levy MM, Carlet JM, Bion J, Parker MM, Jaeschke R et al. Surviving Sepsis Campaign: International guidelines for management of severe sepsis and septic shock: 2008. Crit Care Med. 2008;36:296–327.

61. Levy JH, Tanaka KA, Hursting MJ. Reducing Thrombotic Complications in the Perioperative Setting: An Update on Heparin-Induced Thrombocytopenia. Anesth Analg. 2007;105:570–82.

62. Briggs C, Harrison P, Machin SW. in Michelson AD. Platelets. Second Edition. Platelet Counting. San Diego, CA. Elsevier/Academic Press. 2007;475–483.

63. Koh T, Kabutomori O, Hishiyama M et al. Discrepancy of platelet numbers between automated blood cell analysis and manual counting in patients with thrombocytopenia. Rinsho Byori. 1996;44:889–694.

64. Kunz D. Possibilities and Limitations of Automated Platelet Counting Procedures in the Thrombocytopenic Range. Semin Thromb Hemost. 2001;27:229–236.

65. Lombarts AJ, de Kieviet W. Recognition and prevention of pseudothrombocytopenia and concomitant pseudoleukocytosis. Am J Clin Pathol. 1988;89:634–9.

66. Seegmiller A, Sarode R. Laboratory Evaluation of Platelet Function. Hematol Oncol Clin N Am 21. (2007) 731–742.

67. Jennings LK, White MM. in Michelson AD. Platelets. Second Edition. Platelet Aggregation. San Diego, CA. Elsevier/Academic Press. 2007:495–507.

68. Harrison P, Keeling D. in Michelson AD. Platelets. Second Edition. Clinical tests of platelet function. San Diego, CA. Elsevier/Academic Press. 2007:445–474.

69. Dyszkiewicz-Korpanty A, Quinton R, Yassine J et al. The effect of a pneumatic tube transport system on PFA-100 trade mark closure time and whole blood platelet aggregation. J Thromb Haemost. 2004;2: 354–6.

70. Scheider DJ, Tracy PB, Mann KG, et al. Differential effects of anticoagulants on the activation of platelets ex vivo. Circulation. 1997;96:2877–2883.

71. Hardisty RM, Hutton RA, Montgomery D. Secondary platelet aggregation: A quantitative study. Br J Haematol. 1970;19:307–319.

72. Rochon AG, Shore-Lesserson L. Coagulation Monitoring. Anesthesiology Clin. 2006;24:839–856.

73. Halfdan O, Ingerslev J, Sorensen B. Whole blood laboratory model of thrombocytopenia for use in evaluation of hemostatic interventions. Ann Hematol. 2007;86:217–221.

74. Born GVR. Aggregation of blood platelets by adenosine diphosphate and its reversal. Nature. 1962;194:927–929.

75. Michelson AD, Frelinger AL, Furman MI. Current options in platelet function testing. Am J Cardiol. 2006;98[suppl]:4N–10N.

76. Cattaneo M. Aspirin and Clopidogrel: Efficacy, safety, and the issue of drug resistance. Arterioscler Thromb Vasc Biol. 2004;24:1980–1987.

77. Nuttall GA, Oliver WC, Beynen FM, et al. Determination of normal versus abnormal activated partial thrombo- plastin time and prothrombin time after cardiopulmo- nary bypass. J Cardiothorac Vasc Anesth. 1995;9:355–361.

78. Despotis GJ, Levine V, Saleen R et al. Use of point-of-care test in identification of patients who can benefit from desmopressin during cardiac surgery: A randomised controlled trial. Lancet. 1999;354:106–110.

79. Koscienly J, Ziemer S, Radtke H et al. A practical concept for preoperative identification of patient with impaired primary hemostasis. Clin Appl Thromb Hemost. 2004; 10:195–204.

80. Despotis GJ, Joist JH, Goodnough LT. Monitoring of hemostasis in cardiac surgical patients: Impact of point-of-care testing on blood loss and transfusion outcomes. Clin Chem. 1997;43:1684–1696.

81. Fattorutto M, Pradier O, Shmartz D et al. Does the platelet function analyser (PFA-100) predict blood loss after cardiopulmonary bypass? Br J Anaesth. 2003;90: 692–693.

82. Bhatt DL. Editorial Comment. Aspirin resistance: More than just a laboratory curiosity. J Am Coll Cardiol. 2004; 43(6):1127–1129.

83. Wang TH, Bhatt DL, Topol EJ. Aspirin and clopidogrel resistance: an emerging clinical entity. Eur Heart J. 2006;27(6):647–654.

84. Despotis GJ, Santoro SA, Spitznagel E et al. Prospective evaluation and clinical utility of on-site monitoring of coagulation in patients undergoing cardiac operation. J Thorac Cardiovasc Surg. 1994;107:271–279.

85. Despotis GJ, Grishaber JE, Goodnough LT. The effect of an intraoperative treatment algorithm on physicians' transfusion practice in cardiac surgery [see comments]. Transfusion. 1994;34: 290–296.

86. Kitchens CS. To bleed or not to bleed? is that the question for the PTT? J Thromb Haemost. 2005;3:2607–2611.

87. Lee RI, White PD. A clinical study of the coagulation time of blood. Am J Med Sci. 1913;145:495–503.

88. White GC. The partial thromboplastin time: defining an era in coagulation. J Thromb Hemost. 2003;1:2267–2270.

89. Roizen MF. More preoperative assessment by physicians and less by laboratory tests. N Engl J Med. 2000;342: 204–205.

90. Kitchens CS. Preoperative PT's, PTT's, cost-effectiveness, and health care reform. Radical changes that make good sense. Chest. 1994;106:661–662.

91. von Kaulla KN, Ostendorf P, von Kaulla E. The impedance machine: a new bedside coagulation recording device. J Med. 1975;6:73–88.

92. Hartert H. Blutgerinnungsstudien mit der Thromboelasto- graphie, einem neuen Untersuchungsverfahren. Klin Wochenschr. 1948;26:577–583.

93. Hett DA, Walker D, Pilkington SN et al. Sonoclot analysis. Br J Anaesth. 1995;75:771–776.

94. Saleem A, Blifeld C, Saleh SA et al. Viscoelastic measurement of clot formation: a new test of platelet function. Ann Clin Lab Sci. 1983;13:115–124.

95. McKenzie ME, Gurbel PA, Levine DJ, Serebruany VL. Clinical utility of available methods for determining platelet function. Cardiology. 1999;92:240–247.

96. Ekback G, Carlsson O, Schott U. Sonoclot coagulation analysis: a study of test variability. J Cardiothorac Vase Anesth. 1999;13:393–397.

97. Horlocker TT, Schroeder DR. Effect of age, gender, and platelet count on Sonoclot coagulation analysis in patients undergoing orthopedic operations. Mayo Clin Proc. 1997;72:214–219.

98. Miyashita T, Kuro M. Evaluation of platelet function by Sonoclot analysis compared with other hemostatic variables in cardiac surgery. Anesth Analg. 1998;87:1228–1233.

99. Forestier F, BeHsle S, Contant C, Harel F, Janvier G, Hardy JF. [Reproducibility and interchangeability of the Thromboelastograph, Sonoclot and Hemochron activated coagulation time in cardiac surgery]. Can J Anaesth. 2001;48:902–910.

100. Ganter MT, Monn A, Tavakoli R et al. Monitoring activated clotting time for combined heparin and aprotinin application: in vivo evaluation of a new aprotinin-insensitive test using Sonoclot. Eur J Cardiothorac Surg. 2006;30:278–284

101. Tucci MA, Ganter MT, Hamiel CR, Klaghofer R, Zollinger A, Hofer CK. Platelet function monitoring with the Sonoclot analyzer after in vitro tirofiban and heparin administration. J Thorac Cardiovasc Surg. 2006;131:1314–1322.

102. Zuckerman L, Cohen E, Vaughan J, Woodward E, Caprini J. Comparison of thrombelastography with common coagulation tests. Thrombosis and Haemostasis. 1981;46,752–756.

103. Sorensen B, Ingerslev J. Tailoring haemostatic treatment to patient requirements – an update on monitoring haemostatic response using thrombelastography. Haemophilia. 2005;11:(Suppl. 1)1–6.

104. Goerlinger K. Coagulation management during liver transplatantion. Hämostaseologie. 2006;26(Suppl. 1): S64–S75.

105. Pfanner G, Kilgert K. Obstetric Bleeding complications. Hämostaseologie. 2006;26(Suppl. 1):S56–S63.

106. Shore-Lesserson L. Monitoring anticoagulation and hemostasis in cardiac surgery. Anesthesiol Clin North America. 2003;511–526.

107. Lang T, Bauter A, Braun SL, Tzsch BP, Werner vonPape K, Kolder HJ, Lakner M. Multi-centre investigation on reference ranges for ROTEM thromboelastometry. Blood Coagul Fibrinolysis. 2005;16:301–310.

108. Kozek-Langenecker S. Modern anaesthetic techniques and anticoagulation. Hämostaseologie. 2006;26 (Suppl. 1):S40–S49.

109. Luddington RJ. Thrombelastography/thromboelasto-metry. Clin Lab Haem. 2005;27:81–90.

110. Niemi T, Kuitunen A. Artificial colloids impair haemostasis. An in vitro study using thromboelasto-metry coagulation analysis. Acta Anaesthesiol Scand 2005;49:373–378.

111. Vig S, Chitolie A, Bevan DH, Halliday A, Dormandy J. Thromboelastography: a reliable test? Blood Coagul Fibrinolysis 2001;12:555–561.

112. Kozec-Langenecker S. Management of Massive operative blood loss. Minerva Anestesiol 2007;73:401–415.

113. Koscielny J, Ziemer S, Radtke H, Schmutzler M, Pruss A, Sinha P, Latza et al. A practical Concept for preoperative identification of patients with impaired primary hemostasis. Clin Appl Thrombosis/Hemostasis 2004;10(3):195–20.

Oliver Grottke, Jörg Brokmann and Rolf Rossaint

Management of refractory bleeding

Introduction

Coagulopathy as a source for bleeding is a general disorder in critically ill patients (1). The initial assessment of patients with bleeding problems will focus on how serious the bleeding is and try to identify the underlying source in order to initiate a proper therapy. Clinical examination will help to differentiate between a general coagulopathy and a surgical problem.

If bleeding occurs from multiple sites at the same time, a haemostatic effect should be considered. These bleedings present as slow oozing from non-identifiable sources or delayed after initial adequate haemostasis with soft tissue haematomas. In contrast, bleeding from a single site or sudden onset of bleeding is likely to be due to a local defect. If the patient is haemodynamically stable, imagining techniques including radiography, computed tomography, angiography and ultrasound should be applied to identify the source of bleeding, followed by surgical as well as non-surgical interventions (arterial embolisation, etc.) to limit the ongoing blood loss.

Patients with a suspected coagulation defect should be reevaluated concerning their family history of bleeding to identify inherited haemostatic disorders and to determine exposure to any drugs given before (2). Moreover, many of the medications used in intensive care interfere with haemostasis. Bleeding is multifactorial and includes insufficient synthesis of coagulation factors, dilution as well as consumption of coagulation factors, hy-

pothermia, hypocalcaemia, acidosis and activation of fibrinolysis. If a combination of hypothermia, acidosis and coagulopathy – also called the 'the lethal triad' – is present, surgical control of refractory bleeding is unlikely to be successful (3). Hypothermia is an independent risk factor for bleeding and death, causing an impairment of clotting, a reduction in the synthesis of coagulation factors, altered platelet function, and increased fibrinolysis. Acidosis may develop as a result of reduction in tissue perfusion and consequent release of anaerobic metabolites, compromising the function of platelets and coagulation enzymes. For example, prothrombin activation at pH 7.0 is reduced by 70 % in comparison to pH 7.4. Therefore the management of refractory bleeding should also aim for normothermia, normal pH and normocalcaemia. Thrombocytopenia is one of the most common laboratory abnormalities in critical ill patients (4). A low platelet count may be attributed to several mechanisms and occurs in a variety of clinical settings (sepsis, DIC, ITP, etc.). In a bleeding patient a platelet count less than $50 \times 10^9/l$ is usually an indication for platelet transfusion (5).

In managing refractory bleeding initial laboratory diagnosis is essential and should include the evaluation of routine clotting tests, such as the activated partial thromboplastin time (aPTT), prothrombin time (PT), concentration of fibrinogen and blood cell count (see tab. 1). Although abnormalities in these tests may indicate a coagulation defect, these global tests should be interpreted with caution for several reasons. First of all, the results of PT and aPTT depend on reagent and laboratory processes, e.g. normally the tests are performed at a temperature of 37°C. Secondly, out-of-range results may be due to normal variation for some individuals. Furthermore, coagulation tests vary in sensitivity for reduced levels of coagulation factors. In accordance to these results a systematic review showed that PT has a low predictive value for bleeding (6). The complexity of the cell-based model of the coagulation process explains why global coagulation screening tests are not sensitive markers for clinical haemostasis (7). To identify coagulation abnormalities complementary tests, such as assessment of platelet function (PFA-100), activities of clotting factors and inhibitors, fibrinogen degradation products (FDPs), D-dimers and an examination of the peripheral blood smear may be helpful (8).

Other approaches of diagnosis including thrombelastography might be more appropriate for clinical use, but their value in the management of bleeding needs further investigation. After transfusion, frequent control of laboratories as well as clinical examination are necessary to measure the success of therapy.

Ongoing bleeding will reduce the pool of coagulation factors as well as the level of haemoglobin. Both FFP and haemostatic agents may regenerate the pool of coagulation factors and thus help to terminate refractory bleeding. The intention of this chapter is an attempt to synthesise the evidence for the application of FFP vs. the use of haemostatic agents including bypassing agents such as rFVIIa to overcome refractory bleeding.

Tab. 1 Coagulation tests and their differential diagnosis. Modified from: Critical Care Clinics 21(3), DeLoughery Thomas G, Critical Care Clotting Catastrophies, 531–562, 2005, with permission from Elsevier.

Elevated prothrombin time, normal aPTT

- Factor VII deficiency
- Vitamin K-deficiency
- Therapy with vitamin K-dependent oral anticoagulants
- Sepsis
- Disseminated intravascular coagulation (certain cases)

Normal prothrombin time, elevated aPTT

- Isolated factor deficiency (VIII, IX, XI, XII)
- Specific factor inhibitors
- Heparin therapy
- Lupus inhibitor

Elevated prothrombin time, elevated aPTT

- Multiple coagulation factor deficiencies
- Dilution effect
- Liver disease
- Disseminated intravascular coagulation
- Factor X, V, or II deficiency
- Factor V inhibitors
- Therapy with high heparin levels
- Vitamin K-deficiency
- Low fibrinogen (<0.5 g/l)
- Dysfibrinogemia

Controversial issue 1: Fresh frozen plasma (FFP)

Fresh frozen plasma is human donor plasma separated from whole blood or obtained by plasmapheresis. It is frozen within a specific time period after collection and stored at a temperature below −30°C. Before use FFP must be thawed at 37°C and should be used quickly to avoid hypothermia after transfusion. The volume of a typical unit contains 150–250 ml. FFP contains near-normal physiological levels of all plasma proteins – including procoagulant and inhibitor components of the coagulation cascade such as antithrombin. Coagulation factors are diluted by approximately 15% during the preparation process with anticoagulant solution and further losses might occur during the freezing and thawing process. Also, the activity of coagulation factors depends on the donor's concentration of coagulation factors. For example, levels of von Willebrand factor (VWF) and FVIII levels are ABO blood group-related. Anticoagulants contain varying proportions for trisodium citrate, citric acid, sodium monophosphate, dextrose and adenine. In contrast, solvent-detergent plasma (SD-FFP) contains pooled plasma from 300–500 donors, balancing the variations in factor concentrations. The solvent-detergent treatment for pathogen inactivation causes altered or loss of coagulation factor content. FFP should be transfused ABO-compatible due to the risk of haemolysis with ABO-incompatible FFP. In emergencies AB FFP can be used if the patients ABO blood group is unknown, but AB FFP is in short supply.

FFP has been available since 1941 and its clinical use has grown steadily over the past two decades (9). Conversely, the evidence in favour of transfusing FFP in active bleeding is scarce and the studies are of limited quality. A systematic review by Stanworth et al. identified 57 randomised controlled studies on the use of FFP (10). Out of these 57 studies only 17 compared the use of FFP with no FFP or with colloid/crystalloid solutions in adults. Overall, the review of the literature showed that the studies were of limited quality and were mostly underpowered to show any clinical differences in outcome.

For example, liver diseases are important causes for coagulopathy in ICU patients associated with coagulation factor deficiencies, dysfunction of platelets, abnormalities of fibrinolysis and inhibitors of coagulation. With the exception of one trial, the published studies evaluated prophylactic FFP administration to correct coagulopathy to reduce the risk for bleeding. Only one small RCT compared the clinical effectiveness of FFP with a control group with no FFP in patients with liver disease following an overdose of paracetamol (11). Treatment with FFP had no effect on bleeding morbidity or mortality. However, the sample size of the study was too small and the design was not ideal to detect any differences. Further studies in patients with liver disease were observational and uncontrolled. Youssef et al. investigated in a split retrospective-prospective study enrolling 100 patients with chronic liver disease and no responsiveness to vitamin K substitution. Their main findings showed that large amounts of FFP were necessary to stop bleeding and to correct out-of-range laboratories (12). None of the studies compared the use of FFP with colloid or crystalloids.

DIC (disseminated intravascular coagulation) is a systematic disorder, which is characterised by a derangement of the coagulation system leading to multiple deficiencies in coagulation factors. The prompt identification and management of the underlying disease is the fundamental approach to treat DIC. Due to the consumption of coagulation factors and inhibitors it seems reasonable to substitute the loss of factors by FFP. However, the data on the effectiveness of FFP in these circumstances are rare. In part this observation might be explained by the difficulty to design an appropriate study for this cohort. Gross et al. investigated in a controlled trial the effectiveness of DIC in 33 neonates (13). Neonates were allocated to receive either FFP infusion, exchange transfu-

sion (from whole blood) or no plasma in the control group. No differences in coagulation test or survival rate was observed, but the study was underpowered to show any significant difference.

A single-centre retrospective study from medical ICU patients investigated the benefit of two different FFP doses (FFP 10 ml/kg versus 17 ml/kg) (14). Patients with an INR ≥ 1.5 and no active signs of bleeding were selected. Apart from variability in FFP transfusion practice, a subgroup analysis of matched cases revealed a similar rate of haemorrhage despite FFP transfusion and a higher incidence of acute lung injury during the 48-hour period after transfusion. This finding may be attributed to the possibility that critically ill patients with concurrent inflammation may be more susceptible to transfusion-related acute lung injury (TRALI).

According to international guidelines, the indication for the use of FFP is a prolongation of prothrombin time or activated thromboplastin time of more than 1.5 times accompanied by signs of microvascular bleeding (15). Rather based on evidence from RCTs than on expert opinion, a dose of FFP to raise the coagulation factors above 30 IU/dl is recommended and volumes between 10–20 ml/kg FFP are suggested. Chowdhury et al. assessed the effect of FFP on laboratory coagulation parameters in critically ill patients and showed that coagulation tests are poor predictors for single coagulation factor deficiencies (16). Moreover, they found that a dose of 12.5 ml/kg FFP was not sufficient in most patients for an adequate increment in coagulation factors and that 30 ml/kg FFP were necessary to correct all coagulation factors. This limited efficacy of FFP might be also attributed to the consumption of coagulation factors (17).

FFP transfusion is associated with significant adverse effects. These include TRALI, volume overload and allergic reactions. Due to problems in the reporting and diagnosis of TRALI, to date it is difficult to estimate the real prevalence.

Although active bleeding is usually considered to be an absolute indication for the use of FFP, the current guidelines are not supported by evidence from randomised trials. Despite strict policies for the transfusion of FFP inappropriate use remains a concern (18). Thus, RCTs evaluating the whole benefit of FFP and a comparison of a restrictive versus a liberal transfusion regime are warranted. Studies should include variation in concentrations, address the timing for transfusion and the volume that should be transfused.

Controversial issue 2: Haemostatic agents

Recombinant activated factor VII (rFVIIa)

rFVIIa was originally licensed as a haemostatic agent for use in haemophilia patients with inhibitors to factor VIII or IX (19). Since its first approval in 1999 by the US Food and Drug Administration (FDA), it has also been approved in Europe for factor VII deficiency and Glanzmann's thrombasthenia (GT) with past or present refractoriness to platelet transfusion. rFVIIa exogenously added in pharmacological doses induces haemostasis in the absence of FVIII or FIX by binding to thrombin-activated platelet surfaces, which enhances the generation of thrombin (20). Further, rFVIIa mediates the inhibition of thrombin-activatable fibrinolysis inhibitor, which contributes to the stabilisation of the clot (21). To ensure maximal rFVIIa efficacy, international guidelines recommend to correct acidosis (pH $\geq$ 7.2), avoid severe hypothermia, maintain a platelet count above $50 \times 10^9/l$, a haematocrit of more than 24 % as well as a fibrinogen concentration of at least 0.5–1 g/l before the application of rFVIIa (see fig. 1) (22, 23).

The first successful application with two doses of rFVIIa of 60 µg/kg in a gunshot victim with rFVIIa was reported in 1999 (24). A placebo-controlled international trial by Boffard et al. involving 143 patients with severe blunt trauma showed that the application of three doses (200 µg/kg, 100 µg/kg, 100 µg/kg) of rFVIIa resulted in a significant reduction of red blood cell transfusion, reduction of patients requiring massive transfusion (defined as more than 20 units of red blood cells) and also significantly reduced the incidence of acute respiratory distress syndrome (25). Although not significant, a similar trend of reduced massive transfusion was observed in a parallel study involving 134 patients with severe penetrating trauma. In both studies there was no significant reduction for the need of blood products including FFP, platelets and cryoprecipitate. The observed frequency of adverse events was similar in both groups in either study.

A post-hoc analysis of 30 patients with traumatic injury also revealed no thromboemoblic events or other adverse events (26).

Other studies investigated the early intervention of rFVIIa in patients with intracerebral haemorrhage (ICH). The significant risk of morbidity and mortality in this population, which is in part caused by the expansion of haematoma, makes the application of rFVIIa attractive. A placebo-controlled trial involving 399 patients showed that the application of rFVIIa resulted in a slower increase of haematoma (27). The application of rFVIIa was also associated with a 35 % reduction in mortality and improved the disability score at 90 days. Thromboembolic events were observed in 7 % of the rFVIIa and 2 % of the control group ($p = 0.12$). A subsequent RCT with 841 patients showed a significant reduction in the size of haematoma, but failed to show an effect on mortality and severe disability (28).

A systematic review by Franchini et al. reports on the use of rFVIIa in clinical situations associated with DIC and unresponsiveness to standard treatment (29). They identified 99 patients with signs of DIC in a variety of clinical settings, which were finally successfully treated with rFVIIa as a last rescue option. The majority of published cases were obtained from women with postpartum haemorrhage associated with DIC. Other data came from patients with liver disease (30), pancreatitis (31), dengue haemorrhagic fever (32), cancer (33) and leukaemia (34). Interpretation of these data and the mechanism of rFVIIa suggest a potential role for rFVIIa in the treatment of refractory bleeding associated with DIC. Another review showed the successful application of rFVIIa in patients with von Willebrand disease with severe bleeding and resistance to standard therapy (35).

In the past few years, a growing number of case series and case reports have reported on the successful use of rFVIIa as haemostatic agent in life-threatening bleeding or bleeding resistant to conventional therapy in an array of clinical settings after other therapeutic measures have failed (36). Despite these quite encouraging data, it is not possible to draw any conclusions about the usefulness of rFVIIa in these clinical settings or to derive any dosing recommendations. Furthermore, the effectiveness of rFVIIa may be overestimated due to publication bias. According to Vin-

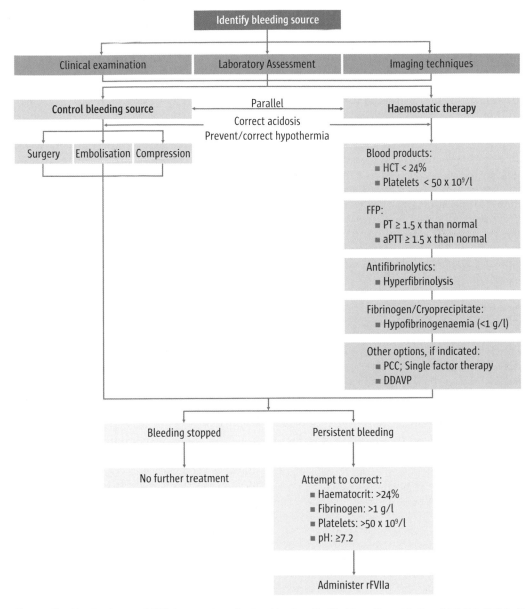

Fig. 1   Algorithm for the use of rFVIIa in managing refractory bleeding. Modified from: Vincent JL, Rossaint R, Roiu B, Ozier Y, Zideman D, Spahn DR. Recommendations on the use of recombinant activated factor VII as an adjunctive treatment for massive bleeding – a European perspective. Crit Care. 2006;10(4):R120.

cent et al. rFVIIa is not a substitute for invasive procedures used to control bleeding (e.g. embolisation), nor should rFVIIa replace the use of traditional blood products (22).

The wide and increasing use of rFVIIa for many off-label indications raises considerable safety issues. Therefore, O'Connell et al. reviewed 168 reports from the U.S. Food and Drug Administration Adverse Reporting System describing thrombembolic events (37). The majority of data showed that thrombembolic events occurred after the application of rFVIIa after unlabelled indication. These events were associated with high mortality and morbidity, but the interpretation of the complications was complicated by concomitant medications, pre-existing medical conditions and indication. Thus, the authors state that RCTs are needed to evaluate both the efficacy and safety in patients without haemophilia.

In conclusion, the available data indicate that rFVIIa might be an option for patients with severe haemorrhage refractory to conventional haemostatic therapy. Further studies are needed to assess its safety, seek to optimise doses and regimes. With regard to the considerable costs involved in the application of rFVIIa further studies should also assess cost-effectiveness. The costs have also been weighted against reduced cost from reduced blood product use, length of stay, morbidity and mortality. After usage of rFVIIa it is essential to closely monitor for bleeding sings as well as thrombotic events.

Prothrombin complex concentrates (PCCs) and single-factor therapy

PCCs contains the vitamin K-dependent factors FII, FVII, FIX and FX. Because of the heterogeneity of available PCCs, the therapeutic amounts of factors vary ("four- versus three-factor concentrates"). Most PCCs also contain heparin and proteins C and S, as well as protein Z of varying concentrations and antithrombin. All plasma products are virally inactivated and have a good safety record. The indications for the use of PCCs are a fast reversal of oral anticoagulation with vitamin K-dependent oral anticoagulants or a known deficiency of the vitamin K-dependent factors in potentially life-threatening bleeding (38). The substitution should be supplemented by intravenous vitamin K to induce the endogenous synthesis of vitamin K-dependent factors. Although some European medical centres favour the use of PCCs in patients with massive bleeding in combination with FFP, a recommendation for this indication cannot be made at this point in time. The clinical diagnosis or a history of heparin-induced thrombocytopenia (HIT) is a contraindication for the use of PCCs. Due to the associated risk of thromboembolic complications frequent clinical examination and laboratory tests are warranted.

The substitution of mono-component factor therapy is required for correcting coagulopathy in patients with acquired or congenital factor deficiencies. In general, a factor activity above 30%–40% is usually sufficient for haemostasis.

Based on the assumption that low fibrinogen levels are associated with an increased risk of bleeding, both cryoprecipitate and fibrinogen are commonly used to correct hypofibrinogenaemia. Although there is no absolute threshold value for diagnosing hypofibrinogenaemia, treatment is usually indicated if the fibrinogen concentration is less than 1 g/l.

Desmopressin (DDAVP)

Desmopressin (1-deamino-8-D-arginine vasopressin) is a synthetic analogue of vasopressin. It induces the release of FVIII and ultralarge VWF multimers from endothelial cells in the circulation in healthy individuals as well as in deficient patients. Plasma concentrations of factor VIII and VWF are up to quadrupled within 30 min after administration. Studies show strong evidence for the use of DDAVP in the prevention of bleeding in patients with certain subtypes of von Willebrand disease and mild haemophilia A (39). Also, DDAVP shortens the bleeding time of most patients with congenital defects of platelet function (40). 18 trials involving 1,295 patients have been performed to evaluate the potential of blood loss after cardiac surgery. Overall, these trials showed only a small effect on perioperative blood loss and had no impact on the need for transfusion or reoperation. Studies from other clinical settings show similar results (41). Although DDAVP shortens skin-bleeding time in patients with acquired defects of platelet function, there are no good data for clinically relevant endpoints (42). On the other hand, a systematic review from Levi et al. showed that DDAVP enhances the risk for thrombotic events in patients with myocardial infarction who underwent cardiac surgery, which might be explained by the secretion of large multimers (43). Adverse events include facial flushing, transient hyponatraemia, and repeated doses of DDAVP may lead to tachyphylaxis.

To conclude, there are definite indications for the use of DDAVP, and the use of this agent might be indicated in patients with refractory bleeding with suspected acquired or inherited platelet function. However, the administration of DDAVP should be carefully undertaken under consideration of the risk/benefit ratio. Furthermore, due to the unpredictable effects of DDAVP a therapeutic trial of administration to assess the level of response is advised.

Summary

The management of refractory bleeding remains an important challenge for the intensivist and requires an interdisciplinary approach. All available resources, including imagining techniques and laboratories should be used to identify the cause of bleeding. Coagulation tests do offer clinical guidance, but have to be interpreted in the clinical context followed by an individual approach of haemostatic therapy.

FFP is indicated in clinical situations with signs of bleeding caused by multi-factor deficiencies after treatment of the underlying disease. The transfusion of FFP should be carefully undertaken under benefit/risk considerations. rFVIIa is a potent haemostatic agent which may be useful to terminate severe bleeding in clinical situations which are not amenable to conventional therapeutics. Though the use of rFVIIa should be applied under the awareness of the current lack of evidence, off-label use and the potential risk of thromboembolic complications.

Key points for clinical practice

- *The decision to transfuse FFP should be tailored to the individual patient depending on clinical and laboratory assessment. The doses of FFP should increase coagulation factors to a predetermined concentration.*
- *rFVIIa should be considered for patients with ongoing bleeding resistant to conventional blood product therapy.*
- *Single-factor deficiencies should be treated with specific plasma fractions, e.g. cryoprecipitate.*
- *PCC is advised in patients on vitamin K-dependent anticoagulation and signs of severe bleeding.*

The authors

Oliver Grottke, MD, MSc[1]
Jörg Brokmann, MD[1]
Rolf Rossaint, MD, PhD[2]
[1]Department of Anaesthesiology | University Hospital Aachen, Germany
[2]Chairman of the Department of Anaesthesiology | University Hospital Aachen, Germany

Address for correspondence
Oliver Grottke
University Hospital Aachen
Department of Anaesthesiology
Pauwelsstraße 30
52074 Aachen, Germany
e-mail: ogrottke@ukaachen.de

References

1. Chakraverty R, Davidson S, Peggs K, Stross P, Garrard C, Littlewood TJ. The incidence and cause of coagulopathies in an intensive care population. Br J Haematol. 1996; 93(2):460-3.
2. Bombeli T, Spahn DR. Updates in perioperative coagulation: physiology and management of thromboembolism and haemorrhage. Br J Anaesth. 2004;93(2): 275-87.
3. Ferrara A, MacArthur JD, Wright HK et al. Hypothermia and acidosis worsen coagulopathy in the patient requiring massive transfusion. Am J Surg. 1990;160(5): 515-18.
4. Mercer KW, Gail Macik B, Williams ME. Hematologic disorders in critically ill patients. Semin Respir Crit Care Med. 2006;27(3):286-96.
5. British Committee for Standards in Haematology, Blood Transfusion Task Force. Guidelines for the use of platelet transfusions. Br J Haematol. 2003;122(1):10-23.
6. Segal JB, Dzik WH. Transfusion Medicine/Hemostasis Clinical Trials Network. Paucity of studies to support that abnormal coagulation test results predict bleeding in the setting of invasive procedures: an evidence-based review. Transfusion. 2005;45(9):1413-25.
7. Hoffman M, Monroe DM 3rd. A cell-based model of hemostasis. Thromb Haemost. 2001;85(6):958-65.
8. DeLoughery TG. --. Crit Care Clin. 2005;21(3):531-62.
9. Stanworth SJ. The Evidence-Based Use of FFP and Cryoprecipitate for Abnormalities of Coagulation Tests and Clinical Coagulopathy. Hematology Am Soc Hematol Educ Program. 2007;2007:179-86.

10. Stanworth SJ, Brunskill SJ, Hyde CJ, McClelland DB, Murphy MF. Is fresh frozen plasma clinically effective? A systematic review of randomized controlled trials. Br J Haematol. 2004;126(1):139–52.

11. Gazzard BG, Henderson JM, Williams R. Early changes in coagulation following a paracetamol overdose and a controlled trial of fresh frozen plasma therapy. Gut. 1975;16(8):617–20.

12. Youssef WI, Salazar F, Dasarathy S, Beddow T, Mullen KD. Role of fresh frozen plasma infusion in correction of coagulopathy of chronic liver disease: a dual phase study. Am J Gastroenterol. 2003;98(6):1391–4.

13. Gross SJ, Filston HC, Anderson JC. Controlled study of treatment for disseminated intravascular coagulation in the neonate. J Pediatr. 1982;100(3):445–8.

14. Dara SI, Rana R, Afessa B, Moore SB, Gajic O. Fresh frozen plasma transfusion in critically ill medical patients with coagulopathy. Crit Care Med. 2005;33(11):2667–71.

15. Practise guidelines for blood component therapy: a report by the American Society of Anesthesiologists Task Force on blood component therapy. Anesthesiology. 1996;84(3):732–47.

16. Chowdhury P, Saayman AG, Paulus U, Findlay GP, Collins PW. Efficacy of standard dose and 30 ml/kg fresh frozen plasma in correcting laboratory parameters of haemostasis in critically ill patients. Br J Haematol. 2004;125(1):69–73.

17. Ciavarella D, Reed RL, Counts RB, Baron L, Pavlin E, Heimbach DM et al. Clotting factor levels and the risk of diffuse microvascular bleeding in the massively transfused patient. Br J Haematol. 1987;67(3):365–8.

18. O'Shaughnessy DF, Atterbury C, Bolton Maggs P, Murphy M, Thomas D et al. British Committee for Standards in Haematology, Blood Transfusion Task Force. Guidelines for the use of fresh-frozen plasma, cryoprecipitate and cryosupernatant. Br J Haematol. 2004;126(1):11–28.

19. Roberts HR, Monroe DM, White GC. The use of recombinant factor VIIa in the treatment of bleeding disorders. Blood. 2004;104(13):3858–64. (Erratum: Blood 2005 15;105(6):2257).

20. Hedner U. Recombinant factor VIIa: its background, development and clinical use. Curr Opin Hematol. 2007; 14(3):225–9.

21. Lisman T, Mosnier LO, Lambert T, Mauser-Bunschoten EP, Meijers JC, Nieuwenhuis HK et al. Inhibition of fibrinolysis by recombinant factor VIIa in plasma from patients with severe hemophilia A. Blood. 2002;99(1):175–9.

22. Vincent JL, Rossaint R, Riou B, Ozier Y, Zideman D, Spahn DR. Recommendations on the use of recombinant activated factor VII as an adjunctive treatment for massive bleeding – a European perspective. Crit Care. 2006;10(4):R120.

23. Martinowitz U, Michaelson M. The Israeli Multidiscipli-

nary rFVIIa Task Force. Guidelines for the use of recombinant activated factor VII (rFVIIa) in uncontrolled bleeding: a report by the Israeli Multidisciplinary rFVIIa Task Force J Thromb Haemost. 2005;3(4):640–8.

24. Kenet G, Walden R, Eldad A, Martinowitz U. Treatment of traumatic bleeding with recombinant factor VIIa. Lancet. 1999;354(9193):1879.

25. Boffard KD, Riou B, Warren B, Choong PI, Rizoli S, Rossaint R et al. NovoSeven Trauma Study Group. Recombinant factor VIIa as adjunctive therapy for bleeding control in severely injured trauma patients: two parallel randomized, placebo-controlled, double-blind clinical trials. J Trauma. 2005;59(1):8–15; discussion 15–8.

26. Kluger Y, Riou B, Rossaint R, Rizoli SB, Boffard KD, Choong PI et al. Safety of rFVIIa in hemodynamically unstable polytrauma patients with traumatic brain injury: post hoc analysis of 30 patients from a prospective, randomized, placebo-controlled, double-blind clinical trial. Crit Care. 2007;11(4):R85.

27. Mayer SA, Brun NC, Begtrup K, Broderick J, Davis S, Diringer MN et al. Recombinant Activated Factor VII Intracerebral Hemorrhage Trial Investigators. Recombinant activated factor VII for acute intracerebral hemorrhage. N Engl J Med. 2005;352(8):777–8.

28. Mayer SA, Brun NC, Begtrup K, Broderick J, Davis S, Diringer MN, Skolnick BE, Steiner T. FAST Trial Investigators. Efficacy and safety of recombinant activated factor VII for acute intracerebral hemorrhage. N Engl Med. 2008; 358(20):2127–37.

29. Franchini M, Manzato F, Salvagno GL, Lippi G. Potential role of recombinant activated factor VII for the treatment of severe bleeding associated with disseminated intravascular coagulation: a systematic review. Blood Coagul Fibrinolysis. 2007;18(7):589–93.

30. Caldwell SH, Chang C, Macik BG. Recombinant activated factor VII (rFVIIa) as a hemostatic agent in liver disease: a break from convention in need of controlled trials. Hepatology. 2004;39(3):592–8.

31. Laffan MA, Tait RC, Blatný J, Espersen K, Grabowska I, Loch-Bakoñska L et al. Use of recombinant activated factor VII for bleeding in pancreatitis: a case series. Pancreas. 2005;30(3):279–84.

32. Chuansumrit A, Tangnararatchakit K, Lektakul Y, Pongthanapisith V, Nimjaroenniyom N, Thanarattanakorn P et al. The use of recombinant activated factor VII for controlling life-threatening bleeding in Dengue Shock Syndrome. Blood Coagul Fibrinolysis. 2004;15(4):335–42.

33. Sallah S, Husain A, Nguyen NP. Recombinant activated factor VII in patients with cancer and hemorrhagic disseminated intravascular coagulation. Blood Coagul Fibrinolysis. 2004;15(7):577–82.

34. Zver S, Andoljsek D, Cernelc P. Effective treatment of life-threatening bleeding with recombinant activated factor VII in a patient with acute promyelocytic leukaemia. Eur J Haematol. 2004;72(6):455–6.

35. Franchini M, Veneri D, Lippi G. The use of recombinant activated factor VII in congenital and acquired von Willebrand disease. Blood Coagul Fibrinolysis. 2006; 17(8):615–9.

36. Levi M, Peters M, Büller HR. Efficacy and safety of recombinant factor VIIa for treatment of severe bleeding: a systematic review. Crit Care Med. 2005;33(4):883–90.

37. O'Connell KA, Wood JJ, Wise RP, Lozier JN, Braun MM. Thromboembolic adverse events after use of recombinant human coagulation factor VIIa. JAMA. 2006; 295(3):293–8.

38. Ansell J, Hirsh J, Poller L, Bussey H, Jacobson A, Hylek E. The pharmacology and management of the vitamin K antagonists: the Seventh ACCP Conference on Antithrombotic and Thrombolytic Therapy. Chest. 2004; 126(3 Suppl):204–233.

39. Mannucci PM. Treatment of von Willebrand's Disease. N Engl J Med. 2004;351:683–694.

40. Cattaneo M. Desmopressin in the treatment of patients with defects of platelet function. Haematologica. 2002;87(11):1122–4.

41. Carless PA, Henry DA, Moxey AJ, O'Connell D, McClelland B, Henderson KM et al. Desmopressin for minimising perioperative allogeneic blood transfusion. Cochrane Database Syst Rev. 2004;(1):CD001884.

42. Mannucci PM, Levi M. Prevention and treatment of major blood loss. N Engl J Med. 2007;356(22):2301–11.

43. Levi M, Cromheecke ME, de Jonge E, Prins MH, de Mol BJ, Briët E et al. Pharmacological strategies to decrease excessive blood loss in cardiac surgery: a meta-analysis of clinically relevant endpoints. Lancet. 1999;354(9194):1940–7.

G. Organisational issues

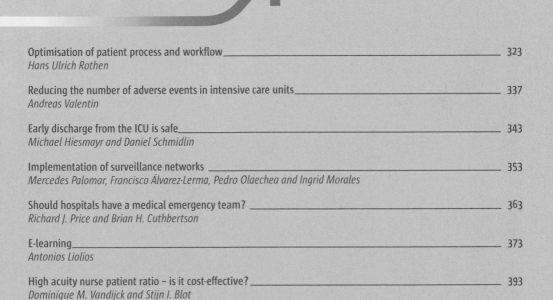

Hans Ulrich Rothen

Optimisation of patient process and workflow

Introduction

For more than thirty years, there has been concern over costs and efficient use of resources in intensive care medicine (1). Rising costs in health care, rational use of resources and even rationing of health care are matters of public interest. In a number of western societies, approximately 10–15 % of the gross national product is used for health care. This share may even increase to 20 % in the United States within the next few years (2). Furthermore, the cost of critical care in the United States represented 13 % of hospital costs, 4 % of national health expenditures, and 0.6 % of the gross domestic product in 2000 (3). Of note, patients with a long stay in the intensive care unit (ICU), although relatively small in number, consume a marked proportion of ICU resources. As an example, approximately ten times as many resources are used per surviving long-term patient as for a surviving short-term patient (4, 5). Such findings suggest that improving the patient process in the ICU and avoiding inappropriate prolonged treatment in patients who ultimately will not survive the hospital stay may help to avoid inappropriate allocation of scarce resources and to reduce unnecessary suffering both for patients and for their relatives.

Organisational issues and quality management have become an important focus of interest in recent years, not only in health care in general (6–10), but also specifically in intensive care medicine (11, 12). Generally, wide variability between individual intensive care units, both with respect to resource use and to outcome, has been described by many (13–16). Such unevenness suggests that there is high variation in the process of caring for critically ill patients and that there might be marked room for improvement in many aspects. However, only limited information exists about factors influencing such variability (15, 17, 18).

The problem

- *Intensive care medicine consumes a high amount of health care resources.*
- *The amount of resource use per patient shows a markedly skewed distribution.*
- *Wide variability exists between individual ICUs, both with respect to severity-adjusted resource use and with respect to outcome.*
- *Such variability suggests that there is great unevenness in patient care processes and that there might be marked room for improvement in many aspects of care in the critically ill, in patient flow through the ICU, and in workflow of critical care professionals.*

In this article we present suggestions for improving the patient process and ultimately for improving productivity. Overall, advances in the patient process may be achieved either by providing more effective or efficient patient care, or by accelerating and streamlining patient flow through the ICU. Aiming at a higher patient flow will generally result in a shorter length of stay in the ICU. This might, however, also lead to restrictions in care of the critically ill. Accordingly, and in order to avoid a concomitant and unwelcome reduction in the quality of care, changes in the patient process should be supplemented by a comprehensive concept of quality management. Finally, a search for opportunities to improve workflow and avoidance of an inappropriate increase in workload should be part of all managerial activities in the ICU.

Other approaches with the potential for improving patient process or workflow, such as regionalisation of critical care (19), and quality assessment through accreditation of ICUs and competency surveillance (20), will not be discussed here.

Optimising the patient process

The patient process in the ICU

The 90° shift

In general, an ICU has three core processes: patient care, education, and research. They are tightly interrelated, and are supplemented by support processes, such as human resource management, logistics, finances and controlling, and information technology. Depending on the type of ICU and characteristics of the hospital, the relative importance of each of the three main processes may vary widely. As an example, teaching and research probably play a minor role in most non-university hospitals. In this chapter, we will thus focus mostly on the central task of an ICU: the patient process, consisting of patient care and patient flow.

Like the employees in many other organisations, medical professionals are accustomed to thinking and acting in functions. In a typical acute care hospital there are, among others, professional groups responsible for nursing care, medical care, physiotherapy, and the hospital's administration. Alternatively or in addition, there might be a department devoted to cardiology, cardiovascular surgery, neurology, neurosurgery, etc. In such an organisation, the patient is "handled" sequentially by members of each group or department (a "silo" approach, see fig. 1). Due to the multiple handovers involved, there is a risk of loss of information and a need for coordination between all areas of responsibility.

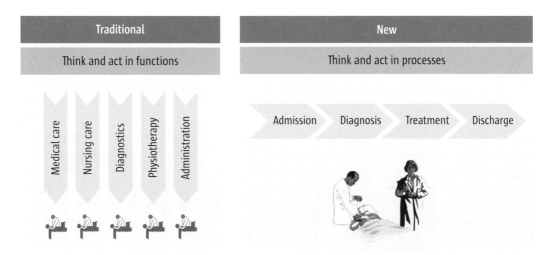

Fig. 1   The 90° shift in the patient process
Traditional: Think and act in functions (nursing care, medical care, diagnostics (laboratory, imaging), therapy, and administration; neurology, cardiology, intensive care medicine, etc.) – the "silo" approach
New: Think and act in processes (admission, diagnosis, treatment, discharge)
Modified from: Etienne M. TQM-Leitfaden für Spitäler [Total quality management – a guideline for hosptials]. Haupt, Bern, Stuttgart, Wien. 2005. ISBN 3-258-6889-5. p.83.

In a new and different approach to patient care, organisations think and act in processes. As the main focus of a hospital is patient care, such processes will include at least admission → diagnostic workup → treatment → discharge. From the perspective of intensive care medicine, organisation and coordination of patient flow (which is a key element in the patient process) should not only include admission of a patient to the ICU, care in the ICU, and discharge from the ICU; rather, a broader approach would seem appropriate. Accordingly, critical care specialists might oversee and participate in the management of patient flow throughout the hospital, beginning with admission to the emergency department or acute care ward and ending with discharge from the hospital (21, 22). As a consequence, the well-known discussion of whether an ICU is "open" or "closed" (23, 24) probably will soon be obsolete, because in the near future the ICU will be "closed but integrative and communicating" (25). Other new models designed to improve patient flow and the process of care include the concept of outreach or medical emergency (rapid response) teams (26, 27), and the creation and extension of high-dependency or intermediate care units in the hospital (28–31).

To allow appropriate flexibility in organisation and to promote a change from the "silo" approach to a focus on the patient process, architectural flexibility is a prerequisite (25). For example, it can be expected that in coming years, the share of high-dependency care beds in acute care hospitals will further and markedly increase. Still, inappropriate design and inflexible set-up of rooms and floors may impede such development.

High-dependency care beds may be located in intensive care units, intermediate care units, step-down/step-up care units, and anaesthesia recovery units. Integrating high-dependency beds in the ICU allows for more flexible adjustment of staffing, monitoring and intensity of care according to the patients' needs (29). Integrating high-dependency care beds in organ-specific departments (e.g. cardiology), on the other hand, may have the advantage of straightforward development of highly specialised patient care (32), but possibly at the cost of limiting the knowledge available for treating patients with multiple, highly complex medical problems. Depending on organisational and architectural structures, the optimal solution will certainly differ between hospitals (31).

Improving the process of care

Overall, there are two main domains of change that can lead to improvements in the process of care in the ICU: organisational issues and medical components (33). Further important elements are the standardisation of care processes and the willingness and ability to learn, not only at a personal level but rather also at an organisational level.

Organisational changes concern, among others, a qualitative or quantitative change in staffing, in assignment of responsibility, and in the structure of the caring team. A number of observational studies have shown that the presence of trained intensivists is associated with improved outcome (34, 35). Accordingly, recommendations for ICU staffing in non-rural areas have been presented, such as those of the Leapfrog Group (36). More than a decade ago, minimal standards also were described for Europe (37).

As compared to these guidelines, an even higher level of physician staffing – both with respect to quality and quantity – is recommended today by the Swiss Society of Intensive Care Medicine (38). This professional society, representing all adult and paediatric/neonatal intensive care specialists of Switzerland, requires that each Swiss ICU be led by a specialist in intensive care medicine. This specialist is required to use at least 80% of his or her total working time (full-time equivalent, FTE) for the unit if the unit has 6 to 8 beds, and even more if the unit is larger. In addition, the guidelines require that the staff include a deputy manager who fulfils certain requirements, such as being a specialist in anaesthesiology or internal medicine and having basic knowledge of critical care medicine. Each ICU must have at least one physician available to the unit around the clock. Finally, for every ICU, a senior staff member educated as a specialist in intensive care medicine (39) has to be available at the bedside within two hours of being called (24 hours a day, 7 days a week). The Swiss guidelines also require minimal standards for nursing personnel, such as 15 full-time equivalent (FTE) staff members for a six-bed

ICU (see also section on workflow, below). At least one-third of the nurses have to possess a certificate as a fully trained critical care nurse.

There are, however, many barriers to implementing such recommendations. As an example, loss of control, loss of income, and increased cost for hospital administration were cited as important barriers to implementing the recommendations of the Leapfrog Group (40). A further hindrance may be the defence of a profession's (physicians, nurses) or a person's traditional right. Possibly even more relevant are potential shortages of ICU professionals, as predicted recently for the United States (41).

Medical components of the process of care include diagnostic or monitoring procedures, use of drugs, and use of technical equipment. These latter components are ideally based on scientific evidence. They form the basis of standards, best practice models and clinical pathways. In critical care medicine, they include, for example, early and aggressive management of sepsis, lung-protective ventilation, and protocols for weaning, sedation, and resuscitation.

As an example, in patients receiving mechanical ventilation, daily interruption of sedative drug infusions decreases the duration of mechanical ventilation and the length of stay in the intensive care unit (42, 43). This daily interruption of sedatives does not result in adverse psychological outcomes, and may even be associated with reductions in post-traumatic stress disorder (44). Recently, a combined protocol for sedation and weaning was described (45). The results of this study suggest that a "wake-up-and-breathe protocol", based on daily spontaneous awakening trials and on daily spontaneous breathing trials, results in better outcomes for mechanically ventilated patients than current standard approaches.

Many barriers to implementing protocol-based treatment exist, however. Examples are lack of early identification of patients at risk (46), lack of adequate monitoring (47), and critical shortages of nursing staff (48). Also, treatment protocols considered standard by many may be challenged by others (49–52) and can change over time (53–56). Finally, continuous presence at the bedside of highly qualified clinicians (see previous paragraphs) with well-established clinical experience and knowledge of pathophysiology of

the critically ill may in many instances outweigh treatment protocols that may have an inherent risk of inappropriateness for a specific clinical situation (57).

To identify relevant areas with the potential for improvement, various techniques can be used. Expert opinion, working groups, and quality circles are well-established examples; another might be the process potential screening method. This tool has recently been used to identify typical hospital processes (58). The instrument consists of a two-dimensional matrix, with 30 quality aspects (e.g. setting goals, use of diagnostic procedures, monitoring) in one dimension, and 16 quality criteria (practicability and feasibility, customer satisfaction, time, agreement with ethical values) in the second dimension. Whether such a concept can be used in daily practice remains to be shown.

Standardisation in the process of care and developments in knowledge may be more easily achieved if the number of procedures is high. Even though it remains difficult in most cases to determine an accurate number for such a minimal threshold, many studies have confirmed a relationship between volume and outcome. One of the first papers exploring this issue was already published more than twenty years ago (59). In it, the outcomes of twelve surgical procedures of varying complexity performed in 1,498 hospitals were analysed to determine whether there is an association between a hospital's volume and its mortality rate. Hospitals having 200 or more of these operations per year had 25–41% lower death rates than hospitals with lower volumes. Similarly, it was recently shown that mechanical ventilation of patients in a hospital with a high case volume is associated with reduced mortality (60). Based on data from that study, it has been suggested that routine transfer of mechanically ventilated patients from low-volume to high-volume hospitals may decrease mortality (19). Indeed, the number needed to treat in this specific model was as low as 16. Of note, other studies did not confirm the association between higher volume and better outcome in some subgroups of critically ill patients (61, 62).

Whether the direct relationship between volume and outcome is due to increased experience, to referrals to institutions with better outcomes, to patient selection, or to some other factor, remains to be shown. If this relationship were due to factors that are basically not related to the size of a unit (quality of staff or of infrastructure, ease of access to care, etc.), then low-volume units might in the end achieve the same outcomes as high-volume ICUs. Finally, regionalisation, as proposed by some, may influence the flow of patients within a health care system, and thus also may affect an institution's accreditation and reputation, as well as physicians' egos and incomes.

Life-long learning is a necessity in medical practice. Learning occurs when understanding gained from prior experience leads to an improvement in a specific activity (63). The learning curve quantitatively describes this relationship. For many activities specific to critical care the curve may be steep, which means that to acquire even basic skills, many trials are necessary (64). Individual learning takes place during daily work, through reading journals, through attending congresses or courses, etc. Continuous learning also occurs by analysis of "errors" (critical incident reporting systems, morbidity-mortality conferences). Finally, the use of simulators may be of increasing importance in critical care teaching and training (65).

Recently, a set of common 'competencies' was developed for specialists in intensive care medicine across Europe (66). The aim of this project was to harmonise existing, but quite diverse, European standards for training and specialist practice (39), while preserving different national methods of delivery of training (67). Ultimately, this will lead to an international consensus on the basic minimum skills expected of doctors completing their training in intensive care. This not only helps to establish intensive care medicine (and hopefully also nursing care) as a medical speciality in its own right, but also might serve as a model for development of other specialities throughout Europe.

Learning should take place not only at the personal, individual level, but also at the organisational level (68). Factors enhancing organisational learning include a flat hierarchy, open communication, a well-developed team culture, the possibility to develop new competencies, and a culture of positive feedback (69). Factors that hinder such learning are a defensive approach to proposed changes in procedures, holding on to norms and privileges, and limiting information exchange. Overall, continuous learning is not only a prerequisite to assure up-to-date, safe and effective care to our patients in the ICU, it is also an important factor to promote innovation and to increase productivity in health care in general.

Patients' and families' needs

It is unchallenged that patient care is the main task in the ICU. Until recently, this probably was even considered the only purpose of critical care by many. Over the last few years, however, there has been an evolution in thinking. Today, the main focus could probably be better described as taking care of the patients' and families' needs. Patient needs include appropriate, state-of-the-art patient care (still the key task in critical care), adequate provision of information, and sound decision-making (70). Family needs include communication with medical and nursing staff, appropriate involvement in decision-making, and emotional support.

Unfortunately, patients' and families' expectations of intensive care medicine and ICU professionals have not generated much scientific interest until now. A few tools for assessing family needs in the ICU have been developed over the years (71–74), and a European multicenter study evaluated what patients and relatives expect from and view as desirable characteristics of physicians practicing intensive care medicine (75). Interestingly, patients and relatives expressed similar views on the importance of knowledge, skills, decision-making and communication in the training of intensive care specialists. Further, priority was given to medical knowledge and skills, and women were more likely to emphasise communication skills.

Meeting the needs of patients and families requires that physicians base their decisions about care for a specific patient (including appropriate, thoughtful end-of-life care) on the wishes and expectations of that individual rather than on their own or other caregivers' morals and expectations. In this respect, it is reassuring that physicians' decisions about patient admission to the ICU are primarily influenced by patients' wishes (76). However, non-medical factors such as a patient's personality or availability of beds have been revealed as further factors, and may be considered ethically inadequate (76). Also, inappropriate admissions of patients to the ICU were perceived as a common problem in a further study (77). Of note, personal experience and religious beliefs may influence the ways in which such decisions are made (78, 79). In addition, although most patients and families believe that the family's opinion should be taken into account in decision-making, for some caregivers this is still an open question (80).

Optimising patient flow

Intensive care units may frequently present a bottleneck to patient flow, and saturation of these services may limit a hospital's responsiveness to new emergencies. In general, patient flow in the ICU consists of two components:
- Admission after planned surgery
- Emergency admission

If surgical planning is reliable, admission of patients after elective surgery to the ICU generally results in a more or less predictable demand on resources. This is mostly due to the fact that length of stay (LOS) in patients admitted to the ICU after elective surgery is usually distributed over a very small range. Even if there is day-to-day and week-to-week variation, such fluctuation in general will be less than in the group of emergency admissions (see tab. 1). Accordingly, an obvious measure in case of high but variable capacity utilisation of an ICU is to reduce any variability in the number of patients admitted after elective surgery. Such variability can be reduced by careful planning and close cooperation with surgical departments (81). In addition, optimising patient flow also may include close cooperation with high-dependency units in the same hospital and with ICUs of other hospitals, ideally organised as a network (82, 83).

In larger ICUs with referrals from various departments and thus a broad patient mix, random fluctuations in the number of patients admitted from different surgical specialities, the emergency department, etc., probably will tend to cancel each other out. Small units, on the other hand, may be more vulnerable to random fluctuation in

Tab. 1 Length of stay in ICU per patient group
N: Number of patients admitted to the ICU January-December 2006. "Surgery other" includes both unplanned admission after elective surgery and admission after emergency surgery. SAPS II: Simplified acute physiology score (130). LOS-ICU: Length of stay in the ICU. Data are means (SD) and percentiles.
Unpublished data from: Department of Intensive Care Medicine, Bern University Hospital, Bern, Switzerland (30-bed multidisciplinary adult ICU).

	Surgery, elective	Surgery, other	Internal medicine
N	1,339	723	1,281
Age (years)	64 (13)	62 (16)	61 (16)
SAPS II (points)	28 (11)	42 (16)	43 (19)
LOS-ICU (days)	1.5 (2.5)	3.0 (5.4)	2.8 (4.8)
■ 10th percentile	0.7	0.5	0.4
■ 25th percentile	0.8	0.7	0.7
■ 50th percentile	0.9	1.1	1.2
■ 75th percentile	1.1	2.8	2.8
■ 90th percentile	2.1	7.7	6.3
■ 95th percentile	4.6	11.2	9.0
■ 99th percentile	12.8	19.9	26.7

the number of admissions or in length of stay. As a consequence, "excess" demand on ICU capacity has to be outsourced more often in such units, for example to the emergency department, recovery rooms, acute care wards, or other hospitals (84). In addition, flexibility in personnel allocation and deployment may help to adjust the ICU's capacity to meet variable needs.

Optimal vs. maximal resource allocation

Optimising the patient process will ultimately help to manage costs in the hospital, and in particular in the ICU (85). At the level of each patient, but also at the level of an ICU, we should keep in mind that there is always a difference between maximal medical care and an economically optimal approach. A general view of this relationship is presented in figure 2. Indeed, economically optimal patient care (see fig. 2, point O) will never be identical to the medically maximal care (point M). Similarly, an economically optimal management of overall resource use of an ICU will never be identical to the medically maximal use of resources in that unit.

The patient process as the key element in a comprehensive concept of quality management

Aiming at an optimised patient process may result in a shorter length of stay of patients in the ICU, but also in restrictions in some aspects of care of the critically ill. To avoid an unwelcome reduction in the quality of care, changes in the patient process should be embedded in an exten-

sive programme of quality management. A wide range of such models are used in the health care setting (86). A concept for quality management was recently also developed by the European Federation of Quality Management (EFQM) (87). It presents a comprehensive model for assessing and improving an organisation, and might well be suitable for the management of an ICU. On the other hand, it is not yet widely used in this latter setting, and for that reason, it will be briefly discussed here.

According to the EFQM model, quality management includes eight principles (see box "The EFQM model"). An organisation is excellent if it achieves outstanding, sustained results in all of them. The model recognises that there are many approaches to achieve such excellence. Overall, the framework is based on nine criteria. Five

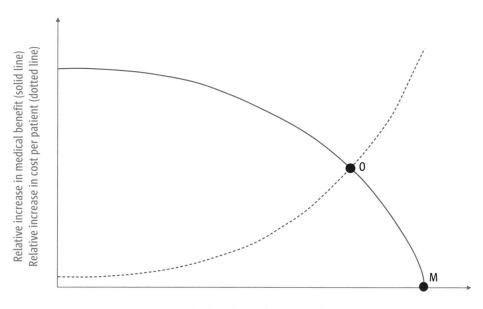

Number of procedures per patient

Fig. 2   Resource use: Physicians' and economists' points of view
The horizontal axis shows the number of measures (e.g. diagnostic and therapeutic procedures) per patient. The vertical axis shows the relative increase in costs and the relative increase in medical benefit per patient. Note that with any increase in the number of measures per patient, the increase in medical benefit will be smaller but the relative increase in resources used gets larger. Pont M: Maximal possible amount of resources used for a specific patient (note that it is possible to use even more procedures for a specific patient, but with no further positive gain in medical benefit). Point O: optimal care, as estimated from an economic point of view.
With permission from: Sachverständigenrat zur Begutachtung der Entwicklung im Gesundheitswesen (1994), Sachstandsbericht 1994, Gesundheitsversorgung und Krankenversicherung 2000. Eigenverantwortung, Subsidiarität und Solidarität bei sich ändernden Rahmenbedingungen, Nomos, Baden-Baden 1994 – ISBN 3-7890-3376-6, S. 205.

of these are named 'enablers' and four are 're-sults'. The 'enabler' criteria cover what an or-ganisation does: *Leadership* driving policy and strategy, delivered through *people, partnerships* and *resources*, and *processes*. The 'results' criteria cover what an organisation achieves: *Perform-ance* (key results), *customers, people* (all individu-als employed by the organisation), and *society* (all those who are affected by the organisation). 'Results' are driven by 'enablers', and 'enablers' are improved using feedback from 'results' (for further details, see (87)). Today, thousands of or-ganisations throughout Europe, covering almost all sectors of activity, are actively practicing the EFQM model.

The EFQM model

The European Federation of Quality Management (EFQM) (87) has developed a comprehensive model to assess and improve an organisation. It includes eight principles:
- *Orientation towards results*
- *Focus on customers*
- *Leadership and constancy of purpose*
- *Management by processes and facts*
- *Development and involvement of employees*
- *Continuous learning, innovation and improvement*
- *Partnership development*
- *Social responsibility*

Another example of a quality concept has been presented recently (88). These authors propose four steps for evaluating and maintaining such a programme:
1. Determine whether the target is changing with periodic data collection
2. Modify behaviour change strategies to regain or sustain improvements
3. Focus on interdisciplinary collaboration
4. Develop and maintain support from the hos-pital leadership

In summary, although care of the critically ill pa-tient is the key mission of an ICU, this task should be viewed as one single element of many respon-sibilities of ICU management. Accordingly, a comprehensive concept of quality management should include many other relevant aspects, and excellence can only be achieved if all of them are appropriately taken into account.

Optimising workflow in the ICU

Assessing workflow and workload in the ICU

Workflow in the ICU is complex. There are many professions involved in care of the critically ill, numerous processes are time-critical, and there are many external influences such as emergency admission, treatment protocols developed by oth-er specialities, etc. Accordingly, there are various shared tasks, overlapping activities, and a great need for acquisition, transfer, and documentation of information. Overall, integration of individual workflows into one single network of patient-cen-tred activity is a challenge (89). Taking into ac-count all these problems, it is surprising that only scant scientific literature exists on this topic (89–91).

Workload, on the other hand, has been eval-uated in many studies. The therapeutic inter-vention scoring system (TISS) and its variants (92–96) are tools that can to some extent be used for this purpose. Other possibilities are, for exam-ple, nursing activities score (NAS) (97), the inten-sive care nursing scoring system (ICNSS) (98), and the time-and-motion (99) and random work sampling studies (100, 101). However, whether workload can be reliably assessed at all has been questioned by some (102, 103).

In this context, nurse (or physician)-to-patient ratio may be considered as a – albeit considerably simplified – surrogate to assess and control work-load. Indeed, nurse-to-patient ratios were found to be inversely related to the risk of postoperative complications or resource use in patients under-going oesophageal resection (104) or hepatectomy (105). The nurse-to-patient ratio was also found to be associated with the duration of respiratory weaning in patients with chronic obstructive pul-monary disease (106) and to be a key determinant of healthcare-associated infection in critically ill patients (107). Similarly, high-intensity ICU phy-sician staffing was associated with reduced ICU and hospital mortality as well as reduced length of stay in the ICU in a number of studies (34). All these findings seem to point at some threshold of workload below which quality of care is impaired. Indeed, based on such findings, minimal stand-ards have been presented (36–38) (see paragraph on process of care, above). There are, however, many barriers to implementing such recommendations (40), and considerable variation in nurse staffing patterns among European countries still exists (15, 108).

Are there adverse effects of excess workload?

As noted in the previous paragraph, excess workload may impair quality of care and patient outcome. This hypothesis is supported by a number of further findings: Fatigue from long hours may impair patient safety (109); risk-adjusted mortality increases with rising workload in neonatal ICUs (110); high workload may explain some of the variations in ICU mortality (111); and finally, eliminating interns' extended work shifts decreases attention failures during night work hours (112).

Excess workload also may result in adverse effects on employees themselves. As an example, extended work shifts may have adverse effects on health and safety among interns (113). Moreover, working conditions may have an influence on the development of burnout syndrome (114–116). Still, it remains unclear whether a higher level of occupational stress (e.g. due to workload, stressful work environment, frequent shifts during off-office hours), personality or lifestyle factors, or other causes typically seen in anaesthesiology and critical care professionals contribute to higher mortality in this group (117).

Optimising workflow

Taking into account the complex workflow and the sometimes high workload described above, it becomes clear that – apart from an appropriate staffing level – open, structured and timely communication plays a paramount role in the ICU. Indeed, many errors in the ICU have been attributed to communication problems (118). Of note, medical professionals seem to be much less aware of such problems than, for example, airline cockpit crews (119).

Measures to improve communication play a crucial role (120). As an example, a patient might pass through several interfaces, starting on the ward, with treatment in the operating room, the intensive care unit, and again returning to the ward. When the shift changes of both physicians

and nurses are added, this may result in a total of more than seven handovers, even in a seemingly straightforward patient path (121). Very often, critical incidents have their roots in communication problems over such interfaces. Using a structured approach whenever possible and sensible helps to improve communication and satisfaction of health care providers (122, 123), as well as between ICU professionals and the patients' relatives (124).

Clinical information systems and information technology play an important, although rather complementary, role in improvement of workflow and specifically also in communication in the ICU (125). Such systems include patient data management systems, clinical decision support systems, picture archiving and communication systems, wireless communication, and handheld computing (126). As recently shown, use of health information technology may indeed have a positive impact on quality, efficiency and cost of medical care (127).

Ultimately, well-structured collaboration between physicians, nurses and all other professionals working in the ICU may not only contribute to enhanced workflow and a better climate in the team, but may also be associated with improved patient outcome (15, 128), the ultimate goal of critical care.

Summary

Organisational issues are an important focus in the management of an ICU. Accordingly, critical care medicine today includes (see also box "Key points for clinical practice"):

- *An optimised patient process:* Admission, monitoring, consistent use of state-of-the-art diagnostic and therapeutic procedures, medically and ethically sound decision-making, discharge of patients or reasonable and thoughtful end-of-life care
- Consideration of both the *patients'* (still the primary focus of all activities) and the *families' needs*
- *Fair distribution and allocation* of limited resources
- *Continuous presence of intensive care professionals* (both nurses with special education in critical care and intensive care specialists) at the bedside. Hopefully, the practice of allowing the most junior physicians to manage the sickest patients will be obsolete in all acute care hospitals very soon.

This is best supported by a comprehensive concept of the quality management of the unit.

Finally, workflow is enhanced by:

- Effective and fair *communication* within the ICU team and with persons from all other concerned medical and therapeutic specialities
- The use of a *clinical information management system* (sometimes also called a patient data management system)

Key points for clinical practice

- *Strive for improvements in the patient process*
  - *Optimise the care processes*
  - *Take into account patients' and families' needs*
  - *Guarantee the continuous presence of ICU professionals at the bedside*
  - *Aim at a fair distribution of limited resources*
- *Adopt a comprehensive concept of quality management for your unit*
- *Improve the workflow*
  - *Promote effective communication within your team and between your team and others*
  - *Use a clinical information management system*

The author

Hans Ulrich Rothen, MD, PhD
   Department of Intensive Care Medicine
   Inselspital Bern
   Bern University Hospital and University of Bern
   3010 Bern, Switzerland
   e-mail: hrothen@insel.ch

References

1. Cullen DJ, Ferrara LC, Briggs BA, Walker PF, Gilbert J. Survival, hospitalization charges and follow-up results in critically ill patients. N Engl J Med. 1976;294:982–7.
2. Kuttner R. Market-based failure – a second opinion on U.S. health care costs. N Engl J Med. 2008;358:549–51.
3. Halpern NA, Pastores SM, Greenstein RJ. Critical care medicine in the United States 1985–2000: an analysis of bed numbers, use, and costs. Crit Care Med. 2004;32:1254–9.
4. Oye RK, Bellamy PE. Patterns of resource consumption in medical intensive care. Chest. 1991;99:685–9.
5. Stricker K, Rothen HU, Takala J. Resource use in the ICU: short- vs. long-term patients. Acta Anaesthesiol Scand. 2003;47:508–15.
6. Bodenheimer T, Fernandez A. High and rising health care costs. Part 4: can costs be controlled while preserving quality? Ann Intern Med. 2005;143:26–31.
7. Darling H. Healthcare cost crisis and quality gap: our national dilemma. Healthc Financ Manage. 2005;59:64–8.
8. Lofgren R, Karpf M, Perman J, Higdon CM. The U.S. health care system is in crisis: implications for academic medical centers and their missions. Acad Med. 2006;81:713–20.
9. Akala FA, El-Saharty S. Public-health challenges in the Middle East and North Africa. Lancet. 2006;367:961–4.
10. Adang EM, Borm GF. Is there an association between economic performance and public satisfaction in health care? Eur J Health Econ. 2007;8:279–85.
11. Bion JF, Heffner JE. Challenges in the care of the acutely ill. Lancet. 2004;363:970–7.
12. Terblanche M, Adhikari NK. The evolution of intensive care unit performance assessment. J Crit Care. 2006;21:19–22.
13. Rapoport J, Teres D, Lemeshow S, Gehlbach S. A method for assessing the clinical performance and cost-effectiveness of intensive care units: A multicenter inception cohort study. Crit Care Med. 1994;22:1385–91.
14. Lassnigg A, Hiesmayr MJ, Bauer P, Haisjackl M. Effect of centre-, patient- and procedure-related factors on intensive care resource utilisation after cardiac surgery. Intensive Care Med. 2002;28:1453–61.
15. Rothen HU, Stricker K, Einfalt J, Bauer P, Metnitz PG, Moreno RP, Takala J. Variability in outcome and resource use in intensive care units. Intensive Care Med. 2007;33:1329–36.
16. Walter KL, Siegler M, Hall JB. How decisions are made to admit patients to medical intensive care units (MICUs): A survey of MICU directors at academic medical centers across the United States. Crit Care Med. 2008;36:414–20.
17. Pollack MM, Patel KM. Need for shift in focus in research into quality of intensive care. Lancet. 2002;359:95–6.
18. Suter PM. Some ICUs save more lives than others: we need to know why! Intensive Care Med. 2005;31:1301–2.
19. Kahn JM, Linde-Zwirble WT, Wunsch H, Barnato AE, Iwashyna TJ, Roberts MS, Lave JR, Angus DC. Potential value of regionalized intensive care for mechanically ventilated medical patients. Am J Respir Crit Care Med. 2008;177:285–91.
20. Barnato AE, Kahn JM, Rubenfeld GD, McCauley K, Fontaine D, Frassica JJ, Hubmayr R, Jacobi J, Brower RG, Chalfin D, Sibbald W, Asch DA, Kelley M, Angus DC. Prioritizing the organization and management of intensive care services in the United States: the PrOMIS Conference. Crit Care Med. 2007;35:1003–11.
21. Hillman K. Critical care without walls. Curr Opin Crit Care. 2002;8:594–9.
22. Dawson D, McEwen A. Critical care without walls: The role of the nurse consultant in critical care. Intensive Crit Care Nurs. 2005;21:334–43.

23. Multz AS, Chalfin DB, Samson IM, Dantzker DR, Fein AM, Steinberg HN, Niederman MS, Scharf SM. A "closed" medical intensive care unit (MICU) improves resource utilization when compared with an "open" MICU. Am J Respir Crit Care Med. 1998;157:1468–73.

24. Treggiari MM, Martin DP, Yanez ND, Caldwell E, Hudson LD, Rubenfeld GD. Effect of intensive care unit organizational model and structure on outcomes in patients with acute lung injury. Am J Respir Crit Care Med. 2007;176:685–90.

25. Regli B, Takala J. The patient process as the basis for the design of an ICU. In: Fink MP, Suter PM, Sibbald WJ Eds. Intensive Care Medicine in 10 years. Update in Intensive Care and Emergency Medicine, Vol 43. Springer Berlin, Heidelberg. 2006. ISBN-10 3-540-26092-7, p.115–32.

26. McGaughey J, Alderdice F, Fowler R, Kapila A, Mayhew A, Moutray M. Outreach and Early Warning Systems (EWS) for the prevention of intensive care admission and death of critically ill adult patients on general hospital wards. Cochrane Database Syst Rev. 2007;CD005529.

27. Winters BD, Pham JC, Hunt EA, Guallar E, Berenholtz S, Pronovost PJ. Rapid response systems: a systematic review. Crit Care Med. 2007;35:1238–43.

28. Nasraway SA, Cohen IL, Dennis RC, Howenstein MA, Nikas DK, Warren J, Wedel SK. Guidelines on admission and discharge for adult intermediate care units. American College of Critical Care Medicine of the Society of Critical Care Medicine. Crit Care Med. 1998;26:607–10.

29. Vincent JL, Burchardi H. Do we need intermediate care units? Intensive Care Med. 1999;25:1345–9.

30. Eachempati SR, Hydo LJ, Barie PS. The effect of an intermediate care unit on the demographics and outcomes of a surgical intensive care unit population. Arch Surg. 2004;139:315–9.

31. Wild C, Narath M. Evaluating and planning ICUs: methods and approaches to differentiate between need and demand. Health Policy. 2005;71:289–301.

32. Fox AJ, Owen-Smith O, Spiers P. The immediate impact of opening an adult high dependency unit on intensive care unit occupancy. Anaesthesia. 1999;54:280–3.

33. Garland A. Improving the ICU: part 2. Chest. 2005;127:2165–79.

34. Pronovost PJ, Angus DC, Dorman T, Robinson KA, Dremsizov TT, Young TL. Physician staffing patterns and clinical outcomes in critically ill patients: a systematic review. JAMA. 2002;288:2151–62.

35. Gajic O, Afessa B, Hanson AC, Krpata T, Yilmaz M, Mohamed SF, Rabatin JT, Evenson LK, Aksamit TR, Peters SG, Hubmayr RD, Wylam ME. Effect of 24-hour mandatory versus on-demand critical care specialist presence on quality of care and family and provider satisfaction in the intensive care unit of a teaching hospital. Crit Care Med. 2008;36:36–44.

36. www.leapfroggroup.org (last accessed 30.01.2008).

37. Ferdinande P. Recommendations on minimal requirements for Intensive Care Departments. Members of the Task Force of the European Society of Intensive Care Medicine. Intensive Care Med. 1997;23:226–32.

38. www.ssicm.org (last accessed 30.01.2008).

39. Barrett H, Bion JF. An international survey of training in adult intensive care medicine. Intensive Care Med. 2005;31:553–61.

40. Kahn JM, Matthews FA, Angus DC, Barnato AE, Rubenfeld GD. Barriers to implementing the Leapfrog Group recommendations for intensivist physician staffing: a survey of intensive care unit directors. J Crit Care. 2007; 22:97–103.

41. Angus DC, Kelley MA, Schmitz RJ, White A, Popovich J Jr. Caring for the critically ill patient. Current and projected workforce requirements for care of the critically ill and patients with pulmonary disease: can we meet the requirements of an aging population? JAMA. 2000;284:2762–70.

42. Kress JP, Pohlman AS, O'Connor MF, Hall JB. Daily interruption of sedative infusions in critically ill patients undergoing mechanical ventilation. N Engl J Med. 2000; 342:1471–7.

43. Jakob SM, Lubszky S, Friolet R, Rothen HU, Kolarova A, Takala J. Sedation and weaning from mechanical ventilation: effects of process optimization outside a clinical trial. J Crit Care. 2007;22:219–28.

44. Kress JP, Gehlbach B, Lacy M, Pliskin N, Pohlman AS, Hall JB. The Long-term Psychological Effects of Daily Sedative Interruption on Critically Ill Patients. Am J Respir Crit Care Med. 2003;168:1457–61.

45. Girard TD, Kress JP, Fuchs BD, Thomason JW, Schweickert WD, Pun BT, Taichman DB, Dunn JG, Pohlman AS, Kinniry PA, Jackson JC, Canonico AE, Light RW, Shintani AK, Thompson JL, Gordon SM, Hall JB, Dittus RS, Bernard GR, Ely EW. Efficacy and safety of a paired sedation and ventilator weaning protocol for mechanically ventilated patients in intensive care (Awakening and Breathing Controlled trial): a randomised controlled trial. Lancet. 2008;371:126–34.

46. Gao H, McDonnell A, Harrison D A, Moore T, Adam S, Daly K, Esmonde L, Goldhill DR, Parry GJ, Rashidian A, Subbe CP, Harvey S. Systematic review and evaluation of physiological track and trigger warning systems for identifying at-risk patients on the ward. Intensive Care Med. 2007;33:667–79.

47. Chan PS, Krumholz HM, Nichol G, Nallamothu BK. Delayed time to defibrillation after in-hospital cardiac arrest. N Engl J Med. 2008;358:9–17.

48. Carlbom DJ, Rubenfeld GD. Barriers to implementing protocol-based sepsis resuscitation in the emergency department – results of a national survey. Crit Care Med. 2007;35:2525–32.

49. Brochard L, Lemaire F. Tidal volume, positive end-expiratory pressure, and mortality in acute respiratory distress syndrome. Crit Care Med. 1999;27:1661–3.

50. Eichacker PQ, Gerstenberger EP, Banks SM, Cui X, Natanson C. Meta-analysis of acute lung injury and acute respiratory distress syndrome trials testing low tidal volumes. Am J Respir Crit Care Med. 2002;166: 1510-4.

51. Deans KJ, Minneci PC, Suffredini AF, Danner RL, Hoffman WD, Ciu X, Klein HG, Schechter AN, Banks SM, Eichacker PQ, Natanson C. Randomization in clinical trials of titrated therapies: unintended consequences of using fixed treatment protocols. Crit Care Med. 2007;35: 1509-16.

52. Tobin MJ, Jubran A. Meta-analysis under the spotlight: Focused on a meta-analysis of ventilator weaning. Crit Care Med. 2008;36:1-7.

53. Sladen RN. Severe sepsis: a bundle still under construction? Can J Anaesth. 2007;54:779-85.

54. Dellinger RP, Levy MM, Carlet JM, Bion J, Parker MM, Jaeschke R, Reinhart K, Angus DC, Brun-Buisson C, Beale R, Calandra T, Dhainaut JF, Gerlach H, Harvey M, Marini JJ, Marshall J, Ranieri M, Ramsay G, Sevransky J, Thompson BT, Townsend S, Vender JS, Zimmerman JL, Vincent JL: Surviving Sepsis Campaign: International guidelines for management of severe sepsis and septic shock: 2008. Intensive Care Med. 2008;34:17-60.

55. Sprung CL, Annane D, Keh D, Moreno R, Singer M, Freivogel K, Weiss YG, Benbenishty J, Kalenka A, Forst H, Laterre PF, Reinhart K, Cuthbertson BH, Payen D, Briegel J. Hydrocortisone therapy for patients with septic shock. N Engl J Med. 2008;358:111-24.

56. Brunkhorst FM, Engel C, Bloos F, Meier-Hellmann A, Ragaller M, Weiler N, Moerer O, Gruendling M, Oppert M, Grond S, Olthoff D, Jaschinski U, John S, Rossaint R, Welte T, Schaefer M, Kern P, Kuhnt E, Kiehntopf M, Hartog C, Natanson C, Loeffler M, Reinhart K. Intensive insulin therapy and pentastarch resuscitation in severe sepsis. N Engl J Med. 2008;358:125-39.

57. Marini JJ. Meta-analysis: Convenient assumptions and inconvenient truth. Crit Care Med. 2008;36:328-9.

58. Ehlers F, Ammenwerth E, Haux R. Process potential screening - an instrument to improve business processes in hospitals. Methods Inf Med. 2006;45:506-14.

59. Luft HS, Bunker JP, Enthoven AC. Should operations be regionalized? The empirical relation between surgical volume and mortality. N Engl J Med. 1979;301:1364-9.

60. Kahn JM, Goss CH, Heagerty PJ, Kramer AA, O'Brien CR, Rubenfeld GD. Hospital volume and the outcomes of mechanical ventilation. N Engl J Med. 2006;355:41-50.

61. Jones J, Rowan K. Is there a relationship between the volume of work carried out in intensive care and its outcome? Int J Technol Assess Health Care. 1995;11: 762-9.

62. Durairaj L, Torner JC, Chrischilles EA, Vaughan Sarrazin MS, Yankey J, Rosenthal GE. Hospital volume-outcome relationships among medical admissions to ICUs. Chest. 2005;128:1682-9.

63. Waldman JD, Yourstone SA, Smith HL. Learning curves in health care. Health Care Manage Rev. 2003;28:41-54.

64. de Oliveira GR, Helayel PE, de Conceicao DG, Garzel IS, Pavei P, Ceccon MS. Learning curves and mathematical models for interventional ultrasound basic skills. Anesth Analg. 2008;106:568-73.

65. Lighthall GK, Barr J. The use of clinical simulation systems to train critical care physicians. J Intensive Care Med. 2007;22:257-69.

66. Bion JF, Barrett H. Development of core competencies for an international training programme in intensive care medicine. Intensive Care Med. 2006;32:1371-83.

67. www.cobatrice.org (accessed 29.01.2008).

68. Stinson L, Pearson D, Lucas B. Developing a learning culture: twelve tips for individuals, teams and organizations. Med Teach. 2006;28:309-12.

69. Schupfer G, Gfrorer R, Schleppers A. [Anaesthetists learn - do institutions also learn? Importance of institutional learning and corporate culture in clinics]. Anaesthesist. 2007;56:983-91.

70. Pronovost PJ, Rodriguez-Paz J, Mohammad Z. Creating competent and caring physicians: ensuring patients are our North Star. Intensive Care Med. 2007;33:1873-5.

71. Macey BA, Bouman CC. An evaluation of validity, reliability and readability of the Critical Care Family Needs Inventory. Heart Lung. 1991;20:398-403.

72. Wasser T, Pasquale MA, Matchett SC, Bryan Y, Pasquale M. Establishing reliability and validity of the critical care family satisfaction survey. Crit Care Med. 2001;29:192-6

73. Heyland DK, Tranmer LE. Measuring family satisfaction with care in the intensive care unit: the development of a questionnaire and preliminary results. J Crit Care. 2001; 16:142-9.

74. Wall RJ, Engelberg RA, Downey L, Heyland DK, Curtis JR. Refinement, scoring, and validation of the Family Satisfaction in the Intensive Care Unit (FS-ICU) survey. Crit Care Med. 2007;35:271-9.

75. The CoBaTrICE Collaboration. The views of patients and relatives of what makes a good intensivist: a European survey. Intensive Care Med. 2007;33:1913-20.

76. Escher M, Perneger TV, Chevrolet JC. National questionnaire survey on what influences doctors' decisions about admission to intensive care. BMJ. 2004; 329:425-$.

77. Giannini A, Consonni D. Physicians' perceptions and attitudes regarding inappropriate admissions and resource allocation in the intensive care setting. Br J Anaesth. 2006;96:57-62.

78. Cardoso T, Fonseca T, Pereira S, Lencastre L. Life-sustaining treatment decisions in Portuguese intensive care units: a national survey of intensive care physicians. Crit Care. 2003;7:R167-75.

79. Sprung CL, Maia P, Bulow HH, Ricou B, Armaganidis A, Baras M, Wennberg E, Reinhart K, Cohen SL, Fries DR,

Nakos G, Thijs LG. The importance of religious affiliation and culture on end-of-life decisions in European intensive care units. Intensive Care Med. 2007;33: 1732–9.

80. Hardart GE, Truog RD. Attitudes and preferences of intensivists regarding the role of family interests in medical decision making for incompetent patients. Crit Care Med. 2003;31:1895–900.

81. McManus ML, Long MC, Cooper A, Mandell J, Berwick DM, Pagano M, Litvak E. Variability in surgical caseload and access to intensive care services. Anesthesiology. 2003;98:1491–6.

82. Takala J. Allocation of ICU resources: first come first serve vs. service when needed. ICU managmement. 2005;5: 51–2.

83. Wilson MJ, Bryan BS. Working with physicians to improve patient throughput. Healthc Exec. 2006;21:22–4,27–8.

84. Van den Berghe G, Albers J, Vahl CF. Is rescheduling surgey a viable solution to triage? ICU managmement. 2005;5:49–50.

85. Lofgren R, Karpf M, Perman J, Higdon CM. The U.S. health care system is in crisis: implications for academic medical centers and their missions. Acad Med. 2006;81: 713–20.

86. Ovretveit J, Staines A. Sustained improvement? Findings from an independent case study of the Jonkoping quality program. Qual Manag Health Care. 2007;16:68–83.

87. www.efqm.org (last accessed 02.02.2008).

88. Curtis JR, Cook DJ, Wall RJ, Angus DC, Bion J, Kacmarek R, Kane-Gill SL, Kirchhoff KT, Levy M, Mitchell PH, Moreno R, Pronovost P, Puntillo K. Intensive care unit quality improvement: a "how-to" guide for the interdisciplinary team. Crit Care Med. 2006;34:211–8.

89. Malhotra S, Jordan D, Shortliffe E, Patel VL. Workflow modeling in critical care: piecing together your own puzzle. J Biomed Inform. 2007;40:81–92.

90. Ali NA, Mekhjian HS, Kuehn PL, Bentley TD, Kumar R, Ferketich AK, Hoffmann SP. Specificity of computerized physician order entry has a significant effect on the efficiency of workflow for critically ill patients. Crit Care Med. 2005;33:110–4.

91. Tang Z, Mazabob J, Weavind L, Thomas E, Johnson TR. A time-motion study of registered nurses' workflow in intensive care unit remote monitoring. AMIA Annu Symp Proc. 2006;759–63.

92. Cullen DJ, Civetta JM, Briggs BA, Ferrara LC. Therapeutic intervention scoring system: a method for quantitative comparison of patient care. Crit Care Med. 1974;2:57–60.

93. Keene AR, Cullen DJ. Therapeutic Intervention Scoring System: update. 1983. Crit Care Med. 1983;11:1–3.

94. Miranda DR, de Rijk A, Schaufeli W. Simplified Therapeutic Intervention Scoring System: the TISS-28 items – results from a multicenter study. Crit Care Med. 1996;24:64–73.

95. Miranda DR, Moreno R, Iapichino G. Nine equivalents of nursing manpower use score (NEMS). Intensive Care Med. 1997;23:760–5.

96. Iapichino G. Daily classification of complexity/level of intensive medical care. Does it allow the monitoring of the managerial process in ICU? Minerva Anestesiol. 2002;68:71–5.

97. Miranda D R, Nap R, de Rijk A, Schaufeli W, Iapichino G. Nursing activities score. Crit Care Med. 2003;31:374–82.

98. Pyykko AK, Ala-Kokko TI, Laurila JJ, Miettunen J, Finnberg M, Hentinen M: Validation of the new Intensive Care Nursing Scoring System (ICNSS). Intensive Care Med. 2004;30:254–9.

99. Tang Z, Mazabob J, Weavind L, Thomas E, Johnson TR. A time-motion study of registered nurses' workflow in intensive care unit remote monitoring. AMIA Annu Symp Proc. 2006;759–63.

100. Oddone E, Guarisco S, Simel D. Comparison of housestaff's estimates of their workday activities with results of a random work-sampling study. Acad Med. 1993;68:859–61.

101. Siegemund M, Rothen HU, Swiss ICU-network. Assessing physicians activities in the ICU using random sampling technique. Intensive Care Med. 2006;32 (Suppl 1):S215.

102. Taylor CJ, Bull F, Burdis C, Ferguson DG. Workload management in A&E: counting the uncountable and predicting the unpredictable. J Accid Emerg Med. 1997; 14:88–91.

103. Hughes M. Nursing workload: an unquantifiable entity. J Nurs Manag. 1999;7:317–22.

104. Amaravadi RK, Dimick JB, Pronovost PJ, Lipsett PA. ICU nurse-to-patient ratio is associated with complications and resource use after esophagectomy. Intensive Care Med. 2000;26:1857–62.

105. Dimick JB, Swoboda SM, Pronovost PJ, Lipsett PA. Effect of nurse-to-patient ratio in the intensive care unit on pulmonary complications and resource use after hepatectomy. Am J Crit Care. 2001;10:376–82.

106. Thorens JB, Kaelin RM, Jolliet P, Chevrolet JC. Influence of the quality of nursing on the duration of weaning from mechanical ventilation in patients with chronic obstructive pulmonary disease. Crit Care Med. 1995;23: 1807–15.

107. Hugonnet S, Chevrolet JC, Pittet D. The effect of workload on infection risk in critically ill patients. Crit Care Med. 2007;35:76–81.

108. Depasse B, Pauwels D, Somers Y, Vincent JL. A profile of European ICU nursing. Intensive Care Med. 1998;24: 939–45.

109. Gaba DM, Howard SK. Patient safety: fatigue among clinicians and the safety of patients. N Engl J Med. 2002;347:1249–55.

110. Tucker J. Patient volume, staffing, and workload in relation to risk-adjusted outcomes in a random

stratified sample of UK neonatal intensive care units: a prospective evaluation. Lancet. 2002;359:99–107.

111. Tarnow-Mordi WO, Hau C, Warden A, Shearer AJ. Hospital mortality in relation to staff workload: a 4-year study in an adult intensive-care unit. Lancet. 2000;356:185–9.

112. Lockley SW, Cronin JW, Evans EE, Cade BE, Lee CJ, Landrigan CP, Rothschild JM, Katz JT, Lilly CM, Stone PH, Aeschbach D, Czeisler CA. Effect of reducing interns' weekly work hours on sleep and attentional failures. N Engl J Med. 2004;351:1829–37.

113. Barger LK, Cade BE, Ayas NT, Cronin JW, Rosner B, Speizer FE, Czeisler CA. Extended work shifts and the risk of motor vehicle crashes among interns. N Engl J Med. 2005;352:125–34.

114. Lederer W, Kinzl JF, Trefalt E, Traweger C, Benzer A. Significance of working conditions on burnout in anesthetists. Acta Anaesthesiol Scand. 2006;50:58–63.

115. Poncet MC, Toullic P, Papazian L, Kentish-Barnes N, Timsit JF, Pochard F, Chevret S, Schlemmer B, Azoulay E. Burnout syndrome in critical care nursing staff. Am J Respir Crit Care Med. 2007;175:698–704.

116. Embriaco N, Azoulay E, Barrau K, Kentish N, Pochard F, Loundou A, Papazian L. High level of burnout in intensivists: prevalence and associated factors. Am J Respir Crit Care Med. 2007;175:686–92.

117. Svardsudd K, Wedel H, Gordh T Jr. Mortality rates among Swedish physicians: a population-based nationwide study with special reference to anesthesiologists. Acta Anaesthesiol Scand. 2002;46:1187–95.

118. Donchin Y, Gopher D, Olin M, Badihi Y, Biesky M, Sprung CL, Pizov R, Cotev S. A look into the nature and causes of human errors in the intensive care unit. Qual Saf Health Care. 2003;12:143–7.

119. Sexton JB, Thomas EJ, Helmreich RL. Error, stress, and teamwork in medicine and aviation: cross sectional surveys. BMJ. 2000;320:745–9.

120. Pronovost PJ, Berenholtz S, Dorman T, Lipsett PA, Simmonds T, Haraden C. Improving communication in the ICU using daily goals. J Crit Care. 2003;18: 71–5.

121. Wurz J, Regli B. In one ear and out the other: communication barriers as a risk factor for critical incidents. Anesth Analg. 2007;104:1319–21.

122. Dodek PM, Raboud J. Explicit approach to rounds in an ICU improves communication and satisfaction of providers. Intensive Care Med. 2003;29:1584–8.

123. McFetridge B, Gillespie M, Goode D, Melby V. An exploration of the handover process of critically ill patients between nursing staff from the emergency department and the intensive care unit. Nurs Crit Care. 2007;12:261–9.

124. Lautrette A, Darmon M, Megarbane B, Joly LM, Chevret S, Adrie C, Barnoud D, Bleichner G, Bruel C, Choukroun G, Curtis JR, Fieux F, Galliot R, Garrouste-Orgeas M, Georges H, Goldgran-Toledano D, Jourdain M, Loubert G, Reignier J, Saidi F, Souweine B, Vincent F, Barnes NK, Pochard F, Schlemmer B, Azoulay E. A communication strategy and brochure for relatives of patients dying in the ICU. N Engl J Med. 2007;356: 469–78.

125. Reng M. The role of information technology in the ICU. In: Kuhlen R, Moreno R, Ranieri M, Rhodes A (eds). 25 years of progress and innovation in intensive care medicine. Medizinisch Wissenschaftliche Verlagsgesellschaft, Berlin. 2007. ISBN 978-3-939069-47-8. p.375–382.

126. Martich GD, van Pelt DC, Lovasik D. Information technology. In: Fink MP, Suter PM, Sibbald WJ, Eds. Intensive care medicine in 10 years. Update in Intensive Care and Emrgency Medicine, Vol 43. Springer, Berlin, Heidelberg, New York, 2006. ISBN 3-540-26092-7. p.133–151.

127. Chaudhry B, Wang J, Wu S, Maglione M, Mojica W, Roth E, Morton SC, Shekelle PG. Systematic review: impact of health information technology on quality, efficiency, and costs of medical care. Ann Intern Med. 2006;144:742–52.

128. Baggs JG, Schmitt MH, Mushlin AI, Mitchell PH, Eldredge DH, Oakes D, Hutson AD. Association between nurse-physician collaboration and patient outcomes in three intensive care units. Crit Care Med. 1999;27: 1991–8.

129. Etienne M. TQM-Leitfaden für Spitäler [Total quality management – a guideline for hosptials]. Haupt, Bern, Stuttgart, Wien. 2005. ISBN 3-258-6889-5. p.83.

130. Le Gall JR, Lemeshow S, Saulnier F. A new Simplified Acute Physiology Score (SAPS II) based on a European/ North American multicenter study. JAMA. 1993;270: 2957–63.

131. Sachverständigenrat zur Begutachtung der Entwicklung im Gesundheitswesen (1994), Sachstandsbericht 1994, Gesundheitsversorgung und Krankenversicherung 2000. Eigenverantwortung, Subsidiarität und Solidarität bei sich ändernden Rahmenbedingungen, Nomos, Baden-Baden. 1994 – ISBN 3-7890-3376-6, S. 205.

Andreas Valentin

Reducing the number of adverse events in intensive care units

Although the classic medical principle of "first do no harm" refers primarily to the balance of risks and benefits of a specific treatment, it also fits a more general approach to the practice of medicine. The combination of complexity and a potential for great harm makes medicine, especially hospital care, as fraught with risk as other high reliability areas like aviation. It is therefore not surprising that several alarming reports have led to an increasing interest in patient safety by the medical profession and the general public. A recent investigation of 21 hospitals in The Netherlands showed that 5.7% of 1.3 million hospital admissions in 2004 resulted in unintentional harm to the patient (1). The concept of patient safety is the assurance that a course of medical treatment will proceed correctly and provide the best possible chance to achieve a desired outcome. This definition is especially important in intensive care medicine. But the complexity of processes and medical conditions dealt with in intensive care units (ICUs) makes the system vulnerable and prone to error (2, 3).

A common definition of error is an occurrence that harms or could have harmed a patient. Research in patient safety is frequently based on this broad definition. Several reasons have brought this approach its current popularity. Probably the most important reason is the attempt to avoid an immediate search for blame and instead to look for the causes of error. An error does not

necessarily lead to patient harm but highlights weak and unsafe steps in the process of care. From this perspective, every error carries the chance to gain an insight into an unsafe practice or even to discover the reason that an error did not lead to an adverse event. In contrast to the more general term "critical incident", an adverse event is an occurrence in which actual harm is done to a patient. This chapter focuses on adverse events in which harm to a patient is due to medical management, rather than the underlying disease (3, 4). Clearly, the goal of reducing the number of adverse events is not controversial. But there are different answers to important questions such as how to detect adverse events, how to deal with them, and how to prevent them. When suitable, a short description of these positions is provided.

What do errors, critical incidents and adverse events have in common?

In patient safety research, as well as in clinical practice, useful information is gained not only by studying actual incidents of harm, but by investigating risky situations or processes. Fortunately, not every error leads to a critical incident or an adverse event. But in many such occurrences, a common characteristic can be found. While health care providers act at the distal end of a process or structure, very often a system is the proximal cause of error (4). Although the failure of a health care professional can be seen as an inevitable consequence of being human, the actual occurrence and outcome of an error is frequently due to the design of one or more systems. System failures range from simple organisational matters, like the maintenance of equipment, to complex issues such as ergonomics (5) or the culture of an institution.

How safe is intensive care?
The scope of the problem

Intensive care is characterised by a complex course of interaction among several medical specialties (6). Considering the tight coupling between the complexity of the system and the high potential for harm (7), most ICUs seem to function very well. But over the last decade, several articles have revealed a serious safety problem in intensive care medicine. In a landmark study, Donchin recorded an average of 178 activities per patient per day and an estimated number of 1.7 errors per patient per day (2). A recent multinational study on sentinel events in intensive care (8) confirmed that reports from single-centre studies reflect a widespread pattern of susceptibility to error in ICUs. In that study, 38.8 events per 100 patient days were detected in five categories – medication; lines, catheters and drains; equipment; airway; and alarms. Although the willing participation of 205 ICUs worldwide shows that patient safety is a serious concern, there is no doubt that a detailed analysis of the causes of error and strategies to prevent it are urgently needed.

Are adverse events preventable?

For everyone who enters the medical profession, it becomes clear very quickly that adverse events can occur even when medical care is managed appropriately. An example is renal insufficiency after appropriate use and dosage of an antibiotic drug. It is therefore necessary to distinguish between nonpreventable and preventable adverse events. Any analysis of an adverse event should make this distinction. If a preventable adverse event is defined as the consequence of an unintercepted serious error in medical care, it will be necessary to prevent not only the future occurrence of the error but also its possible impact. For example, it has been shown that errors made during the administration of drugs occur with considerable frequency (9). But the impact of such an error might be mitigated by restrictions on the amount or concentration of a potentially dangerous drug in a previously prepared syringe.

A first step in prevention –
the recognition of error

A very important step in the prevention of error is the recognition that errors will occur – there is no such thing as an error-free ICU. Only this recognition will make it possible to actively work on preventive strategies and on how to mitigate the impact of errors. Although the detection and analysis of unintended events is often focused on errors of commission, errors of omission are estimated to occur more frequently and to carry a similar potential for harm. Considering a system approach as the appropriate measure to improve patient safety requires knowing the ability of the system to change its performance. Several methods to facilitate detection and reporting of error in ICUs have been put forward (10), and it should be noted that different methods will retrieve different findings (11). There is special interest in error-detection methods based on self-reporting by medical staff (12, 13). One considerable advantage of self-reporting systems is that contextual information is provided by the medical staff directly involved. Another important advantage is the creation of a team culture that relies on an atmosphere of assurance instead of the conventional approach of "blame and shame". It is therefore of utmost importance that medical staff be assured that they can report errors without any fear of reprisal. Since a self-reporting method carries the risk of underreporting, a combination of methods, such as self-reporting and chart review, is likely to be most useful.

A key step – the anticipation of hazards

Although recognizing an error after the fact is an important prerequisite for making improvements, it is obviously preferable to catch safety concerns in advance. This is much more difficult than it sounds and requires continuous awareness and an essential change in perspective. The question is no longer "What went wrong?" but "What might go wrong?" A simple example is the mix-up of medications that can be caused by "look-alike" or "sound-alike" drugs (14). A system in which one drug can be easily confused with another is sure to bring harm to some patient at some point. An anticipatory approach would require staff to identify and review the look-alike and sound-alike drugs in a particular setting and to take action to prevent them being administered erroneously. In ICUs, standard situations such as patient transport, handover, information transfer, and intervention (e.g., intubation) are also important areas for anticipatory safety strategies. For instance, intra-hospital transport of patients through relatively insecure environments poses a high risk (15) and requires an adequately trained staff and appropriate precautions (16). This was highlighted by a report on intra-hospital transfer in which 39 % of 191 incidents were related to equipment failure (e.g., power supply) and 61 % were related to patient/staff management issues (e.g., inadequate monitoring) (17). Obviously, adequate preparation would have avoided or mitigated most of the reported incidents.

What has been shown to reduce adverse events in ICUs?

To answer the question of how to reduce the number of adverse events and thus to measure advances in safety is a difficult undertaking. A simple measurement of event rates does not account for the unknown range of opportunities for harm. A valid measurement of advances in safety would require knowing the denominator (e.g., the population at risk) and the numerator (actual events). Actual harm is not always obvious and may only be detected by active screening (e.g., device-related infection, deep venous thrombosis). Despite this limitation, several interventions have been shown to reduce errors or even to decrease the rate of adverse events associated with particular ICU activities. Important issues are workload and staffing, skills and competency,

communication, and management of standard operations.

Excessive workload, extended working hours, fatigue, and sleep deprivation affect the performance of physicians and nurses (18, 19, 20). These risks are avoidable and have a negative impact not only on patient safety but also on the safety of health care providers (21, 22). Demanding tasks, time pressure and emotional stress add an additional burden for medical staff in ICUs. It is therefore an indisputable duty for ICU managers and hospital administrators to optimise schedule design and ensure appropriate staffing. Landrigan et al. showed that interns in an ICU made 36 % more errors of a serious nature during a traditional work schedule than during an interventional schedule that eliminated extended work shifts (23).

Considering ICUs as complex systems for the management of complex situations, it becomes clear that the actions of operators in these systems require a high level of knowledge, skill, and competence. Guidelines (24) and core competencies (25) for training in intensive care medicine are available. Education and training need to be seen as a continuum ongoing throughout the practice of intensive care. The safety of patient care depends on it. For instance, in an analysis of "line, tube, and drain"-related incidents in critically ill patients, the knowledge and skills of the providers were significant preventive factors (26). Other examples demonstrate that problem-focused education and training programmes in ICUs have a beneficial effect on patient safety. In a recent study, an educational intervention combined with implementation strategies increased the sustained adherence to a guideline for heparin thromboprophylaxis (27). A multicentre study by Pronovost et al. showed an impressive and persistent decrease in catheter-related bloodstream infections after an intervention with strong educational elements (28).

Although ICU staff are frequently confronted with unforeseeable situations, it is obvious that several activities are routine. Every routine procedure in an ICU carries the potential to minimise the causes of error. One of these routine procedures is the handover of patients between care-givers. Since this process is characterised by the communication of complex information under time pressure, a structured approach might support this task. Analogous situations exist in non-medical professional areas and can serve as a model. Catchpole et al. (29) used the expertise from a Formula 1 racing team and from aviation to develop a protocol for the handover between the operating theatre and the ICU. The authors showed that the number of technical errors, inadequate handover information, and duration of handover were reduced by using a protocol focused on leadership, task allocation, rhythm, standardised processes, checklists, awareness, anticipation, and communication.

Changing minds – the creation of a safety culture

One of the characteristics of intensive care medicine is the close collaboration of several medical professionals, particularly between nurses and physicians. This need for collaboration adds complexity to an already complex work environment, but, even more importantly, it adds the potential strengths and opportunities of teamwork among specialists. With respect to patient safety, there are many eyes looking at the same situation but from different perspectives. This is a great opportunity if an atmosphere of trust and respect allows open communication. Different viewpoints give deeper insight into the processes on which the functioning of an ICU is based. This approach requires the transformation of traditional patterns of behaviour, including the assignment of blame, into a new culture focused on systemic improvements in patient safety – from a reactive analysis of error to a proactive design of a safer system. The impact of such cultural changes is difficult to measure (30) but should not be underestimated. In a recent study, Zohar et al. (31) used a measure of health care climate at the hospital and unit levels to investigate the influence of nurse managers and their professional peers on patient safety. Evaluation of climate was based on patient orientation, professional development, and teamwork. The authors found that patient safety was maximised when both hospital and unit climates were positive. Interestingly, a compensatory effect of a positive unit climate was seen when the hospital climate was poor. This observation emphasises the need for cultural change as a key to improved patient safety.

Summary

Patient safety is an essential component in the practice of intensive care medicine. Several reports have demonstrated an urgent need for ICUs to improve the safety of such key processes as the administration of drugs. A very first step in the effort to reduce the number of adverse events is to raise awareness and to recognise error. A more advanced approach includes the active search for hazards and system flaws and requires a sustained cultural change. Open communication and interprofessional exchange of information are essential in the development of such a safety culture. The intensive care community has already proved that patient safety is a top-priority issue. Several interventions have been shown to reduce errors or to decrease the number of adverse events. Important factors are workload and staffing, skills and competency, communication, and management of standard operations.

Key points for clinical practice

- *There is an urgent need for improvement of patient safety in ICUs.*
- *A first step includes raised awareness as well as training in the recognition and management of safety problems.*
- *A change from a destructive "shame and blame" attitude to a proactive safety culture is essential. This requires creating an atmosphere of trust and respect among health care professionals to allow open communication about safety problems.*
- *A system approach is aimed at eliminating hazards due to a flawed design of infrastructure and processes as well as working conditions.*
- *A positive safety culture relies on*
  - *values, attitudes, and patterns of behaviour;*
  - *competencies;*
  - *resources;*
  - *commitment;*
  - *leadership;*
  - *communication founded on mutual trust;*
  - *shared perceptions of the importance of safety; and*
  - *confidence in the efficacy of preventive measures.*

The author

Andreas Valentin, MD
General and Medical ICU
Second Medical Department
KA Rudolfstiftung
Juchgasse 25
1030 Vienna, Austria
e-mail: andreas.valentin@meduniwien.ac.at

References

1. Sheldon T. Dutch study shows that 40% of adverse incidents in hospital are avoidable. BMJ. 2007 May 5; 334(7600):925.

2. Donchin Y, Gopher D, Olin M, Badihi Y, Biesky M, Sprung CL, et al. A look into the nature and causes of human errors in the intensive care unit. Crit Care Med. 1995 Feb;23(2):294–300.

3. Rothschild JM, Landrigan CP, Cronin JW, Kaushal R, Lockley SW, Burdick E, et al. The Critical Care Safety Study: The incidence and nature of adverse events and serious medical errors in intensive care. Crit Care Med. 2005 Aug;33(8):1694–700.

4. Chang A, Schyve PM, Croteau RJ, O'Leary DS, Loeb JM. The JCAHO patient safety event taxonomy: a standardized terminology and classification schema for near misses and adverse events. Int J Qual Health Care. 2005 Apr;17(2):95–105.

5. Donchin Y, Seagull FJ. The hostile environment of the intensive care unit. Curr Opin Crit Care. 2002 Aug;8(4): 316–20.

6. Dodek PM, Raboud J. Explicit approach to rounds in an ICU improves communication and satisfaction of providers. Intensive Care Med. 2003 Sep;29(9):1584–8.

7. Webster CS. The nuclear power industry as an alternative analogy for safety in anaesthesia and a novel approach for the conceptualisation of safety goals. Anaesthesia. 2005 Nov;60(11):1115–22.

8. Valentin A, Capuzzo M, Guidet B, Moreno RP, Dolanski L, Bauer P, et al. Patient safety in intensive care: results from the multinational Sentinel Events Evaluation (SEE) study. Intensive Care Med. 2006 Oct;32(10):1591–8.

9. Calabrese AD, Erstad BL, Brandl K, Barletta JF, Kane SL, Sherman DS. Medication administration errors in adult patients in the ICU. Intensive Care Med. 2001 Oct;27(10): 1592–8.

10. Beckmann U, Bohringer C, Carless R, Gillies DM, Runciman WB, Wu AW, et al. Evaluation of two methods for quality improvement in intensive care: facilitated incident monitoring and retrospective medical chart review. Crit Care Med. 2003 Apr;31(4): 1006–11.

11. Michel P, Quenon JL, de Sarasqueta AM, Scemama O. Comparison of three methods for estimating rates of adverse events and rates of preventable adverse events in acute care hospitals. BMJ. 2004 Jan 24;328(7433): 199.

12. Osmon S, Harris CB, Dunagan WC, Prentice D, Fraser VJ, Kollef MH. Reporting of medical errors: an intensive care unit experience. Crit Care Med. 2004 Mar;32(3):727–33.

13. Schuerer DJ, Nast PA, Harris CB, Krauss MJ, Jones RM, Boyle WA, et al. A new safety event reporting system improves physician reporting in the surgical intensive care unit. J Am Coll Surg. 2006 Jun;202(6):881–7.

14. Medication safety issue brief. Look-alike, sound-alike drugs. Hosp Health Netw. 2005 Oct;79(10):57–8.

15. Gillman L, Leslie G, Williams T, Fawcett K, Bell R, McGibbon V. Adverse events experienced while transferring the critically ill patient from the emergency department to the intensive care unit. Emerg Med J. 2006 Nov;23(11):858–61.

16. Warren J, Fromm RE, Jr., Orr RA, Rotello LC, Horst HM. Guidelines for the inter- and intrahospital transport of critically ill patients. Crit Care Med. 2004 Jan;32(1): 256–62.

17. Beckmann U, Gillies DM, Berenholtz SM, Wu AW, Pronovost P. Incidents relating to the intra-hospital transfer of critically ill patients. An analysis of the reports submitted to the Australian Incident Monitoring Study in Intensive Care. Intensive Care Med. 2004 Aug; 30(8):1579–85.

18. Barger LK, Ayas NT, Cade BE, Cronin JW, Rosner B, Speizer FE, et al. Impact of extended-duration shifts on medical errors, adverse events, and attentional failures. PLoS Med. 2006 Dec;3(12):e487.

19. Gander PH, Purnell HM, Garden A, Woodward A. Work Patterns and Fatigue-Related Risk Among Junior Doctors. Occup Environ Med. 2007 Mar 26.

20. Scott LD, Rogers AE, Hwang WT, Zhang Y. Effects of critical care nurses' work hours on vigilance and patients' safety. Am J Crit Care. 2006 Jan;15(1):30–7.

21. Ayas NT, Barger LK, Cade BE, Hashimoto DM, Rosner B, Cronin JW, et al. Extended work duration and the risk of self-reported percutaneous injuries in interns. JAMA. 2006 Sep 6;296(9):1055–62.

22. Barger LK, Cade BE, Ayas NT, Cronin JW, Rosner B, Speizer FE, et al. Extended work shifts and the risk of motor vehicle crashes among interns. N Engl J Med. 2005 Jan 13;352(2):125–34.

23. Landrigan CP, Rothschild JM, Cronin JW, Kaushal R, Burdick E, Katz JT, et al. Effect of reducing interns' work hours on serious medical errors in intensive care units. N Engl J Med. 2004 Oct 28;351(18):1838–48.

24. Dorman T, Angood PB, Angus DC, Clemmer TP, Cohen NH, Durbin CG, Jr., et al. Guidelines for critical care medicine training and continuing medical education. Crit Care Med. 2004 Jan;32(1):263–72.

25. Bion JF, Barrett H. Development of core competencies for an international training programme in intensive care medicine. Intensive Care Med. 2006 Sep;32(9):1371–83.

26. Needham DM, Sinopoli DJ, Thompson DA, Holzmueller CG, Dorman T, Lubomski LH, et al. A system factors analysis of "line, tube, and drain" incidents in the intensive care unit. Crit Care Med. 2005 Aug;33(8): 1701–7.

27. McMullin J, Cook D, Griffith L, McDonald E, Clarke F, Guyatt G, et al. Minimizing errors of omission: behavioural reinforcement of heparin to avert venous emboli: the BEHAVE study. Crit Care Med. 2006 Mar; 34(3):694–9.

28. Pronovost P, Needham D, Berenholtz S, Sinopoli D, Chu H, Cosgrove S, et al. An intervention to decrease catheter-related bloodstream infections in the ICU. N Engl J Med 2006 Dec. 28;355(26):2725–32.

29. Catchpole KR, de Leval MR, McEwan A, Pigott N, Elliott MJ, McQuillan A, et al. Patient handover from surgery to intensive care: using Formula 1 pit-stop and aviation models to improve safety and quality. Pediatr Anaesth. 2007 May;17(5):470–8.

30. Huang DT, Clermont G, Sexton JB, Karlo CA, Miller RG, Weissfeld LA, et al. Perceptions of safety culture vary across the intensive care units of a single institution. Crit Care Med. 2007 Jan;35(1):165–76.

31. Zohar D, Livne Y, Tenne-Gazit O, Admi H, Donchin Y. Healthcare climate: a framework for measuring and improving patient safety. Crit Care Med. 2007 May;35(5): 1312–7.

Michael Hiesmayr and Daniel Schmidlin

Early discharge from the ICU is safe

Introduction

Availability of intensive care unit capacity

The availability of a sufficient number of intensive care beds is and will be a key factor to allow, on the one hand, major surgery to be performed safely and according to the planned schedule and, on the other, permit timely admission of medical and surgical emergency cases. An additional factor that may exacerbate any shortage of ICU resources is the demographic change in developed countries toward high proportions of older people, leading to an older patient population in most medical fields. Age is identified as an independent risk factor in the majority of analyses regarding fast postoperative recovery and length of stay in the ICU and the hospital.

A sufficient number of ICU beds is not only the result of yearly financial resource allocation but also the result of a continuous process to arrive at a large number of qualified, trained and consistently motivated people (1). Due to the high fixed costs of qualified labour and the relatively low (and only periodically incurred) investment amounts for technical equipment, "empty" yet equipped intensive care units (or other monitoring units) are relatively easily furnished but useless. Considering daily hospital practice: Beds are rare, as is qualified staff, and operating an ICU is expensive for the hospital because of high personnel, drug and technology costs

which typically consume 15–25 % of the total budget of a tertiary care centre. The potential resource shortage may lead to a centralisation of very high risk patients at a few hospitals, thus increasing local knowledge and inducing better intra-hospital processes.

Indicators of inadequate ICU resources are an elevated number of cancelled scheduled operations, refused admission to the ICU, inappropriate timing of discharge, the readmission rate and post-ICU mortality. Another important indicator of adequacy of resources is the proportion of nighttime discharges. These unplanned, "emergency" discharges, typically in response to an acute demand in ICU care, have increased in recent years in areas where ICU beds were limited and are associated with a poorer prognosis (2).

When does a patient receive postoperative intensive care services?

In this article, early discharge from the ICU refers to postoperative/post-interventional patients. Patients with an internal medicine disorder are by definition at a higher risk (also refer to SAPS II) and in most circumstances not in a condition which allows short-term treatment and rapid discharge from the ICU. The situation of patients in the early phase after major surgery is not critical illness but a significant need for attention, medical care and nursing efforts in order to regain and maintain physiologic equilibrium. The elements to be kept within an "acceptable" range are not limited to heart rate and blood pressure but extend to the support of ventilatory mechanics in extubated patients, adequate coughing, pain management, monitoring and treatment of bleeding, control of temperature as well as psychological support in order to decrease anxiety.

Fortunately, due to improved operating techniques as well as common efforts of ICU doctors and nurses, a significant number of postoperative patients regain physiologic stability very quickly. Thus, operation theatre schedules have become increasingly tight, leading to increased pressure to discharge patients rapidly from the ICU. Avoiding prolonged sedation and artificial ventilation helps to save human and financial resources in an environment with a growing proportion of older people. On the other hand, the ICU with its staff, monitors and machinery is thought to play a crucial role for the early postoperative outcome in patients recovering less rapidly.

Besides the return of a physiologic condition, an important prerequisite for early discharge is an adequate mental state. Patients are often uncomfortable due to noise and visual impacts as soon as they regain consciousness and thus are at risk of mental disorders/delirium. It seems wise to shorten ICU stay of conscious patients in order to improve their mental and physical health.

Let us take a look at the regular course of postoperative care following major surgery: Patients often need a phase of intensive postoperative care after major surgery. They have a "scheduled" first admission to the ICU, even if they have undergone an emergency operation. Typically, several hours lie between the begin of surgery and ICU arrival. The relatively unstable phase at arrival in the ICU is not dependent on extubation in the operation theatre, on operations with or without cardiopulmonary bypass, but only on preoperative state and intraoperative events. The better the preoperative condition and the intraoperative course, the easier, faster and more smoothly physiologic parameters return to normal range. The consequence of these facts is that ... a short time of high nursing staff needs in all patients, rapidly decreasing in "easy" cases but with persisting demands in more difficult courses (see also below: Nine Equivalents of Nursing Manpower use Score [NEMS]) (3). A rough estimate says that about 10 % of patients need more than 7 days of ICU stay depending on type of surgery and institutional habits.

What kind of intensive care services does the patient get?

After major surgery, patient needs and the necessary interventions can be divided into those based on human knowledge (application of drug therapy and nursing methods) and those based on the use of certain technologies. Technology is usually easier to obtain and less costly but is useless without the appropriate human resources. Because goal-directed interventions (inducing an elevated level of attention) have a high potential to rapidly improve the postoperative course, it is evident that patient needs are not linearly decreasing. But the availability of human attention per patient is usually constant and the consequent disequilibrium leads to phases of a resource gap inducing a decreased level of care and patient safety.

Due to the significantly higher attribution of doctors and nurses per patient, resource gaps are much rarer in the ICU and account for a lower proportion of total workload than in wards (see fig. 1).

Sunstantial resource gaps on the ward lead not only to higher mortality (3) but also to subsequent, usually urgent, ICU admissions. Readmission to the ICU induces high morbidity and mortality and should be avoided by all means (4).

The role of the ICU in the hospital environment

Patients needing an ICU phase after major interventions have a distinct way to go in order to get former abilities and an equal (or even better) health state (see fig. 2).

If there is not enough time to recover due to any reason, individuals are rapidly transferred to the next sector within or outside the hospital. The faster this happens, the higher the risk for readmission to the former or even a higher dependency level (e.g. from rehabilitation unit directly to ICU). One would also expect that the longer a patient's stay in the intensive care unit the slower this patient should descend the stair (5, 6). Monitoring of readmission rate and post-ICU mortality is mandatory to check for appropriateness of ICU services. The relative contribution of post-ICU mortality constituting 20–35 % of total mortality should not be taken as normal (7). Doctors and nurses caring for critically ill patients over a longer period of time do all know about the difficulties to achieve a slowly downsizing care for their patients after they leave the intensive care unit. Due to the brisk change of nurse-to-patient (and often physician-to-patient) ratio these patients fall, instead of descending properly, down a really steep stair (8).

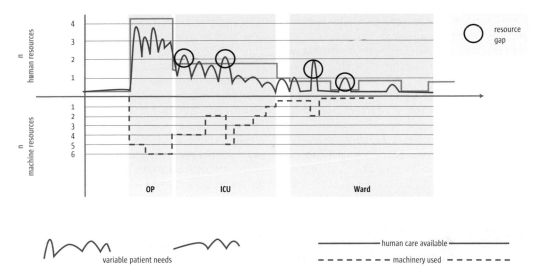

Fig. 1   Workload vs. time profile after major surgery

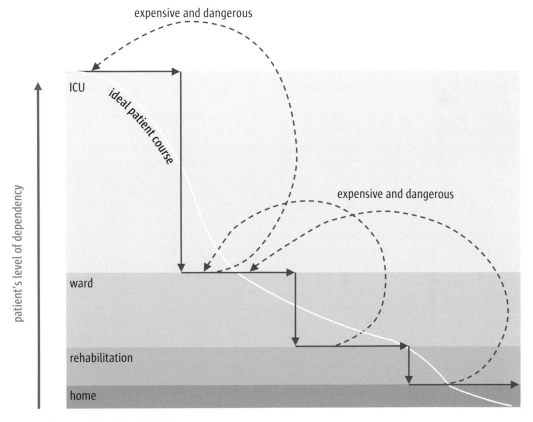

Fig. 2   The steps of care from ICU to home

Patients are the obvious beneficiaries of proper care. But other health care givers such as surgeons need experienced and dedicated intensive care partners who are constantly available in order to increase their patients' safety, avoid unnecessary complications and provide a well-functioning framework for elective surgery. Every surgeon has major concerns: whether there is ICU capacity for the next case, whether his patient does really need prolonged ICU stay, and if so, whether frail patients can remain long enough in the ICU to avoid or to reduce the threat of further complications.

Another significantly concerned party are the ward nurses. They have to cope with the workload of premature discharges and are prone to burn-out and poor teamwork once workload becomes excessive. At present the workload in the ward is not documented very well but is certainly a key to optimise proper delivery of care after major surgery.

Subsequent and usually urgent ICU admissions only occur when "something went wrong" and the resources are insufficient on the ward. Readmission to the ICU induces a high morbidity and mortality and should be avoided by all means (4).

Quantification of human resource utilisation

The extent of nursing care provided can be quantified by several systems, such as the TISS 28 system (5) or the more straightforward NEMS system (3). In both systems a trained nurse is able to provide care for 30 points during a shift, each point being equivalent to 10–12 nursing minutes. The complete NEMS is presented at the end of this article.

Patients after major surgery in an ICU have NEMS scores between 25 and 35 points (3). According to the Swiss Society for Intensive Care Medicine these patients are in category 1A to 1B early on, needing 1.3 to 1.5 nurses per patient, and later step down to category II, needing 1 nurse per 2 patients. The nursing manpower in the postoperative intensive care unit in the tertiary care academic centre (HTG) has been allocated based on a detailed assessment of time needed. We have 0.8 nurses/patient during daytime and 0.5 nurses/patient during nighttime present in the ICU. Nurse allocation is comparable to the figures for Switzerland and to the British "high dependency units" if a mix of patients with a mean NEMS of 28 points is assumed (6). A further refinement has been achieved when combinations of activities have been classified as being of either low (LT) or high (HT) complexity (6). A low level of care or de-creasing level is associated with a good prognosis, whereas a persisting high level or increasing level is associated with a prognosis 3–8 times poorer (8). We are convinced that quantification of workload is important for ICU management issues. It primarily allows assessment of sufficient staffing in order to meet the variable need during day and night shifts as well as during weekdays and weekends. An adequate staffing resource allocation is necessary to deliver proper care and to prevent understaffing-related problems such as higher mortality (7) and burn-out of personnel (9). Clearly, the higher the nursing workload in terms of whatever quantification (see tab. 1), the higher also the attention needed from the physician staff. In other words, higher NEMS usually induce higher SAPS, SOFA (10) or other critical illness quantification scores and, therefore, higher physician resource needs.

Controversial position 1: Pro

Prerequisites for early discharge

We could demonstrate that there is a large variability in duration of artificial ventilation and length of stay in the ICU that is partly explained by structures such as number of personnel and type of ICU but not by severity of patient's disease (11). We also found that the number of available nurse staff was highly variable between units as was the availability of intermediate care beds. Interestingly, one of the ICUs working most efficiently had no intermediate care beds available. Since the first step to a "lower" level of care is taking the patient off the artificial ventilation, early extubation is mandatory for the entire process (12, 13).

It is easy to extubate patients early but the duration until discharge may not be reduced to the

Tab. 1 Interdisciplinary (major interventional cardiology, including cardiac surgery) ICU (HIP) in a non-teaching hospital n = 1,474 patients

ICU stay	less than 48 hours	more than 48 hours
No. of patients	935	539
In-hospital mortality No. (%)	14 (1.5)	45 (8.3)
SAPS II (mean, SD)	20.1 (9.2)	27.1 (12.5)
Log EuroSCORE (where eligible, %)	4.1 (3.8)	10.9 (14.7)

same extent. It is generally accepted that a ventilated patient has to be in an ICU because of the obvious dependency on the technical resources, an extubated patient may need even more attention. It has been observed in one unit in the UK that in the event of a high-risk case load senior nurses tend to be more careful when extubating other patients if there is only a junior nurse available for post-extubation care. Similar behaviour has been scientifically assessed (7).

In the survey (11) cited above we did not only find a large variability in duration of artificial ventilation but that the consecutive duration of stay in the ICU (after extubation) also depends more on local habits than on patient characteristics and/ or (concomitant) sickness.

The pattern found during this multi-centre survey clearly shows that extubation is a smooth and progressive process with a clustering at 6, 12, 15 and 22 hours after admission; discharge from the ICU (see fig. 3) has a staircase pattern in 24-hour intervals for all individual units. The histogram of admission, extubation and discharge (see fig. 4) shows that the most striking time point is discharge. The pattern suggests that external factors govern the process. The nursing workload over time also shows a circadian pattern for patients after cardiac surgery. Only patients with several organs failing will have a constant intensity of nursing care around the clock.

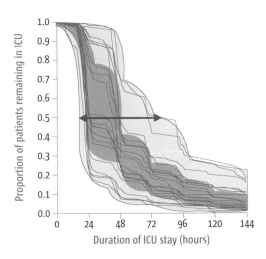

Fig. 3   Proportion of patients staying in the ICU after cardiac surgery
The proportion of surviving patients in the ICU is displayed versus duration since ICU admission. Each line represents one individual ICU. The light grey area indicates the total variability and the dark grey area mainstream behaviour. The arrow indicates the duration range until 50 % of patients have been discharged from the ICU.
With kind permission from Springer Science+Business Media: Intensive Care Med. Effect of centre-, patient- and procedure-related factors on intensive care resource utilisation after cardiac surgery, 28(10), 2002, 1453–61, Lassnigg A, Hiesmayr MJ, Bauer P, Haisjackl M.

Quantification of eligibility for early discharge

Early selection of patients eligible for rapid discharge from the ICU does not seem to be very difficult: Factors such as low comorbidity, patient not too old, fair intra- and postoperative course (small amount of blood loss, haemodynamic stability, rapid recovery from sedation, good pain control) all contribute to a relatively low risk score value (SAPS II or III, APACHE II or III), and therefore should lead to low in-hospital mortality (see tab. 1). Looking at data taken prospectively reveals – not surprisingly – that patients discharged early are less ill and had a better prognosis than those kept in the ICU for more than 48 hours.

As far as cardiac surgical patients are concerned, EuroSCORE is a very helpful tool to estimate patients' need for ICU stay prospectively. In our single centre experience with a rather small number of patients we found a cut-off value of 14 % expected mortality (according to prediction by logistic EuroSCORE) between patients remaining in the ICU for more or less than 48 hours. Estimation of the probable length of stay in the ICU by SAPS II was not reasonably possible in our patients.

The difference between patients discharged early and those with a longer ICU stay is striking when the NEMS is applied to measure nursing workload (see fig. 5).

Patients discharged early not only are the group with a lower workload the first day and those who use human resources markedly less on day 2 (median value of 18 points, see fig. 5), signifying about 180 minutes of qualified work per patient and shift. Patients remaining in the ICU for a longer period are in need of a higher level of nurse attention, i.e. a median value of more than

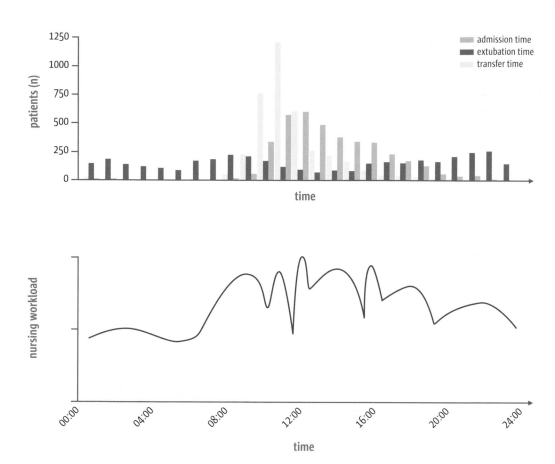

Fig. 4   Time pattern for patient admission, extubation and discharge after cardiac surgery with an estimated nursing workload time pattern

28 NEMS points (roughly 300 minutes per 8-hour shift). It seems evident that such patients cannot be safely transferred to the ward.

Controversial position 2: Con

We draw a simple conclusion from the above: Patients who are at low risk during the pre-, intra- and early postoperative phase in the ICU according to the corresponding scoring systems may be safely discharged. On the other hand, patients at high risk (preoperative and/or postoperatively) indeed almost all need a prolonged ICU stay in order to achieve a good postoperative course.

Being against early discharge in low-risk patients is not an option if sufficient doctor and nursing staff is on duty on the ward. Thus, the most important and challenging patients are those who are in between the two extremes. A sufficiently precise prediction of patients' postoperative course in these individuals is not possible and the responsible doctors and nurses must bear in mind that a certain percentage must return to the ICU within a few days even if the institution has a prudent transfer policy. Cohort data are not sufficiently specific for individuals to avoid unpleasant surprises, especially in elderly patients who may fall down in their room, lose intellectual orientation, experience arrhythmia, heart failure or pulmonary problems. Not to be forgotten are unforeseen complications of the operation/ intervention procedure itself which may lead to readmission to the ICU before or after a second procedure.

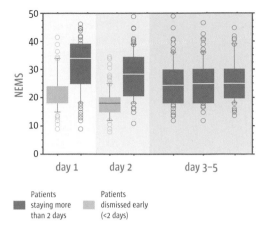

Patients
staying more
than 2 days

Patients
dismissed early
(<2 days)

Fig. 5   Dependence of patient's ability to be discharged
within 48 hours
Interdisciplinary ICU (HIP)
n = 560 patients, 278 discharged within 48 hours,
282 later than 2 days

Moreno et al found already 6 years ago that patient survival on the ward is a result of the health state at the time of discharge from the ICU (see fig. 6) (10).

There is sufficient evidence that an individual can also be discharged from the ICU too early. Either he/she has too many organs still insufficiently working (as represented by a higher Sequential Organ Failure Assessment [SOFA] score), or the workload for the nurses on the ward (as represented by higher NEMS values) is too high, or both. In such cases, early discharge from the ICU is not safe at all but may turn into a life-threatening situation.

Besides low score values, a *conditio sine qua non* is a well-functioning ward with sufficient nursing and physician staff, experienced supervising doctors and regular control of postoperative care. An almost perfect data sharing between the ICU staff and the ward staff is also mandatory to avoid loss of crucial information about the patient's history, operation, drug application and special conditions, needs and wishes. Several groups have sought solutions to diminish the depth of the steps patients have to go down after surgery, as described below.

Strategies to increase number of patients discharged early

There are a few models to make the transitions between the individual units (ICU, ward) smoother and thus improve outcome in patients discharged with a higher level of organ dysfunction and more human resource use.

Patients can be kept in the ICU longer with a decreasing nurse-to-patient ratio within the ICU as patients stabilise. Alternatively an additional structure can be inserted between the ICU and the ward. Such intermediate care units have been shown to be able to deliver a restricted number of specialised tasks and to decrease the length of stay in certain ICUs. The real assessment whether such a structure corresponds more to an ICU or a ward with more nurse manpower always needs to be evaluated carefully. The names do not tell very much. Ideally, an intensivists' consultancy should be available. A further factor is the local proximity of the ward to the ICU. A ward that has immediate access to the ICU personnel in case of deteriorating patient status would be able to accept patients earlier from the ICU when further monitoring or continuous infusion of a single drug appears to be necessary.

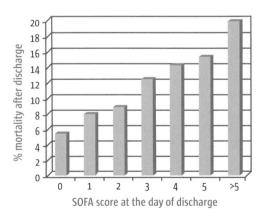

Fig. 6   Percentage of patients dying after discharge from
the ICU. Mortality after discharge from the ICU on
the ward (%).
With kind permission from Springer
Science+Business Media: Intensive Care Med.
Mortality after discharge from intensive care:
the impact of organ system failure and nursing
workload use at discharge, 27(6), 2002, 999–1004,
Moreno R, Miranda DR, Matos R, Fevereiro T.

Another possibility to decrease adverse events, morbidity and mortality on the ward is the creation of a hospital-wide intensive care unit-based medical emergency team to evaluate and treat in-patients deemed at risk of developing an adverse outcome by nursing, paramedical, and/or medical staff as described by the Bellomo group in Australia. The introduction of such teams reduced negative events, morbidity and mortality relevantly whereas additional "high dependency" units did not (14, 15).

An innovative approach could be to create a structured ward team. In a structured ward team an ICU specialist nurse would be part of the ward team 24 hours a day, 7 days a week. This specialist nurse would be involved in identifying deteriorating patients early, supervise intervention and support the nursing staff with specific knowledge and skills. Such an organisation would provide a good backup for junior nurses.

Summary and key points for clinical practice

A short evaluation and "triage" of (postoperative) ICU patients on a daily basis with the help of the corresponding scoring systems (EuroSCORE, NEMS, SOFA, SAPS) is helpful to define patients who may be discharged early and those who certainly should not. It also helps in identifying those patients who are at intermediate risk and in further "classifying" them. The incidence and the reasons for readmissions must be evaluated on a regular basis. Based on these results, measurement of critical elements in patient's state lead to an adequate course of action and to continuous improvement of ward performance. These instruments help doctors and nurses to detect deviations earlier in order to avoid critical situations and, hence, readmission to the ICU "in extremis". The creation of specialised outreach teams in the hospitals seems to be a very promising step in the effort to reduce morbidity and mortality of patients following ICU stays. Readmissions must be avoided by any means, but so must high mortality on the ward.

Which measures are the most helpful at an individual centre is most probably best determined by the centre itself.

Structuring of ICU and ward teams may offer an opportunity to utilise the available human resources more efficiently. The levels of nursing care and the parallel need for physicians in the ICU should be measured for proper allocation of human, technical and other (drugs, surface, logistical) resources.

Major issues

- Knowledge regarding available resources
- Identification of patients to be discharged early
- Knowledge about outcome-related patient risk factors
- Transparency/measurability of workload for ICU doctors and nurses
- Training of doctors and nurses regarding later development of ICU patients
- ICU ward communication: Discharge management/ liaison nurse

Key words

ICU, HDU, fast-track, mortality, risk evaluation, nursing, monitoring

The authors

Michael Hiesmayr, MD[1]
Daniel Schmidlin, MD[2]
   [1]Division of Cardiac-Thoracic and Vascular Anaesthesia & Intensive Care (HTG) | Medical University | Vienna, Austria
   [2]Interdisciplinary ICU | Hirslanden Klinik Im Park (HIP) | Zurich, Switzerland

Address for correspondence
   Daniel Schmidlin
   Hirslanden Klinik Im Park
   Seestrasse 220
   CH-8027 Zurich, Switzerland
   e-mail: daniel.schmidlin@access.unizh.ch

References

1. Talmor D, Shapiro N, Greenberg D, Stone PW, Neumann PJ. When is critical care medicine cost-effective? A systematic review of the cost-effectiveness literature. Crit Care Med. 2006;34(11):2738–47.

2. Goldfrad C, Rowan K. Consequences of discharges from intensive care at night. Lancet 2000;355(9210):1138–42.

3. Reis Miranda D, Moreno R, Iapichino G. Nine equivalents of nursing manpower use score (NEMS). Intensive Care Med. 1997;23(7):760–5.

4. Cohn WE, Sellke FW, Sirois C, Lisbon A, Johnson RG. Surgical ICU recidivism after cardiac operations. Chest. 1999;116(3):688–92.

Appendix

NEMS

Item	Description	Points
1. Basic monitoring (m)	Hourly vital signs, regular record and calculation of fluid balance	9
2. Intravenous medication	Bolus or continuous, not including vasoactive drugs	6
3. Mechanical ventilatory support (R)	Any form of mechanical/assisted ventilation, with or without PEEP (e.g. CPAP), with or without muscle relaxants	12
4. Supplementary ventilatory care (r)	Breathing spontaneously through endotracheal tube; supplementary oxygen any method, except if (3) applies	3
5. Single vasoactive medication (c)	Any vasoactive drug	7
6. Multiple vasoactive medication (C)	More than one vasoactive drug, regardless of type and dose	12
7. Dialysis techniques (d)	All	6
8. Specific interventions in the ICU	Such as endotracheal intubation, introduction of pacemaker, cardioversion, endoscopy, emergency operation in the past 24 h, gastric lavage. The intervention/ procedure is related to the severity of illness of the patient and makes an extra demand upon manpower efforts at the ICU. Routine interventions such as X-rays, echocardiography, ECG, dressings, introduction of venous (e.g. Swan-Ganz) or arterial lines, are not included	5
9. Specific interventions outside the ICU	Such as surgical intervention or diagnostic procedure. The intervention/procedure is related to the severity of illness of the patient and makes an extra demand upon manpower efforts at the ICU	6

5. Miranda DR, de Rijk A, Schaufeli W. Simplified Therapeutic Intervention Scoring System: the TISS-28 items – results from a multicenter study. Crit Care Med. 1996;24(1):64–73.

6. Iapichino G, Radrizzani D, Bertolini G, Ferla L, Pasetti G, Pezzi A, Porta F, Miranda DR. Daily classification of the level of care. A method to describe clinical course of illness, use of resources and quality of intensive care assistance. Intensive Care Med. 2001;27(1):131–6.

7. Tarnow-Mordi WO, Hau C, Warden A, Shearer AJ. Hospital mortality in relation to staff workload: a 4-year study in an adult intensive-care unit. Lancet. 2000;356(9225):185–9.

8. Iapichino G, Radrizzani D, Ferla L, Pezzi A, Porta F, Zanforlin G, Miranda DR. Description of trends in the course of illness of critically ill patients. Markers of intensive care organization and performance. Intensive Care Med. 2002;28(7):985–9.

9. Bakker AB, Le Blanc PM, Schaufeli WB. Burnout contagion among intensive care nurses. J Adv Nurs. 2005;51(3):276–87.

10. Moreno R, Miranda DR, Matos R, Fevereiro T. Mortality after discharge from intensive care: the impact of organ system failure and nursing workload use at discharge. Intensive Care Med. 2001;27(6):999–1004.

11. Lassnigg A, Hiesmayr MJ, Bauer P, Haisjackl M. Effect of centre-, patient- and procedure-related factors on intensive care resource utilisation after cardiac surgery. Intensive Care Med. 2002;28(10):1453–61.

12. Cheng DC, Karski J, Peniston C, Raveendran G, Asokumar B, Carroll J, David T, Sandler A. Early tracheal extubation after coronary artery bypass graft surgery reduces costs and improves resource use. A prospective, randomized, controlled trial. Anesthesiology. 1996;85(6):1300–10.

13. Currey J, Botti M, Browne J. Hemodynamic team decision making in the cardiac surgical intensive care context. Heart Lung. 2003;32(3):181–9.

14. Bellomo R, Goldsmith D, Uchino S, Buckmaster J, Hart G, Opdam H, Silvester W, Doolan L, Gutteridge G. Prospective controlled trial of effect of medical emergency team on postoperative morbidity and mortality rates. Crit Care Med. 2004;32(4):916–21.

15. Jones D, Egi M, Bellomo R, Goldsmith D. Effect of the medical emergency team on long-term mortality following major surgery. Crit Care. 2007;11(1):R12.

Mercedes Palomar, Francisco Álvarez-Lerma, Pedro Olaechea
and Ingrid Morales

Implementation of surveillance networks

Notification systems reveal that nosocomial infections (NI) are key adverse effects in hospitals because of their frequency and impact (1–3). Whatever their basic pathology, critical patients are the most vulnerable to NI. Intensive Care Units (ICU) account for 20–25 % of reported NI (especially those associated with major morbidity and mortality, such as pneumonia and blood stream infection). NI also increase mortality of critically ill patients, especially those with intermediate severity. Furthermore, antibiotic-resistant pathogen rates are on the rise worldwide, as are the related health and economic costs.

ICU-acquired infections are generally related to the use of invasive devices, many of them being preventable. Whatever the detection, registration and reporting method, NI surveillance programs (NISP) are necessary to establish corrective measures. They are relevant only if they aim at improving care (4, 5).

Prevailing NI surveillance systems are based on prevalence and incidence studies (5, 6). Prevalence studies inform on infections present at the time of the study, not about infections already cured. They consume few resources, give a valuable snapshot of a particular moment, but are less accurate and tend to amplify infection rates and antibiotic resistance figures. Instead, incidence studies are time- and effort-consuming, but allow for an assessment of aetiological forces with stronger evidence. This makes them the most used type of study to detect infections in high-risk units such as ICUs, and to evaluate their association with invasive procedures.

Surveillance systems can be local or national. Their development and follow-up can be secured by other services besides the ICU, for instance the departments of infectious diseases or preventive medicine. The methodology can be unit-based or patient-based. The unit-based methodology is easier but has limited stratification possibilities. The patient-based one stratifies infection rates by individual risk factors, is more informative and permits more reliable comparisons with other units/areas/countries. Several American and European ICU surveillance programmes are national or regional (3, 7–9) (NNIS, KISS, ENVIN, France-Rea, etc.). The first programme of its kind started in the United States in 1970, where infection control was made compulsory as a result of

- the Joint Commission For Accreditation of Hospitals (10) (JCAHO) mandate and
- leading guidelines and definitions issued by the Center for Disease Control and Prevention (CDC).

The CDC National Nosocomial Infections Surveillance (NNIS) system yielded standardised methods for collecting and comparing health care-associated infection rates (3, 11). For inter- and intra-hospital comparisons, the NNIS publishes national benchmark infection rates, derived from data sent by participating hospitals. These rates have been used as a reference for other surveillance systems including the European ones.

Objectives of nosocomial infection surveillance in critically ill patients

The objectives of ICU-acquired NI surveillance systems are manifold. They consider four ways of reducing NI rates:

Know the rates of device-related infections acquired in ICU. Surveyed infections are those acquired during an ICU stay. They are related to invasive devices such as mechanical ventilation, urinary and vascular catheters and they are associated to an important morbidity and mortality. Incidence density has been preferred as a frequency indicator, as these ratios permit events (pathologies) to be related to the risk exposure duration.

Identify the most frequent microorganisms responsible for each surveyed infection. It should be noted that the aetiology differs according to the infection under scrutiny (ventilation-associated pneumonia (VAP), blood stream infection related to central venous catheter (BSI-CVC), urinary infection related to urinary catheter (UI)), and also according to the ICU.

Monitor and assess multiresistance markers. Multiresistance indicators were designed for frequent NI pathogens. These multiresistance markers also vary according to the ICUs, they have been related to antibiotic consumption, reservoir existence and cross-transmission (from contaminated patients, or from patients coming from other units or hospitals).

Study of intrinsic risk factors frequency and exposure to extrinsic risk factors. Modifications in the studied population can explain NI rate variations and thus need to be monitored. This monitoring allows units to be compared and time trends to be followed.

Outbreak detection. Outbreaks imply NI rates above endemic levels.

Study of control measures. Effectiveness of control measures needs to be monitored. This information ought to be fed back to the health professionals, in particular on infection risks conveyed through each procedure.

Evaluation of ICU-acquired infection's impact. The NI outcome is assessed in terms of attributed/related mortality and prolongation of ICU/hospital stay.

NI surveillance in critically ill patient improves NI prevention and treatment albeit in a limited (and sometimes controversial) way.

Controversial position 1

NI surveillance programmes strengthen national and local health systems. At national level:

They facilitate agreement upon infection process definitions and study. The advantage of widely accepted, validated and appropriate definitions is well-recognised. The CDC (12) NNIS definitions long were a reference in NI studies. Other European multi-country experiences, such as the HELICS project, improved these definitions in adapting them to different clinical practices in the field to identify these infections (13). In Spain, the EN-VIN-UCI programme yielded and disseminated a manual (14) with the definitions used by the participating ICUs since 1994. They were also included in the proposals for the HELICS project.

They allow agreement upon NI frequency indicators. The medical literature offers a large array of NI frequency indicators. The rate proposed by the national surveillance systems is the "incidence density". It relates controlled infection episodes to risk days (days of exposure to the strongest determinant of a particular infection) (3, 7).

Permit comparison of rates among ICUs, hospitals and countries. Agreed definitions and indicators allow for a comparison of different ICUs/countries (16). Risk stratification, rates calculation and identification of patients' characteristics facilitates such comparison and detection/correction of abnormal situations.

Which are the local pros of NI surveillance programmes? Per se, they are assistance quality markers recognised as such by numerous agencies. Their implementation implies knowledge of markers related to patient safety. In the USA, NISP is an accreditation requirement for hospitals (Joint Comission on Accreditation of Healthcare Organizations) (10). Likewise, NISPs are the basis of strategies meant to improve quality of ICU continuing medical care. Advantages include the following:

Identification of local (unit) departures from national rates. The risk stratification facilitates the design of studies exploring the causes of such deviation and proposing corrective interventions. The NISP information needs to be accessed and analyzed by the ICU professionals. This staff must be involved in strategies to improve care quality. Also, the hospital's administration must contribute the necessary means.

Identification of aetiologies and markers of multiresistance. Corrective strategies must be adapted empirically to each ICU. The knowledge of aetiologies and multiresistance markers is key to establishing NI empirical treatments. Evidence shows that early, appropriate treatment of patients with nosocomial pneumonia and blood stream infections improves survival (16, 17). On this ground, new therapeutic strategies were developed – such as de-escalating therapeutics (18). They encompass the initial treatment of the most frequent pathogens of treated infections, including multiresistant microorganisms. The uneven distribution of resistance prevents the use of standardised antibiotics combinations in all ICUs. Rather, treatments must be adapted locally. Furthermore, changes take place constantly, so the surveillance of the most frequent pathogens and the markers of multiresistance must be done on a continuous basis.

Evaluation of the impact of interventions performed to influence a specific problem. The application of any intervention performed to reduce the rates of a determined infection or of a specific marker of multiresistance must be accompanied by measurement of the effects achieved (rates, mortality, stay at ICU). Knowledge of the impact of an intervention is the best incentive for improving the collaboration of the healthcare personnel in achieving new objectives. Likewise, the application of national campaigns (catheter-related blood stream infections prevention) (19) or international (hand washing) (20) need active surveillance systems to evaluate such interventions.

Early detection of epidemic outbreaks of infections or multiresistant microorganisms. The identification of an epidemic outbreak implies knowledge of the previous rates of a particular infection or of a particular multiresistance marker. The presence of a number higher than expected (more than two times the standard deviation from the previous rates) of a particular infection (catheter-related blood stream infections), the emergence of a new microorganism in the ICU environment (e.g. *Burkholderia cepacea*), or the appearance or increase of a particular marker of multiresistance

(e.g. Methicilin-Resistant *Staphylococcus aureus*, Vancomicine-Resistant *Enterococcus sp*) should launch studies to identify the presence of a particular reservoir, while failure to apply a specific technique or an increase in cross-transmission should start studies to evaluate compliance with basic hygiene rules.

Controversial position 2

Since the beginning of the NNIS surveillance system in the 70s, followed by the European surveillance networks in the mid-90s, some limitations and difficulties have been pointed out on its low practical utility for clinicians. The inclusion of information on a great number of patients of different origin in the same database allows a global view of the situation but offers little local information if the amount contributed per unit is not large enough. Today, reports published by experts defining the rules needed to implement or improve the surveillance networks (21, 22) suggest that such systems have not yet reached the required maturity and reliability. These reports show that national differences in health systems, as well as cultural aspects and the surveillance methods, can influence the obtained results. The reliability and/or the comparability of the information from the surveillance networks that include several areas or countries could be hampered for the following reasons:

Lack of uniformity in the definitions and denominators. Although it has been proposed to standardise the definitions of infections considered of epidemiological interest, as well as the denominators used to compute rates, the interpretation of those definitions is not always uniform. It is particularly complex for surgical infections, some episodes of mechanical ventilation-associated pneumonia and for the denominator used to calculate the rates of catheter-associated bacteremia. These items can partially explain the differences in the rates published by the American and the European networks.

Differences in the type of patients. Since the case mix can be very different per country, but also within countries (24), it is necessary to define and validate the indicators of risk of infection for different types of patients (23), taking into account the variation in the severity and basis pathology of the patients. The EPIC study showed huge differences in severity scores as well as in the ratio of mechanical ventilation between Northern and Southern European countries (25). Since ICUs in Europe are mostly mixed (medical-surgical) and not as specialised as in the US, traditional NI rates including device-associated infection rates cannot sufficiently adjust for differences in case mix. If information per patient is not provided (patient-base surveillance), infection rates different from the true ones can be held for a particular type of patient.

Differences in the methodology of data capture. The quality and the intensity of surveillance vary among hospitals and countries and could explain part of the differences observed in several studies (26). The assignment of budgets allocated to surveillance is not uniform and could influence data quality. Discrepancies in considering the existence or not of an infection are possible if the surveillance is performed by the treating clinician (intensivist, anaesthesist or surgeon), by persons not directly involved in the care of the patient (e.g. infection control nurse) or if the data is collected from the laboratory, clinical course or administrative files without examining the patient or without information from the treating clinician (27–29). Another factor to be considered is the time of observation, for example measuring only the infections appearing during ICU stay or adding the post-discharge ones; this is particularly true for surgical site infections, which can appear during the patient's ICU or hospital stay or even after discharge from the hospital (30). Validity of surveillance data is one of the most crucial factors. So far, the validation of data has been rarely done nor has it been clearly defined what the sensitivity and specificity required by a surveillance network should be (22, 31).

Differences in clinical practice in different places. These differences cover functional as well as architectural aspects (e.g. open vs. closed ICUs, individual rooms, patient/nurse ratio, full-time vs. part-time intensivists, protocols, etc.). They can influence the rates and therefore do not reflect the true figures even when individual patient data is collected.

Differences in legal obligation to participate in surveillance networks. Some legal aspects making the surveillance protocols different between countries must be also considered. Whereas in certain countries the surveillance systems are optional, in others they are compulsory, or there are laws favouring its implementation. Mandatory surveillance carries costs that are not always understood by local governments (32, 33). Different political systems may have different ways of approaching the problem and consequently modify the surveillance results. Furthermore, hospitals participating voluntarily in surveillance networks are generally those most motivated in reducing their infection rates and therefore may have lower rates than hospitals with compulsory surveillance. Moreover, hospitals participating voluntarily may be penalised by publishing their infection rates, whereas non-participating ones, not being subject to surveillance network control, can benefit from not publishing their data.

Differences in the information received by participants and in the publication of results. The information generated by the surveillance networks is of little use if the hospitals which participated in the data collection do not receive feedback quickly and it therefore cannot be used for infection control measures. Although they are rare, there are surveillance networks which include in their programmes the possibility for participating units to analyse their own data and obtain results in real time (e.g. ENVIN in Spain). The Spanish network also provides annual national information, facilitating comparison (7, 14).

There is also controversy on the way the feedback of the information (26, 34, 35) should be performed and on its utility to participating units. It should be noted that the way of expressing the indicators of infections related to device use can lead to confusion. Rates per 100 patients or incidence densities per 1,000 stay days or per 1,000 days of device use are not equivalent. The incidence density per days of exposure to risk factor are the most helpful, but the risk of developing pneumonia of 100 patients ventilated 1 day is not equivalent to the risk of 10 patients ventilated 10 days. Another important issue is publicity in the media; if it is not voluntary (36), it can damage the image of the institution, or can be misinterpreted by those not familiar with the causes of differences among countries and hospitals, discouraging hospitals to take part in surveillance systems.

In summary, epidemiological surveillance networks putting together different regions and countries offer the advantage of providing a great amount of information about rates of nosocomial infections and allow a comparison among different centres, but the wider the networks the greater the likelihood that the collected data diverges from hospitals' local reality and loses its utility for a specific institution.

Conclusions

Ensuring patients' safety during their hospital stay requires mechanisms to determine the incidence of adverse effects, to propose corrective measures and to evaluate them. Effective surveillance involves counting cases and then calculating rates of various infections, analysing this data, and then reporting that data in an appropriate way to personnel involved in patient care.

The need to improve the development, maintenance and use of health surveillance and health information systems is well-recognised. Over the years, the American NNIS system has used standardised definitions, standardised surveillance protocols and risk stratification to calculate infection rates to provide national benchmark infection rates for inter- and intra-hospital comparisons in the USA.

In Europe, several national or regional protocols for the surveillance of ICU-acquired infections were developed, but different case definitions, methodology, indicators or institutional support, hindered inter-country comparisons of NI rates. The creation of an integrated European public health surveillance system, coordinated, comparable, and easy to use, became a priority. In 1994, the European Union financed the HELICS Project (Hospitals in Europe Link for Infection Control through Surveillance). A working group was set up with two representatives from each country (an intensive care unit physician and an epidemiologist from the surveillance network or public health institute), together with members of the European Society of Intensive Care Medicine. The protocols of each country were analysed to assess the feasibility of a retrospective comparison of the indicators between national and regional networks. It was evident that the differences were too significant to allow an international comparison. A new standardised protocol was elaborated after analysis of existing protocols, concerning inclusion criteria, type of surveillance, definitions of infections, risk factors included and indicators measured.

Concerning workload, surveillance can be more or less labour-intensive according to the type of surveillance. The HELICS-ICU protocol (16) offers two types of surveillance: Level 1 or unit-based surveillance and Level 2 or patient-based surveillance. Their main characteristics are summarized in figure 1. Level 1 or unit-based surveillance is a simplified database assuming stratification by type of unit only. It provides limited inter-unit comparability and is rather suited for unit monitoring in time and for regional, national and international trend follow-up. Denominators are collected per unit and consist of the number of patient days for patients staying in the ICU for more than 2 days. Numerators consist in data of patients with ICU-acquired infections only. The main indicators are the site-specific incidence rates (e.g. number of ICU-acquired pneumonia episodes/1,000 patients days), pathogen-specific incidence rates (e.g. number of MRSA pneumonia* 1,000/number of patient days). Limited comparisons are possible through stratification of the rates by ICU type and by the mean percentage of intubated patients in the ICU, an approximation of case mix severity. The simplicity and the low workload of unit-based level 1 surveillance favours continuous participation in order to obtain more extensive data to stabilise the NI indicators and the follow-up time trends.

Level 2 or patient-based surveillance, where risk factor data is collected per patient for all patients staying in the ICU for more than 2 days, whether infected or not, is intended for risk-adjusted comparison of infection rates between ICUs. Individual patient data on extrinsic and intrinsic risk factors is also collected. Level 2 surveillance allows the determination of device-adjusted infection rates, stratification of rates by patient type and risk-adjusted inter-ICU comparisons for benchmarking purposes. These indicators are computed using standardised infection ratios based on composite risk indices that estimate the number of expected infections.

Since ICUs in Europe are mostly mixed (medical-surgical) and not as specialised as in the US, traditional NI rates including device-associated infection rates cannot sufficiently adjust for differences in case mix. Therefore, advanced risk adjustment in Europe requires patient-based surveillance instead of CDC/NNIS unit-based surveillance in which device-adjusted NI rates are stratified by more than 10 different types of units with a homogeneous case mix. Unit based (L1) and patient-based (L2) surveillance can be combined within the same ICU where unit-based surveillance is used continuously to follow trends in the ICU while patient-based surveillance is performed for periodical in-depth interpretation of indicators. For example, all the participating Spanish ICUs conduct unit-based surveillance on a continous basis and perform patient-based surveillance 3 months per year.

Diagnosis differences between units or countries and the possible influence on NI rates can be reduced. The

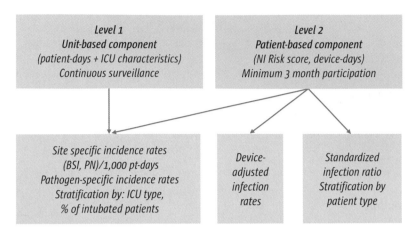

Fig. 1   Indicators per level of surveillance of the HELICS protocol for the surveillance of ICU–acquired infections. BSI: Blood Stream Infection. PN: Pneumonia. NI: Nosocomial Infections.

HELICS project asked if the reported infection had an antimicrobial treatment prescribed for that infection.

Pneumonia definition remains an area of debate, as it is an issue of clinical decision-making. In the absence of a gold standard, efforts are made to improve sensitivity and specificity. Table 1 displays the HELICS criteria for pneumonia definition. With 5 PN categories based on the microbiology diagnostic technique used, the HELICS-ICU definitions offer an option to compare similar pneumonia entities within and between networks. The creation of 5 categories of PN according to the diagnosis criteria permits each practitioner to collect data according to his regular practice and to the coordination level to identify the diagnostic criteria used per country, region and type of hospital. The new HELICS definitions are currently being used in several countries and data collected for analysis at regional, national and European levels since November 2003.

Since 2003, several countries have adapted their national surveillance system to make it compatible with HELICS surveillance and countries without such a system have adopted its methodology. Currently, aggregated surveillance data and inter-EU country comparisons have become available (15, 24). The HELICS-ICU surveillance being centred on patient characteristics and exposure can overlook some of the unit characteristics that can also influence the infection rates, such as staffing (patient to nurse ratio, skills, turnover), architecture of the unit, better-defined case mix, and antimicrobial use. However, the interpretation of differences of HAI rates should be done very carefully. One important aspect of surveillance data is their validity. Several European validation studies have been performed and should be taken into account to develop a protocol applicable to all European networks and individual countries (26, 37).

Since 2005, the HELICS programme has become an integral part of a European initiative called IPSE, with the aim of Improving Patient Safety in Europe. Taking advantage of a large European network and database, it will stimulate applied research and evaluation.

The authors

Mercedes Palomar, MD, PhD[1]
Francisco Álvarez-Lerma, MD, PhD[2]
Pedro Olaechea, MD[3]
Ingrid Morales, MD, MSc[4]
   [1]Intensive Care Unit | University Hospital
   Vall Hebron | Barcelona, Spain
   [2]Intensive Care Unit | University Hospital del
   Mar | Barcelona, Spain
   [3]Intensive Care Unit | Hospital Galdakano |
   Bilbao, Spain
   [4]Unit of epidemiology | Scientific Institute
   of Public Health | Brussels, Belgium

Address for correspondence
   Mercedes Palomar
   ICU. H Vall Hebron
   PºVall Hebron 119–129.
   08035 Barcelona, Spain.
   e-mail: mpalomar@vhebron.net

Tab. 1   Pneumonia definition in HELICS.

Rx criteria	Iwo or more serial chest X-rays or CT-scans with a suggestive image of pneumonia for patients with underlying cardiac or pulmonary disease.
	In patients without underlying cardiac or pulmonary disease one definitive chest X-ray or CT-scan is sufficient
	and at least one of the following symptoms:

Signs and symptoms

Fever > 38°C with no other cause

Leukopenia (< 4,000 WBC/mm3) or leucocytosis (≥ 12,000 WBC/mm3)

and

at least one of the following (or at least two if clinical pneumonia only = PN 4 and PN 5)

- New onset of purulent sputum, or change in character of sputum (color, odor, quantity, consistency)
- Cough or dyspnea or tachypnea
- Suggestive auscultation (rales or bronchial breath sounds), wheezing
- Worsening gas exchange (e.g. O2 desaturation or increased oxygen requirements or increased ventilation demand)

*and (*according to the microbiology diagnostic method used)

Microbiology

Bacteriologic diagnostics	Code
Positive quantitative culture from minimally contaminated lower respiratory tract (LRT) specimen	PN 1*
Broncho-alveolar lavage (BAL) with a threshold of > 10^4 CFU/ml or ≥ 5 % of BAL obtained cells contain intracellular bacteria on direct microscopic exam Gram stain (classified in the diagnostic category BAL).	
Protected brush (PB Wimberley) with a threshold of ≥ 10^3 CFU/ml	
Distal protected aspirate (DPA) with a threshold of ≥ 10^3 CFU/ml	
Positive quantitative culture from possibly contaminated LRT specimen	PN 2*
Quantitative culture of LRT specimen (e.g. endotracheal aspirate) with a threshold of 10^6 CFU/ml	
Alternative microbiology methods:	PN 3
■ Positive blood culture not related to another source of infection ■ Positive growth in culture of pleural fluid ■ Pleural or pulmonary abscess with positive needle aspiration ■ Histological pulmonary exam shows evidence of pneumonia ■ Positive exams for pneumonia with virus or particular microorganism (*Legionella, Aspergillus,* mycobacteria, mycoplasma, *Pneumocystis jiroveci*) ■ Positive detection of viral antigen or antibody from respiratory secretions (e.g. EIA, FAMA, shell vial assay, PCR) ■ Positive direct exam or positive culture from bronchial secretions or tissue ■ Seroconversion (ex: influenza viruses, *Legionella, Chlamydia*) ■ Detection of antigens in urine (Legionella)	
Positive sputum culture or non-quantitative LRT specimen culture	PN 4
No positive microbiology	PN 5

* PN 1 and PN 2 criteria were validated without previous antimicrobial therapy.
** CFU = Colony Forming Units

References

1. Leape LL. Reporting of adverse events. N Engl J Med. 2002; 347: 1633–1638.
2. Burke JP. Infection control. A problem for patient safety. N Engl J Med. 2003;348:651.
3. Center for Infectious Diseases. National Nosocomial Infections Surveillance (NNIS) System Report, data summary from january 1992 to June 2004, issued october 2004. Am J Infect Control. 2004;32:470–85.
4. CDC. Public Health focus: surveillance, prevention and control of nosocomial infections. MMWR. 1992;41: 783–787.
5. Haley RW, Culver DH, White JW, Meade Morgan W, Emori TG, Munn VP, Hooton TM. The efficacy of infection surveillance and control programs in preventing nosocomial infections in US hospitals. Am J Epidemiol. 1985;121:182–205.
6. Humphreys H, Smyth ETM. Prevalence surveys of healthcare-associated infections: what do they tell us, if anything?. Clin Microbiol Infect. 2006;12:2–4.
7. Alvarez-Lerma F, Palomar F, Olaechea P, Otal JJ, Insausti J, Cerdá E, Grupo de Estudio de Vigilancia de Infección Nosocomial en UCI. Estudio Nacional de Vigilancia de Infección Nosocomial en UCI. Informe de los años 2003–2005. Med Intensiva. 2007;31:6–17.
8. Suetens C, Savey A, Lepape A, Morales I, Carlet J, Fabry J. Surveillance des infections nosocomiales en réanimation: Vers une approche consensuelle en Europe. Réanimation. 2003;15:205–213.
9. Geffers C, Gastmeier P, Brauer H, Daschner F, Ruden H. Surveillance of nosocomial infections in ICUs: is postdischarge surveillance indispensable? Infect Control Hosp Epidemiol. 2001;22:157–159.
10. Joint Comisión on Accreditation of Healthcare Organizations: Infection Control. In: JCAHO, Accreditation Manual for Hospitals. Chicago: Joint Commision on Accreditation of Healthcare Organizations. 1990.
11. Culver DH, Horan TC, Gaynes RP, Martone WJ, Jarvis WR, Emori TG, Banerjee SN, Edwards JR, Tolson JS, Henderson TS, Hughes JM and the National Nosocomial Infections Surveillance System. Surgical wound infection rates by wound class, operative procedure, and patient risk index. Am J Med. 1991;91 (Suppl 3B):152–157.
12. Garner JS, Jarvis WR, Emori TG, Horan TC, Hughes JM. CDC definitions for nosocomial infections. Am J Infect Control. 1988;16:128–140.
13. Suetens C, Savey A, Labeeuw J, Morales I and the working group HELICS-ICU. The ICU-HELICS programme: towards European surveillance of hospital-acquired infections in intensive care units. Euro Surveill. 2002;7:127–128.
14. Grupo de Trabajo de Enfermedades Infecciosas de la SEMICYUC (GTEI-SEMICYUC). Estudio Nacional de Vigilancia de Infección Nosocomial en UCI (ENVIN-UCI). Informe de la evolución de la incidencia y características de las infecciones nosocomiales adquiridas en Servicios de Medicina Intensiva (1994–2001). Ed: Jarpyio Editores SA. 2002, Madrid.
15. Suetens C, Lepape A, Palomar M, Hiesmayer M. Impact of risk adjustment on inter-countries comparisons of ICU infections indicators. ESCAIDE. Stockholm, 18–20 October 2007. http://helics.univ-lyon1.fr.
16. Kollef MH, Sherman G, Ward S, Fraser VJ. Inadequate antimicrobial treatment of infections: a risk factor for hospital mortality among critically ill patients. Chest. 1999;115:462–474.
17. Ibrahim EH, Sherman G, Ward S, Fraser VJ, Kollef HK. The influence of inadequate antimicrobial treatment of bloodstream infections on patient in the ICU setting. Chest. 2000;118:146–155.
18. Kollef MH. Hospital-acquired pneumonia and de-escalation of antimicrobial treatment. Crit Care Med. 2001;29: 1473–1475.
19. Pronovost P, Needham D, Berenholtz S, Sinopoli D, Chu H, Cosgrove S et al. An intervention to decrease catheter-related bloodstream infections in the ICU. N Engl J Med. 2006;355(26):2725–32.
20. World Health Organization. World Alliance for patient safety. Forward programme. WHO library-cataloguint in publication date, France, 2004. www: who.int/patientsafety.
21. Pittet D, Allegranzi B, Sax H, Bertinato L, Concia E, Cookson B et al. Considerations for a WHO European strategy on health-care-associated infection, surveillance, and control. Lancet Infect. Dis. 2005;5(4):242–50.
22. Gastmeier P. European perspective on surveillance. J Hosp Infect. 2007;65 Suppl 2:159–64.
23. Zuschneid I, Geffers C, Sohr D, Kohlhase C, Schumacher M, Ruden H et al. Validation of surveillance in the intensive care unit component of the German nosocomial infections surveillance system. Infect Control Hosp Epidemiol. 2007;28(4):496–9.
24. Nosocomial infection rates for interhospital comparison: limitations and possible solutions. A Report from the National Nosocomial Infections Surveillance (NNIS) System. Infect Control Hosp Epidemiol. 1991;12:609–621.
25. Vincent JL, Bihari DJ, Suter PM, Bruining HA, White J, Nicolas-Chanoine MH, Wolff M, Spencer RC, Hemmer M. The prevalence of nosocomial infection in intensive care units in Europe. Results of the European Prevalence of Infection in Intensive Care (EPIC) Study. EPIC International Advisory Committee [see comments]. JAMA. 1995;274: 639–644.
26. Fabry J, Morales I, Metzger MH, Russell I, Gastmeier P. Quality of information: a European challenge. J Hosp Infect. 2007;65 Suppl 2:155–6.
27. Pocormy L, Rovira A, Martin-Baranera M, Gimeno C, Alonso-Tarres C, Vilarasau J. Automatic detection of patients with nosocomial infection by a computer-based

surveillance system: a validation study in a general hospital. Infect. Control Hosp Epidemiol. 2006;27(5): 500–3.

28. Bouam S, Girou E, Brun-Buisson C, Karadimas H, Lepage E. An intranet-based automated system for the surveillance of nosocomial infections: prospective validation compared with physicians' self-reports. Infect Control Hosp Epidemiol. 2003;24 (1):51–5.

29. Sherman ER, Heydon KH, St John KH, Teszner E, Rettig SL, Alexander SK et al. Administrative data fail to accurately identify cases of healthcare-associated infection. Infect Control Hosp Epidemiol. 2006;27(4):332–7.

30. Wilson J, Ramboer I, Suetens C. Hospitals in Europe Link for Infection Control through surveillance (HELICS). Inter-country comparison of rates of surgical site infection- opportunities and limitations. J Hosp Infect. 2007;65 Suppl 2:165–70.

31. McCoubrey J, Reilly J, Mullings A, Pollock KG, Johnston F. Validation of surgical site infection surveillance data in Scotland. J Hosp Infect. 2005;61(3):194–200.

32. Stone PW, Hedblom EC, Murphy DM, Miller SB. The economic impact of infection control: making the business case for increased infection control resources. Am J Infect Control. 2005;33(9):542–7.

33. Stone PW, Braccia D, Larson E. Systematic review of economic analyses of health care-associated infections. Am J Infect Control. 2005;33(9):501–9.

34. McKibben L, Fowler G, Horan T, Brennan PJ. Ensuring rational public reporting systems for health care-associated infections: systematic literature review and evaluation recommendations. Am J Infect Control. 2006; 34(3):142–9.

35. McKibben L, Horan T, Tokars JI, Fowler G, Cardo DM, Pearson ML et al. Guidance on public reporting of healthcare-associated infections: recommendations of the Healthcare Infection Control Practices Advisory Committee. Am J Infect Control. 2005;33(4):217–26.

36. Edmond MB, Bearman GM. Mandatory public reporting in the USA: an example to follow? J Hosp Infect. 2007;65 Suppl 2:182–8.

37. Morales I, Versporten, A, Suetens, C. Factors influencing sensitivity and specificity of the surveillance on ICU-acquired infections. Intensive Care Med. 30. [Supplement1], S137. 2004.

Richard J. Price and Brian H. Cuthbertson

Should hospitals have a medical emergency team?

Introduction

Many patients who suffer an in-hospital cardiac arrest or are admitted urgently to the intensive care unit (ICU) have a preceding period of physiological instability. Such events, in many cases, are therefore predictable. Expert review of these cases has concluded that deranged physiology may be apparent for many hours in advance (1, 2). Often these signs are not identified, or are misinterpreted or mismanaged. In many cases, the most junior doctors managed these patients (3). It is reasonable to believe that early intervention by appropriate individuals may prevent cardiac arrest, death or unplanned ICU admission.

To do this there are two key challenges: firstly to identify these patients at an early stage in their illness and secondly, to provide prompt and effective treatment to prevent these undesirable outcomes. As a system of care, the identification of deterioration is the afferent arm; the delivery of intervention is the efferent arm. There are various models described; the system as a whole, along with supporting administrative, educational and governance structure is known as a Rapid Response System (RRS) (4).

Track and trigger systems – the afferent limb

The afferent limb, identification of the sick patient, is a track and trigger concept. In the context of a RRS, physiological scoring systems are generally used and there are various such scoring systems described (5). One of the many issues with the debate on RRSs is that the various contributory studies have used different scoring systems. Validation of the scoring systems used has been highly variable or non-existent. Some of these track and trigger systems are based around derangement of one of several single parameters: once a single certain threshold is reached (e.g. pulse > 140/min), a response is requested. Others depend on an aggregated score with degrees of derangement in different observations summing to a total score. Again, the constituent observations vary, and in some, laboratory results have been included. In some systems there is a graded response depending on the total score obtained. This is the current recommendation of the National Institute for Clinical Excellence (NICE) in the United Kingdom (UK) (6). The typology and validation of such systems is a separate debate, although is clearly relevant to the resulting delivery of care.

The trigger criteria may also include an option to summon assistance in case of "clinical concern", irrespective of the physiological score. These cases may comprise a considerable proportion of the triggered responses. Cardiac or respiratory arrest also may trigger a response, although in some models, there are two separate systems operating within the same institution, both an RRS and a traditional cardiac arrest team. Sometimes these teams have the same constituent team members performing both roles.

Rapid Response Teams/Medical Emergency Teams – the efferent limb

In concept at least, if patients on a general ward develop critical illness (as identified by deranged physiology), and the resources available (personnel and equipment) do not meet their new needs, a supply-demand mismatch occurs. An approach to prevent further deterioration is to provide early intervention by individuals with critical care competencies. This delivery of care is the efferent limb.

Medical Emergency Teams (METs) were first introduced into the Liverpool Hospital, Sydney, Australia in 1990. Composition of the team varies but is often at least an ICU doctor and nurse and usually others. It has been suggested that a MET ought to have the equipment and skills to establish intensive care level treatment in the ward environment (4). Some would say this was inappropriate (7). Any member of staff can call the MET, medical, nursing or allied professions. This aims to induce a cultural shift within hospitals by empowering ward nurses, or others, to summon critical care expertise rather than the traditional hierarchical system of referral to the junior doctor of the admitting team. The MET is summoned in a similar manner and with comparable urgency to a traditional cardiac arrest team. This enables early treatment through the application of critical care interventions, intensive care admission or follow-up. A further role of an experienced critical care doctor may also be to make the decision to not escalate treatment further or "do not attempt resuscitation" (DNAR) orders. These may be a positive outcome for individual patients especially those who are terminally ill or would not benefit from aggressive treatment. Placement of these orders is a common intervention of a MET.

Critical Care Outreach (CCO) is another means of delivering the intervention arm, and is widely used in the UK. The concept is slightly different and is predominately nurse-led, doctors are not first responders in these systems. Studies of CCO have demonstrated their variable remit (8). Models have included the planned follow-up of discharged ICU patients, planned review of high-risk patients and specialist nursing support (e.g. for tracheostomy care). There may also be the provision of the efferent limb of an RRS.

Rapid Response Systems, as a whole, have been the recommendation of the UK Comprehensive Critical Care Report (9), the UK Resuscitation Council (10) and in the USA, the Institute for Health Improvement (11). Recently, the subject has been reviewed as an expert consensus conference (4), a review by NICE (5), two systematic reviews (7, 12) and a Cochrane review (13). Each of these reviews has generally concluded that the available evidence is weak and that the investigated models of care differ. One of the problems of these reviews is the tendency to combine a variety of models of nurse-led outreach with METs. METs are medically-led and delivered and the model has been similar amongst different study centres. This discussion will only consider the case for and against METs.

The case for Medical Emergency Teams

The rationale for a MET is both obvious and intuitive; that is, to provide a medically-based critical care resource to critically ill patients wherever they may be. The current system in many hospitals involves inevitable delays within a hierarchical system that consists of individuals who may not possess the appropriate skills to treat deteriorating patients. As well as providing for a means of detecting and intervening in critical illness, METs also introduces a system of governance, education and case review to enable quality improvement. The potential of the MET system for detection of medical error has been reported (14).

Thirteen studies have looked at the introduction of METs; two of these are from the same institution. One of the earlier studies compared the first Australian hospital with an MET to two nearby hospitals with conventional cardiac arrest teams (15). This was in a prospective manner over six months. A comparison was made between the hospital with the MET and each of the two control hospitals without. Although the incidences of death and cardiac arrest were unaltered, unanticipated intensive care and high dependency unit (HDU) admissions were reduced. As would be expected, there were differences between the hospital patient populations. Although differences were statistically corrected, this was probably incomplete (16). There were differences in event rates of death and cardiac arrest between the two non-MET (control) hospitals, as well as more DNAR orders in the MET hospital. Overall, the authors reported this study as an interesting provisional finding. The accompanying editorial (16) was positive in outlook, and commented that at least there was no evidence of harm.

Further evidence demonstrating a positive effect of METs comes from several single centre studies, with before-and-after methodologies. An appraisal of the effect of a MET on the incidence of, and mortality from, cardiac arrest by Buist et al. (17) suggested benefit. They found that the corrected odds ratio for a cardiac arrest call following introduction of a MET was 0.50 (0.35–0.73). One limitation of the study however was the use of cardiac arrest *call* as the end-point. This is not the same as a cardiac arrest, nor is it an objective end-point. In their system, there was both a MET and a traditional cardiac arrest team working in the same small institution. The reduction in cardiac arrest calls may have just represented a shift in the call from one system to the other. Additionally, the MET instituted 17 DNAR orders for 124 patients seen in the year. They did report a reduction in the mortality of patients in whom a cardiac arrest call had been made. This is encouraging but it is difficult to place into a wider context given the limitations of the study.

DeVita et al. (18) ran a program to advertise, expand and promote an existing MET. They also looked at the incidence of cardiac arrest calls that occurred as MET calls increased. There was a reduced incidence of cardiac arrest calls from 6.5 to 5.4 per 1,000 admissions (p = 0.02). Attempts to correct for case mix difference were made but not detailed. Similar to Buist et al. (17), there were two systems operating in the same hospital. Again, while the results are superficially encouraging, the use of a cardiac arrest call as an end-point is difficult to interpret. In this study, the proportion of fatal cardiac arrests did not change significantly.

In one of two studies to come from the UK, Goldhill et al. (19) compared ICU patients seen by the MET prior to admission with patients that had not. There was no control over how this occurred. In this study the MET was called a Patient At Risk Team. The composition was similar to an MET and only differed in the suggestion that it should ideally be called by a doctor, not by any member of staff. Patients that had been seen by the PART had a much lower incidence of pre-ICU cardiac arrest (4% *vs.* 30%) and lower mortality. It was only an incidental positive finding in a study that had a different purpose. While this is encouraging, there was no correction for the inevitable case mix differences that may have occurred. Overall, while these studies (15, 17–19) give encouraging suggestions to the potential efficacy of METs they had significant flaws in their design and presentation.

A hospital-wide MET was introduced to the Austin hospital, Melbourne. Two prospective studies were reported which appeared more robust within the limits of the before-and-after study design and both suggested an outcome benefit. One study investigated the incidence of cardiac arrest in the hospital-wide population (20). In the four months prior to a MET there were 63 cardiac arrests with 37 deaths. In the four months afterwards there were 22 cardiac arrests and 16 deaths. Both time periods had similar admission populations of around 21,000. Total in-patient deaths were also reduced from 302 to 222.

They also investigated the effect of the MET on the incidence of specific post-operative complications in major surgical patients (21). These included respiratory failure, renal replacement and severe sepsis. The study again was conducted for the same 4 months before and after introduction. In all, there were around 1,300 procedures in 1,100 patients. Overall, there was a significant reduction in the occurrence of these pre-defined adverse events from 301 per 1,000 patients to 127 per 1,000 patients (relative risk reduction 58%, p < 0.001). There were relative risk reductions of around 80% for each of respiratory failure, stroke, renal replacement and severe sepsis. Emergency ICU admissions were reduced from 89 to 48. The reduction in post-operative death was 37% and this equated to a saving of 23 lives per 1,000 surgical admissions.

A similar before-and-after study has recently been reported from the USA with a MET staffed by physician assistants rather than doctors (22).

These individuals appeared to possess appropriate skills, including intubation with drugs. In the five months before MET there were a mean 7 arrests per 1,000 patients per month. In the 13 months following the introduction of the MET there were 3 arrests per 1,000 patients per month. Interventions performed by the team were summarised and this included endotracheal intubation being performed in 38 of 344 calls. Other authors have similarly listed interventions performed by their METs (20, 21, 23). These were often straightforward with specific skills such as intubation being more unusual; twice in 47 calls (23) and 3 in 99 calls (20). Again, in this recent US study (22), placement of DNAR orders comprised ten percent of their activity.

These studies have demonstrated a positive effect of METs. From an evidence-based medicine perspective, the level of evidence is weak and most of these studies can be considered as Level 2 evidence at most (24), with a significant likelihood of bias. It is known that before-and-after study methodologies commonly show a positive effect of the intervention when one may not be present (25, 26). Although the randomised controlled trial presents a higher level of evidence, it has been suggested in a recent editorial that complex systems of care such as the MET, which require gradual cultural shifts within a hospital structure, are simply not amenable to such methodologies (27). The introduction of an MET may not incur particular cost, risk or difficulty. It could be argued that an MET should be introduced prior to the strongest level of evidence being available, this has been called the proportionality of burden of proof (4).

These studies have concerned only the adult hospital environment. Two studies have now introduced METs into a paediatric setting. An MET was introduced into a major Australian paediatric centre, and there was a non-significant reduction in the incidence of cardiac arrests (28). In the second study (29), again with before-and-after methodology, the introduction of an MET appeared to reduce the combined incidence of cardiac and respiratory arrest from 0.27 per 1,000 (non-ICU) patient days to 0.11 per 1,000 patient days with a risk ratio 0.42. The absolute numbers were small at 36 over the entire study period of 27 months. Statistical significance was only reached with the use of one-tailed testing which is inappropriate and

the result should be treated with caution. Overall, the evidence base in the paediatric setting is not yet comparable.

The case against Medical Emergency Teams

There are two issues to consider. Firstly, is the evidence in favour of METs flawed to the point that it cannot be trusted, i.e. absence of evidence? Secondly, is there good quality evidence to suggest that METs are not beneficial i.e. evidence of absence? In the argument against METs, it is worth considering that there is no particular evidence in favour of the current cardiac arrest team system. At least within the literature, there does not appear to be any suggestion that METs are in some way harmful, although the potential effect on ward level care and skill retention has been raised as an issue (30). The cost of such systems has not been fully described, additional funding may be needed for any personnel required above those who already function as part of a cardiac arrest team. Costs may be saved in reduction of ICU and hospital stay if METs are beneficial.

Is the favourable evidence flawed? Some of the problems of the above studies have already been outlined i.e. the comparability of different hospitals and the use of cardiac arrest calls as an outcome measure. Further problems with the use of before-and-after methodology include seasonal variations, case mix differences and gradual temporal changes in healthcare provision. These can and have been accounted for statistically to a certain degree. The next issue is to ask if these studies have good internal and external validity and appropriate generalisability to allow them to be applied to other centres. The introduction of these systems is generally accompanied by an intensive education period which includes recognition of the sick patient as well as the practicalities of the MET. There may be an MET fellow or MET nurse to provide education and promote the team. Bellomo et al. (21) described that although superficially there appeared to have been 73 lives saved in the surgical population following introduction of the MET, the MET was only called 47 times. The introduction of the MET may be inducing changes in the approach to the recognition of the sick patient beyond that which can be accounted

Is there evidence that METs do not alter outcomes? Within the limits of the same before-and-after study design, there have been two studies that did not demonstrate improvement. Within the UK, Kenward et al. (23) looked at the effect of introduction of an MET on the incidence of cardiac arrest and in-hospital death. The study covered a time period of a year before and after the introduction of MET. Unlike the Australian and US studies, the scoring system used was an aggregate score that led to a graded response. The authors demonstrated validation work on this score in a previously published study (31). In the year with the MET there was no difference in either cardiac arrest (2.4 vs. 2.6 per 1,000 admissions) or in-hospital deaths (19.7 vs. 20.0 per 1,000 admissions). There was not any demonstration of case mix similarity and the negative result again may be due to either case mix differences or random fluctuations. The authors proposed that they had not allowed enough time for the system to bed in and it appears that after the introduction of the MET data collection started immediately.

Several authors have raised this same concept of allowing the MET to establish within hospital culture. The problem of investigating long-term outcome in a before-and-after setting is that changes in medical practices and local facilities may be more likely to occur as time goes on. Two Australian centres have reported longer-term follow-up. Salamonson et al. (32) reported the effects of the first three years of MET activity. Therefore it was not strictly a before-and-after study, rather made the assumption that as time progressed, the MET activity would increase. The number of calls made did increase from 54 in year 1 to 130 in year 3, but the incidence of cardiac arrest and in-hospital death did not change.

Long-term follow up from the Austin hospital has been published recently (33, 34). Overall, the incidence of cardiac arrest was reduced over four years compared to "pre-MET" figures (33). However, when the incidence of in-hospital deaths was compared over discrete one-year periods to the pre-MET figures, an initial reduction in mortality in surgical patients was not sustained and mortality in medical patients appeared to increase (34). The MET was more likely to attend surgical pa-

tients and the authors did suggest that this was a possible reason for the lower comparable mortality seen between medical and surgical patients. The activity of the MET may correlate inversely with the incidence of cardiac arrest (33).

The MERIT (Medical Early Response, Intervention and Therapy) study (35) is the largest and most robust study of METs. It involved 23 Australian hospitals in a prospective cluster-randomised trial. The primary outcome was the composite of unexpected death, cardiac arrest and unplanned ICU admission. Baseline data were collected from all hospitals for two months prior to randomisation and METs were introduced to 12 hospitals. In the control hospitals, data collection continued but no other changes were made and the usual cardiac arrest team continued to function. In the MET hospitals, baseline data collection continued and a 4-month intensive education and introductory program started. The MET was introduced and data collection continued for another six months in all hospitals. In the MET hospitals, there was not any improvement in the composite outcome (unexpected death, cardiac arrest and unplanned ITU admission); 5.3 per 1,000 patients *versus* 5.9 per 1,000 patients in the control hospitals (p = 0.640). Between the baseline and intervention periods, there was a significant reduction in the primary composite outcome only in the *control* (*i.e.* no MET) hospitals 7.1 to 5.9 per 1,000 patients (p = 0.030). The before-and-after reduction in the composite primary outcome in MET hospitals was not statistically significant: 6.6 to 5.3 per 1,000 patients (p = 0.612).

The study has been criticised and may have been underpowered. It was powered to detect a 30% reduction in the composite outcome from 3% to 2.1%, but the baseline incidence of the composite outcome was only 0.68%. Within the control hospitals, 48% of the cardiac arrest calls were not true cardiac arrests or deaths. It has been speculated that this demonstrates MET-like activity in the control hospitals.

The MERIT study used a single parameter scoring system. It demonstrated that this particular system failed to allow early recognition of sick patients. There were, in total, 611 unplanned ICU admissions from the wards in the MET hospitals, yet a MET call was only made for 209 (34%) of these patients. Only 313 (51%) of these 611 patients had MET criteria documented more than

Airway
If Threatened
Breathing
All respiratory arrests Respiratory Rate < 5 breaths per min Respiratory Rate > 36 breaths per min
Circulation
All cardiac arrests Pulse Rate < 40 beats per min Pulse Rate > 36 beats per min Systolic blood pressure < 90mmHg
Neurology
Sudden fall in level of consciousness (fall in Glasgow coma scale of > 2 points) Repeated or extended seizures
Other
Any patient you are seriously worried about that does not fit the above criteria.

Fig. 1   Examples of the MET scoring systems. Reprinted from The Lancet, 365, MERIT Study Investigators. Introduction of the medical emergency team (MET) system: a cluster randomised controlled trial. 2091–7, 2005, with permission from Elsevier.

15 minutes before the event. Of these 313 patients only 95 had a call to the MET made.

Why is there an apparent lack of efficacy? It may be that the MET calling criteria are not appropriately sensitive and specific. The scoring system used in the MERIT study was based on there being a marked derangement of one of several physiological parameters (see fig. 1). Only one of the mentioned studies demonstrated validation work on their scoring system used (23). The scoring systems are designed to summon critical care resource, not necessarily to be a predictor of outcome. To a certain extent, these criteria have been shown to correlate to outcome (36, 37, 38) but the sensitivity remains low (39). Recent systematic reviews of the subject have highlighted deficits in this area (5, 8). There is a variable use of the "worried" category as the basis of the MET call from 23 in

400 calls (40) to 46 of 99 calls (20); this may suggest a lack of sensitivity. The SOCCER (38) study demonstrated that a variety of relatively early signs of derangement may predict adverse events. A recent cohort study has suggested that admission to the ICU from the HDU (41) and mortality in a medical assessment unit (42) may be predicted by comparatively subtle derangements in physiology. Even if the scoring system is appropriate, when the criteria are met, a lack of appropriate utilisation of the MET system has been the comment of several authors and was a finding of the MERIT study. The need for ongoing education and revision of the system has been described even where the MET is established (43, 44). Finally, if the call is made, then all these systems do is to summon a team. Formal training in MET call response has been introduced, along with a more protocolised approach to patient management (40). Although the interventions performed by the METs have been often fairly simple, no author has demonstrated external governance of the actions of the MET.

In the context of a study, the end points assessed, such as death, cardiac arrest or ICU admission, may not have been appropriate. A medical emergency need not always conclude in one of these end points. The reduction in HDU and ITU admissions may not be a reasonable endpoint as perhaps these patients ought to be being admitted to such environments. The introduction of these systems may have involved a prolonged education package. This may have accounted for the benefit seen, particularly within the setting of a single centre with motivated individuals. Finally, it could be argued that METs simply do not work and we need to consider other approaches to this problem; might the answer be in the education of ward doctors and nurses to recognise critical illness and initiate treatment in a timely manner, rather than a system that separates the identification of, and response to, critically ill patients?

Conclusions

Current evidence on METs is varied with some studies suggesting a beneficial effect, and others demonstrating no effect. The majority of studies are of low quality with clear potential sources of bias that may account for either effect. Within the mentioned caveats of the study, the MERIT study (level of evidence 1[+]) is the most robust. Overall this would suggest an evidence of an absence of benefit for METs. Reasons for this may include a lack of sensitivity and specificity of scoring systems, inappropriate staffing, inappropriate or inadequate interventions, incorrect outcomes or a lack of efficacy for MET. Cost-effectiveness has not been studied to date and future efficacy studies must include cost-effectiveness as a key outcome.

Key points for clinical practice

1. *The success of MET systems may depend on each of the constituent components, the physiological scoring system needs to be appropriately sensitive and specific, the call needs to be made and the appropriate individuals need to perform suitable interventions.*

2. *The evidence to date suggests that METs are not efficacious. Further robust research is required before we can be confident in their widespread introduction. In the era after the MERIT study, this is unlikely to occur. Validation of the physiological track-and-trigger and assessment of cost-effectiveness would need to be part of any future assessment.*

3. *We need to learn from our mistakes and in future we must submit new interventions to robust studies of efficacy and cost-effectiveness before implementation. The failure to do this for MET, followed by its widespread implementation despite the lack of evidence, may have denied us a chance to demonstrate efficacy and cost-effectiveness and may now lead to disinvestment in this area.*

The authors

Richard J. Price, FRCA[1]
Brian H. Cuthbertson, MD, FRCA[2]
[1]Specialist Registrar | Intensive Care Unit | Western Infirmary, Glasgow
[2]Consultant and Clinical Senior Lecturer | Health Services Research Unit and Intensive Care Unit | Health Sciences Building and University of Aberdeen | Aberdeen Royal Infirmary | Foresterhill, Aberdeen, UK

Address for correspondence
    Brian H. Cuthbertson
    Consultant and Clinical Senior Lecturer
    Health Services Research Unit and
    Intensive Care Unit
    Health Sciences Research Unit,
    University of Aberdeen
    AB25 2ZD Foresterhill, Aberdeen, UK
    e-mail: b.h.cuthbertson@abdn.ac.uk

References

1. Schein RM, Hazday N, Pena M, Ruben BH, Sprung CL. Clinical antecedents to in-hospital cardiopulmonary arrest. Chest. 1990; 98:1388–1392.
2. Franklin C, Mathew J. Developing strategies to prevent in-hospital cardiac arrest: analysing responses of physicians and nurses in the hours before the event. Crit Care Med. 1994;22:244–247.
3. National Confidential Enquiry into Patient Outcome and Death (NCEPOD). An acute problem? A report of the national confidential enquiry into patient outcome and death. London: NCEPOD 2005.
4. DeVita MA, Bellomo R, Hillman K, Kellum J, Rotondi A, Teres D et al. Findings of the first consensus conference on medical emergency teams. Crit Care Med. 2006;34: 2463–2478.
5. Gao H, McDonnell A, Harrison DA, Moore T, Adam S, Daly K et al. Systematic review and evaluation of physiological track and trigger systems for identifying at risk patients on the ward. Intensive Care Medicine. 2007;33: 667–679.
6. www.nice.org.uk/guidance/index. jsp?action=download&o=35950
7. Cuthbertson BH. Outreach critical care – cash for no questions? Brit J Anaesth. 2003;91:4–5.
8. Esmonde L, McDonnell A, Ball C, Waskett C, Morgan R, Rashidian A et al. Investigating the effectiveness of critical care outreach: a systematic review. Intensive Care Med. 2006;32:1713–1721.
9. Department of Health. Comprehensive Critical Care. A review of adult critical care services. London: Department of Health, 2000.
10. Resuscitation Council (UK). Cardiopulmonary Resuscitation. Standards for Clinical Practice and Training. Resuscitation Council. London 2007.
11. Berwick DM, Calkins DR, McCannon CJ, Hackbarth AD. The 100,000 lives campaign. JAMA. 2006;295;324–327.
12. Winters BD, Cuong Pham J, Hunt EA, Gualler E, Berenholtz S, Pronovost PJ. Rapid response systems: a systematic review. Crit Care Med. 2007;35:1238–1243.
13. McGaughey J, Alderdice F, Fowler R, Kapila A, Mayhew A, Moutray M. Outreach and early warning systems for the prevention of intensive care admission and death of critically ill adult patients on general hospital wards.

Cochrane Database of Systematic Reviews. 2007 (3). CD005529.

14. Braithwaite RS, DeVita MA, Mahidhara R, Simmons RL, Stuart S, Foraida M. Use of medical emergency team (MET) responses to detect medical errors. Qual. Saf. Health Care. 2004;13;255–259.

15. Bristow PJ, Hillman KM, Chey T, Daffurn K, Jacques TC, Norman SL et al. Rates of in-hospital arrests, deaths and intensive care admissions: the effect of a medical emergency team. Med J Aust. 2000;173:236–240.

16. Kerridge RK. The medical emergency team: no evidence to justify not implementing change. Med J Aust. 2000; 173:228–229.

17. Buist MD, Moore GE, Bernard SA, Waxman BP, Anderson JN, Nguyen TV. Effects of a medical emergency team on reduction of and mortality from unexpected cardiac arrests in hospital: preliminary study. BMJ. 2002;324:1–6.

18. DeVita MA, Braithwaite RS, Mahidhara R, Stuart S, Foraida M, Simmons RL. Use of medical emergency team responses to reduce hospital cardiopulmonary arrests Qual. Saf. Health Care. 2004;13;251–254.

19. Goldhill DR, Worthington L, Mulcahy A, Tarling M, Sumner A. The patient-at-risk team: identifying and managing seriously ill ward patients. Anaesthesia. 1999;54;853–860.

20. Bellomo R, Goldsmith D, Uchino S, Buckmaster J, Hart G, Opdam H et al. A prospective before-and-after trial of a medical emergency team. Med J Aust. 2003;179: 283–287.

21. Bellomo R, Goldsmith D, Uchino S, Buckmaster J, Hart G, Opdam H et al. Prospective controlled trial of effect of medical emergency team on postoperative morbidity and mortality rates. Crit Care Med. 2004;32:916–921.

22. Dacey MJ, Mirza ER, Wilcox V, Doherty M, Mello J, Boyer A et al. The effect of a rapid response team on major clinical outcome measures in a community hospital. Crit Care Med. 2007;35:2076–2082.

23. Kenward G, Castle N, Hodgetts T, Shaikhd L. Evalution of a Medical Emergency Team one year after implementation. Resuscitation. 2004;61:257–263.

24. Harbour R, Miller J. A new system for grading recommendations in evidence based guidelines. Br Med J. 2001;323:334–6.

25. Shadish WR, Cook TD, Campbell DT. Experimental and quasi-experimental designs for generalised causal inference. Boston MA: Houghton Mifflin 2001.

26. Cook TD, Campbell DT. Quasi-experimentation: Design and analysis issues for field settings. London: Houghton Mifflin 1979.

27. DeVita MA, Bellomo R. The case of rapid response systems: are randomised controlled trials the right methodology to evaluate systems of care? Crit Care Med. 2007;35:1413–1414.

28. Tibballs J, Kinney S, Duke T, Oakley E, M Hennessy M. Reduction of paediatric in-patient cardiac arrest and death with a medical emergency team: preliminary results. Arch. Dis. Child. 2005;90;1148–1152.

29. Brilli RJ, Gibson R, Luria JW, Wheeler TA, Shaw J, Linam M et al. Implementation of a medical emergency team in a large pediatric teaching hospital prevents respiratory and cardiopulmonary arrests outside the intensive care unit. Pediatr Crit Care Med. 2007; 8:236–246.

30. Al-Khafaji A, Cho SM. Rapid response systems: let's not get carried away! Crit Care Med. 2007;35:2235.

31. Hodgetts TJ, Kenward G, Vlackonikolis I, Payne S, Castle N, Crouch R et al. Incidence, location and reasons for avoidable in-hospital cardiac arrest in a district general hospital. Resuscitation. 2002;54:115–123.

32. Salamonson Y, Kariyawasam A, van Heere B, O'Connor C. The evolutionary process of Medical Emergency Team (MET) implementation: reduction in unanticipated ICU transfers. Resuscitation. 2001;49:135–141.

33. Jones D, Bellomo R, Bates S, Warrillow S, Goldsmith D, Hart G et al. Long term effect of a medical emergency team on cardiac arrests in a teaching hospital. Critical Care. 2005;9:R808–R815.

34. Jones D, Opdam H, Egi M, Goldsmith D, Bates S, Gutteridge G et al. Long-term effect of a Medical Emergency Team on mortality in a teaching hospital. Resuscitation. 2007;74:235–241.

35. MERIT Study Investigators. Introduction of the medical emergency team (MET) system: a cluster randomised controlled trial. Lancet. 2005;365:2091–7.

36. Buist M, Bernard S, Nguyen TV, Moore G, Anderson J. Association between clinically abnormal observations and subsequent in-hospital mortality: a prospective study. Resuscitation. 2004;62:137–141.

37. Bell MB, Konrad D, Granath F, Ekbom A, Martling GR. Prevalance and sensitivity of MET criteria in a Scandinavian University Hospital. Resuscitation. 2006;70:66–73.

38. Jaques T, Harrison GA, McLaws ML, Kilborn G. Signs of critical conditions and emergency responses (SOCCER): a model for prediciting adverse events in an inpatient setting. Resuscitation. 2006;69:175–183.

39. Cretikos M, Chen J, Hillman K, Bellomo R, Finfer S, Flabouris A. The objective medical emergency team activation criteria: A case control study. Resuscitation. 2007;73:62–72.

40. Jones D, Duke G, Green J, Briedis J, Bellomo R, Casamento A et al. Medical Emergency Team syndromes and an approach to their management. Crit Care. 2006;10:R30.

41. Cuthbertson BH, Boroujerdi M, McKie L, Aucott L, Prescott G. Can physiological variables and early warning scoring systems allow early recognition of the deteriorating surgical pediatric patient? Crit Care Med. 2007;35:402–409.

42. Duckitt RW, Buxton-Thomas R, Walker J, Cheek E, Bewick V, Venn R, Forni LG. Worthing physiological scoring system: derivation and validation of a physiological early-warning scoring system for medical admissions. An observational, population based single-centre study. Br J Anaesth. 2007;98:769–774.

43. Jones D, Bates S, Warrillow S, Goldsmith D, Kattula A, Way M et al. Effect of an education programme on the utilization of a medical emergency team in a teaching hospital. Int Med J. 2006;36:231–236.

44. Jones DA, Mitra B, Barbetti J, Choate K, Leong T, Bellomo R. Increasing the use of an existing medical emergency team in a teaching hospital. Anaesth Intensive Care. 2006;34:731–735.

Antonios Liolios

E-learning

Introduction and some definitions

"Get the machine that goes 'ping'! ... Still something missing though ...
Patient! Where's the patient?"
                    Monty Python's "The meaning of life", 1983,
                    labour scene

As new electronic media are continuously added and used for educational purposes the precise definition of electronic learning (or e-learning as it is widely known) has become a challenge (1). Terms synonymous with or related to e-learning in the literature are computer-assisted learning (CAL), computer-aided instruction (CAI), computer-based training (CBT), internet-based learning (IBL), web-based learning (WBL) and many others. As technology evolves, newer terms such as mobile learning (m-learning) (2), podcasting, webcasting, webinar (3) are constantly added, creating a state of confusion as to what exactly e-learning is.

For this article and for the sake of simplicity, our working definition of e-learning will be "learning with the assistance of electronic means".

From this perspective, e-learning can occur via the worldwide web (web) and its communication potential (e-mail, videoconferencing, chatting etc.) or with computer-based interactive teaching applications.

E-learning is called *synchronous* when there is real-time communication between the tutor and students. In this case the teacher and the students interact live and instantly by chat or videoconference, a condition resembling regular classes. E-learning without real-time communication is called *asynchronous*. In this case communication occurs at a later time usually by e-mail, there is a time lag in feedback and the student sets the pace of his study. When the teacher and the student are not in geographic proximity it is called *distant learning*. Finally, the *"blended"* approach is when traditional face-to-face teaching is combined with various forms of e-learning.

It is interesting that the online version of the traditional Merriam-Webster dictionary does not contain the term e-learning (4). In contrast, definitions are available at exclusively online resources such as Webopedia (5) and Wikipedia (6). The excitement about the addition of tutoring-assisting media in education is not new; television and radio have long been used for educational purposes especially in remote areas of Africa (7–9). Furthermore, telemedicine has been used for education and patient care in the remote islands of Greece and other geographically isolated and occasionally inaccessible areas since the 80s (10–13).

Three factors have revolutionised the concept of e-learning in a dramatic way:
- Availability and affordability of computers for the general public
- Increase in computing power and storage (with the consequent capability of multimedia handling)
- Advent and evolution of the internet

Services and data access feasible today were in the realm of imagination or science fiction only a decade ago.

Despite its popularity, convenience and intuitive value, e-learning is not without problems and limitations. In this article we will try to examine both facets of what appears to be the greater stride of humanity towards global advancement of education and knowledge dissemination. Besides discussing the pros and cons of e-learning, we will also view some of today's available e-learning tools for the physician and the health care professional.

Brief historical note

The internet is in essence a method of connecting individual computers or networks to each other. By simply linking their computers, users can exchange data almost instantly. Originally, linking was accomplished via cable/wire, and more recently, via satellite and wireless connections. Linked computers may be standing side by side in the same room or at opposite ends of the globe without appreciable difference in data transfer speed.

The telegraph can be viewed as the predecessor of the internet (14). It uses a binary code (dots and dashes) and its electronic signal standard of ±15 volts is still used in network interface cards today (15).

In 1968 the Defence Advanced Research Projects Agency (DARPA) collaborated with BBN (Bolt, Beranek & Newman) to create the ARPAnet primarily for military purposes. It was the first internet of the kind we know today. In 1970 the first five nodes included the University of California, Los Angeles (UCLA), the University of Stanford, the Santa Barbara University of California, the University of Utah and BBN. Telephone lines and modems were used for data transfer. In 1973 the Transmission Control Protocol/Internet Protocol (TCP/IP) was developed by Vinton Cerf and Robert Kahn, and on January 1, 1984, it was widely accepted for internet communication standardisation. The addition of the Hyper Text Markup Language (HTML) by Tim Berners-Lee permitted the evolution of the web and the appearance of web pages in the form we are familiar with today. The web was opened for free to the general public in 1993. Since then, the evolution of the internet has paralleled that of computing power (15). The introduction of affordable broadband connections for home use has boosted internet dissemination even further (16).

The first article on the role of computers in medical data processing appeared in the PubMed database in 1960 (17), the keyword "internet" in 1991 (18) and "e-learning" in 1999 (19).

Since then we have been witnessing an exponential increase in computer power accompanied by a substantial decrease in cost. One method of evaluating computing power is the concept of million instructions per second (MIPS). It was estimated in 1998 that 100 million MIPS are required to match human brain power; it was also predicted that this goal will be reached in home computers before 2030 (20). Currently, artificial intelligence assists in data acquisition, data processing and medical reasoning in critical care (21).

What is learning?

Learning can be defined as the acquisition, assimilation and application of knowledge. The effectiveness of learning can be evaluated by the ability of the learner to apply the acquired knowledge independently, comprehensively and effectively. For example, a physician taught physical examination should be able to discern pertinent physical findings and to reach the correct diagnosis by combining them without the assistance of an instructor.

Since antiquity, medicine has been considered a blend of science and art; as such, the teacher-student relationship has always been essential. This is reflected in the Hippocratic Oath, where the new physician has to swear that *"To hold him who taught me this art equally dear to me as my parents, to be a partner in life with him, and to fulfil his needs when required"* (22). Furthermore, the practice of clinical medicine is centred on patient contact and interaction with colleagues during rounds, both highly social activities. As basic science has developed, added curricula have created the need for an additional formal didactic approach. Medical students have to sit for increasingly longer periods attending class lectures; it would be years before they would be allowed to synthesise this vast amount of information in front of a real patient. There is where e-learning initially came into play.

Learning in style

Different people cognize and learn differently. Several classifications of the various cognitive learning styles (CLS) have been described.

Different models of CLS can be evaluated with the help of various instruments. The most commonly used are the Visual, Aural, Read/write, and Kinesthetic questionnaire (VARK), Index of Learning Styles (ILS), Myers-Briggs Type Indicator (MBTI) and Cognitive State Analysis (CSA). These questionnaires classify learners as introvert vs. extrovert, sensing vs. intuitive, holistic vs. analytic, verbaliser vs. imager, etc. A detailed description of these topics is beyond the scope of this article, but the importance of these classifications lies in the fact that people with different CLS respond favourably to different teaching modalities.

For example, in the holistic-analytic versus the verbal-imagery type, the holist is synthetic, needs structure and social interaction and constructs a broad picture of the provided knowledge. This type was shown to learn or process information with different effectiveness depending on the teaching approach (aptitude-treatment interaction) (23). The analytic type, on the other hand, needs less structure and tends to examine information in depth. Verbalisers memorise words or verbal associations, and imagers retain mental pictures (24).

Learners can also be classified as visual, auditory, read-write, and kinesthetic depending on the method mostly facilitating individual learning. Most learners exhibit a combination of the four abilities and are classified as multimodal (25).

Based on these classifications, some studies have reported gender differences in the prevailing CLS (26, 27), although others have not confirmed this observation (28). Gender differences have also been reported in portable digital assistant (PDA) use (29) and electronic medical records (EMR) adaptation (30).

The impact of the CLS was shown in various studies in which cognitive style affected performance (31, 32). In a more recent study by McNulty et al., students underwent CAI after taking the MBTI test. The CAI included a discussion forum or an online tutorial. A significant variation in CAI utilisation was seen depending on the CLS profile of each student (for example, "sensing" individuals tended to use CAI more than those classified as "intuitives") (33). Although other studies failed to reveal an association (34, 35) these results demonstrate the potential importance of the underlying CLS when offering e-learning.

Besides CLS, research has shown that short-term memory can register and maintain a limited number of elements. The short-term memory's load during cognition is called cognitive load. If this capacity is exceeded, cognition may be impaired. It is important that learning material is presented in a form minimising cognitive load. This concept is particularly relevant to e-learning as multimedia can handle many modalities which can easily cause information overload (36). Moreover, the cognitive load can affect quality of care (37). Due to their hectic working environment, emergency department physicians are particularly prone to cognitive load and errors; therefore, electronic point-of-care support media should be designed with this perspective (38).

Another important issue is that poor visual-spatial ability may adversely influence cognition and comprehension. In a study involving psychology students undertaking brain anatomy classes with the assistance of 3-D animation, multiple three-dimensional views impeded learning (39).

Multimedia-based e-learning can empower learners to adjust the teaching medium, content and pace to their personal learning style and needs (40). CLS, learning and educational theories and research should be all taken into account when designing, purchasing and implementing e-learning media (41, 42).

Does e-learning work?

One of the major advantages of e-learning is that it can be fun. Graphics, sounds, animation, videos and interactivity impart a flavour of game-playing to the learning process. It is no surprise that after initial hesitation (43), most learners around the globe found e-learning very pleasant and attractive (44–50).

But are there brains beyond the good looks? Does e-learning translate into better outcome? Is e-learning for everyone, everywhere, and does it keep its promises? Is it here to replace or to complement traditional teaching?

The question if e-learning is as effective as human face-to-face teaching has been debated since its introduction. Fascination with technology has sometimes shifted pedagogy out of centre. And as e-learning is expensive to apply and maintain, cost-effectiveness is another major concern.

A large increase in e-learning related studies has been seen in the literature since 1996. Initially, studies were mostly descriptive, but after the initial enthusiasm faded and as e-learning spread more, a shift towards more evaluative studies was seen (51).

E-learning has been successfully used in medical teaching. Evidence-based medicine (EBM) (52), epilepsy genetics training (49), phobia and panic exposure therapy (53), urinalysis interpretation (54), musculoskeletal physical examination skills (55), paediatric developmental psychiatry evaluation (56), neuromuscular blockade management (57), were all taught effectively and enjoyably with e-learning.

Early reports comparing traditional learning with e-learning were not encouraging and this may be attributed to hardware and software limitations of the times (58). Some recent studies mentioned below indicate improved effectiveness of e-learning versus traditional face-to-face, classroom-based teaching.

The efficacy of an e-learning course on the genetics of epilepsy for physicians was compared against reading paper literature. The e-learning group showed a significant increase in knowledge compared to the traditional group (49).

Blood smear making technique was taught to veterinary students. A multimedia tutorial was given to e-learning group as opposed to the control group which attended lectures. After practical exercise both groups were tested and the e-learning group was able to make better smears (59). It should be noted though that the control group was taught in three sessions while the e-learning group received four.

A compact disk-based musculoskeletal assessment of the shoulder and knee joints significantly improved examination and knowledge skills in medical students compared to conventional teaching (55).

Web-based peripheral nervous system teaching to first year medical school students improved exam performance. It is of note that the web-based modality included case studies, review games, simulated interactive patients, flashcards and quizzes (60).

There are also many studies showing at least equivalent effectiveness of e-learning when used as a single modality or combined with traditional teaching.

Online lectures versus traditional lectures on screening for medical students (61), online surgical courses (50), Evidence-Based Medicine (EBM) and Continuing Medical Education (CME) e-learning for physicians (52, 62, 63), physiology laboratory teaching (64) principles of airway management (65), team process skills (66), web-based teaching of internal medicine residents (67), guideline teaching to physicians (68) and interactive dermatology training (69) have all shown at least equal efficiency compared to the traditional educational approach. As expected, exam scores are positively correlated with time spent e-learning (44).

It becomes apparent from the variety of the above-mentioned studies and the broad definition of e-learning that comparative studies between traditional teaching and e-learning are very difficult to conduct and interpret as disparate entities are being compared. Besides the methodological shortcomings of many of the existing studies (descriptive, retrospective, not randomised, small samples), the diversity of what e-learning encompasses does not permit meaningful comparisons; additional research and cost-effectiveness analyses are needed in this area (70, 71).

Some negative aspects of e-learning

The internet can be down and the computer can break at the worst possible moment. Viruses, power failure, file corruption, operating system incompatibilities, all conspire in causing technical problems "far too commonly" as per experienced educators (71), triggering frustration and impeding learning.

While e-learning can be a great educational tool for patients and physicians alike, a significant percentage of medical case teaching and patient information sites are of poor quality, incomplete, outdated and do not abide by the principles of effective learning (72, 73, 74, 75, 76). Furthermore, peer review of e-learning material is not as robust as in print journals (77). The journal "Nature" attempted open, eponymous, online peer review of submitted articles but the initiative received poor response from the authors and was finally abandoned (78).

Social isolation has been quoted as a disadvantage of e-learning and some individuals need to exercise self-discipline in order to complete an e-course (71). Although social isolation is not a feature of blended learning and synchronous e-learning, it may be a necessity for the student who is timid or lives in a geographically remote area.

Cost can be considerable when implementing e-learning especially when the information technology infrastructure of the institution or school is poor. Although savings can increase for the institution and student by the reduction in printed material, classroom requirements and student accommodation, they can be offset by poor course design, software and bandwidth expenses, added faculty time, training requirements and maintenance fees (79). As more online students can be easily recruited, there is always the financial temptation to increase the tutor-to-student ratio with resulting poor course satisfaction and learning.

Finally, not everyone likes computers, the web and studying alone.

As English is the dominant language in the web, it should be kept in mind when implementing e-learning that the language barrier can decrease student performance and retention of information (80, 81).

Although computer knowledge is equivalent to literacy today, there were still computer-illiterate medical students in 2005 Austria where in one medical school 4 % of students had never used a computer before admission and 12 % made little use of available e-learning resources (82).

People still prefer human teaching and live conferences.

Physicians in residency training in Singapore found searching for article and practice guidelines helpful but preferred teaching sessions and print textbooks to e-learning (83). Fully asynchronous e-learning was not popular amongst Belgian occupational medicine postgraduate students as they favoured more communication between themselves and the teachers (84).

Despite having access to tele-education, health care providers preferred face-to-face conferences and received less than 25% of their CME credits from tele-education in one study (85). Barriers to e-learning may include time shortage, unfamiliar-ity with computers, password retrieval frustration and poor software quality (67, 86, 87).

Implementing e-learning can be taxing on the faculty because of the excess workload, inadequate hardware, insufficient training and extra time required (79, 88), e-learning and especially the asynchronous layout may estrange teachers from students, resulting in an online electronic "repository" of knowledge with minimal educational value (89).

Interesting e-learning tools: A brief look

There are many evident advantages of e-learning: It can be more cost-effective and flexible than physically attending a class or course, interactive and teamwork-promoting, self-paced, competence- and problem-based (90, 91), easily updated, more individualised, potentially faster to complete and easier to retain, standardised and easy to document, less paper-dependent, easier to register and ultimately more focused and enjoyable.

We will now move on to some of the unique and interesting applications of e-learning in the medical field after mentioning that with all its embedded links, this article is better read online!

Simulation

"See one, do one, teach one"
Anonymous clinical aphorism about clinical procedures

Human patient simulation

Mannequin-based patient simulation or human patient simulation (HPS) is a modality that has been used for many years in basic and advanced cardiac life support. Increasing computer power and developing software allows physicians to be exposed to various clinical conditions under safe and controlled conditions. Simulation may also provide training standardisation and has been used in bronchoscopy (92), airway management (93), trauma management (94), procedural skills evaluation (95), and critical care training (96, 97). Simulation-trained surgical residents acquired superior crisis management skills compared to traditional lecture-based training in one study (94).

Although HPS has not yet shown to improve outcome, it is a valuable addition to training and skills acquisition especially for aerial critical care transport teams (98) as among others these teams may face severe environmental variations (99).

Fig. 2   Live disaster drill and virtual world side-by-side: A realistic enactment. With kind permission from Springer Science+Business Media: World Journal of Surgery, Simulation for Team Training and Assessment: Case Studies of Online Training with Virtual Worlds, 32, 2008, 161–170, Heinrichs WL, Youngblood P, Harter PM, Dev P.

Virtual reality

Virtual reality (VR) is the digital re-creation of a real environment. Visual, audio and tactile interaction is possible via specially designed interfaces connecting a human to a computer. As opposed to HPS, simulation in VR does not involve any mechanical parts or mannequins.

Virtual patients (VP) have evolved into realistic applications used in critical and high-risk conditions training. They are less expensive than HPS and may allow simultaneous participation from remote locations, although currently they are limited by technical and bandwidth constraints (100) (see fig. 1 and 2). The creation of a virtual hospital and a virtual ICU have been considered for train-

ing and therapeutic purposes (101, 102). VR is also applied in less critical conditions such as surgical and geriatrics training and anatomy teaching (39, 103).

VPs have been used to teach communication skills to medical students. By employing voice recognition, hand, head and gaze tracking, a very

Fig. 1   Screen shot of a virtual world emergency case setting. Each avatar is controlled by a different human trainee who can be remotely located. Vital signs and action options are depicted on the right.
With kind permission from Springer Science+Business Media: World Journal of Surgery, Simulation for Team Training and Assessment: Case Studies of Online Training with Virtual Worlds, 32, 2008, 161–170, Heinrichs WL, Youngblood P, Harter PM, Dev P.

realistic interactive encounter was accomplished between the student and the VP (see fig. 3 and 4). Although limited by technological issues, students rated this experience almost as high as a real patient encounter (104). A system facilitating the creation of web-based VPs is in progress (105).

Although e-learning is not the best choice when teaching communication or interpersonal skills, modern VR applications are slowly bridging the gap (100, 104).

CME and EBM

CME promotes the application of EBM in everyday clinical practice and e-learning appears to be the ideal tool to assist in this direction. Online CME appears to promote guideline application as effectively as face-to-face tuition (62, 63). Currently there are hundreds of online CME providers (106).

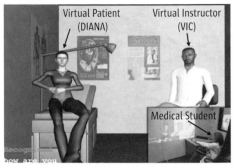

Fig. 4   The virtual patient encounter. Voice recognition is seen at the lower left. The virtual instructor on the right coordinates the diagnosis. Reprinted from: The American Journal of Surgery, 191, Stevens Amy, Hernandez Jonathan, Johnsen Kyle, Dickerson Robert, Raij Andrew, Harrison Cyrus, DiPietro Meredith, Allen Bryan, Ferdig Richard, Foti Sebastian, Jackson Jonathan, Shin Min, Cendan Juan, Watson Robert, Duerson Margaret, Lok Benjamin, et al., The use of virtual patients to teach medical students history taking and communication skills, 806–811, 2006, with permission from Elsevier.

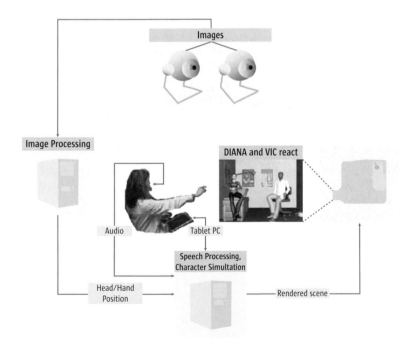

Fig. 3   Medical student-virtual patient interface. Note the two web cameras used to tract the student's head and hand position. Reprinted from: The American Journal of Surgery, 191, Stevens Amy, Hernandez Jonathan, Johnsen Kyle, Dickerson Robert, Raij Andrew, Harrison Cyrus, DiPietro Meredith, Allen Bryan, Ferdig Richard, Foti Sebastian, Jackson Jonathan, Shin Min, Cendan Juan, Watson Robert, Duerson Margaret, Lok Benjamin, et al., The use of virtual patients to teach medical students history taking and communication skills, 806–811, 2006, with permission from Elsevier.

Despite the availability of easy e-access, the recent explosive increase of the medical database created "the information paradox". Although overwhelmed with information, physicians either cannot find the information they need or cannot find it when they need it (107). Furthermore, many CME providers do not clarify the applicability of trial data to the physician's patient population (108) and a large percentage of physicians seeks the opinion of a colleague when confronted with a challenging case (109). Several online databases such as infoPOEM (110), Medscape (111), eMedicine, UptoDate (112) and others have evolved in response for the need of CME, guidelines and accurate and to the point of care information (112).

Recently, the European Union has taken the initiative for EBM standardisation aiming at "just-in-time learning through on-the-job training" (113).

Developing countries may benefit from available online EBM resources although financial restrains and lack of EBM tradition hinder broader acceptance (114, 115).

Telemedicine and tele-education

Norway, and especially its northern part, has a long tradition in telemedicine which has been used since the late 1980s. When the digital era began, telemedicine was further established and teleradiology, digital communication and distant education were implemented. Other disciplines such as teledialysis, telepsychiatry, teledermatology, teleophthalmology and ear-nose-throat (ENT) teleconsultation are also considered (13).

Due to the shortage of US physicians, an e-ICU model was devised where a physician can remotely and continuously direct more than one ICU. This model was developed as digital video and broadband internet services started becoming widely available and affordable. The physician is always available, as opposed to in-house models in which the physician may not be always physically present in the ICU. Furthermore, electronic medical records, alerts, drug interactions, guidelines and even computer-suggested diagnosis may be integrated in the system. There is evidence that the e-ICU may increase ICU quality of care, decrease mortality and lower costs. Interestingly, there is some evidence that the e-ICU may im-

prove outcome even more than the 24-hours-in-house physician model (116–119).

Surgical training has taken advantage of telepresence and teleconferencing. Live surgery performed in an operating room was transmitted to a remote classroom. Medical students gladly accepted the innovation, as they were able to ask more questions and have them answered (120). In another study a user-controlled operating room camera transmitted the surgical procedure to a remote consultant, thus improving collaboration (121).

Psychiatric teleconsultation was found to increase patient compliance, self-reported satisfaction and quality of life in a primary care clinic setting without psychiatrists on site (122). In another randomised study, telepsychiatry was found to be as effective as face-to-face consultation (123).

Teledermatology has been successfully implemented in Australia. A central portal became available for online education, therapy and follow-up (124).

As mentioned before, despite the potential benefits of tele-medicine, it is not utilised by healthcare providers to the anticipated extent. People appear to prefer live, face-to-face lectures and the associated social interaction (85, 125, 126).

Teaching in developing countries

Online training or CBT may be helpful mostly in sub-saharan Africa where discrepancies between burden of disease and health resources can be dramatic (1.3% versus 25%) (115). A malaria training programme implemented for nurses in Gambia was well received (127).

PDAs

PDAs became a commercial success in the 1990s when acceptable levels of cost, utility and portability were met. It is now a common tool in everyday clinical practice.

PDA access to drug references and other electronic resources allowed emergency medicine physicians to answer 87% of their daily practice-generated questions (128). In a study of pediatrics and emergency medicine residents, 82% used their PDA several times daily primarily as a simple medical calculator; most references sought were drug-related (129).

Wireless PDA connection is technically feasible and augments their utility potential (130). In a study involving trauma and critical care fellows, the use of a PDA with online access to a drug reference guide significantly improved antibiotic management. The PDA group was compared to a group of fellows with access to the paper edition of the same guide (131). Interference with medical equipment is always a concern when using wireless devices, especially in the ICU area. Although there is research declaring cell phones interference safe (132), there are reports supporting the restriction of using wireless devices at least 1 metre away from medical equipment (133, 134).

As technology advances, cellular phones, wireless internet access, PDAs, video and photographic cameras fuse into a single device. On the other hand, the wide range of available equipment accommodates the diverse needs of physicians as, depending on their specialty and training level, they have different preferences regarding portable devices (29).

Wikis

Collaborative web pages or wikis, as they are known ("wiki" is the Hawaiian word for "fast") (135), are websites that can be created, altered and edited by everyone. The online encyclopaedia "Wikipedia" was one of the first attempts to create a free-access collaborative learning environment. Although Wikipedia faced criticism regarding its accuracy and reliability in its initial steps, the concept was rapidly established to the point where it currently holds more than 2,284,000 entries in the English language alone (136).

Wikis appear to be very useful for a rapid and brief familiarisation with a topic and may allow easy data access, sharing and updating (137). The limitation is the potential for vandalism or plain inaccuracy. Despite these drawbacks, a study found comparable accuracy between Wikipedia and Encyclopaedia Britannica (138). Access restriction and mandatory user registration may prevent malicious contact although, in a sense, this defies the core principle of a wiki which is unlimited editorial privileges for all.

Webcasting

Educational multimedia content stored in a website can be distributed to users for later review. This process may occur without continuous user monitoring after the initial data transfer is authorised. This is the concept of webcasting, a term coined by combining the words "web" and "broadcasting". The term podcasting has also been used when the popular iPod commercial device is used to display the received media (2). Data distribution for later review is nothing new. The "walkman" (139) was the first device to allow portable audio before the digital era. The major advantage of webcasting and podcasting is user control and accessibility. New data are "pushed" to users via the internet as they become available whenever users connect to the distributing network, thus allowing the use of the requested information "anytime, anywhere" (140). Subscription to a particular podcast is possible via really simple syndication (RSS) (141). Use of interactive material further enhances the allure and utility of podcasting (3, 142). Several prestigious medical journals and critical care organisations have started offering podcast services to their subscribers (143). Podcasting technology is not incredibly complex and is relatively easy to implement (144). Hearing loss is a risk associated with headphone usage and limited daily usage is recommended (145). Furthermore, driving while manipulating a media player is hazardous and should be avoided (146).

Blogs

Blog is another new word created by the contraction of the words "Web" and "Log". In their most popular form, blogs are comment-permitting online diaries. The blogger posts (another word for online printing) a text, sound or video file on a webpage and visitors comment and/or add material to an extent set by the blog administrator. The British Medical Journal has instituted the concept of rapid response which is in essence a blog with online readers' comments after publication of an article. Interesting, although sometimes too lengthy, discussions ensue (109). Video addition to a blog has become easy via commercially available free websites allowing more productive communication and sharing (147).

Scientists have recently discovered blogging and the virtues of collective intelligence (148). Web page creation and web traffic have progressively become less expensive and technically simpler; today, anyone with minimum computer skills can create a blog or a web page at minimal or no cost. To exemplify the above, a blog was created for this very article where it can be discussed in detail. The blog was created in 3 minutes and 5 seconds at no cost (149).

Computer assisted diagnosis

Since the dawn of computers, chess playing and computer-assisted diagnosis (CAD) software have been many software developers' dream (17). Despite the impressive progress in chess software, initial enthusiasm in medicine was followed by the realisation of the inherent limits of CAD.

It appears that the most demanding part of the human diagnostic process is not data combination but data acquisition and evaluation. An experienced physician rapidly identifies the important elements of a detailed history and physical among the numerous irrelevant components presented to him or her and subsequently incorporates them into the differential diagnosis. Computer software depends solely on the data input by a human being. Additionally, abbreviations, medical synonyms, informal and idiomatic expressions are often used in medical communication, making data standardisation and entry problematic.

In an attempt to limit the scope of CAD, specialty-, disease- or condition-specific software has been developed, such as software facilitating optimal extubation timing or decision support for biopsy indication of breast lesions (150, 151).

Isabel, a commercial web-based CAD programme (152), has recently received media attention for its ability to reliably assist in the diagnosis of difficult medical cases. The programme was able to suggest the correct diagnosis in 48 of 50 (96%) cases published in the New England Journal of Medicine when keyword entry was used. It should be noted, however, that the investigator entering the keywords was aware of the correct diagnosis. When the entire case history was entered, accuracy dropped to 74 % (153). The web-based and keyword entry features of the programme allow easy access and continuous updates.

Interestingly, the commercial website Google revealed the correct diagnosis in more than half of the cases published in the same journal (15 of 26 (58%)) (154), sometimes to the surprise of the faculty (155).

Although encouraging, in medical cases "googling" (a new verb (156) for Google usage) is not straightforward. Additional training and expertise are required to maximise its search and retrieval potential (157).

Open access

Paper publishing is expensive and documents are retrieved in a library or by regular mail. Text digitalisation allows journals and textbooks to be delivered online, saving paper costs and increasing convenience and accessibility. This decrease in publishing costs has not yet reached the consumer; many online periodicals and databases are password-protected, requiring a considerable subscription fee. The concept of open access is to have authors pay article processing charges and then make the article available for free access for all. Biomed central is an open access publisher offering 187 peer-reviewed open access journals (158).

Open access articles tend to be cited more often, probably as a result of ease of retrieval and review (159). Despite the self-evident merits of open access, there are concerns that government-mandated and -facilitated open access may ultimately decrease overall journal number and published research quality (160).

Many journals now offer free access to their content after a certain period following publication.

Internet interest groups, online interaction and forums

Peer communication is a common way by which physicians resolve patient-related questions. Consulting a colleague is easy and can offer the often needed human-to-human psychological support (161).

Several discussion groups have emerged facilitating peer communication and learning (162).

The Critical Care Medicine List (CCM-L) is a free, multidisciplinary electronic mail discussion registry with a focus on critical care medicine which was established in 1994 by David Crippen (163). It currently has 1,550 international members and it combines a real-time, online multinational consultative service journal club and discussion group. Membership was associated with an increase to access to information sources, clinical expertise from peers/colleagues, access to information via Medline and use of guidelines and principles of EBM (164).

The efficacy of internet interest groups depends on wide-ranging access to a large, heterogeneous group of members in a position to provide real time feedback to problems and issues as they unfold. CCM-L was one of the first medical bodies to be alerted about the SARS epidemic, as one of the treating physicians from Hong-Kong was also a member (see fig. 5). During several disasters including Sept. 11 and Katrina, members of CCM-L were available to disseminate information and potentially provide assistance to family and friends involved. Members frequently request assistance in unfolding personal emergencies.

The downside of internet interest groups is that they are part of the internet, an exponentially exploding wealth of information in which the veracity and authority of the providers is unknown or unverified. Accordingly, the accuracy of any forthcoming information must analysed by the collective expertise of its members.

Voice-over-IP and video improvement have allowed videoconferences with the use of free software, at no additional cost and in an acceptable quality (165, 166).

Discussion

So is e-learning more than a fashion (167)? Is it an example of gadget-mania or aesthetics taking precedence over utility? Is part of its popularity due to entertainment features such as animation, colours, sounds and videos? Or is it appealing because it promises effortless knowledge assimilation, "Gain without pain"? Learning, especially in medicine, is work, often hard work; can e-learning make it easier?

On 3/28/03 6:21 AM, "Antonios Liolios" wrote

'Hi Tom

Antonios Liolios here from Belgium. Congratulations on your work and may God help you through this.

I was wondering if you have a scanned pic of a pt's CXR which you could share with us.

Sincerely

Antonios Liolios
Belgium'

Lots of them

Tom

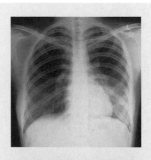

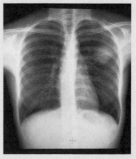

Fig. 5   Internet correspondence between the author and Tom Buckley shortly after SARS erupted in Hong Kong showing patients' chest radiographs

To begin with, when evaluating the literature on the merits and pitfalls of e-learning we should keep in mind that devices, technology and software available even a few years ago could be obsolete today. For example, a 2005 JAMA article on computerised phyfsician order entry (CPOE) concluded that instead of preventing, it may actually facilitate errors. The CPOE system tested was TDS, an antiquated system with poor human-computer interfacing which was withdrawn soon after the study was published (168).

As discussed above, comparing e-learning with traditional face-to-face classroom teaching is not a valid comparison as the methods and means are not equivalent; consequently, and until proper definitions are developed and research is standardised, the results of pertinent studies may not be as meaningful for clinical practice application and investment decisions (169).

E-learning should be viewed as a tool facilitating learning and from this perspective the most meaningful research would be to examine which e-learning modality works better compared to another and for whom (170, 171). Human teaching is still highly appreciated by students who value a good teacher more than elaborate electronic accessories (172).

An additional concern with e-learning is that it may encourage student passivity. When attending a face-to-face lecture, the student has to identify and sort out important material while taking notes, an active mental process. In e-learning the presented educational material is already organised and categorised and is presented without any active filtering and mental engagement required by students (173).

Furthermore, the rush towards e-learning may undermine the basic concepts of medical training and practice which are: physician's responsibility, patient caring and learning from patients (174). It is the patient who is the centre of medical education, not the computer.

Another element of e-learning is the screen and its inherent limitations.

Since the introduction of the computer screen there have been concerns that on-screen reading is not as fast and as effective as reading from paper (175). Although reading angle and head position may have an effect, recent research has shown that screen quality, screen contrast and text language (if different from reader's mother tongue) have the most significant impact on comprehension and information retention (81, 176). Subpixel rendering (ClearType) is a technique improving font display quality in liquid crystal display (LCD) screens; it was shown to improve the accuracy of sentence comprehension when compared to standard LCD displays (177). Despite the advantages in screen technology, however, screen reading remains slower than paper by 10–30% (178). Screen reading is also associated with muscle strain and visual fatigue (179), so it is not surprising that despite the availability of online material, students still tend to print out web pages for study (180).

But screen issues aside, are physicians technophobes and is the medical field in the dark ages of technology (181)? Although this may have been the case in the past (182), things have changed: A 2007 survey undertaken by Manhattan Research, a healthcare research and services firm, revealed that among 1,353 interviewed physicians, almost all had internet access and 50% owned a PDA; since 2005 the use of offline medical journals had dropped by 14%, while the use of online journals had increased by 27% (183). Other studies showed that younger physicians tend to use technology more, but still only a minority uses it while seeing a patient (109). Physicians need technology and software that blends effortlessly with their busy and demanding daily practice, a fact that some software developers tend to forget.

An important consideration when structuring an e-learning programme is to base it on sound pedagogical principles which can be borrowed from fields outside medicine such as cognitive psychology, marketing and management (171, 184). E-learning should be more than "putting notes on the web" or using the scrolling function of the browser as an equivalent to paper page turning (185). When designing e-learning material a multidisciplinary approach involving a clinically active physician, a software developer and an education specialist is ideal (76). When video is added the advice of a media expert may be invaluable.

E-learning curriculum integration should be voluntary and combined with introductory training in order to mitigate the expected faculty and student resistance (186). E-learning should be viewed as a tool supplementing traditional teaching and encouraging cooperative learning

(1). Students with computer difficulties should be identified beforehand and given a computer course (82).

Online material should be carefully secured with updated antivirus, firewall and spyware software. Sensitive data should be saved (backed up) and there should be a plan for alternative action when the system fails or is unavailable (187), as even new generation EMRs have unexpected downtime periods (188). It is not a question of "if" it is going to happen, but "when" it is going to happen. As the internet may facilitate access to copyrighted material, great caution should be exercised in approaching and using it, as costly litigation can ensue if a breach of copyright lawsuit is filed (189).

As e-learning is becoming a part of medical education, computer or PDA possession have became a mandatory admission requirement in several medical schools. Concerns are raised that this policy may hinder the recruitment of financially underprivileged students as the added cost is considerable (190).

Infatuation with the merits of e-learning should not make us oblivious to internet underpenetration and poor computer access in the developing world, the so-called "digital divide". The phenomenon is also seen in the US as large regional variations in e-learning utilisation by practising physicians were seen in one study. From the patients' perspective, it is the old and the poor who suffer the most from this discrepancy (191, 192). There is an ongoing global effort to decrease this gap with the assistance of communication technologies (102, 193, 194).

Present-day middle-aged physicians grew up with textbooks. Even anatomy textbooks consisted of a few images surrounded by dense text, contributing to physicians' "image deprivation". It is not surprising that e-learning is encountering obstacles, delays and even open resistance in its application. New generation physicians are familiar with screen reading and have grown up with the internet and personal computers at their fingertips. It is they who will complete the paradigm shift in medical education and clinical practice.

We live in interesting times.

Some future trends

As most users cannot type blindly (one should learn it!) and there are health hazards associated with keyboard usage (195), a better human-computer interface has been sought for decades. Voice recognition was heralded as a major advancement in computer data entry but despite the encouraging developments it did not find its way into medical practice and teaching (196).

A brain-computer interface using electrocorticographic activity enables humans to move a computer cursor by thinking the task (197, 198). It is hard to even imagine where this technique will lead once perfected and simplified.

A rounds-making robot has been featured in the news and medial literature (199, 200). Robotic telepresence was found to decrease costs and to facilitate physician response time in a major US hospital neurosurgical ICU (201) (see fig. 6).

Accurate wireless hand tracking has recently been introduced in commercial video games (202) and it wouldn't be too imaginative to predict that similar technology will be soon used for interactive VP training.

Ubiquitous computing promises to integrate computer technology seamlessly into our life and offer data access and communication anytime, anywhere ("everyware"). Calm, ubiquitous health (u-health), for all (102, 203, 204).

But what is more important than the technological advances, the new physicians should be prepared for the new world in which they will be part of a team working under managed care and where patients come from a diverse ethnical background, have access to medical knowledge, participate in decision-making and question their physician's authority and judgement.

This is the biggest challenge.

Final conclusions

- *E-learning is another teaching tool as the slide-projector was in the past.*
- *E-learning can be as good as traditional teaching when based on pedagogical principles and combined with human teaching.*
- *E-learning is not for everyone.*
- *It is the patient who is the centre of medical education, not the computer.*

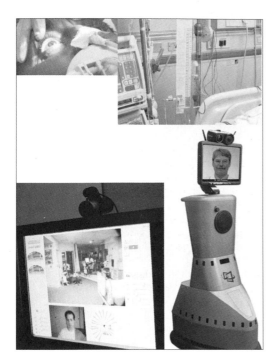

Fig. 6   Paul Vespa, MD, doing his early morning tele-
rounds. The two top pictures show the detail of his
view (patient's pupil reaction and cerebrospinal
fluid drainage colour) and the bottom picture
shows his screen and the robot. Reprinted from:
Surgical Neurology, 67, Paul M. Vespa, Chad Miller,
Xiao Hu, Val Nenov, Farzad Buxey and Neil A. Martin, Intensive care unit robotic telepresence facilitates rapid physician response to unstable patients
and decreased cost in neurointensive care, 331–337,
2007, with permission from Elsevier.

The author

Antonios Liolios, MD
    Medscape Critical Care Editorial Board
    Papageorgiou Hospital ICU
    Thessaloniki, Greece, 56403
    e-mail: aliolios@gmail.com

Acknowledgements

The author would like to thank George Lundberg, MD,
David Cook, MD, George Kazakos, DVM, PhD and Susan
Smith, RN, for their kind input and feedback.

References

All websites have been accessed on March 25th, 2008.

1. Sajeva M. E-learning: Web-based education. Curr Opin
    Anaesthesiol. 2006;19:645–9.
2. Jham BC, Duraes GV, Strassler HE, Sensi LG. Joining the
    podcast revolution. J Dent Educ. 2008;72:278–81.
3. Reynolds PA, Mason R, Eaton KA. Webcasting: casting
    the web more widely. Br Dent J. 2008;204:145–9.
4. http://www.merriam-webster.com/.
5. http://www.webopedia.com/.
6. www.wikipedia.com.
7. Cantrell EG, Craven JL. A trial of television in teaching
    clinical medicine. Br J Med Educ. 1969;3:110–4.
8. Quarmyne AT. Radio and the educational needs of Africa.
    Dev Commun Rep. 1985:3–4.
9. Ofori-ansa K. Africa's search for communication technolo-
    gies for education: a reflection on problems and
    prospects. Dev Commun Rep. 1983:3–5, 13.
10. Tsagaris M, Chatzipantazi P, Tsarouhi A, Ageletopoulos G,
    Amfilohiou A, Tsantoulas D. Outpatient teleclinics: six
    months' experience at the Telemedicine Centre,
    Sismanoglion Hospital of Athens. J Telemed Telecare.
    1996;2 Suppl 1:106–7.
11. Mavrogeni S, Sotiriou D, Thomakos D, Venieris N,
    Panagopoulos P. Telecardiology services in the Aegean
    islands. J Telemed Telecare. 1996;2 Suppl 1:74–6.
12. Balestri R, Cavina E, Aliferis A et al. Telemedicine on a
    small island. J Telemed Telecare. 1999;5 Suppl 1:S50–2.
13. Hartvigsen G, Johansen MA, Hasvold P et al. Challenges in
    telemedicine and eHealth: lessons learned from 20 years
    with telemedicine in Tromso. Medinfo. 2007;12:82–6.
14. Lucky R. The quickening of science communication.
    Science. 2000;289:259–64.
15. Slater WF. Internet history and growth http://www.isoc.
    org/internet/history/2002_0918_Internet_History_and_
    Growth.ppt. 2002.
16. Pombortsis AS. Communication technologies in health
    care environments. Int J Med Inform. 1998;52:61–70.
17. Ledley RS, Lusted LB. The use of electronic computers in
    medical data processing: aids in diagnosis, current
    information retrieval, and medical record keeping. IRE
    Trans Med Electron. 1960;ME-7:31–47.
18. Hankins J. The Internet. Adm Radiol. 1991;10:69–71.
19. Kayser K, Kayser G, Radziszowski D, Oehmann A. From
    telepathology to virtual pathology institution: the new
    world of digital pathology. Rom J Morphol Embryol.
    1999;45:3–9.
20. Moravec H. When will computer hardware match the
    human brain? J Evol and Tech. 1998;1.
21. Dafonte Vazquez JC, Castro Martinez A, Gomez A, Arcay
    Varela B. Intelligent agents technology applied to tasks
    scheduling and communications management in a
    critical care telemonitoring system. Comput Biol Med.
    2007;37:760–73.

22. The Hippocratic Oath http://www.nlm.nih.gov/hmd/greek/greek_oath.html.

23. Bergman LG, Fors UG. Computer-aided DSM-IV-diagnostics – acceptance, use and perceived usefulness in relation to users' learning styles. BMC Med Inform Decis Mak. 2005;5:1.

24. Cook DA. Learning and cognitive styles in web-based learning: theory, evidence, and application. Acad Med. 2005;80:266–78.

25. Lujan HL, DiCarlo SE. First-year medical students prefer multiple learning styles. Adv Physiol Educ. 2006;30:13–6.

26. Wehrwein EA, Lujan HL, DiCarlo SE. Gender differences in learning style preferences among undergraduate physiology students. Adv Physiol Educ. 2007;31:153–7.

27. Dinakar C, Adams C, Brimer A, Silva MD. Learning preferences of caregivers of asthmatic children. J Asthma. 2005;42:683–7.

28. Baykan Z, Nacar M. Learning styles of first-year medical students attending Erciyes University in Kayseri, Turkey. Adv Physiol Educ. 2007;31:158–60.

29. Lottridge DM, Chignell M, Danicic-Mizdrak R, Pavlovic NJ, Kushniruk A, Straus SE. Group differences in physician responses to handheld presentation of clinical evidence: a verbal protocol analysis. BMC Med Inform Decis Mak. 2007;7:22.

30. Menachemi N, Brooks RG. EHR and other IT adoption among physicians: results of a large-scale statewide analysis. J Healthc Inf Manag. 2006;20:79–87.

31. Graff M. Learning from web-based instructional systems and cognitive style. British Journal of Educational Technology. 2003;34.

32. Lynch TG, Woelfl NN, Steele DJ, Hanssen CS. Learning style influences student examination performance. Am J Surg. 1998;176:62–6.

33. McNulty JA, Espiritu B, Halsey M, Mendez M. Personality preference influences medical student use of specific computer-aided instruction (CAI). BMC Med Educ. 2006;6:7.

34. Lynch TG, Steele DJ, Johnson Palensky JE, Lacy NL, Duffy SW. Learning preferences, computer attitudes, and test performance with computer-aided instruction. Am J Surg. 2001;181:368–71.

35. Cook DA, Gelula MH, Dupras DM, Schwartz A. Instructional methods and cognitive and learning styles in web-based learning: report of two randomised trials. Med Educ. 2007;41:897–905.

36. Grunwald T, Corsbie-Massay C. Guidelines for cognitively efficient multimedia learning tools: educational strategies, cognitive load, and interface design. Acad Med. 2006;81:213–23.

37. Workman M, Lesser MF, Kim J. An exploratory study of cognitive load in diagnosing patient conditions. Int J Qual Health Care. 2007;19:127–33.

38. Laxmisan A, Hakimzada F, Sayan OR, Green RA, Zhang J, Patel VL. The multitasking clinician: decision-making and cognitive demand during and after team handoffs in emergency care. Int J Med Inform. 2007;76:801–11.

39. Levinson AJ, Weaver B, Garside S, McGinn H, Norman GR. Virtual reality and brain anatomy: a randomised trial of e-learning instructional designs. Med Educ. 2007;41:495–501.

40. Ruiz JG, Mintzer MJ, Issenberg SB. Learning objects in medical education. Med Teach. 2006;28:599–605.

41. Mas FG, Plass J, Kane WM, Papenfuss RL. Health education and multimedia learning: connecting theory and practice (Part 2). Health Promot Pract. 2003;4:464–9.

42. Mas FG, Plass J, Kane WM, Papenfuss RL. Health education and multimedia learning: educational psychology and health behavior theory (Part 1). Health Promot Pract. 2003;4:288–92.

43. Friedman RB. Top ten reasons the World Wide Web may fail to change medical education. Acad Med. 1996;71:979–81.

44. Cochran A, Edelman LS, Morris SE, Saffle JR. Learner satisfaction with Web-based learning as an adjunct to clinical experience in burn surgery. J Burn Care Res. 2008;29:222–6.

45. Jastrow H, Hollinderbaumer A. On the use and value of new media and how medical students assess their effectiveness in learning anatomy. Anat Rec B New Anat. 2004;280:20–9.

46. Gill A. E-learning and professional development – never too old to learn. Br J Nurs. 2007;16:1084–8.

47. Autti T, Autti H, Vehmas T, Laitalainen V, Kivisaari L. E-learning is a well-accepted tool in supplementary training among medical doctors: an experience of obligatory radiation protection training in healthcare. Acta Radiol. 2007;48:508–13.

48. Hall JL. Distance learning through synchronous interactive television. J Vet Med Educ. 2007;34:263–8.

49. Wehrs VH, Pfafflin M, May TW. E-learning courses in epilepsy – concept, evaluation, and experience with the e-learning course "genetics of epilepsies". Epilepsia. 2007;48:872–9.

50. Ridgway PF, Sheikh A, Sweeney KJ et al. Surgical e-learning: validation of multimedia web-based lectures. Med Educ. 2007;41:168–72.

51. Hammoud M, Gruppen L, Erickson SS et al. To the Point: reviews in medical education online computer assisted instruction materials. Am J Obstet Gynecol. 2006;194:1064–9.

52. Davis J, Chryssafidou E, Zamora J, Davies D, Khan K, Coomarasamy A. Computer-based teaching is as good as face to face lecture-based teaching of evidence based medicine: a randomised controlled trial. BMC Med Educ. 2007;7:23.

53. Gega L, Norman IJ, Marks IM. Computer-aided vs. tutor-delivered teaching of exposure therapy for phobia/panic: randomized controlled trial with pre-registration nursing students. Int J Nurs Stud. 2007;44:397–405.

54. Kim S, Schaad DC, Scott CS, Robins LS, Astion ML. A longitudinal evaluation of an educational software program: a case study of Urinalysis-Tutor. Acad Med. 2001;76:1136–43.

55. Vivekananda-Schmidt P, Lewis M, Hassell AB. Cluster randomized controlled trial of the impact of a computer-assisted learning package on the learning of musculoskeletal examination skills by undergraduate medical students. Arthritis Rheum. 2005;53:764–71.

56. Carroll AE, Schwartz MW. A comparison of a lecture and computer program to teach fundamentals of the Draw-a-Person test. Arch Pediatr Adolesc Med. 2002;156: 137–40.

57. Ohrn MA, van Oostrom JH, van Meurs WL. A comparison of traditional textbook and interactive computer learning of neuromuscular block. Anesth Analg. 1997;84:657–61.

58. Devitt P, Palmer E. Computer-aided learning: an overvalued educational resource? Med Educ. 1999;33:136–9.

59. Preast V, Danielson J, Bender H, Bousson M. Effectiveness of a computer-based tutorial for teaching how to make a blood smear. Vet Clin Pathol. 2007;36:245–52.

60. Allen EB, Walls RT, Reilly FD. Effects of interactive instructional techniques in a web-based peripheral nervous system component for human anatomy. Med Teach. 2008;30:40–7.

61. Spickard A, 3rd, Alrajeh N, Cordray D, Gigante J. Learning about screening using an online or live lecture: does it matter? J Gen Intern Med. 2002;17:540–5.

62. Fordis M, King JE, Ballantyne CM et al. Comparison of the instructional efficacy of Internet-based CME with live interactive CME workshops: a randomized controlled trial. Jama. 2005;294:1043–51.

63. Ryan G, Lyon P, Kumar K, Bell J, Barnet S, Shaw T. Online CME: an effective alternative to face-to-face delivery. Med Teach. 2007;29:e251–7.

64. Dantas AM, Kemm RE. A blended approach to active learning in a physiology laboratory-based subject facilitated by an e-learning component. Adv Physiol Educ. 2008;32:65–75.

65. Bello G, Pennisi MA, Maviglia R et al. Online vs live methods for teaching difficult airway management to anesthesiology residents. Intensive Care Med. 2005;31:547–52.

66. Carbonaro M, King S, Taylor E, Satzinger F, Snart F, Drummond J. Integration of e-learning technologies in an interprofessional health science course. Med Teach. 2008;30:25–33.

67. Cook DA, Dupras DM, Thompson WG, Pankratz VS. Web-based learning in residents' continuity clinics: a randomized, controlled trial. Acad Med. 2005;80:90–7.

68. Bell DS, Fonarow GC, Hays RD, Mangione CM. Self-study from web-based and printed guideline materials. A randomized, controlled trial among resident physicians. Ann Intern Med. 2000;132:938–46.

69. Wahlgren CF, Edelbring S, Fors U, Hindbeck H, Stahle M. Evaluation of an interactive case simulation system in dermatology and venereology for medical students. BMC Med Educ. 2006;6:40.

70. Tallent-Runnels M, Thomas J, Lan W, Cooperm S. Teaching Courses Online: A Review of the Research. Rev Educ Res. 2006;76.

71. Cook DA. Web-based learning: pros, cons and controversies. Clin Med. 2007;7:37–42.

72. Air M, Roman SA, Yeo H et al. Outdated and incomplete: a review of thyroid cancer on the World Wide Web. Thyroid. 2007;17:259–65.

73. Mathur S, Shanti N, Brkaric M et al. Surfing for scoliosis: the quality of information available on the Internet. Spine. 2005;30:2695–700.

74. Huang JY, Discepola F, Al-Fozan H, Tulandi T. Quality of fertility clinic websites. Fertil Steril. 2005;83:538–44.

75. Kim S, Phillips WR, Huntington J et al. Medical case teaching on the web. Teach Learn Med. 2007;19:106–14.

76. Alur P, Fatima K, Joseph R. Medical teaching websites: do they reflect the learning paradigm? Med Teach. 2002;24: 422–4.

77. Ruiz JG, Candler C, Teasdale TA. Peer reviewing e-learning: opportunities, challenges, and solutions. Acad Med. 2007;82:503–7.

78. http://www.nature.com/nature/peerreview/debate/nature05535.html.

79. Boerema C, Stanley M, Westhorp P. Educators' perspective of online course design and delivery. Med Teach. 2007;29:758–65.

80. Karl M, Graef F, Eitner S, Beck N, Wichmann M, Holst S. Comparison between computer-aided testing and traditional multiple choice: an equivalence study. Eur J Dent Educ. 2007;11:38–41.

81. Gulbrandsen P, Schroeder TV, Milerad J, Nylenna M. Paper or screen, mother tongue or English: which is better? A randomized trial. Jama. 2002;287:2851–3.

82. Link TM, Marz R. Computer literacy and attitudes towards e-learning among first year medical students. BMC Med Educ. 2006;6:34.

83. Phua J, Lim TK. Use of traditional versus electronic medical-information resources by residents and interns. Med Teach. 2007;29:400–2.

84. Braeckman LA, Fieuw AM, Van Bogaert HJ. A web- and case-based learning program for postgraduate students in occupational medicine. Int J Occup Environ Health. 2008;14:51–6.

85. Krupinski EA, Lopez AM, Lyman T, Barker G, Weinstein RS. Continuing education via telemedicine: analysis of reasons for attending or not attending. Telemed J E Health. 2004;10:403–9.

86. Gagnon MP, Legare F, Labrecque M, Fremont P, Cauchon M, Desmartis M. Perceived barriers to completing an e-learning program on evidence-based medicine. Inform Prim Care. 2007;15:83–91.

87. Hahne AK, Benndorf R, Frey P, Herzig S. Attitude towards computer-based learning: determinants as revealed by a controlled interventional study. Med Educ. 2005;39:935–43.

88. Zayim N, Yildirim S, Saka O. Instructional Technology Adoption of Medical Faculty in Teaching. Stud Health Technol Inform. 2005;116:255–260.

89. Badge JL, Cann AJ, Scott J. e-Learning versus e-Teaching: Seeing the Pedagogic Wood for the Technological Trees. Biosci Educ Electronic J. 2005;5.

90. Lee L, Brunicardi FC, Scott BG et al. Impact of a novel education curriculum on surgical training within an academic training program. J Surg Res. 2008;145:308–12.

91. Leung WC. Competency based medical training: review. Bmj. 2002;325:693–6.

92. Davoudi M, Colt HG. Bronchoscopy simulation: a brief review. Adv Health Sci Educ Theory Pract. 2008.

93. Kory PD, Eisen LA, Adachi M, Ribaudo VA, Rosenthal ME, Mayo PH. Initial airway management skills of senior residents: simulation training compared with traditional training. Chest. 2007;132:1927–31.

94. Knudson MM, Khaw L, Bullard MK et al. Trauma training in simulation: translating skills from SIM time to real time. J Trauma. 2008;64:255–63; discussion 263–4.

95. Gomoll AH, Pappas G, Forsythe B, Warner JJ. Individual Skill Progression on a Virtual Reality Simulator for Shoulder Arthroscopy: A 3-Year Follow-up Study. Am J Sports Med. 2008.

96. Lighthall GK, Barr J. The use of clinical simulation systems to train critical care physicians. J Intensive Care Med. 2007;22:257–69.

97. Gerlach H, Toussaint S. Between prediction, education, and quality control: simulation models in critical care. Crit Care. 2007;11:146.

98. Lamb D. Could simulated emergency procedures practised in a static environment improve the clinical performance of a Critical Care Air Support Team (CCAST)? A literature review. Intensive Crit Care Nurs. 2007;23:33–42.

99. McGuire NM. Monitoring in the field. Br J Anaesth. 2006;97:46–56.

100. Heinrichs WL, Youngblood P, Harter PM, Dev P. Simulation for team training and assessment: case studies of online training with virtual worlds. World J Surg. 2008;32:161–70.

101. Theodoropoulos A, Kneebone R, Dornan B, Leonard R, Bello F. Development and evaluation of a virtual intensive therapy unit – VITU. Stud Health Technol Inform. 2007;125:467–9.

102. Graschew G, Roelofs TA, Rakowsky S, Schlag PM. Network Design for Telemedicine – e-Health Using Satellite Technology. Stud Health Technol Inform. 2008;131:67–82.

103. Orton E, Mulhausen P. E-learning virtual patients for geriatric education. Gerontol Geriatr Educ. 2008;28:73–88.

104. Stevens A, Hernandez J, Johnsen K et al. The use of virtual patients to teach medical students history taking and communication skills. Am J Surg. 2006;191: 806–11.

105. Zary N, Johnson G, Boberg J, Fors UG. Development, implementation and pilot evaluation of a Web-based Virtual Patient Case Simulation environment – Web-SP. BMC Med Educ. 2006;6:10.

106. http://cmelist.com/list.htm.

107. Smith R. A POEM a week for the BMJ. Bmj. 2002;325:983.

108. Shewchuk RM, Schmidt HJ, Benarous A, Bennett NL, Abdolrasulnia M, Casebeer LL. A standardized approach to assessing physician expectations and perceptions of continuing medical education. J Contin Educ Health Prof. 2007;27:173–82.

109. Bennett NL, Casebeer LL, Zheng S, Kristofco R. Information-seeking behaviors and reflective practice. J Contin Educ Health Prof. 2006;26:120–7.

110. Grad RM, Pluye P, Mercer J et al. Impact of Research-based Synopses Delivered as Daily E-mail: A Prospective Observational Study. J Am Med Inform Assoc. 2008;15:240–245.

111. Lundberg GD. Category I CME credit for reading journal articles on Medscape. MedGenMed. 2004;6:42.

112. Fenton SH, Badgett RG. A comparison of primary care information content in UpToDate and the National Guideline Clearinghouse. J Med Libr Assoc. 2007;95:255–9.

113. Coppus SF, Emparanza JI, Hadley J et al. A clinically integrated curriculum in evidence-based medicine for just-in-time learning through on-the-job training: the EU-EBM project. BMC Med Educ. 2007;7:46.

114. Zaidi Z, Hashim J, Iqbal M, Quadri KM. Paving the way for evidence-based medicine in Pakistan. J Pak Med Assoc. 2007;57:556–60.

115. Mokwena K, Mokgatle-Nthabu M, Madiba S, Lewis H, Ntuli-Ngcobo B. Training of public health workforce at the National School of Public Health: meeting Africa's needs. Bull World Health Organ. 2007;85:949–54.

116. Groves RH Jr, Holcomb BW Jr, Smith ML. Intensive care telemedicine: evaluating a model for proactive remote monitoring and intervention in the critical care setting. Stud Health Technol Inform. 2008;131: 131–46.

117. Wilson LS. Technologies for complex and critical care telemedicine. Stud Health Technol Inform. 2008;131: 117–30.

118. Leong JR, Sirio CA, Rotondi AJ. eICU program favorably affects clinical and economic outcomes. Crit Care. 2005; 9:E22.

119. Breslow MJ, Rosenfeld BA, Doerfler M et al. Effect of a multiple-site intensive care unit telemedicine program on clinical and economic outcomes: an alternative paradigm for intensivist staffing. Crit Care Med. 2004;32:31–8.

120. McIntyre TP, Monahan TS, Villegas L, Doyle J, Jones DB. Teleconferencing surgery enhances effective communication and enriches medical education. Surg Laparosc Endosc Percutan Tech. 2008;18:45–8.

121. Boanca C, Rafiq A, Tamariz F et al. Remote video management for intraoperative consultation and surgical telepresence. Telemed J E Health. 2007;13:603–7.

122. Fortney JC, Pyne JM, Edlund MJ et al. A randomized trial of telemedicine-based collaborative care for depression. J Gen Intern Med. 2007;22:1086–93.

123. O'Reilly R, Bishop J, Maddox K, Hutchinson L, Fisman M, Takhar J. Is telepsychiatry equivalent to face-to-face psychiatry? Results from a randomized controlled equivalence trial. Psychiatr Serv. 2007;58:836–43.

124. Muir J, Lucas L. Tele-dermatology in australia. Stud Health Technol Inform. 2008;131:245–53.

125. Gagnon MP, Duplantie J, Fortin JP, Jennett P, Scott R. A survey in Alberta and Quebec of the telehealth applications that physicians need. J Telemed Telecare. 2007;13:352–6.

126. Binks S, Benger J. Tele-education in emergency care. Emerg Med J. 2007;24:782–4.

127. Dawson AJ, Joof BM. Seeing, thinking and acting against Malaria: a new approach to health worker training for community empowerment in rural Gambia. Rural Remote Health. 2005;5:353.

128. Graber MA, Randles BD, Ely JW, Monnahan J. Answering clinical questions in the ED. Am J Emerg Med. 2008;26:144–7.

129. Khan AN, Frank J, Geria R, Davidson S. Utilization of personal digital assistants (PDAS) by pediatric and emergency medicine residents. J Emerg Med. 2007;32:423–8.

130. Chen YC, Chiu HC, Tsai MD, Chang H, Chong CF. Development of a personal digital assistant-based wireless application in clinical practice. Comput Methods Programs Biomed. 2007;85:181–4.

131. Bochicchio GV, Smit PA, Moore R et al. Pilot study of a web-based antibiotic decision management guide. J Am Coll Surg. 2006;202:459–67.

132. Tri JL, Severson RP, Hyberger LK, Hayes DL. Use of cellular telephones in the hospital environment. Mayo Clin Proc. 2007;82:282–5.

133. van Lieshout EJ, van der Veer SN, Hensbroek R, Korevaar JC, Vroom MB, Schultz MJ. Interference by new-generation mobile phones on critical care medical equipment. Crit Care. 2007;11:R98.

134. Cell phones and electromagnetic interference revisited. Health Devices. 2006;35:449–56.

135. http://en.wikipedia.org/wiki/Wiki.

136. http://wikipedia.org/.

137. Streeter JL, Lu MT, Rybicki FJ. Informatics in radiology: RadiologyWiki.org: the free radiology resource that anyone can edit. Radiographics. 2007;27:1193–200.

138. Giles J. Internet encyclopaedias go head to head. Nature. 2005;438:900–1.

139. Foss TD. iPods are the new Walkmans, only more so. Br J Nurs. 2006;15:185.

140. Boulos MN, Maramba I, Wheeler S. Wikis, blogs and podcasts: a new generation of Web-based tools for virtual collaborative clinical practice and education. BMC Med Educ. 2006;6:41.

141. Johnson L, Grayden S. Podcasts – an emerging form of digital publishing. Int J Comput Dent. 2006;9:205–18.

142. Palmer EJ, Devitt PG. A method for creating interactive content for the iPod, and its potential use as a learning tool: technical advances. BMC Med Educ. 2007;7:32.

143. Savel RH, Goldstein EB, Perencevich EN, Angood PB. The iCritical care podcast: a novel medium for critical care communication and education. J Am Med Inform Assoc. 2007;14:94–9.

144. Rowell MR, Corl FM, Johnson PT, Fishman EK. Internet-based dissemination of educational audiocasts: a primer in podcasting – how to do it. AJR Am J Roentgenol. 2006;186:1792–6.

145. Fligor BJ, Cox LC. Output levels of commercially available portable compact disc players and the potential risk to hearing. Ear Hear. 2004;25:513–27.

146. Chisholm SL, Caird JK, Lockhart J. The effects of practice with MP3 players on driving performance. Accid Anal Prev. 2008;40:704–13.

147. Skiba DJ. Nursing education 2.0: YouTube. Nurs Educ Perspect. 2007;28:100–2.

148. Bonetta L. Scientists enter the blogosphere. Cell. 2007;129:443–5.

149. http://e-learningarticle.blogspot.com/.

150. Mueller M, Wagner CL, Annibale DJ, Knapp RG, Hulsey TC, Almeida JS. Parameter selection for and implementation of a web-based decision-support tool to predict extubation outcome in premature infants. BMC Med Inform Decis Mak. 2006;6:11.

151. Elter M, Schulz-Wendtland R, Wittenberg T. The prediction of breast cancer biopsy outcomes using two CAD approaches that both emphasize an intelligible decision process. Med Phys. 2007;34:4164–72.

152. http://www.isabelhealthcare.com/info/newyorktime.html.

153. Graber ML, Mathew A. Performance of a web-based clinical diagnosis support system for internists. J Gen Intern Med. 2008;23 Suppl 1:37–40.

154. Tang H, Ng JH. Googling for a diagnosis – use of Google as a diagnostic aid: internet based study. Bmj. 2006;333:1143–5.

155. Greenwald R. ... And a diagnostic test was performed. N Engl J Med. 2005;353:2089–90.

156. http://www.merriam-webster.com/dictionary/googling.

157. Ripple AS. Expert googling: best practices and advanced strategies for using google in health sciences libraries. Med Ref Serv Q. 2006;25:97–107.

158. http://www.biomedcentral.com/.

159. Eysenbach G. Citation advantage of open access articles. PLoS Biol. 2006;4:e157.

160. McMullan E. Open access mandate threatens dissemination of scientific information. J Neuroophthalmol. 2008;28:72–4.

161. Smith R. What clinical information do doctors need? Bmj. 1996;313:1062–8.

162. Sanders JC. A comparison of Internet usage between two residency programs in the United Kingdom and the United States. J Clin Anesth. 2002;14:388–94.

163. http://www.ccm-l.org/. http://www.ccm-l.org/.

164. Crippen D, Doig G, Liolios A. Critical care medicine e-mail list: an online survey of a global resource pool. Abstract 32nd SCCM meeting, San Antonio. 2003.

165. Boulos MN, Taylor AD, Breton A. A synchronous communication experiment within an online distance learning program: a case study. Telemed J E Health. 2005;11:583–93.

166. Valaitis R, Akhtar-Danesh N, Eva K, Levinson A, Wainman B. Pragmatists, positive communicators, and shy enthusiasts: three viewpoints on Web conferencing in health sciences education. J Med Internet Res. 2007;9:e39.

167. Campbell JK, Johnson C. Trend spotting: fashions in medical education. Bmj. 1999;318:1272–5.

168. Koppel R, Metlay JP, Cohen A et al. Role of computerized physician order entry systems in facilitating medication errors. Jama. 2005;293:1197–203.

169. Cook DA. The research we still are not doing: an agenda for the study of computer-based learning. Acad Med. 2005;80:541–8.

170. Cook DA, McDonald FS. E-Learning: Is There Anything Special about the "E"? Perspect Biol Med. 2008;51: 5–21.

171. Cook DA. Where are we with Web-based learning in medical education? Med Teach. 2006;28:594–8.

172. Billings-Gagliardi S, Mazor KM. Student decisions about lecture attendance: do electronic course materials matter? Acad Med. 2007;82:S73–6.

173. Walsh CM, Seldomridge LA. Critical thinking: back to square two. J Nurs Educ. 2006;45:212–9.

174. Ludmerer KM, Johns MM. Reforming graduate medical education. Jama. 2005;294:1083–7.

175. Dillon A, McKnight C, Richardson J. Reading from paper versus reading from screens. The Computer Journal. 1988;31:457–464.

176. Shieh KK, Chen MH. Effects of display medium and luminance contrast on concept formation and EEG response. Percept Mot Skills. 2005;100:943–54.

177. Tyrrell R, Gugerty L, Aten T, Edmonds A. The effects of sub-pixel addressing on users' performance and preferences during reading-related tasks. Journal of Vision. 2004;4.

178. Kurniawan SH, Zaphiris P. Reading Online or on Paper: Which is Faster? Abridged Proceedings of the 9th International Conference on Human Computer Interaction New Orleans, LA. 2001.

179. Nakazawa T, Okubo Y, Suwazono Y et al. Association between duration of daily VDT use and subjective symptoms. Am J Ind Med. 2002;42:421–6.

180. Yolton RL, deCalesta D. Pacific's experience with Web-based instruction: bats in the belfry or Webs in the classroom? Optometry. 2000;71:20–8.

181. Rohm BW, Rohm CE Jr. Evolving medical informatics: from diagnosis to prognosis. Int J Electron Healthc. 2004;1:103–11.

182. Morris L, Dumville J, Campbell LM, Sullivan F. A survey of computer use in Scottish primary care: general practitioners are no longer technophobic but other primary care staff need better computer access. Inform Prim Care. 2003;11:5–11.

183. http://www.manhattanresearch.com/products/ Strategic_Advisory/ttp/. 2007.

184. Chan CH, Robbins LI. E-Learning systems: promises and pitfalls. Acad Psychiatry. 2006;30:491–7.

185. Evans C, Gibbons N, Shah K, Griffin DK. Virtual Learning in the Biological Sciences: Pitfalls of Simply "Putting Notes on the Web". 2004.

186. Hege I, Ropp V, Adler M et al. Experiences with different integration strategies of case-based e-learning. Med Teach. 2007;29:791–7.

187. Nelson SB. Not so fast! The dark side of computers in health care. Respir Care. 2004;49:525–30.

188. Lium JT, Tjora A, Faxvaag A. No paper, but the same routines: a qualitative exploration of experiences in two Norwegian hospitals deprived of the paper based medical record. BMC Med Inform Decis Mak. 2008;8:2.

189. Donohue BC, Howe-Steiger L. Understanding the issues of intellectual property in the creation of e-learning courseware. J Vet Med Educ. 2007;34:269–78.

190. Mavis B, Smith JM. Mandatory Microcomputers: Potential Effects on Medical School Recruitment and Admissions. Med Educ Online. 1997;2.

191. Rosenthal DA, Layman EJ. Utilization of information technology in eastern North Carolina physician practices: determining the existence of a digital divide. Perspect Health Inf Manag. 2008;5:3.

192. Schmeida M, McNeal RS. The telehealth divide: disparities in searching public health information online. J Health Care Poor Underserved. 2007;18:637–47.

193. Bukachi F, Pakenham-Walsh N. Information technology for health in developing countries. Chest. 2007;132:1624–30.

194. http://www.digitaldivide.net/.

195. Lincoln AE, Vernick JS, Ogaitis S, Smith GS, Mitchell CS, Agnew J. Interventions for the primary prevention of work-related carpal tunnel syndrome. Am J Prev Med. 2000;18:37–50.

196. Pezzullo JA, Tung GA, Rogg JM, Davis LM, Brody JM, Mayo-Smith WW. Voice Recognition Dictation: Radiologist as Transcriptionist. J Digit Imaging. 2007.

197. Vaughan TM, McFarland DJ, Schalk G et al. The Wadsworth BCI Research and Development Program: at home with BCI. IEEE Trans Neural Syst Rehabil Eng. 2006;14:229–33.

198. Schalk G, Miller KJ, Anderson NR et al. Two-dimensional movement control using electrocorticographic signals in humans. J Neural Eng. 2008;5:75–84.

199. Ellison LM, Pinto PA, Kim F et al. Telerounding and patient satisfaction after surgery. J Am Coll Surg. 2004;199:523–30.

200. Thacker PD. Physician-robot makes the rounds. Jama. 2005;293:150.

201. Vespa PM, Miller C, Hu X, Nenov V, Buxey F, Martin NA. Intensive care unit robotic telepresence facilitates rapid physician response to unstable patients and decreased cost in neurointensive care. Surg Neurol. 2007;67:331–7.

202. www.wii.com.

203. Garde S, Hovenga E, Buck J, Knaup P. Ubiquitous information for ubiquitous computing: expressing clinical data sets with openEHR archetypes. Stud Health Technol Inform. 2006;124:215–20.

204. http://en.wikipedia.org/wiki/Ubiquitous_computing.

Dominique M. Vandijck and Stijn I. Blot

High acuity nurse patient ratio – is it cost-effective?

The optimal level of nurse patient ratios in intensive care is a controversial issue. This chapter provides a summary of the best available evidence in the area of nursing staff and patient safety. As such, it has been demonstrated that a direct link exists between inappropriate nursing staff levels and increased rates of adverse events, mortality, and unfavourable outcome for both, staff and the healthcare system. Otherwise, it has been shown that, to date, there is no substantive literature available that can be used to accurately inform what the optimal nurse patient ratios should be. Besides briefly detailing the frequently used tools to measure nursing workload, advantages as well as some controversial positions will be discussed with regard to potential governmental strategies aimed to improving staffing ratios.

A brief historical overview and backgrounds

Historically, the polio epidemic that broke out in Denmark in 1952 laid the basis of the intensive care revolution. An artificial ventilation technique, previously only used in the operating theatre was now used in the management of these patients. Doing so, lower death rates were observed since continuous monitoring of the vital functions and follow-up by both physicians and nurses was performed. From that moment on,

and in response to the exponential growth of medical interventions and technology, intensive care largely developed, and anticipating the baby-boomer generation to retire, the latter phenomenon is expected to grow even further (1, 2). More and more people will enroll in healthcare, and as patient acuity increases, the condition of a considerable part of them will become too complex to be cared for in general wards. However, as every coin has two sides, these advancements simultaneously created a demand for better skilled and specialised staff (3). Nevertheless, over the years, expenditures in healthcare have increased massively, so controlling budgets became a top priority among policy makers and hospital managers (4). Cost savings were to be made by increasing efficiency while maintaining access and quality of services. Greater emphasis was placed on cost-effectiveness, and in the 1990s, hospital restructuring was a fact resulting in considerable organisational changes (5). As nurses constitute the largest segment of care providers within the healthcare system, nursing costs account for a substantial proportion of the total healthcare budget, making their jobs most vulnerable to pressures to reduce costs. Although, in the early 1990s, there was an overall shortage of nurses, reversal was observed in the mid-1990s; however, there is some question whether nursing

Tab. 1   Nursing staff and patient safety:
Studies reporting an association between lower staffing levels and increased adverse events and mortality

Authors	Year	Reference	Outcome	Measure	Findings
Schultz et al.	1998	(41)	Overall mortality	Nursing hrs per patient per day	↓ nursing hrs associated with ↑ in mortality
Aiken et al.	1999	(42)	30-day mortality	Nurse patient ratio	↑ 15' nursing care per patient per day associated with ↓ 20–30 % of 30d mortality
Aiken et al.	2002	(10)	30-day mortality	Nurse patient ratio of 1:4 vs 1:8 per shift	↑ nurse patient ratio associated with ↓ mortality and failure to rescue
Needleman et al.	2002	(39)	In-hospital mortality	Nursing hrs per patient per day	↑ number of nursing hours of care per day associated with ↓ failure to rescue
Person et al.	2004	(40)	In-hospital mortality	Registered nurses vs licensed ractical nurses	↑ registered nurse staffing associated with ↓ mortality ↑ licensed pratical nurse staffing associated with ↑ mortality

staff increased rapidly enough to keep pace with the demands in the future, and thus ensure access to safe and high-quality delivery of care (6–9). Nowadays, nursing shortages in global and in high acuity specialty nursing fields such as intensive care in particular, presents one of the most significant problems for healthcare administrators, and it is not expected to reverse for several decades (8). This deterioration of the healthcare system has led to concerns, increasingly voiced by nurses, about patient safety, the pressure of working with less than desirable nurse patient ratios, and their subsequent inability to cope with the multiple demands of critically ill patients.

After having further elucidated on the core of the problem, the present book chapter will deal on different, sometimes controversial, aspects related to nursing staff and patient safety, and will detail on what one should understand about optimal nurse patient ratios, as well as on potential approaches to achieve this.

Statement of the problem

Policy makers and healthcare administrators both have the responsibility to ensure effective and efficient intensive care systems. Staffing and productivity are both critical aspects of those systems. Safe and effective staffing with qualified, experienced and professional nurses, including ancillary staff is needed to deliver optimal patient care (i.e. providing care according to the needs of the patient and his relatives), achieve an operationally efficient ICU, and to keep staff satisfied (10). However, induced by healthcare restructuring, healthcare cost containment, and nursing staff downsizing, we have evolved toward a healthcare system that threatens the safety and quality of care, as well as the quality of work life for nurses. Yet, nursing staff are critical to patient safety, as they spend more time caring for the patients than any other single care provider. Clearly, nursing staff decisions should therefore be addressed within the context of patient safety, as well as that of costs. However, the concerns expressed by nurses were largely dismissed as empirical evidence was not available. The American Nurses Association (ANA) recognised this need for empirical data to support and drive staffing decisions (11). Although, the ANA initially failed to demonstrate a significant relationship between quality of care on the one hand and staffing patterns on the other, at present, investigators are now able to support what nurses had been saying, that is, nursing staff influences patient outcomes.

Tab. 2 Nursing staff and patient safety:
Studies reporting an association between lower staffing levels and increased adverse events

Authors	Year	Reference	Outcome	Measure	Findings
Blegen et al.	1998	(24)	Urinary tract infection	Proportion of nurse patient ratio	↑ nurse patient ratio associated with ↓ adverse events up to 87.5 %.
Kovner and Gergen	1998	(16)		Level of nurse staffing	Inverse relation between staffing level and urinary tract infection (p < 0.0001)
Sovie and Jawad	2001	(46)		Nursing hrs per patient per day	↑ nursing hrs associated with ↓ rates of urinary tract infection
Kovner et al.	2002	(17)		Nursing hrs per patient per day	Trend to ↑ urinary tract infection with ↓ nursing hrs (p > 0.05)
Needleman et al.	2002	(39)		Nursing hrs per patient per day	↑ number of nursing hours of care per day associated with ↓ rates of urinary tract infections (p = 0.003)
Kovner and Gergen	1998	(16)	Pneumonia	Level of nurse staffing	Inverse relation between staffing level and pneumonia (p < 0.001)
Amaravadi et al.	2000	(52)		Nurse patient ratio 1:2 vs nurse patient ratio < 1:2	< 1:2 ratio associated with ↑ pneumonia (p = 0.012) and ↑ reintubation (p = 0.001)
Kovner et al.	2002	(17)		Nursing hrs per patient per day	Inverse relation between nursing hrs and pneumonia (p < 0.05)
Needleman et al.	2002	(39)		Nursing hrs per patient per day	↑ number of nursing hours of care per day associated with ↓ rates of pneumonia (p = 0.001)
Unruh et al.	2003	(54)		Proportion of nurse staffing	↓ proportion of nurses associated with ↑ incidence of pneumonia
Cho et al.	2003	(51)		Level/proportion of nursing staff	↑ 1 hr of nursing care per patient per day associated with ↓ 8.9 % in the odds of pneumonia. ↑ 10 % of the proportion of nursing care associated with ↓ 9.5 % in the odds of pneumonia
Blegen and Vaughn	1998	(45)	Shock or cardiac arrest	Proportion of nurse patient ratio	↑ 50 % to 85 % of proportion of nursing care associated with ↓ of rate of adverse events
Needleman et al.	2002	(39)		Nursing hrs per patient per day	↑ number of nursing hours of care per day associated with ↓ rates of shock or cardiac arrest (p = 0.007)
Person et al.	2004	(40)		Nursing staff levels	↑ staffing levels associated with significant ↓ rates of complications

Authors	Year	Reference	Outcome	Measure	Findings
Fridkin et al.	1996	(18)	Sepsis	Nurse patient ratio	Nurse patient ratio is an independent risk factor for catheter sepsis
Amaravadi et al.	2000	(52)		Nurse patient ratio 1:2 vs nurse patient ratio <1:2	< 1:2 ratio associated with ↑ sepsis ($p = 0.04$)
Dimick et al.	2001	(55)		Nurse patient ratio 1:1 or 2 vs nurse patient ratio 1:3 or more	Nurse patient ratio 1:3 or more associated with pulmonary failure ($p = 0.006$)
Berenholtz et al.	2004	(25)		Nursing staff levels	↑ staffing levels associated with ↓ rate of catheter sepsis
Needleman et al.	2002	(39)	Failure to rescue	Nursing hrs per patient per day	↑ number of nursing hours of care per day associated with ↓ rates of failure to rescue in medical and surgical patients ($p = 0.05$, and $p = 0.008$, respectively)
Aiken et al.	2002	(10)		Nurse patient ratio	Each additional patient per nurse associated with ↑ 7 % odds of failure to rescue
Kovner and Gergen	1998	(16)	Thrombosis	Level of nurse staffing	Inverse relation between staffing level and thrombosis ($p < 0.01$)
Kovner et al.	2002	(17)		Nursing hrs per patient per day	Trend to ↑ thrombosis/pulmonary embolisms with ↓ nursing hrs ($p > 0.05$)
Needleman et al.	2002	(39)	Upper gastro-intestinal bleeding	Nursing hrs per patient per day	↑ number of nursing hours of care per day associated with ↓ rates of gastro-intestinal bleeding ($p = 0.007$)
Blegen et al.	1998	(24)	Medication errors	Proportion of nurse patient ratio	↑ proportion of nursing care associated with ↓ medication errors
Blegen and Vaughn	1998	(45)		Level of nursing staff, proportion of nurse patient ratio	↑ 50 % to 85 % of nursing care associated with ↓ rate of adverse events
McGillis Hall et al.	2004	(50)		Nursing staff levels	↓ Proportion of nursing staff associated with ↑ number of medication errors
Thorens et al.	1995	(56)	Duration of weaning from the ventilator	Number and qualifications of nurses ('index of nursing')	Inverse correlation between time on mechanical ventilator and better 'nursing index' ($p = 0.025$)
Blegen and Vaughn	1998	(45)	Patient falls	Proportion of nurse patient ratio	↑ proportion of nursing care associated with ↓ rates of patient falls

Authors	Year	Reference	Outcome	Measure	Findings
Sovie and Jawad	2001	(46)		Nursing hrs per patient per day	↑ nursing hrs associated with ↓ fall rates
Langemo et al.	2003	(48)		Staff mix	↑ Staffing levels associated with ↓ patient falls
Blegen et al.	1998	(24)	Pressure ulcers	Proportion of nurse patient ratio	↑ proportion of nursing care associated with ↓ pressure ulcers
Unruh et al.	2003	(54)		Proportion of nursing staff	↓ proportion of nurses associated with ↑ incidence of pressure sores
Bostick	2004	(53)		Nurse staffing hrs	↑ Nursing staff hrs associated with improvement of stages (1–4) of pressure ulcers
Sovie and Jawad	2001	(46)	Patient satisfaction	Nursing hrs per patient per day	↑ nursing hrs associated with ↑ patient satisfaction
Potter et al.	2003	(47)		Levels of nursing staff	↑ Nursing staff associated with ↑ patient satisfaction

Nursing staff and patient safety

Patient outcomes – mortality and adverse events

During the past decade, the relationship between nursing staff, quality of care and patient outcome became more and more a topic of interest in ICU research. Whereas some authors reported an association between higher staffing levels and favourable patient outcome in terms of adverse events or survival, others could not demonstrate such a relationship (10, 12–43). An extraordinary review of the literature by Spilsbury and Meyer concluded with providing evidence supporting the claim that nursing care indeed makes a difference to patient outcomes (44).

Although there might be some controversy with regard to differences in cohorts under study, five major studies demonstrated that reduced nursing staff were independently linked with unfavourable patient outcome, while two others could not demonstrate such a relationship (10, 31, 39–43) (see tab. 1 and 2). For instance, a study of 168 hospitals, 10,184 nurses, and 232,342 patients who had undergone a surgical procedure, by Aiken and collaborators, showed that as compared to hospitals with higher, those with lower

nurse patient ratios had higher 30-day mortality rates (10). More particularly, it was demonstrated that the risk of death was 14 % and 31 % higher in hospitals with nurse patient ratios of 1:6 or more and 1:8 or more, compared to hospitals with ratios of 1:4 or less. Estimations predicted that excess deaths per 1,000 patients of 5 and 18 for staffed hospitals at 1:4 and 1:8 ratios, respectively. Another landmark paper by Needleman and collaborators studying 799 hospitals covering respectively 5,075,696 and 1,104,659 discharges of medical and surgical patients, showed that both, higher proportion of hours of nursing care and nurse patient ratios, were associated with better care in terms of patient outcome (39).

The relationship between nursing staff and the occurrence of adverse events among patients has been subject of numerous studies (10, 16–18, 24, 25, 39, 40, 45–56) (see tab. 1). For instance, in a cohort of critically ill patients with chronic obstructive pulmonary disease, Thorens and collaborators investigated the impact of reducing nurse patient ratios and the time taken for weaning from mechanical ventilation (56). The authors found that in case of nursing staff reduction, the duration of weaning from mechanical ventilation increased dramatically. A reduction in the number of nurses providing direct patient care, as well as a decrease in nurses adherence with evidence-based guidelines has been shown to have adverse effects on nosocomial infection rates (22, 57–60). The three largest studies to date were conducted by Needleman and collaborators, Cho and collaborators, and Kovner and Gergen (16, 39, 51). Similarly to the findings by Needleman and collaborators, Cho and collaborators found that an increase of either one hour nursing care per patient per day or 10% in the proportion of nurse care per day was associated with an 8.9% and 9.5% decrease in the risk of atelectases and pneumonia, respectively (39, 51). As well, Kovner and Gergen observed that an additional 30 minutes of nursing care per patient per day, resulted in a reduction of the rate of pneumonia by more than 4% (16).

Besides, the total amount of nurses directly involved in patient care, nurse qualifications and years of work experience are important as well. Morrison and collaborators showed that nursing inexperience directly contributed to 10% of all adverse events reported (61). Tourangeau and collaborators found that each additional year of nursing experience could prevent 4 to 6 deaths per 1,000 admissions (62, 63). Lastly, Alonso-Echanove and collaborators reported that patients cared for by less experienced nurses for more than 60% of days on central line intravascular device had 2.6 times higher odds of acquiring intravascular device associated bloodstream infection (64). Based on an extensive review of the literature, we may state that there is sufficient evidence demonstrating that staffing levels have a direct relationship with non-fatal patient outcomes such as pressure ulcers, falls, medication errors, respiratory and urinary infections, and patient complaints.

Staff outcomes – nurse distress

Although nurses have been voicing their concerns regarding patient safety and personal distress in an environment of inadequate numbers of qualified staff, high workloads, mandatory overtime, and fatigue for years, only few authors have studied the direct impact between staffing levels on the one hand and staff outcomes on the other (see tab. 3). Occupational injury, job dissatisfaction, negative stress, decreased concentration, burnout,

and increased personnel turnover were all reported (65, 66). Aiken and collaborators reported a 23% and 15% increase in nurse burnout and job dissatisfaction, for each extra patient added to the 1:4 nurse patient ratio workload (10). Further, in units with workload levels of 80% or above, nurses have lower job satisfaction and higher absenteeism rates, or even think about leaving nursing (67). Contrariwise, higher proportion of staffing is reported to be associated with higher nurse job satisfaction (49, 68, 69). The latter findings are of key importance as nursing shortages that are expected to continue for the next several decades are likely to jeopardise the financial stability of many hospitals and access to healthcare, increase waiting times, and reduce quality of care and the ability of nurses to ensure desirable patient outcomes. Shortages are the most severe in high-acuity areas such as operating theatres, intensive care, neonatal care, and emergency departments all requiring highly skilled nurses, preferably with considerable work experience. If shortages further linger, this could have a counterproductive effect, with the public potentially losing confidence in all involved in the care of the patient, and in the healthcare system as a whole.

System outcomes – resource use and costs

Salient literature described that adverse events resulted in increased healthcare resource utilisation (52, 55, 70–76). The relationship between nurse patient ratios and adverse events in the ICU was investigated by Amaravadi and collaborators (52). They found an approximate increase of 40% in hospital length of stay and a subsequent increase in hospital costs in case nurse patient ratios exceeded 1:2. As well, Dimick and collaborators demonstrated that a lower nurse patient ratio (1:3 or above) increased the risk for re-intubation, and resulted in a 14% increase of hospital costs, compared to a higher nurse patient ratio (1:2 or less) (55). Rothberg and collaborators stated that improving nurse patient ratios is a cost-effective intervention (76). Increasing nurse patient ratios from 1:8 to 1:4 was estimated to cost $ 136,000 per life saved and could save 72,000 lives yearly. Moreover, the authors estimated that savings from reduced length of stays, resulting from the better care delivered, would offset almost half of

Tab. 3   Nursing staff and patient safety:
         Studies reporting an association between staffing levels and nurses psychological well-being

Authors	Year	Reference	Outcome	Measure	Finding
Aiken et al.	2002	(10)	Job dissatisfaction	Nurse patient ratio	Each additional patient per nurse associated with ↑ 15 % odds of job dissatisfaction
McGillis Hall et al.	2003	(49)	Job satisfaction	Staff mix models	Nurses working on units with regulated and unregulated workers ↑ job satisfaction
Verhaeghe et al.	2008	(68)		Number of nurses	↓ Number of nurses or ↓ nurse patient ratio associated with ↑ job satisfaction
O'Brien-Pallas et al.	2004	(67)	Absenteeism	Nurse working time	↑ of 1 hr of overtime per week ↑ the odds of nursing lost-time and sick time
Verhaeghe et al.	2006	(69)		Number of nurses	↓ Number of nurses or ↓ nurse patient ratio associated with ↑ rates of absenteeism
Aiken et al.	2002	(10)	Burnout	Nurse patient ratio	Each additional patient per nurse associated with ↑ 23 % odds of burnout

the increased labour costs. Further, it has been stated that by ensuring appropriate nurse patient ratios and as such preventing patients from developing pressure ulcers and pneumonia, the first of which would lead to annual cost savings of approximately $ 8.5 billion for the United States alone, and the second of which to decreasing the cost of care of about $ 25,000 (51).

Nurse patient ratios

Nursing staff – international comparisons

Nursing staff is one of the most expensive parts of the healthcare budget, so to certain extents the money used to pay nurses can also be used in preventive or educational programmes, or any other effort that produces value to society. Additionally, the optimal level of nursing staff is not simply the number of nurses that would avert the most deaths, and it is difficult to determine exactly what this optimal level should be (77). According to a study by Aiken and collaborators, a nurse patient ratio of 1:4 compared to 1:8 would result in 5 fewer deaths per 1,000 patient admis-

sions on a surgical unit (10). Considering an average length of hospitalisation of 10 days, there would be 240,000 patient hours of care, requiring 60,000 vs. 30,000 nursing hours in the case of nurse patient ratios of 1:4 vs. 1:8, respectively. Taken that one nursing hour costs $ 60, the cost of the 1:4 ratio would be $ 1.8 million more than that for the 1:8 ratio. This would produce a cost of $ 360,000 for each of the 5 averted deaths, which is within the range of an intervention being considered as cost-effective. Notwithstanding this, the latter does not mean that the 1:4 ratio is the optimal one (77). In seeking to address appropriate nursing staff levels in intensive care, comparisons with other countries are desirable. When comparing Western European countries and the US, there are recognised differences in nurse patient ratios; however, numerous differences such as case-mix make interpretation and comparisons often difficult. For instance, the role of ICU nurses in the United Kingdom (UK) is distinct from other countries (78). Actual acuity has to be taken into account, which is observed to be higher for critically ill patients being cared for in the UK as compared to ICUs in Europe, Canada, and the US (79). Also, the UK has one of the lowest number of ICU beds available per hospital population, with less healthcare personnel than their European equivalents (79). Next, nurses in intensive care frequently add new skills and develop practices to enable a more responsible and responsive approach to the increasing and changing demands of critically ill patients (78, 80, 81). Lastly, social, intercultural, political and professional differences may influence appropriate comparisons between healthcare systems and countries. All these aspects need to be considered in relation to the analysis of optimal staffing levels within different environments.

Dependency scoring systems – TISS-76, TISS-28, NEMS, and NAS

Without going into detail, we shortly elaborate on some validated scoring systems widely used by hospital administrators to allocate nurses to patients as fairly as possible. In analysing the appropriateness of identifying optimal nurse patient ratios, the use of dependency scoring systems can provide substantial means to facilitate this process (82). However, although some of these instruments have been demonstrated to give an accurate reflection of nursing workload, a number of deficits raised against using these tools, as they do not reflect the totality of workload within the ICU environment (82–85).

In 1974, the Therapeutic Intervention Scoring System (TISS) including 76 items describing medical and related nursing activities in the ICU, was created by Cullen and collaborators to measure severity of illness in association with the measurement of nursing workload (86). Later, the latter score was simplified into a 28-item score, namely TISS-28 (87). One feature of both versions of TISS is that the scores obtained in relation to the work done by one nurse during three daily shifts are comparable. This is important as it allows comparability within one ICU, between ICUs or between an ICU and other lower dependency units in the hospital (88). Another dependency scoring system is the Nine Equivalents of Nursing Manpower use score (NEMS) (89). Although only consisting of 9 items, NEMS was found to be a suitable therapeutic index to measure nursing workload at the ICU level. More particularly,

the authors recommend NEMS as a predictive tool of workload and planning of nursing staff allocation at the individual patient level (89). As many nursing activities are not necessarily related to the level of patients' acuity or severity of illness, the Nursing Activities Score (NAS) was developed to determine the nursing activities that best describe workload in ICUs by attributing weights to these activities so that the score describes average time consumption instead of severity of illness (90). The latter is of specific value for cost-effectiveness studies as they require accurate evaluation and quantification of nursing activities.

A study by Garfield and collaborators evaluating the use of TISS-28 in a high dependency unit is of particular interest in the analysis of research surrounding the use of dependency scoring systems (91). The authors studied whether the recommended 1:2 nurse patient ratio for such units was accurately reflected in the workload. Interpretation of their findings led the researchers conclude that a 2:3 ratio was a more accurate reflection of the workload.

Optimal nursing staff – potential strategies

Although clear and objective data regarding 'the optimal nurse patient ratio' does not exist, it is commonly perceived that nurse patient ratios are not well-balanced. Several reasons can be argued why hospitals in general might not staff at an optimal level, of which not being paid or subsidised for the quality of care provided is the most important one. In other words, the benefits of improving quality of care are not as large as the costs being spent. Above all, the incentive to do so is almost negligible, as in many cases, all hospitals receive roughly the same payment whether they provide either top or moderate level care. In addition, workload in ICUs is very unpredictable and may rise up or drop down dramatically within only a few hours. Consequently, it is hard to appropriately anticipate this highly variable workload without shunning periods of overstaffing which are scrupulously avoided by the local executive management. Below, three theoretical models will be briefly highlighted (77, 92, 93).

Firstly, specific 'fixed minimum nurse patient ratios' can be established (93). Clearly, minimum ratios provide a clear standard for nursing staff, and enforcement of such a standard is quite straightforward. In theory, a hospital employs nurses according to the overall severity of illness of patients, without going under a previously set minimum of nurses on the floor. The social value of this type of strategy rests on the notion that regulators select the correct minimum ratio. Noteworthy is that, since there are no data reporting the optimal level of nursing staff or relating the benefits of staffing to the costs, it is likely that fixed ratio requirements are too high or too low. Some impending controversial points need to be considered. In this system, the ratios might be too high or too low and hence worsen the effort to reach the optimal staffing level. As well, if a minority of nurses willing to supply labour at the prevailing wage persists, hospitals may be forced to reduce their capacity to maintain staffing ratios. Another critical limitation of ratios is that ratios do not take into account the variability found in hospitals such as available internal and external resources, individual and aggregate patient needs, and the nursing expertise required by the patient population. Next, fixed staffing may not be interpreted as the maximum required staffing, and ratios may potentially lead to an acceptance of minimally safe staffing and patient care instead of best practice staffing and care (93). On the other hand, if hospitals do not receive sufficient state subsidy for the provision of care, they may not be able to afford to increase staffing ratios.

Another strategy includes that hospitals establish 'staffing plans based on the patients' severity of illness' (77). This means that hospitals develop patient classification systems to determine their nursing care requirements and staff accordingly. When compared to fixed minimum staffing ratios, there are several advantages to mention. Patient-acuity based systems recognise that different patients have different needs. Despite this, from a governmental point of view it is rather difficult to enforce such a system, as standard patient classification systems do not exist. Consequently, if applied, hospitals might be inclined to make their own acuity systems which may, probably, not accurately reflect the real level of patient acuity, and therefore, be of questionable validity.

Thirdly, as a response to criticism that hospitals have less financial incentives to work as effectively as possible in terms of delivering top quality of care, policymakers have suggested that in-surance institutions and government healthcare programs should provide greater payments to those that meet or exceed previously determined quality standards. In such a system, called 'pay for performance' system, hospitals would have a direct incentive to invest in achieving better nursing staff levels, if they contribute to the quality of care. The latter is also the greatest benefit of such a system. Nevertheless, a pay for performance system has one major peculiarity as it imposes the need for performance indicators. Above, performance indicators measuring quality of care in an objective manner are scarce and difficult to measure. Moreover, it is easy to imagine that in a system in which hospitals know the indicators they are evaluated on, will strive to achieve the metrics for which they receive greater payment and will ignore those for which reimbursement is less. Lastly, the level of staffing by nurses as a measure of the quality of nursing care can be discussed as well. Other factors, such as effective communication between all healthcare workers, and a positive environment to work in have also been found to positively impact on patients' outcome (94, 95).

Final thoughts, controversial positions and future perspectives

Over years, we have evolved towards a healthcare system in which, correctly, the patient and his relatives expect efficient, effective care and equitable intensive care. Conversely, given the health economic reality, hospitals are expected to work in a more cost-effective manner and to deliver quality care to the community. Further, nurses expect to contribute to quality patient outcomes, organisational goals, and to feel satisfied with their work, their work environment, and their profession. However, healthcare economics has been driving the system to a point where the expectations of patients, families, staff, and organisations may no longer be met. Therefore, comprehensive short and long-term strategies are urgently needed. Some potential strategies described have both, opportunities and drawbacks. At this stage, it is difficult to recommend any single approach as none of these have been evaluated extensively. A place to begin is by ensuring that safe and effective nursing staff is available in all intensive care departments. Nevertheless, and anticipating the increasing demands of the future, high quality data is required to support the design of new staffing models. For instance, given the evidence that inappropriate staffing levels are associated with adverse outcomes, as well as the current and projected shortages of highly skilled nurses, future research should focus on routinely monitoring, in large numbers of hospitals hospital outcomes that are sensitive to levels of nursing staff. Beyond this, hospital administrators, accrediting agencies, insurers, policy makers, and regulators must continue to value and support nurses. They should take action to ensure an adequate supply of nurses in order to enhance and maintain optimal levels of patient safety.

The authors

Dominique M. Vandijck, RN, CCRN, MSc, MA, PhD-candidate[1, 2]

Stijn I. Blot, RN, CCRN, MNSc, PhD, Professor[3, 4]

[1]Ghent University Hospital |
Department of Intensive Care Medicine

[2]Ghent University | Faculty of Medicine and Health Sciences | Interfaculty Centre for Health Economic Research

[3]Ghent University Hospital |
Department of General Internal Medicine and Infectious Diseases

[4]University College Ghent |
Department of Healthcare

Address for correspondence
Dominique M. Vandijck
Ghent University Hospital
Department of Intensive Care Medicine
De Pintelaan 185
9000 Ghent, Belgium
e-mail: Dominique.Vandijck@UGent.be

References

1. Hind M, Jackson D, Andrewes C, Fulbrook P, Galvin K, Frost S. Health care support workers in the critical care setting. Nurs Crit Care. 2000;5:31–9.
2. Buerhaus PI, Staiger DO, Auerbach DI. Implications of an aging registered nurse workforce. JAMA. 2000;283: 2948–54.
3. Rapin M. The ethics of intensive care. Intensive Care Med. 1987;13:300–3.
4. Vandijck DM, Annemans L, Oeyen S, Blot SI, Decruyenaere JM. Cost-effectiveness in critical care. ICU Management. 2007;7:6–8.
5. Vandijck D. Development of an instrument for process orientation measurement in hospitals. Unpublished Master thesis Vlerick Leuven Gent Management School, Ghent. 2006:1–95.
6. Buerhaus PI, Auerbach D. Slow growth in the United States of the number of minorities in the RN workforce. Image J Nurs Sch. 1999;31:179–83.
7. Buerhaus PI, Staiger DO. Managed care and the nurse workforce. JAMA. 1996;276:1487–93.
8. Aiken LH, Sochalski J, Anderson GF. Downsizing the hospital nursing workforce. Health Aff (Millwood). 1996;15:88–92.
9. Spetz J. Hospital employment of nursing personnel. Has there really been a decline? J Nurs Adm. 1998;28:20–7.
10. Aiken LH, Clarke SP, Sloane DM, Sochalski J, Silber JH. Hospital nurse staffing and patient mortality, nurse burnout, and job dissatisfaction. JAMA. 2002;288: 1987–93.
11. American Nurses Association. Nursing fact sheet on quality. Washington, DC: American Nurses Publishing. 1999.
12. Hartz AJ, Krakauer H, Kuhn EM, Young M, Jacobsen SJ, Gay G et al. Hospital characteristics and mortality rates. N Engl J Med. 1989;321:1720–5.
13. Krakauer H, Bailey RC, Skellan KJ, Stewart JD, Hartz AJ, Kuhn EM et al. Evaluation of the HCFA model for the analysis of mortality following hospitalization. Health Serv Res. 1992;27:317–35.
14. Manheim LM, Feinglass J, Shortell SM, Hughes EF. Regional variation in Medicare hospital mortality. Inquiry. 1992;29:55–66.
15. Flood AB, Scott WR, Ewy W. Does practice make perfect? Part II: The relation between volume and outcomes and other hospital characteristics. Med Care. 1984;22: 115–25.
16. Kovner C, Gergen PJ. Nurse staffing levels and adverse events following surgery in U.S. hospitals. Image J Nurs Sch. 1998;30:315–21.
17. Kovner C, Jones C, Zhan C, Gergen PJ, Basu J. Nurse staffing and postsurgical adverse events: an analysis of administrative data from a sample of U.S. hospitals, 1990–1996. Health Serv Res. 2002;37:611–29.
18. Fridkin SK, Pear SM, Williamson TH, Galgiani JN, Jarvis WR. The role of understaffing in central venous catheter-associated bloodstream infections. Infect Control Hosp Epidemiol. 1996;17:150–8.
19. Pronovost PJ, Angus DC, Dorman T, Robinson KA, Dremsizov TT, Young TL. Physician Staffing Patterns and Clinical Outcomes in Critically Ill Patients: A Systematic Review. JAMA. 2002;288:2151–62.

20. Flood SD, Diers D. Nurse staffing, patient outcome and cost. Nurs Manage. 1988;19:34–5, 8–9,42–3.

21. Neidlinger SH, Bostrom J, Stricker A, Hild J, Zhang JQ. Incorporating nursing assistive personnel into a nursing professional practice model. J Nurs Adm. 1993;23:29–37.

22. Archibald LK, Manning ML, Bell LM, Banerjee S, Jarvis WR. Patient density, nurse-to-patient ratio and nosocomial infection risk in a pediatric cardiac intensive care unit. Pediatr Infect Dis J. 1997;16:1045–8.

23. Pronovost PJ, Jenckes MW, Dorman T, Garrett E, Breslow MJ, Rosenfeld BA et al. Organizational characteristics of intensive care units related to outcomes of abdominal aortic surgery. JAMA. 1999;281:1310–7.

24. Blegen MA, Goode CJ, Reed L. Nurse staffing and patient outcomes. Nurs Res. 1998;47:43–50.

25. Berenholtz SM, Pronovost PJ, Lipsett PA, Hobson D, Earsing K, Farley JE et al. Eliminating catheter-related bloodstream infections in the intensive care unit. Crit Care Med. 2004;32:2014–20.

26. Lichtig LK, Knauf RA, Milholland DK. Some impacts of nursing on acute care hospital outcomes. J Nurs Adm. 1999;29:25–33.

27. Robert J, Fridkin SK, Blumberg HM, Anderson B, White N, Ray SM, et al. The influence of the composition of the nursing staff on primary bloodstream infection rates in a surgical intensive care unit. Infect Control Hosp Epidemiol. 2000;21:12–7.

28. Iezzoni LI, Ash AS, Shwartz M, Daley J, Hughes JS, Mackiernan YD. Judging hospitals by severity-adjusted mortality rates: the influence of the severity-adjustment method. Am J Public Health. 1996;86:1379–87.

29. Iezzoni LI, Ash AS, Shwartz M, Mackiernan YD. Differences in procedure use, in-hospital mortality, and illness severity by gender for acute myocardial infarction patients: are answers affected by data source and severity measure? Med Care. 1997;35:158–71.

30. Iezzoni LI, Daley J, Heeren T, Foley SM, Hughes JS, Fisher ES et al. Using administrative data to screen hospitals for high complication rates. Inquiry. 1994;31:40–55.

31. al-Haider AS, Wan TT. Modeling organizational determinants of hospital mortality. Health Serv Res. 1991;26:303–23.

32. Taunton RL, Kleinbeck SV, Stafford R, Woods CQ, Bott MJ. Patient outcomes. Are they linked to registered nurse absenteeism, separation, or work load? J Nurs Adm. 1994;24:48–55.

33. Silber JH, Rosenbaum PR, Schwartz JS, Ross RN, Williams SV. Evaluation of the complication rate as a measure of quality of care in coronary artery bypass graft surgery. JAMA. 1995;274:317–23.

34. Silber JH, Rosenbaum PR. A spurious correlation between hospital mortality and complication rates: the importance of severity adjustment. Med Care. 1997;35:OS77–92.

35. Bradbury RC, Stearns FE, Jr., Steen PM. Interhospital variations in admission severity-adjusted hospital mortality and morbidity. Health Serv Res. 1991;26:407–24.

36. Zimmerman JE, Shortell SM, Rousseau DM, Duffy J, Gillies RR, Knaus WA et al. Improving intensive care: observations based on organizational case studies in nine intensive care units: a prospective, multicenter study. Crit Care Med. 1993;21:1443–51.

37. Mark BA, Salyer J, Wan TT. Market, hospital, and nursing unit characteristics as predictors of nursing unit skill mix: a contextual analysis. J Nurs Adm. 2000;30:552–60.

38. Wan TT, Shukla RK. Contextual and organizational correlates of the quality of hospital nursing care. QRB Qual Rev Bull. 1987;13:61–4.

39. Needleman J, Buerhaus P, Mattke S, Stewart M, Zelevinsky K. Nurse-staffing levels and the quality of care in hospitals. N Engl J Med. 2002;346:1715–22.

40. Person SD, Allison JJ, Kiefe CI, Weaver MT, Williams OD, Centor RM et al. Nurse staffing and mortality for Medicare patients with acute myocardial infarction. Med Care. 2004;42:4–12.

41. Schultz MA, van Servellen G, Chang BL, McNeese-Smith D, Waxenberg E. The relationship of hospital structural and financial characteristics to mortality and length of stay in acute myocardial infarction patients. Outcomes Manag Nurs Pract. 1998;2:130–6.

42. Aiken LH, Sloane DM, Lake ET, Sochalski J, Weber AL. Organization and outcomes of inpatient AIDS care. Med Care. 1999;37:760–72.

43. Shortell SM, Zimmerman JE, Rousseau DM, Gillies RR, Wagner DP, Draper EA et al. The performance of intensive care units: does good management make a difference? Med Care. 1994;32:508–25.

44. Spilsbury K, Meyer J. Defining the nursing contribution to patient outcome: lessons from a review of the literature examining nursing outcomes, skill mix and changing roles. J Clin Nurs. 2001;10:3–14.

45. Blegen MA, Vaughn T. A multisite study of nurse staffing and patient occurrences. Nurs Econ. 1998;16:196–203.

46. Sovie MD, Jawad AF. Hospital restructuring and its impact on outcomes: nursing staff regulations are premature. J Nurs Adm. 2001;31:588–600.

47. Potter P, Barr N, McSweeney M, Sledge J. Identifying nurse staffing and patient outcome relationships: a guide for change in care delivery. Nurs Econ. 2003;21:158–66.

48. Langemo DK, Anderson J, Volden C. Uncovering pressure ulcer incidence. Nurs Manage. 2003;34:54–7.

49. McGillis Hall L. Nursing staff mix models and outcomes. J Adv Nurs. 2003;44:217–26.

50. McGillis Hall L, Doran D, Pink GH. Nurse staffing models, nursing hours, and patient safety outcomes. J Nurs Adm. 2004;34:41–5.

51. Cho SH, Ketefian S, Barkauskas VH, Smith DG. The effects of nurse staffing on adverse events, morbidity, mortality, and medical costs. Nurs Res. 2003;52:71–9.

52. Amaravadi RK, Dimick JB, Pronovost PJ, Lipsett PA. ICU nurse-to-patient ratio is associated with complications and resource use after esophagectomy. Intensive Care Med. 2000;26:1857–62.

53. Bostick JE. Relationship of nursing personnel and nursing home care quality. J Nurs Care Qual. 2004;19:130–6.

54. Unruh L. Licensed nurse staffing and adverse events in hospitals. Med Care. 2003;41:142–52.

55. Dimick JB, Swoboda SM, Pronovost PJ, Lipsett PA. Effect of nurse-to-patient ratio in the intensive care unit on pulmonary complications and resource use after hepatectomy. Am J Crit Care. 2001;10:376–82.

56. Thorens JB, Kaelin RM, Jolliet P, Chevrolet JC. Influence of the quality of nursing on the duration of weaning from mechanical ventilation in patients with chronic obstructive pulmonary disease. Crit Care Med. 1995;23:1807–15.

57. Blot SI, Labeau S, Vandijck D, Van Aken P, Claes B. Evidence-based guidelines for the prevention of ventilator-associated pneumonia: results of a knowledge test among intensive care nurses. Intensive Care Med. 2007;33:1463–7.

58. Labeau S, Vandijck DM, Claes B, Van Aken P, Blot SI. Critical Care Nurses' Knowledge of Evidence-Based Guidelines for Preventing Ventilator-Associated Pneumonia: An Evaluation Questionnaire. Am J Crit Care. 2007;16:371–7.

59. Labeau S, Vereecke A, Vandijck DM, Claes B, Blot SI. Critical care nurses' Knowledge of Evidence-Based Guidelines for Preventing Infections Associated With Central Venous Catheters: An Evaluation Questionnaire. Am J Crit Care. 2008;17:65–71.

60. Vandijck DM, Labeau SO, De Somere J, Claes B, Blot SI, On Behalf Of The Executive Board Of The Flemish Society Of Critical Care N. Undergraduate nursing students' knowledge and perception of infection prevention and control. J Hosp Infect. 2008;68:92–4.

61. Morrison AL, Beckmann U, Durie M, Carless R, Gillies DM. The effects of nursing staff inexperience (NSI) on the occurrence of adverse patient experiences in ICUs. Aust Crit Care. 2001;14:116–21.

62. Tourangeau AE. A theoretical model of the determinants of mortality. ANS Adv Nurs Sci. 2005;28:58–69.

63. Tourangeau AE, Giovannetti P, Tu JV, Wood M. Nursing-related determinants of 30-day mortality for hospitalized patients. Can J Nurs Res. 2002;33:71–88.

64. Alonso-Echanove J, Edwards JR, Richards MJ, Brennan P, Venezia RA, Keen J, et al. Effect of nurse staffing and antimicrobial-impregnated central venous catheters on the risk for bloodstream infections in intensive care units. Infect Control Hosp Epidemiol. 2003;24:916–25.

65. Clarke SP. Hospital work environments, nurse character-istics, and sharps injuries. Am J Infect Control. 2007;35:302–9.

66. Clarke SP. Registered nurse staffing and patient outcomes in acute care: looking back, pushing forward. Med Care. 2007;45:1126–8.

67. O'Brien-Pallas L, Shamian J, Thomson D, Alksnis C, Koehoorn M, Kerr M, et al. Work-related disability in Canadian nurses. J Nurs Scholarsh. 2004;36:352–7.

68. Verhaeghe R, Vlerick P, De Backer G, Van Maele G, Gemmel P. Recurrent changes in the work environment, job resources and distress among nurses: A comparative cross-sectional survey. Int J Nurs Stud. 2008;45:382–92.

69. Verhaeghe R, Vlerick P, Gemmel P, Van Maele G, De Backer G. Impact of recurrent changes in the work environment on nurses' psychological well-being and sickness absence. J Adv Nurs. 2006;56:646–56.

70. Blot SI, Depuydt P, Annemans L, Benoit D, Hoste E, De Waele JJ et al. Clinical and economic outcomes in critical-ly ill patients with nosocomial catheter-related bloodstream infections. Clin Infect Dis. 2005;41:1591–8.

71. Vandijck DM, Blot SI, Decruyenaere JM, Vanholder RC, De Waele JJ, Lameire NH et al. Costs and Length of Stay Associated with Antimicrobial-resistance in Acute Kidney Injury Patients with Bloodstream Infection. Acta Clin Belg. 2008;63:31–8.

72. Vandijck DM, Decruyenaere JM, Labeau SO, Depaemelaere M, Blot SI. Economic impact of catheter-related sepsis in the intensive care unit. ICU Management. 2007;7:10.

73. Vandijck DM, Depaemelaere M, Labeau SO, Depuydt PO, Annemans L, Buyle FM et al. Daily cost of antimicrobial therapy in patients with Intensive Care Unit-acquired, laboratory-confirmed bloodstream infection. Int J Antimicrob Agents. 2008;31:161–5.

74. Vandijck DM, Oeyen S, Decruyenaere JM, Annemans L, Hoste EA. Acute Kidney Injury, Length of Stay, and Costs in Patients Hospitalized in the Intensive Care Unit. Acta Clin Belg. 2007;62:341–5.

75. Oeyen S, Vandijck DM, Benoit DD, Decruyenaere JM, Annemans LH, E.A. Long-term Outcome after Acute Kidney Injury in Critically Ill Patients. Acta Clin Belg. 2007;62:337–40.

76. Rothberg MB, Abraham I, Lindenauer PK, Rose DN. Improving nurse-to-patient staffing ratios as a cost-effective safety intervention. Med Care. 2005;43:785–91.

77. Spetz J. Public policy and nurse staffing: what approach is best? J Nurs Adm. 2005;35:14–6.

78. Endacott R. Staffing intensive care units: a consideration of contemporary issues. Intensive Crit Care Nurs. 1996;12:193–9.

79. Bion J. Rationing intensive care. Bmj. 1995;310:682–3.

80. Cox CL, McGrath A. Respiratory assessment in critical care units. Intensive Crit Care Nurs. 1999;15:226–34.

81. Goodfellow LM. Physical assessment: a vital nursing tool in both developing and developed countries. Crit Care Nurs. Q 1997;20:6–8.

82. Arthur T, James N. Determining nurse staffing levels: a critical review of the literature. J Adv Nurs. 1994;19: 558–65.

83. Campbell T, Taylor S, Callaghan S, Shuldham C. Case mix type as a predictor of nursing workload. J Nurs Manag. 1997;5:237–40.

84. Dickie H, Vedio A, Dundas R, Treacher DF, Leach RM. Relationship between TISS and ICU cost. Intensive Care Med. 1998;24:1009–17.

85. Large WP, Nattrass M, Simpson M. Working towards dependency scoring in critical care. Intensive Care Nurs. 1991;7:214–8.

86. Cullen DJ, Civetta JM, Briggs BA, Ferrara LC. Therapeutic intervention scoring system: a method for quantitative comparison of patient care. Crit Care Med. 1974;2: 57–60.

87. Miranda DR, de Rijk A, Schaufeli W. Simplified Therapeutic Intervention Scoring System: the TISS-28 items – results from a multicenter study. Crit Care Med. 1996;24:64–73.

88. Reis Miranda D. The Therapeutic Intervention Scoring System: one single tool for the evaluation of workload, the work process and management? Intensive Care Med. 1997;23:615–7.

89. Reis Miranda D, Moreno R, Iapichino G. Nine equivalents of nursing manpower use score (NEMS). Intensive Care Med. 1997;23:760–5.

90. Miranda DR, Nap R, de Rijk A, Schaufeli W, Iapichino G. Nursing activities score. Crit Care Med. 2003;31:374–82.

91. Garfield M, Jeffrey R, Ridley S. An assessment of the staffing level required for a high-dependency unit. Anaesthesia. 2000;55:137–43.

92. Annemans L. Course in Health Economy: Healthcare systems and healthcare reform. Ghent University: Academia Press. Ghent. 2002.

93. Malone RE. Nurse staffing ratios: progressive policy changes. J Emerg Nurs. 2003;29:180–2.

94. Aiken LH, Smith HL, Lake ET. Lower Medicare mortality among a set of hospitals known for good nursing care. Med Care. 1994;32:771–87.

95. Knaus WA, Draper EA, Wagner DP, Zimmerman JE. An evaluation of outcome from intensive care in major medical centers. Ann Intern Med. 1986;104:410–8.

Maria Jose Garcia Monge and Peter J.D. Andrews

The role of specialist (neurological critical care) units

Introduction

The earliest intensive care units (ICUs) were developed in the 1950s and 1960s in response to the polio epidemic of that time (1). They rapidly evolved into general ICUs that focused primarily on cardiopulmonary support for critically ill patients. Reports by McIver et al. (2), Gordon (3) and Karimi-Nejad (4) were the first to promote the benefits of airway protection and supported mechanical ventilation for patients after severe head injury. However, by the end of the 1980s despite the adoption of these practices, 30–43 % of patients treated for severe head injuries still died despite treatment in major neurosurgical centres (5).

The past decade has seen the introduction of protocols that involve the regular monitoring and control of intracranial pressure (ICP) and cerebral perfusion pressure (CPP), that have the potential to improve outcome following head injury (6). Although level 1 evidence of their benefits is lacking, they are incorporated into international guidelines, developed using an evidence-based approach and by expert consensus (7, 8, 9).

Critical care is a relatively young specialty and is continuously developing. This evolutionary process includes the development of sub-specialty units, for which there are some effectiveness data, and includes care of postoperative cardiac patients, trauma, and neurological patients. Trauma surgeons compared with non-trauma surgeons have also shown a significant mortality reduc-

tion (10). However the impact of Neurological Intensive or Critical Care Units (NICU) remains controversial (there are no randomised controlled trials to support their effectiveness) and there are concerns that specialty NICUs may increase ICU patient costs.

Traumatic brain injury (TBI) is a leading cause of premature death and disability and remains a major public health problem around the world (11, 12). The economic burden of TBI in the acute-care setting is substantial and treatment outcomes and costs vary considerably by TBI severity and mechanism of injury. Unfortunately, only a few reports of the health economics of intensive care of TBI have been published. Berg (13) reviewed all the articles published for admission for TBI across Europe and found that they numbered 235 patients per 100,000 population, per year and that the average cost per in-patient stay in 2004 ranged from 3,000 Euros in Sweden to 2,800 Euros in Spain.

The high costs and the limited resources available mean that these facilities should only be used when they are likely to improve patient outcome. Appropriate use of the limited neurological intensive care unit (NICU) resource is therefore of considerable importance.

Triage

Chantal et al., investigated whether triage for direct admission of patients with TBI is facilitated by predicting risk of requirement for specialist intervention. In a study involving a cohort of primarily (n = 200) and secondarily (n = 75) referred patients with moderate or severe TBI they showed no strong predictors of raised ICP could be identified, but age and papillary reactivity were significant predictors of surgically removable lesions. In conclusion, these authors showed that it is very difficult to identify patients in need of specialised intervention using baseline characteristics (14) since up to 25 % of patients with severe head injury have evidence of raised ICP in the absence of a surgical lesion, and suffer morbidity and mortality equal to those with surgical lesions (5, 15).

Protocols

There are few data supporting the many complex interventions that comprise NICU care for patients with TBI. However, in common with general ICU introduction of evidence-based protocols implemented by specialist(s), it has been shown to improve outcome.

Patel et al., compared the presentation, therapy and outcome in patients with head injury referred to a regional neurosurgical centre, before and after establishment of protocol-driven therapy. Patients from the two groups were well-matched for admission according to Glasgow Coma Scale Score and extracranial injury. A significant increase in favourable outcomes in the patients with severe head injuries (40.4 % vs. 59.4 %) was observed. The proportion of favourable outcomes was also high (66.6%) in those presenting with evidence of raised ICP in the absence of mass lesion and (60 %) in those that required complex interventions to optimise their recovery. It was concluded that specialist neurocritical care with protocol-driven therapy is associated with a significant improvement in outcome for all patients with severe head injury (16).

Clayton et al. compared the ICU and hospital mortality and length of stay (LOS) in patients before and after implementation of a protocol for their ICU management, based on a protocol by Souter and Andrews in which the maintenance of cerebral perfusion pressure was the primary goal. The protocol also considered the management of ICP. The implementation of the protocol was as-sociated with a reduction in ICU mortality (19.95 vs. 13.5) and in hospital mortality (24.5 vs. 20.8). The LOS remained constant. The group concluded that the introduction of an evidence-based protocol to guide the management of patients with severe head injury has been associated with a significant reduction in both ICU and hospital mortality (17). Elf et al. have shown similar findings (18).

Neuromonitoring

The same general principles that apply to all critically ill patients admitted to an ICU also apply to the treatment of severe head injury patients, however TBI patients frequently suffer from hypotension and hypoxemia between the time of injury and arrival in medical centres (19, 20) and these events are the most common determinants of poor outcome, probably due to secondary brain damage. Blood pressure and oxygenation should therefore be monitored as soon as possible after injury and any deficiencies corrected. In addition, clinical and experimental research strongly supports the argument that monitoring techniques and methods are indispensable in the early detection of further deterioration and to inform specific therapeutic and pharmacological interventions (21). There are many brain specific methods of monitoring which may help us to detect and prevent secondary insults.

Intracranial Pressure (ICP) and Cerebral Perfusion Pressure (CPP)

Intracranial pressure monitoring has not been shown to improve patient outcome in a randomised controlled clinical trial but the risks associated with its use are low and ICP information is considered useful in making therapeutic decisions. ICP monitoring is included in international guidelines (7, 8, 9) and evidence-based protocols previously described. ICP should be monitored in patients with a severe traumatic brain injury (GCS < 8) who also have an abnormal computer tomography (CT) and in those patients with a normal CT but who are older than 40 years old. It should also be monitored in patients with unilateral or bilateral motor posturing or systolic blood pressure < 90 mmHg. Treatment goals are applied to avoid an ICP higher than 25 mmHg and a CPP lower than 50 mmHg (22).

Although many head injury patients are managed using ICP/CPP monitoring, Stocchetti et al. (23) found that there are marked variations between centres in Europe. In a study which involved gathering information about the treatment of 1,005 patients with moderate and severe head injuries in 67 centres in 12 European countries, they showed that ICP and CPP were measured in only 34 % of cases and, in only 37 % of the most severe cases. In patients who were not monitored, ICP increases were less often suspected or identified, but the majority of monitored patients showed ICP increases. In contrast, ICP increases were suspected in fewer than 10 % of the patients not monitored.

Jugular Venous Oximetry (SjvO$_2$)

Desaturations of less than 50 % have been associated with a worse outcome after head injury (24) and increases in arteriojugular content to greater than 9 ml/dl also provides a useful marker of inadequate cerebral blood flow (CBF) and may help guide therapy (25). Cruz et al. carried out a study of 353 patients with severe TBI and diffuse brain swelling on CT. The control group underwent monitoring and management of CPP alone and the experimental group underwent monitoring and management of arteriovenous oxygen difference (AVD) and CPP. At six months post-injury it was shown that GOS had improved in the experimental group (25). Le Roux studied 32 patients with severe brain injury treated for worsening AVD with either mannitol or craniotomy and found that patients with limited improvement in AVD had increased incidence of delayed cerebral infarction and worse outcome at six months post-injury (26).

Continuous SjvO$_2$ monitoring will detect episodes of desaturations associated with raised ICP, hyperventilation and cerebral vasospasm. However, up to half of all measured desaturation below 50 % may be false positive (24) and the major SjvO$_2$ limitation is that it is a global measure of cerebral oxygenation and regional ischaemia may be missed.

Brain Tissue Oximetry (PbrO$_2$)

This technique is a focal method of monitoring tissue oxygenation. A PbrO$_2$ of less than 8–10 mmHg is the threshold below which ischaemic damage develops and which is associated with pathological and neurochemical alterations (27) and a worse outcome (28, 29). Van den Brink et al. reported a series of cases of 101 patients and found that initial PbrO$_2$ values less than 10 mmHg lasting for more than 30 minutes were associated with increased mortality and worse outcomes. A 50 % risk of death was associated with PbrO$_2$ values less than 15 mmHg and lasting 4 hours or longer (26). Valadka et al. reported a prospective case series of 34 patients with severe head injury and found that the likelihood of death increased with increasing duration of time of PbrO$_2$ of less than 15 mmHg. PbrO$_2$ less or equal to 6 mmHg, regardless of its duration, is associated with an increased chance of death (30).

Stiefel et al. conducted consecutive cohort analyses assessing PbrO$_2$ monitoring in paediatrics patients. Prior to its introduction, treatment for such patients following severe TBI involved control of ICP and CPP. After introduction of PbrO$_2$ monitoring, mortality significantly decreased and functional recovery improved. The introduction of PbrO$_2$ monitoring was also associated with fewer ICP and CPP interventions (31).

In common with SjvO$_2$, local PbrO$_2$ changes can be used to assess limits for hyperventilation and thus guide this therapeutic intervention (32). The use of brain tissue monitoring is maturing as a tool to detect and treat secondary brain injury. PbrO$_2$ measurements can provide continuous quantitative data about injury pathophysiology and severity that may help optimise neurointensive care management (33)

Microdialysis

Worsening cerebral damage caused by reduced oxygen delivery below critical thresholds results in failing cellular metabolism, increased production of free radicals, and release of neurotoxic levels of excitatory amino acids (34). Early detection of changes in these chemical markers of ischaemia may help guide management and allow early targeted therapy to reduce the risk of secondary damage in patients at risk. Microdialysis allows detection of these markers at tissue level (35) and which may be undetectable by other monitoring techniques (36).

Near Infrared Spectroscopy (NIRS)

Near infrared spectroscopy is a non-invasive method of estimating regional changes in cerebral oxygenation, but clinical use is limited by its inability to differentiate between intracranial and extracranial changes in blood flow and oxygenation which adversely affects the reliability of the readings (37).

Transcranial Doppler Ultrasound (TCD)

Transcranial Doppler ultrasound is also a form of non-invasive monitoring, which provides indirect information about cerebral blood flow. TCD is very useful in neurointensive care to diagnose high velocity states such as cerebral vasospasm or hyperaemia and to target therapy more appropriately. A limitation is there has been limited success in correlating it with invasive CPP measurements (29) and it is also operator dependent and may be limited by cranial anatomy.

It is hoped that continuous monitoring using multi-modal techniques will help to overcome the limitations of each individual method and will provide a better diagnosis. More specific treatment can then be applied; however, it remains to be determined which parameters are optimal. The use of these techniques requires highly trained personnel to avoid the potential of generating artefacts and possible misinterpretation.

Specialist personnel

There is concern that neurointensive care units (NICU) may increase cost, so it is important to determine if specialist neurological critical care teams (NTC) can improve outcome and if it is cost effective. Varelas et al., assessed the impact of a newly appointed intensivist on NICU patient outcome and found improvement in all patient outcomes studied such as mortality, length of stay (LOS) and discharge following the appointment

(38). Varelas also studied the impact of a neurointensivist on outcomes in head injury and severe stroke patients (39, 40) admitted to a NICU with similar results.

In a similar study Suarez et al., analysed the impact of specialised neurological critical care teams and found that such implementation was associated with reduced length of stay in both the neurosciences critical care unit (4.2 ± 4.0 vs. 3.7 ± 3.4, p < .001) and the hospital (9.9 ± 8.0 vs. 8.4 ± 6.9, p < .0001). They found no difference in readmission rates to the intensive care unit or discharge disposition to home but a significantly reduced hospital mortality (41).

Bershad et al. reported the impact of a neurological critical care team on outcome of critically ill acute ischaemic stroke patients. The presence of a NCT was associated with a decreased length of NCCU stay (2.9 ± 2.0 vs. 3.7 ± 2.9 days, p < 0.01), decreased length of hospital stay (7.5 ± 4.7 vs. 9.9 ± 7.6, p < 0.001), and increased proportion of home discharges (47 % vs. 36 %, p < 0.05). NTC was also associated with a reduction in resource utilisation and improved patient outcomes at hospital discharge (42). Patel et al. have shown similar findings to support the use of specialist personnel (16).

Thus it appears that many studies support the need for an NTC but several factors including the use of patient care protocols may also explain the improvements in patient outcomes, making it difficult to distinguish between the effect of specialist personnel themselves or the care pathways they initiate.

Impact of an NICU on patients' outcomes

To evaluate the benefits of neurological intensive care units (NICU) it is important to analyze their impact on patient outcomes. This has been addressed by a number of groups and the results are summarised in table 1.

Patel et al. (43), analyzed data retrospectively collected from the Trauma Audit and Research Network Database for patients with and without head injury presenting between 1989 and 2003 to assess mortality and cause of death. They found that mortality was increased by 26 % in those patients treated in non-specialty intensive care units. Yang Xuejun et al. compared the clinical outcome

Tab. 1 Studies reporting the impact of admission into a NICU vs. ICU.

Author	Population	Study design	ICU	Nº patients	Mortality
Patel et al. (43)	Severe head injury	Observational database	Neurosurgical ICU vs. Non-neurosurgical	22,216	Increased 26% in Non-neurosurgical ICU
Xuejun et al. (44)	Severe head injury	Prospective randomise study	NICU vs. ICU	200	Decreased from 39% to 25% in NICU
Mirski et al. (45)	ICH	Cohort with historical control	NICU vs. ICU	128	Decreased from 39% to 19% in NICU
Diringer, Edwards (46)	ICH	Cohort with historical control	42 ICUs (2 NICU)	1,038	Increased OR: 3.4 IC: 1.65–7.6 in ICU

of neurointensive care with general critical care in severe head injury. They described a significant increase in good recovery (54%) and significant decrease in mortality in those patients treated in an NICU. They concluded that NICU plays an important role in assessing the neurological state, guiding therapy, evaluating curative effect and estimating the outcome (44).

Mirski and Diringer analysed the impact of NICU treatment of patients with intracerebral haemorrhage (ICH). They found that patients treated in an NICU had a significantly improved mortality, functional outcome at discharge (p < 0.05), a shorter hospital stay (p < 0.01) and lower total cost of care (p < 0.01) than those patients treated in medical or surgical ICUs (45). Diringer and Edwards compared mortality rate after ICH in patients admitted to an NICU with those admitted to a general ICU. The study was an analysis of data collected by Project Impact over three years from 42 participating ICUs (including 2 NIUCs). This group observed that not being in an NICU was associated with an increase in hospital mortality rate, for those patients with a severe ICH (46).

Put together these results strongly suggest that admission to a speciality NICU provides the best care for patients with severe head injury (43). The improved outcome is multifactorial however and may be related to the ability of practitioners to standardise management of common medical problems and organise and manage the ICU environment (47, 48).

Costs/health economics

The best medical practice to ensure continued improvements in patient care whilst controlling rising costs remains a topic of considerable debate (45). Care of the critically ill patient is expensive and it has been estimated that approximately 1% of the USA gross domestic product is directly utilised in ICUs (49). There has been several studies where staffing ICUs with intensivists has been associated with improved outcomes and reduced resource utilisation (49–52) and as we have already reviewed, there also studies where staffing ICUs with a neurological critical care team has lead to a reduction in mortality and improved patient outcomes at hospital discharge (16, 38, 41, 42).

Mirski et al., showed a lower total cost of care for those patients with ICH treated in an NICU. The decreased LOS represented a cost difference of 28% for patients with a craniotomy with or without ICH or coma and of 35% for patients with skull fracture after trauma. In the group of patients with a craniotomy and ICH or coma, the cost savings exceeding $ 5,900 per case.

The cost per neurological critical care patient, managed in NICU was approximately 11% to 29% below that for care in other types of ICU. Imaging use was lower than expected for all modalities and pharmacy costs were also lower, despite the use of all major antibiotics, sedatives, H_2-blokers, antihypertensive, and inotropes. The main pharmacy difference was that medication of lower cost was used more frequently. Such data indicate that knowledgeable use of diagnostic tests (including imaging) and rational use of therapeutic interventions minimises unnecessary expenditure and improves outcomes.

Conclusion

Acute neurological disease processes are a major public health problem around the world and improving patient outcome whilst limiting costs remains a challenge that we must rise to.

Critically ill neurological patients require specialised management using complex monitoring techniques and therapies. A specialised neurological critical care team is necessary to interpret data and guide therapeutic interventions. Sub-specialty trained personnel including an intensivist and specialist nurses following evidence-based protocols have been shown to improve patient outcome and reduce hospital expenditure. There are many studies reporting that patients with severe TBI admitted to NICU fare better than those admitted to general ICUs in terms of outcome, mortality and LOS at a much lower cost.

Therefore, we conclude that there is sufficient evidence to recommend that all critically ill neurological patients should be treated in a specialised ICU.

The authors

Maria Jose Garcia Monge, MD[1]
Peter J.D. Andrews, MD, MB ChB, FRCA[2]
[1]Intensive Care Unit | Hospital:
C.H. Juan Canalejo | A Coruna, Spain
[2]Department of Anaesthesia |
Intensive Care and Pain Management |
University of Edinburgh, UK

Address for correspondence
Peter J.D. Andrews
Western General Hospital
Crewe Road South
EH4 2XU, Edinburgh ,UK
e-mail: p.andrews@ed.ac.uk

References

1. Lassen HCA. A preliminary report on the 1952 epidemic of poliomyelitis in Copenhagen with special reference to the treatment of acute respiratory insufficiency. Lancet. 1953;37.
2. Maciver IN, Lassman LP, Thomson CW, et al. Treatment of severe head injuries. Lancet. 1958;544–550.
3. Gordon E. Controlled respiration in the management of patients with traumatic brain injuries. Acta Anaesthesiol Scand. 1971;15:193–208.
4. Karimi-Nejad A, Frowein RA. The effects of central respiratory disorders on blood and CSF gases. Modern aspects of neurosurgery, vol 1.1.Excerpta Medica, Amsterdam. 1971;pp 74–85.
5. Marshall LF, Gautille T, Klauber MR, Eisemberg HM, Jane JA, Luerssen TG et al. The outcome of severe closed head injuries. J Neurosurg. 1951;75:S28–S36.
6. Kirkpatrick PJ. On guidelines for the management of the severe head injury. J Neurosurg Psychiatry. 1997;62: 109–111.
7. Maas A, Dearden M, Teasdale GM et al. EBIC-guidelines for management of severe head injury in adults. Acta Neurochir. 1997;139:286–294
8. Obrist WD, Langfitt TW, Jaggi JL, et al. Cerebral Blood flow and metabolism in comatose patients with acute head injury. J Neurosurg. 1984;61:241–253
9. Bullock R, Chesnut R, Clifton G, Ghajar J, Marion DW, Narayan RK et al. Guidelines for the management of severe head injury. Brain Trauma Foundation. EurJ Emerg Med. 1996;3:109–127.
10. Haut ER, Chang DC, Efron DT, Cornwell EE 3rd.Injured patients have lower mortality when treated by "full-time" trauma surgeons vs. surgeons who cover trauma "part-time". J Trauma. 2006 Aug;61(2):272–8;discussion 278–9.
11. Jennet B. Epidemiology of head injury. J Neurol Neurosurg. Psychiatry 1996;60:362–369.
12. Masson F. Epidemiology of severe cranial injuries. Ann Fr Anesth Reanim. 2000;19:261–269.
13. Berg J, Tagliaferri F, Servadei F. Cost of trauma in Europe. Eur J Neurol. 2005 Jun;12 Suppl 1:85–90.
14. Hukkelhoven CWPM, Steyerberg EW, Habbena JDF, Maas AIR. Admission of patients with severe and moderate traumatic brain injury to specialized ICU facilities: a search for triage criteria. Intensive Care Med. 2005;3:799–806.
15. Marshall LF, Marshall SB, Klauber MR, Clark MB, Eisenberg HM, Jane JA, et al. A new classification of head injury based on computerised tomography. J Neurotrauma. 1991;75: S4–S20.
16. Patel H, Menon DK, Tebbs S, Hawker R, Hutchinson PJ, Kirkpatrick PJ. Specialist neurocritical care and outcome from head injury. Intensive Care Med. 2002;28:547–553.

17. Clayton TJ, Nelson RJ, Manara AR. Reduction in mortality from severe head injury following introduction of a protocol for intensive care management. Br J Anaesth. 2004;93:761–7.

18. Elf K, Nilsson P, Enblad P. Outcome after traumatic brain injury improved by an organized secondary insult program and standardized neurointensive care. Crit Care Med. 2002 Sep;30(9):2129–34.

19. Chesnut RM, Marshall SB, Piek J, Blunt BA, Klauber MR, Marshall LF.Early and late systemic hypotension as a frequent and fundamental source of cerebral ischemia following severe brain injury in the Traumatic Coma Data Bank. Acta Neurochir. Suppl (Wien) 1993;59:121–5.

20. Gentleman D. Causes and effects of systemic complications among severely head injured patients transferred to a neurosurgical unit.Int Surg. 1992 Oct–Dec;77(4):297–302.

21. Stover JF, Steiger P, Stocker R. Treating intracranial hypertension in patients with severe traumatic brain injury during neurointensive care. Eur Journal of Trauma. 2005;n°4.

22. Guidelines for the management of severe traumatic brain injury, Journal of Neurotrauma. 24 (Supplement 1), May, 2007.

23. Stocchetti N, Penny KI, Dearden M, Braakman R, Cohadon F, Iannotti F et al. Intensive care management of head injured patients in Europe: a survey from the European Brain Injury Consortium. Intensive Care Med. 2001;27:400–406.

24. Sheinberg M, Kanter MJ, Robertson CS, Constant CF, Narayan RK, Grossman RG. Continuous monitoring of jugular venous oxygen saturation in head injuries patients. J Neurosurg. 1992;76:212–71.

25. Cruz J. The first decade of continuous monitoring of jugular bulb oxyhemoglobin saturation: management strategies and clinical outcome. Crit Care Med. 1998;26: 344–51.

26. Le Roux PD, Newell DW, Lam AM et al. Cerebral arteriovenous oxygen differences: a predictor of cerebral infarction and outcome in patients with severe head injury. J Neurosurg. 1997;87:1–8.

27. Sarrafzadeh AS, Kiening KL, Callsen TA et al. Metabolic changes during impending and manifest cerebral hypoxia in traumatic brain injury. Br J Neurosurg. 2003;17:340–6.

28. Van den Brick WA, van Santbrink H, Steyerberg EW, et al. Brain oxygen tension in severe head injury. Neurosurgery. 2000;46:868–76.

29. Fandino j, Stocker R, Prokop S, et al. Cerebral oxygenation and systemic trauma related factors determining neurological outcome after brain injury. J Clin Neurosci. 2000;7:226–33.

30. Valadka AB, Gopinath SP, Contant CF, Uzura M, Robertson CS.Relationship of brain tissue PO2 to outcome after severe head injury. Crit Care Med. 1998 Sep;26(9): 1576–81.

31. Stiefel MF, Spiotta A, Gracias VH et al. Reduced mortality rate in patients with severe traumatic brain injury treated with brain tissue oxygen monitoring. J Neurosurg. 2005;103:805–811.

32. Imberti R, Bellinzona G, Langer M. Cerebral tissue PO$_2$ and SjvO$_2$ changes during moderate hyperventilation in patients with severe traumatic brain injury. J Neurosurg. 2002;96:97–102.

33. Rose JC, Neill JA, Hemphill JC 3rd. Continuous monitoring of the microcirculation in neurocritical care: an update on brain tissue oxygenation. Curr Opin Crit Care. 2006 Apr;12(2):97–102.

34. Siesjö BK. Brain energy metabolism and catecholaminergic activity in hypoxia, hypercapnia and ischemia. J Neural Transm. Suppl. 1978;(14):17–22.

35. Persson L, Hillered L. Chemical monitoring of neurosurgical intensive care patient using intracerebral microdialysis. J Neurosurg. 1992;76:7–80.

36. Bellander BM, Cantais E, Enblad P, Hutchinson P, Nordström CH, Robertson C, Sahuquillo J, Smith M, Stocchetti N, Ungerstedt U, Unterberg A, Olsen NV. Consensus meeting on microdialysis in neurointensive care. Intensive Care Med. 2004 Dec;30(12):2166–9.

37. Owen-Reece H, Smith M, Elwell CE, Goldstone JC. Near infrared spectroscopy. Br J Anaesth. 1999;82:418–26.

38. Varelas PN, Conti MM, Spanaki MV, Potts E, Bradford D, Sunstrom C, Fedder W, Hacein Bey L, Jaradeh S, Gennarelli TA. The impact of a neurointensivist-led team on a semiclosed neurosciences intensive care unit. Crit Care Med. 2004 Nov;32(11):2191–8.

39. Varelas PN, Eastwood D, Yun HJ, Spanaki MV, Hacein Bey L, Kessaris C, Gennarelli TA. Impact of a neurointensivist on outcomes in patients with head trauma treated in a neurosciences intensive care unit. J Neurosurg. 2006 May;104(5):713–9.

40. Varelas PN, Schultz L, Conti M, Spanaki M, Genarrelli T, Hacein-Bey L. The Impact of a Neuro-Intensivist on Patients with Stroke Admitted to a Neurosciences Intensive Care Unit. Neurocrit Care. 2008 Jan 15.

41. Suarez JI, Zaidat OO, Suri MF, Feen ES, Lynch G, Hickman J, Georgiadis A, Selman WR. Length of stay and mortality in neurocritical ill patients: impact of a specialized neurocritical care team. Crit Care Med. 2004 Nov;32(11): 2311–7.

42. Bershad EM, Feen ES, Hernandez OH, Suri MF, Suarez JI.Impact of a Specialized Neurointensive Care Team on Outcomes of Critically Ill Acute Ischemic Stroke Patients. Neurocrit Care. 2008 Jan 15.

43. Patel HC, Bouamra O, Woodford M, King AT, Yates DW, Lecky FE;Trauma Audit and Research Network.Trends in head injury outcome from 1989 to 2003 and the effect of neurosurgical care: an observational study.Lancet. 2005 Oct 29–Nov 4;366(9496):1538–44. Erratum in: Lancet. 2006 Mar 11;367(9513):816.

44. Xuejun Y, Shuyuan Y, Minglu W, Yongzhong G. Prospective survey on neurological intensive care for patients with severe head injury. Chinese Journal of Traumatology. 2001;4(2):93–96.

45. Mirski MA, Chang CW, Cowan R.Impact of a neuroscience intensive care unit on neurosurgical patient outcomes and cost of care: evidence-based support for an intensivist-directed specialty ICU model of care.J Neurosurg Anesthesiol. 2001 Apr;13(2):83–92.

46. Diringer MN, Edwards DF. Admission to a neurologic/ neurosurgical intensive care unit is associated with reduced mortality rate after intracerebral hemorrhage. Crit Care Med. 2001 Mar;29(3):635–40.

47. Gore DC, Prough DS. Impact of intensivists on outcome of critically ill neurological and neurosurgical patients. Crit Care Med. 2004 Nov;32(11):2363–4.

48. Diringer MN. Bringing order to chaos. Crit Care Med. 2004 Nov;32(11):2346.

49. Pronovost PJ, Angus DC, Dorman T et al. Physician staffing patterns and clinical outcome in critically ill patients: A systematic review. JAMA 2002;288:2151–2162.

50. Randolph AG. Reorganizing the delivery of intensive care may improve patient outcome. JAMA. 1999;281:1330–1331.

51. Dimick JB, Pronovost PJ, Heitmiller RF, Lipsett PA. Intensive care unit physician staffing is associated with decreased length of stay, hospital cost, and complications after esophageal resection. Crit Care Med. 2001 Apr;29(4):753–8.

52. Pronovost PJ, Jenckes MW, Droman T et al. Organizational characteristic of intensive care units related to outcomes of abdominal aortic surgery. JAMA. 1999; 281:1310–1317.

53. Suarez JI. Outcome in neurocritical care: advances in monitoring and treatment and effect of a specialized neurocritical care team. Crit Care Med. 2006 Sep; 34(9 Suppl): S232–8.

Rui P. Moreno and Susana Afonso

Building and using outcome prediction models: Should we be lumpers or splitters?

"Every day you may make progress. Every step may be fruitful. Yet there will stretch out before you an ever-lengthening, ever-ascending, ever-improving path. You know you will never get to the end of the journey. But this, so far from discouraging, only adds to the joy and glory of the climb."

Winston Churchill

Introduction

Since their introduction into the field of critical care medicine in the early 1980s, general severity of illness scores and later, the general outcome prognostic models, have been applied to individual patients, providing the attending clinician or the researcher with an individual estimation of severity of illness, similarly to what others had proposed since the 1950s in other fields (1). The first of these systems was the Acute Physiology and Chronic Health Evaluation (APACHE) system (2). Developed in the George Washington University Medical Center in 1981 by William Knaus and co-workers, the APACHE system soon demonstrated its ability to evaluate, in an accurate and reproducible form, the severity of disease in this population (3–5).

Over the next years, simplifications and developments of the model were proposed, such as the Simpli-fied Acute Physiology Score (SAPS) (6) and the APACHE II (7). Apart from quantifying severity, the APACHE II system, published in 1985, introduced the possibility to predict mortality for individual patients, needing for that purpose several additional variables such as the selection of the major reason for Intensive Care Unit (ICU) admission from a list comprising several operative and non-operative diagnoses. Soon, it became apparent that this model, as well as its simplifications and competitors (such as the Mortality Probability Models (MPM) (8), the APACHE III (9), the SAPS II or the MPM II (10)), could only be used to compute the probability of hospital mortality for groups of critically ill patients and not for individual patients. Several reasons have been used to explain this fact, such as the lack of disease-specific variables, inadequate time windows and sampling space for the collection of the variables and the probabilistic nature of the statistical techniques used (11–13).

Apart from the problem of the inapplicability to individual patients, another problem became evident after a few years of use: the choice of the most adequate selection of patients for the reference population. To understand this question, we must realise that all these systems predict what would be the aggregated mortality at hospital discharge of a group of patients, with a certain burden of co-morbid diseases, a certain degree of physiologic dysfunction and a certain acute diagnosis, if they were treated in a virtual Intensive Care Unit (ICU) used to develop the model – the so called development population. At the best of its performance, the system can be only as good as to predict exactly what would be the behavior of a certain group of patients matching exactly a similar group of patients in the development population. This implies that the adequate choice of the development population is a crucial step – probably the most important step – in the development of these systems and models.

In this chapter we will present the actual controversy surrounding the second of these two issues: the selection of the development (or calibration) database and the impact of this choice on the resulting models.

Controversial position 1

The first widely used severity scores and outcome prediction models have all been developed with data collected from patients being cared for in ICUs in the United States of America (USA). This fact holds true especially for all the APACHE models, from the APACHE II to the IV version (7, 9, 14) and to the new MPM III$_0$ model (15). Other widely used models such as the SAPS II (16) and the MPM II models (10) used data from a selected sample of ICUs from Western Europe and the USA.

Apart from easier access to databases, researchers chose this strategy mainly to decrease the variability in the sample and to focus on their main market. It is always easier to work with a more homogeneous sample, where we assume that all the known and unknown factors that affect prognosis present only a random variation in their distribution in the participating ICUs. This homogeneity allows for more precise estimates of the effects of the variables in the outcome of interest (vital status at ICU discharge), creates a bigger market for the developed instruments and allows the set-up of global benchmarking systems in which ICUs can be evaluated based on the observed to predicted mortality ratio in order to generate league tables.

As times passes, all these models present a slow but consistent progressive lack of calibration. Slowly changes in the baseline characteristics of the admitted patients, in the circumstances of ICU admission and in the availability of general and specific therapeutic measures introduced an increasing gap between actual mortality and predicted mortality

(17). Overall, in the last years of the twentieth century, there was an increase in the mean age of the patients admitted to the ICU, with a larger number of chronically sick and immunosuppressed patients and also an increase in the number of admissions due to sepsis (18, 19). At the same time, mortality from major diseases, such as acute myocardial infarction or sepsis decreased steadily and performance consistently improved over the years, with the development and the application of new diagnostic and therapeutic approaches (19), which further impacted on this miscalibration.

So, by focusing in on limited regions of the globe to develop and calibrate the severity scores and the outcome prediction models, researchers that support this approach have had to keep track and to worry not just about changes in baseline epidemiology, but also changes in health delivery and therapeutic options and the resultant changes in outcomes,.

This approach has been followed, for example, by the developers of the APACHE systems (where even several updates in the predictive equations have been performed without changing the name of the score), as described by Zimmerman et al. from the Cerner Corporation that runs the APACHE database (14). Also in some areas of the world country-specific models have been developed and used to great success, such as the ones proposed by Rowan (20) and more recently by Harrison (21) in the UK, or by the Austrian Center of documentation and quality assurance in intensive care medicine (Philipp Metnitz, personnel communication).

The price paid by these researchers is that the results of these methodologies should not and cannot be extrapolated to other settings (e.g. to patients in South America or in Australasia): The genetic background of the patients is different, the epidemiology of diseases is different, lifestyles are different, organisation and delivery of medical care is different and the availability and use of medical technology are different. And these factors can make a difference, as demonstrated very clearly by Paulo Bastos in Brasil, working with the APACHE III system (22, 23).

Controversial position 2

In defence of controversial position 2, several epidemiologists and researchers argue that heterogeneity, although making the work of model developers more difficult, is crucial in order to understand the differences in outcome determinants and outcomes among different regions of the world. So, when building a model, these researchers looked for the database as an instrument to better reflect important differences in patients' and health care systems' baseline characteristics that are known to affect outcome. These include, for example, different genetic markers, different styles of living and a heterogeneous distribution of major diseases within different regions of the world, as well as issues such as access to the health care system in general and to intensive care in particular, or differences in availability and use of major diagnostic and therapeutic measures within the ICUs.

Although the integration of ICUs outside Europe and the US certainly increased the representativeness of the resultant databases, such as the SAPS 3 database developed by Moreno et al. (24) or the Ventila database developed by Esteban et al. (25, 26), it must be acknowledged that the extent to which these databases reflect the case mix of ICUs worldwide cannot be determined yet, since they have not been randomly selected and are consequently not necessarily representative of their respective regions of the world. It is noteworthy, however, to notice that even with major methodological limitations on the local or global representativeness of these databases, they have had a key role in understanding differences among different geographical areas regarding issues such as basic epidemiology of critical care (27), the impact of medical technology on improving outcomes (23), differences in the prevalence and prognostic determinants of severe infection and sepsis (28, 29), compliance with evidence-based advances in respiratory care (30) or the importance of religious affiliation and culture on end-of-life decisions (31).

The construction of these large databases has been accompanied by the development in certain areas of the globe of large registries, now consisting of hundreds of thousands of patients, such as the Intensive Care National Audit and Research Centre (ICNARC) in the United Kingdom, or the Australian and New Zealand Intensive Care Society (ANZICS) Adult Patient Database in Australia and New Zealand. Already, sometimes these databases are truly representative of a given population, by including all the patients in a given region of the world, such as the Scottish Intensive Care Audit Group (SICSAG), reporting data from all the ICUs in the country.

Consequently, apart from their role in documenting patient outcomes and comparing ICUs from different regions using risk-adjusted mortality and generating benchmarking scores, for quality assurance or management purposes (32), these types of instruments and databases have a very important role in research and teaching. They allow researchers to see the differences between different patient groups (24), to try to find the causes for these differences (33, 34) and, most importantly, to try to explain the differences (35). To achieve these aims we must assure that a large degree of heterogeneity remains in the database, a mandatory condition to perform research on the differences.

Conclusion

The choice of an outcome prediction model remains for the clinician or the ICU manager the result of a trade-off between local specificity and comparability and global applicability and comparability. The choice between them remains largely subjective and depends on the reference database that the user wants to use: the US centres participating in the APACHE III database that have been selected to develop the APACHE IV system or a more heterogeneous sample of ICUs across all major regions of the globe as in the SAPS 3 database. The absence of fees regarding the models and the existence of equations specific for each region of the world and for specific groups of patients (e.g. the equations for patients with severe infection and sepsis recently published by our group (29)) should be weighed against paid participation in a continuous database programme, providing a more professional support and analysis and reporting of the data.

For the time being, possibly the best trade-off between these two competing strategies is to move globally but retain a certain degree of local specificity through customisation (36). This option may result in more complex models and more complex data collection and analysis. However, with the widespread use of medical informatics and the forthcoming increase in automatic systems for data registry, validation, storage and analysis, this can be afforded.

No matter which model is chosen, users should keep in mind that the accuracy of these models is dynamic and should be retested periodically, and that when the models' accuracy deteriorates they must be revised and/or updated. It is probable that in the near future this would be an almost automatic process, done by well-managed regional, national or international registries.

So, we forecast that in a couple of years, lumpers and splitters will merge as our instruments will have the ability to zoom, allowing the user to look at large groups on the basis of major characteristics or to focus in on many small groups on the basis of relatively minor characteristics. In conclusion, as the possibilities to compare different databases increase, we will have the duty to think globally and act locally. In the meantime, every day we are making some progress in achieving that aim.

The authors

Rui P. Moreno, MD, PhD
Susana Afonso, MD
 Unidade de Cuidados Intensivos Polivalente |
 Hospital de Santo António dos Capuchos |
 Centro Hospitalar de Lisboa Central, E.P.E. |
 Lisboa, Portugal

Address for correspondence
 Rui P. Moreno
 Unidade de Cuidados Intensivos Polivalente
 Hospital de Santo António dos Capuchos
 Centro Hospitalar de Lisboa Central, E.P.E.
 Alameda de Santo António dos Capuchos
 1169-050 Lisboa, Portugal
 e-mail: r.moreno@mail.telepac.pt

References

1. Apgar V. A proposal for a new method of evaluation of the newborn infant. Anesth Analg. 1953;32:260–7.
2. Knaus WA, Zimmerman JE, Wagner DP, Draper EA, Lawrence DE. APACHE – acute physiology and chronic health evaluation: a physiologically based classification system. Crit Care Med. 1981;9:591–7.
3. Knaus WA, Draper EA, Wagner DP, Zimmerman JE, Birnbaum ML, Cullen DJ, Kohles MK, Shin B, Snyder JV. Evaluating outcome from intensive care: A preliminary multihospital comparison. Crit Care Med. 1982;10:491–6.
4. Knaus WA, Le Gall JR, Wagner DP, Draper EA, Loirat P, Campos RA, Cullen DJ, Kohles MK, Glaser P, Grantihil C, Mercier P, Nicolas F, Nikki P, Shin B, Snyder JV, Wattel F, Zimmerman JE. A comparison of intensive care in the U.S.A. and France. Lancet. 1982;642–6.
5. Wagner DP, Draper EA, Abizanda Campos R et al. Initial international use of APACHE: an acute severity of disease measure. Med Decis Making. 1984;4:297.
6. Le Gall JR, Loirat P, Alperovitch A et al. A Simplified Acute Physiologic Score for ICU patients. Crit Care Med. 1984;12:975–7.
7. Knaus WA, Draper EA, Wagner DP, Zimmerman JE. APACHE II: a severity of disease classification system. Crit Care Med. 1985;13:818–29.
8. Lemeshow S, Teres D, Avrunin J, Gage RW. Refining intensive care unit outcome by using changing probabilities of mortality. Crit Care Med. 1988;16:470–7.
9. Knaus WA, Wagner DP, Draper EA, Zimmerman JE, Bergner M, Bastos PG, Sirio CA, Murphy DJ, Lotring T, Damiano A, Harrell Jr. FE. The APACHE III prognostic system. Risk prediction of hospital mortality for critically ill hospitalized adults. Chest. 1991;100:1619–36.
10. Lemeshow S, Teres D, Klar J, Avrunin JS, Gehlbach SH, Rapoport J. Mortality Probability Models (MPM II) based on an international cohort of intensive care unit patients. JAMA. 1993;270:2478–86.
11. Lemeshow S, Klar J, Teres D. Outcome prediction for individual intensive care patients: useful, misused, or abused? Intensive Care Med. 1995;21:770–6.
12. Carlet J, Montuclard L, Garrouste-Orgeas M. Disaggregating data: from groups to individuals. In: Sibbald WJ, Bion JF, eds. Evaluating Critical Care. Using Health Services Research to Improve Quality. Berlin: Springer, 2001:309–20.
13. Moreno R. From the evaluation of the individual patient to the evaluation of the ICU. Réanimation. 2003;12:47s–8s.
14. Zimmerman JE, Kramer AA, McNair DS, Malila FM. Acute Physiology and Chronic Health Evaluation (APACHE) IV: Hospital mortality assessment for today's critically ill patients. Crit Care Med. 2006;34:1297–310.
15. Higgins TL, Teres D, Copes WS, Nathanson BH, Stark M, Kramer AA. Assessing contemporary intensive care unit outcome: An updated Mortality Probability Admission Model (MPM0-III). Crit Care Med. 2007;35:827–35.
16. Le Gall JR, Lemeshow S, Saulnier F. A new simplified acute physiology score (SAPS II) based on a European/ North American multicenter study. JAMA. 1993;270:2957–63.
17. Moreno R, Matos R. The "new" scores: what problems have been fixed, and what remain. Curr Opin Crit Care. 2000;6:158–65.
18. Angus DC, Linde-Zwirble WT, Lidicker J, Clermont G, Carcillo J, Pinsky MR. Epidemiology of severe sepsis in the United States: analysis of incidence, outcome and associated costs of care. Crit Care Med. 2001;29:1303–10.
19. Martin GS, Mannino DM, Eaton S, Moss M. The epidemiology of sepsis in the United States from 1979 through 2000. N Engl J Med. 2003;348:1546–54.

Building and using outcome prediction models: Should we be lumpers or splitters?

G

20. Rowan KM, Kerr JH, Major E, McPherson K, Short A, Vessey MP. Intensive Care Society's APACHE II study in Britain and Ireland – II: Outcome comparisons of intensive care units after adjustment for case mix by the American APACHE II method. Br Med J. 1993;307:977–81.

21. Harrison DA, Parry GJ, Carpenter JR, Short A, Rowan K. A new risk prediction model for critical care: The Intensive Care National Audit & Research Centre (ICNARC) model. Crit Care Med. 2007;35:1091–8.

22. Bastos PG, Sun X, Wagner DP, Knaus WA, Zimmerman JE, The Brazil APACHE III Study Group. Application of the APACHE III prognostic system in Brazilian intensive care units: a prospective multicenter study. Intensive Care Med. 1996;22:564–70.

23. Bastos PG, Knaus WA, Zimmerman JE, Magalhães Jr A, Wagner DP, The Brazil APACHE III Study Group. The importance of technology for achieving superior outcomes from intensive care. Intensive Care Med. 1996;22:664–9.

24. Metnitz PG, Moreno RP, Almeida E, Jordan B, Bauer P, Campos RA, Iapichino G, Edbrooke D, Capuzzo M, Le Gall JR, SAPS 3 Investigators. SAPS 3. From evaluation of the patient to evaluation of the intensive care unit. Part 1: Objectives, methods and cohort description. Intensive Care Med. 2005;31:1336–44.

25. Esteban A, Frutos-Vivar F, Ferguson ND. The epidemiology of mechanical ventilation. In: Kuhlen R, Moreno R, Ranieri M, Rhodes A, eds. 25 Years of Progress and Innovation in Intensive Care Medicine. Berlin: Medizinisch Wissenschaftliche Verlagsgesellschaft. 2007:93–100.

26. Esteban A, Anzueto A, Frutos F, Alía I, Brochard L, Stewart TE, Benito S, Epstein SK, Apezteguía C, Nightingale P, Arroliga AC, Tobin MJ, for the Mechanical Ventilation International Study Group. Characteristics and Outcomes in Adult Patients Receiving Mechanical Ventilation: A 28-Day International Study. JAMA. 2002;287:345–55.

27. Moreno RP, Metnitz PG, Almeida E, Jordan B, Bauer P, Campos RA, Iapichino G, Edbrooke D, Capuzzo M, Le Gall JR, SAPS 3 Investigators. SAPS 3. From evaluation of the patient to evaluation of the intensive care unit.

Part 2: Development of a prognostic model for hospital mortality at ICU admission. Intensive Care Med. 2005;31:1345–55.

28. Vincent J-L, Sakr Y, Sprung C, Gerlach H, Moreno R, Carlet J, Le Gall J-R, Payen D, Reinhart K, Ranieri VM. Patterns of infection in European Intensive care units: Results of the SOAP study [Abstract]. Am J Respir Crit Care Med. 2004;169:A846.

29. Moreno RP, Metnitz B, Adler L, Hoechtl A, Bauer P, Metnitz PGH, SAPS 3 Investigators. Sepsis mortality prediction based on predisposition, infection and response. Intensive Care Med. 2008;34:496–504.

30. Esteban A, Ferguson ND, Meade MO, Frutos-Vivar F, Apezteguia C, Brochard L, Raymondos K, Nin N, Hurtado J, Tomicic V, Gonzalez M, Elizalde J, Nightingale P, Abroug F, Pelosi P, Arabi Y, Moreno R, Jibaja M, D'Empaire G, Sandi F. Evolution of Mechanical Ventilation in Response to Clinical Research. Am J Respir Crit Care Med. 2008;177:170–7.

31. Sprung CL, Maia P, Bulow H-H, Ricou B, Armaganidis A, Baras M, Wennberg E, Reinhart K, Cohen SL, Fries DR, Nakos G, Thijs LG, the Ethicus Study Group. The importance of religious affiliation and culture on end-of-life decisions in European intensive care units. Intensive Care Med. 2007;33:1732–9.

32. Goldstein H, Spiegelhalter DJ. League tables and their limitations: statistical issues in comparisons of institutional performance. J R Stat Soc A. 1996;159:385–443.

33. Lee WL, Ferguson ND. SOAP and sepsis-Analyzing what comes out in the wash. Crit Care Med. 2006;34:552–4.

34. Rothen HU, Stricker K, Einfalt J, Bauer P, Metnitz PGH, Moreno RP, Takala J. Variability in outcome and resource use in intensive care units. Intensive Care Med. 2007;33:1329–36.

35. Bellomo R, Stow PJ, Hart GK. Why is there such a difference in outcome between Australian intensive care units and others? Current Opinion In Anaesthesiology. 2007;20:100–5.

36. Moreno R, Apolone G. The impact of different customization strategies in the performance of a general severity score. Crit Care Med. 1997;25:2001–8.

José-María Domínguez-Roldán

Specialty of intensive care:
Primary specialty vs. supraspecialty

Introduction

Centralising high-risk patients with qualified caregivers and with the technological resources directed towards the treatment of these patients began to be an essential part of the organisation of daily hospital medical care some decades ago. The grouping of critically ill patients with poor prognoses was one of the care strategies that developed during the time of great military conflicts. During World War II, anaesthesiologists took a prominent role in critical care, grouping together patients with surgical casualties in shock wards (1). It was during the great polio epidemics of the 1950s and 1960s that the need to centralise patients developing respiratory complications became urgent. As a result of this, the first organised areas of intensive treatment for critical patients appeared in the 1960s (2). During that decade, coronary units in Toronto, Kansas and Philadelphia demonstrated their efficiency by reducing morbidity and mortality related to acute myocardial infarction (3).

In these early stages of intensive care unit (ICU) development, assisted ventilation stood out as one of their most relevant features. There were various factors underlying the emergence of the first intensive care units, the most important being the need to centralise patients requiring highly complex care together with the specific technological resources used in their treatment. To this was added the need to group together nursing and medical personnel with specialised training and knowledge in the care of critical patients.

Over the years, intensive care units have been growing in number, becoming an essential area in all hospitals of developing countries. That growth has been influenced by the perception that society has of the effectiveness of intensive care medicine, and also by the requirements of support that other specialties require, such as surgery.

Nowadays, intensive care transcends the traditional borders of medical specialties, and it is not so closely joined to certain techniques like mechanical ventilation. Recently, intensive care medicine took an approach basing patient selection on acuity, severity of the illness and risk of the patient, which challenged the traditional concepts of responsibility for (and ownership of) patients (4).

Fisher defines an intensive care unit as "a hospital area in which an increased concentration of specially trained staff and monitoring equipment allow more detailed and frequent monitoring and more frequent intervention in seriously ill patients" (4). However, the present tendency is to amplify the concept of critical care medicine until it surpasses the limits of the intensive care unit, to include all medical activities performed in any place where there is a seriously ill patient, including emergency departments, ambulance services, disaster zones, etc.

Beside the clinical aspect, the intensive care unit is not only a place for attending to critical patients, but also one of the hospital areas with greater possibilities for the development of clinical research. This assessment is sustained due to the availability of monitoring tools for the patients' physiological parameters, as well as the permanent presence of doctors and nurses in the units.

The management of intensive care units by doctors who are specialists in intensive care medicine or whose primary function is the work of intensive care, has been demonstrated to have a significant influence on the decrease of mortality and survival of patients (5).

The young age of intensive care medicine (ICM) as a medical discipline justifies the existence of some maladjustment between the kind of training needed for the practice of this discipline and the requirements for the certification of professionals. The existence of different models of intensive care medicine around the world (6) also is a reason for this imbalance of requirements. Aside from these factors, and not so many years ago, there still remained the controversy between "closed" intensive care units and the "open units" model. Thus, the relevant definition of the ICU model and type of professional needed to work within it, has conditioned the training and certification of these professionals.

In recent years, different research has shed light on this subject, which could consequently clarify the direction of training for ICU doctors in intensive care units. When compared to ICUs with an "open" model, the efficiency of the ICU in a "closed" system model, where intensivists must be managers, economists, and also have a regular ongoing commitment to the unit, has shown more efficient indicators in some research. Some of these indicators include: decreased ICU length of stay, hospital length of stay, and shorter courses of mechanical ventilation. In ICUs with an "open" model, patient care and responsibility rests on the primary admitting clinician, which leads to diverse medical contributions through multiple referrals or consultations, and are usually organ-system focused (7).

"Closed" units of the intensive care model will bring rationalisation of costs, an increase of clinical efficiency, and consistency in the approach to the family of the patients. The evidence indicates that patient outcomes are improved when intensivists are available around the clock for patient consultation. The effects of full-time work and availability of qualified intensivists has been linked to lower mortality and costs (8). In a retrospective analysis, some authors suggested that a full-time, trained critical care specialist may have made a significant impact on the management of critically ill patients in the hospital (8).

Nevertheless, ICM is not yet a "perfect system" looking for the "perfect professional" who is going to work in ICM. The criticism which ICM is currently receiving will no doubt determine the direction of the professional profile of the future.

1. The intensivist is not always where the severely ill patients are. The critical care patient is not only in the intensive care unit, but also in emergency departments, in the street, at a trauma site, etc. Therefore, it would be necessary to answer the question: "Could society pay a medical specialist to work in all these places?"

2. Intensive care units are very expensive areas. The intensive care unit is the most labour-intensive, technically complex, and expensive part of hospital care. Within hospital services, critical care is regarded as a high resource consumer. Substantial variations in ICU practice, and thus, costs, have been reported, questioning the efficiency of ICUs (9).

3. Another current point of criticism of intensive care as a medical specialty is that ICM is not really adapted to the real demand of assistance of population. The Committee on Manpower for Pulmonary and Critical Care Societies (COMPACCS study) in the US concluded in 2000 that, "if current trends in the utilisation and supply of intensivist services continued, a severe shortage of intensivists would materialise within the next decade". This research also found that two-thirds of critically ill patients did not receive care from intensivists (10) (which in the COMPACCS study also includes pulmonologists who spend some time in ICUs).

Similarities and dissimilarities of intensive care to other medical specialties. Its possible influence in certification and training in ICM

A relevant factor that is going to determine the training and certification of intensive care doctors is the actual legal framework of intensive care. In most European countries, intensive care medicine certification can be obtained as a particular competence (an area of expertise in addition to a primary specialty) with a common training programme for specialists and a board certification in a variety of base disciplines:

- Anaesthesiology
- Surgery
- Cardiac surgery
- Internal medicine
- Cardiology
- Neurology
- Neurosurgery
- Pediatrics
- Pneumonology

The European Directive on Recognition of Professional Qualifications (Directive 2005/36/CE of the European Parliament) (11) does not explicitly identify "intensive care medicine" or "reanimation" as a medical specialty. However, when the most accepted criteria for recognition of a specialty are applied to critical care it seems strange to exclude the recognition of ICM as a medical specialty. For the recognition of a discipline as a medical specialty, the general requirements are:

1. The discipline must be a social need and evidence that practice of the discipline improves patient care and outcomes. At the moment, it would be impossible to imagine great medical centres without the existence of intensive care units that take care of severely ill or high-risk patients. In addition, in developed countries, the attention to a critical patient is a social demand, not only at the hospital level but also in the pre-hospital setting. The treatment of trauma patients, patients with acute cardiac pathologies, or other types of acute patients, is a reality which the citizens of these countries will probably not reject.
2. The discipline must have a body of unique knowledge and not be incorporated into other specialties, that is, what is clearly intensive care management.
3. The discipline must have enough applicability to define a distinguishable clinical practice.
4. The discipline must be able to generate new medical information and contribute to the advancement of medical research (12) (probably one of the stronger areas of intensive care medicine).
5. The discipline must involve specific technologies and procedures in daily practice.
6. Another characteristic of any discipline that wants to be considered as a specialty is the recognition of and adherence to a minimum training period.

Besides the above-mentioned characteristics, and similar to other medical specialties, ICM has some specific features which are relevant to the content of its area of knowledge, and also has significant influence on the professional development and career of doctors in the ICU:

- The attendance to the critical patient shows some distinctive features that differentiate it from other medical specialties. One of them is the requirement of patients for continuous and permanent attention, 24 hours a day, 365 days of the year.
- It is not a procedure-based specialty like most of the surgical specialties.
- It is not an organ-disorder-based specialty, like cardiology or pneumonology. Rather, it is the opposite – critical care includes the management of different organs individually, or, frequently, simultaneously affected organs.
- It is not a population-based specialty, like pediatrics, obstetrics and gynecology. All age groups are included in the clinical population assisted in the ICU.
- Some authors consider ICM a "location-based" specialty (12), like, for example, hospitalists. This assessment can be more or less accurate if the activity of intensivists is considered in the framework of the intensive care unit. However, the future of critical care is not only related to the location of the patient and doctor, but to the severity of the process, the procedures for treatment and the intensivists' attitude toward illness.

ICM is a diverse medical specialty that crosses the "organ approach" which attends to all ages of patients, providing both diverse and commonplace procedures and techniques (see fig. 1), and is mainly located in the intensive Care Units, but can be also performed in different settings where a critical care patient may be located.

In spite of everything mentioned above, the historic recognition of status for the specialty of ICM has not been vindicated. Currently in Europe the official body within the European Union (the European Union of Medical Specialties, UEMS) which is responsible for the harmonisation of medical specialties has not yet considered ICM as an independent medical specialty.

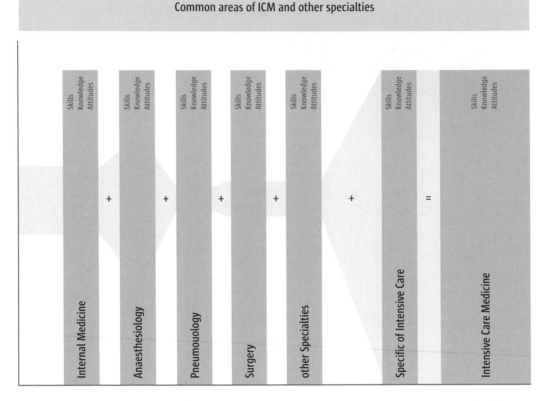

Fig. 1   ICM is a medical specialty that shares knowledge, skills and attitudes with other specialties, like anaesthesiology, pneumonology, etc. These areas plus the specific techniques, area of knowledge, attitudes, set up the structure of ICM.

Present situation of training and certification in intensive care medicine

The legislative heterogeneity that presently exists in the world (specialty, diploma, etc) regarding the kind of certification (primary specialty, supraspecialty, etc.) which allows ICM practice also extends to the models of training (primary specialty, specialty, etc.) used to achieve certification.

From a legal point of view, the level of accreditation for the practice of ICM is also diverse when different countries' legislations are analysed. In some countries, like Spain and Australia, ICM is considered a medical specialty. In other countries, doctors that practice in the ICUs need a certification, or diploma, obtained by not always standardised training periods and exams. Similar variability is observed when the different mod-

els of acquiring ICM skills and knowledge are analysed.

At the international level, the different ways to achieve accreditation (see fig. 2) and training in ICM can be classified as:

■ Primary specialty

ICM as a 'primary specialty' means that a specific programme of acquisition of competences exists independently of training or certification in other specialties. Thus, ICM is a base specialty and can be accessed after undergraduate training. In some countries a primary specialty in ICM is the only model to access certification in ICM. In other countries there is a dual accreditation system. The primary specialty, with a training duration between 60 and 72 months, exists in countries like Spain, Switzerland, Australia and New Zealand.

■ **Subspecialty**

Access to training in the critical care specialty can also be facilitated by a subspecialty model. The subspecialty can be made from different parent disciplines or for a single specialty. In order to access the subspecialty, there must exist specific training to previously/simultaneously acquire the abilities and competencies resulting in the accomplishment of a primary specialty.

▪ **Subspecialty from a single discipline.** This model of training in ICM is mainly developed from anaesthesiology as a parent specialty. Thus, after achieving the certification, anaesthesiologists (or other specialists) can receive special training of variable duration (according to the different regulations of countries), earning the degree of intensivist. Barrett and Bion found (13, 14) that out of thirteen European countries, 34 % provided a single specialty model of training. In 9 of these 13 countries, anaesthesia was the exclusive specialty that allowed access to ICM training.

▪ **Subspecialty from multiple disciplines.** In the United States and four countries in Europe (14), training in ICM can be accessed from multiple base specialties. The main differences between "subspecialty from multiple disciplines" and the supraspecialty is that in the case of supraspecialties, there is a common national curriculum for achieving a diploma as an ICM specialist. Conversely, in the model of "subspecialty" access from multiple specialties there is a variation in the contents of the programmes, duration and standards of training depending on the base specialty. Another difference is that in the "multiple subspecialties" model, access to intensive care training is possible during (in some specialties) or after (in other specialties) base training.

When base specialties (identified as a means to access ICM as a subspecialty) are analysed in an international comparison, notable differences are found. Whereas in Europe the predominant "parent specialty" is anaesthesiology, in the US physicians trained in pulmonary medicine (15) provide the greater part of care in ICUs (16). D.B. Cousin stated in his Lifetime Achievement Award Lecture 2006, "Training

and certifying the intensivists of the future", before the American Society of Critical Care Anaesthesiologists: "*As an anesthesiologist, internist, and intensivist by training and certification, I am a better critical care physician because of my anesthesia training.*" Other authors consider pneumonology or emergency medicine (17) similarly preferential disciplines for accessing ICM.

■ **Supraspecialty**

Multidisciplinary access to ICM training programmes from a range of base disciplines during or after training in the base specialty is the concept of "supraspecialty in ICM". Training may be conducted in a modular system or in a single block, with a common national training curriculum. In Europe, the supraspecialty model currently is the most common method of training in ICM. In the survey developed by ESICM in 2004 (18) involving 41 countries, fifty-four different training programmes in ICM were identified; the supraspecialty model was the most frequently utilised structure of training (39 %). Internal medicine, anaesthesia, surgery, pneumonology are the parent disciplines, more related to ICM as a medical supraspecialty.

"Practice-based" learning, including completion of a training period (3–6 years for ICM), following one of the models mentioned above (supraspecialty, subspecialty, etc.) is a classical approach to acquiring and demonstrating qualification in a medical discipline. However, different and modern models of certification, not based on the traditional place-and-length training but on competence-based training, are emerging.

Intensive care medicine has been one of the pioneer specialties to create a competency-based training programme. The European Society of Intensive Care (ESICM) has developed a competency-based training programme in intensive care for Europe (CoBaTrICE) and other world regions, by using consensus techniques to develop minimum core competencies for specialists in ICM (19). The CoBaTrICE defines the minimum standards of knowledge (20), skills and attitudes required for a doctor to be identified as a specialist in ICM in terms of competency statements.

The first steps of CoBaTriCE collaboration have been made. However, it is only the first part of a

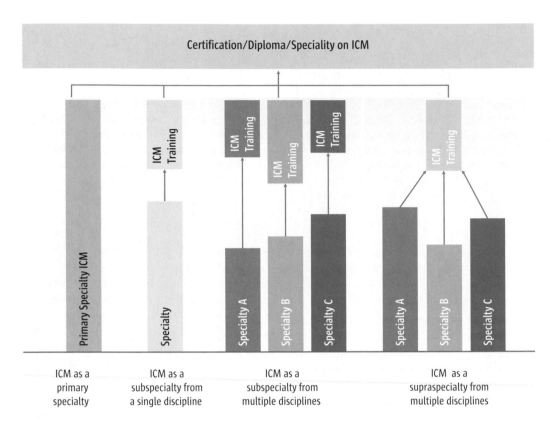

Fig. 2   Different models to access ICM certification/specialisation.

process that should include CoBaTrice as an internationally accepted programme. Moreover, the model certification on competency-based training requires not only the delineation of specific competencies but also the development of specific measurements and indicators of these competencies. Therefore, a competence-based certification system must also be developed.

Advantages and disadvantages of primary specialty versus supraspecialty in ICM

In spite of this broad spectrum of pathways for access to ICM training and certification, some experts consider that current training pathways for intensivists are inefficient and can contribute to a future shortfall in the availability of intensivists (21). This shortage of intensivists is considered very relevant, and a limiting factor to the development of the present model of intensive

care units (22). In 2004 in the United States, the board-certified critical care physicians (directed ICU teams) cared for only one in three ICU patients (23). One of the proposals to address the shortage of critical care doctors should be the possibility of establishing primary residencies in intensive care, which already exist in some countries (21). So, could a change in the pathways of training be a solution for the future of intensive care? What are the advantages and disadvantages of both models?

Supraspecialty in intensive care

The multidisciplinary access to the ICM training programme from a range of parent specialties (supraspecialty) can have some positive elements in comparison with the primary specialty model; however, some disadvantages should also be considered:

Advantages of the ICM supraspecialty model

- One of the strategies to keep a medical discipline alive is to permanently refresh and update that area of knowledge. Multidisciplinary access to intensive care medicine from different medical specialties offers the chance of profiting from many sources of specialist knowledge and skills (24). The background of doctors from other specialties coming to ICM can enrich the area of knowledge and contribute to the increase of diagnostic and therapeutic techniques first developed in other specialties, which could mean an increase in the potential of ICM as a medical specialty.
- In their daily activities, intensive care doctors cross the lines between specialties. One of the main skills of ICU doctors must be a flexible attitude to approach the patient and illness not only from the perspective of an ICU doctor, but also from the view of the other medical specialists who need the support of an intensivist for their patients. A broad-minded position could benefit from the supraspecialty model of training.
- Competence-based training, the most innovative system of definition of knowledge, skills and attitudes in ICM, adapts better to the system of supraspecialty than to the primary specialty model because it facilitates learning of doctors that comes from other specialties where they could have acquired before some of these competences.
- The need to sustain intense clinical activity in acute areas of clinical complexity (with constant mental and physical fatigue) makes it difficult to maintain continuous motivation for improving quality and updating knowledge. However, the approach to ICM as a supraspecialty, and consequently, the possibility of an optional reconversion to the primary specialty may reduce the potential situation of "burn-out" syndrome associated with ICM practice, and may make the daily practice of intensive care easier.
- Following the rules of the "health market", the factors affecting the supply of, and demand for, physician services are complex and dynamic. For the health services administrations, the supraspecialty model could be a more flexible system for adapting to the changing demands on medical specialists. The existence of several potential sources (disciplines/specialties) of physicians could allow specialists to meet a given social demand (25). The dual specialty (in the case of ICM as a supraspecialty, parent specialty plus ICM) could open up additional market options for these physicians.
- The supraspecialty model also offers an advantage to the physician who has opted for ICM training: the previous insight into what ICM involves, and the knowledge gained in the period of training and practice.

Disadvantages of the supraspecialty model

- The intensivists practicing ICM (as a supraspecialty) who come from a primary specialty may tend to bias their clinical activity according to their previous background. Given that most intensive care units are multidisciplinary and non-specialised, this specialisation in organs and pathologies is not suitable in intensive care units where the multidisciplinary ICU should cover the management of the whole spectrum of critical care patients.
- The period of training and acquisition of enough competencies in intensive care is longer if the training is performed as a supraspecialty rather than a primary specialty model. In the international survey of training in adult intensive care, H. Barrett and J.F. Bion observed that the longest periods of training (up to 96 months) are found in some supraspecialty programmes in ICM (14).

Primary specialty model of intensive care

An overview of the advantages and disadvantages of a primary specialty in ICM (entails ICM as a base specialty that can be accessed after undergraduate training, ending with a unique certification in ICM) could consider the following issues:

Advantages of primary specialty in ICM

- One of the main advantages of ICM as a primary specialty is the fact that the medical training is directed specifically toward the exclusive treatment of critical patients or high-risk patients. The concentration of training over a period of four to five years has demonstrated its efficiency in training intensive care specialists. In countries like Australia or Spain, where ICM is a primary specialty, the qualification of these specialists has never been questioned.

- The intensivist is required to be multi-skilled and proficient in all aspects of care for all patients in critical and non-critical situations. This specialist training can be better achieved in long, specific training periods, as in the primary specialty model.

Disadvantages of the primary specialty model

- ICM is a relatively young specialty, and one of the consequences of this is the lack of sufficient comprehension of ICM knowledge in the undergraduate period. Lacking this information could increase the risk of failure for young doctors who choose to specialise in ICM.
- A relevant problem of the ICU primary specialty is the "sustainability" of a life-long career as a professional intensivist. For the intensivist, physical and mental stamina are important qualities. The impact of this potentially highly stressful position, with anti-social working hours, prioritisation of care in a framework of limited and stretched resources (e.g. number of available beds) and making decisions about life and death can have a negative psychological effect. Primary specialty training limits the possibilities of changing to another specialty. Primary specialty makes difficult the change to another job position in the hospital if the training of the doctor is limited to ICM.
- Today, the limited opportunities for private practice of ICM are observable. Consequently, having a primary specialty is associated with the restriction of practising only in the field of ICM. Doctors with ICM as a supraspecialty have the potential of enlarging their areas of practice (to their base specialty) and consequently, to expand to public and private practice. In general, there is a smaller number of positions allocated to the ICU when compared to other job positions or specialties in the hospital. Therefore, the intensivist whose ICU training is achieved as a primary specialty may be limited in terms of future positions.

Summary and key points

It is not simple to give a definite answer to the controversy of primary specialty versus supraspecialty in intensive care medicine. In a general overview, it seems that the supraspecialty model has some advantages over the primary specialty, such as flexibility, "labour market" availability and professional "sustainability".

However, it is evident that the present compartmentalisation of medical specialties needs to develop a more flexible system of training "patient-centered" health care delivery within the rules of the health market.

ICM as a discipline must design a training system to respond to the growing demands of patients and the limitations of the economical resources that sustain the health systems. Intensive care treatment is now an expectation of today's society.

The model of "closed" ICUs seems a good solution for most hospitals, but not for all. Medium-sized hospitals, with medium-size ICUs probably need the profile of a medical mix, which will differ from the staff of specialised ICUs or small ICUs.

Regarding flexibility in the qualification of intensivists, the competence-based training model will probably have a relevant role in the definition of models of ICM training. But for now, the first step is to define the "core", or basic requirements for developing these positions in a large number of ICUs. However, an expansion of the core to a higher level of qualification could contribute to the supply of intensivists for the more specialised intensive care units with greater and more diverse clinical activities.

Alongside the changes occurring due to the competence-based systems, innovative models of acquiring training and certification are emerging. These systems are based on the fact that some specialties share common competencies. Therefore, the first steps of training could include 1–3 years of training in common competences. Subsequent complementary training years (3–4 years) would implement specific competences relevant to the final pathway of the chosen specialty.

Probably, the forces that will decide the future of intensive care training and certification will come from an equilibrium between:

1. The decisions of health authorities
2. The proposals of scientific medical societies of intensive care
3. The demand for specialists in intensive care for a growing population requiring critical care
4. The economic forces that influence the health systems

The author

José-María Domínguez-Roldán, MD, PhD
   Critical Care Department | Hospital Virgen
   del Rocio | Sevilla, España

Address for correspondence
   Jose-Maria Dominguez-Roldan
   Hospital Virgen del Rocio UCI-HRT
   Avda Manuel Siurot s/n
   41013 Sevilla, Spain
   e-mail: jmdominguez@telefonica.net

References

1. Hanson CW, Durbin CG, Maccioli GA, Deutschman CS, Sladen RN, Pronovost PJ, Gattinoni L. The Anesthesiologist in Critical Care Medicine. Past, Present, and Future. Anesthesiology. 2001;95:781–8.

2. Ibsen B. The anesthesit's viewpoint on treatment of respiratory complications in poliomielytis during the epidemic in Copenhagen. Proc Roy Soc Med. 1954;47:72.

3. Hilberman M. The evolution of Intensive Care Units. Crit Care Med. 1975;3:159–165.

4. Fisher MM. Critical care, specialty without frontiers. Crit Care Clin. 1997;13:235–43.

5. Knaus WA, Wagner DP, Zimmerman JE, Draper EA. Variations in mortality and length of stay in intensive care units. Ann Intern Med. 1993;118:753–61.

6. Wunsch H, Rowan KM, Angus DC. International comparisons in critical care: a necessity and challenge. Curr Opin Crit Care. 2007;13:725–31.

7. Multz AS, Chalfin DB, Samson IM, Dantzker DR, Fein AM, Steinberg HN, Niederman MS, Scharf SMA. "Closed" Medical Intensive Care Unit (MICU) Improves Resource Utilization When Compared with an "Open" MICU. Am. J. Respir. Crit. Care Med. 1998;157:1468–1473.

8. Brown, JJ, and G. Sullivan. 1989. Effect on ICU mortality of a full-time critical care specialist. Chest. 1989;96:127–9.

9. Audit Commission. Critical to Success: the place of efficient and effective critical care services within the acute hospital. London: HMSO Publications Centre. 1999.

10. Angus DC, Kelley MA, Schmitz RJ, White A, Popovich J. for the Committee on Manpower for Pulmonary and Critical Care Societies. Current and Projected Workforce Requirements for Care of the Critically Ill and Patients With Pulmonary Disease: Can We Meet the Requirements of an Aging Population? JAMA. 2000;284:2762–2770.

11. Directive 2005/36/EC of the European Parliament and of the Council of 7 September 2005 on the recognition of professional qualifications. Official Journal of the European Union 30.9.2005 L 255/22–L 255/141.

12. Kelley MA. The hospitalist: a new medical specialty? Ann Intern Med. 1999;130:373–5.

13. Bion JF, Ramsay G, Roussos C, Burchardi H. Intensive care training and specialty status in Europe: international comparisons. Task Force on Educational issues of the European Society of Intensive Care Medicine. Intensive Care Med. 1998;24:372–7.

14. Barret H,. Bion JF An international survey of training in adult intensive care medicine. Intensive Care Med. 2005;31:553–61.

15. Evans T, Elliott MW, Ranieri M, Seeger W, Similowski T, Torres A, Roussos C. Pulmonary medicine and (adult) critical care medicine in Europe. Eur Respir J. 2002;19:1202–1206.

16. Hanson CW 3rd, Durbin CG Jr, Maccioli GA, Deutschman CS, Sladen RN, Pronovost PJ, Gattinoni L. The Anesthesiologist in Critical Care Medicine. Past, Present, and Future. Anesthesiology. 2001;95:781–8.

17. Pneumatikos I. Pulmonology or Pulmonary and Critical Care Medicine. A dilemma for the future. Neumon. 2007;20, 125–126.

18. Osborn TM, Alagappan K, Emlet LL, Huang DT, Holliman J, Sthuraman K, Zimmerman JL. The patient care continuum: From the emergency department to the Intensive Care Unit. In: Kuhlen R, Moreno R, Ranieri M, Rhodes A (Eds.). 25 Years of Progress and Innovation in Intensive Care. Medicine MWV Medizinisch Wiss. Berlin, 2007. pp 313–392.

19. CoBaTrICE collaboration, Bion JF, Barrett H. Development of core competencies for an international training programme in intensive care medicine. Intensive Care Med. 2006 32:1371–83.

20. Bion J, Reay H, Bullock A. Training in intensive care. In: Kuhlen R, Moreno R, Ranieri M, Rhodes A (Eds.). 25 Years of Progress and Innovation in Intensive Care. Medicine MWV Medizinisch Wiss. Berlin, 2007. pp 351–358.

21. Fink MP, M. Suter P. The future of our specialty: Critical care medicine a decade from now Crit Care Med. 2006; 34:1811–1816.

22. Cousin DB, Barrett H, Bion JF, Cohen NH. Crisis in critical care: training and certifying future intensivists. Curr Opin Anaesthesiol. 2006;19:107–10.

23. Ewart GW, Marcus L, Gaba MM, Bradner RH, Medina JL, Chandler EB. The critical care medicine crisis: a call for federal action: a white paper from the critical care professional societies. Chest. 2004;125:1518–21.

24. Burchardi H. Regulations of education and training of intensive care medicine in Germany and their structural consequences. Intensive Care Med. 2005; 4:589–90.

25. US Department of Health and Human Services. Health Resources and Services Administration. Report to Congress. The Critical Care Workforce: A Study of the Supply and Demand for Critical Care Physicians. Requested by: Senate Report 108-81.

H. Surgical intensive care and trauma

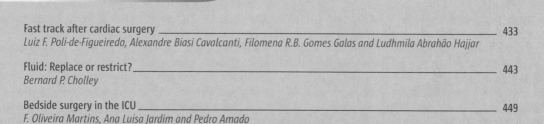

Luiz F. Poli-de-Figueiredo, Alexandre Biasi Cavalcanti,
Filomena R.B. Gomes Galas and Ludhmila Abrahão Hajjar

Fast track after cardiac surgery

Introduction

The concept of fast-track surgery using multimodal perioperative programs was introduced in the
early 1990s to facilitate early discharge from the
hospital and a more rapid resumption of normal
activities of daily living after surgery (1–3). The
aims of "fast-tracking" cardiac surgical patients
include early tracheal extubation and decreased
length of intensive care unit (ICU) and hospital
stay with subsequent cost reduction.

Cost containment and efficient resource use
have forced professionals to rethink their management strategies for cardiac surgery. Fast-tracking
implies the implementation of perioperative patient care to avoid complications related to mechanical ventilation, to improve patient outcome,
and to reduce costs of ICU treatment (2).

Fast-track treatment after cardiac surgery is
composed of three main items:
1. The use of lower anaesthetics dose or faster
   anaesthetic agents;
2. Normothermic temperature management; and
3. Adoption of early extubation protocols.

Other important issues to maximise ICU resources with fast-tracking are to select low risk patients,
to schedule "fast-track" surgeries first so that the
patient can be discharged from the ICU on the
same day, allowing a bed to be used by another
patient (e.g. a high-risk surgical patient) and to
protocolise early steps down to a high dependency
unit with decreased staff-to-patient ratio.

The objective of this chapter is to address controversial issues regarding fast-tracking after cardiac surgery, focusing on early extubation and aggressive postoperative pain management.

Controversial position 1:
Is early extubation safe, cost effective and
does it reduce hospital length of stay after
cardiac surgery?

Early extubation aiming at reducing ICU and
hospital length of stay after heart surgery is not
a new concept. It has been practised since 1977
(4) and the first randomised trial was conducted
in the early 1980s (5). In the 1970s, inhaled anaesthetic agents were predominantly used and,
as a consequence, it was possible to extubate patients early (hours) after heart surgery (2). Since
little cost constraint pressure existed at that time,
the issue of early ICU discharge did not gain

widespread attention and adherence. In the early 1980s, there was a fast-growing shift toward opioid-based anaesthetic protocols. Although this new regimen was clearly associated with better haemodynamic stability, including patients with severely compromised ventricular function (6), the period necessary for awakening was long and demanded ventilation for up to 24 hours in the ICU. The growing emphasis on cost-effective practice has swung our attention back to early extubation.

Early extubation is an essential step for fast-track treatment after heart surgery. Its definition varies widely among studies, but most often is regarded as extubation within 8 hours after surgery (7, 8).

Safety

Two systematic reviews of randomised controlled trials have been conducted to examine the safety of early extubation of adult cardiac surgery patients (9, 10).

Meade et al. identified five randomised controlled trials (624 patients) comparing early versus late extubation once patients were admitted to the ICU (10). Methodological limitations can be detected in all trials, particularly lack of information about allocation list concealment and analysis not following the intention-to-treat principle. Pooled results showed a 13-hour reduction on mechanical ventilation and 12-hour reduction of ICU stay associated with early extubation. Need of re-intubation, myocardial infarction and death were all rare and similar in both groups.

The systematic review by Hawkes et al. (9) reached similar results, except that they included one additional study, by Cheng et al. (7). This trial compared a fast-track anaesthesia plus early extubation versus conventional treatment. Overall, the meta-analysis found reduced length of ICU and hospital stay without difference in morbidity or mortality, in spite of inconclusive power to evaluate adverse events due to low numbers in both groups. In order to unequivocally demonstrate safety equivalence of fast-tracking versus conventional treatment, several thousands of patients would need to be randomised. Such a large trial has little chance of being conducted, although the low rate of adverse events with fast-tracking is reassuring.

Some authors have reported relatively small series of extubation within the operative room (11, 12). However, there seem to be no advantages in terms of ICU or hospital stay with this procedure. On the other hand, adverse event rates may be high (11) and published experience with very early extubation is limited either by the low number of patients or by the absence of randomised controlled studies.

Effect on ICU and hospital length of stay

Several non-randomised studies showed that fast-track treatments, including early extubation, result in a decreased ICU and hospital length of stay (13–15).

A systematic review of randomised trials examined the independent effects of three fast-track treatment items on ICU and hospital stay: low-dose anaesthetics, normothermic management and early extubation protocols (16). Five trials comparing early extubation (within 8 hours postoperatively) with later extubation were included (5, 7, 8, 17, 18). The pooled results of these trials support a modest, but significant, effect of early extubation on length of ICU and hospital stay. No robust evidence was found to support the effect of low-dose anaesthetics or normothermic management on length of stay in the ICU or hospital (16).

Other authors argue that in order to reduce hospital stay and costs, the focus should be on early ICU discharge more than on early extubation (19, 20). Calafiore et al. published their experience with 647 patients discharged on day 0 from 1,194 myocardial revascularisations (19). They found a shortening of hospital stay from 4.9 days in the group not discharged from ICU on day 0 to 4.1 days (p < 0.001). Only 7 (1.1 %) cases were re-admitted to ICU and just 1 patient died (0.2 %). Factors associated with day 0 discharge were elective CABG, first operation, off-pump surgery, no chronic renal failure, no previous stroke, no multi-arterial conduits and no associated carotid endarterectomy.

In a series of 9,054 patients operated on in their institution, Ranucci et al. found that the most important factor to achieve ICU discharge up to the next morning after surgery is the institution of a protocol for early discharge itself

(20). These authors concluded that an essential step in their protocol was the establishment of a step-down unit able to provide care for intermediate complexity patients. These authors did not observe any increase of adverse events or re-admission to ICU in those patients discharged up to 24 hours after surgery.

Cost-effectiveness

Non-randomised studies reported reductions in cost with the adoption of a fast-track strategy after heart surgery (13, 21). Arom et al. estimated a $ 6,000 reduction in hospital charges per patient extubated early (13). Lee et al. found a $ 1,683 sav-

Tab. 1   St Mary's fast-track failure propensity score to be used with nomogram.
Modified from Constantinides VA, Tekkis PP, Fazil A, Kaur K, Leonard R, Platt M et al. Fast-track failure after cardiac surgery: development of a prediction model. Crit Care Med. 2006;34:2875–82.
Instructions: Sum up the points for each factor. Localise this sum in the "Total Score" and find the corresponding probability of fast-track failure straight below. ACS: Acute coronary syndrome; LV: Left ventricular; IABP: Intra-aortic balloon pumping.
Complex procedure was defined as: any combined procedure (valve replacement and CABG), any dual valve or aortic operation, and any other type of operation such as pericardial procedure, tricuspid valve operation, pulmonary embolectomy, or chest wall reconstruction for sternal wound infection.

Risk Factor	Category	Score								
No recent ACS (> 90 days)	Good LV function	0								
	Moderate LV function	0.1								
	Poor LV function	0.2								
Recent ACS (≤ 90 days)	Good LV function	0.05								
	Moderate LV function	0.7								
	Poor LV function	1.2								
Re-do operations	None	0								
	One	0.6								
	More than one	2.8								
Extracardiac arteriopathy	Absent	0								
	Present	1.0								
Preoperative IABP	No	0								
	Yes	1.3								
Serum creatinine, μmol/L	<120	0								
	120–150	0.5								
	>150	2.4								
Complex surgery performed	No	0								
	Yes	1.0								
Operative urgency	Elective/scheduled	0								
	Urgent/emergency	1.2								
Total Score	0	1	2	3	4	5	6	7	8	>9
Probability of fast-track failure (%)	4.9	12.2	27.4	50.6	73.6	88.3	95.4	98.2	99.3	> 99.8

ings in variable direct costs per case (21). However, these studies are limited by the lack of comparable groups except for the fast-track protocol.

Van Mastrigt et al. also evaluated cost-effectiveness in their systematic review of randomised trials (16). They identified seven randomised trials which reported data on costs. However, they were unable to pool their results due to variation in cost categories and time horizon. Unexpectedly, most studies did not find a decrease in costs, although the trial with better methodology (7) reported a significant reduction in costs.

For whom this treatment is intended?
Failure predictors

A prospective study involving 1,084 patients undergoing heart surgery and eligible for a fast-track protocol examined the predictors of fast-track failure (22). After surgery, patients were initially admitted in a fast-track unit. Fast-track failure was defined as patients considered suitable for fast-track management experiencing one of the following outcomes: death (30-day), length of stay in the ICU greater than 48 hours, admission from the fast-track unit to the ICU for additional support, requirement for direct postoperative ICU admission due to development of organ dysfunction pre- or intraoperatively in spite of an initial allocation to fast-track management, and admission to the ICU from the ward having previously being through the fast-track unit. One hundred and sixty-nine cases failed fast-track management (15.6%). Independent predictors for fast-track failure were converted into a score that allows estimation of the probability of failure (see tab. 1). This score may be very helpful in determining which patients may not be included in a fast-track protocol due to a high risk of failure.

A study to determine extubation failure predictors was conducted on a database of 11,330 heart surgeries from a 54-bed cardiothoracic ICU (23). Although this study was not specifically aimed at evaluating fast-track extubation patients, part of the patients in this sample were extubated early, and the study's large size warrants looking at its findings. There were 748 (6.6%) patients who were weaned from mechanical ventilation and subsequently needed re-intubation.

The preoperative predictors of extubation failure were: age of 65 years or more, hospitalisation before surgery, arterial vascular disease, chronic obstructive pulmonary disease, pulmonary hypertension, severe left ventricular dysfunction (ejection fraction < 35%), cardiogenic shock, hematocrit ≤ 34%, blood urea nitrogen ≥ 24 mg/dl, serum albumin ≤ 4.0 g/dl , systemic oxygen delivery ≤ 320 ml/min/m² and redo operations. The operative predictors of extubation failure were the following: surgical procedures involving the thoracic aorta, transfusion of blood products ≥ 10 units and cardiopulmonary bypass time ≥ 120 minutes.

Although advanced age may predict higher risk of extubation failure (23), the elderly population submitted to heart surgery may also be considered for a fast-track protocol, provided other predictors of failure are not present (24, 25). Lee et al. included 114 patients older than 70 years in a fast-track protocol (24). They observed a significant reduction in hospital length of stay. The re-intubation rate was negligible and there were no deaths.

Protocols

The following criteria should be met to proceed to early extubation of heart surgery patients:
- Patient must be awake and cooperative with no evidence of neurologic deficits
- Haemodynamically stable without vasoactive drugs or intra-aortic balloon pump
- Absence of new or uncontrolled arrhythmias
- Chest tube drainage of < 100ml/h for 2 hours
- Arterial pH > 7.35
- PaO_2 > 100 mmHg on FIO_2 < 50%
- Temperature of 35.5–36.5°C

The criteria for day 0 ICU transfer to a step-down unit (i.e. a high dependency unit) are the following:
- At least 2 hours of observation after early extubation
- Stable haemodynamic status
- No significant bleeding
- No arrhythmias
- Normal EKG
- Normal neurological evolution

Controversial position 2:
Is aggressive postoperative pain control safe after cardiac surgery?

Moderate or severe postoperative pain can be detected in up to 50% of cardiac surgery patients (26, 27), in spite of the use of analgesics. Adequate pain management is critical for an uneventful postoperative course, providing haemodynamic stability, reduced myocardial oxygen demand and therefore, less postoperative myocardial ischaemia, a strong predictor of worsened outcome (28). Pain triggers a symphatetic response that causes hypertension, tachycardia and increased myocardial contractility. All those effects lead to a higher oxygen consumption by the vulnerable myocardial cells following cardiac surgery (28).

There are several factors accounting for this high incidence of pain immediately after cardiac surgery. Large incisions, the intraoperative use of rib or sternal retractors, endotracheal and chest tubes, the need for vigorous respiratory and motor physiotherapy, as well as underestimation of pain by assistants and insufficient and/or inadequate use of analgesics. Therefore, pain control is an important issue in the fast-track regimen.

However, widespread achievement of effective analgesia is not been undertaken, largely due to concerns of potential side effects, including opioid-induced ventilatory depression (compromising early extubation), non-steroidal analgesics (renal and ischaemic problems) and regional analgesia (neuroaxial haematoma).

Opioid-based analgesics

Patient-controlled analgesia (PCA) has been widely used for large surgical procedures such as vascular, oncologic and orthopedic surgeries. However, its use in cardiac surgery patients has not been widely adopted, largely due to concerns of respiratory depression (29, 30) and decreased alertness, which may compromise the respiratory physiotherapy so much needed to avoid lung atelectasis and subsequent infection.

Conflicting results have emerged from some prospective trials comparing PCA with opioids and standard nurse-administered analgesia after cardiac surgery. While clear benefits such as less pain and atelectasis were shown in some studies

(31–33), several others have shown that a careful and close pain evaluation and treatment by nurses achieved similar benefits as PCA does (34–37).

It has been observed that bolus administration of an opioid drug is more likely to promote greater respiratory depression than gradual administration (30). Additionally, morphine is much less likely to induce apnea than an equipotent dose of fentanyl, due to its slower onset of action which allows a gradual increase in $PaCO_2$, stimulating breathing.

Two prospective studies addressed the hypothesis that a background infusion of morphine to PCA is beneficial for postoperative pain relief and decreases stress response after cardiac surgery (38, 39). In both studies PCA was very effective in providing postoperative pain after early extubation and no ventilatory compromise was identified. While in one background morphine was beneficial (38), no additional benefit over PCA alone was observed in the other study (39).

Non-steroidal anti-inflammatory drugs

The role of non-steroidal anti-inflammatory drugs (NSAID) for routine postoperative analgesia and for opiod-sparing after cardiac surgery is controversial (40–43). The main concern has been renal function deterioration. However, it has been shown that in patients with normal renal function the use of NSAID for short periods did not affect renal function after cardiac surgery (41, 42). Moreover, effective analgesia associated with decreased opioid need has been demonstrated (42–45). On the other hand, newer agents which inhibit cyclooxygenase-2 were associated with increased major complications after cardiac surgery such as acute myocardial infarction, ischaemic cerebral vascular events and wound infections (46–47). These agents should be avoided.

Regional analgesia

It has been suggested that central neuraxial analgesia may improve outcome after cardiac surgery due to attenuation of stress response and a very effective analgesia (48). Additionally, a reduction in the risk of myocardial infarction has been observed in high-risk patients undergoing non-cardiac surgeries (49). However, the fear of an epidural haematoma inducing paraplegia is the main reason why this technique has not been widely accepted for cardiac surgery patients. Several studies were performed with conflicting results, which were summarised in a meta-analysis performed by Liu et al. (48). They compared patients undergoing coronary artery bypass surgery who were randomised to either general anaesthesia versus general anaesthesia-thoracic epidural analgesia or general anaesthesia-intrathecal analgesia. No differences in the rates of mortality or myocardial infarction after coronary artery bypass grafting with central neuraxial analgesia could be detected. However, neuroaxial anaesthesia was associated to reduced pain scores and faster tracheal extubation, decreased pulmonary complications and cardiac dysrhythmias.

Respiratory depression compromising early extubation and the fast-track regimen is another concern with regional analgesia. However, the use of lower doses of intrathecal morphine provided pain control without compromising early extubation and fast-track protocols (50–55). Morphine injected into the lumbar space offers advantages such as diffusion into the thoracic portions of the spinal cord providing analgesia and reducing the risk of spinal cord injury during catheter insertion, lower doses are required and no catheter is placed in the postoperative period. However, a meta-analysis showed that intrathecal analgesia provided no significant benefits over general anaesthesia regarding mortality, arrhythmias, time for extubation; besides, it provided only a modest decrease in intravenous morphine requirements (48).

The main fear with regional analgesia is the development of neuraxial haematoma and spinal cord injury after spinal puncture, particularly in patients who are fully anticoagulated during cardiopulmonary bypass (56). Although the estimated risk of clinically significant haematoma is very low when the procedure is carried out carefully and benefits could be provided to cardiac surgery patients, the association of neuraxial blockade and full-dose heparin could provoke paraplegia from spinal cord compression by the haematoma, increasing this risk by 100 times in comparison to non-anticoagulated surgical patients (57, 58).

Several precautions are required if the blockage is to be undertaken, including normal coagulation before the procedure, avoidance of multiple punctures, avoidance of surgery at least 24 hours after a puncture accident, and removal of the catheter only under normal blood clotting tests. Very close neurological monitoring is a warrant for an early detection and prompt spinal cord relief by laminectomy (59).

However, several institutions routinely use intrathecal morphine for pain relief after cardiac surgery. Roediger et al. (29) have been using intrathecal morphine since 1998, on more than 4,000 patients without any clinical evidence of haematoma. This controversy is likely to persist for many years.

Key points

- *The aims of "fast-tracking" cardiac surgical patients include early tracheal extubation and decreased length of intensive care unit (ICU) and hospital stay with subsequent cost reduction.*
- *Fast-track treatment after cardiac surgery consists of three main elements:*
  1) *The use of lower anaesthetics dosage or faster anaesthetic agents*
  2) *Normothermic temperature management*
  3) *Adoption of early extubation protocols. Of these, early extubation is the essential step to achieve early ICU and hospital discharge.*
- *Other important issue to maximise ICU resources with fast-tracking is to establish a protocol to guide early step-down to a high dependency unit.*
- *Evidence from systematic reviews of clinical trials shows that early extubation as part of a fast-track protocol leads to reduced ICU and hospital stay, and may reduce costs. Adverse events are uncommon, though available evidence is insufficient to demonstrate equivalence between fast-track and conventional treatment after heart surgery.*
- *Risk factors for fast-track failure have been determined. The St. Mary's fast-track failure score is useful to identify patients who are not suitable to this treatment.*
- *Adequate pain management is critical for an uneventful postoperative course, providing haemodynamic stability, reduced myocardial oxygen demand and therefore, less postoperative myocardial ischaemia*
- *Effective analgesia is precluded largely due to concerns regarding potential side effects, including opioid-induced ventilatory depression (compromising early extubation), non-steroidal analgesics (renal and ischae-*

mic problems) and regional analgesia (neuroaxial hematoma).

- *Conflicting results have emerged from some prospective trials comparing PCA with opioids and standard nurse-administered analgesia after cardiac surgery.*
- *In patients with normal renal function the use of NSAID for short periods did not affect renal function after cardiac surgery. However, COX-2 inhibitors should not be used because of ischaemic events as well as wound infection.*
- *The risk of an epidural hematoma inducing paraplegia is the main reason regional analgesia has not been widely accepted for anticoagulated cardiac surgery patients.*

The authors

Luiz F. Poli-de-Figueiredo, MD[1]
Alexandre Biasi Cavalcanti, MD[2]
Filomena R.B. Gomes Galas, MD[3]
Ludhmila Abrahão Hajjar, MD[4]
[1]Professor of Surgery | Chairman | Department of Surgery | University of Sao Paulo School of Medicine | Sao Paulo, Brazil | Intensivist at Intensive Care Unit | Hospital Albert Einstein | Sao Paulo, Brazil
[2]Intensivist at Intensive Care Unit | Hospital Albert Einstein | Sao Paulo, Brazil
[3]Anaesthesist and Intensivist | Cardiac Postoperative Unit | Heart Institute, InCor | University of São Paulo School of Medicine | Sao Paulo, Brazil
[4]Cardiologist | Cardiac Postoperative Unit | Heart Institute, InCor | University of São Paulo School of Medicine | Sao Paulo, Brazil

Address for correspondence
Luiz F. Poli-de Figueiredo
Faculdade de Medicina
University of São Paulo
Av. Dr. Arnaldo, 455 suite 4215
São Paulo – SP – ZIP 01246–903, Brazil
e-mail: lpoli@uol.com.br

References

1. Cheng DC. Fast-track cardiac surgery: economic implications in postoperative care. J Cardiothorac Vasc Anesth. 1998;12:72–9.

2. Myles PS, Daly DJ, Djaiani G, Lee A, Cheng DC. A systematic review of the safety and effectiveness of fast-track cardiac anesthesia. Anesthesiology. 2003;99: 982–7.

3. White PF, Eng M. Fast-track anesthetic techniques for ambulatory surgery. Curr Opin Anaesthesiol. 2007;20(6): 545–57.

4. Klineberg PL, Geer RT, Hirsh RA, Aukburg SJ. Early extubation after coronary artery bypass graft surgery. Crit Care Med. 1977;5:272–4.

5. Quasha AL, Loeber N, Feeley TW, Ullyot DJ, Roizen MF. Postoperative respiratory care: a controlled trial of early and late extubation following coronary-artery bypass grafting. Anesthesiology. 1980;52:135–41.

6. Stanley TH, Webster LR. Anesthetic requirements and cardiovascular effects of fentanyl-oxygen and fentanyl-diazepam-oxygen anesthesia in man. Anesth Analg. 1978;57:411–6.

7. Cheng DC, Karski J, Peniston C, Raveendran G, Asokumar B, Carroll J, et al. Early tracheal extubation after coronary artery bypass graft surgery reduces costs and improves resource use. A prospective, randomized, controlled trial. Anesthesiology. 1996;85:1300–10.

8. Michalopoulos A, Nikolaides A, Antzaka C, Deliyanni M, Smirli A, Geroulanos S et al. Change in anaesthesia practice and postoperative sedation shortens ICU and hospital length of stay following coronary artery bypass surgery. Respir Med. 1998;92:1066–70.

9. Hawkes CA, Dhileepan S, Foxcroft D. Early extubation for adult cardiac surgical patients. Cochrane Database Syst Rev. 2003;(4):CD003587.

10. Meade MO, Guyatt G, Butler R, Elms B, Hand L, Ingram A et al. Trials comparing early vs late extubation following cardiovascular surgery. Chest. 2001;120(6 Suppl):445S–53S.

11. Montes FR, Sanchez SI, Giraldo JC, Rincon JD, Rincon IE, Vanegas MV, et al. The lack of benefit of tracheal extubation in the operating room after coronary artery bypass surgery. Anesth Analg. 2000;91:776–80.

12. Oxelbark S, Bengtsson L, Eggersen M, Kopp J, Pedersen J, Sanchez R. Fast track as a routine for open heart surgery. Eur J Cardiothorac Surg. 2001;19:460–3.

13. Arom KV, Emery RW, Petersen RJ, Schwartz M. Cost-effectiveness and predictors of early extubation. Ann Thorac Surg. 1995;60:127–32.

14. Chong JL, Grebenik C, Sinclair M, Fisher A, Pillai R, Westaby S. The effect of a cardiac surgical recovery area on the timing of extubation. J Cardiothorac Vasc Anesth. 1993;7:137–41.

15. Foster GH, Conway WA, Pamulkov N, Lester JL, Magilligan DJ, Jr. Early extubation after coronary artery bypass: brief report. Crit Care Med. 1984;12:994–6.

16. van Mastrigt GA, Maessen JG, Heijmans J, Severens JL, Prins MH. Does fast-track treatment lead to a decrease of intensive care unit and hospital length of stay in coronary

artery bypass patients? A meta-regression of randomized clinical trials. Crit Care Med. 2006;34:1624–34.

17. Berdat P, Kipfer B, Fischer G, Neidhart P, Mohacsi P, Althaus U et al. [Conventional heart surgery with the fast-track-method: experiences from a pilot study]. Schweiz Med Wochenschr. 1998;128:1737–42.

18. Reyes A, Vega G, Blancas R, Morato B, Moreno JL, Torrecilla C et al. Early vs conventional extubation after cardiac surgery with cardiopulmonary bypass. Chest. 1997;112:193–201.

19. Calafiore AM, Scipioni G, Teodori G, Di GG, Di MM, Canosa C et al. Day 0 intensive care unit discharge – risk or benefit for the patient who undergoes myocardial revascularization? Eur J Cardiothorac Surg. 2002;21:377–84.

20. Ranucci M, Bellucci C, Conti D, Cazzaniga A, Maugeri B. Determinants of early discharge from the intensive care unit after cardiac operations. Ann Thorac Surg. 2007;83: 1089–95.

21. Lee JH, Kim KH, vanHeeckeren DW, Murrell HK, Cmolik BL, Graber R et al. Cost analysis of early extubation after coronary bypass surgery. Surgery. 1996;120:611–7.

22. Constantinides VA, Tekkis PP, Fazil A, Kaur K, Leonard R, Platt M et al. Fast-track failure after cardiac surgery: development of a prediction model. Crit Care Med. 2006; 34:2875–82.

23. Rady MY, Ryan T. Perioperative predictors of extubation failure and the effect on clinical outcome after cardiac surgery. Crit Care Med. 1999;27:340–7.

24. Lee JH, Graber R, Popple CG, Furey E, Lyons T, Murrell HK et al. Safety and efficacy of early extubation of elderly coronary artery bypass surgery patients. J Cardiothorac Vasc Anesth. 1998;12:381–4.

25. Ott RA, Gutfinger DE, Miller M, Alimadadian H, Codini M, Selvan A et al. Rapid recovery of octogenarians following coronary artery bypass grafting. J Card Surg. 1997;12: 309–13.

26. Watt-Watson J, Stevens B. Managing pain after coronary artery bypass surgery. J Cardiovasc Nursing. 1998;12:39–51.

27. Mueller XM, Tinguely F, Tevaearai HT et al. Pain location, distribution, and intensity after cardiac surgery. Chest. 2000;118: 391–396.

28. Mangano DT, Hollenberg M, Fegert G et al. Perioperative myocardial ischemia in patients undergoing noncardiac surgery – I: incidence and severity during the 4 day perioperative period. The Study of Perioperative Ischemia (SPI) Research Group. J Am Coll Cardiol. 1991; 17:843–50.

29. Roediger L, Larbuisson R, Lamy M. New approaches and old controversies to postoperative pain. European Journal of Anaesthesiology. 2006;23:539–50.

30. Gross JB. When you breath IN you inspire, when you DON'T breath, you … expire. New insights regarding opioid-induced ventilatory depression. Anesthesiology. 2003;99:767–70.

31. Pettersson PH, Lindskog EA, Owall A. Patient-controlled vs. nurse-controlled pain treatment after coronary artery bypass surgery. Acta Anaesth Scand. 2000; 44: 43–7.

32. Boldt J, Thaler E, Lehmann A et al. Pain management in cardiac surgery patients: comparison between standard Mittwoch therapy and patient-controlled analgesia regimen. J Cardiothorac Vasc Anesth. 1998;12:654–8.

33. Gust R, Pecher S, Gust A et al. Effect of patient-controlled analgesia on pulmonary complications after coronary artery bypass grafting. Crit Care Med. 1999;27:2218–23.

34. Tsang J, Brush B. Patient-controlled analgesia in postoperative cardiac surgery. Anaesth Intensive Care. 1999; 27:464–70.

35. Myles PS, Buckland MR, Cannon GB et al. Comparison of patient-controlled analgesia and nurse-controlled infusion analgesia after cardiac surgery. Anaesth Intensive Care. 1994;22:672–8.

36. Searle NR, Roy M, Bergeron G et al. Hydromorphone patient-controlled analgesia (PCA. after coronary artery bypass surgery. Can J Anaesth. 1994;41:198–205.

37. Munro AJ, Long GT, Sleigh JW. Nurse-administered subcutaneous morphine is a satisfactory alternative to intravenous patient-controlled analgesia morphine after cardiac surgery. Anesth Analg. 1998; 87:11–5.

38. Dal D, Kanbak M, Caglar M, Aypar U. A background infusion of morphine does not enhance postoperative analgesia after cardiac surgery. Can J Anaesth. 2003;50:476–9.

39. Guler T, Unlugenc H, Gundogan Z et al. A background infusion of morphine enhances patient-controlled analgesia after cardiac surgery. Can J Anaesth. 2004;51:718–22.

40. Griffin M. Con: non-steroidal anti-inflammatory drugs should not be routinely administered for postoperative analgesia after cardiac surgery. J Cardiothorac Vasc Anesth. 2000;14:735–8.

41. Kulik A, Ruel M, Bourkeb ME et al. Postoperative naproxen after coronary artery bypass surgery: a doubleblind randomized controlled trial. Eur J Cardiothorac Surg. 2004;26:694–700.

42. Hynninen MS, Cheng DC, Hossian IJ. Non-steroidal anti-inflammatory drugs in treatment of postoperative pain after cardiac surgery. Can J Anaesth. 2000;47:1182–7.

43. Ralley FE, Day FJ, Cheng DCH. Pro: non-steroidal anti-inflammatory drugs should be routinely administered for postoperative analgesia after cardiac surgery. J Cardiothorac Vasc Anaesth. 2000;4:731–4.

44. Immer FF, Immer-Bansi AS, Trachsel N. Pain treatment with a COX-2 inhibitor after coronary artery bypass operation: a randomized trial. Ann Thorac Surg. 2003;75:490–5.

45. Fayaz MH, Abel RJ, Pugh SC. Opioid-sparing effects of diclofenac and paracetamol lead to improved outcomes after cardiac surgery. J Cardiothorac Vasc Anesth. 2004;18:742–7.

46. Nussmeier NA, Whelton AA, Brown MT et al. Complications of the COX-2 inhibitors parecoxib and valdecoxib after cardiac surgery. New Eng J Med. 2005; 352:1081–91.

47. Solomon DH, Schneeweiss S, Glynn R. Relationship between selective cyclooxygenase-2 inhibitors and acute myocardial infarction in older adults. Circulation. 2004;109:2068–73.

48. Liu SS, Block BM, Wu CL. Effects of perioperative central neuraxial analgesia on outcome after coronary artery bypass surgery. A Meta-analysis. Anesthesiology. 2004;101:153–61

49. Beattie WS, Badner NH, Choi P. Epidural analgesia reduces postoperative myocardial infarction: a meta-analysis. Anesth Analg. 2001;93:853–8.

50. Bowler I, Djaiani G, Abel R et al. A combination of intrathecal morphine and remifentanil anesthesia for fasttrack cardiac anesthesia and surgery. J Cardiothorac Vasc Anesth. 2002;16:709–14.

51. Shroff A, Rooke GA, Bishop MJ. Effects of intrathecal opioid on extubation time, analgesia, and intensive care unit stay following coronary artery bypass grafting. J Clin Anesth. 1997;9:415–9.

52. Bettex DA, Schmidlin D, Chassot PG, Schmid ER. Intrathecal sufentanil–morphine shortens the duration of intubation and improves analgesia in fast-track cardiac surgery. Can J Anaesth. 2002;49:711–7.

53. Metz S, Schwann N, Hassanein W et al. Intrathecal morphine for off-pump coronary artery bypass grafting. J Cardiothorac Vasc Anesth. 2004;18:451–3.

54. Parlow JL, Steele RG, O'Reilly D. Low-dose intrathecal morphine facilitates early extubation after cardiac surgery: results of a retrospective continuous quality improvement audit. Can J Anaesth. 2005;52:94–9.

55. Zisman E, Shenderey A, Ammar R et al. The effects of intrathecal morphine on patients undergoing minimally invasive direct coronary artery bypass surgery. J Cardiothorac Vasc Anesth. 2005;19:40–3.

56. Turnbull KW. Con: neuraxial block is useful in patients undergoing heparinization for surgery. J Cardiothorac Vasc Anesth. 1996;10:961–2.

57. Ruff RL, Dougherty Jr JH. Complications of lumbar puncture followed by anticoagulation. Stroke. 1981;12:879–81.

58. Ho AM, Chung DC, Joynt GM. Neuraxial blockade and hematoma in cardiac surgery: estimating the risk of a rare adverse event that has not (yet) occurred. Chest. 2000; 117:551–5.

59. Rosen DA, Hawkinberry DW, Rosen KR et al. An epidural hematoma in an adolescent patient after cardiac surgery. Anesth Analg. 2004;98:966–9.

Bernard P. Cholley

Fluid: Replace or restrict?

Introduction

Fluid administration is one of the most widely used therapies in hospitals and clinics. The placement of an IV line is undoubtedly one of the very first interventions in any patient admitted to an acute care unit anywhere in the world. Although the placement of this IV line is generally recognised as a reasonable "first step" for the therapeutic approach, there is little agreement on what should be done regarding fluid administration itself. The type and amount of fluid delivered to the patient depend mainly on empirical practices that vary greatly according to geographical regions, institutions, and even physicians themselves.

The primary goal of fluid therapy is to restore or maintain adequate tissue perfusion. However, in the absence of simple indices attesting that this goal has been reached, patients may well remain underperfused if fluid administration is not sufficient to compensate the deficit or, on the contrary, become congested if fluids are infused beyond the maximum threshold that the cardiovascular system can tolerate.

The present chapter will review the physiological effects of fluid administration on venous return and describe strategies aiming at "optimising" haemodynamics or, conversely, at "restricting" fluids, and analyse their results.

Fluid administration and venous return

When intravenous fluids are given to a patient, most of the volume is distributed in the veins that contain roughly 65 % of the blood volume (1). This additional fluid increases the stressed volume, and thereby the mean systemic pressure, which is the driving force of venous return (see fig. 1). In addition, by recruiting partially collapsed veins, this fluid contributes to reducing venous resistance and further increasing venous return (see fig. 2). The changes induced by fluid infusion are illustrated by the venous return curve that intersects with the cardiac function curve at a point situated higher up towards the right, corresponding to a greater cardiac output value (see fig. 3). Thus, the primary effect of fluid administration is to increase venous return. Since venous return and cardiac output have to be equivalent on average, any increase in venous return is associated with a concomitant increase in stroke volume and cardiac output. This is possible because the heart is built in such a way that it pumps out the blood that returns to it. This ability results from the property of the myofilaments that can increase the force of contraction in response to increased stretching, up to a certain limit (see fig. 4). This property is called the Starling law of the heart (2). From these considerations, it is clear that the best criterion to quantify the effects of fluid therapy is a measure of cardiac output or stroke volume. Fluids are expected to increase systemic flow (stroke volume or cardiac output) and thereby tissue perfusion. The shape of the cardiac function curves tells us that the first millilitres of fluids will have the greatest effect in terms of stroke volume increase (steep portion of the curve) and that after the junction between the steep portion and the plateau, no more improvement in flow will result from additional fluids (see fig. 4). Beyond this "optimal" or "maximal" cardiac output value, any increase in preload will only generate venous con-

gestion and no improvement in tissue perfusion. The congestion will accumulate upstream of the weakest ventricle, usually the right ventricle, leading to systemic oedema, sometimes the left ventricle, resulting in pulmonary oedema. By mea-

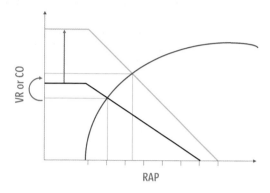

Fig. 3 Effects of fluids on the venous return (VR) curve. After fluids (dashed line), the mean systemic pressure increases, as attested by the shift to the right of x-axis intercept, and venous resistance decreases as reflected by the greater slope of the dashed line. This new VR curve intersects with the cardiac function curve further to the right, which corresponds to a greater cardiac output (CO) value and a greater RAP.

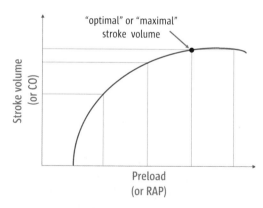

Fig. 1 Schematic representation of the venous reservoir and the effect of fluid administration. Fluids increase the level of stressed volume (volume above the faucet) and therefore the mean systemic pressure (MSP). The pressure gradient between MSP and right atrial pressure (RAP) is the driving force that pushes venous return (VR) back to the right heart.

Fig. 4 Cardiac function curve showing that the first fluid challenge will have the greater effect (steep portion of the curve), whereas repeated challenge will lead to a "plateau". The junction between steep portion and plateau represents the maximal (or optimal) value for stroke volume or cardiac output. Any additional fluid beyond the "optimal" value will only generate congestion and no increase in flow or tissue perfusion.

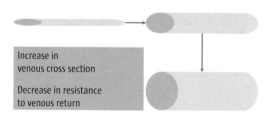

Fig. 2 Effects of fluids on venous size and cross section. The greater the venous cross section the smaller the resistance to venous return.

suring flow changes in response to fluid administration, one can easily detect when the maximal value is reached, indicating when fluid administration is no longer able to improve tissue perfusion and must be stopped to avoid congestion. Subsequent reduction in systemic flow may indicate that the patient might again be able to respond to fluid administration. To be safe, fluid administration must be conducted as rapid administration of small fluid challenges immediately followed by a new measurement of cardiac output or stroke volume. In the examples shown in figures 5 and 6, it is clear that:

1. small aliquots of fluids can have a great effect on stroke volume and systemic flow and
2. the maximum effect may sometimes be reached after very little fluids (250 ml or less), underlining the importance of measuring flow to avoid giving unnecessary fluids.

Haemodynamic optimisation of "high-risk" surgical patients

Some surgical patients are considered at "high risk" for perioperative complications or even death

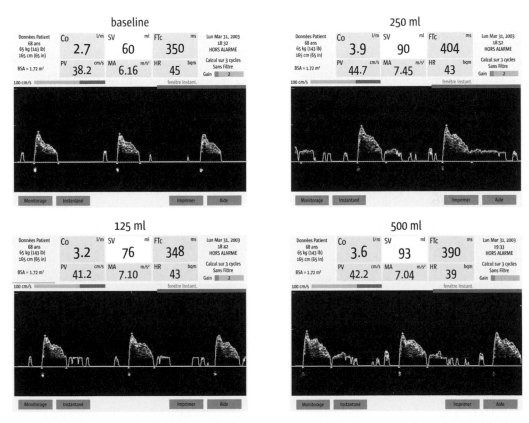

Fig. 5   Representative example of fluid titration conducted using esophageal Doppler to measure stroke volume. The first 125 ml challenge of gelatin improves stroke volume (SV) by 25 % (from 60 to 76 ml). The second 125 ml challenge improves SV by 18 % only. The final 250 ml yield almost no increase in SV (from 90 to 93 ml). 90 ml can be considered as the "optimal" stroke volume value. Fluid administration must be stopped after the last 250 ml that have not resulted in any increase in tissue perfusion. More fluids will be given only if SV decreases by more than 10 % (at least) to avoid venous congestion. From: Mebazaa A, Gheorghiade M, Zannad FM, and Parillo JE (editors).: Acute Heart Failure, 2008, pp 391–6, Chapter 35: esophageal Doppler: noninvasive estilation of stroke volume, Cholley BP. With kind permission of Springer Science and Business Media.

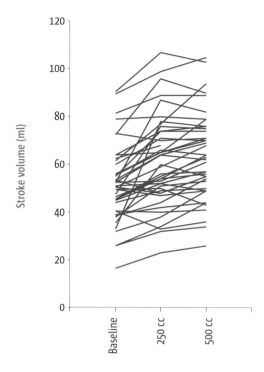

Fig. 6   Individual cardiac function curves of a group of patients prior to surgery illustrating that the first 250 ml have a much greater effect on stroke volume than the second 250 ml: +20 % increase in stroke volume (first challenge) vs. +5 % (second challenge).

by anaesthesiologists, because they have many co-morbidities, advanced age, and/or because they are undergoing difficult surgery. Anaesthetic management of such patients has always been a challenge and many authors have attempted to define the best strategies to reduce perioperative risk.

Introduced in 1988 by Shoemaker (3), the concept of haemodynamic optimisation of high-risk surgical patients has since been tested and altered by many authors. All studies that have tried to achieve haemodynamic optimisation share common characteristics:

1. All aimed at improving perfusion and oxygen delivery to tissues by increasing stroke volume or cardiac output.
2. All used IV fluids as a first step to achieve this goal. Some authors also used red blood cell transfusion or even catecholamine infusion to further increase O_2 delivery.

3. Fluid administration was guided using haemodynamic parameters: mainly cardiac output or stroke volume, but also filling pressures or oxygen venous saturation.

A variety of high-risk surgical populations have been studied. An improvement in outcome has been demonstrated in patients undergoing digestive (4–7), vascular (3, 8), cardiac (9), or orthopedic (10, 11) surgery as well as in multiple trauma patients (12, 13). Many of these studies reported a reduction in post-operative morbidity, but some of them even observed a reduction in mortality. Meta-analyses confirmed that haemodynamic optimisation can reduce postoperative morbidity (14) and even mortality in the most severe patients (15). Even a simple reduction in postoperative morbidity can be of tremendous interest from an economical perspective, especially if this goes along with a reduction in hospital length of stay (16). For example, two studies have found that haemodynamic optimisation of hip fracture patients was able to shorten hospital length of stay, corresponding to significant savings in the cost of care (10, 11). Despite numerous studies suggesting that haemodynamic optimisation is likely to be beneficial in high-risk surgical patients, this is still not yet a standard of care. The main reason is probably that the level of proof is not very high because these studies involved small cohorts of patients in single centres. Two large multicentre trials have failed to confirm that haemodynamic optimisation was effective: one study involved patients that were probably not really at "high risk" of postoperative complications (17) and the second one had haemodynamic endpoints that were questionable (18, 19).

Fluid restriction and surgery

There is apparently a contradiction between the concept of haemodynamic optimisation (fluid titration according to a haemodynamic goal, i.e. maximal stroke volume or cardiac output) and the results of some studies that suggested that fluid restriction (as opposed to liberal administration) was able to shorten length of stay after colonic surgery (20, 21). In those trials, two groups of patients were compared: one group received fluids in order to compensate exactly the pre- and intraoperative losses while the other group received large, uncontrolled amounts of fluids. Not surprisingly, outcome was worse in the group that received uncontrolled fluids. These results have not been confirmed by other trials conducted in colonic surgery (22) and knee arthroplasty (23). It can also be argued that the trials of Brandstrup and Nisanevich did not show the benefit of fluid "restriction", but instead demonstrated the deleterious effect of fluid overload (20, 21). This underlines the necessity of quantitating the effects of intravenous fluids in high-risk patients. The measurement of stroke volume using esophageal Doppler allows fluid titration to reach the maximal value possible for each patient. This will be achieved with very variable volumes of fluids in different patients, which confirms that standardised protocols ("one size fits all") cannot be applied for this purpose. Fluid titration needs to be tailored for each individual. Obtaining the maximal stroke volume or cardiac output value may be excessive and result in "luxury" perfusion. However, this was never found to be deleterious and optimised patients usually had less complications and shorter hospital length of stay than control patients. On the contrary, this strategy may prevent avoidable hypoperfusion in areas with vascular disease. Such intraoperative hypoperfusion may contribute to postoperative organ dysfunction, sometimes leading to complications, prolonged hospital stay or even death. In addition, the measurement of stroke volume also allows to avoid large excess of fluids and subsequent venous congestion, that may also be a source of complications. Interstitial oedema increases the distance between red blood cells and mitochondria, the final destination for oxygen. Healing processes, especially at the level of digestive sutures, might be impaired in cases of excess oedema.

Conclusion

Thus it seems logical to conclude that empirical fluid filling may lead to the double risk of under- or overcompensation of perioperative losses. In the first case, the patient may suffer from insufficient tissue oxygenation in areas where vessels remain poorly perfused. In the second case, the patient might exhibit venous congestion upstream of the ventricle with the poorest pumping ability. Most often, the right ventricle is the weakest, which leads to systemic oedema. Sometimes, left ventricular failure is predominant and can result in pulmonary oedema. There is urgent need for large-scale, well-conducted randomised trials to verify the usefulness of guiding fluid titration using stroke volume or cardiac output measurement. If such strategies confirm a benefit in outcome with a high level of proof, this will demonstrate that a change in our practice may improve patient outcome.

The author

Bernard P. Cholley, MD, PhD
   AP-HP, Hôpital Européen Georges Pompidou
   Université Paris Descartes
   Service d'Anesthésie-Réanimation
   AP-HP, Hôpital Européen Georges Pompidou
   20 rue Leblanc
   75015 Paris, France
   e-mail: bernard.cholley@egp.aphp.fr

References

1. Guyton AC, Guyton AC. Overview of the circulation; medical physics of pressure, flow, resistance, and vascular compliance. Human physiology and mechanisms of disease. Philadelphia: Saunders. 1992: 110–6.
2. Patterson SW, Starling EH. On the mechanical factors which determine the output of the ventricles. J Physiol (Lond). 1914;48:357–79.
3. Shoemaker WC, Appel PL, Kram HB, Waxman K, Lee TS. Prospective trial of supranormal values of survivors as therapeutic goals in high risk surgical patients. Chest. 1988;94:1176–86.
4. Boyd O, Grounds RM, Bennett ED. A randomized clinical trial of the effect of deliberate perioperative increase of oxygen delivery on mortality in high-risk surgical patients. JAMA. 1993;270:2699–707.
5. Wilson J, Woods I, Fawcett J, Whall R, Dibb W, Morris C, et al. Reducing the risk of major elective surgery: randomised controlled trial of preoperative optimisation of oxygen delivery. BMJ. 1999;318:1099–103.
6. Conway DH, Mayall R, Abdul-Latif MS, Gilligan S, Tackaberry C. Randomised controlled trial investigating the influence of intravenous fluid titration using oesophageal Doppler monitoring during bowel surgery. Anaesthesia. 2002;57(9):845–9.
7. Gan TJ, Soppitt A, Maroof M, El-Moalem H, Robertson KM, Moretti E, et al. Goal-directed intraoperative fluid administration reduces length of hospital stay after major surgery. Anesthesiology. 2002;97(4):820–6.

8. Berlauk JF, Abrams JH, Gilmour IJ. Preoperative optimization of cardiovascular hemodynamics improves outcome in peripheral vascular surgery. A prospective, randomized clinical trial. AnnSurg. 1991;214:289–99.

9. Mythen MG, Webb AR. Perioperative plasma volume expansion reduces the incidence of gut mucosal hypoperfusion during cardiac surgery. ArchSurg. 1995;130:423–9.

10. Sinclair S, James S, Singer M. Intraoperative intravascular volume optimisation and length of hospital stay after repair of proximal femoral fracture: randomized controlled trial. BMJ. 1997;315:909–12.

11. Venn R, Steele A, Richardson P, Poloniecki J, Grounds M, Newman P. Randomized controlled trial to investigate influence of the fluid challenge on duration of hospital stay and perioperative morbidity in patients with hip fractures. BrJAnaesth. 2002;88:65–71.

12. Fleming A, Bishop MH, Shoemaker WC, Appel P, Sufficool W, Kuvhenguwha A, et al. Prospective trial of supranormal values as goals of resuscitation in severe trauma. ArchSurg. 1992;127(10):1175–81.

13. Bishop MH, Shoemaker WC, Appel PL, Meade P, Ordog GJ, Wasserberger J, et al. Prospective, randomized trial of survivor values of cardiac index, oxygen delivery, and oxygen consumption as resuscitation end-points in severe trauma. JTrauma. 1995;38:780–7.

14. Bundgaard-Nielsen M, Holte K, Secher NH, Kehlet H. Monitoring of peri-operative fluid administration by individualized goal-directed therapy. Acta Anaesthesiol Scand. 2007 Mar;51(3):331–40.

15. Kern JW, Shoemaker WC. Meta-analysis of hemodynamic optimization in high-risk patients. CritCare Med. 2002; 30(8):1686–92.

16. Fenwick E, Wilson J, Sculpher M, Claxton K. Pre-operative optimisation employing dopexamine or adrenaline for patients undergoing major elective surgery: a cost-effectiveness analysis. IntensiveCare Med. 2002;28(5): 599–608.

17. Takala J, Meier-Hellmann A, Eddleston J, Hulstaert P, Sramek V. Effect of dopexamine on outcome after major abdominal surgery: a prospective, randomized, controlled multicenter study. European Multicenter Study Group on Dopexamine in Major Abdominal Surgery. CritCare Med. 2000;28(10):3417–23.

18. Sandham JD, Hull RD, Brant RF, Knox L, Pineo GF, Doig CJ, et al. A randomized, controlled trial of the use of pulmonary-artery catheters in high-risk surgical patients. NEnglJMed. 2003;348(1):5–14.

19. Cholley BP, Payen D. Pulmonary-artery catheters in high-risk surgical patients. NEnglJMed. 2003;348(20): 2035–7.

20. Brandstrup B, Tonnesen H, Beier-Holgersen R, Hjortso E, Ording H, Lindorff-Larsen K, et al. Effects of intravenous fluid restriction on postoperative complications: comparison of two perioperative fluid regimens: a randomized assessor-blinded multicenter trial. AnnSurg. 2003;238(5):641–8.

21. Nisanevich V, Felsenstein I, Almogy G, Weissman C, Einav S, Matot I. Effect of intraoperative fluid management on outcome after intraabdominal surgery. Anesthesiology. 2005 Jul;103(1):25–32.

22. Holte K, Foss NB, Andersen J, Valentiner L, Lund C, Bie P, et al. Liberal or restrictive fluid administration in fast-track colonic surgery: a randomized, double-blind study. Br J Anaesth. 2007 Oct;99(4):500–8.

23. Holte K, Kristensen BB, Valentiner L, Foss NB, Husted H, Kehlet H. Liberal versus restrictive fluid management in knee arthroplasty: a randomized, double-blind study. Anesth Analg. 2007 Aug;105(2):465–74.

F. Oliveira Martins, Ana Luisa Jardim and Pedro Amado

Bedside surgery in the ICU

Introduction

The best place for surgery is usually the operating room (OR), where there are appropriate resources and generally a procedure can be performed under controlled circumstances. With any patient, but especially in a critically ill patient, the most adequate and ideal place for an interventional procedure is also the OR. When interventional or surgical procedures need to be performed on critically unstable patients with multi-organ dysfunction (MODS) and high levels of organ support, the simple moving of the patient to the OR may be deleterious, with a subsequent degradation in the clinical condition. In some cases these issues can be solved by bringing the OR to the patient bedside in the ICU. This is the so-called bedside surgery in the ICU (1), with the advantages of not having to move the patient to the OR and not impacting on the normal elective operating schedules.

Most of the time, the surgical operation in the ICU is going to be a very simple elective procedure. Rarely, however, urgent resuscitative minimal invasive procedures are required. In this situation the surgeon must minimise operative time and intervention. In the grossly unstable patients, this abbreviated procedure must prevent hypothermia, coagulopathy and metabolic acidosis (lethal triad) and must minimise the activation of the inflammatory cascade of this second hit, preventing the systemic inflammatory response syndrome (SIRS).

Controversial position 1

Today there is a consensus that the critically ill patient in the ICU must be central to all procedures, in a centripetal concept from diagnosis to treatment. Imaging must come to the ICU with ultrasonography (US) and all portable therapies, including endoscopies (oesophago-gastroduodenoscopy, colonoscopy, bronchoscopy) and ERCP (endoscopic retrograde cholangiopancreatography). The same rationale applies to surgical interventional procedures, which must be minimally invasive. Surgical procedures performed for diagnosis or treatment can be undertaken in the ICU in unstable patients too ill to be moved out of the ICU. Most diagnostic surgical procedures are undertaken to diagnose the focus of a severe septic situation or septic shock. With complementary evaluation with US (2), diagnostic peritoneal aspiration (DPA) and diagnostic peritoneal lavage (DPL) by the open technique with mini-laparotomy, or a formal exploratory mini-laparotomy can be performed. It is also possible to perform an exploratory laparoscopy with a millimetric optic port or a standard exploratory laparoscopy with an umbilical port and with an optical trocar (3).

In the case of therapeutic procedures, for instance in the event of trauma, sepsis or abdominal vascular crises, it is important to differentiate emergency life-saving procedures, urgent situations and elective ones.

Emergency procedures

1. Unstable critically ill patients
2. Resuscitative damage control procedures ABC approach
   - Cricothyroidotomy
   - Tracheostomy, percutaneous or surgical
   - Thoracic drainage – hypertensive pneumothorax
   - Thoracic drainage – massive haemothorax
   - Pericardial drainage – cardiac tamponade
   - Pericardial fenestration – cardiac tamponade
   - Resuscitative thoracotomies (left antero-lateral)
3. Control of massive thoracic haemorrhage
4. Control of aortic outflow (aortic cross-clamping in case of massive abdominal bleeding, primary or secondary (post-traumatic or post-operatory)
5. Cardiac tamponade and pulseless electric activity (PEA)
6. Perform internal cardiac massage in case of cardiac asystole (4, 5)
   (After all resuscitative thoracotomies and adequate resuscitation have been performed, the patient is moved to the OR).
   - Repacking of abdominal compartment, after damage control surgery in trauma, to control bleeding in case of recurrent haemorrhage
   - Decompression of abdomen in case of abdominal compartment hypertension and related organ dysfunction or abdominal compartment syndrome (6)
     - Primary
     - Secondary
     - Recurrent
   - External fixation of a pelvic fracture in severe unstable pelvic ring fracture with a haemodynamically unstable patient. Orthopaedic external fixation with a C-Clamp or other external fixation device (7)
   - Extra-peritoneal packing or repacking of the pelvis, in severe pelvic ring fractures with recurrent pelvic haemorrhage, after external fixation, in an unstable patient in shock
   - Cystostomy in case of urethral lesion
   - Fasciotomy in case of compartment syndrome of extremities
     - Fasciotomy of forearm

- Double incision four-compartment fasciotomy of the leg (8)
- Escharotomy – Thoracic circular burns

Urgent procedures

- Percutaneous/surgical tracheostomy
- Thoracic drainage or redrainage for recurrent haemo-/pneumothorax
- Pericardial drainage – pericardial collections
- Re-laparotomy in case of damage control for abdominal trauma to stop bleeding or control contamination.
- Treatment of recurrent abdominal compartment hypertension after decompressive laparostomy (usually Bogota bag). Conversion into a "Vak Pack" procedure (9)
- US-controlled percutaneous drainage of abdominal abcess (10)
- US-controlled mini-laparotomy and marsupialisation of an abdominal or retroperitoneal abscess (11)
- US-controlled percutaneous cholecystotomy in acalculous cholecystitis (12)
- US-controlled minilaparotomy cholecystotomy, cholecystolithotomy and cholecystostomy in litiasic colecistitys
- Single-port laparostomy or middle-line mini-laparotomy for diagnosis of abdominal ischaemia (13)
  - Arterial embolic ischaemia.
  - Arterial thrombosis
  - Venous thrombosis
  - Low-flow situation of splanchnic hypoperfusion

Elective procedures

- Percutaneous tracheostomy (14)
- Scheduled re-laparotomy following abdominal laparotomy and lavage for sepsis
- Scheduled necrosectomy in case of infected pancreatic necrosis. Patient with mini-laparostomy and pancreatic compartment marsupialisation (15)
- Ventrofill progressive centripetal on layer laparorraphy after laparostomy procedures (16)
- PEG – Gastrostomy
- Mini-laparotomy – Stamm gastrotomy
- Mini-laparotomy – Witzell jejunostomy

- Mini-laparotomy – Loop ileostomy to control distal fistulae
  - Post-operative
  - Post-traumatic
  - Colic or enteric fistulae in case of Pancreatitis with infected necrosis and laparostomy
  - Enteric fistulae in cases of laparostomy for abdominal sepsis
  - Enteric fistulae in cases of laparostomy for damage control in abdominal trauma

Ideal bedside surgery protocol (17)

1. The ICU attending and the operating surgeon will be present for the entire surgical procedure
2. Informed consent (when possible)
3. Pre-procedure surgical check-list to be reviewed by the bedside nurse with information of the surgeon General needs are reviewed, as are particular needs for the procedure
4. Pre-procedure anaesthesia check-list
5. Sterile drapes for surgical field
6. Entire surgical team must wear head covering, mask, sterile cover, boots and sterile gloves
7. General anaesthesia: Propofol, Vecuronium, activan, set-up of the ventilator
8. A sterile hand wash should be performed by the operating team
9. Pre-operative antibiotic prophylaxis – Cefazolin or Cefoxitin
10. Chlorhexidine abdominal preparation
11. Wall suction set-up
12. Warm irrigation saline
13. Surgical box:
- Thracheostomy
- Thoracotomy with Finochietto
- Thoracic drainage
- Laparotomy with Gausset and Leriche
  - 2 pick-ups
  - 2 surgical scissors
  - 1 Rigth scissors
  - 10 Kelly haemostatic
  - 2 Farabeauf
  - 2 Crawford
  - 2 Cystic
  - 4 Hallis
  - 4 Kocker
- Laparoscopy

- Minisite 2mm 0° laparoscope
- Minisite disposable 2mm introducer
- Sutures
  - Nylon
  - Vycril
  - Silk
  - Skin staples
  - Goretex vascular suture
- Thoracic
  - Sylastic drains
  - Malecot drains
- Oxygen tubes
- Sterile drapes/Ioban/Opsite – self-adhesive drapes
- Sterile polythene saline bag

14. Electric monopolar coagulator
15. Laparoscopic tower
16. Portable US
17. Portable Rx
18. Portable light set

These minimally invasive surgical bedside procedures have few complications and minimal risks in selected patients. The risks associated with patient transport from ICU to OR are eliminated, in particular in institutions with ORs far from the ICU. This is especially so for haemodynamically unstable patients or those who are on high levels of ventilatory support where loss of the airway can be particularly problematic. These advantages also apply to patients with critical abdominal problems, such as sepsis or trauma, which necessitate laparostomy with repeated abdominal approaches. These multiple transfers to the OR, or conversely, the avoidance of them, increase the risk of nosocomial pneumonia secondary to atelectasis. Bedside surgery in the ICU can also reduce the costs related to OR utilisation, and improve OR schedules for other elective surgical situations with benefits for more patients (18). Bedside surgery should be considered as routine in some elective situations and as mandatory in emergent and urgent crises. In the case of damage control procedures the final definitive surgery should always be performed in the OR.

Bedside anaesthesia

As the critically ill patient is often subjected to many unpleasant experiences and noxious stimuli, a number of measures need to be taken to provide comfort, reduce anxiety and control pain. Bedside ICU surgery has grown both in volume and complexity. It is current practice to perform bedside procedures in the ICU that were traditionally carried out in the operating room (OR) (e.g. minimally invasive tracheostomy, gastrostomy in addition to a number of endoscopic upper GI procedures, colonoscopy and so forth). Open abdomen management is also increasingly more common in severe trauma and intra-abdominal infections.

Decompressive laparotomy to treat ACS, damage control surgery to treat the critically ill patient with abdominal sepsis (e.g. gastrointestinal perforation, anastomotic leak after prior surgery), acute decompensation due to intra-abdominal haemorrhage, re-exploration of a previously open abdomen for washout (peritoneal lavage) or to change or remove intra-abdominal packing, are some of the more complex procedures being performed at the bedside in an ever-increasing number of ICUs. Nevertheless, there is no real consensus on the most appropriate surgical approach. Randomised clinical trials are scarce and the literature on bedside surgery is very limited. Selection of patients to undergo bedside surgery is left up to the clinical judgment of a surgeon experienced in treating this type of patient and who is a member of the multidisciplinary critical care team.

A surgical programme outside the OR (bedside surgery in the ICU) requires careful planning, seamless organisation, close cooperation between the surgeon and the ICU professional staff, with special attention given to the logistic aspects of a programme of this type, to ensure that the bedside procedures are carried out in a safe and effective manner. Bedside anaesthesia should maintain the same high standards of anaesthesia care provided in the OR. The patient's anaesthesia needs and clinical status are not different because of his/her location, but the conditions under which the care is given are different in terms of space and equipment available in an environment outside the OR. The intensivist must possess a cooperative team spirit, in keeping with the very nature of working in an ICU, and an approach oriented on evidence-based, goal-directed care. The key factor is communication amongst all members of the team of which the surgeon naturally is a part.

Guidelines have been developed by the American Society of Anesthesiologists (ASA), "Non-operating Room Anesthetizing Locations" (19). They offer several recommendations, such as a reliable source of O_2 with backup, a suction source, adequate monitoring equipment, and an emergency cart with defibrillator, emergency drugs and other emergency equipment. The ASA has also developed standards with respect to basic anaesthetic monitoring that point out the need for continuous monitoring of oxygenation, ventilation, circulation and temperature (20). Adequate patient monitoring is imperative for the safety of the procedure. All of these requirements are met in the ICU environment. However, it is not enough to simply monitor, we must know how to interpret the data furnished by this monitoring, understand the objectives of the therapy and be trained in how to deal with the critically ill patient, oftentimes suffering from shock or severe sepsis, with no gaps in monitoring and intensive treatment. It is the intensivist who is in the best position to ensure this continuity of care, "armed" with state-of-the-art scientific knowledge in the treatment of the critical patient and various technical skills.

The ICU was, of course, designed for its primary role (treatment of the acute patient) and not as an OR where surgical interventions take place. There are natural constraints in terms of space and equipment and even the staff's vocation that can make these types of procedures difficult. The ICU is definitely not the place for complicated operations. If major blood loss is expected or if extensive exposure is required, the surgery should be carried out in the OR.

Bedside surgery is indicated in two major groups: 1) patients considered too unstable to transport, with the procedure considered to be life-saving; 2) minimally invasive surgical procedures (e.g. serial laparotomies – previously open abdomen for washout –, decompressive laparotomy in ACS, diagnostic laparoscopy in selected cases). Other bedside procedures are minimally invasive types of surgery (tracheostomy, percutaneous endoscopic gastrostomy (PEG) placement, ICV filter placement) and various endoscopic procedures. Jose J. Diaz et al. concluded, in two retrospective studies of critically ill patients, that bedside laparotomy (BSL) was safe for the patient, had a low rate of complications, and improved OR utilisation, thereby reducing costs (21, 22).

Van Natta et al. and Toschlog, Rotondo et al. arrived at similar conclusions with respect to bedside tracheostomy and PEG placement (23, 24). Bedside laparoscopy in the ICU has also been recognised by some authors (25–27) as a diagnostic tool, primarily when intestinal ischaemia is suspected and in septic patients with unknown focus. However, as these were all small series, non-controlled, non-randomised studies, no recommendations can be made. Decision-making is done by the multidisciplinary critical care team experienced in treating these patients, to which the surgeon belongs. Advance planning and communication among all members of the team involved is essential to ensure that the procedure is performed safely.

Bedside anaesthesia (anaesthesia procedures performed at the bedside) requires a thorough knowledge of the patient's overall physical condition and an assessment of the anaesthetic needs for the proposed procedure. The literature on this subject is scarce, although the literature on sedation and analgesia of the critical patient is abundant (SCC-2002 guidelines, sedation and anaesthesia protocols with predetermined endpoints, sedation medication with subjective scales) (28–32). The spectrum of anaesthetic options in bedside surgery ranges from sedation and analgesia to total intravenous anaesthesia (TIVA). Drug selection takes a number of factors into account. In experienced hands, the choice of drugs is less important than the knowledge of how they should be used. Although it would be preferable to use short-acting drugs, the numerous factors that influence the pharmacokinetics and pharmacodynamics of these drugs in the critically ill patient require a professional who is skilled in using them safely. As individual response can vary greatly, the drugs must be carefully titrated and their effects must be monitored.

Anaesthetic options are more limited than in the OR. Since most ICUs do not have adequate gas scavenging systems, inhalational anaesthetics should be avoided due to the environmental pollution they cause. Options are limited to TIVA or regional anaesthetics. In TIVA, propofol is often used as an intravenous hypnotic. Between two other intravenous induction agents, ketamine and etomidate, ketamine preserves haemodynamic stability; its adrenergic effect can increase arterial pressure (AP). Unpleasant dreams and hallucination are important side effects, which can be prevented by concomitant administration of midazolam. Etomidate is an anaesthetic induction agent with a minimal cardiovascular effect, unlike other induction agents. However, its administration, whether by continuous infusion or as a single induction dose has an unfavorable impact on survival of the critical patient. It is therefore strongly recommended that it not be used in critical patients (suppression of adrenal steroid synthesis) (33, 34). The choice of opioids in TIVA follows the same pharmacological principles. Potent opioids with a rapid onset of action and short half-life are usually selected; synthetic opioids from the fentanyl family (fentanyl, sufentanyl, alfentanyl, remifentanyl) are preferred for a patient who is haemodynamically unstable or in renal failure. Neuromuscular blockade is sometimes needed to optimise the surgical field in bedside surgery. Intermediate-acting, non-depolarising muscle relaxants (atracurium, cisatracurium, rocuronium, vecuronium) are usually chosen with routine train-of-four monitoring of the neuromuscular blockade. To avoid awareness in TIVA with neuromuscular paralysis, benzodiazepines along with propofol are used simultaneously to maintain anaesthesia.

Epidural anaesthesia/analgesia

The influence of perioperative epidural analgesia on outcome after major abdominal surgery has been the subject of debate. Meta-analysis of randomised controlled trials (RCTs) has shown that, compared with other analgesic techniques, neuraxial block was associated with a significant decrease in perioperative morbidity and mortality (35–37). On the other hand, a large-scale, randomised multi-centre trial on epidural anaesthesia (the Master Anaesthesia Trial) showed no differences in mortality or morbidity or in the duration of mechanical ventilation or length of stay (LOS) in the ICU in patients who underwent major abdominal surgery. Post-operative analgesia, however, was found to be superior in the epidural group (38, 39). The use of epidural analgesia is limited in the septic patient, due to the risk of severe haematogenic infection (epidural abscess) and the haemodynamic instability caused by the sympathetic blockade and it is contraindicated in patients with coagulation abnormalities.

Monitoring

The relationship between monitoring, safety and patient outcome is sometimes complex. All intensive monitoring of the critical patient is continued in bedside surgery. Cardiorespiratory monitoring includes heart rate, invasive arterial pressure, pulse oximetry, CVP, $ScvO_2$, cardiac output in selected patients. Point-of-care technology bringing the laboratory to the bedside (for assessing blood gases, blood glucose and lactate levels) is an important asset in monitoring these patients. The ICU "cockpit" enables uninterrupted advanced monitoring and treatment of the critical patient, pre-, intra- and postoperatively.

Neurophysiological monitoring

Lately, monitoring of cerebral function to assess depth of anaesthesia has been receiving a lot of attention. Numerous studies have shown that using the Bispectral Index (BIS) to guide administration of anaesthetics results, on average, in less anaesthetic being administered and prevents intraoperative awareness (40–43). There are no published data on this subject using other monitors of cerebral function. Despite the popular idea that TIVA is more frequently associated with intraoperative awareness, the evidence belies this notion (44–46). The Joint Commission on Accreditation of Hospitals Organisation has published a Sentinel Event Alert concerning intraoperative awareness (47); the ASA has also published a practice advisory entitled Intraoperative Awareness and Brain Function Monitoring (48).

More studies are needed in the context of intensive care medicine (many have been extrapolated from OR anaesthesia) to assess the usefulness of this monitor to titrate sedation and anaesthesia (preventing hyper- or hyposedation) both when the critical patient is undergoing bedside general anaesthesia with the use of NMBs (neuromuscular blockers) or when these are used occasionally to facilitate mechanical ventilation.

More controversies

There has been an enormous increase in demand for anaesthesia for sedation or sedation and an-aesthesia in many areas of the hospital for diagnostic or therapeutic procedures, and given the scarcity of supply, it is not always possible to have an anaesthetist present in every circumstance. In the ICU the patient is monitored adequately on a continuous basis; intensivists are experienced in handling sedatives, analgesics, and muscle relaxants, in addition to their training in the treatment of severe acute patients, and there is a body of scientific knowledge that is guided by objectives and in many cases is evidence-based.

A bedside surgery program frees up the anaesthetist to perform in other work settings, improves OR usage, is a cost-effective alternative in selected cases and in the strict indications for bedside surgery. Another advantage of bedside ICU surgery, particularly in the case of the unstable patient, is that is avoids the risks associated with patient transport within the hospital. Transport of the critical patient is a challenge and always demands an assessment of the risks/benefits.

There are discrepancies in the numbers regarding rates of complications associated with intra-hospital transport; in some studies they are low (49), in others significant and described repeatedly in the literature (50–55). Even in the studies that found a very low rate of transport-related complications, their occurrence cannot be dismissed (49). Portable monitors have limited capabilities and artifacts produced by the transport are unavoidable. Although patient transport technology has been upgraded in recent years, intra-hospital transport still takes the patient away from the secure environment of the ICU and exposes him/her to potential complications.

As mentioned earlier, many of these patients have ALI/ARDS. Oftentimes the design and capacity of the ICU ventilator is different from the anaesthetic machine. If the performance of the OR ventilator is inadequate, the ICU ventilator should be used to prevent possible complications. In the OR the patient should be kept on the same mode of ventilation set to the same parameters, something that is not always possible, either because the patient has spontaneous respiration and needs muscle relaxants for the surgery or because the anaesthesia machine does not offer the same mode of ventilation. In these cases, the anaesthetist must be careful during the transition between different ventilatory modes in order to maintain similar tidal volumes and mean airway pressures so as to prevent deterioration of oxygenation and ventilation. These are some of the aspects, among others, that the OR anaesthetist must be aware of and be attentive to. As these problems do not occur in the ICU, they should be taken into consideration when deciding whether to opt for bedside ICU surgery. From this standpoint, bedside ICU surgery enables advanced uninterrupted monitoring of the critical patient and treatment based on an ICU team with state-of-the-art knowledge in the treatment of the critically ill patient, thereby avoiding the risks of transport.

Controversial position 2

The ideal location for any laparotomy or for any surgical procedure is the OR.

There there is an adequate control of infection with positive airflow ventilation, adequate environment, and adequate surgical protocols. In the OR, there are ideal anaesthetic and monitoring resources, and also specifically trained nursing and material and technical devices. Even in respect to unstable patients, the OR is usually not so far from ICU and most of the time any critical ill patient can be transported with secure heamodynamics and ventilatory support.

In emergencies, salvage surgical approaches in the ICU usually do not have good results and often the patient does not survive. Percutaneous thraqueostomy or thoracic or pericardial drainage as resuscitation procedures can be perfomed as an emergency measure, but thoracotomies or laparotomies as resuscitation approaches should not be attempted even in emergency situations.

In urgent situations most patients should be treated in the OR, with all the advantages for the patient and for the institution. In the ICU there is the potential risk of infection conditioned by the environment and sub-optimal local conditions. The ICU usually does not have good technical conditions. The light is deficient and the nurses are usually not trained to perform or assist in surgical procedures. Most of the time there are not enough appropriately trained anaesthetists available in the ICU. A well-trained intensivist with good experience in ventilation does not substitute for a general anaesthetist. The ICU usually has only deficient instrumentation, aspirators are

not as powerful and there is no adequate eletrocoagulation.

For electives procedures it is preferable to take the patient to the OR and schedule the surgery during elective time. Generally this does not significantly compromise elective procedures as these procedures are usuall less time-consuming and can be scheduled during complementary operating lists.

In critically ill patients, the patient must be offered the most specific and quality care to prevent the increased risk of iatrogenic complications which increase morbidity and eventually mortality. It is better to prevent any damage occurring rather than to eventually control it!

The best care for our critically ill patient should always be given in the specific place best suited to their needs.

- Surgery in OR
- Interventional radiology in the radiology department
- Interventional endoscopies in the endoscopy unit

If the patient is too unstable to get out of the ICU, the best approach is to delay the procedure by a few hours, allowing optimisation of the physiologic status.

Summary

There is general agreement that the best place to perform surgical techniques is the OR. There, we have the best resources to perform the appropriate procedures. Nevertheless, sometimes simple elective procedures need to be carried out in the ICU, such as percutaneous tracheostomy or PEG gastrotomy with no need to alter the OR schedule. In other instances there are urgent situations where we cannot wait to go to the OR, e.g. repacking the abdomen for control of bleeding, in cases of damage control or to release a laparostomy in the case of recurrent abdominal compartment syndrome. Similarly, in cases of laparostomy for abdominal sepsis the simple re-laparotomy and abdominal lavage can be performed safely in the ICU. In some situations, such as colecystostomy in acute cholecystitis, the operations should only be performed in the ICU in institutions where the OR is too far from the ICU with patients too unstable to be moved. The same holds true in cases of compartment syndrome from extremities or abdominal compartment syndrome.

The emergency situations of salvage thoracotomy or laparotomy usually should not be performed in the ICU because most of the times it will only change the place of death with increased risk to the team and with no benefit to the patient. Heroic procedures must be avoided. The ICU is not an emergency room and even in an emergency room, it is necessary to have a good triage of patients who benefit from surgical interventional procedures there. Generally, in the most severe situations, it is necessary to have a calm team with security and the right frame of mind to have good results (58). The more serious the situation the simpler the procedures must be and the more calm the team should be.

To perform bedside surgery safely it is necessary to have adequate conditions. There must be a surgeon trained in minimally invasive damage control approaches (59). There must also be an anaesthetist and an intensivist who are comfortable with these situations. There need to be adequate resources, including surgical sets with sutures, staples, sterile drapes, drains. There also needs to be good lighting, adequate suction, electrocoagulators, ultrasonography and portable XR. With all team members trained and with the adequate material many difficult situations in difficult patients can be resolved with good results (60). Sometimes these surgical procedures are a part of the resuscitation process in critically ill patients in the setting of a multidisciplinary centripetal approach where the only protagonist should be the patient.

Key points for clinical practice

The best place for surgical techniques is in the operating room (OR).
Sometimes we can perform bedside surgery in the ICU in simple elective situations, such as percutaneous traqueostomy, PEG gastrostomy or abdominal toilet in sepsis in patients with laparostomy, or in urgent situations such as repacking the abdominal cavity for controlling bleeding after damage control surgery, or releasing a laparostomy in situations of recurrent abdominal hypertension, or to perform a percutaneous cholecystostomy for acute cholcystitis in unstable patients, or performing a fasciotomy in situations of compartment syndrome of extremities, or ultrasound drainage of abdominal infected collections.
- *Bedside surgical procedures must be simple.*
- *We must avoid complex or desperate procedures.*
- *We must have an interested and cooperative team in the ICU with experience in minimally invasive surgical procedures (with surgeon, intensivist, anaestesist and nurses).*
- *We must have good local conditions.*
- *Good lighting, good suction apparatus, adequate surgical material, electrocoagulator, ultrasound, portable Rx.*

The authors

F. Oliveira Martins, MD[1]
Ana Luisa Jardim, MD[2]
Pedro Amado, MD[1]
   [1]Serviço de Cirurgia Geral | Hospital de
   St. António dos Capuchos | Centro Hospitalar
   de Lisboa Central | E.P.E., Lisboa, Portugal
   [2]Unidade de Cuidados Intensivos Polivalente |
   Hospital de St. António dos Capuchos |
   Centro Hospitalar de Lisboa Central | E.P.E.,
   Lisboa, Portugal

Address for correspondence
   F. Oliveira Martins
   Serviço de Cirurgia 6
   Hospital de St. António dos Capuchos
   Centro Hospitalar de Lisboa Central, E.P.E.
   1150 Lisboa, Portugal
   e-mail: spcirurgia@gmail.com

References

1. Tomothy L, Van Natta MD. Elective bed side surgery in critically injured patients is safe and cost-effective. Annals of surgery. 1998. Vol 227 n. 5:618–626.
2. Beagle GL. Bed side diagnostic ultrasound and therapeutic ultrasound-guided procedures in the intensive care setting. Crit care clin. 2000 Jan 16 (1):58–81.
3. Schiappa JM. Bed side laparoscopy. 11th international congress of EAES – Glasgow – June 2003.
4. Boffard K. Emergency department thoracotomy; Manual of definitive surgical trauma care; Second edition 2007.
5. Mattox Kl. Thoracic injury requiring surgery. World S. surg. 1982;7;47–52.
6. Sugrue M. Intra-abdominal pressure: Time for clinical practice guidelines? Intensive Care Med. 2002;28: 389–91.
7. Ertel W, Keel M, Eid K, Platz A, Trentz O. Control of severe haemorrhage using C-clamp and pelvic packing in multiply injured patient with pelvic ring disruption. J. Orthopaedic Trauma. 2001;15;468–74.
8. Mubarak SJ, Owen CA. Double incision fasciotomy of the leg for descompression in compartment syndrome. J Trauma. 1977;59A:184–7.

9. Schein M, Wittman DM, Aprahamian CC, Condon RE. The abdominal compartment syndrome: The physiological and clinical consequences of elevated intra-abdominal pressure. J Am Coll Surg. 1995;180;745–50.

10. Mayberry JC. Bedside open abdominal surgery. Utility and wound management. Crit Care Clin. 2000 Jan; 16(1): 151–72.

11. Begle G.L. Bed side diagnostic ultrasound and therapeutic ultrasound-guide procedures in intensive care setting; Crit Care Clin. 2000 Jan; 16(1);59–81.

12. Boland G, Lee MJ, Mueller PR. Acute cholecystites in the intensive care unit. New Horiz. 1993 May;1(2);246–60.

13. Sberti et al. Investigating intestinal ischaemia following aortic reconstruction. Surgery. 1989.

14. Timothy L et al. Elective bedside surgery in critically injured patient in safe and cost-effective. Annals of Surgery. 1998.

15. Martins O et al. Surgical approach to infected pancreatic necrosis; Annual congress of intensive care medicine, Portugal. Algarve. 2005.

16. Martins O et al. Damage control in sepsis; Annual congress of intensive care medicine, Portugal. Algarve. 2007.

17. Vanderbitt University Medical center. Bedside surgery protocol in trauma, emergency general surgery, surgical critical care. 2005.

18. Timothy L et al. Elective bedside surgery in critical patient in safe and cost-effective; annals of surgery. 1998;vol 227;nº5;618–626.

19. Approved by House of Delegates on October 19, 1994, and last amended on October 15, 2003. Guidelines for nonoperating room anesthetizing locations (www.Asahq.org. standards, guidelines and statements).

20. Approved by the American Society of Anesthesiologists House of Delegates on October 21, 1986 and last amended on October 25, 2005. Standards for basic anesthetic monitoring (www.Asahq.org. standards, guidelines and statements).

21. Diaz JJ, Mauer A, May AK, Miller R, Guy JS, Morris JA. Bedside laparotomy for trauma: are there risks? Surgical Infections. 2004;5:15–20.

22. Diaz JJ, Mejia V, Subhawong AP, Subhawong T, Miller RS, O'Neill PJ et al. Protocol for bedside laparotomy in trauma and emergency general surgery: a low return to the operating room. Am. Surgeon. 2005;71:986–991.

23. Van Natta TL, Morris JA Jr, Eddy VA, Nunn CR, Rutherford EJ, Neuzil D et al. Elective bedside surgery in critically injured patients is safe and cost-effective. Ann Surg. 1998;227:618–24.

24. Toschlog EA, Rotondo M, Briggs S, Sagraves S, Schenarts P, Bard M et al. Intensive care unit bedside surgery: a cost effective approach. Crit Care Med. 2005;33: Abstract Supplement A175.

25. Jaramillo EJ, Treviño JM, Berghoff KR, Franklin MEJr. Bedside diagnostic laparoscopy in the intensive care unit: a 13-year experience. JSLS. 2006;10:155–9.

26. Gagné DJ, Malay MB, Hogle NJ, Fowler DL. Bedside diagnostic minilaparoscopy in the intensive care patient. Surgery. 2002;131:491–6.

27. Rehm CG. Bedside laparoscopy. Critical Care Clinics, Haupt MT, Rehm CG: W.B. Saunders Company, 2000.

28. Jacobi J, Fraser GL, Coursin DB, Riker RR, Fontained, Wittbrodt et al. Clinical practice guidelines for the sustained use of sedatives and analgesics in the critically ill adult. Crit Care Med. 2002;30:119–141.

29. Ibrahim EH, Kollef MH. Using protocols to improve the outcomes of mechanically ventilated patients. Crit Care Clin. 2001;17:989–1001.

30. Brook AD, Ahrens TS; Schaiff R, Prentice D, Sherman G, Shannon W. Effect of a nursing-implemented sedation protocol on the duration mechanical ventilation. Crit Care Med. 1999;27:2609–2615.

31. Devlin JW, Boleski G, Mlynarek M, Nerenz DR, Peterson E, Jankowski M, Horst HM, Zarowitz BJ. Motor activity assessment scale: A valid and reliable sedation scale for use with mechanically ventilated patients in an adult surgical intensive care unit. Crit Care Med. 1999;27: 1271–1275.

32. Kress JP, Pohlman AS, O'Connor MF, Hall JB. Daily interruption of sedative infusions in critically ill patients undergoing mechanical ventilation. N Engl J Med. 2000;342:1471–1477.

33. Lipiner-Friedman D, Sprung CL, Laterre PF, Weiss Y, Goodman SV, Vogeser M et al. Adrenal function in sepsis: The retrospective Corticus cohort study. Crit Care Med. 2007;35:1012–1018.

34. Annane D. ICU physicians should abandon the use of etomidate! Intensive Care Med. 2005;31:325–326.

35. Rodgers A, Walker N, Schug S, Mckee A, Kehlet H, van Zundert A et al. Reduction of post-operative mortality and morbidity with epidural or spinal anesthesia: results from overview of randomized trials. BMJ. 2000;321:1493–7.

36. Ballantyne J, Carr D, deFerranti S, Suarez T, Lau J, Chalmers TC et al. The comparative effects of postoperative analgesic therapies on pulmonary outcome: cumulative meta-analyses of randomized, controlled trials. Anesth Analg. 1998;86:598–612.

37. Beattie W, Badner N, Choi P. Epidural analgesia reduces postoperative myocardial infarction: a meta-analysis. Anesth Analg. 2001;93:853–8.

38. Rigg JR, Jamrozik K, Myles PS, Silbert BS, Peyton PJ, Parsons RW et al. Epidural anesthesia and analgesia and outcome of major sugery: a randomized trial. Lancet. 2002;359:1276–82.

39. Peyton PJ, Myles PS, Silbert BS, Rigg JA, Jamrozik K, Parsons R. Perioperative epidural analgesia and outcome after major abdominal surgery in high-risk patients. Anesth Analg. 2003;96:548.

40. Lennmarken C, Ekman A, Sandin R. Incidence of awareness using BIS-monitoring. Anesth Analg. 2003; 96:S133.

41. Myles PS, Leslie K, McNeil J, Forbes A, Chan MT. Bispectral index monitoring to prevent awareness during anesthesia: the B-Aware randomized controlled trial. Lancet. 2004;363:1757–63.

42. Ekman A, Lindhom M_L, Lennmarken C, Sandin R. Reduction in the incidence of awareness using BIS monitoring. Acta Anaesthesiol Scand. 2004;48:20–6.

43. Liu SS. Effects of bispectral index monitoring on ambulatory anesthesia. A meta-analysis of randomized controlled trials and a cost analysis. Anesthesiology. 2004;101:311–5.

44. Nordstrom O, Engstrom AM, Persson S, Sandin R. Incidence of awareness in total i.v. anaesthesia based on propofol, alfentanil and neuromuscular blockade. Acta Anaesthesiol Scand. 1997;41:978–84.

45. Lequeux PY, Velghe-Lenelle CE, Cantraine F, Sosnowski M, Barvais L. Absence of implicit and explicit memory during propofol/remifentanil anesthesia. Eur J Anesthesiol. 2005;22:333–6.

46. Lequeux PY, Cantraine F, Levarlet M, Barvais L. Absence of explicit and implicit memory in unconscious patients during TCI of propofol. Acta Anaesthesiol Scand. 2003;47: 833–7.

47. http://www.jointcomission.org/Sentinel Events/Sentinel Event Alert/sea_32.htm.

48. A report by the American Society Anesthesiologists task force on intraoperative awareness. Practice advisory for intraoperative awareness and brain function monitoring. Anesthesiology. 2006;104:4.

49. Szem JW, Hydo LJ, Fischer E, Kapur S, Klemperer J, Barie PS. High-risk transport of critically ill patients: safety and outcome of the necessary "road trip" (clinical investigation). Crit Care Med. 1995;23:1660–1666.

50. Beckmann U, Gillies DM, Berenholtz SM, Wu AW, Pronovost P. Incidents relating to the intra-hospital transfer of critically ill patients. An analysis of the reports submitted to the Australian Incident Monitoring Study in Intensive Care. Intensive Care Med. 2004;30: 1579–1585.

51. Hurst JM, Davis K, Johnson DJ, Branson RD, Campbell RS, Branson PS. Cost and complications during in-hospital transport of critically ill patients: a prospective cohort study. J Trauma. 1992;33:582–585.

52. Gervais HW, Eberle B, Konietzke D, Hennes HJ, Dick W. Comparison of blood gases of ventilated patients during transport. Crit Care Med. 1987;15:761–763.

53. Ehrenwerth J, Sorbo S, Hackel A. Transport of critically ill adults. Crit Care Med. 1986;13:543–547.

54. Waydas C, Schneck G, Duswald KH. Deterioration of respiratory function after intrahospital transport of critically ill surgical patients. Intensive Care Med. 1995; 21:784–789.

55. Insel J, Weissman C, Kemper M, Askanazi J, Hyman AI. Cardiovascular changes during transport of critically ill and postoperative patients. Crit Care Med 1986;14: 539–542.

56. Mattox KL. Indication for thoracotomy, deciding to operate; Surgical Clinics N. Am. 1989;69;47–56.

57. Oliveira Martins et al. Damage control surgery; Annual meeting of HUC – UCI. Coimbra. 2007.

58. Kenneth Boffard; Manual of definitive surgical trauma care; second edition. 2007;88–93.

I. Adjunctive issues

Max Jonas, Carl Waldmann and Michael Imhoff

Technology assessment and procurement: 'Monitoring the monitor'

Introduction

Health technologies are defined to include all interventions used to promote health, prevent and treat disease, and to improve rehabilitation and long-term care.

This definition includes instruments, equipment (including disposables), drugs, and procedures used in healthcare delivery such as screening and counselling.

The science of health technology assessment (HTA) has evolved to promote and develop a system which allows judgements to be made on any health technology. These processes significantly focus on appropriate study design and conduct (1).

Background

Health technology assessment as defined above, has a wide mandate to consider:

- Drugs
- Devices
- Procedures
- Surgical techniques
- Counselling, screening

in various settings such as general practice, hospitals and Care homes.

Despite the large area of interest covered by this definition, the approaches to most elements of HTA are similar, with the notable exception of drug-based technologies from the pharmaceutical industry, which are tightly legislated and require assessments ranging from animal studies to large interventional clinical trials. As a complete contrast, medical devices have relatively little legislature surrounding clinical introduction and frequently there is little consensus as to what constitutes adequate assessment. As a result there can be no doubting the need for further developments to the science of HTA. This is especially pertinent with the escalating numbers of devices for which manufacturers make claims relating to patient care. The HTA exercises for these devices stipulate study design and assessment in an attempt to judge and evaluate short- and long-term benefits. There are two questions to answer: Does the device have a positive clinical impact and are the resultant economics affordable in the context of local/national healthcare funding?

The requirement for a balanced approach of science versus economics ensures that the assessment design will draw on expertise from clinicians, engineers, statisticians, economists, ethicists and, of course, lawyers. The important omission from this list are the device manufacturers and those associated with the companies, as industry financed assessment creates difficult pressures and may result in biased trials and assessments.

Under ideal conditions those with a pecuniary interest in the device should be distanced from HTA, but unfortunately there are many trials where the only source of funding that can be identified is from industry rather than government or healthcare agencies. This funding is an important issue, as ultimately one of the major drivers for HTA is the enabling of decisions for priority device purchases within the perspective of budget constraints. This requires quality assessment, free from commercial taint, especially when reflecting on the 11.5 % of the EU GDP – in excess of 700 billion EUR – spent on health technologies. Formal HTA within such a massive budget will create major cost efficiencies and ultimately spread healthcare further.

This review has artificially divided HTA into 6 areas for discussion which would in the real world be running simultaneously:
- Development of technology
- Components of H-T-A
- Return on investment
- Standards & regulatory bodies
- Procurement
- Controversies of principles of assessment

Development of technology

The requirement to develop a new technology is usually market-driven and hopefully also focused on patient need. The patient, however is not the only focus, as development also depends on interaction between clinicians and industry. This is a difficult area because of the sums of money involved in the development of a technology which may generate conflicts of interest in this relationship. Misunderstandings and ethical dangers can be mistaken for technology assessment and can quickly give rise to concerns such as whether industry-sponsored research only is published when the result favours sale of the device or drug manufactured by the company.

Components of HTA

The HTA process has 3 core areas:
- Device safety
- Device performance
- Device cost

Device safety

This is a complex area where there may be safety aspects related to using a device as well as the clinical process and context in which the device is used. Safety also encompasses accuracy of the device, as inappropriate clinical decisions can result from inaccurate measurements. Frequently overlooked is the obverse component of the assessment process which should scrutinise the impact of not using the device.

Assessing the safety of the device or box itself is a statutory requirement and includes elements of electrical safety, detailed multilingual instructions, packaging, compliance with environmental specifications and disposal instructions. All of these issues are dealt with using a European Standard, referred to as the CE mark (La Conformitée Européenne), which certifies that technical manufacturing standards have been met. It is not a functional guarantee that the device or process will be of benefit or be safe in clinical use. In the US the Food and Drug Administration (FDA) fulfils a similar role but in addition, before granting approval for sale in the US, has a remit beyond the technical qualifications of the CE mark and mandates some assessment of clinical operation. The FDA uses clinical experts to review investigational studies relating to the device to ascertain whether the product does what is claimed by the manufacturer and/or presents unreasonable risks to the patient. The FDA classifies devices into three classes according to the risk of potential harm to the user, ranging from Class 1 devices that present minimal risk to the user, e.g. home blood pressure kits, to Class 3 such as dialysis machines or ICU ventilators.

Device performance

Efficacy and effectiveness are used to assess device performance. Efficacy relates to the device's performance under ideal conditions, and effectiveness is performance under normal clinical working conditions. This is an important distinction, as efficacy ratings may indicate the necessity for 'experts' to operate the device, whereas effectiveness relates to the performance limitations under average clinical conditions. Overall, when reviewing technology the new approach should offer improvement over current technologies. This may be because the device can obtain measurements with less risk to the patient, i.e. is less invasive, or has some other aspect which is advantageous.

Efficacy

Assessing efficacy usually means comparison of the device against a known 'gold' standard. When the measurement is well defined, e.g. cardiac output, the efficacy becomes the mathematical correlate of accuracy.

Accuracy is the closeness of the device measurement to the actual value and can be described by:

- Correlation (degree of association between readings)
- Precision (the closeness of repeated measurements)
- Bias (the difference between the means of the measurements)

The repeatability and inaccuracy of the gold standard is important, because if it has a varying accuracy then the limits of agreement between it and the technology under scrutiny become wider, less meaningful and make definitive comparisons difficult, e.g. thermodilution cardiac output vs. other technologies.

Where a gold standard reference does not exist it is necessary to show that the technology has a clinical utility, usually in relationship to patient outcomes. This suggests that the monitor has to be able to detect a variable which when targeted will affect outcome. The efficacy assessment here where there is no gold standard is the determination of sensitivity, specificity and predictive values:

Tab. 1   Sensitivity = A/A+C
Positive predictive value = A/A+B
Specificity = D/B+D
Negative predictive value = D/C+D

	Outcome improved	Outcome not improved
Positive	A	B
Negative	C	D

Effectiveness

Assessment of effectiveness requires clinical trials in which the technology is used as it would be under average conditions. Standard rules of engagement for conducting comparative studies are important to produce valid results and it must be appreciated that there may be issues related to study design.

The two obvious trials are a technology versus control, or the technology with its measurement guiding subsequent therapeutic management. For the former type of trial the data is usually comparative, whereas for the latter the results tend to be clinical outcome-based. For outcome data the ideal measurement is considered to be mortality, but because of the resource implications of numbers needed to power studies for mortality, the use of surrogates such as length of hospital stay or number of complications is common. If using a device to guide therapy, it is important to consider the relative contributions of the device being assessed, as opposed to the therapeutic interventions of the protocol which may be the important determinant of the results.

Device Cost

The economics related to health technologies as stated above, is a key driver for technology assessment. These principles provide a safeguard for a finite and shrinking health budget and represent an attempt to ensure that resources and benefits are spread and do not favour one particular group. The area of cost containment is complex, as in many situations the only costs considered are 'direct' costs relating to the technology and disposables. Frequently the indirect costs such as training and storage are ignored and these may represent a considerable financial load. E.g. a clinical information system may have a monetary cost per bed, but staff training, education and maintenance personnel may generate considerable additional on-costs.

Return on investment (ROI)

The increasing pressure on the cost-effectiveness of care has given ROI analysis increasing importance for the health care professional. The terms and definitions of "return on investment" and "cost-effectiveness" have their origins in the economic literature rather than in medical science. As a consequence, most of our knowledge and the developed methods and principles for measuring ROI come from non-medical applications. The return on investment is the profit that the investment yields. The concept of 'returns', 'profits' and' investment' may appear alien to healthcare and whilst using its industrial sense of giving a perspective for the beneficiary (investor), typically the company, making the investment, in healthcare there are different beneficiaries and different perspectives from which to assess ROI. Under the healthcare paradigm the investor and beneficiary are not always identical and before undertaking a healthcare ROI analysis the perspective has to be defined. Different perspectives in healthcare may include the individual care provider, e.g. the general practitioner, the health care organisation, e.g. a hospital, a health management organisation (HMO), an entire health care system, i.e. the public purse, the employer of the patient, or the individual patient. If the denominator in a ROI analysis is considered to be the perspective, the numerator is the service item being considered. Service items could include a specific medical procedure, e.g. an MRI study, one specific disease episode, the complete treatment for one DRG, or even the entire health coverage for a population. The ultimate goal is to reduce the cost per service item and in principle there are three approaches to potentially reduce cost:

1. Reduction of resource consumption, i.e. the direct cost for an individual service item, e.g. sourcing a medical device that has lower operating costs.
2. Increase of the number of procedures done with the same resource, i.e. reduction of the fixed cost per service, e.g. extended operating hours for expensive imaging equipment (in this case reduction of fixed costs needs to be offset against increased direct costs).
3. Reduction in complications in relation to the delivered service item. This approach is highly specific for healthcare. Typically, complications are expensive, as they require additional treatment, increase the length of stay, and may result in compensation for malpractice. Even a small reduction in the complication rate may have a significant effect on the cost-effectiveness of a service item.

There are also different approaches to ROI analysis using different models and assumptions. The discussion of all methodologies goes beyond the scope of this article, but as a synopsis, there are 5 elements necessary to complete a ROI analysis:

- Analysis of the cost structure of the affected processes
- Asessment of the anticipated changes resulting from the investment
- The actual cost of the new investment
- The potential savings from the investment including a risk analysis
- Calculation of the return on investment

In summary, ROI analysis is feasible even in the highly complex setting of a healthcare institution. In this setting it is necessary to justify the significant investments made for service delivery and show future impact on cost reduction, medical errors, and quality of care. Healthcare ROI analysis is a formidable task and can carry a high level of uncertainty because it was originally not conceived for use in the medical environment. However, used appropriately, it can create a chance to learn more about the processes and cost structure of care.

Standards & regulatory bodies

There are various regulatory bodies that may have a role in the safety of devices, but their terms of reference and legislative powers are country-specific. Listed below are some country-specific regulatory bodies:

UK

- Association of the British Pharmaceutical Industry (ABPI)
- Department of Health
- Medicines and Healthcare Products Regulatory Agency (MHRA)
- National Institute of Clinical Excellence (NICE)

USA

- Centers for Disease Control and Prevention

- The Food and Drug Administration (FDA)
- National Center for Infectious Diseases (NCID)
- National Institutes of Health (NIH)

Germany

- Federal Institute for Drugs and Medical Devices (BfArM)
- Ministry of Health

Italy

- Ministry of Health

Portugal

- The National Institute of Pharmacy and Medicines (Infarmed)

In Europe assessing the safety of the device or box itself is a statutory requirement and includes elements of electrical safety, detailed multilingual instructions, packaging, compliance with environmental specifications and disposal instructions. All of these issues are dealt with using a European standard, referred to as the CE mark (La Conformitée Européenne), which is a technical label for the product required by all European hospitals before procurement. It allows product to be marketed throughout Europe without any additional approval in individual countries. It certifies that technical manufacturing standards have been met. It is not a functional guarantee that the device or process will be of benefit, or be safe, in clinical use.

In the US, the Food and Drug Administration (FDA) fulfils a similar role but in addition, before granting approval for sale in the US, has a remit beyond the technical qualifications of the CE mark and mandates some assessment of clinical operation. The FDA uses clinical experts to review investigational studies relating to the device to ascertain whether the product does what is claimed by the manufacturer and/or presents unreasonable risks to the patient. The FDA classifies devices into three classes according to the risk of potential harm to the user, ranging from Class 1 devices that present minimal risk to the user, e.g. home blood pressure kits, to Class 3, e.g. dialysis machines or ICU ventilators.

In the UK, a regulatory body, the Medicines and Healthcare Regulatory Agency (MHRA) is responsible to the government for ensuring medical devices work, are safe and 'fit for purpose'. This body produces action/alerts when device, or medicine, issues arise and ensures information is publicly available and communicated to all relevant medical personnel. The MHRA is also instrumental in improving access to products and and actively participates in device education, recommending the development of 'driving licences' for technologies such as diathermy units and anaesthetic machines. It is this agency, too, that has the authority to award CE marks and was responsible for warnings about procurement of medical products via web-based auction sites.

The plethora of new health technologies released every year has driven governments and administrators to create bodies such as the National Institute of Clinical Excellence (NICE) in the UK. This body has considerable powers and examines the effectiveness of new technologies in an attempt to help hospitals and health authorities determine priorities. NICE guidance has been applied to the use of technology such as the use of ultrasound for insertion of central venous catheters to drugs used to treat Alzheimer's. It usually will only make recommendations for a technology to be funded if the quality-adjusted life year is less than £ 30,000 (50,000 EUR)

Procurement

Public Procurement is the purchasing of supplies and services by national, regional and local public bodies. Throughout Europe, contracting authorities purchase goods for a wide range of activities, and these large contracts must be advertised throughout Europe. The publication of a green paper in 1996, *'Public Procurement in the EU: Exploring the way forward'*, suggested that public procurement had not measured up to expectations. It proposed an improved procurement system which would improve competition and reduce corruption in the European Union. Subsequent reports concluded that procurement should only be undertaken by specially qualified personnel and information technology should be used to automate ordering, invoice matching and payment. A consistent feature of all these reports were statements encouraging the use of 'competition' to help reduce prices and suggestions that risk could be minimised by standardising on fewer different brands of product.

Procurement law in the European Union dates back to 1957 with the formation of the Common Market in 1957 following the Treaty of Rome. The treaty sets out all the basic laws of the EU such as freedom of movement of goods and workers.

EU legislation demands that member states must translate this European legislation into national legislation, i.e. directives are binding for national governments.

The EC public purchasing rules apply to the all member states and also to the European Economic Area (EEA – Iceland, Norway and Liechtenstein) and to many countries associated with the Union, for instance those covered by Europe Agreements (Bulgaria, Czech Republic, Hungary, Poland, Romania and Slovakia). Agreements have also been made with Turkey, Morocco and Tunisia to develop competitive public procurement practices. Public sector bodies are required to advertise their contract opportunities in the OJEU if the value exceeds the thresholds set by the EU. The OJEU notice reflects business needs and priorities and should achieve a realistic balance between a scope that is wide enough to encourage innovation and a statement of business need to which the market can make a meaningful response; it must also specify achievable timeframes within the EU procurement rules. The rules prescribe how the tenders are advertised and awarded. Currently contracts over certain values are subject to these rules: The tender is advertised in the Supplement to the Official Journal of the European Union (OJEU) and under the EU regulations there are three types of tender procedures available to buyers:

- The open procedure
  This is available in all circumstances and involves a single-stage approach where all candidates may respond to the OJEU advertisement and all offers received must be considered.
- The restricted procedure
  This is available in all circumstances and involves a two-stage approach where candidates who respond to the OJEU advertisement will be considered to have expressed an interest. The buyer will shortlist a number of these who will then be invited to submit offers.
  Where the restricted procedure is used, the buyer must allow a minimum of 37 days from

the date the OJEU notice was despatched to the closing date for receipt of expressions of interest. Once short-listing has taken place, a minimum of 40 days must be allowed for offers to be returned.

- The negotiated procedure
  This is only available in a very limited number of circumstances and is subject to strict conditions. The most common tender used is the restricted procedure, as the open procedure is expensive and time-consuming and there is limited applicability surrounding the negotiated procedure.

Another method of procurement that has recently gained importance is *ProCure21*, a procurement method for publicly funded NHS capital schemes. It is currently being used to deliver community hospitals, primary care centres, mental health units and other acute services such as cardiac care and out-patient units. It stands alongside the Private Finance Initiative (PFI) and the Local Investment Finance Trust (LIFT) initiative to deliver the future of NHS facilities. It is recommended by HM Treasury Guidance and compliant with OGC's Common Minimum Standards policy. It represents current construction industry best practice and helps NHS Trusts guard against the poor practice and results that have been associated with traditional tender procurement. The Department of Health provides ProCure21 for English NHS organisations, but also has provided expertise for similar initiatives in Wales, Northern Ireland and Scotland. The current framework agreement has been extended until September 2010.

It offers a partnering method of construction under the NEC Contract Option 2. An NHS Trust can select a Principal Supply Chain Partner (PSCP) from the ProCure21 framework without having to go through the OJEU tender process. The PSCP will offer a full range of services that will help the trust plan, design, approve, and construct their scheme. Once a final design is agreed both parties agree a guaranteed maximum price before construction starts.

Controversies

The core of HTA relates to the clinical impact of a technology and its affordability in the context of the local healthcare budget. Common examples of devices frequently under HTA scrutiny are patient monitoring technologies.

Patient monitoring is part of a billion-euro industry and naturally represents a commercial arena which is fiercely contested by competing manufacturers. Most of these companies produce devices which duplicate others and so must offer either a functional or cost differential. HTA analysis of any one of these devices should therefore produce a positive clinical impact. Unfortunately for routine monitoring, the evidence for any impact is terrible. For instance, pulse oximetry is considered as standard monitoring for patient management, but a meta-analysis of four trials involving 21,773 patients concluded perioperative monitoring with SpO_2 is unproven. The same is true of most other patient monitors in current use with notable exceptions of the gastric tonometer and oxygen flux measurements, both of which have prognostic value.

One of the major problems in providing a retrospective technology assessment for patient monitoring is that a properly conducted trial could only be done if there were equipoise for the clinicians not to use routinely accepted monitoring.

This would prove impossible given that there are published standards for patient monitoring (Association of Anaesthetists, UK and Ireland, 2007) and elements of monitoring which are considered best practice. Equipoise for not using monitoring requires a high level of physician comfort, which from a custom and practice perspective as well in the current medico-legal climate, does not exist. There is therefore considerable doubt that proper HTA on routine monitoring will ever occur directly.

For patient monitoring what cogent evidence there is can be seen in data from Shoemaker's group in the 1970s which showed that out of 30 monitored variables in common use only flow and oxygen flux had prognostic value. In the subsequent two decades the thermodilution pulmonary artery catheter was the only commonly used method for measuring flow (CO) and oxygen dynamics. A combination of perceived invasiveness, poor publicity and flawed outcome studies, with no clinical protocols, has lead to falling clinical usage and fueled the search for alternative technologies with the 'non-invasive' label. The growth in the CO monitor market combined with conflicting reports of clinical impact has allowed equi-

poise to trial these monitors in various clinical scenarios. The health technology arena has developed rapidly as there is some positive impact data from CO monitor usage with an interesting competitive market developing between the box manufacturers.

Ignoring costs and assuming acceptance of a positive impact, the next phase in HTA would be to compare the devices against a gold standard and each other. The concept of accuracy, i.e. the closeness of the measured vs. the actual value, reflects not only an important attribute of the monitor under scrutiny but also should be considered as a safety feature, which is another HTA component, as inaccuracy may lead to inappropriate clinical decisions.

Once the concept of a positive outcome from clinical usage is suggested and clinical trials undertaken, the issues may become more controversial. The CO monitoring HTA has produced inconsistent trials, inaccurate statistics and unlikely conclusions from clinicians who may have had conflicts of interests when championing a particular monitor using trial data and personal experience. For instance, in comparison with thermodilution as a standard there is an acceptance of statistical values which suggest whether a monitor can be used interchangeably with the gold standard.

The method of analysis is that described by Critchley for comparison of cardiac output monitors. This paper provides the necessary steps to draw conclusions on both statistical and clinical acceptability. This was originally developed for comparison of Doppler and bio-impedance products, however, it is applicable in all situations of comparison, provided the reference monitor (in most cases the PAC) is well characterised and itself proven. In the paper the authors recommend limits of agreement between two methods that are ± 28.3 %. This is often rounded to ± 30 %, and if the values fall within, these values make it possible to state that the comparison device could be a replacement for the reference device.

As an example, the diagram shows results compiled from published papers on a relatively new device in the CO arena from 2005 to 2007. Analysis of some of these papers shows incomplete statistical methods, a failure to report all the results, and some had incomplete discussions with incongruent conclusions. In most cases the data was there to complete the analysis, but assumptions had to be made in some cases. The range of bias values for this new monitor was generally high (–0.26 to +0.8) with several at or greater than 0.5l/min. The limits of agreement clearly show that no study yet published has met the Critchley requirements for substitution of the PAC with the new device (see fig. 1).

The confusion surrounding these results is compounded by the conclusions printed in some peer-reviewed journals. These range from fully supportive – ignoring the statistics – to undecided, to accurate stating poor performance. What is worrying is that there are some clear conflicts of interest relating to several of the authors and include bald published statements by key opinion leaders associated with the products in reputed journals. One such author, in an editorial, suggested that despite results, neither accuracy or inaccuracy was an issue and further stated that "it (the monitor) had certain limitations in its current form that, as far as this author is concerned, do not detract from its potential usefulness in the vast majority of situations". A formal HTA would probably disagree, but what is clear is that the scientific journals have become the marketing tools for competing companies. Even non-partisan and unsuspecting journals can fall prey to such conflicts. One author published an article proposing the use of a particular Doppler monitor in all high-risk surgery. Personal communication with the editor confirmed that attempts were made to remove the references to

the specific manufacturer but leaving a description of the device was equivalent to mentioning the company. More seriously, the senior author failed to declare in the article a financial relationship with the company.

Summary

HTA seeks a positive clinical impact from clinical technologies and considers safety, performance and affordability. As a key point for clinical practice, what HTA doesn't do is to ensure timely and appropriate evidence based for clinical use. There should be greater scrutiny of commercial pressures on authors and a more rigorous review process of the statistics and conclusions. As a final comment, clinical users have to remind themselves that without proper HTA the device you are using is probably the cheapest available.

The authors

Max Jonas, MD
Carl Waldmann, MD
Michael Imhoff, MD
    Section of Technology Assessment and
    Health Informatics (TAHI) of ESICM

Address for correspondence
    Max Jonas
    Consultant and Senior Lecturer

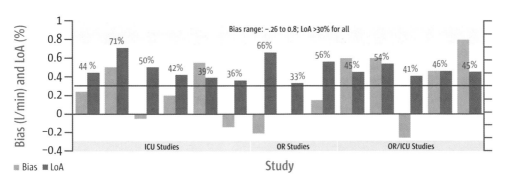

Fig. 1   Histogram plot of 14 published studies of a new monitor showing bias and LoA. All the LoA from this device are outside of accepted values. Despite this some of the articles published conclusions which did not have concur with this evidence and conflicts of interest existed for some of the authors. With permission from Eric Mills.
    LoA = Level of Agreement

General Intensive Care Unit
Southampton General Hospital
Southampton SO16 6YD, UK
e-mail: m.jonas959@btinternet.com

References

1. Sibbald WJ, Inman KJ. Problems in assessing the technology of critical care medicine. Int J Technol Assess Health Care. 1992;8:419–443 (review).

Further reading

Audit Commission Goods for your health. 1996.

Critchley LAH, Critchley JAJH. A meta-analysis of studies using bias and precision statistics to compare cardiac output measurement technologies J Clin Monit. 1999;15:85–91.

European Commission Green Paper. Public procurement In the European union: Exploring the way forward Communication adopted by the Commission on 27th November 1996.

Guyatt GH, Tugwell PX, Feeny DH, Haynes RB, Drummond MA. A framework for clinical evaluation of diagnostic technologies CMAJ. 1986;134:587–594.

Lexchin J, Bero LA, Djulbegovic B, Clark O. Pharmaceutical industry sponsorship and research outcome and quality: systematic review. BMJ. 2003 31st May;11671–170.

Moller JT, Johannessen NW, Espersen K et al. Randomized evaluation of pulse oximetry in 20,802 patients: II. perioperative events and postoperative complications. Anesthesiology. 1993;78:445–453.

NHS ProCure21: http://www.nhs-procure21.gov.uk/content/overview.asp.

NICE. Guidance on the use of ultrasound locating devices for placing central venous catheters. NHS document. Technology Appraisal Guidance No. 49, September 2002.

Pedersen T, Dyrlund Pedersen B, Møller AM. Pulse Oximetry for perioperative monitoring Cochrane Database Syst. Rev 2003 issue 3.

Procurement Policies and standards: http://www.ogc.gov.uk/procurement.

Scales DC, Laupacis A. Health technology assessment in critical care Intensive Care Med. 2007;33:2183–2191.

David Crippen

Controversies in intensive care sedation: Continuous infusions in awake patients and end-of-life sedation

Introduction:
Why is sedation important in the ICU?

The physiologic response to pain, anxiety and discomfort includes an increase in sympathetic activity and musculoskeletal hyperactivity, which can increase oxygen consumption and myocardial oxygen demand in, compromised patients (1). Normally, autonomic hyper-arousal and hypervigilence facilitate appropriate rapid behavioral reaction to threat. Stress-induced levels of cortisol may promote metabolic activation necessary for sustained physical demands necessary to avoid further injury (2). Elevated catecholamine levels increase heart rate and myocardial contractility to bolster cardiac output as potential compensation for injury during "fight of flight" (3). Painful stimulation of somatic afferent nerves is a potent activator of neuroendocrine changes (4). Immediate inhibition of insulin production occurs coincidentally with an increase in glucogon production, resulting in increased blood sugar (hyperglycaemia of stress), free fatty acids, triglycerides and cholesterol to fuel possible "fight or flight". Growth hormone and cortisol secretion increase, providing an antiinflammatory response for potential trauma (5). Aldosterone production acts to conserve salt and water, bolstering intravascular volume in case of potential blood loss (6).

The acute behavioral responses brought about by the activation of these humoral responses by psychological and physical trauma represent evolutionary adaptive responses critical for survival in an uncertain and potentially dangerous environment. These compensatory responses were presumably created at a time in the universe when there were no high technology surrogates for naturally induced environmental stress. Patients in the hybrid operating room and ICU environment undergo stress but no natural environmental threat. Therefore these maladaptations may translate into deleterious haemodynamic and metabolic function. Agitated patients tend to increase peripheral musculoskeletal metabolism, increasing lactate and carbon dioxide production. Both lactate and increased CO_2 are evolutionary signals that danger is approaching, prompting a responsive response to potential jeopardy. Hypercapnea stimulates the sympathetic centers, resulting in tachycardia and mild hypertension (7), and can precipitate panic attacks. During hyperventilation, PCO_2 declines causing cerebral vessels to constrict reflex, further limiting blood flow and oxygen transport to the brain, which can result in cerebral confusion and increased agitation (8). Musculoskeletal hyperactivity also increases oxygen consumption, initiating a reflex in cardiac output. For elderly patients with fixed myocardial blood flow due to coronary artery disease, this increase in myocardial work may result in angina, heart failure or myocardial infarction. Increased catecholamine activity exacerbates this effect.

The solution to ameliorating this therapeutic dilemma lies in selecting effective pharmacologic regimens, administrating optimal doses of medication, and utilising the most effective routes of administration for individualised dilemmas rather than a "shotgun" approach (9). Benzodiazepines are the most commonly used sedatives in critical care. This class of drugs attenuate stress-induced increases in norepinephrine release in the hippocampus, cortex amygdaloid and locus coeruleus region, effectively reducing conditioned fear and generalised anxiety. Variable magnitudes of anterograde amnesia occur as well.

Administering sedative and analgesic medication by the traditional enteral or bolus method can be a problem for this set of patients because the effect cannot be titrated in real time (10). Boluses of medication enter the blood stream, accumulate serum concentration quickly, and then decay with variable and sometimes unpredictable consequences. A good analogy is a home furnace thermostat. The house heats up quickly, and then cools through a "comfort zone" until it gets cold again. The point just before the thermostat turns on again to repeat the next cycle is problematic for patients with unstable or rapidly fluctuating haemodynamics and ventilation. This is when "breakthrough" occurs and the patient is unprotected from the effects of pain and agitation that may precipitate complications.

Safety considerations with continuous infusions of short-acting sedatives

The administration of short-acting sedative agents via continuous infusion minimises fluctuations in drug concentration and permits more consistent and titratable control of anxiety and agitation (11). In the 80s and 90s midazolam was a popular sedative used in continuous infusion but fell out of favor as it was found to increase its length of action with time. Lorazepam is a longer-acting benzodiazepine that also increases its action in time when used in continuous infusion and is rarely used in that mode. The advent of propofol revolutionised the administration of continuous, titrated sedation. Technically, propofol is a sedative-anaesthetic agent with a rapid onset of action

and short duration with a variable amnestic effect (12). Like midazolam, propofol produces a progressive, dose-dependent continuum of anxiolysis, hypnosis, sedation and finally anaesthesia, but unlike midazolam and especially lorazepam, the effects can be titrated and maintained by a rapidly adjustable infusion (13). A major challenge for clinicians is providing adequate sedation, analgesia in the postoperative period without precipitating haemodynamic or ventilatory instability or prolonging recovery time (14).

All of the benzodiazepines reduce ventilatory responses to hypoxia when administered rapidly or in large doses. Benzodiazepine toxicity usually results in an amplification of their therapeutic effects, but rarely ventilatory or cardiac arrest unless large quantities of other cardioactive drugs have been given concurrently (15). Propofol and midazolam have similar side effects and complications. When given concurrently, short-acting sedatives such as propofol and midazolam potentiate the analgesic effect of opiates and increase the incidence of sudden, unexpected hypotension and respiratory depression (16, 17). Propofol has been reported to act like a calcium channel antagonist, producing vasodilitation and hypotension (18) and exhibit primary myocardial depression, exacerbating heart failure in patients with compromised cardiac function (19). It is of the utmost importance that respiratory and haemodynamic function is monitored during infusion of any potent sedative, and that the proper technology is readily available to treat sudden, unexpected decompensations (20).

Much of the research involving the safety of these drugs was done as their use evolved in the 80s and 90s. Ronan and colleagues compared the safety and efficacy of intravenous infusion of propofol versus midazolam when used for 12 to 24 hours in surgical ICU patients. There were no significant differences in pulse oximetry, arterial blood gas, or respiratory parameters during sedation with propofol and midazolam. The drugs produced similar sedation and tolerance to the ICU environment, except that the quality of sedation was better with propofol and the propofol group woke up faster than the midazolam group. The authors concluded that both propofol and midazolam met criteria for the ideal ICU sedative (21).

Addition of analgesia to sedation: The role of fentanyl

There is no reason why combinations of agents cannot promote enhanced benefit. Fentanyl, a synthetic opioid with morphine-like activity has a rapid analgesic and often underappreciated sedative action, (one–two minutes) and short duration (30–40 minutes). Fentanyl can be included as a continuous infusion coincident with midazolam or propofol, adding analgesia and increasing sedative effects. Fentanyl is the ideal agent, promoting less histamine release and significantly less effect on cardiac dynamics than morphine. Fentanyl adds an accurately titratable analgesic and sympatholytic effect to the anxiolytic effects of benzodiazepines and propofol, and is most effectively used in the continuous infusion mode due to its brief span of action.

Like midazolam however, tachyphylaxis occurs quickly and the titrated effect rarely lasts longer than 24 hours in actual practice. The administration of fentanyl plus propofol has the potential to produce unexpected hypotension and respiratory depression (22). This combination should only be used in monitored settings. Occasionally the rapid administration of high doses of fentanyl has resulted in muscular and glotic rigidity during the induction of anaesthesia. This complication is reversible with naloxone or succinyl choline (23).

Reversal of benzodiazepine sedation in real time

The whole point of ICU care is titratability. By their nature, patients in highly monitored environments have unpredictable haemodynamics and ventilation. Their reaction to traditional medications is unpredictable. Since ICU patients are made uncomfortable by the nature of the ICU care plan, it is necessary to offer them some relief from the discomfort and anxiety of ICU care (24). The "usual" dose for a very stable patient may have very unpredictable effects, necessitating the ability to dramatically diminish the effect in real time. This is extremely difficult with long-acting sedatives such as midazolam and especially lorazepam after a day or so of continuous infusion (25).

Benzodiazepine sedation is still used frequently in ICUs. As our ability to titrate sedative effects in real time improves, we must also consider our potential to titrate reversal of their sedation effects. The use of narcotic antagonists such as naloxone has been extensively described in the literature but this agent has no effect on non-narcotic sedatives (26). Flumazenil is an imidazobenzodiazepine that antagonises the effects of benzodiazepine agonists by competitive interaction at the cerebral benzodiazepine receptor site (27, 28). It does not reliably antagonise the effects of other drugs that do not affect benzodiazepine receptors, such as narcotics, barbiturates, cyclic antidepressants, and ethanol.

Flumazenil is a useful consideration for the reversal of benzodiazepine-induced conscious sedation or benzodiazepine overdose. The recommended initial dose of flumazenil for the rapid reversal of benzodiazepine sedative effects is 0.1–0.3 mg administered over 15 seconds. If the desired level of consciousness is not obtained after waiting an additional 45 seconds, a further dose of 0.2 mg can be injected and repeated, if necessary, at 60-second intervals to a maximum total dose of 1 mg (29).

Yoshino et al. investigated the effect of continuous infusion of flumazenil on patients who had general anaesthesia using midazolam as an induction agent and had prolonged recovery after the procedure (30). Fourteen of 54 patients were judged as prolonged recovery and were given 0.25 mg of flumazenil dose. Then, they were randomly divided into the following two groups. In the first group, another 0.25 mg of flumazenil was given 2 hours after the first dose of flumazenil. In the second group, 0.25 mg of flumazenil in 250 ml of lactated Ringer's solution was given continuously for 2 hours after the first flumazenil. All the patients were fully awake after the first flumazenil, but one case of re-sedation occurred in the first group and in none of the patients in the second group. They concluded that continuous infusion of 0.25 mg of flumazenil for 2 hours was effective and effectively avoided the complication of postoperative midazolam re-sedation.

Pregler et al. evaluated the efficacy of intravenous flumazenil in reversing the central effects of midazolam after a general anaesthetic using midazolam for maintenance in 30 ASA I-III inpatients (31). All were interviewed preoperatively and baseline performance on a battery of psychomotor tests was obtained. Parameters measured included an assessment of sleep status, vital signs, responsiveness to verbal stimuli, quality of speech, facial expression, eye coordination, recognition of a picture card, finger-finger-to-nose (FFN) co-ordination and overall discharge readiness. General anaesthesia was induced with midazolam. Midazolam and fentanyl were the primary maintenance agents combined with N_2O and O_2 (70:30) and a limited concentration of isoflurane. In the recovery room the test drug was administered in a double-blinded, randomised manner. Twenty patients received flumazenil, the rest received placebo. Testing was done at times 0, 5, 15, 30, 60, 120, and 180 min in the PACU. Memory testing consisted of recall of study pictures at 180 min and recognition on the first postoperative day. The flumazenil group had a higher mean composite score and better FNN scores at 5, 15, and 30 min (p < 0.01) and identified pictures better at 5 and 15 min (p < 0.004 and 0.04). There were no untoward complications attributable to flumazenil.

The use of flumazenil in the recovery room and ICU carries some risks. Because flumazenil is a short-acting drug, re-sedation frequently occurs following bolus administration, requiring continuous infusion of the drug to maintain awareness. Experiences with flumazenil in the reversal of benzodiazepine-induced sedation in the ICU have been few but promising. Fisher et al. studied mechanically ventilated patients who had been sedated with midazolam and alfentanil for an average of 48 hours (range 6–240 hours) (32). Administration of 0.2–1.0 mg flumazenil IV (mean 0.4 mg) resulted in awakening in 20 of 20 patients. Side effects attributable to flumazenil were minimal, although five patients required immediate extubation due to post-treatment intolerance of their endotracheal tubes secondary to cough. Bodenham et al. published a case report of a mechanically ventilated patient who had received 800 mg midazolam IV over 5 days for sedation and awoke following 0.5 mg flumazenil IV (33). The patient required an infusion of 0.5 mg/h flumazenil for 8 days to prevent re-sedation. None of these patients experienced a serious adverse event.

Certain high-risk populations may experience seizures upon reversal of the central nervous system effects of benzodiazepines especially if the reversal is rapid (34). Seizure activity temporally related to the administration of flumazenil occurred most commonly in patients with seizure disorders who were receiving benzodiazepines as anticonvulsants and in patients presenting to the emergency department with toxic levels of serum cyclic antidepressants (35). Patients with a history of seizures, head trauma, subarachnoid bleeding are particularly at risk. Otherwise, seizures are rare when flumazenil is used to reverse benzodiazepine toxicity in otherwise non-susceptible patients. Acute withdrawal syndrome may occur in patients who have been taking benzodiazepines on a chronic basis, although this complication may be attenuated by the use of closely titrated continuous infusions rather than large boluses (36, 37).

Sedation of awake, non-intubated patients with propofol

By its nature, propofol is extremely potent and short-acting, rendering it ideal for accurate titration of sedative effects for unstable ICU patients (38). Because of its potency and unpredictable anaesthetic effect, a litany of literature citations proclaim its dangers and the logic that propofol should be reserved for intubated patients (39). This restriction has been traditionally enforced by institutional Departments of Anaesthesiology. However, there is accumulating evidence that this restriction is misplaced. Low grade infusions of propofol do not necessarily run a significant risk of unexpected unconsciousness any more than benzodiazepines (40, 41, 42, 43). The issue of titratability trumps the issue of potency when administered in the highly titrated ICU environment by knowledgeable and experienced personnel. If an inadvertent untoward effect appears, the infusion is simply decreased, generating a very rapid effect. In low doses, propofol is an anxiolytic (44). Low doses of propofol act like ethanol, rendering a sense of well-being and comfort without only marginal sedation.

Paradoxically, continuous infusions of midazolam or lorazepam, condoned by the anaesthesiologist lobby, have the potential for much more danger because of their lack of titratability. Midazolam and lorazepam significantly blunt mental status. Midazolam is a potent CNS depressant that gets longer acting the longer it is infused. In 24 hours it is a long-acting drug (45). The only way to titrate it is to bolus against an infusion, and when it is turned off the sedative effect does not rapidly diminish. Fentanyl is probably the next best titratable sedative/analgesic, but only titratable for short periods and with quick tachyphylaxis (46). Judicious titration of fentanyl reversibly ameliorates a pain reflex beneficial to accurately monitor. All these drugs blunt response to the environment, especially in older people, but short-term fentanyl and propofol alone offers quick resolution of these effects when needed. With low doses of continuous propofol infusion, we can make patients comfortable and still maintain a great deal of assessment accuracy. This is very valuable in the ICU, especially the Neuro ICU (47).

By denying judicious propofol use for non-intubated patients in the ICU, the anaesthesiologist lobby has invoked the Principle of Unintended Consequences. By a blunt, one-size-fits-all response to the use of propofol in non-intubated patients, they have generated the exact opposite of their original goal. Instead of a titratable anxiolytic, the effects of which offer transparent neurologic assessment, the intensivist is reduced to a sedative that obtunds in a blanket suppressive effect, yielding an unreliable neurologic exam. So the intensivist must fall back on less accurate means of assessing mental status, fraught with more complications, more CAT scans, more lab and X-ray tests. Neurosurgeons may want to use propofol for their serial neurologic exams but cannot, so patients sometimes get intubated just to get the ability to do accurate hourly neuro checks. The complications of intubation increase, including a predisposition to Ventilator Associated Pneumonia and discomfort (paradoxically increasing the need for more sedation). Neurosurgeons may also refuse to accept suppressive benzodiazepines in their non-intubated patients, and so go bare, allowing the patient to be miserable as the lesser of two evils in order to get accurate serial exams.

The small potential for unstable airways logically seems minimised, but the price for it is a potential increase in non-airway problems. This is unacceptable and preventable. The ICU is a highly monitored area where titrated care occurs. We understand the potential for diminished gag reflex in patients on propofol and how to diminish that potential complication by keeping heads of bed up and close observation (48). We understand how to use titratable drugs and the safety record for propofol in specialised units with adequate nursing

and physicians coverage seems reasonable. We need the option to take care of patients in a titratable manner, or we are no longer an ICU.

Special problems in the sedation of terminally ill patients

As critical care physicians become more aggressive in instituting life support for organ system failure, the possibility of patients not responding increases, and the potential for awake patients preferring death to life support dependency increases with it. For most acute, unstable illnesses, time is needed to see if aggressive treatment will improve the patient's condition. Accordingly, it seems reasonable to give even questionable patients the benefit of any doubt to see if the disease will respond to early aggressive treatment. If it can be seen that organ system failure is not reversible after a "reasonable" period of time, the rationale behind life supporting systems becomes moot, and serves no further useful function (49). It is then that prudent critical care physicians must have the facility to remove life support prolonging only inevitable death (50). Increasingly, some of these patients are aware of their environment.

Modern ICU experience suggests that avoiding institution of a treatment unlikely to achieve a desired clinical effect is easier to assuage than withdrawing it once instituted (51). The expectation of withholding is death from an anticipated dying process. The decision to withdraw might be construed by some, however erroneously, as a "death sentence" by the family. Therefore, in withdrawal of support, two issues require thoughtful discussion with surrogates: The inevitability of eventual death even on life support, and a guarantee of a painless dying process when support is withdrawn.

The technique of weaning artificial ventilation support depends greatly on whether the patient is awake or obtunded. For terminally obtunded patients, support is simply withdrawn, and any apparent evidence of discomfort during the dying process palliated on an as-needed basis. However, for the awake, dying patient, the process is more complex. Patients who opt for death rather than open-ended encumbrance of life support systems such as mechanical ventilators may be alert enough to feel discomfort on discontinuation of these devices. Judiciously administered palliation may hasten the progression but must not be sufficient, in itself, to actually "cause" death. This is a very fine line to tread (52, 53).

For the awake patient, death usually occurs as a direct or indirect result of respiratory failure (54). The mode of discomfort in respiratory failure is dyspnea- the subjective, unpleasant sensation of breathlessness) (55). Dyspnea is qualitatively different from simple tachypnea, which may be present without discomfort (56). There are two fundamental disturbances involved in terminal weaning that can produce the subjective sensation of dyspnea; inability to meet tissue oxygen demands and increased musculoskeletal work required to ventilate. Acute respiratory failure and resultant hypercarbia usually precipitates catecholamine release, systolic hypertension, tachypnea, tachycardia and agitation (57, 58). Hypoxia is not as potent a stimulus for dyspnea as it is an inducer of hyperventilation, which may not be necessarily uncomfortable for the patient and its onset is much slower than increases in PCO_2. This phenomenon was observed in high altitude aviators before the need to augment oxygen was discovered (59, 60).

Extubating the awake dying patient can result in gagging, agitation and panic as the airway collapses as a result of progressive respiratory failure. The most rapid descent into unconsciousness with the least agitation occurs when hypoxia is allowed to progress in the face of normocarbia, allowing the patient to become hypoxic with assisted ventilations to maintain PCO_2 at normal or below-normal levels. Decreasing the FiO_2 promotes hypoxemia and tissue hypoxia but a minimum of agitation as a result of hypercarbia-mediated catecholamine stimulation. Once the patient becomes somnolent from tissue hypoxia, ventilation support can be discontinued, allowing hypoventilation and CO_2 narcosis, further blunting discomfort during the dying process.

Accordingly, during life support withdrawal from the awake, dying patient, the continuance of mechanical ventilation has a strong potential to be palliative. Proprioception from lung and chest wall receptors provides a sense of ventilatory adequacy (61). The work of breathing increases exponentially as tidal volume increases but only linearly as ventilatory frequency increases. Maintenance of effective tidal volumes with mechanical ventilation may lessen the sensation of dyspnea resulting from hypoxia as long as tidal volumes are adequate, but not interfere with an obligatory death spiral from other organ failure.

It is difficult to make weaning from mechanical ventilation totally discomfort-free in the alert dying patient. It is absolutely mandatory that sedation and hypnosis be tailored to ameliorate the helpless feeling of dyspnea in the awake state. Some medications aimed at blunting the sensation of dyspnea work better than others. Benzodiazepines generally do not suppress the unpleasant sensation of breathlessness. In several prospective reports, no significant reduction of breathlessness was found (62, 63) However, In normo or hypocapnic patients with severe COPD, a single dose of 1 mg/kg dihydrocodeine reduced breathlessness by 20 % and improved exercise tolerance by 18 %. Postulated mechanisms of action include: altered central perception of breathlessness, reduction of ventilatory drive, and reduction in oxygen consumption (64, 65). Therefore, narcotic sedatives such as morphine or fentanyl in continuous infusion are very effective in relieving discomfort during a dying process.

Typically one of the most vivid concerns of families is that death, once accepted as inevitable, will progress painlessly. Few patients or families are willing to continue the discomfort of life support systems after a reasonable trial has demonstrated their benefit has come to the point of diminishing returns. When ordinary care is anticipated and supported as extraordinary care is removed, the family can remain at the bedside without fear that the patient will look uncomfortable during the dying process. The family will be able to spend the last moments in a controlled manner, with an understanding of the dying process, thoughtfully titrated.

The author

David Crippen, MD, FCCM
   Associate Professor
   Department of Critical Care Medicine
   University of Pittsburgh Medical Center
   644a Scaife Hall
   3550 Terrace Ave
   PA 15261 Pittsburgh, UK
   e-mail: crippen+@pitt.edu

References

1. Mangano DT, Siliciano D, Hollenberg M et al. Postoperative Myocardial Ischemia. Anesthesiology. 1992:76:342–353.
2. Dimopoulou I, Stamoulis K, Ilias I, Tzanela M, Lyberopoulos P, Orfanos S, Armaganidis A, Theodorakopoulou M, Tsagarakis S. A prospective study on adrenal cortex responses and outcome prediction in acute critical illness: results from a large cohort of 203 mixed ICU patients. Intensive Care Med. 2007 Dec;33(12):2116–21. Epub 2007 Aug 8.
3. Swanson LW. Anatomy of the soul as reflected in the cerebral hemispheres: neural circuits underlying voluntary control of basic motivated behaviors. J Comp Neurol. 2005 Dec 5;493(1):122–31.
4. Hedderich R, Ness TJ. Analgesia for trauma and burns. Crit Care Clin. 1999 Jan;15(1):167–84.
5. Kopelman TR, O'Neill PJ, Kanneganti SR, Davis KM, Drachman DA. The relationship of plasma glucose and glycosylated hemoglobin A1C levels among nondiabetic trauma patients. J Trauma. 2008 Jan;64(1):30–3; discussion 33–4.
6. DeMaria EJ, Lilly MP, Gann DS. Aldosterone secretion following non-hypotensive hemorrhage is potentiated by prior blood loss. J Trauma. 1989 Sep;29(9):1183–90; discussion 1191–2.
7. Donald DE, Shepherd JT. Cardiac receptors: normal and disturbed function. Am J Cardiol. 1979 Oct 22;44(5):873–8.
8. Peebles K, Celi L, McGrattan K, Murrell C, Thomas K, Ainslie PN. Human cerebrovascular and ventilatory CO_2 reactivity to end-tidal, arterial and internal jugular vein PCO_2. J Physiol. 2007 Oct 1;584(Pt 1):347–57. Epub. 2007 Aug 9.
9. Crippen D. Agitation in the ICU: part one Anatomical and physiologic basis for the agitated state. Crit Care. 1999; 3(3):R35-R46.
10. Crippen D. Comfortably numb in the intensive care unit. Crit Care Med. 2006 May;34(5):1558–9.
11. Yoon HD, Yoon ES, Dhong ES, Park SH, Han SK, Koo SH, Kim WK. Low-dose propofol infusion for sedation during local anesthesia. Plast Reconstr Surg. 2002 Mar;109(3):956–63.
12. Miner JR, Bachman A, Kosman L, Teng B, Heegaard W, Biros MH. Assessment of the onset and persistence of amnesia during procedural sedation with propofol. Acad Emerg Med. 2005 Jun;12(6):491–6.
13. Fong JJ, Kanji S, Dasta JF, Garpestad E, Devlin JW. Propofol associated with a shorter duration of mechanical ventilation than scheduled intermittent lorazepam: a database analysis using Project IMPACT. Ann Pharmacother. 2007 Dec;41(12):1986–91. Epub 2007 Oct 23.
14. Lazzaroni M, Bianchi Porro G. Preparation, premedication and surveillance. Endoscopy. 2003 Feb;35(2):103–11. Review.
15. Megarbane B, Gueye P, Baud F. Interactions between benzodiazepines and opioids. Ann Med Interne (Paris). 2003 Nov;154 Spec No 2:S64–72.
16. Blouin RT, Conard PL, Perreault S et al. The effect of flumazenil on midazolam-induced depression of the ventilatory response to hypoxia during isohypercarbia. Anesthesiology. 78(4):635–641. Apr 1993.
17. Wright SW, Chudnofsky CR, Dronen SC et al. Midazolam use in the emergency department. Am J Emerg Med. 1990;8:97–100.
18. Mayer N, Legat K, Weinstabl C et al. Effects of propofol on function of normal, collateral-dependent and ischemic myocardium. Anesth Analg. 1993;76:33–9.
19. Chang KSK, Davis RF. Propofol produces endothelium-independent vasodilation and may act as a Calcium-2 channel blocker. Anesth Analg. 1993;76:24–32.
20. Crippen D. Role of bedside electroencephalography in the adult intensive care unit during therapeutic neuromuscular blockade. Crit Care. 1997;1(1):15–24.
21. Ronan KP, Gallagher TJ, George B et al. Comparison of propofol and midazolam for sedation in intensive care unit patients. Crit Care Med. 1995, 23:286–293.
22. Richman PS, Baram D, Varela M, Glass PS. Sedation during mechanical ventilation: a trial of benzodiazepine and opiate in combination. Crit Care Med. 2006 May; 34(5):1395–401.
23. Svamman FL: Fentanyl -O_2-NO_2 rigidity and pulmonary compliance. Anesth Analg. 1983; 62: 332–334.
24. Crippen DW. Pharmacologic treatment of brain failure and delirium. Crit Care Clin. 1994 Oct;10(4):733–66. Review.
25. Simpson PJ, Eltringham RJ. Lorazepam in intensive care. Clin Ther. 1981;4(3):150–63.
26. Kaplan JL, Marx JA. Effectiveness and safety of intravenous nalmefene for emergency department patients with suspected narcotic overdose: a pilot study. Ann Emerg Med. 1993 Feb;22(2):187–90.
27. Olshaker JS, Flanigan J. Flumazenil reversal of lorazepam-induced acute delirium. J Emerg Med. 2003 Feb;24(2):181–3.
28. Mathieu-Nolf M, Babé MA, Coquelle-Couplet V, Billaut C, Nisse P, Mathieu D. Flumazenil use in an emergency department: a survey. J Toxicol Clin Toxicol. 2001;39(1):15–20.
29. Weinbroum AA, Flaishon R, Sorkine P, Szold O, Rudick V. A risk-benefit assessment of flumazenil in the management of benzodiazepine overdose Drug Saf. 1997 Sep;17(3):181–96.
30. Yoshino A, Nishimura K, Tatsumi K et al. Effect of continuous infusion of flumazenil on unexpected postoperative resedation by midazolam. Masui – Japanese Journal of Anesthesiology. 43(11):1668–74, 1994 Nov.13.
31. Pregler JL, Mok MS, Steen SN. Effectiveness of flumazenil on return of cognitive functions after a general anesthetic. Acta Anaesthesiologica Sinica. 32(3):153–8, 1994 Sep.
32. Fisher GC. Cardiovascular responses to flumazenil induced arousal after arterial surgery. Anaesthesia 44, 104–6, (1989).

33. Bodenham A, Dixon JS, Park GR. Reversal of sedation by prolonged infusion of flumazenil (Anexate, Ro 15–1788), Anaesthesia 43, 376–8, (1988).

34. Spivey WH. Flumazenil and seizures: analysis of 43 cases. [Review] Clinical Therapeutics. 14(2):292–305, 1992 Mar-Apr.

35. Haverkos GP, DiSalvo RP, Imhoff TE. Fatal seizures after flumazenil administration in a patient with mixed overdose. Annals of Pharmacotherapy. 28(12):1347–9, 1994 Dec.

36. Buck KJ, Heim H, Harris RA, Reversal of alcohol dependence and tolerance by a single administration of flumazenil, J Pharmacol Exp Ther. 1991;257:984–9.

37. Hojer J, Baehrendtz S, Magnusson, A et al. A Placebo controlled trial of flumazenil given by continuous infusion in severe benzodiazepine overdosage. Acta Anaesthesiol Csand. 1991 Oct. 35(7): 584–90.

38. Crippen D. Role of bedside electroencephalography in the adult intensive care unit during therapeutic neuromuscular blockade. Crit Care. 1997;1(1):15–24.

39. Angelini G, Ketzler JT, Coursin DB. Use of propofol and other nonbenzodiazepine sedatives in the intensive care unit. Crit Care Clin. 2001 Oct;17(4):863–80.

40. Harrington L. Nurse-administered propofol sedation: a review of current evidence. Gastroenterol Nurs. 2006 Sep-Oct;29(5):371–83; quiz 384–5.

41. Dunn T, Mossop D, Newton A, Gammon A. Propofol for procedural sedation in the emergency department. Emerg Med J. 2007 Jul;24(7):459–61.

42. Bell A, Treston G, McNabb C, Monypenny K, Cardwell R. Profiling adverse respiratory events and vomiting when using propofol for emergency department procedural sedation. Emerg Med Australas. 2007 Oct;19(5):405–10.

43. Girdler NM, Rynn D, Lyne JP, Wilson KE. A prospective randomised controlled study of patient-controlled propofol sedation in phobic dental patients. Anaesthesia. 2000 Apr;55(4):327–33.

44. Pain L, Oberling P, Launoy A, Di Scala G. Effect of nonsedative doses of propofol on an innate anxiogenic situation in rats. Anesthesiology. 1999 Jan;90(1):191–6.

45. Spina SP, Ensom MH. Clinical pharmacokinetic monitoring of midazolam in critically ill patients. Pharmacotherapy. 2007 Mar;27(3):389–98. Review.

46. Chudnofsky CR, Wright SW, Dronen SC, Borron SW, Wright MB. The safety of fentanyl use in the emergency department. Ann Emerg Med. 1989 Jun;18(6):635–9.

47. Mirski MA, Muffelman B, Ulatowski JA, Hanley DF. Sedation for the critically ill neurologic patient. Crit Care Med. 1995 Dec;23(12):2038–53. Review.

48. Scanlon P, Carey M, Power M, Kirby F. Patient response to laryngeal mask insertion after induction of anaesthesia with propofol or thiopentone. Can J Anaesth. 1993 Sep; 40(9):816–8.

49. Afessa B, Keegan MT, Mohammad Z, Finkielman JD, Peters SG. Identifying potentially ineffective care in the sickest critically ill patients on the third ICU day. Chest. 2004 Dec;126(6):1905–9.

50. Cassell J, Buchman TG, Streat S, Stewart RM, Buchman TG. Surgeons, intensivists, and the covenant of care: administrative models and values affecting care at the end of life. Crit Care Med. 2003 Apr;31(4):1263–70.

51. Crippen D, Levy M, Whetstine L, Kuce J et al. Debate: What constitutes 'terminality'and how does itrelate to a Living Will? CritCare. 2000 4:333–338.

52. Crippen D. Terminally weaning awake patients from life sustaining mechanical ventilation: the critical care physician's role in comfortmeasures during the dying process. Clin Intensive Care. 1992;3:206–12.

53. Wein S. Sedation in the imminently dying patient. Oncology. 2000 Apr;14(4):585–92. Review.

54. Twycross RG. Care of the dying. Symptom control. Br J Hosp Med. 1986 Oct;36(4):244–6, 248–9.

55. Zeppetella G. The palliation of dyspnea in terminal disease. Am J Hosp Palliat Care. 1998 Nov–Dec; 15(6): 322–30. Review.

56. Ripamonti C, Bruera E. Dyspnea: pathophysiology and assessment. J Pain Symptom Manage. 1997 Apr;13(4): 220–32. Review.

57. Kaye J, Buchanan F, Kendrick A, Johnson P, Lowry C, Bailey J, Nutt D, Lightman S. Acute carbon dioxide exposure in healthy adults: evaluation of a novel means of investigating the stress response. J Neuroendocrinol. 2004 Mar;16(3):256–64.

58. Modarreszadeh M, Bruce EN. Ventilatory variability induced by spontaneous variations of $PaCO_2$ in humans. J Appl Physiol. 1994 Jun;76(6):2765–75.

59. Cohen PJ, Alexander SC, Smith TC, Reivich M, Wollman H. Effects of hypoxia and normocarbia on cerebral blood flow and metabolism in conscious man. J Appl Physiol. 1967 Aug;23(2):183–9.

60. United States Naval Flight Surgeon's Manual: The Society of U.S. Naval Flight Surgeons. Third Edition 1991: Chapter 1: Physiology of Flight

61. Putensen C, Hering R, Muders T, Wrigge H. Assisted breathing is better in acute respiratory failure. Curr Opin Crit Care. 2005 Feb;11(1):63–8.

62. Woodcock AA, Gross EA, Geddes DM. Drug treatment of breathlessness: contrasting effects of diazepam and promethazine in pink puffers. British Med Journ. 1981; 283:343–346.

63. Shivaram U, Cash M, Finch PJP. Effects of alprazolam on gas exchange, breathing pattern and lung function of COPD patients with anxiety. Respir Care. 1989;34:196–200.

64. Woodcock AA, Gross EA, Gellert A et al. Effects of dihydrocodeine, alcohol, and caffeine on breathlessness and exercise tolerance in patients with chronic obstructive lung disease and normal blood gases. N Engl J Med. 1982;305:1611–1216.

65. Robin ED, Burke CM. Single-patient randomized trial: opiates for intractable dyspnea. Chest 1986;90:888–892.

Jean-Charles Preiser and Philippe Devos

Tight glucose control: Should we target normoglycemia or an intermediate level?

Introduction

The metabolic response to acute stress, observed in critically ill patients, has been entirely revisited since the publication in 2001 of the landmark Leuven study (1), that demonstrated an improved survival following the restoration of normoglycemia (blood glucose value 80–110 mg/dl) by intensive insulin therapy. This "tight glucose control by intensive insulin therapy" (TGCIIT) has received major attention since the publication of the paper in the New England Journal of Medicine, and sometimes led to passionate exchange of views and controversies (2).

Both aspects of TGCIIT, the correction of hyperglycaemia and the large doses of insulin, likely influence synergistically the stress response. Functionally, the lowering of the blood glucose concentration towards "normoglycaemia" will likely prevent dysfunctions of the immune, cardiovascular and neurological systems (3), in agreement with the concept of hyperglycaemia as a mediator rather than a marker of critical illness. However, as recently reviewed (4), the ultimate proof that hyperglycaemia is an independent risk factor for ICU mortality in critically ill patients is lacking. On the other hand the large doses of insulin used in the Leuven study (up to 70 units/day) likely triggered metabolic (related and unrelated to carbohydrates) and non-metabolic effects (2, 3).

Indeed, anabolic, anti-inflammatory and anti-apoptotic properties of insulin have been shown in experimental conditions, as well as improvements in dysfunctions of the endothelial function and of the coagulation. A post-hoc appraisal of the data of the Leuven study (5) suggests that the correction of hyperglycaemia is the predominant factor over insulin therapy, but clearly both factors play a role.

Do the findings of the Leuven study support an universal recommendation of using TGCIIT as a standard therapeutic modality ? Unfortunately, the answer is not clear-cut yet, as the external validity of this study was not confirmed by other prospective trials until now (see tab. 1). The controversy is vivid and yet unresolved. The pros and cons of TGCIIT will be discussed in further details in the next paragraphs.

Controversial position 1: Normoglycaemia should be targeted

This position was commonly heard after the publication of the Leuven I trial in 2001 (1). In this landmark prospective, randomised, controlled study on a large group of patients, major clinical benefits were reported in patients randomised to TGCIIT, when compared to patients randomised to conventional treatment. Of note, the patients in the conventional insulin therapy group received insulin only if glucose concentrations were very high (higher than 215 mg/dl) with the aim of restoring and maintaining blood glucose concentrations between 180 and 200 mg/dl. In the intensive treatment group, insulin was administered to maintain blood glucose levels between 80 and 110 mg/dl. This "genuine TGCIIT" was associated with a decrease of the mortality rate in intensive care unit from 8.0 % to 4.6 % (43 % relative risk reduction, RRR). An even larger benefit was found in long-stayers (mortality reduction from 20.2 % to 10.6 %). In addition, TGCIIT prevented several critical illness-associated complications, including polyneuropathy (relative risk reduction, RRR 44 %), bacteraemia (RRR 46 %), acute renal failure requiring extra-renal epuration (RRR 41 %), need for packed red cell transfusion (RRR 50 %). These remarkable findings were observed in a surgical population, mostly patients admitted to the intensive care unit after cardiac surgery. Of note, in the subset of patients with isolated brain injury intensive insulin therapy protected the central and peripheral nervous system from secondary insults and improved long-term rehabilitation (6).

In a subsequent study performed in a medical intensive care unit, the same investigators also reported a benefit in patients randomised to TGCIIT, as compared to the same conventional treatment. Although this benefit was only found in the patients who stayed in the intensive care unit at least for three days, some, but not all the benefits found in the secondary outcome variables studied in the first study (1) were confirmed (7) (see further discussion below).

The proponents of the generalised use of TGCIIT like to highlight that several recent studies demonstrated that hyperglycaemia is an important risk factor in terms of mortality and morbidity of critically ill patients. For instance, a meta-analysis on myocardial infarction revealed an association between stress hyperglycaemia and increased risk of in-hospital mortality and congestive heart failure or cardiogenic shock (8). Similarly, hyperglycaemia predicted a higher risk of death after stroke and a poor functional recovery in those patients who survived (9). Likewise, hyperglycaemia was also found as a predictor of infectious morbidity in trauma patients (10). In a heterogeneous population of critically ill patients, a retrospective analysis showed that even a mild hyperglycaemia was associated with an increased hospital mortality (11).

Also several retrospective studies compared the outcome of patients before and after the implementation of tight glucose control. For instance, Krinsley et al. (12) reported a 29 % decrease in hospital mortality, and significant reductions in length of ICU stay, incidence of renal failure and need for packed red cell transfusion. Finney et al. (13) have correlated the outcome with the mean level of blood glucose achieved during the stay in the intensive care unit.

These consistent pieces of evidence support the general recommendation of TGCIIT for critically ill patients. The effects of TGCIIT was therefore tested on a larger side than in a single-centre.

Controversial position 2: An intermediate blood glucose level should be targeted

This position essentially emerged after the failure of large multi-centre prospective randomised controlled trials and of several single-centre studies to confirm the results of the Leuven study.

These multi-centre trials include the German VISEP trial (14), the Australian NICE-SUGAR trial (clinicaltrials.gov/ct/show/NCT00220987) and the European GLUCONTROL study (15).

The design and end points of the three prospective randomised controlled trials are detailed in the table 1. Importantly, the VISEP trial was designed to address simultaneously two questions in a group of septic patients (colloids versus cristalloids and TGCIIT), with a factorial design. This trial was stopped after the inclusion of 537 patients in 18 academic tertiary centres in Germany for safety reasons. Large increases in the rate of hypoglycaemia and severe adverse events were not balanced by any significant difference in the 28- nor the 90-day mortality. Similarly, the enrollment of patients in Glucontrol was stopped after the inclusion of 1,109 patients in 21 units for safety reasons and for a high rate of unintended protocol violations, that was not confirmed in the statistical analysis on the final set of 1,101 of the analysable patients (16).

Of note, the retrospective trials (12, 13, 17) consistently reported an association between an im-

Tab. 1 Methodological features of the prospective randomised controlled multi-centre trials on tight glucose control; IIT = intensive insulin therapy, CIT = conventional insulin therapy

	Design	Primary end-point	Number patients required	Target IIT (mg/dl)	Target CIT (mg/dl)
VISEP	2x2 randomisation for blood glucose target and type of fluids	28-day mortality	600	80–110	180–200
Glucontrol	Open label randomised controlled stratified	ICU mortality	factorial design	80–110	140–180
NICE-SUGAR	Open label randomised controlled stratified	90-day mortality	6,100	80–110	140–180

proved outcome an average blood glucose concentration below 140 mg/dl and not 110 mg/dl. Similarly, in diabetic patients after cardiac surgery, Ouattara et al. (18) recently reported that a poor intraoperative glycemic control (defined as a failure to achieve blood glucose levels below 140 mg/dl) was significantly more frequent in patients with severe postoperative morbidity. The opponents to the systematic use of TGCIIT are mainly concerned by the workload and the issue of hypoglycaemia. Implementing TGCIIT is a labour-intensive task, and the availability of sufficient human and technical resources is critical. Actually, the use of the term "normoglycaemia" itself might be misleading, when the range of "normal" blood glucose was defined in fasting healthy subjects and is mainly used to exclude the diagnosis of diabetes. In critically ill or in diabetic patients, such blood glucose range (80–110 mg/dl) may not be normal, nor desirable.

In a recent publication (19) a very typical stepwise approach required to implement a tight glucose control is described. Whichever the desired target blood glucose level the implementation of a systematic algorithm is necessary and should be adapted both by the nursing and the medical staff. Once developed, the protocol can be computerised and must be carefully explained, implying an educational aspect, particularly important in this area that involves every ICU healthcare professional (20). The algorithm will indicate the rate of insulin, but also the time for the next glucose check. The optimal implementation and adaptation of the algorithm cannot be achieved by using a BG target as stringent as "normoglycaemia". Therefore intermediate steps are mandatory.

The increase in the rate of hypoglycaemia is another major concern raised by the implementation of TGCIIT. Very consistent increases in the incidence of hypoglycaemia, by a 4- to 6-factor was reported in the Leuven trials, in VISEP and in Glucontrol. In the latter study, the duration of hypoglycaemia was also higher in the intensive insulin group and the mortality rate was increased in those patients who experienced hypoglycaemia, even when the severity scores at admission did not differ. The increased mortality in patients with hypoglycaemia during TGCIIT was also recently confirmed (21). The possibility that long-lasting hypoglycaemia may be deleterious or even life-threatening cannot be ruled out. Accordingly, any tight glucose control policy will aim to avoid and correct as soon as possible any episode of hypoglycaemia. Using intensive insulin therapy titrated to lower blood glucose to 80–110 mg/dl definitely requires a careful monitoring of the blood glucose, as the classical neurological symptoms can be offset by sedation or by the underlying impairment of the mental status. Now, other risk factors for hypoglycaemia than intensive insulin therapy, such as hepatic, adrenal or renal failure are well-known and documented. Recently, Vriesendorp et al. (22) identified female gender, the presence of pre-existing diabetes, sepsis, the use of continuous veno-venous hemofiltration (especially with bicarbonate-based substitution fluid) as well as a lowering of the infusion rate of nutrition without adjustment of the insulin infusion rate and the administration of insulin by itself as independent risk factors for hypoglycaemia. The physiological response to hypoglycaemia itself can be impaired, as reviewed recently by Cryer et al. (23). Indeed, even asymptomatic episodes of hypoglycaemia can blunt the physiological response of the sympatho-adrenal system, thereby leading to a vicious circle at risk of recurrent hypoglycaemia. Such endocrine dysregulation might increase the risk of harm of intensive insulin therapy. However, the relevance of these findings to ICU patients requires further investigation.

Regarding the consequences of non-life-threatening hypoglycaemia, long-term cognitive and other neurological impairments were sometimes reported (24). Some categories of patients with significant dysfunctions of neoglucogenic organs (liver and kidney), with adrenal failure leading to an impaired responsiveness of counter-regulatory hormones, or with a delayed elimination of insulin (in case of renal failure for instance) could experience longer episodes of hypoglycaemia. The effects of TGCIIT in these subgroups need to be carefully assessed.

Additional issues

Future issues to think about and areas of clinical research will probably include the issues of blood glucose variability, and the search for an accurate delineation of the categories of patients in whom TGCIIT is clearly beneficial.

The detrimental effects of high blood glucose variability was suggested by recent findings in critically ill patients (25). The current implication that could follow the discovery of the importance of keeping glucose as stable as possible favours the use of strict algorithms to maintain glucose within a narrow range. Although several different algorithms are available and validated, indices of glucose variability issue were usually not assessed and not used to compare different protocols.

Some categories of patients could be differentially affected by TGCIIT. In the first Leuven study (1), the absolute mortality and several other outcome variables were dramatically improved in each category of patients. Among these, the patients with myocardial ischaemia and after cardiac surgery may represent a subset of patients particularly susceptible to the deleterious effects of hyperglycaemia (see 26 for a detailed review). In the second Leuven study (7), the results were less clear-cut, as the improvement in vital out-come was only seen in the patients who stayed longer than 3 days, while the mortality tended to increase in the short-stayers randomised to the intensive insulin therapy group. Important outcome variables, ICU and 28-day mortality, requirement for dialysis, incidence of bacteraemia, requirement for prolonged antibiotic therapy, incidence of hyperbilirubinemia and "hyperinflammation" were not improved in the intensive insulin therapy group. These differences between the two Leuven studies could point out subgroups of patients that do no benefit from intensive insulin therapy. In contrast, the other large studies (12, 13, 17) performed in mixed populations concluded that the maintenance of blood glucose below a threshold of 140 mg/dl was consistently associated with an improved outcome, regardless of the category of patients.

Another category of patients that could not benefit from intensive insulin therapy is the subset of patients with pre-existing diabetes, as shown by the aggregation of the results of both Leuven studies. As already alluded, the maintenance of a blood glucose as stable as possible in diabetic patients seems to represent a critical factor (27, 28).

At the present stage, there is then no definite answer to the question of which subgroup is prone to benefit more from intensive insulin therapy than other subgroups. Definitely, interventional studies performed in specific subgroups, or at least subgroup analyses of the large multicentre trials are needed to define the categories of patients that will selectively benefit from intensive insulin therapy. Meanwhile, the use of an intermediate trigger for insulin therapy (140–150 mg/dl) for blood glucose is probably more cautious and is presently recommended (28, 29, 30).

Summary

Tight glucose control by intensive insulin therapy is undoubtedly a labor-intensive and not risk-free therapeutic modality. Although easily accessible and cheap, the implementation of TGCIIT requires a stepwise and multidisciplinary approach. The benefits of the restoration of normoglycaemia was found in one prospective study only, and not confirmed in others. Using a intermediate trigger (140–150 mg/dl) and targeting an intermediate range (80–150 mg/dl) appears to be a safer procedure.

Key points for clinical practice

- Check the equipment available for blood glucose determination and its accuracy.
- A minimal nurse-to-patient ratio of 1-to-2.
- Use existing algorithms for glucose control to develop your own protocol, as a team.
- Choose an easily achievable blood glucose trigger and target first an intermediate blood glucose concentration.
- Record your performances and improve your protocol before targeting a lower blood glucose concentration.

The authors

Jean-Charles Preiser, MD, PhD
Philippe Devos, MD
   Department of General Intensive Care |
   University Hospital of Liege – Sart-Tilman |
   Liege, Belgium

Address for correspondence
   Jean-Charles Preiser
   Department of General Intensive Care
   University Hospital Centre
   Domaine universitaire du Sart-Tilman
   4000 Liege, Belgium
   e-mail: Jean-Charles.Preiser@chu.ulg.ac.be

References

1. Van den Berghe G, Wouters P, Weekers F, Verwaest C, Bruyninckx F, Schetz M et al. Intensive insulin therapy in the critically ill patients. N Engl J Med. 2001;345:1359–67.
2. Devos P, Preiser JC. Current controversies around tight glucose control in critically ill patients. Curr Opin Clin Nutr Metab Care. 2007;10:206–9.
3. Preiser JC, Devos P. Clinical experience with tight glucose control by intensive insulin therapy. Crit Care Med. 2007;35:S503–7.
4. Corstjens AM, van der Horst IC, Zijlstra JG, Groeneveld AB, Zijlstra F, Tulleken JE et al. Hyperglycaemia in critically ill patients: marker or mediator of mortality? Crit Care. 2006;10:216.
5. Van den Berghe G, Wouters PJ, Bouillon R, Weekers F, Verwaest C, Schetz M et al. Outcome benefit of intensive insulin therapy in the critically ill: insulin dose versus glycemic control. Crit Care Med. 2003;31:359–66.
6. Van den Berghe G, Schoonheydt K, Becx P, Bruyninckx F, Wouters PJ. Insulin therapy protects the central and peripheral nervous system of intensive care patients. Neurology. 2005;64:1348–53.
7. Van den Berghe G, Wilmer A, Hermans G, Meersseman W, Wouters PJ, Milants I et al. Intensive insulin therapy in the medical ICU. N Engl J Med. 2006;354:449–61.
8. Capes SE, Hunt D, Malmberg K, Gerstein HC. Stress hyperglycaemia and increased risk of death after myocardial infarction in patients with and without diabetes: a systematic overview. Lancet. 2000;355:773–8.
9. Capes SE, Hunt D, Malmberg K, Pathak P, Gerstein HC. Stress hyperglycemia and prognosis of stroke in nondiabetic and diabetic patients: a systematic overview. Stroke. 2001;32:2426–32.
10. Laird AM, Miller PR, Kilgo RD, et al. Relationship of early hyperglycaemia to mortality in trauma patients. J Trauma. 2004;56:1058–62.
11. Krinsley JS. Association between hyperglycemia and increased hospital mortality in a heterogeneous population of critically ill patients. Mayo Clin Proc. 2003;72:1471–2.
12. Krinsley JS. Effect of an intensive glucose management protocol on the mortality of critically ill adult patients. Mayo Clin Proc. 2004;9:992–1000.
13. Finney SJ, Zekveld C, Elia A, Evans TW. Glucose control and mortality in critically ill patients. JAMA. 2003;290:2041–7.
14. Brunkhorst FM, Engel C, Bloos F, Meier-Hellmann A, Ragaller M, Weiler N et al. Intensive insulin therapy and pentasarchh resuscitation in severe sepsis. N Engl J Med. 2008;358:125–39.
15. Devos P, Preiser JC, Melot C, on behalf of the Glucontrol steering committee. Impact of tight glucose control by intensive insulin therapy on ICU mortality and the rate of hypoglycaemia: final results of the Glucontrol study. Intensive Care Med. 2007;33:S189.
16. Devos P, Ledoux D, Preiser JC, on behalf of the GLUCONTROL Steering Committee. Current practice of glycaemia control in European intensive care units (ICUs). Intensive Care Med. 2005;31:130.
17. Gabbanelli V, Pantanetti S, Donati A, Principi T, Pelaia P. Correlation between hyperglycemia and mortality in a medical and surgical intensive care unit. Minerva Anestesiol. 2005;71:717–25.
18. Ouattara A, Lecomte P, Le Manach Y, Landi M, Jacqueminet S, Platonov I et al. Poor intraoperative blood glucose control is associated with a worsened hospital outcome after cardiac surgery in diabetic patients. Anesthesiology. 2005;103:687–94.
19. Meynaar IA, Dawson L, Tangkau PL, Salm EF, Rijks L. Introduction and evaluation of a computerised insulin protocol. Intensive Care Med. 2007;33:591–6.
20. Holzinger U, Kitzberger R, Fuhrmann V, Schenk P, Kramer L, Funk G et al. ICU-staff education and implementation of an insulin therapy algorithm improve blood glucose control. Intensive Care Med. 2006;31:S202.

21. Krinsley JS, Grover A. Severe hypoglycemia in critically ill patients: risk factors and outcomes. Crit Care Med. 2007;35:2262-7.
22. Vriesendorp TM, DeVries HJ, van Santen S, Moeniralam HS, de Jonge E, Roos YB et al. Predisposing factors for hypoglycemia in the intensive care unit. Crit Care Med. 2006;34:96-101.
23. Cryer PE. Mechanisms of sympathoadrenal failure and hypoglycemia in diabetes. J Clin Invest. 2006;116: 1470-3.
24. Vriesendorp TM, Devries JH, van Santen S, Moeniralam HS, de Jonge E, Roos YB et al. Evaluation of short-term consequences of hypoglycemia in an intensive care unit. Crit Care Med. 2006;34:2714-18.
25. Egi M, Bellomo R, Stachowski E, French CJ, Hart G. Variability of blood glucose concentration and short-term mortality in critically ill patients. Anesthesiology. 2006; 105:244-52.
26. Preiser JC, Devos P, Van den Berghe G. Tight control of glycaemia in critically ill patients. Curr Opin Clin Nutr Metab Care. 2002;5:533-7.
27. Monnier L, Mas E, Ginet C, Michel F, Villon L, Cristol JP et al. Activation of oxidative stress by acute glucose fluctuations compared with sustained chronic hyperglycemia in patients with type 2 diabetes. JAMA. 2006;295:1681-7.
28. Devos P, Preiser JC. Tight blood glucose control: a recommendation applicable to any critically ill patient? Crit Care. 2004;8:427-9.
29. Dellinger RP, Levy MM, Carlet JM, Bion J, Parker MM, Jaeschke R et al. Surviving Sepsis Campaign: International guidelines for management of severe sepsis and septic shock: 2008. Intensive Care Med. 2008;34:17-60.
30. McMahon MM, Miles JM. Glycemic control and nutrition in the intensive care unit. Curr Opin Clin Nutr Metab Care. 2006;9:120-3.

Jan Wernerman

Goals for nutrition support in the ICU

Introduction

ICU nutrition is an important part of critical care and of intensive care medicine. As in all other areas of intensive care medicine, there are areas of controversy also concerning nutrition. Three different controversies will be discussed in this chapter:

1. the overall importance of nutrition,
2. the feasibility of combining enteral and parenteral nutrition, and
3. the use of tight glucose control.

Is nutrition important?

The overall importance of nutrition extends into a grey zone between medicine and philosophy. Basically this comes back to the issue of whether the physiological reactions to stress are useful or not. Within the Darwinistic tradition one looks for an evolutionary advantage in physiology. The question is which insults affecting physiology could have had a sufficient impact to be incorporated into the physiological reaction to stress. In the animal kingdom it is possible to see how individuals survive wounds and infections. If this survival is sufficient to have an evolutionary impact, this clearly brings us into the realm of philosophy. On the other hand, there are many examples of infections that may kill a whole tribe of animals if the sick animal is not separated from the herd, usually by action of predators. So, in summary, there are examples that the physiological adaptation to stress may be an advantage for the individual which should not be interfered with. On the other hand, the adaptation to stress may only be for mild types of stress and not for severe sepsis and multiple organ failure. Usually at the end of the day the position of the individual in this dilemma comes down to philosophy and perhaps even to religion.

Nevertheless, this basic attitude sometimes has a great impact upon our clinical practice. Is nutrition something important or not? Does nitrogen balance, energy deficit, tight glucose control etcetera have any impact whatsoever on outcome? To begin with, it is important to make a few distinctions. Is the individual patient malnourished or not? Will the individual patient be able to support himself within reasonable time or not? If a patient is not malnourished and it is most likely that he/she will be able to support him/herself within reasonable time, it is probably not a nutritional problem. On the other hand, if the patient is overtly malnourished from the start and with a high probability will not be able to support him/herself within a reasonable period of time, then it is definitely a nutritional problem. In the latter case there will probably be very few people argu-ing against it. Most intensive care patients will be somewhere in between these extremes. A practi-cal attitude has been to start up nutrition slowly and wait and see. After 5–7 days of ICU care the number of patients still in the unit is considera-bly reduced due to successful discharges. In ret-rospective, the option to wait and see has been proven to be practical and plausible. For a smaller number of patients a longer period of ICU care is needed, multiple organ failure ensues and nu-trition becomes more important. At this point in time, two difficulties have arisen – the patient now has an accumulated energy deficit and to start en-teral nutrition late is more difficult than to start it early. In many studies focusing on ICU nutrition, the study group is a mixture of short stayers and long stayers. As the short stayers are the major-ity in number, the long stayers will not be visible in a study mixing up the two categories. Further-more, ICU stay means different things in diffe-rent health care systems. If this discussion is lim-ited to patients on ventilator treatment who can-not be fed orally, the group of patients we are dis-cussing becomes more comparable over a broader range of different health care systems.

Part of this discussion stems from studies com-paring parenteral nutrition to standard of care (1). The latter is an acronym for some 500–800 kcal given intravenously as a dextrose solution. The rationale for giving a hypocaloric carbohydrate nutrition is vague. Usually it relates to a wish to provide the obligatory glucose consumption from exogenous sources, also bearing in mind that the stressed subjects usually do not adapt to starva-tion and the decrease in the basal need for glucose seen at starvation. A non-depleted patient can eas-ily tolerate total starvation for a number of days. However, there are individuals with very small gly-cogen reserves who will experience trouble. These individuals are not always easy to detect prospec-tively and therefore it is common to treat every-body with an inexpensive and seemingly harmless treatment. The concept of tight glucose control has, however, put this concept under debate.

On the whole, the attitude towards nutrition, regarding it as important or not, has had a consid-erable impact on the work of the ICU physician. Those who think it is important take an interest in nutrition are knowledgeable and they rarely underfeed patients. Another group of ICU physi-cians feel that nutrition in the ICU often creates more problems than it solves (2). The complica-tion rate attributable to intravenous and enteral nutrition is not negligible. The number of stud-ies proving a positive outcome effect attributable to nutrition is very small and some of them are of debatable quality. Unfortunately, this attitude often coincides with an embarrassingly limited knowledge in nutrition and a tendency to delegate this to other professionals than ICU physicians. Intensive care medicine today is multidisciplinary and to make use of specialised knowledge, wher-ever it is, is quite a task. However, to be unable to integrate it in the total care of the patient is a problem. Whatever external expertise is consult-ed, the consulting physician must be sufficiently knowledgeable to ask the right questions.

The bias of this author is, of course, that nu-trition is important. That avoidance of an energy deficit is important, and that avoidance of nutri-tion-related complications is important. However, it is also essential to continue this debate and to try to promote studies which focus upon the impor-tance of nutrition for long stayers in the ICU.

Is underfeeding harmful?

Recently a number of studies have been published which retrospectively define patients who are un-derfed as compared to an estimated or measured energy expenditure. The studies uniformly report an increase in morbidity and sometimes even mortality related to the accumulated energy deficit (3, 4). Within these studies the patients have been adjusted for the estimated risk of mortality and morbidity, but still the cumulated energy deficit is a predictor of morbidity and mortality. These are observational studies, and the observation is that the major part of the cumulated energy deficit is generated during the first week of ICU stay. Dur-ing this week it is usually difficult to foresee what the length of the ICU stay will turn out to be.

There is basically only one prospective study addressing this issue (5). Methodologically the study is extremely well-performed, but the re-sults are not conclusive. Although the included patients were clearly long stayers and they also exhibited high mortality overall, the temporal pat-tern of the feeding is not disclosed. The results show no difference in mortality, but a difference in length of hospital stay, which, although statistically significant, was of limited clinical importance. At the time of the publication of the study the concept of cumulative energy deficit was not yet introduced, and the results are therefore not presented to highlight that particular aspect. As it is the only prospective study, a recalculation from those data focusing on the energy deficit would be extremely interesting. Other studies in the literature reporting of a combination of enteral and parenteral nutrition usually give full parenteral nutrition on top of enteral nutrition, heavily overfeeding the patients. The scientific value of such studies is next to nothing.

Another aspect that has been presented and advocated is the strategy of permissive hypocaloric feeding. This indicates that patients are deliberately underfed in the ICU. Arguments for that strategy are also retrospective from studies not focusing on the temporal pattern of feeding. For example, the so-called Krishnan study advocating that administration of 33–67% of estimated caloric need gives a survival advantage, totally disregards the length of stay in the ICU, which is the strongest determinant of outcome (6). In general terms it can be said that successful enteral feeding is a strong predictor for a positive outcome also in patients with comparable levels of risk in other parameters (7). As it is also known that even successful enteral feeding very rarely corresponds to the estimated energy expenditure or the measured energy expenditure, the conclusion that the lower-than-estimated administration of calories should be the mechanism for a survival advantage rather than the functioning intestine may in itself be regarded as an important controversy within ICU nutrition. Several new studies are coming up, which will hopefully shed more light on this controversy in the future.

Tight glucose control?

During the last 10-year period, the most cited and discussed contribution to intensive care medicine is tight glucose control. The Leuven experience that a mortality advantage can be expected in ICU long stayers subjected to tight glucose control has been embraced by the ICU community (8, 9). No single publication has had a longer impact upon clinical practice in the ICU as compared to the

first Leuven article in 2001 (8). The controversies relate to the fact that this is a single-centre study and that the nutritional regime is quite ambitious, and to the obvious risk of hypoglycaemia, the potential disadvantage for the short staying medical patients, and the failure of others to reproduce the results.

The advantage of a single-centre study is obvious – the success rate of keeping patients normo-glycemic probably is much higher in Leuven as compared to other centres. Motivation is high, and awareness regarding this treatment is higher than elsewhere. The problem with single-centre studies is, of course, that possible biases on any level of the study are not outbalanced by opposite biases in other participating centres, which is the whole idea behind a multi-centre study trial. On the other hand, in a multi-centre study the motivation among the staff at the different centres may not be as high as it was in Leuven. The confirmatory study from Rochester, Minnesota, unfortunately has historic controls, which does not make the study prospectively randomised (10).

The success of normoglycaemia has been a major discussion point over the past years. The different investigators point out that there may be many different ways to publish the blood sugar values. It may be blood sugars on a defined time point each day, it may be mean or median values of all blood sugar readings, or it may be a mean value derived from the area below the curve. Sometimes also indices are used to reveal outlayer values reflecting hyper glycaemia as well as hypoglycaemia, which is, of course, also very relevant. The GLUCONTROL study was prematurely terminated on the recommendation from the Safety Committee, and one of the arguments was the protocol violation, which reflected the inability to separate the two groups adequately in terms of blood sugar values (11). Until today, the controversy over how blood sugar values should be communicated has not been settled.

The danger of hypoglycaemia was a concern for both the GLUCONTROL study and the VISEP study (12). Both studies were terminated prematurely on recommendation of their respective Safety Committee for high incidence of hypoglycaemia. Both studies show an increased mortality rate in patients with hypoglycaemia, without any immediate time relation to the hypoglycaemia episode. Although the hypoglycaemia episodes were more common in the tight glucose control groups there was no mortality disadvantage for the tight glucose control group overall. The frequency of hypoglycaemia in the GLUCONTROL and VISEP studies is not fundamentally different from the hypoglycaemia episodes in the Leuven studies. It has been discussed extensively whether the hypoglycaemia actually contributed to the mortality or not. Nevertheless, nobody can totally dismiss that hypothesis. For the future, the only solution probably is to have continuous blood glucose monitoring devices and computerised protocols for food and insulin administration if normoglycaemia is to be achieved. Presently many centres have widened the target range for blood sugar.

The feeding regimen during tight glucose control is another matter of controversy, which basically reflects the more philosophical issues addressed earlier in this overview. In a New England Journal of Medicine editorial in conjunction with the Leuven study in medical ICU patients published in 2006, it was even suggested that the ambitious initial nutrition during ICU stay, often involving a combination of enteral and parenteral nutrition, actually created an overmortality, compensated by the tight glucose control (13). This suggestion in the editorial actually reflects the rather great disparities in opinion on this particular point. The issue whether or not to give adequate feeding, in terms of covering the energy expenditure, already early in the course of ICU stay is discussed above, but this discussion spills over into the tight glucose control controversy as well.

In the second Leuven study the intention to treat patients in the treatment group, who were not included among the per protocol patients, staying in the ICU more than 3 days, actually resulted in a tendency toward overmortality (9). The interpretations of this finding differ widely. The investigators favour the interpretation that there was an uneven randomisation, with an overrepresentation of patients who during the initial phase of ICU stay were given a "do not resuscitate" order. In the editorial in the New England Journal of Medicine it was suggested that these patients somehow had a limited physiological reserve making them unsuitable for a tight glucose control schedule (13). Again, whether or not tight glucose control should be postponed until the second/third ICU day, or whether or not it should be instituted immediately, was not resolved. In clinical practice ICU physicians tend to act differently in different centres.

In conclusion

Three controversies within ICU nutrition have been presented and discussed. The core question is whether or not to feed at all. The absence of prospective randomised controlled trials as evidence in favour of feeding may be likened to the absence of any such trials to support the use of a parachute when jumping out of an airplane. Nevertheless the controversy prevails. The second controversy presented is the underfeeding proposal entitled 'permissive hypocaloric feeding'. Here, the observation of successful enteral feeding in ICU patients is interpretated in two different ways. It may be viewed as a favourable prognostic sign related to a functioning organ, or it may be regarded as the cause of the more favourable prognosis. Thirdly, the concept of tight glucose control has developed into a controversy, as the very encouraging results from the initial study have been difficult to reproduce. These three examples are by no means the only controversies within the field of ICU nutrition, but they are a good demonstration of how the shortage of well-designed studies in this area leaves much room for speculations and beliefs.

The author

Jan Wernerman, MD, PhD
　　Professor of Intensive Care Medicine
　　Department of Anaesthesia and
　　Intensive Care Medicine
　　Karolinska University Hospital
　　Huddinge K 32
　　14186 Stockholm, Sweden
　　e-mail: jan.wernerman@karolinska.se

References

1. Heyland DK, Dhaliwal R, Drover JW, Gramlich L, Dodek P. Canadian clinical practice guidelines for nutrition support in mechanically ventilated, critically ill adult patients. JPEN J Parenter Enteral Nutr. 2003;27(5):355–73.
2. Marik PE, Pinsky M. Death by parenteral nutrition. Intensive Care Med. 2003;29(6):867–9.

3. Villet S, Chiolero RL, Bollmann MD et al. Negative impact of hypocaloric feeding and energy balance on clinical outcome in ICU patients. Clin Nutr. 2005;24(4):502–9.

4. Dvir D, Cohen J, Singer P. Computerized energy balance and complications in critically ill patients: An observational study. Clin Nutr. 2005.

5. Bauer P, Charpentier C, Bouchet C, Nace L, Raffy F, Gaconnet N. Parenteral with enteral nutrition in the critically ill. Intensive Care Med. 2000;26(7):893–900.

6. Krishnan JA, Parce PB, Martinez A, Diette GB, Brower RG. Caloric intake in medical ICU patients: consistency of care with guidelines and relationship to clinical outcomes. Chest. 2003;124(1):297–305.

7. Woodcock N, MacFie J. Optimal nutrition support (and the demise of the enteral versus parenteral controversy). Nutrition. 2002;18(6):523–4.

8. van den Berghe G, Wouters P, Weekers F et al. Intensive insulin therapy in the critically ill patients. N Engl J Med. 2001;345(19):1359–67.

9. Van den Berghe G, Wilmer A, Hermans G et al. Intensive insulin therapy in the medical ICU. N Engl J Med. 2006;354(5):449–61.

10. Krinsley JS. Effect of an intensive glucose management protocol on the mortality of critically ill adult patients. Mayo Clin Proc. 2004;79(8):992–1000.

11. Preiser JC, Devos P. Clinical experience with tight glucose control by intensive insulin therapy. Crit Care Med. 2007;35(9 Suppl.):S503–7.

12. Brunkhorst FM, Engel C, Bloos F et al. Intensive insulin therapy and pentastarch resuscitation in severe sepsis. N Engl J Med. 2008;358(2):125–39.

13. Malhotra A: Intensive insulin in intensive care. N Engl J Med. 2006;354(5):516–8.

Richard D. Griffiths and Christina Jones

Pain and stress in the ICU: All in the mind?

We all wish to alleviate pain and reduce stress in our patients but the diversity of analgesic and sedation practice we see across many nations suggests we have not yet got the best approach. As we learn more about memory disturbance and patient experiences and the longer term psychological consequences it is apparent there is more "in the mind" during critical illness than simple waiting to awaken. This review explores the controversy of the meaning of awareness and patient experience within intensive care in terms of their consequences afterwards. We suggest that memory impairment and delusional experiences contribute to a significant longer term psychopathology and that for our patients benefit we require a change in practice within and after intensive care.

Introduction

"All would concede that the ICU environment is not normal. However, our results suggest that patients survive it well and that though their perceptions of their experience are abnormal, this may be no bad thing (1)".

This was the closing statement in an excellent analysis of the recollection of 100 patients following a stay in ICU published in 1979. At that time only 22% were ventilated and 70% of these had no recall, with the rest having only a patchy recall of ventilation. It was apparent that half of the rest suffered some forms of amnesia and 14% of the non-ventilated insisted they had been "on artificial ventilation" and it was only these patients who described pain or discomfort! Almost half of all patients felt they had been confused at some time, one – third had dreams of which 64% were said to be unpleasant. But were they right in thinking this was "no bad thing"? Could there perhaps be a longer term consequence of their "abnormal experience"?

In the early 90's following on from our initial experience of following up and supporting post ICU patients for more than a year (2) we learnt that psychological problems, memory problems, amnesia and unpleasant dreams and vivid delusional experiences often of a persecutory nature (3) might all suggest that there might be "harm in not knowing" (4). It was apparent to us that there was a significant psychological morbidity ranging from anxiety & depression to panic attacks, phobias and post-traumatic stress disorder following critical illness that could be directly related to the pain and stress of unpleasant experiences on a background of clouding of consciousness (5). At the same time we could see similarities and parallels to the distress caused by hallucinations and delusions arising in subjects kept in prolonged dark, solitary isolation exemplified in the book by

Brian Keenan on his experiences as a hostage in Beirut 1986–1991 (6).

Ever since intensive care started we have had the drugs to alleviate pain and reduce stress such that we take sedation and analgesic practice in intensive care for granted and established dogma is rarely challenged. However a glance at practice across many nations soon shows us there is a marked difference in analgesic-sedation approach and therefore presumably a different belief in that dogma (7, 8, 9) and that sedation and analgesic use is double the observed rates of the assessment for analgesic or sedation needs(10). Obviously some of our patients may have undergone surgical trauma or had traumatic injury and others have pain associated with their disease but they are looked after in an advanced, caring environment with many skilled professionals able to provide the reassurance to accompany abundantly available sedative and analgesic agents.

Why then is pain and distress something our patients continue to consistently recall (11)? Numerous studies have shown that following ventilation the overall experience of patients can be varied and may include those that are emotionally challenging and frightening; elicit insecurity, fear and vulnerability, or physical discomforts such as pain, difficulty breathing, ET tube and suctioning, thirst, noise, physical restrictions (12, 13, 14). It should be realised that these are very individual experiences that do not necessarily bear any relationship to the perceptions of the individual's carers or relatives (15).

Is it perhaps because we don't know how to manage physical pain and to use analgesics adequately? Or is it that pain is not the only issue rather there are many adverse stimuli that can cause stress to our patients and we do not fully understand their nature and consequences? One view based upon the experiences during operative procedures is that we allow patients to be aware of the "nasty" things we do and therefore patients are better off more sedated or anaesthetised? This of course ignores the success of regional or local anaesthesia. It assumes that all the things we think very unpleasant are consistently and equally so in everyone all the time? It also makes the assumption that all adverse experiences are real and apparent and could not be delusional. Alternatively understanding what pain and stress means to patients is more complex and perhaps challenges

our pre-conceived ideas about what we consider "adverse".

In this short review we will not discuss physiological mechanisms of stress or the details of analgesia (16, 17, 18) or sedation (19) which are well-covered in authoritative reviews and guidelines but rather suggest that we have to consider more carefully the "mind". This review explores the controversy of the meaning of awareness and patient experience within intensive care in terms of their consequences afterwards.

The controversy

Discomfort and factual recollections of unpleasant events in intensive care seem superficially an obvious precipitant of stress with more factual recall associated with more recall of discomfort (20). The most common source of discomfort after the ET tube (42 %) however was hallucinations (32 %) with pain only in 12 % and these were younger patients. The same group had shown that using a less invasive tracheal suctioning technique halved the recall of tracheal suctioning (41 % to 20 %) but nevertheless those that recalled suctioning still recorded a similar level of discomfort (21). In a large follow-up study in Portugal investigators obtained six month outcome data on 464 out of 1,433 patients admitted (22). Despite the inevitable losses they were able to show that 38 % had no recall of any of their ICU stay. Those that had recall remembered it as calm and friendly in over 93 % of cases. Unreal experiences can be pleasant, unpleasant and sometimes frightening. 51 % experienced dreams and nightmares; of these 14 % were of such a character as to still disturb their life six months later and this along with difficulties in concentrating and remembering recent events were independently associated with a reduced quality of life. That there is a relationship between exposure to stress in the ICU and a poor subsequent health-related quality of life is well-established (23). But what are the most important stressors?

Our current practice suggests we make assumptions about possible stressors?

We assume, understandably but perhaps too readily, that the obvious stressors are the physical pain of the wound, injury or the discomfort of the endotracheal tube yet ignore that their interpretation and integration into memory may be severely impaired by the drugs we use. We assume in determining the level of distress an assessment based upon either the enquiry of a confused, delirious or sedated patient or judgements based upon secondary physiological responses. We assume the patient "response" to a painful procedure is a measure of the discomfort and implied lack of analgesia or worse sedation. We assume that tracheal suctioning is always unpleasant but do not place it in the context of relieving the discomfort of a blocked tube. We assume that the environment is not painful and fail to recognise painful auditory or visual experiences. Loud noise sufficient to startle may be obvious but impaired hearing can lead to distress and misunderstanding of speech and if thirsty the sound of running water can be a torture. We assume the benefits of the analgesics and forget the nausea, bowel dysfunction and feeding problems are not independent of those we use. Above all we wrongly assume the decision we make to analgise and sedate (or restrain a patient if allowed) is based upon a sound risk benefit analysis for the best short and long term interest of the patient and their care.

The central controversy revolves around what we think does harm to our patients

Over the last 20 years we have realised that the experience of the critically ill patient is complicated by the brain impairment manifest in delirium and altered cognition such that the psychological interpretation of real and delusional experiences occurs on the background of disturbed or altered memory and amnesia (24). The implication is that an "adverse" experience may not always have the same meaning, be of similar importance or even be real as compared with a well subject.

Perhaps one of the strongest stressors is that of the fear of dying, harm or injury to oneself or loved ones but this is highly dependent on the context and the ability of the subject to control or influence the perceived outcome. The inability to respond and to act or a lack of control and security of the situation to the extent of loosing all power creates the basis for post-traumatic stress

disorder (PTSD). It is not simply the event but the *lack of personal security* that is critical to developing PTSD. This concept is important to grasp and conceptualise in terms of an experience within the intensive care setting.

The first implication is that something that may seem unpleasant and associated perhaps with fear may not be judged by the patient as such if there is clear personal security or personal control of decisions or the actions result in relief e.g. the personal fear of dying from the inability to breathe is less with a reassuring presence of a nurse and their suctioning of the blocked endotracheal tube.

The recall of pain is influenced by many factors including previous experience, anxiety, lack of sleep (25) and ethnic background (26). An example of this was a young woman who vividly recalled her grandfather dying in a lot of pain. She was admitted to critical care with pneumonia but also needed regular dressings to a leg ulcer and for her the anticipation of the pain of the dressing was so severe that she felt sick for hours before and was so worked up that she needed "Entonox" to cope with the dressing. Teaching this patient relaxation helped the anticipatory anxiety and reduced her overall perception of pain.

For some patients the anxiety, pain and fear are not associated with real memories but delusions. The characters of many delusions are of a persecutory or paranoid nature including fear of harm or death (5). They may be extremely vivid and can be firmly held by the patient to have been true unless appropriate awareness allows them to understand the context. The kinds of experiences that patients describe fall into three broad categories (27):

- benign hallucinatory experiences that are not negative;
- hallucinations with negative or delusional themes (gangsters, aliens, kidnapping, torture);
- "pure" delusions i.e. without hallucinations that are very frightening and heavily imbedded in reality (persecutory or paranoid) such as the nurse who tries to kill them with an injection into their foot.

Many delusions are not apparent or amenable to external influence by carers; such as in the well-behaved patient who had the delusional fear that failing to follow her next instruction by the alien staff would result in herself being replaced by one of the aliens (28). The nature and content of delusional experiences also may have more significance and be more readily recalled depending on the triggers that have elicited the delusion. A study of delusional experiences during a period of high news media exposure of a military conflict occurring just prior to admission to ICU explored this issue (29). It showed that those patients vividly recalling military themes were of an age to have experienced life during the 2nd world war and as such the prior media exposure was priming delusions that had the most impact.

However for some patients delusional experiences are pleasant, for instance gently being rowed around a Scottish Loch by a handsome Laird and in others we have noticed that some patients are able to adapt their delusion and get themselves into a place of safety. One gentleman recalled being tortured as his initial memory for ICU, but after a time he was visited in reality by a friend of his who made films. After this visit his delusion changed and he felt safe because he decided he was involved in the making of a film and so anything that happened could not hurt him. Before this change he recalled a lot of pain, but afterwards he could not recall any.

As we learn more about the recall and experiences of patients it is apparent that brain dysfunction (whether as a result of the disease or secondary to the drugs we use) clouds interpretation through disturbing the senses, distorting memory, misinforming experiences and impairing decision making (30).

Controversial position:
Delusion is worse than reality

To get at what is really an "adverse" experience we need to ask what is meant by a real experience since we are questioning patients about their recall on a background of delirium that affects the majority of our patients (60 to 80%) and has such an impact on outcome, enough to effect mortality (31). This brain failure rightly comes within the framework of multiple organ failure. In a study of 275 mechanically ventilated patients followed up for 6 months, a three-fold increase (Hazard ratio 3.2; 95% CI, 1.4–7.7; p = 0.008) in the risk of death at six months was shown after adjusting

for age, illness severity and co-morbidities. Furthermore we expect precise recall in a background of cognitive impairment where in a cohort of patients similarly studied one third were neuropsychologically impaired at six months (32) and this was strongly associated with delirium at some stage during intensive care.

It proves very hard often to place recall experiences clearly in time. At best many are fragmentary and inconsistent. Over time after ICU, recall changes and may fade. When developing an intensive care memory tool we found the largest change over a 4 month period occurred in the memory of feelings (and the least reliable on retest), then factual recall, while delusional experiences were the most consistently and reliably remembered over time (33). The ability of a memory to be retained and recalled is dependent on a fully functional memory system (which we know may be impaired) and the psychological impact of that memory such that a vivid paranoid delusion may be more strongly recalled than a vague perception or a less significant real event. We have suggested that there are at least two possible processes contributing to memory failure in ICU patients and these were discussed in a detailed review (34). Firstly there is a dampening effect on memory by the illness and drug treatments. Opiates, benzodiazepines, propofol, adrenaline and corticosteroids can all influence memory. Delirium is common and can result in amnesia which is further confounded by sleep disturbance impairing episodic memory consolidation. Secondly we hypothesise that memory for an external event is impaired while that for internal events is enhanced; this attention shift so that they then vividly recall hallucinations and nightmares is a key observation.

Dissociation, where part of a traumatic experience is not consciously recalled, can occur in patients with post traumatic stress disorder (PTSD). However the amnesia many patients experience for factual events in ICU does not seem to fit with dissociation. Our experience with the use of Eye Movement Desensitisation and Reprocessing (EMDR) therapy for PTSD in ICU patients is that these memories are simply not stored and so can not be retrieved at a later stage. This is consistent with our knowledge of cognitive impairment. Extremely frightening parts of delusional memories may however be dissociated. An example of this is a young patient whose whole ICU experience was delusional. He recalled being forced to watch three people being hanged from a tree and then being dragged towards the same tree to be hanged himself. This memory remained very distressing and to increase his sense of safety when processing the trauma the therapist suggested that he should imagine his father being in the situation to keep him safe. He did this but then retrieved a final part of the delusion which had involved his father being hurt and from which he had dissociated as it was too overwhelming. Once this was processed his distress at the whole memory was reduced.

Controversial position: "Knowing" is important and this relates to sedation use?

As mentioned we first raised our concern that a lack of understanding of what has happened in ICU may have harmful consequences some 12 years ago (4) based upon our follow-up and rehabilitation experience. It was picked up by those interested in the "sedation break" concept (35). It was apparent that a break in a patient's autobiography if left unexplained had longer term consequences. At the time we were also exploring the delusional experiences and our limited data also suggested that amnesia and delusional experiences gave a higher risk of PTSD symptoms and suggested that lack of recall of real experiences may be harmful (36). This study showed that PTSD could arise as a result of life threatening delusional experiences in the context of no real memory of ICU and turned the focus on delusional experiences instead of the everyday real experience. This was consistent with our attention shift hypothesis and even suggested that real experiences may not be harmful but even possibly protective. Unfortunately this association between delusional and amnesia was interpreted by some as causal rather than being an observational association and we did not have hard data to causally link them. Amnesia may simply reflect more brain dysfunction but on its own for short periods when the subject has been prepared with an explanation (general anaesthesia) is rarely a problem. Perhaps the more important aspect of amnesia experiences are those early or even before admission to ICU deleting from the patient's

recall the reason for why they are where they are and therefore confounding any subsequent delusional experience.

A recent detailed study in Sweden of stressful experience attempted to relate them to the level of sedation (53). Of 250 patients interviewed face to face a few days after ICU 18% had no recall of ICU or any memory. These patients were significantly older, sicker and more heavily sedated compared to those with memories. Propofol was used in 95% of patients, midazolam in 30% all in combination with opiods and they used the MAAS sedation score which is a motor based score. Unlike previous studies their practice was to have patients less deeply sedated. Of the 206 with memories, 56% remembered the endotracheal tube (ETT) and these had significantly higher (more aware) sedation scores. Almost ¾ describe the discomfort and not being able to speak as bothersome. 80% could remember one bothersome experience with the ETT but this was more related to duration of ventilation than sedation level. Other stressful experiences were as previously reported; e.g. restrictions and thirst. Spells of terror or panic (27%) and nightmares (26%) were less frequently reported but these were regarded as extremely bothersome. Patients with bothersome experiences had significantly longer ICU stays and more emergency admissions, with more periods of wakefulness (higher MAAS score). However those with nightmares had significantly longer ICU stays and ventilation and higher cumulative drug doses, more midazolam and less periods of wakefulness (lower average MAAS scores), but with some episodes of agitation. We are left with the dilemma on one hand with lighter sedation there is more bothersome experience but on deeper sedation there are more distressing hallucinations.

The post-ICU consequences of amnesia, sedation intensity, arousal level and the subsequent development of PTSD were explored in 149 ventilated patients (37). Again 18% had complete amnesia for ICU while only 10% could remember most or all of the time. They too found that factual episodic recall was weakly associated with increased wakefulness and understandably this was more evident nearer the end of the ICU stay. While the experiences are similar 51% had nightmares or hallucinations. There was a 15% incidence of PTSD at six months. Of the various symptom clusters leading to PTSD (re-experiencing, avoidance-emotional numbing, arousal clusters) the highest specificity was to the avoidance-numbing cluster of symptoms. The presence of delirious memories was associated with significantly higher scores in both re-experiencing and avoidance-numbing symptoms. However there was no relationship with the degree of amnesia. The sedation intensity was not related to PTSD, but as in the previous study there was a linear positive relationship with having delirious memories (more sedation more delirious memory). When related to wakefulness episodes, however the relationship suggested that PTSD symptom scores were highest in the middle level of wakefulness and lowest when least aroused or when having the most awake episodes. It has been suggested that the quality of cognitive processing at the time of the traumatic event is important in the development of chronic PTSD. Those individuals who report feeling confusion and feeling overwhelmed as they experienced the traumatic situation are more likely to suffer from chronic PTSD (38). ICU patients may be predisposed to high levels of chronic PTSD because during the traumatic experience their ability to process information is likely to be compromised by a number of factors, either due to the treatment instituted during the ICU stay or due to the critical illness, such as encephalopathy, delirium, sleep deprivation, sedative drugs and opiates. If confused and less awake they are likely to be unable to process the meaning of the events they are experiencing.

We have recently published an observational study of the precipitants of PTSD that confirms the importance of delusional memories (39). Across a number of very diverse European ICUs in four countries 238 post-ventilated patients were studied. Delusional memories were common: 57 % ranging from 44 % to 77 %. The incidence of delirium was 41 % (range 14 %–65 %). Recall of pain and anxiety was not consistent over the follow-up at 2 weeks, 2 months and 3 months with only half the patients showing any consistency in recall of pain for any two time points. Of the 4 of the 22 patients who developed PTSD (18 %) only one patient reported pain and three reported anxiety consistently at all three time points. The rate of defined PTSD was 9.2 % with a range of 3.2 % to 14.8 %. Independent of case mix and illness sever-

ity the factors found to be related to the development of PTSD were recalling of delusional memories, prolonged sedation, a history of pre-existing psychological problems such as anxiety or depression, and physical restraint with no sedation. The incidence of delirium varied between units and its development was more common in patients receiving high daily doses of benzodiazepines or opiates. Only one unit used physical restraint but the association with PTSD cannot be linked to recalling the experience as being traumatic as only one patient could recall being restrained, while over half could recall delusional memories and those that developed PTSD had higher agitation scores. The very inconsistent reporting of pain during the ICU stay draws into question the results of some earlier studies where the reporting was done many months after the events such that the "experience" and its interpretation may have been altered with the passage of time. Much has been made of the number of "adverse" or "traumatic" memories and that more are linked to the development of post traumatic stress disorder by six months (40). However this may be spurious and related to time in ICU and does not address the impact of any particular experience where a single highly frightening experience will have more consequence than several vaguely unpleasant ones. As mentioned earlier there is less reliability when interpreting patient recall of feelings over longer periods, especially pain or discomfort. Psychological disorders such as post traumatic stress disorder are associated with chronic pain (41) and the development of PTSD following critical illness, with increased pain perception, may influence the recall of earlier pain, such as in ICU. Several explanations for this have been postulated, with attention bias to somatic cues being an important contributor.

Clinical practice

How then does this link up with the "sedation-break"?

Having a daily interruption of sedation helps to avoid drug accumulation and in a landmark study significantly reduced the length of mechanical ventilation and ICU stay (42). If there is a concern that our sedative drugs are affecting longer term cognitive function, and in particular memories, it is necessary to question the ideal depth of sedation required so that patients are not traumatised by their experience of ICU yet are not impaired by the formation of delusional memories. In a retrospective study of a proportion of patients that they could contact from the original study the investigators looked at the impact of waking the patient daily while on ICU in terms of their later psychological distress (43). Although the sampling does lay the study open to bias there was a trend towards those patients who were woken daily being less distressed and less likely to develop PTSD than those who were kept continuously sedated and only woken up when finally weaned off a ventilator. These same collaborators have teamed up with those interested in ventilator weaning trials, sedation, and delirium in the Awakening and Breathing Controlled study (ABC) to show that pairing daily awakening trials with breathing trials results in less ventilation, shorter ICU and hospital stay and impressively lower 1 year mortality (44). While the duration of delirium was similar the duration of coma was reduced and less sedative drugs given. Hopefully we can anticipate future data on psychological morbidity and that the long term consequences will be favourable.

The advent of new short acting sedative or analgesic agents allows the titration to achieve the awake yet comfortable patient. Remifentanil, a powerful short acting opiate has allowed greater use of analgesia-based sedation where hypnosis is not the goal in intensive care (45) with the promise of decreased duration of ventilation and stay in intensive care (46). Avoiding prolonged use of benzodiazepines has clear advantages and using an alternative approach in a study comparing dexmedetomidine (a highly selective aplha2-adrenergic receptor agonist) with lorazepam at no extra cost it was possible to achieve a better targeted sedation with more days alive without coma or delirium (47). Interestingly, those patients that were given dexmedetomidine required more fentanyl, confirming the importance of analgesia in preference to hypnotics. While reducing the days in ICU of coma and delirium there was no significant difference in measures of cognitive outcome. In future studies it will be interesting to see if there is any reduction in long term psychological morbidity.

What else might we do apart from awakening patients and reducing the drugs?

Perhaps key to managing the fear, the unknown and the uncertainty is for patients to have confidence in those caring for them combined with a feeling of safety and security through reassurance and comfort. Family members can contribute within ICU and of course are central afterwards during rehabilitation but caution should be exercised when one remembers how traumatised the family and close relations can become. Relatives of critically ill patients can have pathological levels of anxiety and depression and the family social support mechanisms may be near to collapse (48). Fortunately it appeared that the nurses can give important social support within ICU but it leaves the period after ICU with problems. An additional problem for recovering patients is that family members can also develop PTSD. This is not surprising considering the extreme stress and life-threatening experiences they witness but the increased incidence may also reflect familial risks. 33% of family members when interviewed three months after ICU exhibited stress symptoms consistent with a risk of developing PTSD (49). This confirmed our earlier observation during a rehabilitation study that at six months a significant proportion of relatives (49%) expressed very high levels of the symptoms contributing to PTSD (50) and there was a close relationship between symptoms levels in patients and relatives.

In a follow up study of ARDS patients after one year (unfortunately biased by only 50% responding) the relationship between development of PTSD symptoms and health-related quality of life (HRQL) and social support was explored through questionnaires (51). 29% of the 65 patients had high-risk scores for PTSD. Compared with low-scoring patients the "high risk of PTSD" patients had more "traumatic memories" but interesting the only significant difference was more anxiety related to their memories. "High risk of PTSD" patients had more nightmares with only a modest trend to more pain and difficulties with breathing. That anxiety was the most important difference suggests that it was the "fear" factor in the experience that mattered. As expected HRQL was worse than normal controls and this was worse in all main domains in those scoring high for PTSD symptoms, but there was no difference in the physical domains between low and high scoring patients. Perceived social support was significantly higher in low-scoring patients. This study confirms the persistence of mental and psychological impairment longer than physical impairment and confirms that relatives are also intimately involved in the disaster of a critical illness. Whether this lack of social support is primary within the family structure or secondary to the psychological pathology arising in the relatives is unclear and confirms earlier observations. The high incidence of "nightmares" (many ones suspected of being of a delusional and frightening character) is probably related to the long analgesia and sedation these ARDS patients received.

Conclusion

Appropriate analgesia and, where required, sedation are central to pain and stress management but there is a real downside and there is much "in the mind" we must consider. The evidence points to the need for psychological support of patients and relatives during and after ICU as part of rehabilitation (5). The drive to reduce sedation load may hopefully reduce delusional memories and by awakening patients allow them to know more of what goes on. Following on from our experience to help patients recover (24) a novel approach to reduce PTSD is being tested in a randomised control trial. Patient and relative diaries collected during ICU (52) are being tested as a form of cognitive behavioural therapy during recovery to rebuild fragmented memory, contextualise recovery and support the relatives and patients as they rehabilitate.

Key points

- *There is no agreement how best to analgise and sedate intensive care patients.*
- *Memory and recall of experience is greatly disturbed and unreliable.*
- *Frightening and distressing delusional and hallucinatory experiences are consistently associated with longer term psychological morbidity.*
- *Over-sedation and inappropriate analgesia use may confound care.*
- *Psychological support may be needed during recovery*

Key words

Pain, stress, analgesia, sedation, delusions, nightmares, memory, amnesia, delirium, PTSD

The authors

Richard D. Griffiths, BSc, MD, FRCP, FHEA, Prof.
Christina Jones, PhD
    Pathophysiology Unit | Division of Metabolic
    and Cellular Medicine | School of Clinical
    Science | University of Liverpool, UK

Address for correspondence
    Richard D. Griffiths
    Professor of Medicine (Intensive Care)
    Pathophysiology Unit
    School of Clinical Science
    University of Liverpool
    Duncan Building, UCD
    Daulby Street
    L69 3GA Liverpool, UK
    e-mail: rdg@liverpool.ac.uk

References

1. Jones J, Hoggart B, Withey J, Donaghue K, Ellis BW. What the patients say: a study of reactions to an intensive care unit. Intensive Care Medicine. 1979;5:89–92.
2. Jones C, Macmillan RR, Griffiths RD. Providing psychological support for patients after critical illness. Clinical Intensive Care. 1994;5:176–179.
3. Jones C, Griffiths RD, Macmillan RR, Palmer TEA. Psychological problems occurring after intensive care. British Journal of Intensive Care. 1994;4(2):46–53.
4. Griffiths RD, Jones C, MacMillan RR. Where is the harm in not knowing? Care after intensive care. Clinical Intensive Care. 1996;7:144–145.
5. Jones C, Humphris GM, Griffiths RD. Psychological morbidity following critical illness – the rationale for care after intensive care. Clinical Intensive Care. 1998;9:199–205.
6. Keenan, B. An Evil Cradling: The five year ordeal of a hostage. Viking Penguin. 1994 ISBN: 0140236414.
7. Murdoch S, Cohen A. Intensive care sedation: a review of current British practice. Intensive Care Medicine. 2000; 26:922–928.
8. Soliman H, Melot C, Vincent J. Sedative and analgesic practice in the intensive care unit: the result of a European survey. Br J Anaesthesia. 2001;87:186–192.

9. Martin J, Parsch A, Franck M, Wernecke KD, Fischer M, Spies C. Practice of sedation and analgesia in German intensive care units: results of a national survey. Critical Care. 2005;9:R117–R123.

10. Payen JF, Chanques G, Mantz J, Hercule C, Auriant I, Leguillou JL, Binhas M, Genty C, Rolland C, Bosson JL. Current practices in sedation and analegesia for mechanically ventilated critically ill patients: a prospective mulitcenter patient-based study. Anesthesiology. 2007;106:687–95.

11. Desbiens NA, Wu AW, Broste SK, Wenger NS, Connors AF Jr, Lynn J, Yasui Y, Phillips RS, Fulkerson W. Pain and satisfaction with pain control in seriously ill hospitalised adults: Findings from the SUPPORT research investigations. Crit Care Med. 1996;24: 1953–1961.

12. Novaes MAFP, Aronovich A, Ferraz MB, Knobel E. Stressors in ICU: patients' evaluation. Intensive Care Medicine. 1997;23:1282–1285.

13. GranbergA, Bergbom Engberg I, Lundberg D. Patients' experience of being critically ill or severely injured and cared for in an intensive care unit in relation to the ICU syndrome. Part 1. Intensive & Critical Care Nursing. 1998;14:294–307.

14. Rotundi AJ, Chelluri L, Sirio C, Mendelsohn A, Schulz R, Belle S, Im K, Donahue M, Pinsky MR. Patients' recollections of stressful experiences while receiving prolonged mechanical ventilation in an intensive care unit. Crit Care Med. 2002;30:746–52.

15. Novaes MA, Knobel E, Bork AM, Pavao OF, Nogueira-martins LA, Ferraz MB. Stressors in ICU: perception of the patient, relatives and health care team. Intensive Care Med. 1999;25:1421–6.

16. Herr K, Coyne PJ, Key T, Manworren R, McCaffery M, Merkel S, Pelosi-Kelly J, Wild L. Pain assessment in the nonverbal patient: position statement with clinical practice recommendations. Pain Management nursing. 2006;7:44–52.

17. Pun BT, Dunn J. The sedation of critically ill adults: Part 1: Assessment. The first in a two-part series focuses on assessing sedated patients in the ICU. Am J Nurs. 2007;107(7):40–8.

18. Pun BT, Dunn J. The sedation of critically ill adults: part 2: management.Am J Nurs. 2007;107(8):40–9.

19. Jacobi J, Fraser GL, Coursin DB, Riker RR, Fontaine D, Wittbrodt ET, Chalfin DB, Masica MF, Bjerke HS, Coplin WM, Crippen DW, Fuchs BD, Kelleher RM, Marik PE, Nasraway SA Jr, Murray MJ, Peruzzi WT, Lumb PD. Task Force of the American College of Critical Care Medicine (ACCM) of the Society of Critical Care Medicine(SCCM), American Society of Health-System Pharmacists (ASHP), American College of Chest Physicians. Clinical practice guidelines for the sustained use of sedatives and analgesics in the critically ill adult. Crit Care Med. 2002; 30(1):119–41.

20. Van der Leur JP, Van der Schans CP, Loef BG, Deelman BG, Geertzen JHB, Zwaveling JH. Discomfort and factual recollection in intensive care unit patients. Critical Care. 2004;8:R467–R473.

21. Van der Leur JP, Zwaveling JH, Loef BG, Schans CP. Patient recollection of airway suctioning in the ICU: routine versus a minimally invasive procedure. Intensive Care Medicine. 2003;29:433–436.

22. Granja C, Lopes A, Moreira S, Dias C, Costa-Pereira A, Carneiro A. JMIP Study Group. Patients' recollections of experiences in the intensive care unit may affect their quality of life. Critical Care. 2005;9:R96–R109.

23. Schelling G, Richter M, Roozendaal B, Rothenhausler HB, Krauseneck T, Stoll C, Nollert G, Schmidt M, Kapfhammer HP. Exposure to high stress in the intensive care unit may have negative effects on health-related quality-of-life outcomes after cardiac surgery. Crit Care Med. 2003;31:1971–80.

24. Griffiths RD, Jones C. (2007) Seven lessons from 20 years of follow up of intensive care unit survivors. Curr Opin Crit Care. 2007;13:508–513.

25. Haack M, Sanchez E, Mullington J. Elevated inflammatory markers in response to prolonged sleep restriction are associated with increased pain experience in healthy volunteers. Sleep. 2007;30(9):1145–1152.

26. Im E, Chee W, Guevara E, Liu Y, Lim H, Tsai HM, Clark M, Bender M, Suk Kim K, Hee Kim Y, Shin H. Gender and ethnic differences in cancer pain experience: a multiethnic survey in the United States. Nursing research. 2007;56(5):296–306.

27. Skirrow P. Delusional memories of ICU. In: Intensive Care After Care. eds Griffiths RD & Jones C. Butterworth & Heinemann, Oxford UK 2002 pp27–35.

28. Jones C, Griffiths RD, Humphris GM. A case of capgras delusion following critical illness. Intensive Care Medicine 1999;25:1183–1184.

29. Skirrow P, Jones C, Griffiths RD, Kaney S. The impact of current media events on Hallucinatory content: The experience of the intensive care unit (ICU) patient. British Journal of Clinical Psychology 2002;41:87–91.

30. Griffiths RD, Jones C. (2007) Delirium, cognitive dysfunction and posttraumatic stress disorder. Curr Opin in Anaes. 2007;20:124–129.

31. Ely EW, Shintani A, Truman B, Speroff T, Gordon SM, Harrell FE Jr, Inouye SK, Bernard GR, Dittus RS. Delirium as a predictor of mortality in mechanically ventilated patients in the intensive care unit. J Am Med Assoc. 2004;291:1753–1762.

32. Jackson JC, Hart RP, Gordon SM, Shintani A, Truman B, May L, Ely EW. Six-month neuropsychological outcome of medical intensive care unit patients. Crit Care Med. 2003;31:1226–1234.

33. Jones C, Humphris G, Griffiths RD. Preliminary validation of the ICUM tool: a tool for assessing memory of the intensive care experience. Clinical Intensive Care. 2000;11(5);251–255.

34. Jones C, Griffiths RD, Humphris GM. (2000) Disturbed memory and amnesia related to intensive care. Memory. 2000;8(2):79–94.
35. Heffner JE. A wake-up call in the intensive care unit. (Editorial) NEJM. 2000;342:1520–1522.
36. Jones C, Griffiths RD, Humphris G. Acute Post Traumatic Stress Disorder: a new theory for its development after intensive care. Critical Care Medicine. 2001;29:573–580.
37. Weinert CR, Sprenkle M. Post-ICU consequences of patient wakefulness and sedative exposure during mechanical ventilation. Intensive Care Medicine. 2008;34:82–90.
38. Ehlers A, Clark DM. A cognitive model of posttraumatic stress disorder. Behaviour Research & Therapy. 2000; 38(4):319–45.
39. Jones C, Bäckman C, Capuzzo M, Flaatten H, Rylander C, Griffiths RD. Precipitants of Post Traumatic Stress Disorder following intensive care: a hypothesis generating study of diversity in care. Intensive Care Medicine. 2007;33:978–985.
40. Schelling G, Stoll C, Haller M, Briegel J, Manert W, Hummel T, Lenhart A, Heyduck M, Polasek J, Meier M, Preuss U, Bullinger M, Schüffel W, Peter K. Health-related quality of life and posttraumatic stress disorder in survivors of adult respiratory distress syndrome. Crit Care Med. 1998;26:651–9.
41. Asmundson GJG, Coons-MJ, Taylor S, Katz J PTSD and the Experience of Pain: Research and Clinical Implications of Shared Vulnerability and Mutual Maintenance Models. Canadian Journal of Psychiatry. 2002;47(10):930–937.
42. Kress JP, Pohlman AS, O'Connor MF, Hall JB. Daily interruption of sedative infusions in critically ill patients undergoing mechanical ventilation. New England Journal of Medicine. 2000;342:1471–1477.
43. Kress JP, Gehlbach B, Lacy M, Pliskin N, Pohlman AS, Hall JB. The Long-term Psychological Effects of Daily Sedative Interruption on Critically Ill Patients. American Journal of Respiratory and Critical Care Medicine. 2003;168:1457–1461.
44. Girard TD, Kress JP, Fuchs BD, Thomason JWW, Schweickert WD, Pun BT, Taichman DB, Dunn JG, Pohlman AS, Kinniry PA, Jackson JC, Canonico AE, Light RW, Shintani AK, Thompson JL, Gordon SM, Hall JB, Dittus RS, Bernard GR, Ely EW. Efficacy and safety of a paired sedation and ventilator weaning protocol for mechanically ventilated patients in intensive care (Awakening and Breathing Controlled trial): a randomised controlled trial. Lancet. 2008;371:126–34.
45. Park G, Lane M, Rogers S, Bassett P. A comparison of hypnotic and analgesic based sedation in a general intensive care unit. Br J Anaesthesia. 2007;98:76–82.
46. Breen D, Karabinis A, Malbain M, Morais R, Albrecht S, Jarnvig IL, Parkinson P, Kirkham AJ. Decreased duration of mechanical ventilation when comparing analgesia-based sedation using remifentanil with standard hypnotic-based sedation for up to 10 days in intensive care unit patients: a randomised trial. Crit Care. 2005;9:247–8.
47. Pandharipande PP, Pun, BT, Herr DL, Maze M, Girard TD, Miller RR, Shintani AK, Thompson JL, Jackson JC, Deppen SA, Stiles RA, Dittus RS, Bernard GR, Ely EW. Effect of sedation with dexmedetomidine vs lorazepam on acute brain dysfunction in mechanically ventilated patients. The MENDS randomized controlled trial. JAMA. 2007;298; 2644–2653.
48. Jones C, Hussey R, Griffiths RD. Social support in the intensive care unit. Brit. J of Intensive Care. 1991;1(2): 66–69.
49. Azoulay E, Pochard F, Kentish-Barnes N, Chevret S, Aboab J, Adrie C, Annane D, Bleichner G, Bollaert PE, Darmon M, Fassier T, Galliot R, Garrouste-Orgeas M, Goulenok C, Goldgran-Toledano D, Hayon J, Jourdain M, Kaidomar M, Laplace C, Larché J, Liotier J, Papazian L, Poisson C, Reignier J, Saidi F, Schlemmer B. FAMIREA Study Group. Risk of Post-traumatic stress symptoms in family members of intensive care unit patients. Am J Respir Crit Care Med. 2005;171:987–994.
50. Jones C, Skirrow P, Griffiths RD, Humphris G, Ingleby S, Eddleston J, Waldmann C, Gager M. Post-Traumatic stress disorder-related symptoms in relatives of patients following intensive care. Intensive Care Medicine 2004; 30:456–460.
51. Deja M, Denke C, Weber-Carstens S, Schröder J, Pille CE, Hokema F, Falke KJ, Kaisers U. Social support during intensive care unit stay might improve mental impairment and consequently health-related quality of life in survivors of severe acute respiratory distress syndrome. Critical Care. 2006;10:R147–158.
52. Backman C. Patient diaries in ICU. In: Intensive Care After Care. eds Griffiths RD & Jones C. Butterworth & Heinemann, Oxford UK 2002 pp123–129.
53. Samuelson KAM, Lundberg D, Fridlund B. Stressful experience in relation to depth of sedation in mechanically ventilated patients. Nursing in Critical Care. 2007;12:93–104.

Rui Maio, Jorge Cruz and Jose Fernando Teixeira

Controversies on donation after cardiac death

Introduction

When clinical transplantation started, cadaveric organs were recovered from donors declared deceased by cardiopulmonary criteria. Medical advances in sustaining patients on life support, a greater understanding of the neurosciences, and guidelines defining death written by the legal, scientific and medical communities in the late 1960s and early 1970s, produced a shift toward using organs from brain-dead donors (BDD). Additionally, the adoption of brain death eliminated the issue of donor warm ischaemia and its potentially deleterious impact on organ function and survival (1).

The growing disparity between the number of donors and recipients has renewed interest in recovering organs from donors declared dead by cardiopulmonary criteria, known as donation after cardiac death (DCD).

In the United States, for example, although the numbers of organ donors and transplantations have more than doubled over the past 20 years, in 2006 there were about 29,000 solid-organ transplantations and in June 2007, there were about 97,000 people on waiting lists for organ transplantation (2).

In the last decade, the kidney transplant waiting list has increased by more than 260%, yet the number of deceased donor kidney transplants performed has increased by only a modest 16%. Unfortunately, the current supply of deceased donor kidneys cannot meet the increasing demand for donor kidneys and more than 6% of patients on the waiting list die each year while waiting for transplantation (3).

This unprecedented increase in the lists of patients waiting for a transplant in the western world as well as a decrease in the number of BDD in some countries has triggered renewed interest in DCD as a source of organs (4).

Looking for ways to increase the donor pool has also led to the inclusion of kidneys from expanded criteria donors (ECD – over 60 years or aged 50–59 with two of the following three characteristics: cerebrovascular event as cause of death, history of hypertension, or terminal creatinine of 1.5 mg/dl or higher). The acceptance of these broader criteria has increased the donor pool but at some cost in terms of outcomes (5).

In the last 5 years, the most rapid increase in the rate of organ recovery from deceased persons has occurred in the category of DCD. These donors accounted for 6.7% of all deceased donors in 2006 worldwide (30% in the Netherlands, 19% in the UK, 8% in the USA, 5% in Spain).

Several reports have appeared in medical literature showing good long-term function of kidneys from DCD, with graft survival rates similar to kidney transplants from BDD, although primary nonfunction (PNF) and delayed graft function (DGF) rates are higher (6).

Several factors, however, have obstructed the widespread use of organs from DCD, the main one possibly being the preconception on the part of the transplantation community that DCD are marginal or suboptimal donors who provide kidneys with poor renal function. Other problems include legal and ethical ones, as well as the logistics of the procedure.

In summary, donation after cardiac death presents new and complex aspects in vital organ donation. This review highlights the more relevant and controversial ones.

Classification

In 1995, the Maastricht group defined 4 DCD categories. Types I and II, also called "uncontrolled donors", are individuals in whom cardiac death occurs in a sudden manner (in an out-of-hospital setting (Type I) or in the emergency room after unsuccessful cardiopulmonary resuscitation (Type II)), and for whom fulfillment of the legal requirements for donation requires a long time. For these reasons, warm ischaemia is always longer with "uncontrolled" than with "controlled donors." European countries perform the majority of donations of this kind.

Types III and IV are also called "controlled donors." In Type III, the patient is withdrawn from vital support due to terminal illness, organs are retrieved after death is certified, provided there is a previous consent from the patient or the next of kin, the transplantation team is ready, and the donor is usually in a stable condition prior to the cardiac arrest. The warm ischaemia period is therefore short. Most legal and ethical problems concern this type of DCD which has been discussed at length in the United States where nearly all DCD come from this source.

Type IV donors are individuals who suffer a cardiac arrest after being declared brain-dead, or presumed brain-dead patients who suffer a cardiopulmonary arrest prior to the determination of death. This type of donor is the main source of donors in Japan, even after approval of a brain death law (7). In this country (Japan), after the confirmation of brain death, the transplant procurement team has to wait until cardiac arrest occurs. The transplantation team is ready but the donor suffers a long period of instability before cardiac arrest. In western countries, donors who suffer cardiac arrest while in the process of brain death donation are considered "uncontrolled donors" and represent a sporadic source of organs.

The procedure to reach the organ retrieval stage is more complex for Type I donors. For these individuals to be potential donors, cooperation between specially trained and equipped extra-hospital emergency services and a hospital with adequate infrastructures is required (8). Nevertheless, the Type I donor is considered the optimal DCD for several reasons. Firstly, the selection criteria for these donors are very strict with age and ischaemic time limits that ensure good organ quality. Secondly, these donors are individuals who have had a normal lifestyle up until the time of sudden death. And thirdly, they have not been previously admitted to an intensive care unit with the consequent risk of nosocomial infections, nor undergone a period of brain death, during which many neuroendocrine and circulatory alterations take place, with possible detrimental effects to the organs to be transplanted (9).

Outcomes

The unequal distribution of donors in the different categories of DCD programs may explain some of the variation in outcome between published reports. Practice varies between countries and can include the withdrawal of therapy from Type III donors or the inclusion of Type IV donors, practices which occur in the United States or Japan, and this makes comparisons even more difficult.

The different time intervals of each type of DCD must be taken into account in order to assess results properly. There are 3 crucial moments: first, the cardiopulmonary arrest; second, the time of the determination of death, and finally the moment of organ retrieval. Between these stages there are 2 important lapses of time.

The time between cardiopulmonary arrest and the diagnosis of death is short or very short in "controlled donors". Cardiopulmonary arrest is expected and the determination of death is made a few minutes afterwards. In "uncontrolled donors", this lapse of time is longer because cardiopulmonary resuscitation maneuvers are usually performed first. The diagnosis of death is done at least 30 minutes after cardiac arrest. In the case of type I DCD, this interval is much longer.

The interval between the determination of death and organ retrieval is also reduced to a minimum in the case of "controlled donors". The retrieval team is ready and surgery starts immediately after diagnosis of death. In the case of "uncontrolled donors", this period is longer: up to 2–3 hours are needed to fulfill all the legal requirements for organ donation, including the family interview. During this time the organs are perfused using a cardiopulmonary bypass. Japanese DCD have a prolonged period of haemodynamic instability prior to cardiac arrest. Finally, cold ischaemia time is characteristically long in the United States, short in Japan, and intermediate in European countries.

Short-term function of kidneys transplanted from DCD is characterised by a rate of DGF that usually exceeds 70 %

in "uncontrolled donors" and 45 % in "controlled donors". The rate of primary non-function is twice as high as that obtained with BD donors. The lower rate of DGF seen in Type III donors is probably due to the use of stable donors with short warm ischaemia times. In contrast, Japanese donors, with short warm ischaemia but long periods of haemodynamic instability prior to cardiac arrest, show a DGF rate equal to the European groups with long warm ischaemia but no period of haemodynamic instability prior to cardiac arrest.

In a recent study, Locke et al. found that DCD kidneys from donors younger than 50 years of age performed as well as standard criteria donor (SCD) kidneys with regard to long-term graft survival and, moreover, that limiting cold ischaemia time to less than 12 h markedly reduced DGF. DCD kidneys from donors older than 50 years had graft survival rates comparable to ECD kidneys at 5 years (10).

The consequences of ischaemic injury are less critical in kidney transplantation than in liver transplantation; patients receiving kidneys with DGF can be sustained with dialysis while the organ recovers. For this reason, the clinical use of DCD has centered on kidney transplantation. However, DGF predisposes to acute rejection and compromises the long-term survival of the graft.

The clinical experience of using livers from DCD is currently increasing. However, there is an increased rate of PNF, DGF and retransplantation. Biliary strictures proximal to the anastomosis were the most common complication observed and were noted in 50 % of patients. Non-anastomotic proximal duct strictures are traditionally attributed to ischaemic preservation injury.

These results point out the importance of adopting new strategies to prevent the inflammatory response associated with ischaemia reperfusion injury and thus improve the quality of organs recovered after cardiac death. In this setting, the pretreatment of the donor, the pulsatile perfusion of the organs with pharmacological manipulation of the perfusion solution, and the treatment of the recipient with drugs that could modulate the inflammatory response associated with the ischaemia reperfusion injury could improve the quality of organs retrieved after cardiac death (11, 12, 13).

Main controversies of DCD

The main ethical controversies related to the use of organs from DCD are the determination and timing of death, potential conflict of interests for healthcare professionals in ICU, and the need of consent before starting procedures to enhance or-gan viability prior to organ retrieval (14). Arnold and Youngner state that the problems specific to DCD are related to 'time and timing' (15). In this section we will focus on the ethical and legal concerns surrounding DCD.

Controversial position 1:
Irreversibility of cardiopulmonary arrest

The first criterion that has to be considered for the use of a DCD is the concept of the irreversibility of a cardiopulmonary arrest, and therefore, the moment of determination of death when a person can be considered a potential organ donor.

How is irreversibility defined?

Irreversibility is recognised by persistent cessation of function during an appropriate period of observation. Based on cardiopulmonary criteria, death occurs in DCD when respiration and circulation have ceased and cardiopulmonary function *will not resume spontaneously*. This concept of "irreversibility" has also been called the "permanent" cessation of respiration and circulation.

If data show that auto-resuscitation (spontaneous resumption of circulation) cannot occur and if there is no attempt at artificial resuscitation, it can be concluded that respiration and circulation have ceased permanently.

In clinical situations in which death is expected, once respiration and circulation cease (irrespective of electrical cardiac activity), the period of observation needed to determine that circulation will not recur spontaneously (auto-resuscitation) may be only a few minutes. Current data on auto-resuscitation indicate that the relevant event is cessation of circulation, not cessation of electrical activity in the heart.

According to the limited data available, when life-sustaining therapy is withdrawn, spontaneous circulation will not return after 2 minutes of cessation (16).

Some authors argue that a stronger and more precise notion of irreversibility is that the heart cannot be restarted despite standard cardiopulmonary resuscitation (17). This definition is followed by most European protocols of "uncontrolled donors" (18).

How is the permanent absence of circulation determined?

Cessation of functions is recognised by an appropriate clinical examination that reveals the absence of responsiveness, heart sounds, pulse and respiratory effort.

In applying the circulatory criteria of death in non-DCD circumstances, clinical examination alone may be sufficient to determine cessation of circulatory and respiratory functions. However, the urgent time constraints of DCD may require more definitive proof of cessation of these functions with confirmatory tests.

Confirmatory tests (e.g. intra-arterial monitoring or Doppler study) should be performed in accordance with the hospital protocol to assure the family and the hospital professional staff that the patient is dead.

According to Spanish law, death is defined as the absence of a heartbeat for 5 minutes, as demonstrated by the lack of a central pulse and/or a flat electrocardiogram, along with a lack of spontaneous breathing; these events must be recorded after a period of at least thirty minutes of advanced cardiopulmonary resuscitation measures and with a body temperature above 32°C *(RD 2070/1999, Anexo I, art. 3.1)*. Organ preservation maneuvers cannot be commenced until approval has been requested from the local day/night court and this request is granted. However, according to the Spanish Transplantation Bill (*Art. 10.5* and *Anexo I, art. 2* of the *R.D. 2070/1999*), if there is no reply within fifteen minutes of requesting this authorisation, organ preservation maneuvers can be started.

How long should cardiopulmonary arrest persist before organ donation is permitted?

There is serious controversy over when a DCD may be declared dead and organ donation can begin (19). It is in the interest of organ viability to minimise the time between the cessation of circulation and the beginning of organ donation. This process, however, presents a clear conflict between the interests of the dying patient and the interests of the organ recipient(s).

The Pittsburgh Protocol, for example, sets the time interval between onset of asystole and decla-ration of death as 2 minutes, based on data from 108 case observations in which autoresuscitation, or spontaneous resumption of heartbeat, did not occur after 2 minutes of asystole (20). Some authors argue that even if cardiac rhythm can be restored, it will not be restored and is therefore irreversible because resuscitation will not be attempted (21, 22).

The differences between 'not reversed' and 'irreversible', however, are both self-evident and critical to the definition of death. Historically, brain death and cardiopulmonary death have both been defined as irreversible processes, not processes that simply are not going to be treated. Hence, those patients who respond to cardiopulmonary resuscitation with restored heartbeat are not referred to as dead, or previously dead, but as survivors of near-fatal cardiac events. Furthermore, other authorities have pointed out that the brain is not dead at 2 minutes, and some studies have reported restoration of cardiopulmonary function after more than 15 minutes of asystole. The Institute of Medicine has reviewed DCD practice and, while generally supportive of this modality of organ retrieval, their report was particularly concerned with the definitions of death and irreversibility and suggested that 5 minutes was a more reasonable interval, although no data were presented to support this. Weber et al. report that since 1995, organ procurement has not been initiated until 10 minutes after the cessation of heartbeat, in accordance with the Maastricht protocol. This approach establishes a clear demarcation between being a patient and becoming a donor.

Serious harm can result if the time interval is too short. First, it is possible, although unlikely, that patient suffering could occur. Second, it creates an impression, or even a reality, that the needs of the dying patient will be set aside so that the organs can be obtained for someone else. This in turn could result in increased public reluctance to donate, and organ donation efforts can go terribly wrong if appropriate procedures are not followed (23).

Some physicians and nurses at the bedside continue to have concerns about the ethical aspects of their practice that "are numerous, complex and related to the specific roles they play." Some feel uncomfortable about the participation in medical practices that may be required during the transition from end-of-life care to organ donation. For example, in multidisciplinary ICUs, doctors and nurses who care for both potential organ donors and organ recipients may have conflicting interests. They may be uncomfortable recommending the withdrawal of life-sustaining treatment for one patient and hoping to obtain an organ for another (24).

However, the decision to withdraw life-sustaining treatment should be based upon a multi-disciplinary consensus on the futility of continued multi-organ support, and involve senior medical and nursing staff as well as the patient's family. Moreover, it should be unquestionably independent of any subsequent discussion regarding organ donation. All patients in whom the decision to withdraw has been reached should be considered as potential DCD unless specifically contraindicated, and their potential as organ donors should be discussed with a transplant coordinator.

This kind of approach resolves the ethical concerns over the fundamental decision involving the suspension of therapeutic support as it is made by the doctors in attendance regardless of organ retrieval. The possibility of organ donation is an option to be taken into consideration after the decision to withdraw life support. From this perspective, the process is similar to brain death diagnosis which should also be performed regardless of the possibility of withdrawal of organs for transplant.

To avoid obvious conflicts of interest, neither the surgeon who recovers the organs nor any other personnel involved in transplantation must participate in end-of-life care or the declaration of death.

Controversial position 2: Are medical therapies directed at organ preservation acceptable during the dying process?

One of the key elements of organ donation is obtaining consent, either presumed or informed, in accordance with the principle of autonomy and the law of each country. Many protocols for DCD include the need of family consent for donation and for starting invasive interventions that will only benefit the organ recipient(s). Patient and family wishes should be followed as closely as possible (4).

According to the "dead donor rule," donation should not cause or hasten death (25). The re-

covery of organs from DCD must not violate this rule. As currently practiced, DCD inevitably raises more concerns than brain death donation. The process is more complex, and the potential donor is not always dead when life-sustaining measures cease. The intervals between withdrawing care, pronouncing death, and recovering organs are very short.

To minimise the time between declaration of death and organ donation, and to promote organ viability, many protocols involve withdrawal of medical interventions in the operating room so that organ donation can proceed promptly after death. However, the administration of medication and the adoption of measures for the purpose of prematurely ending life must be avoided.

Physicians may have an interest in preserving organ function for transplantation, but measures such as the administration of anticoagulants and vasodilators may not be in the donor's best interest, as they may hasten death, and are thus ethically questionable.

Therapies to maximise organ preservation, such as anticoagulants and phentolamine, should be approached skeptically or avoided altogether because they have the potential to hasten death through hemorrhage, intracranial bleeding, and increased intracranial pressure. In 1997, the Institute of Medicine (IOM) commented that the administration of anticoagulants and vasopressors in settings where they clearly would not hasten death might be acceptable, but that the administration of such medication in circumstances that would hasten death was probably not.

The revised Pittsburgh Protocol specifically prohibits the administration of medications for organ preservation that could potentially cause patient suffering or hasten death.

However, according to the 2005 IOM conference, providing heparin at the time of withdrawal of life-sustaining treatment "is the current standard of care" because "the long-term survival of the transplanted organ may be at risk if thrombi impede circulation to the organ after reperfusion." Theoretically, heparin could hasten death by causing bleeding, but there is no evidence that it does so in practice. Some protocols also call for the advance placement of catheters in large arteries and veins to facilitate the rapid infusion of organ-preservation solutions after death. According to the Code of Practice of doctors in the UK on "Cadaveric organs for transplantation" written in 1983, "After a person is dead there is no legal objection to administering any drugs necessary to maintain the condition of the organs or to conducting the necessary diagnostic tests" (26).

Key points for clinical practice

Donation after cardiac death raises different problems depending on whether the donor is "controlled" or "uncontrolled". In the first case, we have more ethical and legal concerns and in the second, logistic and organisational demands are more relevant. To help clarify these differences we are going to present two protocols in use in clinical practice: one from Spain – Hospital Clinico de Madrid (9) and another from the USA – OPTN/UNOS (27).

"Uncontrolled donors" protocol of Hospital Clínico de Madrid, Spain

This is a complex process the success of which depends on coordination between the different events in a chain. It involves two well-differentiated stages that need to be tightly coordinated.

Extrahospital stage

When the emergency services are notified that an individual has died suddenly or unexpectedly on the street or at home, the sequence of events is the following:

1. Cardiopulmonary resuscitation measures are usually attempted if cardiac arrest is confirmed. Resuscitation has the sole objective of saving the patient's life.
2. The time of cardiopulmonary arrest should be recorded according to the reports of witnesses.
3. If resuscitation maneuvers to recover a heartbeat fail after 30 minutes, the person is declared dead. The cadaver can then be assessed as a potential donor based on specific selection criteria for DCD, according to current legislation.
4. During this time, the potential donor is subjected to mechanical ventilation, external cardiac massage and fluid perfusion (colloids, crystalloids and plasma volume expanders). If

there is bleeding, this is controlled and any other therapeutic measures deemed necessary are taken (placement of chest drains, central catheters, etc.). Cannulation of the femoral artery is better avoided.

5. The team that identifies the possible donor contacts the transplant coordinator and together they perform an initial evaluation. Cadavers with certain characteristics are considered potential donors: younger than 55 years; no thoracic or abdominal bleeding injuries; no external evidence of drug addiction; physical violence excluded as cause of death; external cardiac massage and mechanical ventilation commenced within 15 minutes from the start of cardiac arrest, and continuous cardiac massage, mechanical ventilation, and intravenous saline perfusion during the transfer to the hospital. If the results of this evaluation are favourable, a "DCD code" is activated.
6. According to the code procedure, the emergency (ambulance) services request the help of the police and the hospital is informed of the estimated time of arrival. The cadaver is transported to the hospital in an ambulance escorted by the police at a constant speed of 40–50 km/h.
7. Code activation advises the transplant coordinator, who immediately goes to the hospital. The hospital reception is also informed so that they can expect the arrival of a possible donor and contact the transplant team.
8. Once the hospital has been informed, the emergency department staff gets ready to receive the donor. Hospital security personnel help clear the way for the ambulance and police escort. Simultaneously, the medical team starts to prepare the operating room for the preservation measures.

Hospital stage

On arrival at the emergency room, the attending physician (on call) assumes control of the resuscitation measures. Once death has been pronounced and the death certificate signed, the responsibility for the potential donor is transferred to the transplant coordinator who will reassess the donor according to the general selection criteria and those specific for DCD.

1. Once the decision has been made to continue with the donation process, the following steps are taken:
   - Permission is requested by fax from the local court to start organ preservation maneuvers on the cadaver.
   - Blood is obtained for analytical tests, blood group, Rh, and viral serology. The donor is administered a bolus of heparin (500 IU/kg body weight).
   - The family is located via the police and hospital staff.
2. The cadaver is transferred to the operating room to start the preservation maneuvers, within a time period no longer than 120 minutes since the time of cardiac arrest. The coordinator thus has to strictly monitor the timing of all events.
3. Onset of preservation maneuvers: cardiopulmonary bypass with external oxygenation. This includes:
   - Cannulating the femoral vein and artery of one leg for connection to the extracorporeal circulation system including a membrane oxygenator and temperature exchanger
   - Introducing a Fogarty balloon via the contralateral femoral artery to interrupt blood flow above the level of the superior mesenteric artery
   - Introducing premedication in the extracorporeal circulation pump
   - Obtaining lymph node specimens as soon as possible and submitting them to the immunology laboratory for HLA typing

   Preservation maneuvers should be interrupted in the following situations:
   - When the necessary family consent for donation and/or judicial approval have NOT been obtained
   - If, after 4 hours of bypass, the necessary requisites for organ procurement have not been fulfilled
4. Finally, once family consent has been given, the transplant coordinator requests judicial approval by fax and submits this approval to the local court along with the family authorisation, application for organ procurement, certificate of dh due to cardiac arrest, the clinical record from the emergency room and the extra-hospital emergency service report. A key stage for any type of donation, the family interview is the transplant coordinator's most delicate task, especially in view of the particular characteristics of this type of donor.
5. Once judicial authorisation is obtained, the kidneys are retrieved and, if applicable, the liver, lungs and tissues are also procured. This is followed by the preservation and registration of the organs and tissues following specific protocols.
6. Finally, the court is informed of the end of the organ retrieval procedure.

"Controlled donors" protocol of OPTN/UNOS, USA

Suitable candidate selection

1. A patient who has a non-recoverable and irreversible neurological injury resulting in ventilator dependency but does not fulfill brain death criteria may be a suitable candidate for DCD.
2. Other conditions that may lead to consideration of DCD eligibility include end stage musculoskeletal disease, non-malignant pulmonary disease, and high spinal cord injury.
3. The decision to withdraw life-sustaining measures must be made by the hospital's patient care team and legal next of kin, and documented in the patient chart.
4. The assessment for DCD candidate suitability should be conducted in collaboration with the local Organ Procurement Organization (OPO) and the patient's primary healthcare team. OPO determination of donor suitability may include consulting the OPO medical director and transplant center teams that may be considering donor organs for transplantation.
5. An assessment should be made as to whether death is likely to occur (after the withdrawal of life-sustaining measures) within a time frame that allows for organ donation.

Consent/approval

1. The legal next of kin may consent to procedures or drug administration for the purposes of organ donation (e.g. heparin, regitine, femoral line placement, lymph node excision and bronchoscopy). No donor-related medications shall be administered or donation-related procedures performed without consent.

2. Permission from medical examiner/coroner must be obtained when applicable.
3. There should be a plan for patient care if death does not occur within the established timeframe after the withdrawal of life-sustaining measures. This plan should include logistics and provisions for continued end-of-life care, including immediate notification of the family.
4. For purposes of these model elements, "legal next of kin" shall also include the patient, relatives, a designated healthcare representative, or appropriate surrogate.

Withdrawal of life-sustaining measures/ patient management

1. A timeout is recommended prior to the initiation of the withdrawal of life sustaining measures. The intent of the timeout is to verify patient identification, the respective roles and responsibilities of the patient care team, OPO staff, and organ recovery team personnel.
2. No member of the transplant team shall be present for the withdrawal of life-sustaining measures.
3. No member of the organ recovery team or OPO staff may participate in the guidance or administration of palliative care, or the declaration of death.
4. The location and process for withdrawal of life-sustaining measures (e.g. endotraqueal tube removal, termination of blood pressure support medications) must be determined as a component of the patient management.
5. If applicable, placement of femoral cannulas and administration of pharmacologic agents (e.g. regitine, heparin) for the sole purpose of donor organ function must be detailed in the consent process.

Pronouncement of death

1. The patient care team member that is authorised to declare death must not be a member of the OPO or organ recovery team.
2. The method of declaring cardiac death must comply in every respect with the legal definition of death as an irreversible cessation of circulatory and respiratory functions.

Organ recovery

1. Following the declaration of death by the hospital patient care team, the organ recovery may be initiated.

Conclusions

In 1997, 2000, and 2005, the IOM reviewed and voiced support for donation after cardiac death. In 2005, a conference on DCD concluded that it is "an ethically acceptable practice of end-of-life care, capable of increasing the number of deceased donor organs available for transplantation" (28).

In 2001, a position paper by the Ethics Committee of the Society of Critical Care Medicine put forth recommendations on DCD. These recommendations in many ways mirrored those of the IOM, with the cornerstone remaining protection of the rights and dignity of the donor through informed consent, separation of donor care from the transplantation process, institutional and regular review of DCD policies, and specific training for health care personnel involved in this type of donation. Additionally, the Society of Critical Care Medicine recommended a discussion to educate the recipients on any notable differences in donor-related outcomes associated with receiving organs from DCD donors. Notably, the Society recommended that the observation period after asystole could be as short as 2 minutes and that "above 5 minutes is not recommended."

In January 2007, the Joint Commission (formerly the Joint Commission on Accreditation of Healthcare Organizations) implemented its first accreditation standard for DCD. According to this standard, hospitals with the necessary resources must develop donation policies in conjunction with their medical staff and their organ-procurement organisation that address "opportunities for asystolic recovery" of organs. Since many hospitals have never had an organ donor whose death was declared on the basis of cardiopulmonary criteria, meeting the standard may require new approaches to both organ donation and end-of-life care. The standard, however, requires that relevant hospitals have the policies in place, not that they allow the practice – they can choose to opt out because of concerns about ethics, quality of end-of-life care, or other reasons. When a hospital and its medical staff decide not to provide for DCD and the organ procurement organisation is not in agreement, the hospital must document its efforts to reach a consensus and include its justification for opting out in the donation policy. In addition, as of July 1, 2007, OPTN/UNOS has required all 257 transplant hospitals and 58 organ procurement organisations in the United States to comply with its new rules.

If the number of organ donations after cardiac death continues to increase, more patients will be able to receive transplants. At present, however, these donations remain troubling to some and are not as widely accepted as donations after brain death. Experience has shown that all legal and ethical problems can be solved by reaching agreements with the government, society, and medical community; however, logistical problems are trickier. Broader experience with the recommended practices should help, but concerns are likely to persist.

Regarding the results available and with the introduction of new strategies, DCD may be the best solution for organ shortage and is probably the main source of organs to be explored.

Acknowledgements

The authors would like to thank Mrs Jane Lewis for her help in revising the article.

The authors

Rui Maio, MD, PhD, CETC[1]
Jorge Cruz, MD, MA (Bioethics), CETC[2]
José Fernando Teixeira, MD, FEBVS, CETC[3]
[1]ETCO Councillor | Clinica Universitária Cirurgia 1 | Department of General and Transplantation Surgery | Hospital Santa Maria | Lisboa, Portugal
[2]Institute of Bioethics | Catholic University | Porto, Portugal
[3]Former ETCO president | Department of Vascular Surgery | Hospital São João, Porto, Portugal

Address for correspondence
Jane Lewis
ETCO Executive Officer
e-mail: secretariat@etco.org

References

1. Abt PL, Fisher CA, Shingal AK. Donation after cardiac death in the US: History and use. Jam Coll Surg. 2006;208–255.

2. Stratta RJ, Rohr MS, Sundberg AK et al. Increase kidney transplantation utilizing expanded criteria deceased organ donors with results comparable to standard criteria door transplant. Ann Surg. 2004;239:688–697.

3. Stratta RJ, Rohr MS, Sundberg AK et al. Intermediate-term outcomes with expanded criteria deceased donors in kidney transplantation: a spectrum or specter of quality? Ann Surg. 2006;243:594–601; discussion 601–603.

4. Doig CJ, Rocker G. Retrieving organs from non-heart-beating organ donors: a review of medical and ethical issues. Can J Anesth. 2003;50:1069–76.

5. Port FK, Bragg-Gresham JL, Metzger RA et al. Donor characteristics associated with reduced graft survival: an approach to expanding the pool of kidney donors. Transplantation. 2002, 74:1281–1286.

6. Doshi MD, Hunsicher LG. Short- and long-term outcomes with the use of kidneys and livers donated after cardiac death. Am J Transplant. 2007;7:122–129.

7. Morioka M. Reconsidering brain death: a lesson from Japan's fifteen years of experience. Hastings Cent Rep. 2001;31: 41–6.

8. Arias-Diaz J, Alvarez J, del Barrio MR, Balibrea JL. Non-heart-beating donation: current state of the art. Transplant Proc. 2004 Sep;36 (7): 1891–3

9. Nunez JR. 2st Course on Non-heart-beating donation. 15th Congress of the European Transplant Coordinators Organization. Prague, 2007.

10. Locke JE, Segev D, Warren DS et al. Outcomes of kidneys from donors after cardiac death: Implications for allocation and preservation. Am J Transplantation. 2007;7:1797–1807.

11. Maio R. Ischemia reperfusion lesion in DCD renal transplantation. Doctoral thesis. Lisbon, 2007.

12. Maio R, Figueiredo N, Thiemermann C et al. Donor pre-treatment with erythropoietin – a way to improve the quality of organs from donation after cardiac death. Am J Transplant. 2007;7(Supl 2): 251

13. Maio R, Figueiredo N, Costa P. The advantage of adding PEG to Celsior – a new machine preservation solution for kidneys recovered after cardiac death? Organ, Tissues and Cells. 2007; 2:85–90

14. Bell MD. Non-heart beating organ donation: old procurement strategy – new ethical problems. J Med Ethics. 2003;29:176–81.

15. Arnold RM, Youngner SJ. Time is of the essence: the pressing need for comprehensive non-heart-beating cadaveric donation policies. Transplant Proc. 1995;27:2913–21.

16. DeVita MA. The death watch: certifying death using cardiac criteria. Prog Transplant. 2001;2:58–66.

17. Bartlett ET, Bartlett ET: Differences between death and dying. Journal of Medical Ethics. 1995; 21(5):270–6.

18. Álvarez-Rodríguez J., Del Barrio-Yesa R., Navarro-Izquierdo A. Legal aspects of non-heart-beating-donors. The Madrid solution. Transplant Proc. 1995;27 (5): 2933–4.

19. Daar AS. Non-heart-beating donation: ten evidence- based ethical recommendations. Transplant Proc. 2004;36:1885–1887.

20. University of Pittsburgh Medical Center. Protocol for non-heart-beating organ donation, policy #5107, Patient Care. Updated February 7, 2001.

21. DuBois J. Is organ procurement causing the death of patients? Issues Law Med. 2002;52:7992

22. Menikoff J. The importance of being dead: non-heart-beating organ donation. Issues Law Med. 2002;18:3–20.

23. Norman G. Ethical issues of importance to anesthesiologists regarding organ donation after cardiac death. Curr Opin Organ Transplant. 2005;10:105–109.

24. Steinbrook R. Organ donation after cardiac death. N Engl J Med. 2007;357;3:209–213.

25. Robertson JA. The dead donor rule. Hastings Cent Rep. 1999;29: 6–14.

26. Cadaveric organs for transplantation – a Code of Practice including the diagnosis of brain death. UK Department of Health, 1983.

27. Model elements for controlled DCD recovery protocols. OPTN, 2007.

28. Institute of Medicine. Organ donation: opportunities for action. Washington DC: National Academies Press, 2006.

Ludwig Kramer, Crispiana Cozowicz and Reinhard Kitzberger

Is there a role for extracorporeal support in hepatic failure?

Introduction

Acute liver failure is a life-threatening clinical syndrome following a massive hepatic injury with development of cerebral edema (type A hepatic encephalopathy), frequently progressing to multiorgan failure. Current treatment relies on early orthotopic liver transplantation in patients with the most severe disease, but a considerable proportion of patients will develop irreversible neurological damage and multi-organ failure before a donor organ becomes available. Consequently, methods of stabilising patients on the waiting list as well as therapeutic alternatives to liver transplantation are needed. Randomised studies of extracorporeal detoxification systems so far have not convincingly demonstrated a clear survival benefit. Acute-on-chronic liver failure is another form of hepatic decompensation in the setting of chronic liver disease that carries a similarly grave prognosis. Decompensation can be triggered by bacterial infection, renal dysfunction, bleeding, hypovolaemia, or other causes. Emergent transplantation is impossible; and thus the goal of extracorporeal liver support is metabolic support and detoxification to support recompensation. Unfortunately, patients with acute-on-chronic liver failure are prone to develop treatment-related complications including bleeding, thrombocytopenia and hypotension, making biocompatibility a critical issue. Randomised studies are currently being performed to clarify ongoing contro-

versies regarding survival effects of extracorporeal liver support in acute-on-chronic liver failure.

Definitions of hepatic failure and scope of the problem

Acute liver failure

The terms acute liver failure (ALF) and fulminant hepatic failure (FHF) denote a life-threatening multisystem disease following severe hepatic injury characterised by jaundice, coagulopathy and hepatic encephalopathy (HE) in the absence of pre-existing symptomatic liver disease (37). Among its complications, metabolic brain dysfunction with astrocyte swelling, cerebral vasodilatation and eventual brainstem herniation is a major cause of death. At present, the high mortality of patients progressing to hepatic coma can be reduced only by early orthotopic liver transplantation. Prognostic scores have been developed to identify patients with poor prognosis who require early listing for transplantation. The best known scoring criteria are the King's College Criteria (see tab. 1), which were developed based on a cohort of 588 patients treated between 1972 and 1985 (49). Due to the scarcity of suitable donor organs, considerable

Tab. 1 King's College criteria. Modified from: O'Grady JG, Alexander GJ, Hayllar KM, Williams R. Early indicators of prognosis in fulminant hepatic failure. Gastroenterology 1989;97:439–445 and Bernal W, Donaldson N, Wyncoll D, Wendon J. Blood lactate as an early predictor of outcome in paracetamol-induced acute liver failure: a cohort study. Lancet 2002;359:558–563.

1. Paracetamol intoxication	pH < 7.3 irrespective of encephalopathy intoxication severity after 24 h and fluid resuscitation *or* Arterial lactate concentrations > 3.5 mmol/l following early fluid substitution *or* Arterial lactate concentrations > 3.0 mmol/l following 12 h of fluid substitution *or*
	Encephalopathy III/IV *and* Prothrombin time > 100 s (INR > 6.5) *and* Creatinine > 300 mmol/l (3.4 mg/dl), *all within 24 h*
2. Other aetiologies	Prothrombin time > 100 s (INR > 6.5) or at least three of the following criteria
	▪ Age < 10 or > 40 years ▪ Aetiology hepatitis non-A–E, halothane hepatitis, idiosyncratic drug reaction ▪ Jaundice to encephalopathy time > 7 days ▪ Prothrombin time > 50 s (INR > 3.5) ▪ Serum bilirubin > 300 mmol/l (> 17.4 mg/dl)

INR, international normalised ratio

numbers of patients still succumb to cerebral herniation, infection and multiorgan failure before a donor organ finally becomes available.

Patients with hyperacute liver failure (typically caused by paracetamol intoxication, for definitions see tab. 2) are at the highest risk of cerebral herniation, while they also have the best potential for regeneration. These patients are the most likely candidates to benefit from extracorporeal liver support aiming to ameliorate HE.

Acute-on-chronic liver failure

The term "acute-on-chronic liver failure" was introduced to describe episodes of acute decompensation in patients with pre-existing symptomatic liver disease. Since hepatic decompensation is usually triggered by severe complications including bacterial infection, renal dysfunction or variceal bleeding, mortality is extremely high, and emergent transplantation is impossible. The goal of extracorporeal support in acute-on-chronic liver failure is to stabilise extrahepatic organ dysfunction and support hepatic regen-

eration. Patients with acute-on-chronic liver failure usually have portal hypertension, which makes them particularly prone to treatment-related complications including haemorrhage, ar-

Tab. 2 Definition of acute hepatic failure and its subtypes. Reprinted from: The Lancet, 342, Williams R, Schalm SW and O'Grady JG, Acute liver failure: Redefining the syndromes, 273–275, 1993, with permission from Elsevier.

Subtype of liver failure:	Hyperacute	Acute	Subacute
Encephalopathy	Yes	Yes	Yes
Jaundice to encephalopathy (days)	0–7	8–28	29–72
Cerebral edema	Frequent	Frequent	Rare
Prothrombin time	+++	+++	+
Bilirubin	+	++	+++
Prognosis without transplantation	Moderate	Poor	Poor

terial hypotension and renal dysfunction. Randomised studies employing state-of-the art liver support techologies are currently performed to clarify controversies regarding the effects of extracorporeal liver support in acute-on-chronic liver failure.

Hepatic encephalopathy in ALF:
From "critical mass" to "toxin" hypothesis

Cerebral oedema and hepatic encephalopathy are the most deleterious complications of ALF. The *"critical mass"* hypothesis of acute liver failure is based on the assumption that progressive necrosis of hepatocytes reduces the functional liver mass below a critical threshold, causing encephalopathy, failure of the liver to regenerate and clinical symptoms of decompensation by a lack of life-sustaining factors synthesised by healthy liver. Although never subjected to rigorous scientific scrutiny, the critical mass hypothesis stimulated development of systems employing perfusion of freshly cut liver slices, live hepatocytes and hepatoblastoma cells, even if functional cell mass was usually low (artificial liver support). Only recent technological advances have allowed large-scale isolation and cryopreservation of viable hepatocytes (22). The actual metabolic capacity of cellular components, however, has never been investigated in sufficient detail. In the light of current knowledge, reductions of intracranial pressure during treatment with biological systems are better explained by hypothermia, osmotically active rinsing solutions and correction of iatrogenic hypervolaemia than by the purported metabolic activity of a few grammes of hepatocytes devoid of structural organisation and biliary drainage.

Currently, experimental and clinical evidence strongly favors the *"toxin hypothesis"* in HE, with ammonia, intracellular glutamine and bacterial endotoxin being the most deleterious toxins. The hypothesis of an "endogenous intoxication" therefore explains the emergence of HE and glial swelling in ALF better than the "critical mass hypothesis" (10, 4, 9). Clinical studies have unequivocally demonstrated a causal link between elevated plasma ammonia and subsequent cerebral edema (12, 7, 24). Ammonia is now recognised as the major pathophysiologic factor in the evolution of cerebral edema, as its levels correlate with both intracerebral glutamine concentration and intracranial pressure (45).

Based on the toxin hypothesis, intensive care treatment of ALF has adopted various strategies of extracorporeal detoxification including exchange transfusion, plasmapheresis, high-flux haemodialysis, haemoperfusion, albumin dialysis, and plasma adsorption (23). At least temporary improvement of neurologic function in patients treated with extracorporeal liver support has been observed since the early days of artificial liver support (21).

A brief overview of artificial and bioartificial liver support systems

From haemodialysis to plasmapheresis: Artificial liver support

The success of haemodialysis in the treatment of renal failure has been a constant stimulus for the development of extracorporeal liver support. Small-molecular toxins including ammonia and its equivalent glutamine are effectively removed by standard haemodialysis (1). Up to 63 % of patients with ALF treated by high-permeability haemodialysis in early studies improved neurologically (18, 42), but survival was not improved. At that time, liver transplantation was experimental or not available at all and haemodialysis systems using acetate buffer and cuprophane membranes had poor biocompatibilitiy. Thus, haemodialysis was gradually replaced by systems capable of removing large-molecular toxins, mostly charcoal and resin haemoperfusion (36), exchange transfusion, sorbent dialysis (2) and plasmapheresis (11). None of them improved outcome. The Molecular Adsorbents Recirculating System (MARS, 44), the Prometheus system (19) and single-pass albumin dialysis (41) are the latest developments in the field of artificial liver support. The MARS system has been used extensively and proved to be biocompatible and reduce bilirubin concentrations and also improve short-term mortality. No lasting effects on survival could be demonstrated by a recent meta-analysis (26). Results of a French multi-centre study in patients with acute liver failure are awaited.

The concept of bioartifical liver support

"Bioartifical" liver support systems were originally designed to combine blood detoxification (artificial liver support) with perfusion of extracorporeal hepatocytes (biological liver support), despite the lack of a pathophysiologically sound explanation for the role of extracorporeal hepatocytes. From the experience with liver resection, the minimum quantity of cells required is estimated to be 10–30 % of normal liver mass (1500 g), which was rarely met by existing systems. With most designs employing plasma separation and some involving oxygenators to sustain viability of hepatocytes, the "bioartificial" approach came at the cost of increased complexity, excessive cost, limited biocompatibility, and low mass transfer rates. Almost all bioartifical systems were studied in uncontrolled trials with the goal of bridging for transplantation, which obscured the long-term outcome of extracorporeal treatment (47). The only prospective international multi-centre trial investigating a system containing porcine hepatocytes did not improve outcome, although a subgroup seemed to benefit (17). While most studies were heavily underpowered to elucidate effects on mortality, also a large meta-analysis did not find any efficacy in ALF (27).

Pathophysiologic considerations in extracorporeal treatment

Ammonia/glutamine hypothesis

The pathophysiology of cerebral oedema in ALF is still not fully elucidated. For more than a century, ammonia has been considered the major neurotoxin (13). The "ammonia hypothesis" has been clinically confirmed, as high arterial ammonia levels predicted cerebral herniation and death (12, 7). Importantly, the relation between plasma ammonia levels and severity of HE can be variable, as ammonia exerts neurotoxicity only via the astrocytic synthesis of glutamine. This concept of indirect toxicity also explains the delay of 1–2 days between massive hyperammonaemia and cerebral herniation, representing a window of opportunity for application of extracorporeal liver support. Variations in plasma osmolality caused by rigorous haemodialysis may actually exacerbate

glutamine-induced glial swelling, in particular in patients with hyperacute ALF. Thus, a reasonable approach to extracorporeal treatment should avoid rapid changes in osmolality, which can be prevented by isotonic dialysates and continuous treatment.

Biocompatibility issues in extracorporeal liver support

The systemic inflammatory response syndrome (SIRS) occurs as a response to the release of pro-inflammatory cytokines. SIRS plays an important role in the pathophysiology of ALF by modifying cerebral blood flow, cellular bioenergetics and extrahepatic organ functions. Patients developing SIRS have an increased rate of extrahepatic organ failures, more advanced encephalopathy, and significantly impaired prognosis (38). Systemic inflammation can be massively exacerbated by bioincompatible liver support systems (29). In addition, bioartificial liver support systems containing porcine cells may induce allergic reactions (3). Thus, maximal biocompatibility and optimal anticoagulation are prerequisites for successful extracorporeal treatment. It seems particularly noteworthy that human serum albumin but not hydroxyethyl starch raised systemic vascular resistance in cirrhosis (20), possibly explaining haemodynamic benefits with albumin dialysis (31).

Cerebral hyperaemia and brain oedema

In ALF, wide variations in cardiac output and cerebral blood flow occur (33). Studies of the cerebral circulation consistently show impaired cerebral autoregulation and cerebral hyperperfusion at advanced stages of HE (see tab. 3), possibly induced by increased nitric oxide synthesis (32). These changes could be reproduced in the absence of hepatic necrosis by ammonia infusion in portocavally-shunted animals and appear to be linked to ammonia/glutamine toxicity (8). While some patients may also show a reduction in cerebral blood flow, they appear to be at lower risk of herniation (48). Glutamine-induced astrocytic water accumulation seems to act as an integrative trigger for the development of intracranial hypertension.

Tab. 3   Stages of hepatic encephalopathy (HE) in acute liver failure

HE stage	Clinical characteristics
I	Mood disturbance, mild confusion, slurred speech, disturbance of biorhythm, flapping tremor (asterixis), mood disturbance, mild confusion, slurred speech, disturbance of biorhythm
II	Lethargy or agitation, aggressive mood, moderate confusion, marked flapping tremor
III	Severe confusion or somnolence, arousable on verbal stimuli
IV	Coma, initially arousable on painful stimuli (IVa), not arousable in later stages (IVb), sluggish reaction to light, myoclonus, epileptic fits, signs of intracranial hypertension (IVc)

Vasodilation and the role of hypothermia

Elevated intracellular glutamine levels are associated with increased cerebral blood flow, leading to vasogenic brain edema (9). Vasodilation can be antagonised by hyperventilation and/or administration of thiopental, propofol or indomethacin. To acutely reduce brain oedema, mannitol has been shown to be the best treatment option. Moderate hypothermia is a further strategy which reduces both ammonia uptake and glutamine synthesis; and cooling patients with refractory intracranial hypertension to 32°C was effective in lowering intracranial pressure (25). In addition, intracranial release of inflammatory cytokines was reduced, demonstrating anti-inflammatory effects of hypothermia (25).

Major controversies on liver support strategies in ALF

Why did liver support systems fail to improve survival in ALF?

Extracorporeal systems aiming to improve encephalopathy and sustain hepatic recovery have been investigated for more than 50 years (31). Unfortunately, the goals of reducing mortality were never met (43). It is conceivable that the poor biocompatibility of extracorporeal liver support systems causing coagulopathy, thrombocytopenia and hypotension outweighed their potential benefits in critically ill patients (36, 28). The long-standing uncertainty regarding pathophysiology of HE was a further limitation in devising extracorporeal detoxification systems. Fortunately, the past decade has seen rapid advances in the patho-

physiologic concepts of hepatic encephalopathy (9). Moreover, biocompatibility of extracorporeal detoxification could be improved; and animal models resembling the human syndrome of ALF have been established (5). Thus, modern pathophysiologic concepts of HE are now to be integrated in designing effective ways of extracorporeal liver support.

Is continuous treatment justified?

In contrast to continuous haemofiltration and haemodialysis, most liver support systems employ adsorbents that saturate over time, requiring intermittent treatment. No prospective study has investigated whether continuous detoxification, adding the risks of permanent anticoagulation in patients already prone to bleeding, actually improved outcome. At least patients with grade III/IV encephalopathy and cerebral edema may benefit from continuous treatment; as intermittent haemodialysis caused intracranial pressure to rise (16). In fact, reversal of massive cerebral oedema by continuous liver support and haemofiltration, respectively, has been demonstrated (30, 40) (see fig. 1).

Implications of pathophysiologic advances for artificial and bioartificial liver support

Advances in the pathophysiology of cerebral edema in ALF have challenged many assumptions on which blood detoxification systems were based. Rather than protein-bound and lipophilic large-molecular toxins, increased production and/or impaired metabolism of ammonia, a small, water-

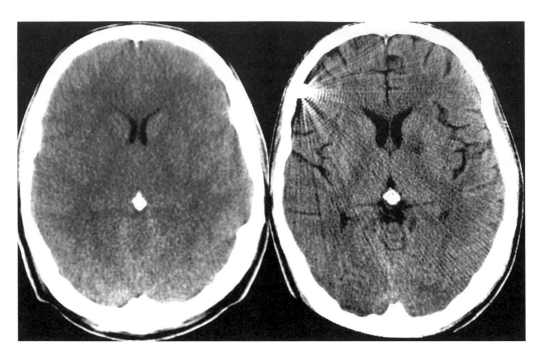

Fig. 1   Effects of early continuous extracorporeal detoxification (FPSA prototype) in a patient with ecstasy/cocaine-induced ALF and refractory cerebral edema. Transplantation was declined due to active injection drug abuse. Comparison of cranial computed tomography scans obtained before (arterial ammonia, 318 μmol/l, left) and after 4 days of continuous treatment (arterial ammonia, < 50 μmol/l) demonstrates restoration of gray-white differentiation and normalisation of sulcal and ventricular width. Note ischaemic infarcts of left internal capsule and occipital cortex and metallic artifact of epidural transducer. Reproduced from: Kramer L, Bauer E, Schenk P, Steininger R, Vigl M, Mallek R. Successful treatment of refractory cerebral oedema in ecstasy/cocaine-induced fulminant hepatic failure using a new high-efficacy liver detoxification device (FPSA-Prometheus). Wien Klin Wochenschr. 2003;115:599–603. With permission from Springer.

soluble molecule, explain most of the dramatic symptoms of acute and chronic encephalopathy, including cerebral herniation. This new knowledge has to be integrated in the clinical management of ALF, which inevitably affects extracorporeal treatment. Given its pivotal importance, effects on ammonia levels need to be reported in all studies investigating extracorporeal treatment.

Ammonia can be effectively removed by haemodialysis at a rate dependent on ammonia concentration, dialyser surface, blood flow and dialysate flow (14). At currently used blood flow rates of 150–200 ml/hr, extracorporeal ammonia clearance is only a fraction of the clearance by a healthy liver, but this may still be sufficient. In liver support systems using plasma separation, mass transfer rates are even lower; only the increase of of extracorporeal blood flow could enhance the rate of ammonia removal. It remains to be shown whether higher flow rates are superior, as they may induce rapid osmolality shifts, hypotension and worsening of cerebral edema. Moreover, shear stress to blood cells and extracorporeal hepatocytes limits biocompatibility. Extracorporeal detoxification could be combined with mild hypothermia and alternative ways of ammonia removal such as acidifying enemas (46), or L-ornithine-L-aspartate (39).

Considering the important role of inflammatory mediators in the pathogenesis of ALF and HE, biocompatibility of extracorporeal systems is a critical factor. Activation of granuloytes and platelets by bioincompatible membranes was associated with bleeding episodes in cirrhotic patients with HE (29). Thus, effective strategies of anticoagulation, use of biocompatible membranes and reduction of extracorporeal volume are required to improve biocompatibility.

The role of biological liver support needs to be clarified in the light of pathophysiological knowledge. Given considerable limitations in flow rates and cell mass, current strategies of biological liver support appear rather insufficient to perform the complex metabolic tasks of the liver. Hepatocyte suspensions and monolayers are characterised by minimal biological activity and short survival periods. Carrier-bound hepatocytes may survive for longer periods but are subjected to limitations in mass transfer rates. Immortalised hepatoma cell lines perform metabolically poorly compared to hepatocytes (35). Protective factors produced by a healthy liver that cannot be replaced by blood products need to be identified to justify biological liver support. This seems particularly relevant with porcine hepatocytes, which may expose patients to biological risks (34). In general, detoxification by haemodialysis, haemofiltration, plasma exchange and artificial liver support seems to be more effective and safer compared to extracorporeal cell perfusion.

Concluding remarks

After over 50 years of progress, strategies of artificial and bioartificial liver support are still not sufficient to fully replace the multiple hepatic functions that are defective in patients with acute and chronic liver failure. There is still no evidence that biological liver support systems can reverse encephalopathy, enhance hepatic regeneration, or improve outcome. Nonetheless, current pathophysiologig knowlegde suggests a role for efficient and biocompatible detoxification, ideally in combination with mild therapeutic hypothermia. Patients developing cerebral edema should preferably be treated by continuous modalities to prevent deleterious shifts in osmolality. Finally, expanding knowledge on the regulation of liver regeneration, differentiation and prevention of apoptosis might ultimately provide clues to effective regenerative treatment for these critically ill patients and hopefully further reduce the need for transplantation in an age of donor organ shortage.

The authors

Ludwig Kramer, MD[1]
Crispiana Cozowicz, MD[2]
Reinhard Kitzberger, MD[2]
[1] Associate Professor of Medicine | Department of Medicine I | Krankenhaus Hietzing | Vienna, Austria
[2] Department of Medicine III | Division of Gastroenterology and Hepatology | Medical University of Vienna, Austria

Address for correspondence
Ludwig Kramer
Department of Medicine I
Krankenhaus Hietzing
Wolkersbergenstrasse 1
1130 Vienna, Austria
e-mail: ludwig.kramer@wienkav.at

References

1. Abouna GM, Ganguly PK, Hamdy HM, Jabur SS, Tweed WA, Costa G. Extracorporeal liver perfusion system for successful hepatic support pending liver regeneration or liver transplantation: a pre-clinical controlled trial. Transplantation. 1999;67:1576–1583.
2. Ash SR, Blake DE, Carr DJ, Carter C, Howard T, Makowka L. Clinical effects of a sorbent suspension dialysis system in treatment of hepatic coma (the BioLogic-DT). Int J Artif Organs. 1992;15:151–161.
3. Baquerizo A, Mhoyan A, Kearns-Jonker M et al. Characterization of human xenoreactive antibodies in liver failure patients exposed to pig hepatocytes after bioartificial liver treatment. Transplantation. 1999;67: 5–18.
4. Basile AS, Saito K, Al-Mardini H, Record CO, Hughes RD, Harrison P, Williams R, Li Y, Heyes MP. The relationship between plasma and brain quinolinic acid levels and the severity of hepatic encephalopathy. Gastroenterology. 1995;108:818–823.
5. Bélanger M, Butterworth RF. Acute liver failure: a critical appraisal of available animal models. Metab Brain Dis. 2005 Dec;20(4):409–423.
6. Bernal W, Donaldson N, Wyncoll D et al. Blood lactate as an early predictor of outcome in paracetamol-induced acute liver failure: A cohort study. Lancet. 2002;359: 558–563.
7. Bhatia V, Singh R, Acharya SK. Predictive value of arterial ammonia for complications and outcome in acute liver failure. Gut. 2006;55:98–104.

8. Blei AT, Olafsson SM, Therrien G, Butterworth R. Ammonia-induced cerebral edema and intracranial hypertension in rats after portocaval anastomosis. Hepatology. 1994;19:80–87.

9. Blei AT. Brain edema and portal-systemic encephalopathy. Liver Transplantation. 2000;6:S14-S20.

10. Butterworth RF, Giuère JF, Michaud J, Lavoie J, Pomeir-Layargues G. Ammonia: A key factor in the pathogenesis of hepatic encephalopathy. Neurochem Pathol. 1987;6:1–12.

11. Clemmesen JO, Kondrup J, Nielsen LB, Larsen FS, Ott P. Effects of high-volume plasmapheresis on ammonia, urea, and amino acids in patients with acute liver failure. Am J Gastroenterol. 2001;96:1217–1223.

12. Clemmesen JO, Larsen FS, Kondrup J, Hansen BA, Ott P. Cerebral herniation in patients with acute liver failure is correlated with arterial ammonia concentration. Hepatology. 1999;29:648–646.

13. Conn HO, Lieberthal MM. The Hepatic Coma Syndromes and Lactulose. Baltimore: Williams & Wilkins, 1979.

14. Cordoba J, Blei AT, Mujais S. Determinants of ammonia clearance by hemodialysis. Artif Organs. 1996; 20:800–803.

15. Cordoba J, Gottstein J, Blei AT. Chronic hyponatremia exacerbates ammonia-induced brain edema in rats after portacaval anastomosis. J Hepatol. 1998;29:589–594.

16. Davenport A, Will EJ, Davison AM. Continuous vs. intermittent forms of haemofiltration and/or dialysis in the management of acute renal failure in patients with defective cerebral autoregulation at risk of cerebral oedema. Contrib Nephrol. 1991;93:225–233.

17. Demetriou AA, Brown RS Jr, Busuttil RW et al. Prospective, randomized, multicenter, controlled trial of a bioartificial liver in treating acute liver failure. Ann Surg. 2004;239:660–667.

18. Denis J, Opolon P, Nusinovici V, Granger A, Darnis F. Treatment of encephalopathy during fulminant hepatic failure by haemodialysis with high permeability membrane. Gut. 1978; 19: 787–793.

19. Falkenhagen D, Strobl W, Vogt G et al. Fractionated plasma separation and adsorption system: a novel system for blood purification to remove albumin bound substances. Artif Organs. 1999;23:81–86.

20. Fernández J, Monteagudo J, Bargallo X, Jiménez W, Bosch J, Arroyo V, Navasa M. A randomized unblinded pilot study comparing albumin versus hydroxyethyl starch in spontaneous bacterial peritonitis. Hepatology. 2005;42: 627–634.

21. Gazzard BG, Weston MJ, Murray-Lyon IM, Flax H, Record CO, Williams R, Portmann B, Langley PG, Dunlop EH, Mellon PJ, Ward MB. Charcoal haemoperfusion in the treatment of fulminant hepatic failure. Lancet. 1974;1: 1301–1307.

22. Gerlach JC, Mutig K, Sauer IM et al. Use of primary human liver cells originating from discarded grafts in a bioreactor for liver support therapy and the prospects of culturing adult liver stem cells in bioreactors: a morphologic study. Transplantation. 2003; 76:781–786.

23. Hughes RD. Hughes RD. Liver support in acute liver failure. Wien Klin Wochenschr. 2003;115:547–548.

24. Jalan R, Bernuau J. Induction of cerebral hyperemia by ammonia plus endotoxin: does hyperammonemia unlock the blood-brain barrier? J Hepatol 2007;47:168–171.

25. Jalan R, Olde Damink SW, Deutz NE, Hayes PC, Lee A. Moderate hypothermia in patients with acute liver failure and uncontrolled intracranial hypertension. Gastroenterology. 2004;127:1338–1346

26. Khuroo MS, Farahat KL. Molecular adsorbent recirculating system for acute and acute-on-chronic liver failure: a meta-analysis. Liver Transpl. 2004;10:1099–1106.

27. Kjaergard LL, Liu J, Als-Nielsen B, Gluud C. Artificial and bioartificial support systems for acute and acute-on-chronic liver failure: a systematic review. JAMA. 2003; 289:217–222

28. Kramer L, Gendo A, Madl C et al. A controlled study of sorbent suspension dialysis in chronic liver disease and hepatic encephalopathy. Int J Artif Organs. 2001;24: 434–442

29. Kramer L, Gendo A, Madl C, Ferrara I, Funk G, Schenk P, Sunder-Plassmann G, Hörl WH. Biocompatibility of a cuprophane charcoal-based detoxification device in cirrhotic patients with hepatic encephalopathy. Am J Kidney Dis. 2000;36:1193–1200

30. Kramer L, Bauer E, Schenk P, Steininger R, Vigl M, Mallek R. Successful treatment of refractory cerebral oedema in ecstasy/cocaine-induced fulminant hepatic failure using a new high-efficacy liver detoxification device (FPSA-Prometheus). Wien Klin Wochenschr. 2003;115: 599–603.

31. Laleman W, Wilmer A, Evenepoel P, Verslype C, Fevery J, Nevens F. Review article: non-biological liver support in liver failure. Aliment Pharmacol Ther. 2006;23:351–333.

32. Larsen FS, Gottstein J, Blei AT. Cerebral hyperemia and nitric oxide synthase in rats with ammonia-induced brain edema. J Hepatol. 2001;34:548–554

33. Larsen FS, Strauss G, Knudsen GM, Herzog TM, Hansen BA, Secher NH. Cerebral perfusion, cardiac output, and arterial pressure in patients with fulminant hepatic failure. Crit Care Med. 2000;28:996–1000.

34. Martin U, Kiessig V, Blusch JH, Haverich A, von der Helm K, Herden T, Steinhoff G. Expression of pig endogenous retrovirus by primary porcine endothelial cells and infection of human cells. Lancet. 1998;352: 692–694.

35. Nyberg SL, Misra SP. Hepatocyte liver-assist systems-a clinical update. Mayo Clin Proc. 1998;73:765–771.

36. O'Grady JG, Gimson AES, O'Brien CJ, Pucknell A, Hughes RD, Williams R. Controlled trials of charcoal hemoperfusion and prognostic factors in fulminant hepatic failure. Gastroenterology. 1988;94:1186–1194.

37. O'Grady JG, Schalm SW, Williams R. Acute liver failure: Redefining the syndromes. Lancet 1993;342:273–275.

38. Rolando N, Wade J, Davalos M, Wendon J, Philpott-Howard J, Williams R. The systemic inflammatory response syndrome in acute liver failure. Hepatology. 2000;32:734–739.

39. Rose C, Michalak A, Rao KV, Quack G, Kircheis G, Butterworth RF. L-ornithine-L-Aspartate lowers plasma and CSF ammonia and prevents cerebral edema in rats with acute liver failure. Hepatology. 1999;30:636–640.

40. Sadamori H, Yagi T, Inagaki M et al. High-flow-rate haemodiafiltration as a brain-support therapy proceeding to liver transplantation for hyperacute fulminant hepatic failure. Eur J Gastroenterol Hepatol. 2002;14:435–439.

41. Sauer IM, Goetz M, Steffen I et al. In vitro comparison of the molecular adsorbent recirculation system (MARS) and single-pass albumin dialysis (SPAD). Hepatology. 2004;39:1408–1414.

42. Silk DB, Trewby PN, Chase RA et al. Treatment of fulminant hepatic failure by polyacrylonitrile-membrane haemodialysis. Lancet. 1977;ii:1–3.

43. Stadlbauer V, Jalan R. Acute liver failure: liver support therapies. Curr Opin Crit Care. 2007,13:215–221.

44. Stange J, Mitzner SR, Risler T et al. Molecular adsorbent recycling system (MARS): clinical results of a new membrane-based blood purification system for bioartificial liver support. Artif Organs. 1999;23:319–330.

45. Tofteng F, Hauerberg J, Hansen BA, Pedersen CB, Jørgensen L, Larsen FS. Persistent arterial hyperammonemia increases the concentration of glutamine and alanine in the brain and correlates with intracranial pressure in patients with fulminant hepatic failure. J Cereb Blood Flow Metab. 2006;26:21–27.

46. Uribe M, Campollo O, Vargas-F et al. Acidifying enemas (lactitol and lactose) vs. nonacidifying enemas (tap water) to treat acute portal-systemic encephalopathy: a double-blind, randomized clinical trial. Hepatology. 1987;7:639–643.

47. Van de Kerkhove MP, Hoekstra R, Chamuleau RA, van Gulik TM. Clinical application of bioartificial liver support systems. Ann Surg. 2004;240:216–230.

48. Wendon JA, Harrison PM, Keays R, Williams R. Cerebral blood flow and metabolism in fulminant liver failure. Hepatology. 1994;19:1407–1413.

49. O'Grady JG, Alexander GJ, Hayllar KM, Williams R. Early indicators of prognosis in fulminant hepatic failure. Gastroenterology. 1989;97:439–445.

50. Bernal W, Donaldson N, Wyncoll D, Wendon J. Blood lactate as an early predictor of outcome in paracetamol-induced acute liver failure: a cohort study. Lancet. 2002;359:558–563.